The Ernst & Young Tax Guide 2006

2006 Tax Calendar

JANUARY

17 ❏ Final estimated tax payment for 2005 due if you did not pay your income tax (or enough of your income tax) for that year through withholding. Use Form 1040-ES.

31 ❏ If you did not pay your last installment of estimated tax by January 17, file your income tax return for 2005 on this date, thereby avoiding any penalty for late payment of the last installment. Use Form 1040 or 1040A.

FEBRUARY

15 ❏ File a new Form W-4 if you can claim exemption from withholding.

MARCH

1 ❏ Farmers and fishermen must file their 2005 income tax return (Form 1040) to avoid an underpayment penalty for the last quarter of 2005 if they were required to but did not pay estimated tax on January 17.

APRIL

17 ❏ File your income tax return for 2005 (Forms 1040, 1040A, or 1040EZ) and pay any tax due.
❏ Make your 2005 IRA contribution.
❏ If you are not extending your return, make your Keogh or SEP-IRA contribution if you have self-employment income.
❏ For an automatic 6-month extension, file Form 4868 and pay any tax that you estimate will be due. Then file Form 1040 or 1040A by October 16. If you get an extension, you can't file Form 1040EZ. (You can use one Form 4868 to file for both your income tax and gift tax extensions.)
❏ Pay the first installment of your 2006 estimated tax if you are not paying your 2006 income tax (or enough of it) through withholding tax.
❏ If you made any taxable gifts during 2005 (more than $11,000 per donee), file a gift tax return for that year (Form 709 or 709-A) and pay any tax due.

JUNE

15 ❏ Pay the second installment of 2006 estimated tax.

30 ❏ Individuals who have signature authority or other authority over certain bank, securities, or other financial accounts in a foreign country must file Form TD F 90-22.1.

SEPTEMBER

15 ❏ Pay the third installment of your 2006 estimated tax.
❏ Last day to make a required minimum contribution to a defined benefit Keogh plan.

OCTOBER

16 ❏ If you requested an automatic 6-month extension to file your 2005 income tax return, file Form 1040 or Form 1040A and pay any tax, interest, and penalty due, and any gift tax return if due.
❏ Last day to make a Keogh or SEP-IRA contribution deductible for calendar year 2005 if you requested a 6-month extension of time to file your tax return.

JANUARY 2007

2 ❏ Last day to establish a Keogh plan for 2006.

The Ernst & Young Tax Guide 2006

By the Tax Partners and Professionals of Ernst & Young LLP

Peter W. Bernstein, Editor

cds
BOOKS

Notice: In the preparation of this book, every effort has been made
to offer the most current, correct, and clearly expressed information available prior to publication: The 2004 version of Internal
Revenue Service Publication 17, Your Federal Income Tax, and
the Internal Revenue Service's draft forms for 2005. Readers
may obtain the 2005 version of Publication 17 and the forms at
www.irs.gov. Note also that inadvertent errors can occur, and tax
rules and regulations often change.

Further, the information in the text is intended to afford general
guidelines on matters of interest to taxpayers. The application and
impact of tax laws can vary widely, however, from case to case,
based upon the specific or unique facts involved. Accordingly, the
information in this book is not intended to serve as legal, accounting, or tax advice. Readers are encouraged to consult with
professional advisors for advice concerning specific matters before
making any decision, and the author and publishers disclaim any
responsibility for positions taken by taxpayers in their individual
cases or for any misunderstanding on the part of readers.

The information in this book is based on the Internal Revenue
Code as of September 2005.

Contents

PART VIII

2005 DRAFT TAX FORMS AND FILLING OUT YOUR TAX RETURN

609

Special Contents

REAL ESTATE INVESTORS' TAX GUIDE

SELF-EMPLOYED ENTREPRENEURS' TAX GUIDE

BUSINESS EXECUTIVES' TAX GUIDE

SENIOR CITIZENS' TAX GUIDE

How to Use This Guide

The Ernst & Young Tax Guide 2006 is an easy-to-use, step-by-step guide to preparing your own tax return. It has been designed with you in mind, and its format should help highlight information to save you time and money.

The book explains, in clear and simple English, important aspects of the tax laws that affect you. It covers what you need to know about your taxes—from how to file your return to how to lower the tax you'll pay next year. Throughout the book, you will find hundreds of examples illustrating how the tax laws work. Sample tax forms and schedules show you how to fill out your return line by line. Here are some of the book's special features and how to use them:

- **Two Books in One.** *The Ernst & Young Tax Guide 2006* is really two books. The first book is the 2004 version of the official Internal Revenue Service tax guide, Publication 17, *Your Federal Income Tax,* which is reproduced here. Published annually, it contains the IRS's position on many of the tax questions taxpayers face. In order to make *The Ernst & Young Tax Guide 2006* available to the public as quickly as possible, we have updated the text of the 2004 version of the IRS guide to take into account developments during 2005. These updates are noted throughout the text. The 2005 IRS Publication 17 can be found at www.irs.gov. The second book is the Ernst & Young guide. Here are comments, explanations, and tax-saving tips on what the IRS tells you—and doesn't tell you. It's no surprise that the IRS doesn't tell you everything, and what it does say often favors the U.S. government. Courts and tax professionals frequently differ with IRS opinions. The Ernst & Young text provides you with this additional material. The two books have been spliced together to give you the most well-rounded tax guide on the market. To distinguish between the two perspectives, the original IRS text appears in black throughout the book, our updates of the IRS text appear in gray, and Ernst & Young's comments appear in the blue boxes or in blue type.

- **TaxSavers, TaxPlanners, TaxAlerts, and TaxOrganizers.** One of the book's biggest attractions is the more than 400 *TaxSavers, TaxPlanners, TaxAlerts,* and *TaxOrganizers* that you'll find appropriately placed throughout the text. *TaxSavers* are tips that help you slash your tax bill this year and next—legally. *TaxPlanners* outline ideas that help you plan better for the upcoming year. *TaxAlerts* point out tax rules and regulations that have just changed or may change in the near future, and they give you important current filing advice about issues you will want to consider as you prepare your return. *TaxOrganizers* point out steps you can take now to make it easier to file your taxes later.

- **Tax Forms.** *The Ernst & Young Tax Guide 2006* contains 2005 draft tax forms. You'll find drafts of many of the federal tax forms that you need in Part VIII, *2005 Draft Tax Forms* and *Filling Out Your Tax Return,* along with tax rate schedules. Please note that draft forms are *not* usable for filing and are included only as a helpful reference. Final 2005 tax forms are easily available at the IRS website, www.irs.gov. Simply click on Forms and Publications and search for the form you need. It is perfectly acceptable to send the forms you print out from the IRS website to the IRS once they have been completed. The 2005 Tax Tables were not yet available when this book went to press in late September 2005, but also can be found at www.irs.gov. A listing of all the tax forms that appear in the book can be found in the Table of Contents.

- **Special Contents.** We've taken great pains to ensure that this book is clearly organized for easy access. If you can't find the section you want in the regular Contents, check the *Special Contents.* All told, there are eight of these—one each for families, homeowners, investors in stocks and bonds, investors in real estate, self-employed entrepreneurs, business executives, senior citizens, and members of the armed forces. Each *Special Contents* contains a listing of the major tax issues for members of that group and tells where you can find the answers in the book. In addition, we have a table of contents at the beginning of each chapter to help you find what you need.

We have drawn from the tax experience of scores of Ernst & Young LLP partners, professionals and staff from all parts of the United States to create this tax guide. Among the major accounting firms, only Ernst & Young LLP publishes a complete tax guide that is available to the general public. It provides the most complete and up-to-date tax information of any tax guide published. You also might be interested in other Ernst & Young publications: *Ernst & Young's Personal Financial Planning Guide,* 5th Edition, a book that walks readers through all the basics of financial planning, including special tactics tied to life's major events, and the *Ernst & Young's Retirement Planning Guide,* a book to help you secure a sound retirement

Changes in the Tax Law You Should Know About

Two new tax laws were enacted in 2005. The most important relating to individual taxpayers was passed just as this book was going to press and contained tax changes relating to Hurricane Katrina. In addition to the changes made by Congress, the IRS also made a number of additional changes to help ease the burden for the millions of hurricane victims. Many of those changes are summarized in the text below but are not covered elsewhere in this book (see Tax Changes Resulting from Hurricane Katrina, below).

The other 2005 tax bill—the Energy Tax Incentives Act of 2005—contains provisions that are relevant to individual taxpayers. But those provisions won't be effective until 2006. (See Chapter 48, Planning Ahead for 2005 and Beyond, for more details.) In addition, there are other tax changes you need to be aware of as you complete your 2005 taxes. Congress passed and President Bush signed into law two significant tax bills in 2004—the Working Families Tax Relief Act of 2004 and the American Jobs Creation Act of 2004. Many provisions of both 2004 laws affect individual income taxes and take effect for the first time in 2005. Both bills contain certain items that were scheduled to be reduced or eliminated,—such as the $1,000 child tax credit, marriage penalty relief, the 10% rate bracket, and the alternative minimum tax exemption—that have been extended beyond their original expiration dates.

The 2004 legislation also offers some new benefits and places some new requirements on taxpayers. One significant new deduction enacted gives taxpayers the ability to choose between deducting their state and local income taxes or their state and local sales taxes—but only in 2004 and 2005 unless further extended by Congress. This is a significant benefit to taxpayers living in states with no income taxes, and also gives taxpayers who do pay a state income tax the option of deducting sales taxes if they are larger than income taxes paid in the year.

The law also imposes stringent new substantiation requirements for vehicles donated to charity after December 31, 2004. The new rules require additional documentation and verification of the value of the automobile in order to support any deduction claimed for the charitable contribution. See Chapter 26, Contributions, for more details on these requirements.

TaxAlert: Tax Changes Resulting from Hurricane Katrina

As a result of the devastation caused by Hurricane Katrina to residents of Louisiana, Alabama, Mississippi and Florida, both Congress and the IRS have made changes to the tax laws and rules in order to help people recover from this disaster. Congress has passed the Katrina Emergency Tax Relief Act of 2005 and the IRS has issued a number of administrative changes. Some of these changes also apply to people outside the area affected by the hurricane.

Also refer to Chapter 26, *Contributions*, and Chapter 27, *Casualty and Theft Losses*, for the general tax rules that apply. Those chapters do not include the latest developments discussed below.

Note: Since the latest changes enacted by Congress, as well as the changes issued by the IRS, were made just as this book was going to press in late September 2005, most of the developments discussed here are not included in Chapters 26 and 27 and elsewhere in this book. Also, it's possible that Congress and the IRS will make further changes that could affect your 2005 taxes. You should check the IRS website at www.irs.gov.

➤ Extensions of Deadlines for Filing and Payments

The deadlines for filing returns and making payments related to income, estate, gift, excise and employment taxes have been extended to February 28, 2006 for those affected by Hurricane Katrina. Earlier the IRS had extended the deadlines to January 3, 2006 but Congress added additional time.

The new deadline generally applies to people in the 64 Louisiana parishes, 52 Mississippi counties, six Alabama counties, and eleven Florida counties affected by Katrina, to file tax returns and submit tax payments with an original or extended due date that fell on or after August 25, 2005. Interest and any late filing or late payment penalties that would otherwise apply are forgiven. This postponement also applies to Katrina relief workers.

➤ Distributions From Employer Plans and IRAs

Penalty-Free Withdrawals from Retirement Plans for Taxpayers Affected by Hurricane Katrina

The 10-percent early withdrawal tax, which usually applies before age 59 1/2, will not apply in the case of a qualified disaster-relief distribution from a 401(k) or other qualified retirement plan, a 403(b) annuity or an IRA made on or after August 25, 2005, and before 2007. A qualified disaster-relief distribution is any distribution made to someone who has sustained a loss as a result of Hurricane Katrina and who lived in the Hurricane Katrina disaster area. The total amount of qualified disaster-relief distributions that an individual can receive that are exempt from the early withdrawal penalty is $100,000.

Extended Rollover Period

While qualified disaster-relief distributions from retirement plans for taxpayers affected by the hurricane are not subject to income tax withholding, they are still subject to income taxes. However, if any portion of a qualified disaster-relief distribution is rolled over during the three-year period beginning the day after the date of the disaster declaration, that amount will not be taxable. For example, if you receive a qualified disaster-relief distribution from a 401(k) plan in 2005, that amount is included in your income (subject to income averaging, discussed below), but is not subject to the 10-percent early withdrawal tax. If you recontribute the amount of the distribution in 2007 to a qualified retirement plan, 403(b) annuity, governmental 457 plan, or IRA, you can file an amended return to claim a refund of the tax you paid on the amount previously included in your income.

Income Averaging for Disaster-Relief Distributions Related to Hurricane Katrina

If you can't recontribute the qualified disaster-relief distribution within three years and you have to pay tax on the amount, the new law provides an additional break. Any amount received as a result of a qualified disaster-relief distribution can be included in your income ratably over the three-year period beginning with the year of distribution, unless you elect not to have the provision apply. So, for example, if you withdrew $90,000 in 2005, you could report $30,000 of income in 2005, another $30,000 of income in 2006 and the final $30,000 in 2007, thus stretching out your tax payments.

Recontributions of Withdrawals for Home Purchases Cancelled Due to Hurricane Katrina

If you took a hardship distribution from a 401(k) plan or 403(b) annuity, or a qualified first-time homebuyer distribution from an IRA after February 28, 2005, and before August 29, 2005, that was supposed to be used to buy a principal residence in the Hurricane Katrina disaster area, but because of the storm could not be, you may get a tax break. As long as the distribution is re-contributed to your pension plan between August 25, 2005, and February 28, 2006, it will be considered a "rollover" and you will not have to pay income tax on the amount withdrawn or an early distribution tax.

Increased Loan Amount from Qualified Retirement Plans for Victims of Hurricane Katrina

Loans from qualified retirement plans are usually limited to $50,000. However, if you are a victim of Hurricane Katrina you are now allowed to borrow up to $100,000 (or your entire balance, if less) before 2007. Furthermore, if you had an outstanding loan on or after August 25, 2005, and if the due date for any repayment is during the period beginning on August 25, 2005, and ending on December 31, 2006, that due date is delayed for one year.

Retirement plans can make loans and hardship distributions to Katrina victims.

The IRS announced that 401(k) and similar employer-sponsored retirement plans can make loans and hardship distributions to victims of Hurricane Katrina and members of their families without being formally amended. Plans can also ignore the limits that normally apply to hardship distributions, thus allowing them, for example, to be used for food and shelter. Plans can also relax any documentation requirements. To qualify, hardship withdrawals must be made by March 31, 2006.

➤ Charitable Contributions

Temporary Suspension of Limitations on Charitable Contributions

Any cash contributions you make during the period beginning on August 28, 2005, and ending on December 31, 2005, to a public charitable organization are not subject to the general percentage limitations based on your adjusted gross income (AGI). Note that this rule applies to all taxpayers and **any** charity, not just those related to Hurricane Katrina. So, a particularly generous individual could contribute 100% of his AGI to charity during this period and deduct it all. Also, any deduction for qualified contributions is not subject to the 3% of AGI disallowance discussed in Chapter 31, *Limit on Itemized Deductions*.

Example: Assume Allan's adjusted gross income (AGI) for 2005 is $100,000, that he made contributions in September 2005 of $70,000 and had other charitable contributions earlier in the year of $40,000, for a total of $110,000 in contributions in 2005. Allan is allowed a deduction of $100,000 for 2005 ($40,000 for his earlier contributions and $60,000 for the qualified contributions). The excess of $10,000 can be carried forward to future years.

Making donations for Katrina victims.

If you wish to make donations to assist victims of Hurricane Katrina you should seek out qualified charities. Qualified charities can be found through a search feature on the IRS website at http://www.irs.gov. Disaster-relief information also can be found at http://www.FirstGov.gov. Publication 3833, Disaster Relief: Providing Assistance Through Charitable Organizations, may be useful for those who want to make contributions or who want to form a new charity.

Increase in Standard Mileage Rate for Charitable Use of Certain Vehicles

Effective for mileage on or after August 25, 2005, and before January 1, 2007, if you use a vehicle for providing donated services to charity solely for the provision of relief related to Hurricane Katrina you can use a rate (rounded to the next highest cent) equal to 70 percent of the business mileage rate in effect on the date of the use, rather than the charitable standard mileage rate of 14 cents per mile, in calculating your charitable contribution deduction. For example, the rate would be 34 cents a mile for the last 4 months of 2005 (70% x 48.5 cents—see **Standard mileage rate increases,** below). A charity can reimburse a volunteer at the actual business mileage rate with no tax consequences to the volunteer.

Tax breaks for leave-based donation programs.

The IRS has provided special relief for employer programs that allow employees to donate their vacation, sick or personal leave in exchange for employer cash payments made to qualified tax-exempt organizations providing relief for the victims of Hurricane Katrina. Employees won't be taxed on leave they donate under such a program in exchange for employer cash payments made before January 1, 2007. Under such a program, you could ask your employer to contribute your unused vacation pay to charity without you being taxed on that money. Of course, you would not get a tax deduction for that contribution. Unlike a similar rule issued after 9/11/01, which allowed contributions to **any** charity, this rule applies only for contributions made to Katrina related charities.

➤ Additional Exemption

Additional Exemption for Housing Hurricane Katrina Displaced Individuals

For 2005 and 2006, you will be entitled to an additional exemption of $500 for each Hurricane Katrina displaced individual for whom you provide housing. You may claim the additional exemption for no more than four individuals. Thus, the maximum additional exemption amount is $2,000. The exemption with respect to any Hurricane Katrina displaced individual may only be claimed one time for all taxable years. So, if you claim this exemption in 2005, you cannot claim it again in 2006.

A Hurricane Katrina displaced individual is an individual who was (as of August 28, 2005) a resident of any Hurricane Katrina disaster area, is displaced from his or her residence located in the disaster area and is provided housing free of charge in your principal residence for a period of 60 consecutive days.

The additional exemption is not subject to the income-based phaseouts applicable to other personal exemptions, and is allowed as a deduction in computing alternative minimum taxable income. It is not allowed for a spouse or dependents.

➤ Casualty Loss Deductions

Suspension of Certain Limitations on Personal Casualty Losses

The new law allows you to claim casualty or theft losses attributable to Hurricane Katrina on or after August 25, 2005, regardless of whether the loss exceeds $100. In addition, personal casualty or theft losses attributable to Hurricane Katrina are deductible without regard to whether the loss is more than 10 percent of your adjusted gross income. Personal casualty or theft losses from Hurricane Katrina are treated as a deduction separate from all other casualty losses. So, if you had other theft or casualty losses, losses attributable to Hurricane Katrina are disregarded for purposes of calculating whether those other losses are more than 10 percent of your adjusted gross income.

Extension of Replacement Period for Nonrecognition of Gain

The law extends from two to five years the replacement period in which you may replace property converted on or after August 25, 2005 (property lost by disaster), in the case of property that is located in the Hurricane Katrina disaster area. Substantially all of the use of the replacement property must be located in this area.

➤ Miscellaneous

Standard mileage rate increases for the last four months of 2005. In response to the recent dramatic gas price increases (which also partially resulted from the hurricane), the optional business standard mileage rate increases by 8¢ to 48.5¢ a mile for all miles driven between September 1 and December 31, 2005, up from 40.5¢ for the first eight months of 2005. The rate for computing deductible medical or moving expenses between September 1 and December 31, 2005, is 22¢ a mile, up from 15¢ for the first eight months of 2005. As discussed earlier, the rate for charitable purposes related to Hurricane Katrina is 70% of the business rate. The rate for other charitable purposes remains at 14¢ a mile.

Special Rule for Determining Earned Income Credit and Refundable Child Credit

In 2005, qualified individuals can elect to calculate the earned income credit and refundable child credit using their earned income from 2004. Qualified individuals are permitted to make the election only if their earned income for 2005 is less than their earned income for 2004. Qualified individuals are individuals who on August 25, 2005, lived in the Hurricane Katrina disaster area and were displaced.

Authority to Make Adjustments Regarding Taxpayer and Dependency Status for Taxpayers Affected by Hurricane Katrina

For 2005 and 2006, the IRS can make any adjustments as may be necessary to ensure that you do not lose any deduction or credit or experience a change of filing status by reason of temporary relocations after Hurricane Katrina or by reason of the receipt of hurricane relief. Such adjustments may include, for example, addressing the application of the residency requirements relating to dependency exemptions in the case of relocations due to Hurricane Katrina.

Forgiveness of Debt

If you were affected by Hurricane Katrina and a debt you have is forgiven by a governmental agency or certain financial entities on or after August 25, 2005 and before 2007, you would not realize taxable income as a result. Other debts that are forgiven generally result in taxable income to you.

IRS/AICPA partnership. The IRS has partnered with the American Institute of Certified Public Accountants (AICPA) to provide assistance to taxpayers at local disaster recovery centers established by the Federal Emergency Management Agency (FEMA). FEMA opens local disaster recovery centers where individuals and businesses may register for disaster aid when the President designates an area to receive federal disaster assistance. CPA volunteers will join the IRS employees assigned to staff these centers.

IRS disaster relief toll-free number. The IRS has set up a special toll-free telephone number for use by people affected by Hurricane Katrina who need help with tax matters. The number is 1-866-562-5227.

What's New for 2005

This section summarizes important tax changes that took effect in 2005. Most of these changes are discussed in more detail throughout this publication.

➤ Elimination of TeleFile.

TeleFile has ben eliminated and will not be available for the filing of 2005 tax returns.

➤ Automatic Extension Now Available for 6 Months

In prior years only a 4-month automatic extension was allowed by filing Form 4868 by April 15. Form 4868 for 2005 now provides for an aurtmatic 6-month extension to October 16, 2006. Form 2688, Application for Additional Extension of Time To File U.S. Individual Income Tax Return, has been eliminated.

➤ Definition of dependent.

Starting in 2005, a dependent is either a qualifying child or a qualifying relative.

Qualifying child. In general, a qualifying child must meet all of the following conditions.

- The child must be your child (including an adopted child, stepchild, or eligible foster child), brother, sister, stepbrother, stepsister, or a descendant of any of them.
- The child must have lived with you for more than half of 2005. But an exception applies, in certain cases, for children of divorced or separated parents.
- At the end of 2005, the child must be under age 19, or under age 24 and a full-time student, or any age and permanently and totally disabled.
- The child must not have provided over half of his or her own support in 2005.

Qualifying relative. In general, a qualifying relative must meet all of the following conditions.

- The person must be either your relative or any other person (other than your spouse) who lived in your home all year as a member of your household. If the person is not your relative, your relationship must not violate local law.
- The person cannot be the qualifying child of another person in 2005 (see above).
- The person must have gross income of less than $3,200. If the person is permanently and totally disabled, certain income from a sheltered workshop may be excluded for this purpose.
- You must have provided over half of the person's support in 2005. But exceptions apply, in certain cases, for children of divorced or separated parents and for a person supported by two or more taxpayers.

The following rules also apply in determining if a person is your dependent.

1. If you are a dependent of another person in 2005, you cannot claim any dependents on your return.
2. If the dependent is married, he or she cannot file a joint return unless the return is filed only as a claim for refund and no tax liability would exist for either spouse if they had filed separate returns.
3. A dependent generally must be a U.S. citizen, U.S. national, or a resident of the United States, Canada, or Mexico.
4. New "tie-breaker" rules apply if a child meets the conditions to be a qualifying child of two or more people and more than one person claims the child as a qualifying child.

Certain tax benefits, such as qualifying widow(er) filing status and medical and dental expenses, can still be claimed based on a person who is not your dependent if the only reason that person is not your dependent is because he or she is a qualifying relative who has gross income of $3,200 or more, or because of items (1) or (2) above.

The definition of "qualifying child" also applies for the following tax benefits changed in 2005.

- Head of household filing status.

In general, you can use head of household filing status only if, as of December 31, 2005, you were unmarried or legally separated (according to your state law) under a decree of divorce or separate maintenance and you paid over half the cost of keeping up a home:

1. That was the main home for all of 2005 of your parent whom you can claim as a dependent. Your parent did not have to live with you.
2. In which you lived for more than half of the year with either of the following:
   a. Your qualifying child (defined above, but without regard to the exception for children of divorced or separated parents). This does not include a qualifying child who is married at the end of 2005 and is not your dependent because he or she either (i) filed a joint return or (ii) is not a U.S. citizen, U.S. national, or a resident of the United States, Canada, or Mexico.
   b. Any other person whom you can claim as a dependent.

You cannot use head of household filing status for a person who is your dependent only because:

- He or she lived with you for all of 2005, or
- You are entitled to claim him or her as a dependent under a multiple support agreement.

The rules under prior law allowing certain married persons living apart from their spouses for the last 6 months of the year to use head of household filing status also apply for 2005.

- Earned income credit (EIC).
- Child tax credit.
- Child and dependent care credit.

➤ Deduction for domestic production activities.

You may be able to deduct up to 3% of your qualified production activities income from the following activities.

1. Construction performed in the United States;
2. Engineering or architectural services performed in the United States for construction projects in the United States; or
3. Any lease, rental, license, sale, exchange, or other disposition of:
   a. Tangible personal property, computer software, and sound recordings that you manufactured, produced, grew, or extracted in whole or in significant part within the United States,
   b. Any qualified film you produced, or
   c. Electricity, natural gas, or potable water you produced in the United States.

The deduction does not apply to income derived from: the sale of food and beverages you prepare at a retail establishment; property you leased, licensed, or rented for use by any related person; or the transmission or distribution of electricity, natural gas, or potable water. This deduction is allowed for alternative minimum tax purposes, but is not allowed in determining net earnings from self-employment.
The deduction is taken on line 35, Form 1040.

➤ Standard mileage rates.

The standard mileage rate for the cost of operating your car increased to 40.5 cents a mile for all business miles driven. The rate is 48.5 cents for use from September through December 2005. See Chapter 28, *Car Expenses and Other Employee Business Expenses.*

The standard mileage rate allowed for use of your car for medical reasons increased to 15 cents a mile. The rate is 22 cents for use from September through December 2005. See Chapter 23, *Medical and Dental Expenses.*

The standard mileage rate allowed for use of your car for determining moving expenses increased to 15 cents a mile. The rate is 22 cents for use from September through December 2005. See Chapter 19, *Moving Expenses.*

➤ Retirement savings plans.

The following paragraphs highlight changes that affect individual retirement arrangements (IRAs) and pension plans.

Traditional IRA income limits.

If you have a traditional IRA and are covered by a retirement plan at work, the amount of income you can have and not be affected by the deduction phaseout increases. The amounts vary depending on filing status. See Chapter 18, *Individual Retirement Arrangements (IRAs).*

Limit on elective deferrals.

The maximum amount of elective deferrals under a salary reduction agreement that could be contributed to a qualified plan increased to $14,000 ($18,000 if you were age 50 or over). However, for SIMPLE plans, the amount increased to $10,000 ($12,000 if you were age 50 or over).

Health savings accounts (HSAs).

You may be able to deduct contributions made to your health savings account (HSA). HSAs are discussed in Publication 969, Health Savings Accounts and Other Tax-Favored Health Plans. You can deduct these contributions on Form 1040, line 25. See Chapter 23, Medical and Dental Expenses.

➤ Educator expenses.

The deduction as an adjustment to gross income for educator expenses has been extended until the end of 2005. The expenses can be deducted on Form 1040, line 23, or Form 1040A, line 16. See Chapter 21, *Education-Related Adjustments.*

➤ Sales tax deduction.

You can again elect to deduct state and local general sales taxes instead of state and local income taxes as an itemized deduction on Form 1040, Schedule A. This deduction will expire at the end of 2005 unless Congress extends it. See Chapter 24, *Taxes You May Deduct,* for more information.

TAXALERT

You have two options with respect to the determination of the sales tax deduction amount. You can deduct the total amount of general state and local sales taxes paid by accumulating receipts showing general sales taxes paid. Alternatively, you may use tables provided by the IRS (available at www.irs.gov). The tables are based on average consumption by taxpayers on a state-by-state basis taking into account filing status, number of dependents, adjusted gross income, and rates of state and local general sales taxation. Taxpayers who use the tables may, in addition to the table amounts, deduct eligible general sales taxes paid with respect to the purchase of motor vehicles, boats, and certain other items. Sales taxes for items that may be added to the tables are not reflected in the tables themselves.

This deduction clearly benefits residents of states with no state income tax. Because it is available to all taxpayers as an option, however, it may benefit others whose sales tax bill for the year exceeds their state income tax (e.g., in low tax jurisdictions or in years where large taxable expenditures are incurred).

The sales tax deduction is a preference for alternative minimum tax (AMT) purposes and may be of little or no value to you if you are subject to the AMT (the AMT is discussed in Chapter 32, How to Figure Your Tax). In such an instance, if you itemize for state tax purposes and claim the sales tax deduction, you may be better off deducting sales tax on the federal return despite the fact that the deduction results in no federal tax savings.

At this time, this deduction is scheduled to expire after 2005.

➤ Hope or lifetime learning credit income limits increased.

The amount of income you can have and still receive a Hope or lifetime learning credit has increased. See Chapter 21, *Education-Related Adjustments,* for more information.

➤ Certain amounts increased.

Some tax items that are indexed for inflation increased for 2005.

Earned income credit (EIC).

The maximum amount of income you can earn and still get the earned income credit increased. The amount depends on your filing status and number of children. The maximum amount of investment income you can have and still be eligible for the credit has increased to $2,700. See Chapter 38, *Other Credits Including the Earned Income Credit.*

Standard deduction.

The standard deduction for taxpayers who do not itemize deductions on Schedule A (Form 1040) has increased. The amount depends on your filing status. See Chapter 22, Standard Deduction.

Exemption amount.

You are allowed a $3,200 deduction for each exemption to which you are entitled. However, your exemption amount could be phased out if you have high income. See Chapter 3, *Personal Exemptions and Dependents.*

Limit on itemized deductions.

Some of your itemized deductions may be limited if your adjusted gross income is more than $145,950 ($72,975 if you are married filing separately). See Chapter 31, *Limit on Itemized Deductions.*

Tax benefits for adoption.

The adoption credit and the maximum exclusion from income of benefits under an employer's adoption assistance program are increased to $10,630. See *Adoption Credit* in Chapter 38, *Other Credits Including the Earned Income Credit,* and Publication 968, Tax Benefits for Adoption.

Social Security and Medicare taxes.

The maximum wages subject to Social Security tax (6.2%) increased to $90,000. All wages are subject to Medicare tax (1.45%).

What's New for 2006

This section summarizes the important changes that take effect in 2006 that could affect your estimated tax payments for 2006. More information on these and other changes can be found in Publication 553, available at www.irs.gov.

➤ Retirement savings plans.

The following paragraphs highlight changes that affect individual retirement arrangements (IRAs) and pension plans.

Traditional IRA income limits.

If you have a traditional IRA and are covered by a retirement plan at work, the amount of income you can have and not be affected by the deduction phaseout increases. The amounts vary depending on filing status.

Limit on elective deferrals.

The maximum amount of elective deferrals under a salary reduction agreement that can be contributed to a qualified plan (other than a SIMPLE plan) increases to $15,000 ($20,000 if you are age 50 or over).

IRA deduction expanded.

The amount you, and your spouse if filing jointly, may be able to deduct as an IRA contribution will remain at $4,000 (but will increase to $5,000 if age 50 or older at the end of 2006). See Chapter 18, *Individual Retirement Arrangements (IRAs),* for more information.

➤ Credits for energy conservation and efficiency measures

Beginning in 2006 there will be new credits for the purchase of various types of energy-saving property.

New tax credits for the purchase of hybrid, fuel cell, advanced lean burn, and other alternative power vehicles. The size of the credit varies depending generally on the weight class of the vehicle and the rated fuel economy. The credit applies to vehicles placed in service after 2005, with termination dates varying with the type of alternative power vehicle. (The prior deduction for certain clean fuel vehicles and refueling property expires at the end of 2005.)

New 30% tax credit for the purchase of qualifying residential solar water heating, photovoltaic equipment, and fuel cell property. The maximum credit is $2,000 (for solar equipment) and $500 for each kilowatt of capacity (for fuel cells). The credit applies for property placed in service after 2005 and before 2008.

New 10% personal tax credit for energy efficient improvements to existing homes. The lifetime maximum credit per taxpayer is $500 and applies for property placed in service after December 31, 2005, and before January 1, 2008.

Personal Exemption Phaseout and Limitation on Itemized Deductions Reduced

In 2006, the personal exemption phaseout and the limitation on itemized deductions, both of which are based on your AGI, will be reduced by one-third. That means that you may be entitled to larger deductions for these items next year.

Roth 401(k) Plans

Beginning in 2006, if your employer's plan allows it, you'll be able to designate part or all of your 401(k) contributions as "Roth 401(k)" contributions. As with a Roth IRA, your contributions to a Roth 401(k) are nondeductible, but all of the income in the plan will be tax free to you when distributed if you meet the same requirements that apply to Roth IRAs—5 years of participation and distribution after age 59, death, disability, or up to $10,000 for a first-time home purchase.

See Chapter 48, Planning Ahead for 2006 and Beyond, for more significant changes taking effect in 2006.

Important 2005 Tax Reminders

Listed below are important reminders and other items that may help you file your 2005 tax return. Many of these items are explained in more detail later in this publication.

➤ **Write in your Social Security number.**

To protect your privacy, Social Security numbers (SSNs) are not printed on the peel-off label that comes in the mail with your tax instruction booklet. This means you must enter your SSN in the space provided on your tax form. If you filed a joint return for 2004 and are filing a joint return for 2005 with the same spouse, enter your names and SSNs in the same order as on your 2004 return. See Chapter 1, *Filing Information.*

➤ **Taxpayer identification numbers.**

You must provide the taxpayer identification number for each person for whom you claim certain tax benefits. This applies even if the person was born in 2005. Generally, this number is the person's Social Security number (SSN). See Chapter 1, *Filing Information.*

➤ **Reporting interest and dividends.**

If you have interest or dividend income of more than $1,500, you have to file Schedule 1 (Form 1040A) or Schedule B (Form 1040) with your tax return. Also, you cannot file Form 1040EZ if you have more than $1,500 of taxable interest income.

➤ **Tax relief for victims of terrorist attacks.**

Under the Victims of Terrorism Tax Relief Act of 2001, the federal income tax liability of those killed in the following attacks is forgiven for certain tax years.

- The April 19, 1995, terrorist attack on the Alfred P. Murrah Federal Building (Oklahoma City).
- The September 11, 2001, terrorist attacks.
- The terrorist attacks involving anthrax occurring after September 10, 2001, and before January 2, 2002.

The Act also exempts from federal income tax certain amounts received by survivors.

For more information, see Publication 3920, Tax Relief for Victims of Terrorist Attacks.

➤ **Benefits for public safety officer's survivors.**

A survivor annuity received by the spouse, former spouse, or child of a public safety officer killed in the line of duty will generally be excluded from the recipient's income regardless of the date of the officer's death. The provision applies to a chaplain killed in the line of duty after September 10, 2001. The chaplain must have been responding to a fire, rescue, or emergency as a member or employee of a fire or police department. See Chapter 13, *Other Income.*

➤ **Parent of a kidnapped child.**

The parent of a child who is presumed by law enforcement authorities to have been kidnapped by someone who is not a family member may be able to take the child into account in determining his or her eligibility for the following.

- Head of household or qualifying widow(er) with dependent child filing status.
- Exemption for dependents.

- Child tax credit.
- Earned income credit.

See Publication 501, Exemptions, Standard Deduction, and Filing Information, and Publication 596, Earned Income Credit (EIC).

➤ **Payments received by Holocaust victims.**

Restitution payments received after 1999 (and certain interest earned on the payments) are not taxable and do not affect the taxability of certain benefits, such as Social Security benefits. For more details, see Chapter 13, *Other Income.*

➤ **Advance earned income credit.**

If a qualifying child lives with you and you expect to qualify for the earned income credit in 2006, you may be able to get part of the credit paid to you in advance throughout the year (by your employer) instead of waiting until you file your tax return. See Chapter 38, *Other Credits Including the Earned Income Credit.*

➤ **Sale of your home.**

Generally, you will only need to report the sale of your home if your gain is more than $250,000 ($500,000 if married filing a joint return). See Chapter 16, *Selling Your Home.*

➤ **Retirement planning services.**

If your employer has a qualified retirement plan, qualified retirement planning services provided for you (or your spouse) by your employer are not included in your income. For more information, see *Retirement Planning Services* under *Fringe Benefits* in Chapter 6, *Wages, Salaries, and Other Income.*

➤ **Individual retirement arrangements (IRAs).**

The following paragraphs highlight important reminders that relate to IRAs. See Chapter 18, *Individual Retirement Arrangements (IRAs),* for details.

IRA for spouse.

A married couple filing a joint return can contribute up to the maximum amount each to their IRAs, even if one spouse had little or no income.

Spouse covered by plan.

Even if your spouse is covered by an employer-sponsored retirement plan, you may be able to deduct contributions to your traditional IRA if you are not covered by an employer plan.

Roth IRA.

You may be able to establish a Roth IRA. In this type of IRA, contributions are not deductible but earnings grow tax free and qualified withdrawals are not taxable. You may also be able to convert a traditional IRA to a Roth IRA, but you must include all or part of the taxable converted amount in income.

➤ **Retirement savings contributions credit.**

If you contribute to an individual retirement arrangement (IRA) or to a retirement plan sponsored by your employer, you may qualify for a tax credit. See *Retirement Savings Contributions Credit* in Chapter 38, *Other Credits Including the Earned Income Credit.*

➤ Foreign source income.

If you are a U.S. citizen with income from sources outside the United States (foreign income), you must report all such income on your tax return unless it is exempt by U.S. law. This is true whether you reside inside or outside the United States and whether or not you receive a Form W-2 or 1099 from the foreign payer. This applies to earned income (such as wages and tips) as well as unearned income (such as interest, dividends, capital gains, pensions, rents and royalties).

If you reside outside the United States, you may be able to exclude part or all of your foreign source earned income. For details, see Publication 54, Tax Guide for U.S. Citizens and Resident Aliens Abroad.

➤ Child tax credit.

You may be able to claim a tax credit for each of your qualifying children under age 17 at the end of the year. See Chapter 36, *Child Tax Credit.*

➤ Health insurance credit.

If you are an eligible individual, you can claim a tax credit equal to 65% of the amount you pay for qualified health insurance coverage. See Chapter 38, *Other Credits Including the Earned Income Credit.*

➤ Joint return responsibility.

Generally, both spouses are responsible for the tax and any interest or penalties on a joint tax return. In some cases, one spouse may be relieved of that responsibility for items of the other spouse that were incorrectly reported on the joint return. For details, see *Joint responsibility* in Chapter 2, *Filing Status.*

➤ Include your phone number on your return.

To promptly resolve any questions we have in processing your tax return, we would like to be able to call you. Please enter your daytime telephone number on your tax form next to your signature.

➤ Third party designee.

You can check the "Yes" box in the "Third Party Designee" area of your return to authorize the IRS to discuss your return with a friend, family member, or any other person you choose. This allows the IRS to call the person you identified as your designee to answer any questions that may arise during the processing of your return. It also allows your designee to perform certain actions. See your income tax package for details.

➤ Payment of taxes.

Make your check or money order payable to "United States Treasury." You can pay your taxes by credit card, using the Electronic Federal Tax Payment System (EFTPS) or, if you file electronically, by electronic funds withdrawal. See Chapter 1, *Filing Information.*

➤ Faster ways to file your return.

The IRS offers fast, accurate ways to file your tax return information without filing a paper tax return. You can use IRS *e-file* (electronic filing). For details, see Chapter 1, *Filing Information.*

➤ Free electronic filing.

You may be able to file your 2005 taxes online for free thanks to an electronic filing agreement. See Chapter 1, *Filing Information.*

➤ Mailing your return.

If you received an envelope with your tax package, please use it. Otherwise, see the last page of this publication for a list of IRS addresses.

➤ Private delivery services.

You may be able to use a designated private delivery service to mail your tax returns and payments. See Chapter 1, *Filing Information,* for more information.

➤ Change of address.

If you change your address, you should notify the IRS. See *Change of Address,* under *What Happens After I File,* in Chapter 1, *Filing Information.*

➤ Refund on a late filed return.

If you were due a refund but you did not file a return, you generally must file your return within 3 years from the date the return was due (including extensions) to get that refund. See Chapter 1, *Filing Information,* for more information.

➤ Privacy Act and paperwork reduction information.

The IRS Restructuring and Reform Act of 1998, the Privacy Act of 1974, and the Paperwork Reduction Act of 1980 require that when we ask you for information we must first tell you what our legal right is to ask for the information, why we are asking for it, how it will be used, what could happen if we do not receive it, and whether your response is voluntary, required to obtain a benefit, or mandatory under the law. A complete statement on this subject can be found in your tax form instruction booklet.

➤ Treasury Inspector General for Tax Administration.

If you want to confidentially report misconduct, waste, fraud, or abuse by an IRS employee, you can call 1-800-366-4484 (1-800-877-8339 for TTY/TDD users). You can remain anonymous.

➤ Photographs of missing children.

The Internal Revenue Service is a proud partner with the National Center for Missing and Exploited Children. Photographs of missing children selected by the Center may appear in this publication on pages that would otherwise be blank. You can help bring these children home by looking at the photographs and calling 1-800-THE-LOST (1-800-843-5678) if you recognize a child.

How to Avoid 25 Common Errors

1 Most importantly, check your math.

2 Double-check that your Social Security number has been correctly written on the return. If you are married, check that your spouse's Social Security number is properly listed, whether filing a joint or separate return.

3 Include your Social Security number on each page of the return so that if a page is misplaced by the IRS, it can be reattached.

4 Check that you have claimed all of your dependents, such as elderly parents who may not live with you. See Chapter 3, *Personal Exemptions and Dependents*.

5 Include on the return the Social Security numbers for all dependents including those born during 2005.

6 If you are single and have a dependent who lives with you, check to see if you qualify for the lower tax rates available to a head of household or surviving spouse.

7 You may be eligible for the earned income credit if you do NOT file as married filing separately. If you have one qualifying child and your earned income and modified adjusted gross income for 2005 are less than $35,263 ($37,263 if you have more than one qualifying child), you may qualify. If you do not have a qualifying child, but are between the ages of 25 and 65, and your earned income for 2005 and modified adjusted gross income are less than $11,750, you may qualify as well. See Chapter 38, *Other Credits Including the Earned Income Credit*.

8 If you are married, check to see if filing separate returns rather than a joint return is more beneficial.

9 Attach all copy Bs of your W-2 forms to your return in order to avoid correspondence with the IRS. If you received a Form 1099-R showing federal income tax withheld, attach copy B of that form as well.

10 You may be eligible to claim the additional standard deductions if you are blind or 65 years of age or older.

11 Be sure to sign your check and write your Social Security number, the form number, and the tax year on the face of any checks made out to the U.S. Treasury. (Example: "000-00-000 — 2005 Form 1040.")

12 Be sure that your Form W-2 and all Form 1099s are correct. If they're wrong, have them corrected as soon as possible so that the IRS's records agree with the amounts you show on your return.

13 If you worked for more than one employer, be sure to claim a credit for any overpaid Social Security taxes withheld from your wages.

14 If you received a state tax refund or a refund of interest you paid on a mortgage in an earlier year, make sure you have not included too much of your refund in your income. These refunds may not be taxable if you did not get a tax benefit from deducting them. If, for example, you used the standard deduction in the year in which the taxes or interest were paid, you do not have to include the refund in income this year.

15 Deductible real property taxes should be distinguished from assessments paid for local benefits, such as repair of streets, sidewalks, sewers, curbs, gutters, and other improvements that tend to benefit specific properties. Assessments of this type generally are not deductible.

16 Make sure to sign and date your return and enter your occupation. If you are filing a joint return, be sure that your spouse also signs as required.

17 Only a portion of your Social Security benefits may be taxable. If your income does not exceed a certain amount, none of it may be taxable.

18 Check last year's tax return to see if there are any items that carry over to this year, such as charitable contributions or capital losses that exceeded the amount you were previously able to deduct.

19 If you can be claimed as a dependent on someone else's return, do not claim a personal exemption on your return. Your standard deduction may be limited as well. See Chapter 22, *Standard Deduction*.

20 Fill out Form 8606, *Nondeductible IRA Contributions*, for your contributions to an IRA account, even if you don't claim any deduction for the contribution.

21 Recheck your basis in the securities that you sold during the year, particularly shares of a mutual fund. Income and capital gains dividends that were automatically reinvested in the fund over the years increase your basis in the mutual fund and thus reduce a gain or increase a loss that you have to report. Also, any "front-end" or purchase fees are still considered part of your cost basis for tax purposes, even though they reduce your investment in a mutual fund.

22 Recheck that you have used the correct column in the Tax Rate Table or the right Tax Rate Schedule for your filing status.

23 Don't miss deadlines: January 2—set up a Keogh plan; April 17—make your IRA contribution; April 17—file your return or request an extension. Check the tax calendar periodically. See the *2006 Tax Calendar*.

24 If you regularly get large refunds, you're having too much withheld and, in effect, giving the IRS an interest-free loan. Increasing the number of allowances you claim on Form W-4 will increase your take-home pay.

25 Keep copies of all documents that you send to the IRS. Use certified mail for all important correspondence to the IRS. Don't forget to keep your records in good shape so that you can find answers to any IRS questions about your return.

50 of the Most Easily Overlooked Deductions

The following list will serve as a reminder of some deductions you can easily overlook when you prepare your return. It is not intended to be all-inclusive, nor applicable to everyone. The circumstances of your situation will determine whether you qualify. See the chapter reference following each item for a complete explanation.

1 Accounting fees for tax preparation services and IRS audits (Chapter 30)

2 Alcoholism and drug abuse treatment (Chapter 23)

3 Amortization of premium on taxable bonds (Chapter 30)

4 Appraisal fees for charitable donations or casualty losses (Chapters 26, 27)

5 Appreciation on property donated to a charity (Chapter 26)

6 Casualty or theft losses (Chapter 27)

7 Cellular telephones (Chapter 30)

8 Cleaning and laundering services when traveling (Chapter 28)

9 Commissions and closing costs on sale of property (Chapter 14)

10 Contact lenses, eyeglasses, and hearing devices (Chapter 23)

11 Contraceptives, if bought with a prescription (Chapter 23)

12 Costs associated with looking for a new job in your present occupation, including fees for résumé preparation and employment of outplacement agencies (Chapter 30)

13 Depreciation of home computers (Chapter 30)

14 Dues to labor unions (Chapter 30)

15 Education expenses to the extent required by law or your employer or needed to maintain or improve your skills (Chapter 30)

16 Employee contributions to a state disability fund (Chapter 24)

17 Employee's moving expenses (Chapter 19)

18 Federal estate tax on income with respect to a decedent (Chapter 30)

19 Fees for a safe-deposit box to hold investments (e.g., stock certificate) (Chapter 30)

20 Fees paid for childbirth preparation classes if instruction relates to obstetrical care (Chapter 23)

21 Fifty percent of self-employment tax (Chapter 1)

22 Foreign taxes paid (Chapter 24)

23 Foster child care expenditures (Chapter 13)

24 Gambling losses to the extent of gambling winnings (Chapter 30)

25 Hospital services fees (laboratory work, therapy, nursing services, and surgery) (Chapter 23)

26 Impairment-related work expenses for a disabled individual (Chapter 30)

27 Improvements to your home (Chapter 16)

28 Investment advisory fees (Chapter 30)

29 IRA trustee's administrative fees billed separately (Chapter 30)

30 Lead paint removal (Chapter 23)

31 Legal fees incurred in connection with obtaining or collecting alimony (Chapter 30)

32 Long-term care insurance premiums (Chapter 23)

33 Margin account interest expense (Chapter 25)

34 Medical transportation, including standard mileage deduction (Chapter 23) and lodging expenses incurred for medical reasons while away from home (Chapter 23)

35 Mortgage prepayment penalties and late fees (Chapter 25)

36 Out-of-pocket expenses relating to charitable activities, including the standard mileage deduction (Chapter 26)

37 Health insurance premiums if self-employed (Chapter 39)

38 Penalty on early withdrawal of savings (Chapter 8)

39 Personal liability insurance for wrongful acts as an employee (Chapter 30)

40 Points on a home mortgage and certain refinancings (Chapter 25)

41 Protective clothing required at work (Chapter 30)

42 Real estate taxes associated with the purchase or sale of property (Chapter 24)

Individual Tax Organizer

The following schedules should help you organize the data you need to prepare your 2005 federal income tax return. They are intended only to provide general guidelines and should not be regarded as all-inclusive.

TAXPAYER INFORMATION

PERSONAL DATA

Your name _____

Your spouse's name _____

Social Security number _____ Spouse's _____

Marital status at year-end: ☐ Married ☐ Single ☐ Widowed after 2003 ☐ Divorced ☐ Married but separated

DEPENDENT CHILDREN

(Qualifying Children)

Name (address if different from yours)	Social Security number	Date of birth	Did you provide more than half of support?	Married filing a joint return?	Full-time student for 5 months or more?	

OTHER DEPENDENTS

(Qualifying Relatives)

Name (address if different from yours)	Social Security number	Relationship	Months lived in your home	Is dependent's income over $3,200	Did you provide more than half of support?

PAYMENTS AND REFUNDS OF INCOME TAXES

	FEDERAL		STATE		CITY	
	Date paid	Amount	Date paid	Amount	Date paid	Amount
2005 estimated payments, including overpayment credited from 2004 return:						
Tax refunds received in 2005[1]						

[1]Do not include interest received on refunds. Detail these amounts in the interest income section of this organizer.

COMPENSATION

Indicate recipient: H=Husband; W=Wife.

H W	Employer name	Gross earnings	Federal income tax withheld	Social Security tax withheld	Medicare tax withheld	State tax withheld	City tax withheld

INTEREST INCOME

Indicate ownership: H=Husband; W=Wife; J=Joint.

Report all interest received by you or for your account on Forms 1099-INT or other statements of total interest received. Failure to record any such income could result in a notice from the IRS.

If the amount of interest reported on Forms 1099-INT includes interest accrued on bonds at the time of purchase, adjustments can be made.

If you invested in a tax-exempt municipal bond fund, note the fund's schedule of percentage income related to each state.

H W J		Amount
	Savings accounts, credit unions, and certificates of deposit:	
	U.S. Savings Bonds and other U.S. government securities:	
	Corporate bonds:	
	Other interest[1]:	
	Tax-exempt interest	
	Interest received on tax refunds:	

[1] If you received interest income from seller-financed mortgages, you will need the payer's name, address, and Social Security number.

DIVIDEND INCOME

Indicate ownership: H=Husband; W=Wife; J=Joint.

Report all dividends received by you or for your account on Forms 1099-DIV or other information statements received. Failure to record any such income could result in a notice from the IRS.

H W J	Name of corporation [identify foreign corporation with (F)]	Indicate T (taxable), C (capital gain), N (nontaxable), U (U.S obligation) X (exempt) Q (qualified)	Dividends received	U.S. taxes withheld

SALE OR PURCHASE OF RESIDENCE

Did you sell your residence during the year or within the last two years?   ☐ Yes   ☐ No
If you answered "Yes," see Chapter 16, *Selling Your Home.*

SALE OF STOCKS AND BONDS

Indicate H-Husband; W-Wife; or J-Joint.

Note: Gross proceeds from sales reported here should reconcile with Forms 1099-B received from your broker. You should explain any discrepancies to prevent an IRS inquiry stemming from their matching program.

H W J	Description (include number of shares, common or preferred, and par value of bonds)	Date Acq.	Date Sold	Gross sales price[1]	Cost or other basis plus expenses of sale[2]	Gain or (loss)[3]

[1] List proceeds of sale or cash received in lieu of fractions on receipt of stock rights or stock dividends.

[2] The basis of stock should be decreased by all nontaxable dividends and increased by any reinvested dividends. See Chapter 14, Basis of Property.

[3] Have you acquired stock, securities, contracts, or options to sell or acquire stock   ☐ Yes   ☐ No
or securities substantially identical to stock or securities sold at a loss within a period
beginning 30 days prior to and ending 30 days after the date of sale? If "Yes," see
the discussion of "Wash Sale" in Chapter 15, Sale of Property.

OTHER TRANSACTIONS

Did you exchange securities for other securities or exchange any investment property for any other property? Did any security held by you or any amounts due you become worthless during the year? Did you sell your vacation home or other property during the year? Did you realize a gain or a loss on property, in whole or in part, by destruction, theft, seizure, or condemnation (including the threat or imminence thereof)? Did you engage in any commodity transactions (including open positions on December 31) during the year? Did you engage in any transactions involving traded options?

If you answered "Yes" to any of these questions, read the applicable portions of this book.

SALE OF OTHER PROPERTY

H W J	Description	Date Acq.	Date Sold	Gross sales price	Cost of other basis, plus expenses of sale	Depreciation or depletion	Gain or (loss)

INSTALLMENT SALES

Did you make sales during the year for which the receipt of all or part of the sales price was deferred until future years?
  If yes, discuss with your tax advisor. ☐ Yes   ☐ No

Did you collect on any installment obligations from sales made prior to 2005? ☐ Yes   ☐ No

For more information, see Chapter 15, *Sale of Property.*

RENT AND ROYALTY INCOME

	Property A		Property B	
Did you actively participate in the operation of the rental activity during the year? For more information on active participation, see Chapter 10, *Rental Income and Expenses.*	☐ Yes	☐ No	☐ Yes	☐ No

Location and description of property[1]
Gross rents and royalties received
Expenses

[1]*If property has been used by you or your family as a personal residence, indicate the total days held for rent but not rented, days rented, and days used by you or your family.*

PARTNERSHIPS (P), SMALL BUSINESS CORPORATIONS (S), AND ESTATES AND TRUSTS (E/T)

Retain all Forms K-1 or other information relating to entity listed below.

P S E/T	H W J	Name	Tax shelter registration number	I.D. number	Income or (loss)

PENSION AND ANNUITY INCOME

Did you receive any payments from a retirement plan? ☐ Yes   ☐ No

If yes, write in the amount received during the year and any taxes withheld. _____

Did you roll over a profit-sharing or retirement plan distribution into another plan? ☐ Yes   ☐ No

What was the starting date of your annuity? _____

What is the amount received in the current taxable year? _____

Did you receive any IRA distributions during the year? ☐ Yes   ☐ No

Retain all Forms 1099-R or other information relating to each distribution.

Did you convert all or any part of a regular IRA into a Roth IRA during 2005? ☐ Yes   ☐ No

If yes, amount converted. _____

OTHER INCOME

Description	Amount
Alimony or legal separation payments received	
Disability payments	
Other tax refunds not shown elsewhere	
Unemployment insurance compensation	
Social security benefits	
Other[1] (describe)	

[1]The types of other income include, but are not limited to, net income from self-employment, director's fees, prizes, cancellation of debts, gambling winnings, jury fees, punitive damages (unless awarded in a wrongful death action where state law so provides), and receiver's fees. Also, include gross income from oil and gas working interests, as well as any expenses relating to them. For more information see Chapter 13, Other Income.

			Amount
Did you receive any income from a foreign source?	☐ Yes	☐ No	
Did you own shares in a mutual fund that retained your share of capital gains and paid the tax on it?	☐ Yes	☐ No	
Did you have any income from farm property?	☐ Yes	☐ No	
Did you have any bartering income?	☐ Yes	☐ No	

DEDUCTIONS

ADJUSTMENTS TO INCOME

Alimony or legal separation payments made in current year

   Recipient's last name _____ and Social Security no. _____

Penalties for early withdrawal of savings

Education Related Expenses

    ☐ Educator Expenses

    ☐ Student Loan Interest

    ☐ Tuition and Fees Deduction

Individual Retirement Arrangements (IRAs)[1]

Did you contribute to your own IRA?	☐ Yes	☐ No
Type:		
☐ Regular		
☐ Roth		
Did you participate in a retirement plan maintained by your employer?	☐ Yes	☐ No
Did your spouse contribute to his/her own IRA?	☐ Yes	☐ No
Did your spouse participate in a retirement plan maintained by his/her employer?	☐ Yes	☐ No
Did you and your spouse contribute to a spousal IRA?	☐ Yes	☐ No

Self-employed Keogh (HR-10) plan	Yours	Spouse's
Amount contributed		
Self-employed health insurance		

Have you incurred moving expenses in connection with starting work at a new permanent location? See Chapter 19, *Moving Expenses*.   ☐ Yes ☐ No

Did you or your spouse receive any disability payments?   ☐ Yes ☐ No

[1]Depending on your (and your spouse's) income level and whether you (or your spouse) are an active participant in an employer-maintained retirement plan, your IRA deduction may be limited.

MEDICAL EXPENSES

Note: You will qualify for a federal deduction only if your total unreimbursed medical expenses exceed 7.5% of your adjusted gross income.

List even if reimbursed	Amount
Medical or health insurance premiums (including amounts paid by payroll deductions)	
Medicare premiums	
Prescription drugs and insulin	
Doctors and dentists	
Hospitals	
Other medical expenses (eyeglasses, contact lenses, hearing aids, travel and lodging expenses)	
Reimbursements for medical expenses through insurance or other sources	( )

Note: If you are divorced or separated, have a child, and paid medical expenses for that child, include these amounts whether or not you are entitled to the dependency exemption. If you were self-employed and had a net profit for the year, were a general partner (or a limited partner receiving guaranteed payments) or if you received wages from an S corporation in which you were a more than 2% shareholder you may be able to deduct the amount paid for health insurance on behalf of yourself, your spouse, and dependents. For more information, see Chapter 23, Medical and Dental Expenses.

TAXES

Item	Amount
Real estate taxes	
Personal property	
Vehicle licenses (allowed in some states). State of	
State or local income taxes (if not listed elsewhere)	
Other taxes (not including income taxes and other taxes listed elsewhere)	
State disability tax	
State and local sales taxes	

Note: Foreign income taxes paid or withheld should be listed by country.

INTEREST EXPENSES

Item	Payee	Amount
Home mortgage paid to financial institutions		
Home mortgage paid to individuals[1]		
Mortgage points on principal residence[2]		
Prepayment penalty on loans		
Brokerage accounts		
Investment interest		
Other (itemize)		

[1] *You need name(s) and social security number(s).*

[2] *Include only points, including loan origination fees, on the purchase or improvement of your principal residence. If you paid points to refinance your mortgage, see Chapter 25,* Interest Expense.

For more information, see Chapter 25, *Interest Expense.*

CHARITABLE CONTRIBUTIONS

In addition to outright gifts of cash or property, deductible contributions also include out-of-pocket expenses incurred for charity, for example, transportation, meals and lodging away from home, and cost and upkeep of special uniforms and equipment required in the performance of donated services. You need a contemporaneous written acknowledgment from the charity to which a contribution or contributions of $250 or more was made during the year. A canceled check does not constitute adequate substantiation for contributions in excess of $250.

If you have sold any property to a charity for less than the property's fair market value, you will need details.

For more information, see Chapter 26, *Contributions*.

CASH CONTRIBUTIONS

Recipient	Amount[1]

If total noncash contributions have a value in excess of $500, you may need the following information:
    the name and address of the donee; the date of the gift; a description of the property, how it was acquired by you, and when it was acquired by you; your tax basis; its value at the time of the donation and how the value was ascertained. Indicate (√) if any property was held by you one year or less.

If you made noncash contributions of property in excess of $5,000 in value, use Form   ☐ Yes   ☐ No
8283, *Noncash Charitable Contributions,* with Section B, *Appraisal Summary,* completed.
If you contributed a motor vehicle to charity see Chapter 26, *Contributions.*

CASUALTY LOSSES

Note: You will qualify for a deduction for a personal casualty loss only if it exceeds 10% of your adjusted gross income and only for the amount *not* covered by insurance reimbursement. See Chapter 27, *Casualty and Theft Losses,* for details.

Casualty losses include such items as losses from automobile collisions; damage from storms, fires, and floods; and damage from vandalism, theft, and other casualties.

A disaster loss is a loss that occurred in an area determined by the President of the United States to warrant federal disaster assistance. See Chapter 27, *Casualty and Theft Losses.*

Describe the casualty loss and its approximate date and location. _____

_____

_____

Indicate (√) type of property: _____ business _____ investment _____ personal

OTHER DEDUCTIONS

Note: In general, you will qualify for a federal deduction only if your total other miscellaneous deductions exceed 2% of your adjusted gross income.

Item	Amount	Item	Amount

Investment expenses:
   Automobile expense
		Educational expense (to maintain or
		   improve skills required by employer)	

Investment counsel fees		Meals and entertainment[1]	
Safe-deposit box		Tax advice/return fees	
Subscriptions		Union dues	
Telephone		Dues for professional organizations	
IRA fees		Business publications	
Other		Office-in-home expenses[2]	
		Other	

[1] *Only 50% of meals and entertainment expenses are deductible.*

[2] *See* Chapter 30, *Miscellaneous Deductions.*

EMPLOYEE BUSINESS EXPENSES

Were you reimbursed for any business expenses incurred in connection with the performance of services for your employer? ☐ Yes ☐ No

If yes, answer the following questions:

A. Are you required to return reimbursement to the extent it exceeds expenses? ☐ Yes ☐ No

B. Are you required to submit itemized supporting documentation to your employer? ☐ Yes ☐ No

If you answered yes to the above questions and your reimbursement does not exceed your expenses, you are generally not required to report the reimbursement and expenses on your return. However, if your reimbursement does not equal your expenses, or if you answered no to questions A and/or B, report below the total reimbursements and expenses for the year. Certain other business expenses, even if not reimbursed, may also be deductible.

Does your employer have an accountable reimbursement plan? See Chapter 28, *Car Expenses and Other Employee Business Expenses.* ☐ Yes ☐ No

Employee business expenses	Amount

Total amount reimbursed. (Do not include any amounts that were reported to you as wages in box 10 of Form W-2.) _____

Do you have substantiation (described below) for travel and entertainment expenses? ☐ Yes ☐ No

Information that must be available includes

- Amounts spent
- Dates of departure and return for each trip and the number of days spent on business
- Dates of entertainment
- Places of entertainment or travel
- Dates and descriptions of business gifts
- Business purposes of the travel, entertainment, or business gifts
- Business relationships with the persons entertained or to whom gifts were made

AUTOMOBILE EXPENSES

Mileage information	Automobile 1	Automobile 2
Number of months used for business during the year		
Total mileage (include personal miles)		
Business mileage portion of the total mileage (indicate separately for 9/1–12/31/05)		
Commuting mileage portion of the total mileage		
Original cost		
Annual lease payments		

Total actual expenses (business and personal for months used for business)

_____

_____

AUTOMOBILE DEPRECIATION

Year, make, model	Cost	Date acquired
Automobile		

Do you have adequate or sufficient evidence to justify the deduction for the vehicles? ☐ Yes ☐ No

If yes, is the evidence written? ☐ Yes ☐ No

CHILD CARE CREDIT

If you incurred any expenses for child or dependent care so that you and your spouse could be gainfully employed or attend an educational institution as a full-time student, complete the table below.

Did your employer provide or reimburse you for the cost of child or dependent care?   □ Yes   □ No

If so, the credit must be reduced by the amount excluded from your income through your employer's dependent care assistance program.

Name of child or dependent	Name, address, and social security number or FEIN of person or organization providing care	Relationship, if any	Period of care		Amount paid
			From	To	

FOREIGN TAXES

List foreign source income and foreign income taxes paid

Country	Income		Taxes Paid	
	Type	Amount	Date paid	Amount

EMPLOYING DOMESTIC HELP

Did you employ domestic help?   □ Yes   □ No

Did you pay more than $1,400 during the year to an individual for services provided in your home?   □ Yes   □ No

If so, you may be required to pay employment taxes see Chapter 42, *What to Do If You Employ Domestic Help.*

Income and Expense Records You Should Keep in Addition to Your Income Tax Return

Some Suggestions That Could Come in Handy

INCOME	RECORDS
❏ **Wages, salaries**	✔ Form W-2
❏ **Interest income**	✔ 1099-INT, 1099-OID or Substitute 1099, such as broker statement or year-end account summary
❏ **Dividend income**	✔ 1099-DIV or Substitute 1099 such as broker statement or year-end account summary
❏ **State tax refunds**	✔ Form 1099-G, state income tax return
❏ **Self-employment income**	✔ Sales slips, invoices, receipts, sales tax reports, business books and records, 1099-MISC
❏ **Capital gains and losses**	✔ 1099-B or Substitute 1099, such as broker statement or year-end account summary showing proceeds from sales of securities or other capital assets. Records must also show your cost or other basis and the expenses of the sale. Your records must show when and how an asset was acquired (including property received as a gift or inheritance), how the asset was used, and when and how it was disposed of. To support the basis of securities, you should keep old account statements, buy/sell execution records, stock dividend and stock split information, and dividend reinvestment records (see Chapter 15, *Sale of Property*).
❏ **IRA distributions**	✔ 1099-R, year-end account summary, Form 8606
❏ **Pension and annuities**	✔ 1099-R, records of contributions
❏ **Rents**	✔ Checkbook, receipts and canceled checks, and other books and records, 1099-MISC
❏ **Partnerships, S corporations**	✔ Schedule K-1, record of unused passive activity losses
❏ **Estates, trusts**	✔ Schedule K-1, copies of last will and testament including codicils, Form 56-Notice Concerning Fiduciary Relationship, Form 1310-Statement of Person Claiming Refund due a Deceased Taxpayer, including death certificate or letters of office, Form 4810-Request for Prompt Assessment Under IRC Section 6501(d), Tax worksheets showing pre- and post-death income allocation, including copies of all 1099s received for the year of death, copies of prior three years' Form 1040, and copies of all prior-year gift tax returns.
❏ **Social Security benefits**	✔ Form SSA-1099
❏ **Royalties**	✔ 1099-MISC
❏ **Unemployment compensation**	✔ 1099-G
❏ **Alimony**	✔ Divorce settlement papers
❏ **Miscellaneous income**	✔ 1099-MISC and other records of amounts receicved

EXPENSE	RECORDS
❏ **Domestic employee expense**	✔ Canceled checks, state unemployment tax payments, see Chapter 42, *What to Do If You Employ Domestic Help*.
❏ **Self-employment expense**	✔ Bills, canceled checks, receipts, bank statements, all business books and records
❏ **IRA contribution**	✔ Year-end account summary, deposit receipt
❏ **Keogh contribution**	✔ Year-end account summary, deposit receipt
❏ **Alimony**	✔ Divorce settlement papers, canceled alimony checks
❏ **Medical and dental expense**	✔ Bills, canceled checks, receipts, pay stubs if employer withholds medical insurance from wages
❏ **Taxes**	✔ Canceled checks, mortgage statements, receipts, Form W-2 ✔ State and local sales tax deduction receipts showing sales taxes paid
❏ **Interest expense**	✔ Bank statements, mortgage statements (Form 1098), canceled checks
❏ **Charitable contributions**	✔ Canceled checks, receipts, detailed description of noncash property contributed, Form 1098-C
❏ **Miscellaneous deductions**	✔ Receipts, canceled checks, or other documentary evidence (See Chapters 27 through 30.)
❏ **Casualty and theft losses**	✔ Description of property, photograph of damaged property, receipts, canceled checks, policy and insurance reports
❏ **Exemptions**	✔ Birth certificates, Social Security numbers

CREDITS	RECORDS
❏ **Child and dependent care**	✔ Receipts, canceled checks and name, address, and identification number of care provider
❏ **Estimated taxes**	✔ Canceled checks
Foreign taxes	✔ Form 1099 DIV
Withheld taxes	✔ Forms W-2 and 1099

PART I

The Income Tax Return

The five chapters in this part provide basic information on the tax system. They take you through the first steps of filling out a tax return—such as deciding what your filing status is, how many exemptions you can take, and what form to file. They also discuss recordkeeping requirements, IRS e-file (electronic filing), certain penalties, and the two methods used to pay tax during the year: withholding and estimated tax. You can find additional information about electronic filing in Chapter 46, *Everything You Need to Know About E-filing*.

1

Filing Information

Note: The 2004 IRS Publication 17 (Your Federal Income Tax) has been updated by Ernst & Young LLP for 2005. Dates and dollar amounts shown are for 2005. Gray type is used to indicate where IRS text has been updated or intentionally omitted. Unrevised IRS text is shown in black type.

Introduction

Unlike the other certainty in life, paying taxes is the one for which you may obtain an extension. Besides explaining when you must file your tax return and what to do if you are unable to get it prepared on time, this chapter provides an introduction to the basic framework within which you file your federal income tax return. It answers a lot of the elementary questions about the procedures and calculations involved in determining your income tax.

This chapter discusses such items as who is required to file and who should file even though he or she is not required to do so. It tells you which forms to use, how to

go about preparing your tax return once you have obtained the correct forms, and where to mail your tax return once it has been completed. In addition, the chapter informs you about the penalties that may be imposed if you do not pay your taxes on time and instructs you on what to do if you discover that a previous tax return is in error. The chapter also explains what the different accounting methods are and which method may be used in preparing your return.

Remember, one of the most important features of this book is Chapter 49, 2005 Draft Federal Tax Forms.

What's New

Who must file. Generally, the amount of income you can receive before you must file a return has been increased. See Table 1-1, Table 1-2, and Table 1-3 for the specific amounts.
[IRS text intentionally omitted]
Mailing your return. You may be mailing your return to a different address this year because the IRS has changed the filing location for several areas. If you received an envelope with your tax package, please use it. Otherwise, see *Where Do I File*, later in this chapter. TeleFile will not be available for 2005 returns.
Form 4868, Application for Automatic Extension of Time to File US Individual Income Tax Return, now provides for an automatic 6-month extension. When you file Form 4868 you will get an auto-

matic extension to file for 6 months, rather than 4 months. You no longer need to File Form 2688 for an additional extension of time.

Reminders

Alternative filing methods. Rather than filing a return on paper, you may be able to file electronically using IRS *e-file*. Create your own personal identification number (PIN) and file a completely paperless tax return. For more information, see *Does My Return Have To Be on Paper*, later.
Change of address. If you change your address, you should notify the IRS. See *Change of Address*, later, under *What Happens After I File.*
Write in your social security number. You must write your so-

cial security number (SSN) in the spaces provided on your tax return. If you file a joint return, write the SSNs in the same order as the names.

Direct deposit of refund. Instead of getting a paper check, you may be able to have your refund deposited directly into your account at a bank or other financial institution. See *Direct Deposit* under *Refunds*, later.

Alternative payment methods. If you owe additional tax, you may be able to pay electronically. See *How To Pay*, later.

Installment agreement. If you cannot pay the full amount due with your return, you may ask to make monthly installment payments. See *Installment Agreement*, later, under *Amount You Owe*.

Service in combat zone. You are allowed extra time to take care of your tax matters if you are a member of the Armed Forces who served in a combat zone, or if you served in the combat zone in support of the Armed Forces. See *Individuals Serving in Combat Zone*, later, under *When Do I Have To File*.

Adoption taxpayer identification number. If a child has been placed in your home for purposes of legal adoption and you will not be able to get a social security number for the child in time to file your return, you may be able to get an adoption taxpayer identification number (ATIN). For more information, see *Social Security Number*, later.

Taxpayer identification number for aliens. If you or your dependent is a nonresident or resident alien who does not have and is not eligible to get a social security number, file Form W-7, Application for IRS Individual Taxpayer Identification Number, with the IRS. For more information, see *Social Security Number*, later.

Third party designee. You can allow the IRS to discuss your tax return with a friend, family member, or any other person you choose by checking the "Yes" box in the *Third party designee* area of your return. For more information, see *Third Party Designee*, later.

This chapter discusses:

- Whether you have to file a return,
- Which form to use,
- How to file electronically,
- When, how, and where to file your return,
- What happens if you pay too little or too much tax,
- What records you should keep and how long you should keep them, and
- How you can change a return you have already filed.

Do I Have To File a Return?

You must file a federal income tax return if you are a citizen or resident of the United States or a resident of Puerto Rico and you meet the filing requirements for any of the following categories that apply to you.

1. Individuals in general. (There are special rules for surviving spouses, executors, administrators, legal representatives, U.S. citizens and residents living outside the United States, residents of Puerto Rico, and individuals with income from U.S. possessions.)
2. Dependents.
3. Children under age 14.
4. Self-employed persons.
5. Aliens.

The filing requirements for each category are explained in this chapter.

The filing requirements apply even if you do not owe tax.

Tip. *Even if you do not have to file a return, it may be to your advantage to do so. See* Who Should File, *later.*

Caution. *File only one federal income tax return for the year regardless of how many jobs you had, how many Forms W-2 you received, or how many states you lived in during the year.*

Individuals—In General

If you are a U.S. citizen or resident, whether you must file a return depends on three factors:

1. Your gross income,
2. Your filing status, and
3. Your age.

To find out whether you must file, see Table 1-1, Table 1-2, and Table 1-3. Even if no table shows that you must file, you may need to file to get money back. (See *Who Should File*, later.)

Gross income. This includes all income you receive in the form of money, goods, property, and services that is not exempt from tax. It also includes income from sources outside the United States (even if you may exclude all or part of it). Common types of income are discussed in *Part Two* of this publication.

Community income. If you are married and your permanent home is in a community property state, half of any income described by state law as community income may be considered yours. This affects your federal taxes, including whether you must file if you do not file a joint return with your spouse. See Publication 555, Community Property, for more information.

Self-employed individuals. If you are self-employed, your gross income includes the amount on line 7 of Schedule C (Form 1040), Profit or Loss From Business, line 1 of Schedule C-EZ (Form 1040), Net Profit From Business, and line 11 of Schedule F (Form 1040), Profit or Loss From Farming. See *Self-Employed Persons*, later, for more information about your filing requirements.

Caution. *If you do not report all of your self-employment income, your social security benefits may be lower when you retire.*

Filing status. Your filing status depends on whether you are single or married and on your family situation. Your filing status is determined on the last day of your tax year, which is December 31 for most taxpayers. See chapter 2 for an explanation of each filing status.

Age. If you are 65 or older at the end of the year, you generally can have a higher amount of gross income than other taxpayers before you must file. See Table 1-1. You are considered 65 on the day before your 65th birthday. For example, if your 65th birthday is on January 1, 2006, you are considered 65 for 2005.

Example
You are 65 years old and earned $11,000 of **taxable income** last year. Your husband, who is 66 years old, received a **pension** of $6,000, all of which was **taxable income.** You and your husband legally separated on December 28. If you had been living together at the end of the year, you would not have had to file an income tax return, because your combined income was less than $18,400. But, because you are living apart and your gross income was more than $9,450, you must file a return.

Surviving Spouses, Executors, Administrators, and Legal Representatives
You must file a final return for a decedent (a person who died) if both of the following are true.

- You are the surviving spouse, executor, administrator, or legal representative.
- The decedent met the filing requirements at the date of death.

For more information on rules for filing a decedent's final return, see chapter 4.

Table 1-1.   2005 Filing Requirements for Most Taxpayers

IF your filing status is...	AND at the end of 2005 you were...*	THEN file a return if your gross income was at least...**
single	under 65	$ 8,200
	65 or older	$ 9,450
married filing jointly***	under 65 (both spouses)	$16,400
	65 or older (one spouse)	$17,400
	65 or older (both spouses)	$18,400
married filing separately	any age	$ 3,200
head of household	under 65	$10,500
	65 or older	$11,750
qualifying widow(er) with dependent child	under 65	$13,200
	65 or older	$14,200

* If you were born on January 1, 1941, you are considered to be age 65 at the end of 2005.

** Gross income means all income you received in the form of money, goods, property, and services that is not exempt from tax, including any income from sources outside the United States (even if you may exclude part or all of it). **Do not** include social security benefits as gross income unless you are married filing a separate return and you lived with your spouse at any time during 2005.

*** If you did not live with your spouse at the end of 2005 (or on the date your spouse died) and your gross income was at least $3,200, you must file a return regardless of your age.

U.S. Citizens and Residents Living Outside the United States

If you are a U.S. citizen or resident living outside the United States, you must file a return if you meet the filing requirements. For information on special tax rules that may apply to you, get Publication 54, Tax Guide for U.S. Citizens and Resident Aliens Abroad. It is available at most U.S. embassies and consulates. Also see *How To Get Tax Help* in the back of this publication.

Explanation
For more information about U.S. citizens living abroad, see Chapter 43, *U.S. Citizens Working Abroad: Tax Treatment of Foreign Earned Income.*

Residents of Puerto Rico

Generally, if you are a U.S. citizen and a resident of Puerto Rico, you must file a U.S. income tax return if you meet the filing requirements. This is in addition to any legal requirement you may have to file an income tax return for Puerto Rico.

If you are a resident of Puerto Rico for the entire year, gross income does not include income from sources within Puerto Rico, except for amounts received as an employee of the United States or a U.S. agency. If you receive income from Puerto Rican sources that is not subject to U.S. tax, you must reduce your standard deduction. As a result, the amount of income you must have before you are required to file a U.S. income tax return is lower than the applicable amount in Table 1-1 or Table 1-2. For more information, see *U.S. taxation* and its discussion, *Standard deduction*, under *The Commonwealth of Puerto Rico* in Publication 570, Tax Guide for Individuals With Income From U.S. Possessions.

Individuals With Income From U.S. Possessions

If you had income from Guam, the Commonwealth of the Northern Mariana Islands, American Samoa, or the Virgin Islands, special rules may apply when determining whether you must file a U.S. federal income tax return. In addition, you may have to file a return with the individual island government. See Publication 570 for more information.

Dependents

If you are a dependent (one who meets the dependency tests in chapter 3), see Table 1-2 to find whether you must file a return. You also must file if your situation is described in Table 1-3.

Responsibility of parent. Generally, a child is responsible for filing his or her own tax return and for paying any tax on the return. But if a dependent child who must file an income tax return cannot file it for any reason, such as age, then a parent, guardian, or other legally responsible person must file it for the child. If the child cannot sign the return, the parent or guardian must sign the child's name followed by the words "By (your signature), parent for minor child."

Child's earnings. Amounts a child earns by performing services are his or her gross income. This is true even if under local law the child's parents have the right to the earnings and may actually have received them. If the child does not pay the tax due on this income, the parent is liable for the tax.

Explanation
For more details about **dependents,** see Chapter 3, *Personal Exemptions and Dependents.*

Children Under Age 14

If a child's only income is interest and dividends (including capital gain distributions and Alaska Permanent Fund dividends) and certain other conditions are met, a parent can elect to include the child's income on the parent's return. If this election is made, the child does not have to file a return. See *Parent's Election To Report Child's Interest and Dividends* in chapter 33.

Self-Employed Persons

You are self-employed if you:

• Carry on a trade or business as a sole proprietor,
• Are an independent contractor,
• Are a member of a partnership, or
• Are in business for yourself in any other way.

Table 1-2.   **2005 Filing Requirements for Dependents**

See chapter 3 to find out if someone can claim you as a dependent.

If your parents (or someone else) can claim you as a dependent, and any of the situations below apply to you, you must file a return. (See Table 1-3 for other situations when you must file.)

In this table, **earned income** includes salaries, wages, tips, and professional fees. It also includes taxable scholarship and fellowship grants. (See *Scholarship and Fellowship Grants* in chapter 13.) **Unearned income** includes investment-type income such as taxable interest, ordinary dividends, and capital gain distributions. It also includes unemployment compensation, taxable social security benefits, pensions, annuities, and distributions of unearned income from a trust. **Gross income** is the total of your earned and unearned income.

Single dependents—Were you **either** age 65 or older **or** blind?

❑ **No.**   You must file a return if **any** of the following apply.
- Your unearned income was more than $800.
- Your earned income was more than $5,000.
- Your gross income was more than the larger of:
  - $800, or
  - Your earned income (up to $4,750) **plus** $250.

❑ **Yes.**   You must file a return if **any** of the following apply.
- Your unearned income was more than $2,050 ($3,300 if 65 or older **and** blind).
- Your earned income was more than $6,250 ($7,500 if 65 or older **and** blind).
- Your gross income was more than $1,250 ($2,500 if 65 or older **and** blind) **plus** the larger of:
  - $800, or
  - Your earned income (up to $4,750) **plus** $250.

Married dependents—Were you **either** age 65 or older **or** blind?

❑ **No.**   You must file a return if **any** of the following apply.
- Your unearned income was more than $800.
- Your earned income was more than $5,000.
- Your gross income was at least $5 and your spouse files a separate return and itemizes deductions.
- Your gross income was more than the larger of:
  - $800, or
  - Your earned income (up to $4,750) **plus** $250.

❑ **Yes.**   You must file a return if **any** of the following apply.
- Your unearned income was more than $1,800 ($2,800 if 65 or older **and** blind).
- Your earned income was more than $6,000 ($7,000 if 65 or older **and** blind).
- Your gross income was at least $5 and your spouse files a separate return and itemizes deductions.
- Your gross income was more than $1,000 ($2,000 if 65 or older **and** blind) **plus** the larger of:
  - $800, or
  - Your earned income (up to $4,750) **plus** $250.

Self-employment can include work in addition to your regular full-time business activities, such as certain part-time work you do at home or in addition to your regular job.

Examples

A person who delivers newspapers would be subject to self-employment tax. A person working at home in a cottage industry—making quilts or pillows, for example—would be subject to self-employment tax. In some instances, it is to your advantage to report income from self-employment, because if you do not already qualify, you will then become eligible for social security benefits. For more information on self-employed persons, see Chapter 39, *If You Are Self Employed: How to File Schedule C.*

You must file a return if your gross income is at least as much as the filing requirement amount for your filing status and age (shown in Table 1-1). Also, you must file Form 1040 and Schedule SE (Form 1040), Self-Employment Tax, if:

1. Your net earnings from self-employment (excluding church employee income) were $400 or more, or

2. You had church employee income of $108.28 or more. (See Table 1-3.)

Use Schedule SE (Form 1040) to figure your self-employment tax. Self-employment tax is comparable to the social security and Medicare tax withheld from an employee's wages. For more information about this tax, get Publication 533, Self-Employment Tax.

TaxSaver

Explanation

You are able to deduct one-half of your self-employment tax for the year in calculating your adjusted gross income. For details see Chapter 24, *Taxes You May Deduct.*

Self-employment tax has two parts: old age, survivor, and disability insurance (OASDI) and Medicare hospital insurance (HI). (The comparable social security tax withheld on an employee's wages consists of these same two parts.) In 2005, the cap on self-employment income subject to OASDI is $90,000. There

Table 1-3.   **Other Situations When You Must File a 2005 Return**

If any of the four conditions listed below apply, you must file a return, even if your income is less than the amount shown in Table 1-1 or Table 1-2.
 	
1.   You owe any special taxes, such as:
 	
   • Social security or Medicare tax on tips you did not report to your employer. (See chapter 7.)
   • Uncollected social security, Medicare, or railroad retirement tax on tips you reported to your employer. (See chapter 7.)
   • Uncollected social security, Medicare, or railroad retirement tax on your group-term life insurance. This amount should be shown in box 12 of your Form W-2.
   • Alternative minimum tax. (See chapter 32.)
   • Additional tax on a qualified retirement plan, including an individual retirement arrangement (IRA). (See chapter 18.)
   • Additional tax on an Archer MSA or health savings account. (See Publication 969, Health Savings Accounts and Other Tax-Favored Health Plans.)
   • Additional tax on a Coverdell ESA or qualified tuition program. (See Publication 970, Tax Benefits for Education.)
   • Recapture of an investment credit or a low-income housing credit. (See the instructions for Form 4255, Recapture of Investment Credit, or Form 8611, Recapture of Low-Income Housing Credit.)
   • Recapture tax on the disposition of a home purchased with a federally-subsidized mortgage. (See chapter 16.)
   • Recapture of the qualified electric vehicle credit. (See chapter 39.)
   • Recapture of an education credit. (See chapter 37.)
   • Recapture of the Indian employment credit. (See the instructions for Form 8845, Indian Employment Credit.)
   • Recapture of the new markets credit. (See Form 8874, New Markets Credit.)
 	
2.   You received any advance earned income credit (EIC) payments from your employer. This amount should be shown in box 9 of your Form W-2. (See chapter 38.)
 	
3.   You had net earnings from self-employment of at least $400. (See *Self-Employed Persons* earlier in this chapter.)
 	
4.   You had wages of $108.28 or more from a church or qualified church-controlled organization that is exempt from employer social security and Medicare taxes. (See Publication 533.)

is no limit on the amount of self-employment income subject to the HI portion of the self-employment tax.

TaxAlert

The 2006 FICA wage base amount has not yet been determined. The 2005 OASDI Trustees Report estimates that the FICA wage base will be $93,000 in 2006. You can confirm the actual wage base for 2006 at http://www.ssa.gov/OACT/COLA/cbb.html

Employees of foreign governments or international organizations. If you are a U.S. citizen who works in the United States for an international organization, a foreign government, or a wholly owned instrumentality of a foreign government, and your employer is not required to withhold social security and Medicare taxes from your wages, you must include your earnings from services performed in the United States when figuring your net earnings from self-employment.

Ministers. You must include income from services you performed as a minister when figuring your net earnings from self-employment, unless you have an exemption from self-employment tax. This also applies to Christian Science practitioners and members of a religious order who have not taken a vow of poverty. For more information, get Publication 517, Social Security and Other Information for Members of the Clergy and Religious Workers.

Aliens

Your status as an alien—resident, nonresident, or dual-status—determines whether and how you must file an income tax return.

The rules used to determine your alien status are discussed in Publication 519, U.S. Tax Guide for Aliens.

Resident alien. If you are a resident alien for the entire year, you must file a tax return following the same rules that apply to U.S. citizens. Use the forms discussed in this publication.

Nonresident alien. If you are a nonresident alien, the rules and tax forms that apply to you are different from those that apply to U.S. citizens and resident aliens. See Publication 519 to find out if U.S. income tax laws apply to you and which forms you should file.

Dual-status taxpayer. If you are a resident alien for part of the tax year and a nonresident alien for the rest of the year, you are a dual-status taxpayer. Different rules apply for each part of the year. For information on dual-status taxpayers, see Publication 519.

Explanation
For more information about foreign citizens living in the United States, see Chapter 44, *Foreign Citizens Living in the United States.*

Who Should File

Even if you do not have to file, you should file a federal income tax return to get money back if any of the following conditions apply.

1. You had federal income tax withheld from your pay.
2. You qualify for the earned income credit. See chapter 38 for more information.
3. You qualify for the additional child tax credit. See chapter 36 for more information.
4. You qualify for the health coverage tax credit. See chapter 39 for more information.

Which Form Should I Use?

You must use one of three forms to file your return: Form 1040EZ, Form 1040A, or Form 1040. (But also see *Does My Return Have To Be on Paper,* later.)

Form 1040EZ

Form 1040EZ is the simplest form to use.
You can use Form 1040EZ if all of the following apply.

1. Your filing status is single or married filing jointly. If you were a nonresident alien at any time in 2005, your filing status must be married filing jointly.
2. You (and your spouse if married filing a joint return) were under age 65 and not blind at the end of 2005. If you were born on January 1, 1941, you are considered to be age 65 at the end of 2005.
3. You do not claim any dependents.
4. Your taxable income is less than $100,000.
5. Your income is only from wages, salaries, tips, unemployment compensation, Alaska Permanent Fund dividends, taxable scholarship and fellowship grants, and taxable interest of $1,500 or less.

6. You did not receive any advance earned income credit (EIC) payments.
7. You do not claim any adjustments to income, such as a deduction for IRA contributions or student loan interest.
8. You do not claim any credits other than the earned income credit.
9. You do not owe any household employment taxes on wages you paid to a household employee.

You must meet all of these requirements to use Form 1040EZ. If you do not, you must use Form 1040A or Form 1040.

Figuring tax. On Form 1040EZ, you can use only the tax table to figure your tax. You cannot use Form 1040EZ to report any other tax.

Form 1040A

If you do not qualify to use Form 1040EZ, you may be able to use Form 1040A.

You can use Form 1040A if all of the following apply.

1. Your income is only from wages, salaries, tips, IRA distributions, pensions and annuities, taxable social security and railroad retirement benefits, taxable scholarship and fellowship grants, interest, ordinary dividends (including Alaska Permanent Fund dividends), capital gain distributions, and unemployment compensation.
2. Your taxable income is less than $100,000.
3. Your adjustments to income are for only the following items.
   a. Educator expenses.
   b. IRA deduction.
   c. Student loan interest deduction.
   d. Tuition and fees deduction.
4. You do not itemize your deductions.
5. Your taxes are from only the following items.
   a. Tax Table.
   b. Alternative minimum tax. (See chapter 32.)
   c. Advance earned income credit (EIC) payments, if you received any. (See chapter 38.)
   d. Recapture of an education credit. (See chapter 37.)
   e. Form 8615, Tax for Children Under Age 14 With Investment Income of More Than $1,600.
   f. Qualified Dividends and Capital Gain Tax Worksheet.
6. You claim only the following tax credits.
   a. The credit for child and dependent care expenses. (See chapter 34.)
   b. The credit for the elderly or the disabled. (See chapter 35.)
   c. The child tax credit. (See chapter 36.)
   d. The additional child tax credit. (See chapter 36.)
   e. The education credits. (See chapter 37.)
   f. The retirement savings contributions credit. (See chapter 39.)
   g. The earned income credit. (See chapter 38.)
   h. The adoption credit. (See chapter 39.)

7. You did not have an alternative minimum tax adjustment on stock you acquired from the exercise of an incentive stock option. (See Publication 525, Taxable and Nontaxable Income.)

You must meet all of the above requirements to use Form 1040A. If you do not, you must use Form 1040.

If you meet the above requirements, you can use Form 1040A even if you received employer-provided adoption benefits or dependent care benefits.

Caution. *If you receive a capital gain distribution that includes unrecaptured section 1250 gain, section 1202 gain, or collectibles (28%) gain, you cannot use Form 1040A. You must use Form 1040.*

Form 1040

If you cannot use Form 1040EZ or Form 1040A, you must use Form 1040. You can use Form 1040 to report all types of income, deductions, and credits.

You may have received Form 1040A or Form 1040EZ in the mail because of the return you filed last year. If your situation has changed this year, it may be to your advantage to file Form 1040 instead. You may pay less tax by filing Form 1040 because you can take itemized deductions, some adjustments to income, and credits you cannot take on Form 1040A or Form 1040EZ.

You must use Form 1040 if any of the following apply.

1. Your taxable income is $100,000 or more.
2. You itemize your deductions.
3. You had income that cannot be reported on Form 1040EZ or Form 1040A, including tax-exempt interest from private activity bonds issued after August 7, 1986.
4. You claim any adjustments to gross income other than the adjustments listed earlier under *Form 1040A.*
5. Your Form W-2, box 12, shows uncollected employee tax (social security and Medicare tax) on tips (see chapter 7) or group-term life insurance (see chapter 6).
6. You received $20 or more in tips in any one month and did not report all of them to your employer. (See chapter 7.)
7. You claim any credits other than the credits listed earlier under *Form 1040A.*
8. You owe the excise tax on insider stock compensation from an expatriated corporation.
9. You have to file other forms with your return to report certain exclusions, taxes, or transactions.

Does My Return Have To Be on Paper?

You may be able to file a paperless return using IRS *e-file* (electronic filing). It's so easy, over 66 million taxpayers preferred *e-file* over filing a paper tax return last year.

This section explains how to *e-file*:

• Using an Authorized IRS *e-file* Provider,

- Using your personal computer, or
- Using a telephone (TeleFile).

TaxPlanner

For more information about e-filing, see Chapter 46, *Everything You Need to Know About E-filing.*

IRS *e-file*

Table 1-4 lists the benefits of IRS *e-file*. IRS *e-file* uses automation to replace most of the manual steps needed to process paper returns. As a result, the processing of *e-file* returns is faster and more accurate than the processing of paper returns. However, as with a paper return, you are responsible for making sure your return contains accurate information and is filed on time.

Using *e-file* does not affect your chances of an IRS examination of your return.

Example
You expect a $3,000 refund. If you can receive your refund in 3 weeks by filing electronically instead of 3 months by filing a paper form, you could save money by investing the refund sooner. Assuming you can earn 3% after tax on your money, you might save $15. However, the company that files your return electronically will usually charge you a separate fee for this service. This should be considered in your decision to file electronically.

Electronic signatures. Create your own personal identification number (PIN) and use a tax professional or file your own paperless return electronically. If you are married filing jointly, you and your spouse will each need to create a PIN and enter these PINs as your electronic signatures.

A PIN is any combination of five numbers, except five zeros. If you use a PIN, there is nothing to sign and nothing to mail—not even your Forms W-2.

To verify your identity, you will be asked to enter your adjusted gross income (AGI) from your originally filed 2004 income tax return, if applicable. Do not use your AGI from an amended return (Form 1040X), math error notice, or other changed amount from the IRS. AGI is the amount shown on your 2004 Form 1040, line 36; Form 1040A, line 21; Form 1040EZ, line 4; and on the TeleFile Tax Record, line I. If you do not have your 2004 income tax return, call the IRS at 1-800-829-1040 to get a free transcript of your account. You will also be asked to enter your date of birth (DOB). Make sure your DOB is accurate and matches the information on record with the Social Security Administration by checking your annual Social Security Statement.

Caution. *You cannot sign your return electronically if you are a first-time filer under age 16 at the end of 2005, or if you are filing Form 3115, 3468 (if attachments are required), 5713, 8283 (if completing Section B), 8332, 8858, or 8885.*

For more details on the PIN method, visit *www.irs.gov/efile* and click on "IRS *e-file* for Individual Taxpayers."

Tip. *An Authorized IRS* e-file *Provider can, with your authorization, generate a PIN for you.*

Forms 8453 and 8453-OL. Your return is not complete without your signature. If you are not eligible or choose not to sign your return electronically, you must complete, sign, and file Form 8453, U.S. Individual Income Tax Declaration for an IRS *e-file* Return, or Form 8453-OL, U.S. Individual Income Tax Declaration for an IRS *e-file* Online Return, whichever applies.

State returns. In most states, you can file an electronic state return simultaneously with your federal return. For more information, check with your local IRS office, state tax agency, tax professional, or the IRS web site at *www.irs.gov/efile*.

Refunds. You can have a refund check mailed to you, or you can have your refund deposited directly to your checking or savings account.

With *e-file*, your refund will be issued in half the time as when filing on paper. If you choose direct deposit, you can receive your refund in as few as 10 days.

Explanation: Direct Deposit Refunds
Direct Deposit refunds will usually be issued 2 to 3 weeks from the date the electronic return is accepted. However, the Treasury Department does not guarantee that a refund will be issued by a specific date or for the anticipated amount. Direct Deposit is quickest when

Table 1-4. **Benefits of IRS *e-file***

Free File Options!	• At least 60 percent of taxpayers are eligible to use free commercial online tax preparation software to *e-file*.
	• Visit *www.irs.gov/efile* to see if you qualify and to access these free services offered by the tax software industry (not the IRS).
Fast! Easy! Convenient!	• Get your refund in half the time as paper filers do, even faster and safer with Direct Deposit—in as few as 10 days.
	• Sign electronically and file a completely paperless return.
	• Receive an electronic proof of receipt within 48 hours that the IRS received your return.
	• If you owe, you can *e-file* and authorize an electronic funds withdrawal or pay by credit card. If you *e-file* before April 17, 2006, you can schedule an electronic funds withdrawal from your checking or savings account as late as April 17, 2006.
	• Prepare and file your federal and state returns together and save time.
Accurate! Secure!	• IRS computers quickly and automatically check for errors or other missing information.
	• The chance of being audited does not differ whether you *e-file* or file a paper tax return.
	• Your bank account information is safeguarded along with other tax return information. The IRS does not have access to credit card numbers.

used in conjunction with e-filing, however it can be used regardless of the method used to file your return.

The following conditions may delay refunds and/or change refund amounts. Direct Deposit elections generally will not be honored in these cases:

1. You owe back taxes, either individual or business.
2. You owe delinquent child support.
3. You have a certain delinquent debt, such as student loans.
4. The last name and Social Security number of the primary taxpayer are not the same as on last year's return. If this is the case, the return will be delayed at least 1 week for rematching.
5. The estimated tax payments reported on the return do not match the estimated tax payments recorded on the IRS master file. This generally occurs when:
   a. The spouse made separate payments and filed a joint return, or vice versa; or
   b. The return was filed before the January 15, 2006, estimated tax payment was credited to the taxpayer's account.
6. You have a Schedule E claiming a deduction for a questionable tax shelter.
7. You are claiming a blatantly unallowable deduction.

TAXPLANNER

A refund anticipation loan (RAL) is a loan made to you based on your expected refund. The loan is a contract between you and a financial institution. Generally, the financial institution will require that you sign an authorization that permits the institution to debit your account after the refund has been credited to it. You can expect to pay a fee to the electronic filer, who, with your permission, submits information to the financial institution, and a fee to the financial institution. These fees are in addition to the tax preparation fee and electronic filing fee. Generally, Direct Deposit takes 2 to 3 weeks before you receive your refund. An RAL could speed up the time for you to have your money by about 2 weeks but at a relatively high "interest cost." For example, if your expected refund is $1,000 and the fee is $30, the "interest cost" to you for the 2 weeks' use of the money comes to over 75% on an annualized basis.

As with a paper return, you may not get all of your refund if you owe certain past-due amounts, such as federal tax, state tax, a student loan, or child support. See *Offset against debts* under *Refunds*, later.

Explanation:
Composition of an Electronic Return

In total, an electronic return contains the same information as a comparable return filed entirely on paper documents. An electronic return consists of:

1. Electronic portion of return—Data transmitted to the IRS electronically
2. Nonelectronic portion of return—Paper documents (filed with the IRS at a later date) that contain information that cannot be electronically transmitted, such as taxpayer signatures and documents prepared by third parties

Electronic Portion of Return

For 2005 returns, most forms and schedules, including Form 1040 and Form 1040A, can be transmitted electronically and are considered the "electronic portion" of the return.

Nonelectronic Portion of Return

Some parts of your return *cannot* be filed electronically, including the following:

- Form 8453, *U.S. Individual Income Tax Declaration for Electronic Filing*, required for all electronic returns
- Copy B Form W-2, Form W-2G, or Form 1099-R, which would normally be attached to the front of a paper return
- Other information documents that are voluntarily being included with the return by the taxpayer as supporting material

Exclusions from Electronic Filing

The following are some of the types of returns that are excluded from electronic filing:

Decedent returns, including joint returns filed by surviving spouses

Returns with a power of attorney currently in effect for the refund to be sent to a third party

Returns subject to community property rules with filing status "Married Filing Separately"

Returns with Social Security numbers within the range 900-00-0000 through 999-99-9998. These are temporary Social Security numbers

TAX ALERT

Many states have mandated tax practitioners to e-file the state return. Subject to certain requirements, the following states have imposed mandatory e-filing: Alabama, California, Connecticut, Massachusetts, Michigan, Minnesota, New Jersey, New York, Oklahoma, Rhode Island (legislation pending) Utah, Virginia, and Wisconsin. **Individuals who file their own returns can file on paper or electronically.**

Refund inquiries. If you do not receive your refund within 3 weeks after your electronically-filed return was accepted by IRS, see *Past-Due Refund*, later.

Balance due. If you owe tax, you must pay it by April 17, 2006, to avoid late-payment penalties and interest. You can make your payment electronically by credit card or by scheduling an electronic funds withdrawal from your checking or savings account.

See *How To Pay*, later, for information on how to pay the balance due.

Using an Authorized IRS *e-file* Provider

Many tax professionals electronically file tax returns for their clients. As a taxpayer, you have two options.

1. You can prepare your return, take it to an Authorized IRS *e-file* Provider, and have the provider transmit it electronically to the IRS.
2. You can have a tax professional prepare your return and transmit it for you electronically.

You may personally enter your PIN or complete Form 8879, IRS *e-file* Signature Authorization, to authorize the provider to enter your PIN on your return.

Note. Tax professionals may charge a fee for IRS *e-file*. Fees may vary depending on the professional and the specific services rendered.

Using Your Personal Computer

You can file your tax return in a fast, easy, convenient way using your personal computer. A computer with a modem or Internet access and tax preparation software are all you need. You can *e-file* from the comfort of your home 24 hours a day, 7 days a week. Best of all, you may qualify for Free File.

If you do not qualify for the Free File options, visit our Partners Page for partners that offer other free or low-cost filing options.

IRS-approved tax preparation software is available for online use on the Internet, for download from the Internet, and in retail stores.

For information on Free File, Partners Page, and tax preparation software, visit our website at *www.irs.gov/efile*.

Using a Telephone (TeleFile)

[IRS text intentionally omitted]

TeleFile is no longer available for 2005 returns. Try to e-file instead.

Through Employers and Financial Institutions

Some businesses offer free *e-file* to their employees, members, or customers. Others offer it for a fee. Ask your employer or financial institution if they offer IRS *e-file* as an employee, member, or customer benefit.

Free Help With Your Return

Free help in preparing your return is available nationwide from IRS-trained volunteers. The Volunteer Income Tax Assistance (VITA) program is designed to help low-income taxpayers and the Tax Counseling for the Elderly (TCE) program is designed to assist taxpayers age 60 or older with their tax returns. Many VITA sites offer free electronic filing and all volunteers will let you know about the credits and deductions you may be entitled to claim. To find a site near you, call 1-800-829-1040. Or to find the nearest AARP TaxAide site, visit AARP's website at *www.aarp.org/taxaide* or call 1-888-227-7669. For more information on these programs, go to *www.irs.gov* and enter keyword "VITA" in the upper right-hand corner.

When Do I Have To File?

April 17, 2006, is the due date for filing your 2005 income tax return if you use the calendar year. For a quick view of due dates for filing a return with or without an extension of time to file (discussed later), see Table 1-5.

If you use a fiscal year (a year ending on the last day of any month except December, or a 52-53-week year), your income tax return is due by the 15th day of the 4th month after the close of your fiscal year.

When the due date for doing any act for tax purposes—filing a return, paying taxes, etc.—falls on a Saturday, Sunday, or legal holiday, the due date is delayed until the next business day.

Filing on time. Your paper return is filed on time if it is mailed in an envelope that is properly addressed, has enough postage, and is postmarked by the due date. If you send your return by registered mail, the date of the registration is the postmark date. The registration is evidence that the return was delivered. If you send a return by certified mail and have your receipt postmarked by a postal employee, the date on the receipt is the postmark date. The postmarked certified mail receipt is evidence that the return was delivered.

Private delivery services. If you use a private delivery service designated by the IRS to send your return, the postmark date generally is the date the private delivery service records in its database or marks on the mailing label. The private delivery service can tell you how to get written proof of this date.

The following are designated private delivery services.

- DHL Express (DHL): DHL Same Day Service, DHL Next Day 10:30 am, DHL Next Day 12:00 pm, DHL Next Day 3:00 pm, and DHL 2nd Day Service.
- Federal Express (FedEx): FedEx Priority Overnight, FedEx Standard Overnight, FedEx 2Day, FedEx International Priority, and FedEx International First.
- United Parcel Service (UPS): UPS Next Day Air, UPS Next Day Air Saver, UPS 2nd Day Air, UPS 2nd Day Air A.M., UPS Worldwide Express Plus, and UPS Worldwide Express.

Caution. *Private delivery services cannot deliver items to P.O. boxes. You must use the U.S. Postal Service to mail any item to an IRS P.O. box address.*

Electronically filed returns. If you use IRS *e-file*, your return is considered filed on time if the authorized electronic return transmitter postmarks the transmission by the due date. An authorized electronic return transmitter is a participant in the IRS *e-file* program that transmits electronic tax return information directly to the IRS.

The electronic postmark is a record of when the authorized electronic return transmitter received the transmission of your electronically filed return on its host system. The date and time in your time zone controls whether your electronically filed return is timely.

Filing late. If you do not file your return by the due date, you may have to pay a failure-to-file penalty and interest. For more information, see *Penalties*, later. Also see *Interest* under *Amount You Owe*.

If you were due a refund but you did not file a return, you generally must file within 3 years from the date the return was due (including extensions) to get that refund.

Nonresident alien. If you are a nonresident alien and earn wages subject to U.S. income tax withholding, your 2005 U.S. income tax return (Form 1040NR or Form 1040NR-EZ) is due by:

- April 17, 2006, if you use a calendar year, or
- The 15th day of the 4th month after the end of your fiscal year if you use a fiscal year.

If you do not earn wages subject to U.S. income tax withholding, your return is due by:

Table 1-5. **When To File Your 2005 Return**

For U.S. citizens and residents who file returns on a calendar year.

	For Most Taxpayers	For Certain Taxpayers Outside the U.S.
No extension requested	April 17, 2006	June 15, 2006
Automatic extension Form 4868 filed, or credit card payment made	October 16, 2006	October 16, 2006

- June 15, 2006, if you use a calendar year, or
- The 15th day of the 6th month after the end of your fiscal year, if you use a fiscal year.

Get Publication 519 for more filing information.

Filing for a decedent. If you must file a final income tax return for a taxpayer who died during the year (a decedent), the return is due by the 15th day of the 4th month after the end of the decedent's normal tax year. In most cases, for a 2005 return, this will be April 17, 2006. See *Final Return for the Decedent* in chapter 4.

Extensions of Time To File

You may be able to get an extension of time to file your return. Special rules apply for those who were:

- Outside the United States, or
- Serving in a combat zone.

Automatic Extension

If you cannot file your 2005 return by the due date, you can get an automatic 6-month extension of time to file.

Example. If your return is due on April 17, 2006, you will have until October 16, 2006, to file.

Caution. *If you do not pay the tax due by the regular due date (generally, April 17), you will owe interest. You may also be charged penalties, discussed later.*

How to get the automatic extension. You can get the automatic extension by:

1. Using IRS *e-file* (electronic filing), or
2. Filing a paper form.

***E-file* options.** There are three ways you can use *e-file* to get an extension of time to file. If you *e-file*, you will get a confirmation number when you complete the transaction. Keep the number with your records.

Complete Form 4868, Application for Automatic Extension of Time To File U.S. Individual Income Tax Return, to use as a worksheet. If you think you may owe tax when you file your return, use *Part II* of the form to estimate your balance due. Do not send Form 4868 to the IRS.

***E-file* by phone.** You can file Form 4868 by phone any time from February 2 through April 17, 2006. You will need to provide certain information from your tax return for 2004. If you wish to make a payment by electronic funds withdrawal, see *Electronic payment options*, under *How To Pay*, later in this chapter.

***E-file* using your personal computer or a tax professional.** You can use a tax software package with your personal computer or a tax professional to file Form 4868 electronically. You will need to provide certain information from your tax return for 2004. If you wish to make a payment by electronic funds withdrawal, see *Electronic payment options*, under *How To Pay*, later in this chapter.

***E-file* and pay by credit card.** You can get an extension by paying part or all of your estimate of tax due by using a credit card. You can do this by phone or over the Internet. You do not file Form 4868. See *Credit card*, under *How To Pay*, later in this chapter.

Filing a paper Form 4868. You can get an extension of time to file by filing a paper Form 4868. Mail it to the address shown in the form instructions.

If you want to make a payment with the form, make your check or money order payable to the "United States Treasury." Write your SSN, daytime phone number, and "2005 Form 4868" on your check or money order.

TAXALERT

The IRS offers some relief to taxpayers unable to pay the amount owed with the filing of Form 4868. The IRS permits Form 4868 to be filed and an automatic 6-month extension obtained even though the tax properly estimated to be due is not paid in full when the form is filed. No late filing penalty will be assessed under these circumstances. However, it is still required that the tax liability shown on Form 4868 be properly estimated based on the information available to the taxpayer. Furthermore, unless at least 90% of the taxpayer's actual tax liability was paid prior to the original due date of the return through withholding or estimated payment, a late payment penalty of 0.5% per month will be assessed for each month from the original due date to the date of payment plus the regular rate of interest on underpayments.

When to file. You must request the automatic extension by the due date for your return. You can file your return any time before the 6-month extension period ends.

TAXSAVER

An extension of time to file will not be valid if it does not show a "proper" estimate of tax liability. A proper estimate is based on all the facts and information you have at the time of filing. If your estimate is found to be improper, your extension will be invalid and you will be subject to failure-to-file penalties. See *Penalties*, later.

Some tax experts contend that you should request the maximum extension allowed for filing your return, arguing that your chances of an audit are reduced, because IRS field agents will have less time to conduct the audit. Other tax experts contend that you're better off filing on April 15, because that way you get lost in the crowd. Both theories are oversimplifications of IRS procedures.

When you file your return. Enter any payment you made related to the extension of time to file on line 69, Form 1040. If you file Form 1040EZ or Form 1040A, include that payment in your total payments on line 9 of Form 1040EZ or line 43 of Form 1040A. Also print "Form 4868" and the amount paid in the space to the left of line 9 or line 43.

[IRS text intentionally omitted]

No further extensions. If you are in the United States, an extension of more than 6 months will not be approved.

TAXPLANNER

An extension of time to file is not an extension of time to pay. If you are unable to pay the full amount of tax due with your tax return because of financial hardship, you should still file the tax return along with a "good faith" payment of as much of the tax due as you can afford to pay. You should complete Form 9465 to request the privilege of paying the remaining tax in installments. This form should be attached to the front of the return when it is filed. However, the IRS will impose a $43 fee for entering into an installment agreement. You can expect a decision back from the IRS within 30 days regarding your installment request; but **you still will be subject to interest and the failure-to-pay penalty on the unpaid tax.**

The IRS will continue to send you a bill for the unpaid tax, interest, and penalty until the total amount is paid. After the tax is completely paid, you can request in writing that the penalty be waived due to reasonable cause because of financial hardship. The IRS has total discretion in waiving penalties and may require you to prove your financial hardship.

If your tax return is already in the formal collection process (i.e., you have been contacted by an IRS official regarding a delinquent tax liability) and you are unable to pay the tax due, you may request an installment agreement with the IRS officer. If he or she agrees, the installment agreement is made using Form 433-D, and you will be required to provide financial information. You may need to seek professional tax advice if this is the case.

Individuals Outside the United States

You are allowed an automatic 2-month extension (until June 15, 2006, if you use the calendar year) to file your 2005 return and pay any federal income tax due if:

1. You are a U.S. citizen or resident, and
2. On the due date of your return:
   a. You are living outside of the United States and Puerto Rico, and your main place of business or post of duty is outside the United States and Puerto Rico, or
   b. You are in military or naval service on duty outside the United States and Puerto Rico.

However, if you pay the tax due after the regular due date (generally, April 17), interest will be charged from that date until the date the tax is paid.

If you served in a combat zone or qualified hazardous duty area, you may be eligible for a longer extension of time to file. See *Individuals Serving in Combat Zone*, later, for special rules that apply to you.

Married taxpayers. If you file a joint return, only one spouse has to qualify for this automatic extension. If you and your spouse file separate returns, this automatic extension applies only to the spouse who qualifies.

How to get the extension. To use this special automatic extension, you must attach a statement to your return explaining what situation qualified you for the extension. (See the situations listed under (2), earlier.)

Extensions beyond 2 months. If you cannot file your return within the automatic 2-month extension period, you may be able to get an additional 4-month extension, for a total of 6 months. Generally, you must file a paper Form 4868 by the end of the automatic extension period (usually June 15) to get this additional 4-month extension. Check the box on line 8 of Form 4868.

This additional 4-month extension of time to file is not a further extension of time to pay. You can use a credit card to pay your estimate of tax due. See *How To Pay*, later in this chapter.

[IRS text intentionally omitted]

No further extension. An extension of more than 6 months will generally not be granted. However, if you are outside the United States and meet certain tests, you may be granted a longer extension. For more information, see *Further extensions* under *When To File and Pay* in Publication 54.

Individuals Serving in Combat Zone

The deadline for filing your tax return, paying any tax you may owe, and filing a claim for refund is automatically extended if you serve in a combat zone. This applies to members of the Armed Forces, as well as merchant marines serving aboard vessels under the operational control of the Department of Defense, Red Cross personnel, accredited correspondents, and civilians under the direction of the Armed Forces in support of the Armed Forces.

Combat zone. For purposes of the automatic extension, the term "combat zone" includes the following areas.

1. The Persian Gulf area, effective January 17, 1991.
2. The qualified hazardous duty area of Bosnia and Herzegovina, Croatia, and Macedonia, effective November 21, 1995.
3. The qualified hazardous duty area of the Federal Republic of Yugoslavia (Serbia/Montenegro), Albania, the Adriatic Sea, and the Ionian Sea north of the 39th parallel, effective March 24, 1999.
4. Afghanistan, effective September 19, 2001.

See Publication 3, Armed Forces' Tax Guide, for information about other tax benefits available to military personnel serving in a combat zone.

Extension period. The deadline for filing your return, paying any tax due, and filing a claim for refund is extended for at least 180 days after the later of:

1. The last day you are in a combat zone or the last day the area qualifies as a combat zone, or
2. The last day of any continuous qualified hospitalization for injury from service in the combat zone.

In addition to the 180 days, your deadline is also extended by the number of days you had left to take action with the IRS when you entered the combat zone. For example, you have 3 1/2 months (January 1–April 15) to file your tax return. Any days left in this period when you entered the combat zone (or the entire 3 1/2 months if you entered it before the beginning of the year) are added to the 180 days. See *Extension of Deadline* in Publication 3 for more information.

The above rules on the extension for filing your return also apply when you are deployed outside the United States (away from your permanent duty station) while participating in a designated contingency operation.

How Do I Prepare My Return?

This section explains how to get ready to fill in your tax return and when to report your income and expenses. It also explains how to complete certain sections of the form. You may find Table 1-6 helpful when you prepare your return.

In most cases, based on what you filed last year, the IRS will mail you Form 1040, Form 1040A, or Form 1040EZ with related instructions. (A TeleFile package will no longer be mailed.) Before you fill in the form, look at the form instructions to see if you need, or would benefit from filing, a different form this year. Also see if you need any additional forms or schedules. You may also want to read *Does My Return Have To Be on Paper*, earlier.

Table 1-6.   Six Steps for Preparing Your Return

1 — Get your records together for income and expenses.
2 — Get the forms, schedules, and publications you need.
3 — Fill in your return.
4 — Check your return to make sure it is correct.
5 — Sign and date your return.
6 — Attach all required forms and schedules.

If you do not receive a tax return package in the mail, or if you need other forms, you can order them or print them from the Internet. See *How To Get Tax Help* in the back of this publication.

Substitute tax forms. You cannot use your own version of a tax form unless it meets the requirements explained in Publication 1167, General Rules and Specifications for Substitute Forms and Schedules.

Form W-2. If you are an employee, you should receive Form W-2 from your employer. You will need the information from this form to prepare your return. See *Form W-2* under *Credit for Withholding and Estimated Tax* in chapter 5.

If you do not receive Form W-2 by January 31, 2006, contact your employer. If you still do not get the form by February 15, the IRS can help you by requesting the form from your employer. When you request IRS help, be prepared to provide the following information.

- Your name, address (including zip code), and phone number.
- Your SSN.
- Your dates of employment.
- Your employer's name, address (including zip code), and phone number.

Form 1099. If you received certain types of income, you may receive a Form 1099. For example, if you received taxable interest of $10 or more, the payer generally must give you a Form 1099-INT. If you have not received it by January 31, 2006, contact the payer. If you still do not get the form by February 15, call the IRS for help.

When Do I Report My Income and Expenses?

You must figure your taxable income on the basis of a tax year. A "tax year" is an annual accounting period used for keeping records and reporting income and expenses. You must account for your income and expenses in a way that clearly shows your taxable income. The way you do this is called an accounting method. This section explains which accounting periods and methods you can use.

Accounting Periods

Most individual tax returns cover a calendar year—the 12 months from January 1 through December 31. If you do not use a calendar year, your accounting period is a fiscal year. A regular fiscal year is a 12-month period that ends on the last day of any month except December. A 52-53-week fiscal year varies from 52 to 53 weeks and always ends on the same day of the week.

You choose your accounting period (tax year) when you file your first income tax return. It cannot be longer than 12 months.

TAXPLANNER

To operate on a fiscal year accounting basis, you must keep your books and records based on that fiscal year. Because most individual taxpayers keep their personal financial records on a calendar year basis, it is easier to use a calendar year period.

It is virtually impossible for an individual to secure permission to change to a fiscal year accounting period without justification. Usually, the justification must be that you are involved in a cyclical business from which self-employment or partnership income flows. Furthermore, in most cases, that income has to be your sole or principal source of income.

More information. For more information on accounting periods, including how to change your accounting period, see Publication 538, Accounting Periods and Methods.

Accounting Methods

Your accounting method is the way you account for your income and expenses. Most taxpayers use either the cash method or an accrual method. You choose a method when you file your first income tax return. If you want to change your accounting method after that, you generally must get IRS approval.

Cash method. If you use this method, report all items of income in the year in which you actually or constructively receive them. Generally, you deduct all expenses in the year you actually pay them. This is the method most individual taxpayers use.

Explanation
Accounting methods are important because they determine when you recognize income and when you deduct expenses for tax purposes. The cash method allows you more flexibility and control over your tax liability.

Individuals who do not own and operate their own business *must* use the cash method. However, the IRS will not permit you to use the cash method if you own your own business and if inventories of unsold goods or materials are on hand at the end of the year.

TAXALERT

IRS officials have expressed the view that you may not use the cash method for any substantial business activity, even one providing only personal or professional services. The law does not support this view. Nevertheless, in conducting audits, the IRS has been aggressive in urging taxpayers to change to the accrual method of accounting.

TAXPLANNER

Generally, most taxpayers who expect to be in the same tax bracket from one year to the next and who want to reduce their current tax bill as much as possible should attempt to defer income to a subsequent year and to take deductions in the current year. (If you suspect you might be in a higher tax bracket in a subsequent year, however, you would want to do just the opposite.)

You might consider lumping together your deductions in a single year. For example, in some states and cities, you may pay property, state, and local income taxes in either December or January, giving you the opportunity to pay 2 years' worth of these taxes in a single calendar year. You can also control when you make charitable contributions. To some extent, you can also control when you make interest payments on a mortgage.

Constructive receipt. Generally, you constructively receive income when it is credited to your account or set apart in any way that makes it available to you. You do not need to have physical possession of it. For example, interest credited to your bank account on December 31, 2005, is taxable income to you in 2005 if you could have withdrawn it in 2005 (even if the amount is not entered in your passbook or withdrawn until 2006).

Garnisheed wages. If your employer uses your wages to pay your debts, or if your wages are attached or garnisheed, the full amount is constructively received by you. You must include these wages in income for the year you would have received them.

Brokerage and other accounts. Profits from a brokerage account, or similar account, are fully taxable in the year you earn them. This is true even if:

1. You do not withdraw the earnings,
2. The credit balance in the account may be reduced or eliminated by losses in later years, or
3. Current profits are used to reduce or eliminate a debit balance from previous years.

Example
You sold your ABC Company stock on December 15, 2005, realizing a gain of $5,000. You did not withdraw the cash in your account until January 6, 2006. The gain is taxable income to you for 2005.

Debts paid for you. If another person cancels or pays your debts (but not as a gift or loan), you have constructively received the amount and generally must include it in your gross income for the year. See *Canceled Debts* in chapter 13 for more information.

Example
Your new employer pays the balance of the mortgage due on your home that is not covered by the selling price so you can move to Florida to work for him. The payments are not intended to be a gift or a loan to you. The amount your employer pays on the mortgage is income to you in the year that he pays it.

Payment to third party. If a third party is paid income from property you own, you have constructively received the income. It is the same as if you had actually received the income and paid it to the third party.

Payment to an agent. Income an agent receives for you is income you constructively received in the year the agent receives it. If you indicate in a contract that your income is to be paid to another person, you must include the amount in your gross income when the other person receives it.

Explanation
The IRS considers you to have received income in the year that your agent receives it, but if a person who is not your agent or creditor receives your income, then you do not have to consider that amount as income until you personally obtain it. The key question is whether you can control the receipt of the income during the year. If you can, the income is taxable to you in that year.

Example
ABC Company mailed you a $500 dividend check on December 9, 2005. The post office inadvertently delivered the check on December 31 to Mr. Wheat on the other side of town. You didn't receive the check until January 6, 2006. The $500 in dividends is taxable to you in 2006, because Mr. Wheat was not your agent. You should carefully explain this turn of events when you prepare your return because the IRS document-matching program will have a Form 1099 from ABC Company that lists the $500 as having been paid to you in 2005.

TAXPLANNER

It is possible to structure a sale of property so that the sale funds are deposited in an escrow account and then disbursed to you in the next tax year. The advantage to you in this arrangement is that you have the security of knowing that the sale proceeds exist, but, at the same time, you're able to defer taxes on the funds until they become income to you in the following tax year. To do this, the escrow arrangement must be agreed on by both the buyer and the seller. The arrangement must follow other specific guidelines as well. You will need to seek professional advice.

Check received or available. A valid check that was made available to you before the end of the tax year is constructively received by you in that year. A check that was "made available to you" includes a check you have already received, but not cashed or deposited. It also includes, for example, your last paycheck of the year that your employer made available for you to pick up at the office before the end of the year. It is constructively received by you in that year whether or not you pick it up before the end of the year or wait to receive it by mail after the end of the year.

No constructive receipt. There may be facts to show that you did not constructively receive income.

Example. Alice Johnson, a teacher, agreed to her school board's condition that, in her absence, she would receive only the difference between her regular salary and the salary of a substitute teacher hired by the school board. Therefore, Alice did not constructively receive the amount by which her salary was reduced to pay the substitute teacher.

Explanation
The IRS does not consider you to have paid an expense if you use a note in lieu of cash to make the payment. In this case, you have only made a promise to pay sometime in the future. However, the IRS considers you to have made a payment if you use cash borrowed from a third party to pay an expense.

Example
If you give a note to your doctor promising to pay him for medical services already rendered, you have not yet paid the expense in the IRS's eyes. However, if you borrow money from your bank and use the cash to pay your doctor, you have paid the expense for tax purposes. Similarly, if you pay by credit card, you have made the payment for tax purposes. Paying by credit card is just like borrowing from a third party. **More information.** For more information on the determination of medical and dental expenses, see Chapter 23, *Medical and Dental Expenses,* and Publication 502, *Medical and Dental Expenses.*

Exception
Individual Retirement Arrangements. If you qualify for a tax-deductible contribution, you may take a deduction for a contribution to an Individual Retirement Arrangement (IRA) in one year, even though you do not make the actual cash contribution to your account until the following year; that is, you may file your tax return showing a deduction for a contribution to your IRA, although you have not yet made the contribution. The deduction is valid as long as you make the contribution on or before April 15 of the following year, even if you get a filing extension. For example, you can make a contribution to an IRA for tax year 2005 on or before April 17, 2006. For more information, see Chapter 18,

Individual Retirement Arrangements (IRAs), and Publication 590, *Individual Retirement Arrangements (IRAs).*

Accrual method. If you use an accrual method, you generally report income when you earn it, rather than when you receive it. You generally deduct your expenses when you incur them, rather than when you pay them.

Income paid in advance. An advance payment of income is generally included in gross income in the year you receive it. Your method of accounting does not matter as long as the income is available to you. An advance payment may include rent or interest you receive in advance and pay for services you will perform later.

A limited deferral until the next tax year may be allowed for certain advance payments. See Publication 538 for specific information.

Additional information. For more information on accounting methods, including how to change your accounting method, get Publication 538.

Social Security Number

You must enter your social security number (SSN) in the space provided on your return. Be sure the SSN on your return is the same as the SSN on your social security card. If you are married, enter the SSNs for both you and your spouse, whether you file jointly or separately.

If you are filing a joint return, write the SSNs in the same order as the names. Use this same order in submitting other forms and documents to the IRS.

Name change. If you changed your name because of marriage, divorce, etc., immediately notify your Social Security Administration (SSA) office so the name on your tax return is the same as the one the SSA has on its records. This will help prevent delays in issuing your refund and safeguard your future social security benefits.

Dependent's social security number. You must provide the SSN of each dependent you claim, regardless of the dependent's age. This requirement applies to all dependents (not just your children) claimed on your tax return.

Exception. If your child was born and died in 2005 and you do not have an SSN for the child, you may attach a copy of the child's birth certificate instead. If you do, enter "DIED" in column (2) of line 6c (Form 1040 or 1040A).

No social security number. File Form SS-5, Application for a Social Security Card, with your local SSA office to get an SSN for yourself or your dependent. It usually takes about 2 weeks to get an SSN. If you or your dependent is not eligible for an SSN, see *Individual taxpayer identification number (ITIN),* later.

If you are a U.S. citizen or resident alien, you must show proof of age, identity, and citizenship or alien status with your Form SS-5. If you are 12 or older and have never been assigned an SSN, you must appear in person with this proof at an SSA office.

Form SS-5 is available at any SSA office, on the Internet at *www.socialsecurity.gov,* or by calling 1-800-772-1213. If you have any questions about which documents you can use as proof of age, identity, or citizenship, contact your SSA office.

If your dependent does not have an SSN by the time your return is due, you may want to ask for an extension of time to file, as explained earlier under *When Do I Have To File.*

If you do not provide a required SSN or if you provide an incorrect SSN, your tax may be increased and any refund may be reduced.

Adoption taxpayer identification number (ATIN). If you are in the process of adopting a child who is a U.S. citizen or resident and cannot get an SSN for the child until the adoption is final, you can apply for an ATIN to use instead of an SSN.

File Form W-7A, Application for Taxpayer Identification Number for Pending U.S. Adoptions, with the IRS to get an ATIN if all of the following are true.

- You have a child living with you who was placed in your home for legal adoption by an authorized placement agency.
- You cannot get the child's existing SSN even though you have made a reasonable attempt to get it from the birth parents, the placement agency, and other persons.
- You cannot get an SSN for the child from the SSA because, for example, the adoption is not final.
- You cannot get an Individual Taxpayer Identification Number (ITIN) (discussed later) for the child.
- You are eligible to claim the child as a dependent on your tax return.

After the adoption is final, you must apply for an SSN for the child. You cannot continue using the ATIN.

See Form W-7A for more information.

Nonresident alien spouse. If your spouse is a nonresident alien and you file a joint or separate return, your spouse must have either an SSN or an ITIN. If your spouse is not eligible for an SSN, see the next discussion.

Individual taxpayer identification number (ITIN). The IRS will issue you an ITIN if you are a nonresident or resident alien and you do not have and are not eligible to get an SSN. To apply for an ITIN, file Form W-7 with the IRS. It usually takes about 4 to 6 weeks to get an ITIN. Enter this number on your tax return wherever your SSN is requested.

Tip. *If you are applying for an ITIN in order to file your tax return, attach your completed tax return to your Form W-7. See the Form W-7 instructions for how and where to file.*

Alien dependent. If your dependent is a nonresident or resident alien who does not have and is not eligible to get an SSN, file Form W-7 with the IRS to apply for an ITIN. Enter this number on your return wherever the dependent's SSN is requested.

Caution. *An ITIN is for tax use only. It does not entitle you or your dependent to social security benefits or change the employment or immigration status of either of you under U.S. law.*

Penalty for not providing social security number. If you do not include your SSN or the SSN of your spouse or dependent as required, you may have to pay a penalty. See the discussion on *Penalties,* later, for more information.

SSN on correspondence. If you write to the IRS about your tax account, be sure to include your SSN (and the name and SSN of your spouse, if you filed a joint return) in your correspondence. Because your SSN is used to identify your account, this helps the IRS respond to your correspondence promptly.

Presidential Election Campaign Fund

This fund was set up to help pay for presidential election campaigns. If you have a tax liability of at least $3, you may have $3 of your tax liability go to this fund by checking the "Yes" box on Form 1040, Form 1040A, or Form 1040EZ. If you are filing a joint return and have a tax liability of at least $6, your spouse may also have $3 go to the fund. If you check "Yes," it will not change the tax you pay or the refund you will receive.

Computations

The following information on entering numbers on your tax return may be useful in making the return easier to complete.

Rounding off dollars. You may round off cents to whole dollars on your return and schedules. If you do round to whole dollars, you must round all amounts. To round, drop amounts under 50 cents and increase amounts from 50 to 99 cents to the next dollar. For example, $1.39 becomes $1 and $2.50 becomes $3.

If you have to add two or more amounts to figure the amount to enter on a line, include cents when adding the amounts and round off only the total.

Example. You receive two Forms W-2: one showing wages of $5,000.55 and one showing wages of $18,500.73. On Form 1040, line 7, you would enter $23,501 ($5,000.55 + $18,500.73 = $23,501.28), not $23,502 ($5,001 + $18,501).

Equal amounts. If you are asked to enter the smaller or larger of two equal amounts, enter that amount.

Example. Line 1 is $500. Line 3 is $500. Line 5 asks you to enter the smaller of line 1 or 3. Enter $500 on line 5.

Negative amounts. If you need to enter a negative amount, put the amount in parentheses rather than using a minus sign. To combine positive and negative amounts, add all the positive amounts together and then subtract the negative amounts.

Attachments

Depending on the form you file and the items reported on your return, you may have to complete additional schedules and forms and attach them to your return.

Tip. *You may be able to file a paperless return using IRS e-file. There's nothing to sign, attach, or mail, not even your Forms W-2.*

Form W-2. Form W-2 is a statement from your employer of wages and other compensation paid to you and taxes withheld from your pay. You should have a Form W-2 from each employer. Be sure to attach a copy of Form W-2 in the place indicated on the front page of your return. Attach it only to the front page of your return, not to any attachments. For more information, see *Form W-2* in chapter 5.

If you received a Form 1099-R, Distributions From Pensions, Annuities, Retirement or Profit-Sharing Plans, IRAs, Insurance Contracts, etc., showing federal income tax withheld, attach a copy of that form in the place indicated on the front page of your return.

Form 1040EZ. There are no additional schedules to file with Form 1040EZ.

Form 1040A. Attach the additional schedules and forms that you had to complete behind the Form 1040A in order by number. If you are filing Schedule EIC, put it last. Do not attach items unless required to do so.

Form 1040. Attach any forms and schedules behind Form 1040 in order of the "Attachment Sequence Number" shown in the upper right corner of the form or schedule. Then arrange all other statements or attachments in the same order as the forms and schedules they relate to and attach them last. Do not attach items unless required to do so.

TAXPLANNER

If you fail to organize your return according to the prescribed sequence numbers, the IRS, upon receipt of your return, will disassemble it and put it back together in the proper order. This procedure may result in the loss of a page of your return, causing some delay in its processing.

Third Party Designee

You can authorize the IRS to discuss your return with a friend, family member, or any other person you choose. If you check the "Yes" box in the *Third party designee* area of your 2005 tax return and provide the information required, you are authorizing:

1. The IRS to call the designee to answer any questions that arise during the processing of your return, and
2. The designee to:
   a. Give information that is missing from your return to the IRS,
   b. Call the IRS for information about the processing of your return or the status of your refund or payments,
   c. Receive copies of notices or transcripts related to your return, upon request, and
   d. Respond to certain IRS notices about math errors, offsets (see *Refunds*, later), and return preparation.

The authorization will automatically end no later than the due date (without any extensions) for filing your 2006 tax return. This is April 16, 2007, for most people.

See your form instructions for more information.

Tip. *If you want to allow the paid preparer who signed your return to discuss it with the IRS, just enter "Preparer" in the space for the designee's name.*

Signatures

You must sign and date your return. If you file a joint return, both you and your spouse must sign the return, even if only one of you had income.

Caution. *If you file a joint return, both spouses are generally liable for the tax, and the entire tax liability may be assessed against either spouse. See chapter 2.*

Tip. *If you e-file your return, you can use an electronic signature to sign your return. See* Does My Return Have To Be on Paper, *earlier.*

If you are due a refund, it cannot be issued unless you have signed your return.

Enter your occupation in the space provided in the signature section. If you file a joint return, enter both your occupation and your spouse's occupation. Entering your daytime phone number may help speed the processing of your return.

When someone can sign for you. You can appoint an agent to sign your return if you are:

1. Unable to sign the return because of disease or injury,
2. Absent from the United States for a continuous period of at least 60 days before the due date for filing your return, or
3. Given permission to do so by the IRS office in your area.

Power of attorney. A return signed by an agent in any of these cases must have a power of attorney (POA) attached that authorizes the agent to sign for you. You can use a POA that states that the agent is granted authority to sign the return, or you can use Form 2848, Power of Attorney and Declaration of Representative. Part I of Form 2848 must state that the agent is granted authority to sign the return.

Unable to sign. If the taxpayer is mentally incompetent and cannot sign the return, it must be signed by a court-appointed representative who can act for the taxpayer.

If the taxpayer is mentally competent but physically unable to sign the return or POA, a valid "signature" is defined under state law. It can be anything that clearly indicates the taxpayer's intent to sign. For example, the taxpayer's "X" with the signatures of two witnesses might be considered a valid signature under a state's law.

Spouse unable to sign. If your spouse is unable to sign for any reason, see *Signing a joint return* in chapter 2.

Child's return. If a child has to file a tax return but cannot sign the return, the child's parent, guardian, or another legally responsible person must sign the child's name, followed by the words "By (your signature), parent for minor child."

Paid Preparer

Generally, anyone you pay to prepare, assist in preparing, or review your tax return must sign it and fill in the other blanks in the paid preparer's area of your return.

A paid preparer can sign the return manually or use a rubber stamp, mechanical device, or computer software program. The preparer is personally responsible for affixing his or her signature to the return.

If the preparer is self-employed (that is, not employed by any person or business to prepare the return), he or she should check the self-employed box in the *Paid Preparer's Use Only* space on the return.

The preparer must give you a copy of your return in addition to the copy filed with the IRS.

If you prepare your own return, leave this area blank. If another person prepares your return and does not charge you, that person should not sign your return.

If you have questions about whether a preparer must sign your return, contact any IRS office.

Explanation

Paid preparer authorization. In the signature area of your 2005 tax return, you are asked whether the IRS can discuss the return with the paid preparer who signed the return. If you check the "Yes" box, you are authorizing:

1) The IRS to call the paid preparer to answer any questions that arise during the processing of your return, and
2) The paid preparer to:
   a) Give information that is missing from your return to the IRS,
   b) Call the IRS for information about the processing of your return or the status of your refund or payments, and
   c) Respond to certain IRS notices that you have shown the preparer. These notices about math errors, offsets (see *Refunds,* later), and return preparation will be sent to you, not the preparer.

The authorization cannot be revoked. However, for your 2005 tax return, it will automatically end no later than the due date (without any extensions) for filing your 2006 tax return. This is April 16, 2007, for most people. See your form instructions for more information.

TaxAlert

A person who is paid to prepare all or a substantial portion of your income tax return must sign it. In addition, the IRS says that a tax consultant who is paid to review a tax return that you have already prepared and signed is also considered a tax return preparer and must sign it.

If an individual who prepares your return refuses to sign it, you are probably dealing with someone you should not rely on. While you could still file the return, you should probably consider using another tax preparer. If you have to pay the first preparer, you should report the matter to the IRS.

Refunds

When you complete your return, you will determine if you paid more income tax than you owed. If so, you can get a refund of the amount you overpaid or, if you file Form 1040 or Form 1040A, you can choose to apply all or part of the overpayment to your next year's (2006) estimated tax. You cannot have your overpayment applied to your 2006 estimated tax if you file Form 1040EZ.

Caution. *If you choose to have a 2005 overpayment applied to your 2006 estimated tax, you cannot change your mind and have any of it refunded to you after the due date (without extensions) of your 2005 return.*

Follow the form instructions to complete the entries to claim your refund and/or to apply your overpayment to your 2006 estimated tax.

Tip. *If your refund for 2005 is large, you may want to decrease the amount of income tax withheld from your pay in 2006. See chapter 5 for more information.*

Explanation

If you choose to apply all or part of your overpayment to your next year's estimated tax, the estimated tax installment payment is considered made on April 15. Your first installment may be reduced accordingly. For more information, see Chapter 5, *Tax Withholding and Estimated Tax,* and Publication 505, *Tax Withholding and Estimated Tax.*

Direct Deposit. Instead of getting a paper check, you may be able to have your refund deposited directly into your account at a bank or other financial institution. Follow the form instructions to request direct deposit.

If the direct deposit cannot be done, the IRS will send a check instead.

Overpayment less than one dollar. If your overpayment is less than one dollar, you will not get a refund unless you ask for it in writing.

Cashing your refund check. Cash your tax refund check soon after you receive it. Checks not cashed within 12 months of the date they are issued will be canceled and the proceeds returned to the IRS.

If your check has been canceled, you can apply to the IRS to have it reissued.

Refund more or less than expected. If you receive a check for a refund you are not entitled to, or for an overpayment that should have been credited to estimated tax, do not cash the check. Call the IRS.

If you receive a check for more than the refund you claimed, do not cash the check until you receive a notice explaining the difference.

If your refund check is for less than you claimed, it should be accompanied by a notice explaining the difference. Cashing the check does not stop you from claiming an additional amount of refund.

If you did not receive a notice and you have any questions about the amount of your refund, you should wait 2 weeks. If you still have not received a notice, call the IRS.

Offset against debts. If you are due a refund but have not paid certain amounts you owe, all or part of your refund may be used to pay all or part of the past-due amount. This includes past-due federal income tax, other federal debts (such as student loans), state income tax, and child and spousal support payments. You will be notified if the refund you claimed has been offset against your debts.

Joint return and injured spouse. When a joint return is filed and only one spouse owes a past-due amount, the other spouse can be considered an injured spouse. An injured spouse can get a refund for his or her share of the overpayment that would otherwise be used to pay the past-due amount.

To be considered an injured spouse, you must:

1. File a joint return, and
2. Have reported income (such as wages, interest, etc.), or
3. Have made and reported tax payments (such as federal income tax withheld from wages or estimated tax payments), or claimed the earned income credit or other refundable credit, and
4. Not be required to pay the past-due amount.

Note. If the injured spouse's permanent home is in a community property state, then the injured spouse must only meet (1) and (4) above. For more information, see Publication 555, Community Property.

If you are an injured spouse, you must file Form 8379, Injured Spouse Claim and Allocation, to have your portion of the overpayment refunded to you. Follow the instructions on the form.

If you have not filed your joint return and you know that your joint refund will be offset, file Form 8379 with your return. You should receive your refund within 14 weeks from the date the paper return is filed or within 11 weeks from the date the return is filed electronically.

If you filed your joint return and your joint refund was offset, file Form 8379 by itself. When filed after offset, it can take up to 8 weeks to receive your refund. Do not attach the previously filed tax return, but do include copies of all Forms W-2 and W-2G for both spouses and any Forms 1099 that show income tax withheld.

Generally, you must file Form 8379 no later than 6 years from the date you are notified of the offset (3 years if the offset was used to pay federal tax debt). A separate Form 8379 must be filed for each tax year to be considered.

Caution. *An injured spouse claim is different from an innocent spouse relief request. An injured spouse uses Form 8379 to request the division of the tax overpayment attributed to each spouse. An innocent spouse uses Form 8857, Request for Innocent Spouse Relief, to request relief from joint liability for tax, interest, and penalties on a joint return for items of the other spouse (or former spouse) that were incorrectly reported on the joint return. For information on innocent spouses, see* Relief from joint liability *under* Filing a Joint Return *in chapter 2.*

Amount You Owe

When you complete your return, you will determine if you have paid the full amount of tax that you owe. If you owe additional tax, you should pay it with your return.

If the IRS figures your tax for you, you will receive a bill for any tax that is due. You should pay this bill within 30 days (or by the due date of your return, if later). See *Tax Figured by IRS* in chapter 32.

Caution. *If you do not pay your tax when due, you may have to pay a failure-to-pay penalty. See* Penalties, *later. For more information about your balance due, see Publication 594, The IRS Collection Process.*

Tip. *If the amount you owe for 2005 is large, you may want to increase the amount of income tax withheld from your pay or make estimated tax payments for 2006. See chapter 5 for more information.*

How To Pay

If you have an amount due on your tax return, you can pay by check, money order, or credit card. If you filed electronically, you also may be able to make your payment electronically.

Tip. *You do not have to pay if the amount you owe is less than $1.*

Check or money order. If you pay by check or money order, make it out to the "United States Treasury." Show your correct name, address, SSN, daytime phone number, and the tax year and form number on the front of your check or money order. If you are filing a joint return, enter the SSN shown first on your tax return.

For example, if you file Form 1040 for 2005 and you owe additional tax, show your name, address, SSN, daytime phone number, and "2005 Form 1040" on the front of your check or money order. If you file an amended return (Form 1040X) for 2004 and you owe tax, show your name, address, SSN, daytime phone number, and "2004 Form 1040X" on the front of your check or money order.

Enclose your payment with your return, but do not attach it to the form. If you filed Form 1040, please complete Form 1040-V, Payment Voucher, and enclose it with your payment and return. Form 1040-V will help us process your payment more accurately and efficiently. Follow the instructions that come with the form.

Do not mail cash with your return. If you pay cash at an IRS office, keep the receipt as part of your records.

Payment not honored. If your check or money order is not honored by your bank (or other financial institution) and the IRS does not receive the funds, you still owe the tax. In addition, you may be subject to a dishonored check penalty.

Electronic payment options. Electronic payment options are convenient, safe and secure methods for paying individual income taxes. There's no check to write, money order to buy, or voucher to mail. Payments can be made 24 hours a day, 7 days a week.

Credit card. You can use your American Express®, Discover®, MasterCard®, or Visa® credit card.

To pay by credit card, call a service provider and follow the recorded instructions. You can also pay by credit card over the Internet using a service provider's web site.

The service providers charge a convenience fee based on the amount you are paying. Fees may vary between the providers. You will be told what the fee is during the transaction and will have the option to continue or end the transaction. You may also obtain the convenience fee by calling the service provider's automated customer service telephone number or visiting their respective web site.

Caution. *Do not add the convenience fee to your tax payment.*

TAXPLANNER

Be careful about paying your taxes by credit card. Most of the payment options demand that you pay a "convenience fee" for using your card. The fees are usually not worth the "frequent flyer miles" you might get on the account. Also, if you won't be paying off your balance right away the interest your credit card charges may be much higher than the interest the IRS charges for late payment.

If you pay by credit card, write the confirmation number you were given at the end of the transaction and the tax payment amount in the upper left corner of page 1 of your tax return.

Service Providers

Official Payments Corporation

To make a payment, call	1-800-2PAY-TAXSM
or	1-800-272-9829
For Customer Service	1-877-754-4413
Web Address	www.officialpayments.com

Link2Gov Corporation

To make a payment, call	1-888-PAY-1040SM
or	1-888-729-1040
For Customer Service	1-888-658-5465
Web Address	www.PAY1040.com

You can *e-file* and pay in a single step by authorizing a credit card payment. This option is available through some tax software packages and tax professionals. You can also pay by credit card using the telephone or the Internet.

Electronic funds withdrawal. You can *e-file* and pay in a single step by authorizing an electronic funds withdrawal from your checking or savings account. This option is available through tax software packages, tax professionals, and TeleFile. If you select this payment option, you will need to have your account number, your financial institution's routing transit number, and account type (checking or savings). You can schedule the payment for any future date up to and including the return due date (April 17, 2006).

Caution. *Be sure to check with your financial institution to make sure that an electronic funds withdrawal is allowed and to get the correct routing and account numbers.*

Electronic Federal Tax Payment System (EFTPS). EFTPS is a free tax payment system that all individual and business taxpayers can use. You can make payments online or by phone.

Here are just a few of the benefits of this easy-to-use system.

- Convenient and flexible. You can use it to schedule payments in advance. For example, you can schedule estimated tax payments (Form 1040-ES) or installment agreement payments weekly, monthly, or quarterly.
- Fast and accurate. You can make a tax payment in minutes. Because there are verification steps along the way, you can check and review your information before sending it.
- Safe and secure. It offers the highest available levels of security. Every transaction receives an immediate confirmation.

For more information or details on enrolling, visit *www.EFTPS.gov* or call EFTPS Customer Service at 1-800-555-4477.

Estimated tax payments. Do not include any 2006 estimated tax payment in the payment for your 2005 income tax return. See chapter 5 for information on how to pay estimated tax.

Interest

Interest is charged on tax you do not pay by the due date of your return. Interest is charged even if you get an extension of time for filing. **Tip.** *If the IRS figures your tax for you, interest cannot start earlier than the 31st day after the IRS sends you a bill. For information, see* Tax Figured by IRS *in chapter 32.*

Interest on penalties. Interest is charged on the failure-to-file penalty, the accuracy-related penalty, and the fraud penalty from the due date of the return (including extensions) to the date of payment. Interest on other penalties starts on the date of notice and demand, but is not charged on penalties paid within 21 calendar days from the date of the notice (or within 10 business days if the notice is for $100,000 or more).

Interest due to IRS error or delay. All or part of any interest you were charged can be forgiven if the interest is due to an unreasonable error or delay by an officer or employee of the IRS in performing a ministerial or managerial act.

A ministerial act is a procedural or mechanical act that occurs during the processing of your case. A managerial act includes personnel transfers and extended personnel training. A decision concerning the proper application of federal tax law is not a ministerial or managerial act.

The interest can be forgiven only if you are not responsible in any important way for the error or delay and the IRS has notified you in writing of the deficiency or payment. For more information, get Publication 556, Examination of Returns, Appeal Rights, and Claims for Refund.

Interest and certain penalties may also be suspended for a limited period if you filed your return by the due date (including extensions) and the IRS does not provide you with a notice specifically stating your liability and the basis for it before the close of the 18-month period beginning on the later of:

- The date the return is filed, or
- The due date of the return without regard to extensions.

For more information, get Publication 556.

TAXPLANNER

If you owe additional tax, it is *not* a good idea to file your return by January 31. As long as you have planned well and have paid enough in estimated taxes to avoid a penalty, you would be better off keeping any other tax you owe in your savings account, where it will earn interest for 2 1/2 months, rather than paying your tax bill early.

Installment Agreement

If you cannot pay the full amount due with your return, you can ask to make monthly installment payments for the full or a partial amount. However, you will be charged interest and may be charged a late payment penalty on the tax not paid by April 17, 2006, even if your request to pay in installments is granted. If your request is granted, you must also pay a fee. To limit the interest and penalty charges, pay as much of the tax as possible with your return. But before requesting an installment agreement, you should consider other less costly alternatives, such as a bank loan.

To ask for an installment agreement, use Form 9465, Installment Agreement Request. You should receive a response to your request within 30 days. But if you file your return after March 31, it may take longer for a reply.

In addition to paying by check or money order, you can use a credit card or EFTPS to make installment agreement payments. See *Credit card* and *Electronic Federal Tax Payment System (EFTPS),* under *How To Pay,* earlier.

Guaranteed availability of installment agreement. The IRS must agree to accept the full payment of your tax liability in installments if, as of the date you offer to enter into the agreement:

1. Your total taxes (not counting interest, penalties, additions to the tax, or additional amounts) do not exceed $10,000,
2. In the last 5 years, you (and your spouse if the liability relates to a joint return) have not:
   a. Failed to file any required income tax return,
   b. Failed to pay any tax shown on any such return, or
   c. Entered into an installment agreement for the payment of any income tax,
3. You show you cannot pay your income tax in full when due,
4. The tax will be paid in full in 3 years or less, and
5. You agree to comply with the tax laws while your agreement is in effect.

Gift To Reduce Debt Held by the Public

You can make a contribution (gift) to reduce debt held by the public. If you wish to do so, make a separate check payable to "Bureau of the Public Debt."

Send your check to:

Bureau of the Public Debt
Department G
P.O. Box 2188
Parkersburg, WV 26106-2188.

Or, enclose your separate check in the envelope with your income tax return. Do not add this gift to any tax you owe.

You can deduct this gift as a charitable contribution on next year's tax return if you itemize your deductions on Schedule A (Form 1040).

Peel-Off Address Label

After you have completed your return, peel off the label with your name and address from the back of your tax return package and place it in the appropriate area of the Form 1040, Form 1040A, or Form 1040EZ you send to the IRS. If you have someone prepare your return, give that person your label to use on your tax return.

If you file electronically and you are not eligible or choose not to sign your return using your PIN, use your label on Form 8453 or 8453-OL. (More information on electronic filing is found earlier in this chapter.)

The label helps the IRS to correctly identify your account. It also saves processing costs and speeds up processing so that refunds can be issued sooner.

Caution. *You must write your SSN in the spaces provided on your tax return.*

Correcting the label. Make necessary name and address changes on the label. If you have an apartment number that is not shown on the label, please write it in. If you changed your name, see the discussion under *Social Security Number,* earlier.

No label. If you did not receive a tax return package with a label, print or type your name and address in the spaces provided at the top of Form 1040 or Form 1040A. If you are married filing a separate return, do not enter your spouse's name in the space at the top. Instead, enter his or her name in the space provided on line 3.

If you file Form 1040EZ and you do not have a label, print or type this information in the spaces provided.

P.O. box. If your post office does not deliver mail to your street address and you have a P.O. box, print your P.O. box number on the line for your present home address instead of your street address.

Foreign address. If your address is outside the United States or its possessions or territories, enter the information on the line for "City, town or post office, state, and ZIP code" in the following order:

1. City,
2. Province or state, and
2. Name of foreign country. (Do not abbreviate the name of the country.)

Follow the country's practice for entering the postal code.

TaxAlert

You are not excused from filing a return because you have not received the proper forms from the IRS. In addition to any IRS office (check the telephone book), you may usually obtain the necessary forms at your local post office, public library, or bank. Forms that you can use to file your return are provided at the back of this book. You may also obtain tax forms via the Internet by visiting the IRS site at www.irs.gov.

Where Do I File?

After you complete your return, you must send it to the IRS. You can mail it or you may be able to file it electronically. See *Does My Return Have To Be on Paper,* earlier.

Mailing your return. If an addressed envelope came with your tax forms package, you should mail your return in that envelope.

If you do not have an addressed envelope or if you moved during the year, mail your return to the address shown at the end of this publication for the area where you now live.

What Happens After I File?

After you send your return to the IRS, you may have some questions. This section discusses concerns you may have about record-keeping, your refund, and what to do if you move.

Where Do You File?

If an envelope addressed to "Internal Revenue Service Center" came with this booklet, please use it. If you do not have one or if you moved during the year, mail your return to the Internal Revenue Service Center shown that applies to you.

 Envelopes without enough postage will be returned to you by the post office. Your envelope may need additional postage if it contains more than five pages or is oversized (for example, it is over ¼" thick). Also, include your complete return address.

IF you live in...	THEN use this address if you:	
	Are not enclosing a check or money order...	Are enclosing a check or money order...
Alabama, Florida, Georgia, Mississippi, North Carolina, Rhode Island, South Carolina, West Virginia	Internal Revenue Service Center Atlanta, GA 39901-0002	Internal Revenue Service Center Atlanta, GA 39901-0102
Maine, Massachusetts, New Hampshire, New York, Vermont	Internal Revenue Service Center Andover, MA 05501-0002	Internal Revenue Service Center Andover, MA 05501-0102
Delaware, Illinois, Indiana, Iowa, Kansas, Michigan, Minnesota, Missouri, Nebraska, North Dakota, South Dakota, Wisconsin	Internal Revenue Service Center Kansas City, MO 64999-0002	Internal Revenue Service Center Kansas City, MO 64999-0102
Connecticut, District of Columbia, Maryland, New Jersey, Pennsylvania	Internal Revenue Service Center Philadelphia, PA 19255-0002	Internal Revenue Service Center Philadelphia, PA 19255-0102
Arkansas, Colorado, Kentucky, Louisiana, New Mexico, Oklahoma, Tennessee, Texas	Internal Revenue Service Center Austin, TX 73301-0002	Internal Revenue Service Center Austin, TX 73301-0102
Alaska, Arizona, California, Hawaii, Idaho, Montana, Nevada, Oregon, Utah, Washington, Wyoming	Internal Revenue Service Center Fresno, CA 93888-0002	Internal Revenue Service Center Fresno, CA 93888-0102
Ohio, Virginia	Internal Revenue Service Center Memphis, TN 37501-0002	Internal Revenue Service Center Memphis, TN 37501-0102
All APO and FPO addresses, American Samoa, nonpermanent residents of Guam or the Virgin Islands*, Puerto Rico *(or if excluding income under Internal Revenue Code section 933),* dual-status aliens, a foreign country: U.S. citizens and those filing Form 2555, 2555-EZ, or 4563	Internal Revenue Service Center Philadelphia, PA 19255-0215 USA	Internal Revenue Service Center Philadelphia, PA 19255-0215 USA

* Permanent residents of Guam should use: Department of Revenue and Taxation, Government of Guam, P.O. Box 23607, GMF, GU 96921; permanent residents of the Virgin Islands should use: V.I. Bureau of Internal Revenue, 9601 Estate Thomas, Charlotte Amalie, St. Thomas, VI 00802.

What Records Should I Keep?

You must keep records so that you can prepare a complete and accurate income tax return. The law does not require any special form of records. However, you should keep all receipts, canceled checks or other proof of payment, and any other records to support any deductions or credits you claim.

If you file a claim for refund, you must be able to prove by your records that you have overpaid your tax.

TaxPlanner

See the detailed listing of tax records to keep at the end of the *Ernst & Young Individual Tax Organizer* in the front of this book.

How long to keep records. You must keep your records for as long as they are important for the federal tax law.

Keep records that support an item of income or a deduction appearing on a return until the period of limitations for the return runs out. (A period of limitations is the period of time after which no legal action can be brought.) For assessment of tax you owe, this generally is 3 years from the date you filed the return. For filing a claim for credit or refund, this generally is 3 years from the date you filed the original return, or 2 years from the date you paid the tax, whichever is later. Returns filed before the due date are treated as filed on the due date.

If you did not report income that you should have reported on your return, and it is more than 25% of the income shown on the return, the period of limitations does not run out until 6 years after you filed the return. If a return is false or fraudulent with intent to evade tax, or if no return is filed, an action can generally be brought at any time.

You may need to keep records relating to the basis of property longer than the period of limitations. Keep those records as long as they are important in figuring the basis of the original or replacement property. Generally, this means for as long as you own the property and, after you dispose of it, for the period of limitations that applies to you. See chapter 14 for information on basis.

Note. If you receive a Form W-2, keep Copy C until you begin receiving social security benefits. This will help protect your benefits in case there is a question about your work record or earnings in a particular year. Review the information shown on your annual (for workers over age 25) Social Security Statement.

Copies of returns. You should keep copies of tax returns you have filed and the tax forms package as part of your records. They may be helpful in amending filed returns or preparing future ones.

If you need a copy of a prior year tax return, you can get it from the IRS. Use Form 4506, Request for Copy of Tax Return. There is a charge for a copy of a return, which you must pay with Form 4506. It may take up to 60 days to process your request.

Transcript of tax return. If you just need information from your return, you can order a transcript by calling 1-800-829-1040, or using Form 4506-T, Request for Transcript of Tax Return. There is no fee for a transcript. Most requests will be processed within 10 business days.

Return transcript. This is available for the current year and the 3 preceding years. A tax return transcript usually contains the information that a third party (such as a mortgage company) requires. You will get the following information from your original return.

- Type of return filed.
- Filing status.
- Tax shown on return.
- Adjusted gross income.
- Mortgage interest.
- Real estate tax deduction.
- Taxable income.
- Number of exemptions.
- Federal income tax withheld.
- Refund per return.
- Earned income credit.
- Self-employment tax paid.

Account transcript. This shows any later changes that you or the IRS made to your original return. In addition to the items shown on a tax return transcript, you will receive the following information.

- Amount of estimated payments.
- Penalty paid or assessed.
- Interest paid or assessed.
- Interest paid to the taxpayer by the IRS.
- Balance due with accruals.

TaxPlanner

We recommend that you keep all your cancelled checks for 6 years. It would be wise to keep your income tax returns permanently. You should keep documents showing your basis in a piece of property for as long as you own that piece of property. If you sell a piece of property, you should keep your records showing your basis in the old property for at least 6 years after the sale.

If you do not keep the requisite records, it may be impossible for you to prove that you incurred deductible expenses or to establish your basis for gain or loss. Without such proof the IRS can deny you a deduction. If you acquire property from an estate or by gift, it is advisable to secure a copy of the valuation of the estate or of the gift tax return so that you can determine the donor's basis in the property that you have been given. When acquiring property from an estate, the basis in the property is generally the fair market value at the date of the decedent's death. When receiving property as a gift, the taxpayer must know the donor's adjusted basis as well as the fair market value at the time of the gift in order to properly determine the basis used in calculating the gain or loss upon disposition. Knowing the donor's basis, you can easily determine your gain or loss when you sell the property. See Chapter 14, *Basis of Property,* for more details on determining gains and losses from the sale of property.

Example

Your parents buy a house for you as a wedding present. You sell the house 10 years later. The only record of the initial transaction is in the county real estate records. You believe there were other costs associated with the purchase but you cannot find any records of them. If you claim the additional unsupported costs and the IRS examines your return for the year of the sale, it's likely that those costs will not be allowed. If you claim the additional costs and do not disclose on your return the lack of records to substantiate them, you could be subject to a penalty.

More information. For more information on recordkeeping, get Publication 552, Recordkeeping for Individuals.

Interest on Refunds

If you are due a refund, you may get interest on it. The interest rates are adjusted quarterly.

If the refund is made within 45 days after the due date of your return, no interest will be paid. If you file your return after the due date (including extensions), no interest will be paid if the refund is made within 45 days after the date you filed. If the refund is not made within this 45-day period, interest will be paid from the due date of the return or from the date you filed, whichever is later.

Accepting a refund check does not change your right to claim an additional refund and interest. File your claim within the period of time that applies. See *Amended Returns and Claims for Refund*, later. If you do not accept a refund check, no more interest will be paid on the overpayment included in the check.

Interest on erroneous refund. All or part of any interest you were charged on an erroneous refund generally will be forgiven. Any interest charged for the period before demand for repayment was made will be forgiven unless:

1. You, or a person related to you, caused the erroneous refund in any way, or
2. The refund is more than $50,000.

For example, if you claimed a refund of $100 on your return, but the IRS made an error and sent you $1,000, you would not be charged interest for the time you held the $900 difference. You must, however, repay the $900 when the IRS asks.

Past-Due Refund

You can check on the status of your 2005 refund if it has been at least 6 weeks from the date you filed your return (3 weeks if you filed electronically). Be sure to have a copy of your 2005 tax return available because you will need to know the filing status, the first SSN shown on the return, and the exact whole-dollar amount of the refund. To check on your refund, do one of the following.

- Go to *www.irs.gov*, and click on "Where's My Refund."
- Call 1-800-829-4477 for automated refund information and follow the recorded instructions.
- Call 1-800-829-1954 during the hours shown in your form instructions.

Change of Address

If you have moved, file your return using your new address.

If you move after you filed your return, you should give the IRS clear and concise written notification of your change of address. Send the notification to the Internal Revenue Service Center serving your old address. You can use Form 8822, Change of Address. If you are expecting a refund, also notify the post office serving your old address. This will help in forwarding your check to your new address (unless you chose direct deposit of your refund).

Be sure to include your SSN (and the name and SSN of your spouse, if you filed a joint return) in any correspondence with the IRS.

What If I Made a Mistake?

Errors may delay your refund or result in notices being sent to you. If you discover an error, you can file an amended return or claim for refund.

Amended Returns and Claims for Refund

You should correct your return if, after you have filed it, you find that:

1. You did not report some income,
2. You claimed deductions or credits you should not have claimed,
3. You did not claim deductions or credits you could have claimed, or
4. You should have claimed a different filing status. (You cannot change your filing status from married filing jointly to married filing separately after the due date of the original return. However, an executor may be able to make this change for a deceased spouse.)

If you need a copy of your return, see *Copies of returns* under *What Records Should I Keep*, earlier in this chapter.

Form 1040X. Use Form 1040X, Amended U.S. Individual Income Tax Return, to correct a return you have already filed. An amended tax return cannot be filed electronically under the *e-file* system.

Completing Form 1040X. On Form 1040X, write your income, deductions, and credits as you originally reported them on your return, the changes you are making, and the corrected amounts. Then figure the tax on the corrected amount of taxable income and the amount you owe or your refund.

If you owe tax, pay the full amount with Form 1040X. The tax owed will not be subtracted from any amount you had credited to your estimated tax.

If you cannot pay the full amount due with your return, you can ask to make monthly installment payments. See *Installment Agreement*, earlier.

If you overpaid tax, you can have all or part of the overpayment refunded to you, or you can apply all or part of it to your estimated tax. If you choose to get a refund, it will be sent separately from any refund shown on your original return.

Filing Form 1040X. After you finish your Form 1040X, check it to be sure that it is complete. Do not forget to show the year of your original return and explain all changes you made. Be sure to attach any forms or schedules needed to explain your changes. Mail your Form 1040X to the Internal Revenue Service Center serving the area where you now live (as shown in the instructions to the form). However, if you are filing Form 1040X in response to a notice you received from the IRS, mail it to the address shown on the notice. Do not use the addresses listed at the end of this publication.

File a separate form for each tax year involved.

Time for filing a claim for refund. Generally, you must file your claim for a credit or refund within 3 years after the date you filed your original return or within 2 years after the date you paid the tax, whichever is later. Returns filed before the due date (without regard to extensions) are considered filed on the due date (even if the due date was a Saturday, Sunday, or legal holiday). These time periods are suspended while you are financially disabled, discussed later.

If the last day for claiming a credit or refund is a Saturday, Sunday, or legal holiday, you can file the claim on the next business day.

If you do not file a claim within this period, you may not be entitled to a credit or a refund.

Late-filed return. If you were due a refund but you did not file a return, you generally must file your return within 3 years from the date the return was due (including extensions) to get that refund. Generally, your return must be postmarked no later than 3 years from the date the return was due (including extensions). For information on postmarks, see *Filing on time*, under *When Do I Have To File*, earlier.

Limit on amount of refund. If you file your claim within 3 years after the date you filed your return, the credit or refund cannot be more than the part of the tax paid within the 3-year period (plus any extension of time for filing your return) immediately before you filed the claim. This time period is suspended while you are financially disabled, discussed later.

Tax paid. Payments, including estimated tax payments, made before the due date (without regard to extensions) of the original return are considered paid on the due date. For example, income tax withheld during the year is considered paid on the due date of the return, April 15 for most taxpayers.

Example 1. You made estimated tax payments of $500 and got an automatic extension of time to August 15, 2003, to file your 2002 income tax return. When you filed your return on that date, you paid an additional $200 tax. On August 17, 2006, you filed an amended return and claimed a refund of $700. Because you filed your claim within 3 years after you filed your original return, you can get a refund of up to $700, the tax paid within the 3 years plus the 4-month extension period immediately before you filed the claim.

Example 2. The situation is the same as in *Example 1*, except you filed your return on October 27, 2003, 2 1/2 months after the extension period ended. You paid an additional $200 on that date. On October 27, 2006, you filed an amended return and claimed a refund of $700. Although you filed your claim within 3 years from the date you filed your original return, the refund was limited to $200, the tax paid within the 3 years plus the 4-month extension period immediately before you filed the claim. The estimated tax of $500 paid before that period cannot be refunded or credited.

If you file a claim more than 3 years after you file your return, the credit or refund cannot be more than the tax you paid within the 2 years immediately before you file the claim.

Example 3. You filed your 2002 tax return on April 15, 2003. You paid taxes of $500. On November 3, 2004, after an examination of your 2002 return, you had to pay an additional tax of $200. On May 15, 2006, you file a claim for a refund of $300. However, because you filed your claim more than 3 years after you filed your return, your refund will be limited to the $200 you paid during the 2 years immediately before you filed your claim.

Financially disabled. The time periods for claiming a refund are suspended for the period in which you are financially disabled. For a joint income tax return, only one spouse has to be financially disabled for the time period to be suspended. You are financially disabled if you are unable to manage your financial affairs because of a medically determinable physical or mental impairment which can be expected to result in death or which has lasted or can be expected to last for a continuous period of not less than 12 months. However, you are not treated as financially disabled during any period your spouse or any other person is authorized to act on your behalf in financial matters.

To claim that you are financially disabled, you must send in the following written statements with your claim for refund.

1. A statement from your qualified physician that includes:
   a. The name and a description of your physical or mental impairment,
   b. The physician's medical opinion that the impairment prevented you from managing your financial affairs,
   c. The physician's medical opinion that the impairment was or can be expected to result in death, or that its duration has lasted, or can be expected to last, at least 12 months,
   d. The specific time period (to the best of the physician's knowledge), and
   e. The following certification signed by the physician: "I hereby certify that, to the best of my knowledge and belief, the above representations are true, correct, and complete."
2. A statement made by the person signing the claim for credit or refund that no person, including your spouse, was authorized to act on your behalf in financial matters during the period of disability (or the exact dates that a person was authorized to act for you).

Exceptions for special types of refunds. If you file a claim for one of the items listed below, the dates and limits discussed earlier may not apply. These items, and where to get more information, are as follows.

- Bad debt. (See *Nonbusiness Bad Debts* in chapter 15.)
- Worthless security. (See *Worthless securities* in chapter 15.)
- Foreign tax paid or accrued. (See Publication 514, Foreign Tax Credit for Individuals.)
- Net operating loss carryback. (See Publication 536, Net Operating Losses (NOLs) for Individuals, Estates, and Trusts.)
- Carryback of certain business tax credits. (See Form 3800, General Business Credit.)
- Claim based on an agreement with the IRS extending the period for assessment of tax.
- Injured spouse claim. (See *Offset against debts*, under *Refunds*, earlier.)

Processing claims for refund. Claims are usually processed shortly after they are filed. Your claim may be accepted as filed, disallowed, or subject to examination. If a claim is examined, the procedures are the same as in the examination of a tax return.

If your claim is disallowed, you will receive an explanation of why it was disallowed.

Taking your claim to court. You can sue for a refund in court, but you must first file a timely claim with the IRS. If the IRS disallows your claim or does not act on your claim within 6 months after you file it, you can then take your claim to court. For information on the burden of proof in a court proceeding, see Publication 556.

The IRS provides a fast method to move your claim to court if:

- You are filing a claim for a credit or refund based solely on contested income tax or on estate tax or gift tax issues considered in your previously examined returns, and
- You want to take your case to court instead of appealing it within the IRS.

When you file your claim with the IRS, you get the fast method by requesting in writing that your claim be immediately rejected. A notice of claim disallowance will then be promptly sent to you.

You have 2 years from the date of mailing of the notice of disallowance to file a refund suit in the United States District Court having jurisdiction or in the United States Court of Federal Claims.

Interest on refund. If you receive a refund because of your amended return, interest will be paid on it from the due date of your original return or the date you filed your original return, whichever is later, to the date you filed the amended return. However, if the refund is not made within 45 days after you file the amended return, interest will be paid up to the date the refund is paid.

Reduced refund. Your refund may be reduced by an additional tax liability that has been assessed against you.

Also, your refund may be reduced by amounts you owe for past-due child support, debts to another federal agency, or for state tax. If your spouse owes these debts, see *Offset against debts*, under *Refunds*, earlier, for the correct refund procedures to follow.

Effect on state tax liability. If your return is changed for any reason, it may affect your state income tax liability. This includes changes made as a result of an examination of your return by the IRS. Contact your state tax agency for more information.

TaxPlanner

The IRS routinely shares information with most states that have state income taxes. If you file an amended federal tax return showing a balance due, you may avoid interest on tax due to the state and any penalties by taking the initiative and filing amended state tax returns when that is appropriate.

Penalties

The law provides penalties for failure to file returns or pay taxes as required.

Civil Penalties

If you do not file your return and pay your tax by the due date, you may have to pay a penalty. You may also have to pay a penalty if you substantially understate your tax, file a frivolous return, or fail to supply your SSN or individual taxpayer identification number. If you provide fraudulent information on your return, you may have to pay a civil fraud penalty.

Filing late. If you do not file your return by the due date (including extensions), you may have to pay a failure-to-file penalty. The penalty is usually 5% for each month or part of a month that a return is late, but not more than 25%. The penalty is based on the tax not paid by the due date (without regard to extensions).

Fraud. If your failure to file is due to fraud, the penalty is 15% for each month or part of a month that your return is late, up to a maximum of 75%.

Return over 60 days late. If you file your return more than 60 days after the due date or extended due date, the minimum penalty is the smaller of $100 or 100% of the unpaid tax.

Exception. You will not have to pay the penalty if you show that you failed to file on time because of reasonable cause and not because of willful neglect.

Paying tax late. You will have to pay a failure-to-pay penalty of 1/2 of 1% (.50%) of your unpaid taxes for each month, or part of a month, after the due date that the tax is not paid. This penalty does not apply during the automatic 4-month extension of time to file period if you paid at least 90% of your actual tax liability on or before the due date of your return and pay the balance when you file the return.

The monthly rate of the failure-to-pay penalty is half the usual rate (.25% instead of .50%) if an installment agreement is in effect for that month. You must have filed your return by the due date (including extensions) to qualify for this reduced penalty.

If a notice of intent to levy is issued, the rate will increase to 1% at the start of the first month beginning at least 10 days after the day that the notice is issued. If a notice and demand for immediate payment is issued, the rate will increase to 1% at the start of the first month beginning after the day that the notice and demand is issued.

This penalty cannot be more than 25% of your unpaid tax. You will not have to pay the penalty if you can show that you had a good reason for not paying your tax on time.

Combined penalties. If both the failure-to-file penalty and the failure-to-pay penalty (discussed earlier) apply in any month, the 5% (or 15%) failure-to-file penalty is reduced by the failure-to-pay penalty. However, if you file your return more than 60 days after the due date or extended due date, the minimum penalty is the smaller of $100 or 100% of the unpaid tax.

Accuracy-related penalty. You may have to pay an accuracy-related penalty if you underpay your tax because:

1. You show negligence or disregard of the rules or regulations, or
2. You substantially understate your income tax.

The penalty is equal to 20% of the underpayment. The penalty will not be figured on any part of an underpayment on which the fraud penalty (discussed later) is charged.

Negligence or disregard. The term "negligence" includes a failure to make a reasonable attempt to comply with the tax law or to exercise ordinary and reasonable care in preparing a return. Negligence also includes failure to keep adequate books and records. You will not have to pay a negligence penalty if you have a reasonable basis for a position you took.

The term "disregard" includes any careless, reckless, or intentional disregard.

Form 1099 series information returns with the amounts of income reported by the payees in their income tax returns. If this document-matching program discloses apparently underreported income, you will receive a notice of additional tax due that may include imposition of a 20% negligence penalty. If you receive an information return showing income paid to you that, through no fault of your own, you did not receive in 2005 or that for some reason is not taxable to you, you should nevertheless report as income on your return the entire amount shown by the information return and subtract from that the amount you believe to be erroneous. Following this procedure usually will avoid automatic generation of the IRS notice and the inconvenience and frustration of corresponding with the IRS to get the matter resolved.

TAXALERT

The penalty in the case of a gross valuation misstatement is 40% of the portion of the underpayment attributable to the misstatement. A gross valuation misstatement is a misstatement with respect to which either the value or adjusted basis claimed on the return for any property is 400% or more of the correct value or adjusted basis. You should keep the necessary documentation in order to avoid the valuation misstatement penalty.

Example
Ted and Joan contributed a property to a charity for which they claimed on their joint return a charitable contribution deduction of $120,000. The property is actually worth only $27,000. Since the value of the property claimed on the return is more than 400% of the correct value, they are subject to a penalty of 40% in the difference between the amount of tax they should have paid if they claimed only $27,000 as a charitable contribution and the amount of tax they actually paid.

Adequate disclosure. You can avoid the penalty for disregard of rules or regulations if you adequately disclose on your return a position that has at least a reasonable basis. See *Disclosure statement*, later.

This exception will not apply to an item that is attributable to a tax shelter. In addition, it will not apply if you fail to keep adequate books and records, or substantiate items properly.

Substantial understatement of income tax. You understate your tax if the tax shown on your return is less than the correct tax. The understatement is substantial if it is more than the larger of 10% of the correct tax or $5,000. However, the amount of the understatement may be reduced to the extent the understatement is due to:

1. Substantial authority, or
2. Adequate disclosure and a reasonable basis.

If an item on your return is attributable to a tax shelter, there is no reduction for an adequate disclosure. However, there is a reduction for a position with substantial authority, but only if you reasonably believed that your tax treatment was more likely than not the proper treatment.

Substantial authority. Whether there is or was substantial authority for the tax treatment of an item depends on the facts and circumstances. Some of the items that may be considered are court opinions, Treasury regulations, revenue rulings, revenue procedures, and notices and announcements issued by the IRS and published in the Internal Revenue Bulletin that involve the same or similar circumstances as yours.

Disclosure statement. To adequately disclose the relevant facts about your tax treatment of an item, use Form 8275, Disclosure Statement. You must also have a reasonable basis for treating the item the way you did.

In cases of substantial understatement only, items that meet the requirements of Revenue Procedure 2003-77 (or later update) are considered adequately disclosed on your return without filing Form 8275.

Use Form 8275-R, Regulation Disclosure Statement, to disclose items or positions contrary to regulations.

Reasonable cause. You will not have to pay a penalty if you show a good reason (reasonable cause) for the way you treated an item. You must also show that you acted in good faith.

Explanation
The IRS's explanation of the penalty for substantial understatement and how to avoid it oversimplifies a very complex situation.

Under regulations issued by the IRS, the following items may generally be considered substantial authority:

- Internal Revenue Code and other statutory provisions
- Temporary and final IRS regulations
- Court cases
- Administrative pronouncements (including revenue rulings and revenue procedures)
- Tax treaties and regulations issued as a result of a treaty
- Congressional intent as reflected in committee reports, joint explanatory statements of managers included in conference committee reports, and statements made in Congress by one of a bill's managers prior to enactment of a bill
- General explanations of tax legislation prepared by the Joint Committee on Taxation (the Blue Book)
- Proposed IRS regulations
- Information or press releases, notices, announcements, and any other similar documents published by the IRS in the *Internal Revenue Bulletin*
- Private letter rulings, technical advice memoranda, actions on decisions, and general counsel memoranda after they have been released to the public, if they are dated after March 12, 1981

Frivolous return. You may have to pay a penalty of $500 if you file a frivolous return. A frivolous return is one that does not include enough information to figure the correct tax or that contains information clearly showing that the tax you reported is substantially incorrect.

You will have to pay the penalty if you filed this kind of return because of a frivolous position on your part or a desire to delay or interfere with the administration of federal income tax laws. This includes altering or striking out the preprinted language above the space provided for your signature.

This penalty is added to any other penalty provided by law.

Explanation
Congress enacted this penalty to attack a great variety of tax protest activities, including:

1. Irregular tax forms not in processible form
2. References to spurious constitutional arguments as a basis for not completing tax forms
3. Unallowable deductions claimed as a protest against military expenses
4. Deliberate use of incorrect Tax Tables
5. Presentation of clearly inconsistent information, such as a taxpayer who lists only two dependents while claiming 99 exemptions for withholding purposes

TaxAlert

Unlike most other penalties, the penalty for filing a frivolous return is not based on your tax liability. The penalty for filing a frivolous return will be assessed immediately and added to any other penalties.

The penalty must be paid in full upon notice and demand from IRS even if you protest the penalty.

Fraud. If there is any underpayment of tax on your return due to fraud, a penalty of 75% of the underpayment due to fraud will be added to your tax.

Joint return. The fraud penalty on a joint return does not apply to a spouse unless some part of the underpayment is due to the fraud of that spouse.

Failure to supply social security number. If you do not include your SSN or the SSN of another person where required on a return, statement, or other document, you will be subject to a penalty of $50 for each failure. You will also be subject to a penalty of $50 if you do not give your SSN to another person when it is required on a return, statement, or other document.

For example, if you have a bank account that earns interest, you must give your SSN to the bank. The number must be shown on the Form 1099-INT or other statement the bank sends you. If you do not give the bank your SSN, you will be subject to the $50 penalty. (You also may be subject to "backup" withholding of income tax. See chapter 5.)

You will not have to pay the penalty if you are able to show that the failure was due to reasonable cause and not willful neglect.

Failure to furnish tax shelter registration number. A person who sells (or otherwise transfers) to you an interest in a tax shelter must give you the tax shelter registration number or be subject to a $100 penalty. If you claim any deduction, credit, or other tax benefit because of the tax shelter, you must attach Form 8271, Investor Reporting of Tax Shelter Registration Number, to your return to report this number. You will have to pay a penalty of $250 for each failure to report a tax shelter registration number on your return. The penalty can be excused if you have a reasonable cause for not reporting the number.

Criminal Penalties
You may be subject to criminal prosecution (brought to trial) for actions such as:

1. Tax evasion,
2. Willful failure to file a return, supply information, or pay any tax due,
3. Fraud and false statements, or
4. Preparing and filing a fraudulent return.

TaxAlert

In addition to any of the other penalties discussed in this section, you can be charged a penalty for paying your tax with a bad check. The penalty may not be imposed if you submit a bad check in good faith and with reasonable cause to believe that it will be paid. The penalty is 2% of the amount of the check or, if the check is less than $750, the lesser of $15 or the amount of the check.

2

Filing Status

Note: The 2004 IRS Publication 17 (Your Federal Income Tax) has been updated by Ernst & Young LLP for 2005. Dates and dollar amounts shown are for 2005. Gray type is used to indicate where IRS text has been updated or intentionally omitted. Unrevised IRS text is shown in black type.

Introduction

One of the first things to determine in preparing your income tax return is your filing status. There are five possible choices: **single, married filing jointly, married filing separately, unmarried head of household,** *and* **qualifying widow or widower with a dependent child.**

Your choice of filing status dictates which Tax Table or Tax Rate Schedule to use in calculating your tax liability; whether you may claim an **exemption** *for a* **dependent** *or whether you may be claimed as a dependent; and how much income you can have before you are taxed at all.*

This chapter helps you determine which filing status to use. There are five filing statuses:

• Single,
• Married Filing Jointly,
• Married Filing Separately,
• Head of Household, and
• Qualifying Widow(er) With Dependent Child.

Tip. *If more than one filing status applies to you, choose the one that will give you the lowest tax.*

Explanation
If your filing status changes during the year, you may not file under one status for one part of that year and under a second status for the remainder of the year. The law requires that your filing status for the entire year be determined by your status on the last day of the tax year. For example, even if you get married on December 31, you are treated as married for the entire year and you may either file as married filing jointly or married filing separately. Choose the one that will produce the lowest tax. (*Note:* If your spouse or a qualifying person died during the year, see the IRS explanation below.)

You must determine your filing status before you can determine your filing requirements (chapter 1), standard deduction (chapter 22), and correct tax (chapter 32). You also use your filing status in determining whether you are eligible to claim certain deductions and credits.

Useful Items

You may want to see:

Publications

☐ **501** Exemptions, Standard Deduction, and Filing Information
☐ **519** U.S. Tax Guide for Aliens
☐ **555** Community Property

Marital Status

In general, your filing status depends on whether you are considered unmarried or married. A marriage means only a legal union between a man and a woman as husband and wife.

TaxPlanner

Under federal law, same sex marriages are not recognized for tax purposes even though they may be valid for state purposes, e.g. Massachusetts. If you are married in such a state you may have to file using a different status for federal and state tax purposes.

Unmarried persons. You are considered unmarried for the whole year if, on the last day of your tax year, you are unmarried or legally separated from your spouse under a divorce or a separate maintenance decree. State law governs whether you are married or legally separated under a divorce or separate maintenance decree.

Divorced persons. If you are divorced under a final decree by the last day of the year, you are considered unmarried for the whole year.

Divorce and remarriage. If you obtain a divorce in one year for the sole purpose of filing tax returns as unmarried individuals, and at the time of divorce you intended to and did remarry each other in the next tax year, you and your spouse must file as married individuals.

Annulled marriages. If you obtain a court decree of annulment, which holds that no valid marriage ever existed, you are considered unmarried even if you filed joint returns for earlier years. You must file Form 1040X, Amended U.S. Individual Income Tax Return, claiming single or head of household status for each tax year affected by the annulment that is not closed by the statute of limitations for filing a tax return. The statute of limitations generally does not expire until 3 years after your original return was filed.

Explanation
Invalid divorces. This is a very confusing subject because courts in different geographic locations disagree with each other. Furthermore, the courts and the IRS have interpreted the law differently.

Generally, you may *not* file a joint return with your second spouse unless the marital relationship with your first spouse has been severed.

While terminating a marriage is usually a matter of obtaining a divorce from a foreign or a domestic court, it is not always that straightforward. When a particular state's law does not recognize the validity of a divorce decree acquired in another jurisdiction, the IRS and the courts disagree over the status of the divorce.

The Second and Third Circuit Courts of Appeals adhere to the so-called rule of validation. Basically, this rule specifies that a divorce in any court's jurisdiction must be recognized for the purposes of tax law. Consequently, under the rule of validation, a valid joint return may be filed with a second spouse. However, the IRS, the Tax Court, and the Ninth Circuit Court of Appeals do not support the rule of validation. Instead, they maintain that a second court possessing jurisdiction may declare a prior divorce invalid. Thus, a return filed jointly by a party of the invalid divorce and a subsequent marriage partner may not be valid. Nevertheless, neither these courts nor the IRS will challenge the validity of a divorce decree until a court of competent jurisdiction has declared the divorce invalid.

Prisoners of war. You are still considered to be married if your spouse is a prisoner of war (POW) or is listed as missing in action (MIA). Even if you subsequently discover that your spouse died in action or in captivity in a prior year, you cannot alter your married filing status on prior income tax returns.

TaxSaver
When to get divorced. December is the better month to get divorced if spouses have similar incomes. In this way, you can file single returns for the entire year. January is the better month to get divorced if one spouse has considerably more income than the other and you both want to save on taxes.

The IRS contends that actions that are designed to control an individual's marital status at the close of the year for tax purposes, such as a year-end tax-motivated divorce followed by immediate remarriage, are shams and should be disregarded for tax purposes. According to the IRS, individuals retain their married status when:

1. A divorce under the laws of a foreign jurisdiction is obtained late in the year
2. At the time of the divorce the parties intend to remarry
3. The remarriage occurs in January of the next year

However, a divorce followed by cohabitation is not necessarily a sham. The IRS has recognized such arrangements and has allowed individuals to claim single filing status as long as they say that they intend to remain divorced and not remarry each other.

TaxPlanner
If you are getting a divorce, you should consider the impact of the alternative minimum tax (AMT) on special types of income. Accelerating these types of income or deferring related deductions may provide a greater benefit while still filing as married filing jointly. See Chapter 32, *How to Figure Your Tax,* for additional discussion of the AMT.

Head of household or qualifying widow(er) with dependent child. If you are considered unmarried, you may be able to file as a head of household or as a qualifying widow(er) with a dependent child. See *Head of Household* and *Qualifying Widow(er) With Dependent Child* to see if you qualify.

Married persons. If you are considered married for the whole year, you and your spouse can file a joint return, or you can file separate returns.

Considered married. You are considered married for the whole year if on the last day of your tax year you and your spouse meet any one of the following tests.

1. You are married and living together as husband and wife.
2. You are living together in a common law marriage that is recognized in the state where you now live or in the state where the common law marriage began.
3. You are married and living apart, but not legally separated under a decree of divorce or separate maintenance.
4. You are separated under an interlocutory (not final) decree of divorce. For purposes of filing a joint return, you are not considered divorced.

Spouse died. If your spouse died during the year, you are considered married for the whole year for filing status purposes.

If you did not remarry before the end of the tax year, you can file a joint return for yourself and your deceased spouse. For the next 2 years, you may be entitled to the special benefits described later under *Qualifying Widow(er) With Dependent Child.*

If you remarried before the end of the tax year, you can file a joint return with your new spouse. Your deceased spouse's filing status is married filing separately for that year.

Married persons living apart. If you live apart from your spouse and meet certain tests, you may be considered unmarried. If this applies to you, you can file as head of household even though you are not divorced or legally separated. If you qualify to file as head of household instead of as married filing separately, your standard deduction will be higher. Also, your tax may be lower, and you may be able to claim the earned income credit. See *Head of Household,* later.

Single

Your filing status is single if, on the last day of the year, you are unmarried or legally separated from your spouse under a divorce or separate maintenance decree, and you do not qualify for another filing status. To determine your marital status on the last day of the year, see *Marital Status,* earlier.

Your filing status may be single if you were widowed before January 1, 2005, and did not remarry in 2005. However, you might be able to use another filing status that will give you a lower tax. See *Head of Household* and *Qualifying Widow(er) With Dependent Child* to see if you qualify.

How to file. You can file Form 1040EZ (if you have no dependents, are under 65 and not blind, and meet other requirements), Form 1040A, or Form 1040. If you file Form 1040A or Form 1040, show your filing status as single by checking the box on line 1. Use the *Single* column of the Tax Table or Section A of the Tax Computation Worksheet to figure your tax.

Married Filing Jointly

You can choose married filing jointly as your filing status if you are married and both you and your spouse agree to file a joint return. On a joint return, you report your combined income and deduct your combined allowable expenses. You can file a joint return even if one of you had no income or deductions.

If you and your spouse decide to file a joint return, your tax may be lower than your combined tax for the other filing statuses. Also, your standard deduction (if you do not itemize deductions) may be higher, and you may qualify for tax benefits that do not apply to other filing statuses.

Tip. *If you and your spouse each have income, you may want to figure your tax both on a joint return and on separate returns (using the filing status of married filing separately). Choose the method that gives the two of you the lower combined tax.*

How to file. If you file as married filing jointly, you can use Form 1040 or Form 1040A. If you have no dependents, are under 65 and not blind, and meet other requirements, you can file Form 1040EZ. If you file Form 1040 or Form 1040A, show this filing status by checking the box on line 2. Use the *Married filing jointly* column of the Tax Table or Section B of the Tax Computation Worksheet to figure your tax.

Explanation
Marriage tax penalty. Marriage partners who earn approximately the same income may pay more tax if they file a joint return or file separate married returns than they would if they filed two single returns. This is known as "the marriage tax penalty."

TAXALERT
Marriage tax penalty relief extended. The 2004 tax act extended "the marriage tax penalty" relief for many taxpayers. Through 2010, the basic standard deduction for joint returns is twice the single standard deduction. In addition, the married filing jointly 10% and 15% rate brackets will be twice the 10% and 15% rate brackets for single filers. This extension partially alleviates the marriage penalty but does not eliminate it.

Explanation
Singles' tax penalty. A single person earning the same **taxable income** as a married person whose spouse has comparatively little taxable income will pay substantially more income tax than the married person. In other words, if you marry someone with little or no taxable income, your tax decreases. This is known as "the singles' tax penalty."

Example
Mary had a total income of $30,000, all from wages for 2005. John had a total income of $300 from interest income for 2005. If John and Mary were married on or before December 31, 2005, their joint tax liability on the gross income of $30,300 would be $1,390. If they married in 2006, their combined tax liabilities in 2005, filing as single taxpayers, would be as follows:

Mary's tax:	$2,905
John's tax:	0
Total:	$2,905

Thus, there is a singles' tax penalty of $1,515. One possible solution would be to get married quickly.

TAXSAVER
When to get married. If you are contemplating a winter marriage and one of you has more income than the other, choose December instead of January if you want to save on your taxes.

Spouse died during the year. If your spouse died during the year, you are considered married for the whole year and can choose married filing jointly as your filing status. See *Spouse died,* earlier, for more information.

Divorced persons. If you are divorced under a final decree by the last day of the year, you are considered unmarried for the whole year and you cannot choose married filing jointly as your filing status.

Filing a Joint Return

Both you and your spouse must include all of your income, exemptions, and deductions on your joint return.

Accounting period. Both of you must use the same accounting period, but you can use different accounting methods. See *Accounting Periods* and *Accounting Methods* in chapter 1.

Joint responsibility. Both of you may be held responsible, jointly and individually, for the tax and any interest or penalty due on your joint return. One spouse may be held responsible for all the tax due even if all the income was earned by the other spouse.

Divorced taxpayer. You may be held jointly and individually responsible for any tax, interest, and penalties due on a joint return filed before your divorce. This responsibility may apply even if your divorce decree states that your former spouse will be responsible for any amounts due on previously filed joint returns.

Relief from joint liability. In some cases, one spouse may be relieved of joint liability for tax, interest, and penalties on a joint return for items of the other spouse that were incorrectly reported on the joint return. You can ask for relief no matter how small the liability.

There are three types of relief available.

1. Innocent spouse relief, which applies to all joint filers.
2. Separation of liability, which applies to joint filers who are divorced, widowed, legally separated, or have not lived together for the 12 months ending on the date election of this relief is filed.
3. Equitable relief, which applies to all joint filers who do not qualify for innocent spouse relief or separation of liability.

You must file Form 8857, Request for Innocent Spouse Relief, to request any of these kinds of relief. Publication 971, Innocent Spouse Relief, explains these kinds of relief and who may qualify for them.

Signing a joint return. For a return to be considered a joint return, both husband and wife generally must sign the return. If your spouse died before signing the return, see *Signing the return* in chapter 4.

Spouse away from home. If your spouse is away from home, you should prepare the return, sign it, and send it to your spouse to sign so that it can be filed on time.

Injury or disease prevents signing. If your spouse cannot sign because of disease or injury and tells you to sign, you can sign your spouse's name in the proper space on the return followed by the words "By (your name), Husband (or Wife)." Be sure to also sign in the space provided for your signature. Attach a dated statement, signed by you, to the return. The statement should include the form number of the return you are filing, the tax year, the reason your spouse cannot sign, and that your spouse has agreed to your signing for him or her.

Signing as guardian of spouse. If you are the guardian of your spouse who is mentally incompetent, you can sign the return for your spouse as guardian.

Spouse in combat zone. If your spouse is unable to sign the return because he or she is serving in a combat zone (such as the Persian Gulf Area, Yugoslavia, or Afghanistan), or a qualified hazardous duty area (Bosnia and Herzegovina, Croatia, and Macedonia), or a contingency operation, and you do not have a power of attorney or other statement, you can sign for your spouse. Attach a signed statement to your return that explains that your spouse is serving in a combat zone. For more information on special tax rules for persons who are serving in a combat zone, or who are in missing status as a result of serving in a combat zone, get Publication 3, Armed Forces' Tax Guide.

Other reasons spouse cannot sign. If your spouse cannot sign the joint return for any other reason, you can sign for your spouse only if you are given a valid power of attorney (a legal document giving you permission to act for your spouse). Attach the power of attorney (or a copy of it) to your tax return. You can use Form 2848, Power of Attorney and Declaration of Representative.

TAXALERT

Contrary to the IRS's assertion, the failure of one spouse to sign a return will not prevent a finding that the return was a joint return. If the facts of the case support the conclusion that the nonsigning spouse gave tacit consent to a joint filing, then a valid joint return exists.

Even when a spouse's signature is forged, a valid joint return can exist. In one case, the IRS challenged the return of a husband who, due to marital difficulties, had an unknown person forge his wife's signature. Even though his wife testified in court that she would not have signed a joint return under any circumstances, the court ruled that the joint return was valid. The court reasoned that the wife's refusal to sign was unrelated to the joint filing status claim. Furthermore, because the couple had always filed jointly in the past and the wife did nothing to indicate her disapproval of her husband's intention to continue to file jointly, the court said she had no grounds to complain after the filing was made. The court's message is: The presence or absence of an authentic signature does not constitute conclusive evidence of the intent to file jointly or singly. In addition, the refusal to sign does not necessarily mean that the intent to file a joint return was nonexistent.

Nonresident alien or dual-status alien. A joint return generally cannot be filed if either spouse is a nonresident alien at any time during the tax year. However, if one spouse was a nonresident alien or dual-status alien who was married to a U.S. citizen or resident at the end of the year, the spouses can choose to file a joint return. If you do file a joint return, you and your spouse are both treated as U.S. residents for the entire tax year. For information on this choice, see chapter 1 of Publication 519.

TAXPLANNER

You may file a joint return and use the more beneficial joint tax rates if you fall into either of the following two categories:

1. As of the close of the tax year, you are a nonresident alien married to a citizen or resident of the United States.
2. You are a nonresident alien at the beginning of the tax year but a resident of the United States at the close of the tax year (*i.e.*, a dual-status taxpayer) and you are married to a citizen or resident of the United States at the end of the tax year.

The catch is that a joint return requires that the worldwide income of both spouses for the entire year be included in taxable income.

Generally, not filing jointly means that separate returns are required. Only the worldwide income of a U.S. citizen and the worldwide income of an alien while a U.S. resident would be included in each person's taxable income. As a result, the alien spouse's income while a nonresident would be excluded. However, the more burdensome married filing separately tax rates must be used.

Married Filing Separately

You can choose married filing separately as your filing status if you are married. This filing status may benefit you if you want to be responsible only for your own tax or if it results in less tax than filing a joint return.

If you and your spouse do not agree to file a joint return, you may have to use this filing status.

You may be able to choose head of household filing status if you live apart from your spouse, meet certain tests, and are considered unmarried (explained later, under *Head of Household*). This can apply to you even if you are not divorced or legally separated. If you qualify to file as head of household, instead of as married filing separately, your tax may be lower, you may be able to claim the earned income credit and certain other credits, and your standard deduction will be higher. The head of household filing status allows you to choose the standard deduction even if your spouse chooses to itemize deductions. See *Head of Household,* later, for more information.

Tip. *Unless you are required to file separately, you should figure your tax both ways (on a joint return and on separate returns). This way you can make sure you are using the filing status that results in the lowest combined tax. However, you will generally pay more combined tax on separate returns than you would on a joint return for the reasons listed under* Special Rules, *later.*

How to file. If you file a separate return, you generally report only your own income, exemptions, credits, and deductions on your individual return. You can claim an exemption for your spouse if your spouse had no gross income and was not the dependent of another person. However, if your spouse had any gross income or was the dependent of someone else, you cannot claim an exemption for him or her on your separate return.

If you file as married filing separately, you can use Form 1040A or Form 1040. Select this filing status by checking the box on line 3 of either form. You also must enter your spouse's social security number and full name in the spaces provided. Use the *Married filing separately* column of the Tax Table or Section C of the Tax Computation Worksheet to figure your tax.

Special Rules

If you choose married filing separately as your filing status, the following special rules apply. Because of these special rules, you will usually pay more tax on a separate return than if you used another filing status that you qualify for.

1. Your tax rate generally will be higher than on a joint return.
2. Your exemption amount for figuring the alternative minimum tax will be half that allowed to a joint return filer.
3. You cannot take the credit for child and dependent care expenses in most cases, and the amount that you can exclude from income under an employer's dependent care assistance program is limited to $2,500 (instead of $5,000 if you filed a joint return). For more information about these expenses, the credit, and the exclusion, see chapter 34.
4. You cannot take the earned income credit.
5. You cannot take the exclusion or credit for adoption expenses in most cases.
6. You cannot take the education credits (the Hope credit and the lifetime learning credit), the deduction for student loan interest, or the tuition and fees deduction.
7. You cannot exclude any interest income from qualified U.S. savings bonds that you used for higher education expenses.
8. If you lived with your spouse at any time during the tax year:
   a. You cannot claim the credit for the elderly or the disabled.
   b. You will have to include in income more (up to 85%) of your social security benefits or equivalent railroad retirement benefits you received, and
   c. You cannot roll over amounts from a traditional IRA into a Roth IRA.
9. The following deductions and credits are reduced at income levels that are half those for a joint return:
   a. The child tax credit,
   b. The retirement savings contributions credit,
   c. Itemized deductions, and
   d. The deduction for personal exemptions.
10. Your capital loss deduction limit is $1,500 (instead of $3,000 if you filed a joint return).
11. If your spouse itemizes deductions, you cannot claim the standard deduction. If you can claim the standard deduction, your basic standard deduction is half the amount allowed on a joint return.

TaxSaver

Consider filing separate returns:

1. If you suspect that your spouse owes the IRS money. If you file a joint return, you will both be liable for any tax due.
2. If you can obtain a larger benefit from a deduction for a net operating loss against separate rather than joint income.
3. If you or your spouse has significant medical or miscellaneous expenses or casualty losses. A larger deduction may be obtained because only medical expenses exceeding 7.5%, miscellaneous expenses exceeding 2%, and personal casualty losses exceeding 10% of adjusted gross income are deductible. Thus, the lower your adjusted gross income, the more medical or miscellaneous expenses or casualty losses will be deductible.

4. If you are getting divorced. Overall tax savings will result when a high-bracket taxpayer deducts his or her alimony payment and an ex-spouse includes that alimony payment in his or her income at a lower marginal rate.
5. If both husband and wife have similar income and deductions.
6. If a spouse wishes to be responsible for only his or her tax liability.

Consider filing a joint return:

1. If only one spouse has income.
2. If, as of the close of the tax year, you are a nonresident alien married to a citizen or resident of the United States, or you are a nonresident alien at the beginning of the tax year but a resident of the United States at the close of the year and you are married to a U.S. citizen or resident of the United States at the end of the year.

Individual retirement arrangements (IRAs). You may not be able to deduct all or part of your contributions to a traditional IRA if you or your spouse was covered by an employee retirement plan at work during the year. Your deduction is reduced or eliminated if your income is more than a certain amount. This amount is much lower for married individuals who file separately and lived together at any time during the year. For more information, see *How Much Can You Deduct* in chapter 18.

Rental activity losses. If you actively participated in a passive rental real estate activity that produced a loss, you generally can deduct the loss from your nonpassive income, up to $25,000. This is called a special allowance. However, married persons filing separate returns who lived together at any time during the year cannot claim this special allowance. Married persons filing separate returns who lived apart at all times during the year are each allowed a $12,500 maximum special allowance for losses from passive real estate activities. See *Limits on Rental Losses* in chapter 10.

Community property states. If you live in Arizona, California, Idaho, Louisiana, Nevada, New Mexico, Texas, Washington, or Wisconsin and file separately, your income may be considered separate income or community income for income tax purposes. See Publication 555.

Joint Return After Separate Returns

You can change your filing status by filing an amended return using Form 1040X.

If you or your spouse (or both of you) file a separate return, you generally can change to a joint return any time within 3 years from the due date of the separate return or returns. This does not include any extensions. A separate return includes a return filed by you or your spouse claiming married filing separately, single, or head of household filing status.

Separate Returns After Joint Return

Once you file a joint return, you cannot choose to file separate returns for that year after the due date of the return.

Explanation

If a husband and wife fail to file for a particular year, they may still file a joint return for that period, even if the return is as much as 3 years overdue. However, once the IRS has notified each spouse individually that

Table 2-1 **Qualifying to File as a Head of Household**

In order to file as a Head of Household you must meet the following requirements:
1) You must maintain as your home a household which for more than half the year is the principal home of:
   a. A dependent who is a qualifying child (see Chapter 3)
      i. If you're divorced and have custody, the child will qualify if he meets the tests for you even if you released your right to a dependency exemption to the noncustodial parent.
   b. A dependent who is a qualifying relative (see Chapter 3) (unless you only qualify due to the multiple support rules).
2) Under a special rule for parents, you can qualify as a head of household if you maintain a home for a parent of yours even if you don't live with the parent. To qualify under this rule, the parent must also qualify to be claimed by you as a dependent.
3) You must be unmarried to claim head of household status. However, if you have lived apart from your spouse for the last six months of the year and your dependent child, stepchild, adopted child, or foster child lives with you and you "maintain" the household, you are treated as unmarried.
4) You cannot be a surviving spouse (who files using the marrieds filing jointly rates).
5) You can not be a nonresident alien at any time during the tax year.

he or she has not filed a return that is more than 3 years overdue, they cannot file a joint return.

Exception. A personal representative for a decedent can change from a joint return elected by the surviving spouse to a separate return for the decedent. The personal representative has 1 year from the due date of the return to make the change. See chapter 4 for more information on filing a return for a decedent.

Head of Household

TaxAlert

The Working Families Tax Relief Act of 2004 modified the definition of "head of household" Under the modified definition, you may qualify to file as Head of Household if:

1. You are unmarried or "considered unmarried" on the last day of the year (cannot be a surviving spouse)
   You are "considered unmarried" if you meet the following requirements:
   (1) You file a separate return.
   (2) You maintain as your home a household, which, for more than half the tax year, is the principal place of abode of a child for whom you are entitled to a dependency deduction, or would have been so entitled but for the release of the exemption by the custodial parent to the noncustodial parent or the allocation of the exemption to the noncustodial parent under a pre-'85 qualified instrument.
   (3) You furnish more than one-half the cost of maintaining the household during the tax year.
   (4) During the last six months of the tax year, your spouse isn't a member of the household.
2. You paid most (more than one-half) of the cost of maintaining as your home a household that is the principal place of abode for most of the year of either:
   A. a qualifying child (defined in Chapter 3 "Personal Exemptions and Dependents") or;
   B. any other person whom the taxpayer is entitled to claim as a dependent (defined in Chapter 3 "Personal Exemptions and Dependents").
   Special rule for parent. You may be eligible to file as head of household even if the parent for whom you can claim an exemption does not live with you. You must pay more than half the cost of keeping up a home that was the main home for the entire year for your father or mother. You are keeping up a main home for your father or mother if you pay more than half the cost of keeping your parent in a rest home or home for the elderly.
   See Table 2-1.

Tip. *If you qualify to file as head of household, your tax rate usually will be lower than the rates for single or married filing separately. You will also receive a higher standard deduction than if you file as single or married filing separately.*

Kidnapped child. A child may qualify you to file as head of household even if the child has been kidnapped. For more information, see Publication 501.

How to file. If you file as head of household, you can use either Form 1040A or Form 1040. Indicate your choice of this filing status by checking the box on line 4 of either form. Use the *Head of a household* column of the Tax Table or Section D of the Tax Computation Worksheet to figure your tax.

Considered Unmarried

You are considered unmarried on the last day of the tax year if you meet all the following tests.

1. You file a separate return, defined earlier under *Joint Return After Separate Returns*.
2. You paid more than half the cost of keeping up your home for the tax year.
3. Your spouse did not live in your home during the last 6 months of the tax year. Your spouse is considered to live in your home even if he or she is temporarily absent due to special circumstances.
4. Your home was the main home of your child, stepchild, or adopted child for more than half the year or was the main home of your foster child for the entire year.
5. You must be able to claim an exemption for the child. However, you can still meet this test if you cannot claim the exemption only because the noncustodial parent is allowed to claim the exemption for the child. See *Exception* under *Support Test for Child of Divorced or Separated Parents* in chapter 3 for situations where the noncustodial parent is allowed to claim the exemption for the child. The general rules for claiming an exemption for a dependent are explained in chapter 3.

Caution. *If you were considered married for part of the year and lived in a community property state (listed earlier under* Married Filing Separately), *special rules may apply in determining your income and expenses. See Publication 555 for more information.*

Nonresident alien spouse. You are considered unmarried for head of household purposes if your spouse was a nonresident alien at any time during the year and you do not choose to treat your nonresident spouse as a resident alien. However, your spouse is not a qualifying person for head of household purposes. You must have another qualifying person and meet the other tests to be eligible to file as a head of household.

Earned income credit. Even if you are considered unmarried for head of household purposes because you are married to a nonresident alien, you are still considered married for purposes of the earned income credit (unless you meet the "considered unmarried" criteria listed earlier). You are not entitled to the credit unless you file a joint return with your spouse and meet other qualifications. See chapter 38 for more information.

Choice to treat spouse as resident. You are considered married if you choose to treat your spouse as a resident alien.

Keeping Up a Home

To qualify for head of household status, you must pay more than half of the cost of keeping up a home for the year. You can determine whether you paid more than half of the cost of keeping up a home by using the *Cost of Keeping Up a Home* worksheet, shown on the next page.

Cost of Keeping Up a Home

	Amount You Paid	Total Cost
Property taxes	$ _____	$ _____
Mortgage interest expense	_____	_____
Rent	_____	_____
Utility charges	_____	_____
Upkeep and repairs	_____	_____
Property insurance	_____	_____
Food consumed on the premises	_____	_____
Other household expenses	_____	_____
Totals	$ _____	$ _____
Minus total **amount you paid**		(_____)
Amount others paid		$ _____

If the total amount you paid is more than the amount others paid, you meet the requirement of paying more than half the cost of keeping up the home.

Costs you include. Include in the cost of upkeep expenses such as rent, mortgage interest, real estate taxes, insurance on the home, repairs, utilities, and food eaten in the home.

Costs you do not include. Do not include in the cost of upkeep expenses such as clothing, education, medical treatment, vacations, life insurance, or transportation. Also, do not include the rental value of a home you own or the value of your services or those of a member of your household.

[Omitted Text]

TaxPlanner

If you are providing some support for your parents—but less than half of their total support—you should investigate targeting your support payments so that you can qualify as a head of household by establishing one of your parents as a dependent. For example, when you are providing funds to your parents for their support, some type of notation should be made on your check that specifically states for whom the money is being provided. In this fashion, you can clearly demonstrate that the 50% support requirement has been satisfied for at least one of your parents.

Temporary absences. You and your qualifying person are considered to live together even if one or both of you are temporarily absent from your home due to special circumstances such as illness, education, business, vacation, or military service. It must be reasonable to assume that the absent person will return to the home after the temporary absence. You must continue to keep up the home during the absence.

Examples

One court has held that a man still qualified for head of household status even though he temporarily moved out of his home after becoming legally separated. The court believed that the man had always intended to return to his home (and, in fact, he did return). The court was also aware that he had been awarded custody of his child.

Another court has held that a man could not claim that he was the head of the household that he maintained for his son where he himself did not live because of fear of his son.

Note: If your child or stepchild is absent from the home less than 6 months under a custody agreement, the absence is considered temporary.

Death or birth. You may be eligible to file as head of household if the individual who qualifies you for this filing status is born or dies during the year. You must have provided more than half of the cost of keeping up a home that was the individual's main home for more than half the year or, if less, the period during which the individual lived.

Example. You are unmarried. Your mother, for whom you can claim an exemption, lived in an apartment by herself. She died on September 2. The cost of the upkeep of her apartment for the year until her death was $6,000. You paid $4,000 and your brother paid $2,000. Your brother made no other payments toward your mother's support. Your mother had no income. Because you paid more than half the cost of keeping up your mother's apartment from January 1 until her death, and you can claim an exemption for her, you can file as a head of household.

Explanation

Except when you are supporting and maintaining your parents, who do not have to live with you, the IRS says that you cannot qualify as head of household unless you live in the home that you are supporting and maintaining. However, some courts have said that you can maintain more than one home and still claim head of household status. The household that qualifies you as a head of household need not be your principal place of abode, but it must be the home where you and members of your household live for an adequate period of time.

Example 1

A woman who owned two homes, hundreds of miles apart, could still claim to be head of household at the home that was the principal place of residence of her adopted son, though she spent only 40% of her time there. For both homes, however, she paid more than half the cost of upkeep.

Example 2

A man could not claim to be head of household, although he paid 80–90% of the household expenses and was a member of a nearby church, because he did not spend a substantial amount of time at the house. He only visited his sisters at the house, either when he was in town on business during the week or when he stopped by for Sunday dinner. The house was owned by his sisters.

Example 3

A woman who spent 85% of her time in one house and 15% in another house that was the principal residence of her daughter and grandchildren was not allowed to claim head of household status. In this case, the houses were less than 2 miles apart and the woman stayed over at her daughter's only when either she or her daughter was ill. Besides, the daughter, not her mother, rented the house, although the daughter used money given to her by her mother to pay the rent.

Example 4

The case of the two-family house. In this case, a husband, wife, and their children lived in one of the house's units and the wife's mother and unwed sister lived in the other unit. The home contained some common areas but also some partitioned areas for the private use of each family unit. A court upheld the wife's mother's claim of head of household status based on her support of her unwed daughter. Even though the mother paid less than half of the total household expenses, she did pay more than half of the expenses attributable to her and her daughter.

Qualifying Widow(er) With Dependent Child

If your spouse died in 2005, you can use married filing jointly as your filing status for 2005 if you otherwise qualify to use that status. The year of death is the last year for which you can file jointly with your deceased spouse. See *Married Filing Jointly,* earlier.

You may be eligible to use qualifying widow(er) with dependent child as your filing status for 2 years following the year your spouse died. For example, if your spouse died in 2004, and you have not remarried, you may be able to use this filing status for 2005 and 2006.

This filing status entitles you to use joint return tax rates and the highest standard deduction amount (if you do not itemize deductions). This status does not entitle you to file a joint return.

How to file. If you file as qualifying widow(er) with dependent child, you can use either Form 1040A or Form 1040. Indicate your filing status by checking the box on line 5 of either form. Use the *Married filing jointly* column of the Tax Table or Section B of the Tax Computation Worksheet to figure your tax.

Eligibility rules. You are eligible to file your 2005 return as a qualifying widow(er) with dependent child if you meet all of the following tests.

1. You were entitled to file a joint return with your spouse for the year your spouse died. It does not matter whether you actually filed a joint return.
2. Your spouse died in 2003 or 2004 and you did not remarry before the end of 2005.
3. You have a child, stepchild, adopted child, or foster child for whom you can claim an exemption.
4. You paid more than half the cost of keeping up a home that is the main home for you and that child for the entire year, except for temporary absences. See *Temporary absences* and *Keeping Up a Home,* discussed earlier under *Head of Household.*

Caution. *As mentioned earlier, this filing status is only available for 2 years following the year your spouse died.*

Example. John Reed's wife died in 2003. John has not remarried. During 2004 and 2005, he continued to keep up a home for himself and his child (for whom he can claim an exemption). For 2003 he was entitled to file a joint return for himself and his deceased wife. For 2004 and 2005 he can file as qualifying widower with a dependent child. After 2005 he can file as head of household if he qualifies.

Death or birth. You may be eligible to file as a qualifying widow(er) with dependent child if the child who qualifies you for this filing status is born or dies during the year. You must have provided more than half of the cost of keeping up a home that was the child's main home during the entire part of the year he or she was alive.

3

Personal Exemptions and Dependents

Note: The 2004 IRS Publication 17 (Your Federal Income Tax) has been updated by Ernst & Young LLP for 2005. Dates and dollar amounts shown are for 2005. Gray type is used to indicate where IRS text has been updated or intentionally omitted. Unrevised IRS text is shown in black type.

Introduction

*In 2005, you are entitled to a $3,200 **deduction** for yourself, your spouse, and each person you support who otherwise qualifies as a dependent. Each year the amount of the personal exemption is adjusted for inflation. This chapter tells you what specific qualifications you have to meet to take these deductions—taking into account recent changes in law as to how a "dependent" is defined. This chapter also informs you about the special rules and procedures that apply to divorced and separated couples with children, widows and widowers, and residents of **community property** states. Perhaps, most important, this chapter suggests when it might not be a good idea to take a deduction, even though you could qualify for it.*

There are two types of dependents: a qualifying child and a qualifying relative.

First, a word about a qualifying child. Beginning in 2005, new legislation has created a uniform definition of a "qualifying child." This uniform definition applies to all of the following tax benefits:

1. Dependency exemption
2. Child tax credit
3. Earned income credit
4 Child and dependent care credit
5. Head of household filing status

Previously, the definition of a qualifying child varied depending on the tax benefit involved. Now that is no longer the case. In order to claim an exemption for a qualifying child, the following four tests must be met:

1. Relationship test
2. Residency test
3. Age test
4. Support test

These tests are discussed in greater detail later on in this chapter. You should be aware, however, that a child who is not a qualifying child might still be a dependent as a qualifying relative.

Other rules apply in determining whether someone is a "qualifying relative." These rules are also discussed in detail later in this chapter. While the changes in the law are important, for most people they will not affect the dependents you can claim.

*The original intent of personal **exemptions** for dependents was to provide tax relief so that even the poorest citizen would be left with enough money after taxes to support themselves and their family. Obviously, a $3,200 deduction can save the taxpayer only a small portion of the income necessary to live. Ironically, the higher your income level and the higher your marginal tax rate, the greater economic benefit you derive from these deductions. A $3,200 deduction is worth $480 to a married couple filing a joint return with a taxable income of $50,000 and a **marginal tax rate** of 15%. The same $3,200 deduction is worth $896 to a married couple filing a joint return with a taxable income over $119,950 and a marginal tax rate of 28%. (Once your adjusted gross income reaches a certain threshold, figuring out what the exemption is worth is more complicated. This chapter explains this in more detail.)*

Also explained in this chapter are the rules that phase out the value of your personal exemptions if your adjusted gross income exceeds certain amounts: $218,950 for married persons filing jointly, $182,450 for heads of household, $145,950 for single taxpayers, and $109,475 for married persons filing separate returns.

Figuring out who should claim whom as a dependent can be a difficult matter. For example, when parents are *divorced, the custodial parent may sign a declaration permitting the noncustodial parent to claim the exemption for the dependent child. Consequently, if the noncustodial parent is in a higher tax bracket, a greater tax benefit can be obtained. Either parent is entitled to claim the medical expenses paid for the child, even if that parent cannot claim the child as a dependent.*

What's New for 2005

Exemption amount. The amount you can deduct for each exemption has increased to $3,200 in 2005 from $3,100 in 2004.

Exemption phaseout. You lose all or part of the benefit of your exemptions if your adjusted gross income is above a certain amount. The amount at which this phaseout begins depends on your filing status. For 2005, the phaseout begins at $109,475 for married persons filing separately, $145,950 for single individuals, $182,450 for heads of household, and $218,950 for married persons filing jointly or qualifying widow(er)s. See *Phaseout of Exemptions*, later.

Definition of a dependent. Beginning in 2005, you will use new rules to determine whether you can claim an exemption for a dependent. A uniform definition for a qualifying child has been created. In order to claim an exemption for a qualifying child, the following four tests must be met:

1. Relationship test
2. Residency test
3. Age test
4. Support test

These tests are discussed in greater detail later on in this chapter. Other rules apply in determining whether someone is a qualifying relative. For most people, these tests will not affect the dependents they can claim.

This chapter discusses exemptions. The following topics will be explained.

- Personal exemptions—You generally can take one for yourself and, if you are married, one for your spouse.
- Exemptions for dependents—You must meet a number of dependency tests for each exemption you claim for a dependent. A dependent is either a qualifying child or a qualifying relative. If you are entitled to claim an exemption for a dependent, that dependent cannot claim a personal exemption on his or her own tax return.
- Phaseout of exemptions—You get less of a deduction when your adjusted gross income goes above a certain amount.
- Social Security number (SSN) requirement for dependents—You must list the Social Security number of any dependent for whom you claim an exemption.

Deduction. Exemptions reduce your taxable income. Generally, you can deduct $3,200 for each exemption you claim in 2005. But, you may lose the benefit of part or all of your exemption if your adjusted gross income is above a certain amount. See *Phaseout of Exemptions*, later.

How you claim an exemption. How you claim an exemption on your tax return depends on which form you file.

If you file Form 1040EZ, the exemption amount is combined with the standard deduction amount and entered on line 5.

If you file Form 1040A or Form 1040, follow the instructions for the form. The total number of exemptions you can claim is the total in the box on line 6d. Also complete line 26 (Form 1040A) or line 42 (Form 1040) by multiplying the total number of exemptions shown in the box on line 6d by $3,200. If your adjusted gross income is more than $109,475, see *Phaseout of Exemptions,* later.

Useful Items

You may want to see:

Publication

☐ **501** Exemptions, Standard Deduction, and Filing Information

Forms (and Instructions)

☐ **2120** Multiple Support Declaration
☐ **8332** Release of Claim to Exemption for Child of Divorced or Separated Parents

Exemptions

There are two types of exemptions: personal exemptions and exemptions for dependents. While each is worth the same amount ($3,200 for 2005), different rules apply to each type.

Personal Exemptions

You are generally allowed one exemption for yourself and, if you are married, one exemption for your spouse. These are called personal exemptions.

Your Own Exemption
You can take one exemption for yourself unless you can be claimed as a dependent by another taxpayer.

Single persons. If another taxpayer is entitled to claim you as a dependent, you cannot take an exemption for yourself. This is true even if the other taxpayer does not actually claim your exemption.

Married persons. If you file a joint return, you can take your own exemption. If you file a separate return, you can take your own exemption only if another taxpayer is not entitled to claim you as a dependent.

Your Spouse's Exemption
Your spouse is never considered your dependent. You may be able to take one exemption for your spouse only because you are married.

An exemption for your spouse is available only if you are married to that person on the last day of your tax year. See Chapter 2, *Filing Status,* for a discussion of the marriage tax penalty, the singles' tax penalty, and a discussion of the best time to marry.

A common-law marriage is recognized for federal tax purposes if it is recognized by the state. Legal advice may be needed to determine if you have a common-law marriage.

Joint return. On a joint return you can claim one exemption for yourself and one for your spouse.

Explanation
Filing a joint return with your spouse will prevent anyone else from claiming him or her as a dependent, even if that person was otherwise entitled to do so. However, filing as married, filing separately can allow someone else to claim your spouse as a dependent.

Example
John and Mary attended college for 6 months during 2005 and were married in November of that year. John earned $12,000 and Mary earned $3,000, during 2005. If the newlyweds file a joint income tax return, they will owe $0 in taxes. However, Mary's parents will then be unable to claim their daughter as a dependent, even though they provided more than half her support that year.

If John and Mary file as married, filing separately, Mary will owe no tax and John will owe $380. In addition, Mary's parents, who are in the 28% tax bracket, will be entitled to claim Mary as a dependent, giving them a tax benefit of $896. Thus, if the newlyweds file separate returns, their overall tax liability combined with that of Mary's parents will be reduced by $516 (the $896 tax savings to Mary's parents less the additional $380 tax John and Mary incur by filing separate returns). If John's parents also provided half of his support in 2005 and can claim him as a dependent, the combined tax liability for everybody involved will be even lower.

You should also consider the tax benefits of the deduction for higher education expenses. You may be able to deduct qualified tuition and related expenses paid during the year for yourself, your spouse, or a dependent, even if you do not itemize. There are eligibility requirements and income limitations that apply. See Chapter 21, *Education-Related Adjustments.*

Separate return. If you file a separate return, you can claim the exemption for your spouse only if your spouse had no gross income, is not filing a return, and was not the dependent of another taxpayer. This is true even if the other taxpayer does not actually claim your spouse's exemption. This is also true if your spouse is a nonresident alien.

Death of spouse. If your spouse died during the year, you generally can claim your spouse's exemption under the rules just explained under *Joint return* and *Separate return.*

If you remarried during the year, you cannot take an exemption for your deceased spouse.

If you are a surviving spouse without gross income and you remarry in the year your spouse died, you can be claimed as an exemption on both the final separate return of your deceased spouse and the separate return of your new spouse for that year. If you file a joint return with your new spouse, you can be claimed as an exemption only on that return.

Divorced or separated spouse. If you obtained a final decree of divorce or separate maintenance by the end of the year, you cannot take your former spouse's exemption. This rule applies even if you provided all of your former spouse's support.

If you're getting divorced near the end of 2005, it may be better to postpone the divorce until January of 2006. In that way, you can claim an exemption for your spouse as well as use the married filing jointly tax rates.

Exemptions for Dependents

You are allowed one exemption for each person you can claim as a dependent. A dependent is either a "qualifying child" or a "qualifying relative."

Explanation
Oddly enough a qualifying child does not have to be your child and your child may be a qualifying relative and *not* a qualifying child.

[IRS text intentionally omitted]

Who Is a Qualifying Child?

What Tests Have to Be Met?

In general, all four of the following tests must be met to claim someone as a qualifying child.

Relationship Test
The child must be your child (including an adopted child, stepchild, or eligible foster child), brother, sister, stepbrother, stepsister, or a descendant of one of these relatives. An adopted child includes a child lawfully placed with you for legal adoption even if the adoption is not final. An eligible foster child is any child who is placed with you by an authorized placement agency or by judgment, decree, or other order of any court of competent jurisdiction.

Residency Test
A child must live with you for more than half of the year. Temporary absences for special circumstances, such as for school, vacation, medical care, military service, or detention in a juvenile facility count as time lived at home. A child who was born or died during the year is considered to have lived with you for the entire year if your home was the child's home for the entire time he or she was alive during the year. Also, exceptions apply, in certain cases, for children of divorced or separated parents and parents of kidnapped children.

Age Test
A child must be under a certain age to be your qualifying child. The child will meet the age test if he hasn't attained the age of 19 as of the close of the calendar year in which your tax year begins (or in

the case of a full-time student, hasn't attained the age of 24), or is permanently and totally disabled at any time during the calendar year. This age test applies to the dependency exemption, head of household filing status, and Earned Income Credit. For purposes of the Child Tax Credit, the child must be under the age of 17 and under the age of 13 (or any age if permanently and totally disabled) for the Credit for Child and Dependent Care Expenses.

Support Test

A child cannot have provided over half of his or her own support during the calendar year. For purposes of the Earned Income Credit only, the support test does not apply. See Special Rules—The Support Test, for more information.

> **Explanation**
> Unlike under prior law, in determining who is a qualifying child, who provides over half the support of the child is not relevant. What is relevant is that the child cannot provide over half of his or her own support during the year.

See Firgure 3-A (a) to see whether you can claim dependency exemption for a qualifying child.

Who Is a Qualifying Relative?

You may also claim a dependency exemption for a qualifying relative. A qualifying relative is:

1. A child or descendant of a child, a brother, sister, stepbrother or stepsister, a father or mother or ancestor of either, a stepfather or stepmother, a niece or nephew, an uncle or aunt, a son-in-law, daughter-in-law, father-in-law, mother-in-law, brother-in-law or sister-in-law, OR any other individual (other than a spouse) who, for the taxable year, has the same principal place of abode as you and is a member of your household. Any of these relationships that were established by marriage are not ended by death or divorce.

> **Explanation**
> For an unrelated person to qualify as your dependent, he or she must live with you at your principal place of residence—not merely at a house that you maintain for the entire year.

2. A person whose gross income for the calendar year is less than the exemption amount ($3,200 in 2005).
3. Someone for whom you provide over one-half of their support for the calendar year.
4. Someone who is not your or any other taxpayer's qualifying child.

See Figure 3-A (b) to see whether you can claim a dependency exemption for a qualifying relative.

Tests That Must Be Met by All Dependents:

In addition to the tests for a qualifying child and a qualifying relative discussed above, the following requirements apply in order to claim a dependency exemption.

The Citizenship/Residency Test

To qualify as a dependent an individual must be a citizen or national of the United States, a resident of the United States, or a resident of Canada or Mexico at some time during the calendar year in which your tax year begins. One exception applies to this rule. If you legally adopt a child who isn't a U.S. citizen or resident (or a resident of Canada or Mexico) at any time during the year, the child won't be ex-

cluded from the definition of dependent under the citizenship/residency test if, for the entire tax year, the child has his or her principal place of abode in your home, and you are a U.S. citizen or national. Your home and household need not be in the United States.

> **Explanation**
> Residents of Puerto Rico do not meet the citizenship test unless they are also U.S. citizens.

Children's place of residence. Children usually are citizens or residents of the country of their parents.

If you were a U.S. citizen when your child was born, the child may be a U.S. citizen although the other parent was a nonresident alien and the child was born in a foreign country. If so, and the other dependency tests are met, you can take the exemption. It does not matter if the child lives abroad with the nonresident alien parent.

> **Example**
> The IRS ruled that a U.S. citizen living in England since the age of 9, who subsequently married an English-woman, could not claim their son, who was born in England, as a dependent. The foreign-born child of a U.S. citizen and a nonresident alien is *not* a citizen or resident of the United States unless the American parent lived in the United States for 10 years before the child's birth. At least 5 of those 10 years must have been subsequent to age 14.

[IRS text intentionally omitted]

The joint return test

An individual can't be treated as a your dependent if the individual files a joint return with his or her spouse for the tax year that begins in the calendar year in which the tax year of the taxpayer begins. A married individual who doesn't file a joint return can be a dependent.

There is one exception to this rule. If no return is actually required, it is immaterial that a joint return is filed for the purpose of getting a refund of tax withheld. The return is considered a refund claim.

Example. You supported your daughter for the entire year while her husband was in the Armed Forces. The couple files a joint return. Even though all the other tests are met, you cannot take an exemption for your daughter.

Example. Your son and his wife each had less than $3,000 of wages and no unearned income. Neither is required to file a tax return. Taxes were taken out of their pay, so they file a joint return to get a refund. You are allowed to take exemptions for your son and daughter-in-law if the other dependency tests are met, even though they file a joint return.

Child May Be a Qualifying Relative

A child who is not your "qualifying child" under the regular tests may still qualify as your dependent "qualifying relative." To claim the dependency exemption for a child who is a qualifying relative, the child cannot be the qualifying child of any other person and the dependency tests of a qualifying relative must be met.

You can claim an exemption for your dependent even if your dependent files a return.

Caution. *If you are entitled to claim an exemption for your dependent, that dependent cannot claim his or her own personal exemption.*

Kidnapped child. You may be eligible to claim the exemption for a child even if the child has been kidnapped. For more information, see Publication 501.

Child born alive. If your child was born alive during the year, and the dependency tests are met, you can claim the exemption. This is true even if the child lived only for a moment. State or local law must treat the child as having been born alive. There must be proof of a live birth shown by an official document, such as a birth certificate.

TAXPLANNER

You can take a dependency exemption for 2005 for a child born on or before December 31, 2005, but not for a baby born January 1, 2006. Plan accordingly!

TAXPLANNER

In addition to the personal exemption, a tax credit may be available for each qualifying child under age 17. The per child credit for 2005 is $1,000.

Stillborn child. You cannot claim an exemption for a stillborn child.
Death of dependent. If your dependent died during the year and otherwise met the dependency tests, you can claim the exemption for your dependent.
   Example. Your dependent mother died on January 15. The dependency tests are met. You can claim the exemption for her on your return.
Housekeepers, maids, or servants. If these people work for you, you cannot claim exemptions for them.
Child tax credit. You may be entitled to a child tax credit for each of your qualifying children for whom you can claim an exemption. For more information, see chapter 36.
[IRS text intentionally omitted]
Temporary absences. A person lives with you as a member of your household even if either (or both) of you are temporarily absent due to special circumstances. Temporary absences due to special circumstances include absences because of illness, education, business, vacation, or military service.
   If the person is placed in a nursing home for an indefinite period of time to receive constant medical care, the absence is considered temporary.
Death or birth. A person who died during the year, but was a member of your household until death, will meet the member of household test. The same is true for a child who was born during the year and was a member of your household for the rest of the year. The test is also met if a child would have been a member except for any required hospital stay following birth.
Local law violated. A person does not meet the member of household test if at any time during your tax year the relationship between you and that person violates local law.
[IRS text intentionally omitted]

Explanation
A dependent must be *either* a relative as described above or a full-time resident in your principal residence. Your child qualifies as a relative, even if the child is illegitimate.
   While your stepchild, stepfather, and stepmother all qualify as relatives, their blood relations do not. Even so, their blood relations may qualify as your dependents if they are full-time residents in your home.
   While your spouse's brother and/or sister qualify as relatives to you, their spouses do not.

Example
Amy is married to Oliver. Amy's sister Laura, along with Laura's husband, Stephen, are relatives of Amy, but only Laura is a relative of Oliver. If Amy and Oliver file a joint tax return, Laura and Stephen may both be claimed as dependents (as relatives) if they otherwise qualify. But if Amy and Oliver file married but separate returns, Stephen would not be considered a relative of Oliver and could only be claimed as a dependent by Oliver if Stephen was a full-time resident in Oliver's personal residence.

Adoption. Even if your adoption of a child is not yet final, the child is considered to be your child if he or she was placed with you for legal adoption by an authorized placement agency. The child also must be a member of your household, but does not have to be a member of your household for the entire year.
   If the child was not placed with you by an authorized placement agency, the child will meet this test only if he or she was a member of your household for your entire tax year.
   Authorized placement agency. An authorized placement agency includes any person or court authorized by state law to place children for legal adoption.

Example
Frank and Lisa are married. Emma, a 5-year-old orphan, is placed by an authorized adoption agency in their home in July 2005. She is a member of the household for the rest of the year. Even though Emma was not a resident of their household for 12 months during 2005, and even though she was not legally adopted by Frank and Lisa until 2006, she may be claimed as Frank and Lisa's dependent for 2005. However, if Emma had not been placed in Frank and Lisa's home by an authorized adoption agency, Frank and Lisa would not be able to claim her as a dependent.

[IRS text intentionally omitted]
Joint return. If you file a joint return, you do not need to show that a person is related to both you and your spouse. You also do not need to show that a person is related to the spouse who provides support.
   For example, your spouse's uncle who receives more than half his support from you may be your dependent, even though he does not live with you. However, if you and your spouse file separate returns, your spouse's uncle can be your dependent only if he is a member of your household and lives with you for your entire tax year.
   Adopted child. If you are a U.S. citizen who has legally adopted a child who is not a U.S. citizen or resident, and the other dependency tests are met, you can take the exemption if your home is the child's main home and the child is a member of your household for your entire tax year.
Foreign students' place of residence. Foreign students brought to this country under a qualified international education exchange program and placed in American homes for a temporary period generally are not U.S. residents and do not meet the citizen or resident test. You cannot claim exemptions for them. However, if you provided a home for a foreign student, you may be able to take a charitable contribution deduction. See *Expenses Paid for Student Living With You* in chapter 26.

Explanation
For more information about taxes for aliens, see Chapter 44, *Foreign Citizens Living in the United States.*

[IRS text intentionally omitted]

Gross Income Test (Applies Only to Qualifying Relative)

Generally, you cannot take an exemption for a qualifying relative if that person had gross income of $3,200 or more for 2005.

If you file on a fiscal year basis, the gross income test applies to the calendar year in which your fiscal year begins.

Gross income defined. All income in the form of money, property, and services that is not exempt from tax is gross income.

In a manufacturing, merchandising, or mining business, gross income is the total net sales minus the cost of goods sold, plus any miscellaneous income from the business.

Gross receipts from rental property are gross income. Do not deduct taxes, repairs, etc. to determine the gross income from rental property.

Gross income includes a partner's share of the gross, not a share of the net partnership income.

Example

Oscar's father retired 5 years ago and receives over half of his support from Oscar. The father is a partner in a real estate partnership, and his share of gross rental income from the partnership is $3,300 before expenses. After expenses, his net rental income is $200. Oscar may not claim his father as a dependent because his father's share of the partnership's gross rental income exceeds the $3,200 exemption amount.

Gross income also includes all unemployment compensation and certain scholarship and fellowship grants. Scholarships received by degree candidates that are used for tuition, fees, supplies, books, and equipment required for particular courses may not be included in gross income. For more information about scholarships, see chapter 13.

Tax-exempt income, such as certain social security payments, is not included in gross income.

Explanation

Gross income also includes (1) gross profit from self-employment, (2) the full gain from the sale of stock or real estate, and (3) the gain on the sale of a personal residence.

Gross income does *not* include (1) tax-free municipal bond interest and (2) gifts received from others.

TAXSAVER

Because tax-free municipal bond interest is not included in gross income, a person who may possibly be claimed by another as a dependent may be better off holding municipal bonds rather than taxable bonds.

Example

Widower Nick, 63 years old, lives with his son and daughter-in-law. His only source of income is earnings from the $60,000 he has to invest. If he invests in a bond yielding 6%, he would receive $3,600 of taxable income. Because that is less than his $5,000 standard deduction, Nick would not have any tax liability. However, Nick's son would not be able to claim his father as a dependent because Nick would have more than $3,200 in gross income.

If Nick invests $30,000 in the 6% bond and $30,000 in a 4% tax-free municipal bond, his annual income would be $3,000 ($1,800 + $1,200), $600 less than if he put all his money in a taxable bond. His son would now be able to claim his father as a dependent, because Nick's gross income ($1,800) would be less than $3,200. However, Nick would now have to file a tax return because his total income is more than $800, the filing requirement threshold for dependents (see Chapter 1, *Filing Information*).

The tax benefit to his son should be compared with Nick's lower yield and increased tax to see which is more beneficial.

Disabled dependents. For this gross income test, gross income does not include income received by a permanently and totally disabled individual for services performed at a sheltered workshop. The availability of medical care must be the main reason the individual is at the workshop. Also, the income must come solely from activities at the workshop that are incident to this medical care. A sheltered workshop is a school operated by certain tax-exempt organizations, or by a state, a U.S. possession, a political subdivision of a state or possession, the United States, or the District of Columbia that provides special instruction or training designed to alleviate the disability of the individual.
[IRS text intentionally omitted]

TAXPLANNER

You are not allowed an exemption for a child who is age 24 or older whose gross income is not less than the exemption amount ($3,200 for 2005). The term "dependent" means that the individual is either a qualifying child or a qualifying relative. A 24-year-old child does not meet the age requirement under the uniform definition of a qualifying child. The 24-year-old child is also not a qualifying relative because the child's income is greater than the exemption amount of $3,200 (for 2005). However, all is not lost if you can't claim an exemption for your child because of this rule. The child can still claim the exemption on his or her return.

Child Who Is a Student

A child who is under age 24 can be a qualifying child as long as he or she is a student.

Student defined. To qualify as a student, your child must be, during some part of each of 5 calendar months during the calendar year (not necessarily consecutive):

1. A full-time student at a school that has a regular teaching staff, course of study, and regularly enrolled body of students in attendance, or
2. A student taking a full-time, on-farm training course given by a school described in (1) above or a state, county, or local government.

Full-time student defined. A full-time student is a person who is enrolled for the number of hours or courses the school considers to be full-time attendance.

School defined. The term "school" includes elementary schools, junior and senior high schools, colleges, universities, and technical, trade, and mechanical schools. It does not include on-the-job training courses, correspondence schools, and night schools.

Example. James, 22, attends college as a full-time student. During the summer, James earned $4,000. If the other dependency tests are met, his parents can take the exemption for James.

Figure 3-A (a) **Can You Claim a Dependency Exemption for a Qualifying Child?**

In order to claim a person as a Qualifying Child all of the following requirements must be met:

1) The person must be your child, stepchild, adopted child, or foster child, or your brother or sister or stepsibling (or a descendant of your brother or sister or stepsibling);
2) The person must live in your home for over half the year;
3) The person must be under 19 years old (or a student under 24);
4) The person must does not provide over half of his or her own support for the year;
5) The person must be a U.S. citizen or a resident of the U.S., Canada, or Mexico;
6) The person must not file a joint return for the year (if the only reason a joint return is filed is to get a refund and no return is otherwise required, this test is satisfied).

In determining whether a person lives in your home for more than half of the year, temporary absences due to special circumstances, including absences due to illness, education, business, vacation, or military service, aren't treated as absences.

For purposes of the above requirements "student" means a full-time student for at least five months of the year.

If an individual may be and is claimed as a qualifying child by two or more taxpayers, special "tie-breaking" rules apply.

Special rules regarding the exemption for a child apply where the parents are divorced or separated.

A person who is not a Qualifying Child may still be a Qualifying Relative.

Figure 3-A (b) **Can You Claim a Dependency Exemption for a Qualifying Relative?**

In order to claim a person as a Qualifying Relative all of the following requirements must be met:

1) The person must be:
   a) your child (a son, daughter, stepson, stepdaughter, eligible foster child or adopted child), or
   b) a descendant of your child , or
   c) your brother, sister, stepbrother, or stepsister, or
   d) your father or mother, or an ancestor of either, or
   e) your nephew or niece, or
   f) your uncle or aunt, or
   g) your son-in-law, daughter-in-law, father-in-law, mother-in-law, brother-in-law, or sister-in-law, or
   h) any unrelated individual whose principal place of abode is your home and is a member your household.
2) The person's gross income for the year must be less than $3,200.
3) You must provide over one-half of the individual's support for the calendar year
4) The person must not be a Qualifying Child of yours or of anyone else
5) The person must be a U.S. citizen or a resident of the U.S., Canada, or Mexico;
6) The person must not file a joint return for the year (if the only reason a joint return is filed is to get a refund and no return is otherwise required, this test is satisfied).

In determining whether a person lives in your home for more than half of the year, temporary absences due to special circumstances, including absences due to illness, education, business, vacation, or military service, aren't treated as absences.

Vocational high school students. People who work on "co-op" jobs in private industry as a part of the school's prescribed course of classroom and practical training are considered full-time students.

Night school. Your child is not a full-time student while attending school only at night. However, full-time attendance at a school can include some attendance at night as part of a full-time course of study.

Explanation
In order to qualify for the full-time student exemption, the child must be enrolled in an institution in which education is the primary purpose.

Example
A hospital providing programs for interns and residents does not qualify. However, a division of the hospital whose primary purpose is the education of students rather than on-the-job training may qualify.

Explanation
For full-time students under the age of 24, the parents must continue to provide over half of the child's support to take the deduction as a qualifying child.

Example
Mr. and Mrs. Johnson's 22-year-old unmarried son, Robert, graduated from college in June 2004 and got a job for the remainder of the year that paid him $10,000 in taxable income. Because Robert was a full-time student for at least 5 months during 2004 and he is under the age of 24, he meets the age test under the definition of qualifying child. Nevertheless, Mr. and

Mrs. Johnson will not be able to take a $3,200 deduction for Robert as their dependent unless they can prove that they provided over half of Robert's support during the entire year. If they are entitled to take the deduction for him, Robert is not entitled to claim an exemption for himself on his return.

Assuming the exemption for Robert is more valuable on his parents' return than on Robert's own return, Robert's parents should document that they did furnish over half their son's support during the year by paying for his tuition and room and board while he was in school. Robert should have used as large a portion of his income as possible for things that do not constitute support. The more money he saved and invested in 2005, the better. Then Mr. and Mrs. Johnson would be entitled to claim Robert as a dependent and take a $3,200 deduction.

On the other hand, if Mr. and Mrs. Johnson are subject to the personal exemption phaseout, claiming Robert as a dependent may not offer any tax savings. In 2005, the personal exemption phaseout begins at $218,950 for joint returns. If Mr. and Mrs. Johnson have an adjusted gross income of $341,550, they would receive no benefit from having Robert as a dependent.

Explanation
The gross income of a married couple residing in a community property state is generally split equally between each spouse for the purposes of the dependency deduction.

Example
Henry Smith provides more than 50% of the support for his son Jim and his daughter-in-law Jan, both of whom are over 19. Jim has no income and is not a student during 2005. Jan earns $7,000. Assuming that the other dependency tests are met, Henry Smith may claim his son Jim as a dependent in a common-law state. In a community property state, however, Henry could not claim Jim as a dependent, because each spouse is treated as having gross income of $3,500 (half of $7,000).

A qualifying relative with income greater than the exemption amount ($3,200 for 2005) cannot be claimed as a dependent. But this income test does not apply to the determination of the exemption allowed for a qualifying child.

Example
Casey Burns provides more than 50% of the support for her child and mother during 2005. Casey's child, Alexis, has a part-time job that pays her $3,600 during 2005. Alexis was under the age of 19 at the end of 2005. Casey's mother, Christina, earned $2,000 in babysitting income and $2,500 from Social Security during 2005. Assuming that Alexis meets all the requirements of qualifying child classification and the other dependency tests, Casey may claim her as a dependent on her 2005 return. Even though Alexis had $400 in income in excess of her exemption amount ($3,600-$3,200), her gross income does not come into play when determining whether she is a dependent of Casey's for 2005. Casey cannot claim her mother as a dependent, even thought she meets the support and other tests of dependency because her mother earned $1,300 more than her exemption amount ($2,000 babysitting income plus $2,500 Social Security minus $3,200 exemption).

Support Test

Generally, you must provide more than half of a person's total support during the calendar year to meet the support test. However, there are special rules that apply in the following two situations.

1. Two or more persons provide support, but no one person provides more than half of a person's total support. See *Multiple Support Agreement,* later.
2. The person supported is the child of divorced or separated parents. See *Support Test for Child of Divorced or Separated Parents,* later.

How to determine if test is met. You figure whether you have provided more than half of a person's total support by comparing the amount you contributed to that person's support with the entire amount of support that person received from all sources. This includes support the person provided from his or her own funds.

You may find *Table 3-1* helpful in figuring whether you provided more than half of a person's support.

Person's own funds not used for support. A person's own funds are not support unless they are actually spent for support.

Example. Your mother received $2,400 in social security benefits and $300 in interest. She paid $2,000 for lodging and $400 for recreation. She put $300 in a savings account.

Even though your mother received a total of $2,700, she spent only $2,400 for her own support. If you spent more than $2,400 for her support and no other support was received, you have provided more than half of her support.

The Support Test—Special Rules

Multiple Support Agreement
Over one-half of support will be treated as received from you if:

1. No one person contributed over one-half of the support,
2. Over one-half of the support was received from two or more persons each of whom, but for the fact that any such person alone did not contribute over one-half of the support, would have been entitled to claim such individual as a dependent for the taxable year,
3. You contributed over 10% of the support, and
4. Each other person who contributed over 10% of the support files a written declaration that they will not claim the supported individual as a dependent for the tax year.

See more details on multiple support agreements below.

Income of Handicapped Dependents
The gross income of an individual who is permanently and totally disabled at any time during the tax year does not include income they earn for services performed at a "sheltered workshop." A "sheltered workshop" is a school which provides special instruction or training that is designed to alleviate the person's disability, and which is operated by an organization that is exempt from income tax under Code Section 501(c) (a not-for-profit organization). In order for the gross income to be exempt from tax, the availability of medical care at the workshop must be the principal reason for the disabled person's attendance there, and the income must arise from an activity that is incidental to the medical care provided by the organization.

Explanation
You may be able to claim someone as a dependent even though you provide support for less than half the year. Support depends on the amount spent, not the length of time over which it is spent. As long as you provide over 50% of the total amount of a person's support for a year, you may claim that person as a dependent.

Child's wages used for own support. You cannot include in your contribution to your child's support any support that is paid for by the child with the child's own wages, even if you paid the wages.

Year support is provided. The year you provide the support is the year you pay for it, even if you do so with borrowed money that you repay in a later year.

Explanation
Only the amount actually spent on support is relevant to the support test. The funds made available for support purposes are not relevant until actually used.

Example 1
The income of a trust for the benefit of a minor was not spent for the minor's support. The parent who provided the funds for the child's support may claim the dependency deduction.

Example 2
According to a court ruling, an individual could claim a dependency deduction for his grandmother even though she received state old-age assistance payments that exceeded the amounts spent by the grandson. The grandmother did not spend all of the payments received from the state for her support. The amount of the state payments that she did spend for her support was less than what was provided to her by her grandson.

If you use a fiscal year to report your income, you must provide more than half of the dependent's support for the calendar year in which your fiscal year begins.

TaxPlanner
You should maintain complete records of expenditures made to support anyone whom you intend to claim as a dependent. Take particular pains to maintain records of support for children of divorced parents and for children who are attending college.

The IRS has established guidelines so that members of a community property state can determine who is entitled to deduct whom as a dependent. For additional information, see IRS Publication 555.

Armed Forces dependency allotments. The part of the allotment contributed by the government and the part taken out of your military pay are both considered provided by you in figuring whether you provide more than half of the support. If your allotment is used to support persons other than those you name, you can take the exemptions for them if they otherwise qualify.

Example. You are in the Armed Forces. You authorize an allotment for your widowed mother that she uses to support herself and your sister. If the allotment provides more than half of their support, you can take an exemption for each of them, if they otherwise qualify, even though you authorize the allotment only for your mother.

Tax-exempt military quarters allowances. These allowances are treated the same way as dependency allotments in figuring support. The allotment of pay and the tax-exempt basic allowance for quarters are both considered as provided by you for support.

Tax-exempt income. In figuring a person's total support, include tax-exempt income, savings, and borrowed amounts used to support that person. Tax-exempt income includes certain social security benefits, welfare benefits, nontaxable life insurance proceeds, Armed Forces family allotments, nontaxable pensions, and tax-exempt interest.

Example 1. You provide $4,000 toward your mother's support during the year. She has earned income of $600, nontaxable social security benefit payments of $4,800, and tax-exempt interest of $200. She uses all these for her support. You cannot claim an exemption for your mother because the $4,000 you provide is not more than half of her total support of $9,600.

Example 2. Your daughter takes out a student loan of $2,500 and uses it to pay her college tuition. She is personally responsible for the loan. You provide $2,000 toward her total support. You cannot claim an exemption for your daughter because you provide less than half of her support.

Social security benefit payments. If a husband and wife each receive payments that are paid by one check made out to both of them, half of the total paid is considered to be for the support of each spouse, unless they can show otherwise.

If a child receives social security benefits and uses them toward his or her own support, the payments are considered as provided by the child.

Support provided by the state (food stamps, housing, etc.). Benefits provided by the state to a needy person generally are considered support provided by the state. However, payments based on the needs of the recipient will not be considered as used entirely for that person's support if it is shown that part of the payments were not used for that purpose.

Foster care payments and expenses. Payments you receive for the support of a foster child from a child placement agency are considered support provided by the agency. Similarly, payments you receive for the support of a foster child from a state or county are considered support provided by the state or county.

If you are not in the trade or business of providing foster care and your unreimbursed out-of-pocket expenses in caring for a foster child were mainly to benefit an organization qualified to receive deductible charitable contributions, the expenses are deductible as charitable contributions, but are not considered support you provided. For more information about the deduction for charitable contributions, see chapter 26. If your unreimbursed expenses are not deductible as charitable contributions, they are considered support you provided.

If you are in the trade or business of providing foster care, your unreimbursed expenses are not considered support provided by you.

Home for the aged. If you make a lump-sum advance payment to a home for the aged to take care of your relative for life and the payment is based on that person's life expectancy, the amount of support you provide each year is the lump-sum payment divided by the relative's life expectancy. The amount of support you provide also includes any other amounts that you provided during the year.

Example
Jane's mother resides in a senior citizens' home that is supported and operated by a church. It cost the church $6,000 last year to support Jane's mother. For Jane to claim her mother as a dependent, she must prove that she has provided more than $6,000 additional support for her mother, over and above the $6,000 provided by the church.

Total Support
To figure if you provided more than half of a person's support, you must first determine the total support provided for that person. Total support includes amounts spent to provide food, lodging, clothing, education, medical and dental care, recreation, transportation, and similar necessities.

Explanation
Money that is not included in gross income, such as certain Social Security benefits, veterans' benefits,

and so on, must be considered in determining support. For example, an amount borrowed by the person, or by you, and spent for support must be included in total support.

Explanation
Generally, the IRS maintains that only expenditures necessary for the essential support—basic food, housing, clothing, education, health, and transportation—qualify toward the 50% support test. Here is a quick list of broad areas in which expenditures will generally constitute support:

> Lodging, including utilities and telephone
> Room and board at a college or private school
> Clothing, laundry, and dry cleaning
> Education, including tuition, books, and supplies
> Medical expenses, including doctor, dentist, and health insurance premiums
> Transportation, including purchase of a car, its maintenance, and gas
> Child care, including babysitters and nursery school
> Charitable contributions on behalf of a dependent
> Payments to an institution for the care of an elderly parent

Courts, however, have been more lenient, and allowed these types of expenditures to count as support:

> Education, music, and dancing lessons
> Child care, summer camp
> Wedding costs, including receptions
> Entertainment, including movies, theater, spending money, toys, and vacations

Generally, the amount of an item of support is the amount of the expense incurred in providing that item. For lodging, the amount of support is the fair rental value of the lodging.

Expenses that are not directly related to any one member of a household, such as the cost of food for the household, must be divided among the members of the household.

Example. Your parents live with you, your spouse, and your two children in a house you own. The fair rental value of your parents' share of lodging is $2,000 a year, which includes furnishings and utilities. Your father receives a nontaxable pension of $4,200, which he spends equally between your mother and himself for items of support such as clothing, transportation, and recreation. Your total food expense for the household is $6,000. Your heat and utility bills amount to $1,200. Your mother has hospital and medical expenses of $600, which you pay during the year. Figure your parents' total support as follows:

	Support provided	
	Father	Mother
Fair rental value of lodging	$1,000	$1,000
Pension spent for their support	2,100	2,100
Share of food (1/6 of $6,000)	1,000	1,000
Medical expenses for mother		600
Parents' total support	**$4,100**	**$4,700**

You must apply the support test separately to each parent. You provide $2,000 ($1,000 lodging, $1,000 food) of your father's total support of $4,100—less than half. You provide $2,600 to your mother ($1,000 lodging, $1,000 food, $600 medical)—more than half of her total support of $4,700. You meet the support test for your mother, but not your father. Heat and utility costs are included in the fair rental value of the lodging, so these are not considered separately.

Lodging defined. If you provide a person with lodging, you are considered to provide support equal to the fair rental value of the room, apartment, house, or other shelter in which the person lives. Fair rental value includes a reasonable allowance for the use of furniture and appliances and for heat and other utilities that are provided.

Fair rental value defined. This is the amount you could reasonably expect to receive from a stranger for the same kind of lodging. It is used instead of actual expenses, such as rent, taxes, interest, depreciation, paint, insurance, utilities, cost of furniture and appliances, etc. In some cases, fair rental value may be equal to the rent paid.

If you provide the total lodging, the amount of support you provide is the fair rental value of the room the person uses, or a share of the fair rental value of the entire dwelling if the person has use of your entire home. If you do not provide the total lodging, the total fair rental value must be divided depending on how much of the total lodging you provide. If you provide only a part and the person supplies the rest, the fair rental value must be divided between both of you according to the amount each provides.

Example. Your parents live rent free in a house you own. It has a fair rental value of $5,400 a year furnished, which includes a fair rental value of $3,600 for the house and $1,800 for the furniture. This does not include heat and utilities. The house is completely furnished with furniture belonging to your parents. You pay $600 for their utility bills. Utilities are not usually included in rent for houses in the area where your parents live. Therefore, you consider the total fair rental value of the lodging to be $6,000 ($3,600 fair rental value of the unfurnished house, $1,800 allowance for the furnishings provided by your parents, and $600 cost of utilities) of which you are considered to provide $4,200 ($3,600 + $600).

Person living in his or her own home. The total fair rental value of a person's home that he or she owns is considered support contributed by that person.

Living with someone rent free. If you live with a person rent free in his or her home, you must reduce the amount you provide for support by the fair rental value of lodging he or she provides you.

TAXSAVER

If your dependent is living in his or her own home, it may be to your mutual advantage for you to acquire a partial interest in the home and thereby become jointly liable for the mortgage and real estate taxes. By doing this, you can include 50% of the mortgage expense and real estate taxes you incur as part of your support calculation.

TAXPLANNER

If your mother lives alone in her own home and you pay the mortgage and real estate taxes for her, no one is entitled to the deduction for mortgage interest expenses or real estate taxes. You pay them, but because you are not personally liable for them, you may not deduct them. Conversely, your mother is personally responsible for them, but she does not pay them and so she may not deduct them.

If you give your mother the cash and she pays the mortgage interest expenses and real estate taxes, she would be entitled to the deductions. However, if you are in a higher tax bracket than your mother, it would be more advantageous for you to take the deductions than for your mother to do so. The higher the tax bracket, the more a deduction is worth.

If the house were transferred into joint ownership and you also became obligated for the mortgage, you

Table 3-1. **Worksheet for Determining Support**

Funds Belonging to the Person You Supported

1. Enter the total funds belonging to the person you supported, including income received (taxable and nontaxable) and amounts borrowed during the year, plus the amount in savings and other accounts at the beginning of the year . . . . **1.**

2. Enter the amount on line 1 that was used for the person's support . . . . **2.**

3. Enter the amount on line 1 that was used for other purposes . . . . **3.**

4. Enter the total amount in the person's savings and other accounts at the end of the year . . . . . **4.**

5. Add lines 2 through 4. (This amount should equal line 1.) . . . . **5.**

Expenses for Entire Household (where the person you supported lived)

6. Lodging (complete line 6a or 6b):
   6a. Enter the amount of rent paid . . . . **6a.**
   6b. Enter the fair rental value of home. If the person you supported owned the home, also include this amount in line 20. . . . . **6b.**

7. Enter the total food expenses . . . . **7.**

8. Enter the total amount of utilities (heat, light, water, etc. not included in line 6a or 6b) . . . . . . **8.**

9. Enter the total amount of repairs (not included in line 6a or 6b) . . . . **9.**

10. Enter the total of other expenses. Do not include expenses of maintaining the home, such as mortgage interest, real estate taxes, and insurance. . . . . **10.**

11. Add lines 6 through 10. These are the total household expenses . . . . **11.**

12. Enter total number of persons who lived in the household . . . . **12.**

Expenses for the Person You Supported

13. Divide line 11 by line 12. This is the person's share of the household expenses . . . . **13.**

14. Enter the person's total clothing expenses . . . . **14.**

15. Enter the person's total education expenses . . . . **15.**

16. Enter the person's total medical and dental expenses not paid for or reimbursed by insurance **16.**

17. Enter the person's total travel and recreation expenses . . . . **17.**

18. Enter the total of the other person's other expenses . . . . **18.**

19. Add lines 14 through 18. This is the total cost of the person's support for the year . . . . **19.**

Did You Provide More Than Half?

20. Enter the amount from line 2, plus the amount from line 6b if the person you supported owned the home. This is the amount the person provided for his or her own support . . . . **20.**

21. Enter the amount others provided for the person's support. Include amounts provided by state, local, and other welfare societies or agencies. Do not include any amounts included on line 1. **21.**

22. Add lines 20 and 21 . . . . **22.**

23. Subtract line 22 from line 19. This is the amount you provided for the person's support . . . . . . **23.**

24. Multiply line 19 by 50% (.50) . . . . **24.**

Is line 23 more than line 24?

Yes. You meet the support test for the person. If the other dependency tests are met, you can claim an exemption for the person.

No. You do not meet the support test for the person. You cannot claim an exemption for the person unless you can do so under a multiple support agreement. See *Multiple Support Agreement* later in this chapter.

---

could deduct the mortgage interest and real estate taxes you paid. In addition, you could claim your mother as a dependent. Arranging things in this manner may realize the greatest tax savings. To take full advantage of the deduction for mortgage interest, you would have to meet the special rules for qualified residence mortgages. See Chapter 25, *Interest Expense.*

Property. Property provided as support is measured by its fair market value. Fair market value is the price that property would sell for on the open market. It is the price that would be agreed upon between a willing buyer and a willing seller, with neither being required to act, and both having reasonable knowledge of the relevant facts.

Capital expenses. Capital items, such as furniture, appliances, and cars, that are bought for a person during the year can be included in total support under certain circumstances.

The following examples show when a capital item is or is not support.

Example 1. You buy a $200 power lawn mower for your 13-year-old child. The child is given the duty of keeping the lawn trimmed. Because a lawn mower is ordinarily an item you buy for personal and family reasons that benefits all members of the household, you cannot include the cost of the lawn mower in the support of your child.

Example 2. You buy a $150 television set as a birthday present for your 12-year-old child. The television set is placed in your child's bedroom. You can include the cost of the television set in the support of your child.

Example 3. You pay $5,000 for a car and register it in your name. You and your 17-year-old daughter use the car equally. Because you own the car and do not give it to your daughter but merely let her use it, you cannot include the cost of the car in your daughter's total support. However, you can include in your daughter's support your out-of-pocket expenses of operating the car for her benefit.

Example 4. Your 17-year-old son, using personal funds, buys a car for $4,500. You provide all the rest of your son's support—$4,000. Since the car is bought and owned by your son, the car's fair market value ($4,500) must be included in his support. The $4,000 support you provide is less than half of his total support of $8,500. You cannot claim an exemption for your son.

TAXSAVER

In Example 4 above, the parents were not able to claim their son as a dependent because the son paid the entire $4,500 to buy the car. However, if the parents had contributed $251 toward the car's purchase, they would then have contributed more than half of their son's support and could claim the son as a dependent and get a $3,200 deduction. Assuming that the parents were in the 28% tax bracket, the deduction was worth $896 to them. The moral of the story is: Contributing to the purchase of a car or a trip in the year in which your child graduates from school may make good tax sense if the contribution assures you of one more year in which you can claim your child as a dependent.

Medical insurance premiums. Medical insurance premiums you pay, including premiums for supplementary Medicare coverage, are included in the support you provide.

Medical insurance benefits. Medical insurance benefits, including basic and supplementary Medicare benefits, are not part of support.

Tuition payments and allowances under the GI Bill. Amounts veterans receive under the GI Bill for tuition payments and allowances while they attend school are included in total support.

Example. During the year, your son receives $2,200 from the government under the GI Bill. He uses this amount for his education. You provide the rest of his support—$2,000. Because GI benefits are included in total support, your son is not your dependent.

Child care expenses. If you pay someone to provide child care or disabled dependent care, you can include these payments in the amount you provided for the support of your child or disabled dependent, even if you claim a credit for the payments. For information on the credit, see chapter 34.

Other support items. Other items may be considered as support depending on the facts in each case.

TAXPLANNER

If you contribute support to a household other than the one in which you live and that household includes more than one person who may qualify as your dependent, you may earmark portions of your support funds for specific persons. This enables you to prove that you have provided more than 50% of the support for a certain member or members of the household. Without written corroboration, it is likely that the monies contributed will be prorated among all the members of the household, which could result in your losing a dependency exemption.

Example
You provide $5,000 of support for your parents. They live in their own apartment and spend $6,000 annually on their joint support.

Unless you specify how much support is designated for each parent, the IRS assumes that half of the money was intended for each parent. Therefore, you won't meet the more than 50% test for either parent.

If you establish in writing that over $3,000 of your funds is support for one of your parents and the balance is for the other, you can claim one dependency deduction.

Do Not Include in Total Support
The following items are not included in total support.

1. Federal, state, and local income taxes paid by persons from their own income.
2. Social security and Medicare taxes paid by persons from their own income.
3. Life insurance premiums.
4. Funeral expenses.
5. Scholarships received by your child if your child is a full-time student.
6. Survivors' and Dependents' Educational Assistance payments used for support of the child who receives them.

Explanation
Savings should not be included in total support.

Example
If a child puts his or her entire after-tax earnings from a part-time job in a savings account or purchases common stock, the child is not considered to have spent any earnings toward self-support.

This is an important point to remember in the year in which a child graduates from school and gets a job for the rest of the year. Whether or not the parents may claim the child as a dependent hinges on whether or not their support payments—tuition, room and board, graduation presents, and so on—exceed the child's earnings that are not put into savings or used to pay taxes.

Multiple Support Agreement

Sometimes no one provides more than half of the support of a qualifying relative. Instead, two or more persons, each of whom would be able to take the exemption but for the support test, together provide more than half of the person's support.

When this happens, you can agree that any one of you who individually provides more than 10% of the person's support, but only one, can claim an exemption for that person. Each of the others must sign a statement agreeing not to claim the exemption for that year. The person who claims the exemption must keep these signed statements for his or her records. A multiple support declaration identifying each of the others who agreed not to claim the exemption must be attached to the return of the person claiming the exemption. Form 2120, Multiple Support Declaration, can be used for this purpose.

Example 1. You, your sister, and your two brothers provide the entire support of your mother for the year. You provide 45%, your sister 35%, and your two brothers each provide 10%. Either you or your sister can claim an exemption for your mother. The other must sign a statement agreeing not to take an exemption for your mother. The one who claims the exemption must attach a Form 2120 or similar declaration to his or her return and must keep the statement signed by the other for his or her records. Because neither brother provides more than 10% of the support, neither can take the exemption and neither has to sign a statement.

Figure 3-B **Who Can You Claim a Dependency Exemption for a Qualifying Child of Divorced or Separated Parents?**

In order to claim a dependency exemption for a qualifying child of divorced or separated parents the following rules apply:

1) Both parents must provide between them more than 50% of the child's support for the year.
2) The exemption goes to the parent having custody of the child unless the custodial parent releases his or her claim to the exemption. (The comparative amount of support provided by each parent isn't relevant.)
3) If each parent has custody for part of the year, the custodial parent is considered to be the one who has custody for the greater portion of the year. If neither parent has custody for more than half the year neither will get the exemption.
4) The release of the exemption by the custodial parent can be executed on an annual basis, for one or more future years or for all future years. You can use Form 8332 for this purpose or a custodial parent may also grant a release by executing a document that conforms to Form 8332.

The above rules only apply to post-1984 divorces and separations. For divorces and separations prior to 1985, the noncustodial parent receives the exemption if the decree or agreement says he should as long as he contributes at least $600 in support of the child.

These rules apply where parents have lived apart at all times during the last six months of the year even if they are not formally divorced and have not entered into a written separation agreement.

Example 2. You and your brother each provide 20% of your mother's support for the year. The remaining 60% of her support is provided equally by two persons who are not related to her. She does not live with them. Because more than half of her support is provided by persons who cannot claim an exemption for her, no one can take the exemption.

Example 3. Your father lives with you and receives 25% of his support from social security, 40% from you, 24% from his brother, and 11% from a friend. Either you or your uncle can take the exemption for your father if the other signs a statement agreeing not to. The one who takes the exemption must attach a Form 2120 or a similar declaration to his return and must keep for his records the signed statement from the one agreeing not to take the exemption.

TAXPLANNER

The multiple support agreement provides a tax-planning opportunity that should not be overlooked. If more than one individual provides at least 10% of the support of a dependent, and if no one individual provides over 50% support, an individual in a higher tax bracket may take the deduction, even if that individual did not provide the most support for the dependent.

Example
Four adult children jointly furnish all of the support for their elderly father. The marginal tax rate for three of the children is 15%, but the fourth child is in the 28% bracket. Therefore, the fourth child should be designated as the one to claim the dependency deduction under the multiple support agreement, even if he or she is providing less support than the other three. The $3,200 deduction is worth $896 to the fourth child but is worth only $480 to any of the other children, because they are taxed at 15%.

Qualifying Child or Qualifying Relative of Parents Who Are Divorced, Separated, or Living Apart

The custodial parent is generally entitled to claim an exemption for a qualifying child or qualifying relative who meets the dependency tests.

The "Tie-Breaker" Rule—Special Rule Relating to Two or More Claiming a Qualifying Child

More than one parent claiming a qualifying child

If the parents do not file a joint return, the child is treated as a qualifying child of the parent with whom the child lived for the longest period of time during the taxable year, or if the child lives with both parents for the same amount of time during the taxable year, the parent with the highest adjusted gross income.

General Rule

If a child may be claimed as a qualifying child by two or more taxpayers during the taxable year, the child will be treated as the qualifying child of the taxpayer who:

1. Is the parent;
2. If more than one taxpayer is the child's parent, the one with whom the child lived for the longest time during the year, or if the time was equal, the parent with the highest adjusted gross income;
3. If no taxpayer is the child's parent, the taxpayer with the highest adjusted gross income.

Custodial parent's release of claim to child's exemption.

A child is treated as being the qualifying child or qualifying relative of the noncustodial parent for a calendar year if:

1. The child receives over one-half of his **support** during the calendar year from his parents;
2. The child's parents satisfy one of the following requirements:
   a. the child's parents are divorced or legally separated under a decree of divorce or separate maintenance;
   b. the child's parents are separated under a written separation agreement; or
   c. the child's parents lived apart at all times during the last six months of the calendar year;
3. the child is in the custody of one or both of his parents for more than one-half of the calendar year; and
4. A decree of divorce or separate maintenance or written separation agreement between the parents applicable to the tax year that begins in that calendar year provides that
   a. the noncustodial parent will be entitled to any deduction for dependents for that child, or
   b. the custodial parent will sign a written declaration form that

the custodial parent won't claim that child as a dependent for the tax year (Form 8332).

[IRS text intentionally omitted]

The term "custodial parent" means the parent with whom a child shared the same principal place of abode for the greater portion of the calendar year. The term "noncustodial parent" means the parent who isn't the custodial parent.

[IRS text intentionally omitted]

Written declaration. The custodial parent may use either Form 8332 or a similar statement (containing the same information required by the form) to make the written declaration to release the exemption to the noncustodial parent. The noncustodial parent must attach the form or statement to his or her tax return.

The exemption can be released for a single year, for a number of specified years (for example, alternate years), or for all future years, as specified in the declaration. If the exemption is released for more than one year, the original release must be attached to the return of the noncustodial parent for the first year, and a copy must be attached for each later year.

Divorce decree or separation agreement made after 1984. If your divorce decree or separation agreement was executed after 1984, the noncustodial parent does not have to attach Form 8332 if both of the following requirements are met.

1. The decree or agreement is signed by the custodial parent and states all of the following:
   a. The custodial parent will not claim the child as a dependent for the year.
   b. The noncustodial parent can claim the child as a dependent without regard to any condition, such as payment of support.
   c. The years for which the noncustodial parent, rather than the custodial parent, can claim the child as a dependent.
2. The noncustodial parent attaches a copy of the following pages of the decree or agreement to his or her tax return.
   a. The cover page (write the other parent's social security number on this page).
   b. The pages that contain the information shown in item (1).
   c. The signature page with the other parent's signature and the date of the agreement.

Caution. *If these requirements are not met, the noncustodial parent must attach to his or her return Form 8332 or a similar statement from the custodial parent releasing the exemption. Failure to attach the requisite form, statement, or written declaration will most likely result in the dependency exemption being denied to the noncustodial parent.*

Child support. All child support payments actually received from the noncustodial parent are considered used for the support of the child.

[IRS text intentionally omitted]

Parents who never married. These special rules for divorced or separated parents also apply to parents who never married.

See Figure 3-B to see who can claim a dependency exemption for a qualifying child of divorced or separated parents.

TAXPLANNER

Due to the education credits (see Chapter 37, *Education Credits*, for information about the Hope Scholarship Credit and the Lifetime Learning Credit), there are situations where the parent may not want to claim an eligible dependent. Education credits phase out for single taxpayers with modified adjusted gross income between $43,000 and $53,000 and for couples filing jointly with modified adjusted gross income between $87,000 and $107,000. The credits are not available to married taxpayers filing separately.

The student may claim the credits, even if the parents paid the expenses, but no one may claim the student as a dependent. The parent must not include the student on his or her tax return, and if the parent is allowed to take a dependency exemption for the student, the student may not claim a dependency exemption on his or her own tax return.

You should not claim your child as your dependent if the education tax credit will provide a greater tax benefit for your child than your tax benefit from the $3,200 exemption amount. The maximum tax benefit for a married couple, in the 28% tax bracket, to claim a child as a dependent is $896.

TAXPLANNER

Generally, the parent in the higher tax bracket should be designated as the parent to claim the dependency exemption for a child, assuming that the parent meets all the tests for claiming the dependency deduction. However, if the person with the highest tax bracket is subject to the phaseout of the personal exemption, the dependency exemption may not benefit that person.

Consider the deduction for higher education expenses. You may be able to deduct qualified tuition and related expenses paid during the year on behalf of a dependent, even if you do not itemize. However, since income limitations apply, it may be more beneficial for the parent in the lower tax bracket to claim the child as a dependent.

Note: The child and dependent care credit and medical expense deductions may be claimed whether or not you can claim the child as a dependent. For more information on the child and dependent care credit, see Chapter 34, *Child and Dependent Care Credit.* For more information on the medical expense deduction see Chapter 23, *Medical and Dental Expenses.*

Phaseout of Exemptions

The amount you can claim as a deduction for exemptions is phased out once your adjusted gross income (AGI) goes above a certain level for your filing status. These levels are as follows:

Filing Status	AGI Level Which Reduces Exemption Amount
Married filing separately	$109,475
Single	145,950
Head of household	182,450
Married filing jointly	218,950
Qualifying widow(er)	218,950

If your AGI exceeds the level for your filing status, use the *Deduction for Exemptions Worksheet* in the instructions for Form 1040 to figure the amount of your deduction for exemptions.

You must reduce the dollar amount of your exemptions by 2% for each $2,500, or part of $2,500 ($1,250 if you are married filing separately), that your AGI exceeds the amount shown above for your filing status. If your AGI exceeds the amount shown by more than $122,500 ($61,250 if married filing separately), the amount of your deduction for exemptions is reduced to zero.

Explanation

The amount you can claim as a deduction for exemptions is completely phased out if your adjusted gross income exceeds the following levels:

Figure 3-C.   **Deduction for Exemptions Worksheet—Line 39**   *Keep for Your Records*

1. Is the amount on Form 1040, line 37, more than the amount shown on line 4 below for your filing status?

☐ No. (STOP) Multiply $3,200 by the total number of exemptions claimed on Form 1040, line 6d, and enter the result on line 42.

☐ Yes. *Continue*

2. Multiply $3,200 by the total number of exemptions claimed on Form 1040, line 6d . . . .   2. _____

3. Enter the amount from Form 1040, line 37 . . . .   3. _____

4. Enter the amount shown below for your filing status.
   * Single—$145,950
   * Married filing jointly or qualifying widow(er)—$218,950
   * Married filing separately—$109,475
   * Head of household—$182,450   } . . . . .   4. _____

5. Subtract line 4 from line 3. If the result is more than $122,500 ($61,250 if married filing separately), (STOP) You **cannot** take a deduction for exemptions . . . .   5. _____

6. Divide line 5 by $2,500 ($1,250 if married filing separately). If the result is not a whole number, increase it to the next higher whole number (for example, increase 0.0004 to 1)   6. _____

7. Multiply line 6 by 2% (.02) and enter the result as a decimal . . . .   7. _____

8. Multiply line 2 by line 7 . . . .   8. _____

9. **Deduction for exemptions**. Subtract line 8 from line 2. Enter the result here and on Form 1040, line 42 . . .   9. _____

Married, filing separately	$170,725
Single	268,450
Head of household	304,950
Married filing jointly and Qualifying widow(er)	341,450

Social Security Numbers for Dependents

You must list the social security number (SSN) of any person for whom you claim an exemption in column (2) of line 6c of your Form 1040 or Form 1040A.

Caution. *If you do not list the dependent's SSN when required or if you list an incorrect SSN, the exemption may be disallowed.*

No SSN. If a person for whom you expect to claim an exemption on your return does not have an SSN, either you or that person should apply for an SSN as soon as possible by filing Form SS-5, Application for a Social Security Card, with the Social Security Administration (SSA). Information about applying for an SSN and Form SS-5 is available at your local SSA office.

It usually takes about 2 weeks to get an SSN. If you do not have a required SSN by the filing due date, you can file Form 4868 for an extension of time to file.

Born and died in 2005. If your child was born and died in 2005, and you do not have an SSN for the child, you may attach a copy of the child's birth certificate instead. If you do, enter "DIED" in column (2) of line 6c of your Form 1040 or Form 1040A.

Alien or adoptee with no SSN. If your dependent does not have and cannot get an SSN, you must list the individual taxpayer identification number (ITIN) or adoption taxpayer identification number (ATIN) instead of an SSN.

Taxpayer identification numbers for aliens. If your dependent is a resident or nonresident alien who does not have and is not eligible to get an SSN, your dependent must apply for an individual taxpayer identification number (ITIN). Write the number in column (2) of line 6c of your Form 1040 or Form 1040A. To apply for an ITIN, use Form W-7, Application for IRS Individual Taxpayer Identification Number.

Taxpayer identification numbers for adoptees. If you have a child who was placed with you by an authorized placement agency, you may be able to claim an exemption for the child. However, if you cannot get an SSN or an ITIN for the child, you must get an adoption taxpayer identification number (ATIN) for the child from the IRS. See Form W-7A, Application for Taxpayer Identification Number for Pending U.S. Adoptions, for details.

TAXORGANIZER

To obtain a Social Security number, fill out form SS-5 located in Chapter 49 and file it with your local Social Security office. If you applied for a Social Security number for your child but failed to receive it by the due date for filing your return, write "Applied For" in the space provided for the number on your return.

TAX ORGANIZER

Records you should keep

Social Security Card
Support test calculations, if your dependent has sufficient income that might jeopardize your claiming him or her as a dependent.

4

Decedents

Note: The 2004 IRS Publication 17 (Your Federal Income Tax) has been updated by Ernst & Young LLP for 2005. Dates and dollar amounts shown are for 2005. Gray type is used to indicate where IRS text has been updated or intentionally omitted. Unrevised IRS text is shown in black type.

Introduction

The death of an individual causes special tax problems that are likely to be unfamiliar and puzzling to the survivors. Among other things, the decedent's will, along with state inheritance laws, can create a bewildering array of questions about how income is to be allocated and which deductions may be claimed and by whom.

This chapter helps you sort out such questions. It is most helpful to a survivor who has to deal with a relatively uncomplicated situation and a small estate. Where the assets are large and the situation is complex, professional assistance is recommended.

TAXALERT

The estate tax will be repealed only during 2010. Unless Congress decides otherwise, the estate tax will be reinstated as of January 1, 2011.

Reminders

Estate tax return. Generally, if the decedent died during 2005, an estate tax return (Form 706) must be filed if the gross estate is more than $1,500,000.

Consistent treatment of estate items. Beneficiaries must generally treat estate items the same way on their individual returns as they are treated on the estate's return. For more information, see *How and When To Report* under *Distributions to Beneficiaries From an Estate* in Publication 559, Survivors, Executors, and Administrators.

This chapter discusses the tax responsibilities of the person who is in charge of the property (estate) of an individual who has died (decedent). It also covers the following topics.

• Filing the decedent's final return.
• Tax effects on survivors.

This chapter does not discuss the requirements for filing an income tax return of an estate (Form 1041). For information on Form 1041, see *Income Tax Return of an Estate—Form 1041* in Publication 559. This chapter also does not discuss the requirements for filing an estate tax return (Form 706). For information, see Form 706 and its instructions.

Explanation

Though this chapter mainly discusses the filing requirement of a final individual income tax return for a decedent, an explanation of the various potential filing requirements may be helpful. Generally, upon an individual's death, there are three types of taxes that should be addressed: estate tax, gift tax, and income tax.

The estate tax is reported on Form 706, *U.S. Estate Tax Return.* Form 706 is a return that is generally based on the value of the net assets of the decedent's "estate" at date of death. The filing deadline for Form 706 is within 9 months after the date of death unless you received an extension of time to file. In 2005, the first $1.5 million of one's estate is generally not taxable because the IRS allows a unified credit that equals the tax calculated on $1.5 million of assets. Therefore, Form 706 is generally required to be filed if your gross estate (the value of the estate *without* subtracting debts and liabilities) is over $1.5 million.

The unified credit amount gradually increases so that by the year 2009 it will equal the tax calculated on $3,500,000 of assets. In 2010, the estate tax is scheduled to be fully repealed.

The repeal of the estate tax, however, is provided to last only for people dying in 2010. After December 31, 2010, the estate tax reverts to 2001 law.

The increase in the unified credit equivalent, the repeal of the estate tax, and the increase in the highest estate tax rate are being phased in as follows:

Year of Death	Highest Estate Tax Rate	Unified Credit Amount
2005	47%	$1,500,000
2006	46%	$2,000,000
2007	45%	$2,000,000
2008	45%	$2,000,000
2009	45%	$3,500,000
2010	N/A	Full Repeal
2011	55% (plus possible surtax)	$1,000,000

Note. The estate tax and gift tax credits are no longer "unified." The estate tax exemption amount changes according to the table above. The gift tax remains level at $1 million.

In addition to the estate tax return, the personal representative of the decedent may be required to file a gift tax return (Form 709) on the decedent's behalf. This return would report any gifts made by the decedent in the year of death and indicate the amount, if any, of gift tax due.

Example
You have made cash gifts using up to $900,000 of your $1 million gift tax exemption in prior years. In 2005 you make another gift of $250,000 in excess of your $11,000 annual gift tax exclusion. $100,000 ($1,000,000 − $900,000) of the gift uses up the last of your $1 million gift tax exemption. You will need to pay gift tax on $150,000 of the gift in 2005.

There are two possible income tax returns that may need to be filed: Form 1040, *U.S. Individual Income Tax Return,* and Form 1041, *U.S. Income Tax Return for Estates and Trusts.* Form 1040 is generally used to report all the income that was earned and received prior to death. Any income that was earned and received after date of death is generally reported by the estate (or the trust, if the asset was held in trust) and is reported on Form 1041. This chapter focuses mainly on Form 1040 issues.

Useful Items

You may want to see:

Publication

☐ **559** Survivors, Executors, and Administrators

Forms (and Instructions)

☐ **56** Notice Concerning Fiduciary Relationship
☐ **1310** Statement of Person Claiming Refund Due a Deceased Taxpayer
☐ **4810** Request for Prompt Assessment Under Internal Revenue Code Section 6501(d)

Personal Representative

A personal representative of an estate is an executor, administrator, or anyone who is in charge of the decedent's property.

Executor. Generally, an executor (or executrix) is named in a decedent's will to administer the estate (property and debts left by the decedent) and distribute properties as the decedent has directed.

Administrator. An administrator (or administratrix) is usually appointed by the court if no will exists, if no executor was named in the will, or if the named executor cannot or will not serve.

Personal representative. In general, an executor and an administrator perform the same duties and have the same responsibilities. Because a personal representative for a decedent's estate can be an executor, administrator, or anyone in charge of the decedent's property, the term personal representative will be used throughout this chapter.

The surviving spouse may or may not be the personal representative, depending on the terms of the decedent's will or the court appointment.

Duties

The primary duties of a personal representative are to collect all of the decedent's assets, pay the creditors, and distribute the remaining assets to the heirs or other beneficiaries.

The personal representative also must perform the following duties.

1. Notify the IRS (as discussed below) that he or she is acting as the personal representative.
2. File any income tax and estate tax return when due. (See *Final Return for the Decedent,* later.)
3. Pay any tax determined up to the date of discharge from duties.
4. Provide the payers of any interest and dividends the name(s) and identification number(s) of the new owner(s). (See *Interest and Dividend Income [Forms 1099],* later.)

For more information on the duties and responsibilities of the personal representative, see *Duties* under *Personal Representative* in Publication 559.

Notifying the IRS. If you are appointed to act in any fiduciary capacity for another, you must file a written notice with the IRS stating this. Form 56 can be used for this purpose. The instructions and other requirements are given on the back of the form.

Explanation
Form 56, *Notice Concerning Fiduciary Relationship,* is used to notify the IRS of the *creation* or *termination* of a fiduciary relationship. If notification is not given to the IRS, notices of taxes due will be sent to the last known address of the decedent. This is considered sufficient notice by the IRS. Therefore Form 56 should be filed in a timely manner so that the personal representative is not considered personally liable for the taxes due, along with possible interest and penalties.

Final Return for the Decedent

The same filing requirements that apply to individuals determine if a final income tax return must be filed for the decedent. Filing requirements are discussed in chapter 1.

Filing to get a refund. A return should be filed to obtain a refund if tax was withheld from salaries, wages, pensions, or annuities, or if estimated tax was paid, even if a return is not required to be filed. See *Claiming a refund,* later. Also, the decedent may be entitled to other credits that result in a refund. See chapters 38 and 39 for additional information on refundable credits and see chapter 36 for information on the child tax credit.

DECEASED   JOHN S. STONE   FEBRUARY 28, 2005

Form 1040
Department of the Treasury—Internal Revenue Service
U.S. Individual Income Tax Return **2005** (99) | IRS Use Only—Do not write or staple in this space.

OMB No. 1545-0074

Label
(See instructions on page 16.)
Use the IRS label.
Otherwise, please print or type.

L A B E L   H E R E

For the year Jan. 1–Dec. 31, 2005, or other tax year beginning   , 2005, ending   , 20

CAR-RT   SORT**CR01
LP   S29   30
JOHN S & JANE M STONE
1992 OAK ST   103
SHERIDAN   WY   82801

I R S

Your social security number
765 00 4321

Spouse's social security number
123 00 4567

▲ You **must** enter your SSN(s) above. ▲

Presidential Election Campaign ▶ Check here if you, or your spouse if filing jointly, want $3 to go to this fund (see page 16) ▶ ☐ **You** ☐ **Spouse**

Checking a box below will not change your tax or refund.

Filing Status

Check only one box.

1 ☐ Single
2 ☐ Married filing jointly (even if only one had income)
3 ☐ Married filing separately. Enter spouse's SSN above and full name here. ▶
4 ☐ Head of household (with qualifying person). (See page 17.) If the qualifying person is a child but not your dependent, enter this child's name here. ▶
5 ☐ Qualifying widow(er) with dependent child (see page 17)

Third Party Designee

Do you want to allow another person to discuss this return with the IRS (see page 56)? ☐ **Yes.** Complete the following. ☑ **No**

Designee's name ▶   Phone no. ▶ (   )   Personal identification number (PIN) ▶

Sign Here

Joint return? See page 17.
Keep a copy for your records.

Under penalties of perjury, I declare that I have examined this return and accompanying schedules and statements, and to the best of my knowledge and belief, they are true, correct, and complete. Declaration of preparer (other than taxpayer) is based on all information of which preparer has any knowledge.

Your signature	Date	Your occupation	Daytime phone number
Jane M. Stone	4/1/06	Engineer	( )
Spouse's signature. If a joint return, **both** must sign. Filing as surviving spouse	Date	Spouse's occupation	

Paid Preparer's Use Only

Preparer's signature ▶	Date	Check if self-employed ☐	Preparer's SSN or PTIN
Firm's name (or yours if self-employed), address, and ZIP code ▶		EIN	
		Phone no. ( )	

Form **1040** (2005)

Determining income and deductions. The method of accounting regularly used by the decedent before death generally determines what income you must include and what deductions you can take on the final return. Generally, individuals use one of two methods of accounting: cash or accrual.

Cash method. If the decedent used the cash method of accounting, include only the items of income actually or constructively received before death and deduct only the expenses the decedent paid before death. For an exception for certain medical expenses not paid before death, see *Decedent* in chapter 23.

Explanation

Actual or constructive receipt of income includes items such as uncashed payroll and **dividend** checks, if they were received or were available to the decedent before death.

Example

If the decedent's payroll check for June 1 through June 15 is available on Wednesday, June 15, but she fails to pick it up and dies on Thursday, June 16, the income is included in the decedent's final individual income tax return. However, if the decedent would not have been paid until Friday, June 17—that date appears on the check and that is the first day it could have been picked up—the income is reported as part of the estate and *not* on the final Form 1040. In the latter case, the income is called *income in respect of the decedent* and is discussed in the following section.

If the decedent was married and lived in a **community property** state—Arizona, California, Idaho, Louisiana, Nevada, New Mexico, Texas, or Washington—half of the combined income and expenses of husband and wife up to the date of death may be attributable to the decedent. Wisconsin has a marital property law that is similar to community property law.

TaxSaver

The person filing the decedent's final return may elect to include as income on that return all of the U.S. Savings Bond interest that had accumulated but had not been reported. If the decedent otherwise had low **taxable income** to report on her final return, this return could be the best one in which to recognize the interest income. To determine whether or not this is advantageous, you have to compare the tax rate of the decedent on the final individual income tax return with the tax rate of the recipient of the bonds. (For a further discussion of this point, see Chapter 8, *Interest Income.*)

Accrual method. If the decedent used an accrual method of accounting, report only those items of income that the decedent accrued, or earned, before death. Deduct those expenses the decedent was liable for before death, regardless of whether the expenses were paid.

Additional information. For more information on the cash and accrual methods, see *Accounting Methods* in chapter 1.

Who must file the return? The personal representative (defined earlier) must file the final income tax return (Form 1040) of the decedent for the year of death and any returns not filed for preceding years. A surviving spouse, under certain circumstances, may have to file the returns for the decedent. See *Joint return,* later.

Example. Samantha Smith died on March 21, 2005, before filing her 2004 tax return. Her personal representative must file her 2004 return by April 15, 2005. Her final tax return is due April 17, 2006.

Explanation

If the decedent had not yet filed a return for the previous year, the personal representative or surviving spouse should prepare and file the return, just as the decedent would have. The only differences are (1) the executor signs the return (see *Signing the Return,* later) and (2) the estimated tax payments that are due after the decedent died are not required to be made. If a joint return is being filed, see the discussion of estimated tax payments under *Joint Return,* later.

For the year of death, the decedent's final return covers income received and deductions paid during the period from January 1 through the date of death (assuming that the decedent was a cash-basis taxpayer).

TAXSAVER

If the decedent was a member of the U.S. Armed Forces and dies while in active service in a combat zone or from wounds, disease, or other injury received in a combat zone, the decedent's income tax liability is forgiven for the tax year in which death occurred.

A decedent's income tax liability is also forgiven for any decedent who was either a military or civilian U.S. employee at death and dies from wounds or injury incurred while a U.S. employee in a terroristic or military action outside the United States.

For additional information, please seek advice from your tax advisor.

TAXSAVER

A surviving spouse may be able to reduce the tax on his or her income by filing a **joint return** with the decedent. Even if a taxpayer died on January 1 with no income earned by that date, the availability of joint tax rates to the surviving spouse could be beneficial. However, if the surviving spouse remarries before the end of the year, the decedent must file as married filing separately.

Filing the return. The word "DECEASED," the decedent's name, and the date of death should be written across the top of the tax return. In the name and address space, you should write the name and address of the decedent and, if a joint return, of the surviving spouse. If a joint return is not being filed, the decedent's name should be written in the name space and the personal representative's name and address should be written in the remaining space.

Example. John Stone died in early 2005. He was survived by his wife, Jane. The top of their final joint return on Form 1040, which includes the required information, is illustrated on the previous page.

Signing the return. If a personal representative has been appointed, that person must sign the return. If it is a joint return, the surviving spouse must also sign it.

If no personal representative has been appointed, the surviving spouse (on a joint return) should sign the return and write in the signature area "Filing as surviving spouse." See *Joint return,* later.

If no personal representative has been appointed and if there is no surviving spouse, the person in charge of the decedent's property must file and sign the return as "personal representative."

TAX ORGANIZER

After a person dies, it may be difficult for the family or personal representative to locate the information necessary to file the final tax return (e.g., charitable contribution receipts, interest deductions, pay stubs, 1099s). However, it is important to make a diligent search and to organize carefully the items located. See chart on page 54 entitled Important Tax-Related Actions to Take After a Death.

Example. Assume in the previous example that no personal representative has been appointed. The bottom of the final joint return, which shows that Jane is filing the return as the surviving spouse, is illustrated on the next page.

Third party designee. You can check the "Yes" box in the Third Party Designee area of the return to authorize the IRS to discuss the return with a friend, family member, or any other person you choose. This allows the IRS to call the person you identified as the designee to answer any questions that may arise during the processing of the return. It also allows the designee to perform certain actions. See your income tax package for details.

Claiming a refund. Generally, a person who is filing a return for a decedent and claiming a refund must file Form 1310 with the return. However, if the person claiming the refund is a surviving spouse filing a joint return with the decedent, or a court-appointed or certified personal representative filing an original return for the decedent, Form 1310 is not needed. The personal representative must attach to the return a copy of the court certificate showing that he or she was appointed the personal representative.

If the personal representative is filing a claim for refund on Form 1040X, Amended U.S. Individual Income Tax Return, or Form 843, Claim for Refund and Request for Abatement, and the court certificate has already been filed with the IRS, attach Form 1310 and write "Certificate Previously Filed" at the bottom of the form.

Example. Mr. Green died before filing his tax return. You were appointed the personal representative for Mr. Green's estate and you file his Form 1040 showing a refund due. You do not need Form 1310 to claim the refund if you attach a copy of the court certificate showing you were appointed the personal representative.

TAXPLANNER

To make sure that refunds are not delayed, it is recommended that Form 1310 be attached to *any* return being filed for a decedent on which a refund is being claimed. This is true despite the fact that Form 1310 may not be required, as discussed above.

Form 1310 can also be submitted to request that a refund check issued jointly to the decedent and surviving spouse be reissued to a surviving spouse.

When and where to file. The final income tax return is due at the same time the decedent's return would have been due had death not occurred. The final return for a decedent who was a calendar year taxpayer is generally due April 15 following the year death occurred. However, when the due date falls on a Saturday, Sunday, or legal holiday, the return is filed timely if filed by the next business day.

TAXPLANNER

The personal representative or surviving spouse may request an extension of time to file the decedent's final income tax return by filing Form 4868. This will give you an additional 4 months to file the return. If additional

Important Tax-Related Actions to Take After a Death	
Action	**Comments**
Obtain at least 10 death certificates from the local county clerk, mortuary, or funeral director.	The executor or personal representative (referred to as the "executor" in this chart) must file the death certificate with the estate tax return (Form 706) for the decedent. Also, death certificates will be needed to claim life insurance proceeds, change title to bank accounts, and transfer title to other assets. Death certificates usually will not be available until a week or two after the death.
Contact life insurance companies to claim the proceeds. The executor can usually find the telephone number in the life insurance policy.	Contact the insurance company as soon as possible. Insurance companies are sometimes slow to respond, and the decedent's family may need the insurance proceeds for support.
Notify the Social Security Administration of the death. Also notify banks and investment brokers.	The telephone number for the Social Security Administration is 1-800-772-1213.
Contact an estate planning or probate attorney to determine what court filings are necessary.	Select an attorney who has at least 5 years of significant experience handling probates and administrations of estates. See the attorney as soon as possible after the death. Referrals to attorneys can be obtained from friends or relatives, or often from a local Bar Association Referral Service.
Contact an accountant regarding all tax filings that will be necessary.	The personal representative or surviving spouse must file a final income tax return for the decedent (Form 1040). No further estimated taxes for the decedent must be paid after the death of the decedent. The "probate estate" (if a probate is necessary) becomes a new taxpayer and the personal representative must file a tax return (Form 1041). The estate may select a fiscal year which may result in beneficial tax deferral. If the decedent created a "revocable living trust" during life, that trust (which becomes irrevocable at death) also becomes a new taxpayer and may also be required to file a Form 1041. However, in certain cases, the probate estate and the trust may file consolidated income tax returns.
Open an estate checking account as soon as possible—deposit all checks due to the decedent and pay all debts and expenses owed (including funeral expenses and taxes) from this account.	It is critical that accurate records are kept. Do not comingle anyone else's income or expenses with the decedent's income and expenses, including income earned and expenses paid after date of death. The executor will need accurate information to report on the decedent's final income tax return, the estate's and/or trust's income tax return, and the estate tax return.
Search through the decedent's desk, office, safe deposit box, and files to locate information which is needed for the tax returns.	Specifically, look for the following: Will, codicils to the Will, trust agreements, addresses, and social security numbers of beneficiaries; checking, savings money market, and CD statements; check book registers, brokerage statements, stock certificates, bonds, retirement plan, and IRA benefit statements; life insurance and annuity policies; the last 3 years of state and federal income tax returns; all prior gift tax returns; property tax bill and deed for real estate; buy-sell or operating agreements for businesses, all outstanding bills (including last illness and funeral bills), and any undeposited checks.
Review the decedent's company retirement and benefit plans, as well as IRA's, with a tax advisor.	The beneficiary of these assets must make certain decisions regarding distributions from these plans and IRA's; and the decisions made can have significant income tax consequnces.

time is required, Form 2688, *Request for Additional Time to File,* may be filed to request an additional 2-month extension. Note that an extension of time to file does not mean an extension of time to pay tax. Hence, any tax liability owed must be paid in full by the due date of the return, excluding extensions. See *When Do I Have to File?* in Chapter 1, *Filing Information.*

You may obtain Form 4868 or Form 2688 via the Internet by visiting the Internal Revenue Service Web site at www.irs.gov.

Generally, you must file the final income tax return of the decedent with the Internal Revenue Service Center for the place where you live. A tax return for a decedent can be electronically filed. A personal representative may also obtain an income tax filing extension on behalf of a decedent.

TAXPLANNER

A representative of a decedent's estate may be held personally liable by the IRS for later-discovered tax deficiencies if the representative has not retained enough of the estate's assets to pay those deficiencies. Therefore, many cautious representatives are slow to distribute the estate's assets to the heirs. Filing Form 4810, *A Request for Prompt Assessment,* may shorten the period in which the IRS may hold the representative responsible for not paying enough tax, thereby potentially allowing the estate's assets to be distributed more promptly. However, the request may trigger an audit of those returns.

Joint return. Generally, the personal representative and the surviving spouse can file a joint return for the decedent and the surviving spouse. However, the surviving spouse alone can file the joint return if no personal representative has been appointed before the due date for filing the joint return for the year of death. This also applies to the return for the preceding year if the decedent died after the close of the preceding tax year and before filing the return for that year. The income of the decedent that was includible on his or her return for the year up to the date of death (as explained under *Determining income and deductions,* earlier) and the income of the surviving spouse for the entire year must be included in the final joint return.

A joint return with the decedent cannot be filed for the year of death if the surviving spouse remarried before the end of the year of the decedent's death. The filing status of the decedent in this instance is married filing separate return.

TAXPLANNER

If you are a surviving spouse and are filing a joint return with the decedent for 2005, you are not relieved of the obligation to make estimated tax payments for 2006 because of the death. See Chapter 5, *Tax Withholding and Estimated Tax,* for more information on estimated tax payments.

TAXSAVER

If the decedent was married, it is important to calculate whether the tax on a joint return would be less than the total tax on two separate returns.

Ordinarily, a joint return would result in the least overall tax for married couples, but only a complete computation will tell you for sure. Remember, the joint return will include all of the income and deductions of the survivor for the entire year, but those of the decedent are included only up to the date of death. If property was owned jointly with the surviving spouse, all of the income after death is required to be reported in the joint return, because it, along with the ownership of the property, passed to the surviving spouse. However, if the property was not owned jointly and passed to an executor at death, the subsequent income on that property would be reported on the income tax return for the estate for which the executor is responsible, and not on the joint return.

Personal representative may revoke joint return election. A court-appointed personal representative may revoke an election to file a joint return that was previously made by the surviving spouse alone. This is done by filing a separate return for the decedent within one year from the due date of the return (including any extensions). The joint return made by the surviving spouse will then be regarded as the separate return of that spouse by excluding the decedent's items and refiguring the tax liability.

Relief from joint liability. In some cases, one spouse may be relieved of joint liability for tax, interest, and penalties on a joint return for items of the other spouse that were incorrectly reported on the joint return. If the decedent qualified for this relief while alive, the personal representative can pursue an existing request, or file a request, for relief from joint liability within two years of the first collection activity against the requesting spouse. For information on requesting this relief, see *Filing a Joint Return* in chapter 2.

How To Report Certain Income

This section explains how to report certain types of income on the final return. The rules on income discussed in the other chapters of this publication also apply to a decedent's final return. See chapters 6 through 17, if they apply.

Interest and Dividend Income (Forms 1099)

A Form 1099 should be received for the decedent reporting interest and dividends earned before death. These amounts must be included on the decedent's final return. A separate Form 1099 should show the interest and dividends earned after the date of the decedent's death and paid to the estate or other recipient that must include those amounts on its return. You can request corrected Forms 1099 if these forms do not properly reflect the right recipient or amounts.

For example, a Form 1099-INT reporting interest payable to the decedent may include income that should be reported on the final income tax return of the decedent, as well as income that the estate or other recipient should report, either as income earned after death or as income in respect of the decedent (discussed later). For income earned after death, you should ask the payer for a Form 1099 that properly identifies the recipient (by name and identification number) and the proper amount. If that is not possible, or if the form includes an amount that represents income in respect of the decedent, report the interest, as shown next under *How to report.*

See *U.S. savings bonds acquired from decedent* in Publication 559 for information on savings bond interest that may have to be reported on the final return.

How to report. If you are preparing the decedent's final return and you have received a Form 1099-INT for the decedent that includes amounts belonging to the decedent and to another recipient (the decedent's estate or another beneficiary), report the total interest shown on Form 1099-INT on Schedule 1 (Form 1040A) or on Schedule B (Form 1040). Next, enter a subtotal of the interest shown on Forms 1099 and the interest reportable from other sources for which you did not receive Forms 1099. Then, show any interest (including any interest you receive as a nominee) belonging to another recipient separately and subtract it from the subtotal. Identify this adjustment as a "Nominee Distribution" or other appropriate designation.

Report dividend income for which you received a Form 1099-DIV, Dividends and Distributions, on the appropriate schedule using the same procedure.

Note. If the decedent received amounts as a nominee, you must give the actual owner a Form 1099, unless the owner is the decedent's spouse. See *General Instructions for Forms 1099, 1098, 5498, and W-2G,* for more information on filing forms 1099.

TAXPLANNER

No matter how hard you try, you will not get the payers of dividends and interest to reflect properly the amounts attributable to the decedent prior to death and the amounts that are paid to the decedent's successor in interest. It is therefore imperative that you follow the example below carefully in order to avoid bothersome inquiries from the IRS.

Example 1

Marty died on June 30, 2005. Marty owned 50 shares of ABC Corporation and 75 shares of XYZ Corporation, both of which paid a $1 per share quarterly dividend on February 1, May 1, August 1, and November 1. Upon Marty's death, all shares were transferred to his estate. XYZ Corporation has properly issued two Forms 1099-DIV. One Form 1099-DIV identifies Marty as the recipient of $150 (the dividends paid to Marty prior to death, from January 1, 2005, to June 30, 2005), and the other identifies Marty's estate as the recipient of

$150 (the dividends paid to the estate, from July 1, 2005, to December 31, 2005). ABC Corporation, however, issued only one Form 1099-DIV, naming Marty as the recipient of the entire year's dividend ($200).

On Marty's final return, you must report total dividends as indicated on all Forms 1099-DIV issued in Marty's name ($150 from XYZ Corporation and $200 from ABC Corporation) on line 5, Part II of Form 1040, Schedule B. Several lines above line 6, write "Subtotal" and enter $350. Below this subtotal, write "Nominee Distribution" and enter $100 (the dividends paid by ABC Corporation to Marty's estate). Indicate the name and EIN of the nominee. Subtract the nominee distribution from the subtotal and report the net result of $250 on line 6. The same reporting procedure would apply to reporting interest. See the example below for an example of the language to put on Schedule B.

Example 2

John Johnson died on July 1, 2005. In January 2006, ABC Bank sent a Form 1099-INT to his executor reflecting interest paid during 2005 of $5,000. Because John was alive for only one-half of 2005, only one-half of the interest will be reported on his final Form 1040 for 2005. The other one-half of the interest will be reported on his estate's income tax return (Form 1041).

Schedule B of John's final Form 1040 should report the $2,500 of interest. Part I, line 1, should be completed as follows:

ABC Bank	$5,000
Less nominee distribution	($2,500)
(estate of John Johnson: EIN:00-0000000)	

Part 1, line 4, would show total interest income of $2,500

The Form 1041 for the estate of John will report the other $2,500 of interest income.

TaxORGANIZER

You should keep a copy of the Forms 1099 that you receive as well as the tax worksheets showing pre- and post-death income for a minimum of 3 years.

Accelerated Death Benefits

Accelerated death benefits are amounts received under a life insurance contract before the death of the insured individual. These benefits also include amounts received on the sale or assignment of the contract to a provider of viatical settlements (life insurance payouts prior to death).

Generally, if the decedent received accelerated death benefits either on his or her own life or on the life of another person, those benefits are not included in the decedent's income. This exclusion applies only if the insured was a terminally or chronically ill individual. For more information, see *Accelerated death benefits* under *Gifts, Insurance, and Inheritances* in Publication 559.

Business Income

This section discusses some of the business income which may have to be included on the final return.

Partnership income. The death of a partner closes the partnership's tax year for that partner. Generally, it does not close the partnership's tax year for the remaining partners. The decedent's distributive share of partnership items must be figured as if the partnership's tax year ended on the date the partner died. To avoid an interim closing of the partnership books, the partners can agree to estimate the decedent's distributive share by prorating the amounts the partner would have included for the entire partnership tax year.

On the decedent's final return, include the decedent's distributive share of partnership items for the following periods.

1. The partnership's tax year that ended within or with the decedent's final tax year (the year ending on the date of death); and
2. The period, if any, from the end of the partnership's tax year in (1) to the decedent's date of death.

TaxALERT

Effective for partnerships with taxable years beginning after December 31, 1997, the partnership's tax year closes with respect to a partner whose entire interest in the partnership is terminated by death. Therefore, the partnership income will have to be allocated between and reported by the decedent and the decedent's successor in interest. The final individual income tax return should include the decedent's share of partnership income and deductions for the partnership's tax year that ends within or with the decedent's last tax year (the year ending on the date of death). The final return must also include income for the period between the end of the partnership's last tax year and the date of death.

The income for the part of the partnership's tax year after the partner's death is reported by the estate or other person who has acquired the interest in the partnership.

Example

Jim, a partner in a law firm, died on December 1, 2005. The tax year for the partnership ends on June 30. Jim's partnership income for the year ending June 30, 2005, of $100,000 will be included on his 2005 individual income tax return. In addition, Jim's final income tax return for 2005 will also include his pro rata portion (154 days) of partnership income and deductions from July 1, 2005, to December 1, 2005, with the remainder to be reported to Jim's successor in interest.

TaxSAVER

Planning for partnership interests can save substantial amounts of income tax. For example, a partner should investigate the possibility of appointing his or her spouse as successor in interest to the partnership so that the income or loss for the year of death can flow onto the survivor's return and thus onto the joint return.

There is another way of ensuring the immediate transfer of the partnership interest to the spouse upon the partner's death so that the income or loss can be reported on the joint return. The spouses may own the partnership interest in joint tenancy. Be sure to check that the partnership will permit this. Also if the executor has the assets and the legal authority to make an immediate distribution of the partnership interest to the spouse all or a portion of the partnership income can be transferred to the final joint return. Prompt action may be necessary. Finally consult with a tax advisor because there may be tax disadvantages to holding property in joint tenancy.

TaxPLANNER

If a decedent had an interest in a passive activity (e.g., a partnership or S corporation) the passive activity rules still apply on the decedent's final individual tax return. For example, the death of a partner does not trigger the deduction of any suspended passive activity losses associated with that partnership. (See Chapter 13, *Other Income*, for more information on passive activity losses.) Generally, the remaining suspended losses may not be transferred to the partner's successor in interest. However, these losses may have to be reduced depending on whether the interest received a step-up in basis. You should consult with your tax advisor for more information.

S corporation income. If the decedent was a shareholder in an S corporation, include on the final return the decedent's share of the S corporation's items of income, loss, deduction, and credit for the following periods.

1. The corporation's tax year that ended within or with the decedent's final tax year (the year ending on the date of death); and
2. The period, if any, from the end of the corporation's tax year in (1) to the decedent's date of death.

Example

Julia Jones was a 20% partner in XYZ Partnership and a 20% shareholder in ABC Corporation, an S corporation. The tax year for both the partnership and the corporation ends on December 31. Julia died on October 1, 2005. Had she lived Julia would have earned $100,000 of ordinary income in 2005 from the partnership and another $100,000 of ordinary income from the corporation.

Julia's final tax return for 2005 will include $75,068 (274 days) of income from ABC Corporation and $75,068 of income from XYZ Partnership. The remaining $24,932 of ABC Corporation and the $24,932 from XYZ Partnership income will be included in the tax return of the successor in interest.

Self-employment income. Include self-employment income actually or constructively received or accrued, depending on the decedent's accounting method. For self-employment tax purposes only, the decedent's self-employment income will include the decedent's distributive share of a partnership's income or loss through the end of the month in which death occurred. For this purpose, the partnership income or loss is considered to be earned ratably over the partnership's tax year. For more information on how to compute self-employment income, see Publication 533, Self-Employment Tax.

Coverdell Education Savings Account (ESA)

Generally, the balance in a Coverdell ESA must be distributed within 30 days after the individual for whom the account was established reaches age 30, or dies, whichever is earlier. The treatment of the Coverdell ESA at the death of an individual under age 30 depends on who acquires the interest in the account. If the decedent's estate acquires the interest, the earnings on the account must be included on the final income tax return of the decedent. If a beneficiary acquires the interest, see the discussion under *Income in Respect of the Decedent*, later.

The age 30 limit does not apply if the individual for whom the account was established, or the beneficiary that acquires the account, is an individual with special needs. This includes an individual who because of a physical, mental, or emotional condition (including a learning disability) requires additional time to complete his or her education.

For more information on Coverdell ESAs, see Publication 970, Tax Benefits for Education.

Archer MSA

The treatment of an Archer MSA, a Medicare Advantage MSA, or a Health Savings Account (HSA), at the death of the account holder, depends on who acquires the interest in the account. If the decedent's estate acquires the interest, the fair market value of the assets in the account on the date of death is included in income on the decedent's final return.

If a beneficiary acquires the interest, see the discussion under *Income in Respect of the Decedent*, later. For more information on Archer MSAs, see Publication 969, *Health Savings Accounts and Other Tax-Favored Health Plans*.

Exemptions, Deductions, and Credits

Generally, the rules for exemptions, deductions, and credits allowed to an individual also apply to the decedent's final income tax return. Show on the final return deductible items the decedent paid (or accrued, if the decedent reported deductions on an accrual method) before death.

Exemptions

You can claim the decedent's personal exemption on the final income tax return. If the decedent was another person's dependent (for example, a parent's), you cannot claim the personal exemption on the decedent's final return.

Standard Deduction

If you do not itemize deductions on the final return, the full amount of the appropriate standard deduction is allowed regardless of the date of death. For information on the appropriate standard deduction, see chapter 22.

Itemized Deductions

If the total of the decedent's itemized deductions is more than the decedent's standard deduction, the federal income tax will generally be less if you claim itemized deductions on the final return. See chapters 23 through 30 for the types of expenses that are allowed as itemized deductions.

> **TAXPLANNER**
>
> Funeral burial and probate expenses are not deductible on the decedent's income tax return. However, these may be deducted on the decedent's estate tax return.

Medical expenses. Medical expenses paid before death by the decedent are deductible, subject to limits, on the final income tax return if deductions are itemized. This includes expenses for the decedent as well as for the decedent's spouse and dependents.
Caution. *Qualified medical expenses are not deductible if paid with a tax-free distribution from an Archer MSA.*

For information on certain medical expenses that were not paid before death, see *Decedent* in chapter 23.

> **TAXSAVER**
>
> The executor or executrix may elect to either claim certain medical and dental expenses as deductions on the estate tax return or as deductions on the decedent's final income tax return. The tax should be computed both ways to see which results in more tax savings.
>
> If an election is made to include the medical and dental expenses on the decedent's income tax return rather than on the federal estate tax return, the execu-

tor or executrix must attach a statement to the income tax return stating that he or she has not claimed the amount as an estate tax deduction and that the estate waives the right to claim the amount as a deduction.

TaxSaver

When death is expected, proper planning can save tax dollars. Deductible expenses, such as interest expense and accounting fees, that are due near the date of death may be paid before death, or after death. Choose the time offering the greater tax benefit. If you arrange to pay the expenses before death, they are deductible on the decedent's final Form 1040 if deductions are itemized. If you arrange to pay them after death, they are deductible on the estate's income tax return. Limitations as to deductibility may apply.

Unrecovered investment in pension. If the decedent was receiving a pension or annuity (with an annuity starting date after 1986) and died without a surviving annuitant, you can take a deduction on the decedent's final return for the amount of the decedent's investment in the pension or annuity contract that remained unrecovered at death. The deduction is a miscellaneous itemized deduction that is not subject to the 2% limit on adjusted gross income. See chapter 30.

Deduction for Losses

A decedent's net operating loss deduction from a prior year and any capital losses (including capital loss carryovers) can be deducted only on the decedent's final income tax return. A net operating loss on the decedent's final income tax return can be carried back to prior years (see Publication 536, *Net Operating Losses (NOLs) for Individuals, Estates, and Trusts*). You cannot deduct any unused net operating loss or capital loss on the estate's income tax return.

TaxSaver

Net operating losses (or carryover losses) from business operations and **capital losses** (or carryover losses) of the decedent may not be carried over to the returns of executors or heirs. However, if a joint return is filed for the year of death, these losses may be used to offset the survivor's income for the entire year. In this case, it may be advantageous for the surviving spouse to incur **capital gains** and/or other income and to offset them with the capital losses and/or net operating losses that cannot be carried forward past the year of the spouse's death.

Example

Your spouse died on June 30, 2005, with $10,000 in **short-term capital losses** from his personal account. Because the maximum capital loss that can be deducted in a year is $3,000, only $3,000 of those losses will be allowed on your 2005 joint return, with no carryover of the remaining $7,000. However, if you could recognize an additional $7,000 in gains before the end of the year, you could use your deceased spouse's remaining $7,000 of losses to offset the gains by filing a joint return. If you waited until a later year to recognize those gains, they would be fully taxable, unless you had incurred other losses to offset them.

Credits

Any of the tax credits discussed in this publication also apply to the final return if the decedent was eligible for the credits at the time of death. These credits are discussed in chapters 34 through 39.

Tax withheld and estimated payments. There may have been income tax withheld from the decedent's pay, pensions, or annuities before death, and the decedent may have paid estimated income tax. To get credit for these tax payments, you must claim them on the decedent's final return. For more information, see *Credit for Withholding and Estimated Tax* in chapter 5.

Explanation

Exemption allowances, the standard deduction, and itemized deductions are not prorated over that part of the year during which a now deceased taxpayer was alive. However, exemptions claimed for **dependents** could be a problem if the decedent did not live long enough during the year to provide the required amount of support. In most situations, potential problems will be alleviated if the surviving spouse files a joint return with the decedent. See Chapter 3, *Personal Exemptions and Dependents,* for more information.

Tax Effect on Others

This section contains information about the effect of an individual's death on the income tax liability of the survivors (including the widow or widower and any beneficiaries) and the estate. A survivor should coordinate the filing of his or her own tax return with the personal representative handling the decedent's estate. The personal representative can coordinate filing status, exemptions, income, and deductions so that the decedent's final return and the income tax returns of the survivors and the estate are all filed correctly.

Explanation
Survivors

If you are a survivor, you may qualify for certain benefits when filing your own income tax return. This section addresses some issues that may apply to you.

Gifts and inheritances. Property received as a gift, bequest, or inheritance is not included in your income. However, if property you receive in this manner later produces income, such as interest, dividends, or rent, that income is taxable to you. If the gift, bequest, or inheritance you receive is the income from property, that income is taxable to you.

If you inherited the right to receive income in respect of the decedent, see *Income in Respect of the Decedent,* later.

TaxAlert

The cost basis of any asset distributed from the decedent's estate (which he/she owned at death) via bequest or inheritance is "stepped up" to the fair market value at the date of the decedent's death or the alternate valuation date. See Chapter 14, *Basis of Property,* for more information.

Furthermore, the asset is deemed to be long-term capital gain property, so any capital appreciation on the asset will be taxed at a 5% or 15% capital gains tax rate.

Exception: If you or your spouse inherits property that you gifted to the decedent within 1 year of death, your basis in the asset is what the decedent's adjusted basis in the asset was immediately before his or her death.

TaxAlert

Fees received by an executor or administrator for duties performed for an estate are includable in the gross income of the executor or administrator but are usually not subject to self-employment tax as long as you are not in the trade or business of being an executor or administrator.

However, a bequest to the executor is not treated as income. It is merely a gift to an heir who also happens to be serving as executor. Therefore, if you are the executor and an heir, you may consider declining to take a fee, in which case you will receive a larger portion of the estate that is not subject to income tax. Contact your tax advisor to assist you in determining which course of action is more beneficial.

Joint return by surviving spouse. A surviving spouse can file a joint return for the year of death and may qualify for special tax rates for the following 2 years. For more information, see *Qualifying Widow(er) With Dependent Child* in chapter 2.

Explanation
After the 2-year period following the date of death, a surviving spouse may still be able to qualify as a **head of household** and use the Tax Table and Tax Rate Schedules for head of household. While not as beneficial as joint return rates, they are better than those for single persons. See Chapter 2, *Filing Status,* for more details.

Decedent as your dependent. If the decedent qualified as your dependent for the part of the year before death, you can claim the exemption for the dependent on your tax return, regardless of when death occurred during the year.

If the decedent was your qualifying child, you may be able to claim the child tax credit. See chapter 36.

Income in Respect of the Decedent

All income that the decedent would have received had death not occurred and that was not properly includible on the final return, discussed earlier, is income in respect of the decedent.

How To Report
Income in respect of a decedent must be included in the income of one of the following.

- The decedent's estate, if the estate receives it.
- The beneficiary, if the right to income is passed directly to the beneficiary and the beneficiary receives it.
- Any person to whom the estate properly distributes the right to receive it.

Tip. *If you have to include income in respect of the decedent in your gross income and an estate tax return was filed for the decedent, you may be able to claim a deduction for the estate tax paid on that income. For more information, see Publication 559.*

Example 1. Frank Johnson owned and operated an apple orchard. He used the cash method of accounting. He sold and delivered 1,000 bushels of apples to a canning factory for $2,000, but did not receive payment before his death. The proceeds from the sale are income in respect of the decedent. When the estate was settled, payment had not been made and the estate transferred the right to the payment to his widow. When Frank's widow collects the $2,000, she must include that amount in her return. It is not to be reported on the final return of the decedent or on the return of the estate.

Example 2. Assume the same facts as in Example 1, except that Frank used an accrual method of accounting. The amount accrued from the sale of the apples would be included on his final return. Neither the estate nor the widow will realize income in respect of the decedent when the money is later paid.

Example 3. Cathy O'Neil was entitled to a large salary payment at the date of her death. The amount was to be paid in five annual installments. The estate, after collecting two installments, distributed the right to the remaining installments to you, the beneficiary. The payments are income in respect of the decedent. None of the payments were includible in Cathy's final return. The estate must include in its income the two installments it received, and you must include in your income each of the three installments as you receive them.

Transferring your right to income. If you transfer your right to income in respect of a decedent, you must include in your income the greater of:

- The amount you receive for the right, or
- The fair market value of the right at the time of the transfer.

Fair market value (FMV). FMV is the price at which the property would change hands between a buyer and a seller, neither having to buy or sell, and both having reasonable knowledge of all necessary facts.

Giving your right to income as a gift. If you give your right to receive income in respect of a decedent as a gift, you must include in your income the fair market value of the right at the time you make the gift.

Example
Tom has a right to receive a payment of $10,000 that represents income in respect of his deceased father (e.g., deferred compensation). He makes a gift of his right to receive the money. He would immediately have to recognize the $10,000 as income on his tax return.

Type of income. The character or type of income that you receive in respect of a decedent is the same as it would be to the decedent if he or she were alive. If the income would have been a capital gain to the decedent, it will be a capital gain to you.

Explanation
Installment obligations. If the decedent had sold property using the installment method and you have the right to collect the payments, use the same gross profit percentage the decedent would have used to figure the part of each payment that represents profit. Include in your income the same profit the decedent would have included had death not occurred. For more information on installment sales, see Publication 537, *Installment Sales.*

If you dispose of an installment obligation acquired from a decedent (other than by transfer to the obligor), the rules explained in Publication 537 for figuring gain or loss on the disposition apply to you.

Example
Andrew sold undeveloped real estate held as an investment in 2003 for $120,000, receiving a note payable in four annual installments of $30,000 each plus inter-

est. Andrew's basis in the land was $40,000. Andrew died before the first installment was due, and the note was transferred to Helen, Andrew's heir. Helen collected the first installment of the note, $30,000, in 2004. When Helen was in need of additional cash in early 2005, she sold the note to a bank for its fair market value of $90,000. For 2004, Helen must recognize gain on the payment she received. Using the same gross profit percentage as the decedent's ($80,000 / $120,000), she would recognize a $20,000 gain, computed as follows:

$$\$30,000 \times \$80,000 / \$120,000 = \$20,000$$

For 2005, Helen must recognize gain on the disposition of the installment obligation. The gain is the difference between her basis and the fair market value at the time of the disposition. Her basis in the obligation is the same as Andrew's ($40,000) less the payment of principal received by her in 2004 ($10,000). Hence, her gain is computed as follows:

$$\$90,000 - (\$40,000 - \$10,000) = \$60,000$$

Whether the gain recognized by Helen on her tax return is **ordinary income** or capital gain depends on what it would have been to Andrew had he lived to collect the payments.

Inherited IRAs. If a beneficiary receives a lump-sum distribution from a traditional IRA he or she inherited, all or some of it may be taxable. The distribution is taxable in the year received as income in respect of a decedent up to the decedent's taxable balance. This is the decedent's balance at the time of death, including unrealized appreciation and income accrued to date of death, minus any basis (nondeductible contributions). Amounts distributed that are more than the decedent's entire IRA balance (including taxable and nontaxable amounts) at the time of death are the income of the beneficiary.

If the beneficiary of a traditional IRA is the decedent's surviving spouse who properly rolls over the distribution into another traditional IRA, the distribution is not currently taxed. A surviving spouse can also roll over tax free the taxable part of the distribution into a qualified plan, section 403(b) annuity, or section 457 plan.

Example. At the time of his death, Greg owned a traditional IRA. All of the contributions by Greg to the IRA had been deductible contributions. Greg's nephew, Mark, was the sole beneficiary of the IRA. The entire balance of the IRA, including income accruing before and after Greg's death, was distributed to Mark in a lump sum. Mark must include the total amount received in his income. The portion of the lump-sum distribution that equals the amount of the balance in the IRA at Greg's death, including the income earned before death, is income in respect of the decedent.

TaxAlert

The IRS has issued final regulations that simplify distribution requirements for IRAs, including distribution from inherited IRAs. Generally speaking, a beneficiary may take distributions from an inherited IRA over his or her own life expectancy. These regulations are effective for distributions for calendar years beginning on or after January 1, 2003.

These regulations also apply to Roth IRAs for post-death distributions.

For more information on inherited IRAs, see Publication 590, *Individual Retirement Arrangements (IRAs)*.

Roth IRAs. Qualified distributions from a Roth IRA are not subject to tax. A distribution made to a beneficiary or to the Roth IRA owner's estate on or after the date of death is a qualified distribution if it is made after the 5-year tax period beginning with the first tax year in which a contribution was made to any Roth IRA of the owner.

Part of any distribution to a beneficiary that is not a qualified distribution may be includible in the beneficiary's income. Generally, the part includible is the earnings in the Roth IRA. Earnings attributable to the period ending with the decedent's date of death are income in respect of the decedent. Additional earnings are the income of the beneficiary.

For more information on Roth IRAs, see Publication 590.

Coverdell education savings account (ESA). If the decedent's spouse or other family member is the designated beneficiary of the decedent's account, the Coverdell ESA becomes that person's Coverdell ESA. It is subject to the rules discussed in Publication 970.

Any other beneficiary (including a spouse or family member who is not the designated beneficiary) must include in income the earnings portion of the distribution. Any balance remaining at the close of the 30-day period is deemed to be distributed at that time. The amount included in income is reduced by any qualified education expenses of the decedent that are paid by the beneficiary within 1 year after the decedent's date of death.

Archer MSA. If the decedent's spouse is the designated beneficiary of the account, the account becomes that spouse's Archer MSA. It is subject to the rules discussed in Publication 969.

Any other beneficiary (including a spouse that is not the designated beneficiary) must include in income the fair market value of the assets in the account on the decedent's date of death. This amount must be reported for the beneficiary's tax year that includes the decedent's date of death. The amount included in income is reduced by any qualified medical expenses for the decedent that are paid by the beneficiary within 1 year after the decedent's date of death.

Other income. For examples of other income situations concerning decedents, see *Specific Types of Income in Respect of a Decedent* in Publication 559.

Deductions in Respect of the Decedent

Items such as business expenses, income-producing expenses, interest, and taxes, for which the decedent was liable but that are not properly allowable as deductions on the decedent's final income tax return will be allowed as a deduction to one of the following when paid.

• The estate; or
• The person who acquired an interest in the decedent's property (subject to such obligations) because of the decedent's death, if the estate was not liable for the obligation.

Explanation

Deductions in respect of the decedent are items that would normally be deductible by the decedent except that he or she had not paid them before death. Typical examples are real estate taxes, state income taxes, and interest expense.

TaxSaver

Expenses in respect of a decedent are deductible on both the estate income tax return (Form 1041) and the estate tax return (Form 706). The estate tax and income tax are two different taxes with two entirely unrelated sets of rules. Taking a deduction on one return does not preclude taking the same deduction on the other return. When death is anticipated, planning the best possible use of double deductions may yield significant tax savings. A professional who specializes in this area should be consulted.

Example

When Oscar died in 2005, he owed accrued interest of $100. The marginal estate tax rate for Oscar's estate is 50%, and the estate's marginal income tax rate is 28%. The deduction on the estate tax return is worth $50 (50% of $100) and the deduction on the estate's income tax return is worth $28. Consequently, $78 of the $100 liability is recovered through tax savings.

On the other hand, less tax savings would be realized if Oscar had paid the $100 of interest before he died. He would have been able to take the interest deduction on his personal income tax return, paying $28 less in taxes, assuming he was in the 28% bracket. When he died, he would have been net out-of-pocket $72, his estate would be $72 less, and therefore his estate tax would be reduced by $36 (50% of $72). Thus, if he had paid the expense, his total tax savings would have been $64—$28 of income tax and $36 of estate tax—instead of the $78 tax saved because he had not paid the interest before he died, thus allowing the double deduction.

Estate Tax Deduction

Income that a decedent had a right to receive is included in the decedent's gross estate and is subject to estate tax. This income in respect of a decedent is also taxed when received by the recipient (estate or beneficiary). However, an income tax deduction is allowed to the recipient for the estate tax paid on the income.

The deduction for estate tax can be claimed only for the same tax year in which the income in respect of the decedent must be included in the recipient's income. (This also is true for income in respect of a prior decedent.)

You can claim the deduction only as a miscellaneous itemized deduction on Schedule A (Form 1040). This deduction is not subject to the 2% limit on miscellaneous itemized deductions as discussed in Chapter 30, *Miscellaneous Deductions*.

If the income in respect of the decedent is capital gain income, you must reduce the gain but not below zero, by any deduction for estate tax paid on such gain. This applies in figuring the following.

• The maximum tax on net capital gain.
• The 50% exclusion for gain on small business stock.
• The limitation on net capital losses.

For more information, see *Estate Tax Deduction* in Publication 559.

TAXPLANNER

The deduction for federal estate tax attributable to income in respect of a decedent is complex. The good news is that the question does not arise if there is no federal estate tax on the decedent's estate. If the amount that each individual can leave estate tax free—$1.5 million in 2005, which is equivalent to the unified credit, and the marital deduction—is large enough to eliminate any federal estate tax liability, there cannot be an income tax deduction for federal estate tax.

If the estate incurs federal estate tax, the recipient of income in respect of a decedent may be entitled to an itemized deduction on his or her income tax return.

To determine the amount that can be deducted, you must first determine if the income and deductions in respect of the decedent result in net income. If so, you must then calculate the additional estate tax attributable to the net income in respect of the decedent.

To determine whether the items in respect of the decedent result in net income, you must deduct the total amount of deductions in respect of the decedent that appears on the estate tax return from the total amount of income in respect of the decedent that appears on that return. To calculate the additional estate tax, you must compare the actual estate tax with the estate tax that would have been paid if the net income in respect of a decedent had not been included. This amount is the deduction. The recipient's claim to the deduction is in the same proportion as his or her share in the total income in respect of the decedent.

Example

Assume that the estate tax return shows that the estate received salary income in respect of a decedent of $2,500 and had a deduction in respect of a decedent of $500 for unpaid real estate tax. The net of these two amounts is $2,000. Recomputation of the estate tax with $2,000 removed from the return shows that the estate tax caused by including these items is $740. If you, as one of two heirs of the estate, collect half of the $2,500 salary, you will be entitled to an income tax itemized deduction of half the $740, or $370.

TAXORGANIZER

Records you should keep.

• Power of appointment (or similar authorization to act as decedent's personal representative)
• Copies of decedent's wills, trust documents, and amendments to same
• Copies of decedent's death certificate
• Copies of all correspondence to and from attorneys, accountants, life insurers, and others related to administration of the estate
• Copies of all tax returns related to the decedent and copies of all source documents used to prepare these returns

5

Tax Withholding and Estimated Tax

Note: The 2004 IRS Publication 17 (Your Federal Income Tax) has been updated by Ernst & Young LLP for 2005. Dates and dollar amounts shown are for 2005. Gray type is used to indicate where IRS text has been updated or intentionally omitted. Unrevised IRS text is shown in black type.

Introduction

April 15 (April 17, 2006 for the 2005 return since the 15th is a Saturday in 2006) is the date by which most people file their income tax return for the previous year, but it is not the day most people actually pay their taxes. The bulk of your taxes is paid during the year, either by your employer's withholding money from your paycheck or by your making **estimated tax** *payments every quarter. The tax system operates on a pay-as-you-go policy, which generally requires that at least 90% of your tax liability be paid during the year.*

The tax law imposes severe penalties if you underwithhold or underpay your estimated taxes. Yet it is clearly not in your best interest to overwithhold or overpay estimated taxes, as the U.S. government does not pay interest on such overpayments. Therefore, it is essential that you estimate your tax liability as accurately as possible so that you neither underpay nor overpay your taxes. This chapter helps you do just that.

Salaries and wages are subject to withholding by your employer regardless of the amount you are paid, the frequency of payment, or the form of payment. Nevertheless, you are entitled to reduce the amount of withholding by filing a completed Form W-4 with your employer. This form takes into account not only your marital status, personal **exemptions,** *and* **dependents,** *but also your estimated* **deductions** *and tax credits. Form W-4 may prove especially beneficial if you have large mortgage deductions or tax-shelter investments.*

*Estimated tax payments cover sources of income not subject to withholding—***self-employment** *income,* **interest, dividends, capital gains,** *and* **trust and estate** *income. While generally your tax withholding and estimated payments have to cover 90% of your tax liability for you to avoid paying some stiff penalties, this is not always the case. This chapter discusses all the important exceptions.*

What's New for 2006

Tax law changes for 2006. When you figure how much income tax you want withheld from your pay and when you figure your estimated tax, consider tax law changes effective in 2006. See *What's New for 2006* in the front of this publication, or get Publication 553, Highlights of 2005 Tax Changes.

TaxAlert

Refer to *Changes in the Tax Law You Should Know About* in the front of the book.

Reminders

Estimated tax safe harbor for higher income taxpayers. If your adjusted gross income was more than $150,000 ($75,000 if you are married filing a separate return), you will have to deposit the smaller of 90% of your expected tax for 2006 or 110% of the tax shown on your 2005 return to avoid an estimated tax penalty.

Payment of estimated tax by electronic funds withdrawal. You may be able to pay your estimated tax by authorizing an automatic withdrawal from your checking or savings account. For more information, see *Payment by Electronic Funds Withdrawal* in chapter 2 of Publication 505.

This chapter discusses how to pay your tax as you earn or receive income during the year. In general, the federal income tax is a pay-as-you-go tax. There are two ways to pay as you go.

- *Withholding.* If you are an employee, your employer probably withholds income tax from your pay. Tax may also be withheld from certain other income, including pensions, bonuses, commissions, and gambling winnings. In each case, the amount withheld is paid to the IRS in your name.
- *Estimated tax.* If you do not pay your tax through withholding, or do not pay enough tax that way, you might have to pay estimated tax. People who are in business for themselves generally will have to pay their tax this way. You may have to pay estimated tax if you receive income such as dividends, interest, capital gains, rent, and royalties. Estimated tax is used to pay not only income tax, but self-employment tax and alternative minimum tax as well.

This chapter explains both of these methods. In addition, it explains the following.

- Credit for withholding and estimated tax. When you file your 2005 income tax return, take credit for all the income tax withheld from your salary, wages, pensions, etc., and for the estimated tax you paid for 2005.
- Underpayment penalty. If you did not pay enough tax during the year either through withholding or by making estimated tax payments, you may have to pay a penalty. The IRS usually can figure this penalty for you. See *Underpayment Penalty* at the end of this chapter.

Useful Items

You may want to see:

Publications

- ☐ **505**   Tax Withholding and Estimated Tax
- ☐ **919**   How Do I Adjust My Tax Withholding?

Forms (and Instructions)

- ☐ **W-4**   Employee's Withholding Allowance Certificate
- ☐ **W-4P**   Withholding Certificate for Pension or Annuity Payments
- ☐ **W-4S**   Request for Federal Income Tax Withholding From Sick Pay
- ☐ **W-4V**   Voluntary Withholding Request
- ☐ **1040-ES** Estimated Tax for Individuals
- ☐ **2210**   Underpayment of Estimated Tax by Individuals, Estates, and Trusts

---

Withholding

This section discusses income tax withholding on these types of income:

- Salaries and wages,
- Tips,
- Taxable fringe benefits,
- Sick pay,
- Pensions and annuities,
- Gambling winnings,
- Unemployment compensation, and
- Certain federal payments, such as social security.

This section explains in detail the rules for withholding tax from each of these types of income.

This section also covers backup withholding on interest, dividends, and other payments.

Salaries and Wages

Income tax is withheld from the pay of most employees. Your pay includes your regular pay, bonuses, commissions, and vacation allowances. It also includes reimbursements and other expense allowances paid under a nonaccountable plan. See *Supplemental Wages,* later, for more information about reimbursements and allowances paid under a nonaccountable plan.

If your income is low enough that you will not have to pay income tax for the year, you may be exempt from withholding. This is explained under *Exemption From Withholding,* later.

Military retirees. Military retirement pay is treated in the same manner as regular pay for income tax withholding purposes, even though it is treated as a pension or annuity for other tax purposes.

Household workers. If you are a household worker, you can ask your employer to withhold income tax from your pay.

Tax is withheld only if you want it withheld and your employer agrees to withhold it. If you do not have enough income tax withheld, you may have to pay estimated tax, as discussed later under *Estimated Tax.*

Farmworkers. Income tax is generally withheld from your cash wages for work on a farm unless your employer both:

- Pays you cash wages of less than $150 during the year, and
- Has expenditures for agricultural labor totaling less than $2,500 during the year.

You can ask your employer to withhold income tax from noncash wages and other wages not subject to withholding. If your employer does not agree to withhold tax, or if not enough is withheld, you may have to pay estimated tax, as discussed later under *Estimated Tax.*

Explanation

Generally, withholding is required on wages, regardless of the amount of wages paid, the frequency of payment, the form of payment (cash, check, stock, or other property), or the manner in which the wage is computed (hourly, weekly, yearly, or even as a percentage of employer profits).

For more information about household workers, see Chapter 42, *What to Do If You Employ Domestic Help.*

Determining Amount of Tax Withheld Using Form W-4

The amount of income tax your employer withholds from your regular pay depends on two things.

- The amount you earn.
- The information you give your employer on Form W-4.

Form W-4 includes three types of information that your employer will use to figure your withholding.

- Whether to withhold at the single rate or at the lower married rate.

• How many withholding allowances you claim. (Each allowance reduces the amount withheld.)
• Whether you want an additional amount withheld.

Note. You must specify a filing status and a number of withholding allowances on Form W-4. You cannot specify only a dollar amount of withholding.

New Job
When you start a new job, you must fill out Form W-4 and give it to your employer. Your employer should have copies of the form. If you need to change the information later, you must fill out a new form.

If you work only part of the year (for example, you start working after the beginning of the year), too much tax may be withheld. You may be able to avoid overwithholding if your employer agrees to use the part-year method. See *Part-Year Method* in chapter 1 of Publication 505 for more information.

Changing Your Withholding
Events during the year may change your marital status or the exemptions, adjustments, deductions, or credits you expect to claim on your return. When this happens, you may need to give your employer a new Form W-4 to change your withholding status or number of allowances.

If the event changes your withholding status or the number of allowances you are claiming, you must give your employer a new Form W-4 within 10 days after either of the following.

• Your divorce, if you have been claiming married status.
• Any event that decreases the number of withholding allowances you can claim.

Generally, you can submit a new Form W-4 whenever you wish to change the number of your withholding allowances for any other reason.

Changing your withholding for 2007. If events in 2006 will decrease the number of your withholding allowances for 2007, you must give your employer a new Form W-4 by December 1, 2006. If the event occurs in December 2006, submit a new Form W-4 within 10 days.

Explanation
You must file a new Form W-4 when it becomes reasonable for you to expect that the estimated deductions or credits you claim on your existing Form W-4 will be less than you anticipated. Conversely, you may file a new Form W-4 when it becomes reasonable to expect that your estimated deductions or credits will be more than you claim on your existing form. Examples of situations that might warrant that you file a new Form W-4 include (1) buying or selling a house, (2) refinancing or paying off a home mortgage, (3) moving to a different city, (4) a substantial increase in medical costs, or (5) change in filing status, or (6) change in number of dependents.

Checking Your Withholding
After you have given your employer a Form W-4, you can check to see whether the amount of tax withheld from your pay is too little or too much. See *Publication 919,* later. If too much or too little tax is being withheld, you should give your employer a new Form W-4 to change your withholding.

Note. You cannot give your employer a payment to cover withholding for past pay periods or a payment for estimated tax.

Completing Form W-4 and Worksheets
Form W-4 has worksheets to help you figure how many withholding allowances you can claim. The worksheets are for your own records. Do not give them to your employer.

Two jobs. If you have income from two jobs at the same time, complete only one set of Form W-4 worksheets. Then split your allowances between the Forms W-4 for each job. You cannot claim the same allowances with more than one employer at the same time. You can claim all your allowances with one employer and none with the other, or divide them any other way.

Example
Bill and Alice are married. Both are employed and expect to file a joint return. When they combine their expected salary and other income and then total their expected deductions and credits on a Form W-4 worksheet, they determine that they are entitled to claim 26 allowances. Bill and Alice must both file separate W-4 forms with their respective employers but may allocate the 26 allowances any way they like. Bill could claim 24 allowances and Alice could claim 2, for example, or each could claim 13 allowances.

Married individuals. If both you and your spouse are employed and expect to file a joint return, figure your withholding allowances using your combined income, adjustments, deductions, exemptions, and credits. Use only one set of worksheets. You can divide your total allowances any way, but you cannot claim an allowance that your spouse also claims.

If you and your spouse expect to file separate returns, figure your allowances using separate worksheets based on your own individual income, adjustments, deductions, exemptions, and credits.

Alternative method of figuring withholding allowances. You do not have to use the Form W-4 worksheets if you use a more accurate method of figuring the number of withholding allowances. See *Alternative method of figuring withholding allowances* under *Completing Form W-4 and Worksheets* in chapter 1 of Publication 505 for more information.

Personal allowances worksheet. Use the Personal Allowances Worksheet on page 1 of Form W-4 to figure your withholding allowances for exemptions and any special allowances that apply.

Example
John and Mary are married and plan to file a joint return. John's wages from his only employer are $55,000. Mary's wages from her only employer are $1,000. Because Mary's wages are $1,000 or less, John may claim a special allowance.

Deductions and adjustments worksheet. Use this worksheet if you plan to itemize your deductions or claim adjustments to your income and you want to reduce your withholding.

Fill out this worksheet to adjust the number of your withholding allowances for deductions, adjustments to income, and tax credits. The Deductions and Adjustments Worksheet is on page 2 of Form W-4. Chapter 1 of Publication 505 explains this worksheet.

Two-earner/two-job worksheet. You may need to complete this worksheet if you have two jobs or a working spouse. You can also add to the amount, if any, on line 8 of this worksheet, any additional withholding necessary to cover any amount you expect to owe other than income tax, such as self-employment tax.

Getting the Right Amount of Tax Withheld
In most situations, the tax withheld from your pay will be close to the tax you figure on your return if you follow these two rules.

• You accurately complete all the Form W-4 worksheets that apply to you.
• You give your employer a new Form W-4 when changes occur.

But because the worksheets and withholding methods do not account for all possible situations, you may not be getting the right amount withheld. This is most likely to happen in the following situations.

- You are married and both you and your spouse work.
- You have more than one job at a time.
- You have nonwage income, such as interest, dividends, alimony, unemployment compensation, or self-employment income.
- You will owe additional amounts with your return, such as self-employment tax.
- Your withholding is based on obsolete Form W-4 information for a substantial part of the year.

Example

Tom is a bachelor living in an apartment. His annual income is $35,000, and he claims the standard deduction when he files his income tax return. He is currently claiming two allowances on his Form W-4. In March 2005, Tom buys a house. As a result of the increased deductions resulting from the purchase, he will itemize his deductions on his 2005 federal income tax return. He estimates that the deductions will total $11,500 and will be made up of mortgage interest, points, real estate tax, and state income tax. He revises his Form W-4 to reflect the change in his status to claim four allowances for the remainder of the year.

Cumulative wage method. If you change the number of your withholding allowances during the year, too much or too little tax may have been withheld for the period before you made the change. You may be able to compensate for this if your employer agrees to use the cumulative wage withholding method for the rest of the year. You must ask in writing that your employer use this method.

To be eligible, you must have been paid for the same kind of payroll period (weekly, biweekly, etc.) since the beginning of the year.

TAXPLANNER

The tax withheld from your salary or wage based on the revised Form W-4 that you file with your employer should be appropriate for your circumstances on an annual basis. However, the new withholding is effective only for pay periods after you file the form, and the total tax withheld for any given year may be significantly less than your actual tax liability. You should estimate your annual tax, as explained later in this chapter, and compare that estimate to the year-to-date tax withheld plus the amounts expected to be withheld based on your revised Form W-4. If that comparison shows a substantial gap, it would be appropriate to file a new Form W-4, claiming fewer allowances or requesting a larger additional amount to be withheld in order to narrow that gap.

TAXPLANNER

You are liable for severe penalties if you complete a Form W-4 with false information in an attempt to reduce your withholding below the amount you are legally allowed. The form should be filled out carefully and accurately so that the amount of your withholding is the least you are legally allowed but enough to avoid underpayment penalties.

On the other hand, contrary to the belief of many taxpayers, there is *not* a penalty for overwithholding.

So much emphasis has been put on the accuracy of various worksheets that some taxpayers may have *increased* their withholding more than they actually want. If you are more comfortable claiming fewer exemptions than you are entitled to so that you can get a nice refund when you file your return, feel free to do so, but remember, it is like giving the government an interest-free loan during the year.

TAXPLANNER

Your Form W-4 should be reviewed periodically as your sources and levels of income change and as your deductible expenses and credits increase or decrease.

Example 1

You have an estimated net loss from a partnership of $2,000, which you would report on Schedule E of your Form 1040. You are not required to make any payments of estimated tax. You may use your $2,000 partnership loss to figure the number of withholding allowances you may claim on your Form W-4.

Example 2

In addition to wages, you have alimony income of $3,000 and an estimated net loss from business of $3,000, which you would report on Schedule C. If you did not have alimony income, you would also otherwise be required to make payments of estimated tax on your alimony income of $3,000. You may not use your business loss to figure your withholding allowances since the loss is already used to offset the alimony income.

Example 3

You have an estimated net loss from your farm of $5,000, which you would report on Schedule F. You would otherwise be required to make payments of estimated tax on rental income of $4,000. To figure your withholding allowances, you may include only $1,000 of your farm loss ($5,000 estimated net loss minus $4,000 income subject to estimated tax).

Example 4

You expect to have itemized deductions of $15,000, which you would report on Schedule A. You also expect to have $9,000 of self-employment income on which you would otherwise have to pay estimated tax. To figure your withholding allowances for Form W-4, you should include only $6,000 of your itemized deductions ($15,000 total itemized deductions minus the $9,000 self-employment income subject to estimated tax). This will, in effect, allow you to withhold through your salary any estimated tax due on your self-employment income. However, you will still be subject to self-employment tax on the $9,000 income.

Rules relating to when you may properly claim withholding allowances. For the purpose of figuring your withholding allowances for estimated deductions and estimated tax credits, *estimated* means the dollar amount of each item you reasonably expect to claim on your 2006 return. That dollar amount should be no more than the sum of the following:

1. The amount of each item shown or expected to be shown on your 2005 return that you also reasonably expect to show on your 2006 return

2. Additional amounts that you can determine for each item for 2006

Additional amounts that can be determined. These are amounts that are not included in (1) and that can be shown to result from identifiable events in 2005 or 2006. Amounts can be shown to result from identifiable events if the amounts relate to payments already made during 2006, to binding obligations to make payments (including payments of taxes) during 2006, and to other events or transactions that have been started and that you can prove at the time you file your Form W-4.

Amounts disallowed by the Internal Revenue Service. Generally, to figure your withholding allowances for 2006, you should not include any amount shown on your 2005 return that has been disallowed by the IRS. If you have not yet filed your 2005 return, you should not include any amount shown on your 2004 return that has been disallowed by the IRS.

Publication 919

To make sure you are getting the right amount of tax withheld, get Publication 919. It will help you compare the total tax to be withheld during the year with the tax you can expect to figure on your return. It also will help you determine how much additional withholding, if any, is needed each payday to avoid owing tax when you file your return. If you do not have enough tax withheld, you may have to pay estimated tax, as explained under *Estimated Tax,* later.

TAXPLANNER

In essence, overwithholding amounts to giving the government a portion of your salary as an interest-free loan. Nevertheless, underwithholding may subject you to stiff non-deductible penalties. It is therefore essential that you estimate your tax liability as accurately as possible so that you neither underwithhold nor overwithhold.

Rules Your Employer Must Follow

It may be helpful for you to know some of the withholding rules your employer must follow. These rules can affect how to fill out your Form W-4 and how to handle problems that may arise.

New Form W-4. When you start a new job, your employer should give you a Form W-4 to fill out. Your employer will use the information you give on the form to figure your withholding beginning with your first payday.

If you later fill out a new Form W-4, your employer can put it into effect as soon as possible. The deadline for putting it into effect is the start of the first payroll period ending 30 or more days after you turn it in.

No Form W-4. If you do not give your employer a completed Form W-4, your employer must withhold at the highest rate, as if you were single and claimed no allowances.

Repaying withheld tax. If you find you are having too much tax withheld because you did not claim all the withholding allowances you are entitled to, you should give your employer a new Form W-4. Your employer cannot repay any of the tax previously withheld.

However, if your employer has withheld more than the correct amount of tax for the Form W-4 you have in effect, you do not have to fill out a new Form W-4 to have your withholding lowered to the correct amount. Your employer can repay the amount that was incorrectly withheld. If you are not repaid, your Form W-2 will reflect the full amount actually withheld.

TAXPLANNER

If you claim 10 or more allowances on your Form W-4 your employer must send it to the IRS. You should not be concerned if, by all reasonable expectations, your deductions and credits entitle you to 10 or more allowances. If you are entitled to 10 or more allowances, you should claim them. However, if you do claim 10 or more allowances, preserve your Form W-4 worksheets and supporting papers. They may be needed to satisfy the IRS that you are entitled to the allowances you are claiming.

Exemption From Withholding

If you claim exemption from withholding, your employer will not withhold federal income tax from your wages. The exemption applies only to income tax, not to social security or Medicare tax.

You can claim exemption from withholding for 2006 only if both the following situations apply.

- For 2005 you had a right to a refund of all federal income tax withheld because you had no tax liability.
- For 2006 you expect a refund of all federal income tax withheld because you expect to have no tax liability.

Student. If you are a student, you are not automatically exempt. See chapter 1 to see whether you must file a return. If you work only part time or only during the summer, you may qualify for exemption from withholding.

Age 65 or older or blind. If you are 65 or older or blind, use one of the worksheets in chapter 1 of Publication 505, under *Exemption From Withholding,* to help you decide whether you can claim exemption from withholding. Do not use either worksheet if you will itemize deductions, claim exemptions for dependents, or claim tax credits on your 2006 return. See *Itemizing deductions or claiming exemptions or credits* in Publication 505.

Claiming exemption from withholding. To claim exemption, you must give your employer a Form W-4. Enter "exempt" on line 7.

Your employer must send the IRS a copy of your Form W-4 if you claim exemption from withholding and your pay is expected to usually be more than $200 a week. If it turns out that you do not qualify for exemption, the IRS will send both you and your employer a written notice.

If you claim exemption, but later your situation changes so that you will have to pay income tax after all, you must file a new Form W-4 within 10 days after the change. If you claim exemption in 2006, but you expect to owe income tax for 2007, you must file a new Form W-4 by December 1, 2006.

TAXSAVER

Many students and retired persons who expect to have no federal income tax liability work part time in occupations in which they receive tips. To avoid unnecessary income tax withholding, you may file a Form W-4 with your employer, certifying that you had no federal income tax liability last year and expect to have none this year as well. Keep in mind that the exemption only applies to income tax withholding, not to Social Security or Medicare tax.

An exemption is good for only one year. You must give your employer a new Form W-4 by February 15 each year to continue your exemption.

Supplemental Wages

Supplemental wages include bonuses, commissions, overtime pay, vacation allowances, certain sick pay, and expense allowances under certain plans. The payer can figure withholding on supplemental wages using the same method used for your regular wages. If these payments are identified separately from your regular wages, your employer or other payer of supplemental wages can withhold income tax from these wages at a flat rate.

Explanation

The IRS has issued proposed regulations to clarify that supplemental wages include any payments by an employer that is other than regular wages. In the case that an employee receives only one type of compensation from an employer, that type of compensation will be regular wages even if the type of compensation is something that would normally be classified as supplemental wages. For example, if an employee receives only stock options as compensation with no other fringe benefits includible as wages, the income on the exercise of the option would generally be regular wages, rather than supplemental wages.

TaxAlert

The current flat rate is 25%. However, once annual supplemental wage payments to an employee exceed $1 million, any additional supplemental wage payments in that year would be subject to withholding at the highest income tax rate (35% for 2006). In proposed regulations, the IRS clarified that the provision for mandatory 35% flat rate withholding on supplemental wage payments in excess of $1 million applies regardless of the withholding method used by the employer for regular wages, and even if the employee has a Form W-4 asserting either exempt status, or claiming a reduced rate of withholding.

Example

Duncan works as an employee of Corporation R. He receives regular wage payments of $200,000 per month in 2005 from Corporation R and income tax is withheld from those wages. In addition, Duncan receives the following payments:

June 30, 2005	$3,000,000 (bonus from Corporation R)
October 31, 2005	$50,000 (sick pay from U, one of the subsidiaries of Corporation R)
December 31, 2005	$100,000 (bonus from T, another subsidiaries of Corporation R)

All payments would be treated as made by one employer. The withholding on the regular monthly wage payment would be based upon Duncan's withholding allowances claimed on Form W-4. For the first $1,000,000 of the $3,000,000 bonus paid on June 30, 2005, income tax may be withheld using the same method used for regular wages. Alternatively, Duncan can elect to withhold income tax at the flat rate of 25% or $250,000. For the rest of the supplemental payments, including the remaining $2,000,000 of the bonus paid on June 30, income tax withheld is required to be calculated at the maximum rate of 35%.

Tax Planner

The mandatory withholding for excess supplemental payments may be problematic for individuals that have substantial deductions, losses and credits, which could otherwise have been taken into account by claiming additional withholding allowances on their Form W-4. Such individuals will have to wait for a refund when they file their return for the year of payment. Alternatively, they may be able to adjust withholding on other compensation or their quarterly estimated tax payments to take into account any excess withholding.

Expense allowances. Reimbursements or other expense allowances paid by your employer under a nonaccountable plan are treated as supplemental wages.

Reimbursements or other expense allowances paid under an accountable plan that are more than your proven expenses are treated as paid under a nonaccountable plan if you do not return the excess payments within a reasonable period of time.

For more information about accountable and nonaccountable expense allowance plans, see *Reimbursements* in chapter 28.

Penalties

You may have to pay a penalty of $500 if both of the following apply.

- You make statements or claim withholding allowances on your Form W-4 that reduce the amount of tax withheld.
- You have no reasonable basis for those statements or allowances at the time you prepare your Form W-4.

There is also a criminal penalty for willfully supplying false or fraudulent information on your Form W-4 or for willfully failing to supply information that would increase the amount withheld. The penalty upon conviction can be either a fine of up to $1,000 or imprisonment for up to one year, or both.

These penalties will apply if you deliberately and knowingly falsify your Form W-4 in an attempt to reduce or eliminate the proper withholding of taxes. A simple error, an honest mistake, will not result in one of these penalties. For example, a person who has tried to figure the number of withholding allowances correctly, but claims seven when the proper number is six, will not be charged a W-4 penalty.

Tips

The tips you receive while working on your job are considered part of your pay. You must include your tips on your tax return on the same line as your regular pay. However, tax is not withheld directly from tip income, as it is from your regular pay. Nevertheless, your employer will take into account the tips you report when figuring how much to withhold from your regular pay.

See chapter 7 for information on reporting your tips to your employer. For more information on the withholding rules for tip income, see Publication 531, Reporting Tip Income.

How employer figures amount to withhold. The tips you report to your employer are counted as part of your income for the month you report them. Your employer can figure your withholding in either of two ways.

- By withholding at the regular rate on the sum of your pay plus your reported tips.
- By withholding at the regular rate on your pay plus a percentage of your reported tips.

Not enough pay to cover taxes. If your regular pay is not enough for your employer to withhold all the tax (including income tax, social security tax, Medicare tax, or railroad retirement tax) due on your pay plus your tips, you can give your employer money to cover the shortage. See *Giving your employer money for taxes* in chapter 7.

Allocated tips. Your employer should not withhold income tax, social security tax, Medicare tax, or railroad retirement tax on any allocated tips. Withholding is based only on your pay plus your reported tips. Your employer should refund to you any incorrectly withheld tax. See *Allocated Tips* in chapter 7 for more information.

Taxable Fringe Benefits

The value of certain fringe benefits you receive from your employer is considered part of your pay. Your employer generally must withhold income tax on these benefits from your regular pay.

For information on fringe benefits, see *Fringe Benefits* under *Employee Compensation* in chapter 6.

Your employer can choose not to withhold income tax on the value of your personal use of an employer-provided car, truck, or other highway motor vehicle. Your employer must notify you if this choice is made.

For more information on withholding on taxable fringe benefits, see chapter 1 of Publication 505.

Sick Pay

Sick pay is a payment to you to replace your regular wages while you are temporarily absent from work due to sickness or personal injury. To qualify as sick pay, it must be paid under a plan to which your employer is a party.

If you receive sick pay from your employer or an agent of your employer, income tax must be withheld. An agent who does not pay regular wages to you may choose to withhold income tax at a flat rate.

However, if you receive sick pay from a third party who is not acting as an agent of your employer, income tax will be withheld only if you choose to have it withheld. See *Form W-4S,* later.

If you receive payments under a plan in which your employer does not participate (such as an accident or health plan where you paid all the premiums), the payments are not sick pay and usually are not taxable.

Union agreements. If you receive sick pay under a collective bargaining agreement between your union and your employer, the agreement may determine the amount of income tax withholding. See your union representative or your employer for more information.

Form W-4S. If you choose to have income tax withheld from sick pay paid by a third party, such as an insurance company, you must fill out Form W-4S. Its instructions contain a worksheet you can use to figure the amount you want withheld. They also explain restrictions that may apply.

Give the completed form to the payer of your sick pay. The payer must withhold according to your directions on the form.

If you do not request withholding on Form W-4S, or if you do not have enough tax withheld, you may have to make estimated tax payments. If you do not pay enough estimated tax or have enough income tax withheld, you may have to pay a penalty.

Pensions and Annuities

Income tax usually will be withheld from your pension or annuity distributions unless you choose not to have it withheld. This rule applies to distributions from:

- A traditional individual retirement arrangement (IRA),
- A life insurance company under an endowment, annuity, or life insurance contract,
- A pension, annuity, or profit-sharing plan,
- A stock bonus plan, and
- Any other plan that defers the time you receive compensation.

The amount withheld depends on whether you receive payments spread out over more than one year (periodic payments), within one year (nonperiodic payments), or as an eligible rollover distribution (ERD). You cannot choose not to have income tax withheld from an ERD.

Explanation
A part of your pension or annuity may not be taxable. See Chapter 11, *Retirement Plans, Pensions, and Annuities,* for information on figuring the nontaxable part. Income tax will not be withheld from the part of your pension or annuity that is nontaxable. Therefore, the tax withheld will be figured on, and cannot be more than, the taxable part.

TaxAlert

A distribution that is eligible for direct rollover treatment (see Chapter 11, *Retirement Plans, Pensions, and Annuities*) but is not directly rolled over is subject to mandatory 20% withholding unless the participant's eligible rollover distributions for the year are expected to be less than $200.

If a participant elects to have a portion of a distribution transferred in a direct rollover and the remainder distributed to him or her, only the portion that is distributed will be subject to the 20% withholding. A plan administrator will not be liable for tax, interest, or penalties for failure to withhold if he or she reasonably relied on information about the participant's plan received from the participant.

TaxPlanner

If property *other than cash* is distributed, withholding must still occur. However, if the distribution consists of cash or other property and securities of the company, withholding need not exceed the sum of the cash and fair market value of property received other than company securities. Consequently, no mandatory withholding occurs where the distribution consists only of securities of the company.

TaxAlert

A written explanation of the direct rollover option and related rules (including the rules governing withholding) must generally be provided to participants not more than 90 days and not less than 30 days before the distribution date. For a series of periodic payments that are eligible for direct rollover, an initial timely notice must be given and an additional notice must be provided at least annually for as long as the payments continue.

Failure to provide such notice could cause the plan to become disqualified under the Internal Revenue Code. The IRS has issued a model notice that plan administrators are allowed to customize by deleting any portions that do not apply to the plan and adding additional information that is not inconsistent with the model notice.

Periodic Payments
Withholding from periodic payments of a pension or annuity is figured in the same way as withholding from salaries and wages. To tell the payer of your pension or annuity how much you want withheld, fill out **Form W-4P,** *Withholding Certificate for Pension or Annuity Payments,* or a similar form provided by the payer. Follow the rules discussed under *Withholding on Salaries and Wages,* earlier, to fill out your Form W-4P.

The withholding rules for pensions and annuities differ from those for salaries and wages in the following ways:

1. If you do not fill out a withholding certificate, tax will be withheld as if you were married and were claiming three withholding allowances.
2. Your certificate will not be sent to the IRS regardless of the number of allowances you claim on it.
3. You can choose not to have tax withheld, regardless of how much tax you owed last year or expect to owe this year. You do not have to qualify for exemption. See *Choosing Not to Have Income Tax Withheld,* later.
4. Tax will be withheld as if you were single and claiming no withholding allowances if:
   a) You do not give the payer your Social Security number (in the required manner), or
   b) The IRS notifies the payer, before any payment or distribution is made, that you gave it an incorrect Social Security number.

Note: Military retirement pay generally is treated in the same manner as wages and not as a pension or annuity for income tax withholding purposes. Military retirees should use Form W-4, not Form W-4P.

TaxAlert

If a series of periodic payments began prior to January 1, 1993, you determine whether post–December 31, 1992, payments are a series of substantially equal periodic payments over a specified period by taking into account all payments, including payments made before January 1, 1993. If the post–December 31, 1992, payments are not a series of substantially equal periodic payments, they will be subject to the direct rollover rules, including mandatory 20% withholding.

Nonperiodic Payments
Tax will be withheld at a 10% rate on any nonperiodic payments you receive.

Because withholding on nonperiodic payments does not depend on withholding allowances or whether you are married or single, you cannot use Form W-4P to tell the payer how much to withhold. But you can use Form W-4P to specify that an additional amount be withheld. You can also use Form W-4P to choose not to have tax withheld or to revoke a choice not to have tax withheld. See *Choosing Not to Have Income Tax Withheld,* later.

Eligible Rollover Distributions
Distributions you receive that are eligible to be rolled over tax-free into qualified retirement or annuity plans are subject to a 20% withholding tax.

An *eligible rollover distribution (ERD)* is any distribution from a qualified pension or tax-sheltered annuity other than:

1. A minimum required distribution, or
2. One of a series of substantially equal periodic pension or annuity payments made over:
   a) Your life (or your life expectancy) or the joint lives of you and your beneficiary (or your life expectancies), or
   b) A specified period of 10 or more years.

The withholding rules for non-ERD distributions are discussed earlier under *Periodic Payments* and *Nonperiodic Payments.*

A distribution is subject to withholding if it is not substantially equal to the periodic payments.

For example, upon retirement you receive 30% of your accrued pension benefits in the form of a single-sum distribution with the balance payable in annuity form. The 30% distribution is an ERD subject to 20% withholding. The annuity payments are periodic payments subject to withholding only if you choose to have withholding taken out.

The payer of a distribution must withhold at a 20% rate on any part of an ERD that is not rolled over directly to another qualified plan. You cannot elect not to have withholding on these distributions.

If tax is withheld on the ERD, it will be withheld only on the taxable part. You must either:

1. Contribute to the new plan (within 60 days from the date of the distribution) an amount equal to the taxable part of the total ERD, including the amount withheld, or
2. Include in your income for the year of the distribution any amount withheld for which you did not make a matching contribution to the new plan.

The matching contribution to cover the withheld amount must be in addition to the rollover of the net amount that you actually received. If all or any portion of an amount equal to the amount withheld is not contributed as a rollover, it must be included in your income to the extent the difference between taxable part of the distribution and actual rollover amount.

Exception to withholding rule. The only way to avoid withholding on an ERD is to have it directly rolled over from the employer's plan to a qualified plan or IRA. This direct rollover is made only at your direction. You must first make sure that the receiving trustee agrees to accept a direct rollover. The transferor trustee must allow you to make such a rollover and provide to you, within a reasonable period of time, written instructions on how to do so. You must also follow spousal consent and other participant and beneficiary protection rules.

TaxSaver

If you receive an eligible rollover distribution from which the mandatory 20% withholding tax has been withheld, and you then decide you wish to roll the distribution over to an IRA within the allowed 60 days, you must come up with the 20% that was withheld from other funds within the 60-day period in order to roll the entire balance over. Otherwise the 20% that has been withheld will be treated as a taxable distribution and ineligible for rollover.

Choosing Not to Have Income Tax Withheld
You can choose not to have income tax withheld from your pension or annuity, whether the payments are periodic or nonperiodic. This rule does not apply to eligible rollover distributions. The payer will tell you how to make this choice. If you use Form W-4P, check the box on line 1 to make this choice. This choice will stay in effect until you decide you want withholding.

The payer will ignore your request not to have income tax withheld if:

1. You do not give the payer your Social Security number (in the required manner), or

2. The IRS notifies the payer, before any payment or distribution is made, that you gave it an incorrect Social Security number.

TAXPLANNER

You should choose to have no tax withheld from nonperiodic payments (total distributions within 1 year) from an employer pension or profit-sharing plan if you intend to defer taxation by putting the money directly into an Individual Retirement Arrangement (IRA).

If you choose not to have any income tax withheld from your pension or annuity, or if you do not have enough withheld, you may have to make estimated tax payments. See *Estimated Tax,* later.

If you do not pay enough tax through either estimated tax or withholding, you may have to pay a penalty. See *Underpayment Penalty,* later in this chapter.

Outside United States. If you are a U.S. citizen or resident alien and you choose not to have tax withheld from pension or annuity benefits, you must give the payer of the benefits a home address in the United States or in a U.S. possession. Otherwise, the payer must withhold tax. For example, the payer would have to withhold tax if you provide a U.S. address for a nominee, trustee, or agent to whom the benefits are to be delivered but do not provide your own home address in the United States or in a U.S. possession.

Revoking a choice not to have tax withheld. If you want to revoke your choice not to have tax withheld, the payer of your pension or annuity will tell you how. If the payer gives you Form W-4P, write "Revoked" by the checkbox on line 1 of the form.

If you get periodic payments and do not complete the rest of the form, the payer will withhold tax as if you were married and claiming three allowances. If you want tax withheld at a different rate, you must complete the rest of the form.

Notice required of payer. The payer of your pension or annuity is required to send you a notice telling you about your right to choose not to have tax withheld.

More information. For more information on taxation of annuities and distributions (including eligible rollover distributions) from qualified retirement plans, see chapter 11. For information on IRAs, see chapter 18. For more information on withholding on pensions and annuities, including a discussion of Form W-4P, see *Pensions and Annuities* in chapter 1 of Publication 505.

Gambling Winnings

Income tax is withheld from certain kinds of gambling winnings at a flat rate.

Gambling winnings of more than $5,000 from the following sources are subject to income tax withholding.

• Any sweepstakes, wagering pool, or lottery.
• Any other wager, if the proceeds are at least 300 times the amount of the bet.

It does not matter whether your winnings are paid in cash, in property, or as an annuity. Winnings not paid in cash are taken into account at their fair market value.

Gambling winnings from bingo, keno, and slot machines generally are not subject to income tax withholding. However, you may need to provide the payer with a social security number to avoid withholding. See *Backup withholding on gambling winnings* in Publica-

tion 505. If you receive gambling winnings not subject to withholding, you may need to pay estimated tax. See *Estimated Tax,* later.

If you do not pay enough tax through withholding or estimated tax payments, you may have to pay a penalty. See *Underpayment Penalty,* later.

Form W-2G. If a payer withholds income tax from your gambling winnings, you should receive a Form W-2G, Certain Gambling Winnings, showing the amount you won and the amount withheld. Report the tax withheld on line 64 of Form 1040.

TAXPLANNER

Gambling losses are deductible, but only to the extent that you have gambling winnings to offset the losses and only if you itemize your deductions. It is very important to keep accurate records to document both your winnings and your losses.

Unemployment Compensation

You can choose to have income tax withheld from unemployment compensation. To make this choice, you will have to fill out Form W-4V (or a similar form provided by the payer) and give it to the payer.

Unemployment compensation is taxable. So, if you do not have income tax withheld, you may have to pay estimated tax. See *Estimated Tax,* later.

If you do not pay enough tax either through withholding or estimated tax, you may have to pay a penalty. See *Underpayment Penalty,* later, for information.

Federal Payments

You can choose to have income tax withheld from certain federal payments you receive. These payments are:

1. Social security benefits,
2. Tier 1 railroad retirement benefits,
3. Commodity credit loans you choose to include in your gross income, and
4. Payments under the Agricultural Act of 1949 (7 U.S.C. 1421 et. seq.), or title II of the Disaster Assistance Act of 1988, as amended, that are treated as insurance proceeds and that you receive because:
   a. Your crops were destroyed or damaged by drought, flood, or any other natural disaster, or
   b. You were unable to plant crops because of a natural disaster described in (a).

To make this choice, you will have to fill out Form W-4V (or a similar form provided by the payer) and give it to the payer.

If you do not choose to have income tax withheld, you may have to pay estimated tax. See *Estimated Tax,* later.

If you do not pay enough tax either through withholding or estimated tax, you may have to pay a penalty. See *Underpayment Penalty,* later, for information.

More information. For more information about the tax treatment of social security and railroad retirement benefits, see chapter 12. Get Publication 225, Farmer's Tax Guide, for information about the tax treatment of commodity credit loans or crop disaster payments.

Backup Withholding

Banks and other businesses that pay you certain kinds of income must file an information return (Form 1099) with the IRS. The information return shows how much you were paid during the year. It also includes your name and taxpayer identification number (TIN). TINs are explained in chapter 1.

These payments generally are not subject to withholding. However, "backup" withholding is required in certain situations. Backup withholding can apply to most kinds of payments that are reported on Form 1099.

The payer must withhold at a flat rate in the following situations.

- You do not give the payer your TIN in the required manner.
- The IRS notifies the payer that the TIN you gave is incorrect.
- You are required, but fail, to certify that you are not subject to backup withholding.
- The IRS notifies the payer to start withholding on interest or dividends because you have underreported interest or dividends on your income tax return. The IRS will do this only after it has mailed you four notices over at least a 120-day period.

See *Backup Withholding* in chapter 1 of Publication 505 for more information.

Penalties. There are civil and criminal penalties for giving false information to avoid backup withholding. The civil penalty is $500. The criminal penalty, upon conviction, is a fine of up to $1,000 or imprisonment of up to 1 year, or both.

Estimated Tax

Estimated tax is the method used to pay tax on income that is not subject to withholding. This includes income from self-employment, interest, dividends, alimony, rent, gains from the sale of assets, prizes, and awards. You also may have to pay estimated tax if the amount of income tax being withheld from your salary, pension, or other income is not enough.

Estimated tax is used to pay both income tax and self-employment tax, as well as other taxes and amounts reported on your tax return. If you do not pay enough through withholding or estimated tax payments, you may have to pay a penalty. If you do not pay enough by the due date of each payment period (see *When To Pay Estimated Tax,* later), you may be charged a penalty even if you are due a refund when you file your tax return. For information on when the penalty applies, see *Underpayment Penalty,* later.

Who Does Not Have To Pay Estimated Tax

If you receive salaries or wages, you can avoid having to pay estimated tax by asking your employer to take more tax out of your earnings. To do this, give a new Form W-4 to your employer. See chapter 1 of Publication 505.

Estimated tax not required. You do not have to pay estimated tax for 2006 if you meet all three of the following conditions.

- You had no tax liability for 2005.
- You were a U.S. citizen or resident for the whole year.
- Your 2005 tax year covered a 12-month period.

You had no tax liability for 2005 if your total tax was zero or you did not have to file an income tax return.

Who Must Pay Estimated Tax?

If you had a tax liability for 2005, you may have to pay estimated tax for 2006.

General rule. You must pay estimated tax for 2006 if both of the following apply.

1. You expect to owe at least $1,000 in tax for 2006 after subtracting your withholding and credits.
2. You expect your withholding and credits to be less than the smaller of:
   a. 90% of the tax to be shown on your 2006 tax return, or
   b. 100% of the tax shown on your 2005 tax return. Your 2005 tax return must cover all 12 months.

TaxPlanner

If you receive a considerable amount of taxable income on which no tax is withheld, you might need to make quarterly estimated tax payments to the IRS.

Some of the most common sources of income not subject to withholding are:

Income from self-employment
Alimony
Interest and dividends
Rent

Even if most or all your income is subject to withholding, you might not be having enough tax withheld to satisfy the IRS—and you might need to pick up the slack by increasing withholding, making estimated tax payments, or both.

TaxAlert

For 2006, you can avoid underpayment penalties by calculating your estimated payments as 100% of your 2005 tax if your adjusted gross income (AGI) was $150,000 or less. If your AGI for 2005 was greater than $150,000, you must have 110% of your 2005 tax paid in. All taxpayers can avoid penalties for underpayment of tax if at least 90% of their *current tax* liability is paid through withholding and estimated tax payments.

Example
Hope Lane's 2006 income tax liability is $45,000. Her adjusted gross income in 2005 was $140,000, while her 2005 tax liability was $30,000. Lane will avoid an underpayment penalty in 2006 if the total amount of tax withheld and estimated tax payments made for 2006 are at least 100% of her 2005 liability, or $30,000.

Each quarter, the calculation for estimated payment purposes may differ depending on which method yields the lesser tax liability. Therefore, the estimated payment for the 1st quarter may be based on your 2005 tax liability while the 2nd quarter estimated payment may be based on 90% of your current year tax liability.

Special rules for farmers, fishermen, and higher income taxpayers. There are exceptions to the general rule for farmers, fishermen, and certain higher income taxpayers. See Figure 5-A and chapter 2 of Publication 505 for more information.

Aliens. Resident and nonresident aliens may also have to pay estimated tax. Resident aliens should follow the rules in this chapter unless noted otherwise. Nonresident aliens should get Form 1040-ES(NR), U.S. Estimated Tax for Nonresident Alien Individuals.

Married taxpayers. To figure whether you must pay estimated tax, apply the rules discussed here to your separate estimated income. If you can make joint estimated tax payments, you can apply these rules on a joint basis.

You and your spouse can make joint estimated tax payments even if you are not living together.

You and your spouse cannot make joint estimated tax payments if:

- You are legally separated under a decree of divorce or separate maintenance,
- Either spouse is a nonresident alien, or
- You and your spouse have different tax years.

Whether you and your spouse make joint estimated tax payments or separate payments will not affect your choice of filing a joint tax return or separate returns for 2006.

Figure 5-A. **Do You Have To Pay Estimated Tax?**

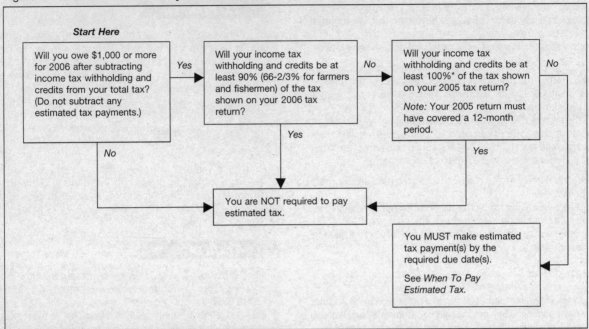

* 110% if less than two-thirds of your gross income for 2005 and 2006 is from farming or fishing and your 2005 adjusted gross income was more than $150,000 ($75,000 if your filing status for 2006 is married filing a separate return).

2005 separate returns and 2006 joint return. If you plan to file a joint return with your spouse for 2006, but you filed separate returns for 2005, your 2005 tax is the total of the tax shown on your separate returns. You filed a separate return if you filed as single, head of household, or married filing separately.

2005 joint return and 2006 separate returns. If you plan to file a separate return for 2006, but you filed a joint return for 2005, your 2005 tax is your share of the tax on the joint return. You file a separate return if you file as single, head of household, or married filing separately.

To figure your share of the tax on the joint return, first figure the tax both you and your spouse would have paid had you filed separate returns for 2005 using the same filing status as for 2006. Then multiply the tax on the joint return by the following fraction.

$$\frac{\text{The tax you would have paid had you filed a separate return}}{\text{The total tax you and your spouse would have paid had you filed separate returns}}$$

Example. Joe and Heather filed a joint return for 2005 showing taxable income of $48,500 and a tax of $6,545. Of the $48,500 taxable income, $40,100 was Joe's and the rest was Heather's. For 2006, they plan to file married filing separately. Joe figures his share of the tax on the 2005 joint return as follows.

Tax on $40,100 based on a separate return	$6,690
Tax on $8,400 based on a separate return	895
Total	$7,585
Joe's percentage of total ($6,690 ÷ $7,585)	88%
Joe's share of tax on joint return ($6,545 × 88%)	$5,760

How To Figure Estimated Tax

To figure your estimated tax, you must figure your expected adjusted gross income, taxable income, taxes, deductions, and credits for the year.

When figuring your 2006 estimated tax, it may be helpful to use your income, deductions, and credits for 2005 as a starting point. Use your 2005 federal tax return as a guide. You can use Form 1040-ES to figure your estimated tax.

You must make adjustments both for changes in your own situation and for recent changes in the tax law. For 2006, there are several changes in the law. Some of these changes are discussed in Publication 553, Highlights of 2005 Tax Changes, or visit the IRS website at *www.irs.gov.*

Form 1040-ES includes a worksheet to help you figure your estimated tax. Keep the worksheet for your records.

For more complete information and examples of how to figure your estimated tax for 2006, see chapter 2 of Publication 505.

TAXPLANNER

A convenient way to figure your estimated tax is to list all your sources of income from last year. Then enter the estimated income from each source for *this* year. Add to this list all new sources of income that you expect this year. Repeat this procedure for all deductions and exemptions. If your itemized deductions are more than the standard deduction, use your itemized deductions. Then compute your estimated tax liability for 2006 based on your estimated taxable income.

After you have calculated your estimated tax liability, add any additional taxes, including self-employment taxes, household employment taxes, and alternative minimum taxes, that you expect to pay for the current year. Then subtract the various tax credits you expect to claim for the current year, and also subtract the income tax you expect to have withheld. The remaining tax liability is your estimated tax.

If your estimated tax exceeds $1,000, equal estimated tax payments generally have to be made on April 15, June 15, September 15, and January 15. Special exceptions, described later in this chapter, may reduce or eliminate this requirement.

When To Pay Estimated Tax

For estimated tax purposes, the year is divided into four payment periods. Each period has a specific payment due date. If you do not pay enough tax by the due date of each of the payment periods, you may be charged a penalty even if you are due a refund when you file your income tax return. The following chart gives the payment periods and due dates for estimated tax payments.

For the period:	Due date:
Jan. 1* through Mar. 31	Apr. 15
April 1 through May 31	June 15
June 1 through Aug. 31	Sept. 15
Sept. 1 through Dec. 31	Jan 15 next year**

*If your tax year does not begin on January 1, see the Form 1040-ES instructions.
**See *January payment,* later.

Saturday, Sunday, holiday rule. If the due date for an estimated tax payment falls on a Saturday, Sunday, or legal holiday, the payment will be on time if you make it on the next day that is not a Saturday, Sunday, or legal holiday. For example, a payment due Saturday, April 15, 2006, will be on time if you make it by Monday, April 17, 2006.

January payment. If you file your 2006 Form 1040 or Form 1040A by January 31, 2007, and pay the rest of the tax you owe, you do not need to make the payment due on January 15, 2007.

Fiscal year taxpayers. If your tax year does not start on January 1, see the Form 1040-ES instructions for your payment due dates.

When To Start

You do not have to make estimated tax payments until you have income on which you will owe the tax. If you have income subject to estimated tax during the first payment period, you must make your first payment by the due date for the first payment period. You can pay all your estimated tax at that time, or you can pay it in installments. If you choose to pay in installments, make your first payment by the due date for the first payment period. Make your remaining installment payments by the due dates for the later periods.

No income subject to estimated tax during first period. If you do not have income subject to estimated tax until a later payment period, you can make your first payment by the due date for that period. You can pay your entire estimated tax by the due date for that period, or you can pay it in installments by the due date for that period and the due dates for the remaining periods. The following chart shows when to make installment payments.

If you first have income on which you must pay estimated tax:	Make a payment by:	Make later installments by:
Before Apr. 1	Apr. 15	June 15 Sept. 15 Jan. 15 next year*
After Mar. 31 and before June 1	June 15	Sept. 15 Jan. 15 next year*
After May 31 and before Sept. 1	Sept. 15	Jan. 15 next year*
After Aug. 31	Jan. 15 next year*	(None)

*See *January payment,* and *Saturday, Sunday, holiday rule* under *When to Pay Estimated Tax,* earlier.

Example

In April 2006, John figured that his estimated tax for 2006 would be $12,000. Accordingly, he made his first 2006 quarterly estimated payment of $3,000 on April 15, 2006, and his second quarterly estimated payment of $3,000 on June 15, 2006. In August, John purchased a new home, and his monthly mortgage payments increased dramatically. Because John could deduct his mortgage interest payments, he reduced his third and fourth quarterly estimated payments due on September 15, 2006, and January 17, 2007, respectively.

How much to pay to avoid a penalty. To determine how much you should pay by each payment due date, see *How To Figure Each Payment,* next. If the earlier discussion of *No income subject to estimated tax during first period* or the later discussion of *Change in estimated tax* apply to you, you may need to read *Annualized Income Installment Method* in chapter 2 of Publication 505 for information on how to avoid a penalty.

Explanation

The discussion that follows shows in detail how to compute your annualized income installment.

Figure your installment for each payment period as follows:

1. Figure your adjusted gross income (AGI), alternative minimum taxable income (AMTI), and adjusted self-employment income (SEI) for the months in 2006 ending before the due date of the payment period. (Your AGI is your actual total income minus your actual adjustments to income for the months in the period.)
2. Multiply each of the amounts in step (1) by
   a) 4, if the payment due date is April 15.
   b) 2.4, if the payment due date is June 15.
   c) 1.5, if the payment due date is September 15.
   d) 1, if the payment due date is January 17, 2007. These amounts are your annualized AGI, AMTI, and SEI.
3. Determine the greater of your
   a) Actual allowable itemized deductions for the months in the period multiplied by the same figure used in step (2), or
   b) Standard deduction for the year.
4. Multiply your exemptions by the 2006 exemption amount.
5. Add the amounts from steps (3) and (4), and subtract the total from your annualized AGI determined in step (2). This amount is your annualized taxable income.
6. Figure the appropriate tax on your annualized taxable income [from step (5)], the alternative minimum tax on your annualized AMTI, and self-employment tax on SEI [from step (2)].
7. Total the amounts figured in step (6).
8. Add any additional taxes that you may owe because of events that occurred during the months in 2006 ending before the due date of the payment period. "Other Taxes" are the ones listed on lines 58–62 of the 2005 Form 1040.
9. Subtract from this total any nonrefundable credits that you may be able to claim because of events that occurred during the months in 2006 ending before the due date of the payment period. These

are the credits that make up the total on line 56 of the 2005 Form 1040. If these credits are more than the total of step (7) plus additional taxes figured in step (8), use zero as the result and go on to the next step.

10. Add to the result of step (9) any of the taxes listed below that you may owe because of events that occurred during the months in 2006 ending before the due date of the payment period:
    a) Tax from recapture of an investment credit
    b) Excise tax on golden parachute payments
11. Subtract the following credits that apply to your situation for the months in 2006 ending before the due date of the payment period:
    a) Credit for federal tax on gasoline and special fuel
    b) Earned income credit
12. Multiply the result of step (12) by
    a) 22.5%, if the payment due date is April 15.
    b) 45%, if the payment due date is June 15.
    c) 67.5%, if the payment due date is September 15.
    d) 90%, if the payment due date is January 19, 2007.
13. Figure the total estimated tax you had to pay by the due date of each of the preceding payment periods. This is the total of the lower of the required installment or the annualized income installment for each payment period.
14. Subtract the step (13) amount from the step (12) amount.

If the annualized income installment for the payment period is less than the required installment, you only need to pay the annualized income installment.

When you pay the annualized income installment for the next payment period, you must add the difference between the required installment for that subsequent payment period (as increased) and the annualized income installment for the previous payment period to the required installment for the next payment period.

How To Figure Each Payment

You should pay enough estimated tax by the due date of each payment period to avoid a penalty for that period. You can figure your required payment for each period by using either the regular installment method or the annualized income installment method. These methods are described in Publication 505. If you do not pay enough each payment period, you may be charged a penalty even if you are due a refund when you file your tax return.

Underpayment penalty. If your estimated tax payment for a previous period is less than one-fourth of your amended estimated tax, you may be charged a penalty for underpayment of estimated tax for that period when you file your tax return. See chapter 4 of Publication 505 for more information.

Change in estimated tax. After you make an estimated tax payment, changes in your income, adjustments, deductions, credits, or exemptions may make it necessary for you to refigure your estimated tax. Pay the unpaid balance of your amended estimated tax by the next payment due date after the change or in installments by that date and the due dates for the remaining payment periods.

Estimated Tax Payments Not Required
You do not have to pay estimated tax if your withholding in each payment period is at least as much as:

• One-fourth of your required annual payment, or
• Your required annualized income installment for that period.

You also do not have to pay estimated tax if you will pay enough through withholding to keep the amount you owe with your return under $1,000.

How To Pay Estimated Tax

There are five ways to pay estimated tax.

• By crediting an overpayment on your 2005 return to your 2006 estimated tax.
• By sending in your payment with a payment-voucher from Form 1040-ES.
• By using the Electronic Federal Tax Payment System (EFTPS). For EFTPS information, see chapter 1.
• By electronic funds withdrawal if you are filing Form 1040 or Form 1040A electronically.
• By credit card using a pay-by-phone system or the Internet.

Crediting an Overpayment
When you file your Form 1040 or Form 1040A for 2005 and you have an overpayment of tax, you can apply part or all of it to your estimated tax for 2006. On line 74 of Form 1040, or line 46 of Form 1040A, enter the amount you want credited to your estimated tax rather than refunded. The amount you have credited should be taken into account when figuring your estimated tax payments.

The credit will be applied to your payments in the order necessary to avoid the penalty for underpayment of estimated tax. You cannot have any of that amount refunded to you until the close of that tax year. You also cannot use that overpayment in any other way.

Explanation
An overpayment that is applied to your estimated tax payment for the current year is considered to have been paid on time even if you are granted an extension and file your previous year's tax return after April 15.

Example
If you get a legal extension on your tax return from April 15 to August 15 and you actually file your return in July, you can apply any overpayment you may have made in the previous year to your estimated tax payments that were due on April 15 and June 15.

Using the Payment-Vouchers
Each payment of estimated tax must be accompanied by a payment-voucher from Form 1040-ES. If you made estimated tax payments last year, you should receive a copy of the 2006 Form 1040-ES in the mail. It will have payment-vouchers preprinted with your name, address, and social security number. Using the preprinted vouchers will speed processing, reduce the chance of error, and help save processing costs.

If you did not pay estimated tax last year, you will have to get Form 1040-ES. After you make your first payment, a Form 1040-ES package with the preprinted vouchers will be mailed to you. Follow the instructions in the package to make sure you use the vouchers correctly.

Use the window envelopes that came with your Form 1040-ES package. If you use your own envelope, make sure you mail your payment-vouchers to the address shown in the Form 1040-ES instructions for the place where you live.

Caution. *Do not use the address shown in the Form 1040 or Form 1040A instructions.*

TaxPlanner
For a copy of Form 1040-ES, see Chapter 50, *2004 Federal Tax Forms and Schedules You Can Use.*

Explanation

The following explanation discusses in detail how to use the payment voucher:

1. Enter your Social Security number, name, and address on the voucher. If this information is preprinted on the voucher, make any corrections that are necessary. Use the preprinted voucher if you have one.

   If you are making joint estimated tax payments, your spouse's name and Social Security number should be included on the voucher. If you make joint payments and you have different last names, separate them with an "and"—for example, "John Brown and Mary Smith."

2. On the right side of the voucher, enter the amount you are paying. If you credited an overpayment on last year's return to your estimated tax for this year, subtract the amount of the overpayment that you want to apply to this payment from the amount you need to pay for the period. The result is the amount you should pay with the voucher. Enter only this amount on line 1 of the voucher. If the amount is zero you do not have to send in a voucher.

3. Tear off the voucher at the perforation.

4. Enclose (but do not staple or otherwise attach) your check or money order with the voucher. Make your check or money order payable to the United States Treasury. Write your Social Security number and "2006 Form 1040-ES" on your check or money order.

5. Fill in the Record of Estimated Tax Payments on your Form 1040-ES package so that you will have a record of your payments.

6. Mail the voucher to the Internal Revenue Service Center for the place where you live. Use the addressed envelope that comes with your voucher or the address for your state shown in the Form 1040-ES package.

If you file a joint return and you are making joint estimated tax payments, please enter the names and social security numbers on the payment voucher in the same order as they will appear on the joint return.

Change of address. You must notify the IRS if you are making estimated tax payments and you changed your address during the year. You must send a clear and concise written statement to the IRS Service Center where you filed your last return and provide all of the following:

• Your full name (and your spouse's full name),
• Your signature (and spouse's signature),
• Your old address (and spouse's old address if different),
• Your new address, and
• Your social security number (and spouse's social security number).

You can use Form 8822, Change of Address, for this purpose.

You can continue to use your old preprinted payment-vouchers until the IRS sends you new ones. However, do not correct the address on the old voucher.

Payment by Electronic Funds Withdrawal or Credit Card

If you want to make estimated payments by electronic funds withdrawal or by credit card, see the Form 1040-ES instructions or *How To Pay Estimated Tax* in Publication 505.

Credit for Withholding and Estimated Tax

When you file your 2005 income tax return, take credit for all the income tax and excess social security or railroad retirement tax withheld from your salary, wages, pensions, etc. Also, take credit for the estimated tax you paid for 2005. These credits are subtracted from your tax. You should file a return and claim these credits, even if you do not owe tax.

If you had two or more employers and were paid wages of more than $90,000 during 2005, too much social security or railroad retirement tax may have been withheld from your wages. See *Credit for Excess Social Security Tax or Railroad Retirement Tax Withheld* in chapter 39.

Withholding

If you had income tax withheld during 2005, you should be sent a statement by January 31, 2006, showing your income and the tax withheld. Depending on the source of your income, you will receive:

• Form W-2, Wage and Tax Statement,
• Form W-2G, Certain Gambling Winnings, or
• A form in the 1099 series.

Forms W-2 and W-2G. You file Form W-2 with your income tax return. File Form W-2G with your return if it shows any federal income tax withheld from your winnings.

You should get at least two copies of each form you receive. Attach one copy to the front of your federal income tax return. Keep one copy for your records. You should also receive copies to file with your state and local returns.

Example

Ted Jones is employed by ABC Company, Inc. His Form W-2 box 2, reflects that he had $10,675.50 in federal tax withheld by ABC Company on wages of $46,958. His state income tax of $2,817.48 withheld for the state of Georgia is reflected in box 17 on the same amount of wages. Box 12 indicates (Code D—Code definitions can be found on the back of the W-2 form) that Ted contributed $2,546.21 to his company's 401(k) plan. That amount of income was not included in the federal or state wages, but it is included in determining how much was withheld from Ted's income for Social Security and Medicare purposes. Refer to boxes 3 and 5. The Social Security tax withheld is in box 4, and the Medicare tax withheld is in box 6. The pension plan box is checked in box 13 and lets Ted (and the IRS) know that he is covered by a pension plan and therefore may be limited in his ability to make deductible IRA contributions.

Form W-2

Your employer should send you a Form W-2 for 2005 by January 31, 2006. You should receive a separate Form W-2 from each employer you worked for.

If you stopped working before the end of the year, your employer could have given you your Form W-2 at any time after you stopped working. However, your employer must send it to you by January 31, 2006.

If you ask for the form, your employer must send it to you within 30 days after receiving your written request or within 30 days after your final wage payment, whichever is later.

If you have not received your Form W-2 on time, you should ask your employer for it. If you do not receive it by February 15, call the IRS.

a Control number			OMB No. 1545-0008	Safe, accurate, FAST! Use	IRS e-file	Visit the IRS website at www.irs.gov/efile.

b Employer identification number (EIN)	1 Wages, tips, other compensation 46,958.00	2 Federal income tax withheld 10,675.50
c Employer's name, address, and ZIP code	3 Social security wages 49,504.21	4 Social security tax withheld 3,069.26
	5 Medicare wages and tips 49,504.21	6 Medicare tax withheld 1,435.62
	7 Social security tips	8 Allocated tips
d Employee's social security number	9 Advance EIC payment	10 Dependent care benefits
e Employee's first name and initial Last name Ted R. Jones	11 Nonqualified plans	12a See instructions for box 12 D 2,546.21
	13 Statutory employee ☐ Retirement plan ☒ Third-party sick pay ☐	12b
	14 Other	12c
		12d
f Employee's address and ZIP code		

15 State Employer's state ID number	16 State wages, tips, etc. 46,958.00	17 State income tax 2,817.48	18 Local wages, tips, etc.	19 Local income tax	20 Locality name

Form **W-2** Wage and Tax Statement **2005**   Department of the Treasury—Internal Revenue Service

Copy B—To Be Filed With Employee's FEDERAL Tax Return.
This information is being furnished to the Internal Revenue Service.

Form W-2 shows your total pay and other compensation and the income tax, social security tax, and Medicare tax that was withheld during the year. Include the federal income tax withheld (as shown on Form W-2) on:

- Line 64 if you file Form 1040,
- Line 39 if you file Form 1040A, or
- Line 7 if you file Form 1040EZ.

Form W-2 is also used to report any taxable sick pay you received and any income tax withheld from your sick pay.

Form W-2G

If you had gambling winnings in 2005, the payer may have withheld income tax. If tax was withheld, the payer will give you a Form W-2G showing the amount you won and the amount of tax withheld.

Report the amounts you won on line 21 of Form 1040. Take credit for the tax withheld on line 64 of Form 1040. If you had gambling winnings, you must use Form 1040; you cannot use Form 1040A or Form 1040EZ.

The 1099 Series

Most forms in the 1099 series are not filed with your return. You should be sent these forms by January 31, 2006. Keep these forms for your records. There are several different forms in this series, including:

- Form 1099-B, Proceeds From Broker and Barter Exchange Transactions,
- Form 1099-DIV, Dividends and Distributions,
- Form 1099-G, Certain Government Payments,
- Form 1099-INT, Interest Income,
- Form 1099-MISC, Miscellaneous Income,
- Form 1099-OID, Original Issue Discount,
- Form 1099-R, Distributions From Pensions, Annuities, Retirement or Profit-Sharing Plans, IRAs, Insurance Contracts, etc.,
- Form SSA-1099, Social Security Benefit Statement, and
- Form RRB-1099, Payments by the Railroad Retirement Board.

If you received the types of income reported on some forms in the 1099 series, you may not be able to use Form 1040A or Form 1040EZ. See the instructions to these forms for details.

Form 1099-R. Attach Form 1099-R to your return if box 4 shows federal income tax withheld. Include the amount withheld in the total on line 64 of Form 1040 or line 39 of Form 1040A. You cannot use Form 1040EZ if you received payments reported on Form 1099-R.

Backup withholding. If you were subject to backup withholding on income you received during 2005, include the amount withheld, as shown on your Form 1099, in the total on line 64 of Form 1040, or line 39 of Form 1040A.

Form Not Correct

If you receive a form with incorrect information on it, you should ask the payer for a corrected form. Call the telephone number or write to the address given for the payer on the form. The corrected Form W-2G or Form 1099 you receive will be marked "Corrected." A special form, Form W-2c, Corrected Wage and Tax Statement, is used to correct a Form W-2.

Form Received After Filing

If you file your return and you later receive a form for income that you did not include on your return, you should report the income and take credit for any income tax withheld by filing Form 1040X, Amended U.S. Individual Income Tax Return.

Separate Returns

If you are married but file a separate return, you can take credit only for the tax withheld from your own income. Do not include any amount withheld from your spouse's income. However, different rules may apply if you live in a community property state.

Community property states are listed in chapter 2. For more information on these rules, and some exceptions, see Publication 555, Community Property.

Fiscal Years

If you file your tax return on the basis of a fiscal year (a 12-month period ending on the last day of any month except December), you must follow special rules to determine your credit for federal income tax withholding. For a discussion of how to take credit for withholding on a fiscal year return, see *Fiscal Years* in chapter 3 of Publication 505.

Explanation
Employees on a fiscal year may suffer a delay in utilizing their credit from withheld taxes. See Chapter 44, *Foreign Citizens Living in the United States,* for an example.

Estimated Tax

Take credit for all your estimated tax payments for 2005 on line 65 of Form 1040 or line 40 of Form 1040A. Include any overpayment from 2004 that you had credited to your 2005 estimated tax. You must use Form 1040 or Form 1040A if you paid estimated tax. You cannot use Form 1040EZ.

Name changed. If you changed your name, and you made estimated tax payments using your old name, attach a brief statement to the front of your tax return indicating:

- When you made the payments,
- The amount of each payment,
- The IRS address to which you sent the payments,
- Your name when you made the payments, and
- Your social security number.

The statement should cover payments you made jointly with your spouse as well as any you made separately.

Separate Returns
If you and your spouse made separate estimated tax payments for 2005 and you file separate returns, you can take credit only for your own payments.

If you made joint estimated tax payments, you must decide how to divide the payments between your returns. One of you can claim all of the estimated tax paid and the other none, or you can divide it in any other way you agree on. If you cannot agree, you must divide the payments in proportion to each spouse's individual tax as shown on your separate returns for 2005.

Divorced Taxpayers
If you made joint estimated tax payments for 2005, and you were divorced during the year, either you or your former spouse can claim all of the joint payments, or you each can claim part of them. If you cannot agree on how to divide the payments, you must divide them in proportion to each spouse's individual tax as shown on your separate returns for 2005.

If you claim any of the joint payments on your tax return, enter your former spouse's social security number (SSN) in the space provided on the front of Form 1040 or Form 1040A. If you divorced and remarried in 2005, enter your present spouse's SSN in that space and write your former spouse's SSN, followed by "DIV," to the left of line 65, Form 1040, or line 40, Form 1040A.

Underpayment Penalty

If you did not pay enough tax either through withholding or by making estimated tax payments, you will have an underpayment of estimated tax and you may have to pay a penalty. Generally, you will not have to pay a penalty for 2005 if any of the following situations applies.

- The total of your withholding and estimated tax payments was at least as much as your 2004 tax (or 110% of your 2004 tax if your adjusted gross income was more than $150,000, $75,000 if your 2005 filing status is married filing separately) and you paid all required estimated tax payments on time.

- The tax balance due on your return is no more than 10% of your total 2005 tax, and you paid all required estimated tax payments on time.
- Your total 2005 tax minus your withholding is less than $1,000.
- You did not have a tax liability for 2004.
- You did not have any withholding taxes and your current year tax less any household employment taxes is less than $1,000.

Special rules apply if you are a farmer or fisherman. See *Farmers and Fishermen* in chapter 4 of Publication 505 for more information.
IRS can figure the penalty for you. If you think you owe the penalty but you do not want to figure it yourself when you file your tax return, you may not have to. Generally, the IRS will figure the penalty for you and send you a bill. However, you must complete Form 2210 and attach it to your return if you think you are able to lower or eliminate your penalty. See chapter 4 of Publication 505.

TAXPLANNER

The safest method of paying enough estimated tax and withholding, and thereby avoiding underpayment penalties, is to use last year's tax. The tax shown on your previous year's tax return less the tax that is expected to be withheld during the current year must be paid in estimated installments throughout the year.

Example
Elizabeth West's 2005 tax return indicates that her 2005 tax liability (including self-employment tax and alternative minimum tax) was $14,000. In 2006, Elizabeth estimates that her tax liability will jump to $24,000 due to several contemplated stock sales that should result in a substantial capital gain. Elizabeth's withholding on her 2006 salary is expected to be $13,000.

Because her withholding of $13,000 during 2006 is not expected to exceed her 2005 tax of $14,000, she should increase her withholding by $1,000 during the year. Even though she will have paid less than 90% of her tax liability for 2006, she will avoid an underpayment penalty because she has paid an amount at least equal to her 2006 tax. If she made this determination early enough in the year, she could accomplish the same result by making four quarterly estimated tax payments of $250.

However, Elizabeth will have to pay an additional $10,000 ($24,000 − $14,000) when she files her 2006 tax return by April 15, 2007. Nevertheless, she will have had the use of this money from the time she sold her stock until the time she filed her 2006 tax return.

Explanation
Underpayment Penalties. You may be penalized for not paying enough tax for a particular installment period. The amount subject to the penalty is the amount by which the required installment, defined as the lesser of items 1 or 2 below, exceeds the amount paid for the quarterly period:

1. 90% of the tax shown on the return (after certain adjustments), allocated evenly to each of quarterly periods; or
2. 100% of the 2005 tax, allocated evenly to each of the quarterly periods (provided the prior year comprised 12 months and a return was filed for such year); if your 2005 adjusted gross income exceeded $150,000, you must have paid 110% of the 2005 tax liability to avoid underpayment penalties for

2006. Note: 100% of prior year tax is the tax liability as shown on the 2005 original return. The tax liability on an amended return is not used for purposes of quarterly estimated payments.

Example

Ms. Green's adjusted gross income in 2005 was $175,000, while her 2005 tax liability was $40,000. Her 2006 income tax liability is $55,000. Ms. Green will avoid an underpayment penalty in 2006 if the total amount of tax withheld and estimated tax payments exceeds 110% of her 2005 tax liability, or $44,000. To avoid a penalty in 2007, she would have to pay in $60,500 (110% of $55,000) since her adjusted gross income also exceeded $150,000 in 2006.

The underpayment penalty may also be avoided by using a special rule based on your annualized income. Under the special rule, no penalty is imposed for a quarter if the cumulative amount paid by the installment date equals or exceeds 90% of the cumulative estimated tax as computed on annualized income.

In general, the annualized method allows you to calculate your quarterly payment based on taxable income received up to the end of the latest quarter, annualized to a 12-month period. You can usually benefit from the annualized method if you do not receive your taxable income evenly throughout the year (e.g., if you are the owner of a ski shop that receives most of its revenue during the winter months).

The use of the methods for determining the underpaid amount, described above, may vary from quarter to quarter to provide the minimum underpayment amount by quarter. Remember, however, that if you pay the annualized income installment, you must add the difference between the amount you pay and the required installment to the required installment for the next period if the annualized income method is not used for the next period.

The tax computed for purposes of determining the quarterly payment required to avoid the underpayment penalty includes the self-employment tax and all other taxes (including the alternative minimum tax), minus any allowable credits.

If the amount paid for a quarterly period is greater than the amount required to avoid penalty, the excess is applied first against underpayments in prior quarters, and then against subsequent underpayments. Any penalty is assessed from the installment due date to the date paid or the original due date of the return, whichever is earlier. The rate of the penalty is the same as the rate of interest for underpayments of tax. However, the penalty is not compounded daily, whereas the interest is.

Special requirements and exceptions are provided for farmers, fishermen, and nonresident aliens.

TaxAlert

The underpayment of estimate tax penalty is not imposed where the total tax liability for the year, reduced by any withheld tax and estimated tax payments, is less than $1,000.

TaxPlanner

You may avoid underpayment penalty before the end of the year by taking a distribution from your IRA account and having enough taxes withheld to cover your underpayment. It is important to remember to repay the entire amount of the distribution, including taxes withheld, within 60 days after the distribution. Otherwise, the distribution is subject to taxes as well as 10% early withdrawal penalty if you are under age 59 1/2.

PART II

Income

The eight chapters in this part discuss many kinds of income. They explain which income is and is not taxed. The chart on the following page lists some of the topics covered in this part. It is divided into (1) items you generally must include in income and (2) items you generally do not include in income.

See *Part Three* for information on gains and losses you report on Schedule D (Form 1040) and for information on selling your home.

INCOME

INCOME GENERALLY INCLUDES:

Alimony (Chapter 20, *Alimony*)

Bartering income (Chapter 13, *Other Income*)

Cancelled debt income (Chapter 13, *Other Income*)

Dividends (Chapter 9, *Dividends and Other Corporate Distributions*)

Gain on the sale of personal items, such as a car (Chapter 13, *Other Income*)

Gambling winnings (Chapter 13, *Other Income*)

Income from an activity not for profit (Chapter 13, *Other Income*)

Interest (Chapter 8, *Interest Income*)

Part of Social Security benefits and equivalent railroad retirement benefits (Chapter 12, *Social Security and Equivalent Railroad Retirement Benefits*)

Pensions and annuities (Chapter 11, *Retirement Plans, Pensions, and Annuities*)

Recoveries of amounts previously deducted (Chapter 13, *Other Income*)

Rental income (Chapter 10, *Rental Income and Expenses*)

Royalties (Chapter 13, *Other Income*)

Tips (Chapter 7, *Tip Income*)

Wages, salaries, and other earnings (Chapter 6, *Wages, Salaries, and Other Earnings*)

Your share of estate and trust income (Chapter 13, *Other Income*)

Your share of partnership and S Corporation income (Chapter 13, *Other Income*)

INCOME GENERALLY DOES NOT INCLUDE:

Accident and health insurance proceeds (Chapter 13, *Other Income*)

Gifts and inheritances (Chapter 13, *Other Income*)

Housing allowance for members of the clergy (Chapter 6, *Wages, Salaries, and Other Earnings*)

Interest on state and local government obligations (Chapter 8, *Interest Income*)

Life insurance proceeds (Chapter 13, *Other Income*)

Military allowances (Chapter 6, *Wages, Salaries, and Other Earnings*)

Part of scholarship and fellowship grants (Chapter 13, *Other Income*)

Part of Social Security benefits and equivalent railroad retirement benefits (Chapter 12, *Social Security and Equivalent Railroad Retirement Benefits*)

Veterans' benefits (Chapter 6, *Wages, Salaries, and Other Earnings*)

Welfare and other public assistance benefits (Chapter 13, *Other Income*)

Workers' compensation and similar payments for sickness and injury (Chapter 13, *Other Income*)

6

Wages, Salaries, and Other Earnings

Note: The 2004 IRS Publication 17 (Your Federal Income Tax) has been updated by Ernst & Young LLP for 2005. Dates and dollar amounts shown are for 2005. Gray type is used to indicate where IRS text has been updated or intentionally omitted. Unrevised IRS text is shown in black type.

Introduction

*Ask most people how much they get paid, and, if they are willing to admit anything, they'll tell you what their salary is. Usually, there's more to income than that. The way the IRS sees it, "**gross income** means all income from whatever source derived." That means that not only is your salary subject to tax but so also are many of the fringe benefits that you might receive—everything from country club membership and employer-provided discounts to a company car. This chapter spells out in greater detail items of compensation that are taxable.*

Some fringe benefits you receive from your employer are tax free. For example, the cost of the first $50,000 of coverage in a group-term life insurance plan will be tax free if all employees in the plan are treated in the same way. But, if your employer, in a moment of detached and disinterested generosity, presents you with a Rolls-Royce as a gift, you will probably have to pay taxes on it. This chapter prepares you—in a tax sense—for whatever lies ahead.

What's New

Elective deferrals. The limit on the amount of your wages you can elect to defer into certain retirement plans (such as section 401(k) plans) increases each year through 2006. If you are age 50 or older, you may be able to make additional catch-up elective deferrals. See *Elective deferrals* in *Retirement Plan Contributions* under *Employee Compensation.*

Reminder

Foreign income. If you are a U.S. citizen or resident alien, you must report income from sources outside the United States (foreign income) on your tax return unless it is exempt by U.S. law. This is true whether you reside inside or outside the United States and whether or not you receive a Form W-2, Wage and Tax Statement, or Form 1099 from the foreign payer. This applies to earned income (such as wages and tips) as well as unearned income (such as interest, dividends, capital gains, pensions, rents, and royalties).

If you reside outside the United States, you may be able to exclude part or all of your foreign source earned income. For details, see Publication 54, Tax Guide for U.S. Citizens and Resident Aliens Abroad.

This chapter discusses compensation received for services as an employee, such as wages, salaries, and fringe benefits. The topics include:

- Bonuses and awards,
- Special rules for certain employees, and
- Sickness and injury benefits.

The chapter explains what income is included in the employee's gross income and what is not included.

Explanation
One of the most important decisions you have to make in determining your correct taxable income is what payments to include. A taxable payment is not limited to cash. It may be property, stock, or other **assets**. Also, you must include in your gross income the fair market value of payments in kind.

Example 1
Your employer provides you with a car that is used for both personal and business purposes. The value of the personal use of the car is included in earnings and it is taxable to you.

Example 2
You assist a group of investors in purchasing a piece of **real estate.** In consideration of your services, the investors award you an unconditional percentage of owner-

ship in the acquired asset. You have invested none of your personal funds. The fair market value of your ownership interest is considered as wages taxable to you in the year the transfer is completed.

Example 3
A farmer receives 50 bushels of wheat as a payment in kind. Unless specifically excluded under a government program, the farmer has income to the extent of the fair market value of the wheat.

Useful Items

You may want to see:

Publications

- ☐ **463**   Travel, Entertainment, Gift, and Car Expenses
- ☐ **503**   Child and Dependent Care Expenses
- ☐ **505**   Tax Withholding and Estimated Tax
- ☐ **525**   Taxable and Nontaxable Income

Explanation
Other useful publications and references include:

- ■ Publication 15, *Circular E, Employer's Tax Guide;* Chapter 5, *Wages and Other Compensation*
- ■ Publication 15-A, *Employer's Supplemental Tax Guide;* Chapter 6, *Employee Fringe Benefits*
- ■ Publication 15-B, *Employer's Tax Guide to Fringe Benefits;* Chapter 1, *Fringe Benefits Overview*

These and other IRS publications are available online at www.irs.gov.

Employee Compensation

This section discusses various types of employee compensation including fringe benefits, retirement plan contributions, stock options, and restricted property.

Explanation
All compensation for personal services, no matter what the form of payment, must be included in gross income. Such compensation is subject to taxes in the year received, unless the taxpayer reports income on the accrual basis.

If you perform services and decide that payment for them should be made to another person, the monies remitted to the third party are taxable to you. The IRS and the courts have long held that "fruits" of a taxpayer's labor are attributable to the "tree" that grew them.

Furthermore, you may not render services and then ask your employer to hold the funds in an attempt to control artificially when the wages will be included in your taxable income.

Example
You are due compensation for work you performed. You advise the payer to hold the money because you will not require the funds immediately. The payer credits the payment due you on the company books. You do not request the money until after the close of the tax year in which the services were rendered.

The IRS may hold that you were in **constructive receipt** of the funds before year's end. The compensation may have to be included in your income for the year in which the payment could have been received, even though you were not actually paid until later.

TaxPlanner

You will have a problem with the IRS if you ask your employer *after* you have performed the work to withhold funds in an attempt to artificially control when the wages will be included in your taxable income. If you make arrangements to defer receipt of income *prior* to commencing work, you may not have a problem as long as the arrangement meets the requirements of the law.

However, if your employer forces you to take your bonus in a later year, then it is not taxable to you until the year in which you receive it.

Example
If at the beginning of the year you arrange to have your employer pay you your year-end bonus over a 5-year period, the IRS will not claim that you were in **constructive receipt** of the entire bonus at year's end. You may even arrange to have your employer add interest to your deferred bonus. You must, however, make these arrangements prior to performance of the work for which the bonus will be paid. However, these types of arrangements must meet a complicated set of requirements, which were included in a 2004 tax act, in order to work.

Form W-2. If you are an employee, you should receive Form W-2 from your employer showing the pay you received for your services. Include your pay on line 7 of Form 1040 or Form 1040A, or on line 1 of Form 1040EZ, even if you do not receive a Form W-2.

Explanation
If a Form W-2 is not received from your employer by the tax filing deadline, Form 4852, substitute for W-2, should be attached to the return.

Child care providers. If you provide childcare, either in the child's home or in your home or other place of business, the pay you receive must be included in your income. If you are not an employee, you are probably self-employed and must include payments for your services on Schedule C (Form 1040), Profit or Loss From Business, or Schedule C-EZ (Form 1040), Net Profit From Business. You are generally not an employee unless you are subject to the will and control of the person who employs you as to what you are to do and how you are to do it.

Baby-sitting. If you baby-sit for relatives or neighborhood children, whether on a regular basis or only periodically, the rules for childcare providers apply to you.

Miscellaneous Compensation

This section discusses different types of employee compensation. **Advance commissions and other earnings.** If you receive advance commissions or other amounts for services to be performed in the future and you are a cash-method taxpayer, you must include these amounts in your income in the year you receive them.

If you repay unearned commissions or other amounts in the same year you receive them, reduce the amount included in your income by the repayment. If you repay them in a later tax year, you can deduct the repayment as an itemized deduction on your Schedule A (Form 1040), or you may be able to take a credit for that year. See *Repayments* in chapter 13.

Explanation
In some cases, an advance payment of a commission or salary may be considered a loan, thus permitting you to delay paying tax on that amount. If the loan is repaid, you will not have to recognize any taxable income. If the loan is forgiven, you will recognize the amount of the loan as compensation in the year in which it was forgiven. See *Canceled Debts* in Chapter 13, *Other Income,* for a complete discussion. Commissions and salaries are considered to be income when they are paid to you or when they are applied as a reduction to your loan account.

The key question is: When may a payment be characterized as a loan? Generally, for a transaction to be considered a loan, a debtor-creditor relationship must exist at the outset. In other words, the lending party expects and will eventually receive monetary repayment. Payment in return for a future obligation to render services is *not* a loan. Thus, an advance on your wages is not a loan. Whether a payment is or is not a loan is usually a question of fact, requiring a review of each case's unique circumstances.

Example
If you receive an advance of your January 2006 salary on December 31, 2005, you will have taxable income in 2005.

TaxSaver
Generally, you should take advantage of your employer's 401(k) plan or 403(b) plan. Your contribution to the plan will not be included in your taxable wages. See Chapter 11, *Retirement Plans, Pensions, and Annuities,* for more information about these plans.

TaxPlanner
You may wish to consider a loan from your employer's qualified pension or annuity plan rather than an advance on your next year's salary. Loans are not considered taxable income to the borrower under most circumstances. See Chapter 11, *Retirement Plans, Pensions, and Annuities,* for rules regarding loans from an employer's qualified pension or annuity plan.

TaxAlert
Owners-employees, such as S corporation shareholders, partners, and sole proprietors are able to borrow from their pension plans without being subject to a penalty tax.

Allowances and reimbursements. If you receive travel, transportation, or other business expense allowances or reimbursements from your employer, see Publication 463. If you are reimbursed for moving expenses, see Publication 521, Moving Expenses.

Back pay awards. Include in income amounts you are awarded in a settlement or judgment for back pay. These include payments made to you for damages, unpaid life insurance premiums, and unpaid health insurance premiums. They should be reported to you by your employer on Form W-2.

Explanation
If you received an amount in settlement or judgment for back wages and liquidated damages (e.g., under Title VII as amended by the 1991 Civil Rights Act), see *Court Awards and Damages* in Chapter 13, *Other Income.* Generally, awards intended to replace lost wages are included in your taxable income.

TaxPlanner
Prior to entering any settlement agreement, you should consult with a tax advisor to ensure that you negotiate the most tax-favorable terms.

Bonuses and awards. Bonuses or awards you receive for outstanding work are included in your income and should be shown on your Form W-2. These include prizes such as vacation trips for meeting sales goals. If the prize or award you receive is goods or services, you must include the fair market value of the goods or services in your income. However, if your employer merely promises to pay you a bonus or award at some future time, it is not taxable until you receive it or it is made available to you.

Employee achievement award. If you receive tangible personal property (other than cash, a gift certificate, or an equivalent item) as an award for length of service or safety achievement, you can generally exclude its value from your income. However, the amount you can exclude is limited to your employer's cost and cannot be more than $1,600 ($400 for awards that are not qualified plan awards) for all such awards you receive during the year. Your employer can tell you whether your award is a qualified plan award. Your employer must make the award as part of a meaningful presentation, under conditions and circumstances that do not create a significant likelihood of it being disguised pay.

However, the exclusion does not apply to the following awards.

- A length-of-service award if you received it for less than 5 years of service or if you received another length-of-service award during the year or the previous 4 years.
- A safety achievement award if you are a manager, administrator, clerical employee, or other professional employee or if more than 10% of eligible employees previously received safety achievement awards during the year.

Example. Ben Green received three employee achievement awards during the year: a nonqualified plan award of a watch valued at $250, and two qualified plan awards of a stereo valued at $1,000 and a set of golf clubs valued at $500. Assuming that the requirements for qualified plan awards are otherwise satisfied, each award by itself would be excluded from income. However, because the $1,750 total value of the awards is more than $1,600, Ben must include $150 ($1,750 – $1,600) in his income.

Government cost-of-living allowances. Cost-of-living allowances generally are included in your income. However, they are not included in your income if you are a federal civilian employee or a federal court employee who is stationed in Alaska, Hawaii, or outside the United States.

Allowances and differentials that increase your basic pay as an incentive for taking a less desirable post of duty are part of your compensation and must be included in income. For example, your compensation includes Foreign Post, Foreign Service, and Overseas Tropical differentials. For more information, see Publication 516, U.S. Government Civilian Employees Stationed Abroad.

Note received for services. If your employer gives you a secured note as payment for your services, you must include the fair market value (usually the discount value) of the note in your income for the year you receive it. When you later receive payments on the note, a proportionate part of each payment is the recovery of the fair market value that you previously included in your income. Do not include that part again in your income. Include the rest of the payment in your income in the year of payment.

If your employer gives you a nonnegotiable unsecured note as payment for your services, payments on the note that are credited toward the principal amount of the note are compensation income when you receive them.

Severance pay. Amounts you receive as severance pay are taxable. A lump-sum payment for cancellation of your employment contract must be included in your income in the tax year you receive it.

Accrued leave payment. If you are a federal employee and receive a lump-sum payment for accrued annual leave when you retire or resign, this amount will be included as wages on your Form W-2.

If you resign from one agency and are reemployed by another agency, you may have to repay part of your lump-sum annual leave payment to the second agency. You can reduce gross wages by the amount you repaid in the same tax year in which you received it. Attach to your tax return a copy of the receipt or statement given to you by the agency you repaid to explain the difference between the wages on the return and the wages on your Forms W-2.

Outplacement services. If you choose to accept a reduced amount of severance pay so that you can receive outplacement services (such as training in résumé writing and interview techniques), you must include the unreduced amount of the severance pay in income.

However, you can deduct the value of these outplacement services (up to the difference between the severance pay included in income and the amount actually received) as a miscellaneous deduction (subject to the 2% limit) on Schedule A (Form 1040).

Sick pay. Pay you receive from your employer while you are sick or injured is part of your salary or wages. In addition, you must include in your income sick pay benefits received from any of the following payers.

- A welfare fund.
- A state sickness or disability fund.
- An association of employers or employees.
- An insurance company, if your employer paid for the plan.

However, if you paid the premiums on an accident or health insurance policy, the benefits you receive under the policy are not taxable.

Social security and Medicare taxes paid by employer. If you and your employer have an agreement that your employer pays your social security and Medicare taxes without deducting them from your gross wages, you must report the amount of tax paid for you as taxable wages on your tax return. The payment is also treated as wages for figuring your social security and Medicare taxes and your social security and Medicare benefits. However, these payments are not treated as social security and Medicare wages if you are a household worker or a farm worker.

Stock appreciation rights. Do not include a stock appreciation right granted by your employer in income until you exercise (use) the right if it satisfies the requirements of new Section 409A of the Internal Revenue Code or if you were vested in it before 2005. When you use the right, you are entitled to a cash or stock payment equal to the fair market value of the corporation's stock on the date of use minus the fair market value on the date the right was granted. You include the cash payment in your income in the year you use the right.

Fringe Benefits

Fringe benefits received in connection with the performance of your services are included in your income as compensation unless you pay fair market value for them or they are specifically excluded by law. Abstaining from the performance of services (for example, under a covenant not to compete) is treated as the performance of services for purposes of these rules.

Accounting period. You must use the same accounting period your employer uses to report your taxable noncash fringe benefits. Your employer has the option to report taxable noncash fringe benefits by using either of the following rules.

- The general rule: benefits are reported for a full calendar year (January 1– December 31).
- The special accounting period rule: benefits provided during the last 2 months of the calendar year (or any shorter period) are treated as paid during the following calendar year. For example,

each year your employer reports the value of benefits provided during the last 2 months of the prior year and the first 10 months of the current year.

Your employer does not have to use the same accounting period for each fringe benefit, but must use the same period for all employees who receive a particular benefit.

You must use the same accounting period that you use to report the benefit to claim an employee business deduction (for use of a car, for example).

Form W-2. Your employer reports your taxable fringe benefits in box 1 (Wages, tips, other compensation) of Form W-2. The total value of your fringe benefits may also be noted in box 12. The value of your fringe benefits may be added to your other compensation on one Form W-2, or you may receive a separate Form W-2 showing just the value of your fringe benefits in box 1 with a notation in box 12.

Accident or Health Plan
Generally, the value of accident or health plan coverage provided to you by your employer is not included in your income. Benefits you receive from the plan may be taxable, as explained later under *Sickness and Injury Benefits.*

> ### Explanation
> This exclusion applies to coverage provided to the tax-payer and the taxpayer's spouse and dependents.

Long-term care coverage. Contributions by your employer to provide coverage for long-term care services are generally not included in your income. However, contributions made through a flexible spending or similar arrangement (such as a cafeteria plan) must be included in your income. This amount will be reported as wages in box 1 of your Form W-2.

Contributions you make to the plan are discussed in Publication 502, Medical and Dental Expenses.
Archer MSA contributions. Contributions by your employer to your Archer MSA generally are not included in your income. Their total will be reported in box 12 of Form W-2 with code R. You must report this amount on Form 8853, Archer MSAs and Long-Term Care Insurance Contracts. File the form with your return.

If your employer does not make contributions to your MSA, you can make your own contributions to your MSA. These contributions are discussed in Publication 969, Health Savings Accounts and Other Tax-Favored Health Plans. Also, see Form 8853.
Health flexible spending arrangement (health FSA). If your employer provides a health FSA that qualifies as an accident or health plan, the amount of your salary reduction, and reimbursements of your medical care expenses and those of your spouse and dependents, are generally not included in your income.
Health reimbursement arrangement (HRA). If your employer provides an HRA that qualifies as an accident or health plan, coverage and reimbursements of your medical care expenses and those of your spouse and dependents are generally not included in your income.

See also *Reimbursement for medical care* under *Other Sickness and Injury Benefits,* later.

Adoption Assistance
You may be able to exclude from your income amounts paid or expenses incurred by your employer for qualified adoption expenses in connection with your adoption of an eligible child. See Publication 968, Tax Benefits for Adoption, for more information.

Adoption benefits are reported by your employer in box 12 of Form W-2 with code T. They are also included as social security and Medicare wages in boxes 3 and 5. However, they are not included as wages in box 1. To determine the taxable and nontaxable amounts, you must complete Part III of Form 8839, Qualified Adoption Expenses. File the form with your return.

De Minimis (Minimal) Benefits
If your employer provides you with a product or service and the cost of it is so small that it would be unreasonable for the employer to account for it, the value is not included in your income. Generally, the value of benefits such as discounts at company cafeterias, cab fares home when working overtime, and company picnics are not included in your income.
Holiday gifts. If your employer gives you a turkey, ham, or other item of nominal value at Christmas or other holidays, do not include the value of the gift in your income. However, if your employer gives you cash, a gift certificate, or a similar item that you can easily exchange for cash, you include the value of that gift as extra salary or wages regardless of the amount involved.

Educational Assistance
You can exclude from your income up to $5,250 of qualified employer-provided educational assistance. The exclusion applies to undergraduate and graduate-level courses. For more information, see Publication 970, Tax Benefits for Education.

Employer-Provided Vehicles
If your employer provides a car (or other highway motor vehicle) to you, your personal use of the car is usually a taxable noncash fringe benefit.

Your employer must determine the actual value of this fringe benefit to include in your income.
Tip. *Certain employer-provided transportation can be excluded from gross income. See the discussion on* Transportation, *later.*

Group-Term Life Insurance
Generally, the cost of up to $50,000 of group-term life insurance coverage provided to you by your employer (or former employer) is not included in your income. However, you must include in income the cost of employer-provided insurance that is more than the cost of $50,000 of coverage.

If your employer provided more than $50,000 of coverage, the amount included in your income is reported as part of your wages in box 1 of your Form W-2. It is also shown separately in box 12 with code C.

> ### Example
> Your employer, ABC Company, pays the premiums on your $150,000 group-term life insurance policy. You are 40 years old. Every $1,000 worth of coverage costs $0.10 per month. Because under the law only $50,000 worth of coverage may be excluded from your income, the cost of the additional $100,000 of life insurance, or $120 [($0.10 × 12 months) × $100], has to be included in your income, even though your employer covers the cost.
>
> If you pay any amount of the $120 directly, you may reduce, dollar for dollar, the amount of the premium that would otherwise be included in your income. Thus, if you paid $50, only $70 ($120 − $50) of the premium would be included in your income.

Group-term life insurance. This insurance is term life insurance protection (insurance for a fixed period of time) that:

- Provides a general death benefit,
- Is provided to a group of employees,
- Is provided under a policy carried by the employer, and
- Provides an amount of insurance to each employee based on a formula that prevents individual selection.

Permanent benefits. If your group-term life insurance policy includes permanent benefits, such as a paid-up or cash surrender value, you must include in your income, as wages, the cost of the permanent benefits minus the amount you pay for them. Your employer should be able to tell you the amount to include in your income.

Accidental death benefits. Insurance that provides accidental or other death benefits but does not provide general death benefits (travel insurance, for example) is not group-term life insurance.

Former employer. If your former employer provides more than $50,000 of group-term life insurance coverage during the year, the amount included in your income is reported as wages in box 1 of Form W-2. Also, it is shown separately in box 12 with code C. Box 12 also will show the amount of uncollected social security and Medicare taxes on the excess coverage, with codes M and N. You must pay these taxes with your income tax return. Include them in your total tax on line 63, Form 1040, and enter "UT" and the amount of the taxes on the dotted line next to line 63.

Two or more employers. Your exclusion for employer-provided group-term life insurance coverage cannot exceed the cost of $50,000 of coverage, whether the insurance is provided by a single employer or multiple employers. If two or more employers provide insurance coverage that totals more than $50,000, the amounts reported as wages on your Forms W-2 will not be correct. You must figure how much to include in your income. Reduce the amount you figure by any amount reported with code C in box 12 of your Forms W-2, add the result to the wages reported in box 1, and report the total on your return.

Figuring the taxable cost. Use the following worksheet to figure the amount to include in your income.

Worksheet 6-1. Figuring the Cost of Group-Term Life Insurance to Include in Income

1. Enter the total amount of your insurance coverage from your employers.. **1.** _____

2. Limit on exclusion for employer-provided group-term life insurance coverage.................................. **2.** $50,000

3. Subtract line 2 from line 1............................ **3.** _____

4. Divide line 3 by $1,000. Figure to the nearest tenth......... **4.** _____

5. Go to Table 6–1. Using your age on the last day of the tax year, find your age group in the left column, and enter the cost from the column on the right for your age group.............. **5.** _____

6. Multiply line 4 by line 5............................... **6.** _____

7. Enter the number of full months of coverage at this cost..... **7.** _____

8. Multiply line 6 by line 7............................... **8.** _____

9. Enter the premiums you paid per month............. **9.** _____

10. Enter the number of months you paid the premiums... **10.** _____

11. Multiply line 9 by line 10.............................. **11.** _____

12. Subtract line 11 from line 8.
   Include this amount in your income as wages........... **12.** _____

Example. You are 51 years old and work for employers A and B. Both employers provide group-term life insurance coverage for you for the entire year. Your coverage is $35,000 with employer A and $45,000 with employer B. You pay premiums of $4.15 a month under the employer B group plan. You figure the amount to include in your income as follows.

Table 6-1

Cost of $1,000 of Group-Term Life Insurance for One Month

Age	Cost
Under 25	$ .05
25 through 29	.06
30 through 34	.08
35 through 39	.09
40 through 44	.10
45 through 49	.15
50 through 54	.23
55 through 59	.43
60 through 64	.66
65 through 69	1.27
70 and older	2.06

Worksheet 6-1. Figuring the Cost of Group-Term Life Insurance to Include in Income—Illustrated

1. Enter the total amount of your insurance coverage from your employers.. **1.** *$80,000*

2. Limit on exclusion for employer-provided group-term life insurance coverage.................................. **2.** *$50,000*

3. Subtract line 2 from line 1............................ **3.** *$30,000*

4. Divide line 3 by $1,000. Figure to the nearest tenth......... **4.** *$30.0*

5. Go to Table 6–1. Using your age on the last day of the tax year, find your age group in the left column, and enter the cost from the column on the right for your age group.............. **5.** *0.23*

6. Multiply line 4 by line 5............................... **6.** *6.90*

7. Enter the number of full months of coverage at this cost.... **7.** *12*

8. Multiply line 6 by line 7............................... **8.** *82.80*

9. Enter the premiums you paid per month............. **9.** *$4.15*

10. Enter the number of months you paid the premiums... **10.** *12*

11. Multiply line 9 by line 10.............................. **11.** *$49.80*

12. Subtract line 11 from line 8.
   Include this amount in your income as wages............ **12.** *$33.00*

Entire cost excluded. You are not taxed on the cost of group-term life insurance if any of the following circumstances apply.

1. You are permanently and totally disabled and have ended your employment.
2. Your employer is the beneficiary of the policy for the entire period the insurance is in force during the tax year.
3. A charitable organization (defined in chapter 26) to which contributions are deductible is the only beneficiary of the policy for the entire period the insurance is in force during the tax year. (You are not entitled to a deduction for a charitable contribution for naming a charitable organization as the beneficiary of your policy.)
4. The plan existed on January 1, 1984, and:
   a. You retired before January 2, 1984, and were covered by the plan when you retired, or
   b. You reached age 55 before January 2, 1984, and were employed by the employer or its predecessor in 1983.

Entire cost taxed. You are taxed on the entire cost of group-term life insurance if either of the following circumstances apply.

- The insurance is provided by your employer through a qualified employees' trust, such as a pension trust or a qualified annuity plan.
- You are a key employee and your employer's plan discriminates in favor of key employees.

Retirement Planning Services

If your employer has a qualified retirement plan, qualified retirement planning services provided to you (and your spouse) by your employer are not included in your income. Qualified services include retirement planning advice, information about your employer's retirement plan, and information about how the plan may fit into your overall individual retirement income plan. You cannot exclude the value of any tax preparation, accounting, legal, or brokerage services provided by your employer.

Transportation

If your employer provides you with a qualified transportation fringe benefit, it can be excluded from your income, up to certain limits. A qualified transportation fringe benefit is:

- Transportation in a commuter highway vehicle (such as a van) between your home and work place,
- A transit pass, or
- Qualified parking.

Cash reimbursement by your employer for these expenses under a *bona fide* reimbursement arrangement is also excludable. However, cash reimbursement for a transit pass is excludable only if a voucher or similar item that can be exchanged only for a transit pass is not readily available for direct distribution to you.

Exclusion limit. The exclusion for commuter highway vehicle transportation and transit pass fringe benefits cannot be more than a total of $105 a month.

The exclusion for the qualified parking fringe benefit cannot be more than $200 a month.

If the benefits have a value that is more than these limits, the excess must be included in your income.

TaxAlert

An exclusion from gross income is allowed for an employee whose employer offers the choice between cash or employer-provided parking, and the employee chooses parking. If you choose cash, the amount offered is includable in your income.

Commuter highway vehicle. This is a highway vehicle that seats at least six adults (not including the driver). At least 80% of the vehicle's mileage must reasonably be expected to be:

- For transporting employees between their homes and work place, and
- On trips during which employees occupy at least half of the vehicle's adult seating capacity (not including the driver).

Transit pass. This is any pass, token, farecard, voucher, or similar item entitling a person to ride mass transit (whether public or private) free or at a reduced rate or to ride in a commuter highway vehicle operated by a person in the business of transporting persons for compensation.

Qualified parking. This is parking provided to an employee at or near the employer's place of business. It also includes parking provided on or near a location from which the employee commutes to work by mass transit, in a commuter highway vehicle, or by carpool. It does not include parking at or near the employee's home.

Explanation
Employer-provided vehicles. If your employer provides a car (or other highway motor vehicle) to you, your personal use of the car is usually a taxable noncash fringe benefit.
Your employer must determine the actual value of this fringe benefit to include in your income.
Note: *Certain employer-provided transportation can be excluded from gross income.*

Retirement Plan Contributions

Your employer's contributions to a qualified retirement plan for you are not included in income at the time contributed. (Your employer can tell you whether your retirement plan is qualified.) However, the cost of life insurance coverage included in the plan may have to be included. See *Group-Term Life Insurance*, earlier, under *Fringe Benefits*.

If your employer pays into a nonqualified plan for you, you generally must include the contributions in your income as wages for the tax year in which the contributions are made. However, if your interest in the plan is not transferable or is subject to a substantial risk of forfeiture (you have a good chance of losing it) at the time of the contribution, you do not have to include the value of your interest in your income until it is transferable or is no longer subject to a substantial risk of forfeiture.

Explanation
Under a *qualified plan,* participating employees may defer taxation on an employer's contributions into their individual accounts or for their vested benefits in qualified plans until some future date of distribution. Additionally, the tax on the income the account generates may be deferred until the money is distributed to the employee.
The same deferred taxation is allowed under a *nonqualified plan* as long as the employee's interest in the plan is simply an unfunded promise to pay by the employer and, after 2005, meets new requirements under a 2004 tax law change. (Whether a plan is qualified or nonqualified depends on whether or not certain statutory requirements are satisfied.)
See Chapter 11, *Retirement Plans, Pensions, and Annuities,* for suggestions about what to do when you receive distributions from qualified plans.

Elective deferrals. If you are covered by certain kinds of retirement plans, you can choose to have part of your compensation contributed by your employer to a retirement fund, rather than have it paid to you. The amount you set aside (called an elective deferral) is treated as an employer contribution to a qualified plan. It is not included in wages subject to income tax at the time contributed. However, it is included in wages subject to social security and Medicare taxes.

Elective deferrals include elective contributions to the following retirement plans.

1. Cash or deferred arrangements (section 401(k) plans).
2. The Thrift Savings Plan for federal employees.
3. Salary reduction simplified employee pension plans (SARSEP).
4. Savings incentive match plans for employees (SIMPLE plans).
5. Tax-sheltered annuity plans (403(b) plans).
6. Section 501(c)(18)(D) plans.
7. Section 457 plans.

Overall limit on deferrals. For 2005, you generally should not have deferred more than a total of $14,000 of contributions to the plans listed in (1) through (6) above. You should not have deferred more than the lesser of your includible compensation or $14,000 of contributions to the plan listed in (7) above (section 457 plan).

TaxAlert

The limit on contributions to 401(k) plans is increased to $15,000 in 2006. Thereafter, the limit is indexed for inflation.

Excess deferrals. Your employer or plan administrator should apply the proper annual limit when figuring your plan contributions. However, you are responsible for monitoring the total you defer to ensure that the deferrals are not more than the overall limit.

If you set aside more than the limit, the excess generally must be included in your income for that year. See Publication 525 for a discussion of the tax treatment of excess deferrals.

Catch-up contributions. You may be allowed catch-up contributions (additional elective deferral) if you are age 50 or older by the end of your tax year.

Stock Options

If you receive a nonstatutory option to buy or sell stock or other property as payment for your services, you usually will have income when you receive the option, when you exercise the option (use it to buy or sell the stock or other property), or when you sell or otherwise dispose of the option. However, if your option is a statutory stock option, you will not have any income until you sell or exchange your stock. Your employer can tell you which kind of option you hold. For details, get Publication 525.

Explanation

A stock option gives you the right to buy a company's stock at a specified price within a designated time period. The price is generally equal to the stock's value on the day you get the option. Generally, stock options are awarded to you by your employer as an alternative method of compensation. The option itself is generally not taxed when it is granted to you. The amount of income and the year when it is included in your taxable income depend on the type of option granted. There are two basic types of stock options: nonqualified stock options and incentive stock options.

Nonqualified stock options (NSOs or NQSOs). Nonqualified stock options do not have some of the favorable tax attributes that incentive stock options (ISOs) have (see below).

A nonqualified stock option is not taxable to you at the time the option is granted, unless the *option* is traded through a public stock exchange. Rather, you are taxed when the option is exercised on the difference between the fixed option price (the exercise price) and the fair market value of the stock on the date you exercise your option. This amount is taxed at ordinary income rates. The basis of the stock received is generally its fair market value on the date you exercise the option. If the stock appreciates thereafter, that gain will be taxable as a capital gain when you sell it.

An advantage of the nonqualified stock option is that you do not have to invest any personal funds when the option is granted or while the option is outstanding. However, if you exercise the option, you will need funds to pay the option price *and* the income tax that will be due on the option spread, the difference between the fair market value on the exercise date and the exercise price.

Incentive stock options (ISOs). Generally, incentive stock options enable you to take advantage of a specific provision of the Internal Revenue Code which gives favorable tax treatment to this type of stock option.

Incentive stock options are not taxable to you at the time the option is granted, nor do you pay tax when the option is exercised. Furthermore, if you do not dispose of the stock within 2 years after the option is granted, and you hold the stock for over 12 months after you exercise the option, any gain will be taxed as a long-term capital gain. However, if you sell the stock within 1 year after the date you exercised the option, or 2 years from the date of grant, the option loses its preferential treatment and the difference between the exercise price and the value at date of exercise is taxed to you as ordinary income.

The spread between the option price and the fair market value of the stock upon exercise of the incentive stock option may be taxed indirectly if you are subject to alternative minimum tax. For a discussion of the alternative minimum tax, see Chapter 32, *How to Figure Your Tax.* For a further discussion of stock options, see Chapter 14, *Basis of Property.*

TaxAlert

The top individual rate on net capital gains of assets held more than 1 year is 15% (5% for taxpayers with income in the lower tax brackets). These lower rates apply to both the regular tax and the alternative minimum tax. For taxpayers with income in the lower brackets, the 5% rate is reduced to zero in 2008.

TaxPlanner

Some employers allow you to use employer stock already owned to finance the exercise of stock options. This exercise method is called a stock swap and allows you to use the stock value without recognizing the gain that would result if you sold the stock and used the proceeds to exercise the stock options. Certain stock holding periods and other restrictions can apply, which should be stipulated in your employer's stock option plan.

TaxSaver

Employee stock purchase plans. Many companies have stock purchase plans that offer participating employees the opportunity to buy company stock at a discount. Employees usually contribute to the plan by authorizing payroll deductions, which are not excludable from gross income.

As an employee, you do not have to pay any tax when the plan's trustee exercises the option and purchases company stock. The stock is credited to your account within the plan.

At a future time, you may request to receive the stock purchased for your account. On distribution, if you immediately sell the stock, any gain will be taxed as ordinary income. The gain will generally be determined by the sale price less the amount you contributed to the plan to buy the stock. Your company should be able to provide you with all relevant information.

However, if after exercising the option you hold it for 2 years from the grant date and over 1 year from the purchase date, any gain will typically be treated as a long-term capital gain (except for the original discount). Again, if you have a capital loss carryover, the fact that the gain is characterized as a capital gain could still result in a tax benefit for you.

Restricted Property

Generally, if you receive property for your services, you must include its fair market value in your income in the year you receive the property. However, if you receive stock or other property that has certain restrictions that affect its value, you do not include the value of the property in your income until it has substantially vested. (You can choose to include the value of the property in your income in the year it is transferred to you.) For details, see *Restricted Property* in Publication 525.

Example

Your employer offers to sell you a parcel of land worth $5,000 for a bargain price of $3,500. You would have to include the $1,500 that the company, in effect, gave you as income for the year. In turn, your cost **basis** for the property would be $5,000, not the $3,500 you actually paid for it.

This example shows the importance of putting a reasonable value on the property you receive from your employer. The lower the value is, the less income you will currently report. However, your basis in the property will also be lower and you will realize a larger gain upon the subsequent sale of the property.

Dividends received on restricted stock. Dividends you receive on restricted stock are treated as compensation and not as dividend income. Your employer should include these payments on your Form W-2.

Explanation

Restricted stock is stock subject to a substantial risk of forfeiture. A substantial risk of forfeiture occurs when your ownership of property is conditional on the performance of substantial services in the future. When you complete these services or when the property may be legally transferred by you, whichever is earlier, you must recognize as income the difference between the fair market value of the property on that date and the amount, if any, you paid for it.

TAXSAVER

If you expect the value of the property to appreciate, you may choose to recognize the income generated by the receipt of the property before any restrictions on your ownership are lifted. This is called an 83(b) election. 83(b) elections must be made within 30 days of when the property is transferred to you. See the instructions in IRS Publication 525. If the property increases in value from the time you have recognized its value as income to the time the risk of forfeiture is removed, the increase will not be taxed at that time. Instead, the tax on that appreciation will be deferred until the property is sold. You may make this choice even if you pay an amount for the property at least equal to its fair market value and therefore recognize zero taxable income currently. You must decide no later than 30 days after you receive the property if you are going to recognize the income while the property is still subject to restrictions.

If you recognize the income and then are forced to forfeit the property, you may deduct as a loss the amount you originally paid for the property, but not the amount of income you recognized as a result of the

election. If you believe that the chances you have of forfeiting the property are high, then you should avoid recognizing the income upfront.

Example 1

On December 10, 2005, your employer sold you a share of stock for $10 that had a fair market value of $110. The stock is subject to a substantial risk of forfeiture until April 1, 2007. Because the stock might have to be forfeited, you do not have to include the $100 difference between your purchase price and the fair market value of the stock in your 2005 taxable income.

Assume you did not recognize the income immediately. On April 1, 2007, the fair market value of a share of stock is $210. You must include $200 ($210 − $10) in your taxable income in 2007. Assuming you are in the 33% tax bracket, your tax is $66.

However, if you chose to recognize the income on the stock immediately, you would include $100 ($110 − $10) in your taxable income for 2005 and would incur tax of $33 if you were in the 33% tax bracket. Having made that choice, you owe no more tax until you sell the stock, at which time you will owe tax on the excess of the selling price over your $110 tax basis for the stock.

Example 2

Assume the same facts as in Example 1, except that after you recognized the income from the property in your 2005 income, you had to forfeit your claim to the property in 2006. You may deduct only the $10 you paid for the stock as a **capital loss**. You do *not* get to claim a loss on the $100 of *income* you previously reported.

Stock you chose to include in income. Dividends you receive on restricted stock you chose to include in your income in the year transferred are treated the same as any other dividends. Report them on your return as dividends. For a discussion of dividends, see chapter 9.

For information on how to treat dividends reported on both your Form W-2 and Form 1099-DIV, see *Dividends received on restricted stock* in Publication 525.

Special Rules for Certain Employees

This section deals with special rules for people in certain types of employment: members of the clergy, members of religious orders, people working for foreign employers, military personnel, and volunteers.

Clergy

If you are a member of the clergy, you must include in your income offerings and fees you receive for marriages, baptisms, funerals, masses, etc., in addition to your salary. If the offering is made to the religious institution, it is not taxable to you.

If you are a member of a religious organization and you give your outside earnings to the organization, you still must include the earnings in your income. However, you may be entitled to a charitable contribution deduction for the amount paid to the organization. See chapter 26.

Housing. Special rules for housing apply to members of the clergy. Under these rules, you do not include in your income the rental value of a home (including utilities) or a designated housing allowance provided to you as part of your pay. However, the exclusion cannot be more than the reasonable pay for your service. If you pay for the utilities, you can exclude any allowance designated for utility cost, up to your actual cost. The home or allowance must be provided as com-

90 INCOME

pensation for your services as an ordained, licensed, or commissioned minister. However, you must include the rental value of the home or the housing allowance as earnings from self-employment on Schedule SE (Form 1040) if you are subject to the self-employment tax. For more information, see Publication 517, Social Security and Other Information for Members of the Clergy and Religious Workers.

Explanation

To qualify for the exclusions from gross income, you must be appropriately ordained, commissioned, or licensed as a minister or other member of the clergy and you must be employed by a religious organization to perform ministerial functions. You qualify as a member of the clergy if you have been appropriately ordained according to the customs of your faith. The exclusion also applies to retired ministers, but not their widows.

Exception

An ordained minister may not claim the exclusions from gross income when the crux of his or her ministry consists of preachings against communism for a non-religious, tax-exempt organization. Such a message is not religious because anticommunism is not an adopted tenet of his or her faith.

Sham churches. The IRS has been cracking down on individuals who declare themselves clergy of newly established churches, arrange to have all their income paid to the church, and then have the church pay their living expenses. The object of such individuals is to take advantage of a church's tax-exempt status and shield income from taxation. Individuals who set up sham churches may be subject to criminal sanctions.

Explanation

Designation requirement. The church or organization that employs you must officially designate the payment as a housing allowance before the payment is made. A definite amount must be designated; the amount of the housing allowance cannot be determined at a later date.

If you are employed and paid by a local congregation, a resolution by a national church agency of your denomination does not effectively designate a housing allowance for you. The local congregation must officially designate the part of your salary that is to be a housing allowance. However, a resolution of a national church agency can designate your housing allowance if you are directly employed by the agency. If no part has been officially designated, you must include your total salary in your income.

Homeowner. If you own your home or are buying it, you can exclude your housing allowance from your income if you spend it for the down payment on the home, for mortgage payments, or for interest, taxes, utilities, repairs, etc. However, you cannot exclude more than the fair rental value of the home plus the cost of utilities, even if a larger amount is designated as a housing allowance. The fair rental value of a home includes the fair rental value of the furnishings in it.

You can deduct on Schedule A (Form 1040) the qualified mortgage interest and real estate taxes you pay on your home even if you use nontaxable housing allowance funds to make the payments. See Chapter 24, *Taxes You May Deduct,* and Chapter 25, *Interest Expense.*

Teachers or administrators. If you are a minister employed as a teacher or administrator by a church school, college, or university, you are performing ministerial services for purposes of the housing exclusion.

However, if you perform services as a teacher or administrator on the faculty of a nonchurch college, you cannot exclude from your income a housing allowance or the value of a home that is provided to you.

Tip. If you live in faculty lodging as an employee of an educational institution or an academic health center, all or part of the value of that lodging may be nontaxable under a different rule. See Faculty lodging in the discussion on meals and lodging in Publication 525.

If you serve as a minister of music or minister of education or serve in an administrative or other function of your religious organization, but are not authorized to perform substantially all of the religious duties of an ordained minister in your church (even if you are commissioned as a **minister of the gospel),** the housing exclusion does not apply to you.

Theological students. The housing exclusion does not apply if you are a theological student serving a required internship as an assistant pastor, unless you are ordained, commissioned, or licensed as a minister.

Traveling evangelists. If you are an ordained minister and are providing evangelistic services, you can exclude amounts received from out-of-town churches that are designated as a housing allowance, provided you actually use them to maintain your permanent home.

Retired members of the clergy. The rental value of a home provided rent free by your church for your past services is not income if you are a retired minister. In addition, the amount of your housing allowance that you spend for utilities, maintenance, repairs, and similar expenses that are directly related to providing a home is not income to you. These amounts are also not included in net earnings from self-employment.

The general convention of a national religious denomination can designate a housing allowance for retired ministers that can be excluded from income. This applies if the local congregations authorize the general convention to establish and maintain a unified pension system for all retired clergy members of the denomination for their past services to the local churches.

A surviving spouse of a retired minister cannot exclude a housing allowance from income.

Pension. A pension or retirement pay for a member of the clergy is usually treated as any other pension or annuity. It must be reported on lines 16a and 16b of Form 1040 or on lines 12a and 12b of Form 1040A.

Members of Religious Orders

If you are a member of a religious order who has taken a vow of poverty, how you treat earnings that you renounce and turn over to the order depends on whether your services are performed for the order.

Services performed for the order. If you are performing the services as an agent of the order in the exercise of duties required by the order, do not include in your income the amounts turned over to the order.

If your order directs you to perform services for another agency of the supervising church or an associated institution, you are considered to be performing the services as an agent of the order. Any wages you earn as an agent of an order that you turn over to the order are not included in your income.

Example. You are a member of a church order and have taken a vow of poverty. You renounce any claims to your earnings and turn over to the order any salaries or wages you earn. You are a registered nurse, so your order assigns you to work in a hospital that is an associated institution of the church. However, you remain under the general direction and control of the order. You are considered to be an agent of the order and any wages you earn at the hospital that you turn over to your order are not included in your income.

Services performed outside the order. If you are directed to work outside the order, your services are not an exercise of duties required by the order unless they meet both of the following requirements.

- They are the kind of services that are ordinarily the duties of members of the order.
- They are part of the duties that you must exercise for, or on behalf of, the religious order as its agent.

If you are an employee of a third party, the services you perform for the third party will not be considered directed or required of you by the order. Amounts you receive for these services are included in your income, even if you have taken a vow of poverty.

Example. Mark Brown is a member of a religious order and has taken a vow of poverty. He renounces all claims to his earnings and turns over his earnings to the order.

Mark is a schoolteacher. He was instructed by the superiors of the order to get a job with a private tax-exempt school. Mark became an employee of the school, and, at his request, the school made the salary payments directly to the order.

Because Mark is an employee of the school, he is performing services for the school rather than as an agent of the order. The wages Mark earns working for the school are included in his income.

Foreign Employer

Special rules apply if you work for a foreign employer.
U.S. citizen. If you are a U.S. citizen who works in the United States for a foreign government, an international organization, a foreign embassy, or any foreign employer, you must include your salary in your income.

Social security and Medicare taxes. You are exempt from social security and Medicare employee taxes if you are employed in the United States by an international organization or a foreign government. However, you must pay self-employment tax on your earnings from services performed in the United States, even though you are not self-employed. This rule also applies if you are an employee of a qualifying wholly owned instrumentality of a foreign government.

Employees of international organizations or foreign governments. Your compensation for official services to an international organization is exempt from federal income tax if you are not a citizen of the United States or you are a citizen of the Philippines (whether or not you are a citizen of the United States).

Your compensation for official services to a foreign government is exempt from federal income tax if all of the following are true.

- You are not a citizen of the United States or you are a citizen of the Philippines (whether or not you are a citizen of the United States).
- Your work is like the work done by employees of the United States in foreign countries.
- The foreign government gives an equal exemption to employees of the United States in its country.

Waiver of alien status. If you are an alien who works for a foreign government or international organization and you file a waiver under section 247(b) of the Immigration and Nationality Act to keep your immigrant status, different rules may apply. See *Foreign Employer* in Publication 525.

Employment abroad. For information on income earned abroad, see Publication 54.

Military

Payments you receive as a member of a military service generally are taxed as wages except for retirement pay, which is taxed as a pension. Allowances generally are not taxed. For more information on the tax treatment of military allowances and benefits, see Publication 3, Armed Forces' Tax Guide.

Military retirement pay. If your retirement pay is based on age or length of service, it is taxable and must be included in your income as a pension on lines 16a and 16b of Form 1040 or on lines 12a and 12b of Form 1040A. Do not include in your income the amount of any reduction in retirement or retainer pay to provide a survivor annuity for your spouse or children under the Retired Serviceman's Family Protection Plan or the Survivor Benefit Plan.

For more information on survivor annuities, see chapter 11.

Disability. If you are retired on disability, see *Military and Government Disability Pensions* under *Sickness and Injury Benefits*, later.

Veterans' benefits. Do not include in your income any veterans' benefits paid under any law, regulation, or administrative practice administered by the Department of Veterans Affairs (VA). The following amounts paid to veterans or their families are not taxable.

- Education, training, and subsistence allowances.
- Disability compensation and pension payments for disabilities paid either to veterans or their families.
- Grants for homes designed for wheelchair living.
- Grants for motor vehicles for veterans who lost their sight or the use of their limbs.
- Veterans' insurance proceeds and dividends paid either to veterans or their beneficiaries, including the proceeds of a veteran's endowment policy paid before death.
- Interest on insurance dividends you leave on deposit with the VA.
- Benefits under a dependent-care assistance program.
- The death gratuity paid to a survivor of a member of the Armed Forces who died after September 10, 2001.

Rehabilitative program payments. VA payments to hospital patients and resident veterans for their services under the VA's therapeutic or rehabilitative programs are not treated as nontaxable veterans' benefits. Report these payments as income on line 21 of Form 1040.

Volunteers

The tax treatment of amounts you receive as a volunteer worker for the Peace Corps or similar agency is covered in the following discussions.
Peace Corps. Living allowances you receive as a Peace Corps volunteer or volunteer leader for housing, utilities, household supplies, food, and clothing are exempt from tax.

Taxable allowances. The following allowances must be included in your income and reported as wages.

- Allowances paid to your spouse and minor children while you are a volunteer leader training in the United States.
- Living allowances designated by the Director of the Peace Corps as basic compensation. These are allowances for personal items such as domestic help, laundry and clothing maintenance, entertainment and recreation, transportation, and other miscellaneous expenses.
- Leave allowances.
- Readjustment allowances or termination payments. These are considered received by you when credited to your account.

Example. Gary Carpenter, a Peace Corps volunteer, gets $175 a month as a readjustment allowance during his period of service, to be paid to him in a lump sum at the end of his tour of duty. Although the allowance is not available to him until the end of his service, Gary must include it in his income on a monthly basis as it is credited to his account.
Volunteers in Service to America (VISTA). If you are a VISTA volunteer, you must include meal and lodging allowances paid to you in your income as wages.

National Senior Services Corps programs. Do not include in your income amounts you receive for supportive services or reimbursements for out-of-pocket expenses from the following programs.

- Retired Senior Volunteer Program (RSVP).
- Foster Grandparent Program.
- Senior Companion Program.

Service Corps of Retired Executives (SCORE). If you receive amounts for supportive services or reimbursements for out-of-pocket expenses from SCORE, do not include these amounts in income.

Volunteer tax counseling. Do not include in your income any reimbursements you receive for transportation, meals, and other expenses you have in training for, or actually providing, volunteer federal income tax counseling for the elderly (TCE).

You can deduct as a charitable contribution your unreimbursed out-of-pocket expenses in taking part in the volunteer income tax assistance (VITA) program. See chapter 26.

Sickness and Injury Benefits

This section discusses sickness and injury benefits including disability pensions, long-term care insurance contracts, workers' compensation, and other benefits.

Disability Pensions

Generally, if you retire on disability, you must report your pension or annuity as income.

Tip. *There is a tax credit for people who are permanently and totally disabled. For information on this credit and the definition of permanent and total disability, see chapter 35.*

For information on disability payments from a governmental program provided as a substitute for unemployment compensation, see chapter 13.

Disability income. Generally, you must report as income any amount you receive for personal injury or sickness through an accident or health plan that is paid for by your employer. If both you and your employer pay for the plan, only the amount you receive that is due to your employer's payments is reported as income. However, certain payments may not be taxable to you. Your employer should be able to give you specific details about your pension plan and tell you the amount you paid for your disability pension. In addition to disability pensions and annuities, you may be receiving other payments for sickness and injury.

Tip. *Do not report as income any amounts paid to reimburse you for medical expenses you incurred after the plan was established.*

Cost paid by you. If you pay the entire cost of a health or accident insurance plan, do not include any amounts you receive from the plan for personal injury or sickness as income on your tax return. If your plan reimbursed you for medical expenses you deducted in an earlier year, you may have to include some, or all, of the reimbursement in your income. See *Reimbursement in a later year* in chapter 23.

Cafeteria plans. Generally, if you are covered by an accident or health insurance plan through a cafeteria plan, and the amount of the insurance premiums was not included in your income, you are not considered to have paid the premiums, and you must include any benefits you receive in your income. If the amount of the premiums was included in your income, you are considered to have paid the premiums, and any benefits you receive are not taxable.

Retirement and profit-sharing plans. If you receive payments from a retirement or profit-sharing plan that does not provide for disability retirement, do not treat the payments as a disability pension. The payments must be reported as a pension or annuity. For more information on pensions, see chapter 11.

Accrued leave payment. If you retire on disability, any lump-sum payment you receive for accrued annual leave is a salary payment. The payment is not a disability payment. Include it in your income in the tax year you receive it.

How to report. If you retired on disability, you must include in income any disability pension you receive under a plan that is paid for by your employer. You must report your taxable disability payments as wages on line 7 of Form 1040 or Form 1040A, until you reach minimum retirement age. Minimum retirement age generally is the age at which you can first receive a pension or annuity if you are not disabled.

Beginning on the day after you reach minimum retirement age, payments you receive are taxable as a pension or annuity. Report the payments on lines 16a and 16b of Form 1040 or on lines 12a and 12b of Form 1040A. The rules for reporting pensions are explained in *How To Report* in chapter 11.

Military and Government Disability Pensions
Certain military and government disability pensions are not taxable.

Service-connected disability. You may be able to exclude from income amounts you receive as a pension, annuity, or similar allowance for personal injury or sickness resulting from active service in one of the following government services.

- The armed forces of any country.
- The National Oceanic and Atmospheric Administration.
- The Public Health Service.
- The Foreign Service.

Conditions for exclusion. Do not include the disability payments in your income if any of the following conditions apply.

1. You were entitled to receive a disability payment before September 25, 1975.
2. You were a member of a listed government service or its reserve component, or were under a binding written commitment to become a member, on September 24, 1975.
3. You receive the disability payments for a combat-related injury. This is a personal injury or sickness that:
   a. Results directly from armed conflict,
   b. Takes place while you are engaged in extra-hazardous service,
   c. Takes place under conditions simulating war, including training exercises such as maneuvers, or
   d. Is caused by an instrumentality of war.
4. You would be entitled to receive disability compensation from the Department of Veterans Affairs (VA) if you filed an application for it. Your exclusion under this condition is equal to the amount you would be entitled to receive from the VA.

Pension based on years of service. If you receive a disability pension based on years of service, you generally must include it in your income. However, if the pension qualifies for the exclusion for a service-connected disability (discussed earlier), do not include in income the part of your pension that you would have received if the pension had been based on a percentage of disability. You must include the rest of your pension in your income.

Retroactive VA determination. If you retire from the armed services based on years of service and are later given a retroactive service-connected disability rating by the VA, your retirement pay for the retroactive period is excluded from income up to the amount of VA disability benefits you would have been entitled to receive. You can claim a refund of any tax paid on the excludable amount (subject to the statute of limitations) by filing an amended return on Form 1040X for each previous year during the retroactive period.

If you receive a lump-sum disability severance payment and are later awarded VA disability benefits, exclude 100% of the severance benefit from your income. However, you must include in your income any lump-sum readjustment or other nondisability severance payment you received on release from active duty, even if you are later given a retroactive disability rating by the VA.

Terrorist attack or military action. Do not include in your income disability payments you receive for injuries resulting directly from a terrorist or military action.

Long-Term Care Insurance Contracts

Long-term care insurance contracts are generally treated as accident and health insurance contracts. Amounts you receive from them (other than policyholder dividends or premium refunds) generally are excludable from income as amounts received for personal injury or sickness. To claim an exclusion for payments made on a *per diem* or other periodic basis under a long-term care insurance contract, you must file Form 8853 with your return.

A long-term care insurance contract is an insurance contract that only provides coverage for qualified long-term care services. The contract must:

- Be guaranteed renewable,
- Not provide for a cash surrender value or other money that can be paid, assigned, pledged, or borrowed,
- Provide that refunds, other than refunds on the death of the insured or complete surrender or cancellation of the contract, and dividends under the contract may be used only to reduce future premiums or increase future benefits, and
- Generally not pay or reimburse expenses incurred for services or items that would be reimbursed under Medicare, except where Medicare is a secondary payer or the contract makes *per diem* or other periodic payments without regard to expenses.

Qualified long-term care services. Qualified long-term care services are:

- Necessary diagnostic, preventive, therapeutic, curing, treating, mitigating, and rehabilitative services, and maintenance and personal care services, and
- Required by a chronically ill individual and provided pursuant to a plan of care as prescribed by a licensed health care practitioner.

Chronically ill individual. A chronically ill individual is one who has been certified by a licensed health care practitioner within the previous 12 months as one of the following.

- An individual who, for at least 90 days, is unable to perform at least two activities of daily living without substantial assistance due to loss of functional capacity. Activities of daily living are eating, toileting, transferring, bathing, dressing, and continence.
- An individual who requires substantial supervision to be protected from threats to health and safety due to severe cognitive impairment.

Limit on exclusion. You can generally exclude from gross income up to $240 a day for 2005. See *Limit on exclusion,* under *Long-Term Care Insurance Contracts,* under *Sickness and Injury Benefits* in Publication 525 for more information.

Workers' Compensation

Amounts you receive as workers' compensation for an occupational sickness or injury are fully exempt from tax if they are paid under a workers' compensation act or a statute in the nature of a workers' compensation act. The exemption also applies to your survivors. The exemption, however, does not apply to retirement plan benefits you receive based on your age, length of service, or prior contributions to the plan, even if you retired because of an occupational sickness or injury.

Caution. *If part of your workers' compensation reduces your social security or equivalent railroad retirement benefits received, that part is considered social security (or equivalent railroad retirement) benefits and may be taxable. For more information, see Publication 915, Social Security and Equivalent Railroad Retirement Benefits.*

Return to work. If you return to work after qualifying for workers' compensation, salary payments you receive for performing light duties are taxable as wages.

Other Sickness and Injury Benefits

In addition to disability pensions and annuities, you may receive other payments for sickness or injury.

Railroad sick pay. Payments you receive as sick pay under the Railroad Unemployment Insurance Act are taxable and you must include them in your income. However, do not include them in your income if they are for an on-the-job injury.

If you received income because of a disability, see *Disability Pensions,* earlier.

Federal Employees' Compensation Act (FECA). Payments received under this Act for personal injury or sickness, including payments to beneficiaries in case of death, are not taxable. However, you are taxed on amounts you receive under this Act as continuation of pay for up to 45 days while a claim is being decided. Report this income on line 7 of Form 1040 or Form 1040A or on line 1 of Form 1040EZ. Also, pay for sick leave while a claim is being processed is taxable and must be included in your income as wages.

Caution. *If part of the payments you receive under FECA reduces your social security or equivalent railroad retirement benefits received, that part is considered social security (or equivalent railroad retirement) benefits and may be taxable. For a discussion of the taxability of these benefits, see* Social security and equivalent railroad retirement benefits *under* Other Income, *in Publication 525.*

You can deduct the amount you spend to buy back sick leave for an earlier year to be eligible for nontaxable FECA benefits for that period. It is a miscellaneous deduction subject to the 2% limit on Schedule A (Form 1040). If you buy back sick leave in the same year you used it, the amount reduces your taxable sick leave pay. Do not deduct it separately.

Other compensation. Many other amounts you receive as compensation for sickness or injury are not taxable. These include the following amounts.

- Compensatory damages you receive for physical injury or physical sickness, whether paid in a lump sum or in periodic payments.
- Benefits you receive under an accident or health insurance policy on which either you paid the premiums or your employer paid the premiums but you had to include them in your income.
- Disability benefits you receive for loss of income or earning capacity as a result of injuries under a no-fault car insurance policy.
- Compensation you receive for permanent loss or loss of use of a part or function of your body, or for your permanent disfigurement. This compensation must be based only on the injury and not on the period of your absence from work. These benefits are not taxable even if your employer pays for the accident and health plan that provides these benefits.

Reimbursement for medical care. A reimbursement for medical care is generally not taxable. However, it may reduce your medical expense deduction. For more information, see chapter 23.

7

Tip Income

Note: The 2004 IRS Publication 17 (Your Federal Income Tax) has been updated by Ernst & Young LLP for 2005. Dates and dollar amounts shown are for 2005. Gray type is used to indicate where IRS text has been updated or intentionally omitted. Unrevised IRS text is shown in black type.

Introduction

Tips are one of the least-reported types of income. Recent estimates have placed the amount of annual tips going to food and beverage industry workers at $18 billion or more annually. However, these employees reported only $7 billion in income from tips on their taxes in 1998. Consequently, in 2000, the IRS announced plans to resume a controversial audit program under which it will conduct employer-only tip examinations and assessments for FICA in cases of "flagrant violations" of tip reporting rules. This audit program focuses on cases of serious noncompliance at businesses in which tipping is customary. Nevertheless, employee reporting requirements and employer withholding requirements have not changed. This chapter spells out the details.

This chapter is for employees who receive tips from customers.

All tips you receive are income and are subject to federal income tax. You must include in gross income all tips you receive directly from customers, tips from charge customers that are paid to you by your employer, and your share of any tips you receive under a tip-splitting or tip-pooling arrangement.

The value of noncash tips, such as tickets, passes, or other items of value are also income and subject to tax.

Explanation
Self-employed individuals may receive cash tips or other income from clients. This additional income is *not* considered income from tips. It is, however, considered self-employment income and must be reported to the IRS on Schedule C. See Chapter 39, *If You Are Self-Employed: How to File Schedule C,* for more information.

Reporting your tip income correctly is not difficult. You must do three things.

1. Keep a daily tip record.
2. Report tips to your employer.
3. Report all your tips on your income tax return.

This chapter will show you how to do these three things and what to do on your tax return if you have not done the first two. This chapter will also show you how to treat allocated tips.

Useful Items

You may want to see:

Publications

- ☐ **531** Reporting Tip Income
- ☐ **1244** Employee's Daily Record of Tips and Report to Employer

Forms (and Instructions)

- ☐ **4137** Social Security and Medicare Tax on Unreported Tip Income
- ☐ **4070** Employee's Report of Tips to Employer

Keeping a Daily Tip Record

Why keep a daily tip record? You must keep a daily tip record so you can:

- Report your tips accurately to your employer,
- Report your tips accurately on your tax return, and
- Prove your tip income if your return is ever questioned.

How to keep a daily tip record. There are two ways to keep a daily tip record. You can either:

1. Write information about your tips in a tip diary, or
2. Keep copies of documents that show your tips, such as restaurant bills and credit card charge slips.

You should keep your daily tip record with your personal records. You must keep your records for as long as they are important for administration of the federal tax law. For information on how long to keep records, see Publication 552, Recordkeeping for Individuals.

If you keep a tip diary, you can use Form 4070A, Employee's Daily Record of Tips. To get Form 4070A, ask the Internal Revenue Service (IRS) or your employer for Publication 1244 or find it at www.irs.gov. Publication 1244 includes a year's supply of Form 4070A. Each day, write in the information asked for on the form.

TAXPLANNER

You are not required to complete Form 4070A as long as you have an alternative method of recording your tips. The IRS issues the form merely to help employees keep track of their income from tips.

Complete written records, however, are essential, particularly if you must later substantiate a claim that you did not receive all the tips your employer alleges were allocated to you.

Examples of documentary evidence are copies of restaurant bills, credit card charges, or charges under any other arrangement containing amounts added by the customer as a tip.

If you do not use Form 4070A, start your records by writing your name, your employer's name, and the name of the business if it is different from your employer's name. Then, each workday, write the date and the following information.

- Cash tips you get directly from customers or from other employees.
- Tips from credit card charge customers that your employer pays you.
- The value of any noncash tips you get, such as tickets, passes, or other items of value.
- The amount of tips you paid out to other employees through tip pools or tip splitting, or other arrangements, and the names of the employees to whom you paid the tips.

Caution. *Do not write in your tip diary the amount of any service charge that your employer adds to a customer's bill and then pays to you and treats as wages. This is part of your wages, not a tip.*

Explanation
An arbitrary fixed charge that your employer adds to the customer's bill is not a tip or gratuity subject to tip reporting and withholding requirements. Even if it is called a tip, the amount an employee is guaranteed from his or her employer is additional wage compensation.

Example
A club does not permit its members to tip its employees but adds 10% to each member's restaurant charges. This additional amount is set aside in a fund and is disbursed monthly to all employees. Because the employer controls the allocation of the funds, they are additional wages, not tips.

However, if a headwaiter receives one lump-sum payment to be distributed to all waiters and waitresses, then the payments are income from tips. The headwaiter would include in his income only the amount he retained, not the total he distributed.

Electronic tip record. You may use an electronic system provided by your employer to record your daily tips. You must receive and keep a paper copy of this record.

Reporting Tips to Your Employer

Why report tips to your employer? You must report tips to your employer so that:

- Your employer can withhold federal income tax and social security and Medicare taxes or railroad retirement tax,
- Your employer can report the correct amount of your earnings to the Social Security Administration or Railroad Retirement Board

(which affects your benefits when you retire or if you become disabled, or your family's benefits if you die), and
- You can avoid the penalty for not reporting tips to your employer (explained later).

TAXSAVER
Your employer usually deducts the withholding due on tips from your regular wages. However, you do not have to have income tax withheld if you can claim exemption from withholding. You can claim exemption only if you had no income tax liability last year and expect none this year. See *Exemption from Withholding* in Chapter 5, *Tax Withholding and Estimated Tax,* for more information.

Example
Many students and retired persons who expect to have no federal income tax liability work part-time in occupations in which they receive tips. To avoid unnecessary income tax withholding, you may file a Form W-4 with your employer, certifying that you had no federal income tax liability last year and expect to have none this year as well.

What tips to report. Report to your employer only cash, check, debit or credit card tips you receive.

If your total tips for any one month from any one job are less than $20, do not report the tips for that month to that employer.

Do not report the value of any noncash tips, such as tickets or passes, to your employer. You do not pay social security and Medicare taxes or railroad retirement tax on these tips.

Example
If you earn only $15 in tips in October, you do not have to report anything to your employer. However, you must still pay federal income tax on the tips when you report them on your tax return. The $15 is never subject to Social Security and Medicare taxes.

TAXPLANNER
If it is not customary to tip for a type of service, the IRS may be willing to concede that additional payments received for normal services may not be tips and may, indeed, be tax-free gifts from the customer. You would have to prove that the services performed did not extend beyond the minimum requirements of the job and that you work in an industry in which extra compensation is not traditional.

This claim would be impossible to sustain in all but the most unusual circumstances. The IRS and the courts generally presume that amounts received for performing services are taxable as compensation.

How to report. If your employer does not give you any other way to report tips, you can use Form 4070. Fill in the information asked for on the form, sign and date the form, and give it to your employer. To get a year's supply of the form, ask the IRS or your employer for Publication 1244 or go to www.irs.gov.

If you do not use Form 4070, give your employer a statement with the following information.

- Your name, address, and social security number.
- Your employer's name, address, and business name (if it is different from the employer's name).

- The month (or the dates of any shorter period) in which you received tips.
- The total tips required to be reported for that period.

You must sign and date the statement. You should keep a copy with your personal records.

Your employer may require you to report your tips more than once a month. However, the statement cannot cover a period of more than one calendar month.

Electronic tip statement. Your employer can have you furnish your tip statements electronically.

TAXPLANNER

Prior to 1999, no provision existed for employees to furnish tip statements to employers in a form other than on paper. The regulations permit either an employer to adopt a system under which some or all of the tipped employees of the employer would furnish their tip statements electronically or the IRS could provide additional methods of demonstrating income from tips. The employer could include in its electronic system any tipped employee(s) working in any location(s).

The entry by the employee in the electronic system on a daily (or more frequent) basis, together with the daily record based on these entries provided by the employer, will satisfy the substantiation requirements.

When to report. Give your report for each month to your employer by the 10th of the next month. If the 10th falls on a Saturday, Sunday, or legal holiday, give your employer the report by the next day that is not a Saturday, Sunday, or legal holiday.

Example 1. You must report your tips received in April 2006 by May 10, 2006.

Example 2. You must report your tips received in May 2006 by June 12, 2006. June 10th is on a Saturday, and the 12th is the next day that is not a Saturday, Sunday, or legal holiday.

Explanation
The amount of tips you report to your employer is treated as income subject to withholding in the month after it has been reported.

Example
If you earn $75 in tips in October, you must report that amount to your employer by November 10. In November your employer will treat the $75 in tips in October as additional compensation subject to federal income tax withholding and Social Security tax.

TAXSAVER

If you earn $25 from tips in December 2005 but do not report it to your employer until January 2006 you may defer recognizing that $25 of income until you file your 2006 tax return.

Final report. If your employment ends during the month, you can report your tips when your employment ends.

Penalty for not reporting tips. If you do not report tips to your employer as required, you may be subject to a penalty equal to 50% of the social security and Medicare taxes or railroad retirement tax you owe on the unreported tips. (For information about these taxes, see *Reporting social security and Medicare taxes on tips not reported to your employer* under *Reporting Tips on Your Tax Return*, later.) The penalty amount is in addition to the taxes you owe.

You can avoid this penalty if you can show reasonable cause for not reporting the tips to your employer. To do so, attach a statement to your return explaining why you did not report them.

TAXALERT

During 1995, the IRS established a *voluntary* program for tip reporting by food and beverage establishments, known as the Tip Reporting Alternative Commitment (TRAC). This program is intended to increase tip reporting and compliance levels by both employees and employers. Under TRAC, an employer agrees to (1) maintain quarterly educational programs that will instruct new employees and update existing employees as to their reporting obligations; (2) comply with all federal tax requirements regarding the maintaining of records, filing of returns, and depositing of taxes; and (3) set up procedures to ensure the accurate recording of all tips. In return, the IRS agrees to base the restaurant's liability for employment taxes solely on reported tips and any unreported tips discovered during an IRS audit of an employee.

During 2000, the IRS announced that it was simplifying its voluntary income from tip compliance agreements and expanding them to all industries where tipping is customary. Under Tip Rate Determination Agreement (TRDA), the IRS and the employer work together to determine the amount of tips that employees generally receive and should report. Under TRAC, the employer agrees to educate employees and establish tip reporting procedures.

Until now, only the gaming, food and beverage, cosmetology, and barber industries were able to make TRDAs with the IRS. The IRS has now developed a TRDA and TRAC for other industries in which tipping is customary. Employers that can participate include taxicab and limousine companies, airport skycap companies, and car wash operations.

In addition to TRDA and TRAC, the IRS will now permit employers in the food and beverage industries to design their own program through Employer's Tip Reporting Alternative Commitment (EmTRAC). This is in lieu of the IRS-developed TRAC. EmTRAC will include the same employer commitments and protections as afforded under TRAC 166-47.

In September of 2004, the IRS announced that it would indefinitely extend its Tip Rate Determination and Education Program. Originally, the program was due to expire in 2005, but due to its success it will continue indefinitely. The program offers employers several voluntary agreement options that assist both employers and employees to comply with tip reporting laws. These options include the Tip Rate Determination Agreement (TRDA), Tip Reporting Alternative Commitment (TRAC) and Employer–designed TRAC (EmTRAC). Each agreement educates employers and employees on federal tax laws regarding tips, simplifies the process for employees to calculate and report their tips and pay taxes, and reduces the likelihood and burden associated with a tip examination.

Employees in the food service industry should be cognizant of the increased diligence by employers and the IRS in reporting tip income. The IRS has issued draft forms of TRAC agreements that can be used as a model for various industries. Employers considering entering into TRAC agreements with the IRS should carefully determine if such an agreement is in their best interest. Consult with your tax advisors for more information.

Giving your employer money for taxes. Your regular pay may not be enough for your employer to withhold all the taxes you owe on your regular pay plus your reported tips. If this happens, you can give your employer money until the close of the calendar year to pay the rest of the taxes.

If you do not give your employer enough money, your employer will apply your regular pay and any money you give to the taxes in the following order.

1. All taxes on your regular pay.
2. Social security and Medicare taxes or railroad retirement tax on your reported tips.
3. Federal, state, and local income taxes on your reported tips.

Any taxes that remain unpaid can be collected by your employer from your next paycheck. If withholding taxes remain uncollected at the end of the year, you may be subject to a penalty for underpayment of estimated taxes. See Publication 505, Tax Withholding and Estimated Tax, for more information.

TaxSaver

If your base wages are not enough to cover your necessary withholding taxes, it may be more beneficial to pay your employer money to cover the withholding deficiency *at the end of the year* instead of making payments to your employer throughout the year. Set aside sufficient cash from tips until the end of the tax year; then, give your employer enough cash to cover the remaining withholding taxes. This approach allows you access to the cash throughout the year and avoids underpayment penalties from not paying in enough taxes during the year.

If you find it easier to manage your cash flow by paying the additional taxes due on a more frequent basis, you can make estimated tax payments or pay the taxes to your employer periodically throughout the year. See Chapter 5, *Tax Withholding and Estimated Tax*, for information on estimated tax.

Caution. Uncollected taxes. *You must report on your tax return any social security and Medicare taxes or railroad retirement tax that remained uncollected at the end of 2005. See* Reporting uncollected social security and Medicare taxes on tips *under* Reporting Tips on Your Tax Return, *later. These uncollected taxes will be shown in box 12 of your 2005 Form W-2 (codes A and B).*

Tip Rate Determination and Education Program

Your employer may participate in the Tip Rate Determination and Education Program. The program was developed to help employees and employers understand and meet their tip reporting responsibilities.

There are two agreements under the program: the Tip Rate Determination Agreement (TRDA) and the Tip Reporting Alternative Commitment (TRAC). In addition, employers in the food and beverage industry may be able to get approval of an employer-designed EmTRAC program. For information on the EmTRAC program, see Notice 2001-1 in Internal Revenue Bulletin No. 2001-2 (or Cumulative Bulletin 2001-1).

If you are employed in the gaming industry, your employer may have a Gaming Industry Tip Compliance Agreement Program. See Revenue Procedure 2003-35 in Internal Revenue Bulletin No. 2003-20.

Your employer can provide you with a copy of the agreement. If you want to learn more about these agreements, contact the local IRS tip coordinator. A list of tip coordinators is available at *www.irs.gov.*

TaxAlert

Effective May 1, 2003, the IRS issued a Revenue Procedure addressing the Gaming Industry Tip Compliance Agreement Program. This program is designed to promote compliance by gaming industry employers and employees with accurate tip income reporting and is intended to reduce disputes with the IRS. The usual duration of any such agreement is three years.

Under the Gaming Industry Tipping Agreement Program, a gaming industry employer and the IRS may work together to reach a Gaming Industry Tip Compliance Agreement that objectively establishes minimum tip rates for tipped employees in specified occupational categories, prescribes a threshold level of participation by the employer's employees, and reduces compliance burdens for the employer and enforcement burdens for the IRS. All employers operating a gaming establishment may participate in the Gaming Industry Tip Compliance Agreement Program. An employee can participate in this type of program only if your employer executes the IRS-prescribed Gaming Industry Tip Compliance Agreement. The employer's participation in this program is voluntary.

If your employer decides to participate in this program, your employer should furnish you with a signed Model Gaming Employee Tip Reporting Agreement. This Agreement will outline the specific reporting requirements by the employee and employer. Further information about the Gaming Industry Tip Compliance Agreement is available in Revenue Procedure 2003-35.

Reporting Tips on Your Tax Return

How to report tips. Report your tips with your wages on line 1, Form 1040EZ, or line 7, Form 1040A or Form 1040.

What tips to report. You must report all tips you received in 2005, including both cash tips and noncash tips, on your tax return. Any tips you reported to your employer for 2005 are included in the wages shown in box 1 of your Form W-2. Add to the amount in box 1 only the tips you did not report to your employer.

Explanation
All voluntary payments received from customers are taxable to the employee. This includes the **fair market value** of any noncash items given to employees.

Example
Tokens given to blackjack dealers in gambling casinos are taxable as income from tips to the dealers.

Caution. *If you received $20 or more in cash and charge tips in a month and did not report all of those tips to your employer, see* Reporting social security and Medicare taxes on tips not reported to your employer, *later.*

Caution. *If you did not keep a daily tip record as required and an amount is shown in box 8 of your Form W-2, see* Allocated Tips, *later.*

If you kept a daily tip record and reported tips to your employer as required under the rules explained earlier, add the following tips to the amount in box 1 of your Form W-2.

• Cash and charge tips you received that totaled less than $20 for any month.
• The value of noncash tips, such as tickets, passes, or other items of value.

Example. John Allen began working at the Diamond Restaurant (his only employer in 2005) on June 30 and received $10,000 in wages during the year. John kept a daily tip record showing that his tips for June were $18 and his tips for the rest of the year totaled $7,000. He was not required to report his June tips to his employer, but he reported all of the rest of his tips to his employer as required.

John's Form W-2 from Diamond Restaurant shows $17,000 ($10,000 wages plus $7,000 reported tips) in box 1. He adds the $18 unreported tips to that amount and reports $17,018 as wages on his tax return.

Reporting social security and Medicare taxes on tips not reported to your employer. If you received $20 or more in cash and charge tips in a month from any one job and did not report all of those tips to your employer, you must report the social security and Medicare taxes on the unreported tips as additional tax on your return. To report these taxes, you must file a return even if you would not otherwise have to file. (You must use Form 1040. You cannot file Form 1040EZ or Form 1040A.)

TAXSAVER

Limit on social security and railroad retirement tax. There are limits on the amount of Social Security and railroad retirement tax that your employer withholds from your wages and reported tips. If you worked for two or more employers in 2005, you may have overpaid one or more of these taxes. You may be eligible for a credit for excess social security tax or railroad retirement tax, discussed in Chapter 38, *Other Credits Including the Earned Income Credit.*

TAXALERT

Since 1994, there has been no limit on the amount of wages and reported tips subject to Medicare tax. The Medicare tax rate is 1.45%. However, only the first $90,000 of wages and tips are subject to Social Security tax in 2005. The Social Security tax rate is 6.2%.

Use Form 4137 to figure these taxes. Enter the tax on line 59, Form 1040, and attach Form 4137 to your return.

Caution. *If you are subject to the Railroad Retirement Tax Act, you cannot use Form 4137 to pay railroad retirement tax on unreported tips. To get railroad retirement credit, you must report tips to your employer.*

Reporting uncollected social security and Medicare taxes on tips. If your employer could not collect all the social security and Medicare taxes or railroad retirement tax you owe on tips reported for 2005, the uncollected taxes will be shown in box 12 of your Form W-2 (codes A and B). You must report these amounts as additional tax on your return. You may have uncollected taxes if your regular pay was not enough for your employer to withhold all the taxes you owe and you did not give your employer enough money to pay the rest of the taxes.

To report these uncollected taxes, you must file a return even if you would not otherwise have to file. You must use Form 1040. (You cannot file Form 1040EZ or Form 1040A.) Include the taxes in your total tax amount on line 63, and write "UT" and the total of the uncollected taxes on the dotted line next to line 63.

TAXSAVER

Tips received while working at a job covered by the Railroad Retirement Tax Act or while working for most state or local governments or for some nonprofit organizations are not subject to Social Security tax and should not be included on Form 4137. See *Employers Subject to the Railroad Retirement Act* in Publication 531.

Allocated Tips

If your employer allocated tips to you, they are shown separately in box 8 of your Form W-2. They are not included in box 1 with your wages and reported tips. If box 8 is blank, this discussion does not apply to you.

What are allocated tips? These are tips that your employer assigned to you in addition to the tips you reported to your employer for the year. Your employer will have done this only if:

- You worked in a restaurant, cocktail lounge, or similar business that must allocate tips to employees, and
- The tips you reported to your employer were less than your share of 8% of food and drink sales.

Explanation

Large food or beverage establishments must report tip allocations to the IRS.

A "large food or beverage establishment" is defined as one where the employer normally employed 10 or more employees on a typical day during the preceding calendar year and where tipping is customary.

How were your allocated tips figured? The tips allocated to you are your share of an amount figured by subtracting the reported tips of all employees from 8% (or an approved lower rate) of food and drink sales (other than carryout sales and sales with a service charge of 10% or more). Your share of that amount was figured using either a method provided by an employer-employee agreement or a method provided by IRS regulations based on employees' sales or hours worked. For information about the exact allocation method used, ask your employer.

Example

The following example shows how a food and beverage establishment might determine what amount to include in the special box provided on each employee's Form W-2.

Lee's is a large food and beverage establishment that for one payroll period had gross receipts of $100,000 and reported tips of $6,200. Directly tipped employees reported $5,700, while indirectly tipped employees reported $500.

Directly tipped employees	Gross receipts for payroll period	Tips reported
Amos	$18,000	$1,080
Mitchell	16,000	880
Charlie	23,000	1,810
Nelson	17,000	800
Ed	12,000	450
Allan	14,000	680
	$100,000	$5,700

The allocation computations would be as follows:

1. Total tips to be allocated: $100,000 (gross receipts) $\times$ 0.08 = $8,000.
2. Tips reported by indirectly tipped employees = $500.
3. Tips to be allocated to directly tipped employees: $8,000 − $500 (indirect employees' tips) = $7,500.
4. Allocation of tips to directly tipped employees:

	Directly tipped employees' share of 8% gross		Gross receipts ratio		Employee share of 8% gross
Amos	$7,500	×	18,000/100,000	=	$1,350
Mitchell	7,500	×	16,000/100,000	=	1,200
Charlie	7,500	×	23,000/100,000	=	1,725
Nelson	7,500	×	17,000/100,000	=	1,275
Ed	7,500	×	12,000/100,000	=	900
Allan	7,500	×	14,000/100,000	=	1,050
					$7,500

5. Calculation of tip shortfall of directly tipped employees:

	Employee share of 8% gross		Tips reported		Employees' shortfall
Amos	$1,350	–	$1,080	=	$270
Mitchell	1,200	–	880	=	320
Charlie	1,725	–	1,810	=	—
Nelson	1,275	–	800	=	475
Ed	900	–	450	=	450
Allan	1,050	–	680	=	370
			Total shortfall		$1,885

Because Charlie has no reporting shortfall, there is no allocation to him.

6. Total tips reported, including reported tips of indirectly tipped employees: $8,000 – $6,200 (total tips reported) = $1,800 (amount allocable among shortfall employees).

7. Allocation of tip shortfall among directly tipped employees:

	Allocable amount		Shortfall ratio		Amount of allocation
Amos	$1 800	×	270/1,885	=	$258
Mitchell	1,800	×	320/1,885	=	305
Nelson	1,800	×	475/1,885	=	454
Ed	1,800	×	450/1,885	=	430
Allan	1,800	×	370/1,885	=	353
			Total		$1,800

These allocated amounts must be reported by the employer on the employees' W-2s in box 8. For example, Amos would have allocated tip income of $258.

TaxPlanner

The reporting requirements for employers are only guidelines and apply only to large food or beverage establishments. Nevertheless, the courts have imposed "industry averages" on taxpayers who had no records or inadequate records.

Example

In a series of cases, the courts held that average tips for taxi drivers come to 10% of gross income. A court was willing to accept a 2% figure for tips only when the driver produced daily logs that showed the amounts of fares and tips. The court believed that the records were true and accurate.

The courts have held that the average tips for barbers and hairdressers range from 2% to 8%.

To estimate the tip income of waiters and waitresses, the IRS has used various methods, based on the total sales of the restaurant. While the courts often adjust the IRS determination, they usually accept any reasonable method the IRS uses. Recent Federal Appeals case law has held that the IRS can assess the restaurant owners for FICA taxes without attempting to first determine the unreported income of each individual employee.

Our advice is: Maintain adequate records of all amounts that you actually receive.

TaxPlanner

If the employee or employer would like to request a tip rate lower than 8%, he or she must file a petition with the district director for the IRS district in which the business is located. The petition must include specific information to justify the lower rate. An employee petition can only be filed with the consent of the majority of the directly tipped employees. The petition must state the total number of directly tipped employees and the number of employees consenting to the petition. The employer must also be notified immediately, and the employer must promptly give the district director a copy of any Form 8027, *Employers Annual Information Return of Tip Income and Allocated Tips,* filed by the employer for the prior 3 years.

Must you report your allocated tips on your return? You must report allocated tips on your tax return unless either of the following exceptions applies.

1. You kept a daily tip record, or other evidence that is as credible and as reliable as a daily tip record, as required under rules explained earlier.
2. Your tip record is incomplete, but it shows that your actual tips were more than the tips you reported to your employer plus the allocated tips.

If either exception applies, report your actual tips on your return. Do not report the allocated tips. See *What tips to report* under *Reporting Tips on Your Tax Return,* earlier.
How to report allocated tips. If you must report allocated tips on your return, add the amount in box 8 of your Form W-2 to the amount in box 1. Report the total as wages on line 7 of Form 1040. (You cannot file Form 1040EZ or Form 1040A.)

Because social security and Medicare taxes were not withheld from the allocated tips, you must report those taxes as additional tax on your return. Complete Form 4137, and include the allocated tips on line 1 of the form. See *Reporting social security and Medicare taxes on tips not reported to your employer* under *Reporting Tips on Your Tax Return,* earlier.

TaxOrganizer

Records you should keep.

- Daily tip record/journal
- Copies of bills and credit card charge slips
- Copies of reports provided to employers related to tip income
- Summary of money given employers to pay any of your taxes on tips not covered by withholding, and receipts from your employer or canceled checks to evidence these payments

8

Interest Income

Note: The 2004 IRS Publication 17 (Your Federal Income Tax) has been updated by Ernst & Young LLP for 2005. Dates and dollar amounts shown are for 2005. Gray type is used to indicate where IRS text has been updated or intentionally omitted. Unrevised IRS text is shown in black type.

Introduction

Interest income is a significant portion of all income earned by Americans. The government takes pains to make sure that all such income is reported by taxpayers. That's why payers of interest, like banks, are required to report to the government the amounts of interest they pay out and to whom. If you do not supply your proper tax identification number—usually your Social Security number—to a payer of interest, tax will automatically be withheld.

Some investments permit you to delay reporting interest income. Such investments may boost the after-tax rate of return on your money, because you may pay tax on the income in a year—a retirement year, for example—when your tax rate is lower. This chapter helps you sort through some of the strategies for postponing taxes on interest income.

Reminder

Foreign-source income. If you are a U.S. citizen with interest income from sources outside the United States (foreign income), you must report that income on your tax return unless it is exempt by U.S. law. This is true whether you reside inside or outside the United States and whether or not you receive a Form 1099 from the foreign payer.

Explanation
You may also have a filing obligation to report your financial interest in or signature authority over any financial accounts in a foreign country, if the aggregate value of these financial accounts exceeds $10,000 at any time during the calendar year. It is important to note that this rule applies to any financial accounts that you hold through a partnership in which you have a greater than 50% ownership interest. You must report that relationship each calendar year by filing TD F 90-22.1 with the Department of the Treasury on or before June 30, of the succeeding year. A substantial penalty may apply if you fail to file this form on time.

This chapter discusses:

• Different types of interest income,
• What interest is taxable and what interest is nontaxable,
• When to report interest income, and
• How to report interest income on your tax return.

In general, any interest that you receive or that is credited to your account and can be withdrawn is taxable income. Exceptions to this rule are discussed later in this chapter.

You may be able to deduct expenses you have in earning this income on Schedule A (Form 1040) if you itemize your deductions. See chapter 30.

Useful Items

You may want to see:

Publications

☐ **537** Installment Sales
☐ **550** Investment Income and Expenses
☐ **1212** List of Original Issue Discount Instruments

Forms (and Instructions)

☐ **Schedule B (Form 1040)** Interest and Ordinary Dividends
☐ **Schedule 1 (Form 1040A)** Interest and Ordinary Dividends for Form 1040A Filers
☐ **3115** Application for Change in Accounting Method
☐ **8815** Exclusion of Interest From Series EE and I U.S. Savings Bonds Issued After 1989
☐ **8818** Optional Form To Record Redemption of Series EE and I U.S. Savings Bonds Issued After 1989

General Information

A few items of general interest are covered here.

Recordkeeping. You should keep a list showing sources and amounts of interest received during the year. Also, keep the forms you receive that show your interest income (Forms 1099-INT, for example) as an important part of your records.

Tax on investment income of a child under age 14. Part of a child's 2005 investment income may be taxed at the parent's tax rate. This may happen if all the following are true.

1. The child was under age 14 at the end of 2005. A child born on January 1, 1992, is considered to be age 14 at the end of 2005.
2. The child had more than $1,600 of investment income (such as taxable interest and dividends) and has to file a tax return.
3. Either parent was alive at the end of 2005.

If all these statements are true, Form 8615, Tax for Children Under Age 14 Who Have Investment Income of More Than $1,600, must be completed and attached to the child's tax return. If any of these statements is not true, Form 8615 is not required and the child's income is taxed at his or her own tax rate.

However, the parent can choose to include the child's interest and dividends on the parent's return if certain requirements are met. Use Form 8814, Parents' Election To Report Child's Interest and Dividends, for this purpose.

For more information about the tax on investment income of children and the parents' election, see chapter 33.

Beneficiary of an estate or trust. Interest you receive as a beneficiary of an estate or trust is generally taxable income. You should receive a Schedule K-1 (Form 1041), Beneficiary's Share of Income, Deductions, Credits, etc., from the fiduciary. Your copy of Schedule K-1 and its instructions will tell you where to report the income on your Form 1040.

Social security number (SSN). You must give your name and SSN to any person required by federal tax law to make a return, statement, or other document that relates to you. This includes payers of interest.

SSN for joint account. If the funds in a joint account belong to one person, list that person's name first on the account and give that person's SSN to the payer. (For information on who owns the funds in a joint account, see *Joint accounts*, later.) If the joint account contains combined funds, give the SSN of the person whose name is listed first on the account.

These rules apply both to joint ownership by a married couple and to joint ownership by other individuals. For example, if you open a joint savings account with your child using funds belonging to the child, list the child's name first on the account and give the child's SSN.

Custodian account for your child. If your child is the actual owner of an account that is recorded in your name as custodian for the child, give the child's SSN to the payer. For example, you must give your child's SSN to the payer of interest on an account owned by your child, even though the interest is paid to you as custodian.

Penalty for failure to supply SSN. If you do not give your SSN to the payer of interest, you may have to pay a penalty. See *Failure to supply social security number* under *Penalties* in chapter 1. Backup withholding also may apply.

Backup withholding. Your interest income is generally not subject to regular withholding. However, it may be subject to backup withholding to ensure that income tax is collected on the income. Under backup withholding, the payer of interest must withhold, as income tax, a percentage of the amount you are paid. For 2006, the percentage is 28%.

Backup withholding may also be required if the Internal Revenue Service (IRS) has determined that you underreported your interest or dividend income. For more information, see *Backup Withholding* in chapter 5.

Reporting backup withholding. If backup withholding is deducted from your interest income, the payer must give you a Form 1099-INT for the year that indicates the amount withheld. The Form 1099-INT will show any backup withholding as "Federal income tax withheld."

Joint accounts. If two or more persons hold property (such as a savings account or bond) as joint tenants, tenants by the entirety, or tenants in common, each person's share of any interest from the property is determined by local law.

the property more easily upon the owner's death. In such cases, no immediate transfer of property interest is intended. In these circumstances, the interest income should be reported solely by the owner who contributed the money.

Example 1

If two brothers, Tom and Bill, have a joint brokerage account in which all the funds were contributed by Tom, with no intention of conferring any immediate benefit on Bill, all of the income should be reported by Tom.

Note: To avoid an IRS deficiency notice issued through its document-matching program, Tom should make sure that his Social Security number is reported on Form 1099-INT.

Example 2

If a husband and wife own bonds as joint tenants, tenants by the entirety, or tenants in common, and they file separate tax returns, each should include his or her share of the income.

Example 3

If a parent does not transfer bonds to his or her child but uses joint tenancy so that ownership of the bonds will pass automatically to the child in case of his or her death, the income belongs to the parent. The parent's Social Security number should be used, and all income should be reported on the parent's return. The same applies to joint savings accounts, other bank accounts, and certificates of deposit.

If a parent does intend to transfer during his or her lifetime some or all of his or her bonds to a child, a proportionate amount of interest should be included in both of their tax returns. Either person's Social Security number may be used.

Note: Bonds, savings accounts, and the like that are in the name of a parent or other adult as custodian under the state's Uniform Gifts or Transfers to Minors Act should use the *child's* Social Security number.

TAXPLANNER

Since only one Social Security number will be recorded by the payer of interest, the IRS's document-matching program may issue deficiency notices when interest income is split between two or more returns. This situation arises because the tax return with the Social Security number shown on the payer's records may not include the full amount of the interest paid. To reduce the chance of receiving an IRS deficiency notice, show both the full amount of the interest paid and a subtraction for "amount attributable to others," including their Social Security numbers, on Schedule B (Form 1040) in the section used for reporting distributions of income.

The person who receives the other part of the interest needn't worry. Although that person includes on his or her return an amount for which he or she does not receive a Form 1099-INT, the IRS rarely questions returns where income in excess of that computed by the government is reported.

Income from property given to a child. Property you give as a parent to your child under the Model Gifts of Securities to Minors Act, the Uniform Gifts to Minors Act, or any similar law, becomes the child's property.

Income from the property is taxable to the child, except that any part used to satisfy a legal obligation to support the child is taxable to the parent or guardian having that legal obligation.

Savings account with parent as trustee. Interest income from a savings account opened for a child who is a minor, but placed in the name and subject to the order of the parents as trustees, is taxable to the child if, under the law of the state in which the child resides, both of the following are true.

1. The savings account legally belongs to the child.
2. The parents are not legally permitted to use any of the funds to support the child.

Form 1099-INT. Interest income is generally reported to you on Form 1099-INT, or a similar statement, by banks, savings and loans, and other payers of interest. This form shows you the interest you received during the year. Keep this form for your records. You do not have to attach it to your tax return.

Report on your tax return the total amount of interest income that you receive for the tax year.

Explanation

The IRS contends that the figures shown on Form 1099 represent the correct amount of interest income paid to you. You have the burden of proof to demonstrate otherwise. If you have a valid reason for claiming that the correct amount is different—write on your return the amount shown on Form 1099 and then immediately show a subtraction (or addition) with an explanation for the adjustment. If you notice an error in the amount of interest stated, you should request that the payer issue a corrected Form 1099.

Example

You buy a bond on 4/1/05, which pays interest once a year on December 31. Because you bought the bond between the interest payment dates, you pay, in addition to the cost of bond, $750 for "purchased interest" (i.e., money to reimburse the seller for the interest that accrued between 1/1/05 and 4/1/05). On 12/31/05, you receive a $3,000 interest payment, which represents interest for the period 1/1/05 through 12/31/05. Since you did not earn the interest from 1/1/05 through 4/1/05, you should not have to pay income tax on this amount. Therefore, on Schedule B (Form 1040), you should report as follows:

XYZ Corporation interest	$3,000
Less amount of purchased interest	(750)

See *Bonds Sold Between Interest Dates* later in this chapter.

TAXORGANIZER

You should keep copies of each Form 1099-INT you receive for a minimum of 3 years. See Chapter 1, *Filing Information,* for more information on recordkeeping.

Interest not reported on Form 1099-INT. Even if you do not receive Form 1099-INT, you must still report all of your taxable interest income. For example, you may receive distributive shares of interest from partnerships or subchapter S corporations. This interest is reported to you on Schedule K-1 (Form 1065) and Schedule K-1 (Form 1120S).

Nominees. Generally, if someone receives interest as a nominee for you, that person will give you a Form 1099-INT showing the interest received on your behalf.

If you receive a Form 1099-INT that includes amounts belonging to another person, see the discussion on nominee distributions under *How To Report Interest Income* in chapter 1 of Publication 550, or see the Schedule 1 (Form 1040A) or Schedule B (Form 1040) instructions.

Incorrect amount. If you receive a Form 1099-INT that shows an incorrect amount (or other incorrect information), you should ask the issuer for a corrected form. The new Form 1099-INT you receive will be marked "Corrected."

Form 1099-OID. Reportable interest income may also be shown on Form 1099-OID, Original Issue Discount. For more information about amounts shown on this form, see *Original Issue Discount (OID)*, later in this chapter.

> **TAXORGANIZER**
>
> You should keep copies of each Form 1099-OID you receive for a minimum of 3 years. See Chapter 1, *Filing Information,* for more information on recordkeeping.

Exempt-interest dividends. Exempt-interest dividends you receive from a regulated investment company (mutual fund) are not included in your taxable income. (However, see *Information-reporting requirement*, next.) You will receive a notice from the mutual fund telling you the amount of the exempt-interest dividends that you received. Exempt-interest dividends are not shown on Form 1099-DIV or Form 1099-INT.

Information-reporting requirement. Although exempt-interest dividends are not taxable, you must show them on your tax return if you have to file. This is an information-reporting requirement and does not change the exempt-interest dividends into taxable income.

Note. Exempt-interest dividends paid from specified private activity bonds may be subject to the alternative minimum tax. See *Alternative Minimum Tax* in chapter 32 for more information. Chapter 1 of Publication 550 contains a discussion on private activity bonds, under *State or Local Government Obligations*.

> **TAXSAVER**
>
> Investment income that is exempt from federal tax may still be taxable on your state tax return. This includes interest and dividends paid or accrued to you on state, municipal, or any other type of debt obligation. However in most states, there are certain federally tax-exempt bonds that are not taxable at the state level. Be sure to check your state filing requirements before you invest in federally tax-exempt obligations. Finally, be aware that interest from certain private activity bonds will result in an adjustment for the Alternative Minimum Tax, even though the interest is not taxable for regular tax. See Chapter 32, *How to Figure Your Tax,* for more information on the Alternative Minimum Tax.

Interest on VA dividends. Interest on insurance dividends that you leave on deposit with the Department of Veterans Affairs (VA) is not taxable. This includes interest paid on dividends on converted United States Government Life Insurance and on National Service Life Insurance policies.

Individual retirement arrangements (IRAs). Interest on a Roth IRA generally is not taxable. Interest on a traditional IRA is tax deferred. You generally do not include it in your income until you make withdrawals from the IRA. See chapter 18.

Taxable Interest

Taxable interest includes interest you receive from bank accounts, loans you make to others, and other sources. The following are some other sources of taxable interest.

Dividends that are actually interest. Certain distributions commonly called dividends are actually interest. You must report as interest so-called "dividends" on deposits or on share accounts in:

- Cooperative banks,
- Credit unions,
- Domestic building and loan associations,
- Domestic savings and loan associations,
- Federal savings and loan associations, and
- Mutual savings banks.

Money market funds. Generally, amounts you receive from money market funds should be reported as dividends, not as interest.

Money market certificates, savings certificates, and other deferred interest accounts. If you open any of these accounts, interest may be paid at fixed intervals of 1 year or less during the term of the account. You generally must include this interest in your income when you actually receive it or are entitled to receive it without paying a substantial penalty. The same is true for accounts that mature in 1 year or less and pay interest in a single payment at maturity. If interest is deferred for more than 1 year, see *Original Issue Discount (OID)*, later.

Interest subject to penalty for early withdrawal. If you withdraw funds from a deferred interest account before maturity, you may have to pay a penalty. You must report the total amount of interest paid or credited to your account during the year, without subtracting the penalty. See *Penalty on early withdrawal of savings* in chapter 1 of Publication 550, for more information on how to report the interest and deduct the penalty.

Money borrowed to invest in money market certificate. The interest you pay on money borrowed from a bank or savings institution to meet the minimum deposit required for a money market certificate from the institution and the interest you earn on the certificate are two separate items. You must report the total interest you earn on the certificate in your income. If you itemize deductions, you can deduct the interest you pay as investment interest, up to the amount of your net investment income. See *Interest Expense* in chapter 3 of Publication 550.

Example. You deposited $5,000 with a bank and borrowed $5,000 from the bank to make up the $10,000 minimum deposit required to buy a 6-month money market certificate. The certificate earned $575 at maturity in 2005, but you received only $265, which represented the $575 you earned minus $310 interest charged on your $5,000 loan. The bank gives you a Form 1099-INT for 2005 showing the $575 interest you earned. The bank also gives you a statement showing that you paid $310 interest for 2005. You must include the $575 in your income. If you itemize your deductions on Schedule A (Form 1040), you can deduct $310, subject to the net investment income limit.

> **TAXPLANNER**
>
> Note that in the example above the $310 in interest is deductible *only* if you itemize your deductions and may be further limited if you have no net investment income (see Chapter 25, *Interest Expense*). If you are not able to fully deduct the interest you pay, you may want to reconsider the investment arrangement.
>
> **Example**
> Assuming the same facts as in the example above, if you are in the top tax bracket, paying 35%, $201 of the $575 interest you earned will go to the IRS, leaving you with only $374. Since you paid $310 in interest charges (for which you receive no tax benefit if you do not itemize) to earn that $374, you have only $64 of after-tax gain on your $5,000 investment, for an after-tax rate of return of 1.28% on this investment.

You should be very interested in the after-tax rate of return on your investments. If your interest income is fully taxable, you may determine your after-tax rate of return in the following manner. First, determine from the Tax Tables (printed in the back of this book) what you expect your highest **marginal tax rate** to be by calculating your total **taxable income** and then determining the highest rate at which it will be taxed. If the rate is, say, 33%, then the IRS gets 33% of your interest income on any investment, and you keep 67%. Thus, if you earn 10% on a bank deposit, your after-tax rate of return is really 6.7% (10% × 67%). See the chart later in this chapter in the *State or Local Government Obligations* section for a comparison of after-tax yields with the yield of municipal bonds. As the chart indicates, you should remember to include your state and local taxes when computing your marginal tax rate.

Gift for opening account. If you receive noncash gifts or services for making deposits or for opening an account in a savings institution, you may have to report the value as interest.

Explanation
Incentive items received (e.g., a toaster from a bank) may be considered income to you, not a tax-free gift. In cases such as this, you may have taxable income.

For deposits of less than $5,000, gifts or services valued at more than $10 must be reported as interest. For deposits of $5,000 or more, gifts or services valued at more than $20 must be reported as interest. The value is determined by the cost to the financial institution.

Example. You open a savings account at your local bank and deposit $800. The account earns $20 interest. You also receive a $15 calculator. If no other interest is credited to your account during the year, the Form 1099-INT you receive will show $35 interest for the year. You must report $35 interest income on your tax return.

Interest on insurance dividends. Interest on insurance dividends left on deposit with an insurance company that can be withdrawn annually is taxable to you in the year it is credited to your account. However, if you can withdraw it only on the anniversary date of the policy (or other specified date), the interest is taxable in the year that date occurs.

Explanation
Remember to distinguish between the insurance dividend and the *interest* on that dividend. An insurance dividend is the amount of your premium that is paid back to you if your insurance company achieves a lower mortality cost on policyholders than it expected. An insurance dividend is treated as an adjustment to your insurance premium and is therefore not taxable income to you unless it exceeds your premium. If you leave this dividend on deposit with the insurance company, however, any interest you receive on it should be included as interest income, just as it would be if you had left the money in the bank.

TAXPLANNER

If you receive Form 1099-INT from an insurance company every year, you may have an untapped source of cash at your disposal. This form usually indicates that insurance dividends paid in prior years are accumulating in a savings account paying *passbook* rates. This money might be better invested in money market funds or other investments paying higher rates. To find out if you have money you did not know about, contact your insurance agent.

Prepaid insurance premiums. Any increase in the value of prepaid insurance premiums, advance premiums, or premium deposit funds is interest if it is applied to the payment of premiums due on insurance policies or made available for you to withdraw.
U.S. obligations. Interest on U.S. obligations, such as U.S. Treasury bills, notes, and bonds, issued by any agency or instrumentality of the United States is taxable for federal income tax purposes.

Explanation
Interest income on U.S. obligations is not subject to *state and local* income tax. Therefore, if your state has a high income tax rate, investing in U.S. obligations, rather than in instruments taxable at the state level, could mean a significant tax savings overall. Nevertheless, interest paid on federal **tax refunds** is taxable by both the state and the federal governments.

Interest on tax refunds. Interest you receive on tax refunds is taxable income.
Interest on condemnation award. If the condemning authority pays you interest to compensate you for a delay in payment of an award, the interest is taxable.

Explanation
The interest on the award is taxable even if the condemning authority is a state or local government. The logic is as follows: The interest arises out of the government's eminent domain activities and not through the exercise of its borrowing power.

Installment sale payments. If a contract for the sale or exchange of property provides for deferred payments, it also usually provides for interest payable with the deferred payments. That interest is taxable when you receive it. If little or no interest is provided for in a deferred payment contract, part of each payment may be treated as interest. See *Unstated Interest and Original Issue Discount* in Publication 537, Installment Sales.

Explanation
Congress has clamped down on a device that was used with great success. The idea was to sell a piece of real estate at an inflated price in order to receive a larger long-term capital gain and, in turn, agree to accept deferred payments carrying a low interest rate. The strategy was to give up interest income taxed at ordinary rates and replace it with a larger long-term capital gain taxed at a lower rate.
Under legislation effective for debt instruments issued after December 31, 1984, payments must be made on a current basis, and certain tests are applied to determine if the interest rate is appropriate. If it isn't, some of each payment is recharacterized as interest. Because the rules are very complex, you should obtain professional assistance when you are negotiating a deal and making the necessary computations.
The rules are not applicable to sales of less than

$250,000, the sale of your principal residence, or sales for less than $1 million of a farm used by the seller as a farm.

However, in these situations, the IRS has the authority to recharacterize a transaction if the stipulated interest rate falls below the published federal rate. In such cases, the IRS would reduce the amount of the capital gain and increase the interest income.

Interest on annuity contract. Accumulated interest on an annuity contract you sell before its maturity date is taxable.

Usurious interest. Usurious interest is interest charged at an illegal rate. This is taxable as interest unless state law automatically changes it to a payment on the principal.

Interest income on frozen deposits. Exclude from your gross income interest on frozen deposits. A deposit is frozen if, at the end of the year, you cannot withdraw any part of the deposit because:

1. The financial institution is bankrupt or insolvent, or
2. The state where the institution is located has placed limits on withdrawals because other financial institutions in the state are bankrupt or insolvent.

The amount of interest you must exclude is the interest that was credited on the frozen deposits minus the sum of:

1. The net amount you withdrew from these deposits during the year, and
2. The amount you could have withdrawn as of the end of the year (not reduced by any penalty for premature withdrawals of a time deposit).

If you receive a Form 1099-INT for interest income on deposits that were frozen at the end of 2005, see *Frozen deposits* under *How To Report Interest Income* in chapter 1 of Publication 550, for information about reporting this interest income exclusion on your tax return.

The interest you exclude is treated as credited to your account in the following year. You must include it in income when you can withdraw it.

Example. $100 of interest was credited on your frozen deposit during the year. You withdrew $80 but could not withdraw any more as of the end of the year. You must include $80 in your income and exclude $20 from your income for the year. You must include the $20 in your income for the year you can withdraw it.

Bonds traded flat. If you buy a bond at a discount when interest has been defaulted or when the interest has accrued but has not been paid, the transaction is described as trading a bond flat. The defaulted or unpaid interest is not income and is not taxable as interest if paid later. When you receive a payment of that interest, it is a return of capital that reduces the remaining cost basis of your bond. Interest that accrues after the date of purchase, however, is taxable interest income for the year it is received or accrued. See *Bonds Sold Between Interest Dates*, later, for more information.

Below-market loans. In general, a below-market loan is a loan on which no interest is charged or on which interest is charged at a rate below the applicable federal rate. See *Below-Market Loans* in chapter 1 of Publication 550 for more information.

Explanation

If you make a below-market loan, you must report as interest income any forgone interest (defined below) arising from that loan. How you should report the income as well as the application of the below-market loan rules and exceptions are described in this section.

If you receive a below-market loan, you may be able to claim a deduction for interest expense in excess of the interest that you actually paid—but only if you use the funds to buy investment property.

Forgone interest. For any period, forgone interest is:

1. The amount of interest that would be payable for that period if interest accrued on the loan at the applicable federal rate and was payable annually on December 31, *minus*
2. Any interest actually payable on the loan for the period.

The **applicable federal rate** is set by the IRS each month and is published in the *Internal Revenue Bulletin*. You can also contact an IRS office to get these rates.

Below-market loans. A below-market loan is a loan on which no interest is charged or on which interest is charged at a rate below the applicable federal rate. A below-market loan is generally recharacterized as an arm's length transaction in which the lender is treated as having made:

1. A loan to the borrower in exchange for a note that requires the payment of interest at the applicable federal rate, and
2. An additional payment to the borrower.

The lender's additional payment to the borrower is treated as a gift, dividend, contribution to capital, payment of compensation, or other payment, depending on the substance of the transaction. The borrower may have to report this payment as taxable income depending on its classification.

Loans subject to the rules. The rules for below-market loans apply to:

Gift loans
Compensation-related loans
Corporation-shareholder loans
Tax avoidance loans
Certain loans to qualified continuing care facilities (made after October 11, 1985)
Certain other below-market loans

Exceptions

The rules for below-market loans do not apply to certain loans on days on which the total outstanding amount of loans between the borrower and lender is $10,000 or less. The rules do not apply on those days to:

1. Gift loans between individuals if the gift loan is not directly used to purchase or carry income-producing assets
2. Compensation-related loans or corporation-shareholder loans if the avoidance of federal tax is not a principal purpose of the loan

A compensation-related loan is any below-market loan between an employer and an employee or between an independent contractor and a person for whom the contractor provided services.

Other loans not subject to the rules. Other loans are excluded from the below-market rules, including:

1. Loans made available by the lender to the general public on the same terms and conditions and that are consistent with the lender's customary business practice.
2. Loans subsidized by a federal, state, or municipal government that are made available under a program of general application to the public.
3. Certain employee-relocation loans.
4. Loans to or from a foreign person, unless the interest income would be effectively connected with the conduct of a U.S. trade or business and would not be exempt from U.S. tax under an income tax treaty.

5. Other loans on which the interest arrangement can be shown to have no significant effect on the federal tax liability of the lender or the borrower.
6. Certain refundable loans to a qualified continuing care facility under a continuing care contract. This exclusion may apply if the lender (resident) or the lender's spouse (resident's spouse) is age 65 or older before the close of the year. In order to qualify for the exclusion from the below-market loan rules, the continuing care facility must also provide the resident-lender (without substantial additional charge) a separate living space, meals, routine medical care, and, when necessary, long-term nursing care. For 2005, the exclusion applies only to the part of the total outstanding loan balance that is $158,100 or less. This threshold is indexed annually for inflation.

If a taxpayer structures a transaction to be a loan not subject to the below-market loan rules, and one of the principal purposes of structuring the transaction in such a way is to avoid federal tax, then the IRS may consider the loan to be a tax-avoidance scheme and, as such, subject to the rules for below-market loans.

All the facts and circumstances are used to determine if the interest arrangement of a loan has a significant effect on the federal tax liability of the lender or borrower. Some factors to be considered are:

- Whether income and deduction items generated by the loan offset each other
- The amount of such items
- The cost to the taxpayer of complying with the below-market loan provisions, if they applied
- Any reasons other than tax avoidance purposes for structuring the transaction as a below-market loan

Gift and demand loans. A gift loan is any below-market loan where the forgone interest is in the nature of a gift. A demand loan is a loan payable in full at any time upon demand by the lender. A lender who makes a gift loan or demand loan is treated as transferring an additional payment to the borrower (as a gift, dividend, etc.) in an amount equal to the forgone interest. The borrower is treated as transferring the forgone interest to the lender and may be entitled to an interest expense deduction depending on the use of the monies borrowed. The lender must report that amount as interest income. These transfers are considered to occur annually, generally on December 31.

Example 1

Jill's grandmother makes an interest-free loan to Jill on July 1 for $50,000. Jill has net investment income from outside sources of $5,000. The applicable federal interest rate is 5% at this time. This loan will be treated as a gift loan. On December 31, Jill will be treated as having paid her grandmother $1,250 in interest and her grandmother must report $1,250 of interest income, even though no money has changed hands.

Special rules for gift loans between individuals that do not exceed $100,000. For gift loans that do not exceed $100,000, the amount of forgone interest that is treated as transferred by the borrower to the lender is limited. This limit is the borrower's net investment income for the year, unless one of the principal purposes of the loan is the avoidance of federal tax. Also, if a borrower has net investment income of $1,000 or less for the year, the borrower's net investment income is considered to be zero and the borrower will have no interest expense deduction.

Example 2

Using the same facts in the above example, assume Jill has $1,100 in net investment income for the year. On December 31, Jill will be treated as having paid her grandmother $1,100 in interest (not $1,250) because of the net investment income limitation. Jill's grandmother would include the $1,100 as interest income.

Term loans. A lender who makes a below-market term loan (a loan that is not a demand loan) is treated as transferring, as a gift, dividend, etc., an additional lump-sum cash payment to the borrower on the date the loan is made. The amount of this payment is the amount of the loan minus the present value of all payments due under the loan. An amount equal to this excess is treated as original issue discount (OID). Accordingly, the OID rules of Section 1272 of the Internal Revenue Code apply. The lender must report the annual part of the OID as interest income. The borrower may be able to deduct some or all of the excess as interest expense depending on the use of the monies borrowed.

Effective dates. These rules apply to term loans made after June 6, 1984, and to demand loans outstanding after that date.

U.S. Savings Bonds

This section provides tax information on U.S. savings bonds. It explains how to report the interest income on these bonds and how to treat transfers of these bonds.

For other information on U.S. savings bonds, write to:

For Series EE and I:
Bureau of the Public Debt
Accrual Services Division
P.O. Box 1328
Parkersburg, WV 26106-1328

For Series HH/H:
Bureau of the Public Debt
Current Income Services Division
HH/H Assistance Branch
P.O. Box 2186
Parkersburg, WV 26106-2186

Or, on the Internet, visit: *www.publicdebt.treas/sav/sav.htm*

Accrual method taxpayers. If you use an accrual method of accounting, you must report interest on U.S. savings bonds each year as it accrues. You cannot postpone reporting interest until you receive it or until the bonds mature. Accrual methods of accounting are explained in chapter 1 under *Accounting Methods*.

Cash method taxpayers. If you use the cash method of accounting, as most individual taxpayers do, you generally report the interest on U.S. savings bonds when you receive it. The cash method of accounting is explained in chapter 1 under *Accounting Methods*.

Series HH Bonds. These bonds were issued at face value. Interest is paid twice a year by direct deposit to your bank account. If you are a cash method taxpayer, you must report interest on these bonds as income in the year you receive it.

Series HH Bonds were first offered in 1980; they were last offered in August 2004. Before 1980, series H bonds were issued. Series H bonds are treated the same as series HH bonds. If you are a cash method taxpayer, you must report the interest when you receive it.

Series H bonds have a maturity period of 30 years. Series HH bonds mature in 20 years.

Series EE and series I bonds. Interest on these bonds is payable when you redeem the bonds. The difference between the purchase price and the redemption value is taxable interest.

Series EE bonds. Series EE bonds were first offered in July 1980. They have a maturity period of 30 years.

Before July 1980, series E bonds were issued. The original 10-year maturity period of series E bonds has been extended to 40 years for bonds issued before December 1965 and 30 years for bonds issued after November 1965. Paper series EE and series E bonds are issued at a discount. Electronic series EE bonds are issued at their face value. The face value plus accrued interest is payable to you at maturity.

Series I bonds. Series I bonds were first offered in 1998. These are inflation-indexed bonds issued at their face amount with a maturity period of 30 years. The face value plus all accrued interest is payable to you at maturity.

Reporting options for cash method taxpayers. If you use the cash method of reporting income, you can report the interest on series EE, series E, and series I bonds in either of the following ways.

1. **Method 1.** Postpone reporting the interest until the earlier of the year you cash or dispose of the bonds or the year they mature. (However, see *Savings bonds traded*, later.)
   Note. Series E bonds issued in 1965 and 1975 matured in 2005. If you have used method 1, you generally must report the interest on these bonds on your 2005 return.
2. **Method 2.** Choose to report the increase in redemption value as interest each year.

You must use the same method for all series EE, series E, and series I bonds you own. If you do not choose method 2 by reporting the increase in redemption value as interest each year, you must use method 1.

Tip. *If you plan to cash your bonds in the same year that you will pay for higher education expenses, you may want to use method 1 because you may be able to exclude the interest from your income. To learn how, see* Education Savings Bond Program, *later.*

Change from method 1. If you want to change your method of reporting the interest from method 1 to method 2, you can do so without permission from the IRS. In the year of change you must report all interest accrued to date and not previously reported for all your bonds.

Once you choose to report the interest each year, you must continue to do so for all series EE, series E, and series I bonds you own and for any you get later, unless you request permission to change, as explained next.

Change from method 2. To change from method 2 to method 1, you must request permission from the IRS. Permission for the change is automatically granted if you send the IRS a statement that meets all the following requirements.

1. You have typed or printed at the top as follows: "Change in Method of Accounting Under Section 6.01 of the Appendix of Rev. Proc. 2002-9 (or later update)."
2. It includes your name and social security number under the label in (1).
3. It identifies the savings bonds for which you are requesting this change.
4. It includes your agreement to:
   a. Report all interest on any bonds acquired during or after the year of change when the interest is realized upon disposition, redemption, or final maturity, whichever is earliest, and
   b. Report all interest on the bonds acquired before the year of change when the interest is realized upon disposition, redemption, or final maturity, whichever is earliest, with the exception of the interest reported in prior tax years.
5. It includes your signature.

You must attach this statement to your tax return for the year of change, which you must file by the due date (including extensions).

You can have an automatic extension of 6 months from the due date of your return for the year of change (excluding extensions) to file the statement with an amended return. At the top of the statement, enter "Filed pursuant to section 301.9100-2." To get this extension, you must have filed your original return for the year of change by the due date (including extensions).

By the date you file the original statement with your return, you must also send a copy to the address below.

Internal Revenue Service
Attention: CC:IT&A (Automatic Rulings Branch)
P.O. Box 7604
Benjamin Franklin Station
Washington, DC 20044

If you use a private delivery service, send the copy to the address below.

Internal Revenue Service
Attention: CC:IT&A (Automatic Rulings Branch),
1111 Constitution Avenue, NW
Room 4516
Washington, DC 20224

Instead of filing this statement, you can request permission to change from method 2 to method 1 by filing Form 3115. In that case, follow the form instructions for an automatic change. No user fee is required.

Explanation

Series E, Series EE, and Series I bonds are unique investments from a tax viewpoint. Since you, as a cash method taxpayer, may decide not to report the increase in value of the bonds as income each year and instead may decide to report the interest income when the bonds are cashed in or when they reach final maturity (whichever is earlier), you can—to an unusual extent—control when the income is recognized. The best time to redeem the bonds is a year in which you have low taxable income and a low tax rate.

Few people choose to report income annually rather than at sale or maturity, but if you do, you would report as income the increase in the redemption value of each bond each year. All you must do is report the income on your tax return. It would be advantageous to report the income annually only if you had an income so low that your personal exemption and itemized deductions or standard deduction might otherwise be wasted. The most likely people to choose this option are children age 14 and over and retired people, both of whom may have low taxable income. (Under the Tax Reform Act of 1986, income received by children under age 14 may be taxed at their parents' rate.) Remember, once you choose to report the income each year, you must obtain permission from the IRS to change your reporting method.

Example

A 70-year-old unmarried man with only $1,500 of other income might wish to report his savings bond interest each year, since his first $9,450 of income (his standard deduction and exemption) is tax free in 2005. If he holds the bonds and reports all the income in the year they mature, his taxable income in that year might be more than $9,450, and he would therefore pay taxes he could have otherwise avoided by reporting a smaller amount of interest each year over the life of the bond.

Explanation

The interest rate on Series EE bonds varies depending upon when the bonds were purchased. The method of calculating the interest rate is different for bonds purchased prior to May 1, 1995, between May 1, 1995, and April 30, 1997, and after May 1, 1997. The interest rate on Series I bonds, the value of which is adjusted with inflation, also changes periodically. The Treasury site at http://www.publicdebt.treas.gov/sav/savtypes has more details.

Millions of Series E and H bonds continue to be held by the public. Most are still earning interest due to extended maturity rates. Some, however, have reached their final maturity and should be exchanged or redeemed.

Prior to September 1, 2004, Series HH bonds could be obtained in exchange for outstanding eligible Series EE bonds and Series E bonds having a combined redemption value of $500 or more. Owners who deferred reporting interest earned on the bonds that they exchange can continue to defer the interest until the year in which the Series HH bonds received in the exchange are redeemed, reach final maturity, or are otherwise disposed of.

Although Series H bonds cannot be exchanged for Series HH bonds (nor can Series E bonds be exchanged for Series EE bonds), the redemption proceeds can be reinvested in new series bonds. However, any previously tax-deferred interest must be reported for federal income tax purposes in the year of redemption.

TAXPLANNER

For most bonds issued prior to May 1997, interest is credited to U.S. savings bonds at specified dates (i.e., there is no proration of interest for bonds cashed during the middle of an interest period). Thus, you should plan ahead to cash in your bonds just after (versus just before) an interest credit date.

Co-owners. If a U.S. savings bond is issued in the names of co-owners, such as you and your child or you and your spouse, interest on the bond is generally taxable to the co-owner who bought the bond.

One co-owner's funds used. If you used your funds to buy the bond, you must pay the tax on the interest. This is true even if you let the other co-owner redeem the bond and keep all the proceeds. Under these circumstances, since the other co-owner will receive a Form 1099-INT at the time of redemption, the other co-owner must provide you with another Form 1099-INT showing the amount of interest from the bond that is taxable to you. The co-owner who redeemed the bond is a "nominee." See *Nominee distributions* under *How To Report Interest Income* in chapter 1 of Publication 550 for more information about how a person who is a nominee reports interest income belonging to another person.

Both co-owners' funds used. If you and the other co-owner each contribute part of the bond's purchase price, the interest is generally taxable to each of you, in proportion to the amount each of you paid.

Community property. If you and your spouse live in a community property state and hold bonds as community property, one-half of the interest is considered received by each of you. If you file separate returns, each of you generally must report one-half of the bond interest. For more information about community property, see Publication 555, Community Property.

Table 8-1. These rules are also shown in Table 8-1.
Ownership transferred. If you bought series E, series EE, or series I bonds entirely with your own funds and had them reissued in your co-owner's name or beneficiary's name alone, you must include in your gross income for the year of reissue all interest that you earned on these bonds and have not previously reported. But, if the bonds were reissued in your name alone, you do not have to report the interest accrued at that time.

This same rule applies when bonds (other than bonds held as community property) are transferred between spouses incident to divorce.

Explanation
If you make a gift of Series E, Series EE, or Series I bonds to a child, remember that it is not possible to transfer the obligation of reporting the interest income that has already accumulated. The interest that has accumulated through the date of the gift must be reported by the donor in the year of the gift. Interest that accumulates from the date of the gift until maturity is reported by the individual receiving the gift.

Purchased jointly. If you and a co-owner each contributed funds to buy series E, series EE, or series I bonds jointly and later have the bonds reissued in the co-owner's name alone, you must include in your gross income for the year of reissue your share of all the interest earned on the bonds that you have not previously reported. The former co-owner does not have to include in gross income at the time of reissue his or her share of the interest earned that was not reported before the transfer. This interest, however, as well as all interest earned after the reissue, is income to the former co-owner.

This income-reporting rule also applies when the bonds are reissued in the name of your former co-owner and a new co-owner. But the new co-owner will report only his or her share of the interest earned after the transfer.

If bonds that you and a co-owner bought jointly are reissued to each of you separately in the same proportion as your contribution to the purchase price, neither you nor your co-owner has to report at that time the interest earned before the bonds were reissued.

Example 1. You and your spouse each spent an equal amount to buy a $1,000 series EE savings bond. The bond was issued to you and your spouse as co-owners. You both postpone reporting interest on the bond. You later have the bond reissued as two $500 bonds, one in your name and one in your spouse's name. At that time neither you nor your spouse has to report the interest earned to the date of reissue.

Example 2. You bought a $1,000 series EE savings bond entirely with your own funds. The bond was issued to you and your spouse as co-owners. You both postpone reporting interest on the bond. You later have the bond reissued as two $500 bonds, one in your name and one in your spouse's name. You must report half the interest earned to the date of reissue.

Transfer to a trust. If you own series E, series EE, or series I bonds and transfer them to a trust, giving up all rights of ownership, you must include in your income for that year the interest earned to the date of transfer if you have not already reported it. However, if you are considered the owner of the trust and if the increase in value both before and after the transfer continues to be taxable to you, you can continue to defer reporting the interest earned each year. You must include the total interest in your income in the year you cash or dispose of the bonds or the year the bonds finally mature, whichever is earlier.

TAXSAVER

If you transfer the bonds to a revocable trust, of which you are considered the owner, you may continue to defer reporting the income. Many individuals use a revocable trust as a substitute for a will. A revocable trust is not required to pay federal income tax on income earned in the trust. Instead, all income (and deductions) is reported on your individual tax return, as if the revocable trust did not exist. In essence, you are treated as if you owned the assets outright. For more details, consult your tax advisor.

The same rules apply to previously unreported interest on series EE or series E bonds if the transfer to a trust consisted of series HH

Table 8-1. **Who Pays the Tax on U.S. Savings Bond Interest**

IF ...	THEN the interest must be reported by ...
you buy a bond in your name and the name of another person as co-owners, using only your own funds	you.
you buy a bond in the name of another person, who is the sole owner of the bond	the person for whom you bought the bond.
you and another person buy a bond as co-owners, each contributing part of the purchase price	both you and the other co-owner, in proportion to the amount each paid for the bond.
you and your spouse, who live in a community property state, buy a bond that is community property	you and your spouse. if you file separate returns, both you and your spouse generally report one-half of the interest.

or series H bonds you acquired in a trade for the series EE or series E bonds. See *Savings bonds traded*, later.

Decedents. The manner of reporting interest income on series E, series EE, or series I bonds, after the death of the owner, depends on the accounting and income-reporting method previously used by the decedent. This is explained in chapter 1 of Publication 550.

Explanation

Income that the decedent had a right to receive at the time of death, but which is included on another's tax return (or the estate tax return), is called "income in respect of the decedent." See Chapter 4, *Decedents,* for more information.

TAXPLANNER

If the final income tax return of the decedent shows a low amount of taxable income, it would be better to include the interest income from the date of purchase of the bonds through the date of death, the choice described in (1). Otherwise, the IRS says that the interest income must be reported by the person who receives the bonds, the choice described in (2).

However, there is a third option. If the bonds are in the name of the decedent alone, their ownership passes to the estate. The estate is a separate taxable entity that files its own income tax return. If the estate has a low amount of taxable income, it might be advisable for the executor to redeem the bonds.

A point to remember is this: The unique method by which interest from U.S. savings bonds are taxed gives you an opportunity to reduce income tax by selecting the person or entity with the lowest tax rate to receive the income.

Example 1

Your uncle, a cash method taxpayer, died and left you a $1,000 Series E bond. He bought the bond for $750 and chose not to report the interest each year. At the date of death, interest of $200 had accrued on the bond and its value of $950 was included in your uncle's estate. Your uncle's executor did not choose to include the $200 accrued interest in your uncle's final income tax return.

You are a cash method taxpayer and do not choose to report the interest each year as it is earned. If you cash the bond when it reaches maturity value of $1,000, you will report $250 interest income—the difference between the maturity value of $1,000 and the original cost of $750. Also, you may deduct (as a miscellaneous de-

duction not subject to the 2% AGI limit) in that year any federal estate tax that was paid on the $200 of interest that was included in your uncle's estate. For more information on this subject, see Chapter 4, *Decedents.*

Example 2

If, in Example 1, the executor had chosen to include the $200 accrued interest in your uncle's final tax return, you would report only $50 as interest when you cashed the bond at maturity. This $50 is the interest earned after your uncle's death.

Example 3

Your aunt died owning Series H bonds that she got in a trade for Series E bonds. (See *Savings bonds traded,* below.) You were the beneficiary of these bonds. Your aunt used the cash method and did not choose to report the interest on the Series E bonds each year as it accrued. Your aunt's executor did not choose to include on her final tax return any interest earned before her death.

The income in respect of a decedent is the sum of the unreported interest on the Series E bonds and the interest, if any, payable on the Series H bonds but not received as of the date of your aunt's death. You must report any interest received during the year as income on your return. The part of the interest that was payable but not received before your aunt's death is income in respect of the decedent and may qualify for the estate tax deduction. For when to report the interest on the Series E bonds traded, see *Savings bonds traded,* below.

TAXPLANNER

There is a limitation on the purchase of Series EE bonds. An individual may purchase only up to $60,000 (face amount) per year. Because bonds are sold for one-half their face value, this means you can spend no more than $30,000 on Series EE bonds per year. You can only buy up to $30,000 of Series I each year, as well.

Savings bonds traded. If you postponed reporting the interest on your series EE or series E bonds, you did not recognize taxable income when you traded the bonds for series HH or series H bonds, unless you received cash in the trade. (You cannot trade series I bonds for series HH bonds. After August 31, 2004, you cannot trade any other series of bonds for series HH bonds.) Any cash you received is income up to the amount of the interest earned on the bonds traded. When your series HH or series H bonds mature, or if you dispose of them before maturity, you report as interest the difference between their redemption value and your cost. Your cost is the sum of the amount you paid for the traded series EE or series E bonds plus any amount you had to pay at the time of the trade.

Example. You own series EE bonds with accrued interest of $523 and a redemption value of $2,723 and have postponed reporting the interest. In 2005, you traded the bonds for $2,500 in series HH bonds and $223 in cash. You must report the $223 as taxable income in 2005, the year of the trade.

Choice to report interest in year of trade. You can choose to treat all of the previously unreported accrued interest on the series EE or series E bonds traded for series HH bonds as income in the year of the trade. If you make this choice, it is treated as a change from method 1. See *Change from method 1* under *Series EE and series I bonds*, earlier.

Form 1099-INT for U.S. savings bonds interest. When you cash a bond, the bank or other payer that redeems it must give you a Form 1099-INT if the interest part of the payment you receive is $10 or more. Box 3 of your Form 1099-INT should show the interest as the difference between the amount you received and the amount paid for the bond. However, your Form 1099-INT may show more interest than you have to include on your income tax return. For example, this may happen if any of the following are true.

- You chose to report the increase in the redemption value of the bond each year. The interest shown on your Form 1099-INT will not be reduced by amounts previously included in income.
- You received the bond from a decedent. The interest shown on your Form 1099-INT will not be reduced by any interest reported by the decedent before death, or on the decedent's final return, or by the estate on the estate's income tax return.
- Ownership of the bond was transferred. The interest shown on your Form 1099-INT will not be reduced by interest that accrued before the transfer.
- You were named as a co-owner and the other co-owner contributed funds to buy the bond. The interest shown on your Form 1099-INT will not be reduced by the amount you received as nominee for the other co-owner. (See *Co-owners*, earlier in this chapter, for more information about the reporting requirements.)
- You received the bond in a taxable distribution from a retirement or profit-sharing plan. The interest shown on your Form 1099-INT will not be reduced by the interest portion of the amount taxable as a distribution from the plan and not taxable as interest. (This amount is generally shown on Form 1099-R, Distributions From Pensions, Annuities, Retirement or Profit-Sharing Plans, IRAs, Insurance Contracts, etc., for the year of distribution.)

For more information on including the correct amount of interest on your return, see *How To Report Interest Income*, later. Publication 550 includes examples showing how to report these amounts.

Tip. *Interest on U.S. savings bonds is exempt from state and local taxes. The Form 1099-INT you receive will indicate the amount that is for U.S. savings bond interest in box 3. Do not include this amount on your state or local income tax return.*

Explanation
When you redeem U.S. savings bonds, the government assumes that the difference between the issue price and the redemption amount is interest paid to you entirely at that time, even though some of the interest may already have been reported by you or someone else. The government will therefore issue a Form 1099-INT to you for the full amount.

If you should not be taxed on the full amount of interest, you should show the full amount as reported on the Form 1099-INT issued by the government on Schedule B (Form 1040) and also show a subtraction for the amount that is not taxable to you. This will help you to avoid IRS deficiency notices.

Education Savings Bond Program

You may be able to exclude from income all or part of the interest you receive on the redemption of qualified U.S. savings bonds during the year if you pay qualified higher educational expenses during the same year. This exclusion is known as the Education Savings Bond Program.

You do not qualify for this exclusion if your filing status is married filing separately.

Form 8815. Use Form 8815 to figure your exclusion. Attach the form to your Form 1040 or Form 1040A.

Qualified U.S. savings bonds. A qualified U.S. savings bond is a series EE bond issued after 1989 or a series I bond. The bond must be issued either in your name (sole owner) or in your and your spouse's names (co-owners). You must be at least 24 years old before the bond's issue date.

Caution. *The issue date of a bond may be earlier than the date the bond is purchased because the issue date assigned to a bond is the first day of the month in which it is purchased.*

Beneficiary. You can designate any individual (including a child) as a beneficiary of the bond.

Verification by IRS. If you claim the exclusion, the IRS will check it by using bond redemption information from the Department of the Treasury.

Qualified expenses. Qualified higher educational expenses are tuition and fees required for you, your spouse, or your dependent (for whom you can claim an exemption) to attend an eligible educational institution.

Qualified expenses include any contribution you make to a qualified tuition program or to a Coverdell education savings account.

Qualified expenses do not include expenses for room and board or for courses involving sports, games, or hobbies that are not part of a degree or certificate granting program.

Eligible educational institutions. These institutions include most public, private, and nonprofit universities, colleges and vocational schools that are accredited and are eligible to participate in student aid programs run by the Department of Education.

Reduction for certain benefits. You must reduce your qualified higher educational expenses by certain tax-free benefits the student may have received. These benefits include:

1. Scholarships that are exempt from tax (see chapter 13 for information on tax-free scholarships), and
2. Any other nontaxable payments (other than gifts, bequests, or inheritances) received for educational expenses, such as:
   a. Veterans' educational assistance benefits,
   b. Benefits under a qualified tuition program, or
   c. Certain employer-provided educational assistance benefits.

Effect of other education benefits. Do not include in your qualified expenses any expenses that were:

- Covered by nontaxable educational benefits paid directly to, or by, the educational institution,
- Used to figure an education credit on Form 8863,
- Used to figure the nontaxable amount of a distribution from a Coverdell ESA, or
- Used to figure the nontaxable amount of a distribution from a qualified tuition program.

Amount excludable. If the total proceeds (interest and principal) from the qualified U.S. savings bonds you redeem during the year are not more than your adjusted qualified higher educational expenses for the year, you may be able to exclude all of the interest. If the proceeds are more than the expenses, you may be able to exclude only part of the interest.

To determine the excludable amount, multiply the interest part of the proceeds by a fraction. The numerator (top part) of the fraction is the qualified higher educational expenses you paid during the year. The denominator (bottom part) of the fraction is the total proceeds you received during the year.

Example. In February 2005, Mark and Joan, a married couple, cashed a qualified series EE U.S. savings bond they bought in April 1997. They received proceeds of $6,892, representing principal of $5,000 and interest of $1,892. In 2005, they paid $4,000 of their daughter's college tuition. They are not claiming an education credit for that amount, and their daughter does not have any tax-free educational assistance. They can exclude $1,098 ($1,892 × ($4,000 ÷ $6,892)) of interest in 2005. They must pay tax on the remaining $794 ($1,892 − $1,098) interest.

TAXPLANNER

Certain high-income taxpayers do not qualify for the tax break on Series EE or Series I bonds for educational purposes. If this is the case, you might consider buying the bonds in your child's name. When the child reaches age 14, he or she may cash them in and will be taxed at his or her rate, rather than yours, which is presumably higher.

Modified adjusted gross income limit. The interest exclusion is limited if your modified adjusted gross income (modified AGI) is:

- $61,200 to $76,200 for taxpayers filing single or head of household, and
- $91,850 to $121,850 for married taxpayers filing jointly or for a qualifying widow(er) with dependent child.

You do not qualify for the interest exclusion if your modified AGI is equal to or more than the upper limit for your filing status.

Modified AGI, for purposes of this exclusion, is adjusted gross income (line 21 of Form 1040A or line 37 of Form 1040) figured before the interest exclusion, and modified by adding back any:

1. Foreign earned income exclusion,
2. Foreign housing exclusion and deduction,
3. Exclusion of income for *bona fide* residents of American Samoa,
4. Exclusion for income from Puerto Rico,
5. Exclusion for adoption benefits received under an employer's adoption assistance program,
6. Deduction for tuition and fees,
7. Deduction for student loan interest, and
8. Deduction for U.S. production activities.

Use the worksheet in the instructions for line 9, Form 8815, to figure your modified AGI. If you claim any of the exclusion or deduction items listed above (except items 6 and 7), add the amount of the exclusion or deduction (except any deduction for tuition and fees or student loan interest) to the amount on line 5 of the worksheet, and enter the total on Form 8815, line 9, as your modified AGI.

If you have investment interest expense incurred to earn royalties and other investment income, see *Education Savings Bond Program* in chapter 1 of Publication 550.

Recordkeeping. If you claim the interest exclusion, you must keep a written record of the qualified U.S. savings bonds you redeem. Your record must include the serial number, issue date, face value, and total redemption proceeds (principal and interest) of each bond. You can use Form 8818, Optional Form To Record Redemption of Series EE and I U.S. Savings Bonds Issued After 1989, to record this information. You should also keep bills, receipts, canceled checks, or other documentation that shows you paid qualified higher educational expenses during the year.

U.S. Treasury Bills, Notes, and Bonds

Treasury bills, notes, and bonds are direct debts (obligations) of the U.S. Government.

Taxation of interest. Interest income from Treasury bills, notes, and bonds is subject to federal income tax, but is exempt from all state and local income taxes. You should receive Form 1099-INT showing the amount of interest (in box 3) that was paid to you for the year.

Payments of principal and interest generally will be credited to your designated checking or savings account by direct deposit through the TREASURY DIRECT system.

Treasury bills. These bills generally have a 4-week, 13-week, or 26-week maturity period. They are issued at a discount in the amount of $1,000 and multiples of $1,000. The difference between the discounted price you pay for the bills and the face value you receive at maturity is interest income. Generally, you report this interest income when the bill is paid at maturity.

Treasury notes and bonds. Treasury notes have maturity periods of more than 1 year, ranging up to 10 years. Maturity periods for Treasury bonds are longer than 10 years. Both notes and bonds generally pay interest every 6 months. Generally, you report this interest for the year paid. For more information, see *U.S. Treasury Bills, Notes, and Bonds* in chapter 1 of Publication 550.

For other information on Treasury notes or bonds, write to:

Treasury Direct
Attn: Customer Information
P.O. Box 9150
Minneapolis, MN 55480-9150

Or, on the Internet, visit: *www. publicdebt.treas.gov*

For information on series EE, series I, and series HH savings bonds, see *U.S. Savings Bonds*, later.

Treasury inflation-indexed securities. These securities pay interest twice a year at a fixed rate, based on a principal amount that is adjusted to take into account inflation and deflation. For the tax treatment of these securities, see *Inflation-Indexed Debt Instruments* under *Original Issue discount (OID)*, in Publication 550.

Explanation
The paragraph above discusses interest income only when a Treasury bill is held until maturity. When a Treasury bill is sold before maturity, the difference between the purchase price and the selling price may be part interest and part **short-term capital gain** or loss.

Example
You buy a $10,000 Treasury bill for $9,760 exactly 100 days before maturity. Thirty days later, you sell the bill for $9,850.

For tax purposes, you have earned a pro rata portion of the discount as interest income for the time you held the bill: 30/100 × ($10,000 − $9,760) = $72. The other $18 you receive over and above the purchase price is a short-term capital gain.

TAXSAVER

U.S. Treasury bills are relatively short-term investments. Their maturity dates vary from a week to a year. Since the interest income in most cases is reported at maturity—unless the bill is sold beforehand—purchasing Treasury bills with a maturity date falling in the following year offers cash basis taxpayers an opportunity to postpone interest income from one year to the next. However, if you borrow money to acquire Treasury bills, your interest expense deduction may also be deferred. See Chapter 23, *Interest Expense,* for an explanation.

Bonds Sold Between Interest Dates

If you sell a bond between interest payment dates, part of the sales price represents interest accrued to the date of sale. You must report that part of the sales price as interest income for the year of sale.

If you buy a bond between interest payment dates, part of the purchase price represents interest accrued before the date of purchase. When that interest is paid to you, treat it as a return of your capital investment, rather than interest income, by reducing your basis in the bond. See *Accrued interest on bonds* under *How To Report Interest Income* in chapter 1 of Publication 550 for information on reporting the payment.

Explanation

Usually, interest on a bond is paid every 6 months. When a bond is sold between interest payment dates, the seller is entitled to payment from the buyer—in addition to payment for the bond itself—for the interest earned since the issuer's last interest payment. This extra payment—often called "purchased interest" on a broker's statement—is interest income to the seller of the bond, reportable for tax purposes as of the date of the sale. The buyer of the bond should record the purchased interest separately from the price of the bond in his or her records. The purchased interest partially offsets the first interest payment made to the buyer.

If the purchased interest is paid in 2005 but the first interest payment is not received until 2006, the buyer should report the purchased interest as an adjustment to interest income in 2006, not in 2005.

Example 1

On April 1, 2005, John bought from George a $10,000 bond yielding 10%. Interest on the bond is paid on January 1 and July 1 of each year. John paid $10,250—$10,000 in principal plus $250 for interest earned from January 1 to April 1. Thus, George received $250 of interest income on April 1, 2005. John received his first interest check on July 1, 2005. Half of that $500 represented a payment of purchased interest, and the other half represented interest income. In order to avoid any IRS notices, John should report the full $500 on Schedule B (Form 1040) and also show a subtraction for $250 of interest that he purchased.

Example 2

Assume the same facts as above, except that John bought the bond from George on October 1, 2005. John received his interest check for $500 on January 1, 2006. Half of it represented repayment of purchased interest, and the other half represented interest income. However, John may *not* deduct the $250 of purchased interest for 2005 but must wait until 2006. On the other hand, George will report his $250 of interest income on his 2005 return, since he received it on October 1, 2005.

Insurance

Life insurance proceeds paid to you as beneficiary of the insured person are usually not taxable. But if you receive the proceeds in installments, you must usually report a part of each installment payment as interest income.

For more information about insurance proceeds received in installments, see Publication 525, Taxable and Nontaxable Income.

Explanation

For more information on life insurance proceeds, see Chapter 13, *Other Income.*

Annuity. If you buy an annuity with life insurance proceeds, the annuity payments you receive are taxed as pension and annuity income from a nonqualified plan, not as interest income. See chapter 11 for information on pension and annuity income from nonqualified plans.

Original Issue Discount (OID)

Original issue discount (OID) is a form of interest. You generally include OID in your income as it accrues over the term of the debt instrument, whether or not you receive any payments from the issuer.

A debt instrument generally has OID when the instrument is issued for a price that is less than its stated redemption price at maturity. OID is the difference between the stated redemption price at maturity and the issue price.

All instruments that pay no interest before maturity are presumed to be issued at a discount. Zero coupon bonds are one example of these instruments.

The OID accrual rules generally do not apply to short-term obligations (those with a fixed maturity date of 1 year or less from date of issue). See *Discount on Short-Term Obligations* in chapter 1 of Publication 550.

De minimis OID. You can treat the discount as zero if it is less than one-fourth of 1% (.0025) of the stated redemption price at maturity multiplied by the number of full years from the date of original issue to maturity. This small discount is known as "de minimis" OID.

Example 1. You bought a 10-year bond with a stated redemption price at maturity of $1,000, issued at $980 with OID of $20. One-fourth of 1% of $1,000 (stated redemption price) times 10 (the number of full years from the date of original issue to maturity) equals $25. Because the $20 discount is less than $25, the OID is treated as zero. (If you hold the bond at maturity, you will recognize $20 ($1,000 − $980) of capital gain.)

Example 2. The facts are the same as in *Example 1*, except that the bond was issued at $950. The OID is $50. Because the $50 discount is more than the $25 figured in *Example 1*, you must include the OID in income as it accrues over the term of the bond.

Debt instrument bought after original issue. If you buy a debt instrument with *de minimis* OID at a premium, the discount is not includible in income. If you buy a debt instrument with *de minimis* OID at a discount, the discount is reported under the market discount rules. See *Market Discount Bonds* in chapter 1 of Publication 550.

Exceptions to reporting OID. The OID rules discussed in this chapter do not apply to the following debt instruments.

1. Tax-exempt obligations. (However, see *Stripped tax-exempt obligations* under *Stripped Bonds and Coupons* in chapter 1 of Publication 550).
2. U.S. savings bonds.
3. Short-term debt instruments (those with a fixed maturity date of not more than 1 year from the date of issue).
4. Obligations issued by an individual before March 2, 1984.
5. Loans between individuals, if all the following are true.
   a. The lender is not in the business of lending money.
   b. The amount of the loan, plus the amount of any outstanding prior loans between the same individuals, is $10,000 or less.
   c. Avoiding any federal tax is not one of the principal purposes of the loan.

Explanation

The IRS interpretation is misleading with respect to tax-exempt obligations issued after September 3, 1982, and acquired after March 1, 1984. Even though interest on such obligations is tax-free, the OID rules will apply in determining the basis of the security in the event of sale, exchange, or maturity. (See the discussion later in this chapter.)

In addition, under the Technical and Miscellaneous Revenue Act of 1988, the original issue discount on a stripped tax-exempt bond may be treated as taxable interest if the stripped bond is sold at a discount rate that is higher than the original issue.

Form 1099-OID. The issuer of the debt instrument (or your broker, if you held the instrument through a broker) should give you Form 1099-OID, Original Issue Discount, or a similar statement, if the total OID for the calendar year is $10 or more. Form 1099-OID will show, in box 1, the amount of OID for the part of the year that you held the bond. It also will show, in box 2, the stated interest that you must include in your income. A copy of Form 1099-OID will be sent to the IRS. Do not file your copy with your return. Keep it for your records.

In most cases, you must report the entire amount in boxes 1 and 2 of Form 1099-OID as interest income. But see *Refiguring OID* shown on Form 1099-OID, later in this discussion, for more information.

Nominee. If someone else is the holder of record (the registered owner) of an OID instrument that belongs to you and receives a Form 1099-OID on your behalf, that person must give you a Form 1099-OID.

Refiguring OID shown on Form 1099-OID. You must refigure the OID shown in box 1 of Form 1099-OID if either of the following apply.

- You bought the debt instrument after its original issue and paid a premium or an acquisition premium.
- The debt instrument is a stripped bond or a stripped coupon (including certain zero coupon instruments).

For information about figuring the correct amount of OID to include in your income, see *Figuring OID on Long-Term Debt Instruments* in Publication 1212.

Explanation
Stripped coupon bonds are coupon bonds that have been separated into component parts. The coupons represent claims for interest payments, which are paid on a periodic basis. The bond itself represents the claim for the repayment of the principal, which occurs at some future time.

Example
A 10-year, $10,000, 9% bond (interest paid semiannually) was issued on January 1, 2005, for $10,000. On April 1, 2005, when the bond had a market price of $9,900, the coupons were stripped from the bond so that they and the bond became separate assets that could be bought and sold in the marketplace. In other words, the holder could have sold the right to receive $450 semiannually for the next 9 3/4 years and could have independently sold the right to receive the $10,000 on January 1, 2015.

Assume that the right to receive 20 semiannual payments is worth $4,100 and the right to receive $10,000 on January 1, 2015, is worth $5,800. The tax treatment to buyer and to seller is as follows:

The seller.
1. Include the accrued interest income of $225 from January 1, 2005, through April 1, 2005, in income.
2. Increase your basis by the $225 to $10,225.
3. Allocate the basis, using **fair market value,** to the coupons [($4,100 ÷ $9,900) × $10,225 = $4,235)] and the bond [($5,800 ÷ $9,900) × $10,225 = $5,990)].

4. Compare the proceeds for what you sell—either the coupons or the bond—with the basis figured above to determine if you've had a gain or a loss.
5. The difference between the basis of what is not sold and the amount that will be received over time is considered an original issue discount (OID). That amount is treated as earned over the life of the asset. Thus, if the coupons were retained, the difference between their basis ($4,235) and the amount that will be received over time ($450 semiannually for 10 years, or $9,000) would be the original issue discount.

In this example, $4,765 in interest income must be included on your returns over the 10 years. The amount to be included in your income for each year is figured by performing a complicated computation, for which you will probably require professional assistance.

Similarly, if the bond were retained, the difference between its basis ($5,990) and the proceeds ($10,000) would be its original issue discount. Again, complicated computations are required to determine the amount included in your income each year.

The buyer. The difference between what you pay and what you will receive over time is the original issue discount. A special computation is necessary to figure how much you should include in income each year.

Form 1099-OID not received. If you had OID for the year but did not receive a Form 1099-OID, see Publication 1212, which lists total OID on certain debt instruments and has information that will help you figure OID. If your debt instrument is not listed in Publication 1212, consult the issuer for further information about the accrued OID for the year.

Refiguring periodic interest shown on Form 1099-OID. If you disposed of a debt instrument or acquired it from another holder during the year, see *Bonds Sold Between Interest Dates*, earlier, for information about the treatment of periodic interest that may be shown in box 2 of Form 1099-OID for that instrument.

Explanation
These rules also apply to debt instruments issued by individuals after March 1, 1984. This will affect individuals who borrow and lend at a discounted rate.

The current law also makes original issue discount the general rule with regard to obligations issued after July 18, 1984, and purchased in the open market. (This law also applies to bonds issued before July 19, 1984, and purchased after April 30, 1993.) If you sell property after December 31, 1984, or buy a bond in the marketplace that was issued after July 18, 1984, or a bond issued prior to July, 1984, and purchased after April 30, 1993, you must determine whether there is original issue discount and, if so, how much. Some of that amount will be included in your ordinary income each year. You will need professional help to make this calculation. For more information, see *Market discount bonds* later in this chapter.

Example
Assume that Jim purchases a publicly traded 6% $1 million bond that was issued after December 31, 1984, for $900,000. The bond has a maturity of 10 years at the time of purchase. Jim will also receive $60,000 in interest each year.

The computation of the amount of original issue discount to be included is as follows:

		Face value	$1,000,000		
		Purchase price	$900,000		
		Length of term	10		
		Coupon rate	6%		

Period	Beginning basis	Total interest income	OID portion	Interest portion	Ending basis
1	$900,000	$69,533	$9,533	$60,000	$909,533
2	909,533	69,634	9,634	60,000	919,166
3	919,166	69,736	9,736	60,000	928,902
4	928,902	69,839	9,839	60,000	938,740
5	938,740	69,943	9,943	60,000	948,683
6	948,683	70,048	10,048	60,000	958,732
7	958,732	70,155	10,155	60,000	968,866
8	968,886	70,262	10,262	60,000	979,148
9	979,148	70,371	10,371	60,000	989,519
10	989,519	70,481	10,481	60,000	1,000,000
		$700,000	$100,000	$600,000	

The total interest income recognized for the first year will be $69,533 ($60,000 interest and $9,533 of OID). Further special computations will be required if the obligation is sold prior to maturity. Professional advice is *absolutely essential* for anyone who needs to make special OID computations.

TaxPlanner

A zero-coupon bond is one that is purchased at a substantial discount and pays no interest during its life.

If you buy a zero-coupon bond, you do not bear the investment risk entailed in reinvesting interest payments received over the life of the bond because there are no such payments. Moreover, since the issue price and the maturity value have been derived from compound interest tables, you may figure what the precise return on your investment will be if the bond is held until it matures. This is true *only* of zero-coupon bonds.

Note: Because you do not receive the interest until a zero-coupon bond matures, the market value of the bond during the holding period can be very volatile as market interest rates change. The longer the maturity is, the more volatile is the price.

Even though the interest on a zero-coupon bond is not paid until maturity, it is included in income each year. Consequently, an individual must pay tax on income that he or she has not yet received. However, if the bonds are owned in your IRA or Keogh plan, this income is not currently taxable. [See Chapter 18, *Individual Retirement Arrangements (IRAs)*, and Education Savings Accounts (ESAs).] The advantage, however, is that you lock in an interest rate.

On the other hand, nontaxable zero-coupon bonds—such as zero-coupon municipal bonds—may be attractive to individuals in a high tax bracket for the obvious reasons that interest rates are locked in and the increase in value each year is not taxable. In this case, you increase your cost basis on the bonds each year by the amount of the original issue discount applicable to that year, even though you don't pay any federal tax on the income. You may, however, have to pay state income taxes. You will need to check your state tax rules.

Example 1

Assume that Jennifer purchases a 10-year $100,000, non-taxable zero-coupon bond on June 28, 2005, for $50,000. The chart below illustrates how the basis of the bond increases over the life of the bond.

Post 7/1/82 debt
Zero-coupon

	Face value	$100,000	
	Purchase price	$50,000	
	Length of term	10	

Period	Beginning basis	OID	Ending basis
1	$50,000	$3,589	$53,589
2	53,589	3,846	57,435
3	57,435	4,122	61,557
4	61,557	4,418	65,975
5	65,975	4,735	70,711
6	70,711	5,075	75,786
7	75,786	5,439	81,225
8	81,225	5,830	87,055
9	87,055	6,248	93,303
10	93,303	6,697	100,000
		$50,000	

The method for determining original issue discount illustrated above is applicable to tax-exempt bonds. The annual increase in basis is determined accordingly. However, the original issue discount computation is *not* the method used for a tax-exempt bond issued before September 4, 1982, and acquired before March 2, 1984. Instead, a rule is used that allocates the discount proportionately over the life of the bond.

Certificates of deposit (CDs). If you buy a CD with a maturity of more than 1 year, you must include in income each year a part of the total interest due and report it in the same manner as other OID.

This also applies to similar deposit arrangements with banks, building and loan associations, etc., including:

• Time deposits,
• Bonus plans,
• Savings certificates,
• Deferred income certificates,
• Bonus savings certificates, and
• Growth savings certificates.

TaxPlanner

A time deposit with a penalty for early withdrawal is one of the few investments that permits you to defer the recognition of income to a subsequent year when the investment matures rather than in the year when the interest accrues. Other examples are U.S. savings bonds and U.S. Treasury bills.

Bearer CDs. CDs issued after 1982 generally must be in registered form. Bearer CDs are CDs that are not in registered form. They are not issued in the depositor's name and are transferable from one individual to another.

Banks must provide the IRS and the person redeeming a bearer CD with a Form 1099-INT.

TaxPlanner

Market discount bonds. A market discount bond is any bond having market discount except:

1. Short-term obligations (those with fixed maturity dates of up to 1 year from the date of issue)
2. Tax-exempt obligations that you bought before May 1, 1993
3. U.S. savings bonds
4. Certain installment obligations

Market discount arises when the value of a debt obligation decreases after its issue date, generally because of an increase in interest rates. If you buy a bond on the secondary market, it may have market discount.

If you dispose of a market discount bond, you generally must recognize the gain as taxable interest income up to the amount of the bond's **accrued market discount,** if:

1. The bond was issued after July 18, 1984, or
2. You purchased the bond after April 30, 1993.

The rest of the gain is capital gain if the bond was a capital asset.

TaxAlert

The gain on the sale of a tax-exempt obligation that is acquired after April 30, 1993, for a price that is less than the face amount of the bond will be treated as *ordinary income* and not as a *capital gain* to the extent of the accrued market discount. Any remaining gain is treated as a capital gain. The gain on the sale of a tax-exempt obligation that is acquired before May 1, 1993, will be treated entirely as a capital gain.

More information. See chapter 1 of Publication 550 for more information about OID and related topics, such as market discount bonds.

State or Local Government Obligations

Interest on a bond used to finance government operations generally is not taxable if the bond is issued by a state, the District of Columbia, a possession of the United States, or any of their political subdivisions.

Bonds issued after 1982 by an Indian tribal government are treated as issued by a state. Interest on these bonds is generally tax exempt if the bonds are part of an issue of which substantially all of the proceeds are to be used in the exercise of any essential government function.

Explanation

Assume that tax-exempt municipal bonds were previously sold to the public at par (face value) at an interest rate lower than the rate demanded by today's investors. Since the interest rate on these bonds is lower than the rate demanded by today's investors, the bonds are trading in the marketplace at a substantial discount from par. This is a market discount. If you buy these bonds now and subsequently realize a gain either when you sell them or when they reach maturity,

you must report the gain as taxable interest income up to the amount of the bonds' accrued market discount and the remaining portion as capital gain if the bond was a capital asset. Similarly, if you realize a capital loss on municipal bonds, it is deductible.

The rule with regard to bonds bought at a premium is different. If you buy a bond for $11,000 that will mature for $10,000 and you hold it until maturity, you may not claim a capital loss or any kind of deduction because the tax law requires that you **amortize** the premium over the life of the bond.

TaxSaver

If you are considering selling a tax-exempt bond and purchasing another tax-exempt bond, keep in mind that for bonds purchased before May 1, 1993, you will not have to treat accrued market discount as ordinary income, but rather as a capital gain. Depending on your tax bracket, this may be a significant consideration since the top capital gains tax rate is 15%, while the top marginal rate is 35%. Further, while most municipal bond interest is not subject to federal tax, capital gain income and accretion of market discount are. You should be aware of this when you are deciding which bonds to buy.

Example

A $10,000, 10-year tax-exempt municipal bond, yielding 8% purchased at par, will provide $800 of tax-free interest each year, and there will be no capital gain on maturity. The total earned for the 10 years is $8,000.

Similarly, a $12,000, 10-year tax-exempt municipal bond with a 5.2% coupon ($624 interest per year) purchased on May 2, 1997, at $10,000 will yield a total of $8,240 over the life of the bond—$624 of tax-free interest each year plus $200 of taxable interest income each year if the bond is held to maturity. This represents the market discount accretion. But the taxable interest income will be subject to tax of up to 35%, so the net earnings for the 10 years may be reduced to $7,540.

TaxPlanner

When you are determining whether to invest in tax-exempt securities, compare the net after-tax income from a tax-exempt investment with a similar taxable investment.

Equivalent Yield Needed from a Taxable Bond

Tax-Exempt Yield	Based on Your Combined Federal and State Marginal Tax Bracket						
	27%	30%	33%	35%	38.6%	42%	44%
4.00	5.48	5.71	5.97	6.15	6.51	6.90	7.14
4.50	6.16	6.43	6.72	6.92	7.33	7.76	8.04
5.00	6.85	7.14	7.46	7.69	8.14	8.62	8.93
5.50	7.53	7.86	8.21	8.46	8.96	9.48	9.82
6.00	8.22	8.57	8.96	9.23	9.77	10.34	10.71
6.50	8.90	9.29	9.70	10.00	10.59	11.21	11.61
7.00	9.59	10.00	10.45	10.77	11.40	12.07	12.50

Interest on arbitrage bonds issued by state or local governments after October 9, 1969, is taxable.

Interest on a private activity bond that is not a qualified bond is taxable. For more information on whether such interest is taxable or tax exempt, see *State or Local Government Obligations* in chapter 1 of Publication 550.

Information reporting requirement. If you must file a tax return, you are required to show any tax-exempt interest you received on your return. This is an information-reporting requirement only. It does not change tax-exempt interest to taxable interest.

When To Report Interest Income

When to report your interest income depends on whether you use the cash method or an accrual method to report income.

Cash method. Most individual taxpayers use the cash method. If you use this method, you generally report your interest income in the year in which you actually or constructively receive it. However, there are special rules for reporting the discount on certain debt instruments. See *U.S. Savings Bonds* and *Original Issue Discount*, earlier.

Example. On September 1, 2003, you loaned another individual $2,000 at 12%, compounded annually. You are not in the business of lending money. The note stated that principal and interest would be due on August 31, 2005. In 2005, you received $2,508.80 ($2,000 principal and $508.80 interest). If you use the cash method, you must include in income on your 2005 return the $508.80 interest you received in that year.

Constructive receipt. You constructively receive income when it is credited to your account or made available to you. You do not need to have physical possession of it. For example, you are considered to receive interest, dividends, or other earnings on any deposit or account in a bank, savings and loan, or similar financial institution, or interest on life insurance policy dividends left to accumulate, when they are credited to your account and subject to your withdrawal. This is true even if they are not yet entered in your passbook.

You constructively receive income on the deposit or account even if you must:

- Make withdrawals in multiples of even amounts,
- Give a notice to withdraw before making the withdrawal,
- Withdraw all or part of the account to withdraw the earnings, or
- Pay a penalty on early withdrawals, unless the interest you are to receive on an early withdrawal or redemption is substantially less than the interest payable at maturity.

Accrual method. If you use an accrual method, you report your interest income when you earn it, whether or not you have received it. Interest is earned over the term of the debt instrument.

Example. If, in the previous example, you use an accrual method, you must include the interest in your income as you earn it. You would report the interest as follows: 2003, $80; 2004, $249.60; and 2005, $179.20.

Coupon bonds. Interest on coupon bonds is taxable in the year the coupon becomes due and payable. It does not matter when you mail the coupon for payment.

How To Report Interest Income

Generally, you report all of your taxable interest income on Form 1040, line 8a; Form 1040A, line 8a; or Form 1040EZ, line 2.

You cannot use Form 1040EZ if your interest income is more than $1,500. Instead, you must use Form 1040A or Form 1040.

Form 1040A. You must complete Schedule 1 (Form 1040A), Part I, if you file Form 1040A and any of the following are true.

- Your taxable interest income is more than $1,500.
- You are claiming the interest exclusion under the Education Savings Bond Program (discussed earlier).

- You received interest from a seller-financed mortgage, and the buyer used the property as a home.
- You received a Form 1099-INT for tax-exempt interest.
- You received a Form 1099-INT for U.S. savings bond interest that includes amounts you reported before 2005.
- You received, as a nominee, interest that actually belongs to someone else.
- You received a Form 1099-INT for interest on frozen deposits.

List each payer's name and the amount of interest income received from each payer on line 1. If you received a Form 1099-INT or Form 1099-OID from a brokerage firm, list the brokerage firm as the payer.

You cannot use Form 1040A if you must use Form 1040, as described next.

Form 1040. You must use Form 1040 instead of Form 1040A or Form 1040EZ if:

- You forfeited interest income because of the early withdrawal of a time deposit,
- You received or paid accrued interest on securities transferred between interest payment dates,
- You had a financial account in a foreign country, unless the combined value of all foreign accounts was $10,000 or less during all of 2005 or the accounts were with certain U.S. military banking facilities,
- You acquired taxable bonds after 1987 and choose to reduce interest income from the bonds by any amortizable bond premium (see *Bond Premium Amortization* in chapter 3 of Publication 550), or
- You are reporting OID in an amount more or less than the amount shown on Form 1099-OID.
- You received tax-exempt interest from private activity bonds issued after August 7, 1986.

Schedule B. You must complete Schedule B (Form 1040), Part I, if you file Form 1040 and any of the following apply.

- Your taxable interest income is more than $1,500.
- You are claiming the interest exclusion under the Education Savings Bond Program (discussed earlier).
- You had a foreign account.
- You received interest from a seller-financed mortgage, and the buyer used the property as a home.
- You received a Form 1099-INT for tax-exempt interest.
- You received a Form 1099-INT for U.S. savings bond interest that includes amounts you reported before 2005.
- You received, as a nominee, interest that actually belongs to someone else.
- You received a Form 1099-INT for interest on frozen deposits.
- You received a Form 1099-INT for interest on a bond that you bought between interest payment dates.
- Statement (4) or (5) in the preceding list is true.

On Part I, line 1, list each payer's name and the amount received from each. If you received a Form 1099-INT or Form 1099-OID from a brokerage firm, list the brokerage firm as the payer.

Form 1099-INT. Your taxable interest income, except for interest from U.S. savings bonds and Treasury obligations, is shown in box 1 of Form 1099-INT. Add this amount to any other taxable interest income you received. You must report all of your taxable interest income even if you do not receive a Form 1099-INT.

If you forfeited interest income because of the early withdrawal of a time deposit, the deductible amount will be shown on Form 1099-INT in box 2. See *Penalty on early withdrawal of savings* in chapter 1 of Publication 550.

Box 3 of Form 1099-INT shows the amount of interest income you received from U.S. savings bonds, Treasury bills, Treasury notes, and Treasury bonds. Add the amount shown in box 3 to any other taxable interest income you received, unless part of the

☐ CORRECTED (if checked)

PAYER'S name, street address, city, state, ZIP code, and telephone no.	Payer's RTN (optional)	OMB No. 1545-0112	
		20**05**	**Interest Income**
		Form **1099-INT**	

PAYER'S Federal identification number	RECIPIENT'S identification number	1 Interest income not included in box 3 $	**Copy B** **For Recipient**
RECIPIENT'S name		2 Early withdrawal penalty $	3 Interest on U.S. Savings Bonds and Treas. obligations $	This is important tax information and is being furnished to the Internal Revenue Service. If you are required to file a return, a negligence penalty or other sanction may be imposed on you if this income is taxable and the IRS determines that it has not been reported.
Street address (including apt. no.)		**4 Federal income tax withheld** $	5 Investment expenses $	
City, state, and ZIP code		6 Foreign tax paid	7 Foreign country or U.S. possession	
Account number (see instructions)		$		

Form **1099-INT**   (keep for your records)   Department of the Treasury - Internal Revenue Service

amount in box 3 was previously included in interest income. If part of the amount shown in box 3 was previously included in your interest income, see *U.S. savings bond interest previously reported*, later.

Box 4 of Form 1099-INT (federal income tax withheld) will contain an amount if you were subject to backup withholding. Report the amount from box 4 on Form 1040EZ, line 7, on Form 1040A, line 39, or on Form 1040, line 64 (federal income tax withheld).

Box 5 of Form 1099-INT shows investment expenses you may be able to deduct as an itemized deduction. See chapter 3 of Publication 550 for more information about investment expenses.

U.S. savings bond interest previously reported. If you received a Form 1099-INT for U.S. savings bond interest, the form may show interest you do not have to report. See *Form 1099-INT for U.S. savings bonds interest*, earlier, under *U.S. Savings Bonds*.

On Schedule B (Form 1040), Part I, line 1, or on Schedule 1 (Form 1040A), Part I, line 1, report all the interest shown on your Form 1099-INT. Then follow these steps.

1. Several lines above line 2, enter a subtotal of all interest listed on line 1.
2. Below the subtotal enter "U.S. Savings Bond Interest Previously Reported" and enter amounts previously reported or interest accrued before you received the bond.
3. Subtract these amounts from the subtotal and enter the result on line 2.

More information. For more information about how to report interest income, see chapter 1 of Publication 550 or the instructions for the form you must file.

Dividends and Other Corporate Distributions

Note: The 2004 IRS Publication 17 (Your Federal Income Tax) has been updated by Ernst & Young LLP for 2005. Dates and dollar amounts shown are for 2005. Gray type is used to indicate where IRS text has been updated or intentionally omitted. Unrevised IRS text is shown in black type.

Introduction

*Most people think they know what **dividends** are. The problem is that the term is commonly used to describe a large number of items that the **IRS** does not consider to be dividends. "Dividends" paid by an insurance company to its policyholders are considered by the IRS to be a return of premiums, not dividends. "Dividends" paid by a savings and loan association to its depositors are considered to be interest, not dividends.*

*So what is a dividend? A **dividend** is a share of a corporation's profits that is distributed to shareholders. This chapter discusses how these distributions as well as other corporate distributions are taxed.*

*If you own stock in a company or shares in a **mutual fund** or **real estate investment trust (REIT)**, you may*

receive dividend distributions. The distributing company or mutual fund will send you a Form 1099-DIV at the end of the year with the total amount of dividends that you must report to the IRS on your income tax return. This chapter explains the difference between the various tax forms you may receive and which forms to keep in your records or attach to your income tax return.

*This chapter also discusses **dividend reinvestment plans (DRIPs)** that reinvest the dividends in the stock generating them. These plans are provided by companies for all their shareholders and should not be confused with retirement plans run by employers for the benefit of their employees.*

Reminder

Foreign income. If you are a U.S. citizen with dividend income from sources outside the United States (foreign income), you must report that income on your tax return unless it is exempt by U.S. law. This is true whether you reside inside or outside the United States and whether or not you receive a Form 1099 from the foreign payer.

TAXSAVER

Foreign dividends. Foreign governments often withhold tax on dividends from foreign corporations before you receive them. For example, if you are a stockholder in a Canadian company that declares a $100 dividend, you might receive only $85 because of a $15 Canadian

withholding tax. Nevertheless, the $100 must be reported on your U.S. income tax return. The $15 of foreign taxes may be claimed either as a foreign tax credit using Form 1116 or as an itemized deduction on Schedule A (Form 1040). It is generally preferable to take the tax credit. For more on this subject, see Chapter 24, *Taxes You May Deduct.*

TAXSAVER

Individuals with $300 or less of foreign taxes paid ($600 for joint filers) are able to take a foreign tax credit for that entire amount. This is an exemption from the limitation of offsetting foreign tax credits against U.S. tax liability. The exemption must be elected each year and is only available if all foreign source income is qualified passive income.

Example

You are a single individual who invests in a mutual fund that holds foreign securities. During 2005, your share of foreign taxes paid by this mutual fund is $250. When you prepare your 2005 tax return, you can claim an exemption from the foreign tax credit limitation and credit the full $250 against your U.S. tax liability.

TaxAlert

Dividends paid on foreign corporation stocks that are readily tradable on U.S. securities markets are eligible for the lower rates. For this purpose, a share will be treated as so traded if an American Depository Receipt (ADR) backed by such share is readily tradable on an established securities market in the United States. Moreover, dividends from corporations incorporated in a U.S. possession or eligible for benefits under a comprehensive income tax treaty with the United States are generally eligible for the lower rate. Dividends paid by foreign personal holding companies, foreign investment companies, and passive foreign investment companies do not qualify for the reduced tax rates.

TaxAlert

Dividends received by an individual shareholder from domestic corporations and "qualified foreign corporations" are treated as net capital gain for purposes of applying the capital gain tax rates for both the regular tax and the alternative minimum tax. Thus, dividends are taxed at a maximum rate of 15%. Taxpayers with income in lower brackets are taxed at 5%.

This reduced tax rate only applies to dividends from common shares held for more than 60 days during the 121-day period beginning 60 days before the ex-dividend period. (The ex-dividend date is the date that determines whether the seller, rather than the buyer, receives the announced dividend.) Hence, this provision combined with the 15% top rate on long-term capital gains makes short-term investing less tax-efficient.

Example

You purchase dividend-paying common stock on February 1 and sell it November 1. The company declares dividends on March 31, June 30, and September 30. The lower tax rates apply to all dividends because you held the stock for more than 60 days out of the 121-day period that began 60 days in advance of each ex-dividend date. If you purchase stock on March 1 and sell it on April 15, a March 31 dividend would *not* qualify for the lower tax rates because you did not hold it for more than 60 days.

TaxAlert

You only need to attach Schedule B and report individual dividends if your total dividend income exceeds $1,500.

This chapter discusses the tax treatment of:

- Ordinary dividends,
- Capital gain distributions,
- Nondividend distributions, and

- Other distributions you may receive from a corporation or a mutual fund.

This chapter also explains how to report dividend income on your tax return.

Dividends are distributions of money, stock, or other property paid to you by a corporation. You also may receive dividends through a partnership, an estate, a trust, or an association that is taxed as a corporation. However, some amounts you receive that are called dividends are actually interest income. (See *Dividends that are actually interest* under *Taxable Interest* in chapter 8.)

Explanation

There are generally two different types of corporations: S corporations and C corporations. The treatment of distributions from S corporations to shareholders differs from that of C corporations to their shareholders.

In this chapter, the IRS is referring to C corporations only, because S corporations do not technically pay dividends. See Chapter 13, *Other Income,* for information on distributions from S corporations.

Most distributions are paid in cash (or check). However, distributions can consist of more stock, stock rights, other property, or services.

Explanation

Any distribution to a shareholder from earnings and profits is generally a dividend. However, a distribution is not a taxable dividend if it is a return of capital to the shareholder. Most distributions are in the form of money, but they may also be in stock or other property.

An interest-free loan or below-market rate loan by a corporation to a stockholder *may* result in taxable dividend income to the stockholder.

Additionally, if you are a stockholder who uses company property for personal use, you are considered to be in **constructive receipt** of a dividend that will be taxable to you and disallowed as a tax deduction to the company. The value of a constructive dividend is the fair market value of the benefit provided to the shareholder.

Example 1

A shareholder's use of a condominium maintained by his solely owned corporation resulted in his receipt of constructive dividends because he maintained the unit as his residence. The taxpayer benefited from the corporation's payments because he did not have to pay any housing costs. The Tax Court determined the portion of the condominium expenses that was allocable to business use and permitted the corporation to deduct that amount. The balance of the expenses was treated as constructive dividends received by the shareholder.

Example 2

A corporation sold real property to its sole shareholder at a price that was lower than the property's fair market value. The result is a constructive dividend to the shareholder of the difference between the fair market value and the purchase price and gain to the corporation.

TaxPlanner

All personal loans from corporations should have written documentation and charge market interest rates. If the corporation does not charge appropriate interest on the personal loans, and if the corporation has sufficient earnings and profits, the unpaid interest will be treated as a constructive dividend of ordinary income to the borrower (individual taxpayer). Failure to correctly report this transaction may subject the borrower to penalties and interest on the underpaid tax.

Useful Items

You may want to see:

Publications

☐ **514** Foreign Tax Credit for Individuals
☐ **550** Investment Income and Expenses
☐ **564** Mutual Fund Distributions

Forms (and Instructions)

☐ **Schedule B (Form 1040)** Interest and Ordinary Dividends
☐ **Schedule 1 (Form 1040A)** Interest and Ordinary Dividends for Form 1040A Filers

TAXORGANIZER

Records you should keep. The following is a list of records that you should keep to substantiate your dividend figures in the event of an IRS or state examination. Generally, we recommend that you retain these records for at least 6 years. However, you should keep records related to dividend reinvestment programs for 6 years after you fully exit the program.

1099-DIV, Dividends and Distributions
Dividend Reinvestment Plan Records
Form 2439, Notice to Shareholders of Undistributed Long-Term Capital Gains
1099s with backup withholding for attachment to your tax return
Form 1096, Annual Summary and Transmittal of U.S. Information Returns
Schedule K-1 (Form 1041), Beneficiary's Share of Income, Deductions, Credits, etc.
Schedule K-1 (Form 1065), Partner's Share of Income, Credits, Deductions, etc.
Schedule K-1 (Form 1120S), Shareholder's Share of Income, Credits, Deductions, etc.

General Information

This section discusses general rules for dividend income.
Tax on investment income of a child under age 14. Part of a child's 2005 investment income may be taxed at the parent's tax rate. This may happen if all of the following are true.

1. The child was under age 14 at the end of 2005. A child born on January 1, 1992, is considered to be age 14 at the end of 2005.
2. The child had more than $1,600 of investment income (such as taxable interest and dividends) and has to file a tax return.
3. At least one of the child's parents was alive at the end of 2005.

If all of these statements are true, Form 8615, Tax for Children Under Age 14 With Investment Income of More Than $1,600, must be completed and attached to the child's tax return. If any of these statements is not true, Form 8615 is not required and the child's income is taxed at his or her own tax rate.

However, the parent can choose to include the child's interest and dividends on the parent's return if certain requirements are met. Use Form 8814, Parents' Election To Report Child's Interest and Dividends, for this purpose.

For more information about the tax on investment income of children and the parents' election, see chapter 33.

Explanation
A parent may elect on Form 8814 to include on his or her return the unearned income of a child under the age of 14 whose income is less than $8,000 and consists solely of interest, dividends, or Alaska Permanent Fund dividends. The election cannot be made if estimated payments were made in your child's name, if your child had an overpayment on his or her 2004 tax return which was applied to 2005, or if your child is subject to backup withholding. (See explanation of backup withholding below.) The election must be made by the due date (including extensions) of the parent's tax return. A separate election must be made for each child whose income the parents choose to report.

On Form 8814, if a child (under age 14) had income over $1,600, it would be taxed as follows: The first $800 would be tax free, the next $800 would be taxed at 10% (5% for dividends), and the amount of income over $1,600 would be taxed at the parents' tax bracket. Note that the same overall tax result is achieved if the election is not made and the child files his or her own tax return. However, the child is required to attach Form 8615 to his or her return, which can be complicated if there is more than one child under age 14 required to file a return.

Beneficiary of an estate or trust. Dividends and other distributions you receive as a beneficiary of an estate or trust are generally taxable income. You should receive a Schedule K-1 (Form 1041), Beneficiary's Share of Income, Deductions, Credits, etc., from the fiduciary. Your copy of Schedule K-1 and its instructions will tell you where to report the income on your Form 1040.

Explanation
In addition to dividends that may be reported on Schedule K-1 (Form 1041) for beneficiaries of estates and trusts, dividends may also be reported to you on a Schedule K-1 (Form 1065) if you are a partner in a partnership or a Schedule K-1 (Form 1120S) if you are a shareholder in an S corporation. Generally, dividends reported on a Schedule K-1 should be entered on Schedule B, Part II, line 5 of Form 1040.

Social security number (SSN). You must give your name and SSN (or individual taxpayer identification number (ITIN)) to any person required by federal tax law to make a return, statement, or other document that relates to you. This includes payers of dividends. If you do not give your SSN or ITIN to the payer of dividends, you may have to pay a penalty.

For more information on SSNs and ITINs, see *Social security number (SSN)* in chapter 8.
Backup withholding. Your dividend income is generally not subject to regular withholding. However, it may be subject to backup

withholding to ensure that income tax is collected on the income. Under backup withholding, the payer of dividends must withhold, as income tax, a percentage of the amount you are paid. For 2006, this percentage is 28%.

Backup withholding may also be required if the Internal Revenue Service (IRS) has determined that you underreported your interest or dividend income. For more information, see *Backup Withholding* in chapter 5.

Stock certificate in two or more names. If two or more persons hold stock as joint tenants, tenants by the entirety, or tenants in common, each person may receive a share of any dividends from the stock. Each person's share is determined by local law.

Explanation
There are many technical problems if stock is jointly registered in two or more names. You should not assume that any income earned is earned jointly. Rather, in cases where no immediate gift transfer of the property is intended, the income should be reported by the owner of the property producing the income. (See *Joint Accounts* in Chapter 8, *Interest Income,* for a complete discussion of this matter.)

TaxPlanner
Because only one recipient's Social Security Number will be recorded by the corporation paying the dividend, the IRS's document-matching program may issue deficiency notices when the income is split between two or more individuals' returns. This situation arises because the income tax return with the Social Security Number shown on the company's records may not include the full amount of the dividend paid.

To reduce the chance of receiving an IRS deficiency notice, show both the full amount of the dividend paid and a subtraction for "amount attributable to others" on Schedule B (Form 1040) in the section used for reporting dividends.

The person who receives the other part of the dividend need not worry. Although that person includes on his or her return an amount for which he or she does not receive a Form 1099-DIV, the IRS rarely questions returns when income in excess of that computed by the government is reported. (See the discussion regarding *Nominees* later in this chapter and *Joint Accounts* in Chapter 8, *Interest Income,* for a further discussion of this matter.)

Form 1099-DIV. Most corporations use Form 1099-DIV, Dividends and Distributions, to show you the distributions you received from them during the year. Keep this form with your records. You do not have to attach it to your tax return.

Dividends not reported on Form 1099-DIV. Even if you do not receive Form 1099-DIV, you must still report all of your taxable dividend income. For example, you may receive distributive shares of dividends from partnerships or subchapter S corporations. These dividends are reported to you on Schedule K-1 (Form 1065) and Schedule K-1 (Form 1120S).

Explanation
The Form 1099 that you receive must be examined carefully. If you receive a Form 1099-DIV, you have received dividends during the year on stock you own. If you receive a Form 1099-INT, you have received interest on a savings account.

TaxOrganizer
While you are not required to attach Form 1099-DIV to your return, it is a good idea to do so if it indicates that you had federal tax withheld from the dividend payment. The amount of federal income tax withheld will be shown in box 4 of Form 1099-DIV. Attaching the form will provide the IRS with a complete picture of how the total amount of your federal income tax withheld was calculated.

Reporting tax withheld. If tax is withheld from your dividend income, the payer must give you a Form 1099-DIV that indicates the amount withheld.

Nominees. If someone receives distributions as a nominee for you, that person will give you a Form 1099-DIV, which will show distributions received on your behalf.

Explanation
A nominee is someone who, in his or her name and with his or her Social Security or federal identification number, receives income that belongs to another person. Form 1099 is used by the nominee to report the amount and type of income received on behalf of the owner.

If you receive a Form 1099 from a nominee, you should cite the source of that income on your tax return as the nominee, not the original payer of the income. If you receive a Form 1099 as a nominee for another person, see the section on nominees under *How to Report Dividend Income,* toward the end of this chapter, for a complete discussion on the filing and reporting requirements of a nominee.

Example
Brokerage Firm A collects your dividend from XYZ Corporation and reports the income to you on Form 1099. You should show the dividend as being received from Brokerage Firm A, *not* from XYZ Corporation.

Form 1099-MISC. Certain substitute payments in lieu of dividends or tax-exempt interest that are received by a broker on your behalf must be reported to you on Form 1099-MISC, Miscellaneous Income, or a similar statement. See *Reporting Substitute Payments* under *Short Sales* in chapter 4 of Publication 550 for more information about reporting these payments.

Incorrect amount shown on a Form 1099. If you receive a Form 1099 that shows an incorrect amount (or other incorrect information), you should ask the issuer for a corrected form. The new Form 1099 you receive will be marked "Corrected."

Dividends on stock sold. If stock is sold, exchanged, or otherwise disposed of after a dividend is declared, but before it is paid, the owner of record (usually the payee shown on the dividend check) must include the dividend in income.

TaxAlert
If stock is sold, exchanged, or otherwise disposed of after a dividend is declared, but before it is paid, the owner of record (usually the payee shown on the dividend check) must report the dividend. Even if the purchase price of the stock goes up because of the amount of the anticipated dividend, the owner of record must report the dividend.

Explanation

Dividends on stock sold. The owner of record on the "record date" for the dividend receives the dividend, not the owner on the date of payment.

The following timeline illustrates when you are entitled to receive dividend payments:

Declaration Date	Ex-Dividend Date	Record Date	Payment Date
The company decides to pay a dividend at some point in the future.	On or after this date, the stock trades without its dividend. If you sell your stock prior to this date, the new owner will generally receive the dividend; if you sell on or after this date, you will generally receive the dividend.	The owner as of the record date is entitled to the declared dividend.	The owner as of the record date receives payment of the dividend *whether or not* he or she still still owns the stock.

TAXPLANNER

If you buy stock on or near the date a dividend is declared, make sure you receive all amounts due. The transaction of the sale may not be recorded in time by the corporation paying the dividend, and the former stock owner may receive payment. If you do not receive a dividend due to you, check with your broker as soon as possible.

If you receive a dividend to which you were not entitled in one year and pay it back in another, it is counted as income in the year received and a deduction in the year repaid. Show the deduction as a negative amount of dividend income on Schedule B (Form 1040). If the repayment is greater than $3,000, however, you may save taxes by recomputing your tax for the prior year and amending your prior year's tax return. Consult your tax advisor.

Dividends received in January. If a regulated investment company (mutual fund) or real estate investment trust (REIT) declares a dividend (including any exempt-interest dividend or capital gain distribution) in October, November, or December payable to shareholders of record on a date in one of those months but actually pays the dividend during January of the next calendar year, you are considered to have received the dividend on December 31. You report the dividend in the year it was declared.

TAXSAVER

You should pay close attention to the timing of your purchase of a mutual fund. For example, if you invest in a fund near the end of the year and the fund shortly thereafter makes a year-end distribution, you will have to pay tax on the distribution even though from your point of view you are simply getting back the capital you just invested in the fund. In effect, all you've done is "bought" taxable income that the fund earned earlier in the year but had not yet paid out to shareholders. Typically, the fund's share price drops by the amount of the distribution. However, your cost basis in the mutual fund will be the predistribution price you paid for the shares.

There is one consolation: Your higher basis will reduce any capital gain on a later sale, or if you sell the fund at a loss, it will increase your capital loss. If you want to limit your tax liability and lower your basis in the shares, you should delay your purchase of fund shares until after the record date for the distribution. Usually a fund can tell you when distributions, if any, for the year are expected. Alternatively, you can consult investment publications, which indicate distribution dates for the previous year. They are usually a pretty good guide to future distribution dates.

Example

ABC Fund declares and distributes a $1 dividend on December 1. If you purchased 1,000 shares at $10 per share on November 30, you will have to report $1,000 of income for 2005. If you bought the shares on December 2, after the record date, you will pay $9 per share and have no taxable income to report. Of course, for the shares bought on November 30, your basis would be $10 per share instead of $9.

TAXPLANNER

If you are thinking of selling shares in a mutual fund, particularly near the end of the year when many funds pay dividends, you should consider redeeming your shares before any upcoming dividend payments are made by the fund. If your shares are worth more than you paid, you can maximize your capital gains on the redemption and avoid paying the higher tax rate due if the dividend is not a qualified dividend. (A dividend generally will qualify for the 15% reduced tax rate if you own the underlying common stock for more than 60 days during the 121-day period beginning 60 days before the "ex-dividend date," the day on which the stock starts trading without its next dividend.) If your shares are worth less than you paid for them, you can minimize your capital losses by selling before the dividend. Remember, the net asset value per share of the fund (that is, the amount you would receive on the redemption of your shares) decreases by the amount of the dividend. For more about mutual funds, see Chapter 40, *Mutual Funds*.

Ordinary Dividends

Ordinary (taxable) dividends are the most common type of distribution from a corporation. They are paid out of the earnings and profits of a corporation and are ordinary income to you. This means they are not capital gains. You can assume that any dividend you receive on common or preferred stock is an ordinary dividend unless the paying corporation tells you otherwise. Ordinary dividends will be shown in box 1a of the Form 1099-DIV you receive.

Qualified Dividends

Qualified dividends are the ordinary dividends that are subject to the same 5% or 15% maximum tax rate that applies to net capital gain. They should be shown in box 1b of Form 1099-DIV you receive.

Qualified dividends are subject to the 15% rate if the regular tax rate that would apply is 25% or higher. If the regular tax rate that would apply is lower than 25%, qualified dividends are subject to the 5% rate.

To qualify for the 5% or 15% maximum rate, all of the following requirements must be met.

1. The dividends must have been paid by a U.S. corporation or a qualified foreign corporation. (See *Qualified foreign corporation* later.)
2. The dividends are not of the type listed later under *Dividends that are not qualified dividends.*
3. You meet the holding period (discussed next).

Holding period. You must have held the stock for more than 60 days during the 121-day period that begins 60 days before the ex-dividend date. The ex-dividend date is the first date following the declaration of a dividend on which the buyer of a stock will not receive the next dividend payment. Instead, the seller will get the dividend.

When counting the number of days you held the stock, include the day you disposed the stock, but not the day you acquired it. See the examples later.

Exception for preferred stock. In the case of preferred stock, you must have held the stock more than 90 days during the 181-day period that begins 90 days before the ex-dividend date if the dividends are attributable to periods totaling more than 366 days. If the preferred dividends are attributable to periods totaling less than 367 days, the holding period in the previous paragraph applies.

Example 1. You bought 5,000 shares of XYZ Corp. common stock on July 1, 2005. XYZ Corp. paid a cash dividend of 10 cents per share. The ex-dividend date was July 9, 2005. Your Form 1099-DIV from XYZ Corp. shows $500 in box 1a (ordinary dividends) and in box 1b (qualified dividends). However, you sold the 5,000 shares on August 4, 2005. You held your shares of XYZ Corp. for only 34 days of the 121-day period (from July 2, 2005, through August 4, 2005). The 121-day period began on May 10, 2005 (60 days before the ex-dividend date), and ended on September 7, 2005. You have no qualified dividends from XYZ Corp. because you did not hold the XYZ stock for more than 60 days.

Example 2. Assume the same facts as in Example 1 except that you bought the stock on July 8, 2005 (the day before the ex-dividend date), and you sold the stock on September 9, 2005. You held the stock for 63 days (from July 9, 2005, through September 9, 2005). The $500 of qualified dividends shown in box 1b of your Form 1099-DIV are all qualified dividends because you held the stock for 61 days of the 121-day period (from July 9, 2005, through September 7, 2005).

Example 3. You bought 10,000 shares of ABC Mutual Fund common stock on July 1, 2005. ABC Mutual Fund paid a cash dividend of 10 cents a share. The ex-dividend date was July 9, 2005. The ABC Mutual Fund advises you that the portion of the dividend eligible to be treated as qualified dividends equals 2 cents per share. Your Form 1099-DIV from ABC Mutual Fund shows total ordinary dividends of $1,000 and qualified dividends of $200. However, you sold the 10,000 shares on August 4, 2005. You have no qualified dividends from ABC Mutual Fund because you did not hold the ABC Mutual Fund stock for more than 60 days.

Holding period reduced where risk of loss is diminished. When determining whether you met the minimum holding period discussed earlier, you cannot count any day during which you meet any of the following conditions.

1. You had an option to sell, were under a contractual obligation to sell, or had made (and not closed) a short sale of substantially identical stock or securities.
2. You were grantor (writer) of an option to buy substantially identical stock or securities.
3. Your risk of loss is diminished by holding one or more other positions in substantially similar or related property.

For information about how to apply condition (3), see Regulations section 1.246-5.

Qualified foreign corporation. A foreign corporation is a qualified foreign corporation if it meets any of the following conditions.

1. The corporation is incorporated in a U.S. possession.

2. The corporation is eligible for the benefits of a comprehensive income tax treaty with the United States that the Treasury Department determines is satisfactory for this purpose and that includes an exchange of information program. For a list of those treaties, see *Table 9-1.*
3. The corporation does not meet (1) or (2) above, but the stock for which the dividend is paid is readily tradable on an established securities market in the United States. See *Readily tradable stock,* later.

Exception. A corporation is not a qualified foreign corporation if it is a foreign personal holding company, foreign investment company, or a passive foreign investment company during its tax year in which the dividends are paid or during its previous tax year.

Readily tradable stock. Any stock (such as common, ordinary stock, or preferred stock) or an American depositary receipt in respect of that stock, is considered to satisfy requirement (3) if it is listed on one of the following securities markets: the New York Stock Exchange, the NASDAQ Stock Market, the American Stock Exchange, the Boston Stock Exchange, the Cincinnati Stock Exchange, the Chicago Stock Exchange, the Philadelphia Stock Exchange, or the Pacific Exchange.

Dividends that are not qualified dividends. The following dividends are not qualified dividends. They are not qualified dividends even if they are shown in box 1b of Form 1099-DIV.

- Capital gain distributions.
- Dividends paid on deposits with mutual savings banks, cooperative banks, credit unions, U.S. building and loan associations, U.S. savings and loan associations, federal savings and loan associations, and similar financial institutions. (Report these amounts as interest income.)
- Dividends from a corporation that is a tax-exempt organization or farmer's cooperative during the corporation's tax year in which the dividends were paid or during the corporation's previous tax year.
- Dividends paid by a corporation on employer securities which are held on the date of record by an employee stock ownership plan (ESOP) maintained by that corporation.
- Dividends on any share of stock to the extent that you are obligated (whether under a short sale or otherwise) to make related

Table 9-1. **Income Tax Treaties**

Income tax treaties that the United States has with the following countries satisfy requirement (2) under *Qualified foreign corporation.*

Australia	Ireland	Romania
Austria	Israel	Russian
Belgium	Italy	Federation
Canada	Jamaica	Slovak
China	Japan	Republic
Cyprus	Kazakhstan	Slovenia
Czech	Korea	South Africa
Republic	Latvia	Spain
Denmark	Lithuania	Sweden
Egypt	Luxembourg	Switzerland
Estonia	Mexico	Thailand
Finland	Morocco	Trinidad and
France	Netherlands	Tobago
Germany	New Zealand	Tunisia
Greece	Norway	Turkey
Hungary	Pakistan	Ukraine
Iceland	Philippines	United
India	Poland	Kingdom
Indonesia	Portugal	Venezuela

payments for positions in substantially similar or related property.

- Payments in lieu of dividends, but only if you know or have reason to know that the payments are not qualified dividends.
- Payments shown in Form 1099-DIV, box 1b, from a foreign corporation to the extent you know or have reason to know the payments are not qualified dividends.

Dividends Used to Buy More Stock

The corporation in which you own stock may have a **_dividend reinvestment plan._** This plan lets you choose to use your dividends to buy (through an agent) more shares of stock in the corporation instead of receiving the dividends in cash. If you are a member of this type of plan and you use your dividends to buy more stock at a price equal to its fair market value, you still must report the dividends as income.

Explanation
Many large publicly held companies allow stockholders to use their dividends to buy more shares of stock *directly* from the company. This type of program eliminates the need to use or pay commissions to an agent or broker. You should keep this cost savings in mind when considering a particular dividend reinvestment plan.

If you are a member of a dividend reinvestment plan that lets you buy more stock at a price less than its fair market value, you must report as dividend income the fair market value of the additional stock on the dividend payment date.

You also must report as dividend income any service charge subtracted from your cash dividends before the dividends are used to buy the additional stock. But you may be able to deduct the service charge. See chapter 30 for more information about deducting expenses of producing income.

In some dividend reinvestment plans, you can invest more cash to buy shares of stock at a price less than fair market value. If you choose to do this, you must report as dividend income the difference between the cash you invest and the fair market value of the stock you buy. When figuring this amount, use the fair market value of the stock on the dividend payment date.

Explanation
Dividend reinvestment plans (often called **DRIPs**)—even those in which employees may make voluntary contributions—should not be confused with retirement plans that invest in company stock. DRIPs are open to all stockholders, not just employees. Dividends are immediately reinvested to buy more shares of that company's stock. DRIPs are also subject to income taxes annually, whereas income in employee retirement plans is typically tax deferred.

DRIPs may cause confusion because some plans permit you to reinvest in shares at a discount, usually about 5%. The discount is included in the amount of dividend taxable to you.

Example
Stock of Company X is selling for $10. You are entitled to $20 in dividends on the stock you hold. Because you are in a DRIP that includes a 5% discount, your dividends will buy 2.105 shares of stock. You will report $21.05 of dividend income.

TaxALERT
The IRS has privately ruled that shareholders who purchase stock solely through a cash purchase plan will *not* be treated as having received a distribution of the discount amount. However, if the shareholders participate in both a DRIP *and* the cash purchase aspects of the plan, they will be treated as having received a taxable distribution of the discount amount of the stock.

TaxPLANNER
Unless you're very careful, you're likely to get an IRS deficiency notice when you take advantage of a dividend reinvestment plan if you hold the shares that are producing the dividends. Problems can occur if you receive two Forms 1099. One will report the dividends paid on shares you hold. The other Form 1099 will report the discount and the dividends paid on the shares held in the plan. Be sure to reconcile the amounts and report the correct total.

Any service charge paid on a dividend reinvestment plan may be taken as an **itemized deduction** on Schedule A of Form 1040 (subject to the 2% of adjusted gross income limitation explained in Chapter 30, *Miscellaneous Deductions*). You should *not* offset your dividend income with the service charge. If you do, you may receive a notice from the IRS.

TaxPLANNER
When you sell shares acquired in a dividend reinvestment plan, you compute the gain or loss in the same way that you normally would by subtracting your cost from the proceeds of the sale. Your cost includes the amount of dividends that have been reinvested. Usually your only record of the shares' cost is the annual statement issued by the administrator of the dividend reinvestment plan. It is imperative to keep these statements as a permanent part of your records. If you don't have this information, you can contact the transfer agent who handles the company's dividend reinvestment plan. You can obtain the name from the company's investor relations office. However, some dividend reinvestment plans charge a fee for re-creating records. Alternatively, you can look up a company's dividend history in Standard & Poor's.

Example
You have accumulated 14 shares of ABC Mutual Fund through a purchase and dividend reinvestments.

Method	Shares	Cost Basis	Date
Purchase	10 shares	$100	6/1/02
Dividend Reinvestments	1 share	$10	12/31/03
	1 share	$15	12/31/04
	2 shares	$25	12/30/05
	14 shares	$150	

If you sold all 14 shares in 2005 for $15 per share, your gain would be $60 ($210 proceeds less $150 basis). Without proof of your dividend reinvestments, however, the IRS could argue that your basis was only the original $100 and your gain was actually $110 ($210 proceeds less $100 cost of original purchase).

Note that a portion of your $60 gain would be long-term, but the gain attributable to the 2 shares purchased on December 30, 2005, through the DRIP would be short-term, because you would not have owned these shares for more than 12 months. The short-term gain would be $5 of the total gain ($30 proceeds on 2 shares less $25 cost).

See Chapter 17, *Reporting Gains and Losses,* to determine how to calculate your gain or loss if you did not sell *all* 14 shares of ABC Mutual Fund at once.

TaxSaver

Dividend reinvestment plans that permit you to invest at less than market price (e.g., whether by discount or reduction in commissions on purchase) may be a very good deal. In effect, you earn a higher yield because you are receiving "extra" shares.

Money Market Funds

Report amounts you receive from money market funds as dividend income. Money market funds are a type of mutual fund and should not be confused with bank money market accounts that pay interest.

TaxPlanner

Dividends paid from money market funds are reported as *dividends*—not interest—even though they represent income the money market fund received on certificates of deposit and other interest-bearing investments. Dividends from money market funds are not eligible for the lower dividend rate. These dividends *must* be shown in the dividend section of Schedule B (Form 1040). If they are not, you're likely to receive a notice from the IRS requesting an explanation.

However, dividends paid or credited by a mutual savings bank, building and loan association, savings and loan association, cooperative banks, or credit unions are considered *interest*—not dividends—for income tax reporting purposes. The Form 1099 that you receive from these organizations tells you which type of income to report and generally instructs you on how to report the income.

Capital Gain Distributions

Capital gain distributions (also called capital gain dividends) are paid to you or credited to your account by regulated investment companies (commonly called mutual funds) and real estate investment trusts (REITs). They will be shown in box 2a of the Form 1099-DIV you receive from the mutual fund or REIT.

Report capital gain distributions as long-term capital gains regardless of how long you owned your shares in the mutual fund or REIT.

Explanation
For 2005, capital gain distributions are reported on Schedule D, line 13. For more information, see Chapter 17, *Reporting Gains and Losses.*

TaxAlert

Although qualifying dividends are taxed at the same rate as capital gains, a taxpayer who has net capital losses and dividend income may not offset those losses against dividends. Net capital losses can be offset against capital gain distributions, however.

Undistributed capital gains of mutual funds and REITs. Some mutual funds and REITs keep their long-term capital gains and pay tax on them. You must treat your share of these gains as distributions, even though you did not actually receive them. However, they are not included on Form 1099-DIV. Instead, they are reported to you on Form 2439, Notice to Shareholder of Undistributed Long-Term Capital Gains.

Report undistributed capital gains shown in box 1a of Form 2439 as long-term capital gains on Schedule D (Form 1040), column (f), line 11. The tax paid on these gains by the mutual fund or REIT is shown in box 2 of Form 2439. You take credit for this tax by including it on Form 1040, line 70, and checking box a on that line. Attach Copy B of Form 2439 to your return, and keep Copy C for your records.

Basis adjustment. Increase your basis in your mutual fund, or your interest in a REIT, by the difference between the gain you report and the credit you claim for the tax paid.

Additional information. For more information on the treatment of distributions from mutual funds, see Publication 564.

Explanation
An investment company or mutual fund that realizes capital gains during the year has the option of whether or not to distribute the capital gains to shareholders of the mutual fund. The two different treatments are reported by shareholders as follows:

Distributed capital gains are reported to shareholders on Form 1099-DIV box 2a. You will receive this amount in cash and must include the entire amount of the distributed capital gains in your calculation of taxable income.

Undistributed capital gains are reported to shareholders on Form 2439. You will *not* receive this amount in cash. Rather, the mutual fund or real estate investment trust (REIT) has retained the capital gains and paid your proportionate share of the tax due. You will include the entire amount of the undistributed capital gains in your calculation of taxable income, but you will also be credited for the tax that the mutual fund paid on your behalf. In addition, you will increase your basis in the stock by the net amount not distributed to you.

Example 1
ABC Mutual Fund elects to distribute all of its 2005 capital gain. *Each shareholder will receive a pro rata share of the distribution in cash.* Each shareholder reports this distribution and pays the appropriate tax. The fund will provide each shareholder with Form 1099-DIV, which contains the amounts to be reported.

Example 2
ABC Mutual Fund elects to treat all of its 2005 capital gain as an undistributed capital gain. *The shareholders receive no cash distribution.* Each shareholder reports his or her share of capital gain and tax paid on his or her behalf by ABC Mutual Fund. These amounts are shown on the Form 2439 that each shareholder receives.

If your share of the capital gain is $1,200 and your share of the tax is $408, the $1,200 is included as capital gain income and the $408 is claimed as a credit on your individual return. Increase your basis in the stock by $792, the net amount not distributed to you ($1,200 less $408).

Explanation
You must report any undistributed gains shown on Form 2439 in addition to any capital gain distributions reported on Form 1099-DIV.

Nondividend Distributions

A nondividend distribution is a distribution that is not paid out of the earnings and profits of a corporation. You should receive a Form 1099-DIV or other statement from the corporation showing the nondividend distribution. On Form 1099-DIV, a nondividend distribution will be shown in box 3. If you do not receive such a statement, you report the distribution as an ordinary dividend.

Basis adjustment. A nondividend distribution reduces the basis of your stock. It is not taxed until your basis in the stock is fully recovered. This nontaxable portion is also called a return of capital. It is a return of your investment in the stock of the company. If you buy stock in a corporation in different lots at different times, and you cannot definitely identify the shares subject to the nondividend distribution, reduce the basis of your earliest purchases first.

When the basis of your stock has been reduced to zero, report any additional nondividend distribution that you receive as a capital gain. Whether you report it as a long-term or short-term capital gain depends on how long you have held the stock. See *Holding Period* in chapter 15.

Example. You bought stock in 1993 for $100. In 1996, you received a nondividend distribution of $80. You did not include this amount in your income, but you reduced the basis of your stock to $20. You received a nondividend distribution of $30 in 2005. The first $20 of this amount reduced your basis to zero. You report the other $10 as a long-term capital gain for 2005. You must report as a long-term capital gain any nondividend distribution you receive on this stock in later years.

Explanation
Some mutual fund dividends may be treated as a tax-free return of capital. This occurs when the mutual fund does not have enough current or accumulated earnings and profits to cover the distribution. In this situation, the distribution is considered to be a "return of capital" (the amount you originally invested) and is nontaxable to the extent of the basis in your shares. (Your basis is generally the price at which you bought the shares plus or minus any adjustments. See Chapter 14, *Basis of Property.*) This amount will be shown in box 3 of Form 1099-DIV.

Although the distribution is tax free, it will reduce your basis in the mutual fund shares. To the extent that the distribution is greater than your basis in your shares, you will be treated as having a gain from the sale or exchange of the shares. This gain must be reported on Schedule D (Form 1040). (See the IRS example directly preceding this explanation.)

TaxOrganizer

It is extremely important to keep accurate records of nontaxable dividends. Most people do not realize that a nontaxable dividend is usually considered a return of purchase price and then a capital gain once your cost

has been recovered. Keep in mind that even nontaxable dividends can become subject to tax at some point.

Liquidating Distributions

Liquidating distributions, sometimes called liquidating dividends, are distributions you receive during a partial or complete liquidation of a corporation. These distributions are, at least in part, one form of a return of capital. They may be paid in one or more installments. You will receive a Form 1099-DIV from the corporation showing you the amount of the liquidating distribution in box 8 or 9.

For more information on liquidating distributions, see chapter 1 of Publication 550.

TaxSaver

If the total liquidating distributions you receive are less than the basis of your stock, you may have a capital loss. You can report a capital loss only after you have received the final distribution in liquidation that results in the redemption or cancellation of the stock. Whether you report the loss as a long-term or short-term capital loss depends on how long you held the stock. See *Holding Period* in Chapter 15, *Sale of Property.*

Example
You own stock in XYZ Corporation with a basis of $100. You received liquidating distributions of $90: $60 in 2004 and $30 in 2005. You report the $10 loss in 2005.

Distributions of Stock and Stock Rights

Distributions by a corporation of its own stock are commonly known as stock dividends. Stock rights (also known as "stock options") are distributions by a corporation of rights to acquire the corporation's stock. Generally, stock dividends and stock rights are not taxable to you, and you do not report them on your return.

Taxable stock dividends and stock rights. Distributions of stock dividends and stock rights are taxable to you if any of the following apply.

1. You or any other shareholder has the choice to receive cash or other property instead of stock or stock rights.
2. The distribution gives cash or other property to some shareholders and an increase in the percentage interest in the corporation's assets or earnings and profits to other shareholders.
3. The distribution is in convertible preferred stock and has the same result as in (2).
4. The distribution gives preferred stock to some common stock shareholders and common stock to other common stock shareholders.
5. The distribution is on preferred stock. (The distribution, however, is not taxable if it is an increase in the conversion ratio of convertible preferred stock made solely to take into account a stock dividend, stock split, or similar event that would otherwise result in reducing the conversion right.)

Explanation
Any transaction having the effect of increasing your proportionate interest in a corporation's assets or earnings and profits may be taxable to you, even though no stock or stock rights are actually distributed.

A number of transactions have the effect of increasing your proportionate interest in a corporation—for example, a change in the conversion ratio on certain classes of stock or a change in the redemption price of certain securities. If such a transaction occurs, you will be informed by the corporation.

The term "stock" includes rights to acquire stock, and the term "shareholder" includes a holder of rights or of convertible securities.

If you receive taxable stock dividends or stock rights, include their fair market value at the time of the distribution in your income.

Example

ABC Company gives its shareholders the option of receiving a dividend as $10 cash or as stock (thus, the distribution will be taxable to *all* shareholders). On February 15, the date of distribution, the value of 1 share of stock is $5. A shareholder who chooses stock in lieu of cash will receive 2 additional shares of stock on February 15. This shareholder will be taxed on $10, the fair market value of the stock, even though no cash was received with which to pay the tax. A shareholder who chooses cash will also be taxed on $10, but this shareholder will have the cash in hand to pay the tax.

Preferred stock redeemable at a premium. If you hold preferred stock having a redemption price higher than its issue price, the difference (the redemption premium) generally is taxable as a constructive distribution of additional stock on the preferred stock. For more information, see chapter 1 of Publication 550.

Basis. Your basis in stock or stock rights received in a taxable distribution is their fair market value when distributed. If you receive stock or stock rights that are not taxable to you, see *Stocks and Bonds* under *Basis of Investment Property* in chapter 4 of Publication 550 for information on how to figure their basis.

Fractional shares. You may not own enough stock in a corporation to receive a full share of stock if the corporation declares a stock dividend. However, with the approval of the shareholders, the corporation may set up a plan in which fractional shares are not issued, but instead are sold, and the cash proceeds are given to the shareholders. Any cash you receive for fractional shares under such a plan is treated as an amount realized on the sale of the fractional shares. You must determine your gain or loss and report it as a capital gain or loss on Schedule D (Form 1040). Your gain or loss is the difference between the cash you receive and the basis of the fractional shares sold.

Example. You own one share of common stock that you bought on January 3, 1997, for $100. The corporation declared a common stock dividend of 5% on June 30, 2005. The fair market value of the stock at the time the stock dividend was declared was $200. You were paid $10 for the fractional-share stock dividend under a plan described in the above paragraph. You figure your gain or loss as follows:

Fair market value of old stock	$200.00
Fair market value of stock dividend (cash received)	+10.00
Fair market value of old stock and stock dividend	$210.00
Basis (cost) of old stock after the stock dividend (($200 ÷ $210) × $100)	$ 95.24
Basis (cost) of stock dividend (($10 ÷ $210) × $100)	+4.76
Total	$100.00
Cash received	$ 10.00
Basis (cost) of stock dividend	−4.76
Gain	$ 5.24

Because you had held the share of stock for more than 1 year at the time the stock dividend was declared, your gain on the stock dividend is a long-term capital gain.

Explanation

It is *not* true that all amounts received with regard to fractional shares are treated as capital gains, as described in the IRS text.

A distinction is made when shareholders have the *option* of receiving cash or other property instead of fractional shares. If shareholders have this option and receive cash in lieu of fractional shares, the value received is treated as dividend income. If the corporation issues cash in lieu of fractional shares of stock for the purpose of saving the trouble, expense, and inconvenience of issuing fractional shares, then the capital gain treatment described above applies. The transaction will be treated as though fractional shares had been received by the shareholders and were then redeemed by the corporation.

Scrip dividends. A corporation that declares a stock dividend may issue you a scrip certificate that entitles you to a fractional share. The certificate is generally nontaxable when you receive it. If you choose to have the corporation sell the certificate for you and give you the proceeds, your gain or loss is the difference between the proceeds and the portion of your basis in the corporation's stock that is allocated to the certificate.

However, if you receive a scrip certificate that you can choose to redeem for cash instead of stock, the certificate is taxable when you receive it. You must include its fair market value in income on the date you receive it.

Other Distributions

You may receive any of the following distributions during the year.

Exempt-interest dividends. Exempt-interest dividends you receive from a regulated investment company (mutual fund) are not included in your taxable income. You will receive a notice from the mutual fund telling you the amount of the exempt-interest dividends you received. Exempt-interest dividends are not shown on Form 1099-DIV or Form 1099-INT.

Explanation

Exempt-interest dividends are reported on line 8b of Form 1040 as tax-exempt interest. While exempt-interest dividends are exempt from federal income taxes, they may be considered an "add-back" for state and local tax purposes. This treatment depends on which state returns you are required to file. Generally, your state may require that you add back to federal adjusted gross income either all or some portion of the amount you entered on line 8b of your 1040. See your state income tax forms for guidance.

Information reporting requirement. Although exempt-interest dividends are not taxable, you must show them on your tax return if you have to file a return. This is an information-reporting requirement and does not change the exempt-interest dividends to taxable income.

Alternative minimum tax treatment. Exempt-interest dividends paid from specified private activity bonds may be subject to the alternative minimum tax. See *Alternative Minimum Tax* in chapter 32 for more information.

Dividends on insurance policies. Insurance policy dividends that

☐ CORRECTED (if checked)

PAYER'S name, street address, city, state, ZIP code, and telephone no.		**1a** Total ordinary dividends $	OMB No. 1545-0110	**Dividends and Distributions**
		1b Qualified dividends $	**20**05 Form **1099-DIV**	
		2a Total capital gain distr. $	**2b** Unrecap. Sec. 1250 gain $	**Copy B** **For Recipient**
PAYER'S Federal identification number	RECIPIENT'S identification number			
RECIPIENT'S name		**2c** Section 1202 gain $	**2d** Collectibles (28%) gain $	This is important tax information and is being furnished to the Internal Revenue Service. If you are required to file a return, a negligence penalty or other sanction may be imposed on you if this income is taxable and the IRS determines that it has not been reported.
		3 Nondividend distributions $	**4** **Federal income tax withheld** $	
Street address (including apt. no.)			**5** Investment expenses $	
City, state, and ZIP code		**6** Foreign tax paid $	**7** Foreign country or U.S. possession	
Account number (see instructions)		**8** Cash liquidation distributions $	**9** Noncash liquidation distributions $	

Form **1099-DIV**   (keep for your records)   Department of the Treasury - Internal Revenue Service

---

the insurer keeps and uses to pay your premiums are not taxable. However, you must report as taxable interest income the interest that is paid or credited on dividends left with the insurance company.

If dividends on an insurance contract (other than a modified endowment contract) are distributed to you, they are a partial return of the premiums you paid. Do not include them in your gross income until they are more than the total of all net premiums you paid for the contract. Report any taxable distributions on insurance policies on Form 1040, line 16b, or Form 1040A, line 12b.

Dividends on veterans' insurance. Dividends you receive on veterans' insurance policies are not taxable. In addition, interest on dividends left with the Department of Veterans Affairs is not taxable.

Patronage dividends. Generally, patronage dividends you receive in money from a cooperative organization are included in your income.

Do not include in your income patronage dividends you receive on:

1. Property bought for your personal use, or
2. Capital assets or depreciable property bought for use in your business. But you must reduce the basis (cost) of the items bought. If the dividend is more than the adjusted basis of the assets, you must report the excess as income.

These rules are the same whether the cooperative paying the dividend is a taxable or tax-exempt cooperative.

Explanation

Patronage dividends are amounts paid by a cooperative organization to one of its patrons (1) on the basis of the quantity or quality of business done with the patron, (2) pursuant to a written obligation in existence before the cooperative received the amounts paid into it by the patron, and (3) determined by reference to net

earnings. In other words, patronage dividends amount to a return of some of the amounts a patron spent with a cooperative. Patronage dividends usually occur with farm cooperatives. Any "refund" or "discount" to the patron is income.

However, if the purchase leading to receipt of the dividend was neither deductible nor considered a capital expense, the dividend really amounts to a discount or a rebate, which is not considered income.

Alaska Permanent Fund dividends. Do not report these amounts as dividends. Instead, report these amounts on Form 1040, line 21, Form 1040A, line 13, or Form 1040EZ, line 3.

TaxSaver

Dividends received on restricted stock. Restricted stock is stock that you get from your employer for services you perform and that is nontransferable and subject to a substantial risk of forfeiture. You do not have to include the value of the stock in your income when you receive it as restricted shares. However, if you get dividends on the restricted stock, you must include them in your income as wages, not dividends. At the time that the restrictions are lifted on the stock and you have full access to the stock, dividends are treated as taxable dividend income.

If you get both a 1099-DIV and a W-2, which includes the dividends on your restricted stock, it is important to report the taxable dividend amount only once on your tax return. To avoid notices generated from the IRS's document-matching program, statements must be included with your return to explain any discrepancies between the amounts reported by you and the amounts indicated on Form 1099-DIV or Form W-2.

TAXPLANNER

Election. You can choose to include in gross income the value of restricted stock as pay for services in the year you receive the stock. Consult with your tax advisor if you are considering this election. If you make this choice, the dividends are treated as any other dividends.

If you elect to include in gross income the value of the restricted stock you have received, you must notify your employer so that dividend payments on the stock are no longer included in your W-2 wages.

How To Report Dividend Income

Generally, you can use either Form 1040 or Form 1040A to report your dividend income. Report the total of your ordinary dividends on line 9a of Form 1040 or Form 1040A. Report qualified dividends on line 9b of that form.

If you receive capital gain distributions, you may be able to use Form 1040A or you may have to use Form 1040. See *Capital gain distributions only* in chapter 17. If you receive nondividend distributions required to be reported as capital gains, you must use Form 1040. You cannot use Form 1040EZ if you receive any dividend income.

Explanation
Use the following decision tree to determine which forms and schedules you may be required to file:

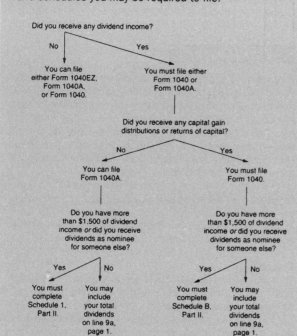

Form 1099-DIV. If you owned stock on which you received $10 or more in dividends and other distributions, you should receive a Form 1099-DIV. Even if you do not receive Form 1099-DIV, you must report all of your taxable dividend income.

See Form 1099-DIV for more information on how to report dividend income.

TAXORGANIZER

You should make sure you keep a copy of all Forms 1099-DIV that you received in the mail. See sample form on page 128.

Form 1040A. You must complete Schedule 1 (Form 1040A), Part II, and attach it to your Form 1040A, if:

1. Your ordinary dividends (Form 1099-DIV, box 1a) are more than $1,500, or
2. You received, as a nominee, ordinary dividends that actually belong to someone else.

List on line 5 each payer's name and the amount of ordinary dividends you received. If you received a Form 1099-DIV from a brokerage firm, list the brokerage firm as the payer.

Enter on line 6 the total of the amounts listed on line 5. Also enter this total on Form 1040A, line 9a.

Explanation
Exempt-interest dividends, which are treated as interest, should not be reported on Schedule 1 of Form 1040A. The amount should be included on line 8b of page 1. See *How to Report Interest Income* in Chapter 8, *Interest Income.*

Form 1040. You must fill in Schedule B, Part II, and attach it to your Form 1040, if:

1. Your ordinary dividends (box 1a of Form 1099-DIV) are more than $1,500, or
2. You received, as a nominee, ordinary dividends that actually belong to someone else.

Explanation
Even if your dividends are less than $1,500, you must report them and, to the extent that they are taxable, pay tax on them. The $1,500 test determines whether or not you must list each dividend payer separately on Schedule B. If your dividends total less than $1,500, you can include a single amount on line 9 of page 1 and avoid completing Schedule B, Part II.

If your ordinary dividends are more than $1,500, you must also complete Schedule B, Part III.

Explanation
Part III of Schedule B refers to a financial interest in a foreign bank, brokerage account, or trust. See the instructions for Schedule B or consult with your tax advisor for additional filing requirements, if applicable.

List on Schedule B, Part II, line 5, each payer's name and the amount of ordinary dividends you received. If your securities are held by a brokerage firm (in "street name"), list the name of the brokerage firm that is shown on Form 1099-DIV as the payer. If your stock is held by a nominee who is the owner of record, and the nominee credited or paid you dividends on the stock, show the name of the nominee and the dividends you received or for which you were credited.

If you receive a Form 1099-DIV that shows your taxpayer identification number and names two or more recipients, or includes amounts belonging to another person, you must file a Form 1099-DIV with the IRS to show the proper distributions of the amounts shown. Complete the form and a Form 1096, Annual Summary and Transmittal of U.S. Information Returns, and file both forms with your Internal Revenue Service Center. Give the other person Copy B of the Form 1099-DIV that you filed as a nominee. On the forms, you should be listed as the "Payer." On Form 1099-DIV, the other owner should be listed as the "Recipient." You are not required, however, to file a Form 1099-DIV to show payments for your spouse. For more information about the reporting requirements and the penalties for failure to file (or furnish) certain information returns, see the Instructions for Forms 1099, 1098, 5498, and W-2G.

Include on line 5 dividends you received, as a nominee, that actually belong to another person (such as your child), even if you later distributed some or all of this income to others. Enter a subtotal of all your dividend income listed on line 5 several lines above line 6. Below the subtotal, write "Nominee Distribution," and show the amounts received as a nominee. Subtract these distributions from the subtotal, and enter the result on line 6.

TAXPLANNER

The complexity of paperwork involved in serving as a nominee makes it clear that you should avoid doing so unless absolutely necessary. If you are a nominee and fail to file the appropriate returns, you could be penalized by the IRS.

Enter on line 6 the total of the amounts listed on line 5. Also enter this total on Form 1040, line 9a.

Qualified dividends. Report qualified dividends (Form 1099-DIV, box 1b) on line 9b of Form 1040 or Form 1040A. Do not include any of the following on line 9b.

- Qualified dividends you received as a nominee. See *Nominees* under *How to Report Dividend Income* in chapter 1 of Publication 550.
- Dividends on stock for which you did not meet the holding period. See *Holding period* earlier under *Qualified Dividends.*
- Dividends on any share of stock to the extent that you are obligated (whether under a short sale or otherwise) to make related payments for positions in substantially similar or related property.
- Payments in lieu of dividends, but only if you know or have reason to know that the payments are not qualified dividends.
- Payments shown in Form 1099-DIV, box 1b, from a foreign corporation to the extent you know or have reason to know the payments are not qualified dividends.

If you have qualified dividends, you must figure your tax by completing the Qualified Dividends and Capital Gain Tax Worksheet in the Form 1040 or 1040A instructions or the Schedule D Tax Worksheet in the Schedule D instructions, whichever applies. Enter qualified dividends on line 2 of the worksheet.

Investment interest deducted. If you claim a deduction for investment interest, you may have to reduce the amount of your qualified dividends that are eligible for the 5% or 15% tax rate. Reduce it by the amount of qualified dividends you choose to include in investment income when figuring the limit on your investment interest deduction. This is done on the Qualified Dividends and Capital Gain Tax Worksheet or the Schedule D Tax Worksheet. For more information about the limit on investment interest, see *Interest Expense* in chapter 25.

Expenses related to dividend income. You may be able to deduct expenses related to dividend income if you itemize your deductions on Schedule A (Form 1040). See chapter 30 for general information about deducting expenses of producing income.

Explanation

Expenses that may be deducted include custody fees, investment advisory fees, depository fees (which are usually applicable to foreign dividends), and service charges relating to dividend income. A more complete discussion of these items appears in Chapter 30, *Miscellaneous Deductions.*

Explanation

Stock sold short. If you borrow stock to make a short sale, you may have to pay the lender an amount to replace the dividends distributed while you maintain your short position. Your treatment of the payment depends on the kind of distribution for which you are reimbursing the lender of the stock.

TAXALERT

Owners whose shares are lent in short sales do not receive the lower capital gains rate on "payments in lieu of dividends," which are often called "substitute" dividends. Brokerages commonly lend stock held in margin accounts to short sellers, but may need to accommodate investors who do not want to receive the unfavorable dividend treatment. If this pertains to your investments, your Form 1099-DIV should indicate the status of your dividends.

See Chapter 15, *Sale of Property,* for an explanation of a short sale.

TAXPLANNER

If you borrow stock to make a short sale, and you pay the lender in lieu of the dividends distributed while you maintain your short position, you can deduct these payments provided you hold the short sale open at least 46 days (more than 1 year in the case of an extraordinary dividend as defined below), and you itemize your deductions. You deduct these expenses as investment interest on Schedule A (Form 1040).

If you close the short sale on or before the 45th day after the date of the short sale (1 year or less in the case of an extraordinary dividend), you cannot deduct the payments made. Instead you must increase the basis of the stock used to close the short sale by that amount.

Exception

The IRS allows a deduction for amounts you pay in place of dividends to the extent of ordinary income received from the lender of the stock for the use of collateral with the short sale. However, this special rule does not apply to payments in place of extraordinary dividends, discussed below.

Explanation

Extraordinary Dividends. If the amount of any dividend you receive on a share of preferred stock equals or exceeds 5% (10% in the case of other stock) of the amount realized on the short sale, the dividend you receive is an extraordinary dividend.

If your payment is made for a liquidating distribution or nontaxable stock distribution, or if you buy more shares equal to a stock distribution issued on the borrowed stock during your short position, you have a capital expense. You must add the payment to the cost of the stock sold short.

See *Short Sales* in Publication 550 for more information about the tax treatment of short sales.

If an individual receives an extraordinary dividend eligible for the capital gain rates with respect to any share of stock, any loss on the sale of the stock is treated as a long-term capital loss to the extent of the dividend. A dividend is treated as investment income for purposes of determining the amount of deductible investment interest only if the taxpayer elects to treat the dividend as not eligible for the capital gain rates.

Example

Ben feels that the market value of XYZ Corporation stock is going to decline, so he sells XYZ stock to Sally. However, Ben does not hold any XYZ stock, so to effect the transaction, Ben's broker borrows XYZ stock from another customer, Robert, to deliver to Sally. Sally is now the stockholder of record.

XYZ Corporation will pay any and all dividends on this stock directly to Sally. However, Robert is entitled to the money, because he merely lent his shares to Ben. Ben, not XYZ Corporation, will pay Robert the amount of the dividend. Ben may deduct the payment as an itemized deduction on Schedule A if he borrows the stock for more than 45 days and has not diminished his risk of loss by, for example, holding an option to buy substantially similar stock. Robert enters that amount on page 1 (Form 1040) as income from Ben.

If Ben returns the stock within 45 days, he will not be able to claim a deduction. The amount paid to Robert increases the basis of the stock sold.

More information. For more information about how to report dividend income, see chapter 1 of Publication 550 or the instructions for the form you must file.

TaxOrganizer

Records you should keep.

- Annual statements from brokerage accounts, mutual funds
- All Forms 1099
- All Forms K-1 (partnership, trust, S corporation)
- All information on purchase of investments and sale of investments

10

Rental Income and Expenses

Note: The 2004 IRS Publication 17 (Your Federal Income Tax) has been updated by Ernst & Young LLP for 2005. Dates and dollar amounts shown are for 2005. Gray type is used to indicate where IRS text has been updated or intentionally omitted. Unrevised IRS text is shown in black type.

Rent is the income received for allowing another person to use property that you own. This income is customarily received in cash. If, in lieu of paying all or part of the rent in cash, a tenant provides you with certain services, the value of those services is rental income to you.

*You may deduct any expenses incurred to repair or to maintain your rental property. However, certain other expenses may not be deducted in the year in which you pay for them; rather, they must be **capitalized** and deducted over a period of years. You may also deduct any **depreciation** taken on your rental property. Depreciation is a noncash expense claimed in order to deduct each year a small part of what you originally paid for the property.*

There are a variety of methods by which you may depreciate property and calculate your tax deduction, and all are explained in this chapter. In 1981, Congress adopted

*the **Accelerated Cost Recovery System (ACRS)**. Then, in 1986, Congress made some additional changes and adopted the **Modified Accelerated Cost Recovery System (MACRS)**. This chapter delves into all the complexities of ACRS and MACRS and outlines strategies that will enable you to benefit from them. It also explains the end of the special depreciation allowance which applied to property placed in service before 2005.*

Typically, you will do better taking a current deduction rather than capitalizing an expense and depreciating an item over time. But, since there are no hard and fast rules as to what must be considered a deductible expense and what must be capitalized, there are plenty of opportunities to be appropriately aggressive and save on your taxes. This chapter explains the rules and the opportunities for tax savings.

Introduction

This chapter discusses rental income and expenses. It covers the following topics.

- Rental income.
- Rental expenses.
- Personal use of dwelling unit (including vacation home).
- Depreciation.
- Limits on rental losses.
- How to report your rental income and expenses.

If you sell or otherwise dispose of your rental property, see Publication 544, Sales and Other Dispositions of Assets.

If you have a loss from damage to, or theft of, rental property, see Publication 547, Casualties, Disasters, and Thefts.

If you rent a condominium or a cooperative apartment, some special rules apply to you even though you receive the same tax treatment as other owners of rental property. See Publication 527, Residential Rental Property, for more information.

Useful Items

You may want to see:

Publications

Forms (and Instructions)

Rental Income

You generally must include in your gross income all amounts you receive as rent. Rental income is any payment you receive for the use or occupation of property. In addition to amounts you receive as normal rent payments, there are other amounts that may be rental income.

When to report. If you are a cash basis taxpayer, report rental income on your return for the year you actually or constructively receive it. You are a cash basis taxpayer if you report income in the year you receive it, regardless of when it was earned. You constructively receive income when it is made available to you, for example, by being credited to your bank account.

For more information about when you constructively receive income, see *Accounting Methods* in chapter 1.

Advance rent. Advance rent is any amount you receive before the period that it covers. Include advance rent in your rental income in the year you receive it regardless of the period covered or the method of accounting you use.

Example. You sign a 10-year lease to rent your property. In the first year, you receive $5,000 for the first year's rent and $5,000 as rent for the last year of the lease. You must include $10,000 in your income in the first year.

Explanation

Some taxpayers have attempted to circumvent the rule requiring advance rent to be included in current income by structuring the payment as a "loan." The courts have generally disallowed this technique and follow this type of transaction with close scrutiny. As a general rule, if such a loan is to be repaid out of future rental proceeds, the loan will probably be considered advance rent.

However, the courts have held that an up-front payment for an option to purchase the property is not considered advance rent and, as such, does not have to be included in income where the agreement provides no provision for returning the money to the renter or applying it to the rent.

Even if there exists a promissory note, the courts will look to the parties' intent, as well as to other factors such as interest charged, whether the loan is secured, and whether the loan payment and rental dates are identified.

Security deposits. Do not include a security deposit in your income when you receive it if you plan to return it to your tenant at the end of the lease. But if you keep part or all of the security deposit during any year because your tenant does not live up to the terms of the lease, include the amount you keep in your income for that year.

If an amount called a security deposit is to be used as a final payment of rent, it is advance rent. Include it in your income when you receive it.

Explanation

Generally, the distinction between advance rent and security deposits depends on the nature of the rights and obligations that are assumed when the deposit is made. If, for example, the landlord has the option either to refund a security deposit or to apply it to a future year's rent, the courts have held that the landlord has unrestricted use of the money and that it is considered advance rent.

In cases in which the landlord is required by law to pay interest on the security deposit, the deposit generally is not considered advance rent.

TAXPLANNER

Landlords often forget whether they have treated a security deposit as a true security deposit or as advance rent. If this happens, the landlord will not be sure how to treat the refund and/or application of the security deposit at the end of the term of the lease. Be sure to note in your records exactly how you are treating the amount for tax purposes so that the tax returns for the year in which the security deposit is returned and/or applied will be easy to prepare.

TAXSAVER

When drawing up a rental agreement, it is helpful to include the following language: "that the security deposit of $xx is not to be used for the last month's rent. . . ." This helps ensure deferred recognition of the security deposit as income until such time as you determine it should not be refunded.

Payment for canceling a lease. If your tenant pays you to cancel a lease, the amount you receive is rent. Include the payment in your income in the year you receive it regardless of your method of accounting.

Explanation

Additionally, the courts have ruled that any payments you receive as consideration for modifying the terms of an existing lease must be treated as **ordinary income.** However, certain expenses incurred as a result of the cancellation or modification of a lease may be currently deductible. For example, attorney fees attributable to the *lessee's* forfeiture and termination of a lease would be currently deductible. On the other hand, if the lessor caused the termination, the expense would usually be amortized over a period of time. You should consult your tax advisor.

TAXSAVER

A payment for cancellation of a lease may be very large, depending on the time left on the lease and the agreement of the parties. As with most types of income to cash basis taxpayers, arranging for the receipt of this payment in a year in which you have a lower **marginal tax rate** may save you taxes.

Expenses paid by tenant. If your tenant pays any of your expenses, the payments are rental income. You must include them in your income. You can deduct the expenses if they are deductible rental expenses. See *Rental Expenses,* later, for more information.

Explanation
When a tenant pays to have capital improvements constructed on the landlord's property and these improvements are *not* made in lieu of rent or other required payments, the value of these improvements is *not* income to the landlord, either when made or on termination of the lease, even though the landlord keeps the improvements at the end of the lease. However, the landlord will have no basis in the improvements and, therefore, cannot depreciate the improvements.

Example 1
Susan rents an apartment to Pam. Pam, at her own expense, constructs a wall to separate the dining area from the living room. At the end of the lease, Pam vacates the apartment, leaving the wall. Susan does not record income at any time, even though she may benefit from the capital improvement.

If Susan must incur an expense to remove the wall and restore the property, it is either deducted from income or capitalized, depending on factors discussed later in this chapter.

Example 2
Ken rents an apartment to Anthony for $550. Anthony pays for plumbing repairs of $150, which he in turn deducts out of his current month's rent. Although Ken has received only $400 from Anthony, he must report the entire rent amount of $550 as income. Ken may also be able to report the $150 for plumbing repairs as a deductible expense.

Other examples of landlord expenses paid by a tenant that would be considered rental income include a tenant's payment of a landlord's real estate taxes, mortgage payments, or income taxes.

TaxPlanner
It would be unusual for an expense paid by a tenant that is the responsibility of the landlord not to be deductible by the landlord as well. But such expenses do exist. Consider, for example, a building code violation fine incurred for some change made in the tenant's space by the tenant without the landlord's consent. The fine is imposed on the landlord, but the violation is the tenant's fault. The tenant pays the penalty, but the landlord still has to declare that amount as income, and, in this case, the landlord probably will not be able to deduct the amount of the fine as an expense. Most penalties are not deductible. If this is a possibility, a clause in the lease making the payment of such a penalty the responsibility of the tenant when the tenant is at fault would probably keep the payment by the tenant from being income to the landlord.

Property or services. If you receive property or services, instead of money, as rent, include the fair market value of the property or services in your rental income.

Explanation
Examples of other types of income treated as rental income include the following:

1. Amounts received from an insurance company under a policy that reimburses a property owner for rent lost because of a fire or other casualty affecting the rental property.
2. Amounts received by subletting a property to another individual. If you did receive such income, you would be able to deduct the rent you are paying to the landlord as an expense. However, you are still not the owner and therefore would not be able to depreciate the property.

If the services are provided at an agreed upon or specified price, that price is the fair market value unless there is evidence to the contrary.
Rental of property also used as a home. If you rent property that you also use as your home and you rent it fewer than 15 days during the tax year, do not include the rent you receive in your income and do not deduct rental expenses. However, you can deduct on Schedule A (Form 1040) the interest, taxes, and casualty and theft losses that are otherwise allowed for nonrental property. See *Personal Use of Dwelling Unit (Including Vacation Home),* later.
Part interest. If you own a part interest in rental property, you must report your part of the rental income from the property.

Rental Expenses

This part discusses repairs and certain other expenses of renting property that you ordinarily can deduct from your rental income. It includes information on the expenses you can deduct if you rent part of your property, or if you change your property to rental use. Depreciation, which you can also deduct from your rental income, is discussed later.

TaxSaver
You may deduct expenses on your rental property during a period in which it is *not* being rented as long as it is actively being held out for rent. This applies to a period between rentals, as well as to the period during which a property is being marketed as a rental property for the first time.

The IRS can disallow these deductions if you are unable to show you were actively seeking a profit and had a reasonable expectation of achieving one. The deduction cannot be disallowed just because your property is difficult to rent.

When to deduct. You generally deduct your rental expenses in the year you pay them.
Vacant rental property. If you hold property for rental purposes, you may be able to deduct your ordinary and necessary expenses (including depreciation) for managing, conserving, or maintaining the property while the property is vacant. However, you cannot deduct any loss of rental income for the period the property is vacant.

Example
You own a rental property that, during 2005, was vacant for about half the year. You had rental income of

$12,000 during the year and ordinary and necessary expenses of $15,000, which resulted in an overall loss of $3,000. As long as you can demonstrate that you have been actively trying to rent the house (e.g., newspaper clippings advertising the property for rent), you would be able to deduct your expenses up to $12,000. The remaining $3,000 of expenses can be carried over to the next year or deducted in the current year if qualified. However, see *Losses from Real Estate Activities,* later in this chapter, for special rules and how to report rental income and expenses. Also see *How to Report Rental Income and Expenses,* later in this chapter.

Pre-rental expenses. You can deduct your ordinary and necessary expenses for managing, conserving, or maintaining rental property from the time you make it available for rent.

Depreciation. You can begin to depreciate rental property when it is ready and available for rent. See *Placed-in-Service Date* under *Depreciation,* later.

Expenses for rental property sold. If you sell property you held for rental purposes, you can deduct the ordinary and necessary expenses for managing, conserving, or maintaining the property until it is sold.

Personal use of rental property. If you sometimes use your rental property for personal purposes, you must divide your expenses between rental and personal use. Also, your rental expense deductions may be limited. See *Personal Use of Dwelling Unit (Including Vacation Home),* later.

Part interest. If you own a part interest in rental property, you can deduct your part of the expenses that you paid.

Repairs and Improvements

You can deduct the cost of repairs to your rental property. You cannot deduct the cost of improvements. You recover the cost of improvements by taking depreciation (explained later).

Separate the costs of repairs and improvements, and keep accurate records. You will need to know the cost of improvements when you sell or depreciate your property.

Repairs. A repair keeps your property in good operating condition. It does not materially add to the value of your property or substantially prolong its life. Repainting your property inside or out, fixing gutters or floors, fixing leaks, plastering, and replacing broken windows are examples of repairs.

If you make repairs as part of an extensive remodeling or restoration of your property, the whole job is an improvement.

Improvements. An improvement adds to the value of property, prolongs its useful life, or adapts it to new uses. Improvements include the following items.

- Putting a recreation room in an unfinished basement.
- Paneling a den.
- Adding a bathroom or bedroom.
- Putting decorative grillwork on a balcony.
- Putting up a fence.
- Putting in new plumbing or wiring.
- Putting in new cabinets.
- Putting on a new roof.
- Paving a driveway.

If you make an improvement to property, the cost of the improvement must be capitalized. The capitalized cost can generally be depreciated as if the improvement were separate property.

Explanation
The examples given by the IRS are not necessarily improvements that must be capitalized. If a so-called im-

provement does not prolong useful life or add to value, it is deductible currently as a repair. It is the "nature" of the repair rather than the "amount" that determines whether it is deductible or not.

Examples
Examples of capitalized expenses are as follows:

- Improvements made to property to comply with government regulations
- Expenditures to place property in a safe condition
- Facelifting to improve property's appearance
- Replacement of flashing around a building's roof
- Replacement of a gravel driveway with a cement driveway
- Replacing a floor
- Replacing or recovering a roof

Examples of deductible expenses are as follows:

- Replacing a portion of a wooden bathroom when damage has been caused by water
- Repainting or repapering a room in a rooming house when it is necessary to keep the area clean and serviceable
- Reinforcing sagging floors
- Resurfacing a parking lot
- Making piecemeal repairs to floors

TaxOrganizer

All records and receipts of your rental expenditures, and what they were specifically for, should be kept for a minimum of three years. This will allow you to substantiate items relating to your rental property if the IRS should have any questions.

It is extremely important to keep accurate records of expenditures segregated for repairs that are currently deductible and improvements that are capitalized. Generally, IRS agents give close attention to repair and maintenance deductions. Sometimes expenditures have completely been disallowed unless the taxpayer can prove each specific amount of repairs.

Other Expenses

Other expenses you can deduct from your rental income include advertising, cleaning and maintenance services, utilities, fire and liability insurance, taxes, interest, commissions for the collection of rent, ordinary and necessary travel and transportation, and other expenses, discussed next.

Explanation
While commissions paid to collect rent are deductible, commissions paid to obtain long-term rentals (greater than a 1-year period) must be capitalized and **amortized** over the life of the lease. Commissions paid to acquire the rental property must be capitalized as part of the basis of that property and recovered when the property is depreciated.

Points paid to acquire a mortgage on the rental property must be amortized over the life of the mortgage.

Other deductible expenses connected to renting include legal costs for dispossessing a tenant, property management fees, and pest control fees.

The "ordinary and necessary travel and transportation" category includes, of course, local transportation. It also covers the cost of meals and lodging on trips to inspect rental property located outside the immediate area. However, for the cost of nonlocal transportation and some other expenses to be deductible, the *primary* purpose of the trip must be to take care of the rental property. (See Chapter 28, *Car Expenses and Other Employee Business Expenses,* for a discussion of how to deduct expenses when you use your Ipersonal automobile in your trade or business.)

Example
If you take a 1-week trip to Florida and spend 1 day inspecting your rental property, *no* nonlocal transportation expenses are deductible. If, on the other hand, 6 of the 7 days are used to repair and attend to the property, *all* nonlocal transportation expenses are deductible. In both cases, local transportation expenses incurred traveling to and from the property are deductible.

Rental payments for property. You can deduct the rent you pay for property that you use for rental purposes. If you buy a leasehold for rental purposes, you can deduct an equal part of the cost each year over the term of the lease.

Example 1
If you pay $1,100 rent for property and collect $1,200 in rent from a third party for the same property, you may deduct the $1,100 you pay. Your profit from the rental activity is $100.

Example 2
If you buy a 10-year lease on property from someone for $1,000, you have to pay the rent that the former owner of the lease had to pay. In turn, you report as income any rent you receive on the property. You may amortize the cost of the lease over 10 years, deducting $100 each year.

Rental of equipment. You can deduct the rent you pay for equipment that you use for rental purposes. However, in some cases, lease contracts are actually purchase contracts. If so, you cannot deduct these payments. You can recover the cost of purchased equipment through depreciation.

Explanation
A lease with an option to buy may be a purchase contract. Generally, if the sum of the rental payments on a lease with an option to buy amounts to a substantial part of what would be the purchase price, and if the option period is clearly less than the useful life of the property, the transaction is treated as a sale. Income is recognized under the installment sale rules. (See Chapter 15, *Sale of Property,* for details.)

If the lease is treated as a sale on the date the lease is entered into, rather than the date the option is exercised, there may be unwanted tax consequences for the landlord. The payments that the landlord receives will be proceeds from the sale of property, and he or she will report the gain on the installment method. The landlord may also have to report imputed interest income (see Chapter 13, *Other Income*). Consequently, the landlord might have more income and fewer deductions than expected.

TAXPLANNER
The rules in this area are complex, but a careful drafting of a property agreement will reduce or eliminate the likelihood that the IRS will consider the lease a sale. Professional help should be obtained.

Insurance premiums paid in advance. If you pay an insurance premium for more than one year in advance, each year you can deduct the part of the premium payment that will apply to that year. You cannot deduct the total premium in the year you pay it.

Local benefit taxes. Generally, you cannot deduct charges for local benefits that increase the value of your property, such as charges for putting in streets, sidewalks, or water and sewer systems. These charges are nondepreciable capital expenditures. You must add them to the basis of your property. You can deduct local benefit taxes if they are for maintaining, repairing, or paying interest charges for the benefits.

TAXSAVER
Whether or not you are offering property for rent, it is important to keep a file on the assessments you pay for sewers, streets, and the like. These add to your cost basis in the property and are important in determining your gain or loss if you ever sell the property. In addition, if you do not rent the property out, the increase in your cost basis for any special assessment may increase your depreciation deduction, depending on the type of assessment.

Travel expenses. You can deduct the ordinary and necessary expenses of traveling away from home if the primary purpose of the trip was to collect rental income or to manage, conserve, or maintain your rental property. You must properly allocate your expenses between rental and nonrental activities. For information on travel expenses, see chapter 28.

To deduct travel expenses, you must keep records that follow the rules in chapter 28.

Local transportation expenses. You can deduct your ordinary and necessary local transportation expenses if you incur them to collect rental income or to manage, conserve, or maintain your rental property.

Generally, if you use your personal car, pickup truck, or light van for rental activities, you can deduct the expenses using one of two methods: actual expenses or the standard mileage rate. For 2005, the standard mileage rate for all business miles is 40 1/2 cents a mile. For more information, see chapter 28.

To deduct car expenses under either method, you must keep records that follow the rules in chapter 28. In addition, you must complete Form 4562, Part V, and attach it to your tax return.

Tax return preparation. You can deduct, as a rental expense, the part of the tax return preparation fees you paid to prepare of Schedule E (Form 1040), Part 1. You can also deduct, as a rental expense, any expense you paid to resolve a tax underpayment related to your rental activities. On your 2005 Schedule E, you can deduct fees paid in 2005 to prepare your 2004 Schedule E, Part I.

TAXORGANIZER
Be sure to keep a detailed diary of expenses for your rental property. Include the following:

- Date and amount paid for maintenance expenses
- Travel expenses to and from rental property (keep

track of number of miles driven or actual car expenses, including the date of travel)
- Amount of tax return preparation fee paid for rental income portion of return (have your tax preparer show the amount separately on his or her invoice)

Not Rented for Profit

If you do not rent your property to make a profit, you can deduct your rental expenses only up to the amount of your rental income. You cannot carry forward to the next year any rental expenses that are more than your rental income for the year. For more information about the rules for an activity not engaged in for profit, see chapter 1 of Publication 535.

Where to report. Report your not-for-profit rental income on Form 1040, line 21. You can include your mortgage interest (if you use the property as your main home or second home), real estate taxes, and casualty losses on the appropriate lines of Form 1040, Schedule A, Itemized Deductions, if you itemize your deductions.

Claim your other rental expenses, subject to the rules explained in chapter 1 of Publication 535, as miscellaneous itemized deductions on Form 1040, Schedule A, line 22. You can deduct these expenses only if they, together with certain other miscellaneous itemized deductions, total more than 2% of your adjusted gross income.

TAXPLANNER

If you move out of your personal residence and rent it, your deductions for **real estate** tax and mortgage interest are shifted from itemized deductions on Schedule A to rental deductions on Schedule E of Form 1040. The only additional deductions you become entitled to are those for operating expenses and depreciation. Since the rental income is included in your gross income, and the amount of additional deductions you are entitled to may be small, renting out your personal residence could increase your taxable income. If you rent out your personal residence with the intention of returning to live in it in the future, a special rule governing the deduction of mortgage interest may benefit you. See *Passive Activity Limits* later in this chapter.

Property Changed to Rental Use

If you change your home or other property, (or a part of it), to rental use at any time other than at the beginning of your tax year, you must divide yearly expenses, such as taxes and insurance, between rental use and personal use.

You can deduct as rental expenses only the part of the expense that is for the part of the year the property was used or held for rental purposes.

For depreciation purposes, treat the property as being placed in service on the conversion date.

You cannot deduct depreciation or insurance for the part of the year the property was held for personal use. However, you can include the home mortgage interest and real estate tax expenses for the part of the year the property was held for personal use as an itemized deduction on Schedule A (Form 1040).

Example. Your tax year is the calendar year. You moved from your home in May and started renting it on June 1. You can deduct as rental expenses seven-twelfths of your yearly expenses, such as taxes and insurance.

Starting with June, you can deduct as rental expenses the amounts you pay for items generally billed monthly, such as utilities.

Renting Part of Property

If you rent part of your property, you must divide certain expenses between the part of the property used for rental purposes and the part of the property used for personal purposes, as though you actually had two separate pieces of property.

You can deduct the expenses related to the part of the property used for rental purposes, such as home mortgage interest and real estate taxes, as rental expenses on Schedule E (Form 1040). You can also deduct as a rental expense a part of other expenses that normally are nondeductible personal expenses, such as expenses for electricity or painting the outside of your house.

You can deduct the expenses for the part of the property used for personal purposes, subject to certain limitations, only if you itemize your deductions on Schedule A (Form 1040).

You cannot deduct any part of the cost of the first phone line even if your tenants have unlimited use of it.

You do not have to divide the expenses that belong only to the rental part of your property. For example, if you paint a room that you rent, or if you pay premiums for liability insurance in connection with renting a room in your home, your entire cost is a rental expense. If you install a second phone line strictly for your tenants' use, all of the cost of the second line is deductible as a rental expense. You can deduct depreciation, discussed later, on the part of the property used for rental purposes as well as on the furniture and equipment you use for rental purposes.

Example

Allison rents a room in her house to Gladys. Every year Allison has the house, including Gladys's room, painted for maintenance purposes. The portion of the paint and labor cost for the rented room is deducted on Schedule E. The portion that does not relate to the rented room is not deductible.

Allison pays mortgage interest and property taxes each year on this home. A percentage of this interest and tax that relates to the rental is deductible on Schedule E and the remaining amount is deductible as an itemized deduction on Schedule A.

How to divide expenses. If an expense is for both rental use and personal use, such as mortgage interest or heat for the entire house, you must divide the expense between the rental use and the personal use. You can use any reasonable method for dividing the expense. It may be reasonable to divide the cost of some items (for example, water) based on the number of people using them. However, the two most common methods for dividing an expense are one based on the number of rooms in your home and one based on the square footage of your home.

TAXPLANNER

As there are various methods of dividing expenses, you should use whichever "reasonable" method provides the best result. For more information, see *How to Divide Expenses,* later in this chapter.

Personal Use of Dwelling Unit (Including Vacation Home)

If you have any personal use of a dwelling unit (including a vacation home) that you rent, you must divide your expenses between rental use and personal use. See *Figuring Days of Personal Use* and *How To Divide Expenses,* later.

If you used your dwelling unit for personal purposes, it may be considered a "dwelling unit used as a home." If it is, you cannot deduct rental expenses that are more than your rental income for the unit. See *Dwelling Unit Used as Home* and *How To Figure Rental Income and Deductions*, later. If your dwelling unit is not considered a dwelling unit used as a home, you can deduct rental expenses that are more than rental income for the unit subject to certain limits. See *Limits on Rental Losses*, later.

Exception for minimal rental use. If you use the dwelling unit as a home and you rent it fewer than 15 days during the year, do not include any of the rent in your income and do not deduct any of the rental expenses. See *Dwelling Unit Used as Home*, later.

TaxSaver

This is one of the very few instances in which the IRS considers income to be nontaxable. You should be on the lookout for opportunities to rent property for less than 15 days to take advantage of this tax loophole. Residents of Augusta, Georgia, for example, have an annual opportunity to rent their houses for a short period during the Masters golf tournament.

Explanation
In general, the tax rules governing the rental of vacation homes and other dwelling units are the same as those governing any rental property. The allowable methods of depreciation, the types of deductible expenditures, and the types of expenditures that should be capitalized are all determined in the same way for both categories of rental property. However, if you or a member of your family uses the vacation home or dwelling unit during the year, the amount of deductible expenses may be limited by special rules.

Here's an easy way to figure out whether or not you have to follow the special rules for reporting rental income outlined later:

Step 1. Determine the number of days the property was rented at **fair market value** during the year. If this number is less than 15, STOP. You may not deduct any rental expenses, and you do not report any rental income. (*Note:* You may always deduct qualified residence interest, taxes, **casualty losses,** and theft losses if you itemize deductions. To do so, simply take the deduction for the entire amount of these items on Schedule A of Form 1040.) If the number of days rented is 15 or more, you must report rental income. Proceed to Step 2.

Step 2. Determine the number of days you personally use the property. If this number does not exceed the greater of (a) 14 days or (b) 10% of the number of days for which the property was rented at fair market value, you are not subject to any special rules. After completing Step 3, you determine your rental income or loss in the same way you would for any type of rental property.

If your personal use of the property exceeds the limits above, you *are* subject to special rules limiting the amount of deductible expenses. After completing Step 3, you determine your rental income or loss using the rules discussed in this section.

Step 3. Allocate *all* expenses between the rental period and the period in which you use the property personally, using the method described in the following section. Expenses allocated to the period of personal use are not deductible, except for interest, taxes, and casualty and theft losses (see Step 1). Then determine your rental income or loss, using either the general rules

for rental property or the special rules regarding the personal use of vacation homes, whichever is appropriate.

Note: See *Days Not Counted as Personal Use,* later, regarding use of a home before or after renting.

Dwelling unit. A dwelling unit includes a house, apartment, condominium, mobile home, boat, vacation home, or similar property. A dwelling unit has basic living accommodations, such as sleeping space, a toilet, and cooking facilities. A dwelling unit does not include property used solely as a hotel, motel, inn, or similar establishment.

Property is used solely as a hotel, motel, inn, or similar establishment if it is regularly available for occupancy by paying customers and is not used by an owner as a home during the year.

Example. You rent a room in your home that is always available for short-term occupancy by paying customers. You do not use the room yourself, and you allow only paying customers to use the room. The room is used solely as a hotel, motel, inn, or similar establishment and is not a dwelling unit.

Explanation
A dwelling unit must provide basic living accommodations, such as sleeping space, a rest room, and cooking facilities. The Tax Court has ruled that a mini–motor home qualifies as a dwelling unit.

An outbuilding used in conjunction with the main building to provide living accommodations, such as a garage, a barn, or a greenhouse, constitutes part of the main dwelling unit. When renting one of these outbuildings, you may deduct expenses only to the extent you have income. You may not deduct a rental loss. This is so because the outbuilding is not considered separate from the main building that is being used as a personal residence or vacation home.

Rental pools and time-shares. Rental pools are agreements under which two or more vacation homes are made available for rent by their owners, who agree to share "at least substantially part of the rental income from the homes regardless [of] which of the vacation homes are actually rented." Under proposed IRS regulations, special rules apply when you are computing income, expense, and personal use days.

Also, under proposed IRS regulations, individuals owning a time-share that they rent are to treat their rental income and expense separately with respect to their unit. Consult your tax advisor.

Dwelling Unit Used as Home

The tax treatment of rental income and expenses for a dwelling unit that you also use for personal purposes depends on whether you use it as a home. (See *How To Figure Rental Income and Deductions,* later.)

You use a dwelling unit as a home during the tax year if you use it for personal purposes more than the greater of:

1. 14 days, or
2. 10% of the total days it is rented to others at a fair rental price.

See *Figuring Days of Personal Use,* later.

If a dwelling unit is used for personal purposes on a day it is rented at a fair rental price, do not count that day as a day of rental use in applying (2) above. Instead, count it as a day of personal use in applying both (1) and (2) above. This rule does not apply when dividing expenses between rental and personal use.

Fair rental price. A fair rental price for your property generally is an amount that a person who is not related to you would be willing to pay. The rent you charge is not a fair rental price if it is substantially less than the rents charged for other properties that are similar to your property.

Examples

The following examples show how to determine whether you used your rental property as a home.

Example 1. You converted the basement of your home into an apartment with a bedroom, a bathroom, and a small kitchen. You rented the basement apartment at a fair rental price to college students during the regular school year. You rented to them on a 9-month lease (273 days). You figured 10% of the total days rented to others at a fair rental price is 27 days.

During June (30 days), your brother stayed with you and lived in the basement apartment rent free.

Your basement apartment was used as a home because you used it for personal purposes for 30 days. Rent-free use by your brother is considered personal use. Your personal use (30 days) is more than the greater of 14 days or 10% of the total days it was rented (27 days).

Example 2. You rented the guest bedroom in your home at a fair rental price during the local college's homecoming, commencement, and football weekends (a total of 27 days). Your sister-in-law stayed in the room, rent free, for the last 3 weeks (21 days) in July. You figured 10% of the total days rented to others at a fair rental price is 3 days.

The room was used as a home because you used it for personal purposes for 21 days. That is more than the greater of 14 days or 10% of the 27 days it was rented (3 days).

Example 3. You own a condominium apartment in a resort area. You rented it at a fair rental price for a total of 170 days during the year. For 12 of those days, the tenant was not able to use the apartment and allowed you to use it even though you did not refund any of the rent. Your family actually used the apartment for 10 of those days. Therefore, the apartment is treated as having been rented for 160 (170 − 10) days. You figure 10% of the total days rented to others at a fair rental price is 16 days. Your family also used the apartment for 7 other days during the year.

You used the apartment as a home because you used it for personal purposes for 17 days. That is more than the greater of 14 days or 10% of the 160 days it was rented (16 days).

Use As Main Home Before or After Renting

For purposes of determining whether a dwelling unit was used as a home, you may not have to count days you used the property as your main home before or after renting it or offering it for rent as days of personal use if:

- You rented or tried to rent the property for 12 or more consecutive months.
- You rented or tried to rent the property for a period of less than 12 consecutive months and the period ended because you sold or exchanged the property.

This special rule does not apply when dividing expenses between rental and personal use.

Figuring Days of Personal Use

A day of personal use of a dwelling unit is any day that the unit is used by any of the following persons.

1. You or any other person who has an interest in it, unless you rent it to another owner as his or her main home under a shared equity financing agreement (defined later).
2. A member of your family or a member of the family of any other person who has an interest in it, unless the family member uses the dwelling unit as his or her main home and pays a fair rental price. Family includes only brothers and sisters, half-brothers and half-sisters, spouses, ancestors (parents, grandparents, etc.) and lineal descendants (children, grandchildren, etc.).
3. Anyone under an arrangement that lets you use some other dwelling unit.
4. Anyone at less than a fair rental price.

TaxSaver

The rule relating to personal use does not apply to use by an in-law of the taxpayer who owns the property. Thus, a son-in-law could lease property at a fair market value to his mother-in-law, and it would not be treated as personal use.

Main home. If the other person or member of the family in (1) or (2) above has more than one home, his or her main home is ordinarily the one he or she lived in most of the time.

Shared equity financing agreement. This is an agreement under which two or more persons acquire undivided interests for more than 50 years in an entire dwelling unit, including the land, and one or more of the co-owners is entitled to occupy the unit as his or her main home upon payment of rent to the other co-owner or owners.

Donation of use of property. You use a dwelling unit for personal purposes if:

- You donate the use of the unit to a charitable organization,
- The organization sells the use of the unit at a fund-raising event, and
- The "purchaser" uses the unit.

TaxPlanner

Although donating your rental property for a certain time period to a charitable organization is considered personal use, you still may be allowed to deduct certain expenses during that time on Schedule A as a charitable contribution. See Chapter 26, *Contributions*, for further details on donating your property.

Examples

The following examples show how to determine days of personal use.

Example 1. You and your neighbor are co-owners of a condominium at the beach. You rent the unit to vacationers whenever possible. The unit is not used as a main home by anyone. Your neighbor uses the unit for 2 weeks every year.

Because your neighbor has an interest in the unit, both of you are considered to have used the unit for personal purposes during those 2 weeks.

Example 2. You and your neighbors are co-owners of a house under a shared equity financing agreement. Your neighbors live in the house and pay you a fair rental price.

Even though your neighbors have an interest in the house, the days your neighbors live there are not counted as days of personal use by you. This is because your neighbors rent the house as their main home under a shared equity financing agreement.

Example 3. You own a rental property that you rent to your son. Your son has no interest in this property. He uses it as his main home. He pays you a fair rental price for the property.

Your son's use of the property is not personal use by you because your son is using it as his main home, he has no interest in the property, and he is paying you a fair rental price.

Example 4. You rent your beach house to Joshua. Joshua rents his house in the mountains to you. You each pay a fair rental price.

You are using your house for personal purposes on the days that Joshua uses it because your house is used by Joshua under an arrangement that allows you to use his house.

Days Used for Repairs and Maintenance

Any day that you spend working substantially full time repairing and maintaining your property is not counted as a day of personal use. Do not count such a day as a day of personal use even if family members use the property for recreational purposes on the same day.

Explanation

If the dwelling unit is rented and you are a guest of the occupant for a brief visit, this will not constitute personal use. Of course, the longer the visit is, the more likely the IRS is to claim you were an occupant rather than a visitor. Certainly, 1 or 2 days should be no problem.

How To Divide Expenses

If you use a dwelling unit for both rental and personal purposes, divide your expenses between the rental use and the personal use based on the number of days used for each purpose. You can deduct expenses for the rental use of the unit under the rules explained in *How To Figure Rental Income and Deductions,* later.

When dividing your expenses follow these rules.

- Any day that the unit is rented at a fair rental price is a day of rental use even if you used the unit for personal purposes that day. This rule does not apply when determining whether you used the unit as a home.
- Any day that the unit is available for rent but not actually rented is not a day of rental use.

Example. Your beach cottage was available for rent from June 1 through August 31 (92 days). Your family uses the cottage during the last 2 weeks in May (14 days). You were unable to find a renter for the first week in August (7 days). The person who rented the cottage for July allowed you to use it over a weekend (2 days) without any reduction in or refund of rent. The cottage was not used at all before May 17 or after August 31.

You figure the part of the cottage expenses to treat as rental expenses as follows.

1. The cottage was used for rental a total of 85 days (92 − 7). The days it was available for rent but not rented (7 days) are not days of rental use. The July weekend (2 days) you used it is rental use because you received a fair rental price for the weekend.
2. You used the cottage for personal purposes for 14 days (the last 2 weeks in May).
3. The total use of the cottage was 99 days (14 days personal use + 85 days rental use).
4. Your rental expenses are 85/99 (86%) of the cottage expenses.

When determining whether you used the cottage as a home, the July weekend (2 days) you used it is personal use even though you received a fair rental price for the weekend. Therefore, you had 16 days of personal use and 83 days of rental use for this purpose. Because you used the cottage for personal purposes more than 14 days and more than 10% of the days of rental use (8 days), you used it as a home. If you have a net loss, you may not be able to deduct all of the rental expenses. See *Property Used as a Home* in the following discussion.

TAXSAVER

The Tax Court allows you to use a different allocation formula for interest and taxes than the one the IRS de-

scribes above. Under the Tax Court formula, interest and taxes are allocated in the ratio of days rented to days in the year instead of in the ratio of days rented to days used. Using the Tax Court ratio results in a smaller amount of interest and taxes being allocated to the rental property, which creates the potential for you to deduct a larger amount of your other rental expenses.

Example

You own a cabin, which you rented for June and July, lived in for 1 month, and tried to rent the rest of the year. Your rental income for the 2 months was $2,800. Your total expenses for the cabin were as follows:

Interest	$1,500
Taxes	900
Utilities	750
Maintenance	300
Depreciation	1,200

	IRS method	Tax Court method
1) Gross rental income	$2,800	$2,800
2) Minus:		
a) Part of interest for rental use ($1,500 × 61/91) ($1,500 × 61/365)	1,005	251
b) Part of taxes for rental use ($900 × 61/91) ($900 × 61/365)	603	150
3) Gross rental income that is more than the interest and taxes for rental	$1,192	$2,399
4) Minus: a) Part of utilities for rental use (61/91)	503	503
b) Part of maintenance for rental use (61/91)	201	201
5) Gross rental income that is more than the interest, taxes, and operating expenses for rental use	$ 488	$1,695
6) Minus: Depreciation limited to the part for rental use ($1,200 × 61/91 = $804) or line 5, whichever is less	$ 488	804
7) Net rental income	$ –0–	$ 891

Both the IRS method and the Tax Court method allocate interest expense and real estate taxes partly to Schedule E (for determining net rental income) and partly to Schedule A (for personal itemized deductions). But examine how these allocations affect Schedule A.

Total interest paid is $1,500. Since the IRS method allocates $1,005 to the rental activity, the $495 balance is allocated to Schedule A. The Tax Court method allocates only $251 to the rental activity, leaving $1,249 for a deduction on Schedule A. Similarly, the IRS method allocates $603 of the $900 in real estate taxes to the rental activity, leaving $297 for Schedule A.

The Tax Court method allocates only $150 to the rental activity, leaving $750 for Schedule A.

	Schedule A deduction		Additional itemized deduction per Tax Court method
	Tax Court method	IRS method	
Interest	$1,249	$495	$ 754
Real estate taxes	750	297	453
			$1,207

Under the Tax Court method, you end up with additional deductions of $1,207, but you also have an additional net rental income of $891. The difference is that you reduce your taxable income by $316 more than under the IRS method. This conclusion assumes that you had enough other itemized deductions to make itemizing worthwhile and that your itemized deductions are not being limited.

The concept illustrated above is also important because rental income is considered to be passive income and, as such, can be used to offset passive losses. For more details, see Chapter 25, *Interest Expense.*

How To Figure Rental Income and Deductions

How you figure your rental income and deductions depends on whether the dwelling unit was used as a home (see *Dwelling Unit Used as Home,* earlier) and, if you used it as a home, how many days the property was rented at a fair rental price.

Property Not Used as a Home
If you do not use a dwelling unit as a home, report all the rental income and deduct all the rental expenses. See *How to Report Rental Income and Expenses,* later.

Your deductible rental expenses can be more than your gross rental income. However, see *Limits on Rental Losses,* later.

Property Used as a Home
If you use a dwelling unit as a home during the year (see *Dwelling Unit Used as Home,* earlier), how you figure your rental income and deductions depends on how many days the unit was rented at a fair rental price.

Rented fewer than 15 days. If you use a dwelling unit as a home and you rent it fewer than 15 days during the year, do not include any rental income in your income. Also, you cannot deduct any expenses as rental expenses.

Rented 15 days or more. If you use a dwelling unit as a home and rent it 15 days or more during the year, you include all your rental income in your income. See *How to Report Rental Income and Expenses,* later. If you had a net profit from the rental property for the year (that is, if your rental income is more than the total of your rental expenses, including depreciation), deduct all of your rental expenses. However, if you had a net loss, your deduction for certain rental expenses is limited.

Use Worksheet 10-1 to figure your deductible expenses.

Explanation
The IRS explanation is correct as far as it goes. However, four areas require clarification:

1. The starting point in determining your rental income is gross rental income, which is defined by the IRS as the gross rent received less expenses incurred to obtain tenants, such as advertising and real estate agent's fees. This definition is important because it enables you to deduct this type of expense *before* taking deductions for interest, taxes, and casualty losses, which might be enough to reduce your rental income to zero. The result may be a larger total deduction. The key point is: Start with gross rent received, deduct your expenses to obtain tenants, and then proceed through the deduction process described above.

2. The total amount of a casualty or theft loss allocated to the rental period is deductible. Ordinarily, a personal casualty or theft loss is deductible only to the extent that it is more than $100 and more than 10% of your **adjusted gross income,** but this is not the case when you are dealing with rental property. Your loss in this case would not be subject to the $100 or 10% floor limitation. (See Chapter 27, *Casualty and Theft Losses,* for further details.)

3. Your basis in the vacation home or other dwelling unit is reduced only by the amount of depreciation actually allowed as a deduction, not by the amount of depreciation allocated to the rental period. This, in effect, decreases any gain you have to recognize if you subsequently sell the property. For more details on sales of **depreciable assets,** see *Depreciation,* later in this chapter.

4. Although the deductions for operating expenses and depreciation may not reduce income below zero, the deductions for interest and real estate taxes may.

TAXSAVER

When you personally use a dwelling unit for more than 14 days or more than 10% of the number of days it is rented at fair market value, it is generally to your advantage to use the Tax Court formula for computing the amount of interest and taxes allocable to the rental period. Doing so usually allows you a greater total deduction, since interest, taxes, and casualty losses may be deducted on Schedule A, even if they are disallowed on Schedule E.

However, when your personal use of the dwelling is less than both 15 days and 10% of the number of days it is rented at fair market value, it is to your advantage to use the IRS method of allocating interest and taxes because the net loss on the rental property will be allowed if your personal use is not substantial. (This assumes that the passive loss rules will not limit your net loss.) In this case, the IRS method does not reduce your total deduction; instead, it decreases your rental income (or increases your rental loss) and hence decreases your adjusted gross income.

Decreasing your adjusted gross income can be important, for the following reasons:

1. For 2005, if your adjusted gross income is in excess of $145,950 ($72,975 if married filing separately), your total itemized deductions will be reduced by 3% of the excess of your adjusted gross income over $145,950 ($72,975 if married filing separately). Therefore, a reduction in adjusted gross income will reduce the effect of this limitation.

2. If your adjusted gross income is above certain thresholds, the amount of personal exemptions you are entitled to may be decreased. Therefore, a reduction in your adjusted gross income may increase the amount you can claim for your personal exemptions.

Worksheet 10-1. **Worksheet for Figuring the Limit on Rental Deductions for a Dwelling Unit Used as a Home**

Use this worksheet only if you answer "yes" to all of the following questions.
- Did you use the dwelling unit as a home this year? (See *Dwelling Unit Used as Home.*)
- Did you rent the dwelling unit 15 days or more this year?
- Is the total of your rental expenses and depreciation more than your rental income?

1. Enter rents received . . . . _____
2.a. Enter the rental portion of deductible home mortgage interest (see instructions) . . . . _____
  b. Enter the rental portion of real estate taxes . . . . _____
  c. Enter the rental portion of deductible casualty and theft losses (see instructions) . . _____
  d. Enter direct rental expenses (see instructions) . . . . _____
  e. **Fully deductible rental expenses.** Add lines 2a–2d . . . . _____
3. Subtract line 2e from line 1. If zero or less, enter zero . . . . _____
4.a. Enter the rental portion of expenses directly related to operating or maintaining the dwelling unit (such as
     repairs, insurance, and utilities) . . . . _____
  b. Enter the rental portion of excess mortgage interest (see instructions) . . . . . _____
  c. Add lines 4a and 4b . . . . _____
  d. **Allowable operating expenses.** Enter the smaller of line 3 or line 4c . . . . _____
5. Subtract line 4d from line 3. If zero or less, enter zero . . . . _____
6.a. Enter the rental portion of excess casualty and theft losses (see instructions) . . . . _____
  b. Enter the rental portion of depreciation of the dwelling unit . . . . _____
  c. Add lines 6a and 6b . . . . _____
  d. **Allowable excess casualty and theft losses and depreciation.** Enter the smaller of line 5 or line 6c . . _____
7.a. **Operating expenses to be carried over to next year.** Subtract line 4d from line 4c . . . . . _____
  b. **Excess casualty and theft losses and depreciation to be carried over to next year.** Subtract line 6d
     from line 6c . . . . _____

Enter the amounts on **lines 2e, 4d, and 6d** on the appropriate lines of Schedule E (Form 1040), Part I.

Worksheet Instructions

Follow these instructions for the worksheet above. If you were unable to deduct all your expenses last year because of the rental income limit, add these unused amounts to your expenses for this year.

Line 2a. Figure the mortgage interest on the dwelling unit that you could deduct on Schedule A (Form 1040) if you had not rented the unit. Do not include interest on a loan that did not benefit the dwelling unit. For example, do not include interest on a home equity loan used to pay off credit cards or other personal loans, buy a car, or pay college tuition. Include interest on a loan used to buy, build, or improve the dwelling unit, or to refinance such a loan. Enter the rental portion of this interest on line 2a of the worksheet.

Line 2c. Figure the casualty and theft losses related to the dwelling unit that you could deduct on Schedule A (Form 1040) if you had not rented the dwelling unit. To do this, complete Form 4684, Casualties and Thefts, Section A, treating the losses as personal losses. On Form 4684, line 17, enter 10% of your adjusted gross income figured without your rental income and expenses from the dwelling unit. Enter the rental portion of the result from Form 4684, line 18, on line 2c of this worksheet. **Note.** Do not file this Form 4684 or use it to figure your personal losses on Schedule A. Instead, figure the personal portion on a separate Form 4684.

Line 2d. Enter the total of your rental expenses that are directly related only to the rental activity. These include interest on loans used for rental activities other than to buy, build, or improve the dwelling unit. Also include rental agency fees, advertising, office supplies, and depreciation on office equipment used in your rental activity.

Line 4b. On line 2a, you entered the rental portion of the mortgage interest you could deduct on Schedule A if you had not rented the dwelling unit. Enter on line 4b of this worksheet the rental portion of the mortgage interest you could not deduct on Schedule A because it is more than the limit on home mortgage interest. Do not include interest on a loan that did not benefit the dwelling unit (as explained in the line 2a instructions).

Line 6a. To find the rental portion of excess casualty and theft losses, use the Form 4684 you prepared for line 2c of this worksheet.

A. Enter the amount from Form 4684, line 10 . . . . . _____
B. Enter the rental portion of **A** . _____
C. Enter the amount from line 2c of this worksheet . _____
D. Subtract **C** from **B**. Enter the result here and on line 6a of this worksheet . . . . . _____

Allocating the limited deduction. If you cannot deduct all of the amount on line 4c or 6c this year, you can allocate the allowable deduction in any way you wish among the expenses included on line 4c or 6c. Enter the amount you allocate to each expense on the appropriate line of Schedule E, Part I.

---

3. The amounts of certain itemized deductions, such as medical expenses, casualty losses, and most miscellaneous itemized deductions, are determined by reference to your adjusted gross income. Decreasing your adjusted gross income potentially increases your itemized deductions for these items.
4. Many states use adjusted gross income as the starting point in computing state taxable income. Using the IRS method may reduce your state tax liability.
5. If you are subject to alternative minimum tax, this method will reduce your alternative minimum taxable income.
6. A reduction in adjusted gross income may reduce the taxable amount of Social Security payments.
7. If you are a participant in a qualified pension plan, a decrease in your adjusted gross income may allow you to deduct contributions to an IRA.

Depreciation

You recover your cost in income producing property through yearly tax deductions. You do this by depreciating the property; that is, by deducting some of your cost on your tax return each year.

Three basic factors determine how much depreciation you can deduct. They are: (1) your basis in the property, (2) the recovery period for the property, and (3) the depreciation method used. You cannot simply deduct your mortgage or principal payments, or the cost of furniture, fixtures and equipment, as an expense.

You can deduct depreciation only on the part of your property used for rental purposes. Depreciation reduces your basis for figuring gain or loss on a later sale or exchange.

You may have to use Form 4562 to figure and report your depreciation. See *How To Report Rental Income and Expenses,* later.

Claiming the correct amount of depreciation. You should claim the correct amount of depreciation each tax year. Even if you did not claim depreciation that you were entitled to deduct, you must still reduce your basis in the property by the full amount of depreciation that you could have deducted. If you did not deduct the correct amount of depreciation for property in any year, you may be able to make a correction for that year by filing Form 1040X, Amended U.S Individual Income Tax Return. If you are not allowed to make the correction on an amended return, you can change your accounting method to claim the correct amount of depreciation. See *Claiming the correct amount of depreciation* in Publication 527 for more information.

Example
Barbara makes improvements in the amount of $10,000 to her rental property. These improvements are capitalized and depreciated over time. In the first year the improvements are put in service, Barbara does not deduct the correct amount of depreciation. She deducts $100 and reduces her basis by that amount, when the actual depreciation amount allowable is $200. If Barbara sells the property at the beginning of the next year, her basis in the property would be $9,800 (not $9,900). This is because even though Barbara only deducted $100 as depreciation, she was *allowed* to take a depreciation deduction of $200 and her adjusted basis should reflect the correct amount of depreciation that should have been taken.

Changing your accounting method to deduct unclaimed depreciation. To change your accounting method, you must file Form 3115, Application for Change in Accounting Method, to get the consent of the IRS. In some instances, you can receive automatic consent. For more information, see chapter 1 of Publication 946.

Land. You can never depreciate the cost of land because land does not wear out, become obsolete, or get used up. The costs of clearing, grading, planting, and landscaping are usually all part of the cost of land and cannot be depreciated.

Explanation
When calculating your depreciation expense, be sure to separate out the cost of land from the cost of the building since land is not depreciable. Taxpayers often forget to separate these costs, and, therefore, the true adjusted basis of the building is often not reflected. These amounts are normally not allocated on your purchase agreement so you must get an estimate of the value of the land by a real estate broker or by your county. For further details, consult your tax advisor.

Depreciation Methods

There are three ways to figure depreciation. The depreciation method you use depends on the type of property and when it was placed in service. For property used in rental activities you use one of the following.

- MACRS (Modified Accelerated Cost Recovery System) for property placed in service after 1986.
- ACRS (Accelerated Cost Recovery System) for property placed in service after 1980 but before 1987.
- Useful lives and either straight line or an accelerated method of depreciation, such as the declining balance method, for property placed in service before 1981.

Caution. *This chapter discusses MACRS only. If you need more information about depreciating property placed in service before 1987, see Publication 534.*

Explanation
Depreciation may perhaps be best understood as a way of deducting the cost of an expenditure over many years. Depreciation is calculated in the same way whether you report income on the **cash** or the **accrual method.**

The period of time over which you depreciate your property has long been the subject of controversy. Different taxpayers, often in the same business, have depreciated the same type of property over widely different periods. Efforts to bring more uniformity to the write-off period resulted in the introduction of the Accelerated Cost Recovery System (ACRS). ACRS was replaced with MACRS (Modified ACRS) by the Tax Reform Act of 1986. Most tangible personal property can be depreciated. Artwork is an exception. It cannot be depreciated because no useful life can be established.

If you placed property in service before 2005, continue to use the same method of figuring depreciation that you used in the past.

Section 179 election. You cannot claim the section 179 deduction for property held to produce rental income. See chapter 2 of Publication 946.

Explanation
Property that does not normally qualify for the Section 179 deduction includes:

1. Property held for the production of income
2. Real property, including buildings and their structures
3. Property acquired from certain groups or persons
4. Certain property you lease to others

Consult your tax advisor.

No deduction greater than basis. The total of all your yearly depreciation deductions cannot be more than the cost or other basis of the property. For this purpose, your yearly depreciation deductions include any depreciation that you were allowed to claim, even if you did not claim it.

Cooperative apartments. If you are a tenant-stockholder in a cooperative housing corporation and rent your cooperative apartment to others, you can deduct depreciation for your stock in the corporation. Your depreciation deduction is your share of the corporation's depreciation. See *Cooperative apartments* in Publication 527 for information on how to figure your depreciation deduction.

Explanation
To qualify as a cooperative housing corporation, four tests must be met:

1. There is only a single class of stock outstanding.
2. Each stockholder must be entitled (solely because he or she owns stock) to occupy a house or an apartment owned or leased by the corporation.
3. There are no distributions to a stockholder that are not out of the corporation's earnings except for partial or complete liquidation.
4. At least 80% of the corporation's gross income is received from the tenant-stockholders.

If you are a tenant-stockholder in a co-op, you compute your depreciation deduction in the following manner:

1. Compute depreciation for all of the depreciable property owned by the corporation, using the following method:
   a) Multiply your cost per share for the corporation stock by the total number of shares outstanding.
   b) Add the total mortgage indebtedness on the property as of the date you purchased your stock to the amount computed in (a).
   c) From the amount determined in (b) subtract the part of the mortgage indebtedness (existing on the date you purchased your stock) allocable to nondepreciable property, such as land. The result is the depreciable basis of the corporation's property.
   d) Compute the depreciation, using the basis calculated in (c) and one of the allowable methods of depreciation discussed later.
2. From the amount of depreciation computed in (1), subtract depreciation on any rental space owned by the corporation that may not be lived in by tenant-stockholders.
3. Divide the number of shares of stock in the corporation you own by the total number of shares outstanding (including shares held by the corporation).
4. Multiply the amount calculated in (2) by the percentage determined in (3). This is your depreciation deduction, which is limited to the adjusted basis of your stock in the corporation.

If you rent your co-op, you may also deduct other rental expenses, such as repairs, maintenance, commissions, and insurance fees, as well as depreciation. Whether or not you rent your co-op, you may deduct your share of the corporation's deductible interest and taxes.

Special Depreciation Allowance No Longer Allowed

You can no longer claim a special depreciation allowance (in addition to your regular MACRS depreciation deduction) for qualified property you placed in service in 2005. The allowance of 50% of the property's depreciable basis which was available for property placed in service before 2005 is no longer available. You may still be able to claim a Section 179 deduction for up to $105,000 of the cost of property placed in service in 2005.

TaxAlert

The 2003 Tax Act increased the bonus depreciation percentage from 30% to 50% for qualified property acquired after May 5, 2003, and before January 1, 2005. In order to qualify for the 50% bonus depreciation, there must have been no binding written contract for the acquisition of the qualified property in effect before May 6, 2003.

The 2004 Tax Act allowed bonus depreciation for qualified property held under a binding written contract in effect before January 1, 2005, and placed in service in 2005.

This deduction is not available for property acquired after 2004.

[IRS text intentionally omitted]

MACRS

Most business and investment property placed in service after 1986 is depreciated using MACRS.

MACRS consists of two systems that determine how you depreciate your property—the General Depreciation System (GDS) and the Alternative Depreciation System (ADS). GDS is used to figure your depreciation deduction for property used in most rental activities, unless you elect ADS.

To figure your MACRS deduction, you need to know the following information about your property:

- Its recovery period,
- Its placed-in-service date, and
- Its depreciable basis.

Personal home changed to rental use. You must use MACRS to figure the depreciation on property you used as your home and changed to rental property in 2005.

Excluded property. You cannot use MACRS for certain personal property placed in service in your rental property in 2005 if it had been previously placed in service before MACRS became effective.

In addition, you may elect to exclude certain property from the application of MACRS. See Publication 946 for more information.

Recovery Periods Under GDS

Each item of property that can be depreciated is assigned to a property class. The recovery period of the property depends on the class the property is in. Under GDS, the recovery period of an asset is generally the same as its property class. The property classes under GDS are:

- 3-year property,
- 5-year property,
- 7-year property,
- 10-year property,
- 15-year property,
- 20-year property,
- Nonresidential real property, and
- Residential rental property.

Recovery periods for property used in rental activities are shown in Table 10-1.

The class to which property is assigned is determined by its class life. Class lives and recovery periods for most assets are listed in *Appendix B* in Publication 946.

Additions or improvements to property. Treat depreciable additions or improvements you make to any property as separate property items for depreciation purposes. The recovery period for an addition or improvement to property begins on the later of:

- The date the addition or improvement is placed in service, or
- The date the property to which the addition or improvement was made is placed in service.

The property class and recovery period of the addition or improvement is the one that would apply to the original property if it were placed in service at the same time as the addition or improvement.

Example. You own a residential rental house that you have been renting since 1986 and that you are depreciating under ACRS. You put an addition onto the house and you placed it in service in 2005. You must use MACRS for the addition. Under GDS, the addition is depreciated as residential rental property over 27.5 years.

Placed-in-Service Date

You can begin to depreciate property when you place it in service in your trade or business or for the production of income. Property is considered placed in service in a rental activity when it is ready and available for a specific use in that activity.

Depreciable Basis

To deduct the proper amount of depreciation each year, you must first determine your basis in the property you intend to depreciate. The basis used for figuring depreciation is your original basis in the property increased by any additions or improvements made to the

Table 10-1. **MACRS Recovery Periods for Property Used in Rental Activities**

Type of Property	MACRS Recovery Period	
	General Depreciation System	Alternative Depreciation System
Computers and their peripheral equipment	5 years	5 years
Office machinery, such as:		
Typewriters		
Calculators		
Copiers	5 years	6 years
Automobiles	5 years	5 years
Light trucks	5 years	5 years
Appliances, such as:		
Stoves		
Refrigerators	5 years	9 years
Carpets	5 years	9 years
Furniture used in rental property	5 years	9 years
Office furniture and equipment, such as:		
Desks		
Files	7 years	10 years
Any property that does not have a class life and that has not been designated by law as being in any other class . . .	7 years	12 years
Roads	15 years	20 years
Shrubbery	15 years	20 years
Fences	15 years	20 years
Residential rental property (buildings or structures) and structural components such as furnaces, water pipes, venting, etc., ...	27.5 years	40 years
Additions and improvements, such as a new roof	The same recovery period as that of the property to which the addition or improvement is made, determined as if the property were placed in service at the same time as the addition or improvement.	

property. Your original basis is usually your cost. However, if you acquire the property in some other way, such as by inheriting it, getting it as a gift, or building it yourself, you may have to figure your original basis in another way. Other adjustments could also affect your basis. See chapter 14.

Example

You use an old truck in your business with an unrecovered cost of $6,000. You trade it in for a new truck and pay an additional $9,000 in cash. You subsequently spend $1,000 to have a heavy-duty component added. Your unadjusted basis is $16,000: the unrecovered cost of the old truck ($6,000) plus the cash paid for the new truck ($9,000) and the heavy-duty component ($1,000). Although you have one adjusted basis for your new truck, you may have to use one method of depreciation for the $6,000 unrecovered cost of the old truck and another method of depreciation for the $10,000. (See the antichurning rules covered in the section *MACRS Depreciation Under ADS* later in this chapter.)

Explanation

If you change personal use property to business or income-producing use property, the depreciable basis of the property would be the lesser of the fair market value at the date of change or the property's adjusted basis.

Example 1

Kelly purchased a house for $80,000. Before changing the property from personal to rental use, she made $6,000 of improvements. On the date of the change from personal to business use, the fair market value of the property was $90,000. The depreciable basis of the property is the lesser of the fair market value of the depreciable property at the date of the change or the property's adjusted basis. Since the adjusted basis of the house ($86,000, which consists of $80,000 cost plus $6,000 of improvements) is less than the fair market value of the house ($90,000), the depreciable basis is $86,000.

Example 2

Alternatively, if the value of the property on the date of the change from personal to business use was $84,000, the depreciable basis would be $84,000 (the lower of the adjusted basis of $86,000 or the fair market value of $84,000).

Conventions

Under MACRS, conventions establish when the recovery period begins and ends. The convention you use determines the number of months for which you can claim depreciation in the year you place property in service and in the year you dispose of the property.

Mid-month convention. A mid-month convention is used for all residential rental property and nonresidential real property. Under this convention, you treat all property placed in service, or disposed of, during any month as placed in service, or disposed of, at the midpoint of that month.

Mid-quarter convention. A mid-quarter convention must be used if the mid-month convention does not apply and the total depreciable basis of MACRS property you placed in service in the last 3 months of a tax year (excluding nonresidential real property, residential rental property, and property placed in service and disposed of in the same year) is more than 40% of the total basis of all such property you place in service during the tax year.

Half-year convention. The half-year convention is used if neither the mid-quarter convention nor the mid-month convention applies. Under this convention, you treat all property placed in service, or disposed of, during a tax year as placed in service, or disposed of, at the midpoint of that tax year.

If this convention applies, you deduct a half-year of depreciation for the first year and the last year that you depreciate the property. You deduct a full year of depreciation for any other year during the recovery period.

Under this convention, you treat all property placed in service, or disposed of, during any quarter of a tax year as placed in service, or disposed of, at the midpoint of the quarter.

Example. During the tax year, Jordan Gregory purchased the following items to use in his rental property. [IRS text intentionally omitted]

- A dishwasher for $400, that he placed in service in January.
- Used furniture for $100, that he placed in service in September.
- A refrigerator for $500, that he placed in service in October.

Jordan uses the calendar year as his tax year. The total basis of all property placed in service in that year is $1,000. The $500 basis of the refrigerator placed in service during the last 3 months of his tax year exceeds $400 (40% × $1,000). Jordan must use the mid-quarter convention instead of the half-year convention for all three items.

Explanation

Under the modified MACRS rules, a half-year convention is used on business personal property placed in service or removed from service during the year. For example, a calendar year taxpayer who has been in business all year computes his or her depreciation as if all property had been acquired on July 1.

If the taxable year is less than 12 months (usually in the case of a new business), the property will be treated as in service during half of the short tax year.

If more than 40% of your business personal property is placed in service in the last 3 months of your tax year, a special averaging convention applies. This is called a mid-quarter convention and requires property placed in service during any quarter of a tax year to be treated as placed in service at the midpoint of such quarter.

Dispositions of business personal property result in a half-year of depreciation.

Residential and nonresidential real property are treated as placed in service (or taken out of service) in the middle of the month and use a mid-month convention rather than the half-year convention described above.

Note that you may also need to compute alternative minimum tax depreciation for purposes of computing your alternative minimum taxable income. See Chapter 32, *How to Figure Your Tax*, for additional information.

MACRS Depreciation Under GDS

You can figure your MACRS depreciation deduction under GDS in one of two ways. The deduction is substantially the same both ways. (The difference, if any, is slight.) You can either:

- Use the percentage from the optional MACRS tables, see Table 10-2, or

- Actually figure the deduction using the depreciation method and convention that apply over the recovery period of the property.

Publication 946 discusses computing depreciation using the proper method and convention.

Using the Optional Tables

You can use the tables in Table 10-2 to compute annual depreciation under MACRS. The tables show the percentages for the first 6 years. The percentages in Tables 10-2-A, 10-2-B, and 10-2-C make the change from declining balance to straight line in the year that straight line will yield a larger deduction. See *Appendix A* of Publication 946 for complete tables.

If you elect to use the straight line method for 5-, 7-, or 15-year property, or the 150% declining balance method for 5- or 7-year property, use the tables in *Appendix A* of Publication 946. [IRS text intentionally omitted]

How to use the tables. The following section explains how to use the optional tables.

Figure the depreciation deduction by multiplying your unadjusted basis in the property by the percentage shown in the appropriate table. Your unadjusted basis is your depreciable basis without reduction for MACRS depreciation previously claimed.

Once you begin using an optional table to figure depreciation, you must continue to use it for the entire recovery period unless there is an adjustment to the basis of your property for a reason other than:

1. Depreciation allowed or allowable, or
2. An addition or improvement that is depreciated as a separate item of property.

If there is an adjustment for a reason other than (1) or (2) (for example, because of a deductible casualty loss), you can no longer use the table. For the year of the adjustment and for the remaining recovery period, figure depreciation using the property's adjusted basis at the end of the year and the appropriate depreciation method, as explained in *MACRS Depreciation Under GDS* in Publication 527.

Tables 10-2-A, 10-2-B, and 10-2-C. The percentages in these tables take into account the half-year and mid-quarter conventions. Use Table 10-2-A for 5-year property, Table 10-2-B for 7-year property, and Table 10-2-C for 15-year property. Use the percentage in the second column (half-year convention) unless you must use the mid-quarter convention (explained earlier). If you must use the mid-quarter convention, use the column that corresponds to the calendar year quarter in which you placed the property in service.

Example 1. You purchased a stove and refrigerator and placed them in service in June. Your basis in the stove is $300 and your basis in the refrigerator is $500. [IRS text intentionally omitted] Both are 5-year property. Using the half-year convention column in Table 10-2-A, you find the depreciation percentage for year 1 is 20%. For that year, your depreciation deduction is $60 ($300 × .20) for the stove and $100 ($500 × .20) for the refrigerator.

For year 2, you find your depreciation percentage is 32%. That year's depreciation deduction will be $96 ($300 × .32) for the stove and $160 ($500 × .32) for the refrigerator.

Example 2. Assume the same facts as in *Example 1*, except you buy the refrigerator in October instead of June. You must use the mid-quarter convention to figure depreciation on the stove and refrigerator. The refrigerator was placed in service in the last 3 months of the tax year and its basis ($500) is more than 40% of the total basis of all property placed in service during the year ($800 × .40 = $320).

Because you placed the refrigerator in service in October, you use the fourth quarter column of Table 10-2-A and find that the depreciation percentage for year 1 is 5%. Your depreciation deduction for the refrigerator is $12.50 ($250 × .05).

Because you placed the stove in service in June, you use the sec-

Table 10-2. **Optional MACRS Tables**

Table 10-2-A. MACRS 5-Year property

Year	Half-year convention	Mid-quarter convention			
		First quarter	Second quarter	Third quarter	Fourth quarter
1	20.00%	35.00%	25.00%	15.00%	5.00%
2	32.00	26.00	30.00	34.00	38.00
3	19.20	15.60	18.00	20.40	22.80
4	11.52	11.01	11.37	12.24	13.68
5	11.52	11.01	11.37	11.30	10.94
6	5.76	1.38	4.26	7.06	9.58

Table 10-2-B. MACRS 7-Year property

Year	Half-year convention	Mid-quarter convention			
		First quarter	Second quarter	Third quarter	Fourth quarter
1	14.29%	25.00%	17.85%	10.71%	3.57%
2	24.49	21.43	23.47	25.51	27.55
3	17.49	15.31	16.76	18.22	19.68
4	12.49	10.93	11.97	13.02	14.06
5	8.93	8.75	8.87	9.30	10.04
6	8.92	8.74	8.87	8.85	8.73

Table 10-2-C. MACRS 15-Year property

Year	Half-year convention	Mid-quarter convention			
		First quarter	Second quarter	Third quarter	Forth quarter
1	5.00%	8.75%	6.25%	3.75%	1.25%
2	9.50	9.13	9.38	9.63	9.88
3	8.55	8.21	8.44	8.66	8.89
4	7.70	7.39	7.59	7.80	8.00
5	6.93	6.65	6.83	7.02	7.20
6	6.23	5.99	6.15	6.31	6.48

Table 10-2-D. Residential Rental Property (27.5-year)

	Use the row for the month of the taxable year placed in service.					
	Year 1	Year 2	Year 3	Year 4	Year 5	Year 6
Jan.	3.485%	3.636%	3.636%	3.636%	3.636%	3.636%
Feb.	3.182	3.636	3.636	3.636	3.636	3.636
Mar.	2.879	3.636	3.636	3.636	3.636	3.636
Apr.	2.576	3.636	3.636	3.636	3.636	3.636
May	2.273	3.636	3.636	3.636	3.636	3.636
Jun.	1.970	3.636	3.636	3.636	3.636	3.636
Jul.	1.667	3.636	3.636	3.636	3.636	3.636
Aug.	1.364	3.636	3.636	3.636	3.636	3.636
Sept.	1.061	3.636	3.636	3.636	3.636	3.636
Oct.	0.758	3.636	3.636	3.636	3.636	3.636
Nov.	0.456	3.636	3.636	3.636	3.636	3.636
Dec.	0.152	3.636	3.636	3.636	3.636	3.636

ond quarter column of Table 10-2-A and find that the depreciation percentage for year 1 is 25%. For that year, your depreciation deduction for the stove is $37.50 ($150 × .25).

Table 10-2-D. Use this table for residential rental property. Find the row for the month that you placed the property in service. Use the percentages listed for that month to figure your depreciation deduction. The mid-month convention is taken into account in the percentages shown in the table.

Example. You purchased a single family rental house and placed it in service in February. Your basis in the house is $160,000.

Using Table 10-2-D, you find that the percentage for property placed in service in February of year 1 is 3.182%. That year's depreciation deduction is $5,091 ($160,000 × .03182).

MACRS Depreciation Under ADS

If you choose, you can use the ADS method for most property. Under ADS, you use the straight line method of depreciation.

Table 10-1 shows the recovery periods for property used in rental activities that you depreciate under ADS. See *Appendix B* in

Publication 946 for other property. If your property is not listed, it is considered to have no class life. Under ADS, personal property with no class life is depreciated using a recovery period of 12 years.

Use the mid-month convention for residential rental property and nonresidential real property. For all other property, use the half-year or mid-quarter convention.

Election. For property placed in service during 2005, you choose to use ADS by entering the depreciation on Form 4562, Part III, line 20.

The election of ADS for one item in a class of property generally applies to all property in that class that is placed in service during the tax year of the election. However, the election applies on a property-by-property basis for residential rental property and non-residential real property.

Once you choose to use ADS, you cannot change your election.

Explanation

The anti-churning rules, as they are designed, are designed to prevent you from taking undue advantage of the new, faster depreciation deduction rates by engaging in transactions in which the real and beneficial ownership interest in the property does not really change. For property originally acquired after 1980 and before 1986, rather than switching to MACRS, you must continue to use the previous method of depreciation only if MACRS will yield greater depreciation deductions in the first year. For property originally acquired prior to 1980, you must continue to use the previous method of accounting in all cases.

Example 1

You own your residence, which you bought in 1976. In 2005, you move out and convert the house to rental property. Although you first put it to business use in 2005, you cannot use MACRS because the property was actually acquired prior to 1980.

Example 2

In 1985, John and Mary acquired assets that they held as community property during their married life. John died in 1988, and his property was included in his estate, which resulted in his half being revalued to current fair market value. John's half of the property can be written off under MACRS, but the IRS says that the anti-churning rules prevent Mary from using MACRS on her revalued half because there was no change of ownership, the property was placed in service after 1980 and before 1986, and the MACRS yields a greater first-year deduction.

Other Rules About Depreciable Property

In addition to the rules about what methods you can use, there are other rules you should be aware of with respect to depreciable property.

Gain from disposition. If you dispose of depreciable property at a gain, you may have to report, as ordinary income, all or part of the gain. See Publication 544, Sales and Other Dispositions of Assets.

Explanation

When you sell an asset for more than your unrecovered cost, you face the problem of recapture, that is, reporting all or part of your gain as ordinary income as opposed to capital gain. If you sell tangible personal property at a gain, your recapture is the lower of your gain or the previous amount of depreciation.

Example

	Case 1	Case 2
1) Cost	$1,000	$1,000
2) Depreciation previously claimed	(600)	(600)
3) Unrecovered cost	$ 400	$ 400
4) Selling price	$ 900	$1,200
5) Gain on sale (4 − 3)	$ 500	$ 800
6) Recapture ordinary income (lower of 2 or 5)	(500)	(600)
7) Possible capital gain (5 − 6)	$ –0–	$ 200

Note that the recapture rules generally do not apply to real property if straight-line depreciation was used. However, a 25% capital gains tax rate may apply to depreciation recapture on real property.

TAXPLANNER

Because the maximum tax rate on ordinary income is 35% and the maximum tax rate on long-term capital gains is generally 15%, the depreciation recaptured may be taxed at a higher rate at the time of the sale.

TAXALERT

Under current law, leasehold improvements must be depreciated under MACRS. You generally must depreciate an addition or improvement to nonresidential real property placed in service over a 39-year period using the straight-line method beginning in the month the addition or improvement is placed in service for assets placed in service after May 12, 1993. Leasehold improvements must be depreciated over the MACRS recovery period even if it exceeds the term of the lease.

However, under the 2004 Tax Act, qualified leasehold improvements placed in service after October 22, 2004, must be depreciated using the straight-line method over a 15-year recovery period. Qualified improvements are any improvements to an interior portion of a building that is nonresidential real property provided:

- The improvement is made under a lease either by the lessee (or sublessee), or by the lessor, of that portion of the building to be occupied exclusively by the lessee (or sublessee);
- The improvement is placed in service more than three years after the date the building was first placed in service; and
- The improvement is not attributable to the enlargement of the building, any elevator or escalator, any structural component benefiting a common area, or the internal structural framework of the building.

TAXORGANIZER

Make sure to keep track of all assets acquired and improvements made related to your rental properties. You should keep records of cost, depreciation method, and amount of depreciation already taken. Therefore, if any of these assets are sold, it will be easier to calculate the gain and recapture amount, if necessary.

Alternative minimum tax. If you use accelerated depreciation, you may have to file Form 6251. Accelerated depreciation can be determined under MACRS, ACRS, and any other method that allows you to deduct more depreciation than you could deduct using a straight line method.

Limits on Rental Losses

Rental real estate activities are generally considered passive activities, and the amount of loss you can deduct is limited. Generally, you cannot deduct losses from rental real estate activities unless you have income from other passive activities. However, you may be able to deduct rental losses without regard to whether you have income from other passive activities if you "materially" or "actively" participated in your rental activity. See *Passive Activity Limits,* later.

Losses from passive activities are first subject to the at-risk rules. At-risk rules limit the amount of deductible losses from holding most real property placed in service after 1986.
Exception. If your rental losses are less than $25,000 and you actively participated in the rental activity, the passive activity limits probably do not apply to you. See *Losses From Rental Real Estate Activities,* later.
Property used as a home. If you used the rental property as a home during the year, the passive activity rules do not apply to that home. Instead, you must follow the rules explained earlier under *Personal Use of Dwelling Unit (Including Vacation Home.)*

At-Risk Rules

The at-risk rules place a limit on the amount you can deduct as losses from activities often described as tax shelters. Losses from holding real property (other than mineral property) placed in service before 1987 are not subject to the at-risk rules.

Generally, any loss from an activity subject to the at-risk rules is allowed only to the extent of the total amount you have at risk in the activity at the end of the tax year. You are considered at risk in an activity to the extent of cash and the adjusted basis of other property you contributed to the activity and certain amounts borrowed for use in the activity. See Publication 925 for more information.

Example
Assume Rob maintains a tax-sheltered investment in which he made an initial investment of $20,000. Assuming Rob had a loss of $6,000 the first year, he would be able to take the loss deduction of $6,000, but the total maximum amount of loss deductions Rob could take in future years could not exceed $14,000 ($20,000 − $6,000).

Passive Activity Limits

In general, all rental activities (except those meeting the exception for real estate professionals, below) are passive activities. For this purpose, a rental activity is an activity from which you receive income mainly for the use of tangible property, rather than for services.
Limits on passive activity deductions and credits. Deductions for losses from passive activities are limited. You generally cannot offset income, other than passive income, with losses from passive activities. Nor can you offset taxes on income, other than passive

income, with credits resulting from passive activities. Any excess loss or credit is carried forward to the next tax year.

For a detailed discussion of these rules, see Publication 925.

You may have to complete Form 8582 to figure the amount of any passive activity loss for the current tax year for all activities and the amount of the passive activity loss allowed on your tax return.

TaxSaver
Note that any passive losses disallowed and carried forward can generally be taken in the year the property is sold. Any passive loss carryforward that has not been utilized at your death is only deductible to the extent that the carryforward loss exceeds the spread between the cost basis of the property that produced the loss and its fair market value on date of death (or alternate valuation date, if so elected by the executor).

Exception for real estate professionals. Rental activities in which you materially participated during the year are not passive activities if, for that year, you were a real estate professional because you met the requirements. For a detailed discussion of the requirements, see Publication 527. For a detailed discussion of material participation, see Publication 925.

Explanation
An activity is considered a rental activity for this exception if:

1. Tangible property is used by customers.
2. Income received is principally for the use of property whether or not there is a lease, service contract, or other arrangement.

An activity is not considered a rental activity for this exception if:

1. The average time the customer uses the property is 7 days or less.
2. The average time the customer uses the property is 30 days or less and personal services have been provided by the owner in connection with the rental.
3. Extraordinary personal services are provided by the owner in connection with the rental.
4. The rental of the activity is incidental to the non-rental.
5. The property is associated with a partnership, S corporation, or joint venture.

Example
Amy owns a time-share condo and rents it to a third party for a week each year. Amy paid for no additional services except for weekly cleaning of the unit through condominium dues. This property is not considered a rental activity.

Losses From Rental Real Estate Activities
If you or your spouse actively participated in a passive rental real estate activity, you can deduct up to $25,000 of loss from the activity from your nonpassive income. This special allowance is an exception to the general rule disallowing losses in excess of income from passive activities. Similarly, you can offset credits from the activity against the tax on up to $25,000 of nonpassive income after taking into account any losses allowed under this exception.

If you are married, filing a separate return, and lived apart from your spouse for the entire tax year, your special allowance cannot be more than $12,500. If you lived with your spouse at any time during the year and are filing a separate return, you cannot use the special allowance to reduce your nonpassive income or tax on nonpassive income.

The maximum amount of the special allowance is reduced if your modified adjusted gross income is more than $100,000 ($50,000 if married filing separately).

Active participation. You actively participated in a rental real estate activity if you (and your spouse) owned at least 10% of the rental property and you made management decisions in a significant and *bona fide* sense. Management decisions include approving new tenants, deciding on rental terms, approving expenditures, and similar decisions.

TaxAlert

A regulation has tightened the "partial disposition" rule, requiring a taxpayer to dispose of "substantially all" of an activity rather than a "substantial part" under an earlier proposed regulation in order to deduct associated carryover suspended losses, that is, losses from this activity that did not get deducted in prior years. You should consult your tax advisor.

More information. See Publication 925 for more information on the passive loss limits, including information on the treatment of unused disallowed passive losses and credits and the treatment of gains and losses realized on the disposition of a passive activity.

TaxSaver

If you rent out your personal residence with the intention of returning to it (say, for example, you are transferred overseas for several years), the mortgage interest on the property may not be subject to the passive loss limitation rules. This can result in significant tax savings.

Example
Rental of a dwelling unit

Rent income	$15,000
Mortgage interest	(7,000)
Real estate tax	(3,000)
Other expenses	(1,000)
Depreciation	(9,000)
Net loss subject to passive loss rules	($5,000)

This loss may be deductible on your tax return, under the active participation $25,000 limitation mentioned earlier.

Rental of a personal residence with intention of returning

Rent income	$15,000
Real estate tax	(3,000)
Other expenses	(1,000)
Depreciation	(9,000)
Net rental (passive) income	$2,000
Mortgage interest (loss **not** subject to passive loss rules)	(7,000)
Net loss from property allowed on tax return	($5,000)

Of this loss, $7,000 (the portion representing qualified residence mortgage interest) may be deductible

against nonpassive income. In addition, the $2,000 net passive income may offset passive losses from other passive activities.

Be aware that the depreciation deduction reduces the cost basis of your property, thereby increasing the gain upon sale of the property.

Explanation
You must meet the active participation standards both in the year in which the loss arose and in the year in which the loss is allowed. Losses that exceed $25,000 carried over from an active participation year can be used in a later year if the taxpayer continues to actively participate.

The $25,000 offset rule does not apply to the losses carried over from prior years where the taxpayer did not actively participate in the rental.

TaxAlert

A tax-saving opportunity exists depending upon how personal property and real property are grouped. Under final regulations, a taxpayer could not treat as a single activity the rental of real property and the rental of personal property (other than personal property provided in connection with real property). Further, effective for tax years beginning in January 1993, it allows a taxpayer to treat as a single activity real property provided in connection with personal property.

Example
An individual who leases $10,000 of real property (e.g., a small structure or other fixture) in connection with renting $150,000 of computer equipment could treat as one activity the rental of both the real property and the personal property.

To make an election to treat all real property as a single activity, a taxpayer must file a statement with his or her original tax return for the tax year the taxpayer is making the election.

TaxPlanner

It may not be beneficial for you to group all of your rental real estate interests together if you have interests in nonrental activities that are also passive. Consult your tax advisor for further details.

How To Report Rental Income and Expenses

If you rent buildings, rooms, or apartments, and provide only heat and light, trash collection, etc., you normally report your rental income and expenses on Form 1040, Schedule E, Part I. However, do not use that schedule to report a not-for-profit activity. See *Not Rented for Profit,* earlier.

If you provide significant services that are primarily for your tenant's convenience, such as regular cleaning, changing linen, or maid service, you report your rental income and expenses on Schedule C (Form 1040), Profit or Loss From Business or Schedule C-EZ, Net Profit From Business (Sole Proprietorship). Significant services do not include the furnishing of heat and light, cleaning of public areas, trash collection, etc. For information, see Publication 334, Tax Guide for Small Business (For Individuals Who Use Schedule C or C-EZ). You also may have to pay self-employment tax on your rental income. See Publication 533, Self-Employment Tax.

Form 1098. If you paid $600 or more of mortgage interest on your rental property to any one person, you should receive a Form 1098, Mortgage Interest Statement, or similar statement showing the interest you paid for the year. If you and at least one other person (other than your spouse if you file a joint return) were liable for, and paid interest on the mortgage, and the other person received the Form 1098, report your share of the interest on Form 1040, Schedule E, line 13. Attach a statement to your return showing the name and address of the other person. In the left margin of Schedule E (Form 1040), next to line 13, enter "See attached."

Schedule E (Form 1040)

Use Form 1040, Schedule E, Part I, to report your rental income and expenses. List your total income, expenses, and depreciation for each rental property. Be sure to answer the question on line 2.

If you have more than three rental or royalty properties, complete and attach as many Schedules E as are needed to list the properties. Complete lines 1 and 2 for each property. However, fill in the "Totals" column on only one Schedule E. The figures in the "Totals" column on that Schedule E should be the combined totals of all Schedules E.

Schedule E, page 2, is used to report income or loss from partnerships, S corporations, estates, trusts, and real estate mortgage investment conduits. If you need to use Schedule E, page 2, use page 2 of the same Schedule E you used to enter the combined totals in Part I.

On Schedule E, page 1, line 20, enter the depreciation you are claiming. You must complete and attach Form 4562 for rental activities only if you are claiming:

- Depreciation on property placed in service during 2005,
- Depreciation on listed property (such as a car), regardless of when it was placed in service, or
- Any car expenses reported on a form other than Schedule C or C-EZ (Form 1040) or Form 2106 or Form 2106-EZ.

Otherwise, figure your depreciation on your own worksheet. You do not have to attach these computations to your return.

Example. On January 1, Justin Cole bought a townhouse and placed it in service as residential rental property. He receives $1,100 a month rental income. His rental expenses for the year are as follows:

Fire insurance (1-year policy)	$ 200
Mortgage interest	5,000
Fee paid to real estate company for collecting monthly rent	572
General repairs	175
Real estate taxes imposed and paid	800

Justin's basis for depreciation of the townhouse is $150,000. He is using MACRS with a 27.5-year recovery period. On April 1, Justin bought a new refrigerator for the rental property at a cost of $2,175. He uses the MACRS method with a 5-year recovery period. [IRS text intentionally omitted]

Justin uses the percentage for January in Table 10-2-D to figure his depreciation deduction for the townhouse. He uses the percentage under "Half-year convention" in Table 10-2-A to figure his de-

preciation deduction for the refrigerator. He must report the depreciation on Form 4562.

Justin figures his net rental income or loss for the townhouse as follows:

Total rental income received ($1,100 × 12)		$13,200
Minus Expenses:		
Fire insurance (1-year policy)	$ 200	
Mortgage interest	5,000	
Rent collection fee	572	
General repairs	175	
Real estate taxes	800	
Total expenses		6,747
Balance		$ 6,453
Minus Depreciation:		
Townhouse ($150,000 × 3.485%)	$5,228	
Refrigerator ($2,175 × 20%)	435	
Total depreciation		5,663
Net rental income for townhouse		$ 790

TaxOrganizer

Records you should keep.

- Rental agreement
- Records of tenant-paid improvements, real estate taxes, mortgage payments, and the like
- A log of how many days a property is rented, used for personal purposes, or vacant
- Proof of advertising vacant properties in newspapers, magazines, and the like
- Lists distinguishing the nature of each repair or improvement
- Receipts for each repair and improvement including date and amount paid
- A log of travel expenses allocating between rental and nonrental purposes
- A schedule showing method of division of expenses if part of property is rented
- Schedule listing depreciable assets with respect to the rental property including amount, date purchased, life of asset, method of depreciation, and depreciation already taken
- Carryforward of passive activity losses not utilized in prior years
- Carryforward of rental losses in excess of $25,000 when actively participating in rental activity
- Form 1098 or other form indicating mortgage interest paid
- Property tax forms and receipts
- Proof of tax preparation fees paid in relation to rental property
- Security deposit information

11

Retirement Plans, Pensions, and Annuities

Note: The 2004 IRS Publication 17 (Your Federal Income Tax) has been updated by Ernst & Young LLP for 2005. Dates and dollar amounts shown are for 2005. Gray type is used to indicate where IRS text has been updated or intentionally omitted. Unrevised IRS text is shown in black type.

Introduction

No matter how welcome retirement may be, you're liable to encounter a host of challenging tax dilemmas that you've never before faced. For starters, the chances are good that you will have some difficulty projecting your tax liabilities. Your income will most likely be different from what it has been, and the way in which you calculate your tax will be different, too. If your **pension** *payments are not subject to mandatory withholding rules, you may have to start making* **estimated tax** *payments or you might elect to have income taxes withheld from*

your pension payments. You'll have to puzzle over the complicated withdrawal requirements for an **Individual Retirement Arrangement (IRA)** *and possibly for a Keogh plan, a pension plan for the* **self-employed.** *If you are entitled to any* **lump-sum distributions,** *you will have to make the difficult decision as to whether to roll over the funds and defer the tax or to pay the tax currently but at the low rates currently permitted by* **10-year income averaging,** *if you are eligible. This chapter helps guide you through this maze of complicated decisions.*

This chapter discusses the tax treatment of distributions you receive from:

- An employee pension or annuity from a qualified plan,
- A disability retirement, and
- A purchased commercial annuity.

What is not covered in this chapter. The following topics are not discussed in this chapter.

The General Rule. This is the method generally used to determine the tax treatment of pension and annuity income from nonqualified plans (including commercial annuities). If your annuity starting date is after November 18, 1996, you generally cannot use the General Rule for a qualified plan. For more information about the General Rule, see Publication 939.

Civil service retirement benefits. If you are retired from the federal government (either regular or disability retirement), see Publication 721, Tax Guide to U.S. Civil Service Retirement Benefits. Publication 721 also covers the information that you need if you are the survivor or beneficiary of a federal employee or retiree who died.

Individual retirement arrangements (IRAs). Information on the tax treatment of amounts you receive from an IRA is in chapter 18.

Useful Items

You may want to see:

Publications

- ☐ **575** Pension and Annuity Income
- ☐ **721** Tax Guide to U.S. Civil Service Retirement Benefits
- ☐ **939** General Rule for Pensions and Annuities

Forms (and Instructions)

- ☐ **W–4P** Withholding Certificate for Pension or Annuity Payments
- ☐ **1099–R** Distributions From Pensions, Annuities, Retirement or Profit-Sharing Plans, IRAs, Insurance Contracts, etc.
- ☐ **4972** Tax on Lump-Sum Distributions
- ☐ **5329** Additional Taxes on Qualified Plans (Including IRAs) and Other Tax-Favored Accounts

Employee Pensions and Annuities

Generally, if you did not pay any part of the cost of your employee pension or annuity and your employer did not withhold part of the cost from your pay while you worked, the amounts you receive each year are fully taxable. You must report them on your income tax return.

Partly taxable payments. If you paid part of the cost of your annuity, you are not taxed on the part of the annuity you receive that represents a return of your cost. The rest of the amount you receive is taxable. Your annuity starting date (defined later) determines which method you must or may use.

If you contributed to your pension or annuity plan, you figure the tax-free and the taxable parts of your annuity payments under either the Simplified Method or the General Rule. If your annuity starting date is after November 18, 1996, and your payments are from a qualified plan, you must use the Simplified Method. Generally, you must use the General Rule only for nonqualified plans.

If your annuity is paid under a qualified plan and your annuity starting date is after July 1, 1986 and before November 19, 1996, you could have chosen to use either the General Rule or the Simplified Method.

TaxAlert

If your annuity starting date is after November 18, 1996, you must use the Simplified Method for payments from a qualified plan unless you have attained age 75 and your annuity payments are guaranteed for at least 5 years.

More than one program. If you receive benefits from more than one program under a single trust or plan of your employer, such as a pension plan and a profit-sharing plan, you may have to figure the taxable part of each separately. For example, benefits from one of your programs could be fully taxable, while the benefits from your other program could be taxable under the General Rule or the Simplified Method. Your former employer or the plan administrator should be able to tell you if you have more than one pension or annuity contract.

Railroad retirement benefits. Part of the railroad retirement benefits you receive is treated for tax purposes like social security benefits, and part is treated like an employee pension. For information about railroad retirement benefits treated as social security benefits, see Publication 915, Social Security and Equivalent Railroad Retirement Benefits. For information about railroad retirement benefits treated as an employee pension, see *Railroad Retirement* in Publication 575.

Credit for the elderly or the disabled. If you receive a pension or annuity, you may be able to take the credit for the elderly or the disabled. See chapter 35.

Explanation

Since this credit is designed to help only those taxpayers with very modest resources, you are ineligible if you receive substantial Social Security benefits or have substantial **adjusted gross income.**

Withholding and estimated tax. The payer of your pension, profit-sharing, stock bonus, annuity, or deferred compensation plan will withhold income tax on the taxable parts of amounts paid to you. You can choose not to have tax withheld except for amounts paid to you that are eligible rollover distributions. See *Eligible rollover distributions* under *Rollovers,* later. You make this choice by filing Form W-4P.

For payments other than eligible rollover distributions, you can tell the payer how to withhold by filing Form W-4P. If an eligible rollover distribution is paid directly to you, 20% will generally be withheld. There is no withholding on a direct rollover of an eligible rollover distribution. See *Direct rollover option* under *Rollovers,* later. If you choose not to have tax withheld or you do not have enough tax withheld, you may have to pay estimated tax.

For more information, see *Pensions and Annuities* under *Withholding* in chapter 5.

Explanation

Unless you elect to have your distribution paid *directly* to an **eligible retirement plan,** the payer of benefits from your pension, profit-sharing, stock bonus, annuity, or other qualified deferred compensation plan is required to withhold an amount equal to 20% of any designated distribution that is an **eligible rollover distribution.** An eligible rollover distribution is any distribution of all or a portion of an employee's balance in a qualified plan or tax-sheltered annuity arrangement which can be rolled over to an IRA or another employer plan. The exceptions to this are (1) any distribution that is one of a series of substantially equal periodic payments made over the life or life expectancy of the employee (or the joint lives or joint life expectancies of the employee and the employee's designated beneficiary) or made over a period of 10 years or more, (2) required minimum distributions, and (3) certain corrective and deemed distributions. An **eligible retirement plan** is generally another **qualified retirement plan,** an **individual retirement account,** an **individual retirement annuity,** a governmental Section 457 plan, or a 403(b) tax-sheltered annuity.

If the payment made to you is not an eligible rollover distribution, the payer will withhold income tax on the taxable amounts paid to you. However, withholding from these payments is not mandatory and you can tell the payer how to withhold by filing Form W-4P, *Withholding Certificate for Pension or Annuity Payments.* If you choose not to have tax withheld, you may have to pay estimated tax.

Loans. If you borrow money from your qualified pension or annuity plan, tax-sheltered annuity program, government plan, or contract purchased under any of these plans, you may have to treat the loan as a nonperiodic distribution unless certain exceptions apply. This means that you must include in income all or part of the amount borrowed. Even if you do not have to treat the loan as a nonperiodic distribution, you may not be able to deduct the interest on the loan in some situations. For details, see *Loans Treated as Distributions* in Publication 575. For information on the deductibility of interest, see chapter 25.

Exception

A loan will not be considered a distribution to the extent that the loan (when added to the outstanding balance of all other loans maintained by the employer) does not exceed the lesser of (1) $50,000 or (2) the greater of either $10,000 or one-half of the participant's vested accrued benefits under the plan. The $50,000 limit is reduced by the excess of the participant's highest outstanding loan balance during the preceding 12-month period, over the outstanding balance at the date of the new loan.

In addition, the exception does not apply unless the

loan by its terms must be repaid within 5 years and re-quires level repayments made not less frequently than quarterly over the term of the loan.

The 5-year rule does not generally apply to loans made in connection with the purchase of a principal residence of a participant.

TaxAlert

Interest on a loan from an employee plan is only de-ductible under the general loan interest rules (dis-cussed in Chapter 25, *Interest Expense*). Even if the interest is deductible under the general rules, it will not be deductible if the loan was made to a key employee or secured by amounts attributable to an employee's salary reduction amounts. It should also be noted that personal loan interest is not deductible.

TaxPlanner

Loans from a retirement plan may be a good way to provide for children's college expenses, a housing down payment, or any other family need. The interest you pay on the loan helps your account grow at an at-tractive rate if the plan credits interest paid on the loan to your account. The downside is that you may earn less in your plan from this interest than you would have had you left money in other investments.

Elective deferrals. Some retirement plans allow you to elect to have your employer contribute part of your compensation to a retirement fund, rather than have it paid to you. You do not pay income tax on this money until you receive it in a distribution from the plan. Gen-erally, you may not defer more than a total of $14,000 ($18,000 for individuals who have attained at least age 50 by year-end) for all qualified plans by which you are covered in 2005 (these amounts increase to $15,000 and $20,000, respectively, in 2006).

Elective deferrals generally include elective contribu-tions to cash or deferred arrangements [known as **401(k) plans**] and elective contributions to Section 501(c)(18)(D) plans, salary reduction simplified em-ployee pension (SARSEP) plans, SIMPLE plans, and 403(b) tax-sheltered annuities.

Certain deferrals (such as cafeteria plan contribu-tions and qualified transportation fringe benefits) that are not included in your gross income are still included in your compensation for purposes of determining your base amount for your 401(k) contributions. Therefore, for example, the amounts contributed to a cafeteria plan will not decrease the tax-deferred amount that can be contributed by the employer at the election of the employee to his or her 401(k) plan.

TaxPlanner

There are several special rules used to determine the limit on employee elective deferrals. If the deferrals are otherwise permitted under these special rules there is an annual limit on elective deferrals—$14,000 for 2005. This is an aggregate limit for each individual that takes into consideration all deferrals by that individual during the year to 401(k) plans, 403(b) tax-sheltered annuities, SIMPLE plans, and SARSEPs. The limit applies even if the employee makes deferrals to plans sponsored by different employers or to differ-

ent types of plans [such as a 401(k) plan and a SIMPLE IRA].

In 2006 the basic limit will increase to $15,000. The dollar limit will be indexed in $500 increments thereafter.

Example

Assume Steve works for Employer A from January 2005 to April 2005 and defers $4,000 to Employer A's 401(k) plan during this time. If Steve leaves in May 2005 to work for Employer B for the remainder of the year, the most Steve could defer to Employer B's 401(k) plan for the remainder of 2005 is $10,000.

Alternatively, assume Steve works for Employer A from January 2005 to August 2005 and defers $5,000 to Employer A's 401(k) plan. In September, Steve leaves to work for Employer B, which sponsors a SIMPLE IRA for its employees. Steve will only be allowed to defer $9,000 to the SIMPLE IRA for 2005—$14,000 aggre-gate limit less $5,000 already deferred to Employer A's 401(k) plan—even though SIMPLE IRAs generally allow employee deferrals of up to $10,000.

TaxAlert

If you are at least 50 years old by the end of the taxable year, you can elect to defer even more to a 401(k) plan, a 403(b) tax-sheltered annuity, a SEP, a SIMPLE plan, or a governmental Section 457 plan. The additional amount of elective contributions that may be made is the lesser of (1) the applicable dollar amount (as de-scribed) or (2) your compensation for the year reduced by any other elective deferrals you made for the year. The applicable dollar amount for catch-up contributions under a 401(k) plan, a 403(b) tax-sheltered annuity, a SEP, or a governmental Section 457 plan is $4,000 for 2005. The applicable dollar amount for catch-up contri-butions under a SIMPLE plan is $2,000 for 2005.

TaxAlert

If you realize that you made excess elective deferrals (the limit for 2005 is $14,000) in any given calendar year, be certain to notify your plan administrator(s) as soon as possible. The excess deferral amount will be taxable to you in the year of the deferral. In addition, if this excess deferral is not distributed to you by the fol-lowing April 15, the excess deferral amount will again be taxed to you when it is ultimately distributed to you upon your retirement or separation from your employer. If the excess deferral is distributed to you by the fol-lowing April 15, however, it will not be taxed a second time when distributed (although the income attribut-able to the excess deferral will be taxed to you in the year of distribution). Excess deferrals in 2005 must be distributed by April 17, 2006.

Matching contributions for the self-employed do not count toward your elective deferral limit. Although employer matching contributions do not generally count against the 2005 $14,000 limit on employee elective deferrals, a special rule previously required self-employed persons to count matching contributions against this limit. For tax years beginning after 1997 (after 1996 for SIMPLE plans), employer matching con-tributions will not count toward a self-employed per-son's elective deferral limit. This rule would typically apply to a partner in a partnership.

TaxPlanner

The benefits of 401(k) plans are substantial. The elective deferrals are not subject to federal, most state, and most local income taxes until they are withdrawn. (They are subject to Social Security and Medicare taxes at the time of deferral, though.) Earnings on elective deferrals are also not subject to income tax until they are withdrawn. An employer matching contribution program (which is deductible to the employer within certain limits) can encourage employees to make elective contributions. Finally, on withdrawal, a lump-sum distribution can escape immediate income tax or excise tax if it is deposited into a rollover account. For more information, see *Rollovers* later in this chapter.

Starting in 2006, the law allows employers to offer "Roth 401(k)" plans to their employees. Under a Roth 401(k), contributions are nondeductible but all the income in the plan is tax-**free** if certain requirements are met at distribution. These requirements are similar to those that apply to Roth IRAs, which are discussed in Chapter 18. However, unlike with Roth IRAs, the ability to contribute to a Roth 401(k) is not limited by the size of your income.

TaxPlanner

403(b) plans (tax-sheltered annuity, or TSA plans), which are available to employees of certain tax-exempt organizations and educational organizations and of state and local governments, offer many of the same benefits that 401(k) plans offer. The elective deferrals are *not* subject to federal income tax, most state income taxes, and most local income taxes, until they are withdrawn. Earnings on elective deferrals are also not subject to income tax until they are withdrawn. Rollovers are permitted for qualifying distributions to help avoid immediate income tax or excise taxes, if applicable. Effective for distributions made after December 31, 2001, eligible rollover distributions from a TSA plan can be rolled over into a qualified retirement plan, another TSA plan, or an IRA.

Prior to 1997, tax-exempt organizations (except for certain grandfathered organizations) were not permitted to adopt 401(k) plans but were able to offer TSA plans. State and local governments (other than rural cooperative plans and certain Indian tribal governments) still cannot provide 401(k) plans to their employees, although they may offer a TSA plan for employees of certain educational organizations.

For information about tax-sheltered annuities, see Publication 571, *Tax-Sheltered Annuity Plans (403(b) Plans) for Employees of Public Schools and Certain Tax-Exempt Organizations.*

TaxSaver

Individuals earning limited amounts of self-employment income may be able to shelter all or a substantial portion of their income by utilizing a SIMPLE IRA. *(Note:* Unless you are self-employed, other than as a partner, SIMPLE IRAs may only be established by your employer.)* Although an individual may only defer $10,000 to a SIMPLE IRA, these deferrals are not limited to a certain percentage of an individual's compensation as is the case with other plans. For example, in 2005 an

individual with $12,500 in self-employment income (e.g., director's fees) could defer $10,000 (or 80%) of the income into a SIMPLE IRA. In addition to the $10,000 employee deferral, either a 3% matching contribution or a 2% employer contribution would be required to satisfy the SIMPLE IRA rules. On the other hand, the same individual could only contribute 25% of the income (after reduction for the 25% contribution itself) into a SEP, or $2,500. (An even better alternative would be a Keogh/401(k) Plan combination. Under that type of plan, you could contribute up to the full 401(k) limit of $14,000.) See the discussion in Chapter 17, *Individual Retirement Arrangements (IRAs),* for more details on the requirements for SIMPLE IRAs. The following illustrates the advantages of using a SIMPLE IRA to defer limited amounts of income.

Example

Amy earned $11,000 in director's fees in 2005, has elected to defer 100% of such income to the SIMPLE IRA, and will utilize the matching contribution. A 25% SEP is shown for comparison. *Note:* This example assumes that Amy has made no other elective deferrals for the year [such as to a 401(k) plan], so the full $14,000 limit on elective deferrals is available.

	SIMPLE IRA	25% SEP
Self-employment income	$11,000	$11,000
Less 1/2 self-employment tax	(777)	(777)
Net self-employment income	$ 10,223	$ 10,223
Times deferral percentage	100%	20%
		(effective)
Elective deferral	(cap) $10,000	$ 2,045
Match of 3%	$ 307	$ 0
Total	$10,307	$ 2,045

TaxAlert

Effective for taxable years beginning after December 31, 2001, and before January 1, 2007, a nonrefundable tax credit is available for eligible individuals, in an amount equal to a percentage (see the table on next page) of their qualified retirement savings contribution, not to exceed $2,000. Only individuals with a joint return with adjusted gross income of $50,000 or less, a head-of-household return of $37,500 or less, or a single return of $25,000 or less are eligible for the credit. The credit is available with respect to elective deferrals to a 401(k) plan, a 403(b) tax-sheltered annuity, or a governmental Section 457 plan, a SIMPLE, or a SEP, and with respect to contributions to a traditional or Roth IRA, and voluntary after-tax employee contributions to a qualified retirement plan or a 403(b) tax-sheltered annuity.

Adjusted Gross Income

Joint Return Over	Not Over	Head of Household Over	Not Over	All Other Cases Over	Not Over	Applicable Percentage
$0	$30,000	$0	$22,500	$0	$15,000	50%
30,000	32,500	22,500	24,375	15,000	16,250	20%
32,500	50,000	24,375	37,500	16,250	25,000	10%
50,000		37,500		25,000		0%

Qualified plans for self-employed individuals. Qualified plans set up by self-employed individuals are sometimes called Keogh or H.R. 10 plans. Qualified plans can be set up by sole proprietors, partnerships (but not a partner), and corporations. They can cover self-employed persons, such as the sole proprietor or partners, as well as regular (common-law) employees.

Distributions from a qualified plan are usually fully taxable because most recipients have no cost basis. If you have an investment (cost) in the plan, however, your pension or annuity payments from a qualified plan are taxed under the Simplified Method. For more information about qualified plans, see Publication 560, Retirement Plans for Small Business.

Section 457 deferred compensation plans. If you work for a state or local government or for a tax-exempt organization, you may be able to participate in a section 457 deferred compensation plan. If your plan is an eligible plan, you are not taxed currently on pay that is deferred under the plan or on any earnings from the plan's investment of the deferred pay. You are taxed on amounts deferred in an eligible state or local government plan only when they are distributed from the plan. You are taxed on amounts deferred in an eligible tax-exempt organization plan when they are distributed or otherwise made available to you.

This chapter covers the tax treatment of benefits under eligible section 457 plans, but it does not cover the treatment of deferrals. For information on deferrals under section 457 plans, see *Retirement Plan Contributions* under *Employee Compensation* in Publication 525.

For general information on these deferred compensation plans, see *Section 457 Deferred Compensation Plans* in Publication 575.

Cost (Investment in the Contract)

Before you can figure how much, if any, of a distribution from your pension or annuity plan is taxable, you must determine your cost (your investment in the contract) in the pension or annuity. Your total cost in the plan includes everything that you paid. It also includes amounts your employer paid that were taxable to you when paid. Cost does not include any amounts you deducted or excluded from income.

From this total cost paid or considered paid by you, subtract any refunds of premiums, rebates, dividends, unpaid loans, or other tax-free amounts you received by the later of the annuity starting date or the date on which you received your first payment.

TaxSaver

You may or may not have any cost (investment) in your plan for unrepaid loans. If you received a loan from a plan but did not repay the loan according to the repayment schedule (a default), the amount of the loan that was in default was probably reported to you as taxable income in the year you failed to make the required payments. The amount of the unrepaid loan that has already been taxed to you reduces the amount that can be distributed to you and should not be included in your cost. However, if you repay part or all of the loan to the plan after the loan has been taxed to you because of a default, your repayments will increase your cost in the plan. Your plan administrator should properly track your loan repayments and determine your cost in the plan.

Your annuity starting date is the later of the first day of the first period for which you received a payment, or the date the plan's obligations became fixed.

Your employer or the organization that pays you the benefits (plan administrator) should show your cost in box 5 of your Form 1099-R.

Foreign employment contributions. If you worked in a foreign country and contributions were made to your retirement plan, special rules apply in determining your cost. See Publication 575.

TaxAlert

Your cost includes contributions by your employer if you were required to include the amounts in your gross income. Under a 2004 Tax Act change, for distributions on or after October 22, 2004, your cost will include only amounts which have been taxed in the U.S. or in a foreign jurisdiction.

Simplified Method

Under the Simplified Method, you figure the tax-free part of each monthly annuity payment by dividing your cost by the total number of expected monthly payments. For an annuity that is payable for the lives of the annuitants, this number is based on the annuitants' ages on the annuity starting date and is determined from a table. For any other annuity, this number is the number of monthly annuity payments under the contract.

Who must use the Simplified Method. You must use the Simplified Method if your annuity starting date is after November 18, 1996, and you receive pension or annuity payments from a qualified plan or annuity, unless you were at least 75 years old and entitled to annuity payments from a qualified plan that are guaranteed for 5 years or more.

Who must use the General Rule. You must use the General Rule if you receive pension or annuity payments from:

- A nonqualified plan (such as a private annuity, a purchased commercial annuity, or a nonqualified employee plan), or
- A qualified plan if you are age 75 or older on your annuity starting date and your annuity payments are guaranteed for at least 5 years.

Annuity starting before November 19, 1996. If your annuity starting date is after July 1, 1986, and before November 19, 1996, you had to use the General Rule for either circumstance described above. You also had to use it for any fixed-period annuity. If you did not have to use the General Rule, you could have chosen to use it. If your annuity starting date is before July 2, 1986, you had to use the General Rule unless you could use the Three-Year Rule.

If you had to use the General Rule (or chose to use it), you must continue to use it each year that you recover your cost.

Who cannot use the General Rule. You cannot use the General Rule if you receive your pension or annuity from a qualified plan and none of the circumstances described in the preceding discussions apply to you. See *Who must use the Simplified Method,* earlier.

More information. For complete information on using the General Rule, including the actuarial tables you need, see Publication 939.

Guaranteed payments. Your annuity contract provides guaranteed payments if a minimum number of payments or a minimum amount (for example, the amount of your investment) is payable even if you and any survivor annuitant do not live to receive the minimum. If the minimum amount is less than the total amount of the payments you are to receive, barring death, during the first 5 years after payments begin (figured by ignoring any payment increases), you are entitled to less than 5 years of guaranteed payments.

Exclusion limit. Your annuity starting date determines the total amount that you can exclude from your taxable income over the years.

Exclusion limited to cost. If your annuity starting date is after 1986, the total amount of annuity income that you can exclude over the years as a recovery of the cost cannot exceed your total cost. Any unrecovered cost at your (or the last annuitant's) death is allowed as a miscellaneous itemized deduction on the final return of the decedent. This deduction is not subject to the 2%-of-adjusted-gross-income limit.

Exclusion not limited to cost. If your annuity starting date is before 1987, you can continue to take your monthly exclusion for as long as you receive your annuity. If you chose a joint and survivor annuity, your survivor can continue to take the survivor's exclusion figured as of the annuity starting date. The total exclusion may be more than your cost.

How to use the Simplified Method. Complete the Simplified Method Worksheet in Publication 575 to figure your taxable annuity for 2005. If the annuity is payable only over your life, use your age at the annuity starting date to determine the total number of expected monthly payments for your annuity. For annuity starting dates beginning in 1998, if your annuity is payable over your life and the lives of other individuals, use the combined ages of you and the youngest survivor annuitant at the annuity starting date. However, if your annuity starting date began before January 1, 1998, the total number of monthly annuity payments expected to be received is based on the primary annuitant's age at the annuity starting date.

Tip. *Be sure to keep a copy of the completed worksheet; it will help you figure your taxable annuity in later years.*

Example. Bill Smith, age 65, began receiving retirement benefits in 2005, under a joint and survivor annuity. Bill's annuity starting date is January 1, 2005. The benefits are to be paid for the joint lives of Bill and his wife Kathy, age 65. Bill had contributed $31,000 to a qualified plan and had received no distributions before the annuity starting date. Bill is to receive a retirement benefit of $1,200 a month, and Kathy is to receive a monthly survivor benefit of $600 upon Bill's death.

Bill must use the Simplified Method to figure his taxable annuity because his payments are from a qualified plan and he is under age 75. Because his annuity is payable over the lives of more than one annuitant, he uses his and Kathy's combined ages and Table 2 at the bottom of the worksheet in completing line 3 of the worksheet. His completed worksheet is shown in Worksheet 10-A.

Bill's tax-free monthly amount is $100 ($31,000 / 310 as shown on line 4 of the worksheet). Upon Bill's death, if Bill has not recovered the full $31,000 investment, Kathy will also exclude $100 from her $600 monthly payment. The full amount of any annuity payments received after 310 payments are paid must be included in gross income.

If Bill and Kathy die before 310 payments are made, a miscellaneous itemized deduction will be allowed for the unrecovered cost on the final income tax return of the last to die. This deduction is not subject to the 2%-of-adjusted gross-income limit.

Tip. *Had Bill's retirement annuity payments been from a nonqualified plan, he would have used the General Rule. He uses the Simplified Method Worksheet because his annuity payments are from a qualified plan.*

Survivors

If you receive a survivor annuity because of the death of a retiree who had reported the annuity under the Three-Year Rule, include the total received in income.

If the retiree was reporting the annuity payments under the General Rule, you must apply the same exclusion percentage to your initial survivor annuity payment called for in the contract. The resulting tax-free amount will then remain fixed. Any increases in the survivor annuity are fully taxable.

If the retiree was reporting the annuity payments under the Simplified Method, the part of each payment that is tax free is the same as the tax-free amount figured by the retiree at the annuity starting date. See *Simplified Method*, earlier.

In any case, if the annuity starting date is after 1986, the total exclusion over the years cannot be more than the cost.

If you are the survivor of an employee, or former employee, who died before becoming entitled to any annuity payments, you must figure the taxable and tax-free parts of your annuity payments using the method that applies as if you were the employee.

Estate tax. If your annuity was a joint and survivor annuity that was included in the decedent's estate, an estate tax may have been paid on it. You can deduct, as a miscellaneous itemized deduction, the part of the total estate tax that was based on the annuity. This deduction is not subject to the 2%-of-adjusted gross-income limit. The deceased annuitant must have died after the annuity starting date. (For details, see section 1.691(d)-1 of the regulations.) This amount cannot be deducted in one year. It must be deducted in equal amounts over your remaining life expectancy.

Explanation

The deduction for an annuity that is included in the decedent's estate has become very rare. Since the exemptions for estate tax have been greatly increased and the marital deduction is now unlimited (and current law now repeals the estate tax effective in 2010), it is unusual for any estate tax to be paid on a joint and survivor annuity. However, some people do qualify.

Example

Alexander dies while receiving an annuity worth $10,000. Alexander's beneficiary will receive $1,000 per year for the next 15 years. The estate tax figured with the annuity included is $4,500 more than when figured without the annuity.

The recipient may claim an itemized deduction (not subject to the 2%-of-adjusted-gross-income limitation) each year of $300 ($1,000/$15,000 × $4,500). In this computation, the $15,000 represents the total dollars that will be received over the 15-year period.

How To Report

If you file Form 1040, report your total annuity on line 16a and the taxable part on line 16b. If your pension or annuity is fully taxable, enter it on line 16b; do not make an entry on line 16a.

If you file Form 1040A, report your total annuity on line 12a and the taxable part on line 12b. If your pension or annuity is fully taxable, enter it on line 12b; do not make an entry on line 12a.

More than one annuity. If you receive more than one annuity and at least one of them is not fully taxable, enter the total amount received from all annuities on Form 1040, line 16a or Form 1040A, line 12a, and enter the taxable part on Form 1040, line 16b, or Form 1040A, line 12b. If all the annuities you receive are fully taxable, enter the total of all of them on Form 1040, line 16b, or Form 1040A, line 12b.

Joint return. If you file a joint return and you and your spouse each receive one or more pensions or annuities, report the total of the pensions and annuities on Form 1040, line 16a, or Form 1040A, line 12a, and report the taxable part on Form 1040, line 16b, or Form 1040A, line 12b.

Explanation

If you receive a distribution and, to avoid the current tax, decide to roll it over into another retirement vehicle such as an IRA, you still are required to show the total amount received on line 16a (or line 12a, Form 1040A). However, on line 16b (or line 12b, Form 1040A) you would show the taxable amount as zero. Also, enter "Rollover" next to line 16b (or line 12b, Form 1040A).

Worksheet 11-A. **Simplified Method Worksheet for Bill Smith**

1. Enter the total pension or annuity payments received this year. Also, add this amount to the total for Form 1040, line 16a, or Form 1040A, line 12a	**1.**	14,400
2. Enter your cost in the plan (contract) at the annuity starting date	**2.**	31,000
Note: *If your annuity starting date was **before** this year and you completed this worksheet last year, skip line 3 and enter the amount from line 4 of last year's worksheet on line 4 below. Otherwise, go to line 3.*		
3. Enter the appropriate number from Table 1 below. **But** if your annuity starting date was **after** 1997 **and** the payments are for your life and that of your beneficiary, enter the appropriate number from Table 2 below	**3.**	310
4. Divide line 2 by the number on line 3	**4.**	100
5. Multiply line 4 by the number of months for which this year's payments were made. If your annuity starting date was **before** 1987, enter this amount on line 8 below and skip lines 6, 7, 10, and 11. Otherwise, go to line 6	**5.**	1,200
6. Enter any amounts previously recovered tax free in years after 1986	**6.**	-0-
7. Subtract line 6 from line 2	**7.**	31,000
8. Enter the **smaller** of line 5 or line 7	**8.**	1,200
9. **Taxable amount for year.** Subtract line 8 from line 1. Enter the result, but not less than zero. Also, add this amount to the total for Form 1040, line 16b, or Form 1040A, line 12b.	**9.**	13,200
Note: *If your Form 1099-R shows a larger taxable amount, use the amount on line 9 instead.*		
10. Add lines 6 and 8	**10.**	1,200
11. **Balance of cost to be recovered.** Subtract line 10 from line 2 . . .	**11.**	29,800

TABLE 1 FOR LINE 3 ABOVE

IF the age at annuity starting date was...	AND your annuity starting date was—	
	before November 19, 1996, enter on line 3...	**after** November 18, 1996, enter on line 3...
55 or under	300	360
56–60	260	310
61–65	240	260
66–70	170	210
71 or older	120	160

TABLE 2 FOR LINE 3 ABOVE

IF the combined ages at annuity starting date were...	THEN enter on line 3...
110 or under	410
111–120	360
121–130	310
131–140	260
141 or older	210

Lump-Sum Distributions

A lump-sum distribution is the distribution or payment in 1 tax year of a plan participant's entire balance from all of the employer's qualified plans of one kind (for example, pension, profit-sharing, or stock bonus plans). A distribution from a nonqualified plan (such as a privately purchased commercial annuity or a section 457 deferred compensation plan of a state or local government or tax-exempt organization) cannot qualify as a lump-sum distribution.

The participant's entire balance from a plan does not include certain forfeited amounts. It also does not include any deductible voluntary employee contributions allowed by the plan after 1981 and before 1987. For more information about distributions that do not qualify as lump-sum distributions, see *Distributions that do not qualify* under *Lump-Sum Distributions* in Publication 575.

TAXALERT

Involuntary distribution requirements. A plan may not distribute your vested accrued benefit to you without your consent (and the consent of your spouse if the qualified joint and survivor annuity rules apply) unless the present value of your accrued benefit is $5,000 or less. Effective for distributions made after December 31, 2001, in determining your accrued benefit for purposes of the $5,000 limitation on involuntary distributions, employers may disregard benefits and related earnings, which are attributable to rollover contributions. Under Department of Labor regulations, involuntary distributions that exceed $1,000 must be rolled over automatically to a designated IRA, unless you affirmatively elect to have the distribution transferred to a different IRA or a qualified plan or to receive it directly.

TaxPlanner

If you change jobs and plan to participate in your new employer's plan, you may want to consider a "plan-to-plan" transfer to the new plan if your new employer co-operates. If an amount is transferred from one qualified plan to another, no amount will be required to be withheld on the amount transferred from your old employer's plan. While there is nothing in the law that requires your new employer to accept transferred amounts, some employers may do this as an accommodation to new employees.

Plan-to-plan transfers have certain advantages over rollovers. See *Rollovers,* later in this chapter. One advantage is that your periods of service for both employers would be counted by the plan for purposes of the 10-year averaging computation.

If you receive a lump-sum distribution from a qualified employee plan or qualified employee annuity and the plan participant was born before January 2, 1936, you may be able to elect optional methods of figuring the tax on the distribution. The part from active participation in the plan before 1974 may qualify as capital gain subject to a 20% tax rate. The part from participation after 1973 (and any part from participation before 1974 that you do not report as capital gain) is ordinary income. You may be able to use the 10-year tax option, discussed later, to figure tax on the ordinary income part.

Use Form 4972 to figure the separate tax on a lump-sum distribution using the optional methods. The tax figured on Form 4972 is added to the regular tax figured on your other income. This may result in a smaller tax than you would pay by including the taxable amount of the distribution as ordinary income in figuring your regular tax.

How to treat the distribution. If you receive a lump-sum distribution, you may have the following options for how you treat the taxable part.

- Report the part of the distribution from participation before 1974 as a capital gain (if you qualify) and the part from participation after 1973 as ordinary income.
- Report the part of the distribution from participation before 1974 as a capital gain (if you qualify) and use the 10-year tax option to figure the tax on the part from participation after 1973 (if you qualify).
- Use the 10-year tax option to figure the tax on the total taxable amount (if you qualify).
- Roll over all or part of the distribution. See *Rollovers,* later. No tax is currently due on the part rolled over. Report any part not rolled over as ordinary income.
- Report the entire taxable part of the distribution as ordinary income on your tax return.

The first three options are explained in the following discussions.

Electing optional lump-sum treatment. You can choose to use the 10-year tax option or capital gain treatment only once after 1986 for any plan participant. If you make this choice, you cannot use either of these optional treatments for any future distributions for the participant.

Taxable and tax-free parts of the distribution. The taxable part of a lump-sum distribution is the employer's contributions and income earned on your account. You may recover your cost in the lump sum and any net unrealized appreciation (NUA) in employer securities tax free.

Cost. In general, your cost is the total of:

- The plan participant's nondeductible contributions to the plan,
- The plan participant's taxable costs of any life insurance contract distributed,

- Any employer contributions that were taxable to the plan participant, and
- Repayments of any loans that were taxable to the plan participant.

You must reduce this cost by amounts previously distributed tax free.

Net unrealized appreciation (NUA). The NUA in employer securities (box 6 of Form 1099-R) received as part of a lump-sum distribution is generally tax free until you sell or exchange the securities. (For more information, see *Distributions of employer securities* under *Taxation of Nonperiodic Payments* in Publication 575.)

Explanation
Employer securities distributed as part of a lump-sum distribution may have increased in value after they were purchased by the trust that is making the distribution. This increase is called "net unrealized appreciation." It is not taxed at the time of the lump-sum distribution.

If you later sell these securities, any gain is taxed as a **long-term capital gain** (i.e., as if held for more than 12 months)—up to the amount of your net unrealized appreciation (NUA). Any gain above this amount is a long-term capital gain only if the employee holds the stock for more than 12 months prior to selling it.

You may also elect not to use this treatment on your tax return and instead treat the NUA as part of your lump-sum distribution. This may be desirable if you have tax losses that can offset the amount of NUA.

You may not claim a loss if you receive stock that is worth less than your total contributions to the plan. You may claim a loss when you sell the stock if it is sold for less than the amount of your own after-tax employee contributions allocated to the shares of stock sold.

Example
Assume that Widget Company's pension trust used the company's contribution for Sarah Jones to purchase 100 shares of Widget Company common stock at $10 per share on January 15, 1998. These securities were given to Sarah Jones as part of a lump-sum distribution on January 3, 2005, when their value had risen to $15 per share. Sarah is taxed on the $10 per share that was contributed by Widget, but she is not taxed on the NUA of $5 per share on January 3, 2005.

If Sarah sold the 100 shares of Widget Company stock on January 12, 2005, for $25 per share, $500 of the gain [($15 − $10) × 100 shares] attributed to NUA would be taxed as long-term capital gain. The balance of the gain of $1,000 [($25 − $5 − $10) × 100 shares] would be taxed as a short-term capital gain, since Sarah did not hold the securities for more than 12 months from the distribution date.

If Sarah had made her own after-tax contributions of $1,700 to the pension trust and received Widget Company stock valued at only $1,000 at the time of the lump-sum distribution, she could not have claimed a loss at that time. However, if she later sold the stock, she would compare her proceeds with $1,700 to determine if she had a gain or a loss on the sale.

TaxPlanner

If you receive only employer securities in an eligible rollover distribution (or employer securities and less than $200 in cash), there is no mandatory 20% withholding requirement. See *Rollovers,* later in this chapter. Therefore, it may be beneficial under some circumstances for you to receive an eligible rollover distribution consisting solely of employer securities and up to $200 in cash rather than all cash or a mix of cash (greater than $200) and employer securities.

Capital Gain Treatment

Capital gain treatment applies only to the taxable part of a lump-sum distribution resulting from participation in the plan before 1974. The amount treated as capital gain is taxed at a 20% rate. You can elect this treatment only once for any plan participant, and only if the plan participant was born before January 2, 1936.

Complete Part II of Form 4972 to choose the 20% capital gain election. For more information, see *Capital Gain Treatment* under *Lump-Sum Distributions* in Publication 575.

10-Year Tax Option

The 10-year tax option is a special formula used to figure a separate tax on the ordinary income part of a lump-sum distribution. You pay the tax only once, for the year in which you receive the distribution, not over the next 10 years. You can elect this treatment only once for any plan participant, and only if the plan participant was born before January 2, 1936.

The ordinary income part of the distribution is the amount shown in box 2a of the Form 1099-R given to you by the payer, minus the amount, if any, shown in box 3. You also can treat the capital gain part of the distribution (box 3 of Form 1099-R) as ordinary income for the 10-year tax option if you do not choose capital gain treatment for that part.

Complete Part III of Form 4972 to choose the 10-year tax option. You must use the special tax rates shown in the instructions for Part III to figure the tax. Publication 575 illustrates how to complete Form 4972 to figure the separate tax.

Rollovers

If you withdraw cash or other assets from a qualified retirement plan in an eligible rollover distribution, you can defer tax on the distribution by rolling it over to another qualified retirement plan or a traditional IRA.

For this purpose, the following plans are qualified retirement plans.

- A qualified employee plan.
- A qualified employee annuity.
- A tax-sheltered annuity plan (403(b) plan).
- An eligible state or local government section 457 deferred compensation plan.

You generally must complete the rollover by the 60th day following the day on which you receive the distribution from your employer's plan. (This 60-day period is extended for the period during which the distribution is in a frozen deposit in a financial institution.) For all rollovers to an IRA, you must irrevocably elect rollover treatment by written notice to the trustee or issuer of the IRA.

Tip. *The IRS may waive the 60-day requirement where the failure to do so would be against equity or good conscience, such as in the event of a casualty, disaster, or other event beyond your reasonable control.*

Eligible rollover distributions. Generally, an eligible rollover distribution is any distribution of all or the balance to your credit in a qualified retirement plan. For information about exceptions to eligible rollover distributions, see Publication 575.

Rollover of nontaxable amounts. You may be able to roll over the nontaxable part of a distribution (such as your after-tax contributions) made to another qualified retirement plan or traditional IRA. The transfer must be made either through a direct rollover to a qualified plan that separately accounts for the taxable and nontaxable parts of the rollover or through a rollover to a traditional IRA.

If you roll over only part of a distribution that includes both taxable and nontaxable amounts, the amount you roll over is treated as coming first from the taxable part of the distribution.

Hardship distributions. Hardship distributions are no longer treated as eligible rollover distributions.

TAXPLANNER

Since hardship distributions are not considered eligible rollover distributions, they are not subject to the mandatory 20% withholding rules that normally apply to eligible rollover distributions. If you are receiving a hardship distribution, you can reduce the amount withheld from the distribution and retain more cash to satisfy the need giving rise to the hardship by filing a Form W-4P with your plan administrator. See the earlier discussion in this chapter on *Withholding and Estimated Tax.*

TAXPLANNER

If you receive a hardship distribution and another event occurs such as your separation from your employer or attainment of age 59 1/2 so that the distribution is permitted without regard to hardship, you should consult your plan administrator to determine the proper treatment under your plan of the distribution. Plans have two alternatives. First, the amount distributed after that event may be treated as *eligible* for rollover treatment. Alternatively, the distribution may be treated as *ineligible* for rollover even though another event has occurred that could entitle the recipient to a distribution without regard to hardship. Plans must be consistent in the treatment of all distributions.

Plans also have alternatives with respect to allocation of basis. If a portion of a distribution that includes a hardship distribution is not includible in gross income (e.g., after-tax contributions), then the portion of the distribution that is not includible in gross income may be allocated to the portion ineligible for rollover or the portion eligible for rollover (or between the two portions) using any reasonable method. Again, plans must be consistent in the treatment of the distributions. Consult your plan administrator for additional information.

Direct rollover option. You can choose to have any part or all of an eligible rollover distribution paid directly to another qualified plan (if permitted) or to a traditional IRA. If you decide on a rollover, it is generally to your advantage to choose this direct rollover option. Under this option, the plan administrator would not withhold tax from any part of the distribution that is directly paid to the other plan.

Withholding tax. If you choose to have all or any part of the distribution paid to you, it is taxable in the year distributed unless you roll it over to another qualified plan or to a traditional IRA within 60 days. The plan administrator must withhold income tax of 20% from the amount of the distribution paid to you. (See *Pensions and Annuities* under *Withholding* in chapter 5.)

Caution. *If you decide to roll over an amount equal to the distribution before withholding, your contribution to the new plan or IRA must include other money (for example, from savings or amounts borrowed) to replace the amount withheld.*

The administrator must give you a written explanation of your distribution options within a reasonable period of time before making an eligible rollover distribution.

TaxPlanner

Remember, if you do not wish to include the property received as part of a distribution in the rollover, you cannot roll over cash in place of the property received (such as stock) unless the actual property is sold. The proceeds from the bona fide sale may then be included in the rollover.

Explanation

Generally, an **eligible rollover distribution** means any distribution of all or any portion of an employee's balance in a qualified plan. Eligible rollover distributions do not include the following.

- Required minimum distributions (e.g., distributions required to be made to more than 5% owners who have attained age 70 1/2)
- Distributions that are part of a series of substantially equal payments that are received at least annually over the life or life expectancy of the employee (or the joint lives or joint life expectancies of the employee and the employee's designated beneficiary) or made over a period of at least 10 years
- Certain corrective distributions made because of the plan's violation of the Internal Revenue Code's limitations
- Loans treated as distributions because they violate the Internal Revenue Code's plan loan rules
- Loans in default that are treated as distributions
- Certain dividends paid on employer securities
- Hardship distributions

Eligible rollover distributions can be rolled over in one of two ways. First, you can transfer funds in a **direct rollover** where the plan trustee transfers some or all of your eligible rollover distribution directly to the trustee of an eligible retirement plan. Second, you can actually receive the distribution and put the money or assets into another qualified plan or IRA within 60 days.

TaxAlert

A qualified plan must allow participants the option of a direct rollover to other qualified plans or an IRA. However, there is nothing in the law that requires your new employer to accept these amounts. If the new employer's plan will not accept these amounts, they could be transferred directly from your old employer's plan to an IRA.

TaxPlanner

A **direct rollover** may be accomplished by the trustee making a wire transfer or mailing a check to the trustee of the recipient plan, or even by providing you with a check and instructing you to deliver it to an eligible retirement plan. However, the check must be made payable only to the trustee or custodian of the eligible retirement plan, not to you. If you do a direct rollover, you can also roll over after-tax contributions to another qualified plan.

Explanation

You cannot be precluded from dividing an eligible rollover distribution by electing to make a direct rollover of a portion of the distribution and to receive a distribution of the remaining portion. However, your employer may preclude you from electing to have a portion of an eligible rollover distribution paid as a direct rollover if that portion is less than $500.

TaxPlanner

Employers may, but need not, exclude eligible rollover distributions that are less than $200 from the direct rollover option. In addition, employers are not required to withhold from distributions of less than $200. It should be noted, however, that amounts of $200 or less may still be eligible for rollover by you within 60 days after receipt (see discussion below).

An employer is not required to allow employees to have a direct rollover paid to more than one recipient plan. Therefore, if you wish to diversify an IRA investment, for example, you can subsequently roll over a distribution to another IRA or utilize an IRA trustee-to-trustee transfer. If an amount is subsequently transferred to a second IRA, it cannot be rolled over again for 1 year. However, there is no limit on direct IRA trustee-to-trustee transfers.

Tip. The withholding requirement on eligible rollover distributions from a qualified plan can be avoided on a distribution received currently simply by having amounts transferred directly to an IRA and then immediately withdrawing them from the IRA.

TaxAlert

Plan administrators are required to give plan participants a written notice explaining the rollover rules, including the direct rollover option and related tax rules. You may consider the decision whether to have your benefits paid in a direct rollover or paid directly to you for at least 30 days after you receive this notice, unless you waive this right.

Explanation

There is a second way amounts can be rolled over. If your funds are not transferred in a direct rollover (e.g., where the plan trustee has made the check payable to you), you may nonetheless roll over some or all of your eligible rollover distribution to an eligible retirement plan. You must complete the rollover by the 60th day following the day on which you receive the distribution. In this case, the plan administrator making the distribution will withhold 20% of the distribution as income tax, and in order to roll over the full distribution, you will have to use other funds to make up the 20% withheld. If you do not make up the amount withheld, you will be taxed on the amount withheld and may also owe a 10% early distribution tax on such amount. See *Tax on Early Distributions* later in this chapter. For this type of rollover, after-tax contributions can only be rolled into an IRA.

TaxSaver

One of the most difficult decisions you have to make when you near retirement is what to do with your qualified pension or profit-sharing plan. There are usually four choices:

1. **Lump-sum distribution.** A lump sum distribution generally will be taxed to you as ordinary income; the after-tax balance can then be invested as you see fit. If you were born before 1936, you may be eligible to pay tax based on 10-year income averaging or capital gain treatment (discussed above).
2. **Annuity.** The qualified plan pays you and/or your surviving spouse an annuity, the value of which is determined by how much of an annuity the lump-sum distribution would have bought from an insurance carrier based on your life expectancy. When you and your spouse die, nothing further is paid. If your plan requires that a joint and survivor annuity be offered to married participants, then, in order to elect out of the annuity alternative, your spouse must consent to another form of distribution, such as a lump-sum distribution.
3. **Rollover to an IRA or other eligible retirement plan.** There is no income tax required to be withheld on any portion of an eligible rollover distribution that is rolled over directly to an IRA or other eligible retirement plan. The principal continues to earn income without tax until it is withdrawn. Withdrawals are taxed at ordinary income rates and are required to begin not later than April 1 of the calendar year following the calendar year in which the employee attains age 70 1/2 (or following the calendar year of retirement in the case of an employer plan where the employee is not a 5% owner). Withdrawals are to be made over the life of such employee or over the lives of such employee and a designated beneficiary (or over a period not extending beyond the life expectancy of such employee or the joint life expectancy of such employee and a designated beneficiary).
4. **Retention in the plan.** If you have more than $5,000 vested in the plan, the plan must permit you to leave your account balance in the qualified plan until you reach age 62 or a stipulated normal retirement age, if later. This may be advantageous if you don't need the money right away depending on the investment return of the plan. If you have less than $5,000 vested in the plan, the plan may require that you receive your account balance in a lump sum whether or not you consent.

Example
You have $100,000 in the company's qualified plan and you will reach the retirement age of 65 shortly. You may have the following options, depending on the plan's distribution provisions:

1. You and your spouse may receive a joint and survivor annuity of $12,000 (based on assumptions used in this example) every year through the year of death of the last to die. Each payment will be subject to tax at ordinary rates, which may be as high as 35%, depending on which tax bracket you're in. The total that you and/or your spouse will receive will depend on your life spans and your actual marginal tax rates in each year that you live. This is the joint and 100% survivor annuity option. Most plans permit more than one annuity option. As an alternative, if your plan permits, you could elect to receive more during your lifetime and have your spouse receive less upon your death, so long as your spouse receives no less than 50% of the amount you receive.
2. You may roll over the entire amount into an IRA or another eligible retirement plan. You will have to begin receiving payments from an IRA, which will be taxed at ordinary income rates, no later than April 1 of the year following the year you reach age 70 1/2.
3. The plan invests solely in a guaranteed insurance contract that has a fixed rate of 8.5% for 2005. This rate may be so attractive that you may elect to defer the receipt of your account balance until a later year, if you qualify.
4. No current tax is paid or withheld if the entire amount is transferred directly over to a qualified plan of a new employer or an IRA. (Remember that while a qualified plan is required to offer the direct rollover option, there is no requirement that another qualified plan accept such rollovers.) You will pay tax when subsequent withdrawals occur.
5. If you will be self-employed during the year in which you retire, you can transfer your qualified pension plan account into a Keogh plan. The virtue of transferring your pension into a Keogh plan instead of an IRA is that, if you were born before 1936, you can be taxed using the 10-year averaging method (discussed above) if you withdraw the money from the Keogh in a lump-sum distribution. You cannot use the 10-year averaging method if you transfer your qualified pension plan account into an IRA. Many people find it easy to arrange to be self-employed in the year in which they retire. If the plan-to-plan transfer is done properly, you can preserve your pre-transfer service from the old plan for purposes of the 5-year minimum participation requirement.

In this example, the choice between options 1, 2, and 3 is tricky and requires analysis under various assumptions of interest rates, life expectancy, medical expenses, current needs, and tax rates. Professional help is necessary and well worth the cost.

Methods 4 and 5 may also save you time and keep your investments consolidated in one account while preserving your option to be taxed using the 10-year averaging method. Consult your tax advisor if you think you qualify for these two alternatives.

Rollover by surviving spouse. You may be able to roll over tax free all or part of a distribution from a qualified retirement plan you receive as the surviving spouse of a deceased employee. The rollover rules apply to you as if you were the employee. You can roll over a distribution into a qualified retirement plan or a traditional IRA.

A beneficiary other than the employee's surviving spouse cannot roll over a distribution.

Alternate payee under qualified domestic relations order. You may be able to roll over all or any part of a distribution from a qualified retirement plan that you receive under a qualified domestic relations order (QDRO). If you receive the distribution as an employee's spouse or former spouse (not as a nonspousal beneficiary), the rollover rules apply to you as if you were the employee. You can roll over the distribution from the plan into a traditional IRA or to another eligible retirement plan. See Publication 575 for more information on benefits received under a QDRO.

Explanation

Any distribution attributable to an employee that is paid to the employee's surviving spouse is treated in the same manner as if the spouse were the employee. The same rule applies if any distribution attributable to an employee is paid to a spouse or a former spouse as an "alternate payee" under a QDRO. A distribution made to the surviving spouse of an employee (or an alternate payee under a QDRO) is an eligible rollover distribution if it meets the requirements explained above. For further details, consult your tax advisor.

TAXPLANNER

Be certain to inform your plan administrator if you wish to change the beneficiary of your qualified retirement plan. Generally, the designated beneficiary on file with your plan administrator will be treated as the beneficiary of your plan even if you have subsequently changed the beneficiary under other agreements, such as a divorce settlement. It is a good idea to review your beneficiary designations each time you have a change in family status (e.g., marriage or divorce). If you have not designated a beneficiary for any salary that, because of death, you will not collect, the money will generally be paid into your estate. In that case, it would be reported as income on the estate's income tax return.

Retirement bonds. If you redeem a retirement bond purchased under a qualified bond purchase plan, you can defer the tax on the amount received that exceeds your basis by rolling it over to an IRA or qualified employer plan as discussed in Publication 590. For more information on the rules for rolling over distributions, see Publication 575.

Special Additional Taxes

To discourage the use of pension funds for purposes other than normal retirement, the law imposes additional taxes on early distributions of those funds and on failures to withdraw the funds timely. Ordinarily, you will not be subject to these taxes if you roll over all early distributions you receive, as explained earlier, and begin drawing out the funds at a normal retirement age, in reasonable amounts over your life expectancy. These special additional taxes are the taxes on:

- Early distributions, and
- Excess accumulation (not receiving minimum distributions).

These taxes are discussed in the following sections.

If you must pay either of these taxes, report them on Form 5329. However, you do not have to file Form 5329 if you owe only the tax on early distributions and your Form 1099-R correctly shows a "1" in box 7. Instead, enter 10% of the taxable part of the distribution on Form 1040, line 60 and write "No" under the heading "Other Taxes" to the left of line 60.

Even if you do not owe any of these taxes, you may have to complete Form 5329 and attach it to your Form 1040. This applies if you meet an exception to the tax on early distributions but box 7 of your Form 1099-R does not indicate an exception.

Tax on Early Distributions

Most distributions (both periodic and nonperiodic) from qualified retirement plans and nonqualified annuity contracts made to you before you reach age 59 1/2 are subject to an additional tax of 10%. This tax applies to the part of the distribution that you must include in gross income.

For this purpose, a qualified retirement plan is:

- A qualified employee plan,
- A qualified employee annuity plan,
- A tax-sheltered annuity plan, or
- A state or local government section 457 deferred compensation plan (to the extent that any distribution is attributable to amounts the plan received in a direct transfer or rollover from one of the other plans listed here).

5% rate on certain early distributions from deferred annuity contracts. If an early withdrawal from a deferred annuity is otherwise subject to the 10% additional tax, a 5% rate may apply instead. A 5% rate applies to distributions under a written election providing a specific schedule for the distribution of your interest in the contract if, as of March 1, 1986, you had begun receiving payments under the election. On line 4 of Form 5329, multiply by 5% instead of 10%. Attach an explanation to your return.

Exceptions to tax. Certain early distributions are excepted from the early distribution tax. If the payer knows that an exception applies to your early distribution, distribution code "2," "3," or "4" should be shown in box 7 of your Form 1099-R and you do not have to report the distribution on Form 5329. If an exception applies but distribution code "1" (early distribution, no known exception) is shown in box 7, you must file Form 5329. Enter the taxable amount of the distribution shown in box 2a of your Form 1099-R on line 1 of Form 5329. On line 2, enter the amount that can be excluded and the exception number shown in the Form 5329 instructions.

Tip. *If distribution code "1" is incorrectly shown on your Form 1099-R for a distribution received when you were age 59 1/2 or older, include that distribution on Form 5329. Enter exception number "11" on line 2.*

General exceptions. The tax does not apply to distributions that are:

- Made as part of a series of substantially equal periodic payments (made at least annually) for your life (or life expectancy) or the joint lives (or joint life expectancies) of you and your designated beneficiary (if from a qualified retirement plan, the payments must begin after your separation from service),
- Made because you are totally and permanently disabled, or
- Made on or after the death of the plan participant or contract holder.

TAXPLANNER

You should carefully consider whether substantially equal periodic distributions commencing before you attain age 59 1/2 would be sufficient to satisfy your income needs. Although these distributions are not subject to the 10% early distribution tax they *will* be subject to this tax if the amount of the distributions is modified (other than by reason of death, disability, or a change in method described below) either before you attain age 59 1/2 or before the end of the calendar 5-year period beginning with the date of the first distribution and after you attain age 59 1/2. In the year the distributions are modified, you will have to pay the 10% penalty tax on all of the distributions you have received to date, plus interest.

TAXALERT

Payments are considered to be substantially equal periodic payments if they are made in accordance with one of three calculations: 1) the required minimum distribution method, 2) the fixed amortization method, or 3) the fixed annuitization method. Because of the rule against modification of substantially equal periodic payments, described above, individuals who chose annuitization or amortization (which require a fixed amount to be withdrawn each year) would have to pay a retroactive penalty on all of the distributions made, if they wanted to reduce the amount of money they received in order to keep their account from being dissipated. The IRS allows individuals who started distributions using the fixed amortization method or the fixed annuitization method to change to the required minimum distribution method once without incurring that penalty.

Additional exceptions for qualified retirement plans.
The tax does not apply to distributions that are:

- From a qualified retirement plan (other than an IRA) after your separation from service in or after the year you reached age 55,
- From a qualified retirement plan (other than an IRA) to an alternate payee under a qualified domestic relations order,
- From a qualified retirement plan to the extent you have deductible medical expenses (medical expenses that exceed 7.5% of your adjusted gross income), whether or not you itemize your deductions for the year,
- From an employer plan under a written election that provides a specific schedule for distribution of your entire interest if, as of March 1, 1986, you had separated from service and had begun receiving payments under the election,
- From an employee stock ownership plan for dividends on employer securities held by the plan, or
- From a qualified retirement plan due to an IRS levy of the plan.

Additional exceptions for nonqualified annuity contracts.
The tax does not apply to distributions that are:

- From a deferred annuity contract to the extent allocable to investment in the contract before August 14, 1982,
- From a deferred annuity contract under a qualified personal injury settlement,
- From a deferred annuity contract purchased by your employer upon termination of a qualified employee plan or qualified employee annuity plan and held by your employer until your separation from service, or
- From an immediate annuity contract (a single premium contract providing substantially equal annuity payments that start within one year from the date of purchase and are paid at least annually).

TaxPlanner

Early distributions from IRAs are also subject to the 10% excise tax. However, the tax does not apply to distributions that are:

- Made after separation from employment if, among other requirements, the individual received unemployment compensation for 12 consecutive weeks by reason of the separation, but only to the extent the distributions do not exceed the amount paid for medical insurance or qualified long-term care insurance during the year,
- Distributions to pay for certain higher education expenses, or
- Distributions used within 120 days to pay qualified acquisition costs on a principal residence of a first-time homebuyer who is the IRA owner, or the spouse, child, grandchild, or ancestor of the IRA owner or spouse.

TaxSaver
Note that the 10% excise tax also does not apply in the year of distribution if you roll over a qualifying distribution (including a direct rollover of an eligible rollover distribution). This is because the tax is applied only to taxable distributions. This helps to make rollovers an even more attractive alternative.

TaxOrganizer
On Form 1099-R, distributions should be coded by the payer without regard to whether a rollover is made or anticipated (except for a direct rollover). Thus, for purposes of Form 1099-R reporting, a rollover that is planned or has already occurred should not be considered an exception to the early distribution penalty.

Example
If Ben Jones withdraws the total balance in his qualified plan, informs the plan administrator that the funds will be rolled over, is under age 59 1/2, and meets no other exception under the early distribution rules, the Form 1099-R should contain a code "1" in Box 7, "Early distribution, no known exception." If Mr. Jones then rolls over his distribution, he should properly report the rollover on his federal income tax return to avoid the early distribution penalty.

Tax on Excess Accumulation
To make sure that most of your retirement benefits are paid to you during your lifetime, rather than to your beneficiaries after your death, the payments that you receive from qualified retirement plans must begin no later than on your required beginning date (defined next). The payments each year cannot be less than the required minimum distribution.

Required beginning date. Unless the rule for 5% owners applies, you must begin to receive distributions from your qualified retirement plan by April 1 of the year that follows the later of:

- The calendar year in which you reach age 70 1/2, or
- The calendar year in which you retire from employment with the employer maintaining the plan.

However, your plan may require you to begin to receive distributions by April 1 of the year that follows the year in which you reach age 70 1/2, even if you have not retired.

For this purpose, a qualified retirement plan includes a:

1. Qualified employee plan,
2. Qualified employee annuity plan,
3. Section 457 deferred compensation plan, or
4. Tax-sheltered annuity plan (for benefits accruing after 1986).

Age 70 1/2. You reach age 70 1/2 on the date that is 6 calendar months after the date of your 70th birthday.

For example, if you are retired and your 70th birthday was on June 30, 2005, you were age 70 1/2 on December 30, 2005. If your 70th birthday was on July 1, 2005, you reached age 70 1/2 on January 1, 2006.

5% owners. If you are a 5% owner of the company maintaining your qualified retirement plan, you must begin to receive distributions by April 1 of the calendar year that follows the year in which you reach age 70 1/2, regardless of when you retire.

Required distributions. By the required beginning date, as explained earlier, you must either:

• Receive your entire interest in the plan (for a tax-sheltered annuity, your entire benefit accruing after 1986), or
• Begin receiving periodic distributions in annual amounts calculated to distribute your entire interest (for a tax-sheltered annuity, your entire benefit accruing after 1986) over your life or life expectancy or over the joint lives or joint life expectancies of you and a designated beneficiary (or over a shorter period).

TaxALERT

The IRS has issued final regulations that provide the life expectancy and distribution period tables to be used for determining required minimum distributions (see Table 11-1).

Table 11-1
Uniform Lifetime Table

The following table is used for determining the distribution period for lifetime distributions to an employee (or IRA owner) in situations in which the employee's (or IRA owner's) spouse is either not the sole designated beneficiary or is the sole designated beneficiary but is not more than 10 years younger than the employee (or IRA owner).

Age	Distribution Period	Age	Distribution Period
70	27.4	93	9.6
71	26.5	94	9.1
72	25.6	95	8.6
73	24.7	96	8.1
74	23.8	97	7.6
75	22.9	98	7.1
76	22.0	99	6.7
77	21.2	100	6.3
78	20.3	101	5.9
79	19.5	102	5.5
80	18.7	103	5.2
81	17.9	104	4.9
82	17.1	105	4.5
83	16.3	106	4.2
84	15.5	107	3.9
85	14.8	108	3.7
86	14.1	109	3.4
87	13.4	110	3.1
88	12.7	111	2.9
89	12.0	112	2.6
90	11.4	113	2.4
91	10.8	114	2.1
92	10.2	115 and older	1.0

Additional information. For more information on this rule, see *Tax on Excess Accumulation* in Publication 575.

Required distributions not made. If the actual distributions to you in any year are less than the required minimum distribution, you are subject to an additional excise tax. The tax equals 50% of the part of the required minimum distribution that was not distributed. You can get this excise tax waived if you establish that the shortfall in distributions was due to reasonable error and that you are taking reasonable steps to remedy the shortfall.

Explanation
All plans (except traditional IRAs) must begin to make minimum distributions to you (unless you are a more than 5% owner) no later than April 1 of the calendar year following the later of:

1. The calendar year in which you reach age 70 1/2, or
2. The calendar year in which you retire.

Traditional IRAs must begin making minimum distributions by April 1 of the calendar year after the calendar year you turn 70 1/2, whether or not you have retired.

Plans can, but are not required to, permit individuals who were receiving minimum distributions on December 31, 1996, but who have not yet retired, to stop receiving distributions until they retire. You should ask your employer or plan administrator if this is permitted under your plan.

Although plans must begin making minimum distributions by the later of the calendar year after you retire or the year after you turn 70 1/2, they are not required to wait until you actually retire. They may begin making minimum distributions in the year after you reach retirement age under the plan. Your plan administrator can provide details on the provisions of your plan.

The required beginning date for an IRA owner is April 1 of the calendar year following the calendar year in which the owner attains age 70 1/2 (see When Must You Withdraw IRA Assets? [Required Minimum Distributions] in Chapter 18, *Individual Retirement Arrangements [IRAs]*).

Distributions to a more than 5% owner must also begin by April 1 of the calendar year after the year in which he or she reaches 70 1/2.

TaxPLANNER

If you work beyond age 70 1/2, it may be advantageous to delay the minimum distributions (if your plan allows) and allow the amounts in the retirement plan to grow on a tax-deferred basis. You may also be able to defer the minimum distributions from your IRA, if you are still working, by transferring your IRA balance to an employer plan sponsored by an employer as long as you're not a 5% or more owner of the employer. The advantage of delaying distributions is reduced for defined benefit plan participants due to a special rule that requires the amount of the minimum distributions to be increased when the participant ultimately retires and begins receiving distributions. Consult your plan administrator or tax advisor for more information on the decision to delay minimum distributions.

TaxPLANNER

Because the penalty for failure to receive required minimum distributions is severe, you must take steps to ensure that you receive these amounts on a timely basis. The minimum distribution rules are particularly onerous for IRA owners who are required to determine their minimum distributions on their own. The IRS has issued final regulations and guidance that will make it easier for IRA owners to meet the minimum required distribution requirements. If a minimum distribution is required with respect to an IRA for a calendar year and the IRA owner is alive at the beginning of the year, the IRA trustee must provide a statement to the IRA owner by January 31 of the calendar year regarding the required minimum distribution in accordance with two alternatives.

Under the first alternative, the IRA trustee must furnish the IRA owner with a statement of the amount of the required minimum distribution with respect to the IRA for the calendar year and the date by which such amount must be distributed. Under the second alternative, the IRA trustee must provide a statement to the IRA owner that: (1) informs the IRA owner that a minimum distribution with respect to the IRA is required for the calendar year and the date by which such amount must be distributed and (2) includes an offer to furnish the IRA owner, upon request, with a calculation of the amount of the required minimum distribution with respect to the IRA for that calendar year. If the IRA owner requests such a calculation, the IRA trustee must calculate the required minimum distribution for the IRA owner and report that amount to the IRA owner. IRA trustees may provide some IRA owners with statements that satisfy the first alternative and other IRA owners with statements that satisfy the second alternative. These reporting requirements were effective beginning with required minimum distributions for 2003.

TAXPLANNER

If you have made after-tax contributions to your employer's retirement plan [e.g., contributions other than pre-tax salary deferrals to a 401(k) plan or 403(b) tax-sheltered annuity], you may be able to satisfy the minimum distribution rules without being taxed for the first year (or possibly the first 2 years) the minimum distributions are required. This may be accomplished by: (1) electing to receive a lump-sum distribution from your retirement plan or IRA by April 1 of the year the minimum distributions are required to begin, (2) retaining the portion of the distribution that represents the tax-free return of your after-tax employee contributions, and (3) electing to roll over the remaining amount of the lump-sum distribution to another qualified retirement plan or IRA.

Example

Assume Dawn reaches age 70 1/2 in 2004 and elects to retire in 2004. Also assume that Dawn has made a total of $40,000 in after-tax employee contributions to her employer's retirement plan over the years and has a balance of $100,000 in the plan as of the end of 2004. Dawn must receive the minimum required distribution for 2004 by April 1, 2005. In addition, she must receive the minimum required distribution for 2005 by December 31, 2005. Assume the minimum required distribution amounts are $15,000 and $20,000 for 2004 and 2005, respectively.

Dawn elects to receive a lump-sum distribution of her entire $100,000 account balance by April 1, 2005; retains $35,000 of this amount attributable to her after-tax employee contributions; and rolls over $65,000 to an IRA within 60 days of the distribution. As a result, she will not be taxed on the $35,000 she did not roll over since this is a nontaxable return of her after-tax employee contributions. More importantly, such nontaxable amounts may be used to satisfy the minimum distribution requirements. In this example, the $35,000 distributed to Dawn by April 1, 2005, equaled the sum of the $15,000 that was required to be distributed by April 1, 2005, and the $20,000 that was required to be distributed to her by December 31, 2005. After the rollover, Dawn would have basis of $5,000 (the balance of her after-tax contributions rolled into the IRA) in her new IRA.

State insurer delinquency proceedings. You might not receive the minimum distribution because of state insurer delinquency proceedings for an insurance company. If your payments are reduced below the minimum due to these proceedings, you should contact your plan administrator. Under certain conditions, you will not have to pay the excise tax.

Form 5329. You must file a Form 5329 if you owe a tax because you did not receive a minimum required distribution from your qualified retirement plan.

Disability Pensions

If you retired on disability, you generally must include in income any disability pension you receive under a plan that is paid for by your employer. You must report your taxable disability payments as wages on line 7 of Form 1040 or Form 1040A until you reach minimum retirement age. Minimum retirement age generally is the age at which you can first receive a pension or annuity if you are not disabled.

Tip. *You may be entitled to a tax credit if you were permanently and totally disabled when you retired. For information on this credit, see chapter 35.*

Beginning on the day after you reach minimum retirement age, payments you receive are taxable as a pension or annuity. Report the payments on Form 1040, lines 16a and 16b or on Form 1040A, lines 12a and 12b.

Tip. *Disability payments for injuries incurred as a direct result of a terrorist attack directed against the United States (or its allies) are not included in income. For more information about payments to survivors of terrorist attacks, see Publication 3920, Tax Relief for Victims of Terrorist Attacks.*

For more information on how to report disability pensions, including military and certain government disability pensions, see chapter 6.

Purchased Annuities

If you receive pension or annuity payments from a privately purchased annuity contract from a commercial organization, such as an insurance company, you generally must use the General Rule to figure the tax-free part of each annuity payment. For more information about the General Rule, get Publication 939. Also, see *Variable Annuities* in Publication 575 for the special provisions that apply to these annuity contracts.

Sale of annuity. Gain on the exchange of an annuity contract is ordinary income to the extent that the gain is due to interest accumulated on the contract and the exchange is for a life insurance or endowment contract. You do not recognize gain or loss on an exchange of an annuity contract solely for another annuity contract if the insured or annuitant remains the same. See *Transfers of Annuity Contracts* in Publication 575 for more information about exchanges of annuity contracts.

TAXSAVER

Annuities are popular investments because the amount you contribute grows over time through the accumulation of earnings. The earnings are not currently taxable to you and are reported as income only in later years, when payments are made from the annuity. The taxable payments are most likely to be made after you've retired. Therefore, an annuity may be a good way in which to earn income and defer taxes. Nowadays, it is more important than ever to investigate the financial strength and credit rating of the insurance company issuing the annuity.

You should realize, though, that income paid from an annuity is treated as ordinary regardless of whether the earnings actually resulted from qualified dividends and/or long-term capital gains, which would be taxed at preferential rates. You should consider this rate difference before you decide to invest in an annuity.

Social Security and Equivalent Railroad Retirement Benefits

Note: The 2004 IRS Publication 17 (Your Federal Income Tax) has been updated by Ernst & Young LLP for 2005. Dates and dollar amounts shown are for 2005. Gray type is used to indicate where IRS text has been updated or intentionally omitted. Unrevised IRS text is shown in black type.

Introduction

Social Security income and equivalent railroad retirement benefits used to be tax free. That hasn't been the case for a while. Now, you may have to pay income tax on amounts you receive. However, figuring out whether the benefits you receive are taxable is not easy. You will *be required to puzzle through complicated rules, obtain information, and make numerous computations. This chapter will simplify your task. Among other things, it includes worksheets to help you make the necessary calculations.*

This chapter explains the federal income tax rules for social security benefits and equivalent tier 1 railroad retirement benefits. It explains:

- How to figure whether your benefits are taxable,
- How to use the social security benefits worksheet (with examples),
- How to report your taxable benefits, and
- How to treat repayments that are more than the benefits you received during the year.

Social security benefits include monthly survivor and disability benefits. They do not include supplemental security income (SSI) payments, which are not taxable.

Equivalent tier 1 railroad retirement benefits are the part of tier 1 benefits that a railroad employee or beneficiary would have been entitled to receive under the social security system. They are commonly called the social security equivalent benefit (SSEB) portion of tier 1 benefits.

If you received these benefits during 2005, you should have received a Form SSA-1099, Social Security Benefit Statement, or Form RRB-1099, Payments by the Railroad Retirement Board, (Form SSA-1042S, Social Security Benefit Statement, or Form RRB-1042S Statement for Nonresident Alien Recipients of: Payments by the Railroad Retirement Board, if you are a nonresident alien). These forms show the amounts received and repaid, and taxes withheld for the year. You may receive more than one of these forms for the same year. You should add the amounts shown on all forms you receive for the year to determine the "total" amounts received and repaid, and taxes withheld for that year. See the *Appendix* at the end of Publication 915 for more information.

Note. *When the term "benefits" is used in this chapter, it applies to both social security benefits and the SSEB portion of tier 1 railroad retirement benefits.*

What is not covered in this chapter. This chapter does not cover the tax rules for the following railroad retirement benefits:

- Non-social security equivalent benefit (NSSEB) portion of tier 1 benefits,
- Tier 2 benefits,
- Vested dual benefits, and
- Supplemental annuity benefits.

For information on these benefits, see Publication 575, Pension and Annuity Income.

This chapter also does not cover the tax rules for foreign social security benefits. These benefits are taxable as annuities, unless they are exempt from U.S. tax or treated as a U.S. social security benefit under a tax treaty.

Useful Items

You may want to see:

Publications

☐ **575** Pension and Annuity Income

☐ **590** Individual Retirement Arrangements (IRAs)
☐ **915** Social Security and Equivalent Railroad Retirement Benefits

Forms (and Instructions)

☐ **1040-ES** Estimated Tax for Individuals
☐ **W-4V** Voluntary Withholding Request

TAXPLANNER

For additional Social Security and retirement information, you may want to consult the following Web sites: www.ssa.gov, www.rrb.gov, and www.seniors.gov.

Are Any of Your Benefits Taxable?

To find out whether any of your benefits may be taxable, compare the base amount for your filing status with the total of:

1. One-half of your benefits, plus
2. All your other income, including tax-exempt interest.

When making this comparison, do not reduce your other income by any exclusions for:

• Interest from qualified U.S. savings bonds,
• Employer-provided adoption benefits,
• Foreign earned income or foreign housing, or
• Income earned by *bona fide* residents of American Samoa or Puerto Rico.

TAXPLANNER

If you want to plan ahead, you can request an estimate of your Social Security benefits by filing Form SSA-7004, *Your Social Security Statement.* Copies of the form can be obtained from your local Social Security office, by calling (800) 772-1213, or by visiting www.ssa.gov on the World Wide Web.

Explanation
Taxation of benefits. In figuring if any of your benefits are taxable, use the amount shown in box 5 of the Form SSA-1099 or Form RRB-1099 you received. If you received more than one form, add together the amount in box 5 of each form.

SSI payments. If you received any SSI payments during the year, do not include these payments in your Social Security benefits received. SSI payments are made under Title XVI of the Social Security Act. They are not taxable for federal income tax purposes.

Form SSA-1099. If you received or repaid Social Security benefits during 2005, you will receive Form SSA-1099, *Social Security Benefit Statement.* An IRS Notice 703 will be enclosed with your Form SSA-1099. This notice includes a worksheet you can use to determine if any of your benefits may be taxable. Keep this notice for your own records. Do **not** mail it to either the Internal Revenue Service or the SSA.

Every person who received Social Security benefits will receive a Form SSA-1099, even if the benefit is combined with another person's in a single check. If you receive benefits on more than one Social Security record, you may get more than one Form SSA-1099.

Form RRB-1099. If you received or repaid the Social Security equivalent portion of tier 1 railroad retirement benefits or special guaranty benefits during 2005, you will receive Form RRB-1099 *Payments by the Railroad Retirement Board.*

Each beneficiary will receive his or her own Form RRB-1099. If you receive benefits on more than one railroad retirement record, you may get more than one Form RRB-1099.

Figuring total income. To figure the total of one-half of your benefits plus your other income, use the worksheet later in this discussion. If the total is more than your base amount, part of your benefits may be taxable.

Explanation
The filing requirements for individuals are based on income, age, and filing status (e.g., married filing jointly, single). See Chapter 1, *Filing Information.*

If you are married and file a joint return for 2005, you and your spouse must combine your incomes and your benefits to figure whether any of your combined benefits are taxable. Even if your spouse did not receive any benefits, you must add your spouse's income to yours to figure whether any of your benefits are taxable.
Tip. *If the only income you received during 2005 was your social security or the SSEB portion of tier 1 railroad retirement benefits, your benefits generally are not taxable and you probably do not have to file a return. If you have income in addition to your benefits, you may have to file a return even if none of your benefits are taxable.*
Base amount. Your base amount is:

• $25,000 if you are single, head of household, or qualifying widow(er),
• $25,000 if you are married filing separately and lived apart from your spouse for all of 2005,
• $32,000 if you are married filing jointly, or
• $-0- if you are married filing separately and lived with your spouse at any time during 2005.

Explanation
Social Security and railroad retirement benefits are partially taxable if your *total income* (defined below) is more than $32,000 for married taxpayers filing jointly and $25,000 for single filers. If you are married filing separately *and* you lived with your spouse at any time during the year, your base amount is $0, which means that your Social Security retirement benefits are partially taxable regardless of your income level. Your *total income* is the sum of your adjusted gross income, tax-exempt income, excluded foreign source income, excluded interest from U.S. savings bonds (interest excluded in connection with the payment of qualified education expenses), and one-half of your Social Security retirement benefits.

Tax-exempt income is *not taxable* for federal purposes, even if you receive Social Security benefits. However, it is one of the items taken into consideration in determining whether or not your income exceeds the threshold amount so that your Social Security benefits are taxable.

TAXSAVER
If you expect your total income (defined above) to exceed the base amount ($32,000 if you are filing a joint

return, $25,000 if you are filing single), you may wish to consider the following strategies.

- *Defer the recognition of income* by investing in U.S. savings bonds. Generally, the increase in value of the bonds issued at a discount (Series E and EE) is not taxable until you surrender the bonds. Additionally, if you hold the bonds until death, your heirs will recognize the income (assuming you did not elect to include in income the annual increase in the value of the bond).
- *Stagger the recognition of income* so that you have alternating years of higher income. Depending on your income level, you could structure income so that your Social Security benefits are taxed every other year. For example, when considering sources of cash flow, surrender U.S. savings bonds, make withdrawals from IRAs, and sell appreciated property in alternate years. You could also schedule the maturity dates of U.S. Treasury notes and bills to ensure that your income is under the base amount in certain years.
- If you have earned income, *consider contributing to your company's 401(k) plan, your not-for-profit 403(b) plan, or a deductible Individual Retirement Arrangement (IRA) account* (see Chapter 18, *Individual Retirement Arrangements (IRAs)*, to determine if you qualify) to decrease your adjusted gross income and also reduce the taxable portion of your social security benefits.

TAXPLANNER

Tax-exempt income is added to your adjusted gross income for purposes of calculating how much, if any, of your Social Security benefits will be subject to tax. Keep this in mind when evaluating the after-tax rate of return of tax-exempt investments vs. taxable investments.

Worksheet. You can use the following worksheet to figure the amount of income to compare with your base amount. This is a quick way to check whether some of your benefits may be taxable.

A. Write in the amount from *box 5* of all your Forms SSA-1099 and RRB-1099. Include the full amount of any lump-sum benefit payments received in 2005, for 2005 and earlier years. (If you received more than one form, combine the amounts from box 5 and write in the total.) .... A._____

Note: *If the amount on line A is zero or less, stop here; none of your benefits are taxable this year.*

B. Enter one-half of the amount on line A............................ B._____

C. Add your taxable pensions, wages, interest, dividends, and other taxable income and write in the total............................... C._____

D. Write in any tax-exempt interest income (such as interest on municipal bonds) plus any exclusions from income (listed earlier) .... D._____

E. Add lines B, C, and D and write in the total .... E._____

Note. *Compare the amount on line E to your base amount for your filing status. If the amount on line E equals or is less than the base amount for your filing status, none of your benefits are taxable this year. If the amount on line E is more than your base amount, some of your benefits may be taxable. You then need to complete Worksheet 1 in Publication 915 (or the Social Security Benefits Worksheet in your tax form instruction booklet).*

Example. You and your spouse (both over 65) are filing a joint return for 2005, and you both received social security benefits during the year. In January 2006, you received a Form SSA-1099 showing net benefits of $7,500 in box 5. Your spouse received a Form SSA-1099 showing net benefits of $3,500 in box 5. You also received a taxable pension of $19,000 and interest income of $500. You did not have any tax-exempt interest income. Your benefits are not taxable for 2005 because your income, as figured in the following worksheet, is not more than your base amount ($32,000) for married filing jointly.

Even though none of your benefits are taxable, you must file a return for 2005 because your taxable gross income ($19,500) exceeds the minimum filing requirement amount for your filing status.

A. Write in the amount from *box 5* of all your Forms SSA-1099 and RRB-1099. Include the full amount of any lump-sum benefit payments received in 2005, for 2005 and earlier years. (If you received more than one form, combine the amounts from box 5 and write in the total.) .... A. $11,000

Note: *If the amount on line A is zero or less, stop here; none of your benefits are taxable this year.*

B. Enter one-half of the amount on line A............................ B.   5,500

C. Add your taxable pensions, wages, interest, dividends, and other taxable income and write in the total............................... C.   19,500

D. Write in any tax-exempt interest income (such as interest on municipal bonds) plus any exclusions from income (listed earlier) .... D.   -0-

E. Add lines B, C, and D and write in the total .... E. $25,000

Note: *Compare the amount on line E to your base amount for your filing status. If the amount on line E equals or is less than the base amount for your filing status, none of your benefits are taxable this year. If the amount on line E is more than your base amount, some of your benefits may be taxable. You then need to complete Worksheet 1 in Publication 915 (or the Social Security Benefits Worksheet in your tax form instruction booklet).*

Who is taxed. The person who has the legal right to receive the benefits must determine whether the benefits are taxable. For example, if you and your child receive benefits, but the check for your child is made out in your name, you must use only your part of the benefits to see whether any benefits are taxable to you. One-half of the part that belongs to your child must be added to your child's other income to see whether any of those benefits are taxable to your child.

TAXORGANIZER

You should maintain a copy of Form(s) SSA-1099, RRB-1099, and Form 1042F for 3 years following the due date (including extensions) of your income tax return.

Repayment of benefits. Any repayment of benefits you made during 2005 must be subtracted from the gross benefits you received in 2005. It does not matter whether the repayment was for a benefit you received in 2005 or in an earlier year. If you repaid more than the gross benefits you received in 2005, see *Repayments More Than Gross Benefits,* later.

Your gross benefits are shown in box 3 of Form SSA-1099 or RRB-1099. Your repayments are shown in box 4. The amount in box 5 shows your net benefits for 2005 (box 3 minus box 4). Use the amount in box 5 to figure whether any of your benefits are taxable.

Tax withholding and estimated tax. You can choose to have federal income tax withheld from your social security benefits and/or the SSEB portion of your tier 1 railroad retirement benefits. If you choose to do this, you must complete a Form W-4V. You can choose withholding at 7%, 10%, 15%, or 25% of your total benefit payment.

If you do not choose to have income tax withheld, you may have to request additional withholding from other income or pay estimated tax during the year. For details, get Publication 505, Tax Withholding and Estimated Tax, or the instructions for Form 1040-ES.

How To Report Your Benefits

If part of your benefits are taxable, you must use Form 1040 or Form 1040A. You cannot use Form 1040EZ.

Reporting on Form 1040. Report your net benefits (the amount in box 5 of your Form SSA-1099 or Form RRB-1099) on line 20a and the taxable part on line 20b. If you are married filing separately and you lived apart from your spouse for all of 2005, also enter "D" to the right of the word "benefits" on line 20a.

Reporting on Form 1040A. Report your net benefits (the amount in box 5 of your Form SSA-1099 or Form RRB-1099) on line 14a and the taxable part on line 14b. If you are married filing separately and you lived apart from your spouse for all of 2005, also enter "D" to the right of the word "benefits" on line 14a.

Benefits not taxable. If none of your benefits are taxable, do not report any of them on your tax return. But if you are married filing separately and you lived apart from your spouse for all of 2005, make the following entries. On Form 1040, enter "D" to the right of the word "benefits" on line 20a and "-0-" on line 20b. On Form 1040A, enter "D" to the right of the word "benefits" on line 14a and "-0-" on line 14b.

TAXORGANIZER

Summary of How to Report Your Benefits

	Form 1040	Form 1040A	Form 1040EZ
Net benefits	Line 20a	Line 14a	Cannot use Form
Taxable benefits	Line 20b	Line 14b	Cannot use Form

How Much Is Taxable?

If part of your benefits are taxable, how much is taxable depends on the total amount of your benefits and other income. Generally, the higher that total amount, the greater the taxable part of your benefits.

Maximum taxable part. Generally, up to 50% of your benefits will be taxable. However, up to 85% of your benefits can be taxable if either of the following situations applies to you.

1. The total of one-half of your benefits and all your other income is more than $34,000 ($44,000 if you are married filing jointly).
2. You are married filing separately and lived with your spouse at any time during 2005.

Explanation

After determining whether or not your Social Security retirement benefits are taxable, you must then determine what percentage (either 50% or 85%) of the total benefit is taxable. If you are filing a joint return and your *total income* (adjusted gross income + tax-exempt income + excluded foreign source income + excluded interest income from U.S. savings bonds + one-half of your Social Security retirement benefits) is less than $44,000 but greater than $32,000, a maximum of 50% of your Social Security retirement benefits is subject to federal tax. If, however, your *total income* exceeds $44,000, up to 85% of your Social Security retirement benefits will be included in income and taxed accordingly.

TAXSAVER

Many states allow a deduction for the amount of Social Security retirement benefits taxed at the federal level. Consult your tax advisor or state income tax authority for details.

Which worksheet to use. A worksheet to figure your taxable benefits is in the instructions for your Form 1040 or Form 1040A. You can use either that worksheet or Worksheet 1 in Publication 915, unless any of the following situations applies to you.

1. You contributed to a traditional individual retirement arrangement (IRA) and you or your spouse is covered by a retirement plan at work. In this situation, you must use the special worksheets in Appendix B of Publication 590 to figure both your IRA deduction and your taxable benefits.
2. Situation (1) does not apply and you take an exclusion for interest from qualified U.S. savings bonds (Form 8815), for adoption benefits (Form 8839), for foreign earned income or housing (Form 2555 or Form 2555-EZ), or for income earned by *bona fide* residents of American Samoa (Form 4563) or Puerto Rico. In this situation, you must use *Worksheet 1* in Publication 915 to figure your taxable benefits.
3. You received a lump-sum payment for an earlier year. In this situation, also complete *Worksheet 2 or 3* and Worksheet 4 in Publication 915. See *Lump-sum election.*

Lump-sum election. You must include the taxable part of a lump-sum (retroactive) payment of benefits received in 2005 in your 2005 income, even if the payment includes benefits for an earlier year.

Tip. *This type of lump-sum benefit payment should not be confused with the lump-sum death benefit that both the SSA and RRB pay to many of their beneficiaries. No part of the lump-sum death benefit is subject to tax.*

Generally, you use your 2005 income to figure the taxable part of the total benefits received in 2005. However, you may be able to figure the taxable part of a lump-sum payment for an earlier year separately, using your income for the earlier year. You can elect this method if it lowers your taxable benefits.

Making the election. If you received a lump-sum benefit payment in 2005 that includes benefits for one or more earlier years, follow the instructions in Publication 915 under *Lump-Sum Election* to see whether making the election will lower your taxable benefits. That discussion also explains how to make the election.

Caution. *Because the earlier year's taxable benefits are included in your 2005 income, no adjustment is made to the earlier year's return. Do not file an amended return for the earlier year.*

TAXPLANNER

Estimated tax. Generally, tax is not withheld on Social Security benefits. This means that you may have to pay estimated tax during the year if these benefits are taxable and you do not have enough taxes withheld from other income. However, you may request to have federal income tax withheld from your benefits at 7%, 10%, 15%, or 25%, but no other percentage or amount is allowed. This request is made by completing Form W-4V, *Voluntary Withholding Request,* and giving it to the agency making the payments. See Chapter 5, *Tax Withholding and Estimated Tax,* for more information on estimated tax.

Examples

The following are a few examples you can use as a guide to figure the taxable part of your benefits.

Example 1. George White is single and files Form 1040 for 2005. He received the following income in 2005:

Fully taxable pension	$18,600
Wages from part-time job	9,400
Taxable interest income	990
Total	$28,990

George also received social security benefits during 2005. The Form SSA-1099 he received in January 2006 shows $5,980 in box 5. To figure his taxable benefits, George completes the worksheet shown here.

Worksheet 1. Figuring Your Taxable Benefits

1. Enter the total amount from box 5 of ALL your Forms SSA-1099 and RRB-1099 5,980

Note. If line 1 is zero or less, stop here; none of your benefits are taxable. Otherwise, go on to line 2.

2. Enter one-half of line 1.. 2,990

3. Enter the total of the amounts from:
Form 1040: Lines 7, 8a, 8b, 9a, 10–14, 15b, 16b, 17–19, and 21.
Form 1040A: lines 7, 8a, 8b, 9a, 10, 11b, 12b, and 13 28,990

4. *Form 1040 filers:* Enter the total of any exclusions/adjustments for:
- Qualified U.S. savings bond interest (Form 8815, line 14),
- Adoption benefits (Form 8839, line 30),
- Foreign earned income or housing (Form 2555, lines 43 and 48, or Form 2555-EZ, line 18), and
- Certain income of bona fide residents of American Samoa (Form 4563, line 15) or Puerto Rico

Form 1040A filers: Enter the total of any exclusions for qualified U.S. savings bond interest (Form 8815, line 14) or for adoption benefits (Form 8839, line 30)................ -0-

5. Add lines 2, 3, and 4 31,980

6. *Form 1040 filers:* Enter the amount from Form 1040, line 36, minus any amounts on Form 1040, lines 33, 34 and 35

Form 1040A filers: Enter the amount from Form 1040A, line 20, minus any amounts on Form 1040A, lines 18 and 19........ -0-

7. Is the amount on line 6 less than the amount on line 5?

No. (STOP) None of your benefits are taxable.
Yes. Subtract line 6 from line 5 31,980

8. If you are:
- Married filing jointly, enter $32,000
- Single, head of household, qualifying widow(er), or married filing separately and you **lived apart** from your spouse for all of 2005, enter $25,000 25,000

Note. If you are married filing separately and you lived with your spouse at any time in 2005, skip lines 8 through 15; multiply line 7 by 85% (.85) and enter the result on line 16. Then go to line 17.

9. Is the amount on line 8 less than the amount on line 7?

No. (STOP) None of your benefits are taxable. Do not enter any amounts on Form 1040, line 20a or 20b, or on Form 1040A, line 14a or 14b. But if you are married filing separately and you lived apart from your spouse for all of 2005, enter -0- on Form 1040, line 20b, or on Form 1040A, line 14b.

Yes. Subtract line 8 from line 7 6,980

10. Enter $12,000 if married filing jointly; $9,000 if single, head of household, qualifying widow(er), or married filing separately and you **lived apart** from your spouse for all of 2005 9,000

11. Subtract line 10 from line 9. If zero or less, enter -0- .... -0-

12. Enter the **smaller** of line 9 or line 10 6,980

13. Enter one-half of line 12.. 3,490

14. Enter the **smaller** of line 2 or line 13 2,990

15. Multiply line 11 by 85% (.85). If line 11 is zero, enter -0-......... -0-

16. Add lines 14 and 15... 2,990

17. Multiply line 1 by 85% (.85).. 5,083

18. Taxable benefits. Enter the **smaller** of line 16 or line 17 .... $2,990

- Enter the amount from line 1 above on Form 1040, line 20a or on Form 1040A, line 14a.

- Enter the amount from line 18 above on Form 1040, line 20b or on Form 1040A, line 14b.

The amount on line 18 of George's worksheet shows that $2,990 of his social security benefits is taxable. On line 20a of his Form 1040, George enters his net benefits of $5,980. On line 20b, he enters his taxable part of $2,990.

Example 2. Ray and Alice Hopkins file a joint return on Form 1040A for 2005. Ray is retired and received a fully taxable pension of $15,500. He also received social security benefits, and his Form SSA-1099 for 2005 shows net benefits of $5,600 in box 5. Alice worked during the year and had wages of $14,000. She made a deductible payment to her IRA account of $1,000. Ray and Alice have two savings accounts with a total of $250 in interest income. They complete Worksheet 1 and find that none of Ray's social security benefits are taxable. They leave lines 14a and 14b of their Form 1040A blank.

Worksheet 1. Figuring Your Taxable Benefits

1. Enter the total amount from box 5 of ALL your Forms SSA-1099 and RRB-1099 5,600

Note. If line 1 is zero or less, stop here; none of your benefits are taxable. Otherwise, go on to line 2.

2. Enter one-half of line 1.. 2,800

3. Enter the total of the amounts from:
Form 1040: Lines 7, 8a, 8b, 9a, 10–14, 15b, 16b, 17–19, and 21.
Form 1040A: lines 7, 8a, 8b, 9a, 10, 11b, 12b, and 13 29,750

4. *Form 1040 filers:* Enter the total of any exclusions/adjustments for:
- Qualified U.S. savings bond interest (Form 8815, line 14),
- Adoption benefits (Form 8839, line 30),
- Foreign earned income or housing (Form 2555, lines 43 and 48, or Form 2555-EZ, line 18), and
- Certain income of bona fide residents of American Samoa (Form 4563, line 15) or Puerto Rico

Form 1040A filers: Enter the total of any exclusions for qualified U.S. savings bond interest (Form 8815, line 14) or for adoption benefits (Form 8839, line 30)................ -0-

5. Add lines 2, 3, and 4 32,550

6. *Form 1040 filers:* Enter the amount from Form 1040, line 36, minus any amounts on Form 1040, lines 33, 34 and 35

Form 1040A filers: Enter the amount from Form 1040A, line 20, minus any amounts on Form 1040A, lines 18 and 19........ 1,000

7. Is the amount on line 6 less than the amount on line 5?

No. (STOP) None of your benefits are taxable.
Yes. Subtract line 6 from line 5 31,550

8. If you are:
- Married filing jointly, enter $32,000
- Single, head of household, qualifying widow(er), or married filing separately and you **lived apart** from your spouse for all of 2005, enter $25,000 32,000

Note. If you are married filing separately and you lived with your spouse at any time in 2005, skip lines 8 through 15; multiply line 7 by 85% (.85) and enter the result on line 16. Then go to line 17.

9. Is the amount on line 8 less than the amount on line 7?

No. (STOP) None of your benefits are taxable. Do not enter any amounts on Form 1040, line 20a or 20b, or on Form 1040A, line 14a or 14b. But if you are married filing separately and you lived apart from your spouse for all of 2005, enter -0- on Form 1040, line 20b, or on Form 1040A, line 14b.

Yes. Subtract line 8 from line 7 .... _____

10. Enter $12,000 if married filing jointly; $9,000 if single, head of household, qualifying widow(er), or married filing separately and you **lived apart** from your spouse for all of 2005 .... _____

11. Subtract line 10 from line 9. If zero or less, enter -0- .... _____

12. Enter the **smaller** of line 9 or line 10 .... _____

13. Enter one-half of line 12 .... _____

14. Enter the **smaller** of line 2 or line 13 .... _____

15. Multiply line 11 by 85% (.85). If line 11 is zero, enter -0- ..... _____

16. Add lines 14 and 15 .... _____

17. Multiply line 1 by 85% (.85) .... _____

18. **Taxable benefits.** Enter the **smaller** of line 16 or line 17 .... _____

- Enter the amount from line 1 above on Form 1040, line 20a or on Form 1040A, line 14a.

- Enter the amount from line 18 above on Form 1040, line 20b or on Form 1040A, line 14b.

Example 3. Joe and Betty Johnson file a joint return on Form 1040 for 2005. Joe is a retired railroad worker and in 2005 received the social security equivalent benefit (SSEB) portion of tier 1 railroad retirement benefits. Joe's Form RRB-1099 shows $10,000 in box 5. Betty is a retired government worker and receives a fully taxable pension of $38,000. They had $2,300 in interest income plus interest of $200 on a qualified U.S. savings bond. The savings bond interest qualified for the exclusion. Thus, they have a total income of $40,300 ($38,000 + $2,300). They figure their taxable benefits by completing Worksheet 1.

Worksheet 1. Figuring Your Taxable Benefits

1. Enter the total amount from box 5 of ALL your Forms SSA-1099 and RRB-1099 10,000

Note. *If line 1 is zero or less, stop here; none of your benefits are taxable. Otherwise, go on to line 2.*

2. Enter one-half of line 1 5,000

3. Enter the total of the amounts from:
Form 1040: Lines 7, 8a, 8b, 9a, 10–14, 15b, 16b, 17–19, and 21.
Form 1040A: lines 7, 8a, 8b, 9a, 10, 11b, 12b, and 13 40,300

4. **Form 1040 filers:** Enter the total of any exclusions/adjustments for:
- Qualified U.S. savings bond interest (Form 8815, line 14),
- Adoption benefits (Form 8839, line 30),
- Foreign earned income or housing (Form 2555, lines 43 and 48, or Form 2555-EZ, line 18), and
- Certain income of bona fide residents of American Samoa (Form 4563, line 15) or Puerto Rico

   Form 1040A filers: Enter the total of any exclusions for qualified U.S. savings bond interest (Form 8815, line 14) or for adoption benefits (Form 8839, line 30) 200

5. Add lines 2, 3, and 4 45,500

6. **Form 1040 filers:** Enter the amount from Form 1040, line 36, minus any amounts on Form 1040, lines 33, 34 and 35

   Form 1040A filers: Enter the amount from Form 1040A, line 20, minus any amounts on Form 1040A, lines 18 and 19 .... -0-

7. Is the amount on line 6 less than the amount on line 5?

   No. (STOP) None of your benefits are taxable.
   Yes. Subtract line 6 from line 5 45,500

8. If you are:
- Married filing jointly, enter $32,000

- Single, head of household, qualifying widow(er), or married filing separately and you **lived apart** from your spouse for all of 2005, enter $25,000 32,000

Note. If you are married filing separately and you lived with your spouse at any time in 2005, skip lines 8 through 15; multiply line 7 by 85% (.85) and enter the result on line 16. Then go to line 17.

9. Is the amount on line 8 less than the amount on line 7?

   No. (STOP) None of your benefits are taxable. Do not enter any amounts on Form 1040, line 20a or 20b, or on Form 1040A, line 14a or 14b. But if you are married filing separately and you lived apart from your spouse for all of 2005, enter -0- on Form 1040, line 20b, or on Form 1040A, line 14b.

   Yes. Subtract line 8 from line 7 13,500

10. Enter $12,000 if married filing jointly; $9,000 if single, head of household, qualifying widow(er), or married filing separately and you **lived apart** from your spouse for all of 2005 12,000

11. Subtract line 10 from line 9. If zero or less, enter -0- 1,500

12. Enter the **smaller** of line 9 or line 10 12,000

13. Enter one-half of line 12 6,000

14. Enter the **smaller** of line 2 or line 13 5,000

15. Multiply line 11 by 85% (.85). If line 11 is zero, enter -0- 1,275

16. Add lines 14 and 15 6,275

17. Multiply line 1 by 85% (.85) 8,500

18. **Taxable benefits.** Enter the **smaller** of line 16 or line 17 .... $6,275

- Enter the amount from line 1 above on Form 1040, line 20a or on Form 1040A, line 14a.

- Enter the amount from line 18 above on Form 1040, line 20b or on Form 1040A, line 14b.

More than 50% of Joe's net benefits are taxable because the income on line 7 of the worksheet ($45,500) is more than $44,000. Joe and Betty enter $10,000 on line 20a, Form 1040, and $6,275 on line 20b, Form 1040.

Deductions Related to Your Benefits

You may be entitled to deduct certain amounts related to the benefits you receive.

Disability payments. You may have received disability payments from your employer or an insurance company that you included as income on your tax return in an earlier year. If you received a lump-sum payment from SSA or RRB, and you had to repay the employer or insurance company for the disability payments, you can take an itemized deduction for the part of the payments you included in gross income in the earlier year. If the amount you repay is more than $3,000, you may be able to claim a tax credit instead. Claim the deduction or credit in the same way explained under *Repayments More Than Gross Benefits,* later.

Legal expenses. You can usually deduct legal expenses that you pay or incur to produce or collect taxable income or in connection with the determination, collection, or refund of any tax.

Legal expenses for collecting the taxable part of your benefits are deductible as a miscellaneous itemized deduction on line 22, Schedule A (Form 1040).

TaxAlert

If your adjusted gross income exceeds $145,950 ($72,975 for married persons filing separately) in 2005, certain itemized deductions claimed on your return may be phased out. See Chapter 30, *Miscellaneous Deductions,* for details.

Repayments More Than Gross Benefits

In some situations, your Form SSA-1099 or Form RRB-1099 will show that the total benefits you repaid (box 4) are more than the gross benefits (box 3) you received. If this occurred, your net benefits in box 5 will be a negative figure (a figure in parentheses) and none of your benefits will be taxable. If you receive more than one form, a negative figure in box 5 of one form is used to offset a positive figure in box 5 of another form for that same year.

If you have any questions about this negative figure, contact your local SSA office or your local RRB field office.

Joint return. If you and your spouse file a joint return, and your Form SSA-1099 or RRB-1099 has a negative figure in box 5, but your spouse's does not, subtract the amount in box 5 of your form from the amount in box 5 of your spouse's form. You do this to get your net benefits when figuring if your combined benefits are taxable.

Example. John and Mary file a joint return for 2005. John received Form SSA-1099 showing $3,000 in box 5. Mary also received Form SSA-1099 and the amount in box 5 was ($500). John and Mary will use $2,500 ($3,000 minus $500) as the amount of their net benefits when figuring if any of their combined benefits are taxable.

Explanation
Social Security benefits are determined on a cash basis, just like most other income of individuals. Accordingly, repayments of prior-year amounts reduce current-year benefits.

TaxSaver

The Social Security Administration (SSA) can reduce your monthly benefits if you have earned income in excess of the threshold amounts and are under retirement age. The retirement earnings test has been eliminated for individuals attaining full retirement age—currently age 65 and 6 months. However, a test remains in effect for individuals ages 62 through full retirement age. A modified test applies for the year an individual reaches age 65 and 6 months. For the year in which an individual reaches full retirement age, each $3 of income earned in 2005 over $31,800 (up from $31,080 in 2004) will reduce your social security benefits by $1. The $31,800 threshold applies only for months prior to attaining full retirement age. There is no limit on earnings beginning the month an individual attains full retirement age. For individuals between the ages of 62 and full retirement age, each $2 of income earned in 2005 over $12,000 (up from $11,640 in 2004) will reduce your Social Security benefits by $1. Other exceptions apply during the initial year you receive Social Security retirement benefits. Consult the SSA for further explanation.

Earned Income Threshold for Early Recipients of Social Security Benefits

	Self-Employed	Not Self-Employed
Included as Income	Net Earnings	Wages
Excluded as Income	Government benefits	Government benefits
	Investment earnings	Investment earnings
	Interest	Interest
	Pensions	Pensions
	Annuities	Annuities
	Capital gains	Capital gains
	IRA distributions	IRA distributions
	Inheritance payments	Inheritance payments

TaxAlert

If you were born after 1937, your "full retirement age" will occur later than age 65. Full retirement age is the age at which full (100%) social security retirement benefits are available. Currently, age 65 and 6 months is considered full retirement age. Beginning with individuals who attained age 62 in the year 2000 (born in 1938), the full retirement age increases over the next 22 years, leveling off at age 67 for individuals who were born in 1960 or later. In other words, the full retirement age for individuals born between 1955 and 1969 will be age 66, plus 2 months for every year after 1954. Refer to the chart below entitled "Scheduled Increases in Social Security Normal Retirement Age."

Scheduled Increases in Social Security Normal Retirement Age

Birth Year	Year Worker Attains Age 62	Normal Retirement Age
1938	2000	65 + 2 months
1939	2001	65 + 4 months
1940	2002	65 + 6 months
1941	2003	65 + 8 months
1942	2004	65 + 10 months
1943	2005	66
1944	2006	66
1945	2007	66
1946	2008	66
1947	2009	66
1948	2010	66
1949	2011	66
1950	2012	66
1951	2013	66
1952	2014	66
1953	2015	66
1954	2016	66
1955	2017	66 + 2 months
1956	2018	66 + 4 months
1957	2019	66 + 6 months
1958	2020	66 + 8 months
1959	2021	66 + 10 months
1960	2022	67
1961 and subsequent years	2023 and later	67

Repayment of benefits received in an earlier year. If the total amount shown in box 5 of all of your Forms SSA-1099 and RRB-1099 is a negative figure, you can take an itemized deduction for the part of this negative figure that represents benefits you included in gross income in an earlier year.

Deduction $3,000 or less. If this deduction is $3,000 or less, it is subject to the 2%-of-adjusted-gross-income limit that applies to certain miscellaneous itemized deductions. Claim it on Schedule A (Form 1040), line 22.

Deduction more than $3,000. If this deduction is more than $3,000, you should figure your tax two ways:

1. Figure your tax for 2005 with the itemized deduction included on Schedule A line 27.
2. Figure your tax for 2005 in the following steps.
   a. Figure the tax without the itemized deduction included on Schedule A line 27.
   b. For each year after 1983 for which part of the negative figure represents a repayment of benefits, refigure your taxable benefits as if your total benefits for the year were reduced by that part of the negative figure. Then refigure the tax for that year.
   c. Subtract the total of the refigured tax amounts in (b) from the total of your actual tax amounts.
   d. Subtract the result in (c) from the result in (a).

Compare the tax figured in methods (1) and (2). Your tax for 2005 is the smaller of the two amounts. If method (1) results in less tax, take the itemized deduction on line 27, Schedule A (Form 1040). If method (2) results in less tax, claim a credit for the amount from step 2(c) above on line 70 of Form 1040 and write "I.R.C. 1341" in the margin to the left of line 70. If both methods produce the same tax, deduct the repayment on Schedule A (Form 1040), line 27.

Explanation

This confusing computation allows you to reduce your current tax by the greater of two amounts: 1) the amount of tax you would save by taking the deduction this year or 2) what you paid in tax the prior year because of including the amount in income.

TaxOrganizer

List of records to keep:

- Copy of Form(s) SSA-1099, RRB-1099, and Form 1042F for 3 years following the due date (including extensions) of your income tax return.
- Copies of all worksheets used to determine taxability of benefits.

13

Other Income

Note: The 2004 IRS Publication 17 (Your Federal Income Tax) has been updated by Ernst & Young LLP for 2005. Dates and dollar amounts shown are for 2005. Gray type is used to indicate where IRS text has been updated or intentionally omitted. Unrevised IRS text is shown in black type.

Introduction

Your salary, interest you earn, dividends received, a gain from the sale of securities—all of these, of course, are taxable income.

Unfortunately, so are a lot of other things: a debt forgiven by a friend, jury pay, a free trip you receive from a travel agency for organizing a group of tourists, and royalties you earn on a book.

The general rule is that anything that enriches you should be included in your gross income, unless it is specifically excluded by the tax law.

Indeed, some things are excluded from taxation. Generally, you don't have to pay income tax on life insurance proceeds that you receive because of the death of the insured. Most gifts and inheritances are tax-free income. The value of the vegetables you grow in your garden and eat yourself is not taxable. This chapter tells you what kind of income is not taxable, and how you can tell the difference.

This chapter includes a discussion on passive activity losses. Passive investments include all rental activities, all limited partnerships, and those other businesses in which the taxpayer is not involved in the operations on a regular, continuous, and substantial basis.

What's New

[IRS text intentionally omitted]

Unlawful discrimination claims. You may be able to take a deduction for attorney fees and court costs paid after October 22, 2004, for actions settled or decided after that date involving a claim of unlawful discrimination, a claim against the United States government, or a claim made under section 1862(b)(3)(A) of the Social Security Act, but only up to the amount included in gross income for the tax year from such claim. For more information, see Publication 525.

Health savings accounts (HSAs). You may be able to make tax-deductible contributions to a health savings account to pay qualified medical expenses. Amounts from HSAs used for qualified medical expenses are not includible in gross income. Amounts from HSAs not used for qualified medical expenses are includible in income. HSAs are discussed in Publication 969, Health Savings Accounts and Other Tax-Favored Health Plans.

Smallpox vaccine injuries. If you are an eligible individual who receives benefits under the Smallpox Emergency Personnel Protection Act of 2003 for a covered injury resulting from a covered countermeasure, you can exclude the payment from your income (to the extent it is not allowed as a medical and dental expense deduction on Schedule A (Form 1040)). Eligible individuals include health care workers, emergency personnel, and first responders in a smallpox emergency, who have received a smallpox vaccination.

This chapter discusses many kinds of income and explains whether they are taxable or nontaxable.

- Income that is taxable must be reported on your tax return and is subject to tax.
- Income that is nontaxable may have to be shown on your tax return but is not taxable.

This chapter begins with discussions of the following income items.

- Bartering.

- Canceled debts.
- Life insurance proceeds.
- Partnership income.
- S Corporation income.
- Recoveries (including state income tax refunds).
- Rents from personal property.
- Repayments.
- Royalties.
- Unemployment benefits.
- Welfare and other public assistance benefits.

These discussions are followed by brief discussions of many income items arranged in alphabetical order.

You must include on your return all income you receive in the form of money, property, and services unless the tax law states that you do not include them. Some items, however, are only partly excluded from income.

Useful Items

You may want to see:

Publications

- ☐ **525** Taxable and Nontaxable Income
- ☐ **544** Sales and Other Dispositions of Assets
- ☐ **550** Investment Income and Expenses

Bartering

Bartering is an exchange of property or services. You must include in your income, at the time received, the fair market value of property or services you receive in bartering. If you exchange services with another person and you both have agreed ahead of time as to the value of the services, that value will be accepted as fair market value unless the value can be shown to be otherwise.

Generally, you report this income on Schedule C, Profit or Loss From Business, or Schedule C-EZ, Net Profit From Business (Form 1040). However, if the barter involves an exchange of something other than services, such as in *Example 3* below, you may have to use another form or schedule instead.

Explanation
The IRS explanation is correct in stating that if you exchange your property and/or services for the property and/or services of another, you have taxable income. However, when you exchange property for property, you generally recognize income only to the extent that the fair market value of the property you receive exceeds your **adjusted basis** in the property you give up (note that an exception to this general rule is for like-kind exchanges). The proper way of determining gain on exchanges of property and your **basis** in the property you receive are discussed in Chapter 14, *Basis of Property,* and Chapter 15, *Sale of Property.*

Example 1. You are a self-employed attorney who performs legal services for a client, a small corporation. The corporation gives you shares of its stock as payment for your services. You must include the fair market value of the shares in your income on Schedule C or Schedule C-EZ (Form 1040) in the year you receive them.

Example 2. You are self-employed and a member of a barter club. The club uses "credit units" as a means of exchange. It adds credit units to your account for goods or services you provide to members, which you can use to purchase goods and services offered by other members of the barter club. The club subtracts credit units from your account when you receive goods or services from other members. You must include in your income the value of the credit units that are added to your account, even though you may not actually receive goods or services from other members until a later tax year.

Example 3. You own a small apartment building. In return for 6 months rent-free use of an apartment, an artist gives you a work of art she created. You must report as rental income on Schedule E, Supplemental Income and Loss (Form 1040), the fair market value of the artwork, and the artist must report as income on Schedule C or Schedule C-EZ (Form 1040) the fair rental value of the apartment.

Form 1099-B from barter exchange. If you exchanged property or services through a barter exchange, Form 1099-B, Proceeds From Broker and Barter Exchange Transactions, or a similar statement from the barter exchange should be sent to you by January 31, 2006. It should show the value of cash, property, services, credits, or scrip you received from exchanges during 2005. The IRS will also receive a copy of Form 1099-B.

Canceled Debts

Generally, if a debt you owe is canceled or forgiven, other than as a gift or bequest, you must include the canceled amount in your income. You have no income from the canceled debt if it is intended as a gift to you. A debt includes any indebtedness for which you are liable or which attaches to property you hold.

If the debt is a nonbusiness debt, report the canceled amount on Form 1040, line 21. If it is a business debt, report the amount on Schedule C or Schedule C-EZ (Form 1040) (or on Schedule F, Profit or Loss From Farming (Form 1040), if the debt is farm debt and you are a farmer).

TAXPLANNER

Family members often make interest-free or below-market interest loans to one another. The IRS may recharacterize these loans as arm's-length transactions and impute interest income to the lender and interest expense to the borrower, which are then reported on their respective tax returns. See Chapter 8, *Interest Income,* for further discussion of below-market loans. You should consult your tax advisor about how to report any below-market loan transactions.

Form 1099-C. If a Federal Government agency, financial institution, or credit union cancels or forgives a debt you owe of $600 or more, you will receive a Form 1099-C, Cancellation of Debt. The amount of the canceled debt is shown in box 2.

Interest included in canceled debt. If any interest is forgiven and included in the amount of canceled debt in box 2, the amount of interest will also be shown in box 3. Whether or not you must include the interest portion of the canceled debt in your income depends on whether the interest would be deductible if you paid it. See *Deductible debt,* under *Exceptions,* later.

If the interest would not be deductible (such as interest on a personal loan), include in your income the amount from Form 1099-C, box 2. If the interest would be deductible (such as on a business loan), include in your income the net amount of the canceled debt (the amount shown in box 2 less the interest amount shown in box 3).

Discounted mortgage loan. If your financial institution offers a discount for the early payment of your mortgage loan, the amount of the discount is canceled debt. You must include the canceled amount in your income.

Mortgage relief upon sale or other disposition. If you are personally liable for a mortgage (recourse debt), and you are relieved of the mortgage when you dispose of the property, you may realize gain or loss up to the fair market value of the property. To the extent the mortgage discharge exceeds the fair market value of the property, it is income from discharge of indebtedness unless it qualifies for exclusion under *Excluded debt,* later. Report any income from discharge of indebtedness on nonbusiness debt that does not qualify for exclusion as other income on Form 1040, line 21.

If you are not personally liable for a mortgage (nonrecourse debt), and you are relieved of the mortgage when you dispose of the property (such as through foreclosure or repossession), that relief is included in the amount you realize. You may have a taxable gain if the amount you realize exceeds your adjusted basis in the property. Report any gain on nonbusiness property as a capital gain.

See *Foreclosures and Repossessions* in Publication 544 for more information.

TaxSaver

Proceed cautiously if the financial institution that holds your mortgage offers you a substantial discount on your loan balance in exchange for a prepayment on it. While this might at first appear very attractive, remember that you will have to pay ordinary income tax on the amount of the discount offered, which may considerably reduce any advantage to you. Your money might be put to better use in investments with a high after-tax yield or in paying off expensive consumer credit.

Stockholder debt. If you are a stockholder in a corporation and the corporation cancels or forgives your debt to it, the canceled debt is a constructive distribution that is generally dividend income to you. For more information, see Publication 542, Corporations.

If you are a stockholder in a corporation and you cancel a debt owed to you by the corporation, you generally do not realize income. This is because the canceled debt is considered as a contribution to the capital of the corporation equal to the amount of debt principal that you canceled.

Exceptions

There are several exceptions to the inclusion of canceled debt in income. These are explained next.

Student loans. Certain student loans contain a provision that all or part of the debt incurred to attend the qualified educational institution will be canceled if you work for a certain period of time in certain professions for any of a broad class of employers.

You do not have income if your student loan is canceled after you agreed to this provision and then performed the services required. To qualify, the loan must have been made by:

1. The Federal Government, a state or local government, or an instrumentality, agency, or subdivision thereof,
2. A tax-exempt public benefit corporation that has assumed control of a state, county, or municipal hospital, and whose employees are considered public employees under state law, or
3. An educational institution:
   a. Under an agreement with an entity described in (1) or (2) that provided the funds to the institution to make the loan, or
   b. As part of a program of the institution designed to encourage students to serve in occupations or areas with unmet needs and under which the services provided are for or under the direction of a governmental unit or a tax-exempt section 501(c)(3) organization.

Section 501(c)(3) organizations are defined in Publication 525.

A loan to refinance a qualified student loan will also qualify if it was made by an educational institution or a tax-exempt 501(a) organization under its program designed as described in (3)(b) above.

Deductible debt. You do not have income from the cancellation of a debt if your payment of the debt would be deductible. This exception applies only if you use the cash method of accounting. For more information, see chapter 5 of Publication 334, Tax Guide for Small Business.

Price reduced after purchase. Generally, if the seller reduces the amount of debt you owe for property you purchased, you do not have income from the reduction. The reduction of the debt is treated as a purchase price adjustment and reduces your basis in the property.

Excluded debt. Do not include a canceled debt in your gross income in the following situations.

- The debt is canceled in a bankruptcy case under title 11 of the U.S. Code. See Publication 908, Bankruptcy Tax Guide.
- The debt is canceled when you are insolvent. However, you cannot exclude any amount of canceled debt that is more than the amount by which you are insolvent. See Publication 908.
- The debt is qualified farm debt and is canceled by a qualified person. See chapter 4 of Publication 225, Farmer's Tax Guide.
- The debt is qualified real property business debt. See chapter 5 of Publication 334.
- The cancellation is intended as a gift.

TaxAlert

You cannot exclude debt you owe to your employer which is forgiven even if it was incurred for purchasing stock.

Education Loan Repayment Assistance

Education loan repayments made to you by the National Health Service Corps Loan Repayment Program (NHSC Loan Repayment Program) or a state education loan repayment program eligible for funds under the Public Health Service Act are not taxable if you agree to provide primary health services in health professional shortage areas. For more information, see Publication 970.

Life Insurance Proceeds

Life insurance proceeds paid to you because of the death of the insured person are not taxable unless the policy was turned over to you for a price. This is true even if the proceeds were paid under an accident or health insurance policy or an endowment contract.

Proceeds not received in installments. If death benefits are paid to you in a lump sum or other than at regular intervals, include in your income only the benefits that are more than the amount payable to you at the time of the insured person's death. If the benefit payable at death is not specified, you include in your income the benefit payments that are more than the present value of the payments at the time of death.

Proceeds received in installments. If you receive life insurance proceeds in installments, you can exclude part of each installment from your income.

To determine the excluded part, divide the amount held by the insurance company (generally the total lump sum payable at the death of the insured person) by the number of installments to be paid. Include anything over this excluded part in your income as interest.

Example
Suppose you receive a $100,000 life insurance death benefit that you elect to receive over 10 annual installments. Any amount that you receive in excess of $10,000 each year will be considered taxable interest income to you.

Surviving spouse. If your spouse died before October 23, 1986, and insurance proceeds paid to you because of the death of your spouse are received in installments, you can exclude up to $1,000 a year of the interest included in the installments. If you remarry, you can continue to take the exclusion.

More information. For more information, see *Life Insurance Proceeds* in Publication 525.

TAXSAVER

Interest option on insurance. If an insurance company pays you only interest on proceeds from life insurance left on deposit with them, the interest you are paid is taxable.

Example
Assume you are a beneficiary of a life insurance death benefit. If under the payment structure of the benefit, you are only receiving the interest, then your entire payment would be considered taxable. The individual (or successor beneficiary) who will be receiving the principal of the benefit would receive it income tax free. Special exclusion ratio rules apply to individuals receiving annuity death benefits in the form of principal and interest.

Surrender of policy for cash. If you surrender a life insurance policy for cash, you must include in income any proceeds that are more than the cost of the life insurance policy. In general, your cost (or investment in the contract) is the total of premiums that you paid for the life insurance policy, less any refunded premiums, rebates, dividends, or unrepaid loans that were not included in your income.

Example
Assuming you terminated a life insurance policy with a cash value of $50,000 and of that amount you only paid $40,000 in net premiums, $10,000 would be considered taxable income to you at that time.

However, if you exchange one life insurance policy for another policy, it is possible that you may not have a taxable transaction. See your tax advisor.

You should receive a Form 1099-R showing the total proceeds and the taxable part. Report these amounts on lines 16a and 16b of Form 1040 or lines 12a and 12b of Form 1040A.

Endowment Contract Proceeds

An endowment contract is a policy under which you are paid a specified amount of money on a certain date unless you die before that date, in which case, the money is paid to your designated beneficiary. Endowment proceeds paid in a lump sum to you at maturity are taxable only if the proceeds are more than the cost of the policy. To determine your cost, subtract any amount that you previously received under the contract and excluded from your income from the total premiums (or other consideration) paid for the contract. Include the part of the lump-sum payment that is more than your cost in your income.

TAXSAVER

There are a number of ways in which insurance proceeds may be paid. The choice may have been made by the deceased, or the choice may belong to the recipient of the proceeds. In either case, proper planning may save tax dollars and increase wealth.

Generally, the insured should not decide how the insurance benefits are to be paid, unless he or she is worried that the beneficiary might squander the money. Absent that, determining the method of payment should be left to the beneficiary, who, after the death of the insured, is in the best position to consider potential investments, as well as tax benefits.

Explanation
Endowment contracts, much like whole life insurance contracts, require you, as the owner, to pay annual premiums in return for a certain sum of cash that is paid when you reach a specified age or upon death. Unless you choose to receive the endowment proceeds in installments, the excess of the proceeds over the cost of the policy is taxable in the year of maturity, *even if the proceeds are not received until a later year.* The excess of the proceeds is taxed as ordinary income, not as capital gain. The cost of the endowment contract is the total amount of the premiums you paid for it, not its cash value at the time of maturity or when you surrender it.

However, if you agree to take the proceeds as an annuity within 60 days after the lump-sum payment becomes available and before you receive any cash, you are not considered to have received the lump sum for tax purposes. The lump sum is taxed as an annuity; that is, you are taxed on the amounts as you receive them each year.

For certain contracts entered into or materially changed after June 21, 1988, you may be required to treat distributions first as income and then as recovery of investment. Distributions are defined for this purpose to include a loan. In certain circumstances, an additional 10% tax will be imposed on the amount that is includable in gross income. Consult your tax advisor to determine if you are subject to this provision.

Public Safety Officer Killed in the Line of Duty

If you are a survivor of a public safety officer who was killed in the line of duty, you may be able to exclude from income certain amounts you receive.

For this purpose, the term public safety officer includes law enforcement officers, firefighters, chaplains, and rescue squad and ambulance crew members. See Publication 559 for more information.

Accelerated Death Benefits

Certain amounts paid as accelerated death benefits under a life insurance contract or viatical settlement before the insured's death are excluded from income if the insured is terminally or chronically ill.

Viatical settlement. This is the sale or assignment of any part of the death benefit under a life insurance contract to a viatical settlement provider. A viatical settlement provider is a person who regularly engages in the business of buying or taking assignment of life insurance contracts on the lives of insured individuals who are terminally or chronically ill and who meets the requirements of section 101(g)(2)(B) of the Internal Revenue Code.

Exclusion for terminal illness. Accelerated death benefits are fully excludable if the insured is a terminally ill individual. This is a person who has been certified by a physician as having an illness or physical condition that can reasonably be expected to result in death within 24 months from the date of the certification.

Exclusion for chronic illness. If the insured is a chronically ill individual who is not terminally ill, accelerated death benefits paid on the basis of costs incurred for qualified long-term care services are fully excludable. Accelerated death benefits paid on a *per diem* or other periodic basis are excludable up to a limit. This limit applies to the total of the accelerated death benefits and any periodic payments received from long-term care insurance contracts. For information on the limit and the definitions of chronically ill individual and long-term care insurance contracts, see *Long-Term Care Insurance Contracts* under *Sickness and Injury Benefits* in chapter 6.

Exception. The exclusion does not apply to any amount paid to a person (other than the insured) who has an insurable interest in the life of the insured because the insured:

- Is a director, officer, or employee of the person, or
- Has a financial interest in the person's business.

Form 8853. To claim an exclusion for accelerated death benefits made on a *per diem* or other periodic basis, you must file Form 8853, Archer MSAs and Long-term Care Insurance Contracts, with your return. You do not have to file Form 8853 to exclude accelerated death benefits paid on the basis of actual expenses incurred.

Partnership Income

A partnership generally is not a taxable entity. The income, gains, losses, deductions, and credits of a partnership are passed through to the partners based on each partner's distributive share of these items. **Schedule K-1 (Form 1065).** Although a partnership generally pays no tax, it must file an information return on Form 1065, U.S. Return of Partnership Income, and send Schedule K-1 (Form 1065) to each partner. In addition, the partnership will send each partner a copy of the Partner's Instructions for Schedule K-1 (Form 1065) to help each partner report his or her share of the partnership's income, deductions, credits, and tax preference items.

Keep Schedule K-1 (Form 1065) for your records. Do not attach it to your Form 1040.

For more information on partnerships, see Publication 541, Partnerships.

Explanation

General. A partnership includes a group, pool, joint venture, or other unincorporated organization that carries on a business or financial operation. Most entities that qualify for partnership treatment can elect out of partnership treatment under the "check-the-box" regulations. See your tax advisor for more information.

Limited liability companies. All states permit the formation of limited liability companies (LLCs). In an LLC, members and designated managers are not personally liable for any debts of the company. The entity will generally be treated as a partnership and, as a result, enjoy the same federal income tax benefits that apply to partnerships. If the entity is appropriately established, LLCs combine the benefits of corporate limited liability with the advantages of partnership taxation. In addition to LLCs, one may consider the formation of a limited liability partnership (LLP). Consult your tax advisor or attorney to find out if these are options for your business in the state you live in.

Reporting income. Because a partnership is not a taxable entity, all tax items are passed through to the partners. A partnership is required to give you a Schedule K-1, Partner's Share of Income, Credits, Deductions, etc. A Schedule K-1 will list your distributive share of income, gains, losses, deductions, and credits that is required to be included in your individual tax return. If, for example, the Schedule K-1 indicates interest income of $100 you will need to include $100 as interest income on your Schedule B, Form 1040. (See Chapter 8, *Interest Income*.)

Basis. Because the partnership's income and losses flow directly through to you, that income or loss will affect your tax basis in the partnership. It is important that you maintain and update this tax-basis calculation every year for two reasons. First, your distributive share of the partnership losses is limited to the adjusted basis of your interest in the partnership at the end of the partnership year in which the losses took place. Second, in the year you sell your partnership interest, you will need to know your tax basis in order to calculate your gain or loss. To determine the adjusted basis of your interest in the partnership, begin with your initial investment and your initial share of your partnership liabilities and make the following adjustments.

Additions to basis

1. Your distributive share of the partnership's taxable income
2. Your share of any tax-exempt income earned by the partnership
3. Your share of the excess of partnership deductions for depletion over the basis of partnership property subject to depletion
4. Any additional capital you contribute
5. Your share of any increase in partnership liabilities

Subtractions from basis

1. Any cash distributions you receive
2. The basis that you take in any property distributed to you by the partnership
3. Your share of oil and gas depletion claimed by the partnership
4. Your distributive share of partnership losses
5. Your share of nondeductible, noncapital expenditures made by the partnership
6. Your share of any decrease in partnership liabilities

The partnership agreement usually covers the distribution of profits, losses, and other items. However, if there is no agreement for sharing a specific item of gain or loss, generally, each partner's distributive share is figured according to the partner's interest in the partnership.

In addition, *special "at-risk" rules apply* to a partnership engaged in any activity.

You may deduct your share of a partnership loss from any activity only up to the total amount that you are at risk in the activity at the end of the partnership's tax year.

The amount you are at risk in an activity is the cash and the adjusted basis of other property you contributed to the activity. Also, you are at risk for any amounts borrowed for use in the activity for which you either are personally liable or have pledged property, except property used in the activity, as security.

Generally, you are not at risk for:

1. Any nonrecourse loans used to finance the activity, to acquire property used in the activity, or to acquire your interest in the activity, unless they are secured by property not used in the activity;

2. Amounts for which you are protected against loss by guarantees, stop-loss agreements, or other similar arrangements; or

3. Amounts borrowed from interested or related parties if your partnership is engaged in certain activities.

For more information on the at-risk rules, see Publication 925, *Passive Activities and At-Risk Rules.*

In addition to the factors discussed above, your amount at risk is affected by the operating results of the activity itself. Income from the activity increases the amount you are at risk. Losses from the activity decrease the amount you are at risk. The at-risk amount is determined at the end of each tax year. Any loss in excess of that amount is disallowed for that year. It may, however, be carried over to future years, and to the extent that you subsequently have amounts at risk, it may be deducted in those years.

Under prior law, a partnership engaged in real estate activity was not subject to the at-risk rules. The Tax Reform Act of 1986 extended the at-risk rules to include real estate activities placed in service after December 31, 1986, but makes exceptions for third-party nonrecourse debt from commercial lenders and certain other parties.

In addition to the at-risk rules, the income from real estate partnerships is also subject to the passive activity rules. See *Passive Activity Limitations and At-Risk Limitations,* at the end of this chapter. Also, consult your tax advisor for further information.

When to report partnership income. Generally, partnership income is treated as paid to you on the last day of the partnership year. (See Chapter 4, *Decedents,* for exceptions relating to partnership interests held by a decedent.) Generally, you must include your distributive share of partnership items on your return for your tax year in which the last day of the partnership year falls. If you receive income from a partnership other than in your capacity as a partner, however, you must report the income in the year in which it was received. For instance, if you sell property to your partnership at a gain, the gain is generally included in income when you receive the sale proceeds, regardless of when your partnership's tax year ends.

Estimated tax payments. A partner must take into account his or her share of the partnership's income or deductions to date at *each* estimated tax payment date. Often, this information is not readily available. If you are a member of a partnership you may protect yourself from underpayment penalties by basing your payments on one of the exceptions described in Chapter 5, *Tax Withholding and Estimated Tax.*

However, if a partner moves from one state to another, and if the states involved follow federal rules, the partnership income or loss should be reported in the state income tax return for the state in which the partner resides when the partnership's year ends.

Sale of partnership interest. If you have a gain or a loss from the sale or exchange of a partnership interest, it is treated as a gain or a loss from the sale of a capital asset. The gain or loss is the difference between the amount you receive and the adjusted basis of your interest in the partnership. If you are relieved of any debts of the partnership, you must include these debts in the amount you receive.

However, you may have ordinary income as well as capital gain or loss on the sale of your partnership interest if the sale involves uncollected accounts receivable or inventory items that have increased in value. Consult your tax advisor for further help.

S Corporation Income

In general, an S corporation does not pay tax on its income. Instead, the income, losses, deductions, and credits of the corporation are passed through to the shareholders based on each shareholder's *pro rata* share. **Schedule K-1 (Form 1120S).** An S corporation must file a return on Form 1120S, U.S. Income Tax Return for an S Corporation, and send Schedule K-1 (Form 1120S) to each shareholder. In addition, the S corporation will send each shareholder a copy of the Shareholder's Instructions for Schedule K-1 (Form 1120S) to help each shareholder report his or her share of the S corporation's income, losses, credits, and deductions.

Keep Schedule K-1 (Form 1120S) for your records. Do not attach it to your Form 1040.

Explanation
Shareholder's return. Generally, S corporation distributions are considered a nontaxable return of your basis in the corporation's stock. However, in certain cases, part of the distributions may be taxable as a dividend or as a long-term or short-term capital gain, or as both. The corporation's distributions may be in the form of cash or property.

All current-year income or loss and other tax items are taxed to you at the corporation's year-end. Generally, the items that are passed through to you as a shareholder will increase or decrease the basis of your S corporation stock as appropriate. Dividends are paid only from prior-year earnings (generally retained earnings from years prior to 1983 or prior to becoming an S corporation). Generally, property (including cash) distributions, except dividend distributions, are considered a return of capital to the extent of your basis in the stock of the corporation. Distributions in excess of basis are treated as a gain from the sale or exchange of property.

You should receive from the S corporation in which you are a shareholder a copy of the Shareholder's Instructions for Schedule K-1 (Form 1120S), together with a copy of Schedule K-1 (Form 1120S), showing your share of the income, credits, and deductions of the S corporation for the tax year. Your distributive share of the items of income, gain, loss, deduction, or credit of the S corporation must be shown separately on your Form 1040. The tax treatment of these items generally is the same as if you had realized or incurred them personally.

Individuals form an S corporation to get the legal benefits of a corporation, such as limited liability, while retaining the tax benefits of an individual. Usually, an S corporation does not pay federal income tax. One exception is a tax on certain gains that is paid by the S corporation, but normally, the individual owners of the corporation pay tax or accrue tax benefits on their personal returns based on the corporation's profits and losses. Income from an S corporation is included in an individual's return as if the S corporation did not exist. Dividends that the S corporation receives are included as dividends on your return on Schedule B (Form 1040). Capital gains are included on Schedule D (Form 1040). Types of income from an S corporation that are not treated specially on an individual's return are combined and included on Schedule E (Form 1040). If you have losses from an S corporation when you are not an active participant in the corporation's business activities, your losses will be subject to the passive activity limitations. See the section on Passive Activity Losses at the end of this chapter.

Estimated tax payments. A shareholder must take into account his or her share of the S corporation's income or deductions to date at *each* estimated tax payment date. Often, this information is not readily available. If you are a member of an S corporation, you may protect yourself from underpayment penalties by basing your payments on one of the exceptions described in Chapter 5, *Tax Withholding and Estimated Tax.*

Generally, an S corporation must have its tax year-end on December 31. However, under certain circumstances, an S corporation may operate on a **fiscal year;** that is, its tax year may end on a date other than December 31. Your return should include all S corporation income for its operating year that ends within your tax year.

Example

If your S corporation's year ends on October 31, your return for 2005 will include the income items for the corporation's entire year that ended October 31, 2005, even though that means including 2 months of 2004.

Deducting losses. You may deduct any losses of the S corporation for the year up to the amount of your basis.

Basis in an S corporation. Your basis in an S corporation at the end of a year is your investment (stock and loans made to the S corporation), with the following adjustments.

Additions to basis

1. Your distributive share of the S corporation's separately and nonseparately stated taxable income
2. Your share of tax-exempt income earned by the S corporation
3. Any additional capital that you contribute
4. Deductions for depletion in excess of the basis of the property
5. A loan to the corporation directly from the shareholder; however, a guarantee of a third-party loan by a shareholder does not qualify as an addition to basis

Subtractions from basis

1. Generally, any cash distributed and the fair market value of property distributed (other than taxable dividends), but not below zero
2. Your distributive share of the S corporation's separately and nonseparately stated items of loss and deduction
3. Your share of nondeductible, noncapital expenditures made by the S corporation
4. Your share of the deductions for depletion for any oil and gas property held by the S corporation to the extent that the deduction does not exceed the proportionate share of the property's adjusted basis allocated to you

Example 1

Your basis in an S corporation is $20,000. The corporation makes a distribution to you of $30,000 in cash or property. You would have to recognize income of $10,000.

Example 2

Your basis in an S corporation is $20,000. If it reports losses of $30,000, you may deduct only $20,000 for

the year. The other $10,000 worth of losses is carried over until you have more basis.

All you need to prepare your individual tax return is the Form K-1 provided by the S corporation. It tells you what the numbers are and where to put them on your Form 1040.

TAXPLANNER

An S corporation is just one of several alternatives to consider as a vehicle to conduct business activities, but it does offer some of the best features of a regular corporation, a partnership, and a sole proprietorship.

1. As in a regular corporation, the stockholders of an S corporation are normally immune from liabilities in excess of their investment.
2. Like a regular corporation, the S corporation structure is convenient for transferring equity to heirs as part of your estate planning and the gradual transition of management and control to your heirs or successors. As shareholders, the heirs then report their proportionate share of S corporation income and losses on their respective tax returns.
3. Like a partnership or sole proprietorship, the S corporation permits the investors to deduct operating losses. Just as important, profits are not taxed twice, as they are in a regular corporation. A regular corporation itself pays taxes, and so do the individuals who receive a share of those profits when dividends are paid. An S corporation is, except in certain circumstances, exempt from taxes—at least at the federal level.

For more information on S corporations and their shareholders, see the instructions for Form 1120S.

Recoveries

A recovery is a return of an amount you deducted or took a credit for in an earlier year. The most common recoveries are refunds, reimbursements, and rebates of deductions itemized on Schedule A (Form 1040). You may also have recoveries of non-itemized deductions (such as payments on previously deducted bad debts) and recoveries of items for which you previously claimed a tax credit.

Tax benefit rule. You must include a recovery in your income in the year you receive it up to the amount by which the deduction or credit you took for the recovered amount reduced your tax in the earlier year. For this purpose, any increase to an amount carried over to the current year that resulted from the deduction or credit is considered to have reduced your tax in the earlier year. For more information, see Publication 525.

Federal income tax refund. Refunds of federal income taxes are not included in your income because they are never allowed as a deduction from income.

State income tax refund. If you received a state or local income tax refund (or credit or offset) in 2005, you generally must include it in income if you deducted the tax in an earlier year. The payer should send Form 1099-G, Certain Government Payments, to you by January 31, 2006. The IRS will also receive a copy of the Form 1099-G. Use the State and Local Income Tax Refund Worksheet in the 2005 Form 1040 Instructions for line 10 to figure the amount (if any) to include in your income.

Explanation

The State and Local Income Tax worksheet can be used to determine the taxable amount of your state and local income tax refund.

State and Local Income Tax Refund Worksheet—Line 10

1. Enter the income tax refund from **Form(s) 1099-G** (or similar statement). But **do not** enter more than the amount on your 2004 Schedule A (Form 1040), line 5 .... 1. _____

2. Enter your total allowable itemized deductions from your 2004 Schedule A (Form 1040), line 28 .... 2. _____

Note. If the filing status on your 2004 Form 1040 was married filing separately and your spouse itemized deductions in 2004, skip lines 3, 4, and 5, and enter the amount from line 2 on line 6.

3. Enter the amount shown below for the filing status claimed on your **2004** Form 1040.
   - Single or married filing separately— $4,850
   - Married filing jointly or qualifying widow(er)— $9,700   } .. 3. _____
   - Head of household— $7,150

4. Did you fill in line 36a on your 2004 Form 1040?
   ☐ **No.** Enter -0-.
   ☐ **Yes.** Multiply the number in the box on line 36a of your 2004 Form 1040 by: $950 if your 2004 filing status was married filing jointly or separately or qualifying widow(er); $1,200 if your 2004 filing status was single or head of household.   4. _____

5. Add lines 3 and 4 .... 5. _____

6. Is the amount on line 5 less than the amount on line 2?
   ☐ **No.** (STOP)   None of your refund is taxable.

   ☐ **Yes.** Subtract line 5 from line 2 .... 6. _____

7. **Taxable part of your refund.** Enter the **smaller** of line 1 or line 6 here and on Form 1040, line 10   7. _____

Mortgage interest refund. If you received a refund or credit in 2005 of mortgage interest paid in an earlier year, the amount should be shown on your Form 1098, box 3, Mortgage Interest Statement. Do not subtract the refund amount from the interest you paid in 2005. You may have to include it in your income under the rules explained in the following discussions.

Interest on recovery. Interest on any of the amounts you recover must be reported as interest income in the year received. For example, report any interest you received on state or local income tax refunds on Form 1040, line 8a.

Explanation
Although the amount of a state tax refund may not be included in gross income, any interest you receive on federal or state refunds is taxable.

Recovery and expense in same year. If the refund or other recovery and the expense occur in the same year, the recovery reduces the deduction or credit and is not reported as income.

Recovery for 2 or more years. If you receive a refund or other recovery that is for amounts you paid in 2 or more separate years, you must allocate, on a *pro rata* basis, the recovered amount between the years in which you paid it. This allocation is necessary to determine the amount of recovery from any earlier years and to determine the amount, if any, of your allowable deduction for this item for the current year. For information on how to compute the allocation, see *Recoveries* in Publication 525.

Itemized Deduction Recoveries

If you recover any amount that you deducted in an earlier year on Schedule A (Form 1040), you generally must include the full amount of the recovery in your income in the year you receive it.

Where to report. Enter your state or local income tax refund on Form 1040, line 10, and the total of all other recoveries as other income on Form 1040, line 21. You cannot use Form 1040A or Form 1040EZ.

Standard deduction limit. You generally are allowed to claim the standard deduction if you do not itemize your deductions. Only your itemized deductions that are more than your standard deduction are subject to the recovery rule (unless you are required to itemize your deductions). If your total deductions on the earlier year return were not more than your income for that year, include in your income this year the lesser of:

- Your recoveries, or
- The amount by which your itemized deductions exceeded the standard deduction.

Example. For 2004, you filed a joint return. Your taxable income was $60,000 and you were not entitled to any tax credits. Your standard deduction was $9,700 and you had itemized deductions of $11,000. In 2005, you received the following recoveries for amounts deducted on your 2004 return:

Medical expenses	$200
State and local income tax refund.....................	400
Refund of mortgage interest	325
Total recoveries	**$925**

None of the recoveries were more than the deductions taken for 2004.

Your total recoveries are less than the amount by which your itemized deductions exceeded the standard deduction ($11,000 − 9,700 = $1,300), so you must include your total recoveries in your income for 2005. Report the state and local income tax refund of $400 on Form 1040, line 10, and the balance of your recoveries, $525, on Form 1040, line 21.

TAXPLANNER
The IRS correctly points out that the recovery of certain amounts you deducted is not income if you did not itemize your deductions in the year in which you paid these expenses. However, if the payer of the refund

submits a Form 1099 or Form 1099-G to the IRS, we suggest that you attach a statement to your return including the item in income and then subtracting it out explaining why the item does not represent taxable income. This may prevent an inquiry from the IRS.

If you were subject to the alternative minimum tax in 2004, you may not have obtained any benefit for all or part of your state income tax deduction. This is because state income taxes are not deductible for purposes of computing the alternative minimum tax. (The alternative minimum tax is explained in Chapter 32, *How to Figure Your Tax.*) You will want to compute carefully the amount of the refund you received in 2005 that did not give you any tax benefit in 2004. Attach a statement in your return explaining why the item does not represent taxable income.

This will require a "with-and-without" computation. If your prior-year tax was not lower *with* the deduction, you did not receive a benefit, and, therefore, the refund is *not* taxable income when received.

If, in 2004, you itemized your deductions and had your itemized deductions scaled back due to a high adjusted gross income (AGI), generally your refund will be included in your income for 2005.

The amount of a refund that would be included in income in the year of receipt is the difference between (1) the prior year's reduced itemized deductions and (2) the reduced itemized deductions (or standard deduction, if greater) that you would have taken had you paid and deducted the proper amount in the first place and received a later refund or recovery.

Example

Tracy had $542,700 of AGI in 2004, paid $40,000 in state income taxes during 2004, and had no other itemized deductions. Tracy had $12,000 of itemized deductions disallowed (3% x $400,000). She received a $5,000 state tax refund in 2005. If Tracy had only paid in the correct $35,000 of state taxes in 2004, she would still have had $12,000 in itemized deductions disallowed. She received a tax benefit to the extent of the $5,000 difference between her $28,000 deduction ($40,000 less $12,000) for 2004 and the $23,000 2004 deduction she would have claimed had she paid in the correct tax in 2004 ($35,000 less $12,000). Thus, the entire $5,000 state tax refund ($28,000 less $23,000) is includable in Tracy's 2005 income.

Standard deduction for earlier years. To determine if amounts recovered in 2005 must be included in your income, you must know the standard deduction for your filing status for the year the deduction was claimed. Standard deduction amounts for 2004, 2003, and 2002 are in Publication 525.

Explanation
The following table can be used as a reference to determine the amount of standard deduction allowed in previous years.

	2004	2003	2002	2001	2000
Single	4,850	4,750	4,700	4,550	4,400
Married filing jointly/ qualifying widower	9,700	9,500	7,850	7,600	7,350
Married filing separately	4,850	4,750	3,925	3,800	3,675
Head of household	7,150	7,000	6,900	6,650	6,450

Example. You filed a joint return for 2004 with taxable income of $45,000. Your itemized deductions were $10,550. The standard deduction that you could have claimed was $9,700. In 2005 you recovered $2,400 of your 2004 itemized deductions. None of the recoveries were more than the actual deductions for 2004. Include $850 of the recoveries in your 2005 income. This is the smaller of your recoveries ($2,400) or the amount by which your itemized deductions were more than the standard deduction ($10,550 − 9,700 = $850).

Explanation
Sometimes you get some money back in a year after you paid and deducted it (e.g., a refund of state income tax or real estate tax). To the extent that you got a tax benefit in the earlier year, and *only* to that extent, you must include the refund in income.

Example
In 2005, Stan and Lori received a refund of $1,000 for real estate taxes they paid in 2004. In 2004, they had $9,850 of itemized deductions, all of which was from their real estate taxes. The 2004 standard deduction was $9,700. Because they only have to report the amount of the refund to the extent they received a tax benefit in 2004, they would include $150 ($9,850 − $9,700) of the refund in income in 2005.

Recovery limited to deduction. You do not include in your income any amount of your recovery that is more than the amount you deducted in the earlier year. The amount you include in your income is limited to the smaller of:

- The amount deducted on Schedule A (Form 1040), or
- The amount recovered.

Example. During 2004 you paid $1,700 for medical expenses. From this amount you subtracted $1,500, which was 7.5% of your adjusted gross income. Your actual medical expense deduction was $200. In 2005, you received a $500 reimbursement from your medical insurance for your 2004 expenses. The only amount of the $500 reimbursement that must be included in your income for 2005 is $200—the amount actually deducted.

Other recoveries. See *Recoveries* in Publication 525 if:

- You have recoveries of items other than itemized deductions, or
- You received a recovery for an item for which you claimed a tax credit (other than investment credit or foreign tax credit) in a prior year.

Rents from Personal Property

If you rent out personal property, such as equipment or vehicles, how you report your income and expenses is generally determined by:

- Whether or not the rental activity is a business, and
- Whether or not the rental activity is conducted for profit.

Generally, if your primary purpose is income or profit and you are involved in the rental activity with continuity and regularity, your rental activity is a business. See Publication 535 for details on deducting expenses for both business and not-for-profit activities.

Reporting business income and expenses. If you are in the business of renting personal property, report your income and expenses on Schedule C or Schedule C-EZ (Form 1040). The form instructions have information on how to complete them.

Reporting nonbusiness income. If you are not in the business of renting personal property, report your rental income on Form 1040, line 21. List the type and amount of the income on the dotted line next to line 21.

Reporting nonbusiness expenses. If you rent personal property for profit, include your rental expenses in the total amount you enter on Form 1040, line 36. Also enter the amount and "PPR" on the dotted line next to line 36.

If you do not rent personal property for profit, your deductions are limited and you cannot report a loss to offset other income. See *Activity not for profit,* under *Other Income,* later.

Repayments

If you had to repay an amount that you included in your income in an earlier year, you may be able to deduct the amount repaid from your income for the year in which you repaid it. Or, if the amount you repaid is more than $3,000, you may be able to take a credit against your tax for the year in which you repaid it. Generally, you can claim a deduction or credit only if the repayment qualifies as an expense or loss incurred in your trade or business or in a for-profit transaction.

Type of deduction. The type of deduction you are allowed in the year of repayment depends on the type of income you included in the earlier year. You generally deduct the repayment on the same form or schedule on which you previously reported it as income. For example, if you reported it as self-employment income, deduct it as a business expense on Schedule C or Schedule C-EZ (Form 1040) or Schedule F (Form 1040). If you reported it as a capital gain, deduct it as a capital loss on Schedule D (Form 1040). If you reported it as wages, unemployment compensation, or other nonbusiness income, deduct it as a miscellaneous itemized deduction on Schedule A (Form 1040).

Repayment of $3,000 or less. If the amount you repaid was $3,000 or less, deduct it from your income in the year you repaid it. If you must deduct it as a miscellaneous itemized deduction, enter it on Schedule A (Form 1040), line 22.

Repayment over $3,000. If the amount you repaid was more than $3,000, you can deduct the repayment (see *Type of deduction,* earlier). However, you can instead choose to take a tax credit for the year of repayment if you included the income under a claim of right. This means that at the time you included the income, it appeared that you had an unrestricted right to it. If you qualify for this choice, figure your tax under both methods and compare the results. Use the method (deduction or credit) that results in less tax.

Method 1. Figure your tax for 2005 claiming a deduction for the repaid amount. If you must deduct it as a miscellaneous itemized deduction, enter it on Schedule A (Form 1040), line 27.

Method 2. Figure your tax for 2005 claiming a credit for the repaid amount. Follow these steps.

1. Figure your tax for 2005 without deducting the repaid amount.
2. Refigure your tax from the earlier year without including in income the amount you repaid in 2005.
3. Subtract the tax in (2) from the tax shown on your return for the earlier year. This is the credit.
4. Subtract the answer in (3) from the tax for 2005 figured without the deduction (Step 1).

If method 1 results in less tax, deduct the amount repaid. If method 2 results in less tax, claim a credit for the amount repaid on Form 1040, line 70, and enter "I.R.C. 1341" next to line 70.

An example of this computation can be found in Publication 525.

Example
For tax year 2004, you were married with no dependents. You filed a joint return with your spouse and reported taxable income of $90,000 (after all deductions and exemptions). Your return showed a tax liability of $15,981, which you paid. In 2005, you had to return $5,000 that you had received and had included in your 2004 gross income. Your marital and filing statuses were the same in 2005 as in 2004, and your taxable income for 2005 is $123,000 (after all deductions and exemptions).

To determine how to treat the repayment on your 2005 return, the following calculations must be performed.

Method 1

2005 taxable income	$123,000
Less: Deduction for repayment	(5,000)
Revised 2005 taxable income	$118,000
Tax using method 1	**$22,830**

Method 2

	2005 taxable income	$123,000
	Recomputed 2005 tax liability	$24,172
(a)	2004 taxable income as previously reported	$ 90,000
	Less: Deduction for repayment	(5,000)
	2004 taxable income w/out repayment	$ 85,000
	Recomputed 2004 tax liability	$14,731
(b)	2004 tax as reported	$ 15,981
	Recomputed 2004 tax liability (w/out repayment)	(14,731)
	Difference	$ 1,250
(c)	Recomputed 2005 tax liability	$ 24,172
	Difference from (b)	(1,250)
	Tax using method 2	**$ 22,922**

To determine which method should be used to account for your repayment in 2005, you must now compare the two methods and choose the one that generates the lower tax liability. In the above example, method 1 generates the lesser tax liability; therefore, you would claim a deduction for the amount repaid by you in 2005 on your 2005 tax return.

Note that these two methods will only result in different tax liabilities if you fall into different marginal tax brackets in each year (e.g., in 2004, you are in the 25% marginal tax bracket and in 2005, you are in the 28% tax bracket).

Repaid social security benefits. If you repaid social security benefits, see *Repayment of benefits* in chapter 12.

Royalties

Royalties from copyrights, patents, and oil, gas, and mineral properties are taxable as ordinary income.

You generally report royalties on Schedule E (Form 1040), Part I. However, if you hold an operating oil, gas, or mineral interest or are in business as a self-employed writer, inventor, artist, etc., report your income and expenses on Schedule C or Schedule C-EZ (Form 1040).

Copyrights and patents. Royalties from copyrights on literary, musical, or artistic works, and similar property, or from patents on inventions, are amounts paid to you for the right to use your work over a specified period of time. Royalties generally are based on the number of units sold, such as the number of books, tickets to a performance, or machines sold.

Oil, gas, and minerals. Royalty income from oil, gas, and mineral properties is the amount you receive when natural resources are extracted from your property. The royalties are based on units, such as barrels, tons, etc., and are paid to you by a person or company who leases the property from you.

Explanation
Income from a working interest in an oil or gas property is reported on Schedule C and is generally subject to self-employment tax, even though you may not actively participate in the operations that produce the income. Such income, however, is not eligible for Individual Retirement Arrangement (IRA) or Keogh plan contributions, because it is not earned by personal services you performed.

Depletion. If you are the owner of an economic interest in mineral deposits or oil and gas wells, you can recover your investment through the depletion allowance. For information on this subject, see chapter 10 of Publication 535, Business Expenses.

Coal and iron ore. Under certain circumstances, you can treat amounts you receive from the disposal of coal and iron ore as payments from the sale of a capital asset, rather than as royalty income. For information about gain or loss from the sale of coal and iron ore, see Publication 544.

Sale of property interest. If you sell your complete interest in oil, gas, or mineral rights, the amount you receive is considered payment for the sale of section 1231 property, not royalty income. Under certain circumstances, the sale is subject to capital gain or loss treatment on Schedule D (Form 1040). For more information on selling section 1231 property, see chapter 3 of Publication 544.

If you retain a royalty, an overriding royalty, or a net profit interest in a mineral property for the life of the property, you have made a lease or a sublease, and any cash you receive for the assignment of other interests in the property is ordinary income subject to a depletion allowance.

Explanation
The sale of most items producing royalty income is treated as a capital transaction. However, this is not true for copyrights and other property created by your personal efforts. The sole purpose of this exception is to prevent people such as authors from receiving capital gain treatment for their literary efforts. For more information, see Chapter 15, *Sale of Property*.

Part of future production sold. If you own mineral property but sell part of the future production, you generally treat the money you receive from the buyer at the time of the sale as a loan from the buyer. Do not include it in your income or take depletion based on it.

When production begins, you include all the proceeds in your income, deduct all the production expenses, and deduct depletion from that amount to arrive at your taxable income from the property.

Explanation
If you are paid royalties or bonuses for the production of oil before production actually begins, you may qualify for a depletion allowance in the year in which the advance royalty or bonus is included in your income. You should consult your tax advisor for further clarification of this point.

Unemployment Benefits

The tax treatment of unemployment benefits you receive depends on the type of program paying the benefits.
Unemployment compensation. You must include in your income all unemployment compensation you receive. You should receive a Form 1099-G, Certain Government Payments, showing the amount paid to you. Generally, you enter unemployment compensation on line 19 of Form 1040, line 13 of Form 1040A, or line 3 of Form 1040EZ.

Types of unemployment compensation. Unemployment compensation generally includes any amount received under an unemployment compensation law of the United States or of a state. It includes the following benefits.

• Benefits paid by a state or the District of Columbia from the Federal Unemployment Trust Fund.
• State unemployment insurance benefits.
• Railroad unemployment compensation benefits.
• Disability payments from a government program paid as a substitute for unemployment compensation. (Amounts received as workers' compensation for injuries or illness are not unemployment compensation. See chapter 6 for more information.)
• Trade readjustment allowances under the Trade Act of 1974.
• Unemployment assistance under the Disaster Relief and Emergency Assistance Act.

Governmental program. If you contribute to a governmental unemployment compensation program and your contributions are not deductible, amounts you receive under the program are not included as unemployment compensation until you recover your contributions.

Repayment of unemployment compensation. If you repaid in 2005 unemployment compensation you received in 2005, subtract the amount you repaid from the total amount you received and enter the difference on line 19 of Form 1040, line 13 of Form 1040A, or line 3 of Form 1040EZ. On the dotted line next to your entry enter "Repaid" and the amount you repaid. If you repaid unemployment compensation in 2005 that you included in income in an earlier year, you can deduct the amount repaid on Schedule A (Form 1040), line 22, if you itemize deductions. If the amount is more than $3,000, see *Repayments,* earlier.

Tax withholding. You can choose to have federal income tax withheld from your unemployment compensation. To make this choice, complete Form W-4V, Voluntary Withholding Request, and give it to the paying office. Tax will be withheld at 10% of your payment.
Caution. *If you do not choose to have tax withheld from your unemployment compensation, you may be liable for estimated tax. For more information on estimated tax, see chapter 5.*

Supplemental unemployment benefits. Benefits received from an employer-financed fund (to which the employees did not contribute) are not unemployment compensation. They are taxable as wages and are subject to withholding for income tax. They may be subject to social security and Medicare taxes. For more information, see *Supplemental Unemployment Benefits* in section 5 of Publication 15-A, Employer's Supplemental Tax Guide. Report these payments on line 7 of Form 1040 or Form 1040A or on line 1 of Form 1040EZ.

Repayment of benefits. You may have to repay some of your supplemental unemployment benefits to qualify for trade readjustment allowances under the Trade Act of 1974. If you repay supplemental unemployment benefits in the same year you receive them, reduce the total benefits by the amount you repay. If you repay the benefits in a later year, you must include the full amount of the benefits received in your income for the year you received them.

Deduct the repayment in the later year as an adjustment to gross income on Form 1040. (You cannot use Form 1040A or Form 1040EZ.) Include the repayment on Form 1040, line 36, and enter "Sub-Pay TRA" and the amount on the dotted line next to line 36. If the amount you repay in a later year is more than $3,000, you may be able to take a credit against your tax for the later year instead of deducting the amount repaid. For more information on this, see *Repayments,* earlier.
Private unemployment fund. Unemployment benefit payments from a private (nonunion) fund to which you voluntarily contribute are taxable only if the amounts you receive are more than your total payments into the fund. Report the taxable amount on Form 1040, line 21.
Payments by a union. Benefits paid to you as an unemployed member of a union from regular union dues are included in your gross income on Form 1040, line 21. However, if the unemployment benefits are paid from a special fund to which you contributed, your payments to the fund are not deductible, and the benefit pay-

ments are includible in your income only to the extent they are more than your contributions.

Guaranteed annual wage. Payments you receive from your employer during periods of unemployment, under a union agreement that guarantees you full pay during the year, are taxable as wages. Include them on line 7 of Form 1040 or Form 1040A or on line 1 of Form 1040EZ.

State employees. Payments similar to a state's unemployment compensation may be made by the state to its employees who are not covered by the state's unemployment compensation law. Although the payments are fully taxable, do not report them as unemployment compensation. Report these payments on Form 1040, line 21.

Welfare and Other Public Assistance Benefits

Do not include in your income governmental benefit payments from a public welfare fund based upon need, such as payments due to blindness. Payments from a state fund for the victims of crime should not be included in the victims' incomes if they are in the nature of welfare payments. Do not deduct medical expenses that are reimbursed by such a fund. You must include in your income any welfare payments that are compensation for services or that are obtained fraudulently.

Persons with disabilities. If you have a disability, you must include in income compensation you receive for services you perform unless the compensation is otherwise excluded. However, you do not include in income the value of goods, services, and cash that you receive, not in return for your services, but for your training and rehabilitation because you have a disability. Excludable amounts include payments for transportation and attendant care, such as interpreter services for the deaf, reader services for the blind, and services to help mentally retarded persons do their work.

Disaster relief grants. Do not include post-disaster grants received under the Disaster Relief and Emergency Assistance Act in your income if the grant payments are made to help you meet necessary expenses or serious needs for medical, dental, housing, personal property, transportation, or funeral expenses. Do not deduct casualty losses or medical expenses that are specifically reimbursed by these disaster relief grants. Unemployment assistance payments under the Act are taxable unemployment compensation. See *Unemployment compensation* under *Unemployment Benefits*, earlier.

Disaster relief payments. You can exclude from income any amount you receive that is a qualified disaster relief payment. A qualified disaster relief payment is an amount paid to you:

1. To reimburse or pay reasonable and necessary personal, family, living, or funeral expenses that result from a qualified disaster,
2. To reimburse or pay reasonable and necessary expenses incurred for the repair or rehabilitation of your home or repair or replacement of its contents to the extent it is due to a qualified disaster,
3. By a person engaged in the furnishing or sale of transportation as a common carrier because of the death or personal physical injuries incurred as a result of a qualified disaster, or
4. By a federal, state, or local government, or agency, or instrumentality in connection with a qualified disaster in order to promote the general welfare.

You can only exclude this amount to the extent any expense it pays for is not paid for by insurance or otherwise. The exclusion does not apply if you were a participant or conspirator in a terrorist action or his or her representative.

A qualified disaster is:

- A disaster which results from a terrorist or military action.
- A Presidentially declared disaster.
- A disaster which results from an accident involving a common carrier, or from any other event, which is determined to be catastrophic by the Secretary of the Treasury or his or her delegate.

For amounts paid under item (4), a disaster is qualified if it is determined by an applicable federal, state, or local authority to warrant assistance from the federal, state, or local government, agency, or instrumentality.

Mortgage assistance payments. Payments made under section 235 of the National Housing Act for mortgage assistance are not included in the homeowner's income. Interest paid for the homeowner under the mortgage assistance program cannot be deducted.

Medicare. Medicare benefits received under title XVIII of the Social Security Act are not includible in the gross income of the individuals for whom they are paid. This includes basic (part A (Hospital Insurance Benefits for the Aged)) and supplementary (part B (Supplementary Medical Insurance Benefits for the Aged)).

Old-age, survivors, and disability insurance benefits (OASDI). OASDI payments under section 202 of title II of the Social Security Act are not includible in the gross income of the individuals for whom they are paid. This applies to old-age insurance benefits, and insurance benefits for wives, husbands, children, widows, widowers, mothers and fathers, and parents, as well as the lump-sum death payment.

Payments to reduce cost of winter energy. Payments made by a state to qualified people to reduce their cost of winter energy use are not taxable.

Nutrition Program for the Elderly. Food benefits you receive under the Nutrition Program for the Elderly are not taxable. If you prepare and serve free meals for the program, include in your income as wages the cash pay you receive, even if you are also eligible for food benefits.

Explanation
Other Sickness and Injury Benefits

In addition to welfare or insurance benefits, you may receive other payments for sickness or injury. Table 13-1 gives a general overview of some of these payments.

Workers' compensation. Amounts you receive as workers' compensation for an occupational sickness or injury are fully exempt from tax if they are paid under a workers' compensation act or a statute in the nature of a workers' compensation act. The exemption also applies to your survivor(s). The exemption from tax, however, does not apply to retirement benefits you receive based on your age, length of service, or prior contributions to the plan, even if you retired because of occupational sickness or injury.

Note. If part of your workers' compensation reduces your social security or equivalent railroad retirement benefits received, that part is considered Social Security (or equivalent railroad retirement) benefits and may be taxable. For more information, see Publication 915, *Social Security and Equivalent Railroad Retirement Benefits*.

Return to work. If you return to work after qualifying for workers' compensation, payments you continue to receive while assigned to light duties are taxable. Report these payments as wages on line 7 of Form 1040 or Form 1040A or on line 1 of Form 1040EZ.

Federal Employees' Compensation Act (FECA). Payments received under this Act for personal injury or sickness, including payments to beneficiaries in case of death, are not taxable. However, you are taxed on amounts you receive under this Act as "continuation of pay" for up to 45 days while a claim is being decided. Report this income on line 7 of Form 1040 or Form 1040A or on line 1 of Form 1040EZ. Also, pay for sick leave while a claim is being processed is taxable and must be included in your income as wages.

The IRS has ruled that the subsidized portion of health benefits provided by an employer to an employee's domestic partner, who does not qualify as a spouse or a dependent, will be taxable as wages to the employee.

You can deduct the amount you spend to "buy back" sick leave for an earlier year to be eligible for nontaxable FECA benefits for that period. It is a miscellaneous deduction subject to the 2% limit on Schedule A (Form 1040). If you buy back sick leave in the same year you use it, the amount reduces your taxable sick leave pay. Do not deduct it separately.

Other compensation. Many other amounts you receive as compensation for injury or illness are not taxable. These include:

- **Compensatory damages** you receive for physical injury or physical illness, whether paid in a lump sum or in periodic payments,
- **Benefits you receive under an accident or health insurance policy** on which either you paid the premiums or your employer paid the premiums but you had to include them in your gross income,
- **Disability benefits** you receive for loss of income or earning capacity as a result of injuries under a "no-fault" car insurance policy, and
- **Compensation you receive for permanent loss or loss of use** of a part or function of your body, or for your permanent disfigurement. This compensation must be based only on the injury and not on the period of your absence from work. These benefits are exempt from tax even if your employer pays for the accident and health plan that provides these benefits.

Only damages received on account of personal physical injury or sickness are nontaxable. Punitive damages will be taxable—other than those received in a wrongful death action where state law stipulates that they are nontaxable. This law is effective for amounts received after August 20, 1996, unless there was a binding settlement in effect on September 13, 1995.

Reimbursement for medical care. A reimbursement for medical care is generally not taxable. However, this reimbursement may reduce your medical expense deduction. For more information, see Chapter 23, *Medical and Dental Expenses.* See Table 13-1.

Other Income

The following brief discussions are arranged in alphabetical order. Income items that are discussed in greater detail in another publication include a reference to that publication.

Activity not for profit. You must include on your return income from an activity from which you do not expect to make a profit. An example of this type of activity is a hobby or a farm you operate mostly for recreation and pleasure. Enter this income on Form 1040, line 21. Deductions for expenses related to the activity are limited. They cannot total more than the income you report and can be taken only if you itemize deductions on Schedule A (Form 1040). See *Not-for-Profit Activities* in chapter 1 of Publication 535 for information on whether an activity is considered carried on for a profit.

Explanation

An activity will be presumed to have been for profit if it results in a profit in at least 3 out of 5 consecutive tax years whether the activity is held individually, in trust, as a partnership, or as an S corporation. However, for the breeding, training, showing, or racing of horses, the activity must result in a profit in at least 2 out of 7 consecutive tax years. If the activity meets this test, it is presumed to be carried on for profit and the limits will not apply.

If you have engaged in an activity for less than 3 years, you can postpone the determination that the activity is not for profit by filing Form 5213, *Election to Postpone Determination.* Get Publication 535, *Business Expenses,* for more information.

It is possible that the IRS may treat you as engaged in a profit-making activity, even if you do not have a profit for 3 or more years during a period of 5 consecutive tax years. The IRS determines the activity's status—for profit or as a hobby—by considering the facts and circumstances surrounding the case. Some factors that will be considered include the following:

1. The manner in which you carry on the activity. For example, do you conduct your actions in a business-like manner (records, activity details, separate bank accounts, etc.)?
2. The expertise possessed by you and your advisors
3. The time and effort you expend in carrying on the activity
4. Any expectation you have that assets used in the activity may appreciate in value
5. Prior success in similar or dissimilar activities
6. Your history of income or loss with respect to the activity
7. The amount of occasional profits, if any, that you earn through the activity
8. Your financial status. For example, the fact that you do not have substantial income from other sources may indicate that you are engaging in the activity for profit
9. Elements of personal pleasure or recreation

These factors are not exclusive, and no one factor or number of factors is determinative.

TAXPLANNER

If an activity does show a profit for any 3 of 5 consecutive years (2 of 7 years for horse farms), there is a presumption by law that you are engaged in the activity for profit. The IRS has the burden of proving that the activity is only a hobby. However, if you do not meet the 3-year test and the IRS determines that the activity is a hobby, then you have the burden of proving your profit motive.

You would normally not file Form 5213, *Election to Postpone Determination with Respect to the Presumption That an Activity Is Engaged in for Profit,* until the IRS has examined records from one of the early years in which you engaged in the activity and has concluded that it is a hobby. Then, to prevent the IRS from assessing a tax on the years under examination, you should file Form 5213.

However, by filing the form, you agree to extend the period for which the IRS may collect additional taxes by disallowing the losses until 2 years after the examination period is over.

Also, by filing, you virtually guarantee that the IRS will carefully examine all years during the period under examination. Because the IRS previously concluded that the activity is a hobby, it is almost certain to reach the same conclusion again.

Alaska Permanent Fund dividend. If you received a payment from Alaska's mineral income fund (Alaska Permanent Fund dividend), report it as income on line 21 of Form 1040, line 13 of Form 1040A, or line 3 of Form 1040EZ. The state of Alaska sends each recipient a document that shows the amount of the payment with the check. The amount is also reported to IRS.

Alimony. Include in your income on Form 1040, line 11, any alimony payments you receive. Amounts you receive for child support are not income to you. Alimony and child support payments are discussed in chapter 20.

TaxPlanner

While alimony payments you receive are taxable, property settlements arising out of divorce are not. You should bear this in mind when considering the tax consequences of a divorce. See Chapter 20, *Alimony*, for more details.

TaxSaver

Receipt of alimony payments is considered compensation for purposes of making an IRA contribution. See Chapter 18, *Individual Retirement Arrangements (IRAs)*, for more details.

Bribes. If you receive a bribe, include it in your income.

Campaign contributions. These contributions are not income to a candidate unless they are diverted to his or her personal use. To be exempt from tax, the contributions must be spent for campaign purposes or kept in a fund for use in future campaigns. However, interest earned on bank deposits, dividends received on contributed securities, and net gains realized on sales of contributed securities are taxable and must be reported on Form 1120-POL, U.S. Income Tax Return for Certain Political Organizations. Excess campaign funds transferred to an office account must be included in the officeholder's income on Form 1040, line 21, in the year transferred.

Cash rebates. A cash rebate you receive from a dealer or manufacturer of an item you buy is not income, but you must reduce your basis by the amount of the rebate.

Example. You buy a new car for $9,000 cash and receive a $400 rebate check from the manufacturer. The $400 is not income to you. Your basis in the car is $8,600. This is your basis on which you figure gain or loss if you sell the car, and depreciation if you use it for business.

Explanation
The IRS realistically views rebates as another way of offering a price reduction to induce you to buy a product. Similarly, the dividends that a life insurance company pays you are a reduction of your premium rather than an addition to your gross income. The same rule applies to any cash rebates you might receive from you credit card company for using its card.

Casualty insurance and other reimbursements. You generally should not report these reimbursements on your return. See Publication 547, Casualties, Disasters, and Thefts, for more information.

Child support payments. You should not report these payments on your return. See Publication 504, Divorced or Separated Individuals, for more information.

Court awards and damages. To determine if settlement amounts you receive by compromise or judgment must be included in your income, you must consider the item that the settlement replaces. Include the following as ordinary income.

1. Interest on any award.
2. Compensation for lost wages or lost profits in most cases.
3. Punitive damages. It does not matter if they relate to a physical injury or physical sickness.
4. Amounts received in settlement of pension rights (if you did not contribute to the plan).
5. Damages for:
   a. Patent or copyright infringement,
   b. Breach of contract, or

Table 13-1. **Are Your Sickness and Injury Benefits Taxable?**

*This table is intended as a general overview. Additional rules may apply depending on your situation. For more information about your benefits, see **Other Sickness and Injury Benefits**.*

Type of Benefit	General Rule
Workers' compensation	Not taxable if paid under a workers' compensation act or a statute in the nature of a workers' compensation act and paid due to a work-related sickness or injury. However, payments received after returning to work are taxable.
Federal Employees' Compensation Act (FECA)	Not taxable if paid because of personal injury or sickness. However, payments received as "continuation of pay" for up to 45 days while a claim is being decided and pay received for sick leave while a claim is being processed are taxable.
Compensatory damages	Not taxable if received for injury or sickness.
Accident or health insurance benefits	Not taxable if you paid the insurance premiums.
Disability benefits	Not taxable if received for loss of income or earning capacity due to an injury covered by a "no-fault" automobile policy.
Compensation for permanent loss or loss of use of a part or function of your body, or for permanent disfigurement	Not taxable if paid due to the injury. The payments must be figured without regard to any period of absence from work.
Reimbursements for medical care	Not taxable—but the reimbursement may reduce your medical expense deduction.

c. Interference with business operations.

6. Back pay and damages for emotional distress received to satisfy a claim under Title VII of the Civil Rights Act of 1964.

Do not include in your income compensatory damages for personal physical injury or physical sickness (whether received in a lump sum or installments).

Explanation

Compensation from a discrimination lawsuit and compensation damages awarded from an Employee Retirement and Income Security Act lawsuit are generally included in your income. Legal fees and expenses paid for such awards after October 22, 2004 are deductible in calculating your adjusted gross income.

Emotional distress. Emotional distress itself is not a physical injury or physical sickness, but damages you receive for emotional distress due to a physical injury or sickness are treated as received for the physical injury or sickness. Do not include them in your income.

If the emotional distress is due to a personal injury that is not due to a physical injury or sickness (for example, employment discrimination or injury to reputation), you must include the damages in your income, except for any damages you receive for medical care due to that emotional distress. Emotional distress includes physical symptoms that result from emotional distress, such as headaches, insomnia, and stomach disorders.

Explanation

Only damages received on account of personal injury or sickness are nontaxable. Punitive damages will be taxable, unless they are received in a wrongful death action for which state law stipulates as of September 13, 1995, that only punitive damages may be awarded. This law is effective for amounts received after August 20, 1996, unless there was a binding settlement in effect on September 13, 1995. If you have a question on whether the award is taxable, you should consult your tax advisor.

TaxSaver

The legal expense that you incur in the process of getting a damage award may be claimed as an itemized deduction (subject to the 2%-of-AGI floor) only if the award is included in your gross income. The same holds true for the deduction in calculating your adjusted gross income for legal fees for "civil rights" type cases created under a 2004 tax act. A "civil rights" type case is one involving claims of discrimination of any sort. If the award is only partially included in your gross income, you may deduct only a proportional amount in legal fees. Thus, if the entire award is excluded from your gross income, none of your legal fees are deductible.

TaxSaver

A technique now being used in large personal injury cases is the so-called structured settlement, in which the defendant's insurance company offers an **annuity** to the injured party instead of a **lump-sum distribution**. The IRS has ruled that the entire amount of the annuity payments may be excluded from the recipient's gross income, even though the recipient is, in effect, receiving interest.

Unlawful discrimination claims. You may be able to take a deduction for attorney fees and court costs paid after October 22,

2004, for actions settled or decided after that date involving a claim of unlawful discrimination, a claim against the United States Government, or a claim made under section 1862(b)(3)(A) of the Social Security Act, but only up to the amount included in gross income for the tax year from such claim. For more information, see Publication 525.

Credit card insurance. Generally, if you receive benefits under a credit card disability or unemployment insurance plan, the benefits are taxable to you. These plans make the minimum monthly payment on your credit card account if you cannot make the payment due to injury, illness, disability, or unemployment. Report on Form 1040, line 21, the amount of benefits you received during the year that is more than the amount of the premiums you paid during the year.

Employment agency fees. If you get a job through an employment agency, and the fee is paid by your employer, the fee is not includible in your income if you are not liable for it. However, if you pay it and your employer reimburses you for it, it is includible in your income.

Energy conservation subsidies. You can exclude from gross income any subsidy provided, either directly or indirectly, by public utilities for the purchase or installation of an energy conservation measure for a dwelling unit.

Energy conservation measure. This includes installations or modifications that are primarily designed to reduce consumption of electricity or natural gas, or improve the management of energy demand.

Dwelling unit. This includes a house, apartment, condominium, mobile home, boat, or similar property. If a building or structure contains both dwelling and other units, any subsidy must be properly allocated.

Estate and trust income. An estate or trust, unlike a partnership, may have to pay federal income tax. If you are a beneficiary of an estate or trust, you may be taxed on your share of its income distributed or required to be distributed to you. However, there is never a double tax. Estates and trusts file their returns on Form 1041, U.S. Income Tax Return for Estates and Trusts, and your share of the income is reported to you on Schedule K-1 (Form 1041).

Explanation

Generally speaking, there are three types of trusts: (1) a trust that is required to distribute all the income it earns during the year (simple trust), (2) a trust that has the choice of whether to distribute all, part, or none of the income (complex trust), and (3) a trust where the person creating the trust is treated as the owner of the trust's assets (grantor trust). The taxability of these trusts varies. A beneficiary of a simple trust must report all the income (though generally not capital gains), whether actually distributed or not, on his or her income tax return (Form 1040). A beneficiary of a complex trust will only report the income of the trust to the extent of distributions actually made by the trust to the beneficiary. The grantor of a grantor trust must report all income gains and deductions on his or her individual income tax return, as they are not taxed on a trust return.

Current income required to be distributed. If you are the beneficiary of an estate or trust that must distribute all of its current income, you must report your share of the distributable net income, whether or not you actually received it.

Example

A beneficiary of a trust that is required to distribute all of its current income receives a Schedule K-1 reporting $100 of interest income. However, the beneficiary has not received any distributions from the trust. The beneficiary must report the $100 of interest income on Schedule B of Form 1040 even though the beneficiary has not received any distributions.

Current income not required to be distributed. If you are the beneficiary of an estate or trust and the fiduciary has the choice of whether to distribute all or part of the current income, you must report:

- All income that is required to be distributed to you, whether or not it is actually distributed, plus
- All other amounts actually paid or credited to you, up to the amount of your share of distributable net income.

Explanation
When an estate earns income before the assets have all been distributed, it is taxed like a complex trust. Many people find this area of estate taxation very confusing, and for good reason. Gifts and inheritances are not gross income to the recipient. However, money or property that you inherit may earn some interest, dividends, or rent while the estate is being settled. It is that income that must be reported either by you or by the estate. Ordinarily, the executor of the estate files an income tax return for the estate, reporting the income, but he or she may shift the tax burden of that income to the beneficiaries if the property has already been distributed to them. See Chapter 4, *Decedents,* for more detail.

TAXALERT
In some instances, adjustments for the alternative minimum tax could flow through a trust to the beneficiary. See Chapter 32, *How to Figure Your Tax,* for more details.

How to report. Treat each item of income the same way that the estate or trust would treat it. For example, if a trust's dividend income is distributed to you, you report the distribution as dividend income on your return. The same rule applies to distributions of tax-exempt interest and capital gains.

The fiduciary of the estate or trust must tell you the type of items making up your share of the estate or trust income and any credits you are allowed on your individual income tax return.

Losses. Losses of estates and trusts generally are not deductible by the beneficiaries.

Exception
There are significant exceptions to the rule that losses of estates and trusts are not deductible by the beneficiaries. When an estate or a trust terminates, the beneficiaries are frequently allowed a deduction for certain expenses that the estate or trust had but was unable to use as a deduction. These items are (1) net operating loss carryovers, (2) certain excess deductions in the year of termination, and (3) capital loss carryovers.

When an estate is terminated, it is not unusual for the attorney's and executor's fees to be paid in the year in which the estate is closed. If these expenses and the net operating loss carryover exceed the estate's income for that year, the excess is deductible by the beneficiaries. This deduction may be claimed only by itemizing deductions on Schedule A (Form 1040). These deductions are subject to the 2% rule on miscellaneous itemized deductions. This means that they are only deductible to the extent that total miscellaneous itemized deductions exceed 2% of AGI.

A capital loss carryover from an estate or a trust may be used in the beneficiaries' current or subsequent returns to reduce capital gains and/or to generate a deduction subject to the limitation that only $3,000 of capital losses in excess of capital gains may be deducted each year.

When to report estate and trust income. You must include your share of the estate or trust income on your return for your tax year in which the last day of the estate on trust tax year falls.

The trustee of the trust on estate will provide you with a Form K-1 that tells you each item of income and deductions, and where they are to be reported on your personal tax return.

TAXSAVER
It may be a good idea if you are the beneficiary of a trust to inform the trustee of your tax situation so that all possible tax-saving alternatives can be explored. Amounts that are *not* required to be distributed currently, according to the terms of the trust, may sometimes be distributed at the discretion of the trustee. There may be substantial tax advantages to the timing, amounts, and methods of such distributions. You and the trustee should consult with a professional who specializes in this area.

TAXPLANNER
If you are receiving trust income, you should consider if it is necessary for you to make estimated tax payments or increase your withholding taxes as a result of this additional income. See Chapter 5, *Tax Withholding and Estimated Tax.*

Grantor trust. Income earned by a grantor trust is taxable to the grantor, not the beneficiary, if the grantor keeps certain control over the trust. (The grantor is the one who transferred property to the trust.) This rule applies if the property (or income from the property) put into the trust will or may revert (be returned) to the grantor or the grantor's spouse.

Generally, a trust is a grantor trust if the grantor has a reversionary interest valued (at the date of transfer) at more than 5% of the value of the transferred property.

TAXALERT
Even though the grantor is taxed on the trust income, the trustee of a grantor trust may need to file Form 1041 if the trust income reaches a level that requires a return. The items of income, deduction, and credit are treated as owned by the grantor, on another person, and are reported on a separate statement (Tax Information Letter) that is attached to Form 1041.

The IRS issued regulations that provide guidance for optional methods of reporting trust income by a grantor trust. For example, alternative methods of reporting include the issuance of a Form 1099 directly from the payer of income to the grantor for inclusion on the grantor's individual tax return; the issuance of a Form 1099 by the trust to the grantor; or the filing of a Form 1041 by the trustee of the grantor trust.

The rules can get complicated, especially if there is more than one grantor. You should consult with your tax advisor for more information.

Expenses paid by another. If your personal expenses are paid for by another person, such as a corporation, the payment may be taxable to you depending upon your relationship with that person and the nature of the payment. But if the payment makes up for a loss caused by that person, and only restores you to the position you were in before the loss, the payment is not includible in your income.

Fees for services. Include all fees for your services in your income. Examples of these fees are amounts you receive for services you perform as:

- A corporate director,
- An executor, administrator, or personal representative of an estate,
- A notary public, or
- An election precinct official.

Nonemployee compensation. If you are not an employee and the fees for your services from the same payer total $600 or more for the year, you may receive a Form 1099-MISC. You may need to report your fees as self-employment income. See *Self-Employed Persons,* in chapter 1, for a discussion of when you are considered self-employed.

Corporate director. Corporate director fees are self-employment income. Report these payments on Schedule C or Schedule C-EZ (Form 1040).

Executor, administrator, or personal representative of an estate. All personal representatives must include in their gross income fees paid to them from an estate. If you are not in the trade or business of being an executor (for instance, you are the executor of a friend's or relative's estate), report these fees on Form 1040, line 21. If you are in the trade or business of being an executor, report these fees as self-employment income on Schedule C or Schedule C-EZ (Form 1040). The fee is not includible in income if it is waived.

Notary public. Report payments for these services on Schedule C or Schedule C-EZ (Form 1040). These payments are not subject to self-employment tax. (See the separate instructions for Schedule SE (Form 1040) for details.)

Election precinct official. You should receive a Form W-2 showing payments for services performed as an election official or election worker. Report these payments on line 7 of Form 1040 or Form 1040A or on line 1 of Form 1040EZ.

Explanation

Self-employment income. Chapter 39, *If You Are Self-Employed: How to File Schedule C,* includes a more comprehensive discussion of self-employment income.

Corporate director fees and executor fees (if you are in the trade or business of being an executor) are considered self-employment income. For both employees and self-employed individuals, the 2005 wage base is $90,000 for Old Age, Survivor, and Disability Insurance (OASDI) and is unlimited for Medicare. The OASDI rate is 12.4% and the Medicare rate is 2.9%. These rates are applied to 92.35% of your self-employment income. Thus, if a person earns self-employment income of $100,000, he or she will pay self-employment tax of $13,838, [i.e., ($90,000 × 15.3%) plus [($100,000 × 92.35%) − $90,000) × 2.9%]; see Schedule SE. However, if your net earnings from self-employment are less than $400, no self-employment tax is payable.

Fees are self-employment income only if you present yourself as being in the trade or business that produces the fees. Therefore, unless you *regularly* appear as a witness, act as an executor or trustee, or judge elections, the fees earned will not be self-employment income subject to self-employment tax.

Clergy fees. Fees received by clergy for performing funerals, marriages, baptisms, or other services must be included in gross income.

TAXSAVER

A member of the clergy, however, can request to be exempt from the self-employment tax on such income by filing Form 4361, *Application for Exemption from Self-Employment Tax for Use by Ministers, Members of Religious Orders, and Christian Science Practitioners.*

TAXPLANNER

Any business that pays you $600 or more in fees should provide you with a Form 1099. A copy of this form should also be filed with the IRS by the business. Individual payers are not required to file this form. However, you are not excused from your responsibility to report the income just because you do not receive a Form 1099.

Professional fees. Fees received by a doctor, lawyer, and so on should be shown on Schedule C, Profit or Loss from Business, not in the Miscellaneous Income section on line 21 of Form 1040. Otherwise, the IRS's document-matching program may generate unwarranted notices, suggesting that you have underpaid your tax.

Explanation

Sole proprietorship (self-employment) income. Unlike a partnership or a regular corporation, a sole proprietorship is not a separate entity. In a sole proprietorship, you and your business are one and the same. You report gross profit or loss for the year from the sole proprietorship on Form 1040, Schedule C (or Schedule C-EZ if you meet certain requirements), and it becomes part of your AGI. In addition to owing income tax on such income, you, as the sole proprietor, will usually be liable for self-employment tax, and you may also be required to make payments of estimated taxes. In order to avoid a penalty for underpayment of estimated taxes you must make estimated tax payments for 2006 if you expect to owe at least $1,000 in tax for 2006 after subtracting your withholding and credits, and you expect your withholding and credits to be less than the smaller of:

1) 90% of the tax to be shown on your 2006 tax return, or
2) 100% of the tax shown on your 2005 tax return (or 110% if your 2005 AGI exceeds $150,000, $75,000 if married filing separately). See Chapter 5, *Tax Withholding and Estimated Tax.*

A net loss from the business can generally be deducted in computing your AGI.

Your profit (or loss) is computed as income less your allowable deductions. Income includes cash, property, and services received by the business from all sources, unless specifically excluded under the tax code. Allowable deductions include all necessary and ordinary expenses incurred in connection with the business. For sole proprietorships in the business of selling goods or inventory, the primary expense will be the cost of goods sold. The cost of goods sold represents the cost of materials, labor, and overhead included in the inventory sold during the year. Other expenses that you deduct on Schedule C include salaries and wages, interest on loans used in the business, rent, depreciation, bad debts, travel and entertainment, insurance, real estate taxes, and so on.

If you operate your own business or have other self-employment income, such as babysitting or selling crafts, see these other publications for more information.

- Publication 334, *Tax Guide for Small Business*
- Publication 535, *Business Expenses*
- Publication 533, *Self-Employment Tax*

TaxSaver

Note: If you receive fees that are self-employment income, you may contribute to a **Keogh plan, Simplified Employee Plan IRA, or SIMPLE IRA.** See Chapter 18, *Individual Retirement Arrangements (IRAs),* for details.

Foster-care providers. Payments you receive from a state, political subdivision, or a qualified foster care placement agency for providing care to qualified foster individuals in your home generally are not included in your income. However, you must include in your income payments received for the care of more than 5 individuals age 19 or older and certain difficulty-of-care payments.

A qualified foster individual is a person who:

1. Is living in a foster family home, and
2. Was placed there by:
   a. An agency of a state or one of its political subdivisions, or
   b. A qualified foster care placement agency.

TaxPlanner

If a foster child lives with you in your home for the entire year, you are entitled to claim the child as a dependent if you provide more than half of his or her support. This is often the case when you care for the children of relatives. By claiming the child as a dependent, you may receive an additional exemption of $3,200 for 2005. Thus, it may be worthwhile for you to calculate whether you are in fact providing more than half the child's support. (See Chapter 34, *Child and Dependent Care Credit,* for details.)

Difficulty-of-care payments. These are additional payments that are designated by the payer as compensation for providing the additional care that is required for physically, mentally, or emotionally handicapped qualified foster individuals. A state must determine that the additional compensation is needed, and the care for which the payments are made must be provided in your home.

You must include in your income difficulty-of-care payments received for more than:

• 10 qualified foster individuals under age 19, or
• 5 qualified foster individuals age 19 or older.

Maintaining space in home. If you are paid to maintain space in your home for emergency foster care, you must include the payment in your income.

Reporting taxable payments. If you receive payments that you must include in your income, you are in business as a foster-care provider and you are self-employed. Report the payments on Schedule C or Schedule C-EZ (Form 1040). See Publication 587, *Business Use of Your Home (Including Use by Daycare Providers),* to help you determine the amount you can deduct for the use of your home.

Found property. If you find and keep property that does not belong to you that has been lost or abandoned (treasure-trove), it is taxable to you at its fair market value in the first year it is your undisputed possession.

Free tour. If you received a free tour from a travel agency for organizing a group of tourists, you must include its value in your income. Report the fair market value of the tour on Form 1040, line 21, if you are not in the trade or business of organizing tours. You cannot deduct your expenses in serving as the voluntary leader of the group at the group's request. If you organize tours as a trade or business, report the tour's value on Schedule C or Schedule C-EZ (Form 1040).

Gambling winnings. You must include your gambling winnings in income on Form 1040, line 21. If you itemize your deductions on Schedule A (Form 1040), you can deduct gambling losses you had during the year, but only up to the amount of your winnings. See chapter 30 for information on recordkeeping.

Lotteries and raffles. Winnings from lotteries and raffles are gambling winnings. In addition to cash winnings, you must include in your income the fair market value of bonds, cars, houses, and other noncash prizes.

Tip. *If you win a state lottery prize payable in installments, see Publication 525 for more information.*

TaxPlanner

If you win a large lottery, proper financial planning can help you minimize the tax bite. You should consult with a financial planner or your tax advisor.

Form W-2G. You may have received a Form W-2G, Certain Gambling Winnings, showing the amount of your gambling winnings and any tax taken out of them. Include the amount from box 1 on Form 1040, line 21. Include the amount shown in box 2 on Form 1040, line 64, as federal income tax withheld.

Explanation

While a winner of the Canadian government lottery does not have to pay Canadian tax on the winnings, a U.S. citizen or resident who wins does have to pay U.S. tax on the amount. Citizens and residents of the United States have to report all income, including foreign income. See Chapter 43, *U.S. Citizens Working Abroad,* and Chapter 44, *Foreign Citizens Living in the United States,* for more information about worldwide income.

TaxPlanner

Because you may not win money gambling until late in the year and gambling losses are deductible only up to the amount of your winnings, you should plan ahead by keeping losing racetrack, lottery, and other gambling tickets. In that way, if you do win, you will be able to itemize your gambling losses. It's also a good idea to keep a diary of gambling losses incurred during the entire year. Note that losses from one kind of gambling are deductible against gains from another kind. These losses are claimed as miscellaneous itemized deductions but are not subject to the 2%-of-AGI floor and are reported on Schedule A, line 27. These losses are also allowed for purposes of the Alternative Minimum Tax (AMT).

Gifts and inheritances. Generally, property you receive as a gift, bequest, or inheritance is not included in your income. However, if property you receive this way later produces income such as interest, dividends, or rents, that income is taxable to you. If property is given to a trust and the income from it is paid, credited, or distributed to you, that income is also taxable to you. If the gift, bequest, or inheritance is the income from the property, that income is taxable to you.

Explanation

Items given to you as an incentive to enter into a business transaction are not tax-free gifts. For example, incentive items such as small appliances or dinnerware given to you by a bank as an incentive to open an account are treated as taxable interest income to you and must be reported at their fair market value.

Inherited pension or IRA. If you inherited a pension or an individual retirement arrangement (IRA), you may have to include part of the inherited amount in your income. See chapter 11 if you inherited a pension. See chapter 18 if you inherited an IRA.

Hobby losses. Losses from a hobby are not deductible from other income. A hobby is an activity from which you do not expect to make a profit. See *Activity not for profit,* earlier.

Caution. *If you collect stamps, coins, or other items as a hobby for recreation and pleasure, and you sell any of the items, your gain is taxable as a capital gain. (See chapter 17.) However, if you sell items from your collection at a loss, you cannot deduct the loss.*

Explanation

While a *net* loss from the sale of stamps, coins, or other items that you collect for a hobby may not be deducted, a loss from the sale of these items may be offset against a gain from the sale of similar items occurring in the same year.

Example

You sell several stamps at a gain of $1,000. You may offset up to $1,000 in losses from the sale of other stamps against this gain. The result is that there is no taxable gain. All of the sales should be listed separately on Schedule D.

TaxSaver

If you are planning to sell an item in your collection that has appreciated in value and your collection also contains an item that has decreased in value, you may want to sell both in the same year to incur the least amount of tax. In short, clean out the junk to establish losses in a year when you have gains.

Holocaust victims restitution. Restitution payments you receive as a Holocaust victim (or the heir of a Holocaust victim) and interest earned on the payments, including interest earned on amounts held in certain escrow accounts or funds, are not taxable. You also do not include them in any computations in which you would ordinarily add excludable income to your adjusted gross income, such as the computation to determine the taxable part of social security benefits. If the payments are made in property, your basis in the property is its fair market value when you receive it.

Excludable restitution payments are payments or distributions made by any country or any other entity because of persecution of an individual on the basis of race, religion, physical or mental disability, or sexual orientation by Nazi Germany, any other Axis regime, or any other Nazi-controlled or Nazi-allied country, whether the payments are made under a law or as a result of a legal action. They include compensation or reparation for property losses resulting from Nazi persecution, including proceeds under insurance policies issued before and during World War II by European insurance companies.

Illegal income. Illegal income, such as money from dealing illegal drugs, must be included in your income on Form 1040, line 21, or on Schedule C or Schedule C-EZ (Form 1040) if from your self-employment activity.

Explanation

It is not necessary for the activity that produces income to be legal for the income to be taxable. Income from illegal activities, such as embezzlement, drug dealing, bookmaking, and bootlegging, is taxable. Al Capone, the notorious Chicago bootlegger during Prohibition, was convicted of income tax evasion because he did not report his illegal income.

Embezzlement income is taxable in the year in which the funds are stolen. If the embezzler pays back the stolen funds in a later year, he on she can claim a deduction in the year of repayment.

Indian fishing rights. If you are a member of a qualified Indian tribe that has fishing rights secured by treaty, executive order, or an Act of Congress as of March 17, 1988, do not include in your income amounts you receive from activities related to those fishing rights. The income is not subject to income tax, self-employment tax, or employment taxes.

TaxAlert

Investment clubs. An investment club is a group of friends, neighbors, business associates, or others who pool limited or stated amounts of funds to invest in stock or other securities. The club may or may not have a written agreement, charter, or bylaws. Usually, the group operates informally with members pledging a regular amount to be paid into the club monthly. Some clubs have a committee that gathers information on securities, selects the most promising, and recommends that the club invest in them. Other clubs rotate the investigatory responsibilities among all their members. Most require all members to vote for or against all investments sales exchanges or other transactions.

How the income from an investment club is reported on your tax return depends on how the club operates. Most clubs operate as partnerships and are treated as such for federal tax purposes. Others operate as corporations, trusts, or associations taxed as corporations.

Members of an investment club should include their share of each type of the club's income on their returns. For example, dividends are reported on Schedule B, Part II, line 5, and capital gains are reported on Schedule D.

The expenses incurred by the club to produce or to collect income, to manage investment property, or to determine any tax due are also reported separately. You may deduct your share of these items on Schedule A as a miscellaneous deduction if you itemize your deductions.

Note: These expenses—along with some others—must exceed 2% of your AGI to be deductible as miscellaneous itemized deductions.

TaxAlert

Depending on how your investment club is organized, it may be required to file a separate partnership, corporation, or trust tax return. More details are explained in IRS Publication 550, some of which follow.

Tax returns and identifying numbers. Investment clubs must file either **Form 1065,** *U.S. Partnership Return of Income;* **Form 1041,** *U.S. Income Tax Return for Estates and Trusts;* or **Form 1120,** *U.S. Corporation Income Tax Return.* Certain small corporations may be able to file **Form 1120-A,** *U.S. Corporation Short-Form Income Tax Return.* See the instructions for Forms 1120 and 1120-A.

Form SS-4. Each club must have an employer identification number (EIN) to use when filing its return. The club's EIN also may have to be given to the payer of dividends. If your club does not have an EIN, use Form SS-4, Application for Employer Identification Number. Mail the completed Form SS-4 to the IRS Center where you file the club's tax return. Form SS-4 can be found in Chapter 50, *2005 Federal Tax Forms and Schedules You Can Use.*

Stock in name of club. When stock is recorded in the name of the investment club, the club must give its own EIN to the payer of dividends.

If the club is a partnership or a trust, the dividends distributed to the partners or beneficiaries must be shown on Form 1065 or Form 1041, respectively. The partners' or the beneficiaries' identifying numbers also must be shown on the return.

If the club is an association taxed as a corporation, any distribution it makes that qualifies as a dividend must be reported on Forms 1096 and 1099-DIV if total distributions to the shareholder are $10 or more for the year.

Stock in name of member. When stock is recorded in the name of one club member, this member must give his or her social security number to the payer of dividends. (When stock is held in the names of two or more club members, the social security number of only one member must be given to the payer.) This member is considered as the record owner for the actual owner of the stock, the investment club. This member is a "nominee" and must file Form 1099-DIV showing the club to be the owner of the dividend, his or her social security number, and the EIN of the club.

Example

In order to avoid any matching notices from the IRS, the nominee should report the dividend income on his or her tax return on line 5, Part II, of Form 1040, Schedule B and then subtract out the nominee distribution.

ABC company	$100
Less: Nominee distribution	($100)

No Social Security coverage for investment club earnings. If an investment club partnership's activities are limited to investing in savings certificates, stock, or securities and collecting interest or dividends for its members' accounts, the members' share of income is not earnings from self-employment. You cannot voluntarily pay the self-employment tax in order to increase your Social Security coverage and ultimate benefits.

For more information about investment clubs, see Publication 550.

Interest on frozen deposits. In general, you exclude from your income the amount of interest earned on a frozen deposit. See *Interest income on frozen deposits* in chapter 8.

Interest on qualified savings bonds. You may be able to exclude from income the interest from qualified U.S. savings bonds you redeem if you pay qualified higher educational expenses in the same year. For more information on this exclusion, see *Education Savings Bond Program* under *U.S. Savings Bonds* in chapter 8.

Job interview expenses. If a prospective employer asks you to appear for an interview and either pays you an allowance or reimburses you for your transportation and other travel expenses, the amount you receive is generally not taxable. You include in income only the amount you receive that is more than your actual expenses.

Jury duty. Jury duty pay you receive must be included in your income on Form 1040, line 21. If you must give the pay to your employer because your employer continues to pay your salary while you serve on the jury, you can deduct the amount turned over to your employer as an adjustment to your income. Include the amount you repay your employer on Form 1040, line 36. Enter "Jury Pay" and the amount on the dotted line next to line 36.

Explanation

Jury fees. This item is often overlooked. Just because a fee is paid by a government body does not mean that it is not subject to tax. However, the Tax Court has ruled that the mileage allowance received by a juror to cover the cost of transportation between the court and his or her home is not included in income. In addition, if you are required to give your jury pay to your employer, you can claim a deduction for the amount paid over. You can claim this deduction whether or not you itemize your deductions. You would report the income on line 21 of Form 1040 and, if you give your jury pay to your employer, report it as an adjustment on line 36 and write "Jury Pay" next to the amount.

Kickbacks. You must include kickbacks, side commissions, push money, or similar payments you receive in your income on Form 1040, line 21, or on Schedule C or Schedule C-EZ (Form 1040), if from your self-employment activity.

Example. You sell cars and help arrange car insurance for buyers. Insurance brokers pay back part of their commissions to you for referring customers to them. You must include the kickbacks in your income.

Health savings accounts (HSAs) and Medical savings accounts (MSAs). You generally do not include in income amounts you withdraw from your HSA, Archer MSA or Medicare Advantage MSA if you use the money to pay for qualified medical expenses. Generally, qualified medical expenses are those you can deduct on Schedule A (Form 1040), Itemized Deductions. For more information about qualified medical expenses, see chapter 23. For more information about HSAs, Archer MSAs or Medicare Advantage MSAs, see Publication 969, Health Savings Accounts and Other Tax-Favored Health Plans.

TAXSAVER

Contributions to an MSA or HSA can also be deductible. See Chapter 23, *Medical and Dental Expenses,* for details.

Prizes and awards. If you win a prize in a lucky number drawing, television or radio quiz program, beauty contest, or other event, you must include it in your income. For example, if you win a $50 prize in a photography contest, you must report this income on Form 1040, line 21. If you refuse to accept a prize, do not include its value in your income.

Explanation

An individual wins a prize in a charitable fundraising raffle and refuses to accept the prize, returning the prize to the charity. The individual need not include the value of the prize as income on his or her return. Likewise, the individual is not entitled to a charitable deduction.

Prizes and awards in goods or services must be included in your income at their fair market value.

Explanation

Fair market value is the price at which property would be exchanged between a willing buyer and a willing seller when neither party is compelled to buy or to sell. When merchandise is received as a prize, fair market value is the suggested retail price, unless some other measure of fair market value can be readily ascertained. Other ways to measure fair market value that have been approved by the courts include the following:

1. **Resale value.** The Tax Court has ruled that, in some cases, the fair market value of an item is what you could realize by selling it.
2. **Value to the recipient.** If you receive a prize that is not something you would ordinarily purchase, the Tax Court has said that you may discount the value of the prize.

Example 1

An individual received a new car as an award from her employer. The Tax Court ruled that the amount to be considered as income was not what the employer had paid for the car but how much the recipient would have realized by selling the car immediately after it was received.

Example 2

Taxpayers received two first-class cruise tickets from a game show. The tickets were nontransferable and had to be used within 1 year. The Tax Court found that the tickets were not something that the taxpayers would normally have acquired but were a luxury that would otherwise have been beyond their means. Accordingly, the Tax Court permitted an amount less than the retail price of the tickets in the taxpayers' gross income.

There is no standardized technique to determine the amount to be included in gross income in cases similar to these. Our advice is this: If you believe that you can justify a value less than normal retail price, it may be worthwhile to include the lower amount in taxable income.

Employee awards or bonuses. Cash awards or bonuses given to you by your employer for good work or suggestions generally must be included in your income as wages. However, certain noncash employee achievement awards can be excluded from income. See *Bonuses and awards* in chapter 6.

TaxSaver

Note received for services. If your employer gives you a negotiable note as payment for your services, you must include the fair market value (usually the discount value) of the note in your income as wages for the year you receive it. When you later receive payments on the note, part of each payment is a recovery of the fair market value that you previously included in your income. Do not include that part in your income again. Include the rest of the payment in your income in the year of payment.

The fair market value of a note is extremely difficult to determine, unless the note may be sold to a third party, and even then its worth may be difficult to determine.

If the issuer of the note is insolvent, the fair market value of the note may be zero. In this case, any money you subsequently get from the issuer is taxed as ordinary income in the year in which you receive it. Similarly, if the value of the note is less than its face value, any amount that you subsequently receive from the issuer that is greater than the recognized value of the note is taxed as ordinary income in the year in which it is received.

A note's fair market value may be less than its face amount if, based on the facts and circumstances at the time the note is issued, it is uncertain that you will be able to collect the face amount. A note may also be considered to be worth less than its face amount if the

interest rate that it pays is below the market rate or the collateral pledged against the note is limited.

If you think the note you receive may be worth more or less than its face value, consult your tax advisor about how to report the transaction.

Pulitzer, Nobel, and similar prizes. If you were awarded a prize in recognition of accomplishments in religious, charitable, scientific, artistic, educational, literary, or civic fields, you generally must include the value of the prize in your income. However, you do not include this prize in your income if you meet all of the following requirements.

- You were selected without any action on your part to enter the contest or proceeding.
- You are not required to perform substantial future services as a condition to receiving the prize or award.
- The prize or award is transferred by the payer directly to a governmental unit or tax-exempt charitable organization as designated by you.

See Publication 525 for more information about the conditions that apply to the transfer.

Qualified tuition programs (QTPs). A qualified tuition program (also known as a 529 program) is a program set up to allow you to either prepay, or contribute to an account established for paying, a student's qualified higher education expenses at an eligible educational institution. A program can be established and maintained by a state, an agency or instrumentality of a state, or an eligible educational institution.

The part of a distribution representing the amount paid or contributed to a QTP is not included in income. This is a return of the investment in the program.

The beneficiary generally does not include in income any earnings distributed from a QTP established and maintained by a state (or an agency or instrumentality of the state) if the total distribution is less than or equal to adjusted qualified higher education expenses. See Publication 970, Tax Benefits for Education, for more information.

Railroad retirement annuities. The following types of payments are treated as pension or annuity income and are taxable under the rules explained in chapter 12.

- Tier 1 railroad retirement benefits that are more than the social security equivalent benefit.
- Tier 2 benefits.
- Vested dual benefits.

Rewards. If you receive a reward for providing information, include it in your income.

Sale of home. You may be able to exclude from income all or part of any gain from the sale or exchange of a personal residence. See chapter 16.

Sale of personal items. If you sold an item you owned for personal use, such as a car, refrigerator, furniture, stereo, jewelry, or silverware, your gain is taxable as a capital gain. Report it on Schedule D (Form 1040). You cannot deduct a loss.

However, if you sold an item you held for investment, such as gold or silver bullion, coins, or gems, any gain is taxable as a capital gain and any loss is deductible as a capital loss.

Example. You sold a painting on an online auction website for $100. You bought the painting for $20 at a garage sale years ago. Report your gain as a capital gain on Schedule D (Form 1040).

Scholarships and fellowships. A candidate for a degree can exclude amounts received as a qualified scholarship or fellowship. A qualified scholarship or fellowship is any amount you receive that is for:

- Tuition and fees to enroll at or attend an educational institution, or
- Fees, books, supplies, and equipment required for courses at the educational institution.

Amounts used for room and board do not qualify for the exclusion.

See Publication 970 for more information on qualified scholarships and fellowship grants.

Payment for services. Generally, you must include in income the part of any scholarship or fellowship that represents payment for past, present, or future teaching, research, or other services. This applies even if all candidates for a degree must perform the services to receive the degree.

For information about the rules that apply to a tax-free qualified tuition reduction provided to employees and their families by an educational institution, see Publication 970.

VA payments. Allowances paid by the Department of Veterans Affairs are not included in your income. These allowances are not considered scholarship or fellowship grants.

Prizes. Scholarship prizes won in a contest are not scholarships or fellowships if you do not have to use the prizes for educational purposes. You must include these amounts in your income on Form 1040, line 21, whether or not you use the amounts for educational purposes.

Stolen property. If you steal property, you must report its fair market value in your income in the year you steal it unless in the same year, you return it to its rightful owner.

Transporting school children. Do not include in your income a school board mileage allowance for taking children to and from school if you are not in the business of taking children to school. You cannot deduct expenses for providing this transportation.

Union benefits and dues. Amounts deducted from your pay for union dues, assessments, contributions, or other payments to a union cannot be excluded from your income.

You may be able to deduct some of these payments as a miscellaneous deduction subject to the 2% limit if they are related to your job and if you itemize deductions on Schedule A (Form 1040). For more information, see *Union Dues and Expenses* in chapter 30.

Strike and lockout benefits. Benefits paid to you by a union as strike or lockout benefits, including both cash and the fair market value of other property, are usually included in your income as compensation. You can exclude these benefits from your income only when the facts clearly show that the union intended them as gifts to you.

Utility rebates. If you are a customer of an electric utility company and you participate in the utility's energy conservation program, you may receive on your monthly electric bill either:

- A reduction in the purchase price of electricity furnished to you (rate reduction), or
- A nonrefundable credit against the purchase price of the electricity.

The amount of the rate reduction or nonrefundable credit is not included in your income.

Passive Activity Limitations and At-Risk Limitations

Explanation

Individuals, estates, trusts, closely held corporations, and personal service corporations are generally prohibited from deducting net losses generated by passive activities. In addition, tax credits from passive activities are generally limited to the tax liability attributable to those activities. Disallowed passive activity losses are suspended and carried forward indefinitely to offset passive activity income generated in future years. Similar carryforward treatment applies to suspended credits.

Note that these rules relate to passive income/losses and do not apply to portfolio income/losses. Portfolio income/losses include interest, dividends, annuities, and royalties, as well as gain or loss from the disposition of income-producing or investment property that is not derived in the ordinary course of a trade or business.

Defining passive activities. A passive activity involves the conduct of any trade or business in which you do not materially participate. You are treated as a material participant only if you are involved in the operations of the activity on a regular, continuous, and substantial basis. If you are not a material participant in an activity but your spouse is, you are treated as being a material participant and the activity is not considered passive.

Seven tests. The IRS has seven tests you can meet to be considered a material participant. If you satisfy one of these tests, you will be considered a material participant in any activity. These tests are:

1. You participate more than 500 hours per taxable year.
2. Your participation during the taxable year constitutes substantially all of the participation of all individuals involved.
3. You participate for more than 100 hours during the taxable year and no one else participates more than you participated.
4. The activity is a significant participation activity (SPA) for the taxable year, and your participation in all SPAs during the taxable year exceeds 500 hours. An SPA is an activity in which an individual participates for more than 100 hours but does not otherwise meet a material participation test.
5. You materially participated in any 5 of the 10 preceding taxable years.
6. The activity is a personal service activity, and you materially participated for any 3 preceding taxable years. A personal service activity involves performance of personal services in the fields of health, law, engineering, architecture, accounting, actuarial sciences, performing arts, consulting, or any other business in which capital is not a material income-producing factor.
7. Based on all the facts and circumstances, your participation is regular, continuous, and substantial during the taxable year.

Defining an activity. The proper grouping of business operations into one or more activities is important in determining the allocation of suspended losses, measuring material participation, separating rental and nonrental activities, and determining when a disposition of an activity has occurred. IRS regulations define an activity as any "appropriate economic unit for measuring gain or loss." What constitutes an "appropriate economic unit" is determined by looking at all facts and circumstances. The regulations list five factors that are to be given the greatest weight. They are:

1. Similarities and differences in types of business
2. The extent of common control
3. The extent of common ownership
4. Geographical location
5. Interdependence between the activities

Generally, taxpayers must be consistent from year to year in determining the business operations that constitute an activity. Consult your tax advisor for more information.

"At-Risk" Limitation Provisions

The deduction for business losses is generally limited to the amount by which you are considered to be "at risk" in the activity. You are considered at risk for the amount of cash you have invested in the venture and the basis of property invested plus certain amounts borrowed for use in the activity.

Borrowed amounts that are considered at risk are (1) loans for which you are personally liable for repayment or (2) loans secured by property, other than that used in the activity. Generally, liabilities that are secured by property within the activity for which you are not otherwise personally liable are not considered to be at risk. An exception: If nonrecourse financing—financing for which you are not personally liable—is secured against real property used in the activity, you may be considered at risk for the amount of financing.

The law provides a broad list of activities (including the holding of real estate acquired after 1986) that are subject to the at-risk provisions. If the "at-risk" provisions apply to you, you should consult with your tax advisor.

Passive Activity Losses

The passive activity rules limit deductions and credits from passive trade or business activities. Deductions attributable to passive activities, to the extent they exceed income from passive activities, generally may not be deducted against other income, such as wages, portfolio income, or business income that is not derived from a passive activity. Deductions that are suspended under these rules are carried forward indefinitely and are treated as deductions from passive activities in succeeding years. Suspended losses are allowed in full when a taxpayer disposes of his or her entire interest in a passive activity to an unrelated person. For dispositions made after January 1, 1995, you must dispose of "substantially all" of a passive activity in order to deduct that same portion. You may also be able to deduct suspended losses in a passive activity if your interest is disposed of in other ways, including abandonment and death of the taxpayer. See *Disposition of Passive Activity,* discussed later. Special rules may apply; you should consult your tax advisor.

Rental Real Estate

As discussed above, generally, a trade or business activity is passive unless the taxpayer *materially participates* in that activity. Rental real estate activities, however, are passive regardless of the level of the taxpayer's participation. A special rule permits the deduction of up to $25,000 of losses from certain rental real estate activities (even though they are considered passive) if the taxpayer actively participates in them. This special rule is available in full to taxpayers with AGI of $100,000 or less and phases out for taxpayers with AGI between $100,000 and $150,000. For further information about rental real estate passive rules, see Chapter 10, *Rental Income and Expenses.*

Real Estate Professionals

Passive activity limitations for certain real estate professionals are more liberal than they used to be. Taxpayers who satisfy certain eligibility thresholds and materially participate in rental real estate activities may treat any losses as losses from a nonpassive activity and may use these losses against all sources of taxable income.

Eligibility. Only individuals and closely held C corporations can qualify for this special rule. An individual taxpayer will qualify for any tax year if more than one-half of the personal services (with more than 750 hours) performed in trades or businesses by the taxpayer during such a tax year are performed in real property trades or businesses in which the taxpayer materially participates. A real property trade or business includes any real property development, redevel-

opment, construction, reconstruction, acquisition, conversion, rental, operation, management, leasing, or brokerage trade or business. Personal services performed as an employee are not considered in determining material participation unless the employee has more than a 5% ownership in the business during any part of the tax year. However, independent contractor realtor services would qualify for this purpose. For closely held C corporations, the eligibility requirements are met if more than 50% of the corporation's gross receipts for the tax year are derived from real property trades or businesses in which the corporation materially participates.

Example 1

During 2005, a self-employed real estate developer earned $100,000 in development fees from projects the developer spent 1,200 hours developing. In addition, the developer incurred rental real estate losses of $200,000 from properties that the developer spent over 800 hours managing during 2005. The developer performs no other personal services during the year and has no other items of income or deduction. Because the developer (1) materially participated in the rental real estate activity, (2) performed more than 750 hours in real property trades or businesses, and (3) performed more than 50% of the developer's total personal service hours in real estate trades or businesses in which the developer materially participated, the developer will have a net operating loss of $100,000 to carry back (and the excess to carry forward) to offset any source of income.

This rule for real estate professionals' passive loss relief is a two-step process. First, you must demonstrate eligibility for the relief provision by achieving the required levels of personal services in real estate trades or businesses. Thereafter, you get relief from the passive loss limitations only for your rental real estate activities for which you satisfy the material participation standards.

For spouses filing joint returns, each spouse's personal services are taken into account separately. However, in determining material participation, the participation of the other spouse is taken into account as required under current law.

Example 2

A husband and wife filing a joint return meet the eligibility requirements if, during the tax year, *one spouse* performs more than 750 hours representing at least half of his or her personal services in a real estate trade or business in which either spouse materially participates.

Aggregation of Activities

Whether a taxpayer *materially participates* in his or her rental real estate activities is determined generally as if each interest of the taxpayer in rental real estate is a separate activity. However, the taxpayer may elect to treat all interest in rental real estate as one activity.

The election permitting a taxpayer to aggregate his or her rental real estate activities for testing for material participation is not intended to alter the rules with respect to material participation through limited partnership interest. Generally, no interest as a limited partner is treated as an interest with respect to which a taxpayer materially participates. However, Treasury regulations provide that a limited partner is considered to materially participate in the activities conducted through the partnership in certain situations where (1) the limited partner is also a general partner at all times during the partnership's tax year, (2) the limited partner materially participates in the activity during any 5 of the preceding 10 years, or (3) the activity is a personal service activity in which the limited partner materially participated for any 3 preceding years.

Losses attributable to limited partnership interests are considered passive, except where regulations provide otherwise. In general, working interests in any oil or gas property held directly or through an entity that does not limit the taxpayer's liability are *not* considered passive, whether or not the taxpayer is a material participant.

The IRS has issued regulations with regard to the aggregation of activities in order to satisfy the material participation tests for real estate professionals. These rules are very complex and hold potential tax traps for the unwary. We recommend that you consult with your tax advisor if you believe that electing to aggregate activities may be beneficial to you.

Example 1

Three brothers own a hardware store as partners. Two of them consider it their full-time job, because it is their only source of income. The third brother lives 200 miles away and is consulted only on major issues. The two brothers who work at the store meet the material participation test. The third brother has a passive investment.

Example 2

Bonnie owns a one-sixteenth interest in four different racehorses. She does not own the stables where the horses are trained and fed. She is not involved in the daily care of the horses. She pays her fair share of the costs and offers advice regarding when and where the horses are to run. Bonnie has significant salary income from a full-time job and from managing her portfolio. Bonnie is probably not a material participant.

Example 3

Andrea is a limited partner in a partnership. She is not a material participant.

Example 4

Chris owns rental property. He has a passive investment.

Exception

An exception to the general rule that does not allow grouping rental activities with business activity is that, in certain instances, passive rental losses can offset income from business activities. For this exception to apply, you must own the same proportionate ownership interest in each activity.

Example

Jack and Jill are married and file a joint return. Jack owns and operates a grocery store that generates net income for the current year. Jill owns the building, of which 25% is rented to Jack's grocery store activity (grocery store rental). The building rental activities generate a net loss in the current year.

Because they file a joint return, Jack and Jill are treated as one taxpayer. Therefore, the sole owner of the grocery store activity is also the sole owner of the rental activity. Consequently, each owner of the business activity has the same proportionate ownership interest in the rental activity. Accordingly, both activities may be grouped together; thus, the net income from Jack's grocery store can be offset by the amount of net loss from Jill's building rental activities. See your tax advisor for more information if you think this exception applies to your situation.

TaxPlanner

You should try to realign your personal finances so that you maximize your interest expense deductions. If you borrowed money to purchase a passive investment, any interest on the loan will be considered part of your passive investment loss. If you are in a real estate limited partnership, you may be able to have all the partners contribute additional capital so that the passive loss is reduced or limited. Your capital contribution could come from your other investments or from a mortgage on a personal residence. If you have untapped appreciation in your personal residence, you can borrow against it and deduct the interest cost subject to certain limitations. Make sure, however, that any mortgage does not exceed the limits applicable to your situation, because such disallowed interest would be considered nondeductible personal interest.

Disposition of Passive Activity

Previously disallowed losses (but not credits) are recognized in full when the taxpayer disposes of his or her entire interest in the passive activity in a fully taxable transaction. However, suspended losses are not deductible when the taxpayer sells the interest to a related party. Rather, the losses remain with the individual (and may offset passive income) until the related purchaser disposes of the interest in a taxable transaction to an unrelated person. Various other types of dispositions trigger suspended losses, including abandonment, death of the taxpayer, gifts, and installment sales of entire interests, although special rules apply.

A sale in a taxable year beginning before January 1, 1987, reported on the installment method and included in income after December 31, 1986, would be considered income from a passive activity.

Example

Bob disposes of rental property in 1987 under the installment sale method and properly reports $2,000 of taxable gain in his 1987 through 2005 tax returns. Bob may treat the 1987 through 2005 gains as income from a passive activity and may offset other passive losses in these years.

TaxAlert: Tax Relief for Victims of Terrorism

President Bush signed into law the Victims of Terrorism Relief Act of 2001 ("Act") on January 23, 2002. The income tax provisions of the Act apply to those people killed in the following attacks:

1. The April 19, 1995, attack on the Alfred P. Murrah Federal Building (**Oklahoma City attack**).

2. The September 11, 2001, attacks on the World Trade Center, the Pentagon, and United Airlines Flight 93 in Somerset County, Pennsylvania (**September 11 attacks**).
3. Terrorist attacks involving anthrax occurring after September 10, 2001, and before January 1, 2002 (**anthrax attacks**).

Income Tax Provisions for Decedents: Income Tax Liability Forgiven for Certain Tax Years

Oklahoma City attack. For those who died from this attack, income tax is forgiven for 1994 and all later years up to and including the year of death.

Example 1
A man was killed in the bombing of the federal building in Oklahoma City on April 19, 1995. His income tax is forgiven for 1994 and 1995.

Example 2
A woman was wounded while walking outside the federal building in Oklahoma City on April 19, 1995. She subsequently died of her wounds in 1996. Her income tax is forgiven for 1994, 1995, and 1996.

September 11 attacks and anthrax attacks. For those who died from these attacks, income tax is forgiven for 2000 and all later years up to and including the year of death.

Amount of tax forgiven. The IRS will forgive the decedent's income tax liability for all years eligible for tax forgiveness. On a joint return, only the decedent's part of the joint income tax liability is eligible for forgiveness. To figure the amount of tax to be forgiven, fill out Worksheet A or Worksheet B in IRS Publication 3920, *Tax Relief for Victims of Terrorist Attacks.*

Minimum amount of relief. The minimum amount of relief is $10,000. If the decedent's total forgiven tax liability is less than $10,000, the difference between $10,000 and the total forgiven tax liability for those years will be treated as a tax payment in the decedent's last tax year. The IRS will refund the difference. Use Worksheet C to figure the additional tax payment, but be sure you first complete Worksheet A or B unless the decedent was not required to file tax returns for the eligible tax years.

Income received after date of death. Generally, income of the decedent received after the date of death must be reported on Form 1041 if the estate has gross income of $600 or more for the tax year. Examples are the decedent's final paycheck or dividends on stock owned by the decedent. However, this income is exempt from income tax and is not included in the Form 1041 if it is received:

- After the date the decedent dies, and
- Before the end of the decedent's tax year (determined without regard to death—generally December 31 for an individual).

For further details, consult your tax advisor and IRS Publication 3920, Tax Relief for Victims of Terrorist Attacks.

Where to File. The IRS has set up a special office for processing returns and claims for tax forgiveness. Use one of the addresses shown below. Where you file the returns depends on whether you use the U.S. Postal Service or a private delivery service.

U.S. Postal Service. File the returns and claims at the following address:

Internal Revenue Service
P.O. Box 4053
Woburn, MA 01888

Private delivery service. Private delivery service cannot deliver to post office boxes. If you use a private delivery service, file the returns and claims at the following address:

Internal Revenue Service
Stop 661
310 Lowell Street
Andover, MA 01810

Income Tax Provisions for Survivors

September 11 Victim Compensation Fund of 2001. Payments from this fund are not included in income.

Qualified Disaster Relief Payments. Qualified disaster relief payments are not included in income. These payments are not subject to income tax, self-employment tax, or employment taxes (social security, Medicare, and federal unemployment taxes). No withholding applies to these payments.

Qualified disaster relief payments include payments you receive (regardless of the source) after September 10, 2001, for the following reasons:

- Reasonable and necessary personal, family, living, or funeral expenses incurred as a result of a terrorist attack.
- Reasonable and necessary expenses incurred for the repair or rehabilitation of a personal residence due to a terrorist attack. (A personal residence can be a rented residence or one you own.)
- Reasonable and necessary expenses incurred for the repair or replacement of the contents of a personal residence due to a terrorist attack.

Qualified disaster relief payments also include the following:

- Payments made by common carriers (for example, American Airlines and United Airlines regarding the September 11 attacks) because of death or physical injury incurred as a result of a terrorist attack.
- Amounts received from a federal, state, or local government in connection with a terrorist attack to those affected by the attack.

CAUTION: Qualified disaster payments do **not** include insurance or other reimbursements for expenses, or income replacement payments, such as payments of lost wages, lost business income, or unemployment compensation.

Disability Payments. For tax years ending after September 10, 2001, disability payments received for injuries incurred as a direct result of a terrorist attack directed against the United States (or its allies), whether inside or outside of the United States, are not included in income.

Death Benefits. Payments received by an individual or the estate of a decedent from the employer of an employee who died as a result of the Oklahoma City or September 11 terrorist attacks, or as a result of the anthrax attacks, are not included in income. **However,** only the amount that exceeds the benefits that would have been payable if the death had occurred for any other reason is excludable.

NOTE: Incidental death benefits paid under a qualified retirement plan are excludable, even if these amounts would have been payable if the death had occurred for any other reason.

TaxPlanner

If you included death benefits in income on a previously filed return and they are now excludable under the above rule, file Form 1040X to amend the return.

Canceled Debt. Canceled debt is not included in your income (or the income of the estate).

If both of the following are true:

You (or the estate) were liable, or became liable, for the debt of a decedent; and

The debt was canceled after September 10, 2001, and before January 1, 2002, because the decedent died as a result of the September 11 attacks or anthrax attacks.

Payments to Survivors of Public Safety Officers. If you are the survivor of a public safety officer who died in the line of duty, the following types of payments are not included in your income:

Bureau of Justice Assistance payments. If you are a surviving dependent of a public safety officer (law enforcement officer or firefighter) who died in the line of duty, do not include in your income the death benefit paid to you by the Bureau of Justice Assistance.

Government plan annuity. If you receive a survivor annuity as the child or spouse (or former spouse) of a public safety officer who was killed in the line of duty, you generally do not have to include it in income. This exclusion applies to the amount of the annuity based upon the officer's service as a public safety officer.

Public Safety Officer Defined. A public safety officer, for the purpose of these exclusions, includes police and law enforcement officers, firefighters, and rescue squads and ambulance crews.

For more information, see Publication 559, *Survivors, Executors, and Administrators,* and Publication 3920, *Tax Relief for Victims of Terrorist Attacks.*

PART III

Gains and Losses

The four chapters in this part discuss investment gains and losses, including how to figure your basis in property. A gain from selling or trading stocks, bonds, or other investment property may be taxed or it may be tax-free, at least in part. A loss may or may not be deductible. These chapters also discuss gains from selling property you personally use—including the special rules for selling your home. Nonbusiness casualty and theft losses are discussed in chapter 27 in Part Five.

Basis of Property

Note: The 2004 IRS Publication 17 (Your Federal Income Tax) has been updated by Ernst & Young LLP for 2005. Dates and dollar amounts shown are for 2005. Gray type is used to indicate where IRS text has been updated or intentionally omitted. Unrevised IRS text is shown in black type.

Introduction

The gain or loss you realize on the disposition of property—whether through a sale or exchange—is measured by the difference between the selling price and your **basis***. In many cases, the basis of an* **asset** *is no more than your cost. However, if you acquire property in exchange for services, by inheritance, or in exchange for other property, different factors besides cost are likely to have a crucial bearing on determining your tax basis.*

This chapter tells you how to calculate the basis of property. Particular attention is given to some of the more complicated situations that may arise. You'll learn, for instance, how to calculate your basis in a particular piece of property by referring to other assets you already hold. To help you determine which expenditures increase your basis in a piece of property and which do not, comprehensive lists of allowable—but often overlooked—expenditures are provided.

This chapter discusses how to figure your basis in property. It is divided into the following sections.

• Cost basis.
• Adjusted basis.
• Basis other than cost.

Your basis is the amount of your investment in property for tax purposes. Use the basis to figure gain or loss on the sale, exchange, or other disposition of property. Also use it to figure deductions for depreciation, amortization, depletion, and casualty losses.

Explanation

This chapter does not reflect the provisions of the law that deal with bankruptcy. If any of your debts were canceled by a creditor or were discharged because you became bankrupt, the basis of your assets might be affected. For information about the effect these provisions may have on basis, see the *Debt Cancellation* section in Publication 908, *Bankruptcy Tax Guide*. Publication 908 discusses the technical rules related to bankruptcy, but here are several key points to remember:

1. The tax treatment of a forgiven debt depends on how the debt arose. For example, a personal loan from a relative, when it was unrelated to a business or an investment, is not taxed if it is forgiven. Instead, it is considered a gift. If the amount is over $11,000 in 2005, the person forgiving the loan might have to file a gift tax return and pay gift tax.
2. On the other hand, a business loan forgiven for business reasons is taxed. In this case, you may pay the tax on a forgiven loan or opt for a reduction in the basis of your assets by an amount equal to the debt forgiven. The result is that you are not able to deduct as much in depreciating the asset. Thus, if it is sold before it is fully depreciated, you have either a larger gain or a smaller loss on the asset than you would if you paid the tax directly. After 1986, a *solvent* taxpayer may make this election only if the loan is "purchase money debt," in which case the forgiveness is treated as a purchase price adjustment of the related asset. You cannot make this election for debt forgiven by your employer.
3. If you declare personal bankruptcy, you are not taxed on any debt you owe that is forgiven or canceled. You also are not taxed on any debt you owe that is forgiven or canceled if a business you own goes into bankruptcy. However, you may be required

to reduce the **net operating loss carryforwards** and **tax credit carryforwards** that otherwise would be available in subsequent years to offset income and reduce your income tax liability. One strategy to avoid losing these tax benefits is to reduce the basis of depreciable property or real property held as inventory, by an amount equal to the debt forgiven.

If you use property for either business or investment purposes and for personal purposes, you must allocate the basis based on the use. Only the basis allocated to the business or investment use of the property can be depreciated.

Your original basis in property is adjusted (increased or decreased) by certain events. If you make improvements to the property, increase your basis. If you take deductions for depreciation or casualty losses, reduce your basis.

Keep accurate records of all items that affect your basis. For more information on keeping records, see chapter 1.

Useful Items

You may want to see:

Publication

- [ ] **15-B** Employer's Tax Guide to Fringe Benefits
- [ ] **525** Taxable and Nontaxable Income
- [ ] **535** Business Expenses
- [ ] **537** Installment Sales
- [ ] **544** Sales and Other Dispositions of Assets
- [ ] **550** Investment Income and Expenses
- [ ] **551** Basis of Assets
- [ ] **564** Mutual Fund Distributions
- [ ] **946** How to Depreciate Property

Cost Basis

The basis of property you buy is usually its cost. The cost is the amount you pay in cash, debt obligations, other property, or services. Your cost also includes amounts you pay for the following items.

- Sales tax.
- Freight.
- Installation and testing.
- Excise taxes.
- Legal and accounting fees (when they must be capitalized).
- Revenue stamps.
- Recording fees.
- Real estate taxes (if you assume liability for the seller).

In addition, the basis of real estate and business assets may include other items.

TAXPLANNER

If you perform services for an entity and in exchange receive stock or a partnership capital interest, the fair market value (FMV) of what you receive is treated as compensation. Your basis in the stock or partnership interest is equal to the amount of compensation reported by you, increased by the amount, if any, paid for the stock or partnership interest. For more information, see Chapter 6, *Wages, Salaries, and Other Earnings.*

TAXSAVER

If you receive an equity interest in a business in exchange for services rendered, you should consider taking a discount on the value of the equity interest. You may do this if the shares are not marketable and/or if they represent only a minority holding.

Loans with low or no interest. If you buy property on a time-payment plan that charges little or no interest, the basis of your property is your stated purchase price minus any amount considered to be unstated interest. You generally have unstated interest if your interest rate is less than the applicable federal rate.

For more information, see *Unstated Interest and Original Issue Discount (OID)* in Publication 537.

Explanation

If you buy personal property or educational services by contract and the carrying charges are separately stated but the interest you pay cannot be determined, the IRS assumes that interest is being charged at the applicable federal rate applied to the average unpaid balance of the contract during the tax year. Your tax basis is determined by subtracting the interest from the total contract cost of the property. You may deduct the interest in the year in which it is, in effect, being paid. But see Chapter 25, *Interest Expense,* for possible limitations on your deductions.

Real Property

Real property, also called real estate, is land and generally anything built on, growing on, or attached to land.

If you buy real property, certain fees and other expenses you pay are part of your cost basis in the property.

Lump sum purchase. If you buy buildings and the land on which they stand for a lump sum, allocate the cost basis among the land and the buildings so you can figure the basis for depreciation on the buildings. Land is not depreciable. Allocate the cost basis according to the respective fair market values (FMVs) of the land and buildings at the time of purchase. Figure the basis of each asset by multiplying the lump sum by a fraction. The numerator is the FMV of that asset and the denominator is the FMV of the whole property at the time of purchase.

Tip. *If you are not certain of the FMVs of the land and buildings, you can allocate the basis according to their assessed values for real estate tax purposes.*

Fair market value (FMV). FMV is the price at which the property would change hands between a willing buyer and a willing seller, neither having to buy or sell, and both having reasonable knowledge of all the necessary facts. Sales of similar property on or about the same date may be helpful in figuring the FMV of the property.

Assumption of mortgage. If you buy property and assume (or buy the property subject to) an existing mortgage on the property, your basis includes the amount you pay for the property plus the amount to be paid on the mortgage.

Explanation

If the real property is used in your trade or business or as a rental, you cannot elect to deduct transfer taxes in lieu of adding them to your basis.

Settlement costs. Your basis includes the settlement fees and closing costs you paid for buying the property. (A fee for buying property is a cost that must be paid even if you buy the property for cash.) Do not include fees and costs for getting a loan on the property in your basis.

The following are some of the settlement fees or closing costs you can include in the basis of your property.

- Abstract fees (abstract of title fees).
- Charges for installing utility services.
- Legal fees (including fees for the title search and preparation of the sales contract and deed).
- Recording fees.
- Survey fees.
- Transfer taxes.
- Owner's title insurance.
- Any amounts the seller owes that you agree to pay, such as back taxes or interest, recording or mortgage fees, charges for improvements or repairs, and sales commissions.

Settlement costs do not include amounts placed in escrow for the future payment of items such as taxes and insurance.

The following are some of the settlement fees and closing costs you cannot include in the basis of property.

- Casualty insurance premiums.
- Rent for occupancy of the property before closing.
- Charges for utilities or other services related to occupancy of the property before closing.
- Charges connected with getting a loan, such as points (discount points, loan origination fees), mortgage insurance premiums, loan assumption fees, cost of a credit report, and fees for an appraisal required by a lender.
- Fees for refinancing a mortgage.

Real estate taxes. If you pay real estate taxes the seller owed on real property you bought, and the seller did not reimburse you, treat those taxes as part of your basis. You cannot deduct them as an expense.

If you reimburse the seller for taxes the seller paid for you, you can usually deduct that amount as an expense in the year of purchase. Do not include that amount in the basis of your property. If you did not reimburse the seller, you must reduce your basis by the amount of those taxes.

Points. If you pay points to get a loan (including a mortgage, second mortgage, line of credit, or a home equity loan), do not add the points to the basis of the related property. Generally, you deduct the points over the term of the loan. For more information on how to deduct points, see *Points* in chapter 25.

Explanation
The following costs increase your tax basis:

1. Interest on debt incurred to finance the construction or production of real property, long-lived personal property with a useful life of 20 years or more, and other tangible property requiring more than 2 years (1 year in the case of property costing more than $1 million) to produce or construct or reach a productive stage. Additionally, interest incurred to finance property produced under a long-term contract increases your tax basis to the extent that income is not reported under the percentage-of-completion method.

   These rules do *not* apply to interest incurred during the construction of real property to be used as your principal residence or second home. (For a definition of principal residence, see Chapter 16, *Selling Your Home.* But see Chapter 25, *Interest Expense,* for other rules affecting how much interest you may be able to deduct on a residence.)

2. The costs of defending or perfecting a title, architect's fees, and financing and finder's fees. Points,

usually up-front payments on a mortgage charged to purchasers or borrowers, may be deducted as interest. See Chapter 25, *Interest Expense,* for more information and the timing of the deduction.

3. Certain start-up costs for a business. These include legal fees for the drafting of documents, accounting fees, and other similar expenses directly associated with the organization of a business. The costs of organizing a partnership, such as the expenses incurred in raising capital, putting together a prospectus, and paying commissions on the sale of investment units, also increase your basis, as does the cost of investigating the creation or acquisition of an active trade or business. See Chapter 39, *If You Are Self-Employed: How to File Schedule C,* for further information.

Some taxpayers who are starting a new business try to deduct the expenses incurred before the business actually begins. The IRS, however, may not accept these as current **deductions,** and it may either require that you deduct the expenses over a number of years or decide that the expenses should increase your basis in the business. You can elect a current deduction for a limited amount (up to $5,000) of start-up expenditures in the tax year in which your trade or business begins. However, this $5,000 amount is reduced (but not below zero) by the amount by which the cumulative cost of start-up expenditures exceeds $50,000. The remainder of the start-up expenditures can be claimed as a deduction ratably over a 15-year period. (Note: these rules only apply to expenses paid or incurred after October 22, 2004. For earlier expenses, no $5,000 first-year deduction was available, and the elective write-off period was only 60 months.) If you currently neither deduct nor amortize an expense, the tax benefit is obtained when the entity is sold or ceases operation. Therefore, it is important to include the election with your tax return for the year in which the costs are first incurred.

Unlike costs of organizing a partnership or starting up its business, costs of selling partnership interests (syndication costs) may not be amortized or deducted. (For further discussion, see *Adjusted Basis,* following.)

TaxSaver

Increasing your tax basis by as much as possible subsequently reduces the amount of gain or increases the amount of loss realized when you dispose of the property.

TaxAlert

Individuals do not derive any tax benefit from **realizing a loss** related to the disposition of personal property. Personal property includes any property that is not considered an investment (such as a refrigerator), as well as any property that is not used in a trade or business.

TaxSaver

If you pay interest, taxes, and other carrying charges on unimproved and unproductive real estate but cannot deduct these expenses because you do not itemize your deductions, consider treating them as **capital expenditures,** which increase your basis and reduce your gain on sale. This election is made on an annual basis and must be renewed each year that you want to continue capitalizing these costs.

Table 14-1. **Examples of Adjustments to Basis**

Increases to Basis	Decreases to Basis

• Capital improvements:
    Putting an addition on your home
    Replacing an entire roof
    Paving your driveway
    Installing central air conditioning
    Rewiring your home
	• Exclusion from income of subsidies for energy conservation measures

• Assessments for local improvements:
    Water connections
    Sidewalks
    Roads
	• Casualty or theft loss deductions and insurance reimbursements

• Casualty losses: Restoring damaged property	• Credit for qualified electric vehicles
	• Postponed gain from the sale of a home

• Legal fees:
    Cost of defending and perfecting a title
    Fees for getting a reduction of an assessment
	• Deduction for clean-fuel vehicles and clean-fuel vehicle refueling property

	• Depreciation and section 179 deduction
• Zoning costs	• Nontaxable corporate distributions
	• Certain canceled debt excluded from income
	• Easements
	• Adoption tax benefits

Example

Jane rents an apartment and has few **itemized deductions.** She borrows money to purchase an unimproved lot in Florida. She incurs $1,000 in interest expense on the borrowed funds and pays $100 in real estate taxes in each of the 5 years she holds the property. If Jane elects to capitalize the interest and taxes, she increases her basis by $5,500 over the 5 years.

TaxOrganizer

You should keep a copy of the closing statement you receive when you are either buying or selling real property.

Points on home mortgage. Special rules may apply to points you and the seller pay when you get a mortgage to buy your main home. If certain requirements are met, you can deduct the points in full for the year in which they are paid. Reduce the basis of your home by any seller-paid points. For more information, see *Points* in chapter 25.

Adjusted Basis

Before figuring gain or loss on a sale, exchange, or other disposition of property or figuring allowable depreciation, depletion, or amortization, you must usually make certain adjustments (increases and decreases) to the basis of the property. The result of these adjustments to the basis is the adjusted basis.

Explanation

Note that you may need to make a separate calculation of basis when figuring your **alternative minimum tax (AMT).** You must take into consideration the impact that AMT adjustments, such as depreciation, have on basis in property. For a discussion of the AMT, see Chapter 32, *How to Figure Your Tax.*

Examples of items that increase or reduce basis are shown in Table 14-1. The following discussions provide information about many of these items.

Increases to Basis

Increase the basis of any property by all items properly added to a capital account. These include the cost of any improvements having a useful life of more than 1 year. Other items added to the basis of property include the cost of extending utility service lines to the property and legal fees, such as the cost of defending and perfecting title and the fees for getting a reduction of an assessment levied against property.

Improvements. Add to your basis in property the cost of improvements if they increase the value of the property, lengthen its life, or adapt it to a different use. For example, improvements include putting a recreation room in your unfinished basement, adding another bathroom or bedroom, putting up a fence, putting in new plumbing or wiring, installing a new roof, or paving your driveway.

TaxSaver

When you sell your home, your gain or loss is measured by the difference between the price you receive on the sale and your basis. Any improvements you have made will have increased your basis and will now decrease your tax liability. It is important that you keep adequate records of all improvements.

1. Replacing the roof
2. Installing permanent storm windows
3. Installing new plumbing
4. Installing a new heating or air-conditioning system
5. Installing a new furnace
6. Restoring a rundown house
7. Landscaping: adding new trees, shrubs, or lawn
8. Building a swimming pool, tennis court, or sauna
9. Constructing or improving a driveway
10. Constructing walks
11. Constructing patios and decks
12. Constructing walls
13. Payment of real estate commissions
14. Payment of legal fees stemming from improvements, zoning, and so on
15. Payment of closing costs
16. Cost of appliances

It is important to distinguish between expenditures that constitute additions to basis and those that constitute repairs. If the asset is used in a trade or a business, repairs are deductible but do not increase its basis. If the asset is personal, the costs of repairs are not deductible and do not increase the asset's basis. (For a more complete discussion of this matter, see Chapter 10, *Rental Income and Expenses*.)

As noted by the IRS, your basis in property is reduced by money you receive as a return of capital. See Chapter 9, *Dividends and Other Corporate Distributions*, for further details.

Example

You buy land and a building for $25,000 for use as a parking lot. You pay $3,000 to have the building torn down, and you sell some of the materials you salvage from it for $5,000. You figure your adjusted basis in the property by taking your $25,000 initial cost, adding the $3,000 you spent for tearing down the building, and subtracting the $5,000 you received for the materials you salvaged. Your adjusted basis for the lot is $23,000. The money you received from the sale of the salvaged materials is not income, and the cost of tearing down the building is not deductible.

TaxOrganizer

You should keep a copy of all invoices you receive for improvements that increase your basis in real property.

Assessments for local improvements. Add to the basis of property assessments for improvements such as streets and sidewalks if they increase the value of the property assessed. Do not deduct them as taxes. However, you can deduct as taxes assessments for maintenance or repairs, or for meeting interest charges related to the improvements.

Example. Your city changes the street in front of your store into an enclosed pedestrian mall and assesses you and other affected property owners for the cost of the conversion. Add the assessment to your property's basis. In this example, the assessment is a depreciable asset.

Explanation

For further discussion of assessments and how to treat them, see Chapter 24, *Taxes You May Deduct*.

Decreases to Basis

Decrease the basis of any property by all items that represent a return of capital for the period during which you held the property. These include the items discussed below.

Casualty and theft losses. If you have a casualty or theft loss, decrease the basis in your property by any insurance proceeds or other reimbursement and by any deductible loss not covered by insurance.

You must increase your basis in the property by the amount you spend on repairs that substantially prolong the life of the property, increase its value, or adapt it to a different use. To make this determination, compare the repaired property to the property before the casualty.

For more information on casualty and theft losses, see chapter 27.

Depreciation and section 179 deduction. Decrease the basis of your qualifying business property by any section 179 deduction you take and the depreciation you deducted, or could have deducted (including any special depreciation allowance), on your tax returns under the method of depreciation you selected.

For more information about depreciation and the section 179 deduction, see Publication 946.

Example. You owned a duplex used as rental property that cost you $40,000, of which $35,000 was allocated to the building and $5,000 to the land. You added an improvement to the duplex that cost $10,000. In February last year, the duplex was damaged by fire. Up to that time, you had been allowed depreciation of $23,000. You sold some salvaged material for $1,300 and collected $19,700 from your insurance company. You deducted a casualty loss of $1,000 on your income tax return for last year. You spent $19,000 of the insurance proceeds for restoration of the duplex, which was completed this year. You must use the duplex's adjusted basis after the restoration to determine depreciation for the rest of the property's recovery period. Figure the adjusted basis of the duplex as follows:

Original cost of duplex			$35,000
Addition to duplex			10,000
Total cost of duplex			$45,000
Minus: Depreciation			23,000
Adjusted basis before casualty			$22,000
Minus: Insurance proceeds		$19,700	
Deducted casualty loss		1,000	
Salvage proceeds		1,300	22,000
Adjusted basis after casualty			$ –0–
Add: Cost of restoring duplex			19,000
Adjusted basis after restoration			$19,000

Your basis in the land is its original cost of $5,000.

Explanation

For additional information on the Section 179 deduction, see Chapter 39, *If You Are Self-Employed: How to File Schedule C*. Also see *How to Depreciate Your Property* in Publication 946.

Explanation

If you discover that you deducted less depreciation than you could have claimed on your prior returns, you should consider filing amended returns to claim a refund if the statute of limitations (generally, 3 years from the date you filed the original return) has not expired. Consult your tax advisor.

Easements. The amount you receive for granting an easement is generally considered to be proceeds from the sale of an interest in real property. It reduces the basis of the affected part of the property. If the amount received is more than the basis of the part of the property affected by the easement, reduce your basis in that part to zero and treat the excess as a recognized gain.

If the gain is on a capital asset, see chapter 17 for information about how to report it. If the gain is on property used in a trade or business, see Publication 544 for information about how to report it.

Credit for qualified electric vehicles. If you claim the credit for a qualified electric vehicle, you must reduce your basis in that vehicle by the maximum credit allowable even if the credit allowed is less than that maximum amount. For information on this credit, see chapter 12 in Publication 535.

Deduction for clean-fuel vehicle and refueling property. If you take the deduction for clean-fuel vehicles or clean-fuel vehicle refueling property, decrease the basis of the property by the amount deducted. For more information about these deductions, see chapter 12 in Publication 535.

Exclusion of subsidies for energy conservation measures. You can exclude from gross income any subsidy you received from a public utility company for the purchase or installation of an energy conservation measure for a dwelling unit. Reduce the basis of the property for which you received the subsidy by the excluded amount. For more information about this subsidy, see chapter 13.

Postponed gain from sale of home. If you postponed gain from the sale of your main home under rules in effect before May 7, 1997, you must reduce the basis of the home you acquired as a replacement by the amount of the postponed gain. For more information on the rules for the sale of a home, see chapter 16.

Basis Other Than Cost

There are many times when you cannot use cost as basis. In these cases, the fair market value or the adjusted basis of the property can be used. Fair market value (FMV) and adjusted basis were discussed earlier.

Property Received for Services

If you receive property for your services, include its FMV in income. The amount you include in income becomes your basis. If the services were performed for a price agreed on beforehand, it will be accepted as the FMV of the property if there is no evidence to the contrary.

Explanation

If you receive property by inheritance or as a gift, special rules apply. The basis of the property you inherit is usually its FMV at the time of the donor's death. (For more details, see *Inherited Property,* discussed later in this chapter.) The basis of property you get as a gift is generally the same as the donor's basis. If, however, the FMV of the property is less than the donor's basis at the time you receive the gift, your basis for the purpose of figuring whether you have a gain or a loss when you sell the property may be the gift's FMV at the time you receive it. (See *Property Received as a Gift,* discussed later in this chapter.)

Restricted property. If you receive property for your services and the property is subject to certain restrictions, your basis in the property is its FMV when it becomes substantially vested. However, this rule does not apply if you make an election to include in income the FMV of the property at the time it is transferred to you, less any amount you paid for it. Property is substantially vested when it is transferable or when it is not subject to a substantial risk of forfeiture (you do not have a good chance of losing it). For more information, see *Restricted Property* in Publication 525.

Explanation

For a full discussion of this subject, see *Property Received for Services* in Chapter 6, *Wages, Salaries, and Other Earnings.*

Bargain purchases. A bargain purchase is a purchase of an item for less than its FMV. If, as compensation for services, you buy goods or other property at less than FMV, include the difference between the purchase price and the property's FMV in your income. Your basis in the property is its FMV (your purchase price plus the amount you include in income).

If the difference between your purchase price and the FMV is a qualified employee discount, do not include the difference in in-

come. However, your basis in the property is still its FMV. See *Employee Discounts* in Publication 15-B.

Examples

Airline, railroad, or subway employees need not include as income free travel provided by their employer if the employer does not incur any substantial additional cost in providing such travel. Employee clothing discounts, discount brokerage fees, and lodging and meal discounts can also qualify as nontaxable compensation. Employees are eligible for such tax-free benefits only if the merchandise or services are also offered to customers in the ordinary course of the employer's business. The amount of the tax-free discount is subject to specific dollar limitations.

Business use of a company car, parking at or near your business premises, business periodicals, and any other property or service provided by your employer can be excluded from your taxable income if you would be allowed to take a business deduction had you paid for the benefit yourself.

Other nontaxable fringe benefits from employers include medical savings account (MSA) or health savings account (HSA) contributions, free medical services, reimbursement of medical expenses, payments of premiums for up to $50,000 of group term life insurance coverage, tuition given to children of university employees, and meals furnished to employees on the employer's business premises for the convenience of the employer.

Taxable Exchanges

A taxable exchange is one in which the gain is taxable or the loss is deductible. A taxable gain or deductible loss also is known as a recognized gain or loss. If you receive property in exchange for other property in a taxable exchange, the basis of the property you receive is usually its FMV at the time of the exchange.

Involuntary Conversions

If you receive replacement property as a result of an involuntary conversion, such as a casualty, theft, or condemnation, figure the basis of the replacement property using the basis of the converted property.

Similar or related property. If you receive replacement property similar or related in service or use to the converted property, the replacement property's basis is the same as the converted property's basis on the date of the conversion, with the following adjustments.

1. Decrease the basis by the following.
   a. Any loss you recognize on the involuntary conversion.
   b. Any money you receive that you do not spend on similar property.
2. Increase the basis by the following.
   a. Any gain you recognize on the involuntary conversion.
   b. Any cost of acquiring the replacement property.

Money or property not similar or related. If you receive money or property not similar or related in service or use to the converted property, and you buy replacement property similar or related in service or use to the converted property, the basis of the replacement property is its cost decreased by the gain not recognized on the conversion.

You can elect to exclude the gain if within 2 years following the year in which the involuntary gain was realized you buy new property that is similar or related in service or use to the old property. If this election is made, a gain will be recognized to the extent that the gain realized exceeds the difference between the cost of the replacement property and the adjusted basis of the old property. The basis of the new property is the cost of the new property decreased by the amount of gain that is not recognized.

For a residence in presidentially declared disaster areas, the replacement period is extended to 4 years after the close of the first year in which the gain on conversion is realized.

Example. The state condemned your property. The adjusted basis of the property was $26,000 and the state paid you $31,000 for it. You realized a gain of $5,000 ($31,000 – $26,000). You bought replacement property similar in use to the converted property for $29,000. You recognize a gain of $2,000 ($31,000 – $29,000), the unspent part of the payment from the state. Your unrecognized gain is $3,000, the difference between the $5,000 realized gain and the $2,000 recognized gain. The basis of the replacement property is figured as follows:

Cost of replacement property	$29,000
Minus: Gain not recognized	3,000
Basis of replacement property	$26,000

Allocating the basis. If you buy more than one piece of replacement property, allocate your basis among the properties based on their respective costs.

When you buy more than one asset for a single amount, such as land with buildings or the operating assets of a business, your costs must be reasonably allocated among the different assets. While the IRS may always question whether or not you have allocated these costs fairly, the IRS is unlikely to do so if the allocation has been contractually agreed to by the parties involved, particularly if you and the seller have adverse interests. Therefore, it may often be to your advantage to have the allocation spelled out in the purchase agreement.

If you are acquiring a trade, business, or investment asset, a favorable allocation of costs may have tax advantages. For example, raw land may not be depreciated, but buildings may. A favorable allocation between land and buildings enables you to claim more depreciation. The costs of specified intangible assets (such as goodwill, covenant-not-to-compete, franchise, etc.) are amortized over a 15-year period. Thus, while you can amortize costs allocated to certain intangible assets, allocating more cost to operating assets instead may create an income tax advantage because of the more rapid depreciation methods available for equipment. However, while the allocation of purchase price to tangible assets (e.g., equipment) will generally produce a favorable income tax result, this allocation can cause state and local sales and use taxes and business property taxes to be imposed on the tangible assets acquired.

If you dispose of a specified intangible asset that was acquired in a transaction, but you retain other specified intangible assets acquired in the same transaction, you may not claim a loss as a result of the disposition. Instead, the bases of the retained specified intangible assets are increased by the amount of the unrecognized loss.

For information about asset allocations, see Chapter 39, *If You Are Self-Employed: How to File Schedule C.*

The residual method must be used to allocate the purchase price of acquired assets. Under the residual method, the amount allocated to the value of goodwill and going concern value is the excess of the purchase price over the FMV of the tangible assets and the other identifiable intangible assets.

For certain types of acquisitions of assets used in a trade or a business, the buyer and seller must file Form 8594 with the IRS, showing how the purchase price was allocated among various classes of assets. For more information, consult your tax advisor.

Basis for depreciation. Special rules apply in determining and depreciating the basis of MACRS property acquired in an involuntary conversion. For information, see *What Is the Basis of Your Depreciable Property?* in chapter 1 of Publication 946.

Nontaxable Exchanges

A nontaxable exchange is an exchange in which you are not taxed on any gain and you cannot deduct any loss. If you receive property in a nontaxable exchange, its basis is generally the same as the basis of the property you transferred. See *Nontaxable Trades* in chapter 15.

Like-Kind Exchanges
The exchange of property for the same kind of property is the most common type of nontaxable exchange. To qualify as a like-kind exchange, the property traded and the property received must be both of the following.

- Qualifying property.
- Like-kind property.

The basis of the property you receive is generally the same as the adjusted basis of the property you gave up. If you trade property in a like-kind exchange and also pay money, the basis of the property received is the adjusted basis of the property you gave up increased by the money you paid.

Basis for depreciation. Special rules apply in determining and depreciating the basis of MACRS property acquired in a like-kind exchange. For information, see *What Is the Basis of Your Depreciable Property?* in chapter 1 of Publication 946.

Qualifying property. In a like-kind exchange, you must hold for investment or for productive use in your trade or business both the property you give up and the property you receive.

Like-kind property. There must be an exchange of like-kind property. Like-kind properties are properties of the same nature or character, even if they differ in grade or quality. The exchange of real estate for real estate and personal property for similar personal property are exchanges of like-kind property.

Example. You trade in an old truck used in your business with an adjusted basis of $1,700 for a new one costing $6,800. The dealer allows you $2,000 on the old truck, and you pay $4,800. This is a like-kind exchange. The basis of the new truck is $6,500 (the adjusted basis of the old one, $1,700, plus the amount you paid, $4,800).

If you sell your old truck to a third party for $2,000 instead of trading it in and then buy a new one from the dealer, you have a taxable gain of $300 on the sale (the $2,000 sale price minus the $1,700 adjusted basis). The basis of the new truck is the price you pay the dealer.

Partially nontaxable exchanges. A partially nontaxable exchange is an exchange in which you receive unlike property or money in addition to like-kind property. The basis of the property you receive is the same as the adjusted basis of the property you gave up, with the following adjustments.

1. Decrease the basis by the following amounts.
    a. Any money you receive.
    b. Any loss you recognize on the exchange.
2. Increase the basis by the following amounts.
    a. Any additional costs you incur.
    b. Any gain you recognize on the exchange.

If the other party to the exchange assumes your liabilities, treat the debt assumption as money you received in the exchange.

Allocation of basis. If you receive like-kind and unlike properties in the exchange, allocate the basis first to the unlike property, other than money, up to its FMV on the date of the exchange. The rest is the basis of the like-kind property.

More information. See *Like-Kind Exchanges* in chapter 1 of Publication 544 for more information.

Property Transferred From a Spouse

The basis of property transferred to you or transferred in trust for your benefit by your spouse is the same as your spouse's adjusted basis. The same rule applies to a transfer by your former spouse that is incident to divorce. However, for property transferred in trust, adjust your basis for any gain recognized by your spouse or former spouse if the liabilities assumed, plus the liabilities to which the property is subject, are more than the adjusted basis of the property transferred.

If the property transferred to you is a series E, series EE, or series I U.S. savings bond, the transferor must include in income the interest accrued to the date of transfer. Your basis in the bond immediately after the transfer is equal to the transferor's basis increased by the interest income includible in the transferor's income. For more information on these bonds, see chapter 8.

At the time of the transfer, the transferor must give you the records needed to determine the adjusted basis and holding period of the property as of the date of the transfer.

For more information about the transfer of property from a spouse, see chapter 15.

Property Received as a Gift

To figure the basis of property you receive as a gift, you must know its adjusted basis to the donor just before it was given to you, its FMV at the time it was given to you, and any gift tax paid on it.

FMV less than donor's adjusted basis. If the FMV of the property at the time of the gift is less than the donor's adjusted basis, your basis depends on whether you have a gain or a loss when you dispose of the property. Your basis for figuring gain is the same as the donor's adjusted basis plus or minus any required adjustments to basis while you held the property. Your basis for figuring loss is its FMV when you received the gift plus or minus any required adjustments to basis while you held the property. See *Adjusted Basis*, earlier.

Example. You received an acre of land as a gift. At the time of the gift, the land had an FMV of $8,000. The donor's adjusted basis was $10,000. After you received the property, no events occurred to increase or decrease your basis. If you later sell the property for $12,000, you will have a $2,000 gain because you must use the donor's adjusted basis at the time of the gift ($10,000) as your basis to figure gain. If you sell the property for $7,000, you will have a $1,000 loss because you must use the FMV at the time of the gift ($8,000) as your basis to figure loss.

If the sales price is between $8,000 and $10,000, you have neither gain nor loss.

Business property. If you hold the gift as business property, your basis for figuring any depreciation, depletion, or amortization deductions is the same as the donor's adjusted basis plus or minus any required adjustments to basis while you hold the property.

FMV equal to or greater than donor's adjusted basis. If the FMV of the property is equal to or greater than the donor's adjusted basis, your basis is the donor's adjusted basis at the time you received the gift. Increase your basis by all or part of any gift tax paid, depending on the date of the gift, explained later.

Also, for figuring gain or loss from a sale or other disposition or for figuring depreciation, depletion, or amortization deductions on business property, you must increase or decrease your basis (the donor's adjusted basis) by any required adjustments to basis while you held the property. See *Adjusted Basis,* earlier.

Gift received before 1977. If you received a gift before 1977, increase your basis in the gift (the donor's adjusted basis) by any gift tax paid on it. However, do not increase your basis above the FMV of the gift at the time it was given to you.

Gift received after 1976. If you received a gift after 1976, increase your basis in the gift (the donor's adjusted basis) by the part of the gift tax paid on it that is due to the net increase in value of the gift. Figure the increase by multiplying the gift tax paid by a fraction. The numerator of the fraction is the net increase in value of the gift and the denominator is the amount of the gift.

The net increase in value of the gift is the FMV of the gift minus the donor's adjusted basis. The amount of the gift is its value for gift tax purposes after reduction by any annual exclusion and marital or charitable deduction that applies to the gift. For information on the gift tax, see Publication 950, Introduction to Estate and Gift Taxes.

Example. In 2005, you received a gift of property from your mother that had an FMV of $50,000. Her adjusted basis was $20,000. The amount of the gift for gift tax purposes was $39,000 ($50,000 minus the $11,000 annual exclusion). She paid a gift tax of $9,000 on the property. Your basis is $26,930, figured as follows:

Fair market value	$50,000
Minus: Adjusted basis	− 20,000
Net increase in value	$30,000
Gift tax paid	$ 9,000
Multiplied by ($30,000 ÷ $39,000)	× .77
Gift tax due to net increase in value	$ 6,930
Adjusted basis of property to your mother	+ 20,000
Your basis in the property	$26,930

Inherited Property

Your basis in property you inherit from a decedent is generally one of the following.

- The FMV of the property at the date of the decedent's death.
- The FMV on the alternate valuation date if the personal representative for the estate elects to use alternate valuation.
- The value under the special-use valuation method for real property used in farming or a closely held business if elected for estate tax purposes.
- The decedent's adjusted basis in land to the extent of the value excluded from the decedent's taxable estate as a qualified conservation easement.

If a federal estate tax return does not have to be filed, your basis in the inherited property is its appraised value at the date of death for state inheritance or transmission taxes.

TaxAlert

The 2001 Tax Act provides that the step-up in basis rules are to be replaced with a carryover basis system in 2010. As of the date of this publication, the carryover basis rules had yet to be determined by Congress.

Explanation

The alternate valuation date is the earlier of the date 6 months after death and the date on which the estate's assets are distributed, sold, exchanged, or disposed of. Alternate valuation may be elected only if it is necessary to file an estate tax return. Furthermore, use of the alternate valuation date must result in a decrease in the estate tax. The election must be made for all property included in the estate.

TaxSaver

Choosing an alternate valuation date may be helpful in reducing estate tax if the market value of the assets in the estate is declining. However, if this is the case, the tax basis of those assets must also be reduced; this means increased income taxes in the future if the market value of the assets rises and they are then sold. Thus, the decision to elect the alternate valuation date to reduce estate tax should be balanced against a possible increase in future income taxes.

For more information, see the instructions to Form 706, United States Estate (and Generation-Skipping Transfer) Tax Return.

Explanation

If a decedent used property that he or she owned for farming, trade, or business purposes at the date of death, the executor of the decedent's estate may, under most conditions, choose the special-use valuation method for that property. This means that the property is included in the decedent's estate at the value based on its *current use* and not at the value based on what its most lucrative use might be. For example, if the land is being used for farming, its value is figured on its worth as farmland and not on what it might be worth if used for industrial purposes.

Certain conditions must be met before you use the special-use valuation method; consult your tax advisor.

The maximum amount that the special-use method can decrease the value of the estate is $870,000 in 2005, increased each year for cost-of-living adjustments.

TaxSaver

In community property states, the basis of the surviving spouse's one-half share of the community property will also receive a step-up in basis, normally to its FMV, at the date of the decedent spouse's death.

TaxOrganizer

If you receive property by inheritance, you should request a copy of the estate tax return from the executor of the estate to determine your basis in the inherited property.

Property Changed to Business or Rental Use

If you hold property for personal use and then change it to business use or use it to produce rent, you can begin to depreciate the property at the time of the change. To do so, you must figure its basis for depreciation. An example of changing property held for personal use to business or rental use would be renting out your former personal residence.

Basis for depreciation. The basis for depreciation is the lesser of the following amounts.

- The FMV of the property on the date of the change.
- Your adjusted basis on the date of the change.

Example. Several years ago, you paid $160,000 to have your house built on a lot that cost $25,000. You paid $20,000 for permanent improvements to the house and claimed a $2,000 casualty loss deduction for damage to the house before changing the property to rental use last year. Because land is not depreciable, you include only the cost of the house when figuring the basis for depreciation.

Your adjusted basis in the house when you changed its use was $178,000 ($160,000 + $20,000 − $2,000). On the same date, your property had an FMV of $180,000, of which $15,000 was for the land and $165,000 was for the house. The basis for figuring depreciation on the house is its FMV on the date of the change ($165,000) because it is less than your adjusted basis ($178,000).

Sale of property. If you later sell or dispose of property changed to business or rental use, the basis you use will depend on whether you are figuring gain or loss.

Gain. The basis for figuring a gain is your adjusted basis in the property when you sell the property.

Example. Assume the same facts as in the previous example except that you sell the property at a gain after being allowed depreciation deductions of $37,500. Your adjusted basis for figuring gain is $165,500 ($178,000 + $25,000 (land) − $37,500).

Loss. Figure the basis for a loss starting with the smaller of your adjusted basis or the FMV of the property at the time of the change to business or rental use. Then make adjustments (increases and decreases) for the period after the change in the property's use, as discussed earlier under *Adjusted Basis.*

Example. Assume the same facts as in the previous example, except that you sell the property at a loss after being allowed depreciation deductions of $37,500. In this case, you would start with the FMV on the date of the change to rental use ($180,000), because it is less than the adjusted basis of $203,000 ($178,000 + $25,000 (land) on that date. Reduce that amount ($180,000) by the depreciation deductions ($37,500). The basis for loss is $142,500 ($180,000 − $37,500).

Stocks and Bonds

The basis of stocks or bonds you buy generally is the purchase price plus any costs of purchase, such as commissions and recording or transfer fees. If you get stocks or bonds other than by purchase, your basis is usually determined by the FMV or the previous owner's adjusted basis, as discussed earlier.

You must adjust the basis of stocks for certain events that occur after purchase. For example, if you receive additional stock from nontaxable stock dividends or stock splits, reduce your basis for each share of stock by dividing the adjusted basis of the old stock by the number of shares of old and new stock. This rule applies only when the additional stock received is identical to the stock held. Also reduce your basis when you receive nontaxable distributions. They are a return of capital.

Example. In 2003 you bought 100 shares of XYZ stock for $1,000 or $10 a share. In 2004 you bought 100 shares of XYZ stock for $1,600 or $16 a share. In 2005 XYZ declared a 2-for-1 stock split. You now have 200 shares of stock with a basis of $5 a share and 200 shares with a basis of $8 a share.

Other basis. There are other ways to figure the basis of stocks or bonds depending on how you acquired them. For detailed information, see *Stocks and Bonds* under *Basis of Investment Property* in chapter 4 of Publication 550.

Identifying stocks or bonds sold. If you can adequately identify the shares of stock or the bonds you sold, their basis is the cost or other basis of the particular shares of stocks or bonds. If you buy and sell securities at various times in varying quantities and you cannot adequately identify the shares you sell, the basis of the securities you sell is the basis of the securities you acquired first. For more information about identifying securities you sell, see *Stocks and Bonds* under *Basis of Investment Property* in chapter 4 of Publication 550.

TaxPlanner

If your portfolio consists of various lots of the same stock acquired at different times and at different costs, some care must be exercised when a sale of a portion of these shares is contemplated. For example, assume that you own five different lots of ABC Motors stock acquired at different times and ranging in cost basis between $40 and $80 per share. If the stock is currently selling for $60 per share and you sell a lot with a basis of $40 per share, you recognize a gain; on the other hand, if you sell a lot having a basis of $80 per share, you sustain a loss. The situation may be far more complicated if the company has paid **stock dividends** or has split its stock one or more times.

It may be advisable to take any shares that you receive as the result of a stock dividend or a stock split and combine them with the shares that gave rise to the dividend or split. Have your broker convert all such related stock certificates into one certificate. Thus, each block of stock having a distinguishable cost basis is separately maintained. Although you are certainly not required to do this, it simplifies your record-keeping task and makes it much easier for you to compute your gain or loss when you sell the shares.

TaxOrganizer

You should keep a copy of your broker confirmation statement as a record for your cost basis in the shares of stock you have purchased during the year.

Explanation

For tax purposes, the selling instructions given to your broken or fund representative must be in writing. Even if stock certificates from a different lot are actually delivered to the transfer agent, you may consider the stock sold as you specified, provided that you identified the shares to be sold and received written confirmation of your orders.

TaxPlanner

Incentive stock options. If the shares you are selling were acquired by exercising an Incentive Stock Option (ISO) with previously owned employer shares, special rules will apply in determining the basis of the ISO shares.

The sale or transfer of stock acquired through the exercise of an ISO within 2 years of the option's grant date and within 1 year of the option's exercise date is known as a "disqualifying disposition." If the sale constitutes a disqualifying disposition of the ISO shares, the lowest basis shares are considered to be sold first, regardless of your effort to identify and sell specific shares. For more information, see Chapter 6, *Wages, Salaries, and Other Earnings,* and Publication 525, *Taxable and Nontaxable Income.*

Charitable contributions. If you own several blocks of appreciated shares, it is generally to your advantage to give away those shares with the lowest tax basis. When you make a contribution of the stock, you should be especially careful to designate which shares are being contributed. Let your stockbroker or transfer agent and the charity know the date you purchased the shares that you are now donating. It's important to take these steps at the time you are making the gift. For more information, see Chapter 26, *Contributions*.

Mutual fund shares. If you sell mutual fund shares you acquired at various times and prices and left on deposit in an account kept by a custodian or agent, you can elect to use an average basis. For more information, see *Average Basis* in Publication 564.

Explanation
For further discussion, see Chapter 17, *Reporting Gains and Losses*. Also, mutual funds are discussed in Chapter 40, *Mutual Funds*.

Bond premium. If you buy a taxable bond at a premium and elect to amortize the premium, reduce the basis of the bond by the amortized premium you deduct each year. See *Bond Premium Amortization* in chapter 3 of Publication 550 for more information. Although you cannot deduct the premium on a tax-exempt bond, you must amortize the premium each year and reduce your basis in the bond by the amortized amount.

Example
On January 15, 2004, Elizabeth purchases for $120,000 a tax-exempt obligation maturing on January 15, 2011, with a stated principal amount of $100,000, payable at maturity. The obligation provides for unconditional payments of interest of $9,000, payable on January 15 of each year. The interest payments on the obligation are qualified stated interest. The amount of bond premium is $20,000 ($120,000 − $100,000).

Based on the remaining payment schedule of the bond and Elizabeth's basis in the bond, Elizabeth's yield is 5.48%, compounded annually. The bond premium that must be amortized on January 15, 2005, is $2,420.55 ($9,000 − $6,579.45). The bond premium amortized is the excess of the qualified stated interest allocable to the period ($9,000) over the product of the adjusted acquisition price at the beginning of the period ($120,000) and Elizabeth's yield (5.48%, compounded annually). However, Elizabeth may not claim the amortization as a deduction on her tax return.

Original issue discount (OID) on debt instruments. You must increase your basis in an OID debt instrument by the OID you include in income for that instrument. See *Original Issue Discount (OID)* in chapter 8.

Tax-exempt obligations. OID on tax-exempt obligations is generally not taxable. However, when you dispose of a tax-exempt obligation issued after September 3, 1982, and acquired after March 1, 1984, you must accrue OID on the obligation to determine its adjusted basis. The accrued OID is added to the basis of the obligation to determine your gain or loss. See chapter 4 of Publication 550.

Explanation
For further discussion of original issue discount, see Chapter 8, *Interest Income*.

TAXSAVER
Automatic investment service and dividend reinvestment plans. If you take part in an automatic investment service, your cost basis per share of stock, including fractional shares, bought by the bank or other agent is your proportionate share of the agent's cost of all shares purchased at the same time plus the same share of the brokerage commission paid by the agent. If you take part in a **dividend** reinvestment plan and you receive stock from the corporation at a discount, your cost is the full FMV of the stock on the dividend payment date. You must include the amount of the discount in your income as an additional dividend.

Special rules apply in determining the basis of stock you acquired through a **stock dividend** or a **stock right. Stock dividends** are distributions by a corporation of its own stock. Usually, stock dividends are not taxable to the shareholder. However, for exceptions to this rule, see Chapter 9, *Dividends and Other Corporate Distributions*. If stock dividends are not taxable, you must allocate your basis for the stock between the old and the new stock in proportion to the FMV of each on the date of the distribution of the new stock.

New and old stock identical. If the new stock you received as a dividend is the same as the old stock on which the dividend is declared, both new and old shares probably have equal FMVs and you can divide the adjusted basis of the old stock by the number of shares of old and new stock. The result is your basis for each share of stock.

Example
You owned one share of common stock that you bought for $45. The corporation distributed two new shares of common stock for each share you held. You then had three shares of common stock, each with a basis of $15 ($45 ÷ 3). If you owned two shares before the distribution, one bought for $30 and the other for $45, you would have six shares after the distribution: three with a basis of $10 each and three with a basis of $15 each.

Explanation
New and old stock not identical. If the new stock you received as a nontaxable dividend is not the same as the old stock on which the dividend was declared, the FMVs of the old stock and the new stock will probably be different, so you should allocate the adjusted basis of your old stock between the old stock and the new stock in proportion to the FMVs of each on the date of the distribution of the new stock.

Example 1
This example shows how to account for stock splits and stock dividends.

	Block 1		
	Shares	Total Cost	Cost per Share
Jan. 15, 2005	100	$3,000	$ 30
2 for 1 stock split	100	−0−	
Dec. 31, 2005	200	$3,000	$ 15
Nov. 30, 2006 10% stock dividend	20		
Dec. 31, 2006	220	$3,000	$13.636

	Block 2		
	Shares	Total Cost	Cost per Share
Nov. 30, 2005	100	$2,000	$ 20
10% stock dividend	10		
Dec. 31, 2005	110	$2,000	$18.182

The original cost of each block of stock must be divided by the number of shares on hand at any given date to arrive at basis per share.

Example 2

This example shows how to account for nontaxable stock dividends with an FMV that is different from the value of the original stock held.

	Shares	Total Cost	Cost per Share	Total FMV	FMV per Share
Feb. 7, 2005 Purchased common stock	1,000	$14,000	$14	$14,000	$14
Aug. 30, 2005 10% stock dividend of preferred stock. FMV of original stock is $22 per share.	100			$1,000	$10

1,000 shares × $14 = $14,000   Cost of originating stock

1,000 shares × $22 = $22,000   Market value of original stock

100 shares × $10 = $1,000   Market value of preferred stock

$22,000/$23,000 × $14,000 = $13,391   Cost of original stock apportioned to such stock

$1,000/$23,000 × $14,000 = $609   Cost of original stock apportioned to the preferred stock

Explanation

If your stock dividend is taxable on receipt, the original basis of your new stock is its FMV on the date of distribution. Your holding period is determined from the date of distribution.

Stock rights are rarely taxable when you receive them. For more information, see Chapter 9, *Dividends and Other Corporate Distributions.*

If you receive stock rights that are taxable, the basis of the rights is their FMV at the time of distribution.

If you receive stock rights that are not taxable and you allow them to expire, they have no basis.

If you exercise or sell the nontaxable stock rights and if, at the time of distribution, the rights had an FMV of 15% or more of the FMV of the old stock, you must divide the adjusted basis of the stock between the stock and the stock rights. Use a ratio of the FMV of each to the FMV of both at the time of distribution of the rights. If the FMV of the stock rights is less than 15%, their basis is zero unless you choose to allocate a part of the basis of the old stock to the rights. You make this allocation on your return for the tax year in which the rights are received.

Basis of new stock. If you exercise the stock rights, the basis of the new stock is its cost plus the basis of the stock rights exercised. The holding period of the new stock begins on the date on which you exercised the stock rights.

Example

You own 100 shares of Tan Company stock, which cost you $22 per share. Tan Company gave you 10 stock rights that would allow you to buy 10 additional shares of stock at $26 per share. At the time the rights were distributed, the stock had a market value of $30, without the rights, and each right had a market value of $3. The market value of the stock rights is less than 15% of the market value of the stock, but you choose to divide the basis of your stock between the stock and the rights. You figure the basis of the rights and the basis of the old stock as follows:

100 shares × $22 = $2,200, basis of old stock

100 shares × $30 = $3,000, market value of old stock

10 rights × $3 = $30, market value of rights

30/3,030 × $2,200 = $21.78, basis of rights

3,000/3,030 × $2,200 = $2,178.22, new basis of old stock

If you sell the stock rights, the basis for figuring gain or loss is $2.178 per right. If you exercise the stock rights, the basis of the new stock you receive is $28.178 per share, the subscription price paid ($26), plus the basis of the stock rights exercised ($2.178 each). The remaining basis of the 100 shares of old stock for figuring gain or loss on a later sale is $2,178.22, or $21.7822 per share.

Explanation

Other basis rules. There are many other special rules you must follow in determining your basis in certain types of property. Here are some examples.

If you receive stock of one corporation in exchange for stock of another corporation in certain types of corporate reorganizations, your basis in the stock received will be equal to the basis of the stock you exchanged.

Certain types of tax credits may reduce basis in whole or in part. For example, if you claim rehabilitation credits on a building, the basis of the property is reduced by the amount of the credit.

If you lease real property on which the lessee makes improvements and the value of such improvements is excluded from income, your basis in the improvements is zero.

If you sell property to charity in a bargain sale, your basis for determining the gain from the sale is reduced by the ratio of the total basis of the property to its FMV.

For more information, you should consult your tax advisor.

15

Sale of Property

Note: The 2004 IRS Publication 17 (Your Federal Income Tax) has been updated by Ernst & Young LLP for 2005. Dates and dollar amounts shown are for 2005. Gray type is used to indicate where IRS text has been updated or intentionally omitted. Unrevised IRS text is shown in black type.

Introduction

Any time you sell or exchange a piece of property at a gain—whether it be your house, a stock you own, or something you use in your trade or business—you usually have to pay taxes on the transaction. That, of course, doesn't mean that sales and exchanges should be avoided, but the manner in which you choose to dispose of an **asset** *may determine how much you will have to pay in taxes. This chapter describes the various options available to you and the tax consequences of each.*

Because the amounts involved in sales and exchanges of property are often quite large relative to other items that make up your income, this chapter merits careful attention. It not only spells out how you deter-

mine the way in which various transactions are taxed but also offers suggestions about how to minimize or defer the tax burdens that you may incur.

In addition, this chapter discusses **bad debts.** *When a borrower cannot repay a loan, it is known as a bad debt. Some loans are made in connection with a trade or a business, some are made for purely personal reasons, and still others are made to make a profit. All sorts of rules have to be followed, and not every bad debt qualifies for a deduction. This chapter spells out what kind of documentation you need to prove that the money you lost was a bona fide debt and that there is no chance of repayment—the two conditions that must be met for you to take a deduction.*

Reminder

Foreign income. If you are a U.S. citizen who sells property located outside the United States, you must report all gains and losses from the sale of that property on your tax return unless it is exempt by U.S. law. This is true whether you reside inside or outside the United States and whether or not you receive a Form 1099 from the payer.

This chapter discusses the tax consequences of selling or trading investment property. It explains:

- What a sale or trade is,
- Figuring gain or loss,
- Nontaxable trades,
- Related party transactions,
- Capital gains or losses,
- Capital assets and noncapital assets,
- Holding period, and
- Rollover of gain from publicly traded securities.

Other property transactions. Certain transfers of property are not discussed here. They are discussed in other IRS publications. These include:

Installment sales, covered in Publication 537, Installment Sales,

Transfers of property at death, covered in Publication 559, Survivors, Executors, and Administrators,

Transactions involving business property, covered in Publication 544, Sales and Other Dispositions of Assets,

Dispositions of an interest in a passive activity, covered in Publication 925, Passive Activity and At-Risk Rules, and

Sales of a main home, covered in chapter 16.

Publication 550, Investment Income and Expenses (Including Capital Gains and Losses), provides more detailed discussion about sales and trades of investment property. Publication 550 includes information about the rules covering nonbusiness bad debts, straddles, section 1256 contracts, puts and calls, commodity futures, short sales, and wash sales. It also discusses investment-related expenses.

TaxSaver

Noncorporate taxpayers who held qualified small business stock (QSBS) for more than 5 years can exclude from gross income 50% of any gain realized from the sale or exchange of the stock. The gain is taxed at a maximum rate of 28%. This exclusion is limited to the greater of:

1. 10 times the taxpayer's basis in the stock; or
2. $10 million in gain from all of the taxpayer's transactions in stock of that corporation (held for more than 5 years).

The rules for determining whether stock is qualified small business stock can be summarized as follows:

- The stock must be newly issued stock and issued after August 10, 1993.
- The stock cannot be acquired in exchange for other stock.
- The issuing corporation must be a C corporation but may not be a cooperative, Domestic International Sales Corporation (DISC), former DISC, real estate investment trust (REIT), regulated investment company (RIC), Real Estate Mortgage Investment Conduit (REMIC), a corporation having a possessions tax credit election in effect nor owning a subsidiary that has a possessions tax credit election in effect.
- At least 80% of the corporation's assets must be used in the active conduct of a qualified trade or business or in the start-up of a future qualified trade or business.
- A qualified trade or business is any business other than one involving the performance of services in the fields of health, law, engineering, architecture, accounting, actuarial science, performing arts, consulting, athletics, financial services, brokerage services, or any other trade or business where the principal asset of the business is the reputation or skill of one or more employees. A qualified trade or business also cannot involve the businesses of banking, insurance, financing, leasing, investing or similar businesses, farming or certain businesses involving natural resource extraction or production, and businesses operating a hotel, motel, restaurant, or similar business.
- The corporation may not have greater than $50 million in gross assets (i.e., the sum of cash plus the aggregate fair market value of other corporate property) at the time the qualified small business stock is issued. If the corporation meets this test at the time of issuance of the stock, a subsequent event that violates this rule will not disqualify stock that previously qualified.

Note: Under certain circumstances, the gain on the sale of publicly traded securities will not be taxed if the proceeds from the sale are used to acquire common stock in a specialized small business investment company (SSBIC) within a 60-day period. See Publication 550, Investment Income and Expenses, for a detailed description of these additional requirements.

TaxAlert

The exclusion of gain from the sale of Qualified Small Business Stock increases to 60% for sales of stock in a corporation that qualifies as an empowerment zone business and the stock was acquired after December 21, 2000. See Publication 954, Tax Incentives for Distressed Communities for more information.

The maximum tax on long-term capital gains for most taxpayers is 15%. This rate applies for both regular and alternative minimum tax purposes.

Although the maximum tax rate on an individual's net long-term capital gains is 15%, a 28% rate applies to the sale of Qualified Small Business Stock. The effective tax rate, after the 50% exclusion, is 14%. Therefore, there is no substantial benefit in having QSBS Stock unless the gain from such sale is rolled over into other QSBS. Under the rollover rules, a taxpayer other than a corporation may elect to roll over capital gains from the sale of QSBS held for more than six months if other small business stock is purchased by the individual during the 60-day period beginning on the date of sale.

Useful Items

You may want to see:

Publications

☐　550　Investment Income and Expenses
☐　564　Mutual Fund Distributions

Forms (and Instructions)

☐　**Schedule D (Form 1040)** Capital Gains and Losses
☐　**8824** Like-Kind Exchanges

Sales and Trades

If you sold property such as stocks, bonds, or certain commodities through a broker during the year, you should receive, for each sale, a Form 1099-B, Proceeds From Broker and Barter Exchange Transactions, or an equivalent statement from the broker. You should receive the statement by January 31 of the next year. It will show the gross proceeds from the sale. The IRS will also get a copy of Form 1099-B from the broker.

Use Form 1099-B (or an equivalent statement received from your broker) to complete Schedule D (Form 1040).

What Is a Sale or Trade?

This section explains what is a sale or trade. It also explains certain transactions and events that are treated as sales or trades.

A sale is generally a transfer of property for money or a mortgage, note, or other promise to pay money.

A trade is a transfer of property for other property or services and may be taxed in the same way as a sale.

Sale and purchase. Ordinarily, a transaction is not a trade when you voluntarily sell property for cash and immediately buy similar property to replace it. The sale and purchase are two separate transactions. But see *Like-kind exchanges* under *Nontaxable Trades,* later.

Example

You sell your car to your brother and buy a new one from a dealer. You have entered into two separate transactions.

Redemption of stock. A redemption of stock is treated as a sale or trade and is subject to the capital gain or loss provisions unless the redemption is a dividend or other distribution on stock.

Dividend versus sale or trade. Whether a redemption is treated as a sale, trade, dividend, or other distribution depends on the circumstances in each case. Both direct and indirect ownership of stock will be considered. The redemption is treated as a sale or trade of stock if:

1. The redemption is not essentially equivalent to a dividend (see chapter 9),
2. There is a substantially disproportionate redemption of stock,
3. There is a complete redemption of all the stock of the corporation owned by the shareholder, or
4. The redemption is a distribution in partial liquidation of a corporation.

Redemption or retirement of bonds. A redemption or retirement of bonds or notes at their maturity is generally treated as a sale or trade.

Surrender of stock. A surrender of stock by a dominant shareholder who retains control of the corporation is treated as a contribution to capital rather than as an immediate loss deductible from taxable income. The surrendering shareholder must reallocate his or her basis in the surrendered shares to the shares he or she retains.

Worthless securities. Stocks, stock rights, and bonds (other than those held for sale by a securities dealer) that became worthless during the tax year are treated as though they were sold on the last day of the tax year. This affects whether your capital loss is long-term or short-term. See *Holding Period*, later.

If you are a cash basis taxpayer and make payments on a negotiable promissory note that you issued for stock that became worthless, you can deduct these payments as losses in the years you actually make the payments. Do not deduct them in the year the stock became worthless.

Explanation
A security is considered worthless when it has no recognizable value. You should be able to establish that the worthless security had value in the year preceding the year in which you take the deduction and that an identifiable event reduced the value to zero, causing the loss in the year in which you deduct it. A drop in the value of a stock, even though substantial, does not constitute worthlessness. The courts have held that if stock is sold for a very nominal sum (e.g., less than 1 cent per share), that is proof of worthlessness.

TAXPLANNER
The deduction for a worthless security must be taken in the year the security becomes worthless, even if it is sold for a nominal sum in the following year. If you do not learn that a security has become worthless until a later year, you should file an amended return for the year in which it became worthless. Because it may be difficult to determine exactly when a stock becomes worthless, the capital loss deduction should be claimed in the earliest year a claim may be reasonably made.

If you hold securities that seem to be on the verge of worthlessness, it may be easier to sell them now and take your capital loss without waiting for proof of worthlessness.

When securities are bought on credit, the timing of the deduction for worthlessness depends on the type of debt you have incurred. If the stock is purchased by giving the seller a note and the stock becomes worthless before the note is paid off, you may deduct the loss only as you make the payments on the note. However, if you borrow the funds from a third party, you may deduct the loss in the year in which the stock becomes worthless. In either case, an accrual basis taxpayer takes the deduction in the year the security becomes worthless.

TAXORGANIZER
You should keep any documents indicating the date on which the security becomes worthless. Examples of sufficient documentation are bankruptcy documents and financial statements.

How to report loss. Report worthless securities on Schedule D (Form 1040), line 1 or line 8, whichever applies. In columns (c) and (d), enter "Worthless." Enter the amount of your loss in parentheses in column (f).

Filing a claim for refund. If you do not claim a loss for a worthless security on your original return for the year it becomes worthless, you can file a claim for a credit or refund due to the loss. You must use Form 1040X, Amended U.S. Individual Income Tax Return, to amend your return for the year the security became worthless. You must file it within 7 years from the date your original return for that year had to be filed, or 2 years from the date you paid the tax, whichever is later. For more information about filing a claim, see *Amended Returns and Claims for Refund* in chapter 1.

Exceptions
While an exchange is generally taxable, the following "exchanges" are not:

• The extension of the maturity date of promissory notes
• The exercise of an option to convert a bond into stock of the issuing corporation, if the conversion privilege is provided for in the bond
• The conversion of security interests to stock in the same corporation subsequent to certain reorganizations (one example: the exchange of common stock for preferred stock)

TAXPLANNER
You may save taxes by carefully planning major sales and exchanges. It may be better to wait until after the end of the year before finalizing a sale so that a gain may be deferred until the next year. Alternatively, you may want to finalize the sale before the end of the year to take advantage of any losses in the current year. Professional advice should be obtained before, not after, a major transaction.

Explanation
Estates. The transfer of property of a decedent to the executor or administrator of the estate, or to the heirs or beneficiaries, generally is not a sale or exchange. No taxable gain or deductible loss results from the transfer.

Easements. Granting or selling an easement usually is not a taxable sale of property. Instead, the amount received for the easement is subtracted from the **basis** of the property. If only a part of an entire tract of property is permanently affected by the easement, only the basis of that part is reduced by the amount received. Any amount received that is more than the basis of the property to be reduced is a taxable gain. The transaction is reported as if it were a sale of the property.

If you transfer a perpetual easement for consideration, the transaction will be treated as a sale of property.

Life estate, etc. The entire amount you realize from disposing of a life interest in property, an interest in property for a set number of years, or an income interest in a trust is a taxable gain if you first got the interest as a gift, inheritance, or transfer in trust. Your basis in the property is considered to be zero. This rule does not apply if all interests in the property are disposed of at the same time.

Example 1

Your father dies, leaving his farm to you for life, with a remainder interest to your younger brother. You decide to sell your life interest in the farm. The entire amount you receive is a taxable gain, and your basis in the farm is disregarded.

Example 2

The facts are the same as in Example 1, except that your younger brother joins you in selling the farm. Because the entire interest in the property is conveyed, your taxable gain is the amount by which your share of the proceeds exceeds your adjusted basis in the farm.

Note: In Example 2, each brother's gain is computed by allocating the tax basis between them. The basis for the entire property—the **fair market value** at the date of the decedent's death—is adjusted for **depreciation** and improvements. Then, using actuarial tables, you compute the value of the life interest and of the **remainder interest** at the date of sale.

The younger brother could sell his remainder interest in the property independently of his brother, using his separate basis in computing his gain or loss on the sale. However, the older brother may not get the benefit of his basis in the property if he sells his life interest separately. The moral of the story is: Sometimes you save on taxes if you get along with your brother.

Sale versus lease. Just because a document says that it is a lease does not necessarily make it a lease for tax purposes. The rules are very complicated and not completely clear. Professional help is advisable. See Publication 544, *Sales and Other Dispositions of Assets.*

Installment sales. Some sales are made under a plan that provides for part or all of the sales price to be paid in a later year. These are called installment sales. If you finance the buyer's purchase of your property instead of the buyer getting a loan or mortgage from a bank, you probably have an installment sale.

You report your gain on an installment sale only as you actually receive payment. You are taxed only on the part of each payment that represents your profit on the sale. In this way, the installment method of reporting income relieves you of paying tax on income that you have not yet collected.

The first step in using the installment method is to find what portion of each installment payment represents a gain. This is determined by calculating the gross profit percentage, which is your gross profit divided by the contract price. Apply this percentage to all payments you receive in a year.

Gross profit is the selling price less the adjusted basis of the property sold. The selling price includes any cash you receive, the fair market value of any property received from the buyer, plus the amount of any existing mortgage on the property that the buyer took subject to or assumed.

Contract price is the selling price less any mortgage encumbrance on the property. However, if the amount of the mortgage is more than the adjusted basis of the property, then the selling price is reduced only by the adjusted basis, so the gross profit percentage is 100%.

Example

In 1987, Able bought commercial **real estate** for $100,000. He put $20,000 down and took out a mortgage for $80,000. By 2005, Able had reduced the mortgage to $40,000 and had an adjusted basis in the real estate of $85,000 (original cost, less depreciation, plus improvements). Able sold the real estate to Baker for $190,000. To pay Able, Baker assumed the rest of the mortgage and made three installment payments of $50,000 each.

Able figures his gross profit as follows:

Selling price	$190,000
Less adjusted tax basis	85,000
Gross profit	$105,000

Able figures his contract price as follows:

Selling price	$190,000
Less mortgage assumed	40,000
Contract price	$150,000

Able's gross profit percentage is 70% (gross profit divided by contract price). Able must report 70% of all contract-price collections as a taxable gain in the year they are received.

TaxSaver

Using the installment sale method may spread out your gain over several years and may result in a lower total tax on your gain.

By taking only a portion of the gain into income each year, you may avoid reaching a higher tax bracket. Even if you are already in the highest bracket, use of the installment sale method may still be beneficial, because taxes may be deferred to later years.

A disadvantage of the installment sale method is that if you are the seller, you do not obtain the sale proceeds immediately and therefore cannot reinvest them elsewhere. Also, a special rule applies to installment obligations arising from a sale of real or personal property if you're a nondealer where the sales price exceeds $150,000. To the extent the total face amount of these obligations arising during any tax year and outstanding at the end of that tax year exceed $5,000,000, interest is payable to the IRS annually on a certain percentage of the deferred tax liability.

TaxSaver

Installment sale treatment is not obligatory. You may elect not to follow the installment sale rules, in which case your total gain is recognized in the year of the sale.

While it is generally advantageous to defer recognition of a gain or part of a gain by using the installment sale method, under certain circumstances, accelerating recognition may result in overall tax savings. For example, if you expect your income in future years to be much higher than it is now or if you currently have a **capital loss** that may be offset by a gain, you may want to recognize your gain immediately.

The law limits the ability to defer tax by restricting use of the installment sale method to certain kinds of property. For example, the installment sale method may not be used for sales of publicly traded stocks or securities. However, you may sell other types of property, such as real property used in your business or for rental, under an installment sale and still defer the tax on the gain.

If you decide not to use the installment sale reporting method, indicate this decision on either Schedule D (Form 1040) or Form 4797 by the date your tax return for the year of the sale is due. (Schedule D is used to report sales of capital assets. Form 4797 is used to report sales of trade or business property and other noncapital assets.) Once you decide not to use the installment sale method, you may change your decision only with the consent of the IRS.

If you choose not to use the installment method and you are a **cash basis** taxpayer, remember that you may discount (reduce the stated value of) any installment payments that you are to receive at a later date. Therefore, the total gain on the sale you report should be discounted because you do not receive the total payment at the time of the sale.

TaxAlert

Sales at a loss do not qualify for installment sale reporting. Also, sales by dealers or by persons who regularly sell personal property on the installment basis no longer qualify for the installment method.

Explanation

The gain you have from an installment sale will be treated as **capital gain** if the property you sold was a capital asset (discussed later). However, if you took depreciation **deductions** on the assets, including the section 179 deduction, part of your gain may be treated as **ordinary income.**

Example

On January 31, 2005, Susan sells property for $4,000 on which she has a $1,000 gain. Half of the gain is taxable at ordinary rates.

If Susan receives the initial $2,000 payment in 2005, she is receiving one-half the proceeds and must report one-half of the gain, or $500. Because the ordinary income portion must be reported first, the entire $500 is treated as an **ordinary gain.** When Susan receives the second $2,000 payment, she reports the second half of the gain, $500, as a capital gain.

Explanation

Any depreciation claimed on personal property must be recaptured as ordinary income in the year of sale, even if there are no payments received in the year of sale. The depreciation recapture for real property is generally limited to the amount by which the depreciation claimed exceeds the amount available under the straight-line method of depreciation. The adjusted basis of the property being sold is increased by the amount of recaptured income that you include in your gross income in the year of sale so that the gain recognized in future years is decreased.

Example

Sam sells tangible personal property to Betty in 2005 for $100,000 to be paid in installments over 5 years, beginning in 2005. Interest is payable at market rates. The property was originally purchased for $30,000. Because of depreciation, it has an adjusted basis of $20,000. There is a gain of $80,000 ($100,000 − $20,000), of which $10,000 is recaptured income to be reported on Sam's 2005 return.

The $10,000 that is included in Sam's income in the year of sale is added to the $20,000 adjusted basis to figure how much income Sam must report using the installment method. Therefore, Sam's gross profit is $70,000 ($100,000 − $30,000). Sam's gross profit percentage is 70%.

On each of the $20,000 payments that Sam receives from 2005 through 2009, $14,000 would be included in his income ($20,000 × 70%).

Explanation

The installment sale rules contain a number of very important limitations.

Sales to a spouse or an 80% controlled entity. If you sell depreciable property to your spouse or to a partnership or corporation of which you own 80% or more, you must report all of the gain in the year of the sale, despite any installment payment schedules set up under the sale agreement. The same rule may also apply to the sale of property to a trust of which you (or your spouse) is a beneficiary.

Sales to other relatives. If you sell property, other than marketable securities, to a related person on an installment basis and that person resells (or makes a gift of) the property within 2 years, you have to recognize any additional gain in the year of the resale.

If you sell marketable securities to a related person and that person resells the property, you have to recognize any additional gain, unless the sale takes place after you have received all the installment payments due to you. There is no 2-year cutoff date as with other kinds of property, noted above. See the special rules regarding publicly traded property, below.

A related person includes your spouse, children, grandchildren, and parents. A related person is also any partnership in which you are a partner, any estates and trusts of which you are a beneficiary, any grantor trusts of which you are treated as an owner, and any corporation in which you own at least half of the total value of the stock.

The normal 3-year statute of limitations for tax assessments by the IRS is extended for resales of installment property by a related person. In these cases, the statute of limitations will not expire until 2 years after you report to the IRS that a resale took place.

Nontaxable trades. Special rules apply to the exchange of like-kind property, which is tax-free. However, nonlike-kind property included in the exchange is taxable. The installment method may be used for the nonlike-kind property.

Like-kind exchanges. For like-kind exchanges involving related parties, both parties must hold the property for more than 2 years for the original exchange to qualify as tax-free. This rule is applicable to both parties to the transaction, even though only one party avails himself or herself of like-kind treatment. Also, real property located in the United States and real property located outside the United States does not qualify as property of a like kind.

Disposing of installment obligations. If you sell property on an installment basis and then later dispose of the installment note, you may have to report a gain or a loss. Generally, the amount of your gain or loss is equal to the difference between your basis in the installment note and the amount you receive when you dispose of the note.

Example

Toni sells real estate on an installment basis for a $200,000 note receivable and has a $120,000 gross profit from the sale. After she collects $100,000 (and reports a profit of $60,000, half her gross profit), she sells the remaining $100,000 note receivable to a bank for $95,000. Toni reports a $55,000 profit in the year of the sale of the note (the remaining $60,000 of gross profit less the $5,000 loss on the sale of the note).

Explanation

A disposition for this purpose is not limited to a sale of the installment note. For example, if you make a sale of property after December 31, 1988, for more than $150,000, and you assign the installment obligation as collateral security for a loan, the IRS will treat this as a disposition. This is because you would have deferred the gain on the sale while obtaining the use of the money through a loan.

Publicly traded property. The installment method cannot be used for sales of publicly traded property, including stock or securities that are traded on an established securities market.

Repossessing property sold under the installment method. If you sell property on an installment plan, you may have to repossess it if, for example, the buyer defaults on his or her obligation. When repossession takes place, you may have to report a gain or a loss. You follow different rules for determining your gain or loss, depending on whether the property being repossessed is personal property or real property.

Personal property. If you repossess personal property sold under an installment plan, you must compare the fair market value of the property recovered with your basis in the installment notes plus any expenses you had in connection with repossession. Under the installment method, your basis is the face value of the note still outstanding less the amount of unreported profit on the original sale. (If you did not use the installment reporting method, your basis is the value of the property at the time of the original sale less payments of principal received to date.)

Your gain or loss is of the same character (short term or long term) as the gain or loss realized on the original sale if you used the installment method. If you did not, any gain resulting from repossession is treated as ordinary income. Any loss is an **ordinary loss** if the property is business property. If it is nonbusiness property, any loss resulting from repossession is treated as a short-term capital loss.

Real property. If you have to repossess your former residence because the buyer defaults and you excluded the gain (see Chapter 16, *Selling Your Home,* for details), no gain or loss is recognized if you resell the house within 1 year of repossession. If the property is not resold within 1 year, you may have to recognize the gain. The amount of tax you may have to pay on the gain will depend on whether the house you repossessed was originally sold before or after May 6, 1997. For houses sold before May 7, 1997, $125,000 of the gain could have been excluded or the gain could have been deferred by acquiring a replacement home. For houses sold after May 6, 1997, up to $250,000 or $500,000 of the gain may be excluded (see Chapter 16, *Selling Your Home,* for more information). You may never deduct a loss on repossession because you may not deduct losses on property used primarily for personal purposes.

Computing your gain or loss on repossessed real property. Generally, your gain or loss on property that you have repossessed equals (1) the total amount of payments you have received under the installment sale minus (2) the amount of taxable gain you have already reported on the installment sale.

The gain you report on the repossessed property is limited, however, to the gross profit you expected on the installment sale less repossession costs and the amount of taxable gain you have already reported on the installment sale. Your basis in the repossessed property is your adjusted basis at the time of the original sale less deferred gain on repossession.

Example

Linda Smith sold a building that was not her personal residence to Ann Carter in 2000 for $100,000, payable in 10 annual installments. Linda's basis in the building was $70,000, and no mortgage was outstanding. The expected gross profit in the sale was $30,000, and the gross profit percentage was 30%.

In 2005, Ann failed to pay the sixth installment. By then, Linda had recognized $15,000 of gain from the $50,000 in payments received. She repossessed the building, incurring legal fees of $1,000 in the process. Linda's gain is computed as follows:

Gain	
Payments received	$50,000
Less: Taxable gain already reported on sale	15,000
Gain subject to limitation	$35,000
Limitation on gain	
Gross profit expected on installment sale	$30,000
Less: Repossession costs	1,000
Less: Taxable gain already reported on sale	15,000
Limitation	$14,000

Linda must report a $14,000 gain on repossession. Her basis in the reacquired building is $49,000, figured by taking $70,000 (her original adjusted basis) and subtracting $21,000 ($35,000 − $14,000), the amount of gain on repossession unrecognized because of the limitation on gain.

TaxPlanner

Computing interest on installment sales. Special rules may apply regarding the amount of interest to be recognized on installment sales of more than $3,000.

If the amount of interest is not specifically stated in the sales agreement or if the stated interest is at an unrealistically low rate, you must calculate unstated or imputed interest. In general, you have unstated interest if (1) the sum of all payments due more than 6 months after the date of sale exceeds (2) the present value of such payments and the present value of any interest payment provided for in the contract. Present value is determined by using a so-called testing rate compounded semiannually. If there is unstated interest, you are required to *impute* interest using the testing rate. The testing rate is calculated by using the applicable federal rate (AFR). The AFR is based on average market yields of U.S. obligations. The AFR may be the short-, medium-, or long-term rate that U.S. obligations are yielding, depending on the length of the contract.

The testing rate is equal to *110% of the AFR* at the time the sale is made. If unstated interest results using the testing rate, then interest must be computed using the testing rate, compounded semiannually.

Example

On June 1, 2005, Nicholas and Alexandra sell their limousine for $45,000, to be paid in three annual installments of $15,000 each on June 1, 2005, May 31, 2006, and May 31, 2007. No interest is stated in the sales contract. Their basis in the car is $35,000.

The imputed interest over the 2 years is $1,630 (3.77% compounded semiannually). This amount must be subtracted from the selling price when the gain on the sale is computed:

Stated selling price	$45,000
Less: unstated interest	1,630
Adjusted selling price	$43,370
Less: Basis	35,000
Gain on sale	$ 8,370
Gross profit percentage: ($8,370 + $43,370)	19.3%

Imputed interest is important to consider for two reasons: (1) It alters the amount of gain on a sale, and (2) it is deductible as an interest expense by the buyer, subject to limitations (see Chapter 25, *Interest Expense),* and must be reported as interest income by the seller.

Note: If all of the installment payments are due within 1 year after the date of sale, it is not necessary to figure your imputed interest. Additionally, payments received within the first 6 months of a sale have no imputed interest. The AFR will be determined by the IRS every month.

TAXORGANIZER

You should keep a copy of your sales agreements, loan agreements, and closing statements associated with any installment sale.

How To Figure Gain or Loss

You figure gain or loss on a sale or trade of property by comparing the amount you realize with the adjusted basis of the property.

Gain. If the amount you realize from a sale or trade is more than the adjusted basis of the property you transfer, the difference is a gain.

Loss. If the adjusted basis of the property you transfer is more than the amount you realize, the difference is a loss.

Adjusted basis. The adjusted basis of property is your original cost or other original basis properly adjusted (increased or decreased) for certain items. See chapter 14 for more information about determining the adjusted basis of property.

Amount realized. The amount you realize from a sale or trade of property is everything you receive for the property. This includes the money you receive plus the fair market value of any property or services you receive. If you received a note or other debt instrument for the property, see *How To Figure Gain or Loss* in chapter 4 of Publication 550 to figure the amount realized.

If you finance the buyer's purchase of your property and the debt instrument does not provide for adequate stated interest, the unstated interest that you must report as ordinary income will reduce the amount realized from the sale. For more information, see Publication 537.

Fair market value. Fair market value is the price at which the property would change hands between a buyer and a seller, neither being forced to buy or sell and both having reasonable knowledge of all the relevant facts.

Example. You trade A Company stock with an adjusted basis of $7,000 for B Company stock with a fair market value of $10,000, which is your amount realized. Your gain is $3,000 ($10,000 − $7,000).

TAXPLANNER

An appraisal by a qualified person is usually accepted by both the courts and the IRS as the fair market value. The appraiser should be familiar with valuation methods accepted in the particular field (real estate, art objects, equipment and machinery, etc.). For real estate, a local appraiser is better qualified than an out-of-towner. In other fields, prior experience in the field is more important. It may be prudent to obtain an appraisal at the date of the transaction, just in case it is needed later.

TAXORGANIZER

You should keep a copy of your appraisal report of any property sold in order to verify its value.

Debt paid off. A debt against the property, or against you, that is paid off as a part of the transaction, or that is assumed by the buyer, must be included in the amount realized. This is true even if neither you nor the buyer is personally liable for the debt. For example, if you sell or trade property that is subject to a nonrecourse loan, the amount you realize generally includes the full amount of the note assumed by the buyer even if the amount of the note is more than the fair market value of the property.

Example. You sell stock that you had pledged as security for a bank loan of $8,000. Your basis in the stock is $6,000. The buyer pays off your bank loan and pays you $20,000 in cash. The amount realized is $28,000 ($20,000 + $8,000). Your gain is $22,000 ($28,000 − $6,000).

Example

You sell property and the buyer pays you $20,000 cash and assumes an existing mortgage on the property of $8,000. You bought the property for $6,000 and added improvements costing $10,000. Your selling expenses were $1,400. Your gain on the sale is figured as follows:

Amount realized		
Cash	$20,000	
Mortgage assumed by buyer	8,000	$28,000
Minus: Adjusted basis		
Cost	$ 6,000	
Improvements	10,000	
Total	$16,000	
Plus: Selling expenses	1,400	$17,400
Gain		**$10,600**

Payment of cash. If you trade property and cash for other property, the amount you realize is the fair market value of the property you receive. Determine your gain or loss by subtracting the cash you pay plus the adjusted basis of the property you trade in from the amount you realize. If the result is a positive number, it is a gain. If the result is a negative number, it is a loss.

Explanation

If you receive a mortgage or a trust note, payments include some interest income in addition to principal.

Example

Assume that a $10,000 installment note with a discounted value of $8,000 is given by an individual to a cash basis taxpayer in payment for a capital asset with a basis of $7,000. The taxpayer recognizes $1,000 ($8,000 − $7,000) as a capital gain. As each installment is paid, eight-tenths ($8,000 ÷ $10,000) of the payment is a return of principal and two-tenths is interest income.

Explanation

If you are an **accrual basis** taxpayer—and most people are not—use the full face value of the note in computing your gain or loss on the sale. Consequently, payments on the note are returns of principal.

If you are a cash basis taxpayer, and if the installment note is given by a corporation and the discounted value of the note is used to compute your gain on the sale of a capital asset, the income to be recognized is a capital gain. If the note is given by an individual, the income is taxable as ordinary income.

Example

A cash basis taxpayer sells a capital asset to a corporation in exchange for a $10,000 note with an interest rate of 5%. Because current interest rates are more than 5% or because of the corporation's low credit status, the note has a discounted value of $8,000, 80% of its face value. The taxpayer uses the $8,000 value to compute gain or loss on the sale. When the corporation later pays the note, the $2,000 difference, which must be reported as income, is treated as a capital gain. If an individual had issued the note, the $2,000 gain to the taxpayer realized on payment of the note would be taxed as ordinary income.

Explanation

Property used partly for business. If you sell or exchange property that you used for both business and personal purposes, the gain or loss on the sale or exchange must be figured as though you had sold two separate pieces of property. You must divide the selling price, selling expenses, and the basis between the business and personal parts. Depreciation is deducted from the basis of the business part. Gain or loss realized on the business part of the property may be treated as capital gain or loss, or as ordinary gain or loss (see Publication 544, *Sales and Other Dispositions of Assets*). Any gain realized on the personal part of the property is a capital gain. A loss on the personal part is not deductible.

No gain or loss. You may have to use a basis for figuring gain that is different from the basis used for figuring loss. In this case, you may have neither a gain nor a loss. See *Basis Other Than Cost* in chapter 14.

TaxSaver

If you plan to give away a capital asset that has depreciated in value, consider selling it and giving away the proceeds instead, particularly if the would-be recipient of the property would likely sell it in the immediate future. By selling, you realize a capital loss and the consequent tax savings. At the same time, the would-be recipient of the property, who might have been unable to claim a capital loss because he or she would have had a different basis in the property, receives assets of the same value, only in cash instead of property.

Nontaxable Trades

This section discusses trades that generally do not result in a taxable gain or deductible loss. For more information on nontaxable trades, see chapter 1 of Publication 544.

Like-kind exchanges. If you trade business or investment property for other business or investment property of a like kind, you do not pay tax on any gain or deduct any loss until you sell or dispose of the property you receive. To be nontaxable, a trade must meet all six of the following conditions.

1. The property must be business or investment property. You must hold both the property you trade and the property you receive for productive use in your trade or business or for investment. Neither property may be property used for personal purposes, such as your home or family car.
2. The property must not be held primarily for sale. The property you trade and the property you receive must not be property you sell to customers, such as merchandise.
3. The property must not be stocks, bonds, notes, choses in action, certificates of trust or beneficial interest, or other securities or evidences of indebtedness or interest, including partnership interests. However, you can have a nontaxable trade of corporate stocks under a different rule, as discussed later.
4. There must be a trade of like property. The trade of real estate for real estate, or personal property for similar personal property is a trade of like property. The trade of an apartment house for a store building, or a panel truck for a pickup truck, is a trade of like property. The trade of a piece of machinery for a store building is not a trade of like property. Real property located in the United States and real property located outside the United States are not like property. Also, personal property used predominantly within the United States and personal property used predominantly outside the United States are not like property.
5. The property to be received must be identified in writing within 45 days after the date you transfer the property given up in the trade.
6. The property to be received must be received by the earlier of:
   a. The 180th day after the date on which you transfer the property given up in the trade, or
   b. The due date, including extensions, for your tax return for the year in which the transfer of the property given up occurs.

Explanation

The term *like kind* refers to a property's nature or character, not its grade or quality. With real estate, for example, whether or not it has been improved is a factor that affects only grade or quality, not its nature. Property held for productive use in a trade or a business may be exchanged for property held for investment.

Examples

Like-kind exchanges include the following:

- Improved for unimproved real estate when exchanged by a person who does not deal in real estate
- A used car for a new one to be used for the same purpose. The following are *not* considered like-kind exchanges:
- Personal property (such as a boat) for real property
- Gold numismatic coins for gold bullion (the IRS ruled that an investment in gold coins was an investment in the coins themselves, while the investment in bullion was an investment in the world gold market)
- Gold bullion for silver bullion
- Male livestock for female livestock

TaxAlert

Depreciable, tangible personal property may be exchanged for either like-kind or like-class property and may qualify for **like-kind exchange treatment.** Like-class properties are depreciable, tangible personal properties within the same "general asset classes" as defined in the Standard Industrial Classification Manual (see Publication 544, *Sales and Other Dispositions of Assets).*

You are not required to make a property-by-property comparison if you

1. Separate the properties into two or more exchange groups, or
2. Transfer or receive more than one property within a single exchange group.

If you trade property with a related party in a like-kind exchange, a special rule may apply. See *Related Party Transactions*, later in this chapter. Also, see chapter 1 of Publication 544 for more information on exchanges of business property and special rules for exchanges using qualified intermediaries or involving multiple properties.

Partly nontaxable exchange. If you receive money or unlike property in addition to like property, and the above six conditions are met, you have a partly nontaxable trade. You are taxed on any gain you realize, but only up to the amount of the money and the fair market value of the unlike property you receive. You cannot deduct a loss.

Example
You exchange real estate held for investment that has an adjusted basis of $8,000 for other real estate that you want to hold for investment. The real estate you receive has a fair market value of $10,000, and you also receive $1,000 in cash. Although the total gain realized on the transaction is $3,000, only $1,000 (cash received) is included in your income.

TaxSaver

Assume that you are to receive property that is worth less than the property you are to give up and you expect to make improvements on the new property. Rather than receive money or unlike property from the other owner to make up the difference in value, you might ask her to make the improvements on her property before the transfer. In that way, you reduce the amount of unlike property included in the exchange and therefore reduce the amount of tax you have to pay on the transfer. What is the incentive for the other owner? Making the improvement might induce you to make the deal.

TaxSaver

If the amount of liabilities you assume in an exchange is less than the amount of liabilities you give up, the difference is treated as cash received. Consequently, if you assume a mortgage that is less than the mortgage you had been carrying on the exchanged property, you recognize gain as if you had received cash for the difference.

If you receive cash but assume more debt than you were relieved of, you cannot offset the cash received with the debt assumed. In this case, you should have the buyer pay down some of the debt you are assuming rather than paying you the cash directly. You may be able to borrow the difference against the property at a later date.

Like property and unlike property transferred. If you give up unlike property in addition to the like property, you must recognize gain or loss on the unlike property you give up. The gain or loss is the difference between the adjusted basis of the unlike property and its fair market value.

Like property and money transferred. If conditions (1)–(6) are met, you have a nontaxable trade even if you pay money in addition to the like property.

Basis of property received. To figure the basis of the property received, see *Nontaxable Exchanges* in chapter 14.

How to report. You must report the trade of like property on Form 8824. If you figure a recognized gain or loss on Form 8824, report it on Schedule D (Form 1040) or on Form 4797, Sales of Business Property, whichever applies.

For information on using Form 4797, see chapter 4 of Publication 544.

TaxSaver

A like-kind exchange is a useful planning tool in deferring tax on appreciated property if you intend to reinvest in a similar property within a relatively short period. No gain or loss is recognized in a deferred like-kind exchange if you meet the following requirements:

1. You must follow specific procedures to identify replacement property within 45 days after relinquishing the old property.
2. You must receive the replacement property within 180 days after relinquishing the old property.
3. You must structure the exchange to comply with one or more of the guidelines described in the final regulations. The reason for this step is that if the exchange does not fall within one of the guidelines, then the exchange could be subject to scrutiny by the IRS.

Taxpayers should design their transactions to comply with one of the following IRS guidelines:

1. You cannot have an immediate ability or unrestricted right to receive money or other property pursuant to the security or guarantee arrangement. However, the replacement property may be secured or guaranteed before you actually receive like-kind replacement property by one or more of the following:
   a. Mortgage, deed of trust, or other security interest in property
   b. Standby letter of credit meeting certain specifications and a guarantee of a third party
2. You may not have an immediate ability or unrestricted right to receive, pledge, borrow, or otherwise obtain the benefits of the cash or cash equivalent held in an escrow account or qualified trust. However, the replacement property may be secured by cash or a cash equivalent if the cash or cash equivalent is held in a qualified escrow account or in a qualified trust.
3. You may not have an immediate ability or unrestricted right to receive, pledge, borrow, or otherwise obtain the benefits of money or other property held by a qualified intermediary. However, you may use a qualified intermediary in a deferred exchange if the qualified intermediary is unrelated to you (see the IRS final regulations for details). A qualified intermediary may be an escrow or title company.

More than one IRS guideline can be used in the same deferred exchange, but the terms and conditions of each must be separately satisfied. You should consult your tax advisor if you are contemplating a like-kind exchange.

Corporate stocks. The following trades of corporate stocks generally do not result in a taxable gain or a deductible loss.

Corporate reorganizations. In some instances, a company will give you common stock for preferred stock, preferred stock for common stock, or stock in one corporation for stock in another corporation. If this is a result of a merger, recapitalization, transfer to a controlled corporation, bankruptcy, corporate division, corporate acquisition, or other corporate reorganization, you do not recognize gain or loss.

Stock for stock of the same corporation. You can exchange common stock for common stock or preferred stock for preferred stock in the same corporation without having a recognized gain or loss. This is true for a trade between two stockholders as well as a trade between a stockholder and the corporation.

Convertible stocks and bonds. You generally will not have a recognized gain or loss if you convert bonds into stock or preferred stock into common stock of the same corporation according to a conversion privilege in the terms of the bond or the preferred stock certificate.

Property for stock of a controlled corporation. If you transfer property to a corporation solely in exchange for stock in that corporation, and immediately after the trade you are in control of the corporation, you ordinarily will not recognize a gain or loss. This rule applies both to individuals and to groups who transfer property to a corporation. It does not apply if the corporation is an investment company.

For this purpose, to be in control of a corporation, you or your group of transferors must own, immediately after the exchange, at least 80% of the total combined voting power of all classes of stock entitled to vote and at least 80% of the outstanding shares of each class of nonvoting stock of the corporation.

If this provision applies to you, you must attach to your return a complete statement of all facts pertinent to the exchange.

Additional information. For more information on trades of stock, see *Nontaxable Trades* in chapter 4 of Publication 550.

Explanation

The statement must include the following information:

- A description of the property transferred, with its cost or other basis
- The kind of stock received, including the number of shares and fair market value
- The principal amount and fair market value of any securities received
- The amount of money received, if any
- A description of any liabilities assumed by the corporation in the transaction, including the corporate business reason for the assumption

Generally, when you transfer property to a corporation that you alone will control in exchange for its stock, no gain or loss is recognized. "Control" means that you or your group of investors owns at least 80% of the outstanding voting stock and at least 80% of the shares of all other classes of outstanding stock. However, if you receive property other than stock, then you may have to recognize a gain equal to that additional property's value. Moreover, if the property you transfer to the corporation has been depreciated, all or a portion of your gain may be ordinary income rather than a capital gain.

Example

You transfer machinery that has an adjusted basis of $10,000 and a fair market value of $25,000 to a corporation that you and your associates will control in exchange for stock worth $20,000 and $5,000 in cash. You realize a $15,000 gain on the transfer of the machinery.

The transfer would have been tax-free if all you had received in return was stock. However, you have to report a gain of $5,000 for the cash received. Furthermore, if you previously claimed $5,000 or more in depreciation on the machinery, all of the $5,000 you received is treated as ordinary income under the depreciation recapture rules. For a complete discussion of depreciation, see Chapter 10, *Rental Income and Expenses*.

Explanation

There has been much litigation over the issue of momentary control—a situation that arises when investors hold the required 80% of stock only briefly and then dispose of a portion of it. Generally, momentary control is not sufficient to ensure preferential tax treatment if there was an agreement or prearranged plan for subsequent disposition of the stock acquired in the exchange.

Condemnations and involuntary exchanges. Condemnation is the process by which private property is legally taken by governments or certain entities, such as public utilities, in exchange for money or property.

If the condemnation award you receive is more than your adjusted basis in the condemned property, you have a gain. This gain may be postponed if you receive similar property instead of cash or if replacement property is purchased with the cash you receive. If you purchase replacement property, it must be put to a use similar to that of the original property. It also must be purchased within 2 years from the close of the first year in which any part of the gain on condemnation is realized. For business real property, the purchase must be made within 3 years.

If the condemnation award you receive is less than your basis in the property, you have a loss. This loss is not deductible if the property was your residence. Your loss, however, may be deducted if the property was used in a trade or a business or for the production of income.

Insurance policies and annuities. You will not have a recognized gain or loss if the insured or annuitant is the same under both contracts and you trade:

1. A life insurance contract for another life insurance contract or for an endowment or annuity contract,
2. An endowment contract for an annuity contract or for another endowment contract that provides for regular payments beginning at a date not later than the beginning date under the old contract, or
3. An annuity contract for another annuity contract.

You also may not have to recognize gain or loss on an exchange of a portion of an annuity contract for another annuity contract. See Revenue Ruling 2003-76 and Notice 2003-51.

Exchanges of contracts not included in this list, such as an annuity contract for an endowment contract, or an annuity or endowment contract for a life insurance contract, are taxable.

Demutualization of life insurance companies. If you received stock in exchange for your equity interest as a policyholder or an annuitant, you generally will not have a recognized gain or loss. See *Demutualization of Life Insurance Companies* in Publication 550.

U.S. Treasury notes or bonds. You can trade certain issues of U.S. Treasury obligations for other issues designated by the Secretary of the Treasury, with no gain or loss recognized on the trade.

Transfers Between Spouses

Generally, no gain or loss is recognized on a transfer of property from an individual to (or in trust for the benefit of) a spouse, or if incident to a divorce, a former spouse. This nonrecognition rule does not apply in the following situations.

- The recipient spouse or former spouse is a nonresident alien.
- Property is transferred in trust. Gain must be recognized to the extent the amount of the liabilities assumed by the trust, plus any liabilities on the property, exceed the adjusted basis of the property.

For other situations, see Publication 550.

Any transfer of property to a spouse or former spouse on which gain or loss is not recognized is treated by the recipient as a gift and is not considered a sale or exchange. The recipient's basis in the property will be the same as the adjusted basis of the giver immediately before the transfer. This carryover basis rule applies whether the adjusted basis of the transferred property is less than, equal to, or greater than either its fair market value at the time of transfer or any consideration paid by the recipient. This rule applies for purposes of determining loss as well as gain. Any gain recognized on a transfer in trust increases the basis.

A transfer of property is incident to a divorce if the transfer occurs within 1 year after the date on which the marriage ends, or if the transfer is related to the ending of the marriage.

Explanation

For transfers of property incident to divorce to a former spouse who is a nonresident alien, gain or loss may be recognized to the spouse who transferred the property based on the fair market value of the property transferred.

Related Party Transactions

Special rules apply to the sale or trade of property between related parties.

TAXPLANNER

Special rules are imposed on taxpayers who try to avoid taxation on property gains by passing the property on to a trust. A special tax is imposed on a trust when the trust sells appreciated property within 2 years of having received it. The property may have been acquired by gift, through a bargain purchase, or as a transfer from another trust. The trust's gain is taxed at the highest rate that the donor of the property would have had to pay had he or she reported the gain on the sale in the same year in which the trust did.

Exception

This special tax is not imposed on a sale or an exchange that occurs within 2 years of the transfer of property if the sale or exchange takes place after the death of the donor of the property.

The purpose of the special tax is to prevent the grantor from taking advantage of a lower tax bracket in a trust. The law assumes, except in the case of death, that if the property is sold within 2 years, this was the plan all along.

Gain on sale or trade of depreciable property. Your gain from the sale or trade of property to a related party may be ordinary income, rather than capital gain, if the property can be depreciated by the party receiving it. See chapter 3 of Publication 544 for more information.

Like-kind exchanges. Generally, if you trade business or investment property for other business or investment property of a like kind, no gain or loss is recognized. See *Like-kind exchanges* earlier under *Nontaxable Trades*.

This rule also applies to trades of property between related parties, defined next under *Losses on sales or trades of property*. However, if either you or the related party disposes of the like property within 2 years after the trade, you both must report any gain or loss

not recognized on the original trade on your return filed for the year in which the later disposition occurs.

Losses on sales or trades of property. You cannot deduct a loss on the sale or trade of property, other than a distribution in complete liquidation of a corporation, if the transaction is directly or indirectly between you and the following related parties.

1. Members of your family. This includes only your brothers and sisters, half-brothers and half-sisters, spouse, ancestors (parents, grandparents, etc.), and lineal descendants (children, grandchildren, etc.).
2. A partnership in which you directly or indirectly own more than 50% of the capital interest or the profits interest.
3. A corporation in which you directly or indirectly own more than 50% in value of the outstanding stock. (See *Constructive ownership of stock*, later.)
4. A tax-exempt charitable or educational organization that is directly or indirectly controlled, in any manner or by any method, by you or by a member of your family, whether or not this control is legally enforceable.

In addition, a loss on the sale or trade of property is not deductible if the transaction is directly or indirectly between the following related parties.

1. A grantor and fiduciary, or the fiduciary and beneficiary, of any trust.
2. Fiduciaries of two different trusts, or the fiduciary and beneficiary of two different trusts, if the same person is the grantor of both trusts.
3. A trust fiduciary and a corporation of which more than 50% in value of the outstanding stock is directly or indirectly owned by or for the trust, or by or for the grantor of the trust.
4. A corporation and a partnership if the same persons own more than 50% in value of the outstanding stock of the corporation and more than 50% of the capital interest, or the profits interest, in the partnership.
5. Two S corporations if the same persons own more than 50% in value of the outstanding stock of each corporation.
6. Two corporations, one of which is an S corporation, if the same persons own more than 50% in value of the outstanding stock of each corporation.
7. An executor and a beneficiary of an estate (except in the case of a sale or trade to satisfy a pecuniary bequest).
8. Two corporations that are members of the same controlled group. (Under certain conditions, however, these losses are not disallowed but must be deferred.)
9. Two partnerships if the same persons own, directly or indirectly, more than 50% of the capital interests or the profit interests in both partnerships.

Multiple property sales or trades. If you sell or trade to a related party a number of blocks of stock or pieces of property in a lump sum, you must figure the gain or loss separately for each block of stock or piece of property. The gain on each item may be taxable. However, you cannot deduct the loss on any item. Also, you cannot reduce gains from the sales of any of these items by losses on the sales of any of the other items.

Indirect transactions. You cannot deduct your loss on the sale of stock through your broker if, under a prearranged plan, a related party buys the same stock you had owned. This does not apply to a trade between related parties through an exchange that is purely coincidental and is not prearranged.

Constructive ownership of stock. In determining whether a person directly or indirectly owns any of the outstanding stock of a corporation, the following rules apply.

Rule 1. Stock directly or indirectly owned by or for a corporation, partnership, estate, or trust is considered owned proportionately by or for its shareholders, partners, or beneficiaries.

Rule 2. An individual is considered to own the stock that is directly or indirectly owned by or for his or her family. Family includes only brothers and sisters, half-brothers and half-sisters, spouse, ancestors, and lineal descendants.

Rule 3. An individual owning, other than by applying rule 2, any stock in a corporation is considered to own the stock that is directly or indirectly owned by or for his or her partner.

Rule 4. When applying rule 1, 2, or 3, stock constructively owned by a person under rule 1 is treated as actually owned by that person. But stock constructively owned by an individual under rule 2 or rule 3 is not treated as owned by that individual for again applying either rule 2 or rule 3 to make another person the constructive owner of the stock.

Property received from a related party. If you sell or trade at a gain property that you acquired from a related party, you recognize the gain only to the extent it is more than the loss previously disallowed to the related party. This rule applies only if you are the original transferee and you acquired the property by purchase or exchange. This rule does not apply if the related party's loss was disallowed because of the wash sale rules described in chapter 4 of Publication 550 under *Wash sales*.

If you sell or trade at a loss property that you acquired from a related party, you cannot recognize the loss that was not allowed to the related party.

Example 1. Your brother sells you stock for $7,600. His cost basis is $10,000. Your brother cannot deduct the loss of $2,400. Later, you sell the same stock to an unrelated party for $10,500, realizing a gain of $2,900. Your reportable gain is $500—the $2,900 gain minus the $2,400 loss not allowed to your brother.

Example 2. If, in *Example 1*, you sold the stock for $6,900 instead of $10,500, your recognized loss is only $700 (your $7,600 basis minus $6,900). You cannot deduct the loss that was not allowed to your brother.

> **Explanation**
> Transactions between a trust and the relative of a trust beneficiary may be indirect related-party transactions. Similarly, the sale of stock by one spouse followed by the purchase by the other spouse of an equal number of the same corporation's shares is an indirect sale between related parties, even though both spouses deal through brokers on the New York Stock Exchange. However, if there is a significant time lapse between the two transactions—a month or more—the transactions are not considered linked.

Capital Gains and Losses

This section discusses the tax treatment of gains and losses from different types of investment transactions.

Character of gain or loss. You need to classify your gains and losses as either ordinary or capital gains or losses. You then need to classify your capital gains and losses as either short term or long term. If you have long-term gains and losses, you must identify your 28% rate gains and losses. If you have a net capital gain, you must also identify any unrecaptured section 1250 gain.

The correct classification and identification helps you figure the limit on capital losses and the correct tax on capital gains. Reporting capital gains and losses is explained in chapter 17.

Capital or Ordinary Gain or Loss

If you have a taxable gain or a deductible loss from a transaction, it may be either a capital gain or loss or an ordinary gain or loss, depending on the circumstances. Generally, a sale or trade of a capital asset (defined next) results in a capital gain or loss. A sale or trade of a noncapital asset generally results in ordinary gain or loss. Depending on the circumstances, a gain or loss on a sale or trade of property used in a trade or business may be treated as either capital

or ordinary, as explained in Publication 544. In some situations, part of your gain or loss may be a capital gain or loss and part may be an ordinary gain or loss.

Capital Assets and Noncapital Assets

For the most part, everything you own and use for personal purposes, pleasure, or investment is a capital asset. Some examples are:

- Stocks or bonds held in your personal account,
- A house owned and used by you and your family,
- Household furnishings,
- A car used for pleasure or commuting,
- Coin or stamp collections,
- Gems and jewelry, and
- Gold, silver, or any other metal.

Any property you own is a capital asset, except the following noncapital assets.

1. Property held mainly for sale to customers or property that will physically become a part of the merchandise that is for sale to customers.
2. Depreciable property used in your trade or business, even if fully depreciated.
3. Real property used in your trade or business.
4. A copyright, a literary, musical, or artistic composition, a letter or memorandum, or similar property:
   a. Created by your personal efforts,
   b. Prepared or produced for you (in the case of a letter, memorandum, or similar property), or
   c. Acquired under circumstances (for example, by gift) entitling you to the basis of the person who created the property or for whom it was prepared or produced.
5. Accounts or notes receivable acquired in the ordinary course of a trade or business for services rendered or from the sale of property described in (1).
6. U.S. Government publications that you received from the government for free or for less than the normal sales price, or that you acquired under circumstances entitling you to the basis of someone who received the publications for free or for less than the normal sales price.
7. Certain commodities derivative financial instruments held by commodities derivatives dealers.
8. Hedging transactions, but only if the transaction is clearly identified as a hedging transaction before the close of the day on which it was acquired, originated, or entered into.
9. Supplies of a type you regularly use or consume in the ordinary course of your trade or business.

> **Example**
> You bought a car for personal use and later sold it for less than you paid for it. The loss is not deductible. However, if you had sold it for more than you paid for it, the gain would be taxable. A loss would be deductible only if, or to the extent that, the car was used for business. If it was sold at a loss, the loss would be deductible. If the car had been stolen, you would have had a theft loss.
> *Note:* In determining the amount of the loss, what you paid for the car would have to be reduced by any depreciation allowed as a deduction. This would reduce the amount of the loss you could claim.
>
> **Explanation**
> While losses on personal property generally are not deductible, losses associated with a trade or a business may be. However, property originally held for personal use

may be converted to business use under certain circumstances (and vice versa). There are very few court cases in this area, and those that exist do not provide much guidance about how long property must be rented before it is considered converted to business use. Each case depends on the specific facts and circumstances. In general, if a residence has been rented for a period of years, there is strong evidence that it has been converted to rental property.

Examples

In one case, a residence was rented out for several months under a bona fide lease. The property could not be reoccupied by the owner during the term of the lease. The owner's motive for leasing the house was to make money. The court held that the property had been converted to rental use.

In another case, a building was remodeled to make it fit for business purposes. This was considered to be strong evidence that the property was being converted to rental use.

Note: There are no clear-cut guidelines for what constitutes conversion to business use. However, simply listing the property with a rental agent is not sufficient. The guidelines in Chapter 16, *Selling Your Home,* may be helpful.

Investment Property

Investment property is a capital asset. Any gain or loss from its sale or trade is generally a capital gain or loss.

Gold, silver, stamps, coins, gems, etc. These are capital assets except when they are held for sale by a dealer. Any gain or loss you have from their sale or trade generally is a capital gain or loss.

TaxPlanner

If you collect gold, silver, stamps, antiques, and the like, you should be aware that losses from the sale or trade of such property generally are not deductible. In order to claim a loss, you must be able to show that your primary purpose in collecting the property was to make a profit. Furthermore, you must show that you were not collecting the items purely as a hobby or for personal enjoyment. Obviously, there may be a very fine line between a hobby and a profit-making activity.

Example

The Tax Court did *not* allow a taxpayer to deduct a loss on the sale of antiques he used to furnish his home. The taxpayer argued that he was speculating on large increases in the value of the antiques. The Tax Court emphasized his personal use of the antiques and noted that most of the taxpayer's sales of antiques were merely a means of financing the acquisition of more antiques.

Stocks, stock rights, and bonds. All of these (including stock received as a dividend) are capital assets except when held for sale by a securities dealer. However, if you own small business stock, see *Losses on Section 1244 (Small Business) Stock* and *Losses on Small Business Investment Company Stock* in chapter 4 of Publication 550.
Personal use property. Property held for personal use only, rather than for investment, is a capital asset, and you must report a gain from its sale as a capital gain. However, you cannot deduct a loss from selling personal use property.

Discounted Debt Instruments

Treat your gain or loss on the sale, redemption, or retirement of a bond or other debt instrument originally issued at a discount or bought at a discount as capital gain or loss, except as explained in the following discussions.

Short-term government obligations. Treat gains on short-term federal, state, or local government obligations (other than tax-exempt obligations) as ordinary income up to your ratable share of the acquisition discount. This treatment applies to obligations that have a fixed maturity date not more than 1 year from the date of issue. Acquisition discount is the stated redemption price at maturity minus your basis in the obligation.

However, do not treat these gains as income to the extent you previously included the discount in income. See *Discount on Short-Term Obligations* in chapter 1 of Publication 550.

Short-term nongovernment obligations. Treat gains on short-term nongovernment obligations as ordinary income up to your ratable share of original issue discount (OID). This treatment applies to obligations that have a fixed maturity date of not more than 1 year from the date of issue.

However, to the extent you previously included the discount in income, you do not have to include it in income again. See *Discount on Short-Term Obligations* in chapter 1 of Publication 550.

Tax-exempt state and local government bonds. If these bonds were originally issued at a discount before September 4, 1982, or you acquired them before March 2, 1984, treat your part of the OID as tax-exempt interest. To figure your gain or loss on the sale or trade of these bonds, reduce the amount realized by your part of the OID.

If the bonds were issued after September 3, 1982, and acquired after March 1, 1984, increase the adjusted basis by your part of the OID to figure gain or loss. For more information on the basis of these bonds, see *Discounted Debt Instruments* in chapter 4 of Publication 550.

Example

On March 1, 1992, Kathy bought a $10,000 tax-exempt state government bond for $9,000 that was originally issued at $8,500 on September 3, 1989. Kathy must treat her part of the original issue discount (OID) as tax-exempt interest. The accumulated OID from the date of issue to the date Kathy purchased the bond was $600. On August 15, 2005, Kathy sold the bond for $9,800. Kathy must report a $100 capital gain on the sale. The market discount in the bond is the original issue price ($8,500) plus the accumulated OID from the date of issue that represented interest to any earlier holders ($600) and minus the price Kathy paid for the bond ($9,000). As a result, the market discount is $100 ($9,100 – $9,000) The remaining difference of $700 ($9,800 – $9,100) is treated as tax-exempt interest.

Any gain from market discount is usually taxable on disposition or redemption of tax-exempt bonds. If you bought the bonds before May 1, 1993, the gain from market discount is capital gain. If you bought the bonds after April 30, 1993, the gain is ordinary income.

You figure the market discount by subtracting the price you paid for the bond from the sum of the original issue price of the bond and the amount of accumulated OID from the date of issue that represented interest to any earlier holders. For more information, see *Market Discount Bonds* in chapter 1 of Publication 550.

A loss on the sale or other disposition of a tax-exempt state or local government bond is deductible as a capital loss.

Explanation

You must accrue OID on tax-exempt state and local government bonds issued after September 3, 1982, and acquired after March 1, 1984. Your adjusted basis at the time of disposition is figured by adding accrued OID to your basis. You must accrue OID on tax-exempt obligations under the same method used for OID on corporate obligations issued after July 1, 1982.

Example

On March 2, 1992, Julie bought a $10,000 tax-exempt state government bond for $9,100 that was originally issued at $8,500 on September 4, 1989. On August 15, 2005, Julie sold the bond for $9,800. Julie previously accrued $500 of OID tax-exempt interest over the period she held the bond. Julie must report a $200 capital gain on the sale of the bond [$9,800 − ($9,100 + $500)].

Redeemed before maturity. If a state or local bond that was issued before June 9, 1980, is redeemed before it matures, the OID is not taxable to you.

If a state or local bond issued after June 8, 1980, is redeemed before it matures, the part of the OID that is earned while you hold the bond is not taxable to you. However, you must report the unearned part of the OID as a capital gain.

Example. On July 1, 1994, the date of issue, you bought a 20-year, 6% municipal bond for $800. The face amount of the bond was $1,000. The $200 discount was OID. At the time the bond was issued, the issuer had no intention of redeeming it before it matured. The bond was callable at its face amount beginning 10 years after the issue date.

The issuer redeemed the bond at the end of 11 years (July 1, 2005) for its face amount of $1,000 plus accrued annual interest of $60. The OID earned during the time you held the bond, $73, is not taxable. The $60 accrued annual interest also is not taxable. However, you must report the unearned part of the OID ($127) as a capital gain.

Long-term debt instruments issued after 1954 and before May 28, 1969 (or before July 2, 1982, if a government instrument). If you sell, trade, or redeem for a gain one of these debt instruments, the part of your gain that is not more than your ratable share of the OID at the time of the sale or redemption is ordinary income. The rest of the gain is capital gain. If, however, there was an intention to call the debt instrument before maturity, all of your gain that is not more than the entire OID is treated as ordinary income at the time of the sale. This treatment of taxable gain also applies to corporate instruments issued after May 27, 1969, under a written commitment that was binding on May 27, 1969, and at all times thereafter.

Long-term debt instruments issued after May 27, 1969 (or after July 1, 1982, if a government instrument). If you hold one of these debt instruments, you must include a part of the OID in your gross income each year that you own the instrument. Your basis in that debt instrument is increased by the amount of OID that you have included in your gross income. See *Original Issue Discount (OID)* in chapter 8 for information about the OID that you must report on your tax return.

If you sell or trade the debt instrument before maturity, your gain is a capital gain. However, if at the time the instrument was originally issued there was an intention to call it before its maturity, your gain generally is ordinary income to the extent of the entire OID reduced by any amounts of OID previously includible in your income. In this case, the rest of the gain is a capital gain.

Market discount bonds. If the debt instrument has market discount and you chose to include the discount in income as it accrued, increase your basis in the debt instrument by the accrued discount to figure capital gain or loss on its disposition. If you did not choose to include the discount in income as it accrued, you must report gain as ordinary interest income up to the instrument's accrued market discount. The rest of the gain is capital gain. See *Market Discount Bonds* in chapter 1 of Publication 550.

A different rule applies to market discount bonds issued before July 19, 1984, and purchased by you before May 1, 1993. See *Market discount bonds* under *Discounted Debt Instruments* in chapter 4 of Publication 550.

Retirement of debt instrument. Any amount that you receive on the retirement of a debt instrument is treated in the same way as if you had sold or traded that instrument.

Notes of individuals. If you hold an obligation of an individual that was issued with OID after March 1, 1984, you generally must include the OID in your income currently, and your gain or loss on its sale or retirement is generally capital gain or loss. An exception to this treatment applies if the obligation is a loan between individuals and all of the following requirements are met.

1. The lender is not in the business of lending money.
2. The amount of the loan, plus the amount of any outstanding prior loans, is $10,000 or less.
3. Avoiding federal tax is not one of the principal purposes of the loan.

If the exception applies, or the obligation was issued before March 2, 1984, you do not include the OID in your income currently. When you sell or redeem the obligation, the part of your gain that is not more than your accrued share of the OID at that time is ordinary income. The rest of the gain, if any, is capital gain. Any loss on the sale or redemption is capital loss.

Explanation

There are other kinds of sales or trades that many individuals enter into. Some of these transactions—short sales, put options, wash sales—are discussed below. The tax rules are very complicated. Professional advice should be obtained if you plan to invest in any of these transactions.

Short sales. A short sale occurs when the seller borrows the property delivered to the buyer and, at a later date, either buys substantially identical property and delivers it to the lender or makes delivery out of such property held by the seller at the time of the sale. The holding period on a short sale is usually determined by the length of time the seller actually holds the property that is eventually delivered to the lender to close the short sale.

Example

Even though you do not own any stock in the Ace Corporation, you contract to sell 100 shares of it, which you borrow from your broker. After 13 months, when the price of the stock has fallen, you buy 100 shares of Ace Corporation stock and immediately deliver them to your broker to close out the short sale. Your gain is treated as a short-term capital gain because your holding period for the delivered property is less than 1 day.

Explanation

Long and short positions. If you have held substantially identical property to the property sold short for 1 year or less on the date of the short sale, the following two rules apply:

1. Any gain on closing a short sale is a short-term gain.
2. The holding period of the substantially identical property begins on the date of the closing of the short sale or on the date of the sale, gift, or other disposition of this property, whichever comes first.

These two rules also apply if you acquire substantially identical property after the originating short sale and before the closing of the short sale.

Example

On February 6, 2004, you bought 100 shares of Able Corporation stock for $1,000. On July 6, 2004, you sold short 100 shares of similar Able stock for $1,600. On November 6, 2004, you purchased 100 more shares of Able stock for $1,800 and used them to close the short sale. On this short sale, you realized a $200 short-term capital loss.

On February 7, 2005, you sold for $1,800 the stock originally bought on February 6, 2004. Although you have actually held this stock for more than 1 year, by using rule 2, the holding period is treated as having begun on November 6, 2004, the date of the closing of the short sale. The $800 gain realized on the sale is therefore a short-term capital gain.

TaxAlert

Short sales take away the tax benefits of long-term holding periods with respect to any substantially identical stock held in a long position, unless you have already met the long-term holding requirement at the time you make the short sale.

Treatment of losses. If, on the date of a short sale of a capital asset, you have held substantially identical property for more than 1 year, any loss you have on the short sale is treated as a long-term capital loss, even though the property used to close the sale was held for 1 year or less.

TaxOrganizer

You should keep a copy of your broker confirmation statement for the purchase of any securities or options. Also, keep a copy of the Form 1099-B provided by your broker for any sales of securities or options.

TaxPlanner

Short sales against the box. Selling short against the box means that you are selling borrowed securities while owning substantially identical securities that you later deliver to close the short sale.

You will generally be required to recognize gain (but not loss) of any appreciated position in stock, a partnership interest, or certain debt instruments that has the effect of eliminating your risk of loss and upside gain potential. You will be treated as making a constructive sale of an appreciated position when you do one of the following: (1) enter into a short sale of the same or substantially identical property; (2) enter into an offsetting contract with respect to the same or substantially identical property (an equity swap, for example); or (3) enter into a futures or forward contract to deliver the same or substantially identical property. In addition, future Treasury regulations are expected to expand these rules to other transactions that have substantially the same effects as the ones described in the Internal Revenue Code.

Exceptions

Certain exceptions apply to these rules. One of the most important is that short sales against the box are effective for tax purposes, so long as the following requirements are met:

1. The transaction is closed within 30 days of the close of the taxable year; and
2. You hold the appreciated financial position throughout the 60-day period beginning on the date such transaction is closed, and you do not enter into certain positions that would diminish the risk of loss during that time.

TaxPlanner

Purchasing put options. Acquiring a put option means that you are buying an option contract to sell 100 shares of stock at a set price during a specific time period. Investors who own appreciated securities that they are not yet ready to sell because of tax reasons often buy put options as a way of protecting their securities against possible price declines.

If the stock price subsequently increases, you obtain the benefit of the price increase less the cost of the put, which expires as worthless. If the stock price declines, however, you may either sell your shares at the put option price or sell the put option separately.

Example

Jim Smith purchased 100 shares of XYZ stock in July 2004 at $25 per share. The selling price in November 2004 was $55. Jim could have sold his shares in November and realized a $30 per-share gain, but it would have been taxed in 2004. Since Jim believed that the stock still had some upward potential and also wanted to postpone recognizing the gain, he bought a put option with an expiration date in March 2005, giving him the right to sell his stock at $55 per share. He locked in his gain and limited his loss to the cost of the put option.

Tax treatment of put options

1. If you sell the put—in lieu of exercising it—the gain or loss is a short-term or long-term capital gain or loss, depending on how long the put has been held.
2. If you neither sell nor exercise the put, the expiration is treated as a sale or an exchange of the put on the expiration date. Whether the loss you incur is a short-term or long-term capital loss depends on how long the put has been held.
3. If you exercise the put, its cost increases your basis in the underlying securities and thus is included in computing your gain or loss at the time of the securities' sale. Whether the gain or loss is short-term or long-term usually depends on the holding period of the underlying stock at the time the put option was acquired.

TaxPlanner

Stock index options. Unlike a put option, which is based on shares in a specific company, a stock index option represents a group of stocks. For example, an index option is available that is keyed to Standard & Poor's 500 stock averages. Investors use stock index options to reduce portfolio exposure to general market or industry fluctuations and to improve their return on investment. Stock index options may also be used to protect current paper gains (gains you have on paper but have not yet realized) and to save taxes when a taxpayer owns appreciated stock that has not been held long enough to qualify for long-term capital gain treatment.

If you expect the stock market to go down, you might purchase stock index put options. If the market does go down, the put options gain in value, perhaps offsetting the loss in any appreciated stock you might hold.

TaxPlanner

Writing covered call options. If you have stock that has appreciated in value but want (1) to defer the gain until the following year and (2) to provide yourself with protection from market declines, consider writing a covered call option with an expiration date next year. A covered call is the selling of an option to purchase shares that you own at a specified price within a set time frame. If the purchaser of the call doesn't exercise it until next year (or lets it lapse), both the amount you receive from selling the call and the proceeds from disposition of the stock are not reported until the following year.

One disadvantage is that you give up the opportunity to benefit from a price increase in the stock you own above the option exercise price.

Example

Bill purchased 100 shares of XYZ stock for $20 per share on December 21, 2003. On December 22, 2004, the stock was selling for $50 per share, but Bill wanted to defer the gain until 2005 and protect himself against a market decline. Bill wrote a covered call option, agreeing to sell his 100 shares for $50 per share at any time within the next 3 months. He received $3 per share for selling this call option. Bill has acquired protection against a market decline because he now has $3 per share in the bank. If the person who bought the option does not exercise it, Bill reports the $3 per share as a short-term capital gain in 2005. If the option is exercised, the $3 per share is added to the $50 per-share exercise price.

If the stock had continued to appreciate, Bill could have bought other shares of the stock in the open market to deliver against the call, or he could have chosen to purchase, or buy back, the option. A short-term loss would have been realized when the option position was closed in either of these two ways.

Explanation

Wash sales. Losses from wash sales or exchanges of stocks or securities are not deductible. However, the gain from these sales is taxable. Commodity futures contracts are not stock or securities and are not covered by the wash sale rule. Any position of a straddle acquired after June 23, 1981, however, is covered by the wash sale rule. This includes futures contracts. See Publication 550, *Investment Income and Expenses.*

A wash sale occurs when you sell stock or securities, and, within 30 days before or after the sale, you buy, acquire in a taxable exchange, or acquire a contract or option to buy substantially identical stock. The substantially identical stock may be acquired by subscription for newly issued stock as well as by buying old stock. However, the unallowable loss is added to the basis of the newly acquired stock or security.

Example

You buy 100 shares of X stock for $1,000. At a later date, you sell these shares for $750. Then, within 30 days of the sale, you acquire 100 shares of the same stock for $800. Your loss of $250 on the sale is not deductible. However, the disallowed loss ($250) is added to the cost of the new stock ($800) to get the basis of the new stock ($1,050).

Explanation

For purposes of the wash sale rule, a short sale is considered complete on the date the short sale is entered into if on that date:

1. You own (or, on or before that date, you enter into a contract or option to acquire) stock or securities identical to those sold short, and
2. You later deliver such stock or securities to close the short sale.

Otherwise, a short sale is not considered complete until the property is delivered to close the sale.

Example

On June 3, you buy 100 shares of stock for $1,000. You sell short 100 shares of the stock for $750 on October 7. On October 8, you buy 100 shares of the same stock for $750. You close the short sale on November 18 by delivering the shares bought on June 3. The $250 loss ($1,000 − $750) is not deductible because the date of entering into the short sale (October 7) is deemed to be the date of sale for wash sale purposes and substantially identical stock was purchased within 30 days from the date of the sale. Therefore, the wash sale rule applies, and the loss is not deductible.

Explanation

Options. Gain or loss from the sale or exchange of a purchased option to buy or sell property that is a capital asset in your hands, or would be if you acquired it, is a capital gain or loss.

If you do not exercise an option to buy or sell, and you have a loss, the option is treated as having been sold or exchanged on the date that it expired.

The capital asset treatment does not apply

1. To a gain from the sale or exchange of an option, if the gain from the sale of the property underlying the option would be ordinary income, or
2. To a dealer in options, if the option is part of inventory, or
3. To a loss from failure to exercise a fixed-price option acquired on the same day the property identified in the option was acquired; such loss is not deductible.

If you grant an option on stocks, securities, commodities, or commodity futures and it is not exercised, the amount you receive (if you are not in the business of granting options) is treated as a short-term capital gain reportable on Schedule D (Form 1040), regardless of the classification of the property in your hands. If the option is exercised, you add the option payment to other amounts you receive to figure the amount you realize on the sale of the property. The classification of your gain or loss is then determined by the type of property you sold.

Your holding period for property acquired under an option to purchase begins on the day after the property was acquired, not the day after the option was acquired.

Commodity futures. A commodity future is a contract for the sale or purchase of some fixed amount of a commodity at a future date for a fixed price. The contracts are treated as either (1) hedges to ensure against unfavorable price changes in a commodity bought or sold in the course of business or (2) capital investments.

Gains and losses on hedging contracts for a commodity purchased in the ordinary course of a trade or a business to ensure the price of, and an adequate supply of, the commodity for use in the business are treated as ordinary business gains and losses.

Straddles. A straddle is a position that offsets an interest an investor has in personal property other than stock. It may take the form of a futures contract, an option, or cash. The purpose of a straddle is to reduce an individual's risk of property loss.

Example

Karen bought an option to have 5,000 bushels of wheat delivered to her in June 2005. At the same time, she bought an option to deliver 5,000 bushels of wheat in July 2005. Karen has a straddle.

Explanation

The treatment of straddles is designed to prevent the deferral of income and the conversion of ordinary income to capital gains.

Example 1

ABC stock is selling at $30. Peter purchases two options on ABC. He purchases a call to buy 100 shares of the stock for $25 per share and a put to sell 100 shares of the stock for $35 per share. As long as the stock does not stay at $30, one of the options will produce a gain and the other one will produce a loss.

Assume that by the end of the year the price of ABC is $34. The value of the call should have increased by $400, and the value of the put should have declined by $400.

Peter cannot recognize the loss on the put until he recognizes the offsetting gain on the call.

Example 2

James purchases 100 shares of BCD stock on August 2, 2004, at $40 per share. On November 1, the BCD sells at $46 per share. James sells a call due in February 2005 for $100. In December, the stock is selling for $50, and James repurchases the call for $400. James has a $300 short-term loss, which he cannot yet deduct. When he sells BCD in the following year, he could have a long-term gain. The loss cannot be deducted until the year in which the call is closed. The holding period of BCD stock is also changed. If James sells BCD in February 2005 for $50 per share, he would have a short-term gain of $700 to report (the $1,000 gain on the stock minus the $300 loss on the call).

Note: There are many special terms, rules, and exceptions to learn if you want to try your luck on these investment strategies. You should study the markets and the tax law very carefully.

TAXPLANNER

Specific types of capital gains can be treated as ordinary income for certain additional financial transactions and certain gains from the sale of a conversion transaction can be treated as ordinary income.

A conversion transaction occurs when substantially all of the expected return from an investment is attributable to the time value of the net investment. In addition, if the transaction falls within one of the following classifications, it will be considered a conversion transaction:

1. Acquiring property and, on a contemporaneous basis, contracting to sell the same property for a determined price
2. Certain straddles
3. Any transaction that is marketed as or sold as producing capital gains
4. Other transactions that the U.S. Treasury Department will describe in future regulations

A special rule exempts options dealers and commodities traders from the above provisions, but anti-abuse rules prevent limited partners or entrepreneurs from unduly profiting by this exception.

The amount of gain that can be considered ordinary income will not exceed the amount of interest that would have accrued on your net investment in the property at a rate equal to 120% of the applicable federal rate for the period of time you held the investment. This amount is then reduced by the amount of ordinary income that was recognized from the conversion transaction and any interest expense in connection with purchasing the property.

Example

Suzanne acquires stock for $10,000 on January 1, 2003, and on that same day agrees to sell it to Rick for $11,500 on January 1, 2005. Assume that the applicable federal rate is 5%. On January 1, 2005, Suzanne delivers the stock to Rick in exchange for $11,500.

This arrangement is a conversion transaction. Thus, $1,236 of Suzanne's gain is ordinary income (120% of 5% compounded for 2 years, applied to an investment of $10,000).

Computation of ordinary gain	
Investment	$10,000
Applicable rate (120% × 5%)	6%
	600
Investment	10,000
Amount after first year	10,600
Applicable rate (120% × 5%)	6%
	636
Amount after first year	10,600
	11,236
Investment	(10,000)
Ordinary income	$1,236

The difference between the ordinary income and the appreciation, $264 ($1,500 − $1,236), is classified as a long-term capital gain.

Additional requirements are imposed on conversion transactions with respect to built-in losses, options dealers, commodities traders, and limited partners and limited entrepreneurs in an entity that deals in options or trades in commodities.

Because the application of these rules is complex, you should consult your tax advisor when considering a potential conversion transaction.

Sale of business. The sale of a business is not usually the sale of one asset. If you sell your business or your interest in a business and need more information, see Publication 544, *Sales and Other Dispositions of Assets*.

Canceling a sale of real property. If you sell real property to an individual and the sales contract gives the buyer the right to return the property to you for the amount paid, you may not have to recognize gain or loss on the sale. You will not recognize gain or loss if the property is returned to you within the same tax year as the sale. However, if the property is returned to you in a future tax year, you must recognize gain or loss in the year of the sale. In the year in which the property is returned to you, your new basis in the property will be equal to the amount of cash, notes, on other property you give back to the buyer.

Lease canceled or sold. If a tenant receives payments for the cancellation of a lease on property used as the tenant's home, a gain is taxed as a capital gain, but any loss is not deductible. If the lease was used in the tenant's trade or business, gain or loss may be capital or ordinary, as explained in Publication 544, *Sales and Other Dispositions of Assets*.

Payments received by a landlord. If a landlord receives payments for cancellation of a lease, they are ordinary income and not capital gains.

Subleases. When you transfer leased property under an arrangement in which the new occupant takes over your monthly lease payments and also pays you an amount each month for relinquishing use of the property, a sublease has been entered into and payments you receive are ordinary income.

Repossession of real property. If real property that is a capital asset in your hands is repossessed by the seller under the terms of the sales contract or by foreclosure of a mortgage, you may have a capital gain or loss. The gain or loss is the difference between your adjusted basis in the property (purchase price with adjustments) and the full amount of your obligation cancelled, plus any money received, in exchange for the property. Losses on repossessions of property held for personal use, however, are not deductible. See Publication 537, *Installment Sales*. Also see the discussion of installment sales in this chapter.

Subdivision of land. If you own a tract of land, and, in order to sell or exchange it, you subdivide it into individual lots or parcels, you may receive capital gains treatment on at least a part of the proceeds if you meet the following four conditions:

1. You are not a dealer in real estate.
2. You have not made any major improvement on the tract while you held it that substantially enhances the value of the lot or parcel sold, and no such improvement will be made as part of the contract of sale with the buyer. A substantial improvement is generally one that increases the value of the property by more than 10%. Some improvements that are considered substantial are structural work on commercial and residential buildings, laying down hard-surface roads, and installing utility services.
3. You have held the land for at least 5 years, unless you got it by inheritance or devise.
4. You did not previously hold the tract or any lot or parcel on such tract mainly for sale to customers in the ordinary course of your trade or business (unless the tract previously would have qualified for this treatment), and, during the same tax year in which the sale occurred, you were not holding any other land for sale to customers in the ordinary course of trade or business. This treatment also applies to S corporations.

Gain on sale of lots. If your land meets these tests, the gain realized on the sale or exchange will be treated in the following manner.

If you sell less than six lots or parcels from the same tract, the entire gain is a capital gain. In figuring the number of lots or parcels sold, two or more adjoining lots sold to a single buyer in a single sale are counted as only one parcel.

When you sell or exchange the sixth lot or parcel from the same tract, the amount by which 5% of the selling price is more than the expenses of the sale is treated as ordinary income, and the rest of any gain will be a capital gain. Five percent of the selling price of all lots sold or ex-

changed from the tract in the tax year in which the sixth lot is sold or exchanged, and in later years, is treated as ordinary income.

If you sell the first six lots of a single tract in 1 year, to the extent of gain, the lesser of 5% of the selling price of each lot sold or the gain is treated as ordinary income. On the other hand, if you sold the first three lots in a single tract in 1 year and the next three lots in the following year, the 5% rule would apply only to the gains realized in the second year.

The selling expenses of the sale must first be deducted from the part of the gain treated as ordinary income, and any remaining expenses must be deducted from the part treated as a capital gain. You may not deduct the selling expenses from other income as ordinary business expenses.

Example 1

You sold five lots from a single tract last year. This year, you sell the sixth lot for $20,000. Your basis for this lot is $10,000, and your selling expenses are $1,500. Your gain is $8,500, all of which is capital gain, figured as follows:

Selling price		$20,000
Minus:		
Basis	$10,000	
Expense of sale	1,500	11,500
Gain from sale of lot		$8,500
5% of selling price	$1,000	
Minus: Expense of sale	1,500	
Gain reported as ordinary income		–0–
Gain reported as capital gain		$8,500

Because the selling expenses are more than 5% of the selling price, none of the gain is treated as ordinary income.

Example 2

Assume in Example 1 that the selling expenses are $800. The amount of gain is $9,200, of which $200 is ordinary income and $9,000 is capital gain, figured as follows:

Selling price		$20,000
Minus:		
Basis	$10,000	
Expense of sale	800	10,800
Gain from sale of lot		$9,200
5% of selling price	$1,000	
Minus: Expense of sale	800	
Gain reported as ordinary income		200
Gain reported as capital gain		$9,000

Explanation

Loss on sale of lots. The 5% rule does not apply to losses. If you sell a lot at a loss, it will be treated as a capital loss if you held it for investment.

For more information on subdivision of land, see Publication 544, *Sales and Other Dispositions of Assets*.

Inventions. An invention is usually a capital asset in the hands of the inventor, whether on not a patent has been applied for or has been obtained. The inventor is the individual whose efforts created the property and who qualifies as the original and first inventor or joint inventor.

If you are an inventor and transfer all substantial rights

to patent property, you may get special tax treatment, as described below, if the transfer is not to your employer or to a related person.

If, for a consideration paid to the inventor, you acquire all the substantial rights to patent property before the invention is reduced to practice (tested and operated successfully under operating conditions), you may, when you dispose of your interest, get special tax treatment, if you are not the employer of the inventor or related to the inventor (as described later). However, if you buy patent property after it is reduced to practice, it may be treated as either a capital or a noncapital asset, depending on the circumstances.

Special tax treatment. If you are the inventor or an individual who acquired all the substantial rights to the patent property before the invention was reduced to practice, and you transfer all the substantial rights or an undivided interest in all such rights, the transfer will be treated as a sale or an exchange of a long-term capital asset. This rule applies even if you have not held the patent property for more than 1 year and whether or not the payments received are made periodically during the transferee's use of the patent or are contingent on the productivity, use, or disposition of the property transferred.

Courts have enforced the substantial rights requirement very strictly. Generally, a patent seller must be able to show that any rights he or she retains are insubstantial in order to treat the sale of rights in the patent property as a long-term capital gain.

The U.S. Courts of Appeals for the Sixth, Seventh, and Ninth Circuits have overturned lower court rulings that allowed patent owners transferring exclusive rights to impose geographical limitations within the United States on the person purchasing the patent. However, the official IRS position is that a transfer of all substantial rights may be limited to one or more countries.

Payment for the patent may be received by the seller in a lump sum, as an installment sale, as a fixed percentage of all future profits from the patent, or as a fee per item produced. All these methods qualify for capital gains treatment, even if the total amount of payment is uncertain.

Transfers between related parties. The special tax treatment does not apply if the transfer is either directly or indirectly between you and certain related parties.

Copyrights. Literary, musical, or artistic compositions, or similar property, are not treated as capital assets if your personal efforts created them or if you got the property in such a way that all or part of your basis in the property is determined by reference to a person whose personal efforts created the property (e.g., if you got the property as a gift). The sale of such property, whether or not it is copyrighted, results in ordinary income.

However, if you get such property, or a copyright to it, in any other way, the amounts you got for granting the exclusive use or right to exploit the work throughout the life of the copyright are treated as being received from the sale of property. It does not matter if the payment is a fixed amount or a percentage of receipts from the sale, performance, exhibition, or publication of the copyright work, on an amount based on the number of copies sold, performances given, or exhibitions made. It also does not matter if the payment is made over the same period as that covering the grantee's use of the copyrighted work.

Deposit in Insolvent or Bankrupt Financial Institution

If you lose money you have on deposit in a qualified financial institution that becomes insolvent or bankrupt, you may be able to deduct your loss in one of three ways.

1. Ordinary loss,
2. Casualty loss, or
3. Nonbusiness bad debt (short-term capital loss).

Ordinary loss or casualty loss. If you can reasonably estimate your loss, you can choose to treat the estimated loss as either an ordinary loss or a casualty loss in the current year. Either way, you claim the loss as an itemized deduction.

If you claim an ordinary loss, report it as a miscellaneous itemized deduction on Schedule A (Form 1040), line 22. The maximum amount you can claim is $20,000 ($10,000 if you are married filing separately) reduced by any expected state insurance proceeds. Your loss is subject to the 2%-of-adjusted-gross-income limit. You cannot choose to claim an ordinary loss if any part of the deposit is federally insured.

If you claim a casualty loss, attach Form 4684, Casualties and Thefts, to your return. Each loss must be reduced by $100. Your total casualty losses for the year are reduced by 10% of your adjusted gross income.

You cannot choose either of these methods if:

1. You own at least 1% of the financial institution,
2. You are an officer of the institution, or
3. You are related to such an owner or officer. You are related if you and the owner or officer are "related parties," as defined earlier under *Related Party Transactions*, or if you are the aunt, uncle, nephew, or niece of the owner or officer.

If the actual loss that is finally determined is more than the amount you deducted as an estimated loss, you can claim the excess loss as a bad debt. If the actual loss is less than the amount deducted as an estimated loss, you must include in income (in the final determination year) the excess loss claimed. See *Recoveries* in Publication 525, Taxable and Nontaxable Income.

TAXPLANNER

Whether you elect to claim a casualty or an ordinary loss in the year in which the requirements for the election are met will depend on a number of factors. First, you must compare the available **casualty loss deduction** (after reducing your loss by $100 plus 10% of your adjusted gross income) to your **ordinary loss deduction** (after adding the loss to other miscellaneous itemized deductions and reducing the total by 2% of adjusted gross income). The ordinary loss election is available on deposits of up to $20,000 ($10,000 if you are married and file a separate return), which are not federally insured. The $20,000 limitation applies to each financial institution, not each deposit or each tax year. This is important if you hold deposits in more than one institution.

The election to claim an ordinary loss, once made, cannot be revoked unless you obtain the consent of the IRS.

You should also consider whether it is better to forgo either election and claim the entire amount as a **capital loss** from a nonbusiness bad debt (see *Nonbusiness Bad Debts*, following). This might be advisable if you have sufficient capital gain income with which to offset the capital loss. Consult with your financial advisor when considering these elections.

Example

Judy Porter estimates that she has incurred a total loss of her $30,000 bank account with an insolvent financial institution. Her account is not federally insured. Judy's adjusted gross income (AGI) is $70,000, and she has no miscellaneous itemized deductions. Judy wants to review the tax consequences of electing to claim the estimated loss as either a casualty loss or an ordinary loss, which is treated as a miscellaneous itemized deduction.

The net deduction available under each method is as follows:

	Casualty loss	Ordinary loss
Estimated loss	$30,000	$20,000*
$100 casualty loss limitation	(100)	n/a
10% AGI limitation	(7,000)	n/a
2% AGI limitation	n/a	(1,400)
Net deduction available	$22,900	$18,600

* Limited to $20,000 per institution.

In addition, if the loss actually sustained by Judy exceeds the amount deducted as an estimated loss, she can claim the excess loss as a bad debt in the year in which that loss is finally determined. Thus, if Judy elects to treat the estimated loss as an ordinary loss and she determines in a subsequent year that her entire balance of $30,000 was lost, she could claim an additional $10,000 deduction for bad debts. This would increase her cumulative deductions under this alternative to a total amount of $28,600.

TaxORGANIZER

You should obtain information and documentation to substantiate when a debt or deposit becomes worthless. The following items are examples of documentation supporting the worthlessness of debts and deposits: bankruptcy filings, news reports, and financial statements.

Nonbusiness bad debt. If you choose to treat the loss as a bad debt, see *How to report bad debts*, later.

Sale of Annuity

The part of any gain on the sale of an annuity contract before its maturity date that is based on interest accumulated on the contract is ordinary income.

Losses on Section 1244 (Small Business) Stock

You can deduct as an ordinary loss, rather than as a capital loss, your loss on the sale, trade, or worthlessness of section 1244 stock. Report the loss on Form 4797, line 10.

Any gain on this stock is capital gain and is reported on Schedule D (Form 1040) if the stock is a capital asset in your hands. See *Losses on Section 1244 (Small Business) Stock* in chapter 4 of Publication 550.

Losses on Small Business Investment Company Stock

See *Losses on Small Business Investment Company Stock* in chapter 4 of Publication 550.

Explanation

While individuals who own certain stock in a small business investment company may be allowed to deduct as an ordinary loss a loss on the sale, exchange, or worthlessness of their stock, the amount that may be claimed is subject to an annual limit of $50,000 ($100,000 on **joint returns**) per taxpayer.

Ordinary loss treatment is generally available only to the original owner. If you obtain stock in a small business corporation or investment company through purchase, gift, inheritance, or the like, you may not claim ordinary losses. Similarly, if small business stock is owned through a partnership, to claim a loss, you must have been a partner when the stock was issued. If you were not a partner at such time and the partnership later distributed the stock to the partners, you may not take an ordinary loss deduction.

To qualify for ordinary loss treatment, you must own Section 1244 stock. This is the stock of a small business corporation or investment company with total capital of under $1 million that meets a *passive income test*. To meet this test, the aggregate of any gross receipts generated over the last 5 years by royalties, rents, dividends, interest, annuities, and sales of stock or securities must be less than 50% of total gross receipts taken in by the corporation in the 5-year period. In addition, the corporation's stock must have been issued for money or property other than securities. Stock that is convertible into other securities of the corporation is not treated as Section 1244 stock.

TaxPLANNER

The loss limitation of $50,000 per taxpayer is an annual limitation. Therefore, if you are considering a sale of Section 1244 stock that is expected to produce a loss of over $50,000, you should consider structuring the transaction so that stock sales will take place in more than 1 year.

Example

Craig, a bachelor, has owned 10,000 shares of qualified small business stock for several years. The stock has a basis of $150,000. He plans to dispose of the stock but expects to realize only $50,000 on the sale. If he sells all 10,000 shares in 2005, he will recognize a $100,000 loss in 1 year. Only $50,000 will be deductible as an ordinary loss. The other $50,000 will be treated as a long-term capital loss. The long-term capital loss can be offset against other capital gains, but the excess can be deducted at the rate of only $3,000 per year.

If Craig sells 5,000 shares in 2005 and 5,000 shares in 2006 and receives the same price, he will still have a total loss of $100,000. Yet, because $50,000 of the loss will be recognized in 2005 and the other $50,000 in 2006, Craig may treat both losses as ordinary losses, which makes the total $100,000 loss fully deductible.

Craig should use Form 4797 to report the Section 1244 loss as a sale of a noncapital asset.

Holding Period

If you sold or traded investment property, you must determine your holding period for the property. Your holding period determines whether any capital gain or loss was a short-term or long-term capital gain or loss.

Long term or short term. If you hold investment property more than 1 year, any capital gain or loss is a long-term capital gain or loss. If you hold the property 1 year or less, any capital gain or loss is a short-term capital gain or loss.

To determine how long you held the investment property, begin counting on the date after the day you acquired the property. The day you disposed of the property is part of your holding period.

Example. If you bought investment property on February 5, 2004, and sold it on February 5, 2005, your holding period is not more than 1 year and you have a short-term capital gain or loss. If you sold it on February 6, 2005, your holding period is more than 1 year and you will have a long-term capital gain or loss.

Securities traded on established market. For securities traded on an established securities market, your holding period begins the day after the trade date you bought the securities, and ends on the trade date you sold them.

Caution. *Do not confuse the trade date with the settlement date, which is the date by which the stock must be delivered and payment must be made.*

Example. You are a cash method, calendar year taxpayer. You sold stock at a gain on December 29, 2005. According to the rules of the stock exchange, the sale was closed by delivery of the stock 3 trading days after the sale, on January 3, 2006. You received payment of the sales price on that same day. Report your gain on your 2005 return, even though you received the payment in 2006. The gain is long term or short term depending on whether you held the stock more than 1 year. Your holding period ended on December 29. If you had sold the stock at a loss, you would also report it on your 2005 return.

Automatic investment service. In determining your holding period for shares bought by the bank or other agent, full shares are considered bought first and any fractional shares are considered bought last. Your holding period starts on the day after the bank's purchase date. If a share was bought over more than one purchase date, your holding period for that share is a split holding period. A part of the share is considered to have been bought on each date that stock was bought by the bank with the proceeds of available funds.

Nontaxable trades. If you acquire investment property in a trade for other investment property and your basis for the new property is determined, in whole or in part, by your basis in the old property, your holding period for the new property begins on the day following the date you acquired the old property.

Property received as a gift. If you receive a gift of property and your basis is determined by the donor's adjusted basis, your holding period is considered to have started on the same day the donor's holding period started.

If your basis is determined by the fair market value of the property, your holding period starts on the day after the date of the gift.

Inherited property. If you inherit investment property, your capital gain or loss on any later disposition of that property is treated as a long-term capital gain or loss. This is true regardless of how long you actually held the property.

Real property bought. To figure how long you have held real property bought under an unconditional contract, begin counting on the day after you received title to it or on the day after you took possession of it and assumed the burdens and privileges of ownership, whichever

happened first. However, taking delivery or possession of real property under an option agreement is not enough to start the holding period. The holding period cannot start until there is an actual contract of sale. The holding period of the seller cannot end before that time.

Stock dividends. The holding period for stock you received as a taxable stock dividend begins on the date of distribution.

The holding period for new stock you received as a nontaxable stock dividend begins on the same day as the holding period of the old stock. This rule also applies to stock acquired in a "spin-off," which is a distribution of stock or securities in a controlled corporation.

Nontaxable stock rights. Your holding period for nontaxable stock rights begins on the same day as the holding period of the underlying stock. The holding period for stock acquired through the exercise of stock rights begins on the date the right was exercised.

Nonbusiness Bad Debts

If someone owes you money that you cannot collect, you have a bad debt. You may be able to deduct the amount owed to you when you figure your tax for the year the debt becomes worthless.

Bad debts that did not come from operating your trade or business are nonbusiness bad debts and are deductible as short-term capital losses. To be deductible, nonbusiness bad debts must be totally worthless. You cannot deduct a partly worthless nonbusiness debt.

Because, in many cases, it may be difficult to determine when a debt loses its value, you should claim a deduction at the earliest time you reasonably believe the debt to be worthless. If you discover you have overlooked a bad debt deduction that you should have taken, amend your return for that year. The statute of limitations for bad debts generally runs 7 years from the due date of the tax return filed for the year in which the debt became worthless.

TaxPlanner

A debt becomes worthless when a prudent person would abandon the effort to collect the debt. This may mean that you expended a lot of effort trying to collect or that you didn't try at all. You have the burden of proving that the debt is worthless.

In most circumstances, it is wise to obtain the opinion of an attorney about whether or not collection efforts are warranted. His or her opinion should be based on objective facts establishing the loss.

Whenever possible, you should also obtain copies of the debtor's financial statements. If they show a positive net worth, then, in order to establish a debt as worthless, you have to demonstrate that the **assets** are not worth what the statements claim or that another creditor has a claim on those assets that takes precedence over yours.

TaxOrganizer

You should document any steps you have taken to recover the amount owed to you. Also, you should get a copy of the debtor's financial statements to substantiate the inability to pay back the loan.

Genuine debt required. A debt must be genuine for you to deduct a loss. A debt is genuine if it arises from a debtor-creditor relationship based on a valid and enforceable obligation to repay a fixed or determinable sum of money.

Basis in bad debt required. To deduct a bad debt, you must have a basis in it—that is, you must have already included the amount in your income or loaned out your cash. For example, you cannot claim a bad debt deduction for court-ordered child support not paid to you by your former spouse. If you are a cash method taxpayer (as most individuals are), you generally cannot take a bad debt deduction for unpaid salaries, wages, rents, fees, interest, dividends, and similar items.

Explanation

The distinction between business and nonbusiness bad debts is generally clear. Business bad debts usually occur because of credit transactions with customers, employees, and others closely related to a trade or a business. The dominant motive in these transactions is to support the business activity. Nonbusiness bad debts frequently arise from casual loans, such as those made to friends or acquaintances. But there is often confusion between business and nonbusiness bad debts in the following areas:

1. **You make loans frequently, but making loans is not a full-time business.** The IRS's position is that business bad debt treatment is limited to those situations in which the taxpayer derives his or her main source of income from credit transactions. Whether or not you are in a trade or business is a question of fact. The greater the regularity of the activity, however, the more likely that a trade or business exists.

Example

You occasionally lend money to individuals starting new businesses. That is an investment activity, not a trade or a business.

2. **You make a loan to a corporation in which you are an employee and a stockholder.** You are allowed a business bad debt deduction if the loan was made primarily to protect your salary. If the loan was made primarily to protect your investment, it is considered a nonbusiness loan. The larger your investment is in a company and the smaller your salary is from it, the greater the chance that a court will determine that a loan you make to the company is for nonbusiness purposes.

TaxPlanner

If you make advances to a corporation you own, the IRS may attempt to recharacterize the advances as equity capital rather than bona fide loans. This might postpone a deduction for a bad debt until the year in which your stock is wholly worthless. Therefore, it is important that you properly document advances you make to the corporation as bona fide loans. Generally, written, interest-bearing instruments with fixed repayment terms will qualify as bona fide debt.

TaxPlanner

If you want a loan to a family member to be considered a bona fide debt, you should document the transaction so that it is clear that both parties expect and intend repayment of the loan.

A child may borrow money from his or her parents for a business venture. To indicate that the borrowed money is not intended as a gift, the parents should draft a note saying who owes whom money. (The parties might check with a lawyer about the exact form the note should take.) If the note calls for partial payments of the debt, each payment should be made on time. This provides evidence that a legitimate creditor-debtor relationship exists. To further support their status as creditors, parents may consider investigating the business in which the child is investing the borrowed money. An arm's-length lender typically makes such an investigation.

It's also a good idea for the note from the parents to provide that the money be repaid with interest. Charging interest provides another bit of evidence that the loan between parents and child is a valid arm's-length transaction. Failure to charge adequate interest can also have important gift and income tax consequences. For details, see Chapter 8, *Interest Income.*

Example 1

Gail lends her son $20,000, which the son then invests in a new business venture. Gail draws up a note that provides for a specific repayment schedule and a stated rate of interest. Collateral is also established on the note to provide Gail with some security. Later, before any payments on the note have been made, the son's business venture fails. Despite repeated efforts to collect the debt, Gail is able to recover only a small amount based on the collateral established at the time of the loan.

Gail may take a bad debt deduction of $20,000, less the amount of collateral she recovered. Gail's son may deduct his loss as a business loss.

Example 2

Assume the same facts as in Example 1 except that Gail does not document the loan. No note is drawn up, and no specific provisions are made about when her son will repay the loan. If the son's business venture fails, he may deduct his loss. The mother, however, may not take a bad debt deduction.

Explanation

Loans in your business. If you are in a business or a profession, you may have bad debts that come from loans you make to your clients. If you are not in the business of lending money and the loans have no close relationship to your business or profession, these bad debts are nonbusiness bad debts.

Mechanics' and suppliers' liens. Workers and material suppliers sometimes file liens against property because of debts owed by a builder or a contractor. If you pay off such a lien to avoid foreclosure and loss of your property, you are entitled to repayment from the builder or contractor. If the debt is uncollectible, you may take a deduction for a bad debt.

Insolvency of contractor. You can take a bad debt deduction for the amount you deposit with a contractor if the contractor becomes insolvent and you are unable to recover (collect) your deposit. If the deposit is for work that is not related to your trade or business, it is a nonbusiness bad debt deduction.

Secondary liability on home mortgage. If you sell your home and the purchaser assumes your mortgage, you may remain secondarily liable for repayment of the mortgage loan. If the purchaser defaults on the loan, you may have to make up the difference if the house is then sold for less than the amount outstanding on the mortgage. You can take a bad debt deduction for the amount you pay to satisfy the mortgage if you cannot collect it from the purchaser.

Corporate securities that become worthless are generally deductible as capital losses. This includes shares of stock, stock rights, bonds, debentures, notes, or certificates, as explained in Chapter 17, *Reporting Gains and Losses.*

TAXPLANNER

Frequently, it is difficult to establish the year in which a corporate security becomes worthless. One guide is a publication called *Capital Changes Reporter,* published by Commerce Clearing House. The section called Worthless Securities provides a current list of companies whose securities have lost their value.

It is even more difficult to determine when a closely held business becomes worthless. It is not necessary for the company to declare bankruptcy. If you are aware that a company is insolvent, you may be able to take a loss. If the business continues to operate and has more than nominal assets, however, it may be only temporarily insolvent. If that is the case, you may not be able to take a loss.

Explanation

Recovery of a bad debt. Any amount recovered for a bad debt deducted in a previous year generally must be included in your income in the year in which the amount was recovered. However, you may exclude the amount recovered up to the amount of the deduction that did not reduce your income subject to tax in the year deducted. Recovery of amounts deducted in previous years is discussed in Chapter 13, *Other Income.*

Example

In 2002, Bill had a $25,000 **long-term capital gain** and a $25,000 bad debt loss. Bill had no **taxable income** for 2002.

In 2005, Bill recovered the entire $25,000 debt. To figure how much he should include in his 2005 income, see the calculations below.

	2002 with bad debt	2002 without bad debt
Income:		
Net long-term capital gain	$25,000	$25,000
Bad debt loss	(25,000)	
Adjusted gross income	—0—	$25,000
Less:		
Standard deductions	—0—	$4,700
Personal exemption	—0—	$3,000
Taxable income	—0—	$17,300

The calculations show that Bill's 2002 taxable income was reduced by $17,300 by including the bad debt. Therefore, $17,300 is included in Bill's taxable income for 2005, the year in which he collected the $25,000 debt.

Explanation

Business bad debts. There are two crucial differences in the treatment of business bad debts and nonbusiness bad debts:

1. Business bad debts are treated as **ordinary losses,** which may be deducted directly from gross income. Nonbusiness bad debts are short-term capital losses and should be shown on Schedule D along with your short-term and long-term gains and losses from other sources. The maximum capital loss that you may use to offset your other income each year is $3,000. See Chapter 17, *Reporting Gains and Losses,* for further information.
2. A business bad debt may be just *partially* worthless and still give rise to a tax deduction. A nonbusiness bad debt has to be totally worthless.

Example

Janet Jones, an accrual basis taxpayer, performs some plumbing work for XYZ Corporation and sends them an invoice for $20,000 in 2004. In 2005, Janet learns that XYZ Corporation will not be able to pay the entire amount of the bill. She may claim a bad debt deduction for the amount of the invoice that is worthless.

Explanation

Some businesses use the **reserve method** of computing bad debt expense in keeping their books. Under this method, an estimate of accounts for services expected to be uncollectible is computed, based on prior years' experience, and the amount is placed in reserve as bad debt expense.

The reserve method is no longer allowed for tax purposes, except for certain financial institutions. Therefore, a business bad debt will be allowed only if it is **specifically charged off** the taxpayer's books during the year. Therefore, if you own a business with a large number of accounts receivable, to maximize your allowable tax deduction, you should carefully review old accounts at year-end to make sure all worthless accounts are written off.

A special rule applies to taxpayers using the accrual method of accounting for amounts to be received for the performance of services: You are not required to include in income any portion of accrued income for services performed that, on the basis of experience, will not be collected. This rule does not apply if interest is required to be paid on a receivable amount or if there is any penalty for failure to pay such amount on time.

The IRS guidelines that spell out how a taxpayer estimates uncollectible amounts for services are somewhat complex. You should consult your tax advisor if these special rules apply to your situation.

Guarantees. If you guarantee payment of another person's debt and then have to pay it off, you may be able to take a bad debt deduction for your loss. It does not matter in what capacity you make the guarantee, whether as guarantor, endorser, or indemnitor.

To qualify for a bad debt deduction, the guarantee must either be entered into with a profit motive or be related to your trade or business or employment.

A worthless debt qualifies as a *nonbusiness bad debt* if you can show that your reason for making the guarantee was to protect your investment or to make a profit. If you make the guarantee as a favor to friends and are not given anything in return, it is considered a gift and you may not take a deduction.

You are justified in taking the deduction if you can show that you *expected* to receive something in return at a future time. The expectation must be reasonable.

Example 1

A taxpayer who ran a successful car rental operation loaned money to her brother-in-law to assist him in starting his own car rental business. The taxpayer received a promissory note due 1 year after the date of the loan, with a stated rate of interest. The brother-in-law's business venture was a flop, and the taxpayer eventually took a bad debt deduction. The court allowed the deduction, pointing out that at the time the loan was made, the brother-in-law was solvent and there was a reasonable expectation that the rental business would serve as a source of repayment.

Example 2

A taxpayer loaned his brother-in-law about $2,000 over a 2-year period to help him support the taxpayer's sister and her children. During the entire period, the brother-in-law was low on cash and his business was failing. There was no record of the loan or any understanding about how it would be repaid. The court ruled that the taxpayer could not take a bad debt deduction because there was no reasonable expectation that the loan would be repaid. Instead, the court said that the $2,000 "loan" should be considered a gift.

How to report bad debts. Deduct nonbusiness bad debts as short-term capital losses on Schedule D (Form 1040).

On Schedule D, Part I, line 1, enter the name of the debtor and "statement attached" in column (a). Enter the amount of the bad debt in parentheses in column (f). Use a separate line for each bad debt.

For each bad debt, attach a statement to your return that contains:

1. A description of the debt, including the amount, and the date it became due,
2. The name of the debtor, and any business or family relationship between you and the debtor,
3. The efforts you made to collect the debt, and
4. Why you decided the debt was worthless. For example, you could show that the borrower has declared bankruptcy, or that legal action to collect would probably not result in payment of any part of the debt.

Filing a claim for refund. If you do not deduct a bad debt on your original return for the year it becomes worthless, you can file a claim for a credit or refund due to the bad debt. To do this, use Form 1040X to amend your return for the year the debt became worthless. You must file it within 7 years from the date your original return for that year had to be filed, or 2 years from the date you paid the tax, whichever is later. For more information about filing a claim, see *Amended Returns and Claims for Refund* in chapter 1.

Additional information. For more information, see *Nonbusiness Bad Debts* in Publication 550. For information on business bad debts, see chapter 11 of Publication 535, Business Expenses.

Rollover of Gain From Publicly Traded Securities

You may qualify for a tax-free rollover of certain gains from the sale of publicly traded securities. This means that if you buy certain replacement property and make the choice described in this section, you postpone part or all of your gain.

You postpone the gain by adjusting the basis of the replacement property as described in *Basis of replacement property*, later. This postpones your gain until the year you dispose of the replacement property.

You qualify to make this choice if you meet all the following tests.

1. You sell publicly traded securities at a gain. Publicly traded securities are securities traded on an established securities market.
2. Your gain from the sale is a capital gain.
3. During the 60-day period beginning on the date of the sale, you buy replacement property. This replacement property must be either common stock or a partnership interest in a specialized small business investment company (SSBIC). This is any partnership or corporation licensed by the Small Business Administration under section 301(d) of the Small Business Investment Act of 1958, as in effect on May 13, 1993.

Amount of gain recognized. If you make the choice described in this section, you must recognize gain only up to the following amount.

1. The amount realized on the sale, minus
2. The cost of any common stock or partnership interest in an SSBIC that you bought during the 60-day period beginning on the date of sale (and did not previously take into account on an earlier sale of publicly traded securities).

If this amount is less than the amount of your gain, you can postpone the rest of your gain, subject to the limit described next. If this amount is equal to or more than the amount of your gain, you must recognize the full amount of your gain.

Limit on gain postponed. The amount of gain you can postpone each year is limited to the smaller of:

1. $50,000 ($25,000 if you are married and file a separate return), or
2. $500,000 ($250,000 if you are married and file a separate return), minus the amount of gain you postponed for all earlier years.

Basis of replacement property. You must subtract the amount of postponed gain from the basis of your replacement property.

How to report and postpone gain. See chapter 4 of Publication 550 for details on how to report and postpone the gain.

16

Selling Your Home

Note: The 2004 IRS Publication 17 (Your Federal Income Tax) has been updated by Ernst & Young LLP for 2005. Dates and dollar amounts shown are for 2005. Gray type is used to indicate where IRS text has been updated or intentionally omitted. Unrevised IRS text is shown in black type.

Introduction

Your home is probably the most valuable asset you own and may increase in value. Consequently, you may have a significant gain—and lots of taxes to pay—when you sell it. Alternatively, some homes will be sold at a loss. Unfortunately, a loss on the sale of your home is generally not deductible. This chapter tells you what you should and shouldn't do when you're considering selling your home.

Your home is probably your best tax shelter. The tax system continues to give many breaks to homeowners. You may deduct the cost of real estate taxes and, subject to certain limitations, the cost of interest paid on your mortgage. (See Chapter 25, Interest Expense, for an explanation of the limitations on deducting home

mortgage interest.) You can completely exclude up to $250,000 of gain ($500,000 if you're married filing jointly) on the sale of your home. Some states continue to allow various types of residential energy conservation and solar energy tax credits against your state income tax liability. Refer to your state's tax return instruction guide to determine if such credits are available.

Any gain you are required to recognize on the sale of a home will be treated as long-term capital gain if the home was held for more than 1 year. The maximum tax rate applicable to net capital gains is 15% (and may be as low as 5%). This is significantly lower than the top tax rate applicable to ordinary income. See Capital Gain Tax Computation in Chapter 17, Reporting Gains and Losses.

What's New

Home acquired in like-kind exchange. You cannot exclude from income a gain from selling your main home after October 22, 2004, if you acquired the home in a like-kind exchange and sold it during the 5-year period beginning with the date you acquired the home. For more information, see *Special Situations*, later.

Home disposed of in like-kind exchange. If you convert your home into business or investment property and then exchange it for other business or investment real estate, you may be able to take advantage of both the $250,000 ($500,000 if you're married filing jointly) exclusion as well as the deferral of any remaining gain under the like-kind exchange rules. For more information, see *Special Situations*, later.

Reminders

Change of address. If you change your mailing address, be sure to notify the IRS using Form 8822, Change of Address. Mail it to the Internal Revenue Service Center for your old address. (Addresses for the Service Centers are on the back of the form.)

Home sold with undeducted points. If you have not deducted all the points you paid to secure a mortgage on your old home, you may be able to deduct the remaining points in the year of the sale. See *Mortgage ending early* under *Points* in chapter 25.

This chapter explains the tax rules that apply when you sell your main home. Generally, your main home is the one in which you live most of the time.

If you sold your main home in 2005, you may be able to exclude from income any gain up to a limit of $250,000 ($500,000 on a joint return in most cases). See *Excluding the Gain*, later. If you can exclude all of the gain, you do not need to report the sale on your tax return.

If you have gain that cannot be excluded, it is taxable. Report it on Schedule D (Form 1040). You may also have to include Form 4797, Sales of Business Property. See *Reporting the Sale*, later.

If you have a loss on the sale, you cannot deduct it on your return.

The main topics in this chapter are:

- Figuring gain or loss,
- Basis,
- Excluding the gain,
- Ownership and use tests, and
- Reporting the sale.

Other topics include:

- Business use or rental of home, and
- Recapturing a federal mortgage subsidy.

Useful Items

You may want to see:

Publications

- [ ] **523** Selling Your Home
- [ ] **530** Tax Information for First-Time Homeowners

Forms (and Instructions)

- [ ] **Schedule D (Form 1040)** Capital Gains and Losses
- [ ] **8822** Change of Address
- [ ] **8828** Recapture of Federal Mortgage Subsidy

Main Home

This section explains the term "main home." Usually, the home you live in most of the time is your main home and can be a:

- House,
- Houseboat,
- Mobile home,
- Cooperative apartment, or
- Condominium.

To exclude gain under the rules of this chapter, you generally must have owned and lived in the property as your main home for at least 2 years during the 5-year period ending on the date of sale.
Land. If you sell the land on which your main home is located, but not the house itself, you cannot exclude any gain you have from the sale of the land.

Example. On March 4, 2005, you sell the land on which your main home is located. You buy another piece of land and move your house to it. This sale is not considered a sale of your main home, and you cannot exclude any gain on the sale of the land.
More than one home. If you have more than one home, you can exclude gain only from the sale of your main home. You must include in income the gain from the sale of any other home. If you have two homes and live in both of them, your main home is ordinarily the one you live in most of the time.

Example 1. You own and live in a house in the city. You also own a beach house, which you use during summer months. The house in the city is your main home.

Example 2. You own a house, but you live in another house that you rent. The rented house is your main home.

Explanation

If you own more than one property, it is important to determine which is your principal, or main, residence. The IRS will not issue a ruling on whether or not a home qualifies as a principal residence. The gain on the sale of your principal residence may be excluded, but the gain on the sale of your non-principal residence or rental property is taxed in the year of the sale.

If you use more than one property as a residence, the determination of which property is your principal residence will be based on all the facts and circumstances. The IRS has said that if you alternate between two properties, the one you use for a majority of time during the year will ordinarily be considered to be your principal residence. However, regulations indicate that other factors are also relevant in determining which property is your principal residence. Those factors include:

- Where you vote,
- The address you use on your tax returns,
- The address you claim to be your residence in other financial dealings,
- Where your children go to school,
- Where you work,
- Where your car is registered,
- Where you belong to social and religious groups.

That the property is currently rented or has been rented in the past does not mean that you may not consider it to be your principal residence. For example, a property that is rented out for a brief period while you are away or while you are trying to sell it should not affect the property's status as your principal residence. In order to exclude the gain, the home's status as your principal residence at the time of sale is no longer relevant as long as it was your principal residence for 2 of the 5 years prior to the date of sale.

Property used partly as your main home. If you use only part of the property as your main home, the rules discussed in this chapter apply only to the gain or loss on the sale of that part of the property. For details, see *Business Use or Rental of Home*, later.

Figuring Gain or Loss

To figure the gain or loss on the sale of your main home, you must know the selling price, the amount realized, and the adjusted basis. Subtract the adjusted basis from the amount realized to get your gain or loss.

$$\begin{array}{r} \text{Selling price} \\ \underline{- \text{ Selling expenses}} \\ \text{Amount realized} \end{array}$$

$$\begin{array}{r} \text{Amount realized} \\ \underline{- \text{ Adjusted basis}} \\ \text{Gain or loss} \end{array}$$

Selling Price

The selling price is the total amount you receive for your home. It includes money, all notes, mortgages, or other debts assumed by the buyer as part of the sale, and the fair market value of any other property or any services you receive.
Payment by employer. You may have to sell your home because of a job transfer. If your employer pays you for a loss on the sale or for your selling expenses, do not include the payment as part of the selling price. Your employer will include it as wages in box 1 of your Form W-2 and you will include it in your gross income as wages on line 7 of Form 1040.

TAXSAVER

Selling your home to your employer. If during 2005 you sold your home directly to your employer at **fair market value,** no portion of the proceeds is treated as additional compensation. Any gain is subject to the regular rules for home sales. However, if your home was sold to your employer at an amount above fair market value, part of the proceeds would be treated as compensation or ordinary income.

Option to buy. If you grant an option to buy your home and the option is exercised, add the amount you receive for the option to the selling price of your home. If the option is not exercised, you must report the amount as ordinary income in the year the option expires. Report this amount on line 21 of Form 1040.

Form 1099-S. If you received Form 1099-S, Proceeds From Real Estate Transactions, box 2 (gross proceeds) should show the total amount you received for your home.

However, box 2 will not include the fair market value of any property other than cash or notes, or any services, you received or will receive. Instead, box 4 will be checked to indicate your receipt (or expected receipt) of these items.

If you can exclude the entire gain, the person responsible for closing the sale generally will not have to report it on Form 1099-S. If you do not receive Form 1099-S, use sale documents and other records to figure the total amount you received for your home.

Amount Realized

The amount realized is the selling price minus selling expenses.
Selling expenses. Selling expenses include:

- Commissions,
- Advertising fees,
- Legal fees, and
- Loan charges paid by the seller, such as loan placement fees or "points."

Explanation
Other selling expenses. The following items are also considered selling expenses: (1) broker's fees, (2) fees for drafting a contract of sale, (3) fees for drafting the deed, (4) escrow fees, (5) geological surveys, (6) maps, (7) title insurance, (8) recording fees, (9) abstracts of title, (10) title certificate, (11) title opinion, and (12) title registration.

Adjusted Basis

While you owned your home, you may have made adjustments (increases or decreases) to the basis. This adjusted basis must be determined before you can figure gain or loss on the sale of your home. For information on how to figure your home's adjusted basis, see *Determining Basis,* later.

Amount of Gain or Loss

To figure the amount of gain or loss, compare the amount realized to the adjusted basis.
Gain on sale. If the amount realized is more than the adjusted basis, the difference is a gain and, except for any part you can exclude, generally is taxable.
Loss on sale. If the amount realized is less than the adjusted basis, the difference is a loss. A loss on the sale of your main home cannot be deducted.

TaxSaver

Loss on sale of a house held for investment. While you cannot deduct a loss on the sale of your home, if you own a house as an investment (and do not use it for personal purposes), you may be able to deduct any loss realized.

Explanation
If you convert your residence to rental property, your basis for purposes of calculating depreciation and a loss on sale is limited to the lesser of your adjusted basis or the value of the residence on the date of con-

version. Your basis, however, for calculating a gain is your adjusted basis less allowable depreciation.

Example
Assume you have a residence with a basis of $150,000, which you convert to business use when its fair market value is $125,000. You would use $125,000 as your basis for calculating depreciation. If you subsequently sold the residence for $130,000 after having deducted $4,000 for depreciation, you would not recognize a gain or loss because a loss results on the gain calculation and a gain results on the loss calculation.

	Gain Calculation	Loss Calculation
Selling price	$130,000	$130,000
Less:		
Adjusted basis	146,000	121,000
Gain/(loss)	($16,000)	$9,000

Jointly owned home. If you and your spouse sell your jointly owned home and file a joint return, you figure your gain or loss as one taxpayer.

Separate returns. If you file separate returns, each of you must figure your own gain or loss according to your ownership interest in the home. Your ownership interest is determined by state law.

Joint owners not married. If you and a joint owner other than your spouse sell your jointly owned home, each of you must figure your own gain or loss according to your ownership interest in the home. Each of you applies the rules discussed in this chapter on an individual basis.

Other Dispositions

The following rules apply to foreclosures and repossessions, abandonments, trades, and transfers to a spouse.
Foreclosure or repossession. If your home was foreclosed on or repossessed, you have a sale.

You figure the gain or loss from the sale in generally the same way as gain or loss from any sale. But the amount of your gain or loss depends, in part, on whether you were personally liable for repaying the debt secured by the home. See Publication 523 for more information.

Form 1099-A and Form 1099-C. Generally, you will receive Form 1099-A, Acquisition or Abandonment of Secured Property, from your lender. This form will have the information you need to determine the amount of your gain or loss and any ordinary income from cancellation of debt. If your debt is canceled, you may receive Form 1099-C, Cancellation of Debt.

Abandonment. If you abandon your home, you may have ordinary income. If the abandoned home secures a debt for which you are personally liable and the debt is canceled, you have ordinary income equal to the amount of the canceled debt. See Publication 523 for more information.

Trading homes. If you trade your old home for another home, treat the trade as a sale and a purchase.

Example. You owned and lived in a home that had an adjusted basis of $41,000. A real estate dealer accepted your old home as a trade-in and allowed you $50,000 toward a new home priced at $80,000. This is treated as a sale of your old home for $50,000 with a gain of $9,000 ($50,000 − $41,000).

If the dealer had allowed you $27,000 and assumed your unpaid mortgage of $23,000 on your old home, your sales price would still be $50,000 (the $27,000 trade-in allowed plus the $23,000 mortgage assumed).

Transfer to spouse. If you transfer your home to your spouse, or to your former spouse incident to your divorce, you generally have no gain or loss. This is true even if you receive cash or other consideration for the home. Therefore, the rules in this chapter do not apply.

More information. If you need more information, see *Transfer to spouse* in Publication 523 and *Property Settlements* in Publication 504, Divorced or Separated Individuals.

Determining Basis

You need to know your basis in your home to determine any gain or loss when you sell it. Your basis in your home is determined by how you got the home. Your basis is its cost if you bought it or built it. If you got it in some other way (inheritance, gift, etc.), its basis is either its fair market value when you got it or the adjusted basis of the person you got it from.

While you owned your home, you may have made adjustments (increases or decreases) to your home's basis. The result of these adjustments is your home's adjusted basis, which is used to figure gain or loss on the sale of your home. See *Adjusted Basis*, later.

You can find more information on basis and adjusted basis in chapter 14 of this publication and in Publication 523.

Cost As Basis
The cost of property is the amount you pay for it in cash, debt obligations, other property, or services.

Purchase. If you buy your home, your basis is its cost to you. This includes the purchase price and certain settlement or closing costs. Generally, your purchase price includes your down payment and any debt, such as a first or second mortgage or notes you gave the seller in payment for the home. If you build, or contract to build, a new home, your purchase price can include costs of construction, as discussed in Publication 523.

Settlement fees or closing costs. When you bought your home, you may have paid settlement fees or closing costs in addition to the contract price of the property. You can include in your basis some of the settlement fees and closing costs you paid for buying the home. You cannot include in your basis the fees and costs for getting a mortgage loan. A fee paid for buying the home is any fee you would have had to pay even if you paid cash for the home.

Chapter 14 lists some of the settlement fees and closing costs that you can include in the basis of property, including your home. It also lists some settlement costs that cannot be included in basis.

Also see Publication 523 for additional items and a discussion of basis other than cost.

Adjusted Basis
Adjusted basis is your basis increased or decreased by certain amounts.

Increases to basis. These include any:

1. Additions and other improvements that have a useful life of more than 1 year,
2. Special assessments for local improvements, and
3. Amounts you spent after a casualty to restore damaged property.

Decreases to basis. These include any:

1. Gain you postponed from the sale of a previous home before May 7, 1997,
2. Deductible casualty losses,
3. Insurance payments you received or expect to receive for casualty losses,
4. Payments you received for granting an easement or right-of-way,
5. Depreciation allowed or allowable if you used your home for business or rental purposes,
6. Residential energy credit (generally allowed from 1977 through 1987) claimed for the cost of energy improvements that you added to the basis of your home,

7. Adoption credit you claimed for improvements added to the basis of your home,
8. Nontaxable payments from an adoption assistance program of your employer that you used for improvements you added to the basis of your home,
9. First-time homebuyer credit (allowed to certain first-time buyers of a home in the District of Columbia), and
10. Energy conservation subsidy excluded from your gross income because you received it (directly or indirectly) from a public utility after 1992 to buy or install any energy conservation measure. An energy conservation measure is an installation or modification that is primarily designed either to reduce consumption of electricity or natural gas or to improve the management of energy demand for a home.

Improvements. These add to the value of your home, prolong its useful life, or adapt it to new uses. You add the cost of additions and other improvements to the basis of your property.

Examples. Putting a recreation room or another bathroom in your unfinished basement, putting up a new fence, putting in new plumbing or wiring, putting on a new roof, or paving your unpaved driveway are improvements. An addition to your house, such as a new deck, a sunroom, or a garage, is also an improvement.

TAXSAVER
Shrubs and trees. The Tax Court has held that shrubbery and trees may qualify as improvements to be added to the basis of your property.

Repairs. These maintain your home in good condition but do not add to its value or prolong its life. You do not add their cost to the basis of your property.

Examples. Repainting your house inside or outside, fixing your gutters or floors, repairing leaks or plastering, and replacing broken window panes are examples of repairs.

Recordkeeping. You should keep records to prove your home's adjusted basis. Ordinarily, you must keep records for 3 years after the due date for filing your return for the tax year in which you sold your home. But if you sold a home before May 7, 1997, and postponed tax on any gain, the basis of that home affects the basis of the new home you bought. Keep records proving the basis of both homes as long as they are needed for tax purposes.

The records you should keep include:

- Proof of the home's purchase price and purchase expenses,
- Receipts and other records for all improvements, additions, and other items that affect the home's adjusted basis,
- Any worksheets you used to figure the adjusted basis of the home you sold, the gain or loss on the sale, the exclusion, and the taxable gain,
- Any Form 2119, Sale of Your Home, that you filed to postpone gain from the sale of a previous home before May 7, 1997, and
- Any worksheets you used to prepare Form 2119, such as the *Adjusted Basis of Home Sold Worksheet* or the *Capital Improvements Worksheet* from the Form 2119 instructions.

TAXORGANIZER
Documenting the basis in your home. The following documentation should be maintained to support the basis in your home upon sale:
- Receipts for all the above listed increases to your cost basis in your house
- Closing statement from purchase of home to support all transfer taxes, attorney's fees, and other fees (survey, inspection, appraisal)

- Annual statements from cooperative housing corporations (co-ops) regarding maintenance payments used to reduce the indebtedness owed by the corporation

TAXPLANNER

Other documents you can use. If you lose your original receipts, other documents may be used to substantiate the cost of improvements to your home. Canceled checks, contracts, before and after photographs, and building permits may be acceptable to the IRS. If all documentation is lost, you should figure your basis by getting estimates of the cost of similar improvements made at the same time you made yours.

For more information on basis and adjusted basis, see Chapter 14, *Basis of Property*.

Excluding the Gain

You may qualify to exclude from your income all or part of any gain from the sale of your main home. This means that, if you qualify, you will not have to pay tax on the gain up to the limit described under *Maximum Exclusion*, next. To qualify, you must meet the ownership and use tests described later.

You can choose not to take the exclusion by including the gain from the sale in your gross income on your tax return for the year of the sale.

Maximum Exclusion

You can exclude up to $250,000 of the gain on the sale of your main home if all of the following are true.

1. You meet the ownership test.
2. You meet the use test.
3. During the 2-year period ending on the date of the sale, you did not exclude gain from the sale of another home.

You can exclude up to $500,000 of the gain on the sale of your main home if all of the following are true.

1. You are married and file a joint return for the year.
2. Either you or your spouse meets the ownership test.
3. Both you and your spouse meet the use test.
4. During the 2-year period ending on the date of the sale, neither you nor your spouse excluded gain from the sale of another home.

TAXPLANNER

Trading up. This provision of the tax law is generally not an advantage for taxpayers who have traded up homes over a long period, rolled over their gains as allowed under prior law, and now must sell a high-priced home and realize a significant profit.

Ownership and Use Tests

To claim the exclusion, you must meet the ownership and use tests. This means that during the **5-year period** ending on the date of the sale, you must have:

1. Owned the home for at least 2 years (the ownership test), and
2. Lived in the home as your main home for at least 2 years (the use test).

Exception. If you owned and lived in the property as your main home for less than 2 years, you can still claim an exclusion in some cases. The maximum amount you can claim will be reduced. See *Reduced Maximum Exclusion*, later.

Example 1—home owned and occupied for 3 years. Amanda bought and moved into her main home in September 2002. She sold the home at a gain on September 15, 2005. During the 5-year period ending on the date of sale (September 16, 2000–September 15, 2005), she owned and lived in the home for 3 years. She meets the ownership and use tests.

Example 2—met ownership test but not use test. Dan bought a home in 1999. After living in it for 6 months, he moved out. He never lived in the home again and sold it at a gain on June 28, 2005. He owned the home during the entire 5-year period ending on the date of sale (June 29, 2000–June 28, 2005). However, he did not live in it for the required 2 years. He meets the ownership test but not the use test. He cannot exclude any part of his gain on the sale, unless he qualified for a reduced maximum exclusion (explained later).

Period of Ownership and Use

The required 2 years of ownership and use during the 5-year period ending on the date of the sale do not have to be continuous.

You meet the tests if you can show that you owned and lived in the property as your main home for either 24 full months or 730 days (365 × 2) during the 5-year period ending on the date of sale.

Explanation
The home you sold must have been owned and lived in as a principal residence by you for 2 of the 5 years prior to its sale. The key terms to remember are "owned" and "lived in" for 2 years.

Temporary absence. Short temporary absences for vacations or other seasonal absences, even if you rent out the property during the absences, are counted as periods of use.

Example. Professor Paul Beard, who is single, bought and moved into a house on August 28, 2002. He lived in it as his main home continuously until January 5, 2004, when he went abroad for a 1-year sabbatical leave. During part of the period of leave, the house was unoccupied, and during the rest of the period, he rented it. On January 6, 2005, he sold the house at a gain.

Because his leave was not a short temporary absence, he cannot include the period of leave to meet the 2-year use test. He cannot exclude any part of his gain, unless he qualifies for a reduced maximum exclusion (explained later). Even if he does qualify for a reduced maximum exclusion, he cannot exclude the part of the gain equal to the depreciation he claimed while renting the house. See *Depreciation after May 6, 1997*, later.

Example
Maurice and Mavis purchase a home in 2004. The following year, Maurice is transferred overseas for 5 years, during which time the house is rented. When Maurice and Mavis return, Maurice's employer sends Maurice to another city in the United States, instead of back to the home purchased in 2004. Maurice and Mavis sell the original house without ever reoccupying it. They are generally not eligible for any exclusion as they did not live in the house at any time during the last 5 years prior to sale.

TAXSAVER
Status of your home. Unlike under prior law, the status of the home when you sell it is irrelevant. Even if you haven't lived in it for 3 years at the time of sale, the exclusion is still available if you meet the 2-year rule.

Ownership and use tests met at different times. You can meet the ownership and use tests during different 2-year periods. However, you must meet both tests during the 5-year period ending on the date of the sale.

Example. In 1996, Helen Jones lived in a rented apartment. The apartment building was later changed to a condominium, and she bought her apartment on December 3, 2002. In 2003, Helen became ill and on April 14 of that year she moved to her daughter's home. On July 12, 2005, while still living in her daughter's home, she sold her apartment.

Helen can exclude gain on the sale of her apartment because she met the ownership and use tests. Her 5-year period is from July 13, 2000, to July 12, 2005, the date she sold the apartment. She owned her apartment from December 3, 2002, to July 12, 2005 (more than 2 years). She lived in the apartment from July 13, 2000 (the beginning of the 5-year period), to April 14, 2003 (more than 2 years).

Cooperative apartment. If you sold stock in a cooperative housing corporation, the ownership and use tests are met if, during the 5-year period ending on the date of sale, you:

1. Owned the stock for at least 2 years, and
2. Lived in the house or apartment that the stock entitles you to occupy as your main home for at least 2 years.

Members of the uniformed services or Foreign Service. You can choose to have the 5-year test period for ownership and use suspended during any period you or your spouse serve on "qualified official extended duty" as a member of the uniformed services or Foreign Service of the United States. This means that you may be able to meet the 2-year use test even if, because of your service, you did not actually live in your home for at least the required 2 years during the 5-year period ending on the date of sale.

If this helps you qualify to exclude gain, you can choose to have the 5-year test period suspended by filing a return for the year of sale that does not include the gain.

Example. David bought and moved into a home in 1997. He lived in it as his main home for 2 1/2 years. For the next 6 years, he did not live in it because he was on qualified official extended duty with the Army. He then sold the home at a gain in 2005. To meet the use test, David chooses to suspend the 5-year test period for the 6 years he was on qualifying official extended duty. This means he can disregard those 6 years. Therefore, David's 5-year test period consists of the 5 years before he went on qualifying official extended duty. He meets the ownership and use tests because he owned and lived in the home for 2 1/2 years during this test period.

Period of suspension. The period of suspension cannot last more than 10 years. You cannot suspend the 5-year period for more than one property at a time. You can revoke your choice to suspend the 5-year period at any time.

For more information about the suspension of the 5-year test period, see *Members of the uniformed services or Foreign Service* in Publication 523.

Exception for individuals with a disability. There is an exception to the use test if during the 5-year period before the sale of your home:

1. You become physically or mentally unable to care for yourself, and
2. You owned and lived in your home as your main home for a total of at least 1 year.

Under this exception, you are considered to live in your home during any time that you own the home and live in a facility (including a nursing home) that is licensed by a state or political subdivision to care for persons in your condition.

If you meet this exception to the use test, you still have to meet the 2-out-of-5-year ownership test to claim the exclusion.

Previous home destroyed or condemned. For the ownership and use tests, you add the time you owned and lived in a previous home that was destroyed or condemned to the time you owned and lived in the home on which you wish to exclude gain. This rule applies if any part of the basis of the home you sold depended on the basis of the destroyed or condemned home. Otherwise, you must have owned and lived in the same home for 2 of the 5 years before the sale to qualify for the exclusion.

Married Persons

If you and your spouse file a joint return for the year of sale, you can exclude gain if either spouse meets the ownership and use tests. (But see *Maximum Exclusion,* earlier.)

Example

In December 2004, Karen, who is single, sells the home she has been living in as a principal residence for the past 4 years and has a gain of $75,000 on the sale. The entire $75,000 qualifies for the exclusion. On December 31, 2004, Karen marries Ray. On January 2, 2005, Ray sells the home he has owned and been living in as a principal residence for over 2 years and has a gain of $350,000 on the sale. Ray can only exclude $250,000 of the gain even if he and Karen file a joint tax return. The $500,000 exclusion does not apply for two reasons. First, Karen sold her home within the 2-year period ending on the date Ray sold his home. Second, Karen did not use Ray's home as her principal residence for at least 2 of the 5 years before the sale.

Example 1–one spouse sells a home. Emily sells her home in June 2005. She marries Jamie later in the year. She meets the ownership and use tests, but Jamie does not. She can exclude up to $250,000 of gain on a separate or joint return for 2005.

Example 2–each spouse sells a home. The facts are the same as in *Example 1* except that Jamie also sells a home in 2005. He meets the ownership and use tests on his home. Emily and Jamie can each exclude up to $250,000 of gain.

Death of spouse before sale. If your spouse died and you did not remarry before the date of sale, you are considered to have owned and lived in the property as your main home during any period of time when your spouse owned and lived in it as a main home.

Home transferred from spouse. If your home was transferred to you by your spouse (or former spouse if the transfer was incident to divorce), you are considered to have owned it during any period of time when your spouse owned it.

Use of home after divorce. You are considered to have used property as your main home during any period when:

1. You owned it, and
2. Your spouse or former spouse is allowed to live in it under a divorce or separation instrument and uses it as his or her main home.

Explanation

This provision removes the old requirement that the home be your residence at the time of sale.

Reduced Maximum Exclusion

You can claim an exclusion, but the maximum amount of gain you can exclude will be reduced, if either of the following is true.

1. You did not meet the ownership and use tests, but the reason you sold the home was:
   a. A change in place of employment,
   b. Health, or
   c. Unforeseen circumstances (as defined later).
2. Your exclusion would have been disallowed because of the rule described in *More Than One Home Sold During 2-Year Period,* later, except that the reason you sold the home was:
   a. A change in place of employment,

b. Health, or

c. Unforeseen circumstances (as defined next).

Use *Worksheet 3* in Publication 523 to figure your reduced maximum exclusion.

Unforeseen circumstances. The sale of your main home is because of an unforeseen circumstance if your primary reason for the sale is the occurrence of an event that you could not reasonably have anticipated before buying and occupying your main home. For more information on unforeseen circumstances, see Publication 523.

More Than One Home Sold During 2-Year Period

You cannot exclude gain on the sale of your home if, during the 2-year period ending on the date of the sale, you sold another home at a gain and excluded all or part of that gain. If you cannot exclude the gain, you must include it in your income.

Exception. You still can claim an exclusion, but the maximum amount of gain you can exclude will be reduced, if the reason you sold the home was:

1. A change in place of employment,
2. Health, or
3. Unforeseen circumstances (as defined earlier).

For more information about this exception, see *More Than One Home Sold During 2-Year Period* in Publication 523.

Business Use or Rental of Home

You may be able to exclude your gain from the sale of a home that you have used for business or to produce rental income. But you must meet the ownership and use tests.

Example 1. On May 29, 1999, Amy bought a house. She moved in on that date and lived in it until May 31, 2001, when she moved out of the house and put it up for rent. The house was rented from June 1, 2001, to March 31, 2003. Amy moved back into the house on April 1, 2003, and lived there until she sold it on January 30, 2005. During the 5-year period ending on the date of the sale (January 31, 2000–January 30, 2005), Amy owned and lived in the house for more than 2 years as shown in the table below.

Five Year Period	Used as Home	Used as Rental
1/31/00–5/31/01	16 months	
6/1/01–3/31/03		22 months
4/1/03–1/30/05	22 months	
	38 months	22 months

Amy can exclude gain up to $250,000. But she cannot exclude the part of the gain equal to the depreciation she claimed for renting the house, as explained after *Example 2*.

Example 2. William owned and used a house as his main home from 1999 through 2002. On January 1, 2003, he moved to another state. He rented his house from that date until April 30, 2005, when he sold it. During the 5-year period ending on the date of sale (May 1, 2000–April 30, 2005), William owned and lived in the house for 32 months (more than 2 years). He must report the sale on Form 4797. He can exclude gain up to $250,000. However, he cannot exclude the part of the gain equal to the depreciation he claimed for renting the house, as explained next.

Depreciation after May 6, 1997. If you were entitled to take depreciation deductions because you used your home for business purposes or as rental property, you cannot exclude the part of your gain equal to any depreciation allowed as a deduction for periods after May 6, 1997. If you can show by adequate records or other evidence that the depreciation deduction allowed was less than the amount allowable, the amount you cannot exclude is the amount allowed.

Property used partly for business or rental. If you used property partly as a home and partly for business or to produce income, see Publication 523.

GAINS AND LOSSES

246 GAINS AND LOSSES

Example

You own a four-unit apartment house. You live in one unit and rent three units. You sell the apartment house for cash. Your records show the following:

Apartment house

Cost	$ 80,000
Capital improvements	20,000
	$100,000
Minus: Depreciation (on three rented units only)	40,000
Adjusted basis	$ 60,000
Selling price	$120,000
Selling expense	8,000

Because one-fourth of the apartment building is your home, you figure the gain on which tax is excluded as follows:

	Personal (1/4)	Rental (3/4)
1) Selling price	$30,000	$90,000
2) Selling expense	2,000	6,000
3) Amount realized (adjusted sales price)	$28,000	$84,000
4) Basis (including improvements)	$25,000	$75,000
5) Depreciation	–0–	40,000
6) Adjusted basis	$25,000	$35,000
7) Gain [(3) minus (6)]	$ 3,000	$49,000
8) Gain not excluded		$49,000
9) Gain excluded	$ 3,000	

The gain of $49,000 on the three-fourths of the building that was rental property is subject to tax in the year of sale. This gain is reported on Form 4797, *Gains and Losses from Sales or Exchanges of Assets Used in a Trade or Business and Involuntary Conversions.* The gain on the one-fourth that was your home is excluded.

TaxSaver

Improvements to rental property. If improvements have been made solely to rental units, their cost should be specifically allocated to the rental part of the property. This allocation will decrease the gain on the business portion of the property, which is taxable in the year of sale.

Keep detailed records of improvements. Be careful to specify whether the improvements were made exclusively to either the business or the personal portion of the residence, or whether they improved the residence as a whole.

Example

Jane Smith purchases a two-family house. The two units in the house are identical. Jane rents one out and uses the other as her personal residence. The house costs $80,000—$20,000 for the land and $60,000 ($30,000 per unit) for the building. Jane remodels the kitchen in the rental unit. The job costs $10,000, which is added to the basis of the rental unit, increasing it to $40,000. Once the unit is rented, depreciation may be claimed on this $40,000 basis.

When the property is sold, the selling price must be apportioned between the business and personal portions of the residence. If, at the time of sale, the adjusted basis of the rental unit, including the amount allocated to land, is $28,000, and if $60,000 of the sell-

ing price is allocated to the rental unit, there would be a taxable gain of $32,000. Without the $10,000 kitchen expense, the adjusted basis would be only $18,000, increasing the currently taxable gain to $42,000.

Explanation

The apportionment of the selling price between the business and personal portions of a house should be based on the relative fair market value of each portion. Substantial improvements made to each portion of the property should be considered in determining the amount of the selling price that is allocated to each part.

Consequently, the allocation of the sales price, as well as the allocation of the cost of the improvements, may affect the amount of gain to be deferred or taxed on the sale of property used partly as your principal home. Evidence to support a particular allocation of the sales price can include a real estate broker's appraisal or the negotiated terms of the sales contract.

Reporting the Sale

Do not report the 2005 sale of your main home on your tax return unless:

- You have a gain and you do not qualify to exclude all of it, or
- You have a gain and you choose not to exclude it.

If you have any taxable gain on the sale of your main home that cannot be excluded, report the entire gain realized on Schedule D (Form 1040). Report it in column (f) of line 1 or line 8 of Schedule D, depending on how long you owned the home. If you qualify for an exclusion, show it on the line directly below the line on which you report the gain. Write "Section 121 exclusion" in column (a) of that line and show the amount of the exclusion in column (f) as a loss (in parentheses).

If you used the home for business or to produce rental income, you may have to use Form 4797 to report the sale of the business or rental part (or the sale of the entire property if used entirely for business or rental in that year). See *Business Use or Rental of Home* in Publication 523.

Installment sale. Some sales are made under arrangements that provide for part or all of the selling price to be paid in a later year. These sales are called "installment sales." If you finance the buyer's purchase of your home yourself, instead of having the buyer get a loan or mortgage from a bank, you probably have an installment sale. You may be able to report the part of the gain you cannot exclude on the installment basis.

Use Form 6252, Installment Sale Income, to report the sale. Enter your exclusion on line 15 of Form 6252.

Seller-financed mortgage. If you sell your home and hold a note, mortgage, or other financial agreement, the payments you receive generally consist of both interest and principal. You must report the interest you receive as part of each payment separately as interest income. If the buyer of your home uses the property as a main or second home, you must also report the name, address, and social security number (SSN) of the buyer on line 1 of either Schedule B (Form 1040) or Schedule 1 (Form 1040A). The buyer must give you his or her SSN and you must give the buyer your SSN. Failure to meet these requirements may result in a $50 penalty for each failure. If you or the buyer does not have and is not eligible to get an SSN, see *Social Security Number* in chapter 1.

More information. For more information on installment sales, see Publication 537, Installment Sales.

Special Situations

The situations that follow may affect your exclusion.

Home acquired in like-kind exchange. You cannot claim the exclusion if:

1. You acquired your home in a like-kind exchange (also known as a section 1031 exchange), and
2. You sold the home:
   a. After October 22, 2004, and
   b. During the 5-year period beginning with the date you acquired the home.

To defer gain from a like-kind exchange, you must have exchanged business or investment property for business or investment property of a like kind. For more information about like-kind exchanges, see Publication 544.

Home disposed of in like-kind exchange. If you convert your home into business or investment property and then exchange it for other business or investment real estate, you may be able to take advantage of both the $250,000 ($500,000 if you're married filing jointly) exclusion as well as the deferral of any remaining gain under the like-kind exchange rules. For more information about like-kind exchanges, see Publication 544.

> ### TAXSAVER
>
> Under a recently issued IRS ruling you can take advantage of both the principal residence gain exclusion and the deferral of gain in a like-kind exchange. For example, assume that you convert your home into rental property after you had owned it and lived in it for 3 years. The cost basis of your home when you exchange it 2 years later is $400,000 but its value is $1 million. (We won't consider depreciation in this example.) You exchange it for another rental property worth $1 million. Your total gain on the exchange is $600,000 ($1 million less $400,000). You can exclude $250,000 of that gain since you meet the ownership and use tests at the date of sale. The balance of the gain ($600,000 − $250,000 or $350,000) is not currently taxable if the like-kind exchange meets the requirements of the tax law. The deferred gain will reduce the cost basis of the new property; so your cost basis in that property will be $650,000 ($1 million less $350,000).

Expatriates. You cannot claim the exclusion if the expatriation tax applies to you. The expatriation tax applies to U.S. citizens who have renounced their citizenship (and long-term residents who have ended their residency) if one of their principal purposes was to avoid U.S. taxes. For more information about the expatriation tax, see chapter 4 of Publication 519, *U.S. Tax Guide for Aliens*.

Home destroyed or condemned. If your home was destroyed or condemned, any gain (for example, because of insurance proceeds you received) qualifies for the exclusion.

Any part of the gain that cannot be excluded (because it is more than the limit) may be postponed under the rules explained in:

- Publication 547, *Casualties, Disasters, and Thefts*, in the case of a home that was destroyed, or
- Chapter 1 of Publication 544, *Sales and Other Dispositions of Assets*, in the case of a home that was condemned.

Sale of remainder interest. Subject to the other rules in this chapter, you can choose to exclude gain from the sale of a remainder interest in your home. If you make this choice, you cannot choose to exclude gain from your sale of any other interest in the home that you sell separately.

Exception for sales to related persons. You cannot exclude gain from the sale of a remainder interest in your home to a related person. Related persons include your brothers and sisters, half-brothers and half-sisters, spouse, ancestors (parents, grandparents, etc.), and lineal descendants (children, grandchildren, etc.). Related persons also include certain corporations, partnerships, trusts, and exempt organizations.

Recapturing (Paying Back) a Federal Mortgage Subsidy

If you financed your home under a federally subsidized program (loans from tax-exempt qualified mortgage bonds or loans with mortgage credit certificates), you may have to recapture (pay back) all or part of the benefit you received from that program when you sell or otherwise dispose of your home. You recapture the benefit by increasing your federal income tax for the year of the sale. You may have to pay this recapture tax even if you can exclude your gain from income under the rules discussed earlier; that exclusion does not affect the recapture tax.

Loans subject to recapture rules. The recapture applies to loans that:

1. Came from the proceeds of qualified mortgage bonds, or
2. Were based on mortgage credit certificates.

The recapture also applies to assumptions of these loans.

When the recapture applies. The recapture of the federal mortgage subsidy applies only if you meet both of the following conditions.

1. You sell or otherwise dispose of your home:
   a. At a gain, and
   b. During the first 9 years after the date you closed your mortgage loan.
2. Your income for the year of disposition is more than that year's adjusted qualifying income for your family size for that year (related to the income requirements a person must meet to qualify for the federally subsidized program).

When recapture does not apply. The recapture does not apply if any of the following situations apply to you:

- Your mortgage loan was a qualified home improvement loan of not more than $15,000,
- The home is disposed of as a result of your death,
- You dispose of the home more than 9 years after the date you closed your mortgage loan,
- You transfer the home to your spouse, or to your former spouse incident to a divorce, where no gain is included in your income,
- You dispose of the home at a loss,
- Your home is destroyed by a casualty, and you repair it or replace it on its original site within 2 years after the end of the tax year when the destruction happened, or
- You refinance your mortgage loan (unless you later meet all of the conditions listed previously under *When the recapture applies*).

Notice of amounts. At or near the time of settlement of your mortgage loan, you should receive a notice that provides the federally subsidized amount and other information you will need to figure your recapture tax.

How to figure and report the recapture. The recapture tax is figured on Form 8828, Recapture of Federal Mortgage Subsidy. If you sell your home and your mortgage is subject to recapture rules, you must file Form 8828 even if you do not owe a recapture tax. Attach Form 8828 to your Form 1040. For more information, see Form 8828 and its instructions.

17

Reporting Gains and Losses

Note: The 2004 IRS Publication 17 (Your Federal Income Tax) has been updated by Ernst & Young LLP for 2005. Dates and dollar amounts shown are for 2005. Gray type is used to indicate where IRS text has been updated or intentionally omitted. Unrevised IRS text is shown in black type.

Introduction

One of the best ways to save tax dollars is to generate long-term capital gains: profits you make from the sale of assets such as stocks, bonds, and real estate. To qualify for long-term capital gains treatment, you have to hold a capital asset for more than 1 year.

The tax benefit of generating long-term capital gains is substantial. Under the tax law, the top tax rate applicable to most long-term capital gains is 15% . Accordingly, you can achieve substantial tax savings by generating

capital gains in lieu of ordinary income. Your net capital gain equals net long-term capital gains less net short-term capital losses. A 28% rate applies to collectibles held over 12 months; a 25% rate applies to real estate gains to the extent of depreciation.

The rate differences between ordinary income and capital gains have a profound effect on tax planning and investing. This chapter will provide you with examples of how the rules work. It also provides advice on year-end planning.

This chapter discusses how to report capital gains and losses from sales, exchanges, and other dispositions of investment property on Schedule D of Form 1040. The discussion includes:

- How to report short-term gains and losses,
- How to report long-term gains and losses,
- How to figure capital loss carryovers,
- How to figure your tax on a net capital gain, and
- An illustrated example of how to complete Schedule D.

If you sell or otherwise dispose of property used in a trade or business or for the production of income, see Publication 544, Sales and Other Dispositions of Assets, before completing Schedule D.

Useful Items

You may want to see:

Publications

- ☐ **537** Installment Sales
- ☐ **544** Sales and Other Dispositions of Assets
- ☐ **550** Investment Income and Expenses

Forms (and Instructions)

- ☐ **Schedule D (Form 1040)** Capital Gains and Losses
- ☐ **4797** Sales of Business Property
- ☐ **6252** Installment Sale Income
- ☐ **8582** Passive Activity Loss Limitations

Reporting Capital Gains and Losses

Report capital gains and losses on Schedule D (Form 1040). Enter your sales and trades of stocks, bonds, etc., and real estate (if required to be reported and not reported on another form or schedule) on line 1 of Part I or line 8 of Part II, as appropriate. Include all these transactions even if you did not receive a Form 1099-B, Proceeds From Broker and Barter Exchange Transactions, or Form 1099-S, Proceeds From Real Estate Transactions (or substitute statement). You can use Schedule D-1 as a continuation schedule to report more transactions.

Explanation

Characterizing your gain or loss. When you sell or dispose of property, you must determine whether your gain or loss is capital or ordinary. Only capital gains and capital losses are reported on Schedule D, while ordinary gains and losses are reported elsewhere. This distinction is significant because (1) you can use capital losses to offset gains only to the extent of capital gains plus $3,000, and (2) net capital gains may be subject to a lower tax rate than ordinary income. Any unused capital losses can be carried over to the next year.

Example

Assume that Alan has $12,000 of capital losses and $4,000 of capital gains in 2005. Alan can deduct only $7,000 of his capital losses in 2005, which is equal to his $4,000 of capital gains plus $3,000. The remaining $5,000 of losses ($12,000 gross losses minus $7,000 of losses used) may be carried over and used in later years, subject to the $3,000 limitation. If

Alan's losses were ordinary, he could have used all of them in 2005, unless subject to other limitations by special provisions of the Internal Revenue Code.

Explanation

Determining your capital gains rate. The capital gains rate depends on the type of property sold, the holding period prior to sale, and your overall income level. Short-term capital gains are subject to your ordinary income rates. Net capital gains are the excess of (1) net long-term capital gains over (2) net short-term capital losses.

Example

Erik bought 3,000 shares of ABC Company on April 1, 2002, when the price of the stock was $20 per share. On May 1, 2005, he sold all of his ABC holdings for $25 per share, realizing a profit of $15,000. Erik files a joint return with his wife with a combined taxable income that places him in the 35% tax bracket. Because he held the ABC stock for more than 12 months, Erik is eligible for the favorable capital gain tax rates. As a 35% taxpayer, his long-term capital gain on ABC stock would be taxed at 15%.

TAXPLANNER

Long-term capital gains vs. ordinary income. The difference between the top marginal rate of 35% and the top rate on net capital gains of 15% is significant—a 20% difference. Accordingly, you should try to generate long-term capital gains, as opposed to ordinary income, whenever possible. It should be noted, however, that the tax law recharacterizes gains from certain conversion transactions into ordinary income. See later in this chapter for an explanation of conversion transactions.

Example

Nancy is in the top 35% marginal tax bracket for 2005 and 2006 and has the following unrealized capital gains and losses:

Stock A: Unrealized short-term capital gain	$ 10,000
Stock B: Unrealized long-term capital loss (15%)	($13,000)
Stock C: Unrealized long-term capital gain (15%)	$ 15,000

Assume that Nancy sells all three stocks in 2005. Nancy will compute her net capital gain for the year as follows:

Net long-term capital gain	$ 2,000
Net short-term capital gain	$10,000
Total gains	$12,000

Nancy has a net capital gain of $12,000. Nancy will pay $300 of tax on her net long-term capital gain ($2,000 × 15%) and $3,500 on her short-term capital gains, which are taxed at her regular 35% rate ($10,000 × 35%). Thus, Nancy will pay a total tax of $3,800 ($300 + $3,500) on her capital gains.

Assume instead that Nancy sells stocks A and B in 2005 but waits until 2006 to sell stock C.

Nancy will have a net long-term capital loss of $3,000 for 2005 ($10,000 gain on stock A, less $13,000 loss on stock B). Nancy will be allowed to off-set the $3,000 capital loss against her ordinary income, giving her a $1,050 tax saving for 2005.

Nancy will also have a $15,000 net long-term capital gain in 2006 from the sale of stock C. This will represent a net capital gain subject to the maximum 15% rate on net capital gains. Nancy will pay $2,250 of tax in 2006 on her net capital gain ($15,000 x 15%).

By using tax planning, Nancy's total liability on her capital gains would be $1,200 ($2,250 for 2006, less $1,050 of tax savings in 2005). As compared to the $3,800 of tax liability without tax planning, Nancy has saved $2,600. Furthermore, Nancy also delayed the payment of the tax by waiting until 2006 to trigger some of her gains.

The tax savings to Nancy may be small relative to the investment ramifications of holding stock C for a longer period. Nancy must therefore balance the potential tax savings against her overall investment strategy.

Explanation

A capital gain or loss results from (1) the sale or exchange of a capital asset or (2) net Section 1231 gains being treated as a capital gain.

Almost everything you own and use for personal purposes or investment purposes is a capital asset. For example, stocks, bonds, jewelry, and household furnishings generally are all capital assets. Most properties held in a business (e.g., inventory, accounts receivable, machinery) are not capital assets. See Chapter 15, *Sale of Property,* for a further elaboration on what constitutes a capital asset.

A net Section 1231 gain is also treated as a capital gain, while a net Section 1231 loss is treated as an ordinary loss. A Section 1231 gain or loss is any gain or loss from the sale or exchange of real property or depreciable personal property used in your trade or business and held by you for more than 1 year. Any depreciation recapture must be separately computed on the sale of depreciable property and reported as ordinary income. Thus, the portion of the gain that is considered depreciation recapture is ordinary income, rather than a Section 1231 gain. The computation of depreciation recapture is discussed in more detail at the end of this chapter.

Section 1231 gains also include recognized gains on the involuntary conversion of (1) property used in a trade or a business and held for more than 1 year, and (2) any capital asset held for more than 1 year and held in connection with a trade or a business or a transaction entered into for profit. Net involuntary conversion losses on these properties are not Section 1231 losses but are deductible as ordinary losses. An involuntary conversion is the loss of property resulting from destruction (complete or partial), theft, seizure, requisition, or condemnation. An involuntary conversion also includes the sale or exchange of property under the threat or imminence of seizure, requisition, or condemnation.

For more information, see Publication 544, *Sales and Other Dispositions of Assets.*

Tax treatment of gains and losses. Once the disposition is properly classified, you can determine whether your gains and losses will be considered ordinary, capital, or nondeductible.

Capital losses resulting from the sale of business or investment property are reported on Schedule D.

These may be used to offset any other capital gains, including capital gains from business and investment property, which are also reported on Schedule D.

Losses on the sale of personal-use property (e.g., a family car) cannot be used to offset capital gains. These losses are not reported on your income tax return. Capital gains on the sale of personal-use property are taxable, however, and are reported on Schedule D.

You must aggregate all of your Section 1231 gains and losses during the year to determine the tax treatment of these items. Net Section 1231 gains are treated as capital, while net Section 1231 losses are treated as ordinary. Under a special look-back rule, if you have a net Section 1231 gain in 2005, the gain will be treated as ordinary income to the extent of any Section 1231 losses in the preceding 5 years (which were not previously used to recharacterize gains). Remember, any gain resulting in depreciation recapture is ordinary income and as a result is not considered in these computations. Fill out Form 4797 to report these items. Ordinary gains and losses are generally included in gross income. The capital gain portion is reported on Schedule D.

Capital gains and losses reported on Schedule D are further classified under long-term and short-term. Net Section 1231 gains are long-term. For other classifications, see the discussion in Chapter 15, *Sale of Property*.

TaxAlert

Recharacterizing capital gains. The Internal Revenue Code contains a provision that recharacterizes capital gains from certain conversion transactions as ordinary income. The purpose of this provision is to prohibit taxpayers from taking advantage of the favorable tax rate on capital gains by entering into transactions that are, in effect, loans but that, because of their form, generate capital gains. In a conversion transaction, the taxpayer is in the economic position of a lender, and substantially all of the taxpayer's return is attributable to the amount of time the investment is held. In order to be a conversion transaction, a transaction must satisfy at least one of the following four criteria: (1) The transaction consists of the acquisition of property by the taxpayer and a substantially contemporaneous agreement to sell the same or substantially identical property in the future; (2) the transaction is a straddle (see Chapter 15, *Sale of Property*); (3) the transaction is one that is marketed or sold to the taxpayer on the basis that it would have the economic characteristics of a loan but the interest-like return would be taxed as capital gain; or (4) the transaction is described in regulations promulgated by the Secretary of the Treasury.

Installment sales. You cannot use the installment method to report a gain from the sale of stock or securities traded on an established securities market. You must report the entire gain in the year of sale (the year in which the trade date occurs).

TaxAlert

Date of installment payments. For purposes of the dates that determine when capital gains are taxed, the date you receive an installment payment is relevant, not the actual date of sale.

Passive activity gains and losses. If you have gains or losses from a passive activity, you may also have to report them on Form 8582. In some cases, the loss may be limited under the passive activity rules. Refer to Form 8582 and its separate instructions for more information about reporting capital gains and losses from a passive activity.

Explanation

For 2005, the gain or loss realized upon the sale or disposition of an interest in a passive activity must be combined with other items of income, expense, gain, or loss from investments in passive activities in order to determine the amount of passive activity losses that will be deductible on Form 1040. See Chapter 13, *Other Income,* for more information.

TaxPlanner

Passive capital gains. If you generate a passive capital gain, you will be allowed to deduct passive losses to the extent of the passive gain as explained above. In addition, that passive capital gain can still be offset by capital losses on Schedule D.

Form 1099-B transactions. If you sold property, such as stocks, bonds, or certain commodities, through a broker, you should receive Form 1099-B or equivalent statement from the broker. Use the Form 1099-B or the equivalent statement to complete Schedule D.

Report the gross proceeds shown in box 2 of Form 1099-B as the gross sales price in column (d) of either line 1 or line 8 of Schedule D, whichever applies. However, if the broker advises you, in box 2 of Form 1099-B, that gross proceeds (gross sales price) less commissions and option premiums were reported to the IRS, enter that net sales price in column (d) of either line 1 or line 8 of Schedule D, whichever applies.

If the net amount is entered in column (d), do not include the commissions and option premiums in column (e).

Form 1099-S transactions. If you sold or traded reportable real estate, you generally should receive from the real estate reporting person a Form 1099-S showing the gross proceeds.

"Reportable real estate" is defined as any present or future ownership interest in any of the following:

1. Improved or unimproved land, including air space,
2. Inherently permanent structures, including any residential, commercial, or industrial building,
3. A condominium unit and its accessory fixtures and common elements, including land, and
4. Stock in a cooperative housing corporation (as defined in section 216 of the Internal Revenue Code).

A "real estate reporting person" could include the buyer's attorney, your attorney, the title or escrow company, a mortgage lender, your broker, the buyer's broker, or the person acquiring the biggest interest in the property.

Your Form 1099-S will show the gross proceeds from the sale or exchange in box 2. Follow the instructions for Schedule D to report these transactions and include them on line 1 or 8 as appropriate.

Reconciling Forms 1099 with Schedule D. Add the following amounts reported to you for 2005 on Forms 1099-B and 1099-S (or on substitute statements):

1. Proceeds from transactions involving stocks, bonds, and other securities, and
2. Gross proceeds from real estate transactions (other than the sale of your main home if you had no taxable gain) not reported on another form or schedule.

If this total is more than the total of lines 3 and 10 of Schedule D, attach a statement to your return explaining the difference.

Nominees. If you receive gross proceeds as a nominee (that is, the gross proceeds are in your name but actually belong to someone else), report on Schedule D, lines 3 and 10, only the proceeds that belong to you. Then add the following amounts reported to you for 2005 on Forms 1099-B and 1099-S (or substitute statements) that you are not reporting on another form or schedule included with your return:

1. Proceeds from transactions involving stocks, bonds, and other securities, and
2. Gross proceeds from real estate transactions (other than the sale of your main home if you are not required to report it).

If the total of (1) and (2) is more than the total of lines 3 and 10, attach a statement to your return explaining the reason for the difference.

Explanation

Amounts reported to you on Form 1099-B are also reported to the IRS. The IRS matches the amounts reported on Forms 1099-B to your return to make sure you reported all of your security sales. The amounts reported on Forms 1099-B should equal the sum of the amounts on lines 3 and 10 in column (d). If not, you will probably receive a letter from the IRS asking you to explain the difference. If the amounts are different, you should attach a schedule to your return explaining why.

TaxOrganizer

Documents you need for Schedule D. Taxpayers who sell stocks, bonds, or other property through a broker should maintain the following documentation in order to facilitate the completion of Schedule D:

* Confirmations received from the broker documenting all sales transactions executed. These can be used to ensure the accuracy of any Forms 1099-B received.
* Confirmations received from the broker documenting all purchase transactions executed. These will be needed to calculate any gains or losses realized upon the sale of the property. The confirmations will also be needed to determine if any gains or losses are long term or short term.

TaxPlanner

Real property tax. The person reporting a real estate transaction is also responsible for including on Form 1099-S the portion of any real property tax that is property allocable to the purchaser. Thus, property tax allocable from the date of sale to year-end is reported on Form 1099-S. Note that if the purchaser agrees to pay the taxes the seller owed on the new home (up to the date of sale), these taxes are not treated as taxes paid by the purchaser but instead are treated as part of the purchaser's cost. Accordingly, these amounts are not included on Form 1099-S as real property tax allocable to the purchaser. Instead, these amounts are included on Form 1099-S as part of the seller's proceeds.

File Form 1099-B or Form 1099-S with the IRS. If you received gross proceeds as a nominee in 2005, you must file a Form 1099-B or Form 1099-S for those proceeds with the IRS. Send the Form 1099-B or Form 1099-S with a Form 1096, Annual Summary and Transmittal of U.S. Information Returns, to your Internal Revenue Service Center by February 28, 2006 (March 31, 2006, if you file Form 1099-B or Form 1099-S electronically). Give the actual owner of the proceeds Copy B of the Form 1099-B or Form 1099-S by January 31, 2006. On Form 1099-B, you should be listed as the "Filer."

The other owner should be listed as the "Recipient." On Form 1099-S, you should be listed as the "Filer." The other owner should be listed as the "Transferor." You do not, however, have to file a Form 1099-B or Form 1099-S to show proceeds for your spouse. For more information about the reporting requirements and the penalties for failure to file (or furnish) certain information returns, see the General Instructions for Forms 1099, 1098, 5498, and W-2G.

Sale of property bought at various times. If you sell a block of stock or other property that you bought at various times, report the short-term gain or loss from the sale on one line in Part I of Schedule D and the long-term gain or loss on one line in Part II. Write "Various" in column (b) for the "Date acquired." See *Comprehensive Example* later in this chapter.

Sale expenses. Add to your cost or other basis any expense of sale such as brokers' fees, commissions, state and local transfer taxes, and option premiums. Enter this adjusted amount in column (e) of either Part I or Part II of Schedule D, whichever applies, unless you reported the net sales price amount in column (d).

For more information about adjustments to basis, see chapter 14.

Explanation

Most property you own and use for personal purposes or for pleasure, such as your house, furniture, and car, falls under the heading of capital asset. A gain on the sale of this kind of property is treated as a capital gain, but no loss is recognized for income tax purposes unless the property was used for business or investment purposes. If you realize a loss on property used for both business and personal purposes, the portion of the loss that is allocated to the business portion of the property may be deductible.

Short-term gains and losses. Capital gain or loss on the sale or trade of investment property held 1 year or less is a short-term capital gain or loss. You report it in Part I of Schedule D. If the amount you report in column (f) is a loss, show it in parentheses.

You combine your share of short-term capital gains or losses from partnerships, S corporations, and fiduciaries, and any short-term capital loss carryover, with your other short-term capital gains and losses to figure your net short-term capital gain or loss on line 7 of Schedule D.

Long-term gains and losses. A capital gain or loss on the sale or trade of investment property held more than 1 year is a long-term capital gain or loss. You report it in Part II of Schedule D. If the amount you report in column (f) is a loss, show it in parentheses.

Explanation

The shortest length of time that qualifies for long-term status is 1 year plus 1 day. Your holding period begins on the day after you buy the property and includes the day you sell it.

Example

Donald pays $1,000 for Corporation X stock on July 1, 2004. His holding period begins on July 2, 2004. Donald sells the stock on July 1, 2005, for $1,500. His holding period runs from July 2, 2004 (the day after he purchased the stock), through July 1, 2005 (the day he sold the stock). Donald has a short-term capital gain of $500 because he has held the stock for exactly 1 year.

Assume instead that Donald sells the stock on July 2, 2005. His holding period runs from July 2, 2004, through July 2, 2005. His holding period is now in excess of 1 year (1 year and 1 day), so Donald's gain will be long term.

You also report the following in Part II of Schedule D:

1. Undistributed long-term capital gains from a regulated investment company (mutual fund) or real estate investment trust (REIT),
2. Your share of long-term capital gains or losses from partnerships, S corporations, and fiduciaries,
3. All capital gain distributions from mutual funds and REITs not reported directly on line 10 of Form 1040A or line 13 of Form 1040, and
4. Long-term capital loss carryovers.

Explanation

Dividends from mutual funds, which are technically known as **regulated investment companies,** are frequently composed of a combination of long-term capital gains and ordinary income. The nature of the gain is determined by how long the mutual fund has held the underlying property that generates the income, not how long you have held the mutual fund shares. Consequently, you may have a long-term capital gain, although you have held the mutual fund shares for less than the required long-term holding period.

Determination of cost basis and holding period. Mutual fund shares may be acquired on various dates, in various quantities, and at various prices. Some individuals may purchase shares through participation in dividend reinvestment or payroll deduction plans. Shares may also be sold on a periodic basis. As a result, individuals often encounter difficulty in determining their cost basis and hence gain or loss on the sale of their mutual fund shares. Under present law, four methods may be used by mutual fund shareholders to determine the cost basis of shares sold. They are:

1. The specific identification method
2. The FIFO (first in, first out) method
3. The single-category method using the average approach
4. The double-category method using the average approach

The specific identification method. In order to *specifically identify* the shares sold, the following requirements must be met:

1. Specific instructions to the broker or agent must be given by the customer, indicating the particular shares to be sold. These instructions must be given at the time of sale or transfer.
2. Written *confirmation* of this request must be received from the broker or agent within a reasonable time after the sale.

The individual shareholder bears the burden of proof that he or she owned and chose to sell the specific shares at the time of sale.

TaxPlanner

Managing gains and losses. This specific identification method provides an investor with the greatest opportunity to manage his or her reported gain or loss. For example, if a shareholder has other capital losses during the year and wishes to generate capital gains, he or she can specifically identify those shares acquired at the *lowest prices* as the shares being sold. One problem with this method, particularly with mutual funds, is the inability of transfer agents to confirm, in writing, specific shares sold to the shareholder.

Explanation

The FIFO method. Under the FIFO (first in, first out) method, the basis of shares acquired first represents the cost of the shares sold. In other words, the *oldest shares* held by the taxpayer are considered to be the first sold. The FIFO method is also a *default* method. If specific identification procedures are not or cannot be followed and the average basis approach (discussed below) is not elected, then the FIFO method will apply.

TaxAlert

Trap for the unwary. In a rising market, the FIFO method produces the *greatest gain* (and least loss) and hence, generally, the most tax.

Explanation

The single- and double-category methods using the average approach. The average basis method must be *elected* by the individual shareholder by attaching a statement to his or her income tax return, for each year the choice applies. The election must indicate whether the single-category method or the double-category method (discussed below) is being used. Once the election is made, it must continue to be used for *all* accounts in the *same* mutual fund. The average method permits the taxpayer to calculate his or her gain or loss based on the average price paid for the shares.

With the single-category method, all shares are included in a single category; that is, the basis of each share is the total adjusted basis of all shares at the time of disposition divided by the total shares. In determining the holding period (long- or short-term), the shares disposed of are considered to be those shares acquired *first* (using a FIFO-type method, discussed earlier).

With the double-category method, all shares in an account are separated into two categories:

1. Short term—shares held for 1 year or less
2. Long term—shares held *more* than 1 year

The average cost for each category is calculated; that is, the basis of each share in a category is the total adjusted basis of all shares in that category divided by the total shares in that category. The shareholder can specify from which category shares are sold. The custodian or agent must confirm this to the shareholder in writing. If no selection is made, the shares in the long-term category are deemed to be sold first. After a share has been held for more than 1 year, it must be transferred from the short-term to the long-term category.

Explanation

Mutual fund dividends. If an individual who purchases shares in a mutual fund receives a capital gain dividend and then sells the shares at a loss within 6 months after purchase, the loss is treated as a *long-term* capital loss to the extent of the capital gain dividend received. Just as important, you may have to pay taxes on a capital gain dividend when you have not had a profit on your investment.

Example

You pay $10,000 for ABC Mutual Fund on June 30. On July 1, ABC Mutual Fund pays you a long-term capital gain dividend of $1,000. The same day, the value of your ABC shares drops to $9,000. You haven't made any money on your investment, but you still have to pay a tax on the capital gain dividend.

TaxSaver

When to generate losses. If at the end of the year you find that you have only short-term capital gains, you might consider generating capital losses by selling assets that have declined in value. Short-term gains are taxed as ordinary income, but you can avoid paying tax on them by offsetting them against both short-term and long-term losses.

Explanation

Sales or load charges. When a person invests in a mutual fund, he or she may be subject to a sales or load charge, which is similar to a commission. When shares are sold or redeemed, the sales or load charge is generally taken into account as part of the purchaser's basis for purposes of computing gain or loss on the sale.

If an investor exchanges shares in a mutual fund for shares in the same "family" or complex of funds, an additional sales or load charge may be waived or reduced if the investor acquires a reinvestment right (i.e., the right to acquire stock of one or more mutual funds without the payment of all or part of the standard load charge) on the original purchase. If such an exchange occurs within 90 days of the original purchase of mutual fund shares, the original sales or load charge will not be included as basis in determining the gain or loss on the exchange. This rule only applies to the extent that the additional sales or load charge is waived or reduced on the exchange. To the extent that the sales or load charge is not treated as basis in computing gain or loss, such a charge will be taken into account on shares subsequently sold.

Example

On January 1, 2005, Kurt Norton purchased 100 shares of mutual fund X for $110, which included a $10 sales or load charge. On January 20, 2005, Kurt exchanged these shares for 50 shares of mutual fund X1, worth $115. Mutual fund X1 is in the same family as mutual fund X. The sales or load charge of $10 on Kurt's purchase of mutual fund X1 was waived. Kurt's gain or loss on the exchange is computed as follows:

Sales price of mutual fund X	$115
Cost basis of mutual fund X	100
Gain (loss)	$ 15

The sales or load charge of $10 on the purchase of mutual fund X did not affect the taxable gain or loss on the exchange but will become part of the basis of mutual fund X1.

For more about mutual funds see Chapter 40, *Mutual Funds.*

The result after combining these items with your other long-term capital gains and losses is your net long-term capital gain or loss (line 15 of Schedule D).

Capital gain distributions only. You do not have to file Schedule D if both of the following are true.

1. The only amounts you would have to report on Schedule D are capital gain distributions from box 2 of Form 1099-DIV (or substitute statement).
2. You do not have an amount in box 2b, 2c, or 2d of any Form 1099-DIV (or substitute statement).

If both of the above statements are true, report your capital gain distributions directly on line 13 of Form 1040 and check the box on line 13. Also, use the Qualified Dividends and Capital Gain Tax Worksheet in the Form 1040 instructions to figure your tax.

You can report your capital gain distributions on line 10 of Form 1040A, instead of on Form 1040, if both of the following are true.

1. None of the Forms 1099-DIV (or substitute statements) you received have an amount in box 2b, 2c, or 2d.
2. You do not have to file Form 1040 for any other capital gains or losses.

Total net gain or loss. To figure your total net gain or loss, combine your net short-term capital gain or loss (line 7) with your net long-term capital gain or loss (line 15). Enter the result on Schedule D Part III, line 16. If your losses are more than your gains, see *Capital Losses,* next. If both lines 15 and 16 are gains and line 43 of Form 1040 is more than zero, see *Capital Gain Tax Rates,* later.

Capital Losses

If your capital losses are more than your capital gains, you can claim a capital loss deduction. Report the deduction on line 13 of Form 1040, enclosed in parentheses.

Example 1

You have capital gains and losses for the year as follows:

	Short-term	Long-term
Gains	$ 700	$ 400
Losses	800	2,000

Your net deductible capital loss is $1,700, which you figure as follows:

Short-term capital losses	$ 800	
Minus: Short-term capital gains	700	
Net short-term capital loss		$ 100
Long-term capital losses	$2,000	
Minus: Long-term capital gains	400	
Net long-term capital loss		$1,600
Net deductible capital loss		$1,700

Your deduction is limited to the lesser of $3,000 ($1,500 if married filing separately) or your capital loss of $1,700.

Example 2

You have a net long-term capital loss of $1,600 and a net short-term capital gain of $450. Your deductible capital loss is $1,150 ($1,600 − $450).

Limit on deduction. Your allowable capital loss deduction, figured on Schedule D, is the lesser of:

1. $3,000 ($1,500 if you are married and file a separate return), or
2. Your total net loss as shown on line 16 of Schedule D.

You can use your total net loss to reduce your income dollar for dollar, up to the $3,000 limit.

Capital loss carryover. If you have a total net loss on line 16 of Schedule D that is more than the yearly limit on capital loss deductions, you can carry over the unused part to the next year and treat it as if you had incurred it in that next year. If part of the loss is still unused, you can carry it over to later years until it is completely used up.

When you figure the amount of any capital loss carryover to the next year, you must take the current year's allowable deduction into account, whether or not you claimed it.

When you carry over a loss, it remains long term or short term. A long-term capital loss you carry over to the next tax year will reduce that year's long-term capital gains before it reduces that year's short-term capital gains.

Figuring your carryover. The amount of your capital loss carryover is the amount of your total net loss that is more than the lesser of:

1. Your allowable capital loss deduction for the year, or
2. Your taxable income increased by your allowable capital loss deduction for the year and your deduction for personal exemptions.

If your deductions are more than your gross income for the tax year, use your negative taxable income in computing the amount in item (2).

Complete the Capital Loss Carryover Worksheet in Publication 550 to determine the part of your capital loss for 2005 that you can carry over to 2006.

Example. Bob and Gloria sold securities in 2005. The sales resulted in a capital loss of $7,000. They had no other capital transactions. Their taxable income was $26,000. On their joint 2005 return, they can deduct $3,000. The unused part of the loss, $4,000 ($7,000 − $3,000), can be carried over to 2006.

If their capital loss had been $2,000, their capital loss deduction would have been $2,000. They would have no carryover.

Use short-term losses first. When you figure your capital loss carryover, use your short-term capital losses first, even if you incurred them after a long-term capital loss. If you have not reached the limit on the capital loss deduction after using the short-term capital loss, use the long-term capital losses until you reach the limit.

Explanation

A net loss may be carried forward until it is exhausted or until the taxpayer dies. This carryforward may be used to reduce your tax when you have a capital gain sometime in the future. Even if you do not have future gains, the carryforward loss may be used to offset taxable income up to $3,000 per year.

Decedent's capital loss. A capital loss sustained by a decedent during his or her last tax year (or carried over to that year from an earlier year) can only be deducted on the final income tax return filed for the decedent. The capital loss limits discussed earlier still apply in this situation. The decedent's estate cannot deduct any of the loss or carry it over to following years.

TAXPLANNER

If the decedent filed a joint return in the year of death, the surviving spouse may offset gains recognized after the decedent's death but before the end of the tax year against the decedent's capital loss carryforward. Therefore, if the surviving spouse has assets that have appreciated in value, he or she should consider selling them in the year of the decedent's death. For a further discussion of this point, see Chapter 4, *Decedents.*

Joint and separate returns. If you and your spouse once filed separate returns and are now filing a joint return, combine your separate capital loss carryovers. However, if you and your spouse once filed a joint return and are now filing separate returns, any capital loss carryover from the joint return can be deducted only on the return of the person who actually had the loss.

Capital Gain Tax Rates

The tax rates that apply to a net capital gain are generally lower than the tax rates that apply to other income. These lower rates are called the maximum capital gain rates.

The term "net capital gain" means the amount by which your net long-term capital gain for the year is more than your net short-term capital loss.

For 2005, the maximum capital gain rates are 5%, 15%, 25%, or 28%. See Table 17-1 for details.

TAXPLANNER

Long-term investment strategies. Investment strategies that emphasize capital appreciation over current income can significantly enhance your after-tax portfolio returns. For example, "buy-and-hold" investors may want to keep growth-oriented investments outside of tax-deferred accounts to benefit from the capital gains tax relief. Long-term gains in a tax-deferred account are taxed at ordinary income rates—currently as high as 35%—when withdrawn. Outside a tax-deferred account, those same long-term gains would be taxed at the more favorable capital gains rate. In addition, new investments in tax-deferred variable annuities will require much longer holding periods to outperform "comparable" investments held in a taxable account. Although mutual funds have not—with some notable exceptions—historically paid considerable attention to the impact of taxes on shareholder returns, more fund families are developing "tax-managed" funds that seek to minimize taxable distributions to shareholders.

To take advantage of the 5% and 15% rates, you should specifically identify shares of securities and/or mutual funds held more than 12 months prior to executing the sale. For tax purposes, the selling instructions given to the broker or fund representative must be in writing. Confirmation of the instructions should be kept in your personal files.

High-income taxpayers who have the option of deferring current compensation may be better off paying tax currently and reinvesting the after-tax proceeds in assets expected to appreciate over the long term. This may apply, for example, in the case of a corporate executive with significant nonqualified stock option holdings where the current option spread—and, thus, the associated current tax liability—is small but the outlook for the company's stock price is favorable.

Tip. *If you figure your tax using the maximum capital gain rates and the regular tax computation results in a lower tax, the regular tax computation applies.*

Example. All of your net capital gain is from selling collectibles, so the capital gain rate would be 28%. Because you are single and your taxable income is $25,000, none of your taxable income will be taxed above the 15% rate. The 28% rate does not apply.

Investment interest deducted. If you claim a deduction for investment interest, you may have to reduce the amount of your net capital gain that is eligible for the capital gain tax rates. Reduce it by the amount of the net capital gain you choose to include in investment income when figuring the limit on your investment interest deduction. This is done on the Schedule D Tax Worksheet or the Qualified Dividends and Capital Gain Tax Worksheet. For more information about the limit on investment interest, see chapter 3 of Publication 550.

TAXPLANNER

Net capital gains. Net capital gains are not included in "investment income" for purposes of determining a

Table 17-1. **What Is Your Maximum Capital Gain Rate?**

IF your net capital gain is from ...	THEN your maximum capital gain rate is ...
Collectibles gain	28%
Gain on qualified small business stock equal to the section 1202 exclusion	28%
Unrecaptured section 1250 gain	25%
Other gain,[1] and the regular tax rate that would apply is 25% or higher	15%
Other gain,[1] and the regular tax rate that would apply is lower than 25%	5%

[1] Other gain means any gain that is not collectibles gain, gain on qualified small business stock, or unrecaptured section 1250 gain.

taxpayer's deduction for investment interest expense. However, you can elect to include capital gains as investment income. This election can be made for all or just a portion of your capital gains. In addition, you can make one election for regular tax purposes and another for alternative minimum tax purposes. If you make such an election, you must reduce the amount of capital gains that are otherwise eligible for the maximum capital gain tax rate by the amount included as investment income.

Collectibles gain or loss. This is gain or loss from the sale or trade of a work of art, rug, antique, metal (such as gold, silver, and platinum bullion), gem, stamp, coin, or alcoholic beverage held more than 1 year.

Gain on qualified small business stock. If you realized a gain from qualified small business stock that you held more than 5 years, you generally can exclude one-half of your gain from income. The taxable part of your gain equal to your section 1202 exclusion is a 28% rate gain. See *Gains on Qualified Small Business Stock* in chapter 4 of Publication 550.

Unrecaptured section 1250 gain. Generally, this is any part of your capital gain from selling section 1250 property (real property) that is due to depreciation (but not more than your net section 1231 gain), reduced by any net loss in the 28% group. Use the Unrecaptured Section 1250 Gain Worksheet in the Schedule D instructions to figure your unrecaptured section 1250 gain. For more information about section 1250 property and section 1231 gain, see chapter 3 of Publication 544.

Explanation
Computing depreciation recapture. If you sell property at a gain, you must generally compute the portion of your gain that is depreciation recapture. Depreciation recapture is treated as ordinary income. The portion of the gain that is not depreciation recapture is treated as a Section 1231 gain. Complete Form 4797 to determine the amount of your gain that is depreciation recapture.

Sale of depreciable personal property. The depreciation recapture rules for depreciable personal property are relatively simple, compared to the rules for real property. Depreciation recapture is the *lesser* of (1) the gain recognized or (2) depreciation taken on the property since 1961. Note that, under these rules, if depreciable personal property is sold at less than its original cost, the full gain will inevitably be depreciation recapture.

Example
In 2001, Alan bought personal property that he used in his trade for $5,000. Alan sold the property for $2,500 in 2005. He had already taken $3,662 in depreciation. Alan computes his gain or loss as follows:

Sales price	$2,500
Purchase price	5,000
Less: Depreciation taken	3,662
Adjusted basis	1,338
Gain on sale	$1,162

Alan's gain on the sale is $1,162, which is less than the $3,662 of depreciation he had taken on the property. Therefore, his depreciation recapture is $1,162. Because this represents the full gain on the sale, no portion of the gain is treated as a Section 1231 gain and all of it will be treated as ordinary income.

Assume instead that the property had appreciated and that Alan sold the property for $6,000:

Sales price	$6,000
Adjusted basis (computed above)	1,338
Gain on sale	$4,662

Because the depreciation Alan took on the property ($3,662) is less than the gain on the sale ($4,662), Alan reports the $3,662 depreciation taken as depreciation recapture. The remaining $1,000 of his gain ($4,662 − $3,662) is treated as a Section 1231 gain.

Explanation

Sale of depreciable real estate. The depreciation recapture rules relating to the sale of real estate are quite complex. These rules depend on (1) when you placed the property in service, (2) what method of depreciation was used, and (3) whether the property was residential rental property or held for business use. It should be noted that no depreciation recapture should occur for real property acquired after 1986 because straight-line depreciation is the only method available for such property.

Real property acquired before 1976. If you acquired the real estate before 1976 and used the straight-line method of depreciation, there is no depreciation recapture on sale. If you used an accelerated method, you must go through a number of computations to determine depreciation recapture.

Step 1. Compute the excess depreciation for post-1975 years, which is the difference between the depreciation deductions you took using an accelerated method and the amount you would have taken had you used the straight-line method for the years you depreciated the property after 1975.

Step 2. Compare this amount to your overall gain on the sale. If your overall gain is less than this amount, then the overall gain is the amount of your depreciation recapture and you can stop here. If the overall gain is greater than the post-1975 excess depreciation, go on to Step 3.

Step 3. Subtract the excess depreciation computed in Step 1 from the total overall gain to compute the remaining gain. Then compute the excess depreciation for the years 1970 through 1975, using the same method as in Step 1. Take the smaller of the remaining gain or the excess depreciation for 1970 through 1975, as computed above.

If the property is *not* residential rental property, then the depreciation recapture is the sum of the excess depreciation computed in Step 1, plus the amount computed in Step 3. If the property is residential rental property, you must then compute the "applicable percentage," which depends on how many full months you owned the property. If you held the property less than 100 months, the applicable percentage is 100%. If you held the property for more than 100 full months, the applicable percentage is 100% minus the number of full months you held the property in excess of 100 months.

Multiply this percentage by the amount calculated in Step 3. Add this result to the amount calculated in Step 1 to get the total amount of gain treated as depreciation recapture.

Property acquired after 1975 and before 1981. Generally, all of the excess accelerated depreciation over straight-line depreciation up to the amount of gain has to be recaptured on sale. Certain kinds of property—government-assisted housing, low-income housing, certain rehabilitation expenses, and Title V loan property—are exempt from this rule. In these special cases, 100% of accelerated depreciation has to be recaptured for the first 100 months the property is held. After that, the recapture percentage declines 1% each month so that after 16 2/3 years there is no further recapture.

Nonresidential real property acquired after 1980 and before 1987. If the accelerated rates under the Accelerated Cost Recovery System (ACRS) are used on commercial real property, the entire amount of depreciation is subject to recapture on sale of the property. This means, in essence, that any gain up to the amount of depreciation previously claimed is treated as ordinary income. However, if straight-line ACRS is used, then none of the depreciation has to be recaptured at the time of sale.

Residential real property acquired after 1980 and before 1987. Any gain on the sale of *residential rental property* is ordinary income if the deductions taken under the accelerated ACRS method of depreciation exceed the depreciation allowed under the 15-year straight-line method of depreciation. However, any gain you incur in excess of the amount you have to recapture is treated as a capital gain. For property acquired after March 15, 1984, the ACRS period is 18 years, and for property acquired after May 8, 1985, the ACRS period is 19 years.

Tax computation using maximum capital gains rates. Use the Qualified Dividends and Capital Gain Tax Worksheet or the Schedule D Tax Worksheet (whichever applies) to figure your tax if you have qualified dividends or net capital gain. You have net capital gain if Schedule D, lines 15 and 16, are both gains.

Schedule D Tax Worksheet. You must use the Schedule D Tax Worksheet in the Schedule D instructions to figure your tax if:

- You have to file Schedule D, and
- Schedule D, line 18 (28% rate gain) or line 19 (unrecaptured section 1250 gain), is more than zero.

See *Comprehensive Example*, later, for an example of how to figure your tax using the Schedule D Tax Worksheet.

Qualified Dividends and Capital Gain Tax Worksheet. If you do not have to use the Schedule D Tax Worksheet (as explained above) and any of the following apply, use the Qualified Dividends and Capital Gain Tax Worksheet in the instructions for Form 1040 or Form 1040A (whichever you file) to figure your tax.

- You received qualified dividends. (See *Qualified Dividends* in chapter 9.)
- You do not have to file Schedule D and you received capital gain distributions. (See *Capital gain distributions only* earlier.)
- Schedule D, lines 15 and 16, are both more than zero.

Comprehensive Example

Emily Jones is single and, in addition to wages from her job, she has income from stocks and other securities. For the 2005 tax year, she had the following capital gains and losses, which she reports on Schedule D. All the Forms 1099 she received showed net sales prices. Her filled-in Schedule D is shown at the end of this chapter.

Capital gains and losses—Schedule D. Emily sold stock in two different companies that she held for less than a year. In June, she sold 100 shares of Trucking Co. stock that she had bought in February. She had an adjusted basis of $650 in the stock and sold it for $900, for a gain of $250. In July, she sold 25 shares of Computer Co. stock that she bought in June. She had an adjusted basis in the stock of $2,500 and she sold it for $2,000, for a loss of $500. She reports these short-term transactions on line 1 in Part I of Schedule D.

Emily had three other stock sales that she reports as long-term transactions on line 8 in Part II of Schedule D. In February, she sold 60 shares of Car Co. for $2,100. She had inherited the Car Co. stock from her father. Its fair market value at the time of his death was $2,500, which became her basis. Her loss on the sale is $400. Because she had inherited the stock, her loss is a long-term loss, regardless of how long she and her father actually held the stock. She enters the loss in column (f) of line 8.

In June, she sold 500 shares of Furniture Co. stock for $14,000. She had bought 100 of those shares in 1994, for $1,000. She had bought 100 more shares in 1996 for $2,200, and an additional 300 shares in 1999 for $1,500. Her total basis in the stock is $4,700. She has a $9,300 ($14,000 − $4,700) gain on this sale, which she enters in column (f) of line 8.

In December, she sold 20 shares of Toy Co. for $4,100. This was qualified small business stock that she had bought in September 2000. Her basis is $1,100, so she has a $3,000 gain which she enters in column (f) of line 8. Because she held the stock more than 5 years, she has a $1,500 section 1202 exclusion. She claims the exclusion on the line below by entering $1,500 as a loss in column (f). She also enters the exclusion as a positive amount on line 2 of the 28% Rate Gain Worksheet.

She received a Form 1099-B (not shown) from her broker for each of these transactions.

Reconciliation of Forms 1099-B. Emily makes sure that the total of the amounts reported in column (d) of lines 3 and 10 of Schedule D is not less than the total of the amounts shown on the Forms 1099-B she received from her broker. For 2005, the total is $23,100.

Capital loss carryover from 2004. Emily has a capital loss carryover to 2005 of $800, of which $300 is short-term capital loss, and $500 is long-term capital loss. She enters these amounts on lines 6 and 14 of Schedule D. She also enters the $500 long-term capital loss carryover on line 5 of the 28% Rate Gain Worksheet. Her filled-in 28% Rate Gain Worksheet is shown at the end of this chapter.

She kept the completed Capital Loss Carryover Worksheet (not illustrated) in her 2004 edition of Publication 550, so she could properly report her loss carryover for the 2005 tax year without refiguring it.

Tax computation. Because Emily has gains on both lines 15 and 16 of Schedule D, she checks the "Yes" box on line 17 and goes to line 18. On line 18 she enters $450 from line 7 of the 28% Rate Gain Worksheet. Because line 18 is greater than zero, she checks the "No" box on line 20 and uses the Schedule D Tax Worksheet to figure her tax.

After entering the gain from line 16 on line 13 of her Form 1040, she completes the rest of Form 1040 through line 43. She enters the amount from that line, $30,000, on line 1 of the Schedule D Tax Worksheet. After filling out the rest of that worksheet, she figures her tax is $3,275. This is less than the $4,165 tax she would have figured without the capital gain tax rates.

28% Rate Gain Worksheet for Emily Jones—Line 18

1. Enter the total of all collectibles gain or (loss) from items you reported on line 8, column (f), of Schedules D and D-1 ... **1.** _0_
2. Enter as a positive number the amount of any section 1202 exclusion you reported on line 8, column (f), of Schedules D and D-1 ... **2.** _1,500_
3. Enter the total of all collectibles gain or (loss) from Form 4684, line 4 (but only if Form 4684, line 15, is more than zero); Form 6252; Form 6781, Part II; and Form 8824 ... **3.** ___
4. Enter the total of any collectibles gain reported to you on:
   - Form 1099-DIV, box 2d;
   - Form 2439, box 1d; and
   - Schedule K-1 from a partnership, S corporation, estate, or trust. } ... **4.** ___
5. Enter your long-term capital loss carryovers from Schedule D, line 14, and Schedule K-1 (Form 1041), line 13c ... **5.** (_500_)
6. If Schedule D, line 7, is a (loss), enter that (loss) here. Otherwise, enter -0- ... **6.** (_550_)
7. Combine lines 1 through 6. If zero or less, enter -0-. If more than zero, also enter this amount on Schedule D, line 18 ... **7.** _450_

Schedule D Tax Worksheet

Complete this worksheet only if line 18 or line 19 of Schedule D is more than zero. Otherwise, complete the Qualified Dividends and Capital Gain Tax Worksheet on page 34 of the Instructions for Form 1040 to figure your tax.

Exception: Do not use the Qualified Dividends and Capital Gain Tax Worksheet **or** this worksheet to figure your tax if:

- Line 15 or line 16 of Schedule D is zero or less **and** you have no qualified dividends on Form 1040, line 9b, **or**
- Form 1040, line 42, is zero or less.

Instead, see the instructions for Form 1040, line 44.

1.	Enter your taxable income from Form 1040, line 43 . . . . **1.**	30,000
2.	Enter your qualified dividends from Form 1040, line 9b . . . . . . **2.** _____	
3.	Enter the amount from Form 4952, line 4g . . **3.** _____	
4.	Enter the amount from Form 4952, line 4e* **4.** _____	
5.	Subtract line 4 from line 3. If zero or less, enter -0- . . . . **5.** _____	
6.	Subtract line 5 from line 2. If zero or less, enter -0- . . . . **6.** _____	
7.	Enter the **smaller** of line 15 or line 16 of Schedule D **7.** 9,350	
8.	Enter the **smaller** of line 3 or line 4 . . . . **8.** _____	
9.	Subtract line 8 from line 7. If zero or less, enter -0- **9.** 9,350	
10.	Add lines 6 and 9 . . . . **10.** 9,350	
11.	Add lines 18 and 19 of Schedule D **11.** 450	
12.	Enter the **smaller** of line 9 or line 11 . . . . **12.** 450	
13.	Subtract line 12 from line 10 . . . . **13.**	8,900
14.	Subtract line 13 from line 1. If zero or less, enter -0-. . . . . **14.**	21,100
15.	Enter the **smaller** of:	
	• The amount on line 1 **or**	
	• $29,700 if single or married filing separately; $59,400 if married filing jointly or qualifying widow(er); or $39,800 if head of household } **15.** 29,700	
16.	Enter the **smaller** of line 14 or line 15 . . . . **16.** 21,100	
17.	Subtract line 10 from line 1. If zero or less, enter -0- **17.** 20,650	
18.	Enter the **larger** of line 16 or line 17 . . . . ▶ **18.** 21,100	
	If lines 15 and 16 are the same, skip lines 19 and 20 and go to line 21. Otherwise, go to line 19.	
19.	Subtract line 16 from line 15 . . . . ▶ **19.** 8,600	
20.	Multiply line 19 by 5% (.05) . . . . **20.**	430
	If lines 1 and 15 are the same, skip lines 21 through 33 and go to line 34. Otherwise, go to line 21.	
21.	Enter the **smaller** of line 1 or line 13 . . . . **21.** 8,900	
22.	Enter the amount from line 19 (if line 19 is blank, enter -0-) **22.** 8,600	
23.	Subtract line 22 from line 21. If zero or less, enter -0-. . . . . ▶ **23.** 300	
24.	Multiply line 23 by 15% (.15) . . . . **24.**	45
	If Schedule D, line 19, is zero or blank, skip lines 25 through 30 and go to line 31. Otherwise, go to line 25.	
25.	Enter the **smaller** of line 9 above or Schedule D, line 19 . . . . **25.** _____	
26.	Add lines 10 and 18 . . . . **26.** _____	
27.	Enter the amount from line 1 above . . . . **27.** _____	
28.	Subtract line 27 from line 26. If zero or less, enter -0-. . . . . **28.** _____	
29.	Subtract line 28 from line 25. If zero or less, enter -0-. . . . . ▶ **29.** _____	
30.	Multiply line 29 by 25% (.25) . . . . **30.** _____	
	If Schedule D, line 18, is zero or blank, skip lines 31 through 33 and go to line 34. Otherwise, go to line 31.	
31.	Add lines 18, 19, 23, and 29 . . . . **31.** 30,000	
32.	Subtract line 31 from line 1 . . . . **32.** 0	
33.	Multiply line 32 by 28% (.28) . . . . **33.**	0
34.	Figure the tax on the amount on **line 18**. Use the Tax Table or Tax Computation Worksheet, whichever applies . . . . **34.**	2,800
35.	Add lines 20, 24, 30, 33, and 34 . . . . **35.**	3,275
36.	Figure the tax on the amount on **line 1**. Use the Tax Table or Tax Computation Worksheet, whichever applies . . . . . **36.**	4,165
37.	**Tax on all taxable income (including capital gains and qualified dividends).** Enter the **smaller** of line 35 or line 36. Also enter this amount on Form 1040, line 44 . . . . **37.**	3,275

*If applicable, enter instead the smaller amount you entered on the dotted line next to line 4e of Form 4952.

SCHEDULE D
(Form 1040)

Department of the Treasury
Internal Revenue Service   (99)

Capital Gains and Losses

► Attach to Form 1040.   ► See Instructions for Schedule D (Form 1040).

► Use Schedule D-1 to list additional transactions for lines 1 and 8.

OMB No. 1545-0074

2005

Attachment
Sequence No. **12**

Name(s) shown on Form 1040

Emily Jones

Your social security number
111 : 00 : 1111

Part I   Short-Term Capital Gains and Losses—Assets Held One Year or Less

(a) Description of property (Example: 100 sh. XYZ Co.)	(b) Date acquired (Mo., day, yr.)	(c) Date sold (Mo., day, yr.)	(d) Sales price (see page D-6 of the instructions)	(e) Cost or other basis (see page D-6 of the instructions)	(f) Gain or (loss) Subtract (e) from (d)
1 100 sh Trucking Co.	2-12-04	6-12-04	900	650	250
25 sh Computer Co.	6-29-04	7-30-04	2,000	2,500	(500)

2 Enter your short-term totals, if any, from Schedule D-1, line 2	**2**		
3 **Total short-term sales price amounts.** Add lines 1 and 2 in column (d)	**3**	2,900	

4 Short-term gain from Form 6252 and short-term gain or (loss) from Forms 4684, 6781, and 8824	**4**	
5 Net short-term gain or (loss) from partnerships, S corporations, estates, and trusts from Schedule(s) K-1	**5**	
6 Short-term capital loss carryover. Enter the amount, if any, from line 8 of your **Capital Loss Carryover Worksheet** on page D-6 of the instructions	**6**	(300)
7 **Net short-term capital gain or (loss).** Combine lines 1 through 6 in column (f)	**7**	550

Part II   Long-Term Capital Gains and Losses—Assets Held More Than One Year

(a) Description of property (Example: 100 sh. XYZ Co.)	(b) Date acquired (Mo., day, yr.)	(c) Date sold (Mo., day, yr.)	(d) Sales price (see page D-6 of the instructions)	(e) Cost or other basis (see page D-6 of the instructions)	(f) Gain or (loss) Subtract (e) from (d)
8 60 sh Car Co.	INHERITED	2-3-04	2,100	2,500	(400)
500 sh Furniture Co.	VARIOUS	6-29-04	14,000	4,700	9,300
20 sh Toy Co.	9-28-99	12-15-04	4,100	1,100	3,000
Section 1202 exclusion					(1,500)

9 Enter your long-term totals, if any, from Schedule D-1, line 9	**9**		
10 **Total long-term sales price amounts.** Add lines 8 and 9 in column (d)	**10**	20,200	

11 Gain from Form 4797, Part I; long-term gain from Forms 2439 and 6252; and long-term gain or (loss) from Forms 4684, 6781, and 8824	**11**	
12 Net long-term gain or (loss) from partnerships, S corporations, estates, and trusts from Schedule(s) K-1	**12**	
13 Capital gain distributions. See page D-1 of the instructions	**13**	
14 Long-term capital loss carryover. Enter the amount, if any, from line 13 of your **Capital Loss Carryover Worksheet** on page D-6 of the instructions	**14**	(500)
15 **Net long-term capital gain or (loss).** Combine lines 8 through 14 in column (f). Then go to Part III on the back	**15**	9,900

For Paperwork Reduction Act Notice, see Form 1040 instructions.   Cat. No. 11338H   Schedule D (Form 1040) 2005

Part III **Summary**

16 Combine lines 7 and 15 and enter the result. If line 16 is a loss, skip lines 17 through 20, and go to line 21. If a gain, enter the gain on Form 1040, line 13, and then go to line 17 below . . | 16 | 9,350

17 Are lines 15 and 16 **both** gains?
☑ **Yes.** Go to line 18.
☐ **No.** Skip lines 18 through 21, and go to line 22.

18 Enter the amount, if any, from line 7 of the **28% Rate Gain Worksheet** on page D-7 of the instructions . . . . ▶ | 18 | 450

19 Enter the amount, if any, from line 18 of the **Unrecaptured Section 1250 Gain Worksheet** on page D-8 of the instructions . . . . ▶ | 19 |

20 Are lines 18 and 19 **both** zero or blank?
☐ **Yes.** Complete Form 1040 through line 43, and then complete the **Qualified Dividends and Capital Gain Tax Worksheet** on page 34 of the Instructions for Form 1040. **Do not** complete lines 21 and 22 below.
☑ **No.** Complete Form 1040 through line 43, and then complete the **Schedule D Tax Worksheet** on page D-9 of the instructions. **Do not** complete lines 21 and 22 below.

21 If line 16 is a loss, enter here and on Form 1040, line 13, the **smaller** of:
● The loss on line 16 or
● ($3,000), or if married filing separately, ($1,500)   . . . . | 21 | ( )

Note. When figuring which amount is smaller, treat both amounts as positive numbers.

22 Do you have qualified dividends on Form 1040, line 9b?
☐ **Yes.** Complete Form 1040 through line 43, and then complete the **Qualified Dividends and Capital Gain Tax Worksheet** on page 34 of the Instructions for Form 1040.
☐ **No.** Complete the rest of Form 1040.

Printed on recycled paper

Schedule D (Form 1040) 2005

PART IV

Adjustments to Income

The four chapters in this part discuss six of the adjustments to income that you can deduct in figuring your adjusted gross income. These chapters cover:

- Contributions you make to traditional individual retirement arrangements (IRAs)—chapter 18,
- Moving expenses you pay—chapter 19,
- Alimony you pay—chapter 20, and
- Educator expenses, student loan interest, and tuition and fees you pay—chapter 21.

Other adjustments to income are discussed in other parts of this or other publications. For details, see Table V below.

Table V. **Other Adjustments to Income**

Use this table to find information about other adjustments to income not covered in this part of the publication.

IF you are looking for more information about the deduction for...	THEN see...
Certain business expenses of reservists, performing artists, and fee-basis officials	Chapter 28.
Contributions to a health savings account	Publication 969, Health Savings Accounts and Other Tax-Favored Health Plans.
One-half of self-employment tax	Chapter 24.
Self-employed health insurance	Chapter 23.
Payments to self-employed SEP, SIMPLE, and qualified plans	Publication 560, Retirement Plans for Small Business.
Penalty on the early withdrawal of savings	Chapter 8.
Contributions to an Archer MSA	Chapter 23.
Reforestation amortization or expense	Chapter 9 of Publication 535, Business Expenses.
Contributions to Internal Revenue Code section 501(c)(18)(D) pension plans	Publication 525, Taxable and Nontaxable Income.
Expenses from the rental of personal property	Chapter 13.
Certain required repayments of supplemental unemployment benefits (sub-pay)	Chapter 13.
Foreign housing costs	Chapter 4 of Publication 54, Tax Guide for U.S. Citizens and Resident Aliens Abroad.
Deduction for clean-fuel vehicle	Chapter 12 of Publication 535, Business Expenses.
Jury duty pay given to your employer	Chapter 13.
Contributions by certain chaplains to Internal Revenue Code section 403(b) plans	Publication 517, Social Security and Other Information for Members of the Clergy and Religious Workers.
Attorney fees and certain costs for actions involving certain unlawful discrimination claims	Publication 525.
Domestic production activities deduction	Instructions for Form 8903

Individual Retirement Arrangements (IRAs)

Note: The 2004 IRS Publication 17 (Your Federal Income Tax) has been updated by Ernst & Young LLP for 2005. Dates and dollar amounts shown are for 2005. Gray type is used to indicate where IRS text has been updated or intentionally omitted. Unrevised IRS text is shown in black type.

Introduction

There are three different IRA options, each with different eligibility requirements and characteristics.

- *Deductible IRAs save YOU taxes this year and every year you make a contribution. If you are eligible, your annual contribution of up to $4,000 ($4,500 if you're 50 by the end of the year) is deductible. In addition, you defer paying taxes on the income earned by the funds in your IRA until withdrawal.*
- *Nondeductible IRAs are known as such because your annual contribution is not deductible. If you are eligible, you can contribute up to $4,000 ($4,500 if you're 50 by the end of the year). You*

can defer paying taxes on the income earned in your IRA until withdrawal.

- *If you are eligible, you can make an annual contribution of up to $4,000 ($4,500 if you're 50 by the end of the year) to a Roth IRA. The contribution is not deductible, but any income earned by the funds in your Roth IRA is tax-exempt upon withdrawal if the Roth IRA meets certain requirements.*

Eligibility requirements for all three kinds of IRAs are described in this chapter.

This chapter also discusses retirement plans for the self-employed—simplified employee pensions (SEPs) (pages 281–282).

What's New for 2005

Modified AGI limit for traditional IRA contributions increased. For 2005, if you are covered by a retirement plan at work, your deduction for contributions to a traditional IRA is reduced (phased out) if your modified adjusted gross income (AGI) is:

- More than $70,000 but less than $80,000 for a married couple filing a joint return or a qualifying widow(er),
- More than $50,000 but less than $60,000 for a single individual or head of household, or
- Less than $10,000 for a married individual filing a separate return.

[IRS text intentionally omitted]

See *How Much Can You Deduct?* under *Traditional IRAs,* later.

What's New for 2006

Traditional IRA contribution and deduction limit. The contribution limit to your traditional IRA for 2006 will be the same as for 2005—the smaller of:

- $4,000, or
- Your taxable compensation for the year.

But, if you reach age 50 by the end of 2006, the most that can be contributed to your traditional IRA for 2006 will increase and will be the smaller of the following amounts:

- $5,000, or
- Your taxable compensation for the year.

Roth IRA contribution limit. If contributions on your behalf are made only to Roth IRAs, your contribution limit for 2006 will generally be the lesser of:

- $4,000, or
- Your taxable compensation for the year.

If you are 50 or older in 2006 and contributions on your behalf are made only to Roth IRAs, your contribution limit for 2006 will generally be the lesser of:

- $5,000, or
- Your taxable compensation for the year.

However, if your modified AGI is above a certain amount, your contribution limit may be reduced.

Modified AGI limit for traditional IRA contributions increased for married couples filing a joint return and qualifying widow(er)s. For 2006, if you are covered by a retirement plan at work, your deduction for contributions to a traditional IRA will be reduced (phased out) if your modified adjusted gross income (AGI) is:

- More than $75,000 but less than $85,000 for a married couple filing a joint return or a qualifying widow(er),
- More than $50,000 but less than $60,000 for a single individual or head of household, or
- Less than $10,000 for a married individual filing a separate return.

[IRS text intentionally omitted]

Reminders

Statement of required minimum distribution. If a minimum distribution is required from your IRA, the trustee, custodian, or issuer that held the IRA at the end of the preceding year must either report the amount of the required minimum distribution to you, or offer to calculate it for you. The report or offer must include the date by which the amount must be distributed. The report is due January 31 of the year in which the minimum distribution is required. It can be provided with the year-end fair market value statement that you normally get each year. No report is required for IRAs of owners who have died.

IRA interest. Although interest earned from your IRA is generally not taxed in the year earned, it is not tax-exempt interest. Do not report this interest on your tax return as tax-exempt interest.

Form 8606. If you make nondeductible contributions to a traditional IRA and you do not file Form 8606, Nondeductible IRAs, with your tax return, you may have to pay a $50 penalty.

Roth IRA. You cannot claim a deduction for any contributions to a Roth IRA. But, if you satisfy the requirements, all earnings are tax free and neither your nondeductible contributions nor any earnings on them are taxable when you withdraw them. See *Roth IRAs,* later.

TaxSaver

Retirement savings through IRAs. Wealth can build up much faster in an IRA or other tax-deferred retirement plan than in your own investment program. Since you do not have to pay income tax as your earnings accumulate within the plan, your investments compound in value more quickly. A person in the 28% tax bracket, for example, could end up with 1.7 times more money after tax on a $4,000 deductible IRA contribution held for 20 years than if he or she did not make the contribution. If the person's **marginal tax rate** drops to 15% in retirement, he or she could have 2 times more money after tax.

Example

If in 2005 you invested $3,000 in an IRA that earns 10% per year, it will be worth $19,375 in 2025 after all

taxes are paid if you are in the 28% bracket. If in 2025 you retire and drop into the 15% tax bracket, your original $4,000 investment will be worth $22,873 after all taxes are paid.

However, if you do not have an IRA, your $4,000 is subject to tax immediately. If you are in the 28% bracket, you are left with only $2,880. Investing that $2,880 in 2005 in a non-IRA investment earning 10%, you will have only $11,569 in 2025 after taxes are paid if you remain in the 28% bracket.

TaxAlert

Note that the highest tax bracket in 2005 is 35%. Under current law, this reduced top individual rate will stay in effect through 2010, and is scheduled to expire after December 31, 2010. Therefore, the savings resulting from an IRA may be different than indicated in this example.

An individual retirement arrangement (IRA) is a personal savings plan that gives you tax advantages for setting aside money for your retirement.

This chapter discusses:

- The rules for a traditional IRA (any IRA that is not a Roth or SIMPLE IRA), and
- The Roth IRA, which features nondeductible contributions and tax-free distributions.

Simplified Employee Pensions (SEPs) and Savings Incentive Match Plans for Employees (SIMPLEs) are not discussed in this chapter. For more information on these plans and employees' SEP-IRAs and SIMPLE IRAs that are part of these plans, see Publications 560 and 590.

Useful Items

You may want to see:

Publications

- ☐ **560** Retirement Plans for Small Business
- ☐ **590** Individual Retirement Arrangements (IRAs)

Forms (and Instructions)

- ☐ **5329** Additional Taxes on Qualified Plans (including IRAs) and Other Tax-Favored Accounts
- ☐ **8606** Nondeductible IRAs

TaxPlanner

Self-employed persons and independent contractors often overlook the benefits available to them from establishing an IRA. The only requirement for contributing to an IRA is that you have not reached age 70 1/2 (*note:* this does not apply to Roth IRAs) and have earned income, which includes income from your business, provided that your personal efforts create a major portion of the business income. Therefore, a self-employed person could establish both a Keogh plan and an IRA. For more information on retirement plans for the self-employed, see Chapter 11, *Retirement Plans, Pensions, and Annuities.*

TAXSAVER

You are a sole proprietor, and you hire your spouse or child to perform bona fide services, such as bookkeeping, as an employee. Assuming that the family member works in a genuine employment relationship, the salary paid is compensation for personal services and should be included in the family member's gross income. The family member's salary is a deductible expense to you. This gross income would entitle that family member to make a contribution to an IRA of up to $4,000.

Your spouse's wages constitute wages subject to Social Security tax, so this strategy may work to your disadvantage.

Be prepared to defend the genuine employment relationship of your spouse against an IRS attack.

Traditional IRAs

In this chapter the original IRA (sometimes called an ordinary or regular IRA) is referred to as a "traditional IRA." Two advantages of a traditional IRA are:

- You may be able to deduct some or all of your contributions to it, depending on your circumstances, and,
- Generally, amounts in your IRA, including earnings and gains, are not taxed until they are distributed.

What Is a Traditional IRA?

A traditional IRA is any IRA that is not a Roth IRA or a SIMPLE IRA.

Who Can Set Up a Traditional IRA?

You can set up and make contributions to a traditional IRA if:

- You (or, if you file a joint return, your spouse) received taxable compensation during the year, and
- You were not age 70 1/2 by the end of the year.

What is compensation? Generally, compensation is what you earn from working. Compensation includes wages, salaries, tips, professional fees, bonuses, and other amounts you receive for providing personal services. The IRS treats as compensation any amount properly shown in box 1 (Wages, tips, other compensation) of Form W-2, Wage and Tax Statement, provided that amount is reduced by any amount properly shown in box 11 (Nonqualified plans).

Scholarship and fellowship payments are compensation for this purpose only if shown in box 1 of Form W-2.

Compensation also includes commissions and taxable alimony and separate maintenance payments.

Self-employment income. If you are self-employed (a sole proprietor or a partner), compensation is the net earnings from your trade or business (provided your personal services are a material income-producing factor) reduced by the total of:

- The deduction for contributions made on your behalf to retirement plans, and
- The deduction allowed for one-half of your self-employment taxes.

Compensation includes earnings from self-employment even if they are not subject to self-employment tax because of your religious beliefs. See Publication 533, Self-Employment Tax, for more information.

What is not compensation? Compensation does not include any of the following items.

- Earnings and profits from property, such as rental income, interest income, and dividend income.
- Pension or annuity income.
- Deferred compensation received (compensation payments postponed from a past year).
- Income from a partnership for which you do not provide services that are a material income-producing factor.
- Any amounts you exclude from income, such as foreign earned income and housing costs.

Explanation

For purposes of figuring out your contribution to your IRA, compensation includes sales commissions, the net income from your business, and partnership income that is subject to self-employment tax. Business and partnership income must be reduced by any contributions to a Keogh or SEP plan you make. Compensation does not include nontaxable amounts, deferred compensation, severance pay, or pension distributions. If you have multiple sources of self-employment income and/or partnership income subject to self-employment tax, all gains and losses from these sources must be aggregated for purposes of computing compensation from self-employment. If the result is a gain, it is added to your wages, possibly permitting you to make a larger deductible contribution to your IRA. If the result of your self-employment activities is a loss, however, you need not account for it in determining your IRA contribution. Income earned outside the United States is compensation to the extent that it is taxable in the United States. Your foreign earned income must be adjusted for any foreign income exclusion. For more information, see Chapter 42, *U.S. Citizens Working Abroad: Tax Treatment of Foreign Earned Income.*

When and How Can a Traditional IRA Be Set Up?

You can set up a traditional IRA at any time. However, the time for making contributions for any year is limited. See *When Can Contributions Be Made,* later.

You can set up different kinds of IRAs with a variety of organizations. You can set up an IRA at a bank or other financial institution or with a mutual fund or life insurance company. You can also set up an IRA through your stockbroker. Any IRA must meet Internal Revenue Code requirements.

Kinds of traditional IRAs. Your traditional IRA can be an individual retirement account or annuity. It can be part of either a simplified employee pension (SEP) or an employer or employee association trust account.

Explanation

The basic difference between the two types of IRA accounts—Individual Retirement Arrangements and Individual Retirement Annuities—lies in the type of investment and the method of funding it. The Individual Retirement Arrangement is generally a type of trust with varied investments, such as stocks, bonds, savings accounts, certificates of deposit, credit union accounts, common trust funds, and **real estate,** among other things. An Individual Retirement Annuity is an investment in an insurance contract.

TaxPlanner

Self-directed IRAs. If you want to actively manage your IRA investments, you may consider setting up a self-directed IRA. To do so, without having to obtain preapproval from the IRS, you may use Form 5305, a model trust form, and Form 5305-A, a model custodial account agreement. However, keep in mind that even if you use these model forms, you still will have to find a financial institution to administer your account.

TaxAlert

In deciding whether or not to create a self-directed IRA, keep in mind that an investment in the following collectibles is disallowed:

- Artworks
- Coins (unless state issued, U.S. minted gold, and silver coins of 1 ounce or less)
- Stamps
- Gems
- Antiques
- Rugs
- Alcoholic beverages
- Metals

How Much Can Be Contributed?

There are limits and other rules that affect the amount that can be contributed and the amount you can deduct. These limits and other rules are explained below.

Community property laws. Except as discussed later under *Spousal IRA limit,* each spouse figures his or her limit separately, using his or her own compensation. This is the rule even in states with community property laws.

Brokers' commissions. Brokers' commissions paid in connection with your traditional IRA are subject to the contribution limit.

TaxAlert

Under a recent IRS letter ruling, if you a pay a so-called "wrap fee" for the management of your IRA, that fee is not subject to the contribution limit even if it also covers the cost of commissions. A wrap-fee is typically based on a percentage of the assets under management.

Trustees' fees. Trustees' administrative fees are not subject to the contribution limit.

Caution. *Contributions to your traditional IRAs reduce your limit for contributions to Roth IRAs. (See* Roth IRAs, *later.)*

General limit. The most that can be contributed to your traditional IRA is the smaller of the following amounts.

- $4,000 ($4,500 if you are 50 or older in 2005). For 2006, this amount remains at $4,000 (but increases to $5, 000 if 50 or older in 2006).
- Your taxable compensation (defined earlier) for the year.

This is the most that can be contributed regardless of whether the contributions are to one or more traditional IRAs or whether all or part of the contributions are nondeductible. (See *Nondeductible Contributions,* later.)

Example 1. Betty, who is 34 years old and single, earned $24,000 in 2005. Her IRA contributions for 2005 are limited to $4,000.

Example 2. John, an unmarried college student working part time, earned $1,500 in 2005. His IRA contributions for 2005 are limited to $1,500, the amount of his compensation.

Spousal IRA limit. If you file a joint return and your taxable compensation is less than that of your spouse, the most that can be contributed for the year to your IRA is the smaller of the following amounts.

1. $4,000 ($4,500 if you are 50 or older in 2005). For 2006, this amount remains at $4,000 (but increases to $5,000 if 50 or older in 2006).
2. The total compensation includible in the gross income of both you and your spouse for the year, reduced by the following two amounts.
   a. Your spouse's IRA contribution for the year to a traditional IRA.
   b. Any contribution for the year to a Roth IRA on behalf of your spouse.

This means that the total combined contributions that can be made for the year to your IRA and your spouse's IRA can be as much as $8,000 ($8,500 if only one of you is 50 or older, or $9,000 if both of you are 50 or older). For 2006, combined total contributions can be as much as $10,000 ($9,000 if only one of you is 50 or older or $10,000 if both of you are 50 or older.

Example 1
A wife holds a job, and her husband does not. The two spouses file a joint return. They may contribute up to $8,000 to their respective IRAs. The contribution can be split between the husband's and wife's accounts in any way they wish, as long as no more than $4,000 is allocated to either account.

Example 2
The working wife died during the year after earning over $8,000. The nonworking husband is allowed to put $4,000 in his spousal IRA for the year, as long as he files a joint return with his deceased wife. A payment cannot be made to the decedent's IRA for the year of death after she dies.

Community property laws should be disregarded when you are determining if you are eligible to make payments to an IRA for your nonworking spouse. Thus, your nonworking spouse is not considered to have earned half your income.

When Can Contributions Be Made?

As soon as you set up your traditional IRA, contributions can be made to it through your chosen sponsor (trustee or other administrator). Contributions to a traditional IRA must be in the form of money (cash, check, or money order). Property cannot be contributed.

Contributions must be made by due date. Contributions can be made to your traditional IRA for a year at any time during the year or by the due date for filing your return for that year, not including extensions. For most people, this means that contributions for 2005 must be made by April 17, 2006, and contributions for 2006 must be made by April 16, 2007.

Age 70 1/2 rule. Contributions cannot be made to your traditional IRA for the year in which you reach age 70 1/2 or for any later year.

You attain age 70 1/2 on the date that is six calendar months after the 70th anniversary of your birth. If you were born on June 30, 1935, the 70th anniversary of your birth is June 30, 2005, and you attained age 70 1/2 on December 30, 2005. If you were born on July 1, 1935, the 70th anniversary of your birth was July 1, 2005, and you attained age 70 1/2 on January 1, 2006.

Designating year for which contribution is made. If an amount is contributed to your traditional IRA between January 1 and April 15, you should tell the sponsor which year (the current year or the previous year) the contribution is for. If you do not tell the sponsor which year it is for, the sponsor can assume, and report to the IRS, that the contribution is for the current year (the year the sponsor received it).

Filing before a contribution is made. You can file your return claiming a traditional IRA contribution before the contribution is actually made. However, the contribution must be made by the due date of your return, not including extensions.

TAXPLANNER

You can make your 2005 IRA contribution as late as April 17, 2006. However, funding your IRA as early as possible maximizes your ending balance. For example, assume you have 20 years until retirement, make the maximum $8,000 contribution for you and your spouse, and the account earns 8%. If you make your contributions at year end, your ending IRA balance will be $366,096. If you make your contributions at the beginning of the year, your ending account balance will be $395,384, an increase of $29,288.

TAXPLANNER

If you do not have the cash available to make your 2005 IRA contribution by April 17, 2005, the deadline for 2005 contributions, you could "borrow" money by distributing part or all of an existing IRA account to yourself and use the money to make your 2005 IRA contribution to a different account. You would have to complete the rollover within 60 days of the withdrawal, meaning that you would have to come up with the funds to complete the rollover or possibly be subject to income tax and the 10% penalty for early withdrawal. *Note:* You may only roll over an IRA fund to a new IRA once in a 1-year period.

Alternatively, if you want the $4,000-per-year IRA deduction but are not particularly concerned about accumulating income tax-free in your IRA, you can take advantage of the 60-day rollover period so that you have some extra spending money for 2 months.

For more information about rollovers, see the discussion later in this chapter.

Contributions not required. You do not have to contribute to your traditional IRA for every tax year, even if you can.

How Much Can You Deduct?

Generally, you can deduct the lesser of:

- The contributions to your traditional IRA for the year, or
- The general limit (or the spousal IRA limit, if it applies).

However, if you or your spouse was covered by an employer retirement plan, you may not be able to deduct this amount. See *Limit If Covered by Employer Plan,* later.

Tip. *You may be eligible to claim a credit for contributions to your traditional IRA. For more information see chapter 39.*

Trustees' fees. Trustees' administrative fees that are billed separately and paid in connection with your traditional IRA are not deductible as IRA contributions. However, they may be deductible as a miscellaneous itemized deduction on Schedule A (Form 1040). See chapter 30.

Brokers' commissions. Brokers' commissions are part of your IRA contribution and, as such, are deductible subject to the limits.

Full deduction. If neither you nor your spouse was covered for any part of the year by an employer retirement plan, you can take a deduction for total contributions to one or more traditional IRAs of up to the lesser of the following amounts.

- $4,000 ($4,500 if you are 50 or older in 2005). For 2006, this amount remains at $4,000 (but increases to $5,000 if you are 50 or older in 2006).
- 100% of your compensation.

This limit is reduced by any contributions made to a 501(c)(18) plan on your behalf.

Spousal IRA. In the case of a married couple with unequal compensation who file a joint return, the deduction for contributions to the traditional IRA of the spouse with less compensation is limited to the lesser of the following amounts.

1. $4,000 ($4,500 if you are 50 or older in 2005). For 2006, this amount remains at $4,000 (but increases to $5,000 if you are 50 or older in 2006).
2. The total compensation includible in the gross income of both spouses for the year reduced by the following three amounts.
   a. The IRA deduction for the year of the spouse with the greater compensation.
   b. Any designated nondeductible contribution for the year made on behalf of the spouse with the greater compensation.
   c. Any contributions for the year to a Roth IRA on behalf of the spouse with the greater compensation.

This limit is reduced by any contributions to a 501(c)(18) plan on behalf of the spouse with less compensation.

Note. If you were divorced or legally separated (and did not remarry) before the end of the year, you cannot deduct any contributions to your spouse's IRA. After a divorce or legal separation, you can deduct only contributions to your own IRA. Your deductions are subject to the rules for single individuals.

Covered by an employer retirement plan. If you or your spouse was covered by an employer retirement plan at any time during the year for which contributions were made, your deduction may be further limited. This is discussed later under *Limit If Covered by Employer Plan.* Limits on the amount you can deduct do not affect the amount that can be contributed. See *Nondeductible Contributions,* later.

Are You Covered by an Employer Plan?

The Form W-2 you receive from your employer has a box used to indicate whether you were covered for the year. The "Retirement plan" box should be checked if you were covered.

Reservists and volunteer firefighters should also see *Situations in Which You Are Not Covered,* later.

If you are not certain whether you were covered by your employer's retirement plan, you should ask your employer.

TAXPLANNER

We recommend that you check your Form W-2 to ensure that the coverage status is accurate. The rules used to determine if you are covered by an employer's plan will depend on the type of plan maintained by your employer. If you are not sure what type of plan your employer maintains, you should ask your employer. The information may also be found in the Summary Plan Description, which can be obtained from your employer. Generally, you will be considered covered if:

1. Your employer maintains a defined benefit pension plan and you meet the plan's eligibility requirements.
2. Your employer maintains a defined contribution money purchase plan, you meet the plan's eligibility

Table 18-1.   Effect of Modified AGI¹ on Deduction If You Are Covered by Retirement Plan at Work

If you are covered by a retirement plan at work, use this table to determine if your modified AGI affects the amount of your deduction.

IF your filing status is...	AND your modified AGI is...	THEN you can take...
single	$50,000 or less	a full deduction.
or	more than $50,000 but less than $60,000	a partial deduction.
head of household	$60,000 or more	no deduction.
married filing jointly	$70,000 or less	a full deduction.
or	more than $70,000 but less than $80,000	a partial deduction.
qualifying widow(er)	$80,000 or more	no deduction.
married filing separately²	less than $10,000	a partial deduction.
	$10,000 or more	no deduction.

¹Modified AGI (adjusted gross income). See *Modified adjusted gross income (AGI)*.
²If you did not live with your spouse at any time during the year, your filing status is considered Single for this purpose (therefore, your IRA deduction is determined under the "Single" column).

requirements, and your employer is required to make a contribution to your account.
3. Your employer maintains a profit-sharing plan and makes a contribution, a forfeiture is allocated to your account, or you make any contribution with respect to a plan year ending with or within your tax year.

Example
Assume that you first became eligible to participate in your employer's profit-sharing plan on July 1, 2005. Your employer makes a contribution for the plan year ending on June 30, 2006. You will not be considered an active participant until 2006, since that is the first tax year during which an allocation was made to your account.

4. Your employer maintains a 401(k), a SEP, or a 403(b) plan, and, if for the year ending with or within your tax year, you elect to defer any compensation.

Federal judges. For purposes of the IRA deduction, federal judges are covered by an employer retirement plan.

For Which Year(s) Are You Covered?
Special rules apply to determine the tax years for which you are covered by an employer plan. These rules differ depending on whether the plan is a defined contribution plan or a defined benefit plan.
Tax year. Your tax year is the annual accounting period you use to keep records and report income and expenses on your income tax return. For almost all people, the tax year is the calendar year.
Defined contribution plan. Generally, you are covered by a defined contribution plan for a tax year if amounts are contributed or allocated to your account for the plan year that ends with or within that tax year.

A defined contribution plan is a plan that provides for a separate account for each person covered by the plan. Types of defined contribution plans include profit-sharing plans, stock bonus plans, and money purchase pension plans.
Defined benefit plan. If you are eligible to participate in your employer's defined benefit plan for the plan year that ends within your tax year, you are covered by the plan. This rule applies even if you:

• Declined to participate in the plan,
• Did not make a required contribution, or

• Did not perform the minimum service required to accrue a benefit for the year.

A defined benefit plan is any plan that is not a defined contribution plan. Defined benefit plans include pension plans and annuity plans.
No vested interest. If you accrue a benefit for a plan year, you are covered by that plan even if you have no vested interest in (legal right to) the account or the accrual.

Situations in Which You Are Not Covered
Unless you are covered under another employer plan, you are not covered by an employer plan if you are in one of the situations described below.
Social security or railroad retirement. Coverage under social security or railroad retirement is not coverage under an employer retirement plan.
Benefits from a previous employer's plan. If you receive retirement benefits from a previous employer's plan, you are not covered by that plan.
Reservists. If the only reason you participate in a plan is because you are a member of a reserve unit of the armed forces, you may not be covered by the plan. You are not covered by the plan if both of the following conditions are met.

1. The plan you participate in is established for its employees by:
   a. The United States,
   b. A state or political subdivision of a state, or
   c. An instrumentality of either (a) or (b) above.
2. You did not serve more than 90 days on active duty during the year (not counting duty for training).

Volunteer firefighters. If the only reason you participate in a plan is because you are a volunteer firefighter, you may not be covered by the plan. You are not covered by the plan if both of the following conditions are met.

1. The plan you participate in is established for its employees by:
   a. The United States,
   b. A state or political subdivision of a state, or
   c. An instrumentality of either (a) or (b) above.
2. Your accrued retirement benefits at the beginning of the year will not provide more than $1,800 per year at retirement.

Limit If Covered by Employer Plan
If either you or your spouse was covered by an employer retirement

Table 18-2. **Effect of Modified AGI[1] on Deduction If You Are NOT Covered by Retirement Plan at Work**

If you are not covered by a retirement plan at work, use this table to determine if your modified AGI affects the amount of your deduction.

IF your filing status is...	AND your modified AGI is...	THEN you can take...
single, head of household, or **qualifying widow(er)**	any amount	a full deduction.
married filing jointly or **separately** with a spouse who *is not* covered by a plan at work	any amount	a full deduction.
married filing jointly with a spouse who *is* covered by a plan at work	$150,000 or less	a full deduction.
	more than $150,000 but less than $160,000	a partial deduction.
	$160,000 or more	no deduction.
married filing separately with a spouse who *is* covered by a plan at work[2]	less than $10,000	a partial deduction.
	$10,000 or more	no deduction.

[1]Modified AGI (adjusted gross income). See *Modified adjusted gross income (AGI)*.
[2]You are entitled to the full deduction if you did not live with your spouse at any time during the year.

plan, you may be entitled to only a partial (reduced) deduction or no deduction at all, depending on your income and your filing status.

Your deduction begins to decrease (phase out) when your income rises above a certain amount and is eliminated altogether when it reaches a higher amount. These amounts vary depending on your filing status.

To determine if your deduction is subject to phaseout, you must determine your modified adjusted gross income (AGI) and your filing status. See *Filing status* and *Modified adjusted gross income (AGI)*, later. Then use Table 18-1 or 18-2 to determine if the phaseout applies.

Social security recipients. Instead of using Table 18-1 or 18-2, use the worksheets in Appendix B of Publication 590 if, for the year, all of the following apply.

- You received social security benefits.
- You received taxable compensation.
- Contributions were made to your traditional IRA.
- You or your spouse was covered by an employer retirement plan.

Use those worksheets to figure your IRA deduction, your nondeductible contribution, and the taxable portion, if any, of your social security benefits.

Deduction phaseout. If you were covered by an employer retirement plan and you did not receive any social security retirement benefits, your IRA deduction may be reduced or eliminated depending on your filing status and modified AGI as shown in Table 18-1.
Tip. *For 2006, if you are covered by a retirement plan at work, your IRA deduction will not be reduced (phased out) unless your modified AGI is:*

- *More than $50,000 but less than $60,000 for a single individual (or head of household),*
- *More than $75,000 but less than $85,000 for a married couple filing a joint return (or a qualifying widow(er)), or*
- *Less than $10,000 for a married individual filing a separate return.*

For a married couple filing a joint return (or a qualifying widow(er)), the upper and lower limits of the phaseout range for 2006 will increase by $5,000 from the limits for 2005.

If your spouse is covered. If you are not covered by an employer retirement plan, but your spouse is, and you did not receive any social security benefits, your IRA deduction may be reduced or eliminated entirely depending on your filing status and modified AGI as shown in Table 18-2.
Filing status. Your filing status depends primarily on your marital status. For this purpose, you need to know if your filing status is single or head of household, married filing jointly or qualifying

widow(er), or married filing separately. If you need more information on filing status, see chapter 2.

Lived apart from spouse. If you did not live with your spouse at any time during the year and you file a separate return, your filing status, for this purpose, is single.

Example

Joe and Mary are both employed. During 2005, Mary's compensation was $55,000, and she was not covered by her employer's retirement plan. Joe's compensation was $25,000, and he was covered by his employer's plan. If Joe and Mary file a joint return, Mary can claim a deduction for an IRA contribution since she is not covered by her employer's retirement plan. However, Joe cannot claim an IRA contribution deduction. If Joe and Mary didn't live together at all during the year and file separate returns, Joe can deduct an IRA contribution of $4,000 (subject to the adjusted gross income limitation), while Mary can deduct $4,000, since she is not covered by her employer's plan.

If they lived together for part of the year and file separate returns, neither can make a deductible IRA contribution.

Modified adjusted gross income (AGI). How you figure your modified AGI depends on whether you are filing Form 1040 or Form 1040A. If you made contributions to your IRA for 2005 and received a distribution from your IRA in 2005, see Publication 590.
Caution. *Do not assume that your modified AGI is the same as your compensation. Your modified AGI may include income in addition to your compensation (discussed earlier), such as interest, dividends, and income from IRA distributions.*

Form 1040. If you file Form 1040, refigure the amount on page 1 "adjusted gross income" line without taking into account any of the following amounts.

- IRA deduction.
- Student loan interest deduction.
- Tuition and fees deduction.
- Foreign earned income exclusion.
- Foreign housing exclusion or deduction.
- Exclusion of qualified savings bond interest shown on Form 8815, Exclusion of Interest From Series EE and I U.S. Savings Bonds

Worksheet 18-1. Figuring Your Modified AGI

Use this worksheet to figure your modified adjusted gross income for traditional IRA purposes.

1. Enter your adjusted gross income (AGI) shown on line 22, Form 1040A, or line 37, Form 1040 figured without taking into account line 17, Form 1040A, or line 32, Form 1040	**1.**	_____
2. Enter any *Student loan interest deduction* from line 18, Form 1040A, or line 33, Form 1040	**2.**	_____
3. Enter any *Tuition and fees deduction* from line 19, Form 1040A, or line 34, Form 1040	**3.**	_____
4. Enter any *Foreign earned income and/or housing exclusion* from line 18, Form 2555-EZ, or line 43, Form 2555	**4.**	_____
5. Enter any *Foreign housing deduction* from line 48, Form 2555	**5.**	_____
6. Enter any *Excluded qualified savings bond interest* shown on line 3, Schedule 1, Form 1040A, or line 3, Schedule B, Form 1040 (from line 14, Form 8815)	**6.**	_____
7. Enter any *Exclusion of employer-provided adoption benefits* shown on line 30, Form 8839	**7.**	_____
8. Enter any Domestic production activities deduction from line 35, Form 1040	**8.**	_____
9. Add lines 1 through 8. This is your **Modified AGI** for traditional IRA purposes	**9.**	_____

Issued After 1989 (For Filers With Qualified Higher Education Expenses).

• Exclusion of employer-provided adoption benefits shown on Form 8839, Qualified Adoption Expenses.

• Domestic production activities deduction.

This is your modified AGI.

Form 1040A. If you file Form 1040A, refigure the amount on page 1 "adjusted gross income" line without taking into account any of the following amounts.

• IRA deduction.
• Student loan interest deduction.
• Tuition and fees deduction.
• Exclusion of qualified savings bond interest shown on Form 8815.
• Exclusion of employer-provided adoption benefits shown on Form 8839.

This is your modified AGI.

Both contributions for 2005 and distributions in 2005. If all three of the following apply, any IRA distributions you received in 2005 may be partly tax free and partly taxable.

• You received distributions in 2005 from one or more traditional IRAs.
• You made contributions to a traditional IRA for 2005.
• Some of those contributions may be nondeductible contributions depending on whether your IRA deduction for 2005 is reduced.

If this is your situation, you must figure the taxable part of the traditional IRA distribution before you can figure your modified AGI. To do this, you can use Worksheet 1-5, Figuring the Taxable Part of Your IRA Distribution, in Publication 590.

If at least one of the above does not apply, figure your modified AGI using Worksheet 18-1 in this chapter.

How to figure your reduced IRA deduction. You can figure your reduced IRA deduction for either Form 1040 or Form 1040A by using the worksheets in chapter 1 of Publication 590. Also, the instructions for Form 1040 and Form 1040A include similar worksheets that you may be able to use instead.

Reporting Deductible Contributions

If you file Form 1040, enter your IRA deduction on line 32 of that form. If you file Form 1040A, enter your IRA deduction on line 17. You cannot deduct IRA contributions on Form 1040EZ.

Nondeductible Contributions

Although your deduction for IRA contributions may be reduced or eliminated, contributions can be made to your IRA up to the general limit or, if it applies, the spousal IRA limit. The difference between your total permitted contributions and your IRA deduction, if any, is your nondeductible contribution.

Example. Mike is 28 years old and single. In 2005, he was covered by a retirement plan at work. His salary was $52,312. His modified AGI was $61,000. Mike made a $4,000 IRA contribution for 2005. Because he was covered by a retirement plan and his modified AGI was over $60,000, he cannot deduct his $4,000 IRA contribution. He must designate this contribution as a nondeductible contribution by reporting it on Form 8606, as explained next.

Explanation

The chief advantage of nondeductible IRA contributions is that since the income compounds on a tax-deferred basis, the ending balance will be substantially larger under an IRA than in a taxable account. In deciding whether to make nondeductible contributions, you should compare the IRA's rate of return against other investments, such as tax-exempt municipal bonds and annuity contracts, and after-tax rates of return on taxable investments. You must also consider the tax effect when you begin taking distributions. The taxation of IRA distributions is discussed below.

Form 8606. To designate contributions as nondeductible, you must file Form 8606.

You do not have to designate a contribution as nondeductible until you file your tax return. When you file, you can even designate otherwise deductible contributions as nondeductible.

You must file Form 8606 to report nondeductible contributions even if you do not have to file a tax return for the year.

Failure to report nondeductible contributions. If you do not report nondeductible contributions, all of the contributions to your traditional IRA will be treated as deductible. All distributions from your IRA will be taxed unless you can show, with satisfactory evidence, that nondeductible contributions were made.

Penalty for overstatement. If you overstate the amount of nondeductible contributions on your Form 8606 for any tax year, you must pay a penalty of $100 for each overstatement, unless it was due to reasonable cause.

Penalty for failure to file Form 8606. You will have to pay a $50 penalty if you do not file a required Form 8606, unless you can prove that the failure was due to reasonable cause.

> ### Explanation
> The law subjecting taxpayers to a $50 fine for failure to file Form 8606 applies retroactively to 1987. If you should have filed Form 8606 for a prior tax year but failed to do so, you should consider amending your return. See Chapter 1, *Filing Information,* for additional details regarding amending your return.

Tax on earnings on nondeductible contributions. As long as contributions are within the contribution limits, none of the earnings or gains on contributions (deductible or nondeductible) will be taxed until they are distributed. See *When Can You Withdraw or Use IRA Assets,* later.

Cost basis. You will have a cost basis in your traditional IRA if you made any nondeductible contributions. Your cost basis is the sum of the nondeductible contributions to your IRA minus any withdrawals or distributions of nondeductible contributions.

Inherited IRAs

If you inherit a traditional IRA, you are called a beneficiary. A beneficiary can be any person or entity the owner chooses to receive the benefits of the IRA after he or she dies. Beneficiaries of a traditional IRA must include in their gross income any taxable distributions they receive.

Inherited from spouse. If you inherit a traditional IRA from your spouse, you generally have the following three choices.

1. Treat it as your own by designating yourself as the account owner.
2. Treat it as your own by rolling it over into your traditional IRA, or to the extent it is taxable, into a:
   a. Qualified employer plan,
   b. Qualified employee annuity plan (section 403(a) plan),
   c. Tax-sheltered annuity plan (section 403(b) plan), or
   d. Deferred compensation plan of a state or local government (section 457 plan).
3. Treat yourself as the beneficiary rather than treating the IRA as your own.

Treating it as your own. You will be considered to have chosen to treat the IRA as your own if:

- Contributions (including rollover contributions) are made to the inherited IRA, or
- You do not take the required minimum distribution for a year as a beneficiary of the IRA.

You will only be considered to have chosen to treat the IRA as your own if:

- You are the sole beneficiary of the IRA, and
- You have an unlimited right to withdraw amounts from it.

However, if you receive a distribution from your deceased spouse's IRA, you can roll that distribution over into your own IRA within the 60-day time limit, as long as the distribution is not a required distribution, even if you are not the sole beneficiary of your deceased spouse's IRA.

Inherited from someone other than spouse. If you inherit a traditional IRA from anyone other than your deceased spouse, you cannot treat the inherited IRA as your own. This means that you cannot make any contributions to the IRA. It also means you cannot roll over any amounts into or out of the inherited IRA. However, you can make a trustee-to-trustee transfer as long as the IRA into which amounts are being moved is set up and maintained in the name of the deceased IRA owner for the benefit of you as beneficiary.

For more information, see the discussion of inherited IRAs under *Rollover From One IRA Into Another,* later.

Can You Move Retirement Plan Assets?

You can transfer, tax free, assets (money or property) from other retirement plans (including traditional IRAs) to a traditional IRA. You can make the following kinds of transfers.

- Transfers from one trustee to another.
- Rollovers.
- Transfers incident to a divorce.

Transfers to Roth IRAs. Under certain conditions, you can move assets from a traditional IRA to a Roth IRA. See *Can You Move Amounts Into a Roth IRA* under *Roth IRAs,* later.

Trustee-to-Trustee Transfer
A transfer of funds in your traditional IRA from one trustee directly to another, either at your request or at the trustee's request, is not a rollover. Because there is no distribution to you, the transfer is tax free. Because it is not a rollover, it is not affected by the 1-year waiting period required between rollovers, discussed later under *Rollover From One IRA Into Another.* For information about direct transfers to IRAs from retirement plans other than IRAs, see Publication 590.

Rollovers
Generally, a rollover is a tax-free distribution to you of cash or other assets from one retirement plan that you contribute (roll over) to another retirement plan. The contribution to the second retirement plan is called a "rollover contribution."

> ### Explanation
> When you receive a property distribution (e.g., shares of stock) from your IRA or a qualified employer plan, you may roll over the property received into an IRA. You are also permitted to sell the property and roll over the sale proceeds into an IRA. You may *not* retain the property distribution and roll over the property's cash equivalent.

Note. An amount rolled over tax free from one retirement plan to another is generally includible in income when it is distributed from the second plan.

Kinds of rollovers to a traditional IRA. You can roll over amounts from the following plans into a traditional IRA:

- A traditional IRA,
- An employer's qualified retirement plan for its employees,
- A deferred compensation plan of a state or local government (section 457 plan), or
- A tax-sheltered annuity plan (section 403(b) plan).

Treatment of rollovers. You cannot deduct a rollover contribution, but you must report the rollover distribution on your tax return as discussed later under *Reporting rollovers from IRAs* and under *Reporting rollovers from employer plans.*

Kinds of rollovers from a traditional IRA. You may be able to roll over, tax free, a distribution from your traditional IRA into a qualified plan. These plans include the federal Thrift Savings Fund (for federal employees), deferred compensation plans of state or local governments (section 457 plans), and tax-sheltered annuity plans (section 403(b) plans). The part of the distribution that you can roll over is the part that would otherwise be taxable (includible in your income). Qualified plans may, but are not required to, accept such rollovers.

Time limit for making a rollover contribution. You generally must make the rollover contribution by the 60th day after the day you receive the distribution from your traditional IRA or your employer's plan.

The IRS may waive the 60-day requirement where the failure to do so would be against equity or good conscience, such as in the event of a casualty, disaster, or other event beyond your reasonable control. For more information, see Publication 590.

Extension of rollover period. If an amount distributed to you from a traditional IRA or a qualified employer retirement plan is a frozen deposit at any time during the 60-day period allowed for a rollover, special rules extend the rollover period. For more information, see Publication 590.

More information. For more information on rollovers, see Publication 590.

Rollover From One IRA Into Another

You can withdraw, tax free, all or part of the assets from one traditional IRA if you reinvest them within 60 days in the same or another traditional IRA. Because this is a rollover, you cannot deduct the amount that you reinvest in an IRA.

Waiting period between rollovers. Generally, if you make a tax-free rollover of any part of a distribution from a traditional IRA, you cannot, within a 1-year period, make a tax-free rollover of any later distribution from that same IRA. You also cannot make a tax-free rollover of any amount distributed, within the same 1-year period, from the IRA into which you made the tax-free rollover.

The 1-year period begins on the date you receive the IRA distribution, not on the date you roll it over into an IRA.

Example. You have two traditional IRAs, IRA-1 and IRA-2. You make a tax-free rollover of a distribution from IRA-1 into a new traditional IRA (IRA-3). You cannot, within 1 year of the distribution from IRA-1, make a tax-free rollover of any distribution from either IRA-1 or IRA-3 into another traditional IRA.

However, the rollover from IRA-1 into IRA-3 does not prevent you from making a tax-free rollover from IRA-2 into any other traditional IRA. This is because you have not, within the last year, rolled over, tax free, any distribution from IRA-2 or made a tax-free rollover into IRA-2.

Exception. There is an exception to the rule that amounts rolled over tax free into an IRA cannot be rolled over tax free again within the 1-year period beginning on the date of the original distribution. The exception applies to a distribution which meets all three of the following requirements.

1. It is made from a failed financial institution by the Federal Deposit Insurance Corporation (FDIC) as receiver for the institution.
2. It was not initiated by either the custodial institution or the depositor.
3. It was made because:
   a. The custodial institution is insolvent, and
   b. The receiver is unable to find a buyer for the institution.

Partial rollovers. If you withdraw assets from a traditional IRA, you can roll over part of the withdrawal tax free and keep the rest of it. The amount you keep will generally be taxable (except for the part that is a return of nondeductible contributions). The amount you keep may be subject to the 10% additional tax on early distributions, discussed later under *What Acts Result in Penalties or Additional Taxes.*

Required distributions. Amounts that must be distributed during a particular year under the required distribution rules (discussed later) are not eligible for rollover treatment.

Inherited IRAs. If you inherit a traditional IRA from your spouse, you generally can roll it over, or you can choose to make the inherited IRA your own. See *Treating it as your own,* earlier.

Not inherited from spouse. If you inherit a traditional IRA from someone other than your spouse, you cannot roll it over or allow it to receive a rollover contribution. You must withdraw the IRA assets within a certain period. For more information, see Publication 590.

Reporting rollovers from IRAs. Report any rollover from one traditional IRA to the same or another traditional IRA on lines 15a and 15b, Form 1040 or lines 11a and 11b, Form 1040A.

Enter the total amount of the distribution on Form 1040, line 15a, or Form 1040A, line 11a. If the total amount on Form 1040, line 15a, or Form 1040A, line 11a, was rolled over, enter zero on Form 1040, line 15b, or Form 1040A, line 11b. If the total distribution was not rolled over, enter the taxable portion of the part that was not rolled over on Form 1040, line 15b, or Form 1040A, line 11b. Put "Rollover" next to Form 1040, line 15b, or Form 1040A, line 11b. See the forms instructions.

If you rolled over the distribution in 2006 or from an IRA into a qualified plan (other than an IRA), attach a statement explaining what you did.

Rollover From Employer's Plan Into an IRA

You can roll over into a traditional IRA all or part of an eligible rollover distribution you receive from your (or your deceased spouse's):

• Employer's qualified pension, profit-sharing or stock bonus plan,
• Annuity plan,
• Tax-sheltered annuity plan (section 403(b) plan), or
• Governmental deferred compensation plan (section 457 plan).

A qualified plan is one that meets the requirements of the Internal Revenue Code.

TAXALERT

Income tax withholding may apply to distributions made from qualified employer plans. Withholding at a rate of 20% is required on a distribution unless it is transferred directly from your employer to an IRA trustee or another employer plan.

The withholding rules do *not* apply to distributions from IRAs [or Simplified Employee Pensions (SEPs), discussed later]. However, if you wish to roll over a qualified plan distribution to an IRA, be sure to transfer the amount directly from your employer's plan to an IRA trustee or another employer plan. Otherwise, 20% of the distribution will be withheld while *100%* of the distribution must be rolled over within 60 days. If you don't have the money to cover the 20% shortage, income taxes (and possibly a 10% penalty) will be due on the amount not rolled over.

For further information, see Chapter 11, *Retirement Plans, Pensions, and Annuities.*

Eligible rollover distribution. Generally, an eligible rollover distribution is any distribution of all or part of the balance to your credit in a qualified retirement plan except the following.

1. A required minimum distribution (explained later under *When Must You Withdraw IRA Assets? (Required Minimum Distributions).*
2. Hardship distributions.
3. Any of a series of substantially equal periodic distributions paid at least once a year over:
   a. Your lifetime or life expectancy,

b. The lifetimes or life expectancies of you and your beneficiary, or

c. A period of 10 years or more.

4. Corrective distributions of excess contributions or excess deferrals, and any income allocable to the excess, or of excess annual additions and any allocable gains.

5. A loan treated as a distribution because it does not satisfy certain requirements either when made or later (such as upon default), unless the participant's accrued benefits are reduced (offset) to repay the loan.

6. Dividends on employer securities.

7. The cost of life insurance coverage.

8. Generally, a distribution to the plan participant's beneficiary.

Explanation
You may withdraw the balance in your IRA and reinvest it in another IRA with no tax consequences if the money is reinvested within 60 days after the funds are distributed. This type of rollover may be done only once in a 1-year period. This rule applies to each separate IRA you own.

Example
You have two or more IRAs. You can roll over a single distribution from each or all of them to a new IRA or to another existing IRA within a 1-year period.

TaxPlanner
If you transfer funds directly between trustees of your IRA and you never actually control or use the account assets, you may transfer your account as often as you like.

All or part of a **lump sum distribution** from a qualified employer benefit plan may be transferred to an IRA. You may affect a partial rollover—and be taxed at **ordinary income** rates—only on the portion of the money not reinvested within 60 days. This portion is not eligible for any special tax treatment, which it might have been had the entire amount in your employer benefit plan been reported as current income. As mentioned earlier, withholding at a rate of 20% is required on a qualified employer plan distribution unless it is transferred directly from your employer to the trustee of an IRA.

TaxAlert
A partial distribution from a qualified plan is eligible for rollover treatment as long as it is *not*:

1. A required minimum distribution (e.g., for individuals who have attained age 70 1/2); or

2. A distribution that is part of a series of substantially equal payments that are received at least annually over life, life expectancy, or a period of at least 10 years.

For more details, see Chapter 11, *Retirement Plans, Pensions, and Annuities*.

TaxPlanner
Not all distributions from qualified employer benefit plans may be rolled over into an IRA. IRAs are specifically prohibited from investing in life insurance contracts. Therefore, if your employer plan distributes to you both cash and a life insurance policy, the value of the life insurance policy (except for your contributions) is currently taxable to you. If this is the case, you should consider rolling over the life insurance contract into another qualified pension, profit-sharing, or stock bonus plan that allows investments in life insurance contracts.

TaxPlanner
A court has held that a tax-free rollover can be made only if the employer's plan and trust are tax-exempt when the distribution is made. In this particular case, the IRS retroactively revoked the tax-exempt status of the trust. This made the distribution ineligible for a rollover.

The IRS believes that once you have made a rollover, you cannot change your mind and report the distribution as taxable income. Presumably you could replicate this effect by taking a distribution from the IRA.

You may roll over a lump-sum distribution from a former spouse's IRA or employee plan that was transferred to you by a divorce decree or written agreement incident to the divorce.

TaxAlert
The IRS has the ability to waive the 60-day rule where there are extenuating circumstances, such as a casualty, disaster, or an egregious error by a financial institution. In certain circumstances the waiver may be automatic; in others you may have to file a request with the IRS. The IRS has been relatively sympathetic to taxpayers and has issued a number of waiver rulings in recent years.

Reporting rollovers from employer plans. Enter the total distribution (before income tax or other deductions were withheld) on Form 1040, line 16a or Form 1040A, line 12a. This amount should be shown in box 1 of Form 1099-R. From this amount, subtract any contributions (usually shown in box 5 of Form 1099-R) that were taxable to you when made. From that result, subtract the amount that was rolled over either directly or within 60 days of receiving the distribution. Enter the remaining amount, even if zero, on Form 1040, line 16b, or Form 1040A, line 12b. Also, enter "Rollover" next to Form 1040, line 16b, or Form 1040A, line 12b.

Converting From Any Traditional IRA to a Roth IRA
You can convert amounts from a traditional IRA into a Roth IRA if, for the tax year you make the withdrawal from the traditional IRA, both of the following requirements are met.

- Your modified AGI (explained later under *Roth IRAs*) is not more than $100,000.
- You are not a married individual filing a separate return.

Note. If you did not live with your spouse at any time during the year and you file a separate return, your filing status, for this purpose, is single.

Required distributions. You cannot convert amounts that must be distributed from your traditional IRA for a particular year (including the calendar year in which you reach age 70 1/2) under the required distribution rules (discussed later).

Inherited IRAs. If you inherited a traditional IRA from someone other than your spouse, you cannot convert it to a Roth IRA.

Income. You must include in your gross income distributions from a traditional IRA that you would have to include in income if you had not converted them into a Roth IRA. You do not include in gross income any part of a distribution from a traditional IRA that is a return of your basis, as discussed later.

If you must include any amount in your gross income, you may have to increase your withholding or make estimated tax payments. See chapter 5.

Recharacterizations

You may be able to treat a contribution made to one type of IRA as having been made to a different type of IRA. This is called recharacterizing the contribution. More detailed information is in Publication 590.

No deduction allowed. You cannot deduct the contribution to the first IRA. Any net income you transfer with the recharacterized contribution is treated as earned in the second IRA.

How to recharacterize a contribution. To recharacterize a contribution, you generally must have the contribution transferred from the first IRA (the one to which it was made) to the second IRA in a trustee-to-trustee transfer. If the transfer is made by the due date (including extensions) for your tax return for the year during which the contribution was made, you can elect to treat the contribution as having been originally made to the second IRA instead of to the first IRA. If you recharacterize your contribution, you must do all three of the following.

- Include in the transfer any net income allocable to the contribution. If there was a loss, the net income you must transfer may be a negative amount.
- Report the recharacterization on your tax return for the year during which the contribution was made.
- Treat the contribution as having been made to the second IRA on the date that it was actually made to the first IRA.

Required notifications. To recharacterize a contribution, you must notify both the trustee of the first IRA (the one to which the contribution was actually made) and the trustee of the second IRA (the one to which the contribution is being moved) that you have elected to treat the contribution as having been made to the second IRA rather than the first. You must make the notifications by the date of the transfer. Only one notification is required if both IRAs are maintained by the same trustee. The notification(s) must include all of the following information.

- The type and amount of the contribution to the first IRA that is to be recharacterized.
- The date on which the contribution was made to the first IRA and the year for which it was made.
- A direction to the trustee of the first IRA to transfer in a trustee-to-trustee transfer the amount of the contribution and any net income (or loss) allocable to the contribution to the trustee of the second IRA. If both IRAs involved in the trustee-to-trustee transfer are maintained by the same trustee, you need only direct that trustee to transfer the contribution.
- The name of the trustee of the first IRA and the name of the trustee of the second IRA.
- Any additional information needed to make the transfer.

Reporting a recharacterization. If you elect to recharacterize a contribution to one IRA as a contribution to another IRA, you must report the recharacterization on your tax return as directed by Form 8606 and its instructions. You must treat the contribution as having been made to the second IRA.

Transfers Incident to Divorce

If an interest in a traditional IRA is transferred from your spouse or former spouse to you by a divorce or separate maintenance decree or a written document related to such a decree, the interest in the IRA, starting from the date of the transfer, is treated as your IRA. The transfer is tax free. For detailed information, see Publication 590.

When Can You Withdraw or Use IRA Assets?

There are rules limiting use of your IRA assets and distributions from it. Violation of the rules generally results in additional taxes in the year of violation. See *What Acts Result in Penalties or Additional Taxes,* later.

Contributions returned before the due date of return. If you made IRA contributions in 2005, you can withdraw them tax free by the due date of your return. If you have an extension of time to file your return, you can withdraw them tax free by the extended due date. You can do this if, for each contribution you withdraw, both of the following conditions apply.

- You did not take a deduction for the contribution.
- You withdraw any interest or other income earned on the contribution. You can take into account any loss on the contribution while it was in the IRA when calculating the amount that must be withdrawn. If there was a loss, the net income earned on the contribution may be a negative amount.

Note. To calculate the amount you must withdraw, see Publication 590.

Caution. *Generally, except for any part of a withdrawal that is a return of nondeductible contributions (basis), any withdrawal of your contributions after the due date (or extended due date) of your return will be treated as a taxable distribution. Excess contributions can also be recovered tax free as discussed under* What Acts Result in Penalties or Additional Taxes, *later.*

Earnings includible in income. You must include in income any earnings on the contributions you withdraw. Include the earnings in income for the year in which you made the contributions, not in the year in which you withdraw them.

Early distributions tax. The 10% additional tax on distributions made before you reach age 59 1/2 does not apply to these tax-free withdrawals of your contributions. However, the distribution of interest or other income must be reported on Form 5329 and, unless the distribution qualifies as an exception to the age 59 1/2 rule, it will be subject to this tax.

TaxPlanner

Withdrawals from IRAs before age 59 1/2 to pay educational expenses. Generally, withdrawals from a traditional or Roth IRA before age 59 1/2 are subject to an additional 10% tax on the part of the distribution included in gross income. You will not be subject to the 10% additional tax, however, if for the year of withdrawal you have paid sufficient qualified higher education expenses for yourself, your spouse, or for your or your spouse's children or grandchildren. This exception does not apply if you use the money to pay for expenses you incurred in a different year.

Qualifications and income limits. There are no specific income limits restricting the use of this provision.

When Must You Withdraw IRA Assets? (Required Minimum Distributions)

You cannot keep funds in your traditional IRA indefinitely. Eventually they must be distributed. If there are no distributions, or if the distributions are not large enough, you may have to pay a 50% excise tax on the amount not distributed as required. See *Excess Accumulations (Insufficient Distributions),* later. The requirements for distributing IRA funds differ depending on whether you are the IRA owner or the beneficiary of a decedent's IRA.

Required minimum distribution. The amount that must be distributed each year is referred to as the required minimum distribution.

Required distributions not eligible for rollover. Amounts that must be distributed (required minimum distributions) during a particular year are not eligible for rollover treatment.

IRA owners. If you are the owner of a traditional IRA, you must start receiving distributions from your IRA by April 1 of the year following the year in which you reach age 70 1/2. April 1 of the year following the year in which you reach age 70 1/2 is referred to as the required beginning date.

Distributions by the required beginning date. You must receive at least a minimum amount for each year starting with the year you reach age 70 1/2 (your 70 1/2 year). If you do not (or did not) receive that minimum amount in your 70 1/2 year, then you must receive distributions for your 70 1/2 year by April 1 of the next year.

If an IRA owner dies after reaching age 70 1/2, but before April 1 of the next year, no minimum distribution is required because death occurred before the required beginning date.

Caution. *Even if you begin receiving distributions before you attain age 70 1/2, you must begin calculating and receiving required minimum distributions by your required beginning date.*

Distributions after the required beginning date. The required minimum distribution for any year after the year you reach 70 1/2 must be made by December 31 of that later year.

TaxPlanner

Explanation
The purpose of an IRA is to provide retirement income. Therefore, when you reach age 70 1/2, you are expected to begin withdrawing the proceeds in your IRA rather than continue to let the funds accumulate and use the IRA as a tool to build your estate. If you don't withdraw the minimum amounts yearly, a 50% nondeductible tax is levied on the amount of the minimum payment left in your IRA.

You must start receiving minimum payments from your IRA by April 1 of the year after the year in which you reach age 70 1/2.

It is only your first distribution (the distribution for the year you reach age 70 1/2) that may be delayed until April 1 of the following year. The second distribution must be made by December 31 of the same year. You must determine what effect the doubling of distributions will have on your tax liability.

Generally, the minimum distribution is based on the joint life expectancy of both you and a survivor who is assumed to be no more than 10 years younger (see IRS Publication 590 or Chapter 11 for the appropriate life expectancy table). Alternatively, if your spouse is more than 10 years younger than you, and your spouse is the beneficiary of your IRA, the minimum distribution is based on your and your spouse's actual joint life expectancy (see IRS Publication 590 for the appropriate life expectancy table). Using this alternate method will result in a lower minimum distribution than the general method due to using a longer life expectancy.

It's worth noting that your IRA fund may continue to grow, even if you are taking the required distributions. For example, if the table used indicates a life expectancy of 20 years, you must withdraw only one-twentieth (5%) of your IRA funds in that year. If the funds in your IRA are earning income at the rate of 10%, your account will continue to grow.

TaxAlert
Once distributions are required, a minimum distribution *must* be made each year based on the age of the IRA owner and the appropriate life expectancy table.

Example 1
Jack Jones, who became 70 1/2 years old on May 1, 2005, has an IRA with a December 31, 2004, balance of $80,000. By looking at tables published by the IRS, he finds that his life expectancy for purposes of his IRA distributions is 26.5 years. This is the life expectancy for a person who is 71, which he will be during 2005. To figure his minimum distribution, he divides the amount in his IRA by 26.5. He must receive a distribution of $3,019 prior to April 3, 2006, to avoid a penalty.

Example 2
In Example 1 above, assume Jack Jones is married and his wife, who is his beneficiary, turns 60 in 2005. Jack can use 27.2 years for his life expectancy since his wife is more than 10 years younger than he is. The distribution required by April 3, 2006, is $2,941.

TaxPlanner
You are always permitted to take more out of your IRA than the minimum amount you calculated.

TaxPlanner
If a participant in an IRA dies, the tax rules that apply to IRA distributions depend on whether the beneficiary is a spouse and whether the participant had reached 70 1/2—the age at which minimum distributions are required from an IRA before death.

If your spouse is a beneficiary. If you die before age 70 1/2 *and* distributions have not yet begun, your spouse could simply retitle your IRA account in his or her name and continue deferring tax, treating your IRA as his or her own (e.g., name new heirs). Otherwise, your spouse would have to begin distributions based on his or her life expectancy by the later of:

- December 31 of the calendar year in which you would have reached age 70 1/2, or
- December 31 of the calendar year that follows the calendar year of your death.

If you live past age 70 1/2 and distributions have begun, your surviving spouse can treat the IRA as his or her own IRA. Otherwise, your spouse would continue receiving minimum distributions over his or her own life expectancy (he or she can always take larger distributions if needed).

If your spouse is not the beneficiary. The options available to a nonspouse beneficiary receiving IRA assets are more limited. Your beneficiary would have to receive distributions from the account:

- By December 31 of the fifth year following the year of your death, or
- In installments intended to last the beneficiary's lifetime (these installments must begin no later than December 31 of the calendar year that follows the calendar year of your death).

However, a nonspouse recipient cannot completely defer income taxes the way that a spouse beneficiary can by simply rolling the money over.

TaxPlanner
There are no minimum required distributions for a Roth IRA during the life of the account owner (see Roth IRAs for more details).

TaxPlanner
Keogh plans. The same withdrawal techniques described in the TaxPlanners above may be used with a Keogh plan, a retirement arrangement that self-employed people may set up.

Employer stock bonus plans and company profit-sharing plans. The main attraction of having your employer put some of your compensation into a stock bonus plan or a company profit-sharing plan is that you are not currently taxed on the contributions to or the earnings in the plan. In addition, these plans have certain advantages that IRAs do not:

1. Borrowing is permitted if the loan is repaid within 5 years.
2. A lump-sum distribution may qualify for 10-year averaging.
3. Minimum distributions can be deferred if you continue to work after age 70 1/2.

Beneficiaries. If you are the beneficiary of a decedent's traditional IRA, the requirements for distributions from that IRA generally depend on whether the IRA owner died before or after the required beginning date for distributions.

More information. For more information, including how to figure your minimum required distribution each year and how to figure your required distribution if you are a beneficiary of a decedent's IRA, see Publication 590.

Are Distributions Taxable?

In general, distributions from a traditional IRA are taxable in the year you receive them.

Exceptions. Exceptions to distributions from traditional IRAs being taxable in the year you receive them are:

• Rollovers,
• Tax-free withdrawals of contributions, discussed earlier, and
• The return of nondeductible contributions, discussed later under *Distributions Fully or Partly Taxable.*

Explanation

IRA distributions are taxed in a manner similar to annuities. If you do not make nondeductible contributions, all distributions from a traditional IRA are taxed as ordinary income. You may not use special 10-year averaging on a lump-sum distribution from your IRA, even if the account is a rollover from a qualified plan. If you made nondeductible contributions, a portion of the distribution may be excludable from income. The excludable amount is computed as follows:

$$\frac{\text{Undistributed Nondeductible Contributions}}{\text{Total of All IRA Balances}} \times \text{Distribution Amount}$$

Example

Assume that Mary has made a $2,000 nondeductible contribution and that her total account balance is $20,000. In 2005, she takes a $5,000 distribution. Her tax-free amount is:

$$\$2,000 / \$20,000 \times \$5,000 = \$500$$

Undistributed nondeductible contributions are obtained from the last Form 8606 you filed. Therefore, make sure you always keep the most recent copy in your files.

Money that you withdraw from your IRA is treated as a distribution to you and may trigger the 10% penalty that is imposed on premature distributions. However, it is possible to "borrow" temporarily from your IRA by taking a distribution and rolling over the funds to the same or to a new IRA within 60 days. That money and any income you earn on it are not considered premature distributions. However, you may not contribute any money that you do earn to your IRA account. Instead, you have to keep that money—and pay tax on it.

Caution. *Although a conversion of a traditional IRA is considered a rollover for Roth IRA purposes, it is not an exception to the rule that distributions from a traditional IRA are taxable in the year you receive them. Conversion distributions are includible in your gross income subject to this rule and the special rules for conversions explained in Publication 590.*

Ordinary income. Distributions from traditional IRAs that you include in income are taxed as ordinary income.

No special treatment. In figuring your tax, you cannot use the 10-year tax option or capital gain treatment that applies to lump-sum distributions from qualified employer plans.

Distributions Fully or Partly Taxable

Distributions from your traditional IRA may be fully or partly taxable, depending on whether your IRA includes any nondeductible contributions.

Fully taxable. If only deductible contributions were made to your traditional IRA (or IRAs, if you have more than one), you have no basis in your IRA. Because you have no basis in your IRA, any distributions are fully taxable when received. See *Reporting taxable distributions on your return,* later.

Partly taxable. If you made nondeductible contributions to any of your traditional IRAs, you have a cost basis (investment in the contract) equal to the amount of those contributions. These nondeductible contributions are not taxed when they are distributed to you. They are a return of your investment in your IRA.

Explanation

A distribution from an IRA is fully taxable, unless it represents a timely withdrawal of an excess contribution, is rolled over into another IRA within the required 60-day period, or represents a return of nondeductible contributions.

If you reach age 59 1/2 and are entitled to withdraw the funds in your IRA without penalty but you decide not to, you are not taxed until an actual distribution is made. However, in the following situations, all or part of your IRA is currently taxed:

1. The occurrence of a prohibited transaction causes the entire amount in your individual retirement *account* to be treated as distributed and therefore taxable to you. For instance, if you lend yourself the money in your IRA, the entire amount in the account is then currently taxable to you. However, if you engage in a prohibited transaction with your individual retirement *annuity,* only the amount of the prohib-

ited transaction is subject to a 5% excise tax (see *Prohibited Transactions*, following).

2. The pledging of an IRA causes the portion pledged to be treated as distributed. For example, if you have an IRA with a value of $7,500 that you pledge as security for a $5,000 bank loan, you are taxed on the $5,000.
3. The pledging of an IRA *annuity* causes the entire account to be treated as distributed.

If you are under age 59 1/2 and distribute part of your IRA in any of the ways described above, a 10% tax penalty is applied to the distributed portion.

Exceptions
The nondeductible 10% penalty tax on premature distributions does not apply if you are disabled and the early distribution is made because of your disability.

Only the part of the distribution that represents nondeductible contributions (your cost basis) is tax free. If nondeductible contributions have been made, distributions consist partly of nondeductible contributions (basis) and partly of deductible contributions, earnings, and gains (if there are any). Until all of your basis has been distributed, each distribution is partly nontaxable and partly taxable.

Form 8606. You must complete Form 8606 and attach it to your return if you receive a distribution from a traditional IRA and have ever made nondeductible contributions to any of your traditional IRAs. Using the form, you will figure the nontaxable distributions for 2005 and your total IRA basis for 2005 and earlier years.

Note. If you are required to file Form 8606, but you are not required to file an income tax return, you still must file Form 8606. Send it to the IRS at the time and place you would otherwise file an income tax return.

Distributions reported on Form 1099-R. If you receive a distribution from your traditional IRA, you will receive Form 1099-R, Distributions From Pensions, Annuities, Retirement or Profit-Sharing Plans, IRAs, Insurance Contracts, etc., or a similar statement. IRA distributions are shown in boxes 1 and 2a of Form 1099-R. A number or letter code in box 7 tells you what type of distribution you received from your IRA.

TAXORGANIZER
Keep Form 1099-R with your records to substantiate IRA distributions and federal income tax withholding.

Withholding. Federal income tax is withheld from distributions from traditional IRAs unless you choose not to have tax withheld. See chapter 5.

Explanation
You may elect at any time not to have taxes withheld on the distribution. Before electing not to withhold, however, you must review your withholdings from other sources and estimated payments. See Chapter 5, *Tax Withholding and Estimated Tax,* for underpayment penalties.

IRA distributions delivered outside the United States. In general, if you are a U.S. citizen or resident alien and your home address is outside the United States or its possessions,

you cannot choose exemption from withholding on distributions from your traditional IRA.

Reporting taxable distributions on your return. Report fully taxable distributions, including early distributions on Form 1040, line 15b, or Form 1040A, line 11b (no entry is required on Form 1040, line 15a, or Form 1040A, line 11a). If only part of the distribution is taxable, enter the total amount on Form 1040, line 15a, or Form 1040A, line 11a, and the taxable part on Form 1040, line 15b, or Form 1040A, line 11b. You cannot report distributions on Form 1040EZ.

What Acts Result in Penalties or Additional Taxes?

The tax advantages of using traditional IRAs for retirement savings can be offset by additional taxes and penalties if you do not follow the rules.

There are additions to the regular tax for using your IRA funds in prohibited transactions. There are also additional taxes for the following activities.

- Investing in collectibles.
- Making excess contributions.
- Taking early distributions.
- Allowing excess amounts to accumulate (failing to take required distributions).

There are penalties for overstating the amount of nondeductible contributions and for failure to file a Form 8606, if required.

Prohibited Transactions
Generally, a prohibited transaction is any improper use of your traditional IRA by you, your beneficiary, or any disqualified person.

Disqualified persons include your fiduciary and members of your family (spouse, ancestor, lineal descendent, and any spouse of a lineal descendent).

The following are examples of prohibited transactions with a traditional IRA.

- Borrowing money from it.
- Selling property to it.
- Receiving unreasonable compensation for managing it.
- Using it as security for a loan.
- Buying property for personal use (present or future) with IRA funds.

Effect on an IRA account. Generally, if you or your beneficiary engages in a prohibited transaction in connection with your traditional IRA account at any time during the year, the account stops being an IRA as of the first day of that year.

Effect on you or your beneficiary. If your account stops being an IRA because you or your beneficiary engaged in a prohibited transaction, the account is treated as distributing all its assets to you at their fair market values on the first day of the year. If the total of those values is more than your basis in the IRA, you will have a taxable gain that is includible in your income. For information on figuring your gain and reporting it in income, see *Are Distributions Taxable*, earlier. The distribution may be subject to additional taxes or penalties.

Taxes on prohibited transactions. If someone other than the owner or beneficiary of a traditional IRA engages in a prohibited transaction, that person may be liable for certain taxes. In general, there is a 15% tax on the amount of the prohibited transaction and a 100% additional tax if the transaction is not corrected.

More information. For more information on prohibited transactions, see Publication 590.

Explanation
The rules relating to prohibited transactions are designed to prevent the manipulation of IRA funds by the person who has set the funds aside for his or her retirement.

A qualified plan run by your employer that engages in a prohibited transaction is subject to a 5% tax on that transaction. Your IRA, which may have been part of your employer's plan, does not lose its tax-exempt status.

Investment in Collectibles

If your traditional IRA invests in collectibles, the amount invested is considered distributed to you in the year invested. You may have to pay the 10% additional tax on early distributions, discussed later. **Collectibles.** These include:

- Art works,
- Rugs,
- Antiques,
- Metals,
- Gems,
- Stamps,
- Coins,
- Alcoholic beverages, and
- Certain other tangible personal property.

Exception. Your IRA can invest in one, one-half, one-quarter, or one-tenth ounce U.S. gold coins, or one-ounce silver coins minted by the Treasury Department. It can also invest in certain platinum coins and certain gold, silver, palladium, and platinum bullion.

Explanation

Although an investment in tangible property, such as art-works, precious metals or gems, antiques, or alcoholic beverages, is not technically a prohibited transaction, the cost of the item is treated as a distribution from your IRA. The amount is included in your income and may be subject to the 10% premature distribution penalty tax.

This rule is designed to prevent you from directing your IRA to invest in property that the trustee could conceivably allow you to keep in your home for your personal enjoyment.

In order to help sell U.S and state issued gold and silver coins, Congress removed the penalty for such coins acquired after October 1, 1986.

Excess Contributions

Generally, an excess contribution is the amount contributed to your traditional IRA(s) for the year that is more than the smaller of the following amounts.

- The maximum deductible amount for the year. For 2005, this is $4,000 ($4,500 if 50 or older).
- Your taxable compensation for the year.

Example

You contribute $8,000 to IRAs you have set up for you and your nonworking spouse. You put $4,050 into your account and $3,950 into your spouse's account. There is a $50 excess contribution to your account. Only $7,950 ($4,000 + $3,950) can be contributed and deducted on your joint income tax return. In order to obtain the full $8,000 contribution, you can withdraw the $50 excess contribution from your account and put it into your spouse's account. This must be done no later than April 17, 2006.

Tax on excess contributions. In general, if the excess contributions for a year are not withdrawn by the date your return for the year is due (including extensions), you are subject to a 6% tax. You must pay the 6% tax each year on excess amounts that remain in your traditional IRA at the end of your tax year. The tax cannot be more than 6% of the value of your IRA as of the end of your tax year. **Excess contributions withdrawn by due date of return.** You will not have to pay the 6% tax if you withdraw an excess contribution made during a tax year and you also withdraw interest or other income earned on the excess contribution. You must complete your withdrawal by the date your tax return for that year is due, including extensions.

How to treat withdrawn contributions. Do not include in your gross income an excess contribution that you withdraw from your traditional IRA before your tax return is due if both the following conditions are met.

- No deduction was allowed for the excess contribution.
- You withdraw the interest or other income earned on the excess contribution.

You can take into account any loss on the contribution while it was in the IRA when calculating the amount that must be withdrawn. If there was a loss, the net income earned on the contribution may be a negative amount.

How to treat withdrawn interest or other income. You must include in your gross income the interest or other income that was earned on the excess contribution. Report it on your return for the year in which the excess contribution was made. Your withdrawal of interest or other income may be subject to an additional 10% tax on early distributions, discussed later.

Explanation

Excess payments you withdraw before the due date of the return are not subject to the 6% excise tax, provided that the full amount of income attributable to the excess contribution is also distributed. The income portion of the distribution is then included in your income in the year in which the excess contribution was made. The withdrawn income may be subject to the 10% tax on premature distributions (see *Early Distributions,* following).

Excess contributions withdrawn after due date of return. In general, you must include all distributions (withdrawals) from your traditional IRA in your gross income. However, if the following conditions are met, you can withdraw excess contributions from your IRA and not include the amount withdrawn in your gross income.

- Total contributions (other than rollover contributions) for 2004 to your IRA were not more than $3,000 ($3,500 if 50 or older).
- You did not take a deduction for the excess contribution being withdrawn.

The withdrawal can take place at any time, even after the due date, including extensions, for filing your tax return for the year.

Explanation

Excess payments may also be adjusted by deducting the correct amount in the current year and applying the excess to the following year's contribution.

Example

If you mistakenly contributed $3,500 to your IRA in 2004, when you were entitled to only a $3,000 contribution, you may reduce your 2005 contribution by the excess $500. If you are entitled to a $4,000 contribution in 2005, you should then contribute no more than $3,500 that year. To make this application work, you must deduct only $3,000 for 2004—not the actual $3,500 you contributed. Although you are still subject to the 6% tax on the $500 excess contribution in 2004, if you reduce the following year's contribution to $3,500, there is no excess contribution remaining in your IRA and no tax would be imposed for 2005.

You would receive a $4,000 deduction for 2005 consisting of the $3,500 you actually contributed in 2005 plus the excess contribution from 2004.

Excess contribution deducted in an earlier year. If you deducted an excess contribution in an earlier year for which the total contributions were not more than the maximum deductible amount for that year ($2,000 for 2001 and earlier years, $3,000 for 2002, 2003 and 2004 ($3,500 for 2002, 2003 and 2004 if 50 or older)), you can still remove the excess from your traditional IRA and not include it in your gross income. To do this, file Form 1040X, Amended U.S. Individual Income Tax Return, for that year and do not deduct the excess contribution on the amended return. Generally, you can file an amended return within 3 years after you filed your return, or 2 years from the time the tax was paid, whichever is later.

Excess due to incorrect rollover information. If an excess contribution in your traditional IRA is the result of a rollover and the excess occurred because the information the plan was required to give you was incorrect, you can withdraw the excess contribution. The limits mentioned above are increased by the amount of the excess that is due to the incorrect information. You will have to amend your return for the year in which the excess occurred to correct the reporting of the rollover amounts in that year. Do not include in your gross income the part of the excess contribution caused by the incorrect information.

Early Distributions

You must include early distributions of taxable amounts from your traditional IRA in your gross income. Early distributions are also subject to an additional 10% tax. See the discussion of Form 5329 under *Reporting Additional Taxes,* later, to figure and report the tax.
Early distributions defined. Early distributions generally are amounts distributed from your traditional IRA account or annuity before you are age 59 1/2.

Age 59 1/2 rule. Generally, if you are under age 59 1/2, you must pay a 10% additional tax on the distribution of any assets (money or other property) from your traditional IRA. Distributions before you are age 59 1/2 are called early distributions.

The 10% additional tax applies to the part of the distribution that you have to include in gross income. It is in addition to any regular income tax on that amount.

Exceptions. There are several exceptions to the age 59 1/2 rule. Even if you receive a distribution before you are age 59 1/2, you may not have to pay the 10% additional tax if you are in one of the following situations.

• You have unreimbursed medical expenses that are more than 7.5% of your adjusted gross income.
• The distributions are not more than the cost of your medical insurance.
• You are disabled.
• You are the beneficiary of a deceased IRA owner.
• You are receiving distributions in the form of an annuity.
• The distributions are not more than your qualified higher education expenses.
• You use the distributions to buy, build, or rebuild a first home.
• The distribution is due to an IRS levy of the qualified plan.

Most of these exceptions are explained in Publication 590.
Note. Distributions that are timely and properly rolled over, as discussed earlier, are not subject to either regular income tax or the 10% additional tax. Certain withdrawals of excess contributions after the due date of your return are also tax free and therefore not subject to the 10% additional tax. (See *Excess contributions withdrawn after due date of return,* earlier.) This also applies to transfers incident to divorce, as discussed earlier.

The IRS has identified three methods available for determining whether distributions from an IRA are considered to be "substantially equal periodic payments."

1. **The "straight life expectancy" method:** To use this method, you divide the balance in the individual retirement account at the end of each year by the owner's life expectancy or joint and survivor life expectancy, as determined from tables published by the IRS. Under this method, distributions may vary from year to year due to:
   (a) account balance changes resulting from earnings and distributions during the year, and
   (b) changes in the owner's life expectancy as the owner gets older.
2. **The amortization method:** This method involves determining an annuity payment based on the balance in the individual retirement account, the beneficiary's life expectancy, and an assumed interest rate. Under this method, you would essentially be able to choose among various distribution amounts: IRS rules allow you to select from several interest rate assumptions and between two published life expectancy tables. However, once the annuity amount has been determined, it will not change from year to year.
3. **The annuity factor method:** This method involves determining an annuity payment by dividing the balance in the individual retirement account by an annuity factor derived from a reasonable mortality table using a reasonable rate of interest. As under the amortization method, once determined, the annuity amount will not change.

TaxAlert

Note that the substantially equal periodic payment exception (described above) is applied on an IRA-by-IRA basis. Therefore, an IRA owner who wants the flexibility in the future to increase the annual withdrawal amounts can divide an existing IRA into several IRAs before distributions begin. Substantially equal periodic distributions could be taken prior to 59 1/2 from only one of the IRAs. In the future, if additional payments are needed, distributions could be taken from one or more of the other IRAs.

Taxpayers have the ability to make a one-time switch from either the amortization method or annuity factor method to the straight life expectancy method. The one-time switch may be beneficial if you are locked into a fixed payment under either the amortization or annuity factor methods and your account has dropped in value. By using the one-time switch to the straight life expectancy method, a new lower payment can be calculated based on the lower account balance. You should consult your tax advisor for additional details.

The straight life expectancy method (method 1, above) is the easiest to use but will result in the smallest annual distribution. The amortization and annuity factor methods result in larger distributions and are more difficult to compute, respectively, than the straight life expectancy method.

Since the rules regarding substantially equal periodic payments are complex and substantial penalties apply for failure to comply, you should consult your tax advisor when planning to take early distributions from your IRA(s).

Additional 10% tax. The additional tax on early distributions is 10% of the amount of the early distribution that you must include in your gross income. This tax is in addition to any regular income tax resulting from including the distribution in income.

Nondeductible contributions. The tax on early distributions does not apply to the part of a distribution that represents a return of your nondeductible contributions (basis).

More information. For more information on early distributions, see Publication 590.

Excess Accumulations (Insufficient Distributions)

You cannot keep amounts in your traditional IRA indefinitely. Generally, you must begin receiving distributions by April 1 of the year following the year in which you reach age 70 1/2. The required minimum distribution for any year after the year in which you reach age 70 1/2 must be made by December 31 of that later year.

Tax on excess. If distributions are less than the required minimum distribution for the year, you may have to pay a 50% excise tax for that year on the amount not distributed as required.

Request to excuse the tax. If the excess accumulation is due to reasonable error, and you have taken, or are taking, steps to remedy the insufficient distribution, you can request that the tax be excused.

If you believe you qualify for this relief, do the following.

- File Form 5329 with your Form 1040.
- Pay any tax you owe on excess accumulations.
- Attach a letter of explanation.

If the IRS approves your request, it will refund the excess accumulations tax you paid.

Exemption from tax. If you are unable to take required distributions because you have a traditional IRA invested in a contract issued by an insurance company that is in state insurer delinquency proceedings, the 50% excise tax does not apply if the conditions and requirements of Revenue Procedure 92-10 are satisfied.

TaxAlert

If you cannot receive required distributions from your IRA because your insurance company is in state insurer delinquency proceedings, consult a tax advisor to see if you can avoid the 50% excise tax.

More information. For more information on excess accumulations, see Publication 590.

Reporting Additional Taxes

Generally, you must use Form 5329 to report the tax on excess contributions, early distributions, and excess accumulations. If you must file Form 5329, you cannot use Form 1040A or Form 1040EZ.

Filing a tax return. If you must file an individual income tax return, complete Form 5329 and attach it to your Form 1040. Enter the total amount of additional taxes due on Form 1040, line 60.

Not filing a tax return. If you do not have to file a tax return but do have to pay one of the additional taxes mentioned earlier, file the completed Form 5329 with the IRS at the time and place you would have filed your Form 1040. Be sure to include your address on page 1 and your signature and date on page 2. Enclose, but do not attach, a check or money order payable to the United States Treasury for the tax you owe, as shown on Form 5329. Enter your social security number and "2005 Form 5329" on your check or money order.

Form 5329 not required. You do not have to use Form 5329 if either of the following situations exist.

- Distribution code 1 (early distribution) is correctly shown in box 7 of all Forms 1099-R. If you do not owe any other additional tax on a distribution, multiply the taxable part of the early distribution by 10% and enter the result on Form 1040, line 60. Put "No" to the left of line 60 to indicate that you do not have to file Form 5329. However, if you also owe any other additional tax on a distribution, do not enter this 10% additional tax directly on your Form 1040. You must file Form 5329 to report your additional taxes.

• You rolled over a distribution from a qualified retirement plan.

Roth IRAs

Regardless of your age, you may be able to establish and make nondeductible contributions to a retirement plan called a Roth IRA. **Contributions not reported.** You do not report Roth IRA contributions on your return.

What Is a Roth IRA?

A Roth IRA is an individual retirement plan that, except as explained in this chapter, is subject to the rules that apply to a traditional IRA (defined earlier). It can be either an account or an annuity. Individual retirement accounts and annuities are described in Publication 590.

To be a Roth IRA, the account or annuity must be designated as a Roth IRA when it is set up. A deemed IRA can be a Roth IRA, but neither a SEP-IRA nor a SIMPLE IRA can be designated as a Roth IRA.

Unlike a traditional IRA, you cannot deduct contributions to a Roth IRA. But, if you satisfy the requirements, qualified distributions (discussed later) are tax free. Contributions can be made to your Roth IRA after you reach age 70 1/2 and you can leave amounts in your Roth IRA as long as you live.

When Can a Roth IRA Be Set Up?

You can set up a Roth IRA at any time. However, the time for making contributions for any year is limited. See *When Can You Make Contributions*, later under *Can You Contribute to a Roth IRA*.

Can You Contribute to a Roth IRA?

Generally, you can contribute to a Roth IRA if you have taxable compensation (defined later) and your modified AGI (defined later) is less than:

• $160,000 for married filing jointly or qualifying widow(er),
• $10,000 for married filing separately and you lived with your spouse at any time during the year, or
• $110,000 for single, head of household, or married filing separately and you did not live with your spouse at any time during the year.

Tip. *You may be eligible to claim a credit for contributions to your Roth IRA. For more information, see chapter 39.*

Is there an age limit for contributions? Contributions can be made to your Roth IRA regardless of your age.

Can you contribute to a Roth IRA for your spouse? You can contribute to a Roth IRA for your spouse provided the contributions satisfy the spousal IRA limit (discussed in *How Much Can Be Contributed* under *Traditional IRAs*), you file jointly, and your modified AGI is less than $160,000.

Compensation. Compensation includes wages, salaries, tips, professional fees, bonuses, and other amounts received for providing personal services. It also includes commissions, self-employment income, and taxable alimony and separate maintenance payments.

Modified AGI. Your modified AGI for Roth IRA purposes is your adjusted gross income (AGI) as shown on your return modified as follows.

1. Subtract conversion income. This is any income resulting from the conversion of an IRA (other than a Roth IRA) to a Roth IRA.

2. Add the following deductions and exclusions:
   a. Traditional IRA deduction,
   b. Student loan interest deduction,
   c. Tuition and fees deduction,
   d. Foreign earned income exclusion,
   e. Foreign housing exclusion or deduction,
   f. Exclusion of qualified savings bond interest shown on Form 8815,
   g. Exclusion of employer-provided adoption benefits shown on Form 8839, and
   h. Domestic production activities deduction.

You can use Worksheet 18-2 to figure your modified AGI.

How Much Can Be Contributed?

The contribution limit for Roth IRAs depends on whether contributions are made only to Roth IRAs or to both traditional IRAs and Roth IRAs.

Roth IRAs only. If contributions are made only to Roth IRAs, your contribution limit generally is the lesser of the following amounts.

• $4,000 ($4,500 if you are 50 or older in 2005). For 2006, this amount remains the same at $4,000 (but increases to $5,000 if 50 or older in 2006).
• Your taxable compensation.

However, if your modified AGI is above a certain amount, your contribution limit may be reduced, as explained later under *Contribution limit reduced*.

Roth IRAs and traditional IRAs. If contributions are made to both Roth IRAs and traditional IRAs established for your benefit, your contribution limit for Roth IRAs generally is the same as your limit would be if contributions were made only to Roth IRAs, but then reduced by all contributions (other than employer contributions under a SEP or SIMPLE IRA plan) for the year to all IRAs other than Roth IRAs.

This means that your contribution limit is the lesser of the following amounts.

• $4,000 ($4,500 if you are 50 or older in 2005). For 2006, $4,000 ($5,000 if 50 or older in 2006) minus all contributions (other than employer contributions under a SEP or SIMPLE IRA plan) for the year to all IRAs other than Roth IRAs.
• Your taxable compensation minus all contributions (other than employer contributions under a SEP or SIMPLE IRA plan) for the year to all IRAs other than Roth IRAs.

However, if your modified AGI is above a certain amount, your contribution limit may be reduced, as explained later under *Contribution limit reduced*.

Contribution limit reduced. If your modified AGI is above a certain amount, your contribution limit is gradually reduced. Use Table 18-3 to determine if this reduction applies to you.

Figuring the reduction. If the amount you can contribute to your Roth IRA is reduced, see Publication 590 for how to figure the reduction.

When Can You Make Contributions?

You can make contributions to a Roth IRA for a year at any time during the year or by the due date of your return for that year (not including extensions).

Tip. *You can make contributions for 2005 by the due date (not including extensions) for filing your 2005 tax return. This means that most people can make contributions for 2005 by April 17, 2006.*

Explanation: Roth IRAs
Roth IRAs are tax-free retirement-savings vehicles. By permitting tax-free withdrawals, contributions made early in your working life receive the greatest tax benefit.

Worksheet 18-2. **Modified Adjusted Gross Income for Roth IRA Purposes**

Use this worksheet to figure your modified adjusted gross income for Roth IRA purposes.

1. Enter your adjusted gross income (Form 1040, line 37, or Form 1040A, line 22)	**1.** _____
2. Enter any income resulting from the conversion of an IRA (other than a Roth IRA) to a Roth IRA	**2.** _____
3. Subtract line 2 from line 1	**3.** _____
4. Enter any traditional IRA deduction (Form 1040, line 32, or Form 1040A, line 17)	**4.** _____
5. Enter any student loan interest deduction (Form 1040, line 33, or Form 1040A, line 18)	**5.** _____
6. Enter any tuition and fees deduction (Form 1040, line 34, or Form 1040A, line 19)	**6.** _____
7. Enter any foreign earned income and/or housing exclusion (Form 2555, line 43, or Form 2555-EZ, line 18)	**7.** _____
8. Enter any foreign housing deduction (Form 2555, line 48)	**8.** _____
9. Enter any exclusion of bond interest (Form 8815, line 14)	**9.** _____
10. Enter any exclusion of employer-provided adoption benefits (Form 8839, line 30)	**10.** _____
11. Enter any Domestic production activities deduction (Form 1040, line 35)	**11.** _____
12. Add the amounts on lines 3 through 11	**12.** _____

13. Enter:
 • $160,000 if married filing jointly or qualifying widow(er)
 • $10,000 if married filing separately and you lived with your spouse at any time during the year
 • $110,000 for all others .... **13.** _____

Next. Is the amount on line 12 more than the amount on line 13?

Yes. See the *Note* below.

No. The amount on line 12 is your *modified AGI* for Roth IRA purposes. (If you're calculating your modified adjusted gross income for purposes of determining whether you can convert from a traditional IRA to a Roth IRA, reduce this amount by any minimum required distributions from IRAs included on Form 1040, line 15a or Form 1040A, line 11a.)

Note. If the amount on line 12 is more than the amount on line 13 and you have other income or loss items, such as social security income or passive activity losses, that are subject to AGI-based phaseouts, you can refigure your AGI solely for the purpose of figuring your modified AGI for Roth IRA purposes. Refigure your AGI without taking into account any income from conversions. (If you receive social security benefits, use *Worksheet 1* in *Appendix B* of Publication 590 to refigure your AGI.) Then go to list item (2) under *Modified AGI* or line 4 above in *Worksheet 18-2* to refigure your modified AGI. If you do not have other income or loss items subject to AGI-based phaseouts, your modified AGI for Roth IRA purposes is the amount on line 12.

Example 1

John is 25 years old on January 1, 2005. On January 1 of each year, he contributes $4,000 to a Roth IRA. The account earns 8% per year. John retires on January 1, 2045, at age 65 (immediately after he makes his last Roth IRA contribution). He will have accumulated $1,122,667 toward retirement—all available tax free.

Example 2

Jim is also 25 years old on January 1, 2005. Rather than make his $4,000 Roth contribution on January 1 of each year, he waits until April 15 of the next year to make his contribution. His account also earns 8% per year. In order to retire with the same amount as John, he must wait until April 15, 2046, to retire. Alternatively, if he retires on January 1, 2045, he will only have accumulated $1,009,333 toward retirement—$113,334 less than John.

Example 3

Mary is 16 years old and earns wages of $4,000 in 2005. Her father gifts her $4,000, which she uses to open a Roth IRA on December 31, 2005. If the account earns 8% per year, it will be worth approximately $188,000 (tax free) if she retires at age 66.

What If You Contribute Too Much?

A 6% excise tax applies to any excess contribution to a Roth IRA.

Excess contributions. These are the contributions to your Roth IRAs for a year that equal the total of:

1. Amounts contributed for the tax year to your Roth IRAs (other than amounts properly and timely rolled over from a Roth IRA or properly converted from a traditional IRA, as described later) that are more than your contribution limit for the year, plus
2. Any excess contributions for the preceding year, reduced by the total of:
   a. Any distributions out of your Roth IRAs for the year, plus
   b. Your contribution limit for the year minus your contributions to all your IRAs for the year.

Withdrawal of excess contributions. For purposes of determining excess contributions, any contribution that is withdrawn on or before the due date (including extensions) for filing your tax

Table 18-3. **Effect of Modified AGI on Roth IRA Contribution**

This table shows whether your contribution to a Roth IRA is affected by the amount of your modified adjusted gross income (modified AGI).

IF you have taxable compensation and your filing status is...	AND your modified AGI is...	THEN...
married filing jointly, or **qualifying widow(er)**	less than $150,000	you can contribute up to $4,000 ($4,500 if age 50 or older in 2005). For 2006, this amount is $4,000 ($5,000 if 50 or older in 2006).
	at least $150,000 but less than $160,000	the amount you can contribute is reduced as explained under *Contribution limit reduced* in Publication 590.
	$160,000 or more	you cannot contribute to a Roth IRA.
married filing separately and you lived with your spouse at any time during the year	zero (-0-)	you can contribute up to $4,000 ($4,500 if age 50 or older in 2005). For 2006, this amount is $4,000 ($5,000 if 50 or older in 2006).
	more than zero (-0-) but less than $10,000	the amount you can contribute is reduced as explained under *Contribution limit reduced* in Publication 590.
	$10,000 or more	you cannot contribute to a Roth IRA.
single, head of household, or **married filing separately** and you did not live with your spouse at any time during the year	less than $95,000	you can contribute up to $4,000 ($4,500 if age 50 or older in 2005). For 2006, this amount is $4,000 ($5,000 if 50 or older in 2006).
	at least $95,000 but less than $110,000	the amount you can contribute is reduced as explained under *Contribution limit reduced* in Publication 590.
	$110,000 or more	you cannot contribute to a Roth IRA.

return for the year is treated as an amount not contributed. This treatment applies only if any earnings on the contributions are also withdrawn. The earnings are considered to have been earned and received in the year the excess contribution was made.

Applying excess contributions. If contributions to your Roth IRA for a year were more than the limit, you can apply the excess contribution in one year to a later year if the contributions for that later year are less than the maximum allowed for that year.

Can You Move Amounts Into a Roth IRA?

You may be able to convert amounts from either a traditional, SEP, or SIMPLE IRA into a Roth IRA. You may be able to recharacterize contributions made to one IRA as having been made directly to a different IRA. You can roll amounts over from one Roth IRA to another Roth IRA.

Conversions
You can convert a traditional IRA or a SIMPLE IRA to a Roth IRA. The conversion is treated as a rollover, regardless of the conversion method used. Most of the rules for rollovers, described earlier under *Rollover From One IRA Into Another* under *Traditional IRAs,* apply to these rollovers. However, the 1-year waiting period does not apply.

Conversion methods. You can convert amounts from a traditional IRA to a Roth IRA in any of the following ways.

- **Rollover.** You can receive a distribution from a traditional IRA and roll it over (contribute it) to a Roth IRA within 60 days after the distribution.
- **Trustee-to-trustee transfer.** You can direct the trustee of the traditional IRA to transfer an amount from the traditional IRA to the trustee of the Roth IRA.

- **Same trustee transfer.** If the trustee of the traditional IRA also maintains the Roth IRA, you can direct the trustee to transfer an amount from the traditional IRA to the Roth IRA.

Same trustee. Conversions made with the same trustee can be made by redesignating the traditional IRA as a Roth IRA, rather than opening a new account or issuing a new contract.

TAXPLANNER

You can choose to change a Roth Conversion IRA back into a regular IRA and once again convert the regular IRA back into a Roth IRA. Generally, you can only do this once in a calendar year. Such a change can be beneficial in a situation where you converted a regular IRA into a Roth IRA at a time when stock market values were high and then they subsequently dropped significantly. You can avoid paying tax on the "vanished" profits by recharacterizing the Roth IRA as a regular IRA and then converting back to a Roth IRA when stock values are lower.

TAXPLANNER

Even if you're past the age when minimum required distributions (MRDs) from traditional IRAs have begun, you can still convert the IRA to a Roth IRA, thereby eliminating the requirement to make additional lifetime distributions from the account. *Note: You cannot roll over the current-year MRD to a Roth IRA as part of a conversion.*

Partial conversions are permissible. You can also convert one or more separate IRAs. However, in determining the tax consequences of a partial conversion—whether from a single IRA or separate accounts—normal IRA distribution rules apply. Thus, the tax consequences depend on the value of *all* IRAs, as well as your total nondeductible contributions to all IRAs.

Example

Suppose you have two IRAs, each with a current value of $50,000. One was funded entirely with deductible contributions, while the other was funded entirely with nondeductible contributions totaling $20,000. If you converted either IRA in full, you would recognize $40,000 of income. *Note that this result occurs regardless of the IRA converted.*

Value of IRA converted	$50,000
Total nondeductible contributions	$20,000 (a)
Percentage of the total value of all IRAs converted	50% (b)
Nondeductible contributions deemed rolled over (a) × (b)	($10,000)
Gross income inclusion	($40,000)

Whether to convert or not can be a perplexing issue. It depends on many factors, such as your income tax bracket at the time of conversion versus your tax bracket in the future (e.g., during retirement), investment rates of return, your age and life expectancy, whether you have sufficient funds *outside of your IRA* with which to pay the taxes attributable to the conversion, and to what extent you'll need the funds in your IRA during retirement (vs. accumulating wealth primarily for your heirs). Like many complex financial decisions, it pays to run the numbers. Consult with your financial advisor about whether a Roth IRA conversion makes sense for you.

Converting from a SIMPLE IRA. Generally, you can convert an amount in your SIMPLE IRA to a Roth IRA under the same rules explained earlier under *Converting From Any Traditional IRA to a Roth IRA.*

However, you cannot convert any amount distributed from the SIMPLE IRA during the 2-year period beginning on the date you first participated in any SIMPLE IRA plan maintained by your employer.

More information. For more detailed information on conversions, see Publication 590.

Failed Conversions

If, when you converted amounts from a traditional IRA or SIMPLE IRA into a Roth IRA, you expected to have modified AGI of less than $100,000 and a filing status other than married filing separately, but your expectations did not come true, you have made a failed conversion.

Results of failed conversions. If the converted amount (contribution) is not recharacterized (explained earlier), the contribution will be treated as a regular contribution to the Roth IRA and subject to the following tax consequences.

- A 6% excise tax per year will apply to any excess contribution not withdrawn from the Roth IRA.
- The distributions from the traditional IRA must be included in your gross income.
- The 10% additional tax on early distributions may apply to any distribution.

How to avoid. You must move the amount converted (including all earnings from the date of conversion) into a traditional IRA by the due date (including extensions) for your tax return for the year during which you made the conversion to the Roth IRA. You do not have to include this distribution (withdrawal) in income. See *Recharacterizations,* earlier, for more information.

Rollover From a Roth IRA

You can withdraw, tax free, all or part of the assets from one Roth IRA if you contribute them within 60 days to another Roth IRA. Most of the rules for rollovers, explained earlier under *Rollover From One IRA Into Another* under *Traditional IRAs,* apply to these rollovers.

Are Distributions Taxable?

You do not include in your gross income qualified distributions or distributions that are a return of your regular contributions from your Roth IRA(s). You also do not include distributions from your Roth IRA that you roll over tax free into another Roth IRA. You may have to include part of other distributions in your income. See *Ordering rules for distributions,* later.

What are qualified distributions? A qualified distribution is any payment or distribution from your Roth IRA that meets the following requirements.

1. It is made after the 5-year period beginning with the first taxable year for which a contribution was made to a Roth IRA set up for your benefit, and
2. The payment or distribution is:
   a. Made on or after the date you reach age 59 1/2,
   b. Made because you are disabled,
   c. Made to a beneficiary or to your estate after your death, or
   d. To pay up to $10,000 (lifetime limit) of certain qualified first-time homebuyer amounts. See Publication 590 for more information.

Additional tax on distributions of conversion contributions within 5-year period. If, within the 5-year period starting with the first day of your tax year in which you convert an amount from a traditional IRA to a Roth IRA, you take a distribution from a Roth IRA, you may have to pay the 10% additional tax on early distributions. You generally must pay the 10% additional tax on any amount attributable to the part of the amount converted (the conversion contribution) that you had to include in income. A separate 5-year period applies to each conversion. See *Ordering rules for distributions,* later, to determine the amount, if any, of the distribution that is attributable to the part of the conversion contribution that you had to include in income.

Additional tax on other early distributions. Unless an exception applies, the taxable part of other distributions from your Roth IRA(s) that are not qualified distributions is subject to the 10% additional tax on early distributions. See Publication 590 for more information.

Ordering rules for distributions. If you receive a distribution from your Roth IRA that is not a qualified distribution, part of it may be taxable. There is a set order in which contributions (including conversion contributions) and earnings are considered to be distributed from your Roth IRA. Regular contributions are distributed first. See Publication 590 for more information.

Explanation

The Roth IRA includes a special ordering rule that allows early withdrawals (before age 59 1/2), also known as non-qualified distributions. This rule provides that amounts withdrawn are first considered to come from contributions. After all original contributions have been withdrawn, remaining amounts are considered to have arisen from earnings within the IRA. Distribution of these amounts are taxable and could be subject to an early withdrawal penalty. Early withdrawals from a Roth IRA, therefore, are tax free and penalty free as long as the taxpayer is withdrawing contributions, not accumulated earnings.

Must you withdraw or use Roth IRA assets? You are not required to take distributions from your Roth IRA at any age. The minimum distribution rules that apply to traditional IRAs do not apply to Roth IRAs while the owner is alive. However, after the death of a Roth IRA owner, certain of the minimum distribution rules that apply to traditional IRAs also apply to Roth IRAs.

TAXPLANNER

There are no minimum required distributions (MRDs) for a Roth IRA *during the life of the account owner.* This means that your account can stay intact for as long as you live, allowing investment earnings to grow on a tax-free basis. In addition, if you're married, your spouse—if named the beneficiary of the account—can "step into your shoes" (e.g., by establishing a Roth IRA rollover account) and continue to defer distributions during the remainder of his or her lifetime.

Following your death (or the death of your surviving spouse if he or she were named the account beneficiary and rolled over the account after your death), the normal post-mortem MRD rules would apply (see *Required Distributions* earlier). Since there is technically no required beginning date for making MRDs from a Roth IRA during your life, the schedule of required distributions after your death would be determined by your designated beneficiary who can receive distributions over his or her remaining life expectancy, so long as the first MRD is made by December 31 in the year following the year of your death. The ability to delay distributions until after your death, and then have the account gradually distributed tax free to heirs over their lifetimes, creates a useful way to transfer wealth from one generation to another.

More information. For more detailed information on Roth IRAs, see Publication 590.

Explanation:
Simplified Employee Pensions (SEPs)

A simplified employee pension is a written plan that allows an employer to make contributions toward an employee's retirement without becoming involved in more complex retirement plans. If you are self-employed, you can contribute to your own SEP.

The SEP rules permit an employer to contribute and deduct each year to each participating employee's SEP up to 25% of the employee's compensation (up to $210,000) or $42,000, whichever is less (for 2005). If you are self-employed, special rules apply when figuring the maximum deduction for these contributions. In determining the percentage limit on contributions, compensation is net earnings from self-employment, taking into account the contributions to the SEP.

TAXSAVER

Even if your employer makes contributions to a SEP for your account, you can make contributions to your own IRA. The IRA deduction rules, previously discussed, apply to any amounts you contribute to your IRA.

TAXSAVER

A self-employed person can claim a deduction to a SEP as long as the contribution is made by the due date of the return, including extensions. Even if you failed to set up a plan by December 31, you can still establish a SEP after the end of the year and make a timely payment.

TAXALERT

SEPs permitting salary reduction contributions cannot be established after 1996, although SEPs that allowed elective deferrals before 1997 (SARSEPs) can continue to do so.

Explanation:
Savings Incentive Match Plans for Employees (SIMPLE)

Your employer can establish a type of retirement plan called the savings incentive match plan for employees. In general, employers with 100 or fewer employees earning at least $5,000 and who do not maintain another employer-sponsored retirement plan are eligible to set up SIMPLE plans. SIMPLE plans, which are not subject to some of the complicated rules that apply to other types of retirement plans, can be adopted as an IRA or as a part of a 401(k) plan. All employees who earn more than $5,000 a year must be eligible to participate, and self-employed individuals may also participate in SIMPLE plans. In general, contributions to a SIMPLE plan are not taxable until withdrawn.

The employer generally must either match elective employee contributions dollar for dollar up to 3% of compensation or make a "nonelective" contribution of 2% of compensation on behalf of each eligible employee. No other contributions may be made to a SIMPLE account. Contributions to a SIMPLE account generally are deductible by the employer; however, matching contributions are deductible only if made by the due date (including extensions) of the employer's tax return.

TAXALERT

The limit on maximum annual elective deferrals to a SIMPLE plan will increase as follows:

Year	Regular Amount	"Catch-up*" Amount
2005	10,000	12,000
2006	10,000**	12,500**

*For taxpayers who reach age 50 before the end of the plan year.

**Adjusted for inflation.

Employers are given a 2-year grace period to maintain a SIMPLE plan once they are no longer eligible to participate.

19

Moving Expenses

Note: The 2004 IRS Publication 17 (Your Federal Income Tax) has been updated by Ernst & Young LLP for 2005. Dates and dollar amounts shown are for 2005. Gray type is used to indicate where IRS text has been updated or intentionally omitted. Unrevised IRS text is shown in black type.

Introduction

The good news about moving expenses is that you usually may deduct them if you move because you change jobs. The not-so-good news is that, because no two moves are alike, there are several tests you must meet in order to claim the deductions. Disagreements with the IRS over moving expenses are frequent.

Moving expenses are deducted from your gross income in arriving at your adjusted gross income (AGI). This can be advantageous, since you do not have to complete Schedule A-Itemized Deductions in order to receive the benefit of the deduction.

In general, meals bought in connection with a move, expenses related to searching for a residence or living in temporary quarters, and expenses incurred in selling, purchasing, or leasing a residence in connection with a move are not deductible expenses.

If you are interested in deducting as much of your move as possible, the first rule you should follow is to keep adequate records of all your moving-related expenditures. Receipts, plus a log of your activities, will generally suffice. The other ins and outs of moving expenses are detailed in this chapter.

What's New

Standard mileage rate. The standard mileage rate for moving expenses has been increased from 14 cents a mile in 2004 to 15 cents a mile through August 2005 (22 cents per mile after August). See *Travel by car* under *Deductible Moving Expenses.*

Reminder

Change of address. If you change your mailing address, be sure to notify the IRS using Form 8822, Change of Address. Mail it to the Internal Revenue Service Center for your old address. Addresses for the Service Centers are on the back of the form.

This chapter explains the deduction of certain expenses of moving to a new home because you changed job locations or started a new job. It includes the following topics.

- Who can deduct moving expenses.
- What moving expenses are deductible.
- What moving expenses are not deductible.
- How a reimbursement affects your moving expense deduction.
- How and when to report moving expenses.
- Special rules for members of the Armed Forces.

You may be able to deduct moving expenses whether you are self-employed or an employee. Your expenses generally must be related to starting work at your new job location. However, certain retirees and survivors may qualify to claim the deduction even though they are not starting work at a new job location. See *Who Can Deduct Moving Expenses.*

Moves to locations outside the United States. This chapter does not discuss moves outside the United States. If you are a United States citizen or resident alien who moved outside the United States or its possessions because of your job or business, see Publication 521, Moving Expenses, for special rules that apply to your move.

Useful Items

You may want to see:

Publication

☐ **521** Moving Expenses

Forms (and Instructions)

☐ **3903** Moving Expenses
☐ **8822** Change of Address

Who Can Deduct Moving Expenses

You can deduct your moving expenses if you meet all three of the following requirements.

1. Your move is closely related to the start of work.
2. You meet the distance test.
3. You meet the time test.

After you have read these rules, you may want to use *Figure 19-B* to help you decide if you can deduct your moving expenses.

Different rules may apply if you are a member of the Armed Forces or a retiree or survivor moving to the United States. These rules are discussed later in this chapter.

Related to Start of Work

Your move must be closely related, both in time and in place, to the start of work at your new job location.

Closely related in time. You can generally consider moving expenses incurred within 1 year from the date you first reported to work at the new location as closely related in time to the start of work. It is not necessary that you arrange to work before moving to a new location, as long as you actually do go to work.

If you do not move within 1 year of the date you begin work, you ordinarily cannot deduct the expenses unless you can show that circumstances existed that prevented the move within that time.

Example. Your family moved more than a year after you started work at a new location. You delayed the move for 18 months to allow your child to complete high school. You can deduct your moving expenses.

> ### Explanation
> You must make the actual move within a year of starting a new job, unless circumstances prevent you from doing so. Although not moving your family so that your child may complete high school in the same school is an acceptable reason, not moving because you haven't sold your home is not. Good intentions are not enough.

Closely related in place. You can generally consider your move closely related in place to the start of work if the distance from your new home to the new job location is not more than the distance from your former home to the new job location. If your move does not meet this requirement, you may still be able to deduct moving expenses if you can show that:

1. You are required to live at your new home as a condition of your employment, or
2. You will spend less time or money commuting from your new home to your new job location.

> ### Explanation
> Assume that your new home is 60 miles from your new job but that your former home was only 55 miles from your new job. If you want to deduct your moving expenses, you must give the IRS an acceptable reason why you now drive farther than you would have if you hadn't moved. An acceptable reason might be that from your new home you are able to use a freeway or a commuter train or bus that saves you time and/or money, whereas before you had to drive across town on local streets all the way to work.

Home defined. Your home means your main home (residence). It can be a house, apartment, condominium, houseboat, house trailer, or similar dwelling. It does not include other homes owned or kept up by you or members of your family. It also does not include a seasonal home, such as a summer beach cottage. Your former home means your home before you left for your new job location. Your new home means your home within the area of your new job location.

Retirees or survivors. You may be able to deduct the expenses of moving to the United States or its possessions even though the move is not related to the start of work at a new job location. You must have worked outside the United States or be a survivor of someone who did. See *Retirees or Survivors Who Move to the United States,* later.

Distance Test

Your move will meet the distance test if your new main job location is at least 50 miles farther from your former home than your old main job location was from your former home. For example, if your old main job location was 3 miles from your former home, your new main job location must be at least 53 miles from that former home. You can use *Worksheet 19-1* to see if you meet this test.

The distance between a job location and your home is the shortest of the more commonly traveled routes between them. The distance test considers only the location of your former home. It does not take into account the location of your new home. See *Figure 19-A.*

Example. You moved to a new home less than 50 miles from your former home because you changed main job locations. Your old main job location was 3 miles from your former home. Your new main job location is 60 miles from that home. Because your new main job location is 57 miles farther from your former home than the distance from your former home to your old main job location, you meet the distance test.

> ### Explanation
> The key is that your new job location must be at least 50 miles farther from your former home than your old job location. The IRS doesn't care how far away you live from your new office in absolute terms. To be able to deduct moving expenses, your new job has to be 50 miles farther from your former home than your old job used to be.
>
> ### Example
> Even though you may now live 55 miles from your office, the fact that your office is only 45 miles more from your old home than it used to be means that you will not be able to deduct your moving expenses.
>
> You can tell whether you meet the distance test simply by subtracting the total miles from your *old* home to the old job from the total miles from the old home to the new job. The difference must be 50 miles or greater.

First job or return to full-time work. If you go to work full time for the first time, your place of work must be at least 50 miles from your former home to meet the distance test.

If you go back to full-time work after a substantial period of part-time work or unemployment, your place of work must also be at least 50 miles from your former home.

> ### TAXSAVER
> First-time job seekers, such as high school and college graduates, and people reentering the labor force after a substantial period of unemployment may deduct moving expenses.
>
> You must move from a former principal home to a new principal home, which means that you must have a principal home from which to move. According to one court, a college graduate could not deduct his expenses to move to his new job location because his student residence was not his principal home.

Figure 19-A. **Illustration of Distance Test**

DISTANCE TEST IS MET

Your new main job location is at least 50 miles farther from your former residence than your old main job location was.

DISTANCE TEST IS NOT MET

Your new main job location is not at least 50 miles farther from your former residence than your old main job location was.

Explanation

Two months of unemployment is not long enough to qualify as a substantial period of unemployment. If you had only a brief break in employment, you must meet the same distance requirement that you would if you had been working continuously.

Armed Forces. If you are in the Armed Forces and you moved because of a permanent change of station, you do not have to meet the distance test. See *Members of the Armed Forces*, later.

Main job location. Your main job location is usually the place where you spend most of your working time. If there is no one place where you spend most of your working time, your main job location is the place where your work is centered, such as where you report for work or are otherwise required to "base" your work.

Explanation

Your principal place of work is usually the place where you spend the most time working. An employee's principal place of work is the employer's plant, office, shop, store, or other property.

Example

A member of a railroad crew spends most of his working time aboard a train. His principal place of work is his home terminal, station, or other central point where he reports in, checks out, or receives instructions.

Union members. If you work for several employers on a short-term basis and you get work under a union hall system (such as a construction or building trades worker), your main job location is the union hall.

More than one job. If you have more than one job at any time, your main job location depends on the facts in each case. The more important factors to be considered are:

• The total time you spend at each place,

• The amount of work you do at each place, and
• How much money you earn at each place.

Example

A consultant working on an assignment in Detroit—a city that was not his main job location—was allowed by the Tax Court to deduct moving expenses when, at the request of his employer, he moved from Canton, Ohio, to Dallas, Texas, even though he continued the consulting assignment in Detroit. The Tax Court's rationale was that Detroit was only a temporary place of work and that the moving expenses arose from a shift from one principal place of work—Canton—to another—Dallas.

Time Test

To deduct your moving expenses, you also must meet one of the following two time tests.

1. The time test for employees.
2. The time test for self-employed persons.

Both of these tests are explained below. See *Table 19-1* for a summary of these tests.

Time Test for Employees

If you are an employee, you must work full time for at least 39 weeks during the first 12 months (39-week test) after you arrive in the general area of your new job location. Full-time employment depends on what is usual for your type of work in your area.

For purposes of this test, the following four rules apply.

1. You count only your full-time work as an employee, not any work you do as a self-employed person.
2. You do not have to work for the same employer for all 39 weeks.
3. You do not have to work 39 weeks in a row.
4. You must work full time within the same general commuting area for all 39 weeks.

Table 19–1. **Satisfying the Time Test for Employees and Self-Employed Persons**

IF you are...	THEN you satisfy the time test by meeting the...
an employee	39-week test for employees.
both self-employed and an employee, but unable to satisfy the 39-week test for employees	78-week test for self-employed persons.
both self-employed and an employee at the same time	78-week test for a self-employed person or the 39-week test for an employee. Your principal place of work determines which test applies.
self-employed	78-week test for self-employed persons.

Explanation

The courts have held that the mere enrollment in an employment registry does not by itself constitute full-time employment.

Example

A registered nurse moved to California, where she enrolled with a nursing registry that facilitated the employment of nurses. Even though it may be the customary method to obtain a job in a hospital in California, the mere enrollment in the registry does not establish the taxpayer as a full-time employee.

Temporary absence from work. You are considered to have worked full time during any week you are temporarily absent from work because of illness, strikes, lockouts, layoffs, natural disasters, or similar causes. You are also considered to have worked full time during any week you are absent from work for leave or vacation provided for in your work contract or agreement.

Example

A government employee moved to Washington, D.C., from Honolulu but took a temporary leave of absence from her job to go to Texas to continue her studies. The Tax Court ruled that she could not deduct her moving expenses to Washington D.C. since her location during the time of her leave was not in the "general location" of her new workplace.

A person on leave is still considered to be a full-time employee and must meet the distance requirements as though he or she were actually working at his or her new business location. In this example, the employee would have had to remain in Washington, D.C., for the required 39 weeks in the year (see below) following her move from Honolulu for her moving expenses to have been deductible.

Seasonal work. If your work is seasonal, you are considered to be working full time during the off-season only if your work contract or agreement covers an off-season period of less than 6 months. For example, a school teacher on a 12-month contract who teaches on a full-time basis for more than 6 months is considered to have worked full time for the entire 12 months.

Explanation

According to the IRS, a seasonal employee under contract for less than 39 weeks of work does not meet the 39-week test unless the contract is extended and the employee actually works the required additional time or is prevented from doing so involuntarily, for example, because of illness, natural disaster, or a similar cause.

Time Test for Self-Employed Persons

If you are self-employed, you must work full time for at least 39 weeks during the first 12 months and for a total of at least 78 weeks during the first 24 months (78-week test) after you arrive in the general area of your new job location.

For purposes of the time test for self-employed persons, the following three rules apply.

1. You count any full-time work you do either as an employee or as a self-employed person.
2. You do not have to work for the same employer or be self-employed in the same trade or business for the 78 weeks.
3. You must work within the same general commuting area for all 78 weeks.

Self-employment. You are self-employed if you work as the sole owner of an unincorporated business or as a partner in a partnership carrying on a business. You are not considered self-employed if you are semiretired, are a part-time student, or work only a few hours each week.

Full-time work. You can count only those weeks during which you work full time as a week of work. Whether you work full time during any week depends on what is usual for your type of work in your area.

Example

You are a self-employed dentist and maintain office hours 4 days a week. You are considered to perform services full time if maintaining office hours 4 days a week is not unusual for other self-employed dentists in the area.

If you were both an employee and self-employed, see *Table 19-1* for the requirements.

Joint Return

If you are married and file a joint return and both you and your spouse work full time, either of you can satisfy the full-time work test. However, you cannot add the weeks your spouse worked to the weeks you worked to satisfy that test.

TAXSAVER

If you file separate returns, each person must meet the time test individually and deduct only his or her own expenses.

The time test may be met by either spouse if a joint return is filed. However, weeks worked by both husband and wife cannot be added together to meet the time test.

If you and your spouse are living together, and if both of you have been working full-time but one of you loses your job, you obtain the maximum tax benefits by filing a joint return. This is the case even if you reside in a **community property** state. Moving expenses paid by both husband and wife may be aggregated and are deductible in full.

Time test not yet met. You can deduct your moving expenses on your 2005 tax return even though you have not yet met the time test by the date your 2005 return is due. You can do this if you expect to meet the 39-week test in 2006, or the 78-week test in 2006 or 2007. If you deduct moving expenses but do not meet the time test in 2006, or 2007, you must either:

1. Report your moving expense deduction as other income on your Form 1040 for the year you cannot meet the test, or
2. Amend your 2005 return.

If you do not deduct your moving expenses on your 2005 return and you later meet the time test, you can file an amended return for 2005 to take the deduction.

Example

You arrive in the general area of your new job location September 1, 2005. You deduct moving expenses on your 2005 return, the year of the move, even though you have not met the time test by the date your return is due. If you do not meet the 39-week test by September 1, 2006, you must either:

1. Report as income on your 2006 return the amount you deducted as moving expenses on your 2005 return, or
2. Amend your 2005 return.

Exceptions to the Time Test

You do not have to meet the time test if one of the following applies.

1. You are in the Armed Forces and you moved because of a permanent change of station. See *Members of the Armed Forces,* later.
2. Your main job location was outside the United States and you moved to the United States because you retired. See *Retirees or Survivors Who Move to the United States,* later.
3. You are the survivor of a person whose main job location at the time of death was outside the United States. See *Retirees or Survivors Who Move to the United States,* later.
4. Your job at the new location ends because of death or disability.
5. You are transferred for your employer's benefit or laid off for a reason other than willful misconduct. For this exception, you must have obtained full-time employment and you must have expected to meet the test at the time you started the job.

Explanation

The courts have held and the IRS agrees that if, after moving for job-related purposes, you are fired or laid off, involuntarily lose your job (for other than willful misconduct), or are required to move again by your employer before the 39 weeks are up, you are still able to deduct your moving expenses. Death and disability also exempt a taxpayer from the 39-week requirement. However, if you voluntarily take a leave of absence—even if employment benefits continue—you may not count the leave period toward the 39 weeks.

Example

A taxpayer who terminated his employment voluntarily after working in his new location only 37 weeks (even though he did so in order to start a different job elsewhere) was not allowed the deduction for his original moving costs.

TAXSAVER

Since you have 2 years to fulfill the time requirement, you should assume that you will meet it and deduct moving expenses in the year in which you incur them. Even if you expect to incur more moving expenses later, do not wait to deduct those that you already have incurred. Any later expenses that qualify may be deducted in a subsequent year.

If you fail to meet the time test later, you may either file an amended return and repay any tax due along with interest or report as income the amount you previously deducted. In some cases, the 2-year period may be extended.

Example

A woman was allowed to deduct moving expenses incurred 30 months after her transfer because she waited until her child finished school before moving her family. The IRS rule is: You have to demonstrate that there is a good reason for the delay.

Members of the Armed Forces

If you are a member of the Armed Forces on active duty and you move because of a permanent change of station, you do not have to meet the distance and time tests, discussed earlier. You can deduct your unreimbursed moving expenses.

A permanent change of station includes:

• A move from your home to your first post of active duty,
• A move from one permanent post of duty to another, and
• A move from your last post of duty to your home or to a nearer point in the United States. The move must occur within 1 year of ending your active duty or within the period allowed under the Joint Travel Regulations.

Spouse and dependents. If a member of the Armed Forces dies, is imprisoned, or deserts, a permanent change of station for the spouse or dependent includes a move to:

• The place of enlistment,
• The member's, spouse's, or dependent's home of record, or
• A nearer point in the United States.

If the military moves you and your spouse and dependents to or from separate locations, the moves are treated as a single move to your new main job location.

More information. For more information on moving expenses for members of the Armed Forces, and instructions for completing Form 3903, see *Members of the Armed Forces* in Publication 521.

Retirees or Survivors Who Move to the United States

If you are a retiree who was working abroad or a survivor of a decedent who was working abroad and you move to the United States or one of its possessions, you do not have to meet the time test, discussed earlier. However, you must meet the requirements discussed below under *Retirees who were working abroad* or *Survivors of decedents who were working abroad.*

Caution. *If you are living in the United States, retire, and then move and remain retired, you cannot claim a moving expense deduction for that move.*

United States defined. For this section of this chapter, the term "United States" includes the possessions of the United States.

Retirees who were working abroad. You can deduct moving expenses for a move to a new home in the United States when you permanently retire. However, both your former main job location and your former home must have been outside the United States.

Permanently retired. You are considered permanently retired when you cease gainful full-time employment or self-employment. If, at the time you retire, you intend your retirement to be permanent, you will be considered retired though you later return to work. Your intention to retire permanently may be determined by:

1. Your age and health,
2. The customary retirement age for people who do similar work,
3. Whether you receive retirement payments from a pension or retirement fund, and
4. The length of time before you return to full-time work.

Survivors of decedents who were working abroad. If you are the spouse or the dependent of a person whose main job location at the time of death was outside the United States, you can deduct moving expenses if the following five requirements are met.

1. The move is to a home in the United States.
2. The move begins within 6 months after the decedent's death. (When a move begins is described later.)
3. The move is from the decedent's former home.
4. The decedent's former home was outside the United States.
5. The decedent's former home was also your home.

When a move begins. A move begins when one of the following events occurs.

1. You contract for your household goods and personal effects to be moved to your home in the United States, but only if the move is completed within a reasonable time.

2. Your household goods and personal effects are packed and on the way to your home in the United States.
3. You leave your former home to travel to your new home in the United States.

Deductible Moving Expenses

If you meet the requirements discussed earlier under *Who Can Deduct Moving Expenses*, you can deduct the reasonable expenses of:

1. Moving your household goods and personal effects (including in-transit or foreign-move storage expenses), and
2. Traveling (including lodging but not meals) to your new home.

Caution. *You cannot deduct any expenses for meals.*

Reasonable expenses. You can deduct only those expenses that are reasonable for the circumstances of your move. For example, the cost of traveling from your former home to your new one should be by the shortest, most direct route available by conventional transportation. If, during your trip to your new home, you stop over, or make side trips for sightseeing, the additional expenses for your stopover or side trips are not deductible as moving expenses.

Travel by car. If you use your car to take yourself, members of your household, or your personal effects to your new home, you can figure your expenses by deducting either:

1. Your actual expenses, such as gas and oil for your car, if you keep an accurate record of each expense, or
2. The standard mileage rate of 15 cents a mile through August 2005 (22 cents a mile after August 2005).

Whether you use actual expenses or the standard mileage rate to figure your expenses, you can deduct parking fees and tolls you paid in moving. You cannot deduct any part of general repairs, general maintenance, insurance, or depreciation for your car.

Member of household. You can deduct moving expenses you pay for yourself and members of your household. A member of your household is anyone who has both your former and new home as his or her home. It does not include a tenant or employee, unless that person is your dependent.

Figure 19-B. **Can You Deduct Expenses for a Non-Military Move Within the United States?**[1]

[1] Members of the Armed Forces for special rules that apply to them.

[2] Your move must be closely related to the start of work at your new job location. See *Related to Start of Work*.

[3] If you deduct expenses and do not meet this test later, you must either file an amendment tax return or report your moving expense deduction as other income. See *Time test not yet met*.

[4] If you become self-employed during the first 12 months, answer YES if your time as a full-time employee added to your time as a self-employed person equals or will equal at least 78 weeks in the first 24 months (including 39 weeks in the first twelve months) after you arrived in the new area.

Location of move. There are different rules for moving within or to the United States than for moving outside the United States. This chapter only discusses moves within or to the United States. The rules for moves outside the United States can be found in Publication 521.

Household Goods and Personal Effects

You can deduct the cost of packing, crating, and transporting your household goods and personal effects and those of the members of your household from your former home to your new home.

If you use your own car to move your things, see *Travel by car*, earlier.

You can deduct any costs of connecting or disconnecting utilities required because you are moving your household goods, appliances, or personal effects.

You can deduct the cost of shipping your car and household pets to your new home.

You can deduct the cost of moving your household goods and personal effects from a place other than your former home. Your deduction is limited to the amount it would have cost to move them from your former home.

Caution. *You cannot deduct the cost of moving furniture you buy on the way to your new home.*

Explanation

Moving furniture that was in storage at the time of the move is deductible as long as the actual cost of moving it does not exceed what the cost of moving it would have been had the furniture been located at your former home.

Example

You are a resident of North Carolina and have been in college pursuing a degree for the last 4 years. Because of the small size of your apartment, you stored some of your furniture with your parents in Georgia.

You get a job in Washington, D.C. It costs you $1,100 to move the furniture from Georgia to Washington, D.C. If the furniture in Georgia had been shipped from North Carolina, your former home, it would have cost only $600. You may deduct only $600 of the $1,100 charge.

Note: If you lived in a dormitory or other rented quarters in North Carolina but you went home to Georgia for the summers, were considered an out-of-state or nonresident student in North Carolina, and otherwise maintained most of the major elements of residency (voting, automobile registration, charge accounts, etc.) in Georgia, you could argue that Georgia was your former home. In that case, all moving expenses would be deductible.

Explanation
A yacht is not considered a part of your household goods or personal effects. The rationale given by the courts is that Congress intended moving expenses to cover only items that you must move from your old home to a new location. To be deductible as a moving expense, an item must be, according to the courts, "intimately associated" with your home. A yacht is not.

However, the courts have upheld the deductibility of costs associated with moving a sailboat that the taxpayer owned for 4 years and frequently used. The taxpayer proved that he was "intimately associated" with the boat. This "intimate association" enabled the boat to be characterized as a "personal effect," thereby making all expenses associated with moving it deductible.

Storage expenses. You can include the cost of storing and insuring household goods and personal effects within any period of 30 consecutive days after the day your things are moved from your former home and before they are delivered to your new home.

Travel Expenses

You can deduct the cost of transportation and lodging for yourself and members of your household while traveling from your former home to your new home. This includes expenses for the day you arrive.

You can include any lodging expenses you had in the area of your former home within one day after you could no longer live in your former home because your furniture had been moved.

You can deduct expenses for only one trip to your new home for yourself and members of your household. However, all of you do not have to travel together or at the same time. If you use your own car, see *Travel by car*, earlier.

Explanation
The courts allowed the cost of an escort as a moving expense when a taxpayer's mobile home broke down en route—the breakdown was attributable solely to the move. The charge for moving a mobile home by a professional mover is deductible. However, the replacement cost of tires for the mobile home does not qualify as a deductible moving expense. The reason is that new tires are essentially capital improvements.

TaxAlert

Travel expenses from your former home to your new home are only deductible as moving expenses when incurred after obtaining employment in the area to which you are moving.

Nondeductible Expenses

You cannot deduct the following items as moving expenses.

• Any part of the purchase price of your new home.

Explanation
No deduction is allowed for the costs of selling your former home (or settling an unexpired lease) and purchasing your new home (or the acquisition of a new lease).

• Car tags.
• Driver's license.
• Expenses of buying or selling a home.
• Expenses of getting or breaking a lease.
• Home improvements to help sell your home.
• Loss on the sale of your home.

Explanation
Under no circumstances is a loss on the sale of your personal residence deductible as a moving expense, or as any other kind of expense, even if the move forced you to sell at a loss. However, if any portion of your home was used for income-producing purposes, then the portion of the loss allocable to such use may be deductible. For more information see Chapter 16, *Selling Your Home*.

Although you may not deduct property taxes and interest as moving expenses, you may claim them as itemized deductions.

• Losses from disposing of memberships in clubs.
• Meal expenses.
• Mortgage penalties.
• Pre-move house-hunting expenses.
• Real estate taxes.
• Refitting of carpets and draperies.
• Security deposits (including any given up due to the move).
• Storage charges except those incurred in transit and for foreign moves.
• Temporary living expenses.

Explanation
Many moving costs represent real economic losses to you but are not deductible as moving expenses when you are computing your **taxable income**. These nondeductible moving costs are simply considered personal expenses, whether or not you are reimbursed for them. If you itemize your deductions, you might be able to deduct some costs that are not deductible as moving expenses.

Mortgage penalties that are loan prepayment penalties are usually deductible as interest. Real estate taxes are deductible. In many states, automobile tags are deductible as personal property taxes. A portion of your driver's license may be deductible as automobile transportation expenses.

You may not deduct the cost of buying new drapes.

House-hunting trips and temporary housing expenses are not deductible. Also, the cost of meals incurred in connection with a move are not deductible. In addition, expenses associated with the purchase, sale, or lease of a residence are not deductible.

Example 1
The IRS has ruled that the costs associated with the transfer of a U.S. government employee were not deductible, since the employee initiated the transfer, even when the transfer was in the interest of the government. The transfer must be a requirement of the employer and not merely for the benefit of the employee.

Example 2
A taxpayer replaced carpeting and drapes at her newly leased apartment because of her husband's allergies. The costs were for the comfort of the taxpayer rather than moving expenses. A deduction was not allowed.

No double deduction. You cannot take a moving expense deduction and a business expense deduction for the same expenses. You must decide if your expenses are deductible as moving expenses or as business expenses. For example, expenses you have for travel, meals, and lodging while temporarily working at a place away from your regular place of work may be deductible as business expenses if you are considered away from home on business. Generally, your work at a single location is considered temporary if it is realistically expected to last (and does in fact last) for 1 year or less. See *Temporary Assignment or Job* in chapter 28 for information on deducting your expenses.

TAXSAVER

If you are denied a deduction for moving expenses on the grounds that the move is only temporary (generally a year or less), you may still deduct your expenses for travel, meals, and lodging while away from home as business expenses.

Example
A professor who went on a 10-month sabbatical for post-doctoral research training could not deduct the expense of moving his household and personal goods. He could, however, deduct his traveling expenses, as well as the cost of his meals and lodging, while away.

TAXPLANNER

If you are a nonresident alien temporarily in the United States earning taxable income for performing personal services, you can also deduct moving expenses to the United States if you meet both the time test and the distance test, explained earlier in this chapter. However, if you deduct moving expenses to the United States, you can not also deduct travel expenses while temporarily away from you foreign home because moving expenses are based on a change of your principal place of business.

How and When To Report

This section explains how and when to report your moving expenses and any reimbursements or allowances you received for your move.
Form 3903. Use Form 3903 to figure your moving expense deduction.
Where to deduct. Deduct your moving expenses on line 26 of Form 1040. The amount of moving expenses you can deduct is shown on line 5 of Form 3903.
Caution. *You cannot deduct moving expenses on Form 1040EZ or Form 1040A.*
Reimbursements. If you receive a reimbursement for your moving expenses, how you report this amount and your expenses depends on whether the reimbursement is paid to you under an accountable plan or a nonaccountable plan.
For more information on reimbursements, see Publication 521.

TAXSAVER

If your employer purchases your former residence, the real estate commission that is avoided is not income to you, although the gain on the sale of the residence is taxed as a **capital gain**, subject to the capital gain exclusion rules, discussed in Chapter 16, *Selling Your Home.*
Any reimbursement by your employer for a loss on the sale of your home must be included in your income. You may not deduct the loss on your home, though you may deduct the amount attributable to the real estate commission, if any, as a selling expense.
If your employer purchases your former home from you at **fair market value** and there is a subsequent decline in its worth, the loss is sustained by your employer. The home's drop in value does not affect you.
If your employer purchases your former home from you at *more* than fair market value, the excess is ordinary taxable income to you and not capital gain. You could not exclude that excess from your income, even if you purchased a new home for more than you got in total for the old one.

Explanation
Some employers use third-party relocation service companies to buy your home from you. If the third party pays any direct home-selling costs that are normally imposed on the seller by local law and/or custom, then you will be treated as having received taxable income.

Example
An employer agreed to pay home-selling costs but required that the employee repay them if he terminated employment within a stipulated period of time. The IRS held that an enforceable debt was created and that the employee had taxable income to report when the debt was cancelled (or not paid). The employer must report the income on Form W-2.

When To Deduct Expenses

You may have a choice of when to deduct your moving expenses and report any reimbursement.
Expenses not reimbursed. If you were not reimbursed, deduct your allowable moving expenses either in the year you incurred them or in the year you paid them.
Example. In December 2004, your employer transferred you to another city in the United States, where you still work. You are single and were not reimbursed for your moving expenses. In 2004, you paid for moving your furniture and you deducted these expenses on your 2004 tax return. In January 2005, you paid for travel to the new city. You can deduct these additional expenses on your 2005 tax return.
Expenses reimbursed. If you are reimbursed for your expenses, you may be able to deduct your expenses either in the year you incurred them or in the year you paid them. If you use the cash method of accounting, you can choose to deduct the expenses in the year you are reimbursed even though you paid the expenses in a different year.
If you are reimbursed for your expenses in a year after you paid the expenses, you may want to delay taking the deduction until the

year you receive the reimbursement. If you do not choose to delay your deduction until the year you are reimbursed and you deduct moving expenses that will be reimbursed, you must include the reimbursement in your income.

Explanation

Your employer may give you a flat amount of money to cover all your moving expenses, some of which may not be deductible. The IRS says that the employer must apply the reimbursement first to the deductible moving expenses that are not subject to withholding and then deduct withholding and social security tax from the remainder.

TAX PLANNER

If your move is a result of a qualified assignment by your employer for a year or less, and you receive reimbursement for your daily expenses (or a per diem allowance), your reimbursement for moving expenses may not be fully tax-free to you. Though your flight, hotel and meal costs while traveling for business may be considered tax-free, the reimbursement from your employer for cost associated with the movement of household goods and storage would be fully taxable to you when received.

TAXALERT

Be sure to take into account reimbursement for nondeductible expenses when you are figuring your **estimated tax** payments.

Choosing when to deduct. If you use the cash method of accounting, which is used by most individuals, you can choose to deduct moving expenses in the year your employer reimburses you if:

1. You paid the expenses in a year before the year of reimbursement, or
2. You paid the expenses in the year immediately after the year of reimbursement but by the due date, including extensions, for filing your return for the reimbursement year.

TAXSAVER

You generally deduct your moving expenses in the year in which you pay them. However, if you receive a reimbursement in one year and don't pay the expenses until the next year, you still may deduct the expenses in the earlier year, as long as you pay them before the due date, including extensions, for filing your return for the year of reimbursement. You should deduct your expenses in the year in which you will save the most taxes.

Report your moving expense deduction on Form 3903.

How to make the choice. You choose to deduct moving expenses in the year you received reimbursement by taking the deduction on your return, or amended return, for that year.

Caution. *You cannot deduct any moving expenses for which you received a reimbursement that was not included in your income. (Reimbursements are discussed in Publication 521.)*

TAXORGANIZER

Records You Should Keep
- Receipts for:
  Professional mover's fees
  Rental of moving truck and/or equipment
  Storage and insurance of household goods and personal effects
  Cost of lodging while traveling from former home to new home
  Parking fees and tolls during move
- Mileage for use of car or actual expenses (gas and oil) while traveling from former home to new home

20

Alimony

Note: The 2004 IRS Publication 17 (Your Federal Income Tax) has been updated by Ernst & Young LLP for 2005. Dates and dollar amounts shown are for 2005. Gray type is used to indicate where IRS text has been updated or intentionally omitted. Unrevised IRS text is shown in black type.

Introduction

This chapter discusses alimony and child support and the complicated tax rules and regulations that apply.

Designing a divorce decree, a separation agreement, or a support decree is rarely an easy task. Marital settlements are so diverse and so complex that no two situations are the same. One common element, however, is likely to be the payment of **alimony***—an amount subject to one of these settlement agreements that is not considered* **child support** *or a property settlement and that meets certain specific tests. If certain circumstances are met, alimony is a deduction from gross income for the spouse who pays it and included in the income of the spouse who receives it.*

Alimony may take many different forms. The payment by one spouse of the other spouse's share of mortgage and other costs for jointly owned property may be considered alimony. The payment of life insurance premiums on policies irrevocably assigned to a spouse may also be considered alimony. Alimony may even include the payment of medical and dental expenses. This chapter discusses what should and should not be considered an alimony payment.

The Deficit Reduction Act of 1984 completely restructured the alimony rules. The old rules still apply to alimony payments made under pre-1985 divorce and separation agreements—unless those agreements have been specifically modified. For related information refer to dependency exemption (see Chapter 3, Personal Exemptions and Dependents), the child care credit (see Chapter 34, Child and Dependent Care Credit), head of household status (see Chapter 2, Filing Status), the earned income credit (see Chapter 38, Other Credits Including the Earned Income Credit), and the retirement savings credit (also see Chapter 38).

This chapter discusses the rules that apply if you pay or receive alimony. It covers the following topics:

- What payments are alimony,
- What payments are not alimony, such as child support,
- How to deduct alimony you paid,
- How to report alimony income you received, and
- Whether you must recapture the tax benefits of alimony. Recapture means adding back in your income all or part of a deduction you took in a prior year.

Alimony is a payment to or for a spouse or former spouse under a divorce or separation instrument. It does not include voluntary payments that are not made under a divorce or separation instrument.

Alimony is deductible by the payer and must be included in the spouse's or former spouse's income. Although this chapter is generally written for the payer of the alimony, the recipient can use the information to determine whether an amount received is alimony.

To be alimony, a payment must meet certain requirements. Different requirements apply to payments under instruments executed after 1984 and to payments under instruments executed before 1985. This chapter discusses the rules for payments under instruments executed after 1984. For the rules for payments under pre-1985 instruments, see Publication 504, Divorced or Separated Individuals.

Explanation
An outline of alimony rules that apply to divorce and separation instruments executed before 1985 and not modified after 1984 is shown on page 305. Note that 2004 was the last year the information on pre-1985 instruments was included in IRS Publication 504. However, information on applying the pre-1985 rules can be found on the IRS's website at www.irs.gov.

[IRS text intentionally omitted]

Use Table 20-1 in this chapter as a guide to determine whether certain payments are considered alimony.

Definitions. The following definitions apply throughout this chapter.

Spouse or former spouse. Unless otherwise stated in the following discussions about alimony, the term "spouse" includes former spouse.

Divorce or separation instrument. The term "divorce or separation instrument" means:

1. A decree of divorce or separate maintenance or a written instrument incident to that decree,
2. A written separation agreement, or

Table 20-1. Alimony Requirements (Instruments Executed After 1984)

Payments ARE alimony if all of the following are true:	Payments are NOT alimony if any of the following are true:
Payments are required by a divorce or separation instrument.	Payments are not required by a divorce or separation instrument.
Payer and recipient spouse do not file a joint return.	Payer and recipient spouse file a joint return.
Payment is in cash (including checks or money orders).	Payment is: • Not in cash, • A noncash property settlement, • Spouse's part of community income, or • To keep up the payer's property.
Payment is not designated in the instrument as not alimony.	Payment is designated in the instrument as not alimony.
Spouses legally separated under a decree of divorce or separate maintenance are not members of the same household.	Spouses legally separated under a decree of divorce or separate maintenance are members of the same household.
Payments are not required after death of the recipient spouse.	Payments are required after death of the recipient spouse.
Payment is not treated as child support.	Payment is treated as child support.
These payments are deductible by the payer and includible in income by the recipient.	*These payments are neither deductible by the payer nor includible in income by the recipient.*

3. A decree or any type of court order requiring a spouse to make payments for the support or maintenance of the other spouse. This includes a temporary decree, an interlocutory (not final) decree, and a decree of alimony *pendente lite* (while awaiting action on the final decree or agreement).

Useful Items

You may want to see:

Publication

☐ **504**   Divorced or Separated individuals

General Rules

The following rules apply to alimony regardless of when the divorce or separation instrument was executed.

Payments not alimony. Not all payments under a divorce or separation instrument are alimony. Alimony does not include any of the following.

1. Child support.
2. Noncash property settlements.
3. Payments that are your spouse's part of community income. (See *Community Property* in Publication 504.)
4. Payments to keep up the payer's property.
5. Use of property.

1. Any payment not required by the decree or agreement
2. Any payment that does not arise out of the marital relationship but that is required by the decree or agreement, such as repayment of a loan to your spouse
3. Any payment you make before the decree or agreement
4. Any payment you agreed to make before the decree or agreement and paid later
5. Any payment you make after your former spouse's remarriage
6. Any payment you make after your divorced spouse's death, even though required by the decree or agreement
7. Any payment you make that is part of a property settlement

Payments to a third party. Cash payments (including checks and money orders) to a third party on behalf of your spouse under the terms of your divorce or separation instrument may be alimony if they otherwise qualify. These include payments for your spouse's medical expenses, housing costs (rent, utilities, etc.), taxes, tuition, etc. The payments are treated as received by your spouse and then paid to the third party.

Life insurance premiums. Alimony includes premiums you must pay under your divorce or separation instrument for insurance on your life to the extent your spouse owns the policy.

Explanation
The ownership of a life insurance policy must be assigned to your former spouse before you may deduct the premiums you pay as alimony. In addition, your former spouse must be the irrevocable beneficiary of the policy. Your children may be irrevocable contingent beneficiaries.

If your children are the beneficiaries of a life insurance policy and your former spouse is a contingent beneficiary, you still control the policy. The premiums you pay on it are not considered alimony.

For the premiums to be considered alimony, your former spouse's benefit from the life insurance policy must be measurable in dollars. If your former spouse would benefit from the policy only under certain contingencies, the economic advantage cannot be measured and your premiums would not be considered alimony.

Payments for jointly owned home. If your divorce or separation instrument states that you must pay expenses for a home owned by you and your spouse or former spouse, some of your payments may be alimony.

Mortgage payments. If you must pay all the mortgage payments (principal and interest) on a jointly owned home, and they otherwise qualify, you can deduct one-half of the total payments as alimony. If you itemize deductions and the home is a qualified home, you can claim half of the interest in figuring your deductible interest. Your spouse must report one-half of the payments as alimony received. If your spouse itemizes deductions and the home is a qualified home, he or she can claim one-half of the interest on the mortgage in figuring deductible interest.

Taxes and insurance. If you must pay all the real estate taxes or insurance on a home held as tenants in common, you can deduct one-half of these payments as alimony. Your spouse must report one-half of these payments as alimony received. If you and your spouse itemize deductions, you can each claim one-half of the real estate taxes and none of the home insurance.

If your home is held as tenants by the entirety or joint tenants, none of your payments for taxes or insurance are alimony. But if you itemize deductions, you can claim all of the real estate taxes and none of the home insurance.

Other payments to a third party. If you made other third-party payments, see Publication 504 to see whether any part of the payments qualifies as alimony.

Instruments Executed After 1984

The following rules for alimony apply to payments under divorce or separation instruments executed after 1984.

Exception for instruments executed before 1985. There are two situations where the rules for instruments executed after 1984 apply to instruments executed before 1985.

1. A divorce or separation instrument executed before 1985 and then modified after 1984 to specify that the after-1984 rules will apply.
2. A temporary divorce or separation instrument executed before 1985 and incorporated into, or adopted by, a final decree executed after 1984 that:
   a. Changes the amount or period of payment, or
   b. Adds or deletes any contingency or condition.

[IRS text intentionally omitted]

Example 1. In November 1984, you and your former spouse executed a written separation agreement. In February 1985, a decree of divorce was substituted for the written separation agreement. The decree of divorce did not change the terms for the alimony you pay your former spouse. The decree of divorce is treated as executed before 1985. Alimony payments under this decree are not subject to the rules for payments under instruments executed after 1984.

Example 2. Assume the same facts as in *Example 1* except that the decree of divorce changed the amount of the alimony. In this example, the decree of divorce is not treated as executed before 1985.

The alimony payments are subject to the rules for payments under instruments executed after 1984.

Explanation
For divorce decrees and separation agreements executed after 1984 (and, in certain cases, decrees or agreements executed before 1985 which have been modified), payments may not be deductible, even if there is a legal obligation to make them. Payments would be deductible only if all the other requirements were fulfilled.

TAXPLANNER

Don't overlook the opportunity to use the new rules on an old divorce.

Example
Bob and Mary were divorced in 1975, with Mary agreeing to pay Bob $2,000 per month in qualifying alimony payments. Mary was a stockbroker earning top dollars in 1975. Bob had never had a full-time job. In 2005, Mary's fortunes are not so rosy, whereas Bob is a top Los Angeles real estate broker.

Bob and Mary could agree that, in 2005, Mary will pay less money to Bob but that it won't be considered alimony. If Mary's marginal tax bracket has dropped to 15% and Bob's tax bracket is 35%, Mary could pay Bob as little as 65% of what her normal payment is ($1,300), and both would win. Mary would be out-of-pocket less than the $1,700 after tax she would have were she to deduct the usual $2,000 payment at her 15% bracket; Bob would receive the same amount after taxes ($1,300) than if he had received the $2,000 as taxable alimony at his 35% bracket.

Alimony requirements. A payment to or for a spouse under a divorce or separation instrument is alimony if the spouses do not file a joint return with each other and all the following requirements are met.

1. The payment is in cash.
2. The instrument does not designate the payment as not alimony.
3. The spouses are not members of the same household at the time the payments are made. This requirement applies only if the spouses are legally separated under a decree of divorce or separate maintenance.
4. There is no liability to make any payment (in cash or property) after the death of the recipient spouse.
5. The payment is not treated as child support.

Each of these requirements is discussed next.

Payments must be in cash. Only cash payments, including checks and money orders, qualify as alimony. The following do not qualify as alimony.

- Transfers of services or property (including a debt instrument of a third party or an annuity contract).
- Execution of a debt instrument by the payer.
- The use of property.

TAXPLANNER

According to the IRS, an annuity contract given to a spouse is a transfer of property and not a cash payment. Therefore, the spouse giving the annuity contract would not be entitled to a deduction for alimony. The spouse receiving the annuity contract has the same investment cost as the spouse giving it. The only taxable income to the receiving spouse would be the amounts received in excess of cost.

If you are the alimony payer and you want to ensure a tax deduction, you can use distributions from an annuity contract that you own to make future alimony payments rather than transfer the annuity contract to your spouse.

Payments to a third party. Cash payments to a third party under the terms of your divorce or separation instrument can qualify as a cash payment to your spouse. See *Payments to a third party* under *General Rules*, earlier.

Also, cash payments made to a third party at the written request of your spouse qualify as alimony if all the following requirements are met.

1. The payments are in lieu of payments of alimony directly to your spouse.
2. The written request states that both spouses intend the payments to be treated as alimony.
3. You receive the written request from your spouse before you file your return for the year you made the payments.

Explanation
Medical and dental expenses. If you paid your spouse's medical and dental expenses under a decree or agreement, you may deduct them as alimony. However, a payment of unusually large medical expenses in a given year might trigger excess front-loading rules. The result could be that you lose the deduction for payments under the recapture rules (see a discussion of recapture rules later), even though they are required as part of the divorce or separation agreement.

Your spouse must report these payments as alimony received and may include them as medical expenses if he or she is itemizing deductions.

Note: The spouse who pays the medical bills saves tax by claiming the amounts as alimony rather than as medical expenses. Alimony is fully deductible from adjusted gross income, whether or not the payer itemizes deductions. For medical expenses, only those exceeding 7.5% of adjusted gross income (AGI) are deductible (or those exceeding 10% of AGI for alternative minimum tax purposes).

TaxSaver

If you pay medical insurance premiums on behalf of a former spouse, you may be entitled to an additional deduction. Your former spouse may be able to deduct those payments as medical expenses.

Example
A husband who had not been directly ordered by the courts to carry medical insurance for his former wife but who was ordered to pay her reasonable medical expenses was allowed to deduct premiums paid as alimony. (He could not deduct the premiums as a medical expense.) His former wife had to include the amount that her former husband paid for the insurance premiums as income. Both parties treated as alimony the premiums and any actual medical expenses paid that were not reimbursed by insurance payments.

Note: The husband may have created a larger deduction for alimony by taking out an insurance policy on his former wife, since he may deduct the cost of the premiums (his out-of-pocket cost) whether or not his former wife incurs any actual medical expenses. Conversely, the former wife may pay a tax on an amount from which she derives no direct benefit.

Payments designated as not alimony. You and your spouse can designate that otherwise qualifying payments are not alimony. You do this by including a provision in your divorce or separation instrument that states the payments are not deductible as alimony by you and are excludable from your spouse's income. For this purpose, any instrument (written statement) signed by both of you that makes this designation and that refers to a previous written separation agreement is treated as a written separation agreement. If you are subject to temporary support orders, the designation must be made in the original or a later temporary support order.

Your spouse can exclude the payments from income only if he or she attaches a copy of the instrument designating them as not alimony to his or her return. The copy must be attached each year the designation applies.

Spouses cannot be members of the same household. Payments to your spouse while you are members of the same household are not alimony if you are legally separated under a decree of divorce or separate maintenance. A home you formerly shared is considered one household, even if you physically separate yourselves in the home.

You are not treated as members of the same household if one of you is preparing to leave the household and does leave no later than 1 month after the date of the payment.

Exception. If you are not legally separated under a decree of divorce or separate maintenance, a payment under a written separation agreement, support decree, or other court order may qualify as alimony even if you are members of the same household when the payment is made.

Explanation
Separated and living apart. The courts have traditionally held that spouses living under the same roof are not separated. However, some courts have looked to the facts and circumstances surrounding each case to determine whether or not spouses living in the same house who seldom see each other and who incur duplicate living expenses are, in fact, separated. The Appeals Courts have been reluctant to deal with the highly personalized questions that must be asked to determine whether or not the parties are truly living apart.

Liability for payments after death of recipient spouse. If you must continue to make payments for any period after your spouse's death, the part of the payment that would continue is not alimony whether made before or after the death. If all of the payment would continue, then none of the payments made before or after the death are alimony.

The divorce or separation instrument does not have to expressly state that the payments cease upon the death of your spouse if, for example, the liability for continued payments would end under state law.

Example. You must pay your former spouse $10,000 in cash each year for 10 years. Your divorce decree states that the payments will end upon your former spouse's death. You must also pay your former spouse or your former spouse's estate $20,000 in cash each year for 10 years. The death of your spouse would not terminate these payments under state law.

The $10,000 annual payments are alimony. But because the

$20,000 annual payments will not end upon your former spouse's death, they are not alimony.

Substitute payments. If you must make any payments in cash or property after your spouse's death as a substitute for continuing otherwise qualifying payments, the otherwise qualifying payments are not alimony. To the extent that your payments begin, accelerate, or increase because of the death of your spouse, otherwise qualifying payments you made may be treated as payments that were not alimony. Whether or not such payments will be treated as not alimony depends on all the facts and circumstances.

Example 1. Under your divorce decree, you must pay your former spouse $30,000 annually. The payments will stop at the end of 6 years or upon your former spouse's death, if earlier.

Your former spouse has custody of your minor children. The decree provides that if any child is still a minor at your spouse's death, you must pay $10,000 annually to a trust until the youngest child reaches the age of majority. The trust income and corpus (principal) are to be used for your children's benefit.

These facts indicate that the payments to be made after your former spouse's death are a substitute for $10,000 of the $30,000 annual payments. $10,000 of each of the $30,000 annual payments is not alimony.

Example 2. Under your divorce decree, you must pay your former spouse $30,000 annually. The payments will stop at the end of 15 years or upon your former spouse's death, if earlier. The decree provides that if your former spouse dies before the end of the 15-year period, you must pay the estate the difference between $450,000 ($30,000 × 15) and the total amount paid up to that time. For example, if your spouse dies at the end of the tenth year, you must pay the estate $150,000 ($450,000 − $300,000).

These facts indicate that the lump-sum payment to be made after your former spouse's death is a substitute for the full amount of the $30,000 annual payments. None of the annual payments are alimony. The result would be the same if the payment required at death were to be discounted by an appropriate interest factor to account for the prepayment.

TAXALERT

A recent court decision denied an alimony deduction because the taxpayer was required to make payments to his children in the same amount as the alimony if his ex-wife died. The agreement stated that the alimony payments ended at death; however, the alimony was set up as installment payments and if the ex-wife died before all payments were made, the remaining payments were to be paid to the children. Although no post-death payments were actually made, the alimony deduction was still disallowed.

Child support. A payment that is specifically designated as child support or treated as specifically designated as child support under your divorce or separation instrument is not alimony. The designated amount or part may vary from time to time. Child support payments are neither deductible by the payer nor taxable to the recipient.

Specifically designated as child support. A payment will be treated as specifically designated as child support to the extent that the payment is reduced either:

1. On the happening of a contingency relating to your child, or
2. At a time that can be clearly associated with the contingency.

A payment may be treated as specifically designated as child support even if other separate payments are specifically designated as child support.

TAXPLANNER

Since child support payments are considered fixed, any reductions in child support that are not part of the original decree or a subsequent court-approved modified divorce decree are considered reductions in alimony, not child support. Therefore, be sure to have the court approve any child support reductions so that you can continue to deduct the full alimony payments.

Example
After a taxpayer remarried, his son from his previous marriage began to live with him. The taxpayer and his former wife agreed that, as a result, his child support payments should be eliminated. Even though both former spouses agreed that the payment reductions applied to child support, the courts held that they applied to alimony because the taxpayer and his former spouse did not obtain a modification of their divorce decree in court.

Contingency relating to your child. A contingency relates to your child if it depends on any event relating to that child. It does not matter whether the event is certain or likely to occur. Events relating to your child include the child's:

• Becoming employed,
• Dying,
• Leaving the household,
• Leaving school,
• Marrying, or
• Reaching a specified age or income level.

Clearly associated with a contingency. Payments are presumed to be reduced at a time clearly associated with the happening of a contingency relating to your child only in the following situations.

1. The payments are to be reduced not more than 6 months before or after the date the child will reach 18, 21, or local age of majority.
2. The payments are to be reduced on two or more occasions that occur not more than 1 year before or after a different one of your children reaches a certain age from 18 to 24. This certain age must be the same for each child, but need not be a whole number of years.

In all other situations, reductions in payments are not treated as clearly associated with the happening of a contingency relating to your child.

Either you or the IRS can overcome the presumption in the two situations above. This is done by showing that the time at which the payments are to be reduced was determined independently of any contingencies relating to your children. For example, if you can show that the period of alimony payments is customary in the local jurisdiction, such as a period equal to one-half of the duration of the marriage, you can treat the amount as alimony.

Explanation
Child Support in Agreements Executed Before 1985
Child support amounts may not be inferred for payments made under agreements executed before 1985 and not revised. You may not assume that portions of the alimony payments are used by a former spouse for support of a child. The U.S. Supreme Court has held that payments are not treated as child support pay-

ments unless they are expressly designated as such in the governing document.

Child Support in Agreements Executed After 1984

Child support amounts *may* be inferred for payments made under agreements executed or revised after 1984, even if such payments are not specifically earmarked. However, such payments will be reduced upon certain contingencies related to the child. Such contingencies would include the child attaining a certain age or income level, dying, marrying, leaving school, leaving the spouse's household, or getting a job.

Payments that are reduced at a time that can clearly be associated with a contingency will be treated as child support. For example, if a payment was to stop at a certain calendar date that just happened to be the child's nineteenth birthday, that payment would be considered child support.

The parent who has custody of the child is entitled to take the dependency exemption for the child, as long as the parents themselves could have claimed the exemption had they filed a joint return. This will not apply if

1. There is a multiple support agreement in effect specifying who gets the exemption.
2. The custodial parent relinquishes the exemption in writing (using language in IRS Form 8332). The Working Families Tax Relief Act of 2004 provides an alternative to a signed declaration. If the noncustodial parent is allowed the exemption in the divorce agreement, then no signed form is required. The noncustodial parent should attach a copy of the portion of the agreement supporting the exemption claimed.
3. There is an executed, pre-1985 divorce or separation agreement in effect that provides that the noncustodial parent who also furnishes at least $600 of child support can claim the exemption.

Note: The custodial parent is still entitled to claim the dependent care credit, even if he or she relinquishes the dependency exemption to the noncustodial parent.

A parent can deduct medical expenses that he or she paid directly for a child's benefit, even though the dependency exemption for the child is claimed by the other parent. This is the case as long as a multiple-support agreement is not in effect.

TAXPLANNER

In 2005, *single* taxpayers with adjusted gross income over $145,950 and taxpayers filing as head of household with adjusted gross income exceeding $182,450 will not receive the full benefit of the deduction for personal exemptions. Taxpayers with adjusted gross income above these thresholds will have the amount of each personal and dependent exemption simultaneously reduced at a rate of 2% for each $2,500 (or fraction thereof) by which adjusted gross income exceeds the applicable threshold. In other words, each personal and dependent exemption is fully phased out for single taxpayers with adjusted gross income of $268,450 and for heads of households with adjusted gross income of $304,950. As a result, the former spouse with less adjusted gross income may receive a greater

tax benefit from claiming the children as dependents than would the spouse with higher income.

How To Deduct Alimony Paid

You can deduct alimony you paid, whether or not you itemize deductions on your return. You must file Form 1040. You cannot use Form 1040A or Form 1040EZ.

Enter the amount of alimony you paid on Form 1040, line 31a. In the space provided on line 31b, enter your spouse's social security number.

If you paid alimony to more than one person, enter the social security number of one of the recipients. Show the social security number and amount paid to each other recipient on an attached statement. Enter your total payments on line 31a.

Caution. *If you do not provide your spouse's social security number, you may have to pay a $50 penalty and your deduction may be disallowed.*

Explanation
Even if the validity of a divorce decree is questioned, your spouse must include periodic payments that you make under such a divorce decree in income. You may deduct the payments as alimony. A divorce decree is valid for tax purposes until a court having proper jurisdiction declares it invalid.

The IRS generally recognizes a state court as having proper jurisdiction if that court has personal jurisdiction over the parties involved or if that court has jurisdiction over the subject matter of the action.

Example 1
In the process of separating, a husband and wife entered into a support agreement under a state court. The husband later obtained a Mexican divorce that said nothing about the support agreement. The state considered the divorce to be valid. Even though the Mexican divorce decree made no mention of the support payments, the payments were considered alimony because the original state support agreement had never been invalidated.

Example 2
A husband who obtained a Mexican divorce was later sued by his former wife for support payments and for a legal separation under state law. The state court granted the former wife the support payments. The Mexican divorce was not recognized by the state, but the payments were considered to be alimony.

How To Report Alimony Received

Report alimony you received on Form 1040, line 11. You cannot use Form 1040A or Form 1040EZ.

Caution. *You must give the person who paid the alimony your social security number. If you do not, you may have to pay a $50 penalty.*

Recapture Rule

If your alimony payments decrease or terminate during the first 3 calendar years, you may be subject to the recapture rule. If you are subject to this rule, you have to include in income in the third year part of the alimony payments you previously deducted. Your spouse can deduct in the third year part of the alimony payments he or she previously included in income.

The 3-year period starts with the first calendar year you make a payment qualifying as alimony under a decree of divorce or separate maintenance or a written separation agreement. Do not include any time in which payments were being made under temporary support orders. The second and third years are the next 2 calendar years, whether or not payments are made during those years.

The reasons for a reduction or termination of alimony payments that can require a recapture include:

• A change in your divorce or separation instrument,
• A failure to make timely payments,
• A reduction in your ability to provide support, or
• A reduction in your spouse's support needs.

When to apply the recapture rule. You are subject to the recapture rule in the third year if the alimony you pay in the third year decreases by more than $15,000 from the second year or the alimony you pay in the second and third years decreases significantly from the alimony you pay in the first year.

TaxSaver

If the payments are spread out equally over the 3 years, they are all deductible. Also, payments in year 3 may be more beneficial than those made in year 2 because that may ensure that the payments in year 3 do not decrease by more than $15,000 from the payments in year 2.

When you figure a decrease in alimony, do not include the following amounts.

1. Payments made under a temporary support order.
2. Payments required over a period of at least 3 calendar years of a fixed part of your income from a business or property, or from compensation for employment or self-employment.
3. Payments that decrease because of the death of either spouse or the remarriage of the spouse receiving the payments.

Figuring the recapture. You can use Worksheet A in Publication 504 to figure recaptured alimony.

Including the recapture in income. If you must include a recapture amount in income, show it on Form 1040, line 11 ("Alimony received"). Cross out "received" and enter "recapture." On the dotted line next to the amount, enter your spouse's last name and social security number.

Deducting the recapture. If you can deduct a recapture amount, show it on Form 1040, line 31a ("Alimony paid"). Cross out "paid" and enter "recapture." In the space provided, enter your spouse's social security number.

Other Alimony Issues and Rules

Explanation
Transfer of property. If property is transferred in settlement of marital rights, the spouse making the transfer does not recognize either gain or loss on the transfer, whether the property has appreciated or declined in value. The transfer is treated like a gift, and the spouse receiving the property takes the basis of the transferring spouse. This is true even if the spouse receiving the property pays cash and the transaction is cast in the form of a sale.

The following are exceptions to the nonrecognition rules:

1. Transfer of an installment note to a trust will cause the deferred gain to be recognized
2. Transfer of property subject to liabilities in excess of basis will cause the excess to be recognized

TaxPlanner

The transfer between spouses of a note receivable that arose from an installment sale will not be considered a disposition for purposes of accelerating the reporting of previously deferred income. Instead, the recipient of the installment note will have the same tax posture as the spouse who made the transfer.

Explanation
Transfer of business property. The law is silent on the status of unrealized income from normal business accounts receivable that may be transferred. There is no recapture of investment tax credit or depreciation on the transfer of business property. The spouse making the transfer must provide permanent records of cost basis, accumulated depreciation, holding period, and investment-credit recapture potential to the other spouse. There is no penalty for failure to do so, however.

TaxAlert

There is a new property transfer provision for tax years beginning after December 31, 2004. Under the new 2004 law, any disallowed losses due to the cost basis of business property are carried over to the spouse or former spouse in a tax-free transfer of S corporation stock incident to divorce. Under prior law, the losses suspended due to basis limitations could not be transferred.

TaxPlanner

A spouse who is to receive property with a tax basis substantially less than its current value should carefully evaluate the tax consequences of disposing of it. The recipient may be subject to tax from recapture of investment tax credit and depreciation and should obtain the advice of competent counsel on such matters.

Example
As part of the divorce property settlement, Kyle gives Mary a computer that he used for 4 years in his sole proprietorship business. Kyle paid $5,000 for the computer, claimed investment credit on it, and claimed depreciation of $3,950. Since the computer ceased to be business property when it was given to Mary, she must recapture part of the investment credit claimed by Kyle. Further, Mary must pay ordinary income tax on her profit if she sells the computer for more than $1,050. See Chapter 17, *Reporting Gains and Losses*, and Chapter 38, *Other Credits Including the Earned Income Credit*.

Explanation
Trust property. If income-producing property is placed in trust to pay alimony, the alimony payments are not included or deducted from income. This rule applies whether the alimony payments are made out of the trust income or principal. Trust distributions must be

reported as income by your spouse. If your obligation to pay alimony is stated in a divorce decree, other court order, or written separation agreement, your spouse reports the distributions as alimony on line 11 of Form 1040. If your obligation is not so stated, your spouse reports the income distributions as income received from a trust, on Schedule E (Form 1040).

You may also set up a trust to pay both alimony and child support. If your former spouse remarries and you are no longer required to pay alimony, the trust may continue disbursing monies for child support.

TaxPlanner

If a trust that is set up to disburse alimony payments holds municipal bonds, the distributions to the former spouse are nontaxable to the extent that they are attributable to the trust's municipal bond income. Also, if the distributions from the trust exceed the trust's income, the excess distribution of trust principal is not taxable.

Explanation
Insurance, endowment, or annuity. If an insurance or endowment policy or an annuity contract is purchased to discharge alimony or support called for in a divorce decree, the payer does not include in, or deduct from income, payments made under the contract. The recipient must include the payments in income.

Annulments. Generally, state laws blur the distinction between a divorce and an annulment. The rules on alimony often apply to an annulment decree as well as to a divorce decree. You should examine the law of the state in which you reside to determine if this is the case.

Example
In New York, a marriage was annulled due to the wife's insanity. The husband was required to provide for her care and maintenance. Since under the general rules of law the annulment would be considered a divorce, the husband's payments were treated as alimony.

TaxPlanner

Expenses of a home. If part of an alimony award is used to pay such expenses as real estate taxes, insurance, mortgage interest, and utilities for a home owned by a divorced couple, the facts in each case determine the amount deductible by one spouse and includable by the other spouse. Two facts to consider are the type of ownership and the kinds of expenses that must be paid. The spouse making the payments will only be entitled to a deduction if he or she has an ownership interest in the home. However, in each case, the payments must cover a period of more than 10 years or otherwise qualify as periodic payments if made pursuant to a pre-1985 agreement.

Ownership
You should check your state law, ownership documents, and your divorce decree to determine what type of ownership you have.

1. **Joint tenants or tenants by the entirety.** You and your former spouse own a home jointly as **tenants by the entirety** or **joint tenants** with a right of survivorship. You are both jointly and individually responsible for the entire mortgage balance. If your divorce decree states that your former spouse is to pay the mortgage (principal and interest) on the property from money that he or she receives from you as support, then your former spouse must include one-half of each principal and interest payment as income from alimony and you may deduct one-half of each principal and interest payment as alimony.

   Your former spouse may deduct one-half of the interest if your former spouse itemizes deductions on Schedule A (Form 1040). If you itemize your deductions, it is not clear how your share of the interest should be handled. It may be deductible under the home mortgage rules if your children live there and you are not already deducting interest on two personal residences. Or it might be considered investment interest, since as far as you are concerned, the property is now just an investment. Lastly, it could be personal interest and therefore not deductible.

2. **Tenants in common.** If you and your former spouse own a home **as tenants in common**, your former spouse owns half of the property. Therefore, you may deduct as alimony amounts you pay on your former spouse's half of the property for principal, interest, insurance, and taxes. Your former spouse must include these amounts in income.

   If your former spouse itemizes deductions on Schedule A (Form 1040), he or she may deduct as taxes and interest the part you paid for real estate taxes and interest on your former spouse's half of the property. He or she may not deduct amounts for insurance. Insurance is a nondeductible personal expense.

   Amounts you paid on your half of the property are not deductible as alimony, nor are they includable in income by your former spouse. If you itemize your deductions on Schedule A (Form 1040), you may deduct the part you pay for real estate taxes and interest on your half of the property. You may not deduct insurance payments on your half of the property.

3. **Your former spouse owns the home.** If the home is owned by your former spouse, under a decree or agreement you pay the real estate taxes, mortgage payments, and insurance premiums on it, you may deduct these payments as alimony. Your former spouse must include these payments in income.

   If your former spouse itemizes deductions on Schedule A (Form 1040), he or she may deduct the part of each payment that is for taxes and interest on the mortgage.

4. **You own the home.** If the home you own is lived in rent-free by your former spouse, you may not deduct your mortgage payments or the fair rental value of the home as alimony. However, if you itemize your deductions, you may deduct on Schedule A (Form 1040) any real estate taxes and interest you pay on the property.

Rent. If, under a divorce or separate maintenance decree or written separation agreement, you must pay rent to a third-party lessor to provide housing for your spouse or former spouse, you may deduct the rent payments as alimony. Your former spouse must include these payments in income.

Utilities. If your former spouse is the one who has the right to use the home, regardless of the type of ownership, you may deduct as alimony the amount you pay for utilities under a decree or agreement. Your former spouse must include these amounts in income.

Property ownership. There are many consequences of property ownership that must be considered in a divorce settlement. Any payments made pursuant to a divorce decree by you for the mortgage, property taxes, insurance, and so on are considered alimony *only* if the house belongs to your former spouse. If you transfer your interest in the property to your children, payments to cover their portion of the mortgage payments would be treated as child support, not alimony.

Sale of property. If you sell property that you and your spouse own jointly, you must report your share of the recognized gain or loss on your income tax return for the year of the sale. Your share of the gain or loss is determined by your state law governing ownership of property. For more information on how to report the gain or loss, see IRS Publication 544.

Example
John and Mary owned a home that cost them $150,000. In their divorce, the court decree holds that Mary can remain in the home until their son, who is 10 years old, reaches 18. Mary must pay rent to John for using his half of the house. In 2005, the house is sold and John and Mary together receive $250,000.

Upon sale of the home, Mary is subject to tax on the gain on the home sale. Assuming she meets the requirements, she can exclude up to $250,000 of her portion of the total gain. See Chapter 16, *Selling Your Home.*

John was a landlord during the rental years and probably claimed related expenses and depreciation on his tax return. If the rent charged was reasonable, John could deduct any losses, subject to the restrictions on passive activities.

Upon sale, John is subject to tax on his entire portion of the gain.

TAXPLANNER

Other aspects of obtaining a divorce. IRS Publication 504, *Divorced or Separated Individuals,* examines more closely some of the tax aspects of obtaining a divorce, including the tax treatment of costs incurred in working out a settlement.

Court costs and legal fees related to the divorce are not deductible. However, the portion of these fees attributable to obtaining alimony is deductible as an itemized deduction, since it is an expense associated with the production of income. Any additional costs incurred to obtain alimony are also deductible, as are costs for tax advice.

Be sure to have itemized invoices for professional services. Deductible items should be specifically listed on any bill. You may claim only the deductible portion of your own legal expenses. You may not deduct the legal expenses of your spouse. Those expenses also may not be considered alimony payments.

Some part of your legal fees may give you a tax benefit, even though the fees are not spent for obtaining alimony or tax advice. For example, if part of your legal fees may be allocated to obtaining property, the tax basis of the property should be increased by the amount of such fees. If the property is business property, you will have larger **depreciation** deductions and a smaller gain if the property is sold.

There are several additional aspects that you should consider in a year in which you become divorced:

1. **Revising Form W-4.** Form W-4 should be changed if you are no longer able to claim as many withholding allowances due to your change in marital status. This may occur because you no longer file a joint return with your former spouse. It also may occur if you are not entitled to a dependency exemption for one or more of your children. When you revise your Form W-4, your employer adjusts your tax withholding to reflect the changes in your marital status or number of dependents.
2. **Estimated taxes on alimony.** If you are receiving alimony, you may be required to make estimated tax payments, since alimony is not covered by withholding. (See Chapter 5, *Tax Withholding and Estimated Tax.*)
3. **Allocating joint estimated tax payments between you and your former spouse.** If you and your former spouse are divorced during the year and have been making joint estimated tax payments, the payments you have already made may be applied to either person's separate return or may be divided between you, as the two of you see fit. If no allocation can be agreed on, the estimated payments should be applied between the separate returns in proportion to the taxes due on each.

Example
Your return shows a tax liability of $5,100. Your former spouse's return shows a tax liability of $2,300. You would be entitled to apply 69% [$5,100 ÷ ($5,100 + $2,300)] of your total joint estimated payments against your tax liability.

4. **Retirement plans.** An employee's interest in a qualified retirement plan can be allocated between a current and a former spouse by a qualified domestic relations order. Benefits so allocated are taxed to the current and former spouses when the payments are actually received.

   If the benefits are received by anyone other than the employee or the current or former spouses, the benefits are taxed to the employee, not the recipient.
5. **Federal income taxes withheld.** Taxes withheld from your income are treated the same way as the income that generates them. If salary is split equally between you and your spouse because of community property rules, then the tax withholding is also divided evenly between the two of you.
6. **Alimony and your IRA.** All taxable alimony or separate maintenance payments received by an individual under a decree of divorce or separate maintenance are treated as eligible compensation for making IRA contributions. See Chapter 18, *Individual Retirement Arrangements (IRAs),* for details.
7. **Stock options.** If you transfer nonqualified stock options you received from your employer to your

spouse in a divorce, there would be no tax at that time. When the options are exercised your spouse will be taxed on the difference between the exercise price of the option and the value of the stock.

Instruments Executed Before 1985

Here is an outline of the old alimony rules that apply to divorce or separation instruments executed *before* 1985 and *not* changed after 1984.

Payments you make under a court decree of divorce or separation are included in the income of your spouse or former spouse and may be deducted as alimony by you if they are:

1. Required under a decree of divorce or separation, or a written instrument incident to that decree
2. Based on a marital or family relationship
3. Paid after the date the decree became effective
4. Periodic instead of a lump sum

Payments made before the divorce decree or separate maintenance agreement issued by the court do not qualify as alimony. The divorce need not be final for the payments to be considered alimony, but the payments must be ordered by the court and, if made under pre-1985 agreements, must satisfy a legal obligation arising from the marriage.

Payments you make under a written separation agreement executed after August 16, 1954, or materially altered or modified after that date, are included in the income of your spouse and may be deducted as alimony by you if they are:

1. Based on a marital or family relationship
2. Paid after the agreement is put into effect and while you and your spouse are separated and living apart
3. Paid during a tax year for which you do not file a **joint return** with the spouse who gets these payments
4. Periodic instead of a lump sum

To be binding, a written agreement must state the amount of the support payments, the length of time over which the payments are to be made, and the items of support covered by the payments. The agreement does not have to mention specifically that the couple is separated.

The written separation agreement must be accepted by both parties. One spouse may not merely designate payments as alimony. The courts have held that a letter from a husband to a wife defining various payments as support do not meet the requirements of a written agreement, even if the payments are accepted by the wife. The agreement takes effect when it has been signed by both parties, no matter what the date is on the agreement.

Example

A wife signed a separation agreement and sent it to her husband. The husband signed it before a notary public but did not return it to the wife for several months. The husband, who had been out of the country, began sending the wife support payments before she received the signed agreement. The court held that the agreement became effective when signed by the husband. All payments were viewed as alimony.

Explanation

Payments you make under a decree for support or any type of court order, including a temporary decree, entered into after March 1, 1954, or changed by a court after that date, are included in the income of your spouse and may be deducted as alimony by you if they are:

1. Required under the decree or court order
2. Paid while you and your spouse are separated and living apart
3. Paid during a tax year for which you do not file a joint return with the spouse who gets these payments
4. Periodic instead of a lump sum

Payments you make under a decree for support or any type of court order qualify as alimony, even though the decree is not pursuant to a divorce or **legal separation** agreement. These payments must be specified as being for a spouse, not a child.

Spouses separated under an interlocutory decree retain the relationship of husband and wife, even though payments made pursuant to this type of decree qualify as alimony. However, if payments are being made under an interlocutory decree issued prior to March 1, 1954, and that decree has not yet been revised, the payments are not considered alimony.

Temporary alimony. If you do not file a joint return, you may deduct periodic payments you make under a decree of alimony *pendente lite* (while awaiting action on the final decree or agreement) entered after March 1, 1954. Your spouse must include the payments in income.

Remarriage of former spouse. You may not deduct payments you make under a divorce decree to your former spouse after the spouse remarries, if you have no legal obligation to continue to make the payments. Legal obligation to continue to make the payments would be determined under the law of the state in which your divorce was granted. However, your former spouse must still report the payments as miscellaneous income (not alimony), unless it can be shown that they were gifts, were payments on a loan, or were otherwise excludable from income.

Example 1

In 1984, you were divorced from your spouse. The divorce decree calls for you to pay your former spouse $400 a month as alimony. In April 1997, your former spouse remarried, but you were not aware of this, and you continued to make the payments.

Under the state law in which you got your divorce, your legal obligation to make the payments ends if your former spouse remarries. Even though you were unaware that your former spouse remarried, you cannot deduct the payments you made after April 1997. However, your former spouse must include the payments in gross income.

Example 2

Assume the same facts as in Example 1, except that you were aware of your former spouse's remarriage and you continued to make the payments but considered them a gift. In this situation, your former spouse does not have to include the payments made after April 1997 in gross income, and you may not deduct them.

Explanation

Periodic payments in a community property state to a separated spouse are deductible as alimony only if they are more than that spouse's part of the **community income**.

Example

You live in a community property state. You are separated, and your spouse has no income. Under a written support agreement, you pay your spouse periodic payments of $12,000 of your $20,000 total yearly community income. Under your state law, earnings of a spouse living separate and apart from the other spouse continue as community property. On your separate returns, each of you must report $10,000 gross income (half of the total community income). In addition, your spouse must report $2,000 as alimony received on line 11 of Form 1040. You may deduct $2,000 as alimony paid on line 31a of Form 1040.

Note: If you did *not* make any payments to your spouse or notify him or her of the amount of the community income, the IRS can require that you report the entire $20,000 as your income.

Explanation

A couple's property continues to be considered community property by the IRS until a final divorce is granted. This is true, even though some states—Louisiana, for example—might retroactively recognize the date of separation as the time when property is no longer shared. Consequently, until a final divorce is granted, a spouse should treat as alimony only those payments that are more than his or her share of the community income. Furthermore, alimony paid to a former spouse is generally considered as having been paid from community income when you and your current spouse file separate returns.

Example

A California resident was divorced and remarried. His new wife was a **nonresident alien**, and they filed separate tax returns. The courts held that he could deduct only half of the alimony payments made to his former wife because he failed to prove that the alimony payments were made from separate income property that he did not share with his new wife. Therefore, his new wife was, in effect, paying half of his alimony payments to his former wife. Her payments were not deductible as alimony.

Explanation

Periodic payments are payments of a fixed amount (e.g., $400 a month) for an indefinite period or payments of an indefinite amount (e.g., 10% of a salary that changes from year to year) for either a fixed or an indefinite period. They need not be made at regular intervals.

Even if a state court describes payments made under a divorce decree as payments for property rights, they may be periodic payments if they are made to fulfill a legal support obligation.

Installment payments that you make to take care of your alimony obligation (the amount you must pay under the decree) generally are not considered periodic payments if the total obligation is stated in the decree or agreement. They may not be deductible at all, or they may be only partly deductible, depending mainly on the period over which you must make the payments.

In general, courts have held that if an amount specified in the divorce decree can be determined by arithmetical means, it is considered a principal sum. Payments to reach a principal sum are installment payments, not periodic payments, and generally are not deductible as alimony if they are paid over a period of 10 years or less. The following are property settlement payments, not periodic payments:

- Repayment of a debt between husband and wife in equal annual installments
- Repayment on an annual basis of the wife's interest in community property retained by the husband

Example

A woman purchased a residence in her name. Her former husband had the right to use the residence for his lifetime. The woman was not allowed to deduct the fair rental value of the property as alimony, and the man did not have to include the value in his income as periodic payments. The IRS ruled that, according to state law, the woman was making a one-time transfer of property to her former husband. Such a transfer does not qualify as alimony.

Explanation

If the period stated is 10 years or less, the payments generally are not considered periodic, and, therefore, you may not deduct them. However, if the payments are subject to certain specific contingencies, they are deductible periodic payments, even though under the decree they are for a specified period of 10 years or less. Alimony payments are considered subject to contingencies if they are to end or change in amount on:

1. The death of either spouse
2. The remarriage of the spouse receiving them
3. A change in the economic status (amount of money on property owned) of either spouse

The contingency may be set forth in the terms of the decree or agreement, or it may be imposed by local law. The payments must be in the nature of alimony or an allowance for support.

Example

Under the terms of a settlement agreement approved by the divorce decree, you agreed to pay your former spouse $19,000. Of this amount, you paid $14,000 as soon as the decree was entered. You pay the remaining $5,000 for 25 months at $200 a month. The payments will stop if your former spouse dies or remarries. You may not deduct the $14,000 that is a lump-sum payment, and your former spouse does not include it in income. Because the monthly payments of $200 will stop if your former spouse dies or remarries, they are periodic payments. You may deduct them, and your former spouse must include them in income.

Explanation

If the period stated is more than 10 years and the payments are not subject to contingencies, you may deduct a certain amount of each installment payment paid during the year as a periodic payment and your spouse must include it in income. The amount is limited to 10% of the total amount to be paid over the entire time called for by the decree. This 10% limit applies to installment payments made on a timely basis and to amounts due in a future tax year but paid in advance. The limit does not apply to amounts due in a prior tax year, but paid in a later tax year. If the payments are made for more than 10 years and are subject to contingencies, you may deduct them in full as periodic payments.

Example
Your decree states that you must pay your former spouse $150,000 in installments of $20,000 a year for 5 years and $5,000 a year for the following 10 years. The payments are not subject to any contingencies. You may deduct only 10% of the $150,000, or $15,000, during each of the first 5 years. During the last 10 years, you may deduct the entire $5,000 you pay each year.

Explanation
The 10% rule is relevant only when the amounts of alimony payments required by the divorce decree are not paid evenly over the specified payment period. The intention of the 10% rule is to prevent property settlements from being disguised as alimony. Alimony is deductible; a property settlement is not. The 10% rule does not apply if the payments would cease on the occurrence of certain contingencies.

TAXPLANNER
Although you may deduct only 10% of the total amount of fixed payments in any one year, you may be able to claim a greater deduction than you would normally if you alter the timing of the payments.

Example 1
A husband is obligated to pay $160,000 over a 15-year period by paying $20,000 a year for the first 5 years and $6,000 a year for the last 10 years. Because he may deduct only 10% of the total fixed amount in any one year, only $16,000 (10% of $160,000) of the $20,000 paid in each of the first 5 years is deductible. The $4,000-per-year difference ($20,000 paid less $16,000 deductible) is not deductible by the husband or taxable to his former spouse.

In the fifth year, however, the husband makes a payment of only $16,000, instead of the required $20,000. That entire amount is deductible, since it is not more than 10% of the total amount due. If in the sixth year of payments he makes a $10,000 payment (the $6,000 he owes for that year plus the $4,000 from the year before), he may again deduct the entire amount. The $10,000 payment is less than the 10% limitation. Also, back alimony is not subject to the 10% rule. Thus, by shifting the timing of his payments, the husband may take a greater deduction.

Note: The 10% rule does apply to the advance payment of alimony. If in the above example the husband wants to make the $6,000-a-year payments for years 6, 7, and 8 in the sixth year, he may deduct only $16,000 (10% of the total amount due) of the $18,000 paid.

Example 2
Mr. Oldster got behind in his alimony payments. He made a lump-sum settlement of the amounts he owed, as well as future alimony. The amount paid was less than the total amount due and was also less than the amount of delinquent alimony. Since there was no designation of the amounts, he was allowed to deduct the total payment as back alimony.

TAXPLANNER
There are certain circumstances in which what appears to be a lump-sum payment may, in fact, be deductible as alimony.

According to an IRS ruling, a lump-sum payment to a former spouse for the remaining portion of alimony payments to which he or she is entitled qualifies as alimony.

Example
A couple divorced, and the divorce decree stipulated that the wife pay $81,000 in alimony, $3,600 per year for 22 1/2 years. After 10 years, the husband could elect to receive the present value of the remaining payments. Since the payments spanned more than 10 years, they were considered periodic. However, because of the 10% limitation rule, the husband had to include only $8,100, 10% of the total payments received over the 22 1/2 years, in his income for the year in which he received the lump-sum payment [(10% × $3,600) × 22.5].

Note: This opinion was given by the IRS before 1985.

TAXPLANNER
For installment payments to qualify as periodic payments, the last payment must be made more than 10 years after the decree became effective. There have been numerous errors made in implementing the effective dates of agreements and the ending of the 10-year period.

Example
According to a divorce decree, a husband must make payments at the beginning of each month for 120 months, beginning with the month after the decree becomes final. If the decree became final on December 15, 1984, the first payment was due January 1, 1985. The one hundred twentieth and final payment is due December 1, 1994—14 days short of 10 years. Since the payment period falls short of the 10-year-plus requirement, the payments are not deductible as alimony.

Exception
The 10-year rule will not apply to an agreement executed before 1985 if it has been modified after 1984 and expressly provides that the new rules will apply. If a pre-1985 agreement has been modified and there is a change in the term of payment, the new alimony rules enacted in 1984 will apply when expressly indicated.

21

Education-Related Adjustments

Note: The 2004 IRS Publication 17 (Your Federal Income Tax) has been updated by Ernst & Young LLP for 2005. Dates and dollar amounts shown are for 2005. Gray type is used to indicate where IRS text has been updated or intentionally omitted. Unrevised IRS text is shown in black type.

Introduction

This chapter discusses the education-related adjustments you can deduct in figuring your adjusted gross income. These include certain educator expenses and interest paid on qualified student loans as well as certain amounts paid for tuition and other education expenses. Students and teachers alike will find this information interesting, relevant, and, hopefully, money-saving as well. In addition to these education adjustments that can lower your tax bill, see Chapter 37, Education Credits and Other Education Benefits.

What's New

Educator expenses. The provision for educator expenses was to have expired at the end of 2003, but the Working Families Tax Relief Act of 2004 extended this provision until the end of 2005. You can deduct up to $250 of qualified expenses as an adjustment to gross income in 2005. See *Educator Expenses* for more information.

Student loan interest deduction. Final regulations, issued May 7, 2004, made the following changes to the rules for deducting student loan interest. These changes apply to interest due and paid on qualified student loans after December 31, 1997.

Longer period allowed for loan disbursement. The 60-day safe harbor for disbursing loan proceeds used to pay qualified education expenses has been increased to 90 days before and 90 days after the academic period to which the expenses relate. See *Reasonable period of time* for more information.

Interest paid by a third party may be deductible. The person legally obligated to make interest payments on a student loan may be able to deduct interest payments on that loan made by someone else (third party). For more information, see *Expenses paid by others*.

Tip. *If you are affected by either of these changes, you may want to file Form 1040X, Amended U.S. Individual Income Tax Return, to correct a return you have already filed. Generally, you must file your claim for a refund within 3 years after the date you filed your original return or within 2 years after the date you paid the tax, whichever is later.*

[IRS text intentionally omitted]

TaxSaver

In 2005 the amount of qualified education expenses you can take into account in figuring your tuition and fees deduction increases to $4,000 if your modified adjusted gross income (MAGI) is not more than $65,000 ($130,000 if you are married filing jointly). If your MAGI is larger than $65,000 ($130,000), but is not more than $80,000 ($160,000 if you are married filing jointly), your maximum tuition and fees deduction is $2,000. No tuition and fees deduction is allowed if your MAGI is larger than $80,000 ($160,000).

Unlike other deductions that phase out depending on your level of adjusted gross income (AGI), this deduction does not get phased out—instead it is lost completely at the upper income level. If your modified adjusted gross income (MAGI) is even $1 above the $160,000 level if you are married and file a joint return ($80,000 for others) no deduction is allowed. This makes it critical that you manage your MAGI if you might otherwise be entitled to this deduction.

This deduction will expire at the end of 2005 unless Congress acts to extend it.

This chapter discusses the education-related adjustments you can deduct in figuring your adjusted gross income.

This chapter covers:

• Educator expenses,
• Student loan interest deduction, and
• The tuition and fees deduction.

Explanation

Chapter 37, *Education Credits and Other Education Tax Benefits,* discusses other education-related items that you may be able to claim.

Useful Items

You may want to see:

Publication

☐   **970**   Tax Benefits for Education

Educator Expenses

If you were an eligible educator in 2005, you can deduct up to $250 of qualified expenses you paid in 2005. If you and your spouse are filing jointly and both of you were eligible educators, the maximum deduction is $500. However, neither spouse can deduct more than $250 of his or her qualified expenses.

Eligible educator. An eligible educator is a kindergarten through grade 12 teacher, instructor, counselor, principal, or aide in a school for at least 900 hours during a school year.

Qualified expenses. Qualified expenses include ordinary and necessary expenses paid in connection with books, supplies, equipment (including computer equipment, software, and services), and other materials used in the classroom. An ordinary expense is one that is common and accepted in your educational field. A necessary expense is one that is helpful and appropriate for your profession as an educator. An expense does not have to be required to be considered necessary.

Qualified expenses do not include expenses for home schooling or for nonathletic supplies for courses in health or physical education.

You must reduce your qualified expenses by the following amounts.

- Tax-free interest on U.S. series EE and I savings bonds (Form 8815). See *Figuring the Tax-Free Amount* in chapter 10 of Publication 970.
- Tax-free portion of a distribution from a qualified tuition program (QTP). See *Figuring the Taxable Portion of a Distribution* in chapter 8 of Publication 970.
- Tax-free portion of a distribution from a Coverdell education savings account (ESA). See *Figuring the Taxable Portion of a Distribution* in chapter 7 of Publication 970.
- Any reimbursements you received for these expenses that were not reported to you in box 1 of your Form W-2.

How the deduction is claimed. To claim the deduction, enter the allowable amount on line 23 of Form 1040, or line 16 of Form 1040A.

TaxAlert

This special deduction was to have expired at the end of 2003 but has been extended until the end of 2005.

Student Loan Interest Deduction

Generally, personal interest you pay, other than certain mortgage interest, is not deductible on your tax return. However, if your modified adjusted gross income (MAGI) is less than $65,000 ($135,000 if filing a joint return) there is a special deduction allowed for paying interest on a student loan (also known as an education loan) used for higher education. For most taxpayers, MAGI is the adjusted gross income as figured on their federal income tax return before subtracting any deduction for student loan interest. This deduction can reduce the amount of your income subject to tax by up to $2,500 in 2005. Table 21-1 summarizes the features of the student loan interest deduction.

Table 21-1.   **Student Loan Interest Deduction at a Glance**

Do not rely on this table alone. Refer to the text for more details.

Feature	Description
Maximum benefit	You can decrease your income subject to tax by up to $2,500.
Loan qualifications	Your student loan • must have been taken out solely to pay qualified education expenses, and • cannot be from a related person or made under a qualified employer plan.
Student qualifications	The student must be • you, your spouse, or your dependent, and • enrolled at least half-time in a degree program.
Time limit on deduction	You can deduct interest paid during the remaining period of your student loan.
Phaseout	The amount of your deduction depends on your income level.

Student Loan Interest Defined

Student loan interest is interest you paid during the year on a qualified student loan. It includes both required and voluntary interest payments.

Qualified Student Loan

This is a loan you took out solely to pay qualified education expenses (defined later) that were:

- For you, your spouse, or a person who was your dependent (defined in chapter 3) when you took out the loan,
- Paid or incurred within a reasonable period of time before or after you took out the loan, and
- For education provided during an academic period for an eligible student.

Loans from the following sources are not qualified student loans.

- A related person.
- A qualified employer plan.

Reasonable period of time. Qualified education expenses are treated as paid or incurred within a reasonable period of time before or after you take out the loan if they are paid with the proceeds of student loans that are part of a federal postsecondary education loan program.

Even if not paid with the proceeds of that type of loan, the expenses are treated as paid or incurred within a reasonable period of time if both of the following requirements are met.

1. The expenses relate to a specific academic period, and
2. The loan proceeds are disbursed within a period that begins 90 days before the start of that academic period and ends 90 days after the end of that academic period.

If neither of the above situations applies, the reasonable period of time usually is determined based on all the relevant facts and circumstances.

Academic period. An academic period includes a semester, trimester, quarter, or other period of study (such as a summer school session) as reasonably determined by an educational institution. In the case of an educational institution that uses credit hours or clock hours and does not have academic terms, each payment period can be treated as an academic period.

Eligible student. This is a student who was enrolled at least half-time in a program leading to a degree, certificate, or other recognized educational credential.

Enrolled at least half-time. A student was enrolled at least half-time if the student was taking at least half the normal full-time work load for his or her course of study.

The standard for what is half of the normal full-time work load is determined by each eligible educational institution. However, the standard may not be lower than any of those established by the Department of Education under the Higher Education Act of 1965.

Loan from a related person. You cannot deduct interest on a loan you get from a related person. Related persons include:

- Your spouse,
- Your brothers and sisters,
- Your half brothers and half sisters,
- Your ancestors (parents, grandparents, etc.),
- Your lineal descendants (children, grandchildren, etc.), and
- Certain corporations, partnerships, trusts, and exempt organizations.

Loan from a qualified employer plan. You cannot deduct interest on a loan made under a qualified employer plan or under a contract purchased under such a plan.

Qualified Education Expenses

Generally, for purposes of the student loan interest deduction, these expenses are the total costs of attending an eligible educational institution, including graduate school. They include amounts paid for the following items.

- Tuition and fees.
- Room and board.
- Books, supplies, and equipment.
- Other necessary expenses (such as transportation).

The cost of room and board qualifies only to the extent that it is not more than the greater of the following amounts.

- The allowance for room and board, as determined by the eligible educational institution, that was included in the cost of attendance (for federal financial aid purposes) for a particular academic period and living arrangement of the student.
- The actual amount charged if the student is residing in housing owned or operated by the eligible educational institution.

Eligible educational institution. An eligible educational institution is any college, university, vocational school, or other postsecondary educational institution eligible to participate in a student aid program administered by the Department of Education. It includes virtually all accredited, public, nonprofit, and proprietary (privately owned profit-making) postsecondary institutions.

Certain educational institutions located outside the United States also participate in the U.S. Department of Education's Federal Student Aid (FSA) programs. See chapter 4 of Publication 970 for more information.

For purposes of the student loan interest deduction, an eligible educational institution also includes an institution conducting an internship or residency program leading to a degree or certificate from an institution of higher education, a hospital, or a health care facility that offers postgraduate training.

An educational institution must meet the above criteria only during the academic period(s) for which the student loan was incurred.

The deductibility of interest on the loan is not affected by the institution's subsequent loss of eligibility.

Tip. *The educational institution should be able to tell you if it is an eligible educational institution.*

Adjustments to qualified education expenses. You must reduce your qualified education expenses by certain tax-free items (such as the tax-free part of scholarships and fellowships). See chapter 4 of Publication 970 for details.

Include As Interest

In addition to simple interest on the loan, certain loan origination fees, capitalized interest, interest on revolving lines of credit, and interest on refinanced student loans can be student loan interest if all other requirements are met.

Loan origination fee. This is a one-time fee charged by the lender for the use of money, which is treated as interest accrued over the life of the loan. This payment cannot be for property or services provided by the lender, such as commitment fees or processing costs.

Capitalized interest. This is unpaid interest on a student loan that is added by the lender to the outstanding principal balance of the loan.

Interest on revolving lines of credit. This interest, which includes interest on credit card debt, is student loan interest if the borrower uses the line of credit (credit card) only to pay qualified education expenses. See *Qualified Education Expenses,* earlier.

Interest on refinanced student loans. This includes interest on both:

- Consolidated loans—loans used to refinance more than one student loan of the same borrower, and
- Collapsed loans—two or more loans of the same borrower that are treated by both the lender and the borrower as one loan.

Caution. *If you refinance a qualified student loan for more than your original loan and you use the additional amount for any purpose other than qualified education expenses, you cannot deduct any interest paid on the refinanced loan.*

Voluntary interest payments. These are payments made on a qualified student loan during a period when interest payments are not required, such as when the borrower has been granted a deferment or the loan has not yet entered repayment status.

Do Not Include As Interest

You cannot claim a student loan interest deduction for:

- Interest you paid on a loan if under the terms of the loan, you are not legally obligated to make interest payments.
- Loan origination fees that are payments for property or services provided by the lender, such as commitment fees or processing costs.

Can You Claim the Deduction

Generally, you can claim the deduction if all four of the following requirements are met.

- Your filing status is any filing status except married filing separately.
- No one else is claiming an exemption for you on his or her tax return.
- Your modified adjusted gross income (MAGI) is less than $65,000 ($135,000 if you file a joint return). For details on figuring your MAGI, see chapter 4 of Publication 970.
- You paid interest on a qualified student loan.

Expenses paid by others. If you are the person legally obligated to make interest payments and someone else makes a payment of interest on your behalf, you are treated as receiving the payments from the other person and, in turn, paying the interest. See chapter 4 of Publication 970 for more information.

No Double Benefit Allowed

You cannot deduct as interest on a student loan any amount you can deduct under any other provision of the tax law (for example, home mortgage interest).

Who Can Claim a Dependent's Expenses

You can deduct interest paid on a student loan for your dependent only if you:

- Are legally obligated to make the interest payments,
- Actually made the payments during the tax year, and
- Claim an exemption for your dependent on your tax return.

You are not considered to have made student loan interest payments actually made by your dependent, regardless of whether your dependent is legally liable for the loan.

How Much Can You Deduct

Your student loan interest deduction for 2005 is generally the smaller of:

- $2,500, or
- The interest you paid in 2005.

The amount determined above is phased out (gradually reduced) if your MAGI is between $50,000 and $65,000 ($105,000 and $135,000 if you file a joint return). You cannot take a student loan interest deduction if your MAGI is $65,000 or more ($135,000 or more if you file a joint return). For details on figuring your MAGI, see chapter 4 of Publication 970.

How Do You Figure the Deduction

Generally, you figure the deduction using the Student Loan Interest Deduction Worksheet in the Form 1040 or Form 1040A instructions. However, if you are filing Form 2555, 2555-EZ, or 4563, or you are excluding income from sources within Puerto Rico, you must complete Worksheet 4-1 in chapter 4 of Publication 970.

To help you figure your student loan interest deduction, you should receive Form 1098-E, Student Loan Interest Statement. Generally, an institution (such as a bank or governmental agency) that received interest payments of $600 or more during 2005 on one or more qualified student loans must send Form 1098-E (or acceptable substitute) to each borrower by January 31, 2006.

For qualified student loans taken out before September 1, 2004, the institution is required to include on Form 1098-E only payments of stated interest. Other interest payments, such as certain loan origination fees and capitalized interest, may not appear on the form you receive. However, if you pay qualifying interest that is not included on Form 1098-E, you can also deduct those amounts. For information on allocating payments between interest and principal, see chapter 4 of Publication 970.

To claim the deduction, enter the allowable amount on line 33 (Form 1040), or line 18 (Form 1040A).

Tuition and Fees Deduction

You may be able to deduct qualified education expenses paid during the year for yourself, your spouse, or a dependent. You cannot claim this deduction if your filing status is married filing separately or if another person can claim an exemption for you as a dependent on his or her tax return. The qualified expenses must be for higher education, as explained later under *What Expenses Qualify*.

The tuition and fees deduction can reduce your income subject to tax by up to $4,000. It is available through 2005.

Table 21-2 summarizes the features of the tuition and fees deduction.

Tip. *You may be able to take a credit for your education expenses instead of a deduction. You can choose the one that will give you the lower tax. See chapter 37 for details about the credit.*

Can You Claim the Deduction

The following rules will help you determine if you can claim the tuition and fees deduction.

Who Can Claim the Deduction
Generally, you can claim the tuition and fees deduction if all three of the following requirements are met.

1. You paid qualified education expenses of higher education.
2. You paid the education expenses for an eligible student.
3. The eligible student is yourself, your spouse, or a dependent for whom you claim an exemption (defined in chapter 3) on your tax return.

Qualified education expenses are defined in the next column under *What Expenses Qualify*. Eligible students are defined later under *Who Is an Eligible Student*.

Who Cannot Take the Deduction
You cannot take the tuition and fees deduction if any of the following apply.

- Your filing status is married filing separately.
- Another person can claim an exemption for you as a dependent on his or her tax return. You cannot take the deduction even if the other person does not actually claim that exemption.
- Your modified adjusted gross income (MAGI) is more than $80,000 ($160,000 if filing a joint return).
- You were a nonresident alien for any part of the year and did not elect to be treated as a resident alien for tax purposes. More information on nonresident aliens can be found in Publication 519, U.S. Tax Guide for Aliens.
- You or anyone else claims a Hope or lifetime learning credit in 2005 with respect to expenses of the student for whom the qualified education expenses were paid.

Table 21-2. **Tuition and Fees Deduction at a Glance**

Do not rely on this table alone.
Refer to the text for more details.

Question	Answer
What is the maximum benefit?	You can decrease your income subject to tax by up to $4,000.
Where is the deduction taken?	As an adjustment to income on Form 1040, line 34, or 1040A, line 19.
For whom must the expenses be paid?	A student enrolled in an eligible educational institution who is either: • you, • your spouse, or • your dependent for whom you claim an exemption.
What tuition and fees are deductible?	Tuition and fees required for enrollment or attendance at an eligible postsecondary educational institution, but not including personal, living, or family expenses, such as room and board.

What Expenses Qualify

The tuition and fees deduction is based on qualified education expenses you pay for yourself, your spouse, or a dependent for whom you claim an exemption on your tax return. Generally, the deduction is allowed for qualified education expenses paid in 2005 in connection with enrollment at an institution of higher education during 2005 or for an academic period (defined earlier under *Student Loan Interest Deduction*) beginning in 2005 or in the first 3 months of 2006.

Payments with borrowed funds. You can claim a tuition and fees deduction for qualified education expenses paid with the proceeds of a loan. You use the expenses to figure the deduction for the year in which the expenses are paid, not the year in which the loan is repaid. Treat loan payments sent directly to the educational institution as paid on the date the institution credits the student's account.

Student withdraws from class(es). You can claim a tuition and fees deduction for qualified education expenses not refunded when a student withdraws.

Qualified Education Expenses

For purposes of the tuition and fees deduction, qualified education expenses are tuition and certain related expenses required for enrollment or attendance at an eligible educational institution.

Eligible educational institution. An eligible educational institution is any college, university, vocational school, or other postsecondary educational institution eligible to participate in a student aid program administered by the Department of Education. It includes virtually all accredited, public, nonprofit, and proprietary (privately owned profit-making) postsecondary institutions. The educational institution should be able to tell you if it is an eligible educational institution.

Certain educational institutions located outside the United States also participate in the U.S. Department of Education's Federal Student Aid (FSA) programs. See chapter 6 of Publication 970 for more information.

Related expenses. Student-activity fees and fees for course-related books, supplies, and equipment are included in qualified education expenses only if the fees and expenses must be paid to the institution as a condition of enrollment or attendance.

No Double Benefit Allowed

You cannot do any of the following.

- Deduct qualified education expenses you deduct under any other provision of the law, for example, as a business expense,
- Deduct qualified education expenses for a student on your income tax return if you or anyone else claims a Hope or lifetime learning credit for that same student in the same year,
- Deduct qualified education expenses that have been used to figure the tax-free portion of a distribution from a Coverdell education savings account (ESA) or a qualified tuition program (QTP). For a QTP, this applies only to the amount of tax-free earnings that were distributed, not to the recovery of contributions to the program. See *Figuring the Taxable Portion of a Distribution* in chapter 7 (Coverdell ESA) and in chapter 8 (QTP) of Publication 970.
- Deduct qualified education expenses that have been paid with tax-free interest on U.S. savings bonds (Form 8815). See *Figuring the Tax-Free Amount* in chapter 10 of Publication 970.
- Deduct qualified education expenses that have been paid with tax-free scholarship, grant, or employer-provided educational assistance. See the following section on *Adjustments to qualified education expenses*.

Adjustments to qualified education expenses. If you paid qualified education expenses with certain tax-free funds, you cannot claim a deduction for those amounts. You must reduce the qualified expenses by the amount of any tax-free educational assistance and refunds you received.

Tax-free educational assistance. This includes:

- Tax-free part of scholarships and fellowships (see chapter 1 of Publication 970),
- Pell grants (see chapter 1 of Publication 970),
- Employer-provided educational assistance (see chapter 11 of Publication 970),
- Veterans' educational assistance (see chapter 1 of Publication 970), and
- Any other nontaxable (tax-free) payments (other than gifts or inheritances) received as educational assistance.

Refunds. Qualified education expenses do not include expenses for which you, or someone else who paid qualified education expenses on behalf of a student, receive a refund. (For information on expenses paid by a dependent student or third party, see *Who Can Claim a Dependent's Expenses*, later.)

If a refund of expenses paid in 2005 is received before you file your tax return for 2005, simply reduce the amount of the expenses paid by the amount of the refund received. If the refund is received after you file your 2005 tax return, see *When Must the Deduction Be Repaid (Recaptured)*, in chapter 6 of Publication 970.

You are considered to receive a refund of expenses when an eligible educational institution refunds loan proceeds to the lender on behalf of the borrower. Follow the above instructions according to when you are considered to receive the refund.

Amounts that do not reduce qualified education expenses. Do not reduce qualified education expenses by amounts paid with funds the student receives as:

- Payment for services, such as wages,
- A loan,
- A gift,
- An inheritance, or
- A withdrawal from the student's personal savings.

Do not reduce the qualified education expenses by any scholarship or fellowship reported as income on the student's tax return in the following situations.

- The use of the money is restricted to costs of attendance (such as room and board) other than qualified education expenses.
- The use of the money is not restricted and is used to pay education expenses that are not qualified (such as room and board).

Expenses That Do Not Qualify

Qualified education expenses do not include amounts paid for:

- Insurance,
- Medical expenses (including student health fees),
- Room and board,
- Transportation, or
- Similar personal, living, or family expenses.

This is true even if the amount must be paid to the institution as a condition of enrollment or attendance.

Sports, games, hobbies, and noncredit courses. Qualified education expenses generally do not include expenses that relate to any course of instruction or other education that involves sports, games or hobbies, or any noncredit course. However, if the course of instruction or other education is part of the student's degree program, these expenses can qualify.

Comprehensive or bundled fees. Some eligible educational institutions combine all of their fees for an academic period into one amount. If you do not receive or do not have access to an allocation showing how much you paid for qualified education expenses and how much you paid for personal expenses, such as those listed above, contact the institution. The institution is required to make this allocation and provide you with the amount you paid (or were billed) for qualified education expenses on Form 1098-T, Tuition Statement. See *How Do You Figure the Deduction*, later, for more information about Form 1098-T.

Who Is an Eligible Student

For purposes of the tuition and fees deduction, an eligible student is a student who is enrolled in one or more courses at an eligible educational institution. The student must have either a high school diploma or a General Educational Development (GED) credential.

Who Can Claim a Dependent's Expenses

Generally, to claim the tuition and fees deduction for qualified education expenses for a dependent, you must:

- Have paid the expenses, and
- Claim an exemption for the student as a dependent.

Table 21-3 summarizes who can claim the deduction.

How Much Can You Deduct

The maximum tuition and fees deduction in 2005 is $4,000, $2,000, or $0, depending on the amount of your modified adjusted gross income (MAGI). For details on figuring your MAGI, see chapter 6 of Publication 970.

How Do You Figure the Deduction
Generally, you figure the deduction using the Tuition and Fees Deduction Worksheet in the Form 1040 or Form 1040A instructions. However, if you are filing Form 2555, Form 2555-EZ, or Form 4563, or if you exclude income from sources within Puerto Rico, you must complete the worksheet in chapter 6 of Publication 970.

To help you figure your tuition and fees deduction, you should receive Form 1098-T, Tuition Statement. Generally, an eligible educational institution (such as a college or university) must send Form 1098-T (or acceptable substitute) to each enrolled student by January 31, 2006.

To claim the deduction, enter the allowable amount on Form 1040, line 34, or Form 1040A, line 19.

TaxPlanner

While eligible taxpayers can claim a deduction in 2005 for up to $4,000 of qualified higher education expenses, qualified expenses must be incurred in connection with an academic term which began in 2005 or which will begin during the first 3 months of 2006. To be an eligible taxpayer in 2005, you must meet a number of requirements and must not have adjusted gross income in excess of $65,000 if single or $135,000 if married filing jointly to claim the $4,000 deduction. You may claim a deduction for up to $2,000 of qualified expenses if your adjusted gross income is more than $65,000 but not more than $80,000 if single, or more than $135,000 but not more than $160,000 if married filing jointly.

Table 21-3. **Who Can Claim a Dependent's Expenses?**

Do not rely on this table alone. See Who Can Claim a Dependent's Expenses *in chapter 6 of Publication 970.*

IF your dependent is an eligible student and you...	AND...	THEN...
claim an exemption for your dependent	**you** paid all qualified education expenses for your dependent	only **you** can deduct the qualified education expenses that you paid. Your dependent cannot take a deduction.
claim an exemption for your dependent	**your dependent** paid all qualified education expenses	**no one** is allowed to take a deduction.
do not claim an exemption for your dependent, but are **eligible** to	**you** paid all qualified education expenses	**no one** is allowed to take a deduction.
do not claim an exemption for your dependent, but are **eligible** to	**your dependent** paid all qualified education expenses	**no one** is allowed to take a deduction.
are **not** eligible to claim an exemption for your dependent	**you** paid all qualified education expenses	only your **dependent** can deduct the amount you paid. The amount you paid is treated as a gift to your dependent.
are **not** eligible to claim an exemption for your dependent	**your dependent** paid all qualified education expenses	only your **dependent** can take a deduction.

PART V

Standard Deduction and Itemized Deductions

After you have figured your adjusted gross income, you are ready to subtract the deductions used to figure taxable income. You can subtract either the standard deduction or itemized deductions. Itemized deductions are deductions for certain expenses that are listed on Schedule A (Form 1040). The ten chapters in this part discuss the standard deduction, each itemized deduction, and the limit on some of your itemized deductions if your adjusted gross income exceeds certain amounts. See chapter 22 for the factors to consider when deciding whether to subtract the standard deduction or itemized deductions.

GENERALLY TAKE THE STANDARD DEDUCTION **IF:**	ITEMIZE YOUR DEDUCTIONS **IF:**
• Your standard deduction is more than the total itemized deductions you can claim (Chapters 22, *Standard Deduction,* and 31, *Limit on Itemized Deductions*).	• You cannot take the standard deduction (Chapter 22, *Standard Deduction*).
YOU GENERALLY CANNOT TAKE THE STANDARD DEDUCTION IF:	• You had large uninsured medical and dental expenses (Chapter 23, *Medical and Dental Expenses*),
• You are filing a tax return with a short tax year,	• You paid taxes and interest on your home (Chapter 24, *Taxes You May Deduct,* and Chapter 25, *Interest Expense*),
• You were a nonresident or a dual-status alien during the year (Chapter 22, *Standard Deduction*), or	• You made large charitable contributions (Chapter 26, *Contributions*),
• You are married filing separately, and your spouse itemizes deductions.	• You had large uninsured casualty or theft losses (Chapter 27, *Casualty and Theft Losses*),
	• You had employee business expenses (Chapter 28, *Car Expenses and Other Employee Business Expenses*),
	• You had employee educational expenses (Chapter 29, *Tax Benefits for Work-Related Education*), or
	• You had various miscellaneous expenses (Chapter 30, *Miscellaneous Deductions*),
	and
	• Your total itemized deductions are more than the standard deduction you can claim (Chapter 22, *Standard Deduction*).

Standard Deduction

Note: The 2004 IRS Publication 17 (Your Federal Income Tax) has been updated by Ernst & Young LLP for 2005. Dates and dollar amounts shown are for 2005. Gray type is used to indicate where IRS text has been updated or intentionally omitted. Unrevised IRS text is shown in black type.

Introduction

Taxpayers who do not itemize their deductions are eligible for the standard deduction. However, you should determine whether itemizing deductions or taking the applicable standard deduction produces greater tax savings. In determining the amount of your standard deduction, you must consider many factors, including filing status, age, blindness, unearned income, and whether or not someone is claiming you as an exemption. Higher deductions are allowed if you or your spouse is over age 65 or is totally or partially blind. On the other hand, if another taxpayer can claim you as a dependent, your standard deduction may be limited. This chapter, which includes several useful worksheets, will help you to figure out what your standard deduction is.

What's New

Increase in standard deduction. The standard deduction for most taxpayers who do not itemize deductions on Schedule A of Form 1040 is higher in 2005 than it was in 2004. The amount depends on your filing status. There are tables at the end of this chapter to help you figure your standard deduction for 2005.

TaxAlert

The basic standard deduction amount for married couples filing joint returns has been increased to twice the basic standard deduction amount for single returns. The Working Families Relief Act has extended the increased standard deduction for married couples for the years 2005–2010. This mitigates the so-called "marriage penalty," where a married couple filing a joint return paid more in taxes than two single individuals with the same income.

This chapter discusses:

- How to figure the amount of your standard deduction,
- The standard deduction for dependents, and
- Who should itemize deductions.

Most taxpayers have a choice of either taking a standard deduction or itemizing their deductions. The standard deduction is a dollar amount that reduces the amount of income on which you are taxed.

The standard deduction is a benefit that eliminates the need for many taxpayers to itemize actual deductions, such as medical expenses, charitable contributions, and taxes, on Schedule A of Form 1040. The standard deduction is higher for taxpayers who are 65 or older or blind. If you have a choice, you should use the method that gives you the lower tax.

Tip. *You benefit from the standard deduction if your standard deduction is more than the total of your allowable itemized deductions.*

Persons not eligible for the standard deduction. Your standard deduction is zero and you should itemize any deductions you have if:

- You are married and filing a separate return, and your spouse itemizes deductions,
- You are filing a tax return for a short tax year because of a change in your annual accounting period, or
- You are a nonresident or dual-status alien during the year. You are considered a dual-status alien if you were both a nonresident and resident alien during the year.

Note. If you are a nonresident alien who is married to a U.S. citizen or resident at the end of the year, you can choose to be treated as a U.S. resident. (See Publication 519, U.S. Tax Guide for Aliens.) If you make this choice, you can take the standard deduction.

Explanation

Married persons who file separate returns must be consistent in claiming the standard deduction or itemizing deductions. If one spouse itemizes deductions, the other spouse must also itemize deductions and cannot claim the standard deduction.

A tax return filed for a decedent through the date of death is not considered a short tax year so that the decedent is entitled to the full standard deduction.

Example

Mike and Denise are married. Each of them has a very successful business, and this year they plan to file separate income tax returns. Denise is very detail-oriented and keeps accurate records of all her itemized deductions. Mike has never cared much for what he considers tedious accounting, and would be happy to avoid this chore by claiming the standard deduction on his return ($5,000 in 2005 for a married taxpayer filing separately). If Denise itemizes deductions on her 2005 return, however, Mike will not be eligible to claim the standard deduction.

Example

John Thomas dies on June 15, 2005. John's final tax return will cover the period from January 1 through June 15.

The full amount of the standard deduction may be claimed on John's final return.

Caution. *If an exemption for you can be claimed on another person's return (such as your parents' return), your standard deduction may be limited. See* Standard Deduction for Dependents, *later.*

TAXPLANNER

The key word is *can.*

You cannot forgo an otherwise allowable dependent exemption in order to increase that dependent's standard deduction.

Standard Deduction Amount

The standard deduction amount depends on your filing status, whether you are 65 or older or blind, and whether an exemption can be claimed for you by another taxpayer. Generally, the standard deduction amounts are adjusted each year for inflation. The standard deduction amounts for most taxpayers for 2005 are shown in Table 22-1.

Decedent's final return. The amount of the standard deduction for a decedent's final tax return is the same as it would have been had the decedent continued to live. However, if the decedent was not 65 or older at the time of death, the higher standard deduction for age cannot be claimed.

Higher Standard Deduction for Age (65 or Older)

If you do not itemize deductions, you are entitled to a higher standard deduction if you are age 65 or older at the end of the year. You are considered 65 on the day before your 65th birthday. Therefore, you can take a higher standard deduction for 2005 if you were born before January 2, 1941.

Use Table 22-2 to figure the standard deduction amount.

Higher Standard Deduction for Blindness

If you are blind on the last day of the year and you do not itemize deductions, you are entitled to a higher standard deduction as shown in Table 22-2. You qualify for this benefit if you are totally or partly blind.

Partly blind. If you are partly blind, you must get a certified statement from an eye doctor or registered optometrist that:

- You cannot see better than 20/200 in the better eye with glasses or contact lenses, or
- Your field of vision is not more than 20 degrees.

If your eye condition will never improve beyond these limits, the statement should include this fact. You must keep the statement in your records.

If your vision can be corrected beyond these limits only by contact lenses that you can wear only briefly because of pain, infection, or ulcers, you can take the higher standard deduction for blindness if you otherwise qualify.

Spouse 65 or Older or Blind

You can take the higher standard deduction if your spouse is age 65 or older or blind and:

- You file a joint return, or
- You file a separate return and can claim an exemption for your spouse because your spouse had no gross income and an exemption for your spouse could not be claimed by another taxpayer.

Caution. *You cannot claim the higher standard deduction for an individual other than yourself and your spouse.*

TAXSAVER

Itemizing vs. standard deduction. In calculating your taxable income, you should use the larger of your itemized deductions or your standard deduction. By doing some planning, it may be possible to use the standard deduction in some years and to itemize deductions in others.

Example

In December 2005, Bill and Barbara Chapman add up their itemized deductions for 2005 and find that the total is only $3,900. At that time, they receive an annual real estate tax bill for $4,050, which can be paid anytime before January 31, 2006. A religious organization that the Chapmans are affiliated with is also requesting a $2,050 contribution for its building fund. If the Chapmans make both expenditures in 2005, they will receive no tax benefit from these tax-deductible expenditures because their itemized deductions would total $10,000, the same as their standard deduction. If they make the expenditures in 2006, they might generate more than the standard deduction for that year. Postponing would be a better strategy.

TAXPLANNER

If it is too late to postpone 2005 deductions, you may want to consider whether you should defer items that would otherwise qualify as itemized deductions in 2005 to 2006. The standard deduction will not change in 2006 for married taxpayers that file jointly (except for an inflation adjustment). If you would not obtain a benefit from claiming an itemized deduction in 2005 (because your total itemized deductions will be less than the 2005 standard deduction), you may be able to obtain a benefit from claiming that item in 2006. Review this carefully or speak with your tax advisor before proceeding because only certain itemized deductions may be deferred.

Examples

The following examples illustrate how to determine your standard deduction using Tables 22-1 and 22-2.

Example 1. Larry, 46, and Donna, 33, are filing a joint return for 2005. Neither is blind. They decide not to itemize their deductions. They use Table 22-1. Their standard deduction is $10,000.

Example 2. Assume the same facts as in Example 1, except that Larry is blind at the end of 2005. Larry and Donna use Table 22-2. Their standard deduction is $11,000.

Example 3. Bill, 72, and Terry, 66, are filing a joint return for 2005. Neither is blind. They decide not to itemize their deductions. They use Table 22-2. Their standard deduction is $12,000.

Standard Deduction for Dependents

The standard deduction for an individual for whom an exemption can be claimed on another person's tax return is generally limited to the greater of:

Table 22-1. Standard Deduction Chart for Most People*

If Your Filing Status is...	Your Standard Deduction is...
Single or Married filing separate return	$5,000
Married filing joint return or Qualifying widow(er) with dependent child	10,000
Head of household	7,300

*Do not use this chart if you were 65 or older or blind, or if someone else can claim an exemption for you (or your spouse if married filing jointly). Use Table 22-2 or 22-3 instead.

Table 22-2. Standard Deduction Chart for People Age 65 or Older or Blind*

Check the correct number of boxes below. Then go to the chart.

You   65 or older ☐   Blind ☐
Your spouse, if claiming   65 or older ☐   Blind ☐
spouse's exemption
Total number of boxes you checked ☐

IF your filing status is...	AND the number in the box above is...	THEN your standard deduction is...
Single	1	$6,250
	2	7,500
Married filing joint return or Qualifying widow(er) with dependent child	1	11,000
	2	12,000
	3	13,000
	4	14,000
Married filing separate return	1	6,000
	2	7,000
	3	8,000
	4	9,000
Head of household	1	8,550
	2	9,800

*If someone else can claim an exemption for you (or your spouse if married filing jointly), use Table 22-3, instead.

 If you are married filing a separate return and your spouse itemizes deductions, or if you are a dual-status alien, you cannot take the standard deduction even if you were 65 or older or blind.

Table 22-3. Standard Deduction Worksheet for Dependents*

If you were 65 or older or blind, check the correct number of boxes below. Then go to the worksheet.

You   65 or older ☐   Blind ☐
Your spouse, if claiming   65 or older ☐   Blind ☐
spouse's exemption
Total number of boxes you checked ☐

1.	Enter your earned income (defined below). If none, enter −0−.	1. _____
2.	Additional amount	2. $250
3.	Add lines 1 and 2.	3. _____
4.	Minimum amount.	4. $800
5.	Enter the larger of line 3 or line 4.	5. _____
6.	Enter the amount shown below for your filing status. • Single or Married filing separately— $5,000 • Married filing jointly or Qualifying widow(er) with dependent child— $10,000 • Head of household—$7,300	6. _____
7. Standard deduction. a. Enter the smaller of line 5 or line 6. If under 65 and not blind, stop here. This is your standard deduction. Otherwise, go on to line 7b. b. If 65 or older or blind, multiply $1,250 ($1,000 if married or qualifying widow(er) with dependent child) by the number in the box above. c. Add lines 7a and 7b. This is your standard deduction for 2005.		7a. _____ 7b. _____ 7c. _____

Earned income includes wages, salaries, tips, professional fees, and other compensation received for personal services you performed. It also includes any amount received as a scholarship that you must include in your income.

*Use this worksheet only if someone else can claim an exemption for you (or your spouse if married filing jointly).

• $800, or
• The individual's earned income for the year plus $250 (but not more than the regular standard deduction amount, generally $5,000).

However, if the individual is 65 or older or blind, the standard deduction may be higher.

If an exemption for you (or your spouse if you are filing jointly) can be claimed on someone else's return, use Table 22-3 to determine your standard deduction.

Explanation

Although the reduction in the standard deduction available to your dependent children is well publicized, the reduction for dependent parents is not so well known.

Example

Assume that your 61-year-old widowed mother has $6,800 of interest income. If she is not your dependent, she has no tax liability. Her $5,000 standard deduction plus her $3,200 personal exemption eliminate her taxable income. As your dependent, her standard deduction drops to $800 and she loses her personal exemption entirely. Her taxable income would be $6,000 and her tax would be $600. You might pay less tax because of the additional $3,200 dependent exemption (assuming your exemptions are not phased out because your income is too high), but no one will benefit from the remaining unused standard deduction of $4,200 ($5,000 − $800).

Earned income defined. Earned income is salaries, wages, tips, professional fees, and other amounts received as pay for work you actually perform.

For purposes of the standard deduction, earned income also includes any part of a scholarship or fellowship grant that you must include in your gross income. See *Scholarship and Fellowship Grants* in chapter 1 of Publication 970 for more information on what qualifies as a scholarship or fellowship grant.

Example 1. Michael is single. His parents claim an exemption for him on their 2005 tax return. He has interest income of $780 and wages of $150. He has no itemized deductions. Michael uses Table 22-3 to find his standard deduction. He enters $150 (his earned income) on line 1, $400 ($150 plus $250) on line 3, $800 (the larger of $400 and $800) on line 5, and $5,000 on line 6. The amount of his standard deduction, on line 7a, is $800 (the smaller of $800 and $5,000).

Example 2. Joe, a 22-year-old full-time college student, is claimed on his parents' 2005 tax return. Joe is married and files a separate return. His wife does not itemize deductions on her separate return.

Joe has $1,500 in interest income and wages of $3,800. He has no itemized deductions. Joe finds his standard deduction by using Table 22-3. He enters his earned income, $3,800, on line 1. He adds lines 1 and 2 and enters $4,050 on line 3. On line 5 he enters $4,050, the larger of lines 3 and 4. Since Joe is married filing a separate return, he enters $5,000 on line 6. On line 7a he enters $4,050 as his standard deduction because it is smaller than $5,000, the amount on line 6.

Example 3. Amy, who is single, is claimed on her parents' 2005 tax return. She is 18 years old and blind. She has interest income of $1,300 and wages of $2,900. She has no itemized deductions. Amy uses Table 22-3 to find her standard deduction. She enters her wages of $2,900 on line 1. She adds lines 1 and 2 and enters $3,150 on line 3. On line 5 she enters $3,150, the larger of lines 3 and 4. Since she is single, Amy enters $5,000 on line 6. She enters $3,150 on line 7a. This is the smaller of the amounts on lines 5 and 6. Because she checked one box in the top part of the worksheet, she enters $1,250 on line 7b. She then adds the amounts on lines 7a and 7b and enters her standard deduction of $4,400 on line 7c.

Who Should Itemize

You should itemize deductions if your total deductions are more than the standard deduction amount. Also, you should itemize if you do not qualify for the standard deduction, as discussed earlier under *Persons not eligible for the standard deduction.*

You should first figure your itemized deductions and compare that amount to your standard deduction to make sure you are using the method that gives you the greater benefit.

Caution. *You may be subject to a limit on some of your itemized deductions if your adjusted gross income (AGI) is more than $145,950 ($72,975 if you are married filing separately). See chapter 31 and the instructions for Schedule A (Form 1040), line 28, for more information on figuring the correct amount of your itemized deductions.*

TAXALERT

If you're over the limit. Allowable itemized deductions (other than medical expenses, casualty and theft losses, and investment interest) are reduced by an amount equal to 3% of a taxpayer's adjusted gross income in excess of $145,950 ($72,975 for married persons filing a separate return). However, these allowable itemized deductions are not reduced by more than 80%. You should consider this limitation, if applicable, in determining the benefits from itemizing deductions. See Chapter 31, *Limit on Itemized Deductions,* for more details.

When to itemize. You may benefit from itemizing your deductions on Schedule A (Form 1040) if you:

- Do not qualify for the standard deduction, or the amount you can claim is limited,
- Had large uninsured medical and dental expenses during the year,
- Paid interest and taxes on your home,
- Had large unreimbursed employee business expenses or other miscellaneous deductions,
- Had large uninsured casualty or theft losses,
- Made large contributions to qualified charities, or
- Have total itemized deductions that are more than the standard deduction to which you otherwise are entitled.

These deductions are explained in chapters 23–30.

If you decide to itemize your deductions, complete Schedule A and attach it to your Form 1040. Enter the amount from Schedule A, line 28, on Form 1040, line 40.

Electing to itemize for state tax or other purposes. Even if your itemized deductions are less than the amount of your standard deduction, you can elect to itemize deductions on your federal return rather than take the standard deduction. You may want to do this, for example, if the tax benefit of being able to itemize your deductions on your state tax return is greater than the tax benefit you lose on your federal return by not taking the standard deduction. To make this election, you must enter "IE" (itemized elected) on the dotted line next to line 40 (Form 1040).

TAXPLANNER

Another reason to itemize even when your deductions are less than the standard deduction may apply if you are subject to the alternative minimum tax (AMT). The entire standard deduction is disallowed for AMT purposes. If you instead itemize your deductions, some of those deductions, such as charitable contributions or mortgage interest, may reduce your AMT and therefore your tax bill. For more information about the AMT, see the special section in Chapter 32, *How to Figure Your Tax.*

Caution. *If you are married filing a separate return and your spouse itemizes deductions, or if you are a dual-status alien, you cannot take the standard deduction even if you were 65 or older or blind.*

Changing your mind. If you do not itemize your deductions and later find that you should have itemized—or if you itemize your deductions and later find you should not have—you can change your return by filing Form 1040X, Amended U.S. Individual Income Tax Return. See *Amended Returns and Claims for Refund* in chapter 1 for more information on amended returns.

Married persons who filed separate returns. You can change methods of taking deductions only if you and your spouse both make the same changes. Both of you must file a consent to assessment for any additional tax either one may owe as a result of the change.

You and your spouse can use the method that gives you the lower total tax, even though one of you may pay more tax than you would have paid by using the other method. You both must use the same method of claiming deductions. If one itemizes deductions, the other should itemize because he or she will not qualify for the standard deduction. (See *Persons not eligible for the standard deduction,* earlier.)

Medical and Dental Expenses

Note: The 2004 IRS Publication 17 (Your Federal Income Tax) has been updated by Ernst & Young LLP for 2005. Dates and dollar amounts shown are for 2005. Gray type is used to indicate where IRS text has been updated or intentionally omitted. Unrevised IRS text is shown in black type.

Introduction

Deductible medical expenses include payments for the diagnosis, cure, mitigation, treatment, and prevention of disease. Payments with respect to any part or function of the body are allowed, as are payments for the prevention or alleviation of mental illness. You may include even your cab or bus fare to the doctor's office. But you may not include expenditures that are merely beneficial to your general health or purely cosmetic medical procedures—like vacation costs or hair transplants, for example.

While almost any medical expense qualifies for the deduction, it's difficult to take an actual **deduction** *on your tax return, and it's getting more difficult. Your medi-cal expenses must total more than 7.5% of your* **adjusted gross income** *before you can take any deduction. In other words, someone with an adjusted gross income of $30,000 in 2005 has to have more than $2,250 of medical expenses before he or she may deduct any of them.*

Note: *Your 2005 itemized deductions may be subject to certain overall limitations if your adjusted gross income exceeds $145,950 ($72,975 if married filing separately). However, deductions for medical expenses are not subject to overall limitation. See Chapter 31, Limit on Itemized Deductions, for more information on this subject.*

What's New

Standard mileage rate. The standard mileage rate allowed for out-of-pocket expenses for a car when you use it for medical reasons is 15 cents a mile through August 2005 (22 cents after August 31, 2005). See *Transportation* under *What Expenses Are Includible.*

Health Savings Accounts (HSAs). In 2005, you may be able to make tax-deductible contributions to a health savings account to pay qualified medical expenses. Health savings accounts are discussed in Publication 969, Health Savings Accounts and Other Tax-Favored Health Plans. Flexible Spending—Under new IRS rules, your employer may allow you to use your 2005 pre-tax Flexible Spending Account to reimburse expenses incurred up until March 15, 2006.

Reminders

Health coverage tax credit. There is a credit for health insurance premiums paid by certain workers who are displaced by for-eign trade or who are receiving a pension from the Pension Benefit Guaranty Corporation. For more information, see *Health Coverage Tax Credit* in chapter 39.

This chapter will help you determine:

• What medical expenses are,
• What expenses you can include this year,
• How much of the expenses you can deduct,
• Whose medical expenses you can include,
• What medical expenses are includible,
• How you treat reimbursements,
• How to report the deduction on your tax return,
• How to report impairment-related work expenses, and
• How to report health insurance costs if you are self-employed.

Useful Items

You may want to see:

Publication

☐ 502   Medical and Dental Expenses
☐ 969   Health Savings Accounts and Other Tax-Favored Health Plans

Form (and Instructions)

☐ Schedule A (Form 1040)   Itemized Deductions

What Are Medical Expenses?

Medical expenses are the costs of diagnosis, cure, mitigation, treatment, or prevention of disease, and the costs for treatments affecting any part or function of the body. They include the costs of equipment, supplies, and diagnostic devices needed for these purposes.

Medical care expenses must be primarily to alleviate or prevent a physical or mental defect or illness. Medical expenses include dental expenses. Do not include expenses that are merely beneficial to general health, such as vitamins or a vacation.

Medical expenses include the premiums you pay for insurance that covers the expenses of medical care, and the amounts you pay for transportation to get medical care. Medical expenses also include amounts paid for qualified long-term care services and limited amounts paid for any qualified long-term care insurance contract.

TaxAlert

Marijuana and other controlled substances. The IRS has ruled that the cost of marijuana or any other federally controlled substance, even if recommended by a physician in a state whose laws permit such purchase and use, is not deductible. The U.S. Supreme Court has, in effect, upheld this ruling.

What Expenses Can You Include This Year?

You can include only the medical and dental expenses you paid this year, regardless of when the services were provided. If you pay medical expenses by check, the day you mail or deliver the check generally is the date of payment. If you use a "pay-by-phone" or "online" account to pay your medical expenses, the date reported on the statement of the financial institution showing when payment was made is the date of payment. If you use a credit card, include medical expenses you charge to your credit card in the year the charge is made, not when you actually pay the amount charged.

TaxPlanner

Timing your medical expenses. Medical expenses don't usually lend themselves to tax planning. However, because a medical deduction is available *only* in the year of payment, you may be able to maximize your deduction if you can control the timing of your payment.

To determine the most beneficial year of payment, you need to assess your situation prior to the end of the year. If it is clear that your current-year medical expenses will not exceed the nondeductible floor—7.5% of your adjusted gross income—try to defer payment of any medical bills until after year-end. You may be able to salvage a deduction next year.

If you can schedule major or minor surgery in non-emergency cases, you should compare this year's medical deductions with what they are liable to be next year to choose the more beneficial time. It is the date of payment—not the date of surgery—that determines the year in which you may deduct the expense. Remember, putting the charge on a credit card counts as payment at that time.

If you suspect that your adjusted gross income is going to drop substantially next year, defer the payment of medical bills. However, if you think your adjusted gross income is going to skyrocket next year, pay those bills now and try to salvage a deduction.

Exception

Prepaid medical expenses generally are not deductible until the year of treatment.

Separate returns. If you and your spouse live in a noncommunity property state and file separate returns, each of you can include only the medical expenses each actually paid. Any medical expenses paid out of a joint checking account in which you and your spouse have the same interest are considered to have been paid equally by each of you, unless you can show otherwise.

Community property states. If you and your spouse live in a community property state and file separate returns, any medical expenses paid out of community funds are divided equally. Each of you should include half the expenses. If medical expenses are paid out of the separate funds of one spouse, only the spouse who paid the medical expenses can include them. If you live in a community property state, are married, and file a separate return, see Publication 555, Community Property.

How Much of the Expenses Can You Deduct?

You can deduct only the amount of your medical and dental expenses that is more than 7.5% of your adjusted gross income (Form 1040, line 37).

In this chapter, the term "7.5% limit" is used to refer to 7.5% of your adjusted gross income. The phrase "subject to the 7.5% limit" is also used. This phrase means that you must subtract 7.5% (.075) of your adjusted gross income from your medical expenses to figure your medical expense deduction.

Example. Your adjusted gross income is $40,000, 7.5% of which is $3,000. You paid medical expenses of $2,500. You cannot deduct any of your medical expenses because they are not more than 7.5% of your adjusted gross income.

TaxPlanner

If your spouse's medical expenses exceed yours. You should consider filing separate returns whenever the medical expenses of either spouse substantially exceed those of the other spouse. Compute and compare your tax liability if you and your spouse were to file jointly with the potential tax liability if you were to file separately before deciding which filing status to choose.

Whose Medical Expenses Can You Include?

You can generally include medical expenses you pay for yourself as well as those you pay for someone who was your spouse or your dependent either when the services were provided or when you paid for them. There are different rules for decedents and for individuals who are the subject of multiple support agreements.

Spouse. You can include medical expenses you paid for your spouse. To include these expenses, you must have been married either at the time your spouse received the medical services or at the time you paid the medical expenses.

Example 1. Mary received medical treatment before she married Bill. Bill paid for the treatment after they married. Bill can include these expenses in figuring his medical expense deduction even if Bill and Mary file separate returns.

If Mary had paid the expenses, Bill could not include Mary's expenses in his separate return. Mary would include the amounts she paid during the year in her separate return. If they filed a joint return, the medical expenses both paid during the year would be used to figure their medical expense deduction.

Example 2. This year, John paid medical expenses for his wife, Louise, who died last year. John married Belle this year and they file a joint return. Because John was married to Louise when she received the medical services, he can include those expenses in figuring his medical deduction for this year.

Dependent. You can include medical expenses you paid for your dependent. For you to include these expenses, the person must have been your dependent either at the time the medical services were provided or at the time you paid the expenses. A person generally qualifies as your dependent for purposes of the medical expense deduction if the person is a dependent as described in chapter 3, but with three modifications: (1) the gross income test does not apply for qualifying relatives; (2) the rule that a joint return filer can't be a dependent does not apply; and (3) the rule that a dependent is ineligible to have dependents also does not apply. [IRS text intentionally omitted]

You can include the medical expenses of any person who is your dependent even if you cannot claim an exemption for him or her on your return.

Example. In 2004 your son was your dependent. In 2005 he no longer qualified as your dependent. However, you paid $800 in 2005 for medical services provided to your son in 2004 when he was your dependent. You can include the $800 in your medical expenses for 2005. You cannot include this amount in your 2004 medical expenses.

TAXPLANNER

If you pay medical expenses for others. If you pay medical expenses on behalf of someone other than yourself, your spouse, or your dependent and your payment is made directly to the provider of the medical service, the payment is not deductible for income tax purposes. However, your payment will not be considered a gift to the individual either. An unlimited gift tax exclusion is available for qualifying medical expenses paid on any individual's behalf directly to the provider of the medical service. This exclusion is also available for transfers that would otherwise be subject to the generation-skipping transfer tax. The generation-skipping transfer tax, imposed at a flat 47% rate in 2005 in addition to any gift or estate tax incurred, is applied to transfers that are made to persons two or more generations below the donor. The flat rate goes down (and up) over the next years as follows:

2006	46%
2007–2009	45%
2010	0%
2011+	55%

You should consult your tax advisor if you are interested in pursuing this type of tax planning.

Example

A grandparent pays medical expenses directly to the hospital on a grandchild's behalf. The payments will reduce the grandparent's taxable estate and will not be subject to gift tax or generation-skipping transfer tax. This could result in significant tax savings.

Adopted child. You can include medical expenses that you paid for a child before adoption, if the child qualified as your dependent when the medical services were provided or when the expenses were paid.

If you pay back an adoption agency or other persons for medical expenses they paid under an agreement with you, you are treated as having paid those expenses provided you clearly substantiate that the payment is directly attributable to the medical care of the child.

But if you pay the agency or other person for medical care that was provided and paid for before adoption negotiations began, you cannot include them as medical expenses.

Tip. *You may be able to take a credit or exclusion for other expenses related to adoption. See Publication 968, Tax Benefits for Adoption, for more information.*

Child of divorced or separated parents. [IRS text intentionally omitted] A child of parents who are divorced, separated, or who lived apart during the last six months of the calendar year is considered the dependent of both of his parents for medical expense deduction purposes, if the child received over half of his support from his parents and was in the custody of one or both parents for over half of the calendar year.

For rules regarding what expenses you can include this year, see *What Expenses Can You Include This Year,* earlier.

In figuring your deduction for medical expenses, you can include the medical expenses of your dependents. The definition of dependent for this purpose includes only two tests—a support test and a member of household or relationship test.

The gross income test, the joint return test, and the citizenship/residency test, which are discussed in Chapter 3, apply to determine whether you are entitled to an exemption for that dependent, but only the support test and the member of household or relationship test apply to determine whether an individual is your dependent for medical expense deduction purposes.

Under a multiple support agreement, one of several persons providing support to an individual is considered to satisfy the support test with regard to that individual. If, because of a multiple support agreement, you are treated as satisfying the support test with respect to an individual who satisfies the member of household or relationship test for you, that individual is your dependent for purposes of the medical expense deduction. In that case, in figuring your deduction for medical expenses, you may include the medical expenses you pay for that individual, regardless of whether the other tests for the dependency exemption are satisfied.

Any medical expenses paid to you by others who joined you in the agreement cannot be included as medical expenses by anyone. However, you can include the entire unreimbursed amount you paid for medical expenses.

Example. You and your three brothers each provide one-fourth of your mother's total support. Under a multiple support agreement, you treat your mother as your dependent. You paid all of her medical expenses. Your brothers repaid you for three-fourths of these expenses. In figuring your medical expense deduction, you can include only one-fourth of your mother's medical expenses. Your brothers cannot include any part of the expenses. However, if you and your brothers share the nonmedical support items and you separately pay all of your mother's medical expenses, you can include the amount you paid for her medical expenses in your medical expenses.

Decedent

Medical expenses paid before death by the decedent are included in figuring any deduction for medical and dental expenses on the decedent's final income tax return. This includes expenses for the decedent's spouse and dependents as well as for the decedent.

The survivor or personal representative of a decedent can choose to treat certain expenses paid by the decedent's estate for the decedent's medical care as paid by the decedent at the time the medical services were provided. The expenses must be paid within the 1-year period beginning with the day after the date of death. If you are the survivor or personal representative making this choice, you must attach a statement to the decedent's Form 1040 (or the decedent's amended return, Form 1040X) saying that the expenses have not been and will not be claimed on the estate tax return. **Caution.** *Qualified medical expenses paid before death by the decedent are not deductible if paid with a tax-free distribution from any Archer MSA or health savings account.*

Amended returns and claims for refund are discussed in chapter 1. **What if you pay medical expenses of a deceased spouse or dependent?** If you paid medical expenses for your deceased spouse or dependent, include them as medical expenses on your Form 1040 in the year paid, whether they are paid before or after the decedent's death. The expenses can be included if the person was your spouse or dependent either at the time the medical services were provided or at the time you paid the expenses.

What Medical Expenses Are Includible?

Use Table 23-1 in this chapter as a guide to determine which medical and dental expenses you can include on Schedule A (Form 1040). See Publication 502 for information about other expenses you can include.

TaxPlanner

If the IRS challenges your deduction. In case the IRS challenges your deduction of medical expenses, you should keep the following information in order to support your claim for medical expenses incurred:

- Receipts and canceled checks evidencing payment of medical expenses
- A permanent record of the name and address of the provider of medical care, the amount of the expenses, and the date paid
- Documentation that the expense was to obtain medical treatment, that medicine was prescribed, and that the expense was incurred on a doctor's recommendation

After reviewing the checklist, you may still be wondering whether a particular expense is deductible or not. The most comprehensive listing of items that you may and may not include when figuring your medical expenses appears in Publication 502, *Medical and Dental Expenses.*

Examples
Here are more examples of items that have been held to be deductible:

- A wig, if it is essential to your mental health and not just for enhancing your personal appearance
- Cosmetic surgery that is medically necessary (meaningfully promotes the proper function of the body or prevents or treats illness or disease) or needed to correct a deformity related to an injury, disease, or congenital abnormality and not just for enhancing personal appearance
- Special diet food that is necessary and prescribed by a doctor to the extent that the cost exceeds the amount spent for normal nutritional needs
- Orthopedic shoes in excess of the cost of normal shoes
- Fees paid to someone to accompany and guide a blind person
- Costs attributable to a dog or other animal that assists individuals with physical disabilities
- Fees paid for a note taker for a deaf person
- Legal fees to obtain guardianship over a mental patient who has refused to accept therapy voluntarily
- Fees paid for childbirth preparation classes if instruction relates to obstetrical care
- Costs of a weight loss program for treatment of a specific disease, such as hypertension or obesity
- Costs of a wheelchair lift and its installation in a van
- Reasonable costs for home modifications or improvements to accommodate a handicapped person's condition when incurred for the purpose of medical care or directly related to medical care
- Legal fees necessary to authorize medical treatment for mental illness
- Expenses incurred for radial keratotomy (i.e., eye surgery to correct nearsightedness)

TaxSaver

Weight loss programs. The IRS has recently ruled that individuals who suffer from specific physician-diagnosed diseases such as obesity and hypertension may deduct, as a medical expense, uncompensated costs of participation in weight loss programs. Costs associated with weight loss programs to improve general health and appearance are not deductible. Whether the cost of the program is deductible or not, the costs of low-calorie foods purchased while in the program are not deductible.

TaxSaver

Physical and dental exams. The cost of periodic physical and dental exams can be included as a deductible medical expense. Usually, these expenses are too small to be deductible because only expenses over 7.5% of your adjusted gross income can be deducted. However, in years where other medical expenses have been incurred, the inclusion of these expenses in calculating your medical expense deduction can lead to tax savings.

TaxSaver

Drugs that may be obtained without a prescription (aspirin, cold remedies, skin ointments, etc.) are not deductible, even though they may be recommended or prescribed by a physician. The IRS has ruled, however, that participants in an employer sponsored health plan (such as a flexible spending account) may claim reimbursement from the plan for nonprescription drugs.

Table 23-1.   **Medical and Dental Expenses Checklist**

You can include:	You cannot include:

• Bandages
• Birth control pills prescribed by your doctor
• Capital expenses for equipment or improvements to your home needed for medical care (see Publication 502)
• Certain fertility enhancement procedures (see Publication 502)
• Certain weight-loss expenses for obesity
• Diagnostic devices
• Expenses of an organ donor
• Eye surgery—to promote the correct function of the eye
• Guide dogs or other animals aiding the blind, deaf, and disabled
• Hospital services fees (lab work, therapy, nursing services, surgery, etc.)
• Lead-based paint removal (see Publication 502)
• Legal abortion
• Legal operation to prevent having children such as a vasectomy
• Long-term care contracts, qualified (see Publication 502)
• Meals and lodging provided by a hospital during medical treatment
 	
• Medical and hospital insurance premiums
• Medical services fees (from doctors, dentists, surgeons, specialists, and other medical practitioners)
• Oxygen equipment and oxygen
• Part of life-care fee paid to retirement home designated for medical care
• Prescription medicines (prescribed by a doctor) and insulin
• Psychiatric and psychological treatment
• Social Security tax, Medicare tax, FUTA, and state employment tax for worker providing medical care (see *Wages for nursing services*, below)
• Special items (artificial limbs, false teeth, eye-glasses, contact lenses, hearing aids, crutches, wheelchair, etc.)
• Special education for mentally or physically disabled persons (see Publication 502)
• Stop-smoking programs
• Transportation for needed medical care
• Treatment at a drug or alcohol center (includes meals and lodging provided by the center)
• Wages for nursing services (see Publication 502)
	• Baby sitting and childcare
	• Bottled water
	• Contributions to Archer MSAs or HSAs (see Publication 969)
	• Diaper service
	• Expenses for your general health (even if following your doctor's advice) such as—
	   —Health club dues
	   —Household help (even if recommended by a doctor)
	   —Social activities, such as dancing or swimming lessons
	   —Trip for general health improvement
	• Flexible spending account reimbursements for medical expenses (if contributions were on a pre-tax basis) (see Publication 502)
	• Funeral, burial, or cremation expenses
	• Health savings account payments for medical expenses (see Publication 502)
	• Illegal operation or treatment
	• Life insurance or income protection policies, or policies providing payment for loss of life, limb, sight, etc.
	• Maternity clothes
	
	• Medical insurance included in a car insurance policy covering all persons injured in or by your car
	• Medicine you buy without a prescription
	• Nursing care for a healthy baby
	• Prescription drugs you brought in (or ordered shipped) from another country, in most cases (see Publication 502)
	• Nutritional supplements, vitamins, herbal supplements, "natural medicines," etc., unless recommended by a medical practitioner as a treatment for a specific medical condition diagnosed by a physician
	• Surgery for purely cosmetic reasons (see Publication 502)
	• Toothpaste, toiletries, cosmetics, etc.
	• Teeth whitening
	• Weight-loss expenses not for the treatment of obesity or other disease

TaxPlanner

Medical fees and school tuition. Some schools include a fee for medical care in the amount charged for tuition. Because you may deduct only the amount allocated to medical care if it is separately stated, an itemized bill should be requested.

Explanation

Whether or not an expense is deductible is determined by the nature of the services rendered, not by the qualifications and/or experience of the person rendering them. For example, the services do not necessarily need to be performed by a nurse, as long as the services rendered are generally considered nursing services. These include services connected with caring for the patient's condition, such as giving medication or changing bandages, as well as bathing and grooming the patient.

Examples

The courts allowed deductions for payments to a daughter for the care of her arthritic mother to the extent that they were for medical care.

In another instance, the courts allowed a deduction for the compensation paid to a "personal attendant" who was not a registered or a practical nurse. The deduction was permitted because the invalid was recovering from surgery and was in need of constant attendance.

TaxPlanner

Two choices, one deduction. An expense may qualify for more than one tax benefit. For instance, a payment may qualify for the child care credit (see Chapter 34, *Child and Dependent Care Credit),* or it may be considered a medical expense. However, the same expense generally may not be used for both benefits. You should analyze each benefit based on your marginal tax rate and your medical expense deduction limitation (7.5% of adjusted gross income) to determine how best to classify the expense.

TaxSaver

Capital expenses. You may include in medical expenses all or part of the amounts you pay for special equipment installed in your home, or for improvements, if the main reason for the purchase is for medical care. The amount of your medical expense deduction, however, will depend on the extent to which the equipment or improvement has increased the value of the property. To the extent a capital improvement adds value to your home, it increases the cost basis of your home. Any amount paid above the added value is currently deductible as a medical expense. A U.S. District Court held that this deduction is available in the year the home becomes habitable. So if a home is built over a period of years, the amount paid over the added value is all deductible in the year you can move into it, making it easier to get above the 7.5% adjusted gross income (AGI) threshold.

Example

You have a heart ailment. On your doctor's advice, you install an elevator in your home so that you will not need to climb stairs. The elevator costs $2,000. According to competent appraisals, the elevator increases the value of your home by $1,400. The $600 difference is a medical expense. However, you may include the total cost of $2,000 in medical expenses if the elevator does not increase the value of your home.

TaxSaver

Appraisals. The cost of an appraisal obtained to determine the increase in value of your home is also deductible, but not as a medical expense. The appraisal cost is an expense associated with the determination of your tax liability and can be included as a miscellaneous itemized deduction. See Chapter 30, *Miscellaneous Deductions*.

Explanation

Operating and upkeep expenses. If a capital expense qualifies as a medical expense, amounts paid for operation or upkeep also qualify as a medical expense, as long as the medical reason for the capital expense still exists. These expenses are medical expenses even if none or only part of the original expense was deductible.

Example

Assume the same facts as in the above example, except that the elevator increased the value of your home by $2,000. In this case, you are not entitled to a medical deduction for the cost of the elevator. However, the costs of electricity to operate the elevator and repairs to maintain it are deductible, as long as the medical reason for the elevator exists.

Exception

An exception to the general rule exists for expenditures incurred to accommodate the condition of a physically handicapped person that generally do not increase the value of a personal residence. These expenses are deductible in full as a medical expense. Examples of expenses made for the primary purpose of accommodating a personal residence to the handicapped condition of a taxpayer, the taxpayer's spouse, or dependents who reside there include:

- Construction of entrance or exit ramps to the residence
- Widening doorways at entrances or exits to the residence
- Widening or otherwise modifying hallways and interior doorways
- Installing railings, support bars, or other modifications to bathrooms
- Lowering or making other modifications to kitchen cabinets and equipment
- Altering the location or otherwise modifying electrical outlets and fixtures
- Installing porch lifts and other forms of lifts (an elevator, however, may also add to the fair market value of the residence, and any deduction would have to be decreased to that extent)
- Modifying fire alarms, smoke detectors, and other warning systems
- Modifying stairs
- Adding handrails or grab bars, whether or not in bathrooms
- Modifying hardware on doors
- Modifying areas in front entrance and exit doorways
- Grading of ground to provide access to the residence

According to the IRS, other similar expenditures may also be incurred in accommodating a personal residence to the handicapped condition of a taxpayer or a dependent. However, only reasonable costs for accommodating a handicapped person's condition will be considered incurred for the purpose of medical care. Additional costs attributable to personal desires are not deductible.

Example

You are physically handicapped and confined to a wheelchair. You incur expenses to widen doorways and lower kitchen cabinets in your residence to permit access by you. These expenses are deductible, subject to the 7.5% threshold discussed above.

TaxPlanner

Medically related capital improvements. If you have to make a medically related capital improvement, you should request a written recommendation from your doctor. In addition, obtain a reliable written appraisal from a real estate appraiser or a valuation expert. Be prepared to prove to what extent the value of your property was or was not increased.

TaxPlanner

Swimming pools. It is often difficult to obtain a medical deduction for the installation of a swimming pool. The IRS has held that swimming pools generally fall within the category of recreational or luxury items and will look at various facts when it is determining the deduction for the cost of a swimming pool, including:

- Whether the primary purpose of the pool is for medical care
- Whether the expenditure is related to medical care
- Whether the pool does more than serve the convenience and/or comfort of the taxpayer

You should contact your tax advisor if you intend to install a swimming pool for medical reasons.

Insurance Premiums

You can include in medical expenses insurance premiums you pay for policies that cover medical care. Policies can provide payment for:

- Hospitalization, surgical fees, X-rays, etc.,
- Prescription drugs,
- Replacement of lost or damaged contact lenses,
- Membership in an association that gives cooperative or so-called "free-choice" medical service, or group hospitalization and clinical care, or
- Qualified long-term care insurance contracts (subject to additional limitations). See *Qualified Long-term Care Insurance Contracts* in Publication 502.

If you have a policy that provides more than one kind of payment, you can include the premiums for the medical care part of the policy if the charge for the medical part is reasonable. The cost of the medical part must be separately stated in the insurance contract or given to you in a separate statement.

Note. When figuring the amount of insurance premiums you can deduct on Schedule A, do not include any health coverage tax credit advance payments shown in box 1 of Form 1099-H. Also, if you are claiming the health coverage tax credit, subtract the amount shown on line 4 of Form 8885 (reduced by any advance payments shown on line 6 of that form) from the total insurance premiums you paid.

TAXALERT

You can now treat premiums paid for qualified long-term care insurance as a deductible medical expense subject to dollar limits based on your age at the close of the taxable year.

Age:	Annual deductible limit:
40 or less	$270
Over 40 but not more than 50	510
Over 50 but not more than 60	1020
Over 60 but not more than 70	2,720
Over 70	3,400

Explanation
Amounts you pay to receive medical care from a health maintenance organization (HMO) are treated as medical insurance premiums.

TAXSAVER

Cafeteria plans. Employees who pay all or part of their medical insurance premiums via employer plans should ask their employer to investigate a flexible spending arrangement, which is sometimes referred to as a cafeteria plan.

Example
You are in the 28% tax bracket, and you pay $2,000 to cover your medical insurance premiums. Because medical expenses are deductible only if they exceed 7.5% of your adjusted gross income, chances are that you are not able to deduct your payments for medical insurance.

If your company offers medical insurance as part of a cafeteria plan, you may opt to have your wages reduced by $2,000 under a salary reduction plan to cover the cost of the insurance. The cut in wages reduces your income tax, producing a federal tax savings in this case of $560. Additional tax savings may also be enjoyed because of lower state income taxes and reduced FICA taxes.

Employer-sponsored health insurance plan. Do not include in your medical and dental expenses on Schedule A (Form 1040) any insurance premiums paid by an employer-sponsored health insurance plan unless the premiums are included in box 1 of your Form W-2. Also, do not include on Schedule A (Form 1040) any other medical and dental expenses paid by the plan unless the amount paid is included in box 1 of your Form W-2.

Example. You are a federal employee participating in the Federal Employee Health Benefits (FEHB) program. Your share of the FEHB premium is paid with pre-tax dollars. Because you are an employee whose insurance premiums are paid with money that is never included in your gross income, you cannot deduct the premiums paid with that money.

Long-term care services. Contributions made by your employer to provide coverage for qualified long-term care services under a flexible spending or similar arrangement must be included in your income. This amount will be reported as wages in box 1 of your Form W-2.

Health reimbursement arrangement (HRA). If you have medical expenses that are reimbursed by a health reimbursement arrangement, you cannot include those expenses in your medical expenses. This is because an HRA is funded solely by the employer.

Medicare A. If you are covered under social security (or if you are a government employee who paid Medicare tax), you are enrolled in Medicare A. The payroll tax paid for Medicare A is not a medical expense. If you are not covered under social security (or were not a government employee who paid Medicare tax), you can voluntarily enroll in Medicare A. In this situation you can include the premiums paid for Medicare A as a medical expense.

Medicare B. Medicare B is a supplemental medical insurance. Premiums you pay for Medicare B are a medical expense. If you applied for it at age 65 or after you became disabled, you can include in medical expenses the monthly premiums you paid. If you were over age 65 or disabled when you first enrolled, check the information you received from the Social Security Administration to find out your premium.

Prepaid insurance premiums. Premiums you pay before you are age 65 for insurance for medical care for yourself, your spouse, or your dependents after you reach age 65 are medical care expenses in the year paid if they are:

- Payable in equal yearly installments, or more often, and
- Payable for at least 10 years, or until you reach age 65 (but not for less than 5 years).

Unused sick leave used to pay premiums. You must include in gross income cash payments you receive at the time of retirement for unused sick leave. You also must include in gross income the value of unused sick leave that, at your option, your employer applies to the cost of your continuing participation in your employer's health plan after you retire. You can include this cost of continuing participation in the health plan as a medical expense.

If you participate in a health plan where your employer automatically applies the value of unused sick leave to the cost of your continuing participation in the health plan (and you do not have the option to receive cash), do not include the value of the unused sick leave in gross income. You cannot include this cost of continuing participation in that health plan as a medical expense.

Meals and Lodging

You can include in medical expenses the cost of meals and lodging at a hospital or similar institution if a principal reason for being there is to get medical care. See *Nursing home,* later.

You may be able to include in medical expenses the cost of lodging not provided in a hospital or similar institution. You can include the cost of such lodging while away from home if all of the following requirements are met.

- The lodging is primarily for and essential to medical care.
- The medical care is provided by a doctor in a licensed hospital or in a medical care facility related to, or the equivalent of, a licensed hospital.
- The lodging is not lavish or extravagant under the circumstances.
- There is no significant element of personal pleasure, recreation, or vacation in the travel away from home.

The amount you include in medical expenses for lodging cannot be more than $50 for each night for each person. You can include lodging for a person traveling with the person receiving the medical care. For example, if a parent is traveling with a sick child, up to $100 per night can be included as a medical expense for lodging. Meals are not included.

Example 1

A businessman who became ill while out of town was allowed to deduct the costs of his meals and hotel room when, due to a shortage of hospital rooms, he was required to move into a hotel. He had not recovered sufficiently to return home. The courts found that the test of deductibility was *not* the nature of the institution (i.e., whether it was a hospital or a similar institution) but the condition of the individual and the nature of the services.

Example 2

The parents of a mentally ill son rented an apartment to be close to the son's clinic. They were not allowed to deduct its costs because no care was received in the apartment, and the apartment had not been altered in any way to facilitate their son's treatment. Therefore, the court held that the parents had not incurred any expenses for their son's care in the apartment.

Nursing home. You can include in medical expenses the cost of medical care in a nursing home, home for the aged, or similar institution, for yourself, your spouse, or your dependents. This includes the cost of meals and lodging in the home if a principal reason for being there is to get medical care.

Do not include the cost of meals and lodging if the reason for being in the home is personal. You can, however, include in medical expenses the part of the cost that is for medical or nursing care.

Transportation

You can include in medical expenses amounts paid for transportation primarily for, and essential to, medical care.

You can include:

- Bus, taxi, train, or plane fares, or ambulance service,
- Transportation expenses of a parent who must go with a child who needs medical care,
- Transportation expenses of a nurse or other person who can give injections, medications, or other treatment required by a patient who is traveling to get medical care and is unable to travel alone, and
- Transportation expenses for regular visits to see a mentally ill dependent, if these visits are recommended as a part of treatment.

TAXALERT

The IRS has ruled that transportation costs and registration fees for attending a medical conference on a chronic disease suffered by a dependent are deductible medical expenses. The cost of meals and lodging cannot be deducted.

Explanation

Although the IRS has repeatedly denied *any* deduction for commuting expenses to get to one's place of work—even for disabled individuals—under certain circumstances, a deduction may be permitted for transportation required for medical reasons.

Example

If, at your doctor's advice, you take a job for the purposes of occupational therapy, you may deduct your commuting expenses. Because the employment is prescribed therapy, the expense of going to and from work is incurred in the course of obtaining occupational therapy and thus is deductible as medical transportation.

Explanation

The courts have, however, allowed a deduction for the costs of meals as well as lodging and transportation between a taxpayer's home and the out-of-state clinic where treatment was obtained when the trip was made for medical reasons. The meals were considered to be part of the transportation costs. In addition, because the taxpayer's husband had to accompany his spouse on the trip, his food costs en route were also deductible.

The expenses of a move to a different climate may be deductible if the principal purpose of the move is to alleviate an illness.

TAXALERT

The Tax Court has recently ruled that a couple could not deduct depreciation as a medical expense for a modified van in which they transported their disabled son, who had spina bifida. The Court said that depreciation is not a medical expense. They did allow the cost of necessary modifications to the van.

Car expenses. You can include out-of-pocket expenses, such as the cost of gas and oil, when you use your car for medical reasons. You cannot include depreciation, insurance, general repair, or maintenance expenses.

If you do not want to use your actual expenses, for 2005 you can use a standard rate of 15 cents a mile through August 2005 (22 cents a mile after August 31, 2005) for use of a car for medical reasons.

You can also include parking fees and tolls. You can add these fees and tolls to your medical expenses whether you use actual expenses or use the standard mileage rate.

Example. Bill Jones drove 2,800 miles before September 2005 for medical reasons. He spent $200 for gas, $5 for oil, and $50 for tolls and parking. He wants to figure the amount he can include in medical expenses both ways to see which gives him the greater deduction.

He figures the actual expenses first. He adds the $200 for gas, the $5 for oil, and the $50 for tolls and parking for a total of $255.

He then figures the standard mileage amount. He multiplies the 2,800 miles by 15 cents a mile for a total of $420. He then adds the $50 tolls and parking for a total of $470.

Bill includes the $470 of car expenses with his other medical expenses for the year because the $470 is more than the $255 he figured using actual expenses.

Transportation expenses you cannot include. You cannot include in medical expenses the cost of transportation expenses in the following situations.

- Going to and from work, even if your condition requires an unusual means of transportation.
- Travel for purely personal reasons to another city for an operation or other medical care.
- Travel that is merely for the general improvement of one's health.

Disabled Dependent Care Expenses

Some disabled dependent care expenses may qualify as either:

- Medical expenses or
- Work-related expenses for purposes of taking a credit for dependent care. (See chapter 34.)

You can choose to apply them either way as long as you do not use the same expenses to claim both a credit and a medical expense deduction.

Explanation
Special care for the handicapped. The costs of sending a mentally or physically handicapped person to a special school or home, including certain advance payments for lifetime care, may be included in medical expenses. See Publication 502, *Medical and Dental Expenses,* for more information about medical care expenses for a handicapped person. Enter the amount you paid for special care on line 1, Schedule A (Form 1040).

The distinguishing characteristic of a special school is the content of its curriculum, which must be designed to enable the student to compensate for or overcome a handicap in order to prepare him or her for future normal education and living. Thus, any expenses for therapy that helps your child's adaptation are deductible medical expenses. In addition, the expenses of your child's schooling at a "special school" for mentally or physically disabled individuals are deductible (including the cost of an ordinary education) if the resources of the school are the reason for your child's presence and the educational services provided are rendered only as an incident to the medical care provided. For instance, schools that provide special services for children with mental and/or physical disabilities, such as schools for the teaching of Braille or lip reading are special schools because the primary purpose of the schools is alleviating or treating a physical handicap. Similarly, schools with special programs for treating severe learning, mental, psychological or emotional disorders or dyslexia are special schools. The curriculum of a special school may include some ordinary education, but this must be incidental to the primary purpose of the school.

If a handicapped person attends a school that is not a special school, only those costs that are specifically attributable to medical care are deductible expenses. A school that offers small classes and individual attention does not qualify as a special school.

Example
In addition to the regular tuition for a private school, the parents of a handicapped child paid a special fee for a language development program designed to help students with learning disabilities. Although no deduction was allowed for the regular tuition, the cost of the special course was deductible as a medical expense.

Figure 23-A. Is Your Excess Medical Reimbursement Taxable?

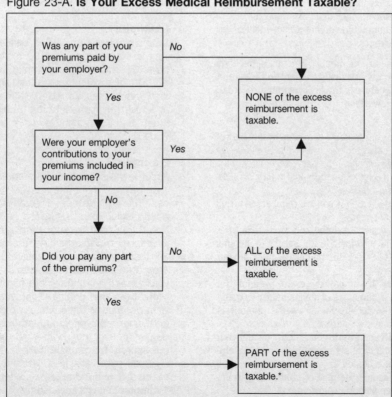

*See *Premiums paid by you and your employer* in this chapter.

However, if an ordinary school is willing to develop a special program that meets your child's needs, the school will qualify as a special school, since the determination of whether a school is a special school is made on the basis of your child's curriculum, not the curriculum of the school as a whole.

How Do You Treat Reimbursements?

You can include in medical expenses only those amounts paid during the taxable year for which you received no insurance or other reimbursement.

Insurance Reimbursement

You must reduce your total medical expenses for the year by all reimbursements for medical expenses that you receive from insurance or other sources during the year. This includes payments from Medicare.

Even if a policy provides reimbursement for only certain specific medical expenses, you must use amounts you receive from that policy to reduce your total medical expenses, including those it does not provide reimbursement for.

Example. You have insurance policies which cover your hospital and doctors' bills but not your nursing bills. The insurance you receive for the hospital and doctors' bills is more than their charges. In figuring your medical deduction, you must reduce the total amount you spent for medical care by the total amount of insurance you received even if the policies do not cover some of your medical expenses.

Health reimbursement arrangement (HRA). A health reimbursement arrangement is an employer-funded plan that reimburses employees for medical care expenses and allows unused amounts to be carried forward. An HRA is funded solely by the employer and the reimbursements for medical expenses, up to a maximum dollar amount for a coverage period, are not included in your income.

Other reimbursements. Generally, you do not reduce medical expenses by payments you receive for:

- Permanent loss or loss of use of a member or function of the body (loss of limb, sight, hearing, etc.) or disfigurement to the extent the payment is based on the nature of the injury without regard to the amount of time lost from work, or
- Loss of earnings.

You must, however, reduce your medical expenses by any part of these payments that is designated for medical costs. See *How Do You Figure and Report the Deduction on Your Tax Return*, later.

For how to treat damages received for personal injury or sickness, see *Damages For Personal Injuries*, later.

You do not have a medical deduction if you are reimbursed for all of your medical expenses for the year.

Excess reimbursement. If you are reimbursed more than your medical expenses, you may have to include the excess in income. You may want to use Figure 23-A to help you decide if any of your reimbursement is taxable.

Premiums paid by you. If you pay the entire premium for your medical insurance or all of the costs of a plan similar to medical insurance, you generally do not include an excess reimbursement in your gross income.

Premiums paid by you and your employer. If both you and your employer contribute to your medical insurance plan and your employer's contributions are not included in your gross income, you must include in your gross income the part of your excess reimbursement that is from your employer's contribution.

Explanation

You can figure the percentage of the excess reimbursement you must include in gross income using the following formula.

$$\frac{\text{Amount paid by employer}}{\text{Total annual cost of policy}} = \frac{\text{Percent of excess}}{\text{reimbursement that is taxable}}$$

Example

You are covered by your employer's medical insurance policy. The annual premium is $2,000. Your employer pays $600 of that amount and the balance of $1,400 is taken out of your wages. The part of any excess reimbursement you receive under the policy that is from your employer's contributions is figured as follows:

$$\frac{\$600}{\$2000} = 30\%$$

You must include in your gross income 30% (.30) of any excess reimbursement you received for medical expenses under the policy.

Insurance reimbursements. Reimbursements from insurance or other sources received during the year in which the medical expense is paid reduce the medical deduction to the extent of the reimbursement.

If total reimbursements exceed total medical expenses for the year, the excess reimbursement may have to be included in income. The determining factor of whether or not the excess reimbursement has to be included in income depends on who paid the premium for the insurance policy.

If you pay the entire premium for medical insurance, none of the excess reimbursement is includible in income. On the other hand, if you share the cost of the premium with, for example, your employer, the part of the excess reimbursement attributable to the employer's contribution to the premium must be included in income.

Example 1

John's annual medical insurance premium is $3,000. John's employer pays $900 of the premium, and John pays $2,100 of the premium. In 2004, John incurs $5,000 of medical expenses, and his insurance company reimburses him $5,500, an excess reimbursement of $500. The amount of the excess reimbursement that must be included in John's income is $150 ($900/$3,000 × $500).

Example 2

Assume the same facts as in the example above, except John pays for the entire medical insurance premium himself. The $500 excess insurance reimbursement would *not* be included in income.

Premiums paid by your employer. If your employer or your former employer pays the total cost of your medical insurance plan and your employer's contributions are not included in your income, you must report all of your excess reimbursement as other income.

More than one policy. If you are covered under more than one policy, the costs of which are paid by both you and your employer, you must first divide the medical expense among the policies to figure the excess reimbursement from each policy. Then divide the policy costs to figure the part of any excess reimbursement that is from your employer's contribution.

Example. You are covered by your employer's health insurance policy. The annual premium is $1,200. Your employer pays $300, and the balance of $900 is deducted from your wages. You also paid the entire premium ($250) for a personal health insurance policy.

During the year, you paid medical expenses of $3,600. In the same year, you were reimbursed $2,400 under your employer's policy and $1,600 under your personal policy.

You figure the part of any excess reimbursement you receive that is from your employer's contribution as follows:

Step 1.

Reimbursement from employer's policy	$2,400
Reimbursement from your policy	1,600
Total reimbursement	*$4,000*
Amount of medical expenses from your policy ([$1,600 ÷ $4,000] × $3,600 total medical expenses)	$1,440
Amount of medical expenses from your employer's policy ([$2,400 ÷ $4,000] × $3,600 total medical expenses)	2,160
Total medical expenses	*$3,600*
Excess reimbursement from your employer's policy ($2,400 − $2,160)	$240

Step 2. Because both you and your employer contributed to the cost of this policy, you must divide the cost to determine the excess reimbursement from your employer's contribution.

Employer's contribution in relation to the annual cost of the policy ($300 ÷ $1,200)	25%
Amount to report as other income on line 21, Form 1040 (25% × $240)	*$60*

Example

John pays $1,800 and his employer pays $600 toward the $2,400 annual premium for health insurance policy No. 1. Additionally, John pays the entire premium, $500, for health insurance policy No. 2. During 2004, John paid $7,200 of medical expenses and in the same year was reimbursed $5,000 under the first policy and $3,000 under the second policy.

The portion of excess reimbursement attributable to the employer's contribution is computed as follows:

Reimbursement from policy No. 1	$5,000
Reimbursement from policy No. 2	3,000
Total reimbursement	$8,000
Amount of reimbursed medical expenses from policy No. 1 ($5,000/$8,000 × $7,200 total medical expenses)	$4,500
Amount of reimbursed medical expenses from policy No. 2 ($3,000/$8,000 × $7,200 total medical expenses)	2,700
Total medical expenses	$7,200
Excess reimbursement from policy No. 1 ($5,000 − $4,500)	$ 500

The employer's contribution to the annual cost of policy No. 1 is 25% ($600/$2,400). Consequently, John must include $125 in income for 2003 ($500 × 25%).

None of the excess reimbursement from policy No. 2, $300 ($3,000 − $2,700), must be included in income, because John paid the entire premium of the policy.

See Publication 502 to figure the amount of the excess reimbursement you must include in gross income.

Reimbursement in a later year. If you are reimbursed in a later year for medical expenses you deducted in an earlier year, you must report the reimbursement as income up to the amount you previously deducted as medical expenses.

However, do not report as income the reimbursement you received up to the amount of your medical deductions that did not reduce your tax for the earlier year. For more information about the recovery of an amount that you claimed as an itemized deduction in an earlier year, see *Itemized Deduction Recoveries* in chapter 13.

Medical expenses not deducted. If you did not deduct a medical expense in the year you paid it because your medical expenses were not more than 7.5% of your adjusted gross income, or because you did not itemize deductions, do not include the reimbursement up to the amount of the expense in income. However, if the reimbursement is more than the expense, see *Excess reimbursement,* earlier.

Example. Last year, you had medical expenses of $500. You cannot deduct the $500 because it is less than 7.5% of your adjusted gross income. If, in a later year, you are reimbursed for any of the $500 in medical expenses, you do not include that amount in your gross income.

Damages for Personal Injuries

If you receive an amount in settlement of a personal injury suit, part of that award may be for medical expenses that you deducted in an earlier year. If it is, you must include that part in your income in the year you receive it to the extent it reduced your taxable income in the earlier year. See *Reimbursement in a Later Year*, discussed earlier.

Future medical expenses. If you receive an amount in settlement of a damage suit for personal injuries, part of that award may be for future medical expenses. If it is, you must reduce any future medical expenses for these injuries until the amount you received has been completely used.

How Do You Figure and Report the Deduction on Your Tax Return?

Once you have determined which medical care expenses you can include, you figure and report the deduction on your tax return.

What Tax Form Do You Use?

You figure your medical expense deduction on lines 1–4 of Schedule A, Form 1040. You cannot claim medical expenses on Form 1040A or Form 1040EZ. If you need more information on itemized deductions or you are not sure if you can itemize, see chapters 22 and 31.

Enter the amount you paid for medical and dental expenses on line 1, Schedule A (Form 1040). This should be your expenses that were not reimbursed by insurance or any other sources.

You can deduct only the amount of your medical and dental expenses that is more than 7.5% of your adjusted gross income shown on line 37, Form 1040. For an example, see the partial Schedule A.

Impairment-Related Work Expenses (Business or Medical)

If you are disabled, you can take a business deduction for expenses that are necessary for you to be able to work. If you take a business deduction for these impairment-related work expenses, they are not subject to the 7.5% limit that applies to medical expenses.

You are disabled if you have:

• A physical or mental disability (for example, blindness or deafness) that functionally limits your being employed, or
• A physical or mental impairment (for example, a sight or hearing impairment) that substantially limits one or more of your major life activities, such as performing manual tasks, walking, speaking, breathing, learning, or working.

Impairment-related expenses defined. Impairment-related expenses are those ordinary and necessary business expenses that are:

• Necessary for you to do your work satisfactorily,
• For goods and services not required or used, other than incidentally, in your personal activities, and
• Not specifically covered under other income tax laws.

Where to report. If you are self-employed, deduct the business expenses on the appropriate form (Schedule C, C-EZ, E, or F) used to report your business income and expenses.

If you are an employee, complete Form 2106, Employee Business Expenses, or Form 2106-EZ, Unreimbursed Employee Business Expenses. Enter on line 27, Schedule A (Form 1040) that part of the amount on line 10 of Form 2106, or line 6 of Form 2106-EZ, that is related to your impairment. Enter the amount that is unrelated to your impairment on line 20, Schedule A (Form 1040). Your impairment-related work expenses are not subject to the 2%-of-adjusted-gross-income limit that applies to other employee business expenses.

Example. You are blind. You must use a reader to do your work. You use the reader both during your regular working hours at your place of work and outside your regular working hours away from your place of work. The reader's services are only for your work. You can deduct your expenses for the reader as business expenses.

TaxSaver

While most miscellaneous itemized deductions are only allowed to the extent that the aggregate of such deductions exceeds 2% of your adjusted gross income, "impairment-related work expenses" are *not* subject to this limitation.

Example 1
You are confined to a wheelchair. Sometimes you must go out of town on business. Your friend or spouse goes with you to help with such things as carrying your luggage or getting up steps. You do not pay your helper a salary, but you do pay for your helper's travel, meals, and lodging while on such trips. You have learned how to take care of yourself and to do your job in your hometown without a helper. Because the expenses for the transportation, meals, and lodging of your helper are directly related to doing your job, you may deduct them as miscellaneous deductions on Form 1040.

Example 2
Assume the same facts as in the example above, except you are dependent on your friend's help at home as well as while traveling on business. The expenses of the friend are medical expenses, not business expenses.

If, in the above example, your spouse goes with you on the out-of-town business trips, you may deduct as medical expenses only the out-of-pocket costs for your spouse's transportation. Expenses for your spouse's meals and lodging are not deductible.

Health Insurance Costs for Self-Employed Persons

If you were self-employed and had a net profit for the year, were a general partner (or a limited partner receiving guaranteed payments), or received wages from an S corporation in which you were

a more than 2% shareholder (who is treated as a partner), you may be able to deduct, as an adjustment to income, up to 100% of the amount paid for medical and qualified long-term care insurance on behalf of yourself, your spouse, and dependents.

TaxAlert

If you are self-employed and have a net profit for the year, you can now deduct up to 100% of the amount you pay for health insurance on behalf of yourself, your spouse, and dependents. This deduction cannot be greater than the taxpayer's net earnings from his or her trade or business.

You may also be able to deduct premiums if you received wages from an S corporation in which you were a more-than-2%-shareholder. Eligible premiums will be shown in Box 14 of your W-2.

The insurance plan must be established under your trade or business, and you cannot take this deduction to the extent that the amount of the deduction is more than your earned income from that trade or business.

You cannot take this deduction for any month in which you were eligible to participate in any subsidized health plan maintained by your employer or your spouse's employer. This rule is applied separately to plans that provide long-term care insurance and plans that do not provide long-term care insurance.

If you qualify to take the deduction, use the Self-Employed Health Insurance Deduction Worksheet in the Form 1040 instructions to figure the amount you can deduct. But, if any of the following applies, do not use the worksheet.

- You had more than one source of income subject to self-employment tax.
- You file Form 2555, Foreign Earned Income, or Form 2555-EZ, Foreign Earned Income Exclusion.
- You are using amounts paid for qualified long-term care insurance to figure the deduction.

If you cannot use the worksheet in the Form 1040 instructions, use the worksheet in Publication 535, Business Expenses, to figure your deduction.

Note. When figuring the amount you may deduct for insurance premiums, do not include any advance payments shown in box 1 of Form 1099-H, Health Coverage Tax Credit (HCTC) Advance Payments. Also, if you are claiming the health coverage tax credit, subtract the amount shown on line 4 of Form 8885 (reduced by any advance payments shown on line 6 of that form) from the total insurance premiums you paid.

Where to report. You take this deduction on Form 1040, line 29. If you itemize your deductions and do not claim 100% of your self-employed health insurance on line 29, include any remaining premiums with all other medical care expenses on Schedule A (Form 1040), subject to the 7.5% limit. See chapter 7 of Publication 535, Business Expenses, for more information.

SCHEDULES A&B (Form 1040) Department of the Treasury Internal Revenue Service (99)	Schedule A—Itemized Deductions (Schedule B is on back) ▶ Attach to Form 1040. ▶ See Instructions for Schedules A and B (Form 1040).		OMB No. 1545-0074 20**05** Attachment Sequence No. **07**
Name(s) shown on Form 1040 Bill and Helen Jones			Your social security number 000 00 0000

Medical and Dental Expenses					
		Caution. Do not include expenses reimbursed or paid by others.			
	1	Medical and dental expenses (see page A-2)	**1**	3,434	
	2	Enter amount from Form 1040, line 38	**2** 33,000		
	3	Multiply line 2 by 7.5% (.075).	**3**	2,475	
	4	Subtract line 3 from line 1. If line 3 is more than line 1, enter -0-		**4**	959

24

Taxes You May Deduct

Note: The 2004 IRS Publication 17 (Your Federal Income Tax) has been updated by Ernst & Young LLP for 2005. Dates and dollar amounts shown are for 2005. Gray type is used to indicate where IRS text has been updated or intentionally omitted. Unrevised IRS text is shown in black type.

Introduction

You have been allowed to deduct taxes you pay—other than your federal income tax—ever since the nation's income tax was first enacted. The underlying theory is that taxes are an involuntary expenditure and therefore should be deducted from an individual's **gross income.** *But there is a practical consideration as well: The payment of state and local taxes makes it more difficult for an individual to meet the federal tax bill.*

The taxes you may deduct include two of the most significant. They are state and local taxes you pay on property you own and on your income.

You can also choose to deduct your state and local sales taxes instead of deducting state and local income taxes. This choice is especially meaningful for people who live in states that impose no state income tax, such as Alaska, Florida, Nevada, South Dakota, Texas, Washington, and Wyoming. Taxes you pay to a foreign government may also be deducted. These and other taxes that you may deduct from your federal income tax are described in this chapter.

Note: Your 2005 itemized deductions may be subject to certain limitations if your adjusted gross income exceeds $145,950 ($72,975 if married filing separately). See Chapter 31, Limit on Itemized Deductions, for more information on the deduction limitations.

Reminder

General sales tax deduction. You can elect to deduct state and local general sales taxes instead of state and local income taxes as an itemized deduction on Schedule A (Form 1040). This deduction expires after 2005.

Limit on itemized deductions. If your adjusted gross income is more than $145,950 ($72,975 if you are married filing separately), the overall amount of your itemized deductions may be limited. See chapter 31 for more information about this limit.

This chapter discusses which taxes you can deduct if you itemize deductions on Schedule A (Form 1040). It also explains which taxes you can deduct on other schedules or forms and which taxes you cannot deduct.

This chapter covers:

• Income taxes (state, local, and foreign),
• General sales taxes (state and local),
• Real estate taxes (state, local, and foreign),
• Personal property taxes (state and local), and
• Taxes and fees you cannot deduct.

Use Table 24-1 as a guide to determine which taxes you can deduct.

At the end of the chapter is a section that explains which form you use to deduct the different types of taxes.

Business taxes. You can deduct certain taxes only if they are ordinary and necessary expenses of your trade or business or of pro-

ducing income. For information on these taxes, see Publication 535, Business Expenses.

State or local taxes. These are taxes imposed by the 50 states, U.S. possessions, or any of their political subdivisions (such as a county or city), or by the District of Columbia.

Indian tribal government. An Indian tribal government that is recognized by the Secretary of the Treasury as performing substantial government functions will be treated as a state for this purpose. Income taxes, real estate taxes, and personal property taxes imposed by that Indian tribal government (or by any of its subdivisions that are treated as political subdivisions of a state) are deductible.

Foreign taxes. These are taxes imposed by a foreign country or any of its political subdivisions.

Useful Items

You may want to see:

Publications

☐ **514** Foreign Tax Credit for Individuals
☐ **530** Tax Information for First-Time Homeowners

Forms (and Instructions)

☐ **Schedule A (Form 1040)** Itemized Deductions
☐ **Schedule E (Form 1040)** Supplemental Income and Loss
☐ **Form 1116** Foreign Tax Credit

Table 24-1. **Which Taxes Can You Deduct?**

	You Can Deduct	You Cannot Deduct
Income Taxes	State and local income taxes. Foreign income taxes. Employee contributions to state funds listed under *Contributions to state benefit funds.* One-half of self-employment tax paid.	Federal income taxes. Employee contributions to private or voluntary disability plans. State and local general sales taxes (if you choose to deduct state and local income taxes).
General Sales Taxes	State and local general sales taxes.	State and local income taxes (if you choose to deduct state and local general sales taxes).
Real Estate Taxes	State and local real estate taxes. Foreign real estate taxes. Tenant's share of real estate taxes paid by cooperative housing corporation.	Taxes for local benefits (with exceptions). Trash and garbage pickup fees (with exceptions). Rent increase due to higher real estate taxes. Homeowners association charges.
Personal Property Taxes	State and local personal property taxes.	Import duties.
Other Taxes	Taxes that are expenses of your trade or business or of producing income. Taxes on property producing rent or royalty income. Occupational taxes. See chapter 30.	State and local sales and use taxes. Federal excise taxes, such as telephone taxes (see *Taxes and Fees You Cannot Deduct*). Per capita taxes.
Fees and Charges	Fees and charges that are expenses of your trade or business or of producing income.	Fees and charges that are not expenses of your trade or business or of producing income, such as fees for driver's licenses, car inspections, parking, or charges for water bills (see *Taxes and Fees You Cannot Deduct*). Fines and penalties.

Tests To Deduct Any Tax

The following two tests must be met for any tax to be deductible by you.

- The tax must be imposed on you.
- The tax must be paid during your tax year.

The tax must be imposed on you. Generally, you can deduct only taxes that are imposed on you.

Generally, you can deduct property taxes only if you are the property owner. If your spouse owns property and pays real estate taxes on it, the taxes are deductible on your spouse's separate return or on your joint return.

The tax must be paid during your tax year. If you are a cash basis taxpayer, you can deduct only those taxes actually paid during your tax year. If you pay your taxes by check, the day you mail or deliver the check is the date of payment, provided the check is honored by the financial institution. If you use a pay-by-phone account, the date reported on the statement of the financial institution showing when payment was made is the date of payment. If you contest a tax liability and are a cash basis taxpayer, you can deduct the tax only in the year it is actually paid.

If you use an accrual method of accounting, see Publication 538, Accounting Periods and Methods, for more information.

Income Taxes

This section discusses the deductibility of state and local income taxes (including employee contributions to state benefit funds) and foreign income taxes.

State and Local Income Taxes

You can deduct state and local income taxes. You can elect to deduct state and local general sales taxes instead of state and local income taxes.

Exception. You cannot deduct state and local income taxes you pay on income that is exempt from federal income tax, unless the exempt income is interest income. For example, you cannot deduct the part of a state's income tax that is on a cost-of-living allowance that is exempt from federal income tax.

What To Deduct

Your deduction may be for withheld taxes, estimated tax payments, or other tax payments as follows.

Withheld taxes. You can deduct state and local income taxes withheld from your salary in the year they are withheld. For 2005, these taxes will be shown in boxes 17 and 19 of your Form W-2. You may also have state or local income tax withheld on Form W-2G (box 14), Form 1099-MISC (box 16), or Form 1099-R (boxes 10 and 13).

Estimated tax payments. You can deduct estimated tax payments you made during the year to a state or local government. However, you must have a reasonable basis for making the estimated tax payments. Any estimated state or local tax payments you make that are not reasonably determined in good faith at the time of payment are not deductible. For example, you made an estimated state income tax payment. However, the estimate of your state tax liability shows that you will get a refund of the full amount of your estimated payment. You had no reasonable basis to believe you had any additional liability for state income taxes and you cannot deduct the estimated tax payment.

Refund applied to taxes. You can deduct any part of a refund of prior-year state or local income taxes that you chose to have credited to your 2005 estimated state or local income taxes.

Do not reduce your deduction by either of the following items.

- Any state or local income tax refund (or credit) you expect to receive for 2005.
- Any refund of (or credit for) prior year state and local income taxes you actually received in 2005.

However, part or all of this refund (or credit) may be taxable. See *Refund (or credit) of state or local income taxes*, later.

Explanation
Generally, all state, county, city, and municipal income taxes are deductible in the year in which you pay them—including the state and local taxes applicable to interest income that is not taxable at the federal level.

Example
You have the following income:

Salary	$18,000
Municipal bond income (exempt from federal tax but taxable by your state)	2,000
Total income	$20,000

If your state income tax is $1,000, then 10%, or $100, is attributable to the federally exempt income. Nevertheless, you may deduct the entire $1,000 on your federal return.

TaxPlanner

Municipal bonds. Municipal bonds issued by your state frequently are not subject to your state's income tax, whereas obligations for other states usually are subject to the state tax.

Be sure to use your effective state rate after the federal tax benefit when you are deciding between investing in a state tax-exempt municipal bond or an obligation that is subject to your state's tax.

TaxPlanner

Deducting expenses. If you deduct an expense when you pay it rather than when the expense is incurred, as most people do, you may deduct the following:

1. State income tax withheld from salary in 2005
2. State **estimated tax** payments made in 2005 for 2005
3. Fourth-quarter state estimated tax payment for 2004 made in January 2005
4. State income tax paid with your 2004 state income tax return filed in 2005
5. State income tax paid in 2005 with a request for a filing extension for your 2004 state income tax return
6. Additional state income tax paid in 2005 as a result of an **audit** or an amended return

In most states, the fourth-quarter estimated tax payment is due in January of the following year. A January 2006, payment for the last quarter of 2005 is deductible on your 2006 return. If, however, the payment is made by December 31, 2005, it is deductible on your 2005 return. If you can accelerate your payment by a few weeks, you can accelerate your **deduction** for state income taxes by a full year.

TaxAlert

Taxpayers have been denied deductions when state estimated tax payments made on December 31 were substantially in excess of their actual tax liability. To be assured of a deduction, you must be able to prove that the tax payment was based on a reasonable estimate of your actual tax bill. Also, be sure not to prepay your state taxes if you're in an alternative minimum tax position. See Chapter 32, *How to Figure Your Tax*.

TaxOrganizer

You should keep cancelled checks for payments of state estimated income tax (or any deductible tax) in order to support your claim for deductible taxes.

Separate federal returns. If you and your spouse file separate state, local, and federal income tax returns, you each can deduct on your federal return only the amount of your own state and local income tax.

Joint state and local returns. If you and your spouse file joint state and local returns and separate federal returns, each of you can deduct on your separate federal return part of the state and local income taxes. You can deduct only the amount of the total taxes that is proportionate to your gross income compared to the combined gross income of you and your spouse. However, you cannot deduct more than the amount you actually paid during the year. You can avoid this calculation if you and your spouse are jointly and individually liable for the full amount of the state and local income

taxes. If so, you and your spouse can deduct on your separate federal returns the amount you each actually paid.

Joint federal return. If you file a joint federal return, you can deduct the total of the state and local income taxes both of you paid.

TaxPlanner

If you file joint state returns and separate federal returns. If you plan on filing a joint state return with your spouse and separate federal returns, and if you are both jointly and individually liable for the full amount of the state tax, the state tax should be paid, to the extent possible, by the person in the higher separate federal income tax bracket. (For advice on filing jointly or separately, see Chapter 2, *Filing Status*.)

Contributions to state benefit funds. As an employee, you can deduct mandatory contributions to state benefit funds that provide protection against loss of wages. Mandatory payments made to the following state benefit funds are deductible as state income taxes on Schedule A (Form 1040), line 5.

- California Nonoccupational Disability Benefit Fund.
- New Jersey Nonoccupational Disability Benefit Fund.
- New Jersey Unemployment Compensation Fund.
- New York Nonoccupational Disability Benefit Fund.
- Rhode Island Temporary Disability Benefit Fund.
- Washington State Supplemental Worker's Compensation Fund.
- West Virginia Unemployment Compensation Fund.

Caution. *Employee contributions to private or voluntary disability plans are not deductible.*

Refund (or credit) of state or local income taxes. If you receive a refund of (or credit for) state or local income taxes in a year after the year in which you paid them, you may have to include the refund in income on Form 1040, line 10, in the year you receive it. This includes refunds resulting from taxes that were overwithheld, applied from a prior year return, not figured correctly, or figured again because of an amended return. If you did not itemize your deductions in the previous year, do not include the refund in income. If you deducted the taxes in the previous year, include all or part of the refund on Form 1040, line 10, in the year you receive the refund. For a discussion of how much to include, see *Recoveries* in chapter 13.

Explanation

If you received a refund of taxes that you paid in an earlier year, such as 2003 or 2004, do not use that refund to reduce your deduction for taxes that you paid during 2005.

However, if you receive a refund of taxes in the same year in which you paid the taxes, you would use the refund to reduce your deduction for taxes.

Example

You paid $4,000 of estimated state income taxes for 2004 in four equal payments. You made your fourth payment in January 2005. You were not subject to state income tax withholding in 2004. In 2005, you received a $400 tax refund based on your 2004 state income tax return. One hundred dollars (25% of $400) of the refund is attributable to your 2005 payment. Your deduction for state and local income taxes paid in 2005 includes $900 ($1,000 − $100) plus any other payments you made during 2005 and any amount withheld during 2005. The amount of your state tax refund to be reported as income in 2005 would be $300 ($400 − $100).

TaxSaver

Reducing the amount of the reported refund will reduce your adjusted gross income. If your adjusted gross income is lower, you may benefit from greater itemized deductions.

TaxPlanner

If you subtract part of the refund from your other tax payments, the income reported by you will not match the amount reported to the IRS by the state on Form 1099-G. You may then receive a notice proposing an additional assessment of tax. You may avoid the notice by attaching an explanation to your return.

Explanation

An overpayment of state income tax that is to be credited against the estimated state tax for the following year is treated as though it were refunded to you. The overpayment may then be deducted as an estimated tax payment.

Example

Your 2004 state return showed an overpayment of $500, which you indicated was to be credited against your 2005 state estimated tax declaration. In addition, you made three quarterly state estimated tax payments of $500 each during 2005. On your 2005 Form 1040, you report a tax refund of $500 on line 10 and a deduction on Schedule A of $2,000.

TaxOrganizer

When you receive your Form 1099-G from your state or local government, keep it as documentation of your refund.

Foreign Income Taxes

Generally, you can take either a deduction or a credit for income taxes imposed on you by a foreign country or a U.S. possession. However, you cannot take a deduction or credit for foreign income taxes paid on income that is exempt from U.S. tax under the foreign earned income exclusion or the foreign housing exclusion. For information on these exclusions, see Publication 54, Tax Guide for U.S. Citizens and Resident Aliens Abroad. For information on the foreign tax credit, see Publication 514.

Explanation

If you have income from foreign sources, you may be required to pay foreign taxes on that income, or foreign taxes may be withheld on that income before you receive it.

TaxPlanner

Credit for foreign taxes. It is usually better to take a credit for foreign taxes than to deduct them as itemized deductions. Credits reduce your U.S. tax on a dollar-for-dollar basis, whereas a deduction just reduces the amount of income subject to tax. However, if your foreign tax credit is limited and must be carried over to future years, you may want to consider taking a deduction now instead of waiting for a credit. See Chapter 43, *U.S. Citizens Working Abroad: Tax Treatment of Foreign Earned Income,* for more information on foreign tax credit limitations. The following example shows how a credit is usually more advantageous.

Example

You and your spouse had **adjusted gross income** of $90,000 in 2005, $20,000 of which was from foreign sources. You file a joint return and have no **dependents.** You had to pay $2,000 in foreign income taxes on dividend income received from sources within a foreign country. If your itemized deductions are otherwise $9,700, your added deduction for the foreign income tax reduces your U.S. tax by $500. If, however, you choose to claim a credit for the $2,000 foreign tax, your U.S. tax is reduced by the full $2,000. Therefore, you have an additional tax benefit of $1,500 by taking the credit.

TaxPlanner

If you invest in stock of a foreign company. If you have invested in stock of a foreign company and the stock is being held by your stockbroker, ask him or her for the information that permits you to determine your foreign tax credit. In most instances, monthly statements received from brokers show only the *net* amount of foreign dividends received, *after* the foreign income tax has been deducted.

Credit for foreign taxes is available without limitation, if all your foreign income is from passive sources (interest, dividends, royalties, etc.) and the taxes are $300 or less ($600 or less if you are married filing jointly). See Chapter 38, *Other Credits Including the Earned Income Credit,* for more information about the foreign tax credit.

Example

Your brokerage statement shows foreign dividend income of $850. Upon inquiry, you determine that foreign income taxes of $150 have been withheld. Therefore, you should report $1,000 ($850 + $150) of dividend income. You then may be entitled to take a foreign tax credit of $150 or an itemized deduction of $150.

TaxOrganizer

For your files, you should keep your broker's statement showing any amount of foreign taxes paid.

General Sales Taxes

You can elect to deduct state and local general sales taxes, instead of state and local income taxes, as an itemized deduction on Schedule A (Form 1040). You can deduct either your actual expenses or an amount figured using the Optional State Sales Tax Tables in Publication 600 (or Publication 600-A for Alaska residents). If you use the Optional State Sales Tax Tables, you may be able to add to the table amount any state and local general sales tax you paid on motor vehicles, boats, and other items specified in Publication 600. See the Instructions for Schedule A (Form 1040) for details.

A 2004 tax act now allows a deduction for state and local sales tax if you don't deduct state and local income taxes. This election makes sense if your sales taxes are greater than your income taxes. To prove your actual sales taxes, if you don't use the Optional State Sales Tax Table amounts in Publication 600 (available at www.irs.gov, you have to keep track of all your purchases during the year. This deduction is especially useful for people who live in states with no income taxes, such as Nevada and Texas.

Real Estate Taxes

Deductible real estate taxes are any state, local, or foreign taxes on real property levied for the general public welfare. You can deduct these taxes only if they are based on the assessed value of the real property and charged uniformly against all property under the jurisdiction of the taxing authority.

Deductible real estate taxes generally do not include taxes charged for local benefits and improvements that increase the value of the property. They also do not include itemized charges for services (such as trash collection) to specific property or people, even if the charge is paid to the taxing authority. For more information about taxes and charges that are not deductible, see *Real Estate–Related Items You Cannot Deduct*, later.

Tenant-shareholders in a cooperative housing corporation. Generally, you can deduct your share of the real estate taxes the corporation paid or incurred on the property. The corporation should provide you with a statement showing your share of the taxes. For more information, see *Special Rules for Cooperatives* in Publication 530.

Explanation
Generally, you may deduct only those real estate taxes assessed against property that you own.

Examples
No deduction was allowed for real estate taxes when:

- A taxpayer paid, under court order, real estate taxes on his aunt's house, in which he resided.
- A guarantor paid real estate taxes on foreclosed property.
- The executor of an estate paid real estate taxes on a residence belonging to the estate, which she was occupying.
- A tenant-shareholder in a cooperative housing corporation paid his proportionate share of real estate taxes levied on recreational facilities owned and maintained by another corporation.
- A husband paid real estate taxes on property previously transferred to his wife. He had guaranteed payment if his wife defaulted but was not otherwise obligated. He will not be able to claim a deduction unless his wife actually defaults.
- The Tax Court held that a couple could not claim deductions for real property taxes paid by the husband for property owned by the S corporations that the couple owned.
- The Tax Court has held that sons could not deduct real estate taxes they paid on a house owned by their father and uncle because they did not have a beneficial interest in the property under California law.

You may, however, deduct real estate taxes when you have a beneficial interest in property, if the payment is made to protect that interest.

Real estate documents you need. You should keep a copy of your real estate tax bill in order to support your claim for the real estate tax deduction. Also, if you purchased a new house during the year, you should keep the closing statement. Typically, the closing statement will show the amount of taxes you paid to the seller at the time of the purchase.

Buyers and sellers of real estate. If you bought or sold real estate during the year, the real estate taxes must be divided between the buyer and the seller.

The buyer and the seller must divide the real estate taxes according to the number of days in the real property tax year (the period to which the tax imposed relates) that each owned the property. The seller is treated as paying the taxes up to, but not including, the date of sale. The buyer is treated as paying the taxes beginning with the date of sale. This applies regardless of the lien dates under local law. Generally, this information is included on the settlement statement provided at the closing.

If you (the seller) cannot deduct taxes until they are paid because you use the cash method of accounting, and the buyer of your property is personally liable for the tax, you are considered to have paid your part of the tax at the time of the sale. This lets you deduct the part of the tax to the date of sale even though you did not actually pay it. However, you must also include the amount of that tax in the selling price of the property. The buyer must include the same amount in his or her cost of the property.

You figure your deduction for taxes on each property bought or sold during the real property tax year as follows.

Worksheet 24.1.

1. Enter the total real estate taxes for the real property tax year .... _____

2. Enter the number of days in the real property tax year that you owned the property .... _____

3. Divide line 2 by 365 .... _____

4. Multiply line 1 by line 3. This is your deduction. Enter it on Schedule A (Form 1040), line 6 .... _____

Note. Repeat steps 1 through 4 for each property you bought or sold during the real property tax year.

Real estate taxes for prior years. Do not divide delinquent taxes between the buyer and seller if the taxes are for any real property tax year before the one in which the property is sold. Even if the buyer agrees to pay the delinquent taxes, the buyer cannot deduct them. The buyer must add them to the cost of the property. The seller can deduct these taxes paid by the buyer. However, the seller must include them in the selling price.

Examples. The following examples illustrate how real estate taxes are divided between buyer and seller.

Example 1. Dennis and Beth White's real property tax year for both their old home and their new home is the calendar year, with payment due August 1. The tax on their old home, sold on May 7, was $620. The tax on their new home, bought on May 3, was $732. Dennis and Beth are considered to have paid a proportionate share of the real estate taxes on the old home even though they did not actually pay them to the taxing authority. On the other hand, they can claim only a proportionate share of the taxes they paid on their new property even though they paid the entire amount.

Dennis and Beth owned their old home during the real property tax year for 126 days (January 1 to May 6, the day before the sale). They figure their deduction for taxes on their old home as follows.

TAXES ON OLD HOME

1. Enter the total real estate taxes for the real property tax year............... $620

2. Enter the number of days in the real property tax year that you owned the property... 126

3. Divide line 2 by 365.. .345

4. Multiply line 1 by line 3. This is your deduction. Enter it on Schedule A (Form 1040), line 6 .... $214

Since the buyers of their old home paid all of the taxes, Dennis and Beth also include the $214 in the selling price of the old home. (The buyers add the $214 to their cost of the home.)

Dennis and Beth owned their new home during the real property tax year for 243 days (May 3 to December 31, including their date of purchase). They figure their deduction for taxes on their new home as follows.

TAXES ON NEW HOME

1. Enter the total real estate taxes for the real property tax year............... $732

2. Enter the number of days in the real property tax year that you owned the property... 243

3. Divide line 2 by 365.. .666

4. Multiply line 1 by line 3. This is your deduction. Enter it on Schedule A (Form 1040), line 6 .... $488

Since Dennis and Beth paid all of the taxes on the new home, they add $244 ($732 paid less $488 deduction) to their cost of the new home. (The sellers add this $244 to their selling price and deduct the $244 as a real estate tax.)

Dennis and Beth's real estate tax deduction for their old and new homes is the sum of $214 and $488, or $702. They will enter this amount on Schedule A (Form 1040), line 6.

Example 2. George and Helen Brown bought a new home on May 3, 2005. Their real property tax year for the new home is the calendar year. Real estate taxes for 2004 were assessed in their state on January 1, 2005. The taxes became due on May 31, 2005, and October 31, 2005.

The Browns agreed to pay all taxes due after the date of purchase. Real estate taxes for 2004 were $680. They paid $340 on May 31, 2005, and $340 on October 31, 2005. These taxes were for the 2004 real property tax year. The Browns cannot deduct them since they did not own the property until 2005. Instead, they must add $680 to the cost of their new home.

In January 2006, the Browns receive their 2005 property tax statement for $752, which they will pay in 2006. The Browns owned their new home during the 2005 real property tax year for 243 days (May 3 to December 31). They will figure their 2006 deduction for taxes as follows.

1. Enter the total real estate taxes for the real property tax year............... $752

2. Enter the number of days in the real property tax year that you owned the property... 243

3. Divide line 2 by 365.. .666

4. Multiply line 1 by line 3. This is your deduction. Claim it on Schedule A (Form 1040), line 6 .... $501

The remaining $251 ($752 paid less $501 deduction) of taxes paid in 2006, along with the $680 paid in 2005, is added to the cost of their new home.

Because the taxes up to the date of sale are considered paid by the seller on the date of sale, the seller is entitled to a 2005 tax deduction of $931. This is the sum of the $680 for 2004 and the $251 for the 122 days the seller owned the home in 2005. The seller must

also include the $931 in the selling price when he or she figures the gain or loss on the sale. The seller should contact the Browns in January 2006 to find out how much real estate tax is due for 2005.

Form 1099-S. For certain sales or exchanges of real estate, the person responsible for closing the sale (generally the settlement agent) prepares Form 1099-S, Proceeds From Real Estate Transactions, to report certain information to the IRS and to the seller of the property. Box 2 of the form is for the gross proceeds of the sale and should include the portion of the seller's real estate tax liability that the buyer will pay after the date of sale. The buyer includes these taxes in the cost basis of the property, and the seller both deducts this amount as a tax paid and includes it in the sales price of the property.

For a real estate transaction that involves a home, any real estate tax the seller paid in advance but that is the liability of the buyer appears on Form 1099-S, box 5. The buyer deducts this amount as a real estate tax, and the seller reduces his or her real estate tax deduction (or includes it in income) by the same amount. See *Refund (or rebate)*, later.

Explanation

Frequently, when property is sold, the amount of the real estate taxes for the "real property tax year" is not yet known, so an allocation is made on the closing statement at the time of sale based on the tax bill for the preceding year.

If the actual real estate tax bill for the real property tax year is greater than the amount used in the original allocation, the seller is entitled to a deduction greater than that shown on the real estate closing statement. The difference between the deductible amount and the amount allocated on the closing statement is considered additional proceeds of the sale.

The buyer is entitled to deduct his or her allocable share of the actual bill. The excess of the amount that he or she pays over (1) the deductible amount and (2) the amount paid or received at the closing is added to the cost of the property.

TAXPLANNER

When to deduct real estate taxes. If the real estate taxes are actually paid after the year of the sale, the seller may deduct his or her share of the taxes either in the year of the sale or in the year in which the tax is paid, whichever produces the greatest tax advantage.

The situation is slightly different for the buyer. If the buyer is liable for payment of the tax, he or she may deduct his or her allocated share of the tax only in the year in which the payment is made. If the seller is liable for payment of the tax, the buyer may deduct his or her allocated share either in the year of the sale or in the year of payment.

Taxes placed in escrow. If your monthly mortgage payment includes an amount placed in escrow (put in the care of a third party) for real estate taxes, you may not be able to deduct the total amount placed in escrow. You can deduct only the real estate tax that the third party actually paid to the taxing authority. If the third party does not notify you of the amount of real estate tax that was paid for you, contact the third party or the taxing authority to find the proper amount to show on your return.

TAXPLANNER

When to accelerate a tax payment. Most lenders arrange for payment of taxes out of escrow accounts on the tax due date. When the due date is shortly after the end of the calendar year, it may be advantageous to accelerate the payment in order to get the deduction for payment a year earlier.

Example
Real estate taxes of $1,200 for the year 2005 become due and payable on February 1, 2006. The taxpayer made monthly escrow payments of $100 each during 2005. If the taxes were paid from the escrow account on the February 1, 2006, due date, the $1,200 is a 2006 deduction. However, if the taxes were paid by December 31, 2005, the $1,200 is a 2005 deduction.

TAX*ORGANIZER*

Escrow statements. Be sure to keep your yearly escrow statement, which should indicate the amount of real estate taxes paid from the escrow account.

Tenants by the entirety. If you and your spouse held property as tenants by the entirety and you file separate federal returns, each of you can deduct only the taxes each of you paid on the property.

Divorced individuals. If your divorce or separation agreement states that you must pay the real estate taxes for a home owned by you and your spouse, part of your payments may be deductible as alimony and part as real estate taxes. See *Taxes and insurance* in chapter 20 for more information.

Minister's and military personnel housing allowances. If you are a minister or a member of the uniformed services and receive a housing allowance that you can exclude from income, you still can deduct all of the real estate taxes you pay on your home.

Refund (or rebate). If you receive a refund or rebate in 2005 of real estate taxes you paid in 2005, you must reduce your deduction by the amount refunded to you. If you receive a refund or rebate in 2005 of real estate taxes you deducted in an earlier year, you generally must include the refund or rebate in income in the year you receive it. However, you only need to include the amount of the deduction that reduced your tax in the earlier year. For more information, see *Recoveries* in chapter 13.

Tip. *If you did not itemize deductions in the year you paid the tax, do not report the refund as income.*

Real Estate–Related Items You Cannot Deduct

Payments for the following items generally are not deductible as real estate taxes.

- Taxes for local benefits.
- Itemized charges for services (such as trash and garbage pickup fees).
- Transfer taxes (or stamp taxes).
- Rent increases due to higher real estate taxes.
- Homeowners' association charges.

Taxes for local benefits. Deductible real estate taxes generally do not include taxes charged for local benefits and improvements tending to increase the value of your property. These include assessments for streets, sidewalks, water mains, sewer lines, public parking facilities, and similar improvements. You should increase the basis of your property by the amount of the assessment.

Local benefit taxes are deductible only if they are for maintenance, repair, or interest charges related to those benefits. If only a part of the taxes is for maintenance, repair, or interest, you must be able to show the amount of that part to claim the deduction. If you cannot determine what part of the tax is for maintenance, repair, or interest, none of it is deductible.

Taxes for local benefits may be included in your real estate tax bill. If your taxing authority (or mortgage lender) does not furnish you a copy of your real estate tax bill, ask for it. You should use the rules above to determine if the local benefit tax is deductible.

Explanation
Real property taxes are deductible if they are levied for the welfare of the general public and are levied at a proportionate rate against all property within the taxing jurisdiction.

Real property taxes should be distinguished from assessments paid for local benefits, such as repair of streets, sidewalks, sewers, curbs, gutters, and other improvements that tend to benefit specific properties. Assessments of this type generally are not deductible.

A property owner often has the option of paying a special assessment in one payment or spreading the assessment over a period of years. In either case, the assessment itself is not deductible. However, payment of certain special assessments may increase the tax basis of your home. (See Chapter 14, *Basis of Property,* for a full discussion of this matter.) If an assessment on business or investment property is paid in installments, any interest charged is deductible. If the property is personal rather than business property, the interest would not be deductible. See Chapter 25, *Interest Expense.*

The IRS and the courts have held that the following *are* deductible as real property taxes:

- Assessments for the repair and resurfacing of streets, but not the lengthening or widening of them
- Wheeling, West Virginia, police and fire department charges imposed on owners of buildings and **tangible personal property**

If you pay real estate taxes this year but you are not itemizing your deductions, see Chapter 14, *Basis of Property.*

Different rules apply to real estate taxes paid during the period in which you are making improvements intended for business use. These rules are discussed in Chapter 25, *Interest Expense.*

Itemized charges for services. An itemized charge for services to specific property or people is not a tax, even if the charge is paid to the taxing authority. For example, you cannot deduct the charge as a real estate tax if it is:

- A unit fee for the delivery of a service (such as a $5 fee charged for every 1,000 gallons of water you use),
- A periodic charge for a residential service (such as a $20 per month or $240 annual fee charged to each homeowner for trash collection), or
- A flat fee charged for a single service provided by your government (such as a $30 charge for mowing your lawn because it was allowed to grow higher than permitted under your local ordinance).

Caution. *You must look at your real estate tax bill to determine if any nondeductible itemized charges, such as those just listed, are included in the bill. If your taxing authority (or mortgage lender) does not furnish you a copy of your real estate tax bill, ask for it.*

Exception. Service charges used to maintain or improve services (such as trash collection or police and fire protection) are deductible as real estate taxes if:

- The fees or charges are imposed at a like rate against all property in the taxing jurisdiction,
- The funds collected are not earmarked; instead, they are commingled with general revenue funds, and
- Funds used to maintain or improve services are not limited to or determined by the amount of these fees or charges collected.

Explanation

If the cost of providing certain services, such as garbage collection or sanitary measures, is paid for out of the general real estate tax fund, the entire amount of your real estate tax bill is deductible. If, however, the amount charged for such services is separately stated or paid into a specific fund, that amount is not deductible.

Transfer taxes (or stamp taxes). Transfer taxes and similar taxes and charges on the sale of a personal home are not deductible. If they are paid by the seller, they are expenses of the sale and reduce the amount realized on the sale. If paid by the buyer, they are included in the cost basis of the property.

Rent increase due to higher real estate taxes. If your landlord increases your rent in the form of a tax surcharge because of increased real estate taxes, you cannot deduct the increase as taxes.

Homeowners' association charges. These charges are not deductible because they are imposed by the homeowners' association, rather than the state or local government.

Personal Property Taxes

Personal property tax is deductible if it is a state or local tax that is:

- Charged on personal property,
- Based only on the value of the personal property, and
- Charged on a yearly basis, even if it is collected more or less than once a year.

A tax that meets the above requirements can be considered charged on personal property even if it is for the exercise of a privilege. For example, a yearly tax based on value qualifies as a personal property tax even if it is called a registration fee and is for the privilege of registering motor vehicles or using them on the highways.

If the tax is partly based on value and partly based on other criteria, it may qualify in part.

Example. Your state charges a yearly motor vehicle registration tax of 1% of value plus 50 cents per hundredweight. You paid $32 based on the value ($1,500) and weight (3,400 lbs.) of your car. You can deduct $15 (1% × $1,500) as a personal property tax because it is based on the value. The remaining $17 ($.50 × 34), based on the weight, is not deductible.

Explanation

Most state automobile license fees are not based on the value of the automobile and, therefore, are not deductible as personal property taxes.

Taxes and Fees You Cannot Deduct

Many federal, state, and local government taxes are not deductible because they do not fall within the categories discussed earlier. Other taxes and fees, such as federal income taxes, are not deductible because the tax law specifically prohibits a deduction for them. See Table 24-1.

Taxes and fees that are generally not deductible include the following items.

- *Estate, inheritance, legacy, or succession taxes.* However, you can deduct the estate tax attributable to income in respect of a decedent if you, as a beneficiary, must include that income in your gross income. In that case, deduct the estate tax as a miscellaneous deduction that is not subject to the 2%-of-adjusted-gross-income limit. For more information, see chapter 4.
- *Federal income taxes.* This includes taxes withheld from your pay.
- *Fines.* You cannot deduct penalties for violation of any law, including forfeiture of related collateral deposits.
- *Gift taxes.*
- *License fees.* You cannot deduct license fees for personal purposes (such as marriage, driver's, and dog license fees).
- *Per capita taxes.* You cannot deduct state or local per capita taxes.
- *Social security.* This includes social security, Medicare, or railroad retirement taxes withheld from your pay.
- *Social security and other employment taxes for household workers.* However, the social security and other employment taxes you pay on the wages of a household worker may qualify as medical or child care expenses. For more information, see chapters 23 and 34.

Explanation

Other taxes that are *not* deductible include the following:

1. Federal and state excise taxes on telephone service
2. Federal gasoline taxes
3. Federal excise taxes on tobacco products and alcoholic beverages
4. Federal excise taxes on automobiles with low gas mileage (the "gas guzzler" tax)
5. Foreign taxes on income earned by U.S. citizens and U.S. **resident aliens** who qualify for the foreign **earned income** exclusion
6. Passport fees
7. Occupancy taxes
8. Penalties assessed as taxes

Many taxes and fees other than those listed above are also nondeductible, unless they are ordinary and necessary expenses of a business or income producing activity. For other nondeductible items, see *Real Estate–Related Items You Cannot Deduct*, earlier.

Where To Deduct

You deduct taxes on the following schedules.

State and local income taxes. These taxes are deducted on Schedule A (Form 1040), line 5, even if your only source of income is from business, rents, or royalties. You must check box a on line 5. If you deduct these taxes, you cannot elect to deduct general sales taxes.

General sales tax deduction. These taxes are deducted on Schedule A (Form 1040), line 5. If you elect to deduct these taxes, you cannot deduct state and local income taxes. You must check box b on line 5.

Foreign income taxes. Generally, income taxes you pay to a foreign country or U.S. possession can be claimed as an itemized deduction on Schedule A (Form 1040), line 8, or as a credit against your U.S. income tax on Form 1040, line 47. To claim the credit, you may have to complete and attach Form 1116. For more information, see chapter 39, the Form 1040 instructions, or Publication 514.

Real estate taxes and personal property taxes. These taxes are deducted on Schedule A (Form 1040), lines 6 and 7, unless they are paid on property used in your business in which case they are deducted on Schedule C or Schedule F (Form 1040). Taxes on property that produces rent or royalty income are deducted on Schedule E (Form 1040).

Self-employment tax. Deduct one-half of your self-employment tax on Form 1040, line 27.

Other taxes. All other deductible taxes are deducted on Schedule A (Form 1040), line 8.

25

Interest Expense

Note: The 2004 IRS Publication 17 (Your Federal Income Tax) has been updated by Ernst & Young LLP for 2005. Dates and dollar amounts shown are for 2005. Gray type is used to indicate where IRS text has been updated or intentionally omitted. Unrevised IRS text is shown in black type.

Introduction

Interest expense is the amount of money you pay for the use of borrowed money. Depending on the use of the borrowed funds, certain types of interest expense may be deducted from your income.

To calculate your deduction, you must first separate your borrowings into five categories: (1) amounts used for investments generating portfolio income (interest, dividends, etc.), (2) amounts used for investment in passive activities (see Chapter 13, Other Income), (3) amounts used to purchase or improve a personal residence, (4) amounts used in an active trade or business, and (5) amounts used for personal reasons. However, remember that no portion of your personal interest expense is deductible.

The interest paid on the other four categories of borrowings are subject to different rules regarding deductibility. This chapter will explain those rules and how to account for the use of your borrowings.

Your 2004 itemized deductions may be subject to certain limitations if your adjusted gross income exceeds $145,950 ($72,975 for married persons filing separately). This general limitation does not apply to investment interest expense, but it does apply to home mortgage interest expense. See Chapter 31, Limit on Itemized Deductions, for more information on this subject.

Reminders

Personal interest. Personal interest is not deductible. Examples of personal interest include interest on a loan to purchase an automobile for personal use and credit card and installment interest incurred for personal expenses.

But you may be able to deduct interest you pay on a qualified student loan. For details, see Publication 970, Tax Benefits for Education.

Limit on itemized deductions. If your adjusted gross income is more than $145,950 ($72,975 if you are married filing separately), the overall amount of your itemized deductions may be limited. See chapter 31 for more information about this limit.

This chapter discusses interest. Interest is the amount you pay for the use of borrowed money.

Explanation
Loan payments generally are divided between principal and interest. In the absence of any specific division, partial payments are presumed to apply first to interest and then to principal. However, if a single payment is made in full settlement of an outstanding debt, the payment is first applied to the remaining principal balance and then to interest.

The types of interest you can deduct as itemized deductions on Schedule A (Form 1040) are:

• Home mortgage interest, including certain points, and
• Investment interest.

This chapter explains these deductions. It also explains where to deduct other types of interest and lists some types of interest you cannot deduct.

Use Table 25-1 to find out where to get more information on various types of interest, including investment interest.

Useful Items

You may want to see:

Publication

☐ **936** Home Mortgage Interest Deduction

Home Mortgage Interest

Generally, home mortgage interest is any interest you pay on a loan secured by your home (main home or a second home). The loan may be a mortgage to buy your home, a second mortgage, a line of credit, or a home equity loan.

You can deduct home mortgage interest only if you meet all the following conditions.

- You must file Form 1040 and itemize deductions on Schedule A (Form 1040).
- You must be legally liable for the loan. You cannot deduct payments you make for someone else if you are not legally liable to make them. Both you and the lender must intend that the loan be repaid. In addition, there must be a true debtor-creditor relationship between you and the lender.

Explanation

Interest paid to a related person is deductible, as long as it is paid for a bona fide debt. For example, parents may deduct interest paid on amounts borrowed from their minor children if the interest is otherwise deductible. If the borrower is not legally liable for the debt, or if there is no intent for the loan to be repaid, it is not a bona fide debt and interest payments are not deductible.

To deduct interest that you pay, the interest must be your liability. When two or more persons are jointly liable for the payment of interest, the person actually making the interest payment is entitled to the entire deduction.

It is not necessary to have a fixed percentage interest rate applied to the money that you have borrowed for the interest to be deducted. What is necessary is that the amount of interest paid can be definitely determined. It is usually based on a written agreement between the lender and the borrower.

Low-interest and interest-free loans, which were once popular between family members, now have severe limitations applied to them. See Chapter 8, *Interest Income*.

- The mortgage must be a secured debt on a qualified home. (Generally, your mortgage is a secured debt if you put your home up as collateral to protect the interests of the lender. The term "qualified home" means your main home or second home. For details, see Publication 936.)

Explanation

To be fully deductible as home mortgage interest, the interest must be on a debt that is secured by property that is a qualified residence. A qualified residence is property that is owned by you and used as a principal or second residence. A residence may, among other things, be a house, a cooperative apartment, a condominium, a house trailer, or a houseboat. To be considered a qualified residence, a houseboat must include basic living accommodations, including sleeping space, a toilet, and cooking facilities.

TAXPLANNER

You may treat a home currently under construction as a qualified home for a period of up to 24 months if it becomes a qualifying residence as of the time that it is ready for occupancy.

Amount Deductible

In most cases, you will be able to deduct all of your home mortgage interest. Whether you can deduct all of it depends on the date you took out the mortgage, the amount of the mortgage, and your use of its proceeds.

Fully deductible interest. If all of your mortgages fit into one or more of the following three categories at all times during the year, you can deduct all of the interest on those mortgages. (If any one mortgage fits into more than one category, add the debt that fits in each category to your other debt in the same category.)

The three categories are:

1. Mortgages you took out on or before October 13, 1987 (called grandfathered debt).

Explanation

All mortgage indebtedness existing on October 13, 1987 (grandfathered debt), is treated as acquisition indebtedness, regardless of the amount. The interest on this indebtedness is fully deductible.

Individuals who refinanced and increased their mortgage indebtedness before October 14, 1987, may have greater interest deductions than those individuals who waited until later because new or refinanced indebtedness is limited in amount, as explained in this chapter.

Example 1

When you are refinancing pre–October 14, 1987, mortgage debt, the amount that exceeds the existing debt does not qualify as grandfathered debt. The excess may be treated as home acquisition or home equity indebtedness, but the total qualifying indebtedness cannot exceed the fair market value of the residence. Grandfathered debt refinanced after October 13, 1987, generally retains its status as grandfathered debt only for the remaining term of the original debt.

Example 2

An original mortgage note incurred prior to October 14, 1987, to purchase a qualified residence had been reduced to $100,000 in 2005, when the value of the residence was $175,000. If this mortgage is refinanced, $100,000 of the new mortgage note is treated as grandfathered debt. Up to $75,000 may be treated as home acquisition or home equity indebtedness. If the indebtedness exceeds the value of the residence ($175,000), the excess must be allocated in accordance with the use of the excess amount.

2. Mortgages you took out after October 13, 1987, to buy, build, or improve your home (called home acquisition debt), but only if throughout 2005 these mortgages plus any grandfathered debt totaled $1 million or less ($500,000 or less if married filing separately).

Explanation

This limitation applies only to loans incurred to purchase, construct, or improve a home.

TAXPLANNER

Is your loan large enough? When you are purchasing or constructing a home, consider your future financial needs carefully. The original loan can never be refinanced to increase the amount available for this limitation.

If you believe that you will need money for personal uses in the near future, you may want to increase the original mortgage at the time of acquisition or improvement to meet those future needs. Otherwise, if you later obtain a home equity loan, the interest on only $100,000 of the loan ($50,000 if married filing separately) is deductible as mortgage interest.

Additionally, interest paid on a home equity loan where the loan proceeds were used for personal use, and not for home improvements, is not deductible under the Alternative Minimum Tax rules.

3. Mortgages you took out after October 13, 1987, other than to buy, build, or improve your home (called home equity debt), but only if throughout 2005 these mortgages totaled $100,000 or less ($50,000 or less if married filing separately) and totaled no more than the fair market value of your home reduced by (1) and (2).

TaxSaver

The benefits of home equity loans. Many taxpayers are taking home equity loans as a means of paying off their credit card balances, automobile loans, and other types of consumer expenditures. There are two major benefits of home equity borrowing:

1. Interest on up to $100,000 of home equity loans ($50,000 if married filing separately) is tax deductible for federal income tax purposes, whereas personal interest is not.
2. Home equity loans are less expensive than other types of credit. For example, the rate for home equity loans may be 7% or less. In comparison, the interest rates for credit cards and unsecured personal loans can exceed 18%.

Although home equity loans present several benefits, you should remember that if you are unable to pay off the loan, your house is in jeopardy—not the items that you purchased with the borrowed funds. In addition, not all home equity debt interest is deductible for alternative minimum tax purposes.

The dollar limits for the second and third categories apply to the combined mortgages on your main home and second home.

Explanation
According to the IRS, the fair market value of your home cannot be less than the adjusted purchase price on the last day of the taxable year.

Example
John Joyce purchases a home in August 2005 for $150,000. He makes improvements costing $10,000 to the home during 2005, but these improvements add only $5,000 to the value of the home.

Although the value of the home at the end of 2005 is only $155,000, John is allowed to use $160,000, the cost of the home plus improvements, as the fair market value.

TaxSaver

If your mortgage is above the limit. If part of your mortgage is in excess of the qualified mortgage limitation and you have investments that produce taxable income, you could sell some of your investments and use the proceeds to reduce your mortgage principal in order to meet the quali-

fied mortgage limitation. You could then re-borrow the funds and trace them to the purchase of new investments. Interest expense on the newly invested loan proceeds remains fully deductible, subject to the investment income limitations discussed later in this chapter. Remember to consider transaction costs of switching investments and the "wash sale" rule discussed in Chapter 15, *Sale of Property.* For additional information, consult your tax advisor.

See *Part II* of Publication 936 for more detailed definitions of grandfathered, home acquisition, and home equity debt.

Explanation
A second home may also be a qualified residence. A second home may be one that you do not occupy, a home that you occupy part of the year, or a home that you rent out. If the home is rented out, it is subject to the use requirements relating to vacation homes. It qualifies as your home only if you used it more than the greater of:

1. 14 days, or
2. 10% of the number of days during the year that it was rented at a fair rental or held out for sale.

If a dwelling is not rented at any time during the year, it may be treated as a qualified residence, even if it is not used by you. For this purpose, the IRS states that "rented" includes holding the residence out for rental or for resale.

Example
Mary owns a vacation home in northern Michigan. Because of business pressures, she is unable to use the home in 2004 or 2005 and lists the home for sale on November 1, 2005.

The house qualifies as a residence in 2004. It is not considered her residence in 2005, because Mary did not use the house for more than the greater of 14 days or 10% of the number of days it was held out for sale (10% × 61 days = 6 days).

TaxPlanner

If, in the above example, members of Mary's family use the home for 15 days in 2005, she will be considered to have used it for the same period of time and the home will be considered her residence. Members of Mary's family include her brothers or sisters, husband, children and grandchildren, and parents or grandparents.

TaxPlanner

If you own more than two homes, you may not deduct interest on the mortgages secured by more than two of these homes during any one year as home mortgage interest.

You must include your main residence as one of the homes. You may choose any one of your other homes as a qualified residence and may change this choice for each tax year.

However, you cannot choose to treat one home as a second residence for part of a year and another home as a second residence for the remainder of the year if both of these homes were owned by you during the entire year and neither home was your main residence during that year.

You can use Figure 25-A to check whether your home mortgage interest is fully deductible.

Figure 25-A. **Is My Home Mortgage Interest Fully Deductible?**

(Instructions: Include balances of ALL mortgages secured by your main home and second home.

[1]You must itemize deductions on Schedule A (Form 1040) and be legally liable for the loan. The loan must be a secured debt on a qualified home. See *Home Mortgage Interest.*

[2]If all mortgages on your main or second home exceed the home's fair market value, a lower limit may apply. See *Home equity debt limit* under *Home Equity Debt* in *Part II* of Publication 936.

[3]Amounts over the $1,000,000 limit ($500,000 if married filing separately) qualify as home equity debt if they are not more than the total home equity debt limit. See Publication 936 for more information about grandfathered debt, home acquisition debt, and home equity debt.

[4]See Table 25-1 for where to deduct other types of interest payments.

Limits on deduction. You cannot fully deduct interest on a mortgage that does not fit into any of the three categories listed above. If this applies to you, see *Part II* of Publication 936 to figure the amount of interest you can deduct.

Special Situations

This section describes certain items that can be included as home mortgage interest and others that cannot. It also describes certain special situations that may affect your deduction.

Late payment charge on mortgage payment. You can deduct as home mortgage interest a late payment charge if it was not for a specific service performed in connection with your mortgage loan.

Explanation

The Tax Court in one case broadly interpreted the phrase *specific services* and ruled that a taxpayer was not allowed to deduct late charges on a home mortgage loan as mortgage interest. The Court determined in that case that the late charges related to the specific service of collecting the late payment. Furthermore, the formula used in calculating the late charge did not resemble standard interest computations, because the late charge was the same whether the payment was 1 day or 1 year late.

Mortgage prepayment penalty. If you pay off your home mortgage early, you may have to pay a penalty. You can deduct that penalty as home mortgage interest provided the penalty is not for a specific service performed or cost incurred in connection with your mortgage loan.

Sale of home. If you sell your home, you can deduct your home mortgage interest (subject to any limits that apply) paid up to, but not including, the date of sale.

Example. John and Peggy Harris sold their home on May 7. Through April 30, they made home mortgage interest payments of $1,220. The settlement sheet for the sale of the home showed $50 interest for the 6-day period in May up to, but not including, the date of sale. Their mortgage interest deduction is $1,270 ($1,220 + $50).

Prepaid interest. If you pay interest in advance for a period that goes beyond the end of the tax year, you must spread this interest over the tax years to which it applies. You can deduct in each year only the interest that qualifies as home mortgage interest for that year. However, see *Points,* later.

Example 1

When Dan borrowed $10,000 on a mortgage on November 1, 2005, he prepaid 16 months of interest ($1,600). The $1,600 of prepaid interest is considered to be paid, and therefore deductible, equally over the 16-month period ($100 per month). Dan should deduct $200 in 2005, $1,200 in 2006, and $200 in 2007.

Example 2

On March 27, Eric signed a mortgage note for $1,200 and agreed to repay it in 12 equal installments, beginning on April 28. Interest of $96 was subtracted from the face value of the note, and Eric received $1,104. If Eric uses the cash method of accounting, as most people do, interest is considered to be paid in 12 installments of $8 each ($96 ÷ 12). Eric may deduct $72 ($8 × 9 months) for the first year and $24 ($8 × 3 months) in the following year.

No deduction is permitted for the interest if payment for an installment period is not made. Therefore, if Eric were to miss two installment payments in the first year, he could deduct only $56 ($8 × 7 months).

Mortgage interest credit. You may be able to claim a mortgage interest credit if you were issued a mortgage credit certificate (MCC) by a state or local government. Figure the credit on Form 8396, Mortgage Interest Credit. If you take this credit, you must reduce your mortgage interest deduction by the amount of the credit.

For more information on the credit, see chapter 39.

Ministers' and military housing allowance. If you are a minister or a member of the uniformed services and receive a housing allowance that is not taxable, you can still deduct your home mortgage interest.

Mortgage assistance payments. If you qualify for mortgage assistance payments for lower-income families under section 235 of the National Housing Act, part or all of the interest on your mortgage may be paid for you. You cannot deduct the interest that is paid for you.

No other effect on taxes. Do not include these mortgage assistance payments in your income. Also, do not use these payments to reduce other deductions, such as real estate taxes.

Divorced or separated individuals. If a divorce or separation agreement requires you or your spouse or former spouse to pay home mortgage interest on a home owned by both of you, the payment of interest may be alimony. See the discussion of *Payments for jointly-owned home* in chapter 20.

Redeemable ground rent. If you make annual or periodic rental payments on a redeemable ground rent, you can deduct them as mortgage interest.

Payments made to end the lease and to buy the lessor's entire interest in the land are not ground rents. You cannot deduct them. For more information, see Publication 936.

Nonredeemable ground rent. Payments on a nonredeemable ground rent are not mortgage interest. You can deduct them as rent if they are a business expense or if they are for rental property.

Rental payments. If you live in a house before final settlement on the purchase, any payments you make for that period are rent and not interest. This is true even if the settlement papers call them interest. You cannot deduct these payments as home mortgage interest.

Mortgage proceeds invested in tax-exempt securities. You cannot deduct the home mortgage interest on grandfathered debt or home equity debt if you used the proceeds of the mortgage to buy securities or certificates that produce tax-free income. "Grandfathered debt" and "home equity debt" are defined earlier under *Amount Deductible.*

Refunds of interest. If you receive a refund of interest in the same tax year you paid it, you must reduce your interest expense by the amount refunded to you. If you receive a refund of interest you deducted in an earlier year, you generally must include the refund in income in the year you receive it. However, you need to include it only up to the amount of the deduction that reduced your tax in the earlier year. This is true whether the interest overcharge was refunded to you or was used to reduce the outstanding principal on your mortgage.

If you received a refund of interest you overpaid in an earlier year, you generally will receive a Form 1098, Mortgage Interest Statement, showing the refund in box 3. For information about Form 1098, see *Mortgage Interest Statement,* later.

For more information on how to treat refunds of interest deducted in earlier years, see *Recoveries* in chapter 13.

Example

During 2005, Andrea paid $2,000 in interest on her adjustable rate mortgage. On December 31, 2005, a $200 interest refund for 2005 was credited to her account. Andrea's net deduction for interest on her loans is $1,800 ($2,000 paid minus $200 refunded).

Refunds of interest paid must be included in income if they represent a return of interest deducted in a prior year. If you receive a refund in 2005 for interest paid in 2004 and *did not itemize* your deductions in 2004, the refund should *not be included* in your 2005 income. If you receive the refund in 2005 and you *did itemize* your deductions in 2004, the refund is generally *included* in your 2005 income to the extent the deduction reduced your tax in 2004.

Points

The term "points" is used to describe certain charges paid, or treated as paid, by a borrower to obtain a home mortgage. Points may also be called loan origination fees, maximum loan charges, loan discount, or discount points.

A borrower is treated as paying any points that a home seller pays for the borrower's mortgage. See *Points paid by the seller,* later.

Explanation

Usually, for federally regulated mortgage loans, points will be designated on the Uniform Settlement Statement (also known as Form HUD-1) as "loan origination fee," "loan discount," "discount points," or simply "points."

General rule. You generally cannot deduct the full amount of points in the year paid. Because they are prepaid interest, you generally deduct them ratably over the life (term) of the mortgage.

However, see *Deduction allowed in year paid,* and *Home improvement loan.*

Explanation

Deducting points. Generally, taxpayers are prohibited from deducting prepaid interest in the year of payment. Rather, they must capitalize the prepaid interest and deduct it ratably over the life of the loan.

However, as discussed below, an exception exists for taxpayers who buy, build, or improve their principal residences and pay "points" in order to obtain a lower interest rate on their loans. The term "points" is a fee paid by the borrower that is like prepaid interest. To be deductible, the charge must represent interest paid for the use of money and must be *paid before* the time for which it represents a charge for the use of the money. Furthermore, the home must be the taxpayer's principal residence. You should note that the IRS has ruled that you can elect *not* to currently deduct points and to amortize them over the life of a loan. Such an election may be advantageous if the deduction does not benefit you in the year of purchase (e.g., you're not itemizing your deductions).

Deduction allowed in year paid. You can fully deduct points in the year paid if you meet all the following tests. (You can use Figure 25-B as a quick guide to see whether your points are fully deductible in the year paid.)

1. Your loan is secured by your main home. (Your main home is the one you live in most of the time.)
2. Paying points is an established business practice in the area where the loan was made.
3. The points paid were not more than the points generally charged in that area.
4. You use the cash method of accounting. This means you report income in the year you receive it and deduct expenses in the year you pay them. (If you want more information about this method, see *Accounting Methods* in chapter 1.)
5. The points were not paid in place of amounts that ordinarily are stated separately on the settlement statement, such as appraisal fees, inspection fees, title fees, attorney fees, and property taxes.
6. The funds you provided at or before closing, plus any points the seller paid, were at least as much as the points charged. The funds you provided do not have to have been applied to the points. They can include a down payment, an escrow deposit, earnest money, and other funds you paid at or before closing for any purpose. You cannot have borrowed these funds from your lender or mortgage broker.
7. You use your loan to buy or build your main home.
8. The points were computed as a percentage of the principal amount of the mortgage.
9. The amount is clearly shown on the settlement statement (such as the Uniform Settlement Statement, Form HUD-1) as points charged for the mortgage. The points may be shown as paid from either your funds or the seller's.

Note. If you meet all of these tests, you can choose to either fully deduct the points in the year paid, or deduct them over the life of the loan.

Home improvement loan. You can also fully deduct in the year paid points paid on a loan to improve your main home, if tests (1) through (6) are met.

Caution. Second home. *You cannot fully deduct in the year paid points you pay on loans secured by your second home. You can deduct these points only over the life of the loan.*

Refinancing. Generally, points you pay to refinance a mortgage are not deductible in full in the year you pay them. This is true even if the new mortgage is secured by your main home.

However, if you use part of the refinanced mortgage proceeds to improve your main home and you meet the first six tests listed under *Deduction allowed in year paid,* earlier, you can fully deduct the part of the points related to the improvement in the year you paid them with your own funds. You can deduct the rest of the points over the life of the loan.

Example 1. In 1992, Bill Fields got a mortgage to buy a home. In 2005, Bill refinanced that mortgage with a 15-year $100,000 mortgage loan. The mortgage is secured by his home. To get the new loan, he had to pay three points ($3,000). Two points ($2,000) were for prepaid interest, and one point ($1,000) was charged for services, in place of amounts that ordinarily are stated separately on the settlement statement. Bill paid the points out of his private funds, rather than out of the proceeds of the new loan. The payment of points is an established practice in the area, and the points charged are not more than the amount generally charged there. Bill's first payment on the new loan was due July 1. He made six payments on the loan in 2005 and is a cash basis taxpayer.

Bill used the funds from the new mortgage to repay his existing mortgage. Although the new mortgage loan was for Bill's continued ownership of his main home, it was not for the purchase or improvement of that home. He cannot deduct all of the points in 2005. He can deduct two points ($2,000) ratably over the life of the loan. He deducts $67 [($2,000 ÷ 180 months) × 6 payments] of the points in 2005. The other point ($1,000) was a fee for services and is not deductible.

Example 2. The facts are the same as in *Example 1,* except that Bill used $25,000 of the loan proceeds to improve his home and $75,000 to repay his existing mortgage. Bill deducts 25% ($25,000 ÷ $100,000) of the points ($2,000) in 2005. His deduction is $500 ($2,000 × 25%).

Bill also deducts the ratable part of the remaining $1,500 ($2,000 − $500) that must be spread over the life of the loan. This is $50 [($1,500 ÷ 180 months) × 6 payments] in 2005. The total amount Bill deducts in 2005 is $550 ($500 + $50).

Explanation

According to the IRS, points paid when you refinance an existing mortgage must be deducted ratably over the life of the new loan. They are not fully deductible in the year in which they were paid because they were not paid in connection with the improvement or purchase of a home, even though the original loan met the requirements for deductibility. Points paid on a refinanced mortgage are fully deductible in the year paid to the extent the additional loan proceeds are used for home improvement and the points are paid with funds you provide. If only a portion of the loan proceeds is used for home improvement, then only a corresponding portion of the points is fully deductible in the year paid. The balance of the points is deducted ratably over the life of the loan.

However, an Eighth Circuit Court decision allowed a full immediate deduction for points paid by taxpayers in obtaining a permanent mortgage on their home, the proceeds of which were used to pay off a short-term, 3-year mortgage with a balloon payment and a recently obtained home improvement loan secured by a second mortgage. The court indicated that the permanent mortgage obtained was sufficiently "in connection with" the original purchase of the home.

TaxAlert

The IRS has disagreed with this court decision and still argues that points paid for a loan to refinance a mort-

Figure 25-B. **Are My Points Fully Deductible This Year?**

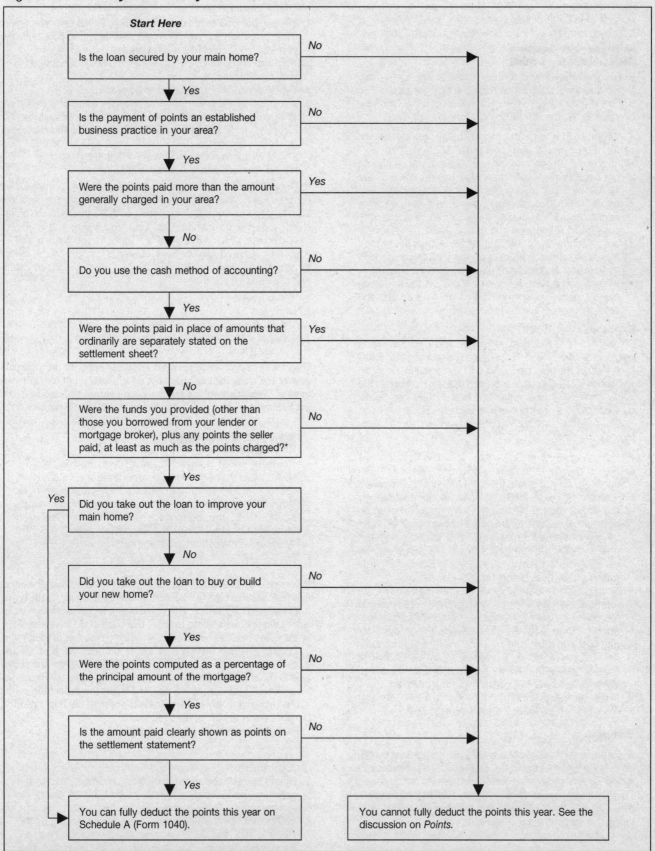

*The funds you provided do not have to have been applied to the points. They can include a down payment, an escrow deposit, earnest money, and other funds you paid at or before closing for any purpose.

gage on a taxpayer's principal residence are not deductible. Therefore, the IRS will not follow the decision outside of the Eighth Circuit (Arkansas, Iowa, Minnesota, Missouri, Nebraska, North Dakota, and South Dakota).

TaxPlanner

Before you refinance. Before you refinance your home mortgage, you should consider both tax and financial factors.

For the interest to remain fully deductible, the following tax-related factors should be considered:

- Whether the term of the mortgage should be extended beyond the original term.
- In general, the total of all mortgage balances should not exceed the lesser of the fair market value of the house or $1.1 million ($1 million acquisition debt and $100,000 home equity debt) or, if married filing separately, $550,000. However, see previous discussion of refinanced grandfather debt if you have a pre–October 14, 1987, mortgage. Other limitations may also apply. See limits on the deduction of mortgage interest, discussed previously in this chapter.
- When a loan is either refinanced or paid off, the remaining balance points being amortized on the old loan (the one being refinanced) can be taken as an itemized deduction.

Example

On January 1, 2000, Tom refinanced and paid $3,000 in points for a 15-year loan. He was taking a deduction for $200 each year for the points paid ($3,000 ÷ 15 years). He again refinanced in 2005 at a lower interest rate. The balance of the points from the original refinanced loan $2,000 can be deducted in 2005 since the loan was paid off.

The financial factors you may also want to consider include the following:

- If there are refinancing costs, you should determine how many months it would take to recoup these costs. To do so, divide the total amount of estimated refinancing costs (deductible and nondeductible) by the anticipated reduction in your monthly mortgage payment (i.e., the difference between your existing monthly payment of principal and interest and the new monthly payment). If you will recover your refinancing costs before you sell your home, then refinancing may be a smart thing to do.
- You should evaluate whether the current value of the after-tax savings from a lower interest rate exceeds the up-front cost of refinancing. Specifically, consider such factors as taxes, present value, and opportunity costs (lost income on funds used to pay refinancing charges). Software programs can assist you in evaluating whether it may be beneficial to refinance. You may also want to consult your tax advisor.
- If refinancing extends the life of your payments you also need to evaluate the total interest cost.

Example

If you are in your 10th year of a 30-year mortgage, you may be paying more interest in the long term if you refinance to a new 30-year mortgage, even if the interest rate is lower. Typically interest amounts are higher in the beginning years of a loan and more of your payment goes toward interest rather than principal in the beginning years.

Deduction allowed ratably. If you do not meet the tests above under *Deduction allowed in year paid,* the loan is not a home improvement loan, or you choose not to deduct your points in full in the year paid, you can deduct the points ratably (equally) over the life of the loan if you meet all the following tests.

1. You use the cash method of accounting. This means you report income in the year you receive it and deduct expenses in the year you pay them. Most individuals use this method.
2. Your loan is secured by a home. (The home does not need to be your main home.)
3. Your loan period is not more than 30 years.
4. If your loan period is more than 10 years, the terms of your loan are same as other loans offered in your area for the same or longer period.
5. Either your loan amount is $250,000 or less, or the number of points is not more than:
   a. 4, if your loan period is 15 years or less, or
   b. 6, if your loan period is more than 15 years.

Original issue discount. If you do not qualify to either deduct the points in the year paid or deduct them ratably over the life of the loan, or if you choose not to use either of these methods, the points reduce the issue price of the loan. This reduction results in original issue discount, which is discussed in chapter 5 of Publication 535.

Amounts charged for services. Amounts charged by the lender for specific services connected to the loan are not interest. Examples of these charges are:

- Appraisal fees,
- Notary fees,
- Preparation costs for the mortgage note or deed of trust,
- Mortgage insurance premiums, and
- VA funding fees.

You cannot deduct these amounts as points either in the year paid or over the life of the mortgage. For information about the tax treatment of these amounts and other settlement fees and closing costs, get Publication 530, Tax Information for First-Time Homeowners.

TaxPlanner

Pointers about points. To get a deduction for points, make sure that the loan document clearly establishes that the points were not paid for any specific services that the lender performed or agreed to perform in connection with the borrower's account under the loan contract. Charges should be separately itemized on the financing and settlement statements.

Points paid by the seller. The term "points" includes loan placement fees that the seller pays to the lender to arrange financing for the buyer.

Treatment by seller. The seller cannot deduct these fees as interest. But they are a selling expense that reduces the amount realized by the seller. See chapter 16 for information on the sale of your home.

Treatment by buyer. The buyer reduces the basis of the home by the amount of the seller-paid points and treats the points as if he or she had paid them. If all the tests under *Deduction allowed in year paid,* earlier, are met, the buyer can deduct the points in the year paid. If any of those tests is not met, the buyer deducts the points over the life of the loan.

For information about basis, see chapter 14.

Explanation

Points paid by the seller, including those charged to the seller, in connection with the buyer's home mortgage loan are considered points paid by the buyer. Therefore, points paid by the seller may be fully deductible by the buyer in the year paid (see discussion of *Points* above). As a reminder, your basis in the home needs to be reduced by the amount of seller-paid points.

Funds provided are less than points. If you meet all the tests in *Deduction allowed in year paid,* earlier, except that the funds you provided were less than the points charged to you (test 6), you can deduct the points in the year paid, up to the amount of funds you provided. In addition, you can deduct any points paid by the seller.

Example 1. When you took out a $100,000 mortgage loan to buy your home in December, you were charged one point ($1,000). You meet all the tests for deducting points in the year paid, except the only funds you provided were a $750 down payment. Of the $1,000 charged for points, you can deduct $750 in the year paid. You spread the remaining $250 over the life of the mortgage.

Example 2. The facts are the same as in *Example 1,* except that the person who sold you your home also paid one point ($1,000) to help you get your mortgage. In the year paid, you can deduct $1,750 ($750 of the amount you were charged plus the $1,000 paid by the seller). You spread the remaining $250 over the life of the mortgage. You must reduce the basis of your home by the $1,000 paid by the seller.

Excess points. If you meet all the tests in *Deduction allowed in year paid,* earlier, except that the points paid were more than are generally paid in your area (test 3), you deduct in the year paid only the points that are generally charged. You must spread any additional points over the life of the mortgage.

Mortgage ending early. If you spread your deduction for points over the life of the mortgage, you can deduct any remaining balance in the year the mortgage ends. However, if you refinance the mortgage with the same lender, you cannot deduct any remaining balance of spread points. Instead, deduct the remaining balance over the term of the new loan.

A mortgage may end early due to a prepayment, refinancing, foreclosure, or similar event.

Example. Dan paid $3,000 in points in 1995 that he had to spread out over the 15-year life of the mortgage. He had deducted $2,000 of these points through 2004.

Dan prepaid his mortgage in full in 2005. He can deduct the remaining $1,000 of points in 2005.

Limits on deduction. You cannot fully deduct points on a mortgage unless the mortgage fits into one of the categories listed earlier under *Fully deductible interest.* See Publication 936 for details.

Mortgage Interest Statement

If you paid $600 or more of mortgage interest (including certain points) during the year on any one mortgage, you generally will receive a Form 1098, Mortgage Interest Statement, or a similar statement from the mortgage holder. You will receive the statement if you pay interest to a person (including a financial institution or a cooperative housing corporation) in the course of that person's trade or business. A governmental unit is a person for purposes of furnishing the statement.

The statement for each year should be sent to you by January 31 of the following year. A copy of this form will also be sent to the IRS.

TAXORGANIZER

When you receive Form 1098, the form which lists your mortgage interest and applicable points paid during the year, keep it with your other important tax documents.

Explanation
An individual who "takes back" a mortgage indebtedness when selling a residence is not required to prepare a Form 1098 or otherwise notify the debtor of the amount of interest paid. He or she must include the interest income on his or her tax return as seller-financed mortgage interest income and report the payer's name and amount received.

The statement will show the total interest you paid during the year. If you purchased a main home during the year, it will also show the deductible points paid during the year, including seller-

paid points. However, it should not show any interest that was paid for you by a government agency.

As a general rule, Form 1098 will include only points that you can fully deduct in the year paid. However, certain points not included on Form 1098 also may be deductible, either in the year paid or over the life of the loan. See *Points,* earlier, to determine whether you can deduct points not shown on Form 1098.

Prepaid interest on Form 1098. If you prepaid interest in 2005 that accrued in full by January 15, 2006, this prepaid interest may be included in box 1 of Form 1098. However, you cannot deduct the prepaid amount for January 2006 in 2005. (See *Prepaid interest,* earlier.) You will have to figure the interest that accrued for 2006 and subtract it from the amount in box 1. You will include the interest for January 2006 with the other interest you pay for 2006. See *How To Report,* later.

Refunded interest. If you received a refund of mortgage interest you overpaid in an earlier year, you generally will receive a Form 1098 showing the refund in box 3. See *Refunds of interest,* earlier.

Investment Interest

This section discusses the interest expenses you may be able to deduct as an investor.

If you borrow money to buy property you hold for investment, the interest you pay is investment interest. You can deduct investment interest subject to the limit discussed later. However, you cannot deduct interest you incurred to produce tax-exempt income. Nor can you deduct interest expenses on straddles.

Investment interest does not include any qualified home mortgage interest or any interest taken into account in computing income or loss from a passive activity.

Investment Property

Property held for investment includes property that produces interest, dividends, annuities, or royalties not derived in the ordinary course of a trade or business. It also includes property that produces gain or loss (not derived in the ordinary course of a trade or business) from the sale or trade of property producing these types of income or held for investment (other than an interest in a passive activity). Investment property also includes an interest in a trade or business activity in which you did not materially participate (other than a passive activity).

Partners, shareholders, and beneficiaries. To determine your investment interest, combine your share of investment interest from a partnership, S corporation, estate, or trust with your other investment interest.

Allocation of Interest Expense

If you borrow money for business or personal purposes as well as for investment, you must allocate the debt among those purposes. Only the interest expense on the part of the debt used for investment purposes is treated as investment interest. The allocation is not affected by the use of property that secures the debt.

Limit on Deduction

Generally, your deduction for investment interest expense is limited to the amount of your net investment income.

You can carry over the amount of investment interest that you could not deduct because of this limit to the next tax year. The interest carried over is treated as investment interest paid or accrued in that next year.

You can carry over disallowed investment interest to the next tax year even if it is more than your taxable income in the year the interest was paid or accrued.

Net Investment Income
Determine the amount of your net investment income by subtracting your investment expenses (other than interest expense) from your investment income.

Investment income. This generally includes your gross income from property held for investment (such as interest, dividends, annuities, and royalties). Investment income does not include Alaska Permanent Fund dividends. It also does not include qualified dividends or capital gain distributions unless you choose to include them.

Choosing to include qualified dividends. Investment income generally does not include qualified dividends (discussed in chapter 9). However, you can choose to include all or part of your qualified dividends in investment income.

You make this choice by completing Form 4952, line 4g, according to its instructions.

If you choose to include any amount of your qualified dividends in investment income, you must reduce your qualified dividends that are eligible for the lower capital gains tax rates by the same amount.

Choosing to include net capital gain. Investment income generally does not include net capital gain from disposing of investment property (including capital gain distributions from mutual funds). However, you can choose to include all or part of your net capital gain in investment income.

You make this choice by completing Form 4952, line 4g, according to its instructions.

If you choose to include any amount of your net capital gain in investment income, you must reduce your net capital gain that is eligible for the lower capital gains tax rates by the same amount.

Tip. *Before making either choice, consider the overall effect on your tax liability. Compare your tax if you make one or both of these choices with your tax if you do not.*

Explanation
Qualified dividends will not be treated as "investment income" for purposes of determining the limitation on the deductibility of investment interest expense, unless you elect to treat the dividends as not eligible for the favorable capital gains rates.

TaxPlanner

While it may be possible to borrow in order to acquire dividend-paying stocks, it will be necessary to analyze your entire portfolio to determine if the interest expense deduction will be limited due to insufficient investment income from other sources.

Explanation
A deduction is allowed for interest paid on indebtedness incurred to purchase or hold investment property. Investment property includes any property producing interest, dividends, annuities, royalties, or certain gains.

Example
If you borrow money to purchase both taxable securities and tax-free investments (such as state municipal bonds), the interest income from the tax-free bonds is not taxable. Accordingly, the interest expense paid on the loan allocable to the tax free bonds is not deductible. The interest income from the tax-free bonds, since it is not taxable, does not count as investment income for purposes of calculating the limitation.

Explanation
The amount of investment interest that may be deducted is limited to the amount of investment income less allowable expenses, other than interest, that are directly connected with the production of investment income. Investment income does not include qualified dividends or long-term capital gains unless you make an election to treat them as not eligible for the favorable capital gains rates. The allowable expenses include those expenses that are deducted on

your tax return, after the 2% of adjusted gross income limitation on miscellaneous deductions. (For more information, see Chapter 30, *Miscellaneous Deductions*.)

If the investment interest paid exceeds investment income, the excess may be carried forward to offset investment income in future years.

No deduction is allowed for interest paid on indebtedness incurred to hold obligations that are exempt from federal taxation.

Example 1
In 2004, Lorraine borrows $83,000 to purchase White Company securities. During the same year, she earns $30,000 of net investment income and incurs $10,000 of interest expense on her loan. Lorraine can deduct the $10,000 interest expense as investment interest on Schedule A (Form 1040).

Example 2
George and Lisa Johnson, who file a joint return, have the following income and deductions in 2005:

Salary	$30,000
Interest income from a state municipal bond	$500
Interest income	20,000
Short-term capital gain	5,000
Adjusted gross income	$55,000
Investment advisory fees	$2,000
Investment interest expense	$31,000

Their deduction for investment interest is figured as follows:

Investment income	$25,000
Direct investment expense ($2,000 − 2% of $55,000)	900
Net investment income ($25,000 − $900)	$24,100
Investment interest deduction	$24,100

The $6,900 ($31,000 − $24,100) of investment interest expense that is not allowed as a deduction in 2005 may be carried forward to 2006.

TaxAlert

Net long-term capital gains from the disposition of investment property and qualified dividends are not treated as investment income for purposes of computing the limitation on investment interest deductions. You may, however, elect to include net long-term capital gain and qualified dividend amounts in investment income for this purpose if you also reduce by the same amount the net long-term capital gain and qualified dividends that are eligible for the special maximum capital gains rates. Short-term capital gains may still be included in the computation of investment income. For an additional discussion of reporting gains and losses, see Chapter 17, *Reporting Gains and Losses.*

Explanation
The 2% limitation on miscellaneous deductions applies first to deductions other than investment expenses.

Example
In Example 2 above, if George and Lisa Johnson also had tax preparation fees of $500, the $1,100 (2% limitation) would reduce this amount first. The remainder, $600, would then reduce the investment expense, leaving $1,400 to be subtracted from investment income.

Explanation

Deduct interest on margin accounts on Schedule A (Form 1040) for the year in which you paid it. Interest on these accounts is considered paid when the broker is paid or when the interest becomes available to the broker through your account.

Deduct interest on money borrowed to buy a money market certificate on Schedule A (Form 1040). You must include the total interest you earn on the certificate in your income.

Example

You deposited $5,000 with a bank and borrowed another $5,000 from the same bank to make up the $10,000 minimum deposit required to buy a 6-month money market certificate. The certificate earned $250 at maturity in 2005, but you received only $100, which represents the $250 you earned minus $150 interest charged on your $5,000 loan. The bank gives you a Form 1099-INT, Statement of Recipients of Interest Income, showing the $250 interest you earned. The bank also gives you a statement showing that you paid $150 interest for 2005. You must include the $250 in your income. You may deduct $150 on Schedule A (Form 1040) if you itemize your deductions.

TAXPLANNER

The amount that you forfeit to a bank or a savings institution as a penalty for premature withdrawal of funds from an account is deductible from your **gross income** in figuring your **adjusted gross income**. You need not itemize to get this deduction.

Investment income of child reported on parent's return. Investment income includes the part of your child's interest and dividend income that you choose to report on your return. If the child does not have qualified dividends, Alaska Permanent Fund dividends, or capital gain distributions, this is the amount on line 6 of Form 8814, Parents' Election To Report Child's Interest and Dividends.

Child's qualified dividends. If part of the amount you report is your child's qualified dividends, that part (which is reported on line 9b of Form 1040 or Form 1040A) generally does not count as investment income. However, you can choose to include all or part of it in investment income, as explained under *Choosing to include qualified dividends,* earlier.

Your investment income also includes the amount on Form 8814, line 6, (or, if applicable, the amount figured next under *Child's Alaska Permanent Fund dividends).*

Child's Alaska Permanent Fund dividends. If part of the amount you report is your child's Alaska Permanent Fund dividends, that part does not count as investment income. To figure the amount of your child's income that you can consider your investment income, start with the amount on Form 8814, line 6. Multiply that amount by a percentage that is equal to the Alaska Permanent Fund dividends divided by the total amount of interest and dividend income on Form 8814, lines 1a and 2. Subtract the result from the amount on Form 8814, line 6.

Child's capital gain distributions. If part of the amount you report is your child's capital gain distributions, that part (which is reported on Schedule D, line 13 or Form 1040, line 13) generally does not count as investment income. However, you can choose to include all or part of it in investment income, as explained in *Choosing to include net capital gain,* earlier.

Your investment income also includes the amount on Form 8814, line 6, (or, if applicable, the amount figured under *Child's Alaska Permanent Fund dividends,* earlier).

Investment expenses. Investment expenses include all income-producing expenses (other than interest expense) relating to invest-

ment property that are allowable deductions after applying the 2% limit that applies to miscellaneous itemized deductions. Use the smaller of:

1. The investment expenses included on Schedule A (Form 1040), line 22, or
2. The amount on Schedule A, line 26.

Losses from passive activities. Income or expenses that you used in computing income or loss from a passive activity are not included in determining your investment income or investment expenses (including investment interest expense). See Publication 925, Passive Activity and At-Risk Rules, for information about passive activities.

Form 4952

Use Form 4952, Investment Interest Expense Deduction, to figure your deduction for investment interest.

Exception to use of Form 4952. You do not have to complete Form 4952 or attach it to your return if you meet all of the following tests.

- Your investment interest expense is not more than your investment income from interest and ordinary dividends minus any qualified dividends.
- You have no other deductible investment expenses.
- You have no disallowed investment interest expense from 2004.

If you meet all of these tests, you can deduct all of your investment interest.

More Information

For more information on investment interest, see *Investment Expenses* in chapter 3 of Publication 550.

Items You Cannot Deduct

Some interest payments are not deductible. Certain expenses similar to interest also are not deductible. Nondeductible expenses include the following items.

- Personal interest (discussed later).
- Service charges (however, see *Other Expenses* in chapter 30).
- Annual fees for credit cards.
- Loan fees.
- Credit investigation fees.
- FHA mortgage insurance premiums and VA funding fees.
- Interest to purchase or carry tax-exempt securities.

Explanation

While the general rule is that interest paid on a debt incurred to purchase or carry tax-exempt obligations is not deductible, this does not mean that if you hold tax-exempt obligations, all interest expense deductions are disallowed. The courts have consistently held that there must be a sufficiently direct relationship between the incurring of the debt and the carrying of the tax-exempt obligation before the interest is disallowed. However, if you have significant interest expense and municipal bond income, you may lose your interest deductions.

The IRS has ruled that a direct relationship between debt and the purchase of tax-exempt obligations exists when the debt proceeds are used for, and are directly traceable to, the purchase of tax-exempts. A direct relationship between debt and the carrying of tax-exempt obligations exists when tax-exempts are used as collateral for a loan.

If only part of a debt you have is related to the holding of tax-exempt obligations, only that part of the interest paid is disallowed.

Example

Barry and Tricia borrow $10,000 from a bank and invest $2,500 of the proceeds in tax-exempt obligations.

In this case, 25% ($2,500 × $10,000) of the interest they pay on the loan is not deductible as investment interest.

TAXPLANNER

Don't worry about whether or not you use debt to acquire or carry tax-exempt obligations if your investment in tax-exempts is "insubstantial." The IRS defines "insubstantial" as being less than 2% of the average **adjusted basis** of your portfolio investments and business assets.

Penalties. You cannot deduct fines and penalties paid to a government for violations of law, regardless of their nature.

TAXPLANNER

If you used borrowed funds to pay interest. To get an interest deduction when you use borrowed funds to pay interest, you need to be careful in structuring the transaction. Generally, the IRS says that meeting an interest obligation by giving a new note or increasing the amount due on an old note does *not* constitute payment. A deduction would be allowed only when the renewed note is paid. If, however, you borrow the money to pay the interest from a *different creditor,* the interest deduction would be allowed.

Nevertheless, the Tax Court allowed an interest deduction when the purpose of the second loan was not limited to the payment of interest on the first loan and the taxpayer showed that he could have paid the interest with other funds. You can't be too cautious in this area. Borrow from a second lender whenever possible.

TAXPLANNER

Margin interest. Stockbrokers charge you interest on a margin account—an account in which you place the money you have borrowed from your broker to purchase stocks or bonds. For the interest to be deductible, there must be a subsequent payment to your broker in cash. Alternatively, you may specifically allocate proceeds from dividends, interest, or stock sales to cover the interest. Merely charging the account does not constitute payment.

Personal Interest

Personal interest is not deductible. Personal interest is any interest that is not home mortgage interest, investment interest, business interest, or other deductible interest. It includes the following items.

- Interest on car loans (unless you use the car for business).
- Interest on federal, state, or local income tax.
- Finance charges on credit cards, retail installment contracts, and revolving charge accounts incurred for personal expenses.
- Late payment charges by a public utility.

TAXPLANNER

When you are faced with the necessity of purchasing both a house and a large-ticket consumer item (e.g., a car), you should consider the tax nature of the debt, particularly the value of the deductible interest on ac-quisition debt compared to loans that are repaid with nondeductible interest. Your future plans to purchase consumer items should play an important role in your mortgage and other financing decisions. In addition, if you plan ahead, you can avoid the additional costs of refinancing your mortgage or taking out a home equity loan in order to make your consumer purchases.

Example 1
Suppose you plan to finance the purchase of a car next year. If you take out a longer-term mortgage with lower payments than you might otherwise have done, you can apply the difference to your car payments. This will enable you to reduce the term of your car loan, which most likely will be financed at a higher rate than your mortgage and paid for with nondeductible interest.

Example 2
You are considering purchasing a new house and a new car within a relatively short time period. You may want to decrease your down payment on the house so that there will be extra cash available for a down payment on the car. By making a larger down payment on the car, your nondeductible interest, the interest paid on the car loan, will be less. Conversely, by decreasing your down payment on the house, you gain a tax benefit in the form of higher mortgage interest deductions.

Tip. *You may be able to deduct interest you pay on a qualified student loan. For details, see Publication 970.*

Explanation
Student loan interest deduction. You can claim a deduction for interest paid on qualified education loans that include indebtedness incurred for your benefit or the benefit of your spouse, or any dependent at the time the indebtedness is incurred. Qualified loans also include refinancings or consolidations of the original loans. You can claim this deduction whether or not you itemize your deductions.

The deduction is allowed only for interest paid on a qualified education loan. No deduction is allowed for individuals claimed as dependents on another taxpayer's return for the tax year.

The maximum deduction is $2,500 in 2005.

The deduction is phased out for individual single taxpayers with modified adjusted gross income (AGI) of $50,000–$65,000 and for couples filing jointly with modified AGI of $105,000–$135,000.

TAXSAVER

What loans cannot include in order to qualify. Education loans include loans covering both tuition and room and board. However, loans cannot include educational expenses that are paid through amounts from an employer educational assistance program or from amounts withdrawn from a Coverdell education savings account or qualified tuition programs. It is unclear how students or the IRS will be able to separate these expenses from the total loans received and payments made on those loans.

The U.S. Treasury is authorized to require lenders to report to borrowers the amount that constitutes deductible student loan interest. The government has also devised a method for borrowers to certify to lenders that loan proceeds are being used to pay for qualified educational expenses.

As with the education tax credits, this deduction is another factor to consider in determining whether or not a working student should be claimed as a dependent. Parents with income above the income thresholds cannot claim this deduction.

For further information about claiming the student loan interest deduction and a worksheet, see Chapter 49, *Filling Out Form 1040,* line 33, Student Loan Interest Deduction. Also see student loan interest deduction in Chapter 20, *Alimony.*

Explanation

Interest you pay on loans acquired to purchase life insurance is also personal interest and generally is not deductible under current law.

TaxPlanner

If you have loans outstanding for personal purposes, consider paying off these loans and substituting a different form of indebtedness.

Example

You have a $5,000 indebtedness on your credit card account. The funds were used for various personal purposes, and the interest is not deductible. You also have a $5,000 certificate of deposit (CD) that matures in 2005. Use the $5,000 from the maturity of the CD to pay off the credit card indebtedness. If you wish, you may borrow new funds for investment in a new CD. The interest on the new borrowings will be investment interest. The rules for deducting investment interest expense are more lenient than those for personal interest. Be sure to calculate the amount you would earn after taxes on such a borrowing or investment.

Allocation of Interest

If you use the proceeds of a loan for more than one purpose (for example, personal and business), you must allocate the interest on the loan to each use. However, you do not have to allocate home mortgage interest if it is fully deductible, regardless of how the funds are used.

You allocate interest (other than fully deductible home mortgage interest) on a loan in the same way as the loan itself is allocated. You do this by tracing disbursements of the debt proceeds to specific uses. For details on how to do this, see chapter 5 of Publication 535.

Explanation

There are five types of interest expense, each of which has different limitations on deductibility:

1. Personal interest is not deductible (except for a limited amount of student loan interest described earlier in this chapter). Personal interest generally includes interest on credit card debts and on automobile loans. If you have to incur debt, try to make the debt related to either trade or business interest, investment interest, passive activity interest, or qualified residence interest.
2. Trade or business interest is fully deductible. Generally, it is interest on debt that relates to your trade or business. However, trade or business interest is *not* deductible if it is in connection with the trade or business of performing services as an employee.
3. Investment interest deductions may be limited because the deduction cannot exceed your net investment income for the taxable year. Any excess investment interest that is not deductible in the taxable year may be deducted in following years.
4. Passive activity interest is interest that is used to offset passive activity income. Generally, a passive activity is any interest in a real estate or other activity in which you do not materially participate. For tax purposes, you are considered a material participant if you are involved in the operations of the activity on a regular, continuous, and substantial basis. For additional discussion, see Chapter 13, *Other Income.*
5. Interest on a debt secured by a qualified residence is deductible within the limitations discussed earlier in this chapter.

TaxSaver

When interest on debt used for investment exceeds investment income, the remaining investment interest may be deducted if it is qualified residence interest.

Example

In 2005, you purchase corporate bonds for $200,000, using a 6.0% home equity loan. Your investment income is $5,000.

Interest on your home equity loan	$12,000
Interest on portion of loan up to $100,000	$6,000
Balance investment interest expense	$6,000
Deductible investment interest equal to investment income	$5,000
Investment interest expense carryover to 2005	$1,000

TaxSaver

Interest on debt used for a passive activity is subject to the same deduction rules as other passive activity expenses.

Example 1

Phil borrowed money to purchase a one-fourth interest in a partnership that manages an apartment building. In 2005, Phil paid $16,000 interest on the loan. His share of income and expenses was $60,000 and $40,000, respectively. Phil's passive income is $4,000 ($60,000 − $40,000 − $16,000). If his share of the partnership's expenses had been $50,000 instead of $40,000, Phil's $16,000 in interest expense would have resulted in a passive loss of $6,000 ($60,000 − $50,000 − $16,000). This loss can be carried over to future years in which there is additional passive income or when the investment is sold.

Example 2

Karen Moore has the following income and expenses in 2005:

Wages	$79,000
Interest	$18,000
Short-term capital gain from sale of stock	$2,000
Long-term capital gain taxed at 15%	$1,000
Adjusted gross income (AGI)	$100,000

Investment interest expense	$21,000
Investment fees	$2,500
Unreimbursed employee expenses	$1,000

Karen's total miscellaneous itemized deductions are $3,500 ($2,500 + $1,000). After considering the 2% floor limitation, her allowable miscellaneous itemized deductions are $1,500 [$3,500 − (2% × $100,000 AGI)]. Therefore, Karen's net investment income is $18,500 [($18,000 + $2,000) − $1,500]. Because the long-term capital gain is taxed at 15%, it is not considered investment income. Karen could elect to treat the gain as ordinary income and would then be allowed to treat the $1,000 as investment income. Note that, in computing the allowable deductions, the noninvestment expenses were disallowed *before* the investment expenses.

Explanation
The proceeds of loans, other than qualified mortgage loans, which were used for mixed purposes, must be allocated to each applicable category.

Example
Joan borrows $100,000 on September 1, 2005, at an interest rate of 12% and deposits the funds in one checking account. Joan uses the money to purchase investment securities ($30,000 on September 1), a personal automobile ($30,000 on October 1), and equipment for her business ($40,000 on November 1). Joan pays interest of $1,000 at the end of each month.

Under the allocation rules, the interest on the loan is considered investment interest unless the proceeds are traceable to other purposes. The allocation is made as follows:

	Investment interest		Personal interest		Business interest	
September	100%	$1,000	—		—	
October	70%	700	30%	$300	—	
November	30%	300	30%	300	40%	$400
December	30%	300	30%	300	40%	400
Total		$2,300		$900		$800

When repayments of the debt are made, the repayment amounts are allocated first to nondeductible personal expenditures, then to investment and passive activity expenditures, and then to business expenditures.

TAXSAVER

The accounting for interest expense on loans used for mixed purposes is extremely complex.

To simplify your tax records, establish separate loan and bank accounts for each category of expenditure.

TAXSAVER

Interest on a qualified mortgage loan is not required to be allocated and is fully deductible when paid.

Although borrowing against your residence may ensure deductibility of the interest expense, the residence serves as collateral on the loan and may be foreclosed in the event of default.

As a reminder, interest paid on a home equity loan where the proceeds are not used to buy, build, or improve your home is not deductible under the Alternative Minimum Tax rules.

Table 25-1.   Where To Deduct Your Interest Expense

IF you have ...	THEN deduct it on ...	AND for more information go to ...
Deductible student loan interest	Form 1040, line 33 or Form 1040A, line 18	Publication 970
Deductible home mortgage interest and points reported on Form 1098	Schedule A (Form 1040), line 10	Publication 936
Deductible home mortgage interest *not* reported on Form 1098	Schedule A (Form 1040), line 11	Publication 936
Deductible points *not* reported on Form 1098	Schedule A (Form 1040), line 12	Publication 936
Deductible investment interest (other than interest incurred to produce rents or royalties)	Schedule A (Form 1040), line 13	Publication 550
Deductible business interest (non-farm)	Schedule C or C-EZ (Form 1040)	Publication 535
Deductible farm business interest	Schedule F (Form 1040)	Publications 225 and 535
Deductible interest incurred to produce rents or royalties	Schedule E (Form 1040)	Publications 527 and 535
Personal interest	Not Deductible	

How To Report

You must file Form 1040 to deduct any home mortgage interest expense on your tax return. Where you deduct your interest expense generally depends on how you use the loan proceeds. See Table 25-1 for a summary of where to deduct your interest expense.

Home mortgage interest and points. Deduct the home mortgage interest and points reported to you on Form 1098 on Schedule A (Form 1040), line 10. If you paid more deductible interest to the financial institution than the amount shown on Form 1098, show the larger deductible amount on line 10. Attach a statement explaining the difference and print "See attached" next to line 10.

Deduct home mortgage interest that was not reported to you on Form 1098 on Schedule A (Form 1040), line 11. If you paid home mortgage interest to the person from whom you bought your home, show that person's name, address, and taxpayer identification number (TIN) on the dotted lines next to line 11. The seller must give you this number and you must give the seller your TIN. A Form W-9 can be used for this purpose. Failure to meet any of these requirements may result in a $50 penalty for each failure. The TIN can be either a social security number, an individual taxpayer identification number (issued by the Internal Revenue Service), or an employer identification number. See *Social Security Number* in chapter 1 for more information about TINs.

TaxAlert

Seller-financed mortgages. If you pay interest on a seller-financed mortgage, you are required to include the following information on line 11 of Schedule A (Form 1040):

- The seller's Social Security number or identification number
- The seller's name and address

You must also provide the seller with your Social Security or identification number. Obviously, the best time to exchange this information is at the closing. However, this rule also applies to prior agreements. If you do not have the seller's identification number, or have not provided the seller with your Social Security number, you should meet the requirements as soon as possible to reduce the potential for penalties.

If you can take a deduction for points that were not reported to you on Form 1098, deduct those points on Schedule A (Form 1040), line 12.

More than one borrower. If you and at least one other person (other than your spouse if you file a joint return) were liable for and paid interest on a mortgage that was for your home, and the other person received a Form 1098 showing the interest that was paid during the year, attach a statement to your return explaining this. Show how much of the interest each of you paid, and give the name and address of the person who received the form. Deduct your share of the interest on Schedule A (Form 1040), line 11, and print "See attached" next to the line.

If you are the payer of record on a mortgage on which there are other borrowers entitled to a deduction for the interest shown on the Form 1098 you received, deduct only your share of the interest on Schedule A (Form 1040), line 10. You should let each of the other borrowers know what his or her share is.

Mortgage proceeds used for business or investment. If your home mortgage interest deduction is limited but all or part of the mortgage proceeds were used for business, investment, or other deductible activities, see Table 25-1. It shows where to deduct the part of your excess interest that is for those activities.

Investment interest. Deduct investment interest, subject to certain limits discussed in Publication 550, on Schedule A (Form 1040), line 13.

Amortization of bond premium. There are various ways to treat the premium you pay to buy taxable bonds. See *Bond Premium Amortization* in Publication 550.

TaxSaver

Premiums on taxable bonds. There are various ways to treat the premium you pay to buy taxable bonds. You may deduct amortizable bond premiums directly from interest income. This could be beneficial whether or not you itemize your deductions.

Explanation

Premiums on tax-exempt bonds. You must amortize the premium and reduce the basis of tax-exempt bonds. However, you may not deduct the amortized premium. See Publication 535, *Business Expenses*.

Market discounts. You may be able to deduct only some of the interest expense incurred to acquire or carry marketable bonds with market discounts. For debt obligations issued after July 18, 1984, the interest expense deduction will be limited to the sum of:

1. Interest income from marketable bonds
2. The interest expense in excess of interest income in (1) and accrued market discount

The disallowed interest expense is deferred until the bond is sold or matures and is deducted then. The interest limitation does not apply to tax-exempt obligations purchased before May 1, 1993, U.S. savings bonds, obligations with a maturity of 1 year or less, and certain installment obligations.

Example

Sam acquires a $100,000, 9% interest-bearing bond for $90,000 on January 2, 2005. The bond was originally issued at face value in 1998. It matures in 2015, 10 years after Sam purchased it. Sam borrowed money to acquire the bond. In 2005, Sam paid $10,200 in interest on the debt. The allowable interest deduction for the year is figured as follows:

(a)	Interest expense	$10,200
(b)	Interest income ($100,000 × 9%)	(9,000)
(c)	Net interest expense	$1,200
(d)	Accrued market discount ($10,000 ÷ 10 yrs.)	(1,000)
(e)	Net interest expense in excess of accrued market discount	$200

Total allowable interest expense is $9,200 [(b) + (e)]. The remaining $1,000 will be allowed as a deduction in the year in which the bond matures or is sold.

Sam may elect to include the accrued market discount in income for the tax years to which it's attributable, thus allowing all interest expense to be deductible. If Sam makes this election, it will apply to all market discount bonds he acquires.

See the discussion in this chapter regarding limitations on the deduction of investment interest.

Income-producing rental or royalty interest. Deduct interest on a loan for income-producing rental or royalty property that is not used in your business in Part I of Schedule E (Form 1040).

Example. You rent out part of your home and borrow money to make repairs. You can deduct only the interest payment for the rented part in Part I of Schedule E (Form 1040). Deduct the rest of the interest payment on Schedule A (Form 1040) if it is deductible home mortgage interest.

26

Contributions

Note: The 2004 IRS Publication 17 (Your Federal Income Tax) has been updated by Ernst & Young LLP for 2005. Dates and dollar amounts shown are for 2005. Gray type is used to indicate where IRS text has been updated or intentionally omitted. Unrevised IRS text is shown in black type.

Introduction

Americans give billions of dollars to charity each year. One explanation for that generosity may be that the federal government encourages charitable giving. It has long been the policy of the government to allow individuals tax **deductions** *for charitable contributions they make. In effect, Uncle Sam is contributing part of every dollar you give to charity.*

Even so, there are lots of rules governing charitable contributions, and it's important that you know them. This chapter tells you how to maximize your allowable

charitable deductions and minimize your taxes. You'll learn why, for example, you might want to consider giving shares of stock instead of cash to your favorite charity. Just as important, the chapter tells you how to document your contributions.

Your 2005 itemized deductions may be subject to certain limitations if your adjusted gross income exceeds $145,950 ($72,975 if married filing separately).

For more information on this subject see Chapter 31, Limit on Itemized Deductions.

TaxAlert

See the special section in the front of this guide for information on tax changes relating to Hurricane Katrina.

What's New

Donations of vehicles. As a result of the American Jobs Creation Act of 2004, your deduction for contributions of cars, boats, and airplanes to charity may be substantially limited. Under the new law, your deduction will depend on what the charity does with the vehicle. If it sells the vehicle, your deduction will be limited to the sales proceeds, regardless of what you thought the fair market value might be. The new law also imposes new detailed recordkeeping and receipt requirements for this type of contribution. For more details see the Tax Alert below on Donations of Vehicles—NEW REQUIREMENTS.

Tsunami relief. Donations that you made in January of 2005 for tsunami relief could have been deducted on your 2004 tax return. If you deducted those contributions in 2004 you cannot deduct them again in 2005. If you did not deduct them in 2004, you can deduct them on your 2005 tax return.

Reminders

Disaster relief. You can deduct contributions earmarked for flood relief, hurricane relief, or other disaster relief to a qualified organization (defined later under *Organizations That Qualify To Receive Deductible Contributions*). However, you cannot deduct contributions earmarked for relief of a particular individual or family.

Written acknowledgment required. You can claim a deduction for a contribution of $250 or more only if you have a written acknowledgment of your contribution from the qualified organization or if you have certain payroll deduction records. For more information, see *Records To Keep,* later in this chapter.

Payment partly for goods or services. A qualified organization must give you a written statement if you make a payment that is more than $75 and is partly a contribution and partly for goods or services. The statement must tell you that you can deduct only the amount of your payment that is more than the value of the goods or services you received. It must also give you a good faith estimate of the value of those goods or services. See *Contributions From Which You Benefit,* later in this chapter, for more information.

Limit on itemized deductions. If your adjusted gross income is more than $145,950 ($72,975 if you are married filing separately), the overall amount of your itemized deductions may be limited. See chapter 31 for more information about this limit.

This chapter explains how to claim a deduction for your charitable contributions. It discusses:

- Organizations that are qualified to receive deductible charitable contributions,
- The types of contributions you can deduct,
- How much you can deduct,
- What records to keep, and
- How to report your charitable contributions.

A charitable contribution is a donation or gift to, or for the use of, a qualified organization. It is voluntary and is made without getting, or expecting to get, anything of equal value.

Form 1040 required. To deduct a charitable contribution, you must file Form 1040 and itemize deductions on Schedule A. The amount of your deduction may be limited if certain rules and limits explained in this chapter apply to you.

Useful Items

You may want to see:

Publications

- [ ] **78** Cumulative List of Organizations
- [ ] **526** Charitable Contributions
- [ ] **561** Determining the Value of Donated Property

Forms (and Instructions)

- [ ] **Schedule A (Form 1040)** Itemized Deductions
- [ ] **8283** Noncash Charitable Contributions

Organizations That Qualify To Receive Deductible Contributions

You can deduct your contributions only if you make them to a qualified organization. To become a qualified organization, most organizations other than churches and governments, as described below, must apply to the IRS.

Tip. *You can ask any organization whether it is a qualified organization, and most will be able to tell you. Or you can check IRS Publication 78, which lists most qualified organizations. You may find Publication 78 in your local library's reference section, or on the internet at* www.irs.gov. *You can also call the IRS Tax Exempt/Government Entities Customer Service at 1-877-829-5500 to find out if an organization is qualified.*

Types of Qualified Organizations

Generally, only the five following types of organizations can be qualified organizations.

1. A community chest, corporation, trust, fund, or foundation organized or created in or under the laws of the United States, any state, the District of Columbia, or any possession of the United States (including Puerto Rico). It must be organized and operated only for one or more of the following purposes.
   a. Religious.
   b. Charitable.
   c. Educational.
   d. Scientific.
   e. Literary.
   f. The prevention of cruelty to children or animals.

   Certain organizations that foster national or international amateur sports competition also qualify.

Examples
Contributions to the following U.S. and political subdivisions have been allowed:

- Contributions to the National Park Foundation
- Money donated to a state by an individual to defray expenses of hosting a governor's conference
- Contributions to a state for a parade incidental to a presidential inauguration

The IRS has ruled that the following are *not deductible* as contributions:

- Payments made to a state hospital for the purpose of reimbursing the state for the care of a person confined in the hospital do not constitute contributions made to a state for exclusively public purposes.
- The amount spent by a tenant for additions or improvements to government-owned housing is not deductible as a charitable contribution. Such amounts represent a nondeductible personal, living, or family expense.

2. War veterans' organizations, including posts, auxiliaries, trusts, or foundations, organized in the United States or any of its possessions.
3. Domestic fraternal societies, orders, and associations operating under the lodge system.

   Note. Your contribution to this type of organization is deductible only if it is to be used solely for charitable, religious, scientific, literary, or educational purposes, or for the prevention of cruelty to children or animals.

4. Certain nonprofit cemetery companies or corporations.

   Note. Your contribution to this type of organization is not deductible if it can be used for the care of a specific lot or mausoleum crypt.

5. The United States or any state, the District of Columbia, a U.S. possession (including Puerto Rico), a political subdivision of a state or U.S. possession, or an Indian tribal government or any of its subdivisions that perform substantial government functions.

   Note. To be deductible, your contribution to this type of organization must be made solely for public purposes.

Examples. Qualified organizations include:

- Churches, a convention or association of churches, temples, synagogues, mosques, and other religious organizations.
- Most nonprofit charitable organizations such as the Red Cross and the United Way.
- Most nonprofit educational organizations, including the Boy and Girl Scouts of America, colleges and universities, museums, and day-care centers if substantially all the child care provided is to enable individuals (the parents) to be gainfully employed and the services are available to the general public. However, if your contribution is a substitute for tuition or other enrollment fee, it is not deductible as a charitable contribution, as explained later under *Contributions You Cannot Deduct*.
- Nonprofit hospitals and medical research organizations.
- Utility company emergency energy programs, if the utility company is an agent for a charitable organization that assists individuals with emergency energy needs.
- Nonprofit volunteer fire companies.
- Public parks and recreation facilities.
- Civil defense organizations.

Certain foreign charitable organizations.

Under income tax treaties with Canada, Israel, and Mexico, you may be able to deduct contributions to certain Canadian, Israeli, or Mexican charitable organizations. Generally, you must have income from sources in that country in order to claim the charitable contribution deduction. For additional information on the deduction of contributions to Canadian charities, see Publication 597, Information on the United States–Canada Income Tax Treaty. If you need more information on how to figure your contribution to Mexican and Israeli charities, see Publication 526.

Table 26-1. **Examples of Charitable Contributions—A Quick Check**

Use the following lists for a quick check of contributions you can or cannot deduct. See the rest of this chapter for more information and additional rules and limits that may apply.

Deductible As Charitable Contributions	Not Deductible As Charitable Contributions
Money or property you give to: • Churches, synagogues, temples, mosques, and other religious organizations • Federal, state, and local governments, if your contribution is solely for public purposes (for example, a gift to reduce the public debt) • Nonprofit schools and hospitals • Public parks and recreation facilities • Salvation Army, Red Cross, CARE, Goodwill Industries, United Way, Boy Scouts, Girl Scouts, Boys and Girls Clubs of America, etc. • War veterans groups Costs you pay for a student living with you, sponsored by a qualified organization Out-of-pocket expenses when you serve a qualified organization as a volunteer	Money or property you give to: • Civic leagues, social and sports clubs, labor unions, and chambers of commerce • Foreign organizations (except certain Canadian, Israeli, and Mexican charities) • Groups that are run for personal profit • Groups whose purpose is to lobby for law changes • Homeowners' associations • Individuals • Political groups or candidates for public office Cost of raffle, bingo, or lottery tickets Dues, fees, or bills paid to country clubs, lodges, fraternal orders, or similar groups Tuition Value of your time or services Value of blood given to a blood bank

Explanation

Any organization can tell you if it is a qualified organization.

Generally, charitable contributions must be made to organizations to be deductible. However, the courts have upheld contributions made to certain individuals on the grounds that the contribution was made to him or her as an agent for the organization. Consider the following cases in which deductions were allowed:

• An individual established a scholarship fund consisting of a personal checking account. Recipients were picked by school principals on the basis of need and scholastic merit. Each check was signed by the donor and made payable jointly to the scholar and the school. The donor was not involved in the selection process.
• A host family acting as a caretaker for an individual under a Department of Public Welfare/Medical Assistance Program is entitled to deduct as a charitable contribution any unreimbursed out-of-pocket expenses incurred in supporting a participant.
• A taxpayer directed his bank to send a check to a specifically named missionary. He instructed the bank to inform the missionary that the check was for Presbyterian mission work. The Tax Court held that this was really a contribution to the church through the missionary as an agent for the church.

Exception

The Supreme Court ruled that funds transferred by parents directly to their sons while they served as unpaid missionaries were not charitable contributions "for the use of" the church, even though the funds were requested by the church.

Contributions You Can Deduct

Generally, you can deduct your contributions of money or property that you make to, or for the use of, a qualified organization. A gift or contribution is "for the use of" a qualified organization when it is held in a legally enforceable trust for the qualified organization or in a similar legal arrangement.

If you give property to a qualified organization, you generally can deduct the fair market value of the property at the time of the contribution. See *Contributions of Property,* later in this chapter.

Your deduction for charitable contributions is generally limited to 50% of your adjusted gross income, but in some cases 20% and 30% limits may apply. See *Limits on Deductions,* later.

Table 26-1 lists some examples of contributions you can deduct and some that you cannot deduct.

Explanation

Fair market value generally is the price that property would sell for on the open market. It takes into account many factors that affect the value of property on the date of the contribution.

Example

If you give used clothing to the Salvation Army, the fair market value is the price that typical buyers actually pay for clothing of this age, condition, style, and use. Usually, such items are worth far less than what you paid for them.

TAXPLANNER

Determining fair market value. A valuable tool for determining fair market value is IRS Publication 561, *Determining the Value of Donated Property.* The publication helps donors and appraisers determine the value of property given to qualified organizations and includes the kind of information you must have to support the charitable deduction you claim on your return.

A sale or purchase of similar property reasonably close to the date of your contribution is usually the best indication of fair market value. Replacement cost and opinions of experts are also valid methods for determining value.

IRS Publication 561 discusses pitfalls to be avoided in determining the value of donated property. Some pitfalls and how to avoid them are the following:

1. The best evidence of fair market value depends on actual transactions, not on some artificial estimate.
2. Do not consider unexpected events occurring after your donation of property in making the valuation. Generally, you should only consider facts known at the time of the gift.
3. Past events are not necessarily reliable in predicting future earnings and fair market value. For example, a taxpayer contributes all rights in a patent to a charitable organization. The patent has a history of high earnings, but the current trend reflects declining earnings. In this case, more emphasis should be placed on the earnings trend rather than on the earnings history.

The cost of an appraisal is not deductible as a charitable contribution, but it may be claimed as a miscellaneous itemized deduction.

A description of property for which a deduction of more than $500 is claimed must be attached to your return along with a Form 8283. Additionally, you are required to obtain a qualified appraisal for certain noncash donations. A qualified appraisal must be made by an independent party. The charity or any person or entity related to the charity cannot render the appraisal. Appraisals are required for the donation of property with a claimed value in excess of $5,000. If you make gifts of two or more items of similar property during the year, the claimed value of all of those items will be added together in determining whether the $5,000 limit is exceeded. For contributions of property in excess of $500,000 the appraisal must be attached to your return.

The appraisal may not be made by the organization receiving the gift, the party from whom the taxpayer acquired the property, the taxpayer, or certain persons related to any of these persons.

The appraisal fee cannot be based on a percentage of the appraised value of the gift.

Form 8283, containing an acknowledgment of receipt of the property by the receiving organization and a certification by the appraiser, must be filed with the tax return on which the deduction is taken.

Special Rules and Limitations: The appraisal rules may be different for certain types of property. In general, the above appraisal rules do not apply to contributions of intellectual property (e.g., patents, copyrights, trademarks, etc.), certain stock in trade or inventory held for sale in the normal course of business, publicly traded securities, and certain "qualified vehicles" (i.e., motor vehicles, boats, and airplanes).

Example

In a Tax Court case upheld on appeal, the IRS disallowed a deduction for the contribution of nonpublicly traded stock in a prominent tax-preparation corporation because the taxpayers failed to get and attach an appraisal to their return.

TAXALERT

Donations of Vehicles—NEW REQUIREMENTS

Under the American Jobs Creation Act of 2004, donations of vehicles are now subject to new requirements and limitations beginning in 2005. In general, to be fully deductible, the charity must either (1) use the vehicle in a significant way in performing its regularly conducted activities, or (2) materially improve the vehicle's condition (e.g., through major repairs that significantly increase the vehicle's value—minor repairs, routine maintenance and cleaning are not considered material improvements). If the charity sells the vehicle without any significant intervening use or material improvement, the deduction cannot exceed the gross proceeds received by the charity from the sale. In other words, if the charity sells the vehicle, your deduction will be limited to its sales proceeds.

You can't take a deduction for a contribution of a motor vehicle, boat, or airplane unless it is substantiated by a contemporaneous (i.e., within 30 days of the contribution, or sale if the vehicle is sold) written acknowledgment by the charity receiving the gift which contains

1. The name and taxpayer identification number of the donor,
2. The vehicle identification number or similar number,
3. If the vehicle is to be used or improved by the charity: a certification of the intended use or material improvement of the vehicle and the intended duration of the use, and a certification that the vehicle will not be sold before the completion of such use or improvement,
4. If the vehicle is sold without the intervening use or improvement: a certification that the vehicle was sold in an arm's-length transaction between unrelated parties, the gross proceeds from the sale, and a statement that the deductible amount may not exceed the amount of such gross proceeds.

The charity will use new Form 1098-C for this purpose.

Examples

Example 1. As part of its regularly conducted activities, an organization delivers meals to needy individuals. The use requirement would be met if the organization actually used a donated qualified vehicle to deliver food to the needy. Use of the vehicle to deliver meals substantially furthers a regularly conducted activity of the organization. However, the use also must be significant, which depends on the nature, extent, and frequency of the use. If the organization used the vehicle only once or a few times to deliver meals, the use would not be considered significant. If the organization used the vehicle to deliver meals every day for one year the use would be considered significant. If the organization drove the vehicle 10,000 miles while delivering meals, such use likely would be considered significant. However, use of a vehicle in such an activity for one week or for several hundreds of miles generally would not be considered a significant use.

Example 2. An organization uses a donated qualified vehicle to transport its volunteers. The use would not be significant merely because a volunteer used the vehicle over a brief period of time to drive to or from the organization's premises. On the other hand, if at the time the organization accepts the contribution of a qualified vehicle, the organization intends to use the vehicle as a regular and ongoing means of transport for volunteers of the organization, and such vehicle is so used, then the significant use test likely would be met.

Example 3. The following example is a general illustration of the provision. A taxpayer makes a charitable contribution of a used automobile in good running condition and that needs no immediate repairs to a charitable organization that operates an elder care facility. The charitable organization accepts the vehicle and immediately provides the donor a written acknowledgment containing the name and TIN of the donor, the vehicle identification number, a certification that it intends to retain the vehicle for a year or longer to transport the facility's residents to community and social events and deliver meals to the needy, and a certification that the vehicle will not be transferred in exchange for money, other property, or services before completion of such use by the organization. A few days after receiving the vehicle, the charitable organization commences to use the vehicle three times a week to transport some of its residents to various community events, and twice a week to deliver food to needy individuals. The organization continues to regularly use the vehicle for these purposes for approximately one year and then sells the vehicle. Under the provision, the charity's use of the vehicle constitutes a significant intervening use prior to the sale by the organization, and the donor's deduction is not limited to the gross proceeds received by the organization.

Intellectual Property

Due to the inherent difficulties in valuing intellectual property, such as patents, copyrights, trademarks, trade names, trade secrets, know-how, software, similar property, or applications or registrations of such property, the American Jobs Creation Act of 2004 contained significant revisions to the rules for deducting contributions of intellectual property, effective for contributions made after June 3, 2004. Under the new rules, the deduction for a contribution of intellectual property is generally limited to the lesser of the taxpayer's basis in the property or the fair market value of the property.

Additionally, you would be allowed to deduct additional amounts in the year of contribution or in subsequent tax years based on a specified percentage of the "qualified donee income" received or accrued by the charitable recipient for the contributed property. Qualified donee income is only the income properly allocable to the intellectual property itself, rather than to the activity in which such property is used.

If you make a qualified intellectual property contribution, the deduction allowed for each tax year ending on or after the date of the contribution is increased by the applicable percentage of qualified income for the contribution that is properly allocable to that year. The amount of the additional deduction allowed per year phases out over the 12 years following the contribution.

The calculation of the charitable contribution deduction is very complex. You should consult with your tax advisor if you're considering donating intellectual property to charity.

TAXALERT

Accurate assessments. It is very important to get an accurate assessment of donated property because you may be liable for a special penalty if you overstate its value. You may be liable for the penalty if the value claimed on your return is more than 200% of the correct amount.

The penalty is 20% of the tax underpayment attributable to the overvaluation and may increase to 40% if the value claimed is 400% or more of the correct amount.

Contributions From Which You Benefit

If you receive a benefit as a result of making a contribution to a qualified organization, you can deduct only the amount of your contribution that is more than the value of the benefit you receive.

If you pay more than fair market value to a qualified organization for merchandise, goods, or services, the amount you pay that is more than the value of the item can be a charitable contribution. For the excess amount to qualify, you must pay it with the intent to make a charitable contribution.

Example 1. You pay $65 for a ticket to a dinner-dance at a church. All of the proceeds of the function go to the church. The ticket to the dinner-dance has a fair market value of $25. When you buy your ticket, you know that its value is less than your payment. To figure the amount of your charitable contribution, you subtract the value of the benefit you receive ($25) from your total payment ($65). You can deduct $40 as a contribution to the church.

Example 2. At a fund-raising auction conducted by a charity, you pay $600 for a week's stay at a beach house. The amount you pay is no more than the fair rental value. You have not made a deductible charitable contribution.

Exceptions

A deduction for a charitable contribution was *not* permitted in the following instances:

- A person contributed a computer to a university, and the donor reserved the right to use the computer for 12 weeks per year.
- A person released frontage to a county for widening a road in order to obtain the required approval by the county planning commission of the development plan for certain lots prior to their sale. (However, the cost of the frontage is part of the total cost **basis** of the remaining property for determining the gain or loss on the sale of the property.)
- The amount paid by a taxpayer to purchase building bonds issued by a church was not a gift made to the church. However, if the taxpayer had subsequently given the bonds to the church, he would have been entitled to a charitable deduction for their fair market value at the time of the gift.
- A person made contributions to a nonprofit organization formed by parents of pupils attending a private school. The organization provided school bus transportation for members' children. The contributions served a private rather than a public interest.
- A taxpayer paid a fee to a nonprofit corporation for the privilege of taking up residence in a home operated by the corporation. This fee, along with a required entrance fee, entitled the taxpayer to lifetime care in the home. The fee represented a personal expense.

Athletic events. If you make a payment to, or for the benefit of, a college or university and, as a result, you receive the right to buy tickets to an athletic event in the athletic stadium of the college or university, you can deduct 80% of the payment as a charitable contribution.

If any part of your payment is for tickets (rather than the right to buy tickets), that part is not deductible. In that case, subtract the price of the tickets from your payment. 80% of the remaining amount is a charitable contribution.

Example 1. You pay $300 a year for membership in an athletic scholarship program maintained by a university (a qualified organization). The only benefit of membership is that you have the right to buy one season ticket for a seat in a designated area of the stadium at the university's home football games. You can deduct $240 (80% of $300) as a charitable contribution.

Example 2. The facts are the same as in Example 1 except that your $300 payment included the purchase of one season ticket for the stated ticket price of $120. You must subtract the usual price of a ticket ($120) from your $300 payment. The result is $180. Your deductible charitable contribution is $144 (80% of $180).

Charity benefit events. If you pay a qualified organization more than fair market value for the right to attend a charity ball, banquet, show, sporting event, or other benefit event, you can deduct only the amount that is more than the value of the privileges or other benefits you receive.

If there is an established charge for the event, that charge is the value of your benefit. If there is no established charge, your contribution is that part of your payment that is more than the reasonable value of the right to attend the event. Whether you use the tickets or other privileges has no effect on the amount you can deduct. However, if you return the ticket to the qualified organization for resale, you can deduct the entire amount you paid for the ticket.

Caution. *Even if the ticket or other evidence of payment indicates that the payment is a "contribution," this does not mean you can deduct the entire amount. If the ticket shows the price of admission and the amount of the contribution, you can deduct the contribution amount.*

Example. You pay $40 to see a special showing of a movie for the benefit of a qualified organization. Printed on the ticket is "Contribution—$40." If the regular price for the movie is $8, your contribution is $32 ($40 payment − $8 regular price).

Explanation

The IRS requires that charities determine the fair market value of benefits offered in exchange for contributions in advance of the solicitation and state in the solicitation, as well as in the receipt, tickets, or other documents, what portion of the contribution is deductible. The charity may advise donors that the full amount of a contribution is deductible if any of the following applies:

- The fair market value of all the benefits received in conjunction with the contribution is not more than the lesser of 2% of the payment or $83.
- The contribution is at least $41.50, and the only benefits received in connection with the payment are token items, such as bookmarks, calendars, key chains, mugs, posters, and T-shirts bearing the organization's name or logo (i.e., low-cost articles with a cost not in excess of $8.30).
- The charity distributes unordered items to patrons. The distributed item must be accompanied by a request for a contribution and by a statement that the item can be retained whether or not a contribution is made. The aggregate cost per patron of these items cannot exceed $8.30.

Example 1

In 2005, a nonprofit broadcast organization sends its patrons a listener's guide for 1 year in return for a contribution of $41.50 or more. The cost of the production and distribution of the listener's guide is $7 per year per patron, and its fair market value is $10. The listener's guide is not available to nonmembers by paid subscription or through newsstand sales. Because the cost of the listener's guide is $7 and it is received in return for a contribution of $41.50 or more, the broadcast organization may advise its patrons that the full amount of the payment is a deductible contribution. However, if the cost of the publication exceeds $8.30, the charitable organization would be required to inform its patrons of the amount by which they should reduce their charitable deductions.

Membership fees or dues. You may be able to deduct membership fees or dues you pay to a qualified organization. However, you can deduct only the amount that is more than the value of the benefits you receive. You cannot deduct dues, fees, or assessments paid to country clubs and other social organizations. They are not qualified organizations.

Certain membership benefits can be disregarded. Both you and the organization can disregard certain membership benefits you get in return for an annual payment of $75 or less to the qualified organization. You can pay more than $75 to the organization if the organization does not require a larger payment for you to get the benefits. The following benefits are covered under this rule.

1. Any rights or privileges, other than those discussed under *Athletic events,* earlier, that you can use frequently while you are a member, such as:
   a. Free or discounted admission to the organization's facilities or events,
   b. Free or discounted parking,
   c. Preferred access to goods or services, and
   d. Discounts on the purchase of goods and services.
2. Admission, while you are a member, to events that are open only to members of the organization, if the organization reasonably projects that the cost per person (excluding any allocated overhead) is not more than $8.30.

Token items. You can deduct your entire payment to a qualified organization as a charitable contribution if both of the following are true.

- You get a small item or other benefit of token value.
- The qualified organization correctly determines that the value of the item or benefit you received is not substantial and informs you that you can deduct your payment in full.

Written statement. A qualified organization must give you a written statement if you make a payment to it that is more than $75 and is partly a contribution and partly for goods or services. The statement must tell you that you can deduct only the amount of your payment that is more than the value of the goods or services you received. It must also give you a good faith estimate of the value of those goods or services.

The organization can give you the statement either when it solicits or when it receives the payment from you.

Exception. An organization will not have to give you this statement if one of the following is true.

1. The organization is:
   a. The type of organization described in (5) under *Types of Qualified Organizations,* earlier, or
   b. Formed only for religious purposes, and the only benefit you receive is an intangible religious benefit (such as admission to a religious ceremony) that generally is not sold in commercial transactions outside the donative context.
2. You receive only items whose value is not substantial. See *Token items,* earlier.
3. You receive only membership benefits that can be disregarded, as described earlier.

Expenses Paid for Student Living With You

You may be able to deduct some expenses of having a student live with you. You can deduct qualifying expenses for a foreign or American student who:

1. Lives in your home under a written agreement between you and a qualified organization as part of a program of the organization to provide educational opportunities for the student,
2. Is not your dependent or relative, and
3. Is a full-time student in the twelfth or any lower grade at a school in the United States.

Tip. *You can deduct up to $50 a month for each full calendar month the student lives with you. Any month when conditions (1) through (3) above are met for 15 days or more counts as a full month.*

For additional information, see *Expenses Paid for Student Living With You* in Publication 526.

Mutual exchange program. You cannot deduct the costs of a foreign student living in your home under a mutual exchange program through which your child will live with a family in a foreign country.

> **Explanation**
>
> The deduction is limited to amounts that you actually spend for the well-being of the student during the taxable year while the student is a member of the household and a full-time student. Amounts you pay for the student's books, tuition, food, clothing, transportation, medical and dental care, and entertainment qualify for the deduction. Depreciation on your home, the fair market value of lodging at your home, or similar items are not considered an amount spent by you and are not deductible.
>
> If you are compensated or reimbursed for the costs of having a student live with you, you may not take a deduction for any part of these costs.

Out-of-Pocket Expenses in Giving Services

You may be able to deduct some amounts you pay in giving services to a qualified organization. The amounts must be:

- Unreimbursed,
- Directly connected with the services,
- Expenses you had only because of the services you gave, and
- Not personal, living, or family expenses.

> **Explanation**
>
> Unreimbursed out-of-pocket expenses incurred in rendering services to qualified charities are considered contributions made "to" the charitable entities rather than "for the use of" the charitable entities, and, as such, the deduction may be subject to the 50% limit rather than the 30% limit. See *Limits on Deductions,* later, to determine if further limitations apply.

Table 26-2 contains questions and answers that apply to some individuals who volunteer their services.

Conventions. If you are a chosen representative attending a convention of a qualified organization, you can deduct actual unreimbursed expenses for travel and transportation, including a reasonable amount for meals and lodging, while away from home overnight in connection with the convention. However, see *Travel,* later.

You cannot deduct personal expenses for sightseeing, fishing parties, theater tickets, or nightclubs. You also cannot deduct travel, meals and lodging, and other expenses for your spouse or children.

You cannot deduct your expenses in attending a church convention if you go only as a member of your church rather than as a chosen representative. You can deduct unreimbursed expenses that are directly connected with giving services for your church during the convention.

Uniforms. You can deduct the cost and upkeep of uniforms that are not suitable for everyday use and that you must wear while performing donated services for a charitable organization.

Foster parents. You may be able to deduct as a charitable contribution some of the costs of being a foster parent (foster care provider) if you have no profit motive in providing the foster care and are not, in fact, making a profit. A qualified organization must designate the individuals you take into your home for foster care.

You can deduct expenses that meet both of the following requirements.

1. They are unreimbursed out-of-pocket expenses to feed, clothe, and care for the foster child.
2. They must be mainly to benefit the qualified organization.

> **Explanation**
>
> You may deduct reasonable, unreimbursed out-of-pocket expenses you spend for underprivileged children to attend athletic events, movies, or dinners. It must be part of an event sponsored on behalf of a qualifying organization. Expenses for yourself are not deductible.

Unreimbursed expenses that you cannot deduct as charitable contributions may be considered support provided by you in determining whether you can claim the foster child as a dependent. For details see chapter 3.

Example. You cared for a foster child because you wanted to adopt her, not to benefit the agency that placed her in your home. Your unreimbursed expenses are not deductible as charitable contributions.

Car expenses. You can deduct unreimbursed out-of-pocket expenses, such as the cost of gas and oil, which are directly related to the use of your car in giving services to a charitable organization. You cannot deduct any part of general repair and maintenance expenses, depreciation, registration fees, or the costs of tires or insurance.

If you do not want to deduct your actual expenses, you can use a standard mileage rate of 14 cents a mile to figure your contribution.

> **TaxAlert**
>
> As this book was going to press, changes in the standard mileage rate were being considered. See the special section on tax changes relating to Hurricane Katrina at the front of this book.

You can deduct parking fees and tolls whether you use your actual expenses or the standard mileage rate.

You must keep reliable written records of your car expenses. For more information, see *Car expenses* under *Records To Keep,* later.

Travel. Generally, you can claim a charitable contribution deduction for travel expenses necessarily incurred while you are away from home performing services for a charitable organization only if there is no significant element of personal pleasure, recreation, or vacation in the travel. This applies whether you pay the expenses directly or indirectly. You are paying the expenses indirectly if you make a payment to the charitable organization and the organization pays for your travel expenses.

The deduction for travel expenses will not be denied simply because you enjoy providing services to the charitable organization. Even if you enjoy the trip, you can take a charitable contribution deduction for your travel expenses if you are on duty in a genuine and substantial sense throughout the trip. However, if you have only nominal duties, or if for significant parts of the trip you do not have any duties, you cannot deduct your travel expenses.

Example 1. You are a troop leader for a tax-exempt youth group and you help take the group on a camping trip. You are responsible for overseeing the setup of the camp and for providing adult supervision for other activities during the entire trip. You participate in the activities of the group and really enjoy your time with them. You oversee the breaking of camp and you help transport the group home. You can deduct your travel expenses.

Example 2. You sail from one island to another and spend 8 hours a day counting whales and other forms of marine life. The project is sponsored by a charitable organization. In most circumstances, you cannot deduct your expenses.

Example 3. You work for several hours each morning on an archaeological dig sponsored by a charitable organization. The rest of the day is free for recreation and sightseeing. You cannot take a charitable contribution deduction even though you work very hard during those few hours.

Example 4. You spend the entire day attending a charitable organization's regional meeting as a chosen representative. In the evening you go to the theater. You can claim your travel expenses as charitable contributions, but you cannot claim the cost of your evening at the theater.

Daily allowance (per diem). If you provide services for a charitable organization and receive a daily allowance to cover reasonable travel expenses, including meals and lodging while away from home overnight, you must include in income the amount of the allowance that is more than your deductible travel expenses. You can deduct your necessary travel expenses that are more than the allowance.

Deductible travel expenses. These include:

- Air, rail, and bus transportation,
- Out-of-pocket expenses for your car,
- Taxi fares or other costs of transportation between the airport or station and your hotel,
- Lodging costs, and
- The cost of meals.

Because these travel expenses are not business-related, they are not subject to the same limits as business-related expenses. For information on business travel expenses, see *Travel Expenses* in chapter 28.

Contributions You Cannot Deduct

There are some contributions you cannot deduct, such as those made to individuals and those made to nonqualified organizations. (See *Contributions to Individuals* and *Contributions to Nonqualified Organizations*, next). There are others you can deduct only part of, as discussed later under *Contributions From Which You Benefit*.

Contributions to Individuals

You cannot deduct contributions to specific individuals, including the following.

- Contributions to fraternal societies made for the purpose of paying medical or burial expenses of deceased members.
- Contributions to individuals who are needy or worthy. This includes contributions to a qualified organization if you indicate that your contribution is for a specific person. But you can deduct a contribution that you give to a qualified organization that in turn helps needy or worthy individuals if you do not indicate that your contribution is for a specific person.
- Payments to a member of the clergy that can be spent as he or she wishes, such as for personal expenses.
- Expenses you paid for another person who provided services to a qualified organization.

Example. Your son does missionary work. You pay his expenses. You cannot claim a deduction for your son's unreimbursed expenses related to his contribution of services.

- Payments to a hospital that are for services for a specific patient. You cannot deduct these payments even if the hospital is operated by a city, a state, or other qualified organization.

TaxPlanner

Direct contributions to needy individuals. Direct contributions to needy or worthy individuals are not deductible. But, if you can show that the economic benefit derived by the specific individual is less than the contribution to the organization in whose care the individual is placed, the excess may be deductible.

Example

An individual made a contribution to a school for crippled children that her son attended. The donor required that a portion of her contribution be used to purchase a wheelchair for the exclusive use of her son. She was allowed a deduction for a charitable contribution for the amount by which the contribution exceeded the cost of the wheelchair. (The cost of the wheelchair may qualify as a medical expense.)

Contributions to Nonqualified Organizations

You cannot deduct contributions to organizations that are not qualified to receive tax-deductible contributions, including the following.

1. Certain state bar associations if:
   a. The state bar is not a political subdivision of a state,
   b. The bar has private, as well as public, purposes, such as promoting the professional interests of members, and
   c. Your contribution is unrestricted and can be used for private purposes.
2. Chambers of commerce and other business leagues or organizations.
3. Civic leagues and associations.
4. Communist organizations.
5. Country clubs and other social clubs.
6. Foreign organizations other than:
   a. A U.S. organization that transfers funds to a charitable foreign organization if the U.S. organization controls the use of the funds or if the foreign organization is only an administrative arm of the U.S. organization, or

---

Example

A contribution to the U.S. Red Cross is deductible, even though some portion of the contribution may be used outside the United States. If you make a contribution to a U.S. organization *directing* that it be sent to a foreign charitable organization to be used abroad, a deduction may not be allowed because the real recipient is not a domestic organization.

---

   b. Certain Canadian, Israeli, or Mexican charitable organizations. See *Certain foreign charitable organizations* under *Organizations That Qualify To Receive Deductible Contributions*, earlier.

Explanation

The Canadian, Mexican, and Israeli tax treaties provide that contributions to charitable organizations (other than charitable contributions to a college or a university at which you or a member of your family is or was enrolled) are subject to the U.S. percentage limits on charitable contributions, applied to your income from sources in each of these countries.

The organizations must meet the qualifications that U.S. charitable organizations must meet. The organization can tell you if it qualifies for deductible charitable contributions.

---

7. Homeowners' associations.
8. Labor unions. But you may be able to deduct union dues as a miscellaneous itemized deduction, subject to the 2%-of-adjusted-gross-income limit, on Schedule A (Form 1040). See chapter 30.
9. Political organizations and candidates.

Contributions From Which You Benefit

If you receive or expect to receive a financial or economic benefit as a result of making a contribution to a qualified organization, you cannot deduct the part of the contribution that represents the value of the benefit you receive. These contributions include the following.

- Contributions for lobbying. This includes amounts that you earmark for use in, or in connection with, influencing specific legislation.
- Contributions to a retirement home that are clearly for room, board, maintenance, or admittance. Also, if the amount of your contribution depends on the type or size of apartment you will occupy, it is not a charitable contribution.
- Costs of raffles, bingo, lottery, etc. You cannot deduct as a charitable contribution amounts you pay to buy raffle or lottery tickets or to play bingo or other games of chance. For information on how to report gambling winnings and losses, see chapter 13 and chapter 30.

Table 26-2. **Volunteers' Questions and Answers**

If you do volunteer work for a qualified organization, the following questions and answers may apply to you. All of the rules explained in this chapter also apply. See, in particular, Out-of-Pocket Expenses *in Giving Services.*

Question	Answer
I do volunteer work 6 hours a week in the office of a qualified organization. The receptionist is paid $6 an hour to do the same work I do. Can I deduct $36 a week for my time?	No, you cannot deduct the value of your time or services.
The office is 30 miles from my home. Can I deduct any of my car expenses for these trips?	Yes, you can deduct the costs of gas and oil that are directly related to getting to and from the qualified organization where you are a volunteer. If you don't want to figure your actual costs, you can deduct 14 cents for each mile.
I volunteer as a Red Cross nurse's aide at a hospital. Can I deduct the cost of uniforms that I must wear?	Yes, you can deduct the cost of buying and cleaning your uniforms if the hospital is a qualified organization, the uniforms are not suitable for everyday use, and you must wear them when volunteering.
I pay a babysitter to watch my children while I do volunteer work for a qualified organization. Can I deduct these costs?	No, you cannot deduct payments for child care expenses as a charitable contribution, even if they are necessary so you can do volunteer work for a qualified organization. (If you have child care expenses so you can work for pay, see chapter 34.)

- Dues to fraternal orders and similar groups. However, see *Membership fees or dues,* earlier, under *Contributions From Which You Benefit.*
- Tuition, or amounts you pay instead of tuition, even if you pay them for children to attend parochial schools or qualifying nonprofit day-care centers. You also cannot deduct any fixed amount you may be required to pay in addition to the tuition fee to enroll in a private school, even if it is designated as a "donation."

Explanation

Tuition-type payments disguised as a charitable contribution are not deductible. Certain rules have been established by the IRS to determine whether an item is a tuition payment or a charitable contribution.

No deduction for a charitable contribution is allowed if *at least one* of the following conditions exists:

1. A contract under which a taxpayer agrees to make a "contribution," and that contract contains provisions ensuring the admission of the taxpayer's child;
2. A plan allowing taxpayers either to pay tuition or to make "contributions" in exchange for schooling;
3. The designation of a contribution for the direct benefit of a particular child;
4. The otherwise unexplained denial of admission or readmission to a school of children of taxpayers who are financially able but who do not contribute.

Other factors that are considered in deciding if a contribution is deductible include the following:

1. The absence of a significant tuition charge;
2. Substantial or unusual pressure to contribute applied to parents of students;
3. Contribution appeals made as part of the admissions or enrollment process;
4. The absence of significant potential sources of revenue for operating the school other than contributions by parents of students;
5. The contribution amounts are the same for all families or are paid pursuant to published guidelines for donations.

Value of Time or Services

You cannot deduct the value of your time or services, including:

- Blood donations to the Red Cross or to blood banks, and
- The value of income lost while you work as an unpaid volunteer for a qualified organization.

TAXPLANNER

Services to a charitable organization. If you contribute *your* services to a charitable organization, you are not permitted to take a charitable deduction for the value of your time or services. However, you are entitled to take a charitable deduction if you acquire the right to services to be performed by another and then gratuitously transfer that right to the charity.

Example

You purchase a series of six golf lessons from a local golf professional. Because you are unable to use the lessons, you donate them to your church for use in their raffle. The cost of the six lessons is deductible as a charitable contribution.

Personal Expenses

You cannot deduct personal, living, or family expenses, such as:

- The cost of meals you eat while you perform services for a qualified organization unless it is necessary for you to be away from home overnight while performing the services, or
- Adoption expenses, including fees paid to an adoption agency and the costs of keeping a child in your home before adoption is final. However, you may be able to claim a tax credit for these expenses and exclude from your gross income adoption expenses paid or reimbursed by your employer. See *Adoption Credit* in chapter 39 and Publication 968, Tax Benefits for Adoption.

You also may be able to claim an exemption for the child. See *Adoption* in chapter 3.

Appraisal Fees

Fees that you pay to find the fair market value of donated property are not deductible as contributions. You can claim them, subject to the 2%-of-adjusted-gross-income limit, as miscellaneous deductions on Schedule A (Form 1040). See chapter 30.

Contributions of Property

If you contribute property to a qualified organization, the amount of your charitable contribution is generally the fair market value of the property at the time of the contribution. However, if the property has increased in value, you may have to make some adjustments to the amount of your deduction. See *Giving Property That Has Increased in Value,* later.

Explanation
If you permit a charitable organization to use your property without charge (or at a minimal rate), no charitable deduction is allowed.

TaxSaver
The IRS, however, will allow charitable deductions for the cost of operation, maintenance, and repair of property directly related to the charitable organization's use of the property.

If you donate the use of your yacht to the church for use in their raffle, no income tax deduction is allowed for the rental value or other value of the donated use. Direct operating costs, such as fuel, used in connection with the donated use are allowable as a charitable contribution.

For information about the records you must keep and the information you must furnish with your return if you donate property, see *Records To Keep* and *How To Report,* later.

TaxAlert
The American Jobs Creation Act of 2004 changes some of the rules for reporting contributions of certain non-cash property. The new law extends to all C corporations the requirement currently applicable to an individual, closely held corporation, personal service corporation, partnership, or S corporation, that the donor must obtain a qualified appraisal of the property if the deduction claimed exceeds $5,000. In addition, the new law provides that if the amount of the contribution of property exceeds $500,000, the donor (whether an individual, partnership, or corporation) must attach a qualified appraisal to the tax return. *Note that the new rules apply to contributions made after June 3, 2004.*

Partial interest in property. Generally, you cannot deduct a charitable contribution (not made by a transfer in trust) of less than your entire interest in property.

Right to use property. A contribution of the right to use property is a contribution of less than your entire interest in that property and is not deductible. For exceptions and more information, see *Partial Interest in Property Not in Trust* in Publication 561.

Explanation
This rule does not apply to a contribution of a partial interest in property if that interest is your entire interest in the property, such as an income interest.

Nevertheless, there are some situations in which you may claim a deduction for a charitable contribution that is less than your entire interest in the property.

1. **Undivided part of your entire interest.** A contribution of an undivided part of your entire interest in property must consist of a part of each and every substantial interest or right you own in the property and must extend over the entire term of your interest in the property.

Example 1
If you own 100 acres of land and give 50 acres to a qualified organization, you may deduct the charitable contribution.

A court allowed a taxpayer a deduction when a 10% undivided interest in 44 works of art was donated to an art museum. The art museum did not take physical possession of the works of art at any time within a period that extended for more than a year after the donation. It was held that the art museum clearly had the right to possession for 10% of the days in the year and the fact that the museum did not exercise that right was not relevant.

2. **Remainder interest in a personal home or farm.** You may take a charitable deduction for a gift to a qualified organization of a **remainder interest** in a personal home or a farm if the gift is irrevocable.

Example 2
If you transfer a remainder interest in your home to your church but keep the right to live there for life, you may take a deduction for the value of the remainder interest transferred.

3. **Valuation of a partial interest in property.** The amount of the deduction for a charitable contribution of a partial interest in property is the fair market value of the partial interest at the time of the contribution. If the contribution is a remainder interest in real property, **depreciation** (figured on the **straight-line** method) and **depletion** of the property must be taken into account in determining its value. This future value must be further discounted at a rate set by the government. The rate is published each month, and you may use the rate for the month in which the contribution is made or, if you elect, the rate in either of the preceding 2 months. You should use the rate that produces the largest charitable deduction.

No deduction is allowed for the value of an interest in property transferred in trust unless the donor's entire interest is contributed to a qualified organization or unless the interest is an income interest or a remainder interest.

TaxPlanner
A deduction for a charitable contribution of an income interest in property made by a transfer in trust is allowed if the income interest is either a guaranteed **annuity** interest or a **unitrust** interest. A unitrust interest is the irrevocable right to receive payment of a fixed percentage of the net fair market value of the trust **assets** determined on a yearly basis, while an annuity interest is a right to receive a fixed percentage of the initial fair market value of the new assets.

A deduction for a charitable contribution of a remainder interest in trust is allowed if the trust is (1) a **pooled income fund,** (2) a charitable remainder annuity trust, or (3) a charitable remainder unitrust.

The use of these trusts may be very beneficial both to the individual and to the individual's favorite charity. Individuals with substantial wealth should consult their tax and legal advisors about using these mechanisms.

Future interests in tangible personal property. You can deduct the value of a charitable contribution of a future interest in tangible personal property only after all intervening interests in and rights to the actual possession or enjoyment of the property have either expired or been turned over to someone other than yourself, a related person, or a related organization.

Future interest. This is any interest that is to begin at some future time, regardless of whether it is designated as a future interest under state law.

Determining Fair Market Value

This section discusses general guidelines for determining the fair market value of various types of donated property.

Fair market value is the price at which property would change hands between a willing buyer and a willing seller, neither having to buy or sell, and both having reasonable knowledge of all the relevant facts. Publication 561 contains a more complete discussion.

Used clothing and household goods. Generally, the fair market value of used clothing and household goods is far less than its original cost.

For used clothing, you should claim as the value the price that buyers of used items actually pay in used clothing stores, such as consignment or thrift shops. See *Household Goods* in Publication 561 for information on the valuation of household goods, such as furniture, appliances, and linens.

Example. Dawn Greene donated a coat to a thrift store operated by her church. She paid $300 for the coat 3 years ago. Similar coats in the thrift store sell for $50. The fair market value of the coat is reasonably determined to be $50. Dawn's donation is limited to $50.

Cars, boats, and aircraft. If you contribute a car, boat, or aircraft to a charitable organization, you must determine its fair market value. But the amount you may actually deduct may be less than the fair market value of the car, boat, or aircraft if the charitable organization sells it for less than fair market value. If the charity uses the vehicle appropriately, as discussed above in Determining Fair market value, you may be able to deduct its fair market value. [Omitted Text]

Certain commercial firms and trade organizations publish used car pricing guides, commonly called "blue books," containing complete dealer sale prices or dealer average prices for recent model years. The guides may be published monthly or seasonally and for different regions of the country. These guides also provide estimates for adjusting for unusual equipment, unusual mileage, and physical condition. The prices are not "official" and these publications are not considered an appraisal of any specific donated property. But they do provide clues for making an appraisal and suggest relative prices for comparison with current sales and offerings in your area.

[IRS text intentionally omitted]

Large quantities. If you contribute a large number of the same item, fair market value is the price at which comparable numbers of the item are being sold.

Giving Property That Has Decreased in Value

If you contribute property with a fair market value that is less than your basis in it, your deduction is limited to its fair market value. You cannot claim a deduction for the difference between the property's basis and its fair market value.

Giving Property That Has Increased in Value

If you contribute property with a fair market value that is more than your basis in it, you may have to reduce the fair market value by the amount of appreciation (increase in value) when you figure your deduction.

Your basis in property is generally what you paid for it. See chapter 14 if you need more information about basis.

Different rules apply to figuring your deduction, depending on whether the property is:

1. Ordinary income property, or
2. Capital gain property.

Ordinary income property. Property is ordinary income property if its sale at fair market value on the date it was contributed would have resulted in ordinary income or in short-term capital gain. Examples of ordinary income property are inventory, works of art created by the donor, manuscripts prepared by the donor, and capital assets held 1 year or less.

Amount of deduction. The amount you can deduct for a contribution of ordinary income property is its fair market value less the amount that would be ordinary income or short-term capital gain if you sold the property for its fair market value. Generally, this rule limits the deduction to your basis in the property.

Example. You donate stock that you held for 5 months to your church. The fair market value of the stock on the day you donate it is $1,000, but you paid only $800 (your basis). Because the $200 of appreciation would be short-term capital gain if you sold the stock, your deduction is limited to $800 (fair market value less the appreciation).

Explanation
Ordinary income property. If, on the date it was contributed, the sale of the property would have resulted in ordinary income or a short-term capital gain to the donor, it is ordinary income property. Examples of ordinary income property include inventory, letters, and memoranda given by the person who prepared them (or the person for whom they were prepared) and any property that was acquired and held for 1 year or less.

Example
You contribute inventory to your church with a fair market value of $20,000 and a cost of $8,000. Because the inventory is property that had previously been held for sale in the ordinary course of business, you would have recognized ordinary income of $12,000 had the property been sold. Therefore, your contribution of $20,000 is reduced by $12,000. Your deduction is limited to $8,000.

Capital gain property. Property is capital gain property if its sale at fair market value on the date of the contribution would have resulted in long-term capital gain. It includes capital assets held more than 1 year, as well as certain real property and depreciable property used in your trade or business and, generally, held more than 1 year.

Amount of deduction—general rule. When figuring your deduction for a gift of capital gain property, you usually can use the fair market value of the gift.

Exceptions. In certain situations, you must reduce the fair market value by any amount that would have been long-term capital gain if you had sold the property for its fair market value. Generally, this means reducing the fair market value to the property's cost or other basis.

Example
An individual purchased stock in 1983 for $1,000. He contributed it to his church in 2005, at which time it was worth $20,000. His charitable contribution deduction is $20,000, the fair market value at the date of the contribution.

Explanation
You usually may deduct a gift of capital gain property at its fair market value. However, your deduction is limited to your adjusted basis in the property in the following instances:

1. If the capital gain property is contributed to certain private foundations. (A private foundation generally receives only small or no contributions from the general public.)

TAX ALERT

Contributions to private foundations. Contributions of qualified appreciated stock to private foundations are deductible at full market value subject to the 20% limitation, discussed later. If, on the date of contribution, market quotes are readily available and the sale of the stock would result in a long-term capital gain, it is qualified appreciated stock. An example would be shares of IBM that qualify for long-term capital gain treatment.

2. If you choose the 50% limit instead of the special 30% limit, discussed later (see *Limit on Deductions,* later).
3. If the property contributed is **tangible personal property** that is put to an unrelated use by the charity, that is, a use that is unrelated to the purpose or function of the charitable organization for which it was granted its tax-exempt status.

Example
If a painting you contribute to an educational institution is placed in the organization's library for display and study by art students, the use is *not* an unrelated use. But, if the painting is sold and the proceeds are used by the organization for educational purposes, the use is unrelated and your deduction is limited to the painting's cost.

TAX PLANNER

Before you donate a gift of tangible personal property, attempt to determine whether the use will be related to the charitable organization's exempt function. In such circumstances, ask the charitable organization to prepare a statement of intended use and retain it in your tax return file.

TAX SAVER

If you donate appreciated securities that you have held for more than a year, not only can you take a deduction based on the fair market value of the securities, but you will also avoid paying tax on the appreciation. Consequently, the cost of your contribution is reduced by the tax deduction you claim and the tax you avoided by not selling the property. In most cases, the charity does not incur any tax when it sells the property. Be careful, though, if the securities are the subject of a tender offer or other purchase agreement. The Tax Court has ruled that a gift of securities subject to such an agreement will result in income to the donor for the gain.

Example
You own stock worth $1,000. When you bought the stock more than a year ago, it cost you $100. If you sell the stock and donate the $1,000 to your favorite charity, you incur capital gains tax—possibly as much as $135, depending on what tax bracket you're in. If you contribute the stock directly to the charity, the $900 gain is not subject to tax if the stock was held for more than a year.

TAX SAVER

To get the maximum tax benefit from a contribution of appreciated property, be sure that the property qualifies for long-term capital gain treatment if it is sold.

Example
You purchased stock for $1,000 on January 12, 2004. The stock was donated to your church on January 8, 2005, at which time it was worth $3,000. Because the $2,000 of appreciation would have been a short-term capital gain if you had sold the stock, your deduction is limited to $1,000. If, however, you had waited to make

your donation to the church until January 13, 2005, and the stock was still worth $3,000, you would have been able to deduct $3,000.

TAXALERT

You can recognize a charitable contribution for the full fair market value of appreciated property for both regular and alternative minimum tax purposes.

Bargain sales. A bargain sale of property to a qualified organization (a sale or exchange for less than the property's fair market value) is partly a charitable contribution and partly a sale or exchange. A bargain sale may result in a taxable gain.

Explanation

The calculation of the gain on a bargain sale requires that you properly allocate your tax basis in the property sold. For example, consider the following facts:

Asset:	FMV	$1,000	
	Adjusted basis	$ 500	
Sold to ABC Charity for		$ 500	
Gain to taxpayer		$ 250	(Calculated as follows:)

$\dfrac{\text{Sale price}}{\text{FMV}} \times \text{Adjusted basis}$

$\dfrac{\$500}{\$1,000} \times \$500 - \$250$ allocated adjustment basis

Gain = amount received − allocated adjusted basis

Gain = $500 − $250

Gain = $250

Charitable deduction is $500

More information. For more information on donated appreciated property, see *Giving Property That Has Increased in Value* in Publication 526.

When To Deduct

You can deduct your contributions only in the year you actually make them in cash or other property (or in a later carryover year, as explained later under *Carryovers*). This applies whether you use the cash or an accrual method of accounting.

Time of making contribution. Usually, you make a contribution at the time of its unconditional delivery.

Checks. A check that you mail to a charity is considered delivered on the date you mail it.

Credit card. Contributions charged on your bank credit card are deductible in the year you make the charge.

Pay-by-phone account. If you use a pay-by-phone account, the date you make a contribution is the date the financial institution pays the amount. This date should be shown on the statement the financial institution sends to you.

Stock certificate. A gift to a charity of a properly endorsed stock certificate is completed on the date of mailing or other delivery to the charity or to the charity's agent. However, if you give a stock certificate to your agent or to the issuing corporation for transfer to the name of the charity, your gift is not completed until the date the stock is transferred on the books of the corporation.

Promissory note. If you issue and deliver a promissory note to a charitable organization as a contribution, it is not a contribution until you make the note payments.

Option. If you grant an option to buy real property at a bargain price to a charitable organization, you cannot take a deduction until the organization exercises the option.

Borrowed funds. If you make a contribution with borrowed funds, you can deduct the contribution in the year you make it, regardless of when you repay the loan.

Limits on Deductions

If your total contributions for the year are 20% or less of your adjusted gross income, you do not need to read this section. The limits discussed here do not apply to you.

The amount of your deduction is limited to 50% of your adjusted gross income and may be limited to 30% or 20% of your adjusted gross income, depending on the type of property you give and the type of organization you give it to. These limits are described below.

If your contributions are more than any of the limits that apply, see *Carryovers,* later.

50% Limit

This limit applies to the total of all charitable contributions you make during the year. This means that your deduction for charitable contributions cannot be more than 50% of your adjusted gross income for the year.

Generally, the 50% limit is the only limit that applies to gifts to organizations listed below under *50% limit organizations*. But there is one exception. A 30% limit also applies to these gifts if they are gifts of capital gain property for which you figure your deduction using fair market value without reduction for appreciation. (See *Special 30% Limit for Capital Gain Property,* later.)

50% limit organizations. You can ask any organization whether it is a 50% limit organization and most will be able to tell you. Or you can check IRS Publication 78, or the IRS website (www.irs.gov), or call the IRS Tax Exempt/Government Entities Customer Service at the number listed earlier under *Organizations that Qualify To Receive Deductible Contributions.* The following is a partial list of the types of organizations that are 50% limit organizations.

- Churches and conventions or associations of churches.
- Educational organizations with a regular faculty and curriculum that normally have a regularly enrolled student body attending classes on site.
- Hospitals and certain medical research organizations associated with these hospitals.
- Publicly supported charities.
- Private operating foundations.
- Private nonoperating foundations that make qualifying distributions of 100% of contributions within 2 1/2 months following the year they receive the contributions.
- Certain private foundations whose contributions are pooled in a common fund, the income and principal of which are paid to public charities.

30% Limit

A 30% limit applies to the following gifts.

- Gifts to all qualified organizations other than 50% limit organizations. This includes gifts to veterans' organizations, fraternal societies, nonprofit cemeteries, and certain private nonoperating foundations.
- Gifts for the use of any organization. However, if these gifts are of capital gain property, they are subject to the 20% limit, described later, rather than the 30% limit.

Student living with you. Amounts you spend on behalf of a student living with you are subject to the 30% limit. These amounts are considered a contribution for the use of a qualified organization.

Special 30% Limit for Capital Gain Property

A special 30% limit applies to gifts of capital gain property to 50% limit organizations. (For gifts of capital gain property to other organizations, see *20% Limit,* later.) However, the special 30% limit does not apply when you choose to reduce the fair market value of the property by the amount that would have been long-term capital gain if you had sold the property. Instead, only the 50% limit applies.

Two separate 30% limits. This special 30% limit for capital gain property is separate from the other 30% limit. Therefore, the deduction of a contribution subject to one 30% limit does not reduce the amount you can deduct for contributions subject to the other 30% limit. However, the total you deduct cannot be more than 50% of your adjusted gross income.

Example. Your adjusted gross income is $50,000. During the year, you gave capital gain property with a fair market value of $15,000 to a 50% limit organization. You do not choose to reduce the property's fair market value by its appreciation in value. You also gave $10,000 cash to a qualified organization that is not a 50% limit organization. The $15,000 gift of property is subject to the special 30% limit. The $10,000 cash gift is subject to the other 30% limit. Both gifts are fully deductible because neither is more than the 30% limit that applies ($15,000 in each case) and together they are not more than the 50% limit ($25,000).

For more information, see the rules for electing the 50% limit for capital gain property under *How To Figure Your Deduction When Limits Apply* in Publication 526.

20% Limit

This limit applies to all gifts of capital gain property to or for the use of qualified organizations (other than gifts of capital gain property to 50% limit organizations).

Explanation
An organization can tell you whether contributions to it qualify for the 50%, 30%, or 20% limit.

Contributions to any charitable organization are limited to 50% of your adjusted gross income. This includes a gift of an income interest in trust to a charitable organization.

How to figure your deduction. To figure your deduction, first you consider gifts to charitable organizations that qualify for the 50% limit. Second, you consider gifts to which the 20% and 30% limits apply. Third, you consider gifts of capital gain property to which the special 30% limit for capital gain property applies.

Example 1
Your adjusted gross income is $50,000 for 2005. On September 1, 2005, you gave your church $2,000 cash plus land, with a fair market value of $30,000 and a basis to you of $10,000. You had held the land for investment for more than 1 year. You also gave $5,000 cash to a private foundation to which the 30% limit applies. Because your allowable contributions—$32,000 ($2,000 + $30,000)—to an organization to which the 50% limit applies are more than $25,000 (50% of $50,000), your deductions subject to the 30% limit are not allowable. The $2,000 cash donated to the church is considered first. The deduction for the gift of land does not have to be reduced by the appreciation in value and is limited to $15,000 (30% × $50,000). The unused part ($15,000) may be carried over for 5 years. Therefore, in 2005, your deduction is limited to $17,000 ($2,000 + $15,000). The $5,000 contribution to the private foundation may also be carried over for 5 years.

Example 2
Your 2005 adjusted gross income was $50,000. During the year, you gave $5,000 cash to a private foundation, to which the 30% limit applies. You made no other charitable contributions. The entire $5,000 is deductible, because 30% of $50,000 is greater than $5,000.

TAXPLANNER
Contributions of inventory property that was acquired during the taxable year in which the gift was made are not subject to the percentage limitation rules. The cost of these items is claimed as part of the cost of goods sold.

TAXPLANNER
To ease the restrictions on charitable contribution limitations, you may consider making a series of smaller gifts over several years rather than one or two large gifts per year.

Carryovers

You can carry over your contributions that you are not able to deduct in the current year because they exceed your adjusted-gross-income limits. You can deduct the excess in each of the next 5 years until it is used up, but not beyond that time. For more information, see *Carryovers* in Publication 526.

Explanation
For contributions made to private non-operating foundations that are in excess of 30% of your adjusted gross income, or 20% for capital gain property, you may continue to deduct the excess in each of the next 5 years until it is used up.

You may not carry over gifts to certain veterans' organizations, fraternal societies, and nonprofit cemetery companies to which the 20% limit applies.

For other contributions in excess of the percentage limitations, you may deduct the amount carried over in the following year to the extent that it is not more than the applicable percentage of your adjusted gross income for that year less the amount donated to qualified organizations during that year. In other words, current-year contributions are considered *before* prior-year carryovers. The excess can be carried over for 5 years.

The carryover amounts retain their respective limitation percentages in the carryover year.

Excess contributions can be carried over only to subsequent returns of the person who made the gift. However, if the person who made the gift dies, the carryover is lost.

Example 1
You had adjusted gross income of $20,000 in 2004. During the year, you contributed $11,000 cash to your church.

You deducted $10,000 in 2004 (50% of $20,000) and carried over $1,000. In 2005, you had adjusted gross income of $20,000 and contributed $9,000 during the year. You can deduct the entire amount that you carried over from 2004. However, if you had contributed $9,500 during 2005, you could deduct only $500 of the $1,000 you carried over, carrying over the balance of $500 to 2006.

Example 2
Your adjusted gross income for 2005 and 2006 is $50,000 and $20,000, respectively. During 2005, you contributed long-term capital gain property valued at $25,000 to your church. In 2005, you deducted $15,000 (30% of $50,000) and carried over $10,000. In 2006, however, your carryover deduction is limited to 30% of $20,000, or $6,000; the remaining $4,000 will have to be carried over to 2007.

Explanation

If a gift of long-term capital gain property subject to the 30% limitation is made and, for some unforeseen reasons, cannot be utilized entirely in the current year or in carryover years, you may elect to reduce its value by 100% of the gain and deduct the lower net value of the gift under the 50% limitation.

Example

Julia Walsh makes a contribution of long-term capital gain property that cost her $40,000 and now has a fair market value of $50,000. Julia dies during the taxable year. Her adjusted gross income on her final return is $80,000.

Without the election mentioned above, Julia's deduction would be limited to $24,000 (30% × $80,000). However, if the value of the property is reduced by $10,000, the deduction is increased to $40,000.

Records To Keep

You must keep records to prove the amount of the cash and noncash contributions you make during the year. The kind of records you must keep depends on the amount of your contributions and whether they are cash or noncash contributions.

TaxOrganizer

If the IRS raises questions. In case the IRS questions your charitable contribution deductions, you should keep the following information to support your claim for charitable contribution deductions:

- Canceled checks evidencing payments of charitable contributions.
- Receipts (letter or other written communication) from the charitable organization showing the name of the organization, the date of the contribution, and the amount of the contribution. The IRS now allows the use of e-mail receipts.
- Other reliable written records that include the information described above (records may be considered reliable if they were made at or near the time of the contribution, were regularly kept by you, or if, in the case of small donations, you have emblems, buttons, or other tokens that are regularly given to persons making small cash contributions).
- Copies of appraisals (if you are claiming a deduction in excess of $5,000) or other determinations of the market value of the contribution.

Note. An organization generally must give you a written statement if it receives a payment from you that is more than $75 and is partly a contribution and partly for goods or services. (See *Contributions From Which You Benefit* under *Contributions You Can Deduct*, earlier.) Keep the statement for your records. It may satisfy all or part of the record-keeping requirements explained in the following discussions.

Cash Contributions

Cash contributions include those paid by cash, check, credit card, or payroll deduction. They also include your out-of-pocket expenses when donating your services.

For a contribution made in cash, the records you must keep depend on whether the contribution is:

- Less than $250, or
- $250 or more.

Amount of contribution. In figuring whether your contribution is $250 or more, do not combine separate contributions. For example, if you gave your church $25 each week, your weekly payments do not have to be combined. Each payment is a separate contribution.

If contributions are made by payroll deduction, the deduction from each paycheck is treated as a separate contribution.

If you made a payment that is partly for goods and services, as described earlier under *Contributions From Which You Benefit*, your contribution is the amount of the payment that is more than the value of the goods and services.

Contributions of Less Than $250

For each cash contribution that is less than $250, you must keep one of the following items.

1. A canceled check, or a legible and readable account statement that shows:
   a. If payment was by check: the check number, amount, date posted, and to whom paid.
   b. If payment was by electronic funds transfer: the amount, date posted, and to whom paid.
   c. If payment was charged to a credit card: the amount, transaction date, and to whom paid.
2. A receipt (or a letter or other written communication) from the charitable organization showing the name of the organization, the date of the contribution, and the amount of the contribution.
3. Other reliable written records that include the information described in (2). Records may be considered reliable if they were made at or near the time of the contribution, and were regularly kept by you, or if, in the case of small donations, you have emblems, buttons, or other tokens that are regularly given to persons making small cash contributions.

Car expenses. If you claim expenses directly related to the use of your car in giving services to a qualified organization, you must keep reliable written records of your expenses. Whether your records are considered reliable depends on all the facts and circumstances. Generally, they may be considered reliable if you made them regularly and at or near the time you had the expenses.

Your records must show the name of the organization you were serving and the date each time you used your car for a charitable purpose. If you use the standard mileage rate of 14 cents a mile, your records must show the miles you drove your car for the charitable purpose. If you deduct your actual expenses, your records must show the costs of operating the car that are directly related to a charitable purpose.

TaxAlert

As this book was going to press, changes in the standard mileage rate for charitable purposes were being considered. See the special section on tax changes relating to Hurricane Katrina at the front of this book.

See *Car expenses,* earlier, under *Out-of-Pocket Expenses in Giving Services,* for the expenses you can deduct.

Contributions of $250 or More

You can claim a deduction for a contribution of $250 or more only if you have an acknowledgment of your contribution from the qualified organization or certain payroll deduction records.

If you made more than one contribution of $250 or more, you must have either a separate acknowledgment for each or one acknowledgment that shows your total contributions.

Written acknowledgments. You are required to obtain a contemporaneous written acknowledgment from any charitable organization to which a contribution of $250 or more is made in order to deduct that contribution. *Contemporaneous* for this purpose means that you must obtain the written acknowledgment on or before the earlier of (1) the date on which your 2005 return is actually filed or (2) the due date for the return, including extensions. An e-mail receipt qualifies as a written acknowledgment.

A canceled check does not constitute adequate substantiation for a cash contribution of the amount. The written acknowledgment will have to state the amount of cash and a description (but not the value) of any property other than cash contributed. It must also state whether the charitable organization provided any goods or services in consideration for the contribution, and, if so, a description and good faith estimate of the value of goods or services provided. If the goods or services provided as consideration for the contribution consist solely of intangible religious benefits, a statement to that effect will have to be included in the written acknowledgment.

Note that the primary responsibility lies with you, not the charitable organization, to request and maintain the required substantiation in your records.

For any contribution over $75 for which the charity provides goods or services, such as a dinner, the charity must provide a statement to the donor that reports the estimated value of the goods or services received by the donor in exchange for the contribution. A payment to a charity is deductible only to the extent that it exceeds the value of any goods or services received in return.

Separate payments. In general, separate payments are not combined for purposes of the substantiation requirement. Therefore, you could deduct separate contributions of less than $250 from each paycheck or make monthly payments to a charity without running afoul of the requirement. However, you could not, for example, simply write multiple checks on the same day in order to avoid substantiation. Similarly, separate payments made at different times with respect to different fundraising events are not totaled in order to determine whether the charity must inform the donor of the value of any benefit received in return for a donation in excess of $75.

Acknowledgment. The acknowledgment must meet these tests.

1. It must be written.
2. It must include:
   a. The amount of cash you contributed,
   b. Whether the qualified organization gave you any goods or services as a result of your contribution (other than certain token items and membership benefits), and
   c. A description and good faith estimate of the value of any goods or services described in (b). If the only benefit you received was an intangible religious benefit (such as admission to a religious ceremony) that generally is not sold in a commercial transaction outside the donative context, the acknowledgment must say so and does not need to describe or estimate the value of the benefit.
3. You must get it on or before the earlier of:

   a. The date you file your return for the year you make the contribution, or
   b. The due date, including extensions, for filing the return.

Payroll deductions. If you make a contribution by payroll deduction, you do not need an acknowledgment from the qualified organization. But if your employer deducted $250 or more from a single paycheck, you must keep:

- A pay stub, Form W-2, or other document furnished by your employer that proves the amount withheld, and
- A pledge card or other document from the qualified organization that states the organization does not provide goods or services in return for any contribution made to it by payroll deduction.

Out-of-pocket expenses. If you render services to a qualified organization and have unreimbursed out-of-pocket expenses related to those services, you can satisfy the written acknowledgment requirement just discussed if:

1. You have adequate records to prove the amount of the expenses, and
2. By the required date, you get an acknowledgment from the qualified organization that contains:
   a. A description of the services you provided,
   b. A statement of whether or not the organization provided you any goods or services to reimburse you for the expenses you incurred,
   c. A description and a good faith estimate of the value of any goods or services (other than intangible religious benefits) provided to reimburse you, and
   d. A statement of any intangible religious benefits provided to you.

Noncash Contributions

For a contribution not made in cash, the records you must keep depend on whether your deduction for the contribution is:

1. Less than $250,
2. At least $250 but not more than $500,
3. Over $500 but not more than $5,000, or
4. Over $5,000 but not more than $500,000,
5. Over $500,000, or
6. A vehicle donation.

Amount of contribution. In figuring whether your contribution is $250 or more, do not combine separate contributions. If you received goods or services in return, as described earlier in *Contributions From Which You Benefit*, reduce your contribution by the value of those goods or services. If you figure your deduction by reducing the fair market value of the donated property by its appreciation, as described earlier in *Giving Property That Has Increased in Value*, your contribution is the reduced amount.

Deductions of Less Than $250
If you make any noncash contribution, you must get and keep a receipt from the charitable organization showing:

1. The name of the charitable organization,
2. The date and location of the charitable contribution, and
3. A reasonably detailed description of the property.

Tip. *A letter or other written communication from the charitable organization acknowledging receipt of the contribution and containing the information in (1), (2), and (3) will serve as a receipt.*

You are not required to have a receipt where it is impractical to get one (for example, if you leave property at a charity's unattended drop site).
Additional records. You must also keep reliable written records for each item of donated property. Your written records must include the following information.

- The name and address of the organization to which you contributed.
- The date and location of the contribution.

- A description of the property in detail reasonable under the circumstances. For a security, keep the name of the issuer, the type of security, and whether it is regularly traded on a stock exchange or in an over-the-counter market.
- The fair market value of the property at the time of the contribution and how you figured the fair market value. If it was determined by appraisal, keep a signed copy of the appraisal.
- The cost or other basis of the property if you must reduce its fair market value by appreciation. Your records should also include the amount of the reduction and how you figured it. If you choose the 50% limit instead of the special 30% limit on certain capital gain property, you must keep a record showing the years for which you made the choice, contributions for the current year to which the choice applies, and carryovers from preceding years to which the choice applies. See *How To Figure Your Deduction When Limits Apply* in Publication 526 for information on how to make the capital gain property election.
- The amount you claim as a deduction for the tax year as a result of the contribution, if you contribute less than your entire interest in the property during the tax year. Your records must include the amount you claimed as a deduction in any earlier years for contributions of other interests in this property. They must also include the name and address of each organization to which you contributed the other interests, the place where any such tangible property is located or kept, and the name of any person in possession of the property, other than the organization to which you contributed.
- The terms of any conditions attached to the gift of property.

Deductions of At Least $250 But Not More Than $500

If you claim a deduction of at least $250 but not more than $500 for a noncash charitable contribution, you must get and keep an acknowledgment of your contribution from the qualified organization. If you made more than one contribution of $250 or more, you must have either a separate acknowledgment for each or one acknowledgment that shows your total contribution.

The acknowledgment must contain the information in items (1) through (3) listed under *Deductions of Less Than $250,* earlier, and your written records must include the information listed in that discussion under *Additional records.*

The acknowledgment must also meet these tests.

1. It must be written.
2. It must include:
   a. A description (but not necessarily the value) of any property you contributed,
   b. Whether the qualified organization gave you any goods or services as a result of your contribution (other than certain token items and membership benefits), and
   c. A description and good faith estimate of the value of any goods or services described in (b). If the only benefit you received was an intangible religious benefit (such as admission to a religious ceremony) that generally is not sold in a commercial transaction outside the donative context, the acknowledgment must say so and does not need to describe or estimate the value of the benefit.
3. You must get it on or before the earlier of:
   a. The date you file your return for the year you make the contribution, or
   b. The due date, including extensions, for filing the return.

Deductions Over $500

You are required to give additional information if you claim a deduction over $500 for noncash charitable contributions. See *Records To Keep* in Publication 526 for more information.

Explanation

A receipt is not required if you deposit property at a charity's unattended drop site unless you claim that the property is worth more than $250. However, you must maintain a written record of the contribution, listing the items contributed and the date and location of the contribution.

You are required to file Form 8283, *Noncash Charitable Contributions,* if you claim a deduction of over $500 for noncash contributions. Additionally, there are special rules for noncash contributions in excess of $5,000 and $500,000, as well as donations of vehicles, discussed previously in this chapter.

For contributions having a fair market value of more than $500 but not more than $5,000, the donor must provide the following information:

- The name and address of the charitable organization
- The description of the donated property
- The date of the contribution
- The date it was acquired by the donor
- How it was acquired by the donor
- The donor's cost or adjusted basis (except for publicly traded securities or property held for more than 12 months)
- The fair market value of the contribution
- The method used to determine the fair market value (e.g., appraisal, thrift shop value, catalog, market quote, or comparable sales)

Form 8283 must be filed with the tax return on which the deduction is taken.

For contributions in excess of $500,000 you must attach a copy of the qualified appraisal to your return.

Qualified Conservation Contribution

If the gift was a qualified conservation contribution, your records must also include the fair market value of the underlying property before and after the gift and the conservation purpose furthered by the gift. See *Qualified conservation contribution* in Publication 561 for more information.

How To Report

Enter your cash contributions (including out-of-pocket expenses) on Schedule A (Form 1040), line 15.

Enter your noncash contributions on Schedule A (Form 1040), line 16.

If your total deduction for all noncash contributions for the year is over $500, you must also file Form 8283. See *How To Report* in Publication 526 for more information.

Casualty and Theft Losses

Note: The 2004 IRS Publication 17 (Your Federal Income Tax) has been updated by Ernst & Young LLP for 2005. Dates and dollar amounts shown are for 2005. Gray type is used to indicate where IRS text has been updated or intentionally omitted. Unrevised IRS text is shown in black type.

Introduction

Almost anytime something you own is stolen, damaged, or destroyed in an accident or by an act of nature and you are not compensated by insurance, you are eligible for a tax **deduction.** *The loss need not be connected in any way to your trade or business, and it may include such personal items as jewelry, furs, and antiques. That's small comfort if everything you own has been demolished in a terrible earthquake or a devastating hurricane, but it's something.*

In order to claim a **casualty loss deduction,** *you must first prove that the casualty occurred. The most difficult task is substantiating the value of the property you have lost. That gorgeous necklace that your grandmother gave you may be worth a substantial amount, but, unless you can prove it, you're going to have a difficult time claiming a tax deduction if it is stolen. (Of course, even if you can prove the value your deduction is generally limited to your cost basis.) Recordkeeping and documentation are extremely important.*

No matter how good your records are, you must first pass two general limitations on the amount of your casualty and theft loss. First, you may not deduct the first $100 of any loss. Second and more significant, you are able to deduct personal casualty and theft losses only when the total amount you lost in any year (reduced by $100 per casualty) exceeds 10% of your **adjusted gross income.** *(The rules for deducting business losses are different. They are also discussed in this chapter.)*

This chapter spells out which casualty losses are deductible. You'll also learn about the details that should be considered in deciding when to take your deduction. Most importantly, this chapter discusses the records and other evidence you need to support any claim that you make.

Generally, for 2005, your itemized deductions are limited if your adjusted gross income exceeds $145,950 ($72,975 for married persons filing separately). However, this additional limitation does not apply to casualty or theft losses.

TaxAlert

See the special section in the front of this guide for information on tax changes relating to Hurricane Katrina.

This chapter explains the tax treatment of personal (not business related) casualty losses, theft losses, and losses on deposits.

Explanation

This chapter, however, does include a discussion on what to do if a loss is partly business and partly personal. For example, if your basement flooded and damage occurred to both personal property and business property from your home office located in the basement, the loss would be partly business and partly personal. See *Property used partly for business and partly for personal purposes,* later in this chapter.

The chapter also explains the following topics.

• How to figure the amount of your loss.
• How to treat insurance and other reimbursements you receive.
• The deduction limits.
• When and how to report a casualty or theft.

Explanation

This chapter also discusses the special rules for disaster area losses.

Forms to file. When you have a casualty or theft, you have to file Form 4684. You will also have to file one or both of the following forms.

• Schedule A (Form 1040), Itemized Deductions
• Schedule D (Form 1040), Capital Gains and Losses

Explanation

For details on which form to use, see *How to Report Gains and Losses,* later in this chapter.

Condemnations. For information on condemnations of property, see *Involuntary Conversions* in chapter 1 of Publication 544.

Workbook for casualties and thefts. Publication 584 is available to help you make a list of your stolen or damaged personal-use property and figure your loss. It includes schedules to help you figure the loss on your home, its contents, and your motor vehicles.

TAXPLANNER

Publication 584-B is available to help you make a list of your stolen or damaged business or income-producing property and figure your loss.

Other sources of information. For information on a casualty or theft loss of business or income-producing property, see Publication 547.

Useful Items

You may want to see:

Publications

☐ **544**   Sales and Other Dispositions of Assets
☐ **547**   Casualties, Disasters, and Thefts
☐ **584**   Casualty, Disaster, and Theft Loss Workbook (Personal-Use Property)

Forms (and Instructions)

☐ **Schedule A (Form 1040)**   Itemized Deductions
☐ **Schedule D (Form 1040)**   Capital Gains and Losses
☐ **4684**   Casualties and Thefts

Casualty

A casualty is the damage, destruction, or loss of property resulting from an identifiable event that is sudden, unexpected, or unusual.

- A sudden event is one that is swift, not gradual or progressive.
- An unexpected event is one that is ordinarily unanticipated and unintended.
- An unusual event is one that is not a day-to-day occurrence and that is not typical of the activity in which you were engaged.

Deductible losses. Deductible casualty losses can result from a number of different causes, including the following.

- Car accidents (but see *Nondeductible losses,* next, for exceptions).

Explanation
Damage resulting from faulty but not intentionally reckless driving is a casualty loss. Damage incurred while an automobile was operated by an unauthorized person is also a casualty loss.

The following are examples of casualty losses involving automobiles:

- The loss of an automobile that fell through the ice while the taxpayer was ice fishing
- Damage to an automobile starter caused by a child who pressed the starter button while the automobile's engine was operating

- Earthquakes.
- Fires (but see *Nondeductible losses,* next, for exceptions).
- Floods.
- Government-ordered demolition or relocation of a home that is unsafe to use because of a disaster as discussed under *Disaster Area Losses* in Publication 547.
- Mine cave-ins.
- Shipwrecks.
- Sonic booms.
- Storms, including hurricanes and tornadoes.
- Terrorist attacks
- Vandalism.
- Volcanic eruptions

Explanation
Losses caused by a person's own negligence are deductible, as are losses that occur even though they could have been foreseen or prevented. The courts have also *allowed* casualty loss deductions in the following cases:

Animals and insects
- Damage caused by a mass attack of southern pine beetles capable of destroying a tree in 5 to 10 days
- Death of a horse by swallowing the lining of a hat

Drought
- Cracking of foundation walls due to soil shrinkage
- Death of trees and plants within 3 to 4 months as a result of extraordinary drought

Earthquakes and landslides
- Collapse of a garage wall due to subsoil hydraulic action
- Damage caused by a mine cave-in (a deduction was allowed even though the landslide was reasonably foreseeable)

Household
- Bursting of hot water boiler caused by air obstruction in water pipes
- Damage to furniture dropped 16 floors by movers
- Damage caused by a flood due to faulty construction (however, the cost of repairing the defect was not deductible)

Lightning
- Any damage by lightning

Personal belongings
- Damage to a diamond ring inadvertently dropped in a kitchen garbage disposal
- Damage to a ring caused by a husband slamming a car door on his wife's finger

Septic tank
- Damage by a tractor plowing the ground

Storms
- Damage to a beach due to abnormal rains
- Damage to a home by ice and snow
- Damage to a beach house that was caused by a hurricane but was not discovered until 2 years later, when the floorboards and porch buckled (the loss was deductible in the year in which the damage was discovered)
- Property damage due to unusually high water levels caused by storms

Trees, shrubs, and landscaping

- Damage caused by accidental application of chemical weed killer to a lawn
- Damage to trees caused by blizzards and snowstorms
- Loss of trees, shrubs, and grass due to fire

Vandalism

- Damage to household appliances caused by vandals who broke into a house under construction
- Damage and destruction of art objects by vandals

Nondeductible losses. A casualty loss is not deductible if the damage or destruction is caused by the following.

- Accidentally breaking articles such as glassware or china under normal conditions.
- A family pet.
- A fire if you willfully set it or pay someone else to set it.
- A car accident if your willful negligence or willful act caused it. The same is true if the willful act or willful negligence of someone acting for you caused the accident.
- Progressive deterioration (explained next).

Progressive deterioration. Loss of property due to progressive deterioration is not deductible as a casualty loss. This is because the damage results from a steadily operating cause or a normal process, rather than from a sudden event. The following are examples of damage due to progressive deterioration.

- The steady weakening of a building due to normal wind and weather conditions.
- The deterioration and damage to a water heater that bursts. However, the rust and water damage to rugs and drapes caused by the bursting of a water heater does qualify as a casualty.

Explanation

The following also do *not* qualify as casualty losses: damage from faulty construction that caused walls and floors to settle, dry rot to a wooden sloop, and the decline in value of a piece of land affected by gradual deterioration. However, the breaking up of a driveway caused by weather conditions over a 4-month period has been allowed.

- Most losses of property caused by droughts. To be deductible, a drought-related loss generally must be incurred in a trade or business or in a transaction entered into for profit.

Explanation

A water well that ran dry because of a drought may not be deducted as a casualty loss. The courts have also *disallowed* deductions for casualty losses in the following cases:

Animals and insects

- Damage to shrubs eaten by a horse
- Damage to an antique vase by a cat
- Damage to a fur coat by moths
- Loss of a valuable dog that strayed off

Automobiles

- Damage to a fuel pump and muffler caused by high stones in a road (the taxpayer was unable to prove that it was more than wear and tear)
- Damage caused by a tire blowout due to overloading

- Damage caused by exposure to saltwater
- The forced sale of an automobile due to divorce
- Damage caused by potholes in the road

Earthquakes and landslides

- Any additional loss in value due to buyer resistance (a deduction is allowed only for physical damage)

Household items

- Sale of household items by a storage company (the sale was not an unexpected occurrence)

Personal belongings

- The loss of a ring from the owner's finger
- The accidental disposal of tissues in which two rings were wrapped
- The accidental dropping of eyeglasses or a watch
- The loss of baggage and contents in transit

Shipwreck

- The snapping of a propeller on a yacht that was not the result of a shipwreck or other casualty

Trees, shrubs, and landscaping

- Damage to trees from Dutch elm disease (the disease is progressive and not sudden or unexpected)
- The gradual suffocation of a root system over a 16-month period
- Damage to palm trees caused by lethal yellowing

- Termite or moth damage.
- The damage or destruction of trees, shrubs, or other plants by a fungus, disease, insects, worms, or similar pests. However, a sudden destruction due to an unexpected or unusual infestation of beetles or other insects may result in a casualty loss.

Explanation

The following are also *not* considered casualty losses: damage to trees and plants caused by moths, damage caused by rat infestation, the death of a horse from colic, and the loss of livestock due to disease.

Theft

A theft is the taking and removing of money or property with the intent to deprive the owner of it. The taking of property must be illegal under the laws of the state where it occurred and it must have been done with criminal intent.

Explanation

A theft loss is deducted in the year of discovery, not the year of the theft, unless they both occur in the same year. If, in the year of discovery, an insurance claim exists and there is a reasonable expectation of recovering the cost of the asset from the insurance company, no deduction is permitted. Losses on securities which resulted from malfeasance of officers or directors—such as in the case of Enron—are not considered theft losses. Instead the loss is treated as a capital loss.

Theft includes the taking of money or property by the following means.

- Blackmail.
- Burglary.

- Embezzlement.
- Extortion.
- Kidnapping for ransom.
- Larceny.
- Robbery.
- Threats.

Examples

- A taxpayer from New York was allowed a deduction for a theft loss for money given to fortune-tellers. Under New York law, fortune-telling is a crime. The taxpayer's testimony and receipts were sufficient proof of the amounts paid to the fortune-tellers.
- A moving company placed an individual's belongings in storage until a price dispute could be resolved. A court ruled that because there was a reasonable likelihood that the individual would recover his property, no theft loss was allowed.

The taking of money or property through fraud or misrepresentation is theft if it is illegal under state or local law.

Decline in market value of stock. You cannot deduct as a theft loss the decline in market value of stock acquired on the open market for investment if the decline is caused by disclosure of accounting fraud or other illegal misconduct by the officers or directors of the corporation that issued the stock. However, you can deduct as a capital loss the loss you sustain when you sell or exchange the stock or the stock becomes completely worthless. You report a capital loss on Schedule D (Form 1040). For more information about stock sales, worthless stock, and capital losses, see chapter 4 of Publication 550.

Mislaid or lost property. The simple disappearance of money or property is not a theft. However, an accidental loss or disappearance of property can qualify as a casualty if it results from an identifiable event that is sudden, unexpected, or unusual. Sudden, unexpected, and unusual events are defined earlier.

Example. A car door is accidentally slammed on your hand, breaking the setting of your diamond ring. The diamond falls from the ring and is never found. The loss of the diamond is a casualty.

Explanation

Another type of loss you may experience is seizure, requisition, or condemnation. For example, the government might seize your home in order to build a new highway. For further discussion, see Chapter 14, *Basis of Property,* and Chapter 15, *Sale of Property.*

Loss on Deposits

A loss on deposits can occur when a bank, credit union, or other financial institution becomes insolvent or bankrupt. If you incurred this type of loss, you can choose one of the following ways to deduct the loss.

- As a casualty loss.
- As an ordinary loss.
- As a nonbusiness bad debt.

Explanation

For more information see *Special Treatment for Losses on Deposits in Insolvent or Bankrupt Financial Institutions* in the instructions for Form 4684.

Casualty loss or ordinary loss. You can choose to deduct a loss on deposits as a casualty loss or as an ordinary loss for any year in which you can reasonably estimate how much of your deposits you have lost in an insolvent or bankrupt financial institution. The choice is generally made on the return you file for that year and applies to all your losses on deposits for the year in that particular financial institution. If you treat the loss as a casualty or ordinary loss, you cannot treat the same amount of the loss as a nonbusiness bad debt when it actually becomes worthless. However, you can take a nonbusiness bad debt deduction for any amount of loss that is more than the estimated amount you deducted as a casualty or ordinary loss. Once you make this choice, you cannot change it without approval of the Internal Revenue Service.

If you claim an ordinary loss, report it as a miscellaneous itemized deduction on line 22 of Schedule A (Form 1040). The maximum amount you can claim is $20,000 ($10,000 if you are married filing separately) reduced by any expected state insurance proceeds. Your loss is subject to the 2%-of-adjusted-gross-income limit. You cannot choose to claim an ordinary loss if any part of the deposit is federally insured.

Explanation

If you choose to treat the loss as a casualty loss, it is subject to $100 per event and 10% of your adjusted gross income limitations (see *Deduction Limits,* later).

Example

In 2005, Molly had an adjusted gross income of $25,000 and a loss on deposits of $7,100.

Casualty loss (minus $100 floor)	$7,000
Less: 10% of AGI (10% × $25,000)	2,500
Itemized deduction	$4,500

For 2005, Molly would have a $4,500 itemized deduction with no further tax deduction in the following tax year.

Nonbusiness bad debt. If you do not choose to deduct the loss as a casualty loss or as an ordinary loss, you must wait until the year the actual loss is determined and deduct the loss as a nonbusiness bad debt in that year.

Explanation

A nonbusiness bad debt arises from loans between an individual and those not connected with the individual's business. If you elect to treat the loss as a nonbusiness bad debt, the loss is treated as a short-term capital loss. Capital losses, net of capital gains, are subject to the $3,000 ($1,500 for married persons filing separately) capital loss limitation in any 1 year, with any excess over the annual limit being deductible in following tax years. See Chapter 17, *Reporting Gains and Losses,* for a further explanation of the limitations regarding the deductibility of capital losses.

Example

If Molly chose to treat her loss on deposits as a nonbusiness bad debt, she would have a $3,000 loss in 2005, a $3,000 loss in 2006, and $1,100 loss in 2007, assuming no other capital gains or losses in these years. Her total allowable loss is $7,100.

How to report. The kind of deduction you choose for your loss on deposits determines how you report your loss. If you choose:

- Casualty loss—report it on Form 4684 first and then on Schedule A (Form 1040).
- Ordinary loss—report it on Schedule A (Form 1040) as a miscellaneous itemized deduction.
- Nonbusiness bad debt—report it on Schedule D (Form 1040).

More information. For more information, see *Special Treatment for Losses on Deposits in Insolvent or Bankrupt Financial Institutions* in the instructions for Form 4684.

Explanation
Deducted loss recovered. If you recover an amount you deducted as loss in an earlier year, you may have to include the amount recovered in your income for the year of recovery. If any part of the original deduction did not reduce your tax in the earlier year, you do not have to include that part of the recovery in your income. For more information, see *Recoveries* in Publication 525.

Proof of Loss

To deduct a casualty or theft loss, you must be able to prove that you had a casualty or theft. You must be able to support the amount you claim for the loss as discussed next.

Casualty loss proof. For a casualty loss, your records should show all the following.

- The type of casualty (car accident, fire, storm, etc.) and when it occurred.
- That the loss was a direct result of the casualty.
- That you were the owner of the property or, if you leased the property from someone else, that you were contractually liable to the owner for the damage.
- Whether a claim for reimbursement exists for which there is a reasonable expectation of recovery.

Theft loss proof. For a theft loss, your records should show all the following.

- When you discovered that your property was missing.
- That your property was stolen.
- That you were the owner of the property.
- Whether a claim for reimbursement exists for which there is a reasonable expectation of recovery.

TaxPlanner

It is important that you have records that will prove your deduction. If you do not have the actual records to support your deduction, you can use other satisfactory evidence that is sufficient to establish your deduction. **Proving a theft took place.** For a loss from theft to be deductible, you must be able to prove that a theft has taken place. Therefore, if you think a theft may have occurred, you should file a report with the police and attach a copy of the police report to your return. The report should tell of any evidence of breaking and entering and of any witness to the removal of the property. It is not necessary that the police investigate the alleged incident. **Supporting evidence.** If you are going to claim a deduction for a casualty or theft loss, it is important that you gather as much supporting evidence as possible. Newspaper clippings about a storm, police reports, and insurance reports may all be helpful in proving the nature of the casualty or theft and when it occurred. You have the burden of proof to establish that a casualty occurred and that your loss was a direct result of the casualty.

Example
The Tax Court disallowed a casualty loss deducted for flood damage because the taxpayer failed to corroborate his testimony or provide reliable substantiation of the amount of loss, such as an inventory of damaged personal items and receipts for repairs to his residence.

Explanation
If there is no positive proof that a theft occurred, all details and evidence should be presented. If evidence points to a theft, the Tax Court has allowed a deduction. However, if the evidence points to a mysterious (unexplained) disappearance, deductions may be disallowed. **If the property is leased.** Losses are deductible only by the owner of the property, unless the property is leased and the lessee is obligated to repair casualty damage to the property.

Examples
- If you purchase an automobile for your son or daughter and put the title to the automobile in the child's name, any casualty or theft loss is deductible by the child—not by you.
- If you damage another person's property, you may not deduct any payments you make to restore or replace that property.
- Members of social clubs may not deduct an assessment to repair hurricane damage to club property.

Amount of Loss

Figure the amount of your loss using the following steps.

1. Determine your adjusted basis in the property before the casualty or theft.
2. Determine the decrease in fair market value of the property as a result of the casualty or theft.
3. From the smaller of the amounts you determined in (1) and (2), subtract any insurance or other reimbursement you received or expect to receive.

Explanation
Calculate your loss, taking into consideration any reimbursements you may receive. Your loss is limited to the lesser of your cost or the reduction in fair market value.

Proof of the amount of a casualty loss is as important as proving the existence of the casualty. There are numerous court cases in which the taxpayers have shown the existence of a casualty but failed to establish a loss amount and were therefore denied a casualty loss deduction.

Example 1
A ruby ring valued at $5,000 is stolen from your house. The ring was purchased by your grandfather in 1950 for $500 and was handed down through two generations by means of nontaxable gifts. The amount of the loss is limited to $500, the cost of the ring to your grandfather.

Example 2
A homeowner was not entitled to a casualty loss deduction resulting from hurricane damage to trees lo-

cated on his property. A real estate agent's appraisal was not accepted as adequate proof of decline in the fair market value of the property. Thus, the decrease in the fair market value of the property as a result of the casualty was zero.

TaxPlanner

Establishing the amount of your loss may be difficult, but the time you spend documenting the loss may be of great value in reducing your tax. You should make a list of all stolen, lost, damaged, or destroyed items as soon after the theft, disaster, or casualty as possible. IRS Publication 584, *Disaster and Casualty Loss Workbook,* may be useful. It has schedules to help you calculate a loss on your home and its contents and on your automobile, van, truck, or motorcycle.

It is equally important to retain records that help you establish the adjusted basis of valuable property. In other words, you should keep as supporting documentation receipts and documents establishing the original purchase price, costs of improvements, portions sold, or earlier losses in the value of the property.

In one court opinion, a taxpayer was denied a casualty loss deduction because she failed to establish either her basis in or the fair market value of the property.

Determining the decrease in market value of household items and personal belongings is often difficult. A certain percentage of the original cost of an item has often been used both by the IRS and by the courts to determine the fair market value of a particular item. Therefore, if you can produce evidence of the original cost of the items that were lost or damaged, you may help your case.

For personal-use property and property used in performing services as an employee, apply the deduction limits, discussed later, to determine the amount of your deductible loss.

Explanation
Gain from reimbursement. If your reimbursement is more than your adjusted basis in the property, you have a gain. This is true even if the decrease in the fair market value of the property is smaller than your adjusted basis.

If you have a gain, you may have to pay tax on it or you may be able to postpone reporting the gain. See *Insurance and Other Reimbursements,* later.

Leased property. If you are liable for casualty damage to property you lease, your loss is the amount you must pay to repair the property minus any insurance or other reimbursement you receive or expect to receive.

Explanation
Business or income-producing property. If you have business or income-producing property, such as rental property, and it is stolen or completely destroyed, the decrease in fair market value is not considered. Your loss is figured as follows: Your adjusted basis in the property minus any salvage value minus any insurance or other reimbursement you receive or expect to receive.

Adjusted Basis

Adjusted basis is your basis in the property (usually cost) increased or decreased by various events, such as improvements and casualty losses. For more information, see chapter 14.

TaxPlanner

Separate computations. Generally, if a single casualty or theft involves more than one item of property, you must figure the loss on each item separately; then combine the losses to determine the total loss from that casualty or theft.

Exception for personal-use real property. In figuring a casualty loss on personal-use real property, the entire property (including any improvements, such as buildings, trees, and shrubs) is treated as one item. Figure the loss using the smaller of the following:

- The decrease in fair market value of the entire property
- The adjusted basis of the entire property

Decrease in Fair Market Value

Fair market value (FMV) is the price for which you could sell your property to a willing buyer when neither of you has to sell or buy and both of you know all the relevant facts.

The decrease in FMV is the difference between the property's fair market value immediately before and immediately after the casualty or theft.

FMV of stolen property. The FMV of property immediately after a theft is considered to be zero, since you no longer have the property.

Example
Several years ago, you purchased silver dollars at face value for $150. This is your adjusted basis in the property. Your silver dollars were stolen this year. The fair market value of the coins was $1,000 when stolen, and insurance did not cover them. Your theft loss is $150, the lesser of the adjusted basis in the property ($150), or the decrease in fair market value of the property ($1,000).

Recovered stolen property. Recovered stolen property is your property that was stolen and later returned to you. If you recover property after you had already taken a theft loss deduction, you must refigure your loss using the smaller of the property's adjusted basis (explained earlier) or the decrease in FMV from the time just before it was stolen until the time it was recovered. Use this amount to refigure your total loss for the year in which the loss was deducted.

If your refigured loss is less than the loss you deducted, you generally have to report the difference as income in the recovery year. But report the difference only up to the amount of the loss that reduced your tax. For more information on the amount to report, see *Recoveries* in chapter 13.

Example
Your personal automobile is stolen. You paid $7,000 for it, and, on the day it was stolen, it had a fair market value of $5,500. Several days later, your automobile is found damaged and abandoned. The fair market value

is reduced to $3,000 because of the damage. Your loss is $2,500. The decrease in market value ($5,500 – $3,000) is less than your cost of $7,000. Therefore, your deduction is limited to $2,500.

Figuring Decrease in FMV—Items To Consider
To figure the decrease in FMV because of a casualty or theft, you generally need a competent appraisal. But other measures can also be used to establish certain decreases.

Appraisal. An appraisal to determine the difference between the FMV of the property immediately before a casualty or theft and immediately afterward should be made by a competent appraiser. The appraiser must recognize the effects of any general market decline that may occur along with the casualty. This information is needed to limit any deduction to the actual loss resulting from damage to the property.

Several factors are important in evaluating the accuracy of an appraisal, including the following.

- The appraiser's familiarity with your property before and after the casualty or theft.
- The appraiser's knowledge of sales of comparable property in the area.
- The appraiser's knowledge of conditions in the area of the casualty.
- The appraiser's method of appraisal.

TaxPlanner
You may be able to use an appraisal that you used to get a federal loan (or a federal loan guarantee) as the result of a Presidentially declared disaster to establish the amount of your disaster loss. For more information on disasters, see *Disaster Area Loss,* under *When to Report Gains and Losses,* later.

TaxSaver
Damaged trees. If a casualty occurs that damages or destroys trees or shrubs on your residential property and you do not plan to repair or replace them, make sure that the appraiser's valuation documenting the decrease in the value of the property considers the estimated cleanup costs.

Explanation
An appraisal obtained for the purpose of getting a loan of federal funds or a loan guarantee from the federal government as a result of a disaster declared by the President could also be used to establish the amount of a disaster loss. Consult your tax advisor to be certain you comply with IRS guidelines.

Appraisal fee. The appraisal fee is not a part of the casualty or theft loss. It is an expense in determining your tax liability. You can deduct it as a miscellaneous deduction subject to the 2%-of-adjusted-gross-income limit on Schedule A (Form 1040). See *Costs of photographs and appraisals,* below. For information about miscellaneous deductions, see Chapter 30, *Miscellaneous Deductions.*

TaxSaver
If you have property appraised because you have a casualty loss and the loss turns out not to be deductible because it does not exceed 10% of your adjusted

gross income (see *10% Rule,* under *Deduction Limits,* later), the cost of the appraisal is still deductible as a miscellaneous deduction subject to the 2%-of-adjusted-gross-income limit on Schedule A (Form 1040).

Cost of cleaning up or making repairs. The cost of repairing damaged property is not part of a casualty loss. Neither is the cost of cleaning up after a casualty. But you can use the cost of cleaning up or making repairs as a measure of the decrease in FMV if you meet all the following conditions.

- The repairs are actually made.
- The repairs are necessary to bring the property back to its condition before the casualty.
- The amount spent for repairs is not excessive.
- The repairs take care of the damage only.
- The value of the property after the repairs is not, due to the repairs, more than the value of the property before the casualty.

Explanation
Courts have held that cleanup expenses are deductible in the following circumstances:

- Replanting of damaged trees necessary to restore the property to its approximate value before the casualty
- Removing destroyed or damaged trees and shrubs, less any salvage value received
- Replacing a windstorm-damaged carport

Note: Losses must be reduced by the $100 deductible limit and any money paid by an insurance company (see *$100 Rule,* under *Deduction Limits,* later).

TaxSaver
If the fair market value of your property is decreased. If the repairs do not bring the property back to its condition before the casualty, it may be that the decrease in fair market value is greater than the cost of the repairs. The greater loss is deductible.

Example
As a result of a boating accident, the fair market value of your boat drops from $6,000 to $2,500. You originally paid $5,000 for the boat. You spend $2,000 on repairs, which actually increase the market value of the boat to $4,800. Nevertheless, you are entitled to a deduction of $3,500, which is the decrease in market value as a result of the casualty ($6,000 – $2,500).

Landscaping. The cost of restoring landscaping to its original condition after a casualty may indicate the decrease in FMV. You may be able to measure your loss by what you spend on the following.

- Removing destroyed or damaged trees and shrubs minus any salvage you receive.
- Pruning and other measures taken to preserve damaged trees and shrubs.
- Replanting necessary to restore the property to its approximate value before the casualty.

Explanation
The IRS takes the position that ornamental trees and shrubbery are an integral part of the **real property** and have no separate value. Therefore, the loss from damage

to landscaping is measured by the decline in the fair market value of the entire property, not of an individual tree.

This treatment generally works to your advantage. If you originally planted the trees, your basis in them is probably substantially less than the decline in their fair market value. However, because the trees are regarded as an integral part of the property, your basis for figuring your loss is not just your basis for the trees but your basis for the entire property.

Example
You purchased a lot 10 years ago for $12,000 and spent $2,000 for shrubs and saplings. The entire property is now worth $20,000. A fire destroys all of the now mature shrubs and trees and reduces the market value of the property to $11,000. You are entitled to a deduction of $9,000. Even though you paid only $2,000 for the trees, you paid $14,000 for the entire property. Because the decline in value of $9,000 is less than your basis of $14,000, you may deduct the entire decrease in fair market value.

TaxSaver

Storm damage. After a storm, damaged or fallen mature trees are often replaced with saplings. You should argue that the replacements—the saplings—are worth less than the fallen trees and a loss greater than the cost of the saplings should be allowed. It pays to be aggressive when claiming casualty losses for trees. Even though the IRS does not compute the amount of a loss by assigning values to individual trees or shrubs, that should not stop you from doing so to bolster your claim.

Car value. Books issued by various automobile organizations that list your car may be useful in figuring the value of your car. You can modify the book's retail value by such factors as mileage and the condition of your car to figure its value. The prices are not official, but they may be useful in determining value and suggesting relative prices for comparison with current sales and offerings in your area. If your car is not listed in the books, determine its value from other sources. A dealer's offer for your car as a trade-in on a new car is not usually a measure of its true value.

Figuring Decrease in FMV—Items Not To Consider
The following items are generally not considered when establishing the decrease in the FMV of your property.
Replacement cost. The cost of replacing stolen or destroyed property is not part of a casualty or theft loss.

Example
You bought a new chair 4 years ago for $300. In April, a fire destroyed the chair. You estimate that it would cost $500 to replace it. If you had sold the chair before the fire, you estimate that you could have received only $100 for it because it was 4 years old. The chair was not insured. Your loss is $100, the fair market value of the chair before the fire. It is not $500, the replacement cost.

Cost of protection. The cost of protecting your property against a casualty or theft is not part of a casualty or theft loss. For example, you cannot deduct the amount you spend on insurance or to board up your house against a storm.

Explanation
If the property is business property, these expenses are deductible as business expenses.

If you make permanent improvements to your property to protect it against a casualty or theft, add the cost of these improvements to your basis in the property. An example would be the cost of a dike to prevent flooding.

Explanation
Burglar alarms. The costs of protecting your property against potential casualty are not deductible. This includes such items as burglar alarms and smoke detectors.

Related expenses. Any incidental expenses you have due to a casualty or theft, such as expenses for the treatment of personal injuries, for temporary housing, or for a rental car, are not part of your casualty or theft loss.

TaxSaver
Incidental expenses may be deductible as business expenses if the damaged or stolen property is business property.

However, money spent for temporary lodging at a hotel or an apartment while your residence is being repaired or rebuilt, the cost of water purchased due to well contamination, the cost of putting up a fence around a fire-damaged residence, and the towing of an automobile to a garage for repairs are all personal expenses that may not be deducted.

Sentimental value. Do not consider sentimental value when determining your loss. If a family portrait, heirloom, or keepsake is damaged, destroyed, or stolen, you must base your loss only on its FMV.
Decline in market value of property in or near casualty area. A decrease in the value of your property because it is in or near an area that suffered a casualty, or that might again suffer a casualty, is not to be taken into consideration. You have a loss only for actual casualty damage to your property. However, if your home is in a federally declared disaster area, see *Disaster Area Losses* in Publication 547.

Explanation
Taxpayers have been unable to take deductions for such things as a decline in market value of a house because it is near a newly opened highway or because of the stigma of a previous fire. There must be actual physical damage to the property that is the immediate and direct result of a casualty. However, a court case has held that an owner could deduct as a casualty loss the decrease in fair market value due to permanent buyer resistance resulting from changes made to the neighborhood following a flood.

Costs of photographs and appraisals. Photographs taken after a casualty will be helpful in establishing the condition and value of the property after it was damaged. Photographs showing the condition of the property after it was repaired, restored, or replaced may also be helpful.

Appraisals are used to figure the decrease in FMV because of a casualty or theft. See *Appraisal*, earlier, under *Figuring Decrease in FMV—Items To Consider*, for information about appraisals.

The costs of photographs and appraisals used as evidence of the value and condition of property damaged as a result of a casualty are not a part of the loss. You can claim these costs as a miscellaneous itemized deduction subject to the 2%-of-adjusted-gross-income limit on Schedule A (Form 1040). For information about miscellaneous deductions, see chapter 30.

TaxOrganizer

Photographs or videotapes of your home and its contents may be useful in other ways as well. First, they may provide evidence of value before the casualty. Recent photos, or tapes, for example, may be used to prove that the property was in good condition prior to the casualty. Second, they may assist you in determining what items are missing or were destroyed in a fire or theft. People often do not have an accurate inventory of household items. Photos or tapes serve as useful reminders.

The photographs or videotapes should be updated annually and kept outside your house, preferably in a safe-deposit box. They may be even more important in dealing with your insurance claim than they are in helping you with the IRS.

Insurance and Other Reimbursements

If you receive an insurance payment or other type of reimbursement, you must subtract the reimbursement when you figure your loss. You do not have a casualty or theft loss to the extent you are reimbursed.

If you expect to be reimbursed for part or all of your loss, you must subtract the expected reimbursement when you figure your loss. You must reduce your loss even if you do not receive payment until a later tax year. See *Reimbursement Received After Deducting Loss,* later.

Failure to file a claim for reimbursement. If your property is covered by insurance, you must file a timely insurance claim for reimbursement of your loss. Otherwise, you cannot deduct this loss as a casualty or theft loss. However, this rule does not apply to the portion of the loss not covered by insurance (for example, a deductible).

Example. You have a car insurance policy with a $500 deductible. Because your insurance did not cover the first $500 of an auto collision, the $500 would be deductible (subject to the deduction limits discussed later). This is true even if you do not file an insurance claim, since your insurance policy would never have reimbursed you for the deductible.

Gain from reimbursement. If your reimbursement is more than your adjusted basis in the property, you have a gain. This is true even if the decrease in the FMV of the property is smaller than your adjusted basis. If you have a gain, you may have to pay tax on it, or you may be able to postpone reporting the gain. See Publication 547 for more information on how to treat a gain from a reimbursement for a casualty or theft.

Explanation

You do not have to report a gain that results from a reimbursement that exceeds your basis in the lost, damaged, or destroyed property if you use the entire reimbursement to purchase property that is either similar or related in use to the original property. Instead, the recognition of the gain is postponed until the replacement property is sold. Your basis in the replacement property is its cost minus any postponed gain. With a home, the gain may not be taxable under the new rules for exclusion of gain on home sales (see the rules discussed in Chapter 16, *Selling Your Home*).

You are allowed a certain amount of time to select and purchase the replacement property. This time period begins on the day of the casualty or theft and ends 2 years after the close of the tax year in which the reimbursement is received. Thus, if your house was robbed on August 1, 2002, and your insurance company reimbursed you for your loss on May 1, 2003, you would have until December 31, 2005, to repair or replace the damaged goods. If the cost of the replacement property is less than the reimbursement received, the unspent part of the reimbursement must be recognized as a gain.

Types of Reimbursements

The most common type of reimbursement is an insurance payment for your stolen or damaged property. Other types of reimbursements are discussed next. Also see the Instructions for Form 4684.

Employer's emergency disaster fund. If you receive money from your employer's emergency disaster fund and you must use that money to rehabilitate or replace property on which you are claiming a casualty loss deduction, you must take that money into consideration in computing the casualty loss deduction. Take into consideration only the amount you used to replace your destroyed or damaged property.

Example. Your home was extensively damaged by a tornado. Your loss after reimbursement from your insurance company was $10,000. Your employer set up a disaster relief fund for its employees. Employees receiving money from the fund had to use it to rehabilitate or replace their damaged or destroyed property. You received $4,000 from the fund and spent the entire amount on repairs to your home. In figuring your casualty loss, you must reduce your unreimbursed loss ($10,000) by the $4,000 you received from your employer's fund. Your casualty loss before applying the deduction limits discussed later is $6,000.

Explanation

If you have use and occupancy insurance for your business and are reimbursed for loss of business income, it does not reduce your casualty or theft loss. However, the reimbursement is considered income and is taxed in the same way as your other business income.

Cash gifts. If you receive excludable cash gifts as a disaster victim and there are no limits on how you can use the money, you do not reduce your casualty loss by these excludable cash gifts. This applies even if you use the money to pay for repairs to property damaged in the disaster.

Example. Your home was damaged by a hurricane. Relatives and neighbors made cash gifts to you which were excludable from your income. You used part of the cash gifts to pay for repairs to your home. There were no limits or restrictions on how you could use the cash gifts. Because it was an excludable gift, the money you received and used to pay for repairs to your home does not reduce your casualty loss on the damaged home.

Insurance payments for living expenses. You do not reduce your casualty loss by insurance payments you receive to cover living expenses in either of the following situations.

- You lose the use of your main home because of a casualty.
- Government authorities do not allow you access to your main home because of a casualty or threat of one.

Inclusion in income. If these insurance payments are more than the temporary increase in your living expenses, you must include the excess in your income. Report this amount on line 21 of Form 1040. However, if the casualty occurs in a Presidentially declared disaster area, none of the insurance payments are taxable. See *Qualified disaster relief payments,* under *Disaster Area Losses* in Publication 547.

A temporary increase in your living expenses is the difference between the actual living expenses you and your family incurred during the period you could not use your home and your normal living expenses for that period. Actual living expenses are the reasonable and necessary expenses incurred because of the loss of your main home. Generally, these expenses include the amounts you pay for the following.

- Rent for suitable housing.
- Transportation.
- Food.
- Utilities.
- Miscellaneous services.

Normal living expenses consist of these same expenses that you would have incurred but did not because of the casualty or the threat of one.

Example. As a result of a fire, you vacated your apartment for a month and moved to a motel. You normally pay $525 a month for rent. None was charged for the month the apartment was vacated. Your motel rent for this month was $1,200. You normally pay $200 a month for food. Your food expenses for the month you lived in the motel were $400. You received $1,100 from your insurance company to cover your living expenses. You determine the payment you must include in income as follows.

1) Insurance payment for living expenses.....................................$1,100

2) Actual expenses during the month
you are unable to use your home because
of the fire..1,600

3) Normal living expenses....................................725

4) Temporary increase in living expenses:
Subtract line 3 from line 2 875

5) Amount of payment includible in income:
Subtract line 4 from line 1 .... $225

Tax year of inclusion. You include the taxable part of the insurance payment in income for the year you regain the use of your main home or, if later, for the year you receive the taxable part of the insurance payment.

Example. Your main home was destroyed by a tornado in August 2003. You regained use of your home in November 2004. The insurance payments you received in 2003 and 2004 were $1,500 more than the temporary increase in your living expenses during those years. You include this amount in income on your 2004 Form 1040. If, in 2005, you receive further payments to cover the living expenses you had in 2003 and 2004, you must include those payments in income on your 2005 Form 1040.

Disaster relief. Food, medical supplies, and other forms of assistance you receive do not reduce your casualty loss unless they are replacements for lost or destroyed property. These items are not taxable income to you.

Tip. *Qualified disaster relief payments you receive for expenses you incurred as a result of a Presidentially declared disaster, are not taxable income to you. For more information, see* Disaster Area Losses *in Publication 547.*

Disaster unemployment assistance payments are unemployment benefits that are taxable.

Generally, disaster relief grants received under the Disaster Relief and Emergency Assistance Act are not includible in your income. See *Disaster Area Losses* in Publication 547.

Reimbursement Received After Deducting Loss

If you figured your casualty or theft loss using your expected reimbursement, you may have to adjust your tax return for the tax year in which you receive your actual reimbursement. This section explains the adjustment you may have to make.

Actual reimbursement less than expected. If you later receive less reimbursement than you expected, include that difference as a loss with your other losses (if any) on your return for the year in which you can reasonably expect no more reimbursement.

Example. Your personal car had a FMV of $2,000 when it was destroyed in a collision with another car in 2004. The accident was due to the negligence of the other driver. At the end of 2004, there was a reasonable prospect that the owner of the other car would reimburse you in full. You subtracted the expected reimbursement when you figured your loss. You did not have a deductible loss in 2004.

In January 2005, the court awarded you a judgment of $2,000. However, in July it became apparent that you will be unable to collect any amount from the other driver. You can deduct the loss in 2005 subject to the limits discussed later.

TaxPlanner

Even though there is no formal IRS ruling, many IRS auditors tend to disallow any deduction for the unreimbursed amount if you are fully insured and settle your claim with the insurance carrier for less than the amount of the loss by signing a proof of loss statement. The proof of loss statement sets the value of the loss between you and the insurance company. Generally, the IRS auditor will only allow a deduction of the unreimbursed loss if he or she is convinced that you have attempted all reasonable remedies against the insurer.

Actual reimbursement more than expected. If you later receive more reimbursement than you expected after you claimed a deduction for the loss, you may have to include the extra reimbursement in your income for the year you receive it. However, if any part of the original deduction did not reduce your tax for the earlier year, do not include that part of the reimbursement in your income. You do not refigure your tax for the year you claimed the deduction. For more information, see *Recoveries* in chapter 13.

Example

Last year, a hurricane destroyed your motorboat. Your loss was $3,000, and you estimated that your insurance would cover $2,500 of it. Because you did not itemize deductions on your return last year, you could not deduct the loss. When the insurance company reimburses you for the loss, you do not report any of the reimbursement as income. This is true even if it is for the full $3,000 because you did not deduct the loss on your return. The loss did not reduce your tax.

Caution. *If the total of all the reimbursements you receive is more than your adjusted basis in the destroyed or stolen property, you will have a gain on the casualty or theft. If you have already taken a deduction for a loss and you receive the reimbursement in a later year, you may have to include the gain in your income for the later year. Include the gain as ordinary income up to the amount of your deduction that reduced your tax for the earlier year. See Publication 547 for more information on how to treat a gain from the reimbursement of a casualty or theft.*

Actual reimbursement same as expected. If you receive exactly the reimbursement you expected, you do not have any amount to include in your income or any loss to deduct.

Example. In December 2005, you had a collision while driving your personal car. Repairs to the car cost $950. You had $100 deductible collision insurance. Your insurance company agreed to reimburse you for the rest of the damage. Because you expected a reimbursement from the insurance company, you did not have a casualty loss deduction in 2005.

Due to the $100 rule (discussed later under *Deduction Limits*), you cannot deduct the $100 deductible you paid. When you receive the $850 from the insurance company in 2006, do not report it as income.

Example

A taxpayer suffered a casualty loss from vandalism and filed a claim with her insurance company in the year of the loss. The insurance company denied any liability for the damage. Consequently, the taxpayer filed suit against the insurance company. A court held that the taxpayer could not deduct the loss in the year in which it was incurred, because a reasonable possibility of recovery still existed. No deduction was allowed while the suit against the insurance company was still pending.

Single Casualty on Multiple Properties

Personal property. If a single casualty or theft involves more than one item of personal property, you must figure the loss on each item separately. Then combine the losses to determine your total loss from that casualty or theft. Personal property is any property that is not real property.

Example. A fire in your home destroyed an upholstered chair, an oriental rug, and an antique table. You did not have fire insurance to cover your loss. (This was the only casualty or theft you had during the year.) You paid $750 for the chair and you established that it had a FMV of $500 just before the fire. The rug cost $3,000 and had a FMV of $2,500 just before the fire. You bought the table at an auction for $100 before discovering it was an antique. It had been appraised at $900 before the fire. You figure your loss on each of these items as follows:

	Chair	Rug	Table
1) Basis (cost)	$750	$3,000	$100
2) FMV before fire	$500	$2,500	$900
3) FMV after fire	–0–	–0–	–0–
4) Decrease in FMV	$500	$2,500	$900
5) Loss (smaller of (1) or (4))	$500	$2,500	$100
6) Total loss			$3,100

Real property. In figuring a casualty loss on personal-use real property, treat the entire property (including any improvements, such as buildings, trees, and shrubs) as one item. Figure the loss using the smaller of the adjusted basis or the decrease in FMV of the entire property.

Example. You bought your home a few years ago. You paid $160,000 ($20,000 for the land and $140,000 for the house). You also spent $2,000 for landscaping. This year a fire destroyed your home. The fire also damaged the shrubbery and trees in your yard. The fire was your only casualty or theft loss this year. Competent appraisers valued the property as a whole at $200,000 before the fire, but only $30,000 after the fire. (The loss to your household furnishings is not shown in this example. It would be figured separately on each item, as explained earlier under *Personal property*.) Shortly after the fire, the insurance company paid you $155,000 for the loss. You figure your casualty loss as follows:

1) Adjusted basis of the entire property (land, building, and landscaping)	$162,000
2) FMV of entire property before fire	$200,000
3) FMV of entire property after fire	30,000
4) Decrease in FMV of entire property	$170,000
5) Loss (smaller of (1) or (4))	$162,000
6) Subtract insurance	155,000
7) Amount of loss after reimbursement	$ 7,000

Deduction Limits

After you have figured your casualty or theft loss, you must figure how much of the loss you can deduct. If the loss was to property for your personal use or your family's use, there are two limits on the amount you can deduct for your casualty or theft loss.

1. You must reduce each casualty or theft loss by $100 ($100 rule).
2. You must further reduce the total of all your casualty or theft losses by 10% of your adjusted gross income (10% rule).

You make these reductions on Form 4684.

These rules are explained next and *Table 27-1* summarizes how to apply the $100 rule and the 10% rule in various situations. For more detailed explanations and examples, see Publication 547.

Property used partly for business and partly for personal purposes. When property is used partly for personal purposes and partly for business or income-producing purposes, the casualty or theft loss deduction must be figured separately for the personal-use part and for the business or income-producing part. You must figure each loss separately because the $100 rule and the 10% rule apply only to the loss on the personal-use part of the property.

Explanation

Business or income-producing property. A loss on business property, property that earns you rent or royalty income, or other income-producing property is not subject to either the $100 rule or the 10% rule. For business or income-producing property, you must figure your loss separately for each item that is stolen, damaged, or destroyed. If casualty damage occurs both to a building and to trees on the same piece of property, the loss is measured separately for each.

Total loss of business or income-producing property. If you have business or income-producing property that is completely lost because of a casualty or theft, your deductible loss is your basis in the property minus any salvage value and minus any insurance or other reimbursement you receive or expect to receive. It does not matter what the decrease in fair market value is.

Example

You owned machinery that you used in your business. The machinery had an adjusted basis of $25,000 when it was completely destroyed by fire. Its fair market value just before the fire was $20,000. Because this was business property, and because it was completely destroyed, your deductible loss is your adjusted basis in the machinery, $25,000, decreased by salvage value and by any insurance or other reimbursement. Fair market value is not considered when you are figuring your loss, even though it is less than your basis in the machinery.

Explanation

Partial loss of business or income-producing property. If business or income-producing property is damaged but not completely destroyed in a casualty, the loss is the decrease in value because of the casualty or your adjusted basis in the property, whichever is less. From this amount (the lesser of your adjusted basis or the decrease in value), you must subtract any insurance or other reimbursement you receive or expect to receive.

TAXSAVER

If your car is stolen. If your automobile is stolen or destroyed, you may be able to deduct more than the value listed in one of the various books issued by auto-

Table 27-1.   How To Apply the Deduction Limits for Personal-Use Property

	$100 Rule	10% Rule
General Application	You must reduce each casualty or theft loss by $100 when figuring your deduction. Apply this rule after you have figured the amount of your loss.	You must reduce your total casualty or theft loss by 10% of your adjusted gross income. Apply this rule after you reduce each loss by $100 (the $100 rule).
Single Event	Apply this rule only once, even if many pieces of property are affected.	Apply this rule only once, even if many pieces of property are affected.
More Than One Event	Apply to the loss from each event.	Apply to the total of all your losses from all events.
More Than One Person— With Loss From the Same Event (other than a married couple filing jointly)	Apply separately to each person.	Apply separately to each person.
Married Couple— With Loss From the Same Event / Filing Jointly	Apply as if you were one person.	Apply as if you were one person.
Filing Separately	Apply separately to each spouse.	Apply separately to each spouse.
More Than One Owner (other than a married couple filing jointly)	Apply separately to each owner of jointly owned property.	Apply separately to each owner of jointly owned property.

mobile organizations. If you use the automobile for business, you must make a separate calculation of the business and personal portions of the loss. This may produce a larger loss.

Example

Blair Hunt's automobile, which cost $8,000, is stolen. The "blue book"—one of the books published by automobile organizations—values his automobile at $5,000. Blair used the automobile for business 40% of the time and deducted $800 of depreciation expense.

	Business portion	Personal portion
Value before theft	$2,000	$3,000
Value after theft	–0–	–0–
Decrease in value	$2,000	$3,000
Adjusted basis:		
Original cost	$3,200	$4,800
Depreciation	(800)	–0–
Adjusted basis	$2,400	$4,800

Blair's casualty loss before the $100 limitation is $5,400, computed as follows:

Business portion—adjusted basis	$2,400
Personal portion—the lower of the decrease in value or the adjusted basis	3,000
Total	$5,400

TAXSAVER

By reporting the business loss on Schedule C (if self-employed), you can reduce your self-employment income and, hence, your self-employment tax.

$100 Rule

After you have figured your casualty or theft loss on personal-use property, you must reduce that loss by $100. This reduction applies to each total casualty or theft loss. It does not matter how many pieces of property are involved in an event. Only a single $100 reduction applies.

Explanation

The $100 rule and the 10% rule do not apply if the loss is on business property, property that earns you rent or royalty income, or other income-producing property.

Example. A hailstorm damages your home and your car. Determine the amount of loss, as discussed earlier, for each of these items. Since the losses are due to a single event, you combine the losses and reduce the combined amount by $100.

Single event. Generally, events closely related in origin cause a single casualty. It is a single casualty when the damage is from two or more closely related causes, such as wind and flood damage caused by the same storm.

Explanation

A single casualty may also damage two or more pieces of property, such as a hailstorm that damages both your home and your car parked in your driveway.

10% Rule

You must reduce the total of all your casualty or theft losses on personal-use property by 10% of your adjusted gross income. Apply this rule after you reduce each loss by $100. If you have both gains and losses from casualties or thefts, see *Gains and losses,* later in this discussion.

Example 1. In June, you discovered that your house had been burglarized. Your loss after insurance reimbursement was $2,000. Your adjusted gross income for the year you discovered the theft is $29,500. You first apply the $100 rule and then the 10% rule. Figure your theft loss deduction as follows.

1) Loss after insurance	$2,000
2) Subtract $100	100
3) Loss after $100 rule	$1,900
4) Subtract 10% × $29,500 AGI	2,950
5) **Theft loss deduction**	–0–

You do not have a theft loss deduction because your loss after you apply the $100 rule ($1,900) is less than 10% of your adjusted gross income ($2,950).

Explanation

More than one loss. If you have more than one casualty or theft loss during your tax year, reduce each loss by any reimbursement and by $100. Then you must reduce the total of *all* your losses by 10% of your adjusted gross income.

Example 2. In March, you had a car accident that totally destroyed your car. You did not have collision insurance on your car, so you did not receive any insurance reimbursement. Your loss on the car was $1,200. In November, a fire damaged your basement and totally destroyed the furniture, washer, dryer, and other items stored there. Your loss on the basement items after reimbursement was $1,700. Your adjusted gross income for the year that the accident and fire occurred is $25,000. You figure your casualty loss deduction as follows.

	Car	Basement
1) Loss...	$1,200	$1,700
2) Subtract $100 per incident	100	100
3) Loss after $100 rule...	$1,100	$1,600
4) Total loss		$2,700
5) Subtract 10% × $25,000 AGI..		2,500
6) **Casualty loss deduction**		**$ 200**

Gains and losses. If you had both gains and losses from casualties or thefts to personal-use property, you must compare your total gains to your total losses. Do this after you have reduced each loss by any reimbursements and by $100.

Explanation
Note, however, you should do the above calculation before you have reduced the losses by 10% of your adjusted gross income.

Caution. *Casualty or theft gains do not include gains you choose to postpone. See Publication 547 for information on the postponement of gain.*

Losses more than gains. If your losses are more than your recognized gains, subtract your gains from your losses and reduce the result by 10% of your adjusted gross income. The rest, if any, is your deductible loss.

Example
Your theft loss after reducing it by reimbursements and by $100 is $2,700. Your casualty gain is $700. Because your loss is more than your gain, you must reduce your $2,000 net loss ($2,700 − $700) by 10% of your adjusted gross income.

Gains more than losses. If your recognized gains are more than your losses, subtract your losses from your gains. The difference is treated as capital gain and must be reported on Schedule D (Form 1040). The 10% rule does not apply to your gains.

Example 1
Your theft loss after reducing it by reimbursements and by $100 is $600. Your casualty gain is $1,600. Because your gain is more than your loss, you must report the $1,000 net gain ($1,600 − $600) on Schedule D.

Example 2
During 2005, a storm completely destroyed your summer cottage, resulting in a casualty gain of $5,000 after you were reimbursed by your insurance company. Later in the year, your home was broken into on two separate occasions. Jewelry, silverware, and other items of personal property were stolen each time. The loss (after applying the $100 rule) on the first theft was $900 and on the second theft was $4,000. Your 2005 adjusted gross income is $25,000.

1) Loss on first theft......................................	$ 900
2) Plus: loss on second theft................................	4,000
3) Total losses	$4,900
4) Gain on cottage..	5,000
5) Net gain for 2004	$100

The $100 gain will be reported on Form 4684. See *Insurance and Other Reimbursements*, regarding recognition of gains discussed earlier.

When To Report Gains and Losses

If you receive an insurance or other reimbursement that is more than your adjusted basis in the destroyed or stolen property, you have a gain from the casualty or theft. You must include this gain in your income in the year you receive the reimbursement, unless you choose to postpone reporting the gain as explained in Publication 547.

If you have a loss, see *Table 27-2.*

Loss on deposits. If your loss is a loss on deposits in an insolvent or bankrupt financial institution, see *Loss on Deposits,* earlier.

Casualty loss. Generally, you can deduct a casualty loss only in the tax year in which the casualty occurred. This is true even if you do not repair or replace the damaged property until a later year.

Theft loss. You generally can deduct a theft loss only in the year you discover your property was stolen. You must be able to show that there was a theft, but you do not have to know when the theft occurred. However, you should show when you discovered that your property was missing.

Disaster Area Loss

If you have a casualty loss from a disaster that occurred in a Presidentially declared disaster area, you can choose to deduct the loss on your tax return or amended return for either of the following years.

• The year the disaster occurred.
• The year immediately preceding the year the disaster occurred.

TaxSaver
If you were affected by one of the 2005 Presidentially declared disasters, such as the severe flooding, debris flows, and mudslides in California or the severe winter storms and flooding in Indiana, you may get speedier action on your return by writing on the front of the return that a disaster loss is being claimed.

TaxPlanner
If you are not in need of an immediate tax refund, you may want to wait to file until near the April 15 deadline. By waiting, you may be able to determine which tax year provides greater tax savings from the deduction and to choose that year to claim the loss. For more information, consult your tax advisor.

Explanation
A loss in a Presidentially declared disaster area may be deducted on the tax return for the year in which the disaster occurs or in the immediately preceding tax year if certain requirements are met. First, the loss must have been from a disaster in an area that the President says needs federal assistance. Second, the tax return for the preceding year must be amended by the date it is due (with extensions), or, if that date has already passed, by the date the tax return for the year of the disaster is due (without extensions). In both instances, extensions are allowed. Generally, you would have until April 15, 2006, to amend a 2004 return to report a 2005 disaster loss. An amended return is filed on Form 1040X. A listing of federal disaster areas may be obtained from your newspaper, from local officials, or from the Federal Emergency Management Agency's Web site (www.fema.gov/disasters).

TaxPlanner
To determine whether you should claim the disaster loss on your current year's return or on your return for the preceding year, you should calculate the tax effects of claiming the loss in both years. Once you make a choice, it becomes irrevocable 90 days after you file your return.

Table 27-2. **When To Deduct a Loss**

IF you have a loss...	THEN deduct it in the year...
from a casualty,	the loss occurred.
in a Presidentially declared disaster area,	the disaster occurred or the year immediately before the disaster.
from a theft,	the theft was discovered.
on a deposit treated as a:	
• casualty,	• a reasonable estimate can be made.
• bad debt,	• deposits are totally worthless.
• ordinary loss,	• a reasonable estimate can be made.

Postponed tax deadlines. The IRS may postpone for up to 1 year certain tax deadlines of taxpayers who are affected by a Presidentially declared disaster. The tax deadlines the IRS may postpone include those for filing income and employment tax returns, paying income and employment taxes, and making contributions to a traditional IRA or Roth IRA.

If any tax deadline is postponed, the IRS will publicize the postponement in your area by publishing a news release, revenue ruling, revenue procedure, notice, announcement, or other guidance in the Internal Revenue Bulletin (IRB).

Who is eligible. If the IRS postpones a tax deadline, the following taxpayers are eligible for the postponement.

- Any individual whose main home is located in a covered disaster area (defined next).
- Any business entity or sole proprietor whose principal place of business is located in a covered disaster area.
- Any relief worker affiliated with a recognized government or philanthropic organization who is assisting in a covered disaster area.
- Any individual, business entity, or sole proprietor whose records are needed to meet a postponed deadline, provided those records are maintained in a covered disaster area. The main home or principal place of business does not have to be located in the covered disaster area.
- Any estate or trust that has tax records necessary to meet a postponed tax deadline, provided those records are maintained in a covered disaster area.
- The spouse on a joint return with a taxpayer who is eligible for postponements.
- Any other person determined by the IRS to be affected by a Presidentially declared disaster.

Covered disaster area. This is an area of a Presidentially declared disaster area in which the IRS has decided to postpone tax deadlines for up to 1 year.

Abatement of interest and penalties. The IRS may abate the interest and penalties on underpaid income tax for the length of any postponement of tax deadlines.

More information. For more information, see *Disaster Area Losses* in Publication 547.

How To Report Gains and Losses

Use Form 4684 to report a gain or a deductible loss from a casualty or theft. If you have more than one casualty or theft, use a separate Form 4684 to determine your gain or loss for each event. Combine the gains and losses on one Form 4684. Follow the form instructions as to which lines to fill out. In addition, you must use the appropriate schedule to report a gain or loss. The schedule you use depends on whether you have a gain or loss.

If you have a:	Report it on:
Gain	Schedule D (Form 1040)
Loss	Schedule A (Form 1040)

Adjustments to basis. If you have a casualty or theft loss, you must decrease your basis in the property by any deductible loss and any insurance or other reimbursement. Amounts you spend to restore your property after a casualty increase your adjusted basis. See *Adjusted Basis* in chapter 14 for more information.

Net operating loss (NOL). If your casualty or theft loss deduction is more than your income, you may have an NOL. You can use an NOL to lower your tax in an earlier year, allowing you to get a refund for tax you have already paid. Or, you can use it to lower your tax in a later year. You do not have to be in business to have an NOL from a casualty or theft loss. For more information, see Publication 536, Net Operating Losses (NOLs) for Individuals, Estates, and Trusts.

TaxPlanner

If your loss exceeds your income. If your casualty loss exceeds your income, you should fill out Form 1045, *Application for Tentative Refund,* to see whether you have a net operating loss. When filling out this form, treat your casualty losses as business deductions rather than nonbusiness deductions. If your casualty loss results in a net operating loss, then your net operating loss can be carried back to offset your taxable income, and you may get a refund of prior-year taxes.

For example, a 2005 net operating loss caused by a casualty loss should be carried back first to 2002, any remaining loss should be carried back to 2003, and then to 2004. If any loss still remains, it can be carried forward for the next 20 years. Alternatively, you may elect on your 2005 tax return not to carry back your net operating loss but carry it forward only. See the discussion in Chapter 39, *If You Are Self-Employed: How to File Schedule C,* and you may also want to consult your tax advisor. You should compare the refund available from a carryback to the expected tax benefits in the future in order to determine whether you should make the election.

Explanation

Effective for losses occurring in 1998 or later, Congress changed the carryback period for most net operating losses from 3 years to 2 years and the carryforward period from 15 years to 20 years. However, the carryback period for net operating losses caused by casualty and theft losses remains at 3 years.

TaxOrganizer

List of records you should keep:

- Documentation of date, time, and place of occurrence of the casualty or theft
- Police reports
- Insurance reports including evidence of amount of reimbursement, if any
- Original receipts (if applicable)
- Repair bills
- Form 1099 (if applicable)
- Any appraisals or valuations supporting property value
- An inventory of stolen, lost, damaged, or destroyed items
- Pictures of damaged items (if any)
- Any type of supporting evidence such as newspaper clippings about a storm

Car Expenses and Other Employee Business Expenses

Note: The 2004 IRS Publication 17 (Your Federal Income Tax) has been updated by Ernst & Young LLP for 2005. Dates and dollar amounts shown are for 2005. Gray type is used to indicate where IRS text has been updated or intentionally omitted. Unrevised IRS text is shown in black type.

Introduction

If you are traveling on business and your employer does not reimburse your expenses, you may deduct many of them on your income tax return. If you use your automobile partly for business purposes, you may be able to deduct some of your operating expenses. If you entertain a business associate at a restaurant or nightclub, you may be able to deduct that expense, too. Within strict limits, business gifts are also deductible.

You must be able to prove the business purpose, as well as the amount of the expense, to claim a deduction for employee expenses. All expenses should be substantiated with receipts and records indicating the time, place, and business nature of the expense. This chapter explains business-related expenses for travel, transportation, entertainment, and gifts that you may deduct on your income tax return. It also discusses the reporting and record-keeping requirements for these expenses.

What's New

Standard mileage rate. The standard mileage rate for the cost of operating your car through August 2005 is 40.5 cents a mile for all business miles. The rate is 48.5 cents a mile from September 1, 2005 through December 31, 2005.

Car expenses and use of the standard mileage rate are explained under *Transportation Expenses,* later.

TAXALERT

For 2005, you can exclude up to $200 per month of employer-provided parking, even if you choose it instead of cash or your employer reduces your compensation to provide the parking. The $200 is indexed for inflation. Alternatively, for 2005, you can exclude up to $105 per month for a transit pass and transportation in a commuter highway vehicle.

Standard mileage rate method. You can use the standard mileage rate to figure the deductible costs of operating up to four cars at the same time. Before 2004, you could not use the standard mileage rate if you used two or more cars at the same time. See *Standard Mileage Rate,* later.

[IRS text intentionally omitted]

TaxAlert

The special 50% and 30% depreciation allowances for the purchase of a new car used for business purposes is not available for cars purchased on or after January 1, 2005.

Meal expenses when subject to "hours of service" limits. Generally, you can deduct only 50% of your business-related meal expenses while traveling away from your tax home for business purposes. You can deduct a higher percentage if the meals take place during or incident to any period subject to the Department of Transportation's "hours of service" limits. (These limits apply to certain workers who are under certain federal regulations.) The percentage is 70% for 2005. See *Exceptions to the 50% Limit* under *50% Limit,* later.

You may be able to deduct the ordinary and necessary business-related expenses you have for:

- Travel,
- Entertainment,
- Gifts, or
- Transportation.

An ordinary expense is one that is common and accepted in your field of trade, business, or profession. A necessary expense is one that is helpful and appropriate for your business. An expense does not have to be required to be considered necessary.

This chapter explains:

- What expenses are deductible,
- What records you need to prove your expenses,
- How to treat any expense reimbursements you may receive, and
- How to report your expenses on your return.

Explanation

All employee-related expenses and certain transportation expenses are classified as miscellaneous itemized deductions. Included in this category are expenses incurred by employees that are fully or partially reimbursed or not reimbursed at all by their employer. Also included are any expenses for traveling away from home or for transportation.

The total of all miscellaneous itemized expenses (including those mentioned previously, as well as those discussed in Chapter 30, *Miscellaneous Deductions*) must be over 2% of a taxpayer's adjusted gross income.

TaxAlert

On October 4, 2004, President Bush signed a bill extending the provisions that allowed eligible educators to take a deduction from gross income for certain expenses. The annual deduction is limited to $250 and covers expenses paid or incurred for books, supplies, computer equipment, and supplementary material used by the eligible educator in the classroom. See Chapter 20 for further information.

TaxPlanner

If you were an eligible educator and your expenses were greater than $250, you can deduct the additional amount as an itemized deduction subject to the 2% limit.

Who does not need to use this chapter. If you are an employee, you will not need to read this chapter if all of the following are true.

1. You fully accounted to your employer for your work-related expenses.
2. You received full reimbursement for your expenses.
3. Your employer required you to return any excess reimbursement and you did so.
4. There is no amount shown with a code "L" in box 12 of your Form W-2, Wage and Tax Statement.

If you meet these four conditions, there is no need to show the expenses or the reimbursements on your return. See *Reimbursements,* later, if you would like more information on reimbursements and accounting to your employer.

Tip. *If you meet these conditions and your employer included reimbursements on your Form W-2 in error, ask your employer for a corrected Form W-2.*

Useful Items

You may want to see:

Publications

- ☐ **463**   Travel, Entertainment, Gift, and Car Expenses
- ☐ **535**   Business Expenses
- ☐ **1542**   Per Diem Rates

Forms (and Instructions)

- ☐ **Schedule A (Form 1040)**   Itemized Deductions
- ☐ **Schedule C (Form 1040)**   Profit or Loss From Business
- ☐ **Schedule C-EZ (Form 1040)**   Net Profit From Business
- ☐ **Schedule F (Form 1040)**   Profit or Loss From Farming
- ☐ **Form 2106**   Employee Business Expenses
- ☐ **Form 2106-EZ**   Unreimbursed Employee Business Expenses

---

Travel Expenses

If you temporarily travel away from your tax home, you can use this section to determine if you have deductible travel expenses. This section discusses:

- Traveling away from home,
- Tax home,
- Temporary assignment, and
- What travel expenses are deductible.

It also discusses the standard meal allowance, rules for travel inside and outside the United States, and deductible convention expenses.

Travel expenses defined. For tax purposes, travel expenses are the ordinary and necessary expenses (defined earlier) of traveling away from home for your business, profession, or job.

You will find examples of deductible travel expenses in Table 28-1.

Example 1

The courts held that a stockholder of a corporation could not deduct the expense of operating his personal automobile while performing services for the corporation. The stockholder was not an employee or officer of the corporation. He was not reimbursed for his expenses. The courts held that the stockholder's interest in the corporation was too remote for the expense to be an ordinary business expense.

Example 2

A government employee was allowed to deduct unreimbursed expenses incurred in the use of his private airplane for business purposes. He was also allowed to depreciate the business portion of the airplane's use.

TAXPLANNER

For you to deduct a business expense, a board resolution or a policy statement from the company that employs you should indicate that you may have to incur certain expenses for which you will not be reimbursed in order for you to fulfill your job.

TAXPLANNER

You are able to deduct only 50% of most business meal and entertainment costs. Other allowable unreimbursed entertainment expenses will be grouped with certain other of your miscellaneous itemized deductions. You will be allowed a tax deduction to the extent that all these deductions exceed 2% of your adjusted gross income.

Traveling Away From Home

You are traveling away from home if:

1. Your duties require you to be away from the general area of your tax home (defined later) substantially longer than an ordinary day's work, and
2. You need to sleep or rest to meet the demands of your work while away from home.

This rest requirement is not satisfied by merely napping in your car. You do not have to be away from your tax home for a whole day or from dusk to dawn as long as your relief from duty is long enough to get necessary sleep or rest.

Example 1. You are a railroad conductor. You leave your home terminal on a regularly scheduled round-trip run between two cities and return home 16 hours later. During the run, you have 6 hours off at your turnaround point where you eat two meals and rent a hotel room to get necessary sleep before starting the return trip. You are considered to be away from home.

Example 2. You are a truck driver. You leave your terminal and return to it later the same day. You get an hour off at your turnaround point to eat. Because you are not off to get necessary sleep and the brief time off is not an adequate rest period, you are not traveling away from home.

Members of the Armed Forces. If you are a member of the U.S. Armed Forces on a permanent duty assignment overseas, you are not traveling away from home. You cannot deduct your expenses for meals and lodging. You cannot deduct these expenses even if you have to maintain a home in the United States for your family members who are not allowed to accompany you overseas. If you are transferred from one permanent duty station to another, you may have deductible moving expenses, which are explained in chapter 19.

A naval officer assigned to permanent duty aboard a ship that has regular eating and living facilities has a tax home aboard ship for travel expense purposes.

Travel to family home. If you (and your family) do not live at your tax home, you cannot deduct the cost of traveling between your tax home and your family home. You also cannot deduct the cost of meals and lodging while at your tax home. See *Example 1* that follows.

If you are working temporarily in the same city where you and your family live, you may be considered as traveling away from home. See *Example 2,* below.

Example 1. You are a truck driver and you and your family live in Tucson. You are employed by a trucking firm that has its terminal in Phoenix. At the end of your long runs, you return to your home terminal in Phoenix and spend one night there before returning home. You cannot deduct any expenses you have for meals and lodging in Phoenix or the cost of traveling from Phoenix to Tucson. This is because Phoenix is your tax home.

Example 2. Your family home is in Pittsburgh, where you work 12 weeks a year. The rest of the year you work for the same employer in Baltimore. In Baltimore, you eat in restaurants and sleep in a rooming house. Your salary is the same whether you are in Pittsburgh or Baltimore.

Because you spend most of your working time and earn most of your salary in Baltimore, that city is your tax home. You cannot deduct any expenses you have for meals and lodging there. However, when you return to work in Pittsburgh, you are away from your tax home even though you stay at your family home. You can deduct the cost of your round trip between Baltimore and Pittsburgh. You can also deduct your part of your family's living expenses for meals and lodging while you are living and working in Pittsburgh.

Example 1

A famous baseball player was not allowed to deduct expenses for meals and lodging in Los Angeles, California, even though he maintained a home in another state. The court found his tax home to be Los Angeles, since it was his principal place of business.

Example 2

A member of the Marine Corps was stationed in Japan. His family remained in California, since they were not allowed to accompany him to his principal place of duty. The marine was not allowed to deduct travel expenses. His tax home was Japan, his principal place of duty. See *Members of the Armed Forces,* later.

Explanation

Where you earn the most money is the principal test for deciding where your tax home is.

Example

The IRS required a taxpayer to claim as his tax home a city away from the home in which his family resided. He earned 75% of his income in the city away from his family and 25% of his income in the city where his family lived. Since his tax home was different from his personal residence, he could deduct travel expenses incurred while living with his family.

Explanation

The distance between your residence and your place of employment is not a factor in determining whether expenses away from home are being incurred.

Example

The courts ruled that a taxpayer's personal decision to live a great distance from the location of his permanent employment did not render his meal and lodging expenses deductible. His place of business was his tax home.

Tax Home

To determine whether you are traveling away from home, you must first determine the location of your tax home.

Generally, your tax home is your regular place of business or post of duty, regardless of where you maintain your family home. It includes the entire city or general area in which your business or work is located.

If you have more than one regular place of business, your tax home is your main place of business. See *Main place of business or work,* later.

If you do not have a regular or a main place of business because of the nature of your work, then your tax home may be the place where you regularly live. See *No main place of business or work,* later.

If you do not have a regular place of business or post of duty and there is no place where you regularly live, you are considered a transient (an itinerant) and your tax home is wherever you work. As a transient, you cannot claim a travel expense deduction because you are never considered to be traveling away from home.

Main place of business or work. If you have more than one place of business or work, consider the following when determining which one is your main place of business or work.

1. The total time you ordinarily spend in each place.
2. The level of your business activity in each place.
3. Whether your income from each place is significant or insignificant.

Example. You live in Cincinnati where you have a seasonal job for 8 months each year and earn $25,000. You work the other 4 months in Miami, also at a seasonal job, and earn $9,000. Cincinnati is your main place of work because you spend most of your time there and earn most of your income there.

No main place of business or work. You may have a tax home even if you do not have a regular or main place of business or work. Your tax home may be the home where you regularly live.

Factors used to determine tax home. If you do not have a regular or main place of business or work, use the following three factors to determine where your tax home is.

1. You perform part of your business in the area of your main home and use that home for lodging while doing business in the area.
2. You have living expenses at your main home that you duplicate because your business requires you to be away from that home.
3. You have not abandoned the area in which both your historical place of lodging and your claimed main home are located; you have a member or members of your family living at your main home; or you often use that home for lodging.

If you satisfy all three factors, your tax home is the home where you regularly live. If you satisfy only two factors, you may have a tax home depending on all the facts and circumstances. If you satisfy only one factor, you are a transient; your tax home is wherever you work and you cannot deduct travel expenses.

Example
After a taxpayer's employment in Cape Canaveral, Florida, was terminated, the taxpayer obtained temporary contract jobs in Virginia, Florida, North Carolina, Vermont, and Alabama. The Tax Court rejected the IRS assertion that the taxpayer had no tax home and allowed deductions for travel, meals, and lodging because he maintained a "tax home" in Cape Canaveral. The court noted that such deductions were allowed because the taxpayer returned to his Cape Canaveral home during periods of unemployment, and the taxpayer had a valid business purpose for maintaining his permanent address.

Example. You are single and live in Boston in an apartment you rent. You have worked for your employer in Boston for a number of years. Your employer enrolls you in a 12-month executive training program. You do not expect to return to work in Boston after you complete your training.

During your training, you do not do any work in Boston. Instead, you receive classroom and on-the-job training throughout the United States. You keep your apartment in Boston and return to it frequently. You use your apartment to conduct your personal business. You also keep up your community contacts in Boston. When you complete your training, you are transferred to Los Angeles.

You do not satisfy factor (1) because you did not work in Boston. You satisfy factor (2) because you had duplicate living expenses. You also satisfy factor (3) because you did not abandon your apartment in Boston as your main home, you kept your community contacts, and you frequently returned to live in your apartment. You have a tax home in Boston.

Explanation
According to the IRS, a home is a "regular place of abode in a real and substantial sense." The criteria are as follows:

1. You work in the same vicinity as your claimed abode and use it while doing business.
2. Your living expenses incurred at your claimed abode are duplicated when you're away on business.
3. You (a) have not abandoned the vicinity in which your place of lodging and claimed abode are both located; (b) have a family member or members (marital or lineal) currently residing at your claimed abode; or (c) use the claimed abode frequently.

If you maintain no fixed home, the burden of proof is on you to show the business portion of your daily expenses.

Example 1
You are an outside salesperson with a sales territory covering several states. Your employer's main office is in Newark, New Jersey, but you do not conduct any business there. Your work assignments are temporary, and you have no way of knowing where your future assignments will be located. You have a room in your married sister's house in Dayton, Ohio. You stay there for one or two weekends a year, but you do no work in the area. You do not pay your sister for the use of the room.

You do not satisfy any of the three factors listed earlier. You are a transient and have no tax home.

Example 2
A traveling salesman could not establish Reno, Nevada, as his tax home, even though he maintained a post office box and a bank account there, had dealings with a local stockbroker, bought an automobile there, stored his personal belongings there, and filed an income tax return from the city. He did not maintain a permanent place in Reno but stayed in hotels while he was there. Since no tax home was established, he could deduct only the business portion of his daily expenses. However, no expenses were allowed, since he did not maintain the necessary records.

Example 3
A traveling saleswoman maintained a room in her sister's home at a nominal rent. She worked for an employer in the same city, who paid her a per diem when she was away from that city. She had established a home for travel expense purposes.

Example 4
A college professor held a tenured position at a university located in Texas. While studying for her Ph.D. in Hawaii, she maintained a credit union account, a

houseboat on which she paid property taxes, a post office box, and a library card in Texas and also stored almost all of her possessions there. She returned to the university after receiving her degree. The court ruled that her stay was not for an indefinite period, and she was able to deduct her lodging expenses in Hawaii.

Temporary Assignment or Job

You may regularly work at your tax home and also work at another location. It may not be practical to return to your tax home from this other location at the end of each workday.

Temporary assignment vs. indefinite assignment. If your assignment or job away from your main place of work is temporary, your tax home does not change. You are considered to be away from home for the whole period you are away from your main place of work. You can deduct your travel expenses if they otherwise qualify for deduction. Generally, a temporary assignment in a single location is one that is realistically expected to last (and does in fact last) for one year or less.

However, if your assignment or job is indefinite, the location of the assignment or job becomes your new tax home and you cannot deduct your travel expenses while there. An assignment or job in a single location is considered indefinite if it is realistically expected to last for more than one year, whether or not it actually lasts for more than one year.

If your assignment is indefinite, you must include in your income any amounts you receive from your employer for living expenses, even if they are called travel allowances and you account to your employer for them. You may be able to deduct the cost of relocating to your new tax home as a moving expense. See chapter 19 for more information.

Example 1
A construction worker who had been regularly employed near his home took a job in a city 250 miles away when construction got very slow in his hometown. He lived in his own trailer at the new job location. The job was expected to last 16 months, after which he planned to return home to his family. He frequently visited his hometown and continued to search for work there. *Previously,* the IRS had ruled that the worker was temporarily away from his home and *could* deduct his meals and lodging. However, under the most recent ruling, the worker's meals and lodging expenses would *not* be deductible because the assignment was expected to last longer than a year.

Example 2
A worker sold his residence in his home city, ceased to search for work there, and bought a new home at a new job location. The IRS ruled that the worker's stay was indefinite. He could not deduct the cost of his meals and lodging.

Example 3
Bill Horton, a professional hockey player, was allowed to deduct the cost of meals and lodging while playing hockey in San Diego, California. The Tax Court ruled that his tax home was in Michigan, where he maintained his house. A limited contract and the seasonal nature of the hockey profession caused the court to classify the San Diego job as temporary.

Example 4
A professional gambler spent equal amounts of time each year in Tampa and Gainesville, Florida; engaged

in an equal amount of activity in both places; derived equal amounts of income in both places; and rented an apartment in each location. The court ruled that the activities were not temporary because they were "seasonal and recurring" activities. Therefore, the costs of both apartments were not deductible.

Exception for federal crime investigations or prosecutions. If you are a federal employee participating in a federal crime investigation or prosecution, you are not subject to the one-year rule. This means you may be able to deduct travel expenses even if you are away from your tax home for more than one year.

For you to qualify, the Attorney General must certify that you are traveling:

1. For the federal government,
2. In a temporary duty status, and
3. To investigate or prosecute, or provide support services for the investigation or prosecution of, a federal crime.

You can deduct your otherwise allowable travel expenses throughout the period of certification.

Determining temporary or indefinite. You must determine whether your assignment is temporary or indefinite when you start work. If you expect an assignment or job to last for one year or less, it is temporary unless there are facts and circumstances that indicate otherwise. An assignment or job that is initially temporary may become indefinite due to changed circumstances. A series of assignments to the same location, all for short periods but that together cover a long period, may be considered an indefinite assignment.

Explanation
If employment away from home in a single location is realistically expected to last for more than 1 year, or if there is no realistic expectation that the employment will last for 1 year or less, the employment is indefinite regardless of whether it actually exceeds 1 year.

Employment is temporary if work away from home in a single location is realistically expected to last (and does in fact last) for 1 year or less, in the absence of any facts and circumstances indicating otherwise.

TaxAlert

Employment away from home in a single location lasting more than 1 year is not treated as temporary. However, if employment away from home was initially expected to be for 1 year or less, and then expectations changed for it to be for more than 1 year, the employment will be considered temporary up to the point that the time length expectations changed.

Example 1
A taxpayer accepts work in a city 250 miles from the city in which she is regularly employed. She expects the work to be completed in 18 months but in fact completes the work in 10 months. The taxpayer's travel expenses are not deductible because the taxpayer's employment is indefinite. Even though the work actually lasted less than 1 year, the employment is still indefinite because the taxpayer realistically expected the work to last longer than 1 year.

Example 2
The facts are the same except that the taxpayer expects the work to be completed in 9 months. After 8 months,

however, the taxpayer is asked to remain for 7 more months (for an actual stay of 15 months). The taxpayer's travel expenses are deductible only during the first 8 months of employment because only during those months did the taxpayer realistically expect the employment to be temporary.

Going home on days off. If you go back to your tax home from a temporary assignment on your days off, you are not considered away from home while you are in your hometown. You cannot deduct the cost of your meals and lodging there. However, you can deduct your travel expenses, including meals and lodging, while traveling between your temporary place of work and your tax home. You can claim these expenses up to the amount it would have cost you to stay at your temporary place of work.

If you keep your hotel room during your visit home, you can deduct the cost of your hotel room. In addition, you can deduct your expenses of returning home up to the amount you would have spent for meals had you stayed at your temporary place of work.

Probationary work period. If you take a job that requires you to move, with the understanding that you will keep the job if your work is satisfactory during a probationary period, the job is indefinite. You cannot deduct any of your expenses for meals and lodging during the probationary period.

What Travel Expenses Are Deductible?

Once you have determined that you are traveling away from your tax home, you can determine what travel expenses are deductible.

You can deduct ordinary and necessary expenses you have when you travel away from home on business. The type of expense you can deduct depends on the facts and your circumstances.

Explanation
Ordinarily, you can deduct expenses that you incurred to produce or collect income, or to manage, conserve, or maintain property held for producing income only on Schedule A (Form 1040). Therefore, you must itemize your deductions to claim these expenses. See Chapter 30, *Miscellaneous Deductions.*

To be deductible, an expense must be closely associated with an activity that is expected to produce income or must be incurred maintaining property that is held to produce income. Such expenses are deductible only if you itemize.

Travel and other costs of attending investment seminars are specifically disallowed.

Example 1
Transportation expenses to attend a stockholders' meeting are not deductible, unless you can demonstrate that you played a fairly substantial role in the meeting. Otherwise, it is not clear that the expenses were incurred to produce income.

Example 2
The courts held that an individual who spent his lunch hour at brokerage houses could not deduct his travel expenses because he could not establish the relationship between his visits and his investment activities.

Table 28-1 summarizes travel expenses you may be able to deduct. You may have other deductible travel expenses that are not covered there, depending on the facts and your circumstances.

When you travel away from home on business, you should keep records of all the expenses you have and any advances you receive from your employer. You can use a log, diary, notebook, or any other written record to keep track of your expenses. The types of expenses you need to record, along with supporting documentation, are described in Table 28-2, later.

Separating costs. If you have one expense that includes the costs of meals, entertainment, and other services (such as lodging or transportation), you must allocate that expense between the cost of meals and entertainment and the cost of other services. You must have a reasonable basis for making this allocation. For example, you must allocate your expenses if a hotel includes one or more meals in its room charge.

Travel expenses for another individual. If a spouse, dependent, or other individual goes with you (or your employee) on a business trip or to a business convention, you generally cannot deduct his or her travel expenses.

Employee. You can deduct the travel expenses of someone who goes with you if that person:

1. Is your employee,
2. Has a *bona fide* business purpose for the travel, and
3. Would otherwise be allowed to deduct the travel expenses.

Business associate. If a business associate travels with you and meets the conditions in (2) and (3) above, you can deduct the travel expenses you have for that person. A business associate is someone with whom you could reasonably expect to actively conduct business. A business associate can be a current or prospective (likely to become) customer, client, supplier, employee, agent, partner, or professional advisor.

Bona fide business purpose. A *bona fide* business purpose exists if you can prove a real business purpose for the individual's presence. Incidental services, such as typing notes or assisting in entertaining customers, are not enough to make the expenses deductible.

Example. Jerry drives to Chicago on business and takes his wife, Linda, with him. Linda is not Jerry's employee. Linda occasionally types notes, performs similar services, and accompanies Jerry to luncheons and dinners. The performance of these services does not establish that her presence on the trip is necessary to the conduct of Jerry's business. Her expenses are not deductible.

Jerry pays $115 a day for a double room. A single room costs $90 a day. He can deduct the total cost of driving his car to and from Chicago, but only $90 a day for his hotel room. If he uses public transportation, he can deduct only his fare.

TaxAlert
The tax law denies a deduction for travel expenses paid or incurred for a spouse, dependent, or other individual accompanying you on business travel, unless certain requirements are met. For the expenses to be deductible, your traveling companion must (1) be a bona fide employee of the person paying or reimbursing the expenses; (2) be traveling for a bona fide business purpose; and (3) have expenses that are otherwise deductible. The denial of the deduction does not apply to expenses that would otherwise qualify as deductible moving expenses.

Meals and Incidental Expenses
You can deduct the cost of meals in either of the following two situations.

1. It is necessary for you to stop for substantial sleep or rest to properly perform your duties while traveling away from home on business.
2. The meal is business-related entertainment.

You can deduct incidental expenses if requirement (1) above is met.

Table 28-1. **Travel Expenses You Can Deduct**
This chart summarizes expenses you can deduct when you travel away from home for business purposes.

IF you have expenses for...	THEN you can deduct the costs of...
transportation	travel by airplane, train, bus, or car between your home and your business destination. If you were provided with a ticket or you are riding free as a result of a frequent traveler or similar program, your cost is zero. If you travel by ship, see *Luxury Water Travel* and *Cruise ships* (under *Conventions*) in Publication 463 for additional rules and limits.
taxi, commuter bus, and airport limousine	fares for these and other types of transportation that take you between: • The airport or station and your hotel, and • The hotel and the work location of your customers or clients, your business meeting place, or your temporary work location.
baggage and shipping	sending baggage and sample or display material between your regular and temporary work locations.
car	operating and maintaining your car when traveling away from home on business. You can deduct actual expenses or the standard mileage rate as well as business-related tolls and parking. If you rent a car while away from home on business, you can deduct only the business-use portion of the expenses.
lodging and meals	your lodging and meals if your business trip is overnight or long enough that you need to stop for sleep or rest to properly perform your duties. Meals include amounts spent for food, beverages, taxes, and related tips. See *Meals and incidental expenses* for additional rules and limits.
cleaning	dry cleaning and laundry.
telephone	business calls while on your business trip. This includes business communication by fax machine or other communication devices.
tips	tips you pay for any expenses in this chart.
other	other similar ordinary and necessary expenses related to your business travel. These expenses might include transportation to or from a business meal, public stenographer's fees, computer rental fees, and operating and maintaining a house trailer.

Business-related entertainment is discussed under *Entertainment Expenses,* later. The following discussion deals with meals that are not business-related entertainment and with incidental expenses.

Lavish or extravagant. You cannot deduct expenses for meals that are lavish or extravagant. An expense is not considered lavish or extravagant if it is reasonable based on the facts and circumstances. Expenses will not be disallowed merely because they are more than a fixed dollar amount or take place at deluxe restaurants, hotels, nightclubs, or resorts.

50% limit on meals. You can figure your meal expenses using either of the following two methods.

1. Actual cost.
2. The standard meal allowance.

Both of these methods are explained below. But, regardless of the method you use, you generally can deduct only 50% of the unreimbursed cost of your meals.

TaxAlert

Meal expenses when subject to hours of service limits. Generally, you can deduct only 50% of your business-related meal expenses while traveling away from your tax home for business purposes. If you consume the meals during or incident to any period subject to the Department of Transportation's hours of service limits, you can deduct a higher percentage. The percentage is 70% for 2005, 75% for 2006 and 2007 and 80% for 2008 and thereafter.

Individuals subject to the Department of Transportation's hours of service limits include the following persons:

1. Certain air transportation workers (such as pilots, crew, dispatchers, mechanics, and control tower operators) who are under Federal Aviation Administration regulations.
2. Interstate truck operators and bus drivers who are under Department of Transportation regulations.
3. Certain railroad employees (such as engineers, conductors, train crews, dispatchers, and control operations personnel) who are under Federal Railroad Administration regulations.
4. Certain merchant mariners who are under Coast Guard regulations.

For more information on business meal expenses, see Publication 463.

If you are reimbursed for the cost of your meals, how you apply the 50% limit depends on whether your employer's reimbursement plan was accountable or nonaccountable. If you are not reimbursed, the 50% limit applies whether the unreimbursed meal expense is for business travel or business entertainment. The 50% limit is explained later under *Entertainment Expenses*. Accountable and non-accountable plans are discussed later under *Reimbursements*.

Actual cost. You can use the actual cost of your meals to figure the amount of your expense before reimbursement and application of the 50% deduction limit. If you use this method, you must keep records of your actual cost.

Standard meal allowance. Generally, you can use the "standard meal allowance" method as an alternative to the actual cost method. It allows you to use a set amount for your daily meals and incidental expenses (M&IE), instead of keeping records of your actual costs. The set amount varies depending on where and when you travel. In this chapter, "standard meal allowance" refers to the federal rate for M&IE, discussed later under *Amount of standard meal allowance*. If you use the standard meal allowance, you still must keep records to prove the time, place, and business purpose of your travel. See *Recordkeeping*, later.

> *Incidental expenses.* The term "incidental expenses" means:

- Fees and tips given to porters, baggage carriers, bellhops, hotel maids, stewards or stewardesses and others on ships, and hotel servants in foreign countries,
- Transportation between places of lodging or business and places where meals are taken, if suitable meals cannot be obtained at the temporary duty site, and
- Mailing costs associated with filing travel vouchers and payment of employer-sponsored charge card billings.

Incidental expenses do not include expenses for laundry, cleaning and pressing of clothing, lodging taxes, or the costs of telegrams or telephone calls.

> *Incidental expenses only method.* You can use an optional method (instead of actual cost) for deducting incidental expenses only. The amount of the deduction is $3 a day for incidental expenses paid or incurred for travel away from home in 2005. You can use this method only if you did not pay or incur any meal expenses. You cannot use this method on any day that you use the standard meal allowance.

Caution. *Federal employees should refer to the Federal Travel Regulations at www.gsa.gov, click on "Travel" then on "Federal Travel Regulation (FTR) Overview" for changes affecting their claims for reimbursement of these expenses.*

50% limit may apply. If you use this method for meal expenses and you are not reimbursed or you are reimbursed under a nonaccountable plan, you can generally deduct only 50% of the standard meal allowance. If you are reimbursed under an accountable plan and you are deducting amounts that are more than your reimbursements, you can deduct only 50% of the excess amount. The 50% limit is explained later under *Entertainment Expenses*. Accountable and nonaccountable plans are discussed later under *Reimbursements*.

Caution. *There is no optional standard lodging amount similar to the standard meal allowance. Your allowable lodging expense deduction is your actual cost.*

> *Who can use the standard meal allowance.* You can use the standard meal allowance whether you are an employee or self-employed, and whether or not you are reimbursed for your traveling expenses.

Use of the standard meal allowance for other travel. You can use the standard meal allowance to figure your meal expenses when you travel in connection with investment and other income-producing property. You can also use it to figure your meal expenses when you travel for qualifying educational purposes. You cannot use the standard meal allowance to figure the cost of your meals when you travel for medical or charitable purposes.

Amount of standard meal allowance. The standard meal allowance is the federal M&IE rate. The rate is $31 a day for 2005, for most small localities in the United States.

Most major cities and many other localities in the United States are designated as high-cost areas, qualifying for higher standard meal allowances. Locations qualifying for these rates are listed in Publication 1542.

You can also find this information on the Internet at *www.gsa.gov*, click on "Per Diem Rates," then click on "Find Rates for Fiscal Year," then on "2005" for the period January 1, 2005–September 30, 2005, and "2006" for the period October 1, 2005–December 31, 2005. However, you can apply the rates in effect before October 1, 2005, for expenses of all travel within the United States for 2005 instead of the updated rates. You must consistently use either the rates for the first 9 months for all of 2005 or the updated rates for the period of October 1, 2005, through December 31, 2005.

If you travel to more than one location in one day, use the rate in effect for the area where you stop for sleep or rest. If you work in the transportation industry, however, see *Special rate for transportation workers*, later.

TaxPlanner

Whether or not you receive meal money from your employer, you may claim the standard meal allowance and therefore minimize your record-keeping problems. If you are self-employed, you may also claim the standard meal allowance.

Standard meal allowance for areas outside the continental United States. The standard meal allowance rates do not apply to travel in Alaska, Hawaii, or any other locations outside the continental United States. The federal per diem rates for these locations are published monthly in the *Maximum Travel Per Diem Allowances for Foreign Areas*.

You can access foreign per diem rates at: *www.state.gov/m/a/als/prdm*.

Your employer may have these rates available, or you can purchase the publication from the:

Superintendent of Documents
U.S. Government Printing Office
P.O. Box 371954
Pittsburgh, PA 15250-7954

You can also order it by calling the Government Printing Office at 1-866-512-1800.

Special rate for transportation workers. You can use a special standard meal allowance if you work in the transportation industry. You are in the transportation industry if your work:

1. Directly involves moving people or goods by airplane, barge, bus, ship, train, or truck, and
2. Regularly requires you to travel away from home and, during any single trip, usually involves travel to areas eligible for different standard meal allowance rates.

If this applies to you, you can claim a $41 a day standard meal allowance ($46 for travel outside the continental United States) with respect to meal and incidental expenses paid or incurred for 2005.

Using the special rate for transportation workers eliminates the need for you to determine the standard meal allowance for every area where you stop for sleep or rest. If you choose to use the special rate for any trip, you must use the special rate (and not use the regular standard meal allowance rates) for all trips you take that year.

Travel for days you depart and return. For both the day you depart for and the day you return from a business trip, you must prorate the standard meal allowance (figure a reduced amount for each day). You can do so by one of two methods.

1. Method 1: You can claim 3/4 of the standard meal allowance, or
2. Method 2: You can prorate using any method that you consistently apply and that is in accordance with reasonable business practice.

Example. Jen is employed in New Orleans as a convention planner. In March, her employer sent her on a 3-day trip to Washington, DC, to attend a planning seminar. She left her home in New Orleans at 10 a.m. on Wednesday and arrived in Washington, DC, at 5:30 p.m. After spending two nights there, she flew back to New Orleans on Friday and arrived back home at 8:00 p.m. Jen's employer gave her a flat amount to cover her expenses and included it with her wages.

Under Method 1, Jen can claim 2 1/2 days of the standard meal allowance for Washington, DC: 3/4 of the daily rate for Wednesday and Friday (the days she departed and returned), and the full daily rate for Thursday.

Under Method 2, Jen could also use any method that she applies consistently and that is in accordance with reasonable business practice. For example, she could claim 3 days of the standard meal allowance even though a federal employee would have to use method 1 and be limited to only 2 1/2 days.

Travel in the United States

The following discussion applies to travel in the United States. For this purpose, the United States includes the 50 states and the District of Columbia. The treatment of your travel expenses depends on how much of your trip was business related and on how much of your trip occurred within the United States. See *Part of Trip Outside the United States,* later.

Trip Primarily for Business
You can deduct all your travel expenses if your trip was entirely business related. If your trip was primarily for business and, while at your business destination, you extended your stay for a vacation, made a personal side trip, or had other personal activities, you can deduct your business-related travel expenses. These expenses include the travel costs of getting to and from your business destination and any business-related expenses at your business destination.

Example. You work in Atlanta and take a business trip to New Orleans. On your way home, you stop in Mobile to visit your parents. You spend $1,070 for the 9 days you are away from home for travel, meals, lodging, and other travel expenses. If you had not stopped in Mobile, you would have been gone only 6 days, and your total cost would have been $920. You can deduct $920 for your trip, including the round-trip transportation to and from New Orleans. The deduction for your meals is subject to the 50% limit on meals mentioned earlier.

Trip Primarily for Personal Reasons
If your trip was primarily for personal reasons, such as a vacation, the entire cost of the trip is a nondeductible personal expense. However, you can deduct any expenses you have while at your destination that are directly related to your business.

A trip to a resort or on a cruise ship may be a vacation even if the promoter advertises that it is primarily for business. The scheduling of incidental business activities during a trip, such as viewing videotapes or attending lectures dealing with general subjects, will not change what is really a vacation into a business trip.

rental properties. If the primary purpose of the trip is to search for rental properties, all travel expenses can be deducted.

TAXORGANIZER

Careful records should be maintained when family members are along on business trips. If a spouse or other family member on a trip serves a business purpose, care should be taken to document that fact. Otherwise, the incremental travel expenses attributed to the additional person may not be deducted. Receipts and a diary of your activities will be of assistance in documenting the purpose of your trip.

Part of Trip Outside the United States
If part of your trip is outside the United States, use the rules described later under *Travel Outside the United States* for that part of the trip. For the part of your trip that is inside the United States, use the rules for travel in the United States. Travel outside the United States does not include travel from one point in the United States to another point in the United States. The following discussion can help you determine whether your trip was entirely within the United States.

Public transportation. If you travel by public transportation, any place in the United States where that vehicle makes a scheduled stop is a point in the United States. Once the vehicle leaves the last scheduled stop in the United States on its way to a point outside the United States, you apply the rules under *Travel Outside the United States.*

Example. You fly from New York to Puerto Rico with a scheduled stop in Miami. You return to New York nonstop. The flight from New York to Miami is in the United States, so only the flight from Miami to Puerto Rico is outside the United States. Because there are no scheduled stops between Puerto Rico and New York, all of the return trip is outside the United States.

Private car. Travel by private car in the United States is travel between points in the United States, even when you are on your way to a destination outside the United States.

Example. You travel by car from Denver to Mexico City and return. Your travel from Denver to the border and from the border back to Denver is travel in the United States, and the rules in this section apply. The rules under *Travel Outside the United States* apply to your trip from the border to Mexico City and back to the border.

Travel Outside the United States

If any part of your business travel is outside the United States, some of your deductions for the cost of getting to and from your destination may be limited. For this purpose, the United States includes the 50 states and the District of Columbia.

How much of your travel expenses you can deduct depends in part upon how much of your trip outside the United States was business related.

See chapter 1 of Publication 463 for information on luxury water travel.

Travel Entirely for Business or Considered Entirely for Business
You can deduct all your travel expenses of getting to and from your business destination if your trip is entirely for business or considered entirely for business.

Travel entirely for business. If you travel outside the United

States and you spend the entire time on business activities, you can deduct all of your travel expenses.

Travel considered entirely for business. Even if you did not spend your entire time on business activities, your trip is considered entirely for business if you meet at least one of the following four exceptions.

Exception 1 - No substantial control. Your trip is considered entirely for business if you did not have substantial control over arranging the trip. The fact that you control the timing of your trip does not, by itself, mean that you have substantial control over arranging your trip.

You do not have substantial control over your trip if you:

1. Are an employee who was reimbursed or paid a travel expense allowance,
2. Are not related to your employer, and
3. Are not a managing executive.

"Related to your employer" was defined earlier in this chapter under *Who cannot use the standard meal allowance.*

A "managing executive" is an employee who has the authority and responsibility, without being subject to the veto of another, to decide on the need for the business travel.

A self-employed person generally has substantial control over arranging business trips.

Exception 2 - Outside United States no more than a week. Your trip is considered entirely for business if you were outside the United States for a week or less, combining business and nonbusiness activities. One week means seven consecutive days. In counting the days, do not count the day you leave the United States, but do count the day you return to the United States.

Exception 3 - Less than 25% of time on personal activities. Your trip is considered entirely for business if:

1. You were outside the United States for more than a week, and
2. You spent less than 25% of the total time you were outside the United States on nonbusiness activities.

For this purpose, count both the day your trip began and the day it ended.

Exception 4 - Vacation not a major consideration. Your trip is considered entirely for business if you can establish that a personal vacation was not a major consideration, even if you have substantial control over arranging the trip.

Travel Primarily for Business

If you travel outside the United States primarily for business but spend some of your time on nonbusiness activities, you generally cannot deduct all of your travel expenses. You can only deduct the business portion of your cost of getting to and from your destination. You must allocate the costs between your business and nonbusiness activities to determine your deductible amount. These travel allocation rules are discussed in chapter 1 of Publication 463.

Tip. *You do not have to allocate your travel expense deduction if you meet one of the four exceptions listed earlier under* Travel considered entirely for business. *In those cases, you can deduct the total cost of getting to and from your destination.*

Explanation
A business day is established if, during any part of the day, you are required to be present at a business-related event. Weekends falling between business days may be considered business days, but if they fall at the end of your business meetings and you remain for personal reasons, they are not business days. Transportation days are business days when you travel to your destination on a direct route.

TaxPlanner

If, in order to take advantage of lower plane fares, your employer reimburses your travel expenses for staying overnight on Saturday at the end of a business trip, the meals and lodging costs for Saturday can be deducted by your employer and excluded from your income to the extent the costs do not exceed the cost savings. The IRS privately ruled that these travel expenses relating to the Saturday night away are deductible even though the day is spent sightseeing.

Travel Primarily for Personal Reasons

If you travel outside the United States primarily for vacation or for investment purposes, the entire cost of the trip is a nondeductible personal expense. If you spend some time attending brief professional seminars or a continuing education program, you can deduct your registration fees and other expenses you have that are directly related to your business.

Conventions

You can deduct your travel expenses when you attend a convention if you can show that your attendance benefits your trade or business. You cannot deduct the travel expenses for your family.

If the convention is for investment, political, social, or other nonbusiness purposes, you cannot deduct the expenses.

Caution. *Your appointment or election as a delegate does not, in itself, determine whether you can deduct travel expenses. You can deduct your travel expenses only if your attendance is connected to your own trade or business.*

Convention agenda. The convention agenda or program generally shows the purpose of the convention. You can show your attendance at the convention benefits your trade or business by comparing the agenda with the official duties and responsibilities of your position. The agenda does not have to deal specifically with your official duties and responsibilities; it will be enough if the agenda is so related to your position that it shows your attendance was for business purposes.

Explanation
To determine whether a trip is primarily for business, the courts have used the following guidelines:

1. The amount of time spent on personal activity compared with the amount of time spent on business activity.
2. The location of the convention (the setting of a convention at a resort does not mean that the expense is disallowed, but a more businesslike setting increases the strength of your case).
3. The attitude of your sponsor toward the purpose of the meeting.

The courts must also be satisfied that the primary purpose of the convention is business related.

Conventions held outside the North American area. See chapter 1 of Publication 463 for information on conventions held outside the North American area.

Explanation
The amount of expenses you incur when you travel on an ocean liner or cruise ship may not be fully de-

ductible. If you attend a convention while aboard the cruise ship, you may still deduct up to $2,000 per individual per calendar year if the following requirements are met:

1. The meeting must be directly related to the active conduct of a business.
2. The cruise ship must be registered in the United States and may travel only to ports in the United States or its possessions.
3. You attach to your return a written statement signed by you that includes:
   a) The total days of the trip, excluding the days of transportation to and from the cruise ship port;
   b) The number of hours each day that you devoted to scheduled business activities, and
   c) A program of the scheduled business activities of the meeting.
4. You attach to your return a written statement signed by an officer of the organization or group sponsoring the meeting that includes:
   a) A schedule of the business activities of each day of the meeting, and
   b) The number of hours you attended the scheduled business activities.

Example

You have a business meeting in Puerto Rico and choose to travel by ship. You spend 6 days on the cruise ship from the time you depart until the time you return. The total cost of the 6-day cruise package is $3,000. You may deduct only $2,000 of the $3,000 costs.

Entertainment Expenses

You may be able to deduct business-related entertainment expenses you have for entertaining a client, customer, or employee.

You can deduct entertainment expenses only if they are both ordinary and necessary (defined earlier) and meet one of the following two tests.

1. Directly-related test.
2. Associated test.

Both of these tests are explained in Publication 463.

Caution. *The amount you can deduct for entertainment expenses may be limited. Generally, you can deduct only 50% of your unreimbursed entertainment expenses. This limit is discussed later under* 50% *Limit.*

Club dues and membership fees. You cannot deduct dues (including initiation fees) for membership in any club organized for:

1. Business,
2. Pleasure,
3. Recreation, or
4. Other social purpose.

This rule applies to any membership organization if one of its principal purposes is either:

1. To conduct entertainment activities for members or their guests, or
2. To provide members or their guests with access to entertainment facilities.

The purposes and activities of a club, not its name, will determine whether or not you can deduct the dues. You cannot deduct dues paid to:

1. Country clubs,
2. Golf and athletic clubs,
3. Airline clubs,
4. Hotel clubs, and
5. Clubs operated to provide meals under circumstances generally considered to be conducive to business discussions.

Entertainment. Entertainment includes any activity generally considered to provide entertainment, amusement, or recreation. Examples include entertaining guests at nightclubs; at social, athletic, and sporting clubs; at theaters; at sporting events; on yachts; or on hunting, fishing, vacation, and similar trips.

You cannot deduct expenses for entertainment that are lavish or extravagant. If you buy a ticket to an entertainment event for a client, you generally cannot deduct more than the face value of the ticket, even if you paid a higher price.

Gift or entertainment. Any item that might be considered either a gift or entertainment generally will be considered entertainment. However, if you give a customer packaged food or beverages that you intend the customer to use at a later date, treat it as a gift.

If you give a customer tickets to a theater performance or sporting event and you do not go with the customer to the performance or event, you have a choice. You can treat the cost of the tickets as either a gift expense or an entertainment expense, whichever is to your advantage.

You can change your treatment of the tickets at a later date by filing an amended return. Generally, an amended return must be filed within 3 years from the date the original return was filed or within 2 years from the time the tax was paid, whichever is later.

If you go with the customer to the event, you must treat the cost of the tickets as an entertainment expense. You cannot choose, in this case, to treat the cost of the tickets as a gift expense.

Separating costs. If you have one expense that includes the costs of entertainment, and other services (such as lodging or transportation), you must allocate that expense between the cost of entertainment and the cost of other services. You must have a reasonable basis for making this allocation. For example, you must allocate your expenses if a hotel includes entertainment in its lounge on the same bill with your room charge.

A meal as a form of entertainment. Entertainment includes the cost of a meal you provide to a customer or client, whether the meal is a part of other entertainment or by itself. A meal expense includes the cost of food, beverages, taxes, and tips for the meal. To deduct an entertainment-related meal, you or your employee must be present when the food or beverages are provided.

Caution. *You cannot claim the cost of your meal both as an entertainment expense and as a travel expense.*

Taking turns paying for meals or entertainment. If a group of business acquaintances take turns picking up each others' meal or entertainment checks without regard to whether any business purposes are served, no member of the group can deduct any part of the expense.

Trade association meetings. You can deduct expenses for entertainment that are directly related to, and necessary for, attending business meetings or conventions of certain exempt organizations if the expenses of your attendance are related to your active trade or business. These organizations include business leagues, chambers of commerce, real estate boards, trade associations, and professional associations.

Explanation

The courts have held that costs of entertaining fellow employees are not deductible, even though the entertaining may have contributed to high morale and increased productivity.

Additional information. For more information on entertainment expenses, including discussions of the directly related and associated tests, see chapter 2 of Publication 463.

50% Limit

In general, you can deduct only 50% of your business-related meal and entertainment expenses. (If you are subject to the Department of Transportation's "hours of service" limits, you can deduct a higher percentage. See *Individuals subject to "hours of service" limits,* later.)

The 50% limit applies to employees or their employers, and to self-employed persons (including independent contractors) or their clients, depending on whether the expenses are reimbursed.

Figure 28-A summarizes the general rules explained in this section.

The 50% limit applies to business meals or entertainment expenses you have while:

1. Traveling away from home (whether eating alone or with others) on business,
2. Entertaining customers at your place of business, a restaurant, or other location, or
3. Attending a business convention or reception, business meeting, or business luncheon at a club.

TAXPLANNER

The tax law denies a deduction for amounts paid or incurred for membership in any club organized for business, pleasure, recreation, or other social purpose.

Included expenses. Expenses subject to the 50% limit include:

- Taxes and tips relating to a business meal or entertainment activity,
- Cover charges for admission to a nightclub,
- Rent paid for a room in which you hold a dinner or cocktail party, and
- Amounts paid for parking at a sports arena.

However, the cost of transportation to and from a business meal or a business-related entertainment activity is not subject to the 50% limit.

Application of 50% limit. The 50% limit on meal and entertainment expenses applies if the expense is otherwise deductible and is not covered by one of the exceptions discussed later in this section.

The 50% limit also applies to certain meal and entertainment expenses that are not business related. It applies to meal and entertainment expenses incurred for the production of income, including rental or royalty income. It also applies to the cost of meals included in deductible educational expenses.

When to apply the 50% limit. You apply the 50% limit after determining the amount that would otherwise qualify for a deduction. You first determine the amount of meal and entertainment expenses that would be deductible under the other rules discussed in this chapter.

Example 1. You spend $100 for a business-related meal. If $40 of that amount is not allowable because it is lavish and extravagant, the remaining $60 is subject to the 50% limit. Your deduction cannot be more than $30 (.50 × $60).

Example 2. You purchase two tickets to a concert and give them to a client. You purchased the tickets through a ticket agent. You paid $150 for the two tickets, which had a face value of $60 each ($120 total). Your deduction cannot be more than $60 (.50 × $120).

Explanation

Although entertaining a client or a business associate often makes sound business sense, entertainment deductions have sometimes been abused. For this reason, Congress has imposed limitations on the deductibility of entertainment expenses. Only 50% of otherwise allowable entertainment expenses are deductible. The 50% disallowance generally applies to all taxpayers, regardless of the nature of the business. Even before the 50% disallowance, entertainment expenses are subject to stringent record-keeping requirements and must pass one of two tests:

1. **Directly related test.** The expenditure is directly related to the active conduct of your business.
2. **Associated with test.** The expenditure is associated with the active conduct of your business, and the entertainment directly precedes or follows a substantial, bona fide business discussion.

Business meals—those that have a business purpose as opposed to a social and personal one—are not subject to these entertainment rules if they occur in surroundings conducive to business discussion, the taxpayer or an employee of the taxpayer is present when the food or beverages are served, and the expenses are properly substantiated.

Deductions for entertainment or business meals may not be taken if such expenses are considered lavish or extravagant.

Example

State police officers who are required to eat meals while on duty in public places were permitted to deduct expenses for these meals. The court found that the officers were significantly restricted by their employment regarding the time and place they were permitted to eat and that the meals were often subject to business-related interruptions.

Explanation

Entertainment directly related to business. The directly related test is satisfied if all of the following are true:

- You expect to derive income or some other specific business benefit (other than mere goodwill) at some indefinite future time. However, it is not necessary to demonstrate that you actually receive the benefit.
- You actively engage in a business meeting, discussion, or other bona fide business transaction with the person being entertained.
- Your principal purpose of the combined business-entertainment activity is the *active conduct* of your business. It is not necessary to devote more time to business than to the entertainment to meet this requirement.

Certain entertainment activities generally do not meet the directly related test unless proven otherwise. If you are not present for the entertainment, if the group entertained includes persons other than business associates (such as spouses), or if there are substantial distractions (as may occur in nightclubs, theaters, sporting events, and vacation resorts), your activity may fail the directly related test.

The IRS gives taxpayers some relief from these strict rules when the activity is clearly in a business setting. For example, expenditures made to further your business by providing a hospitality room at a convention are treated as entertainment expenses directly related to business. Additionally, situations in which no meaningful personal or social relationship exists between you and the persons entertained are often considered to have occurred in a business setting. For example, entertaining business and civic leaders at the opening of a new hotel or theatrical production—for the purpose of obtaining business publicity rather than creat-

Figure 28-A. **Does the 50% Limit Apply to Your Expenses?**

There are exceptions to these rules. See *Exceptions to the 50% Limit.*

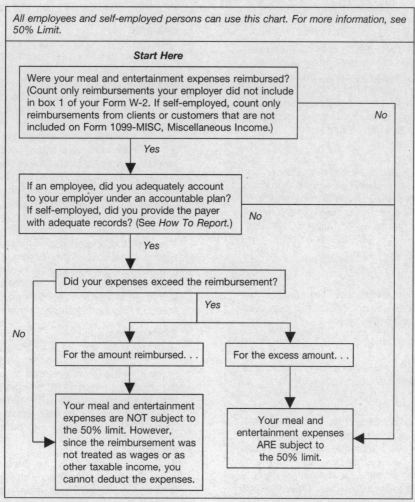

All employees and self-employed persons can use this chart. For more information, see 50% Limit.

Start Here

Were your meal and entertainment expenses reimbursed? (Count only reimbursements your employer did not include in box 1 of your Form W-2. If self-employed, count only reimbursements from clients or customers that are not included on Form 1099-MISC, Miscellaneous Income.) — No

Yes ↓

If an employee, did you adequately account to your employer under an accountable plan? If self-employed, did you provide the payer with adequate records? (See *How To Report.*) — No

Yes ↓

Did your expenses exceed the reimbursement? — No

Yes ↓

For the amount reimbursed. . .

For the excess amount. . .

Your meal and entertainment expenses are NOT subject to the 50% limit. However, since the reimbursement was not treated as wages or as other taxable income, you cannot deduct the expenses.

Your meal and entertainment expenses ARE subject to the 50% limit.

---

ing or maintaining goodwill—is a deductible entertainment expense directly related to business.

Example

An attorney paid for the costs of an annual fishing trip with three business associates who were sources of referrals to his law practice. He also used his cabin 75% of the time for entertaining business clients. The attorney could not prove that substantial and bona fide business discussions occurred during the fishing trip or on any of the occasions when business clients used the cabin. He showed that, at most, he had just a generalized expectation of deriving income or other business benefits at some indefinite future time from those entertained. As a result, he was denied deductions for these expenses because they did not meet the directly related test.

Explanation

Entertainment associated with business. If an entertainment expenditure does not meet the directly related requirements, it may still be deductible if it passes the associated with test. An entertainment activity passes the associated with test only if it satisfies two conditions:

- The activity has a clear business purpose.
- The entertainment directly precedes or follows a substantial, bona fide business discussion.

The desire to obtain new business and the intent to maintain an existing business relationship—goodwill— are objectives that have a clear business purpose. A substantial, bona fide business discussion occurs when you actively engage in a business transaction to obtain some business benefit and the business meeting, negotiation, or discussion is substantial in relation to the entertainment. However, it is not necessary to spend more time on business than on entertainment.

Example

Bonnie McDonald, an independent consultant, spends 4 hours delivering a new management program to a group of executives in her client's New Orleans office. After the meeting, Bonnie takes the group to the French Quarter for dinner and a show. Dixieland jazz is played throughout dinner.

The entertainment passes the associated with test and is therefore deductible (subject to the 50% limitation) because Bonnie is maintaining a business relationship and the entertainment follows a substantial business meeting. The expense would not pass the directly related test because (1) goodwill generally does not qualify and (2) substantial distractions exist.

Explanation
Entertainment directly precedes or follows a substantial business discussion if it occurs on the same day. If the entertainment and business discussion do not occur on the same day, the facts and circumstances of each case determine whether or not the entertainment and the business discussion occur close enough in time so that the expenses can be deducted.

Example
A group of business associates come to Denver and hold substantial discussions with a taxpayer. Entertainment for the business guests on the evening prior to or after the day of the business discussions is generally regarded as directly preceding or following the business discussion. Therefore, 50% of the entertainment expenses are deductible.

Explanation
Deducting goodwill entertainment. Generally, entertaining for goodwill alone is not deductible. However, you may deduct goodwill expenditures when:

- The goodwill occurs during a quiet business lunch or dinner.
- The goodwill precedes or follows a substantial business discussion (i.e., passes the associated with test).

Example 1
Liz Brown, a partner of a management consulting firm, plans a dinner party in a New York City hotel. She invites a number of current and prospective clients. Business is only casually discussed; her main goal is to cultivate goodwill. The expense for the dinner party is not deductible. The goodwill is a clear business purpose, but the dinner is not preceded or followed by a substantial business discussion.

Example 2
After considering the tax cost of the nondeductible goodwill expenses, Liz Brown holds a second dinner party, but she adds a formal presentation, which is substantial in relation to the time spent cultivating goodwill. The costs of the refreshments and dinner qualify as goodwill entertainment, since the entertainment is associated with business and the goodwill (the business purpose) is preceded by a substantial business discussion (the presentation). As a result, 50% of the qualifying expenses are deductible.

Explanation
Out-of-pocket entertaining costs at clubs and lodges. Congress has made it clear that out-of-pocket entertainment costs—that otherwise qualify as directly related or associated with business expenses—may still be partially deducted, even if they are incurred at an entertainment facility. Again, 50% of such costs may not be deducted.

An entertainment facility is usually **real property,** such as a fishing camp, a ski lodge, an apartment, or a hotel suite, that may also include personal property, such as a yacht, an airplane, or an automobile. You may own or rent the facility or just be a member of a club or organization, such as a country club or a sporting group, that provides use of a facility.

Example
Mike Franklin, a sports equipment manufacturer, takes a customer to a hunting lodge on an overnight trip. Immediately after the trip, the customer discusses products and market projections. The discussion ends with the customer placing his semiannual order.

In this instance, 50% of the costs of the meals, hunting rights, drinks in the nightclub, and transportation to and from the lodge are deductible. These costs qualify as entertainment associated with business and followed by a substantial business discussion (i.e., the expenses pass the associated with test). Because 50% of the entertainment costs would have been deductible if not incurred at an entertainment facility, they are also deductible even though the hunting lodge is an entertainment facility. These costs are not directly associated with the operation and maintenance of the place. However, the cost of the lodging is associated with the operation and maintenance of the facility. Therefore, the lodging expense, though partially deductible if incurred at a nonentertainment facility (e.g., a hotel instead of the hunting lodge), is not deductible.

Explanation
Deductions for the costs of tickets to cultural, theatrical, or sporting events are severely limited. In addition to meeting the directly related or associated with tests, the allowable portion of the ticket cost is limited to the face value of the ticket. The allowable portion of the ticket cost must be further reduced because only 50% of the allowable expense may be deducted.

Example
You pay a scalper $150 for three tickets to a sporting event. The face value of each ticket is $20. Your deduction is limited to $30 ($20 face value × three tickets × 50%).

Explanation
A similar rule also applies to the cost of luxury skyboxes at sports arenas. Costs for the business use of a suite, an apartment, an automobile, or an airplane are generally deductible. Personal use of an entertainment facility may be considered compensation, and the individual may be subject to tax.

Exceptions to the 50% Limit
Generally, business-related meal and entertainment expenses are subject to the 50% limit. Figure 28-A can help you determine if the 50% limit applies to you.

Your meal or entertainment expense is not subject to the 50% limit if the expense meets either of the following exceptions.
Employee's reimbursed expenses. If you are an employee, you are not subject to the 50% limit on the amount of expenses for which your employer reimburses you under an accountable plan. Accountable plans are discussed later under *Reimbursements.*

Exceptions
Entertainment test exceptions. Expenses incurred in the following situations generally are not subject to the directly related and associated with tests:

- Business meals in surroundings normally considered conducive to a business discussion.

- Recreational and social activities primarily benefiting employees (e.g., company picnics, office Christmas parties, and golf outings).
- Business meetings of employees, stockholders, agents, or directors.
- Attendance at a business meeting of a tax-exempt business league (e.g., a chamber of commerce, a board of trade, or a professional organization).
- Employee entertainment or recreation that is treated as compensation on the employee's income tax return and as wages for withholding purposes.
- Nonemployee entertainment or recreation that is treated as income on the nonemployee's tax return and reported to him or her on an informational return (Form 1099).

Exceptions to the 50% limit. Expenses incurred in the following situations are not subject to the 50% disallowance provision:

- Reimbursed meal or entertainment expenses.
- Employer-paid recreational expenses for employees (e.g., a holiday party).
- Entertainment taxable to the recipient.
- Entertainment expenses made available to the general public.
- Entertainment expenses related to charitable fundraising sports events.

Individuals subject to "hours of service" limits. You can deduct a higher percentage of your meal expenses while traveling away from your tax home if the meals take place during or incident to any period subject to the Department of Transportation's "hours of service" limits. The percentage is 70% for 2005, and it gradually increases to 80% by the year 2008.

Individuals subject to the Department of Transportation's "hours of service" limits include the following persons.

1. Certain air transportation workers (such as pilots, crew, dispatchers, mechanics, and control tower operators) who are under Federal Aviation Administration regulations.
2. Interstate truck operators and bus drivers who are under Department of Transportation regulations.
3. Certain railroad employees (such as engineers, conductors, train crews, dispatchers, and control operations personnel) who are under Federal Railroad Administration regulations.
4. Certain merchant mariners who are under Coast Guard regulations.

Gift Expenses

If you give gifts in the course of your trade or business, you can deduct all or part of the cost. This section explains the limits and rules for deducting the costs of gifts.

$25 limit. You can deduct no more than $25 for business gifts you give directly or indirectly to any one person during your tax year. A gift to a company that is intended for the eventual personal use or benefit of a particular person or a limited class of people will be considered an indirect gift to that particular person or to the individuals within that class of people who receive the gift.

If you give a gift to a member of a customer's family, the gift is generally considered to be an indirect gift to the customer. This rule does not apply if you have a *bona fide*, independent business connection with that family member and the gift is not intended for the customer's eventual use.

If you and your spouse both give gifts, both of you are treated as one taxpayer. It does not matter whether you have separate businesses, are separately employed, or whether each of you has an independent connection with the recipient. If a partnership gives gifts, the partnership and the partners are treated as one taxpayer.

Incidental costs. Incidental costs, such as engraving on jewelry, or packaging, insuring, and mailing, are generally not included in determining the cost of a gift for purposes of the $25 limit.

A cost is incidental only if it does not add substantial value to the gift. For example, the cost of gift wrapping is an incidental cost. However, the purchase of an ornamental basket for packaging fruit is not an incidental cost if the value of the basket is substantial compared to the value of the fruit.

Exceptions. The following items are not considered gifts for purposes of the $25 limit.

1. An item that costs $4 or less and:
   a. Has your name clearly and permanently imprinted on the gift, and
   b. Is one of a number of identical items you widely distribute. Examples include pens, desk sets, and plastic bags and cases.
2. Signs, display racks, or other promotional material to be used on the business premises of the recipient.

Explanation
Business gifts are subject to close scrutiny. The IRS views this area as one of potential abuse. Business gifts are subject to strict substantiation requirements. The date of the gift and the name of the recipient must be noted in your records to uphold the deduction.

The business gift limitations do not apply to the following types of donations:

- Fellowship grants or scholarships.
- Achievement prizes and awards.
- Death benefits to an employer's survivors.

Examples
The cost of beer offered by a service station owner to entice customers into his service station was allowed as a business gift deduction. The courts held that the expenses were directly related to the active conduct of his business and were incurred to sell additional goods and services.

Wine samples distributed in connection with a public offering of stock were allowed as a business gift subject to the $25 per recipient limitation.

Gift or entertainment. Any item that might be considered either a gift or entertainment generally will be considered entertainment. However, if you give a customer packaged food or beverages that you intend the customer to use at a later date, treat it as a gift.

If you give a customer tickets to a theater performance or sporting event and you do not go with the customer to the performance or event, you have a choice. You can treat the cost of the tickets as either a gift expense or an entertainment expense, whichever is to your advantage.

You can change your treatment of the tickets at a later date by filing an amended return. Generally, an amended return must be filed within 3 years from the date the original return was filed or within 2 years from the time the tax was paid, whichever is later.

If you go with the customer to the event, you must treat the cost of the tickets as an entertainment expense. You cannot choose, in this case, to treat the cost of the tickets as a gift expense.

TaxPlanner

It is usually to your advantage to define a particular item as an entertainment expense rather than as a gift. Although entertainment expenses are subject to the 50% limitation, there is no fixed dollar limitation on the deduction, though the expenses must be considered ordinary and necessary.

Transportation Expenses

This section discusses expenses you can deduct for business transportation when you are not traveling away from home as defined earlier. These expenses include the cost of transportation by air, rail, bus, taxi, etc., and the cost of driving and maintaining your car.

Transportation expenses include the ordinary and necessary costs of all of the following.

- Getting from one workplace to another in the course of your business or profession when you are traveling within your tax home. (Tax home is defined earlier under *Travel Expenses.*)
- Visiting clients or customers.
- Going to a business meeting away from your regular workplace.
- Getting from your home to a temporary workplace when you have one or more regular places of work. These temporary workplaces can be either within the area of your tax home or outside that area.

Transportation expenses do not include expenses you have while traveling away from home overnight. Those expenses are travel expenses, which are discussed earlier. However, if you use your car while traveling away from home overnight, use the rules in this section to figure your car expense deduction. See *Car Expenses,* later.

Illustration of transportation expenses. Figure 28-B illustrates the rules for when you can deduct transportation expenses when you have a regular or main job away from your home. You may want to refer to it when deciding whether you can deduct your transportation expenses.

Temporary work location. If you have one or more regular work locations away from your home and you commute to a temporary work location in the same trade or business, you can deduct the expenses of the daily round-trip transportation between your home and the temporary location, regardless of distance.

If your employment at a work location is realistically expected to last (and does in fact last) for one year or less, the employment is temporary unless there are facts and circumstances that would indicate otherwise.

If your employment at a work location is realistically expected to last for more than 1 year or if there is no realistic expectation that the employment will last for 1 year or less, the employment is not temporary, regardless of whether it actually lasts for more than 1 year.

If employment at a work location initially is realistically expected to last for 1 year or less, but at some later date the employment is realistically expected to last more than 1 year, that employment will be treated as temporary (unless there are facts and circumstances that would indicate otherwise) until your expectation changes. It will not be treated as temporary after the date you determine it will last more than 1 year.

If the temporary work location is beyond the general area of your regular place of work and you stay overnight, you are traveling away from home. You may have deductible travel expenses as discussed earlier in this chapter.

Explanation
If your employment at a work location is realistically expected to (and does in fact) last for 1 year or less, the employment is temporary unless there are facts and circumstances that would indicate otherwise. If your employment at a work location is realistically expected to last for more than 1 year, or if there is no realistic expectation that the employment will last for 1 year or less, the employment is not temporary, regardless of whether it actually lasts for more than 1 year. If employment at a work location initially is realistically expected to last for 1 year or *less,* but at some later date the employment is realistically expected to last *more* than 1 year, that employment will be treated as temporary (unless there are facts and circumstances that would indicate otherwise) until the date you determine it will last more than 1 year. It will not be treated as temporary after the date you determine it will last more than 1 year.

No regular place of work. If you have no regular place of work but ordinarily work in the metropolitan area where you live, you can deduct daily transportation costs between home and a temporary work site outside that metropolitan area.

Generally, a metropolitan area includes the area within the city limits and the suburbs that are considered part of that metropolitan area.

You cannot deduct daily transportation costs between your home and temporary work sites within your metropolitan area. These are nondeductible commuting expenses.

TAXPLANNER

The IRS has ruled that a taxpayer may deduct the expenses of daily transportation between his or her residence and any temporary work site as long as he or she has a regular work site.

Based on this ruling by the IRS, the Tax Court allowed a logger to deduct his expenses of traveling between his residence and various cutting sites because the court held the logger's residence was his *regular* place of business.

However, in response to this decision by the Tax Court, the IRS issued a new ruling that stated that daily transportation expenses incurred in going between a taxpayer's residence and a work location are nondeductible commuting expenses unless one of the following three exceptions applies:

1. A taxpayer may deduct daily transportation expenses incurred in going between the taxpayer's residence and a temporary work location *outside* the metropolitan area where the taxpayer lives and normally works. However, unless paragraph (2) or (3) below applies, daily transportation expenses incurred in going between the taxpayer's residence and a temporary work location *within* that metropolitan area are nondeductible commuting expenses.
2. If a taxpayer has one or more *regular* work locations away from the taxpayer's residence, the taxpayer may deduct daily transportation expenses incurred in going between the taxpayer's residence and a temporary work location in the same trade or business, regardless of the distance.
3. If a taxpayer's residence is the taxpayer's *principal* place of business (as opposed to a regular place of business), the taxpayer may deduct daily transportation expenses incurred in going between the residence and another work location in the same trade or business, regardless of whether the other work location is regular or temporary and regardless of the distance.

Explanation
It is important to note the difference between a principal place of business and a regular place of business. A principal place of business is determined by a facts and circumstances test. Among the facts and circumstances to be taken into account in determining an individual's principal place of business are the following:

1. The portion of total income from business activities that is attributable to activities at each location.
2. The portion of time spent in business activities in each location.
3. The facilities available to the taxpayer at each location.

Figure 28-B. **When Are Transportation Expenses Deductible?**
Most employees and self-employed persons can use this chart.
(Do not use this chart if your home is your principal place of business.
See *Office in the home*.)

Home: The place where you reside. Transportation expenses between your home and your main or regular place of work are personal commuting expenses.

Regular or main job: Your principal place of business. If you have more than one job, you must determine which one is your regular or main job. Consider the time you spend at each, the activity you have at each, and the income you earn at each.

Temporary work location: A place where your work assignment is realistically expected to last (and does in fact last) one year or less. Unless you have a regular place of business, you can only deduct your transportation expenses to a temporary work location <u>outside</u> your metropolitan area.

Second job: If you regularly work at two or more places in one day, whether or not for the same employer, you can deduct your transportation expenses of getting from one workplace to another. You cannot deduct your transportation costs between your home and a second job on a day off from your main job.

The regular place of business standard is less stringent than the principal place of business standard. A regular place of business is defined as any location at which the taxpayer works or performs services on a regular basis.

Two places of work. If you work at two places in one day, whether or not for the same employer, you can deduct the expense of getting from one workplace to the other. However, if for some personal reason you do not go directly from one location to the other, you cannot deduct more than the amount it would have cost you to go directly from the first location to the second.

Transportation expenses you have in going between home and a part-time job on a day off from your main job are commuting expenses. You cannot deduct them.

Example 1
A doctor who practiced at a private clinic could not deduct the automobile expenses incurred on his regular and emergency trips between his home and the hospital. Under the hospital rules, the doctor was required to visit the hospital daily, as well as to spend a day on call each month. The court ruled that since the hospital was an integral and regular place of business for the doctor, his travel was a nondeductible commuting expense.

Example 2
A doctor could not deduct the cost of traveling between his office at home and the clinic where he practiced. Although he kept his medical and business records in his office in the home, he didn't see patients there. The court ruled that it was neither a principal business office nor a focal point for his medical practice and disallowed the deduction.

Example 3
A doctor who maintained two separate offices was denied a deduction for the costs of commuting between his residence and the places where he conducted his medical practices. He was, however, permitted to deduct commuting costs between his offices and to the hospital where he made his rounds.

Example 4

A college professor who maintained a home office was not allowed to deduct transportation expenses from his home to the college. The court determined that the focal point of his activities was the college at which he taught.

Exception

A police officer was allowed to claim a deduction for automobile expenses traveling to and from work because he was under orders to consider himself at work from the moment he left home until he returned.

Example

A teacher could not deduct the expenses for an automobile she used to carry books and teaching materials to her classes, even though she could not store them at the school. She also used her automobile on days on which she came to school just to attend meetings. It took an hour to drive to school. Getting there by alternative means of transportation took 1 1/2 hours and was very inconvenient. The court concluded that she would have driven even if she didn't have to transport books and that her expenses were merely commuting costs and not deductible.

Armed Forces reservists. A meeting of an Armed Forces reserve unit is a second place of business if the meeting is held on a day on which you work at your regular job. You can deduct the expense of getting from one workplace to the other as just discussed under *Two places of work.*

You usually cannot deduct the expense if the reserve meeting is held on a day on which you do not work at your regular job. In this case, your transportation generally is considered a nondeductible commuting expense. However, you can deduct your transportation expenses if the location of the meeting is temporary and you have one or more regular places of work.

If you ordinarily work in a particular metropolitan area but not at any specific location and the reserve meeting is held at a temporary location outside that metropolitan area, you can deduct your transportation expenses.

If you travel away from home overnight to attend a guard or reserve meeting, you can deduct your travel expenses. These expenses are discussed earlier under *Travel Expenses.*

If you travel more than 100 miles away from home in connection with your performance of services as a member of the reserves, you may be able to deduct some of your reserve-related travel costs as an adjustment to income rather than as an itemized deduction. See *Armed Forces reservists traveling more than 100 miles from home* under *Special Rules,* later.

Commuting expenses. You cannot deduct the costs of taking a bus, trolley, subway, or taxi, or of driving a car between your home and your main or regular place of work. These costs are personal commuting expenses. You cannot deduct commuting expenses no matter how far your home is from your regular place of work. You cannot deduct commuting expenses even if you work during the commuting trip.

Example. You had a telephone installed in your car. You sometimes use that telephone to make business calls while commuting to and from work. Sometimes business associates ride with you to and from work, and you have a business discussion in the car. These activities do not change the trip from personal to business. You cannot deduct your commuting expenses.

Parking fees. Fees you pay to park your car at your place of business are nondeductible commuting expenses. You can, however, deduct business-related parking fees when visiting a customer or client.

Advertising display on car. Putting display material that advertises your business on your car does not change the use of your car from personal use to business use. If you use this car for commuting or other personal uses, you still cannot deduct your expenses for those uses.

Car pools. You cannot deduct the cost of using your car in a nonprofit car pool. Do not include payments you receive from the passengers in your income. These payments are considered reimbursements of your expenses. However, if you operate a car pool for a profit, you must include payments from passengers in your income. You can then deduct your car expenses (using the rules in this chapter).

Hauling tools or instruments. Hauling tools or instruments in your car while commuting to and from work does not make your car expenses deductible. However, you can deduct any additional costs you have for hauling tools or instruments (such as for renting a trailer you tow with your car).

Union members' trips from a union hall. If you get your work assignments at a union hall and then go to your place of work, the costs of getting from the union hall to your place of work are nondeductible commuting expenses. Although you need the union to get your work assignments, you are employed where you work, not where the union hall is located.

Office in the home. If you have an office in your home that qualifies as a principal place of business, you can deduct your daily transportation costs between your home and another work location in the same trade or business. (See chapter 30 for information on determining if your home office qualifies as a principal place of business.)

Examples of deductible transportation expenses. The following examples show when you can deduct transportation expenses based on the location of your work and your home.

Example 1. You regularly work in an office in the city where you live. Your employer sends you to a one-week training session at a different office in the same city. You travel directly from your home to the training location and return each day. You can deduct the cost of your daily round-trip transportation between your home and the training location.

Example 2. Your principal place of business is in your home. You can deduct the cost of round-trip transportation between your qualifying home office and your client's or customer's place of business.

Example 3. You have no regular office, and you do not have an office in your home. In this case, the location of your first business contact is considered your office. Transportation expenses between your home and this first contact are nondeductible commuting expenses. Transportation expenses between your last business contact and your home are also nondeductible commuting expenses. Although you cannot deduct the costs of these first and last trips, you can deduct the costs of going from one client or customer to another.

Car Expenses

If you use your car for business purposes, you may be able to deduct car expenses. You generally can use one of the two following methods to figure your deductible expenses.

- Standard mileage rate.
- Actual car expenses.

If you use actual car expenses to figure your deduction for a car you lease, there are rules that affect the amount of your lease payments that you can deduct. See *Leasing a car* under *Actual Car Expenses,* later.

In this chapter, "car" includes a van, pickup, or panel truck.

Explanation

Fixed and variable rate. Under certain circumstances, employees' business expenses for car expenses will be deemed substantiated when their employer reimburses such expenses with a mileage allowance different from the 40.5-cents-per-mile standard mileage rate (48.5 cents per mile after August 2005).

Tip. *You may be entitled to a tax credit for an electric vehicle (see chapter 39) or a deduction from gross income for a part of the cost of a clean-fuel vehicle that you place in service during the year. The vehicle must meet certain requirements, and you do not have to use it in your business to qualify for the credit or the deduction. For more information, see chapter 12 of Publication 535.*

Rural mail carriers. If you are a rural mail carrier, you may be able to treat the amount of qualified reimbursement you received as the amount of your allowable expense. Because the qualified reimbursement is treated as paid under an accountable plan, your employer should not include the amount of reimbursement in your income.

If your vehicle expenses are more than the amount of your reimbursement, you can deduct the unreimbursed expenses as an itemized deduction on Schedule A (Form 1040).

A "qualified reimbursement" is the amount of reimbursement you receive that meets both of the following conditions.

1. It is given as an equipment maintenance allowance (EMA) to employees of the U.S. Postal Service.
2. It is at the rate contained in the 1991 collective bargaining agreement. Any later agreement cannot increase the qualified reimbursement amount by more than the rate of inflation.

See your employer for information on your reimbursement.
Caution. *If you are a rural mail carrier and received a qualified reimbursement, you cannot use the standard mileage rate.*

Standard Mileage Rate

You may be able to use the standard mileage rate to figure the deductible costs of operating your car for business purposes. For 2005, the standard mileage rate is 40.5 cents a mile for all business miles.

Caution. *If you use the standard mileage rate for a year, you cannot deduct your actual car expenses for that year.*

You generally can use the standard mileage rate regardless of whether you are reimbursed and whether any reimbursement is more or less than the amount figured using the standard mileage rate. See *Reimbursements* under *How To Report,* later.

Choosing the standard mileage rate. If you want to use the standard mileage rate for a car you own, you must choose to use it in the first year the car is available for use in your business. Then in later years, you can choose to use either the standard mileage rate or actual expenses.

If you want to use the standard mileage rate for a car you lease, you must use it for the entire lease period. For leases that began on or before December 31, 1997, the standard mileage rate must be used for the entire portion of the lease period (including renewals) that is after 1997.

If you choose to use the standard mileage rate, you are considered to have chosen not to use the depreciation methods under the Modified Accelerated Cost Recovery System (MACRS). This is because the standard mileage rate includes an allowance for depreciation that is not expressed in terms of years. If you change to the actual expenses method in a later year, but before your car is fully depreciated, you have to estimate the remaining useful life of the car and use straight line depreciation. For more information about depreciation included in the standard mileage rate, see the exception in *Methods of depreciation* under *Depreciation Deduction* in chapter 4 of Publication 463.

Standard mileage rate not allowed. You cannot use the standard mileage rate if you:
1. Use the car for hire (such as a taxi),
2. Use five or more cars at the same time (as in fleet operations),
3. Claimed a depreciation deduction for the car using any method other than straight line depreciation,
4. Claimed a section 179 deduction on the car,
5. Claimed the special depreciation allowance on the car,
6. Claimed actual car expenses after 1997 for a car you leased, or
7. Are a rural mail carrier who received a qualified reimbursement. (See *Rural mail carriers,* earlier.)

Five or more cars. If you own or lease five or more cars that are used for business at the same time, you cannot use the standard mileage rate for the business use of any car. However, you may be able to deduct your actual expenses for operating each of the cars in your business. See *Actual Car Expenses* in chapter 4 of Publication 463 for information on how to figure your deduction.

You are not using five or more cars for business at the same time if you alternate using (use at different times) the cars for business.
Example 1. Marcia, a salesperson, owns three cars and two vans

that she alternates using for calling on her customers. She can use the standard mileage rate for the business mileage of the three cars and the two vans because she does not use them at the same time.

Example 2. Maureen owns a car and four vans that are used in her housecleaning business. Her employees use the vans and she uses the car to travel to various customers. Maureen cannot use the standard mileage rate for the car or the vans. This is because all five vehicles are used in Maureen's business at the same time. She must use actual expenses for all vehicles.

Parking fees and tolls. In addition to using the standard mileage rate, you can deduct any business-related parking fees and tolls. (Parking fees that you pay to park your car at your place of work are nondeductible commuting expenses.)

TaxAlert

Employer-provided parking. For 2005, you can exclude up to $200 per month of employer-provided parking, even if you choose it instead of cash or your employer reduces your compensation to provide the parking. The $200 is indexed for inflation.

Actual Car Expenses

If you do not use the standard mileage rate, you may be able to deduct your actual car expenses.

Tip. *If you qualify to use both methods, you may want to figure your deduction both ways to see which gives you a larger deduction.*

Actual car expenses include:

Depreciation	Lease payments	Registration fees
Garage rent	Licenses	Repairs
Gas	Oil	Tires
Insurance	Parking fees	Tolls

Business and personal use. If you use your car for both business and personal purposes, you must divide your expenses between business and personal use. You can divide your expense based on the miles driven for each purpose.

Example. You are a contractor and drive your car 20,000 miles during the year: 12,000 miles for business use and 8,000 miles for personal use. You can claim only 60% (12,000 ÷ 20,000) of the cost of operating your car as a business expense.

Explanation

To claim a deduction for car expenses properly, you must establish that you are entitled to the deduction because the car was used at least partially for business. The deduction will be allowed only to the extent of business use. If you can establish that you are entitled to the deduction but are unable to establish the precise amount of the deduction, the court will apply its own best judgment to make an approximation of the business portion of the expenses.

Example 1

A doctor who is constantly on emergency call may not deduct all of his automobile expenses and depreciation. He must calculate how much of the automobile's use is business and how much is personal. The business portion is deductible.

Example 2

A construction worker who kept a log book of miles driven but failed to distinguish between business and personal mileage was not allowed to take any deduction.

Example 3

A salesman was able to prove that he used his automobile exclusively for business except for his round trip to and from work of 16 miles. However, he was unable to establish how many miles were dedicated to business use. The court concluded that his business use was 75% and his personal use was 25%.

Interest on car loans. If you are an employee, you cannot deduct any interest paid on a car loan. This interest is treated as personal interest and is not deductible. However, if you are self-employed and use your car in that business, see chapter 5 of Publication 535. **Tip.** *If you use a home equity loan to purchase your car, you may be able to deduct the interest. See chapter 25 for more information.*

TaxPlanner

If an employee who owns a home finances the purchase of an automobile through a loan secured by the home, the interest would be fully deductible as home mortgage interest if the employee is within the $100,000 home equity indebtedness rules.

Taxes paid on your car. If you are an employee, you can deduct personal property taxes paid on your car if you itemize deductions. Enter the amount paid on line 7 of Schedule A (Form 1040). (See chapter 24 for more information on taxes.) If you are not an employee, see your form instructions for information on how to deduct personal property taxes paid on your car.

Sales taxes. Generally, sales taxes on your car are part of your car's basis and are recovered through depreciation, discussed later. However, to the extent the car is not used in your trade or business, you can choose to deduct that part of the sales tax on your car as part of your state and local sales tax deduction on Schedule A (Form 1040). You can only choose to deduct state and local sales taxes as an itemized deduction if you choose not to deduct state and local income taxes.

Fines and collateral. You cannot deduct fines and collateral you pay for traffic violations.

Depreciation and section 179 deductions. Generally, the cost of a car, plus sales tax and improvements, is a capital expense. Because the benefits last longer than one year, you generally cannot deduct a capital expense. However, you can recover this cost through the section 179 deduction (the deduction allowed by section 179 of the Internal Revenue Code), the special depreciation allowance, and depreciation deductions. By using depreciation, you recover the cost over more than one year by deducting part of it each year. The section 179 deduction, the special depreciation allowance, and the depreciation deduction are discussed in more detail in chapter 4 of Publication 463.

Explanation

For more information on the Section 179 deduction, see Chapter 39, *If You Are Self-Employed: How to File Schedule C.*

For more information on depreciation, see Chapter 10, *Rental Income and Expenses.*

Generally, there are limits on these deductions. Special rules apply if you use your car 50% or less in your work or business.

TaxAlert

The special 50% and 30% depreciation allowances for the purchase of a new car used for business purposes is not available for cars purchased on or after January 1, 2005.

EXPLANATION
Severe limitations on deductions apply on luxury automobiles and automobiles used for both business and personal purposes.

Passenger automobile. The total initial-year depreciation deduction (including section 179 expense) you can take for a passenger automobile (that is not a truck, van, or an electric vehicle) that you use in your business and first place in service in 2005 is $2,960.

Caution. The limits are reduced if the business use of the vehicle is less than 100%.

Electric vehicle. The total initial-year depreciation deduction (including section 179 expense) you can take for an electric vehicle that you use in your business and first place in service in 2005 is $8,880.

Caution. The limits are reduced if the business use of the vehicle is less than 100%.

Truck or van. The total initial-year depreciation deduction (including section 179 expense) you can take for a truck or van (such as a minivan or a sports utility vehicle built on a truck chassis) that you use in your business and first place in service in 2005 is higher than for other passenger vehicles. The maximum amount allowable is $3,260.

Caution. The limits are reduced if the business use of the vehicle is less than 100%.

Explanation
If qualified business use of a vehicle purchased after 1986 is over 50%, then you can claim 200% declining balance depreciation over a 5-year period. Declining balance depreciation is described in Chapter 10, *Rental Income and Expenses.* Qualified business use means direct use in your trade or business, including your job. It does not include looking after your investments. However, if you use your automobile more than 50% in your trade or business, you can then use accelerated 5-year depreciation for the part used for looking after your investments.

If qualified business use is 50% or less, depreciation must be calculated on a straight-line basis over 5 years, with a proration of the maximum deduction. Although a 5-year life rate is used, only a half-year's depreciation is deductible in the first year. The other half-year is not deductible until the sixth year. Again, depreciation in excess of the allowed amounts is carried over to future years to depreciate fully the business portion of the asset.

Example
You buy an automobile in 2005 and use it 60% for business, 10% for looking after your investments, and 30% for personal use. You can deduct 70% of your depreciation, calculated using accelerated depreciation. If you use your automobile only 45% for business and 25% for looking after your investments, you can still deduct 70%, but it must be computed on a straight-line basis.

Leasing a car. If you lease a car, truck, or van that you use in your business, you can use the standard mileage rate or actual expenses to figure your deductible car expense.

Deductible payments. If you choose to use actual expenses, you can deduct the part of each lease payment that is for the use of the car in your business. You cannot deduct any part of a lease payment that is for personal use of the car, such as commuting.

You must spread any advance payments over the entire lease period. You cannot deduct any payments you make to buy a car, even if the payments are called lease payments.

If you lease a car for 30 days or more, you may have to reduce your lease payment deduction by an "inclusion amount." For information on reporting lease inclusion amounts, see *Leasing a Car* in chapter 4 of Publication 463.

TaxPlanner

If you buy an automobile (for personal use) and finance it, you cannot deduct any of the interest charges. If you finance the car by taking out a home equity loan, the interest may be deductible as home mortgage interest. See Chapter 8, *Interest Income.* However, if you are **self-employed** and use your car in your trade or business, you may deduct 100% of the business portion of the interest charges. If you simply use your car as an **employee,** you may pay less tax by leasing a car rather than buying it because you can deduct your lease payments subject to the business use rules discussed elsewhere in this chapter.

Leasing an automobile. Deducting employee business expenses for the cost of a leased automobile is similar to doing so for an automobile you own. You may deduct the portion of the total lease payments that is attributable to business use, using the ratio of business miles to total miles to make the calculation. This deduction represents the depreciation and financing costs. Normal operating costs and maintenance (if not included in the lease) and business parking may also be deducted.

The luxury automobile rules are intended to impose the same unfavorable treatment for leased automobiles as for purchased automobiles. If you lease an automobile for business use, you can deduct the lease payments and operating expenses for that business use. If you lease an automobile and the value exceeds certain levels, you are deemed to have received additional income.

Note: You must recapture a portion of your lease payment deductions and report them as income if your business use of the automobile falls below 50%.

See Publication 463, *Travel, Entertainment, Gift and Car Expenses,* for further details and the tables for computing the lease adjustments.

Sale, Trade-In, or Other Disposition
If you sell, trade in, or otherwise dispose of your car, you may have a taxable gain or a deductible loss. This is true whether you used the standard mileage rate or actual car expenses to deduct the business use of your car. Publication 544 has information on sales of property used in a trade or business, and details on how to report the disposition.

Explanation
Unreimbursed automobile expenses are deductible only as miscellaneous itemized deductions. Employees formerly classified as "outside sales representatives" are also subject to this provision.

As a result, these expenses will be deductible only to the extent that, when aggregated with your other miscellaneous itemized deductions, they exceed 2% of your adjusted gross income.

TAXSAVER

In some cases, you may be able to deduct a greater mileage rate than the IRS customarily permits. For example, the courts have allowed truck drivers who were reimbursed at a greater rate than the standard rate to deduct the greater rate. The truck drivers had kept detailed weekly records of their trucks' operating costs.

TAXSAVER

If you own an expensive business automobile, the standard mileage rate is probably inadequate to cover your operating costs. You should keep detailed records of your total expenses so that you may claim a larger deduction than you would be able to claim by using the standard mileage rate.

Recordkeeping

If you deduct travel, entertainment, gift, or transportation expenses, you must be able to prove (substantiate) certain elements of the expense. This section discusses the records you need to keep to prove these expenses.

If you keep timely and accurate records, you will have support to show the IRS if your tax return is ever examined. You will also have proof of expenses that your employer may require if you are reimbursed under an accountable plan. These plans are discussed later under *Reimbursements*.

TAXPLANNER

Good record-keeping is a good business practice and a must for tax purposes. A clear and consistent set of records is the first step in justifying your expense deduction. Reasonable estimates of expenses are no longer acceptable, even if the estimate is moderate in relation to the income generated.

Form 4562, which is used to show your automobile depreciation, specifically asks whether you have evidence to support your business use percentage.

You must maintain adequate records or sufficient evidence, either written or oral, that will corroborate your own statement. Sufficient evidence includes account books, trip sheets, expense reports, appointment calendars, statements of witnesses, and certain accountings to an employer. Contemporaneous logs are no longer required, but a report made at the event would be more credible than records prepared at a later date.

If you are required to turn in the original copies of your receipts and logbooks to your employer, you should make copies for yourself. If the confidentiality of names is a consideration, special arrangements might have to be made with your employer to make necessary information available if and when it is needed.

When records are lost in circumstances beyond your control, such as destruction by fire, flood, earthquake, or other casualty, the IRS is more lenient in accepting reconstructed records and secondary evidence than it is when records are not available because of carelessness or mysterious disappearance.

Example

Travel expense records were lost during a change of residence resulting from marital problems. The court ruled that marital difficulties did not constitute a casualty warranting the use of reconstructed records.

How To Prove Expenses

Table 28-2 is a summary of records you need to prove each expense discussed in this chapter. You must be able to prove the elements listed across the top portion of the chart. You prove them by having the information and receipts (where needed) for the expenses listed in the first column.

Caution. *You cannot deduct amounts that you approximate or estimate.*

You should keep adequate records to prove your expenses or have sufficient evidence that will support your own statement. You must generally prepare a written record for it to be considered adequate. This is because written evidence is more reliable than oral evidence alone. However, if you prepare a record in a computer memory device with the aid of a logging program, it is considered an adequate record.

What Are Adequate Records?
You should keep the proof you need in an account book, diary, statement of expense, or similar record. You should also keep documentary evidence that, together with your records, will support each element of an expense.

Documentary evidence. You generally must have documentary evidence, such as receipts, canceled checks, or bills, to support your expenses.

Exception. Documentary evidence is not needed if any of the following conditions apply.

1. You have meals or lodging expenses while traveling away from home for which you account to your employer under an accountable plan and you use a per diem allowance method that includes meals and/or lodging. (Accountable plans and per diem allowances are discussed later under *Reimbursements*.)
2. Your expense, other than lodging, is less than $75.
3. You have a transportation expense for which a receipt is not readily available.

TAXALERT

The tax law disallows an otherwise allowable deduction for any expense for traveling, entertainment, gifts, or listed property, unless the expense is substantiated by adequate records. Taxpayers are required to maintain documentary evidence (such as receipts) for (1) any lodging expenditure and (2) any other expenditure of $75 or more.

Adequate evidence. Documentary evidence ordinarily will be considered adequate if it shows the amount, date, place, and essential character of the expense.

Table 28-2. **How To Prove Certain Business Expenses**

IF you have expenses for...	THEN you must keep records that show details of the following elements...			
	Amount	**Time**	**Place or Description**	**Business Purpose and Business Relationship**
Travel	Cost of each separate expense for travel, lodging, and meals. Incidental expenses may be totaled in reasonable categories such as taxis, daily meals for traveler, etc.	Dates you left and returned for each trip and number of days spent on business.	Destination or area of your travel (name of city, town, or other designation).	Purpose: Business purpose for the expense or the business benefit gained or expected to be gained. Relationship: N/A
Entertainment	Cost of each separate expense. Incidental expenses such as taxis, telephones, etc., may be totaled on a daily basis.	Date of entertainment. (Also see *Business Purpose*.)	Name and address or location of place of entertainment. Type of entertainment if not otherwise apparent. (Also see *Business Purpose*.)	Purpose: Business purpose for the expense or the business benefit gained or expected to be gained. For entertainment, the nature of the business discussion or activity. If the entertainment was directly before or after a business discussion: the date, place, nature, and duration of the business discussion, and the identities of the persons who took part in both the business discussion and the entertainment activity.
Gifts	Cost of the gift.	Date of the gift.	Description of the gift.	Relationship: Occupations or other information (such as names, titles, or other designations) about the recipients that shows their business relationship to you. For entertainment, you must also prove that you or your employee was present if the entertainment was a business meal.
Transportation	Cost of each separate expense. For car expenses, the cost of the car and any improvements, the date you started using it for business, the mileage for each business use, and the total miles for the year.	Date of the expense. For car expenses, the date of the use of the car.	Your business destination.	Purpose: Business purpose for the expense. Relationship: N/A

For example, a hotel receipt is enough to support expenses for business travel if it has all of the following information.

1. The name and location of the hotel.
2. The dates you stayed there.
3. Separate amounts for charges such as lodging, meals, and telephone calls.

A restaurant receipt is enough to prove an expense for a business meal if it has all of the following information.

1. The name and location of the restaurant.
2. The number of people served.
3. The date and amount of the expense.

If a charge is made for items other than food and beverages, the receipt must show that this is the case.

Canceled check. A canceled check, together with a bill from the payee, ordinarily establishes the cost. However, a canceled check by itself does not prove a business expense without other evidence to show that it was for a business purpose.

TAXPLANNER

You must maintain detailed records and report the required information on your tax return if you wish to claim a deduction for expenses that exceed reimbursements. You must keep these records, even though you do not have to give the completely detailed information to your employer because reimbursements by your employer meet the IRS per diem standards.

Duplicate information. You do not have to record information in your account book or other record that duplicates information shown on a receipt as long as your records and receipts complement each other in an orderly manner.

You do not have to record amounts your employer pays directly for any ticket or other travel item. However, if you charge these items to your employer, through a credit card or otherwise, you must keep a record of the amounts you spend.

Timely-kept records. You should record the elements of an expense or of a business use at or near the time of the expense or use and support it with sufficient documentary evidence. A timely-kept record has more value than a statement prepared later when generally there is a lack of accurate recall.

You do not need to write down the elements of every expense on the day of the expense. If you maintain a log on a weekly basis which accounts for use during the week, the log is considered a timely-kept record.

If you give your employer, client, or customer an expense account statement, it can also be considered a timely-kept record. This is true if you copy it from your account book, diary, statement of expense, or similar record.

Proving business purpose. You must generally provide a written statement of the business purpose of an expense. However, the degree of proof varies according to the circumstances in each case. If the business purpose of an expense is clear from the surrounding circumstances, then you do not need to give a written explanation.

Confidential information. You do not need to put confidential information relating to an element of a deductible expense (such as the place, business purpose, or business relationship) in your account book, diary, or other record. However, you do have to record the information elsewhere at or near the time of the expense and have it available to fully prove that element of the expense.

What If I Have Incomplete Records?
If you do not have complete records to prove an element of an expense, then you must prove the element with:

1. Your own written or oral statement, containing specific information about the element, and
2. Other supporting evidence that is sufficient to establish the element.

Destroyed records. If you cannot produce a receipt because of reasons beyond your control, you can prove a deduction by reconstructing your records or expenses. Reasons beyond your control include fire, flood, and other casualty.

Separating and Combining Expenses
This section explains when expenses must be kept separate and when expenses can be combined.

Separating expenses. Each separate payment is generally considered a separate expense. For example, if you entertain a customer or client at dinner and then go to the theater, the dinner expense and the cost of the theater tickets are two separate expenses. You must record them separately in your records.

Combining items. You can make one daily entry in your record for reasonable categories of expenses. Examples are taxi fares, telephone calls, or other incidental travel costs. Meals should be in a separate category. You can include tips for meal-related services with the costs of the meals.

Expenses of a similar nature occurring during the course of a single event are considered a single expense. For example, if during entertainment at a cocktail lounge, you pay separately for each serving of refreshments, the total expense for the refreshments is treated as a single expense.

Allocating total cost. If you can prove the total cost of travel or entertainment but you cannot prove how much it cost for each person who participated in the event, you may have to allocate the total cost among you and your guests on a pro rata basis. An allocation would be needed, for example, if you did not have a business relationship with all of your guests.

If your return is examined. If your return is examined, you may have to provide additional information to the IRS. This information could be needed to clarify or to establish the accuracy or reliability of information contained in your records, statements, testimony, or documentary evidence before a deduction is allowed.

How Long To Keep Records and Receipts
You must keep records as long as they may be needed for the administration of any provision of the Internal Revenue Code. Generally,

this means you must keep your records that support your deduction (or an item of income) for 3 years from the date you file the income tax return on which the deduction is claimed. A return filed early is considered filed on the due date. For a more complete explanation, get Publication 583, Starting a Business and Keeping Records.

> **Explanation**
> If you use your automobile less than 50% for business and claim actual expenses, you must keep those records for at least 6 years (the straight-line, useful life depreciation period).

Reimbursed for expenses. Employees who give their records and documentation to their employers and are reimbursed for their expenses generally do not have to keep copies of this information. However, you may have to prove your expenses if any of the following conditions apply.

1. You claim deductions for expenses that are more than reimbursements.
2. Your expenses are reimbursed under a nonaccountable plan.
3. Your employer does not use adequate accounting procedures to verify expense accounts.
4. You are related to your employer, as defined earlier under *Who cannot use the standard meal allowance.*

See the next section, *How To Report,* for a discussion of reimbursements, adequate accounting, and nonaccountable plans.

> **Explanation**
> If you have expenses greater than your reimbursement and want to deduct them, you are required to put a statement in your tax return showing the total of all expenses you incurred and all reimbursements you received for that year. This information may be given in broad categories, such as transportation, meals and lodging while **away from home overnight,** entertainment expenses, and other business expenses. The statement must show the total of any charges paid or borne directly by your employer through credit cards or any other means. See *Records* for more details.
>
> **Self-employed** persons and independent contractors must be able to show that the expenses were directly related to, or associated with, their business.
>
> **Example**
> An accountant was not allowed to deduct expenses incurred at a country club because she failed to indicate the business purpose of the activities that generated the expenses and she did not maintain a detailed record of the persons entertained on each occasion. Lacking any documentation to the contrary, a court concluded that there was a likelihood that the expenses were at least partially personal.

Additional information. Chapter 5 of Publication 463 has more information on recordkeeping, including examples.

How To Report

This section explains where and how to report the expenses discussed in this chapter. It discusses reimbursements and how to treat them under accountable and nonaccountable plans. It also explains rules for fee-basis officials, certain performing artists, Armed Forces reservists, and certain disabled employees. This section ends with an illustration of how to report travel, entertainment, gift, and car expenses on Form 2106-EZ.

Explanation

Employees receiving the standard meal allowance under a nonaccountable plan (discussed below) may claim 50% of the standard meal allowance as a miscellaneous itemized deduction, subject to the 2% limitation. Reimbursements under accountable plans are not included in the employee's taxable compensation. Therefore, such employees receive no deduction, and the 50% limitation applies to the employer's deduction.

Self-employed. You must report your income and expenses on Schedule C or C-EZ (Form 1040) if you are a sole proprietor, or on Schedule F (Form 1040) if you are a farmer. You do not use Form 2106 or 2106-EZ. See your form instructions for information on how to complete your tax return. You can also find information in Publication 535 if you are a sole proprietor, or in Publication 225, Farmer's Tax Guide, if you are a farmer.

Both self-employed and an employee. If you are both self-employed and an employee, you must keep separate records for each business activity. Report your business expenses for self-employment on Schedule C, C-EZ, or F (Form 1040), as discussed earlier. Report your business expenses for your work as an employee on Form 2106 or 2106-EZ, as discussed next.

Employees. If you are an employee, you generally must complete Form 2106 to deduct your travel, transportation, and entertainment expenses. However, you can use the shorter Form 2106-EZ instead of Form 2106 if you meet all of the following conditions.

1. You are an employee deducting expenses attributable to your job.
2. You were not reimbursed by your employer for your expenses (amounts included in box 1 of your Form W-2 are not considered reimbursements).
3. If you are claiming car expenses, you use the standard mileage rate.

For more information on how to report your expenses on Forms 2106 and 2106-EZ, see *Completing Forms 2106 and 2106-EZ*, later.

Gifts. If you did not receive any reimbursements (or the reimbursements were all included in box 1 of your Form W-2), the only business expense you are claiming is for gifts, and the rules for certain individuals (such as performing artists) discussed later under *Special Rules*, do not apply to you, do not complete Form 2106 or 2106-EZ. Instead, claim the amount of your deductible gifts directly on line 20 of Schedule A (Form 1040).

Statutory employees. If you received a Form W-2 and the "Statutory employee" box in box 13 was checked, you report your income and expenses related to that income on Schedule C or C-EZ (Form 1040). Do not complete Form 2106 or 2106-EZ.

Statutory employees include full-time life insurance salespersons, certain agent or commission drivers, traveling salespersons, and certain homeworkers.

Example 1

John Smith, a salesman working on behalf of a principal, solicits orders from wholesalers and restaurants for merchandise intended for resale. John reports his income and expenses on Schedule C as a statutory employee.

Example 2

An agent-driver engaged in distributing meat, vegetables, bakery goods, beverages (other than milk), or dry cleaning services is classified as a statutory employee.

Caution. *If you are entitled to a reimbursement from your employer but you do not claim it, you cannot claim a deduction for the expenses to which that unclaimed reimbursement applies.*

Explanation

While you may not claim a deduction for an expense that your employer would reimburse, you may be entitled to a deduction for a work-related expense that you feel was necessary to do your job but that your employer does not reimburse.

Example

You are a technician who works in a laboratory in which your employer requires you to wear a certain type of uniform while on the job. The uniform is unsuitable for street wear. Your employer refuses to reimburse you for the cost of the uniform. You are entitled to deduct the expense on your own income tax return.

Reimbursement for personal expenses. If your employer reimburses you for nondeductible personal expenses, such as for vacation trips, your employer must report the reimbursement as wage income in box 1 of your Form W-2. You cannot deduct personal expenses.

Reimbursements

This section explains what to do when you receive an advance or are reimbursed for any of the employee business expenses discussed in this chapter.

If you received an advance, allowance, or reimbursement for your expenses, how you report this amount and your expenses depends on whether the reimbursement was paid to you under an accountable plan or a nonaccountable plan.

This section explains the two types of plans, how per diem and car allowances simplify proving the amount of your expenses, and the tax treatment of your reimbursements and expenses.

TAXSAVER

If the various requirements discussed below are met, reimbursements are excluded from the employee's gross income for income tax as well as employment tax purposes. Amounts considered paid under a nonaccountable plan are subject to income tax as well as to employment taxes. A tax deduction is allowable as a miscellaneous itemized deduction, subject to applicable limitations, for employee business expenses reimbursed under a nonaccountable plan.

No reimbursement. You are not reimbursed or given an allowance for your expenses if you are paid a salary or commission with the understanding that you will pay your own expenses. In this situation, you have no reimbursement or allowance arrangement, and you do not have to read this section on reimbursements. Instead, see *Completing Forms 2106 and 2106-EZ*, later, for information on completing your tax return.

TAXSAVER

You may claim a deduction for business expenses even if you don't receive specific reimbursements from your employer. You should have your employer supply you with a written document explaining that your compensation plan is based on the expectation that you will incur various travel, transportation, automobile, entertainment, and business gift expenses.

Travel, transportation, automobile expenses, entertainment, business gifts, and other expenses should be reported as miscellaneous deductions on Schedule A of Form 1040.

If you are repeatedly spending money for business expenses, it is probably advantageous for you to make an arrangement with your employer to adjust your salary and/or commission downward and to give you an expense allowance. This could help you justify your deductions if you are subject to an IRS examination.

Reimbursement, allowance, or advance. A reimbursement or other expense allowance arrangement is a system or plan that an employer uses to pay, substantiate, and recover the expenses, advances, reimbursements, and amounts charged to the employer for employee business expenses. Arrangements include per diem and car allowances.

A per diem allowance is a fixed amount of daily reimbursement your employer gives you for your lodging, meal, and incidental expenses when you are away from home on business. (The term "incidental expenses" is defined earlier under *Meals and Incidental Expenses*.) A car allowance is an amount your employer gives you for the business use of your car.

Your employer should tell you what method of reimbursement is used and what records you must provide.

Accountable Plans

To be an accountable plan, your employer's reimbursement or allowance arrangement must include all three of the following rules.

1. Your expenses must have a business connection—that is, you must have paid or incurred deductible expenses while performing services as an employee of your employer.
2. You must adequately account to your employer for these expenses within a reasonable period of time.
3. You must return any excess reimbursement or allowance within a reasonable period of time.

See *Adequate Accounting* and *Returning Excess Reimbursements*, later.

Explanation

For a reimbursement or other expense allowance arrangement to be an accountable plan, it must satisfy the substantiation requirement. Generally, for each expense item and for each business use, the employee must report the amount, time, place, and business purpose.

Example 1

An employer proposed to reimburse its district manager's business expenses in lieu of paying additional salary. This would result in a portion of the district manager's salary being recharacterized as paid under a reimbursement or other expense allowance arrangement, and, thus, it would fail the reimbursement requirement. Therefore, the reimbursements would be subject to employment taxes since they would not be paid under an arrangement that is an accountable plan.

Example 2

Where a taxpayer did not substantiate expenses or return excess allowance amounts, such amounts were paid under a nonaccountable plan and, thus, were includible in gross income.

Exception 1

The substantiation requirement for expense amounts related to business meals and lodging can be satisfied by using a per diem allowance. Per diem reimbursements of such expenses are not included in taxable income to the extent of the government rate.

Exception 2

The substantiation requirement for expenses relating to the business use of an employee's private automobile can be satisfied by using the standard mileage rate (40.5 cents per business mile or 48.5 cents after August 31, 2005) or the fixed-and-variable-rate allowance. Under the fixed-and-variable-rate allowance method, an employer reimburses an employee's business mileage expenses using a flat rate or a stated schedule of fixed and variable rate payments that incorporates specific rules to approximate the employee's actual automobile expenses.

An excess reimbursement or allowance is any amount you are paid that is more than the business-related expenses that you adequately accounted for to your employer.

The definition of reasonable period of time depends on the facts and circumstances of your situation. However, regardless of the facts and circumstances of your situation, actions that take place within the times specified in the following list will be treated as taking place within a reasonable period of time.

- You receive an advance within 30 days of the time you have an expense.
- You adequately account for your expenses within 60 days after they were paid or incurred.
- You return any excess reimbursement within 120 days after the expense was paid or incurred.
- You are given a periodic statement (at least quarterly) that asks you to either return or adequately account for outstanding advances and you comply within 120 days of the statement.

TaxAlert

It is imperative that the substantiation be done and that excess amounts be returned within a reasonable period of time. If the reasonable time requirement is not met, the unsubstantiated or excess amounts are treated as reimbursements under a nonaccountable plan.

Employee meets accountable plan rules. If you meet the three rules for accountable plans, your employer should not include any reimbursements in your income in box 1 of your Form W-2. If your expenses equal your reimbursement, you do not complete Form 2106. You have no deduction since your expenses and reimbursement are equal.

Tip. *If your employer included reimbursements in box 1 of your Form W-2 and you meet all three rules for accountable plans, ask your employer for a corrected Form W-2.*

Accountable plan rules not met. Even though you are reimbursed under an accountable plan, some of your expenses may not meet all three rules. Those expenses that fail to meet all three rules for accountable plans are treated as having been reimbursed under a nonaccountable plan (discussed later).

TaxPlanner

A plan providing per diem allowances or mileage allowances that are reasonably calculated not to exceed the employee's expenses will satisfy the requirement for the return of excess reimbursement, even though the employee is not required to return the excess allowance. However, the employee must return the portion of the allowance attributable to unsubstantiated days or miles of travel.

Example

An employee receives a monthly mileage allowance of $162, based on anticipated business miles of 400 per month, reimbursed at the rate of 40.5 cents per mile. The 40.5-cent-per-mile rate is reasonably calculated not to exceed the employee's expenses. The employee travels and substantiates only 300 business miles. The requirement to return the excess is satisfied if the employee is required to return the $40.50 (100 miles × 40.5 cents) advance allowance that is attributable to the 100 unsubstantiated business miles. (The cents-per-mile rate after August 31, 2005 is 48.5¢).

Reimbursement of nondeductible expenses. You may be reimbursed under your employer's accountable plan for expenses related to that employer's business, some of which are deductible as employee business expenses and some of which are not deductible. The reimbursements you receive for the nondeductible expenses do not meet rule (1) for accountable plans, and they are treated as paid under a nonaccountable plan.

Example. Your employer's plan reimburses you for travel expenses while away from home on business and also for meals when you work late at the office, even though you are not away from home. The part of the arrangement that reimburses you for the nondeductible meals when you work late at the office is treated as paid under a nonaccountable plan.

Tip. *The employer makes the decision whether to reimburse employees under an accountable plan or a nonaccountable plan. If you are an employee who receives payments under a nonaccountable plan, you cannot convert these amounts to payments under an accountable plan by voluntarily accounting to your employer for the expenses and voluntarily returning excess reimbursements to the employer.*

Adequate Accounting

One of the three rules for an accountable plan is that you must adequately account to your employer for your expenses. You adequately account by giving your employer a statement of expense, an account book, a diary, or a similar record in which you entered each expense at or near the time you had it, along with documentary evidence (such as receipts) of your travel, mileage, and other employee business expenses. (See Table 28-2, earlier, for details you need to enter in your record and documents you need to prove certain expenses.)

You must account for all amounts you received from your employer during the year as advances, reimbursements, or allowances. This includes amounts you charged to your employer by credit card or other method. You must give your employer the same type of records and supporting information that you would have to give to the IRS if the IRS questioned a deduction on your return. You must pay back the amount of any reimbursement or other expense allowance for which you do not adequately account or that is more than the amount for which you accounted.

Per Diem and Car Allowances

If your employer reimburses you for your expenses using a per diem or car allowance, you can generally use the allowance as proof of the amount of your expenses. A per diem or car allowance satisfies the adequate accounting requirements for the amount of your expenses only if all four of the following conditions apply.

1. Your employer reasonably limits payments of your expenses to those that are ordinary and necessary in the conduct of the trade or business.
2. The allowance is similar in form to and not more than the federal rate (discussed later).
3. You prove the time (dates), place, and business purpose of your expenses to your employer (as explained in Table 28-2) within a reasonable period of time.

4. You are not related to your employer (as defined next). If you are related to your employer, you must be able to prove your expenses to the IRS even if you have already adequately accounted to your employer and returned any excess reimbursement.

If the IRS finds that an employer's travel allowance practices are not based on reasonably accurate estimates of travel costs (including recognition of cost differences in different areas for per diem amounts), you will not be considered to have accounted to your employer. In this case, you must be able to prove your expenses to the IRS.

Related to employer. You are related to your employer if:

1. Your employer is your brother or sister, half brother or half sister, spouse, ancestor, or lineal descendant,
2. Your employer is a corporation in which you own, directly or indirectly, more than 10% in value of the outstanding stock, or
3. Certain relationships (such as grantor, fiduciary, or beneficiary) exist between you, a trust, and your employer.

You may be considered to indirectly own stock, for purposes of (2), if you have an interest in a corporation, partnership, estate, or trust that owns the stock or if a member of your family or your partner owns the stock.

The federal rate. The federal rate can be figured using any one of the following methods.

1. For per diem amounts:
   a. The regular federal per diem rate.
   b. The standard meal allowance.
   c. The high-low rate.
2. For car expenses:
   a. The standard mileage rate.
   b. A fixed and variable rate (FAVR).

Regular federal per diem rate. The regular federal per diem rate is the highest amount that the federal government will pay to its employees for lodging, meal, and incidental expenses (or meal and incidental expenses only) while they are traveling away from home in a particular area. The rates are different for different locations. Your employer should have these rates available. (Employers can get Publication 1542, which gives the rates in the continental United States for the current year.)

The standard meal allowance. The standard meal allowance (discussed earlier) is the federal rate for meals and incidental expenses (M&IE). The rate for most small localities in the United States is $31 a day for 2005. Most major cities and many other localities qualify for higher rates. The rates for all localities within the continental United States are listed in Publication 1542.

You receive an allowance only for meals and incidental expenses when your employer does one of the following.

- Provides you with lodging (furnishes it in kind).
- Reimburses you, based on your receipts, for the actual cost of your lodging.
- Pays the hotel, motel, etc., directly for your lodging.
- Does not have a reasonable belief that you had (or will have) lodging expenses, such as when you stay with friends or relatives or sleep in the cab of your truck.
- Figures the allowance on a basis similar to that used in computing your compensation, such as number of hours worked or miles traveled.

High-low rate. This is a simplified method of computing the federal per diem rate for travel within the continental United States. It eliminates the need to keep a current list of the per diem rate for each city.

Under the high-low method, the per diem amount for travel during January through September of 2005 is $204 (including $46 for M&IE) for certain high-cost locations. All other areas have a per diem amount of $129 (including $36 for M&IE). (Employers can get Publication 1542 (Revised May 2005), which gives the areas eligible for the $204 per diem amount under the high-low method for all or part of this period.)

Caution. *Effective October 1, 2005, the per diem rate under this method for certain high-cost locations changed after this book went to press. The rate for all other locations also changed. However, an employer can continue to use the rates described in the preceding paragraph for the remainder of 2005 if those rates and locations are used consistently during October, November, and December for all employees. Employers who did not use the high-low method during the first 9 months of 2005 cannot begin to use it before 2006. See* Revenue Procedure 2005-10 *for more information. Also see Publication 1542 (on the Internet at www.irs.gov) for any changes to these rates.*

Prorating the standard meal allowance on partial days of travel. The standard meal allowance is for a full 24-hour day of travel. If you travel for part of a day, such as on the days you depart and return, you must prorate the full-day M&IE rate. This rule also applies if your employer uses the regular federal per diem rate or the high-low rate.

You can use either of the following methods to figure the federal M&IE for that day.

1. *Method 1:*
   a. For the day you depart, add 3/4 of the standard meal allowance amount for that day.
   b. For the day you return, add 3/4 of the standard meal allowance amount for the preceding day.
2. *Method 2:* Prorate the standard meal allowance using any method that you consistently apply and that is in accordance with reasonable business practice.

The standard mileage rate. This is a set rate per mile that you can use to compute your deductible car expenses. For 2005, the standard mileage rate is 40 1/2 cents a mile for all business miles through August and 48.5 cents a mile after August 31, 2005. This rate is adjusted periodically.

Fixed and variable rate (FAVR). This is an allowance your employer may use to reimburse your car expenses. Under this method, your employer pays an allowance that includes a combination of payments covering fixed and variable costs, such as a cents-per-mile rate to cover your variable operating costs (such as gas, oil, etc.) plus a flat amount to cover your fixed costs (such as depreciation (or lease payments), insurance, etc.). If your employer chooses to use this method, your employer will request the necessary records from you.

Reporting your expenses with a per diem or car allowance. If your reimbursement is in the form of an allowance received under an accountable plan, the following two facts affect your reporting.

1. The federal rate.
2. Whether the allowance or your actual expenses were more than the federal rate.

The following discussions explain where to report your expenses depending upon how the amount of your allowance compares to the federal rate.

Allowance less than or equal to the federal rate. If your allowance is less than or equal to the federal rate, the allowance will not be included in box 1 of your Form W-2. You do not need to report the related expenses or the allowance on your return if your expenses are equal to or less than the allowance.

However, if your actual expenses are more than your allowance, you can complete Form 2106 and deduct the excess amount on Schedule A (Form 1040). If you are using actual expenses, you must be able to prove to the IRS the total amount of your expenses and reimbursements for the entire year. If you are using the standard meal allowance or the standard mileage rate, you do not have to prove that amount.

Example. Nicole drives 10,000 miles a year for business. Under her employer's accountable plan, she accounts for the time (dates), place, and business purpose of each trip. Her employer pays her a mileage allowance of 20 cents a mile.

Since Nicole's $4,050 expenses computed under the standard mileage rate (10,000 miles × 40 1/2 cents) are more than her $2,000 reimbursement (10,000 miles × 20 cents), she itemizes her deductions to claim the excess expenses. Nicole completes Form 2106 (showing all of her expenses and reimbursements) and enters $2,050 ($4,050 − $2,000) as an itemized deduction. Note: The mileage rate is 48.5 cents after August 31, 2005.

Allowance more than the federal rate. If your allowance is more than the federal rate, your employer must include the allowance amount up to the federal rate in box 12 of your Form W-2. This amount is not taxable. However, the excess allowance will be included in box 1 of your Form W-2. You must report this part of your allowance as if it were wage income.

If your actual expenses are less than or equal to the federal rate, you do not complete Form 2106 or claim any of your expenses on your return.

However, if your actual expenses are more than the federal rate, you can complete Form 2106 and, generally, deduct those excess expenses. You must report on Form 2106 your reimbursements up to the federal rate (as shown in box 12 of your Form W-2) and all your expenses. You should be able to prove these amounts to the IRS.

Example. Joe lives and works in Austin. His employer sent him to San Diego for 4 days and paid the hotel directly for Joe's hotel bill. The employer reimbursed Joe $60 a day for his meals and incidental expenses. The federal rate for San Diego is $51 a day.

Joe can prove that his actual meal expenses totaled $325. His employer's accountable plan will not pay more than $60 a day for travel to San Diego, so Joe does not give his employer the records that prove that he actually spent $325. However, he does account for the time, place, and business purpose of the trip. This is Joe's only business trip this year.

Joe was reimbursed $240 ($60 × 4 days), which is $36 more than the federal rate of $204 ($51 × 4 days). The employer includes the $36 as income on Joe's Form W-2 in box 1. The employer also enters $204 in box 12 of Joe's Form W-2, along with a code L.

Joe completes Form 2106 to figure his deductible expenses. He enters the total of his actual expenses for the year ($325) on Form 2106. He also enters the reimbursements that were not included in his income ($204). His total deductible expense, before the 50% limit, is $121. After he figures the 50% limit on his unreimbursed meals and entertainment, he will include the balance, $61, as an itemized deduction.

Returning Excess Reimbursements

Under an accountable plan, you are required to return any excess reimbursement for your business expenses to the person paying the reimbursement or allowance. Excess reimbursement means any amount for which you did not adequately account within a reasonable period of time. For example, if you received a travel advance and you did not spend all the money on business-related expenses, or if you do not have proof of all your expenses, you have an excess reimbursement.

"Adequate accounting" and "reasonable period of time" were discussed earlier.

Travel advance. You receive a travel advance if your employer provides you with an expense allowance before you actually have the expense, and the allowance is reasonably expected to be no more than your expense. Under an accountable plan, you are required to adequately account to your employer for this advance and to return any excess within a reasonable period of time.

If you do not adequately account for or do not return any excess advance within a reasonable period of time, the amount you do not account for or return will be treated as having been paid under a nonaccountable plan (discussed later).

Unproved amounts. If you do not prove that you actually traveled on each day for which you received a per diem or car allowance (proving the elements described in Table 28-2), you must return this unproved amount of the travel advance within a reasonable period of time. If you do not do this, the unproved amount is considered paid under a nonaccountable plan (discussed later).

Per diem allowance more than federal rate. If your employer's accountable plan pays you an allowance that is higher than the federal rate, you do not have to return the difference between the two rates for the period you can prove business-related travel expenses. However, the difference will be reported as wages on your Form W-2. This excess amount is considered paid under a nonaccountable plan (discussed later).

Example. Your employer sends you on a 5-day business trip to Phoenix and gives you a $300 ($60 × 5 days) advance to cover your meals and incidental expenses. The federal per diem for meals and incidental expenses for Phoenix is $47. Your trip lasts only 3 days. Under your employer's accountable plan, you must return the $120 ($60 × 2 days) advance for the 2 days you did not travel. You do not have to return the $39 difference between the allowance you received and the federal rate for Phoenix ($60 − $47) × 3 days). However, the $39 will be reported on your Form W-2 as wages.

Nonaccountable Plans

A nonaccountable plan is a reimbursement or expense allowance arrangement that does not meet one or more of the three rules listed earlier under *Accountable Plans.*

In addition, even if your employer has an accountable plan, the following payments will be treated as being paid under a nonaccountable plan.

- Excess reimbursements you fail to return to your employer.
- Reimbursement of nondeductible expenses related to your employer's business. See *Reimbursement of nondeductible expenses* earlier under *Accountable Plans.*

If you are not sure if the reimbursement or expense allowance arrangement is an accountable or nonaccountable plan, ask your employer.

Reporting your expenses under a nonaccountable plan. Your employer will combine the amount of any reimbursement or other expense allowance paid to you under a nonaccountable plan with your wages, salary, or other pay. Your employer will report the total in box 1 of your Form W-2.

You must complete Form 2106 or 2106-EZ and itemize your deductions to deduct your expenses for travel, transportation, meals, or entertainment. Your meal and entertainment expenses will be subject to the 50% limit discussed earlier under *Entertainment Expenses.* Also, your total expenses will be subject to the 2%-of-adjusted-gross-income limit that applies to most miscellaneous itemized deductions.

Example. Kim's employer gives her $500 a month ($6,000 for the year) for her business expenses. Kim does not have to provide any proof of her expenses to her employer, and Kim can keep any funds that she does not spend.

Kim is being reimbursed under a nonaccountable plan. Her employer will include the $6,000 on Kim's Form W-2 as if it were wages. If Kim wants to deduct her business expenses, she must complete Form 2106 or 2106-EZ and itemize her deductions.

Completing Forms 2106 and 2106-EZ

This section briefly describes how employees complete Forms 2106 and 2106-EZ. Table 28-3 explains what the employer reports on Form W-2 and what the employee reports on Form 2106. The instructions for the forms have more information on completing them.

Form 2106-EZ. You may be able to use the shorter Form 2106-EZ to claim your employee business expenses. You can use this form if you meet all three of the following conditions.

1. You are an employee deducting expenses attributable to your job.
2. You were not reimbursed by your employer for your expenses (amounts included in box 1 of your Form W-2 are not considered reimbursements).
3. If you claim car expenses, you use the standard mileage rate.

Car expenses. If you used a car to perform your job as an employee, you may be able to deduct certain car expenses. These are generally figured on Form 2106, Part II, and then claimed on Form 2106, Part I, line 1, Column A. Car expenses using the standard mileage rate can also be figured on Form 2106-EZ by completing Part II and Part I, line 1.

Transportation expenses. Show your transportation expenses that did not involve overnight travel on Form 2106, line 2, Column A, or on Form 2106-EZ, Part I, line 2. Also include on this line business expenses you have for parking fees and tolls. Do not include expenses of operating your car or expenses of commuting between your home and work.

Employee business expenses other than meals and entertainment. Show your other employee business expenses on Form 2106, lines 3 and 4, Column A, or Form 2106-EZ, lines 3 and 4. Do not include expenses for meals and entertainment on those lines. Line 4 is for expenses such as gifts, educational expenses (tuition and books), office-in-the-home expenses, and trade and professional publications.

Tip. *If line 4 expenses are the only ones you are claiming, you received no reimbursements (or the reimbursements were all included in box 1 of your Form W-2), and the* Special Rules *discussed later do not apply to you, do not complete Form 2106 or 2106-EZ. Claim these amounts directly on Schedule A (Form 1040), line 20. List the type and amount of each expense on the dotted lines and include the total on line 20.*

Meal and entertainment expenses. Show the full amount of your expenses for business-related meals and entertainment on Form 2106, line 5, Column B. Include meals while away from your tax home overnight and other business meals and entertainment. Enter 50% of the line 8 meal and entertainment expenses on Form 2106, line 9, Column B.

If you file Form 2106-EZ, enter the full amount of your meals and entertainment on the line to the left of line 5 and multiply the total by 50%. Enter the result on line 5.

Hours of service limits. If you are subject to the Department of Transportation's "hours of service" limits, use 70% instead of 50% for meals while away from your tax home.

Reimbursements. Enter on line 7 of Form 2106 the amounts your employer (or third party) reimbursed you that were not included in box 1 of your Form W-2. (You cannot use Form 2106-EZ.) This includes any reimbursement reported under code L in box 12 of Form W-2.

Allocating your reimbursement. If you were reimbursed under an accountable plan and want to deduct excess expenses that were not reimbursed, you may have to allocate your reimbursement. This is necessary if your employer pays your reimbursement in the following manner:

1. Pays you a single amount that covers meals and/or entertainment, as well as other business expenses, and
2. Does not clearly identify how much is for deductible meals and/or entertainment.

You must allocate the reimbursement so that you know how much to enter on Form 2106, line 7, Column A and Column B.

Example. Rob's employer paid him an expense allowance of $5,000 this year under an accountable plan. The $5,000 payment consisted of $2,000 for airfare and $3,000 for entertainment and car expenses. The employer did not clearly show how much of the $3,000 was for the cost of deductible entertainment. Rob actually spent $6,500 during the year ($2,000 for airfare, $2,000 for entertainment, and $2,500 for car expenses).

Since the airfare allowance was clearly identified, Rob knows that $2,000 of the payment goes in Column A, line 7 of Form 2106. To allocate the remaining $3,000, Rob uses the worksheet from the instructions for Form 2106. His completed worksheet follows.

Table 28-3. **Reporting Travel, Entertainment, Gift, and Car Expenses and Reimbursements**

IF the type of reimbursement (or other expense allowance) arrangement is under:	THEN the employer reports on Form W-2:	AND the employee reports on Form 2106: *
An accountable plan with:		
Actual expense reimbursement: Adequate accounting made <u>and</u> excess returned.	No amount.	No amount.
Actual expense reimbursement: Adequate accounting and return of excess both required <u>but</u> excess not returned.	The excess amount as wages in box 1.	No amount.
Per diem or mileage allowance up to the federal rate: Adequate accounting made <u>and</u> excess returned.	No amount.	All expenses and reimbursements only if excess expenses are claimed. Otherwise, form is not filed.
Per diem or mileage allowance up to the federal rate: Adequate accounting and return of excess both required <u>but</u> excess not returned.	The excess amount as wages in box 1. The amount up to the federal rate is reported only in box 12—it is not reported in box 1.	No amount.
Per diem or mileage allowance exceeds the federal rate: Adequate accounting up to the federal rate only <u>and</u> excess not returned.	The excess amount as wages in box 1. The amount up to the federal rate is reported only in box 12—it is not reported in box 1.	All expenses (and reimbursement reported on Form W-2, box 12) only if expenses in excess of the federal rate are claimed. Otherwise, form is not required.
A nonaccountable plan with:		
Either adequate accounting or return of excess, or both, not required by plan	The entire amount as wages in box 1.	All expenses.
No reimbursement plan:	The entire amount as wages in box 1.	All expenses.

* You may be able to use Form 2106-EZ. See *Completing Forms 2106 and 2106-EZ.*

1. Enter the total amount of reimbursements your employer gave you that were not reported to you in box 1 of Form W-2 .... $3,000
2. Enter the total amount of your expenses for the periods covered by this reimbursement 4,500
3. Of the amount on line 2, enter your total expense for meals and entertainment 2,000
4. Divide line 3 by line 2. Enter the result as a decimal (rounded to at least three places) .... .444
5. Multiply line 1 by line 4. Enter the result here and in Column B, line 7 1,332
6. Subtract line 5 from line 1. Enter the result here and in Column A, line 7 .... $1,668

On line 7 of Form 2106, Rob enters $3,668 ($2,000 airfare and $1,668 of the $3,000) in Column A and $1,332 (of the $3,000) in Column B.

After you complete the form. After you have completed your Form 2106 or 2106-EZ, follow the directions on that form to deduct your expenses on the appropriate line of your tax return. For most taxpayers, this is line 20 of Schedule A (Form 1040). However, if you are a government official paid on a fee basis, a performing artist, an Armed Forces reservist, or a disabled employee with impairment-related work expenses, see *Special Rules,* later.

Limits on employee business expenses. Your employee business expenses may be subject to any of the three limits described next. These limits are figured in the following order on the specified form.

1. Limit on meals and entertainment. Certain meal and entertainment expenses are subject to a 50% limit. Employees figure this limit on line 9 of Form 2106 or line 5 of Form 2106-EZ. See *50% Limit* under *Entertainment Expenses,* earlier.

2. Limit on miscellaneous itemized deductions. Employees deduct employee business expenses (as figured on Form 2106 or 2106-EZ) on line 20 of Schedule A (Form 1040). Most miscellaneous itemized deductions, including employee business expenses, are subject to a 2%-of-adjusted-gross-income limit. This limit is figured on line 25 of Schedule A (Form 1040).

3. Limit on total itemized deductions. If your adjusted gross income (line 37 of Form 1040) is more than $145,950 ($72,975 if you are married filing separately), the total of certain itemized deductions, including employee business expenses, may be limited. See chapter 22 for more information on this limit.

Special Rules

This section discusses special rules that apply to government officials who are paid on a fee basis, performing artists, Armed Forces reservists, and disabled employees with impairment-related work expenses.

Officials paid on a fee basis. Certain fee-basis officials can claim their employee business expenses whether or not they itemize their other deductions on Schedule A (Form 1040).

Fee-basis officials are persons who are employed by a state or local government and who are paid in whole or in part on a fee basis. They can deduct their business expenses in performing services in that job as an adjustment to gross income rather than as a miscellaneous itemized deduction.

If you are a fee-basis official, include your employee business expenses from line 10 of Form 2106 or line 6 of Form 2106-EZ on line 24 of Form 1040.

Expenses of certain performing artists. If you are a performing artist, you may qualify to deduct your employee business expenses as an adjustment to gross income rather than as a miscellaneous itemized deduction. To qualify, you must meet all of the following requirements.

1. During the tax year, you perform services in the performing arts as an employee for at least two employers.
2. You receive at least $200 each from any two of these employers.
3. Your related performing-arts business expenses are more than 10% of your gross income from the performance of those services.
4. Your adjusted gross income is not more than $16,000 before deducting these business expenses.

Special rules for married persons. If you are married, you must file a joint return unless you lived apart from your spouse at all times during the tax year.

If you file a joint return, you must figure requirements (1), (2), and (3) separately for both you and your spouse. However, requirement (4) applies to your and your spouse's combined adjusted gross income.

Where to report. If you meet all of the above requirements, you should first complete Form 2106 or 2106-EZ. Then you include your performing-arts-related expenses from line 10 of Form 2106 or line 6 of Form 2106-EZ on line 24 of Form 1040.

If you do not meet all of the above requirements, you do not qualify to deduct your expenses as an adjustment to gross income. Instead, you must complete Form 2106 or 2106-EZ and deduct your employee business expenses as an itemized deduction on line 20 of Schedule A (Form 1040).

Armed Forces reservists traveling more than 100 miles from home. If you are a member of a reserve component of the Armed Forces of the United States and you travel more than 100 miles away from home in connection with your performance of services as a member of the reserves, you can deduct your travel expenses as an adjustment to gross income rather than as a miscellaneous itemized deduction. The amount of expenses you can deduct as an adjustment to gross income is limited to the federal per diem rate (for lodging, meals, and incidental expenses) and the standard mileage rate (for car expenses) plus any parking fees, ferry fees, and tolls. The federal rate is explained earlier under *Per Diem and Car Allowances.*

Member of a reserve component. You are a member of a reserve component of the Armed Forces of the United States if you are in the Army, Navy, Marine Corps, Air Force, or Coast Guard Reserve, the Army National Guard of the United States, the Air National Guard of the United States, or the Reserve Corps of the Public Health Service.

How to report. If you have reserve-related travel that takes you more than 100 miles from home, you should first complete Form 2106 or Form 2106-EZ. Then include your expenses for reserve travel over 100 miles from home, up to the federal rate, from line 10 of Form 2106 or line 6 of Form 2106-EZ on line 24 of Form 1040. Subtract this amount from the total on line 10 of Form 2106 or line 6 of Form 2106-EZ and deduct the balance as an itemized deduction on line 20 of Schedule A (Form 1040).

You cannot deduct expenses of travel that does not take you more than 100 miles from home as an adjustment to gross income. Instead, you must complete Form 2106 or 2106-EZ and deduct those expenses as an itemized deduction on line 20 of Schedule A (Form 1040).

Impairment-related work expenses of disabled employees. If you are an employee with a physical or mental disability, your impairment-related work expenses are not subject to the 2%-of-adjusted-gross-income limit that applies to most other employee business expenses. After you complete Form 2106 or 2106-EZ, enter your impairment-related work expenses from line 10 of Form 2106 or line 6 of Form 2106-EZ on line 27 of Schedule A (Form 1040), and identify the type and amount of this expense on the dotted line next to line 27. Enter your employee business expenses that are unrelated to your disability from line 10 of Form 2106 or line 6 of Form 2106-EZ on line 20 of Schedule A.

Impairment-related work expenses are your allowable expenses for attendant care at your workplace and other expenses you have in connection with your workplace that are necessary for you to be able to work. For more information, see chapter 23.

Illustrated Example
Bill Wilson is an employee of Fashion Clothing Co. in Manhattan, NY. In a typical week, Bill leaves his home on Long Island on Monday morning and drives to Albany to exhibit the Fashion line for 3 days to prospective customers. Then he drives to Troy to show Fashion's new line of merchandise to Town Department Store, an old customer. While in Troy, he talks with Tom Brown, purchasing agent for Town Department Store, to discuss the new line. He later takes John Smith of Attire Co. out to dinner to discuss Attire Co.'s buying Fashion's new line of clothing.

Bill purchased his car on January 3, 2002. He uses the standard mileage rate for car expense purposes. He records his total mileage, business mileage, parking fees, and tolls for the year. Bill timely records his expenses and other pertinent information in a travel expense log (not shown). He obtains receipts for his expenses for lodging and for any other expenses of $75 or more.

During the year, Bill drove a total of 25,000 miles of which 20,000 miles were for business. He answers all the questions in Part II of Form 2106-EZ. He figures his car expense to be $8,100 (20,000 business miles × 40 .5 cents standard mileage rate).

His total employee business expenses are shown in the following table.

Type of Expense	Amount
Parking fees and tolls	$ 325
Car expenses	8,100
Meals	2,632
Lodging, laundry, dry cleaning	8,975
Entertainment	1,870
Gifts, education, etc.	430
Total	**$22,332**

Bill received an allowance of $3,600 ($300 per month) to help offset his expenses. Bill did not have to account to his employer for the reimbursement, and the $3,600 was included as income in box 1 of his Form W-2.

Because Bill's reimbursement was included in his income and he is using the standard mileage rate for his car expenses, he files Form 2106-EZ with his tax return. His filled-in form is shown on the next page.

Explanation
Note: This example does not take into account the increase in the cents-per-mile rate to 48.5 as of September 1, 2005.

TaxOrganizer

Records you should keep. If you deduct expenses for traveling away from home, you must be able to substantiate the expenses by keeping adequate evidence.

Adequate Evidence. Evidence is ordinarily considered adequate if it shows the amount, date, place, and essential character of the expense.

For example, a hotel receipt is sufficient to prove an expense for business travel if it has all of the following information:

1. The name and location of the hotel
2. The dates of your stay
3. Itemization of separate charges such as lodging, meals, and telephone calls

A restaurant receipt is enough to prove an expense for a business meal if it has all of the following:

1. The name and location of the restaurant
2. The number of people served
3. The date and amount of expense

Generally, you must have documentary evidence, such as receipts, canceled checks or bills, to support your expenses. A canceled check, together with a bill from the payee, ordinarily establishes the cost. However, a canceled check alone does not prove a business expense without other evidence to show that it was for a business purpose.

Exceptions. Evidence not needed if:

1. You have meals or lodging expenses while traveling away from home for which you account to your employer under an accountable plan and you use a per diem allowance method that includes meals and/or lodging.
2. Your expense, other than lodging, is less than $75.
3. You have transportation expense for which a receipt is not readily available.

If a charge is made for an item other than food and beverage, the receipt must show that this is the case.

Incomplete Records. If you do not have complete records to prove an element of expense, then you must prove the element by:

1. Your own statement, whether written or oral, that contains specific information about the element, and
2. Other supporting evidence that is sufficient to establish the element.

In addition, it is helpful to keep an account book, diary, or similar record that includes the following:

- Amount of each separate expense,
- Time and place of travel or entrainment,
- Number of days away from home spent on business, and
- Business purpose of the expense.

Form **2106-EZ**	**Unreimbursed Employee Business Expenses**	OMB No. 1545-1441

Department of the Treasury
Internal Revenue Service   (99)

► **Attach to Form 1040.**

2005

Attachment
Sequence No. **54A**

Your name	Occupation in which you incurred expenses	Social security number
Bill Wilson	Sales	555 : 00 : 5555

You May Use This Form Only if All of the Following Apply.

• You are an employee deducting ordinary and necessary expenses attributable to your job. An ordinary expense is one that is common and accepted in your field of trade, business, or profession. A necessary expense is one that is helpful and appropriate for your business. An expense does not have to be required to be considered necessary.

• You **do not** get reimbursed by your employer for any expenses (amounts your employer included in box 1 of your Form W-2 are not considered reimbursements for this purpose).

• If you are claiming vehicle expense, you are using the standard mileage rate for 2005.

Caution: *You can use the standard mileage rate for 2005 **only if: (a)** you owned the vehicle and used the standard mileage rate for the first year you placed the vehicle in service, **or (b)** you leased the vehicle and used the standard mileage rate for the portion of the lease period after 1997.*

Part I	**Figure Your Expenses**		
1	Vehicle expense using the standard mileage rate. Complete Part II and multiply line 8a by 40.5¢ (.405)	**1**	8,100
2	Parking fees, tolls, and transportation, including train, bus, etc., that **did not** involve overnight travel or commuting to and from work	**2**	325
3	Travel expense while away from home overnight, including lodging, airplane, car rental, etc. **Do not** include meals and entertainment	**3**	8,975
4	Business expenses not included on lines 1 through 3. **Do not** include meals and entertainment	**4**	430
5	Meals and entertainment expenses: $ __4,502__ × 50% (.50) (Employees subject to Department of Transportation (DOT) hours of service limits: Multiply meal expenses incurred while away from home on business by 70% (.70) instead of 50%. For details, see instructions.)	**5**	2,251
6	**Total expenses.** Add lines 1 through 5. Enter here and on **Schedule A (Form 1040), line 20.** (Armed Forces reservists, fee-basis state or local government officials, qualified performing artists, and individuals with disabilities: See the instructions for special rules on where to enter this amount.)	**6**	20,081

Part II	**Information on Your Vehicle.** Complete this part **only** if you are claiming vehicle expense on line 1.

7   When did you place your vehicle in service for business use? (month, day, year) ►   __1__ / __3__ / __02__

8   Of the total number of miles you drove your vehicle during 2005, enter the number of miles you used your vehicle for:

   a Business __20,000__   **b** Commuting (see instructions) __2,600__   **c** Other __2,400__

9   Do you (or your spouse) have another vehicle available for personal use? . . . . ☑ **Yes** ☐ **No**

10   Was your vehicle available for personal use during off-duty hours? . . . . ☑ **Yes** ☐ **No**

11a   Do you have evidence to support your deduction? . . . . ☑ **Yes** ☐ **No**

  b   If "Yes," is the evidence written? . . . . ☑ **Yes** ☐ **No**

For Paperwork Reduction Act Notice, see page 3.   Cat. No. 20604Q   Form **2106-EZ** (2005)

Tax Benefits for Work-Related Education

Note: The 2004 IRS Publication 17 (Your Federal Income Tax) has been updated by Ernst & Young LLP for 2005. Dates and dollar amounts shown are for 2005. Gray type is used to indicate where IRS text has been updated or intentionally omitted. Unrevised IRS text is shown in black type.

Introduction

Educational expenses are generally considered to be personal in nature. The law, however, does recognize that certain educational expenses are necessary for you in your business or as an employee. Deductions may be allowed for these expenses, as well as for reasonable expenses incurred in acquiring the education.

It's often difficult to determine if work-related educational expenses are deductible. You do not necessarily have to earn a new degree for such expenses to be claimed. On the other hand, earning a degree doesn't necessarily make the expenses deductible. The expenses do have to meet certain tests. For example, they are deductible if the education either maintains or improves skills required in your trade or business or if the courses are required for you to retain your current job. The expenses are not deductible if they are spent on education that is required for you to meet the minimum educational requirements of your position. In addition, travel as a form of education is not deductible.

This chapter discusses work-related educational expenses. You'll learn that you may deduct not only your fees for educational instruction but also a number of other expenses that you incur because you are simultaneously working and in school.

Work-related educational expenses of an employee and other miscellaneous itemized deductions are deductible only to the extent that they exceed 2% of adjusted gross income.

It is also important to note that your 2005 itemized deductions may be subject to certain other limitations if your adjusted gross income exceeds $145,950 ($72,975 if married filing separately). See Chapter 31, Limit on Itemized Deductions, for more information on this subject.

For a discussion of education credits and other education benefits—such as employer provided educational programs and qualified tuition programs—see Chapter 37, Education Credits.

What's New

Standard mileage rate. Generally, if you claim a business deduction for work-related education and you drive your car to and from school, the amount you can deduct in 2005 is 40.5 cents per mile (through August 31, 48.5 cents per mile afterwards), up from 37.5 cents per mile in 2004. See *Transportation Expenses* under *What Expenses Can Be Deducted*, for more information.

Reminder

Limit on itemized deductions. If your adjusted gross income is more than $145,950 ($72,975 if you are married filing separately), the overall amount of your itemized deductions may be limited. See chapter 31 for more information about this limit.

This chapter discusses work-related education expenses that you may be able to deduct as business expenses.

To claim such a deduction, you must:

1. Be working,
2. Itemize your deductions on Schedule A (Form 1040) if you are an employee,

3. File Schedule C (Form 1040) or Schedule F (Form 1040) if you are self-employed, and

4. Have expenses for education that meet the requirements discussed under *Qualifying Work-Related Education*.

If you are an employee and able to itemize your deductions, you may be able to claim a deduction for the expenses you pay for your work-related education. Your deduction will be the amount by which your qualifying work-related education expenses plus other job and certain miscellaneous expenses is greater than 2% of your adjusted gross income. See chapter 30.

If you are self-employed, you deduct your expenses for qualifying work-related education directly from your self-employment income.

Your work-related education expenses may also qualify you for other tax benefits, such as the tuition and fees deduction (see chapter 21) and the Hope and lifetime learning credits (see chapter 37). You may qualify for these other benefits even if you do not meet the requirements listed above.

Also, keep in mind that your work-related education expenses may qualify you to claim more than one tax benefit. Generally, you may claim any number of benefits as long as you use different expenses to figure each one.

Tip. *When you figure your taxes, you may want to compare these tax benefits so you can choose the method(s) that give you the lowest tax liability. First, figure your taxes using the expenses as business deductions. Then, figure your taxes again using any of the other deductions and credits for which you qualify. You may find that a combination of credit(s) and deduction(s) gives you the lowest tax.*

Useful Items

You may want to see:

Publications

☐ **463** Travel, Entertainment, Gift, and Car Expenses
☐ **970** Tax Benefits for Education

Forms (and Instructions)

☐ **2106** Employee Business Expenses
☐ **2106-EZ** Unreimbursed Employee Business Expenses
☐ **Schedule A (Form 1040)** Itemized Deductions

Qualifying Work-Related Education

You can deduct the costs of qualifying work-related education as business expenses. This is education that meets at least one of the following two tests.

1. The education is required by your employer or the law to keep your present salary, status, or job. The required education must serve a *bona fide* business purpose of your employer.

2. The education maintains or improves skills needed in your present work.

However, even if the education meets one or both of the above tests, it is not qualifying work-related education if it:

1. Is needed to meet the minimum educational requirements of your present trade or business, or

2. Is part of a program of study that will qualify you for a new trade or business.

You can deduct the costs of qualifying work-related education as a business expense even if the education could lead to a degree.

Use Figure 29-A (see next page) as a quick check to see if your education qualifies.

Explanation

In order to be deductible, work-related educational expenses must relate to your current occupation.

Example

A college student obtaining employment through his or her college cooperative program or work/study program is not engaged in a trade or a business. His or her college fees are not deductible as a work-related education expense, because they are incurred in preparation for an occupation.

A full-time student does not have a trade or a business and may not deduct the cost of courses toward a college degree, even though the student may be employed full-time during the summer months.

TaxPlanner

The IRS does not explicitly allow or disallow work-related educational expenses for a semi-retired person. Therefore, it appears that educational expenses to maintain skills are deductible, even though the individual has reduced the scope of his or her trade or business.

An individual who abandons a former profession for a period of years and acquires a *new* profession may not deduct courses related to resuming his or her original profession.

A fully retired individual is not considered to have a trade or a business and is not entitled to a deduction for work-related educational expenses.

Example

Gaby, an engineer, decides to teach math at a local high school. After teaching for a few years, she decides to resume her former career in engineering. Gaby takes refresher courses at a local college. The costs of these courses are *not* work-related educational expenses.

TaxPlanner

This chapter discusses when educational expenses may be deducted because they are work related. Eligible taxpayers may be able to claim a deduction for up to $4,000 of qualified tuition and related expenses in 2005 regardless of whether those expenses would be considered to be work-related. For additional information, see Chapter 21, *Education-Related Adjustments,* section on Tuition and Fees Deductions, and IRS Publication 970.

Education Required by Employer or by Law

Once you have met the minimum educational requirements for your job, your employer or the law may require you to get more education. This additional education is qualifying work-related education if all three of the following requirements are met.

1. It is required for you to keep your present salary, status, or job,

2. The requirement serves a business purpose of your employer, and

3. The education is not part of a program that will qualify you for a new trade or business.

Example 1

As a result of a corporate downsizing policy, you are taking courses to be retrained in another trade or business. If this education qualifies you to enter a new trade or business, even with the same employer, the costs are nondeductible.

Figure 29-A. **Does Your Work-Related Education Qualify?**

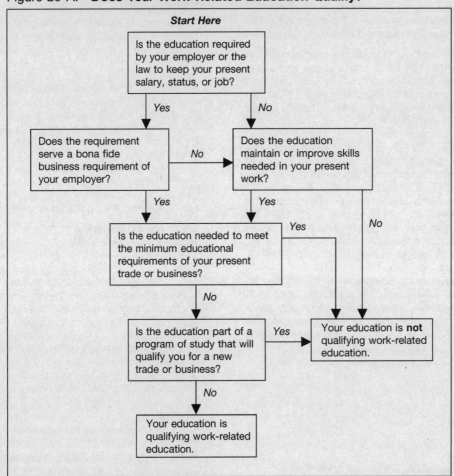

Example 2

Your employer is restructuring its workforce. The company has said that additional education is required for you to retain your current job. Because the education serves a business purpose of your employer and is necessary for you to maintain your current position, the additional educational expenses are deductible.

When you get more education than your employer or the law requires, the additional education can be qualifying work-related education only if it maintains or improves skills required in your present work. See *Education To Maintain or Improve Skills.*

Example. You are a teacher who has satisfied the minimum requirements for teaching. Your employer requires you to take an additional college course each year to keep your teaching job. If the courses will not qualify you for a new trade or business, they are qualifying work-related education even if you eventually receive a master's degree and an increase in salary because of this extra education.

Education To Maintain or Improve Skills

If your education is not required by your employer or the law, it can be qualifying work-related education only if it maintains or improves skills needed in your present work. This could include refresher courses, courses on current developments, and academic or vocational courses.

Example. You repair televisions, radios, and stereo systems for XYZ Store. To keep up with the latest changes, you take special courses in radio and stereo service. These courses maintain and improve skills required in your work.

Examples

The following are examples of educational expenses that were *deductible* because the courses maintained or improved skills:

- A tax attorney attended an out-of-town tax forum. The course was valuable for her in maintaining current knowledge of the tax laws.
- An engineering aide took night courses that improved his skills but were not required by his employer.
- A concert harpist took music lessons. The costs were deductible as she was maintaining or improving her skills.
- A doctor, engaged in the private practice of psychiatry, undertook a program of study and training at an accredited psychoanalytic institute that enabled him to qualify to practice psychoanalysis. The expenditures were deductible because the study and training maintained or improved skills required in the doctor's trade or business and didn't qualify the doctor for a new trade or business.
- A farmer could deduct the cost of a welding course that improved his welding skills. Welding skills were

necessary in the farming operation to keep the machinery repaired.
- An ordained minister could deduct the cost of undergraduate courses in psychology, education, and business. The court determined that the courses maintained and improved the skills that he needed to lead a congregation competently: counseling, teaching, and managing the financial affairs of the church.
- An attorney who has already passed the bar and is working as a tax lawyer can deduct the cost of obtaining a master in laws of taxation (LLM).
- A CPA practicing in the area of taxation can deduct the cost of obtaining a masters in taxation graduate degree provided it is not a requirement for taking the CPA exam.

Maintaining skills vs. qualifying for new job. Education to maintain or improve skills needed in your present work is not qualifying education if it will also qualify you for a new trade or business.

Examples

- A bookkeeper who was also a tax return preparer returned to school and earned a bachelor's degree in accounting. The degree qualified her to sit for the certified public accounting examination. The costs incurred in earning the degree are not deductible because the courses were intended to obtain a new degree rather than to improve or maintain her skills; the new degree qualified her for a new trade or business.
- A quality control foreman took courses in business law, corporate strategy and business policies, and business finance. The costs were held to be nondeductible because they were only remotely related to his duties.

Temporary absence. If you stop working for a year or less in order to get education to maintain or improve skills needed in your present work and then return to the same general type of work, your absence is considered temporary. Education that you get during a temporary absence is qualifying work-related education if it maintains or improves skills needed in your present work.

Example. You quit your biology research job to become a full-time biology graduate student for one year. If you return to work in biology research after completing the courses, the education is related to your present work even if you do not go back to work with the same employer.

Indefinite absence. If you stop work for more than a year, your absence from your job is considered indefinite. Education during an indefinite absence, even if it maintains or improves skills needed in the work from which you are absent, is considered to qualify you for a new trade or business. Therefore, it is not qualifying work-related education.

Explanation
While the IRS defines a temporary leave of absence as a period of 1 year or less, the courts have been more lenient, approving deductions for educational expenses for a leave of more than 1 year. The cases turn on whether or not the taxpayer's intention is to reenter the same trade or business, regardless of whether or not it is with a new employer.

Examples
- A manager who quit his job to pursue a 2-year master of business administration program but who expected to reenter the same trade or business was allowed to deduct the cost of his courses.

- A parochial schoolteacher ended her employment to raise a family. Over the next 23 years, she attended several different colleges until she was awarded a bachelor's degree in education. The following fall, she began employment again as a full-time teacher. The court determined that when she left the parochial school, there was no indication that she was on a leave of absence or that she planned to resume teaching in the future. Consequently, the court denied the deduction for the educational expenses.

Education To Meet Minimum Requirements

Education you need to meet the minimum educational requirements for your present trade or business is not qualifying work-related education. The minimum educational requirements are determined by:

1. Laws and regulations,
2. Standards of your profession, trade, or business, and
3. Your employer.

Example
You have completed 2 years of a 3-year law school curriculum and are hired by a law firm to do legal research and to perform other functions on a full-time basis. As a condition of employment, you are required to obtain a law degree and to pass the state bar examination. You complete the law school education by attending night classes and take a bar review course in order to prepare for the bar examination. The law courses and the bar review course are considered the minimum educational requirements needed to qualify for your trade or business, and thus the costs of such courses are not deductible. However, courts have held that you may amortize over your life expectancy fees paid to state bar admission authorities.

Once you have met the minimum educational requirements that were in effect when you were hired, you do not have to meet any new minimum educational requirements. This means that if the minimum requirements change after you were hired, any education you need to meet the new requirements can be qualifying education. **Caution.** *You have not necessarily met the minimum educational requirements of your trade or business simply because you are already doing the work.*

Example 1. You are a full-time engineering student. Although you have not received your degree or certification, you work part time as an engineer for a firm that will employ you as a full-time engineer after you finish college. Although your college engineering courses improve your skills in your present job, they are also needed to meet the minimum job requirements for a full-time engineer. The education is not qualifying work-related education.

Example 2. You are an accountant and you have met the minimum educational requirements of your employer. Your employer later changes the minimum educational requirements and requires you to take college courses to keep your job. These additional courses can be qualifying work-related education because you have already satisfied the minimum requirements that were in effect when you were hired.

Requirements for Teachers
States or school districts usually set the minimum educational requirements for teachers. The requirement is the college degree or the minimum number of college hours usually required of a person hired for that position.

If there are no requirements, you will have met the minimum

educational requirements when you become a faculty member. You generally will be considered a faculty member when one or more of the following occurs.

1. You have tenure.
2. Your years of service count toward obtaining tenure.
3. You have a vote in faculty decisions.
4. Your school makes contributions for you to a retirement plan other than social security or a similar program.

Example 1. The law in your state requires beginning secondary school teachers to have a bachelor's degree, including 10 professional education courses. In addition, to keep the job, a teacher must complete a fifth year of training within 10 years from the date of hire. If the employing school certifies to the state Department of Education that qualified teachers cannot be found, the school can hire persons with only 3 years of college. However, to keep their jobs, these teachers must get a bachelor's degree and the required professional education courses within 3 years.

Under these facts, the bachelor's degree, whether or not it includes the 10 professional education courses, is considered the minimum educational requirement for qualification as a teacher in your state.

If you have all the required education except the fifth year, you have met the minimum educational requirements. The fifth year of training is qualifying work-related education unless it is part of a program of study that will qualify you for a new trade or business.

Example 2. Assume the same facts as in *Example 1* except that you have a bachelor's degree and only six professional education courses. The additional four education courses can be qualifying work-related education. Although you do not have all the required courses, you have already met the minimum educational requirements.

Example 3. Assume the same facts as in *Example 1*, except that you are hired with only 3 years of college. The courses you take that lead to a bachelor's degree (including those in education) are not qualifying work-related education. They are needed to meet the minimum educational requirements for employment as a teacher.

Example 4. You have a bachelor's degree and you work as a temporary instructor at a university. At the same time, you take graduate courses toward an advanced degree. The rules of the university state that you can become a faculty member only if you get a graduate degree. Also, you can keep your job as an instructor only as long as you show satisfactory progress toward getting this degree. You have not met the minimum educational requirements to qualify you as a faculty member. The graduate courses are not qualifying work-related education.

TAXSAVER

It's possible to maximize an education deduction by carefully limiting pre-employment education to minimum job requirements. Courses taken after employment is secured may then be deductible as maintaining or improving skills.

Example 1

Denise Thomas is starting her final semester of courses that will enable her to be a registered nurse. She needs 6 credit hours of nursing courses to reach the required level of education. In addition to the 6 credit hours, Denise also wants to take an advanced nursing course. To reduce her taxes, Denise should complete the minimum job requirements for nursing. If she takes the advanced nursing course after she qualifies to be a nurse and secures a nursing position, the cost of the advanced nursing course is deductible.

Example 2

Robert Taylor is a recent law school graduate and is considering the pursuit of a full-time graduate law (LLM)

---

program in international law. To qualify for a deduction, Robert should secure employment as a lawyer and complete the minimum requirements for practicing law (i.e., bar admission) before starting any graduate program. After meeting these minimum requirements for practicing law, Robert may begin a graduate law program in international law and deduct the related educational expenses.

Certification in a new state. Once you have met the minimum educational requirements for teachers for your state, you are considered to have met the minimum educational requirements in all states. This is true even if you must get additional education to be certified in another state. Any additional education you need is qualifying work-related education. You have already met the minimum requirements for teaching. Teaching in another state is not a new trade or business.

Example. You hold a permanent teaching certificate in State A and are employed as a teacher in that state for several years. You move to State B and are promptly hired as a teacher. You are required, however, to complete certain prescribed courses to get a permanent teaching certificate in State B. These additional courses are qualifying work-related education because the teaching position in State B involves the same general kind of work for which you were qualified in State A.

Education That Qualifies You for a New Trade or Business

Education that is part of a program of study that will qualify you for a new trade or business is not qualifying work-related education. This is true even if you do not plan to enter that trade or business.

If you are an employee, a change of duties that involves the same general kind of work is not a new trade or business.

Example 1. You are an accountant. Your employer requires you to get a law degree at your own expense. You register at a law school for the regular curriculum that leads to a law degree. Even if you do not intend to become a lawyer, the education is not qualifying because the law degree will qualify you for a new trade or business.

Example 2. You are a general practitioner of medicine. You take a 2-week course to review developments in several specialized fields of medicine. The course does not qualify you for a new profession. It is qualifying work-related education because it maintains or improves skills required in your present profession.

Explanation

A change of duties is limited to employees. It does not pertain to self-employed individuals.

The IRS defines the phrase "the same general type of work" very narrowly. The burden is on the taxpayer to prove that he or she has not qualified for a new trade or business. However, teachers are generally given more latitude (see the following section, *Teaching and Related Duties*).

A deduction as a work-related expense has not been allowed for law school educational expenses, even if they are required by an employer. The courts have specifically disallowed a deduction for law school for employees in the following trades or businesses: accountant, insurance claims adjuster, industrial arts teacher, engineer, probation officer, patent examiner, mathematics teacher, IRS agent, hospital administrator, doctor, philosophy professor, and computer systems analyst.

Exceptions

Nevertheless, the courts have *allowed deductions* in some special cases:

- A night manager of a supermarket took food management courses at a local university. The courses elevated his rank within the management structure and also qualified him for a day manager position. The court held that the general management progression did not represent a change in business, and the court allowed the deductions.
- An engineer whose duties were changing to include more management and administrative skills took courses and received a degree in business management and administration. The courses were deductible because the education did not qualify him for a new trade or a business but was directly related to his current position. The courses also allowed him to maintain and improve skills required by his employer.
- Costs incurred in becoming a specialist within your trade or business are deductible.

TAXSAVER

You may be able to deduct expenses incurred in gaining a specialty within a trade or a business if the expenses are delayed until after you have established yourself in the trade or business.

Example

A dentist engaged in general practice returned to dental school for full-time postgraduate study in orthodontics while continuing her practice on a part-time basis. After completing her postgraduate training, she limited her practice to orthodontic patients. The expenses incurred by the dentist in her studies were deductible because they improved her skills as a dentist and did not qualify her for a new trade or business.

Example 3. While working in the private practice of psychiatry, you enter a program to study and train at an accredited psychoanalytic institute. The program will lead to qualifying you to practice psychoanalysis. The psychoanalytic training does not qualify you for a new profession. It is qualifying work-related education because it maintains or improves skills required in your present profession.

Explanation

Payment for psychoanalysis that is required as part of your training to be a psychoanalyst may be a deductible educational expense necessary for professional training. The law specifically permits an itemized deduction for the cost of psychoanalytic training undertaken by psychiatrists as education expenses, because the training maintains or improves skills required in their trade or business and does not qualify them for a new trade or business. The courts have also allowed deductions for expenses incurred by a clinical psychologist in studying to become a psychoanalyst and expenses incurred by a psychiatrist for psychoanalytic training as a condition to accepting the directorship of a child study center.

However, when a psychiatric residency was undertaken to qualify a taxpayer for a new profession, the expenses were not deductible.

Bar or CPA Review Course

Review courses to prepare for the bar examination or the certified public accountant (CPA) examination are not qualifying work-related education. They are part of a program of study that can qualify you for a new profession.

Explanation

Bar review courses are not deductible, even if you are currently practicing in one state and are seeking admission to the bar in another state. However, you may be able to deduct the cost of graduate courses (LLM). See earlier examples under *Education to Maintain or Improve Skills,* and *Education to Meet Minimum Requirements.*

Teaching and Related Duties

All teaching and related duties are considered the same general kind of work. A change in duties in any of the following ways is not considered a change to a new business.

1. Elementary school teacher to secondary school teacher.
2. Teacher of one subject, such as biology, to teacher of another subject, such as art.
3. Classroom teacher to guidance counselor.
4. Classroom teacher to school administrator.

Explanation

If you are an employed teacher who meets the minimum education requirements of one state, you may deduct the cost of required courses to qualify as a teacher in another state. Changing employers and locations is not a significant change of duties and does not create a new trade or business. Likewise, deductions have been allowed for a Canadian teacher taking courses to qualify to teach in the United States. However, the IRS has ruled that the position of elementary school teacher does not involve the same general type of work and is not the same trade or business as a university professor.

Example

Lynn Arnold left her position as an elementary music teacher to obtain a Ph.D. degree in music. After obtaining her degree, she took a job as an assistant professor in the music department of a university. Lynn cannot deduct the expenses of getting her Ph.D.

What Expenses Can Be Deducted

If your education meets the requirements described earlier under *Qualifying Work-Related Education,* you can generally deduct your education expenses as business expenses. If you are not self-employed, you can deduct business expenses only if you itemize your deductions.

You cannot deduct expenses related to tax-exempt and excluded income.

Deductible expenses. The following education expenses can be deducted.

1. Tuition, books, supplies, lab fees, and similar items.
2. Certain transportation and travel costs.
3. Other education expenses, such as costs of research and typing when writing a paper as part of an educational program.

Nondeductible expenses. You cannot deduct personal or capital expenses. For example, you cannot deduct the dollar value of vacation time or annual leave you take to attend classes. This amount is a personal expense.

Unclaimed reimbursement. If you do not claim reimbursement that you are entitled to receive from your employer, you cannot deduct the expenses that apply to the reimbursement.

Example. Your employer agrees to pay your education expenses if you file a voucher showing your expenses. You do not file a voucher, and you do not get reimbursed. Because you did not file a voucher, you cannot deduct the expenses on your tax return.

Transportation Expenses

If your education qualifies, you can deduct local transportation costs of going directly from work to school. If you are regularly employed and go to school on a temporary basis, you can also deduct the costs of returning from school to home.

Attendance on a temporary basis. You go to school on a temporary basis or are considered to go on a temporary basis if either of the following situations applies to you.

1. Your attendance at school is realistically expected to last 1 year or less and does indeed last for 1 year or less.
2. Initially your attendance at school is realistically expected to last 1 year or less, but at a later date your attendance is reasonably expected to last more than 1 year. Your attendance will be considered temporary up to the date you determine it will last more than 1 year.

Note. If you are in either situation (1) or (2) above, your attendance is not temporary if facts and circumstances indicate otherwise.

Attendance not on a temporary basis. You do not go to school on a temporary basis if any of the following situations apply to you.

1. Your attendance at school is realistically expected to last more than 1 year. It does not matter how long you actually attend.
2. Initially your attendance at school is realistically expected to last 1 year or less, but at a later date your attendance is reasonably expected to last more than 1 year. Your attendance is not temporary after the date you determine it will last more than 1 year.

Deductible Transportation Expenses

If you are regularly employed and go directly from home to school on a temporary basis, you can deduct the round-trip costs of transportation between your home and school. This is true regardless of the location of the school, the distance traveled, or whether you attend school on nonwork days.

Transportation expenses include the actual costs of bus, subway, cab, or other fares, as well as the costs of using your car. Transportation expenses do not include amounts spent for travel, meals, or lodging while you are away from home overnight.

Example 1. You regularly work in a nearby town, and go directly from work to home. You also attend school every work night for 3 months to take a course that improves your job skills. Since you are attending school on a temporary basis, you can deduct your daily round-trip transportation expenses in going between home and school. This is true regardless of the distance traveled.

Example 2. Assume the same facts as in *Example 1* except that on certain nights you go directly from work to school and then home. You can deduct your transportation expenses from your regular work site to school and then home.

Example 3. Assume the same facts as in *Example 1* except that you attend the school for 9 months on Saturdays, nonwork days. Since you are attending school on a temporary basis, you can deduct your round-trip transportation expenses in going between home and school.

Example 4. Assume the same facts as in *Example 1* except that you attend classes twice a week for 15 months. Since your attendance in school is not considered temporary, you cannot deduct your transportation expenses in going between home and school. If you go directly from work to school, you can deduct the one-way transportation expenses of going from work to school. If you go from work to home to school and return home, your transportation expenses cannot be more than if you had gone directly from work to school.

Using your car. If you use your car (whether you own or lease it) for transportation to school, you can deduct your actual expenses or use the standard mileage rate to figure the amount you can deduct. The standard mileage rate for 2005 is 40.5 cents per mile. Whichever method you use, you can also deduct parking fees and tolls. See chapter 28 for information on deducting your actual expenses of using a car.

Travel Expenses

You can deduct expenses for travel, meals (see *50% Limit on Meals*, later), and lodging if:

1. You travel overnight to obtain qualifying work-related education, and
2. The main purpose of the trip is to attend a work-related course or seminar.

Travel expenses for qualifying work-related education are treated the same as travel expenses for other employee business purposes. For more information, see chapter 28.

Caution. *You cannot deduct expenses for personal activities, such as sightseeing, visiting, or entertaining.*

Mainly personal travel. If your travel away from home is mainly personal, you cannot deduct all of your expenses for travel, meals, and lodging. You can deduct only your expenses for lodging and 50% of your expenses for meals during the time you attend the qualified educational activities.

Whether a trip's purpose is mainly personal or educational depends upon the facts and circumstances. An important factor is the comparison of time spent on personal activities with time spent on educational activities. If you spend more time on personal activities, the trip is considered mainly educational only if you can show a substantial nonpersonal reason for traveling to a particular location.

Example 1. John works in Newark, New Jersey. He traveled to Chicago to take a deductible 1-week course at the request of his employer. His main reason for going to Chicago was to take the course.

While there, he took a sightseeing trip, entertained some friends, and took a side trip to Pleasantville for a day.

Since the trip was mainly for business, John can deduct his round-trip airfare to Chicago. He cannot deduct his transportation expenses of going to Pleasantville. He can deduct only the meals (subject to the 50% limit) and lodging connected with his educational activities.

Example 2. Sue works in Boston. She went to a university in Michigan to take a course for work. The course is qualifying work-related education.

She took one course, which is one-fourth of a full course load of study. She spent the rest of the time on personal activities. Her reasons for taking the course in Michigan were all personal.

Sue's trip is mainly personal because three-fourths of her time is considered personal time. She cannot deduct the cost of her round-trip train ticket to Michigan. She can deduct one-fourth of the meals (subject to the 50% limit) and lodging costs for the time she attended the university.

Example 3. Dave works in Nashville and recently traveled to California to take a 2-week seminar. The seminar is qualifying work-related education.

While there, he spent an extra 8 weeks on personal activities. The facts, including the extra 8-week stay, show that his main purpose was to take a vacation.

Dave cannot deduct his round-trip airfare or his meals and lodging for the 8 weeks. He can deduct only his expenses for meals (subject to the 50% limit) and lodging for the 2 weeks he attended the seminar.

TAXSAVER

Through careful planning and documentation, as well as recognition of the stringent tests applied by the courts, it's possible to mix business with pleasure and deduct some or all of your travel expenses. If you travel away from home primarily to obtain education, your expenditures for the education, as well as for travel, meals, and lodging while away from home, are deductible. It is helpful to be able to prove that the location you are visiting is unique and that, if education is involved, the education cannot be obtained elsewhere.

However, if you engage in some personal activity while on the trip, such as sightseeing, social visiting, entertaining, or other recreation, your expenses attributable to those personal activities are nondeductible personal expenses.

If your travel away from home is primarily personal, your expenditures for travel, meals, and lodging (other than meals and lodging during the time spent participating in deductible educational pursuits) are not deductible.

Whether a particular trip is primarily personal or primarily educational depends on all the facts and circumstances of each case, including the time devoted to personal activity as compared with the time devoted to educational pursuits. It is important to maintain good documentation regarding the types of expenses incurred and in what capacity they were incurred.

Example

Shannon, a hair stylist, decides to attend a 4-day workshop on the latest trends of hair coloring and styling that is offered in Tampa, Florida, 400 miles from her home. Her primary purpose in going to Tampa is to take the course, but she also takes a side trip to Orlando (a couple of hours away from Tampa) for 2 days. Shannon's transportation expenses to Tampa are deductible, but her transportation to Orlando is not. Additionally, her expenses for meals and lodging while away from home must be allocated between her educational pursuits and her personal activities. Those expenses that are entirely personal, such as sightseeing in Orlando, are not deductible.

The cost of deductible meals must be reduced by 50%.

Cruises and conventions. Certain cruises and conventions offer seminars or courses as part of their itinerary. Even if the seminars or courses are work related, your deduction for travel may be limited. This applies to:

1. Travel by ocean liner, cruise ship, or other form of luxury water transportation, and
2. Conventions outside the North American area.

For a discussion of the limits on travel expense deductions that apply to cruises and conventions, see *Luxury Water Travel* and *Conventions* in Publication 463.

50% limit on meals. You can deduct only 50% of the cost of your meals while traveling away from home to obtain qualifying work-related education. You cannot have been reimbursed for the meals.

Employees must use Form 2106 or Form 2106-EZ to apply the 50% limit.

Travel as Education

You cannot deduct the cost of travel as a form of education, even if it is directly related to your duties in your work or business.

Example. You are a French language teacher. While on sabbatical leave granted for travel, you traveled through France to improve your knowledge of the French language. You chose your itinerary and most of your activities to improve your French language skills. You cannot deduct your travel expenses as education expenses. This is true even if you spent most of your time learning French by visiting French schools and families, attending movies or plays, and engaging in similar activities.

Explanation

The cost of travel is not a deductible educational expense when the educational aspect of a trip is the trip itself. However, if you establish an ordinary and necessary business need for the travel, such as research that can only be done in a specific location or a specific seminar, then a deduction may be allowed for travel expenses.

TaxSaver

Student Loan Interest Expense. You may be able to deduct interest you pay on a qualified student loan. If you qualify, you can take this deduction whether or not the education is work related and even if you do not itemize deductions on Schedule A (Form 1040). For more information on the deduction of student loan interest, see Publication 970.

TaxAlert

Interest expense of up to $2,500 paid during 2005 on qualified student loans may be deducted from your income in determining your adjusted gross income. For more information, see Chapter 21, *Education-Related Adjustments,* section on Student Loan Interest Deduction.

No Double Benefit Allowed

You cannot do any of the following.

- Deduct work-related education expenses as business expenses if you deduct these expenses under any other provision of the law, for example, as a tuition and fees deduction. See chapter 21.
- Deduct work-related education expenses paid with tax-free scholarship, grant, or employer-provided educational assistance. See *Adjustments to Qualifying Work-Related Education Expenses*, next.

Adjustments to Qualifying Work-Related Education Expenses
If you pay qualifying work-related education expenses with certain tax-free funds, you cannot claim a deduction for those amounts. You must reduce the qualifying expenses by the amount of any tax-free educational assistance you received.

Tax-free educational assistance includes:

- The tax-free part of scholarships and fellowships (see chapter 1 of Publication 970),
- Pell grants (see chapter 1 of Publication 970),
- Employer-provided educational assistance (see chapter 11 of Publication 970),
- Veterans' educational assistance (see chapter 1 of Publication 970), and
- Any other nontaxable (tax-free) payments (other than gifts or inheritances) received for education expenses.

Do not reduce the qualifying work-related education expenses by amounts paid with funds the student receives as:

- Payment for services, such as wages,
- A loan,
- A gift,
- An inheritance, or
- A withdrawal from the student's personal savings.

Also, do not reduce the qualifying work-related education expenses by any scholarship or fellowship reported as income on the student's return or any scholarship which, by its terms, cannot be applied to qualifying work-related education expenses.

Reimbursements

How you treat reimbursements depends on the arrangement you have with your employer.

There are two basic types of reimbursement arrangements—accountable plans and nonaccountable plans. You can tell the type of plan you are reimbursed under by the way the reimbursement is reported on your Form W-2.

For information about how to treat reimbursements under both accountable and nonaccountable plans, see *Reimbursements* in chapter 28.

Deducting Business Expenses

Self-employed persons and employees report business expenses differently.

The following information explains what forms you must use to deduct the cost of your qualifying education as a business expense.

Self-Employed Persons

If you are self-employed, you must report the cost of your qualifying work-related education on the appropriate form used to report your business income and expenses (generally Schedule C, C-EZ, or F). If your educational expenses include expenses for a car or truck, travel, or meals, report those expenses the same way you report other business expenses for those items. See the instructions for the form you file for information on how to complete it.

TAXSAVER

From a tax perspective, it is more beneficial to report educational expenses on Schedules C, C-EZ, or F as appropriate. Reporting expenses on these forms will lower your adjusted gross income. As a result, a greater percentage of your itemized deductions may be allowed and the education expenses will not be subject to any itemized deduction limitations. In addition, reporting the expenses on Schedules C, C-EZ, or F will reduce your self-employment tax.

Employees

If you are an employee, you can deduct the cost of qualifying work-related education only if you:

1. Did not receive any reimbursement from your employer,
2. Were reimbursed under a nonaccountable plan (amount is included in box 1 of Form W-2), or
3. Received reimbursement under an accountable plan, but the amount received was less than your expenses.

If either (1) or (2) applies, you can deduct the total qualifying cost. If (3) applies, you can deduct only the qualifying costs that were more than your reimbursement.

In order to deduct the cost of your qualifying work-related education as a business expense, include the amount with your deduction for any other employee business expenses on Schedule A (Form 1040), line 20. (Special rules for expenses of certain performing artists and fee-basis officials and for impairment-related work expenses are explained later.) This deduction is subject to the 2%-of-adjusted-gross-income limit that applies to most miscellaneous itemized deductions. See chapter 30.

Form 2106 or 2106-EZ. To figure your deduction for employee business expenses, including qualifying work-related education, you generally must complete Form 2106 or Form 2106-EZ.

Form not required. Do not complete either Form 2106 or Form 2106-EZ if:

- All reimbursements, if any, were included in box 1 of your Form W-2, and
- You are not claiming travel, transportation, meal, or entertainment expenses.

If you meet both of these requirements, enter the expenses directly on Schedule A (Form 1040), line 20. (Special rules for expenses of certain performing artists and fee-basis officials and for impairment-related work expenses are explained later.)

Using Form 2106-EZ. This form is shorter and easier to use than Form 2106. Generally you can use this form if:

- All reimbursements, if any, were included in box 1 of your Form W-2, and
- You are using the standard mileage rate if you are claiming vehicle expenses.

If you do not meet both of these requirements, use Form 2106.

Performing Artists and Fee-Basis Officials

If you are a qualified performing artist, or a state (or local) government official who is paid in whole or in part on a fee basis, you can deduct the cost of your qualifying work-related education as an adjustment to gross income rather than as an itemized deduction.

Include the cost of your qualifying work-related education with any other employee business expenses on Form 1040, line 24. You do not have to itemize your deductions on Schedule A (Form 1040), and, therefore, the deduction is not subject to the 2%-of-adjusted-gross-income limit. You must complete Form 2106 or 2106-EZ to figure your deduction, even if you meet the requirements described earlier under *Form not required*.

For more information on qualified performing artists, see Publication 463.

Impairment-Related Work Expenses

If you are disabled and have impairment-related work expenses that are necessary for you to be able to get qualifying work-related education, you can deduct these expenses on Schedule A (Form 1040), line 27. They are not subject to the 2%-of-adjusted-gross-income limit. To deduct these expenses, you must complete Form 2106 or 2106-EZ, even if you meet the requirements, described earlier, under *Form not required*.

For more information on impairment-related work expenses, see Publication 463.

Recordkeeping

You must keep records as proof of any deduction claimed on your tax return. Generally, you should keep your records for 3 years from the date of filing the tax return and claiming the deduction.

For specific information about keeping records of business expenses, see *Recordkeeping* in chapter 28.

TAXORGANIZER

Records you should keep.

- Job descriptions and other employer-provided materials that would set forth the educational requirements of your job
- Tuition statements and canceled checks
- Receipts for books, supplies, lab fees, and the like
- Records of travel, transportation, lodging, and meal expenses related to education and training activity

Miscellaneous Deductions

Note: The 2004 IRS Publication 17 (Your Federal Income Tax) has been updated by Ernst & Young LLP for 2005. Dates and dollar amounts shown are for 2005. Gray type is used to indicate where IRS text has been updated or intentionally omitted. Unrevised IRS text is shown in black type.

Introduction

This chapter covers a variety of expenses, some of which are deductible on your tax return and some of which are not. Deductible expenses can be broadly broken down into three categories: deductible employee expenses, deductible expenses of producing or collecting income, and other deductible expenses. The general rule is that you may deduct any "ordinary and necessary" expense that is related to your trade or business, that is connected

with producing or collecting other taxable income, or that is paid to determine your tax. Note, however, that your deductions may be limited depending on the type of the expense and your income level. (See discussion below regarding Deductions Subject to the 2% Limit *and Chapter 31,* Limit on Itemized Deductions, *for more information.)*

Nondeductible expenses, by definition, are all expenses

that are not deductible. These expenses are typically personal in nature. The nondeductible expenses discussed in this chapter are not all-inclusive, but rather reflect the more common expenses that people may think are (or should be) deductible.

With proper planning, you may be able to deduct more than you think. Be sure to take note of the special comments throughout this chapter with respect to documenting the appropriateness of your deductions, and check out the list at the front of the book for 50 of the Most Easily Overlooked Deductions to be sure you haven't missed anything.

Reminder

Limit on itemized deductions. For 2005, if your adjusted gross income is more than $145,950 ($72,975 if you are married filing separately), you may have to reduce the amount of certain itemized deductions, including most miscellaneous deductions. See chapter 31 for more information.

This chapter explains which expenses you can claim as miscellaneous itemized deductions on Schedule A (Form 1040). You must reduce the total of most miscellaneous itemized deductions by 2% of your adjusted gross income. This chapter covers the following topics.

- Deductions subject to the 2% limit.
- Deductions not subject to the 2% limit.
- Expenses you cannot deduct.

You must keep records to verify your deductions. You should keep receipts, canceled checks, financial account statements, and other documentary evidence. For more information on recordkeeping, get Publication 552, Recordkeeping for Individuals.

Useful Items

You may want to see:

Publications

☐ **529** Miscellaneous Deductions
☐ **535** Business Expenses
☐ **587** Business Use of Your Home (Including Use by Day-Care Providers)
☐ **946** How To Depreciate Property

Forms (and Instructions)

☐ **2106** Employee Business Expenses
☐ **2106-EZ** Unreimbursed Employee Business Expenses

Deductions Subject to the 2% Limit

You can deduct certain expenses as miscellaneous itemized deductions on Schedule A (Form 1040). You can claim the amount of expenses that is more than 2% of your adjusted gross income. You figure your deduction on Schedule A by subtracting 2% of your adjusted gross income from the total amount of these expenses. Your adjusted gross income is the amount on line 37, Form 1040.

Generally, you apply the 2% limit after you apply any other deduction limit. For example, you apply the 50% (or 70%) limit on business-related meals and entertainment (discussed in chapter 28) before you apply the 2% limit.

Explanation
2% limitation. First, you must determine which expenses are deductible. Next, you must calculate the amount that is deductible, taking into account any limitation for certain types of expenses (e.g., 50% for meals and entertainment). The sum of all of your allowable miscellaneous deductions is then reduced by 2% of your adjusted gross income (AGI) on Schedule A.

Example
Assume an individual's adjusted gross income is $45,000 in 2005. This person paid $1,500 in 2005 for the preparation of his 2004 income tax returns and also had $200 of unreimbursed business-related meal expenses in 2005. Both of these expenses are deductible. The $1,500 tax preparation fee is fully deductible, whereas only 50% of the $200 meal expense is deductible. Therefore, total miscellaneous deductions are $1,600 ($1,500 + (50% × $200). However, 2% of the individual's AGI is $900 ($45,000 × 2%), so he is permitted a deduction of only $700 ($1,600 of total allowable deductions reduced by 2% of AGI, or $900).

Deductions subject to the 2% limit are discussed in the three categories in which you report them on Schedule A.

1. Unreimbursed employee expenses (line 20).
2. Tax preparation fees (line 21).
3. Other expenses (line 22).

Impairment-related work expenses. If you have a physical or mental disability, certain expenses you incur that allow you to work may not be subject to the 2% limit. See *Impairment-Related Work Expenses* under *Deductions Not Subject to the 2% Limit*, later.

Performing artists. If you are a qualified performing artist, you may be able to deduct your employee business expenses as an adjustment to income rather than as a miscellaneous itemized deduction. See *Special Rules* in chapter 28 if you need more information about this exception.

State and local government officials paid on a fee basis. If you performed services as an employee of a state or local government and you were paid in whole or in part on a fee basis, you can claim your trade or business expenses in performing those services as an adjustment to income, rather than as a miscellaneous deduction. See *Officials Paid on a Fee Basis* under *Deductions Not Subject to the 2% Limit*, later.

Armed Forces reservists. If you are a member of a reserve component of the Armed Forces of the United States, and you travel more than 100 miles away from home in connection with your performance of services as a member of the reserves, you may be able to deduct some of your reserve-related travel costs as an adjustment to gross income rather than as an itemized deduction. For more information, see *Armed Forces Reservists Traveling More Than 100 Miles From Home*, under *Deductions Not Subject to the 2% Limit*, later.

Educators. If you were an eligible educator in 2005, you can deduct up to $250 of qualified expenses you paid in 2005 as an adjustment to income rather than as an itemized deduction. See *Educator Expenses* in chapter 21.

Unreimbursed Employee Expenses (Line 20)

You can deduct only unreimbursed employee expenses that are:

1. Paid or incurred during your tax year,
2. For carrying on your trade or business of being an employee, and
3. Ordinary and necessary.

An expense is ordinary if it is common and accepted in your type of trade or business. An expense is necessary if it is appropriate and helpful to your trade or business.

Explanation
Unreimbursed employee business expenses. If you are an employee and have business expenses either that are not reimbursed or that are more than the amount reimbursed by your employer, you can generally deduct them only as a miscellaneous deduction (subject to the 2% adjusted gross income limit) on Schedule A (Form 1040).

TAXPLANNER

If you can get your employer to reimburse you for what would otherwise be unreimbursed business expenses, in lieu of an equal amount of future salary, you should do so. You benefit at no additional cost to your employer because reimbursed employee business expenses for which you have adequately accounted to your employer are deductible by your employer the same as wages. However, the reimbursement for those expenses is not included on your Form W-2 as income, so your tax liability should be less. This only works if you give up your right to receive payment in the event you don't incur any business expenses.

Examples of unreimbursed employee expenses are listed next. The list is followed by discussions of additional unreimbursed employee expenses.

- Business bad debt of an employee.
- Education that is work related. (See chapter 29.)
- Legal fees related to your job.
- Licenses and regulatory fees.
- Malpractice insurance premiums.
- Medical examinations required by an employer.
- Occupational taxes.
- Passport for a business trip.
- Subscriptions to professional journals and trade magazines related to your work.
- Travel, transportation, entertainment, and gifts related to your work. (See chapter 28.)

Explanation
Business bad debt of an employee. A business bad debt is a loss from a debt created or acquired in your trade or business, or a loss when there is a very close relationship between the debt and your trade or business when the debt is created (e.g., as an employee, your main motive for creating the debt is a business reason). For example, if an employee makes a bona fide loan to his employer in order to keep his job, and the company fails to pay the debt, the employee has a business bad debt. See Publication 535 for more information on business bad debts.

Explanation
Business travel and entertainment. Generally, only 50% of the amount spent for business meals (including meals away from home on overnight business) and entertainment will be deductible. This limit must be applied before arriving at the amount subject to the 2% of AGI limitation.

TAXALERT

You are not allowed to deduct the travel expenses of family members, even if there is a business purpose for their presence on the trip, unless the family member is also an employee. If your employer reimburses you for travel expenses, the portion of the expense attributable to family members who are not employees of the company may be included in your W-2 income. See Chapter 28, *Car Expenses and Other Employee Business Expenses*, for more information about travel expenses.

TAXALERT

The deduction percentage for meals consumed while away from home by individuals subject to hours of service limitations of the Department of Transportation, such as interstate truck and bus drivers, certain railroad employees, and certain merchant marines, is 70% in 2005. The deduction percentage will increase to 75% in 2006 and 2007 and to 80% by 2008. Note that you must apply this percentage before applying the 2% of AGI limitation.

TAXORGANIZER

Records you should keep. Adequate records should be kept for the amount of your travel and entertainment expenses—the time and place they occurred, the business purpose of the expenses, and the business relationship to the persons entertained—in order for you to substantiate your deduction.

Explanation
Business gifts. You can deduct no more than $25 for business gifts to any one person per year. See Chapter 28, *Car Expenses and Other Employee Business Expenses*, for more information.

Business Liability Insurance
You can deduct insurance premiums you paid for protection against personal liability for wrongful acts on the job.

Damages for Breach of Employment Contract
If you break an employment contract, you can deduct damages you pay your former employer that are attributable to the pay you received from that employer.

Depreciation on Computers or Cellular Telephones
You can claim a depreciation deduction for a computer or cellular telephone that you use in your work as an employee if its use is:

1. For the convenience of your employer, and
2. Required as a condition of your employment.

Explanation
"For the convenience of your employer" means that your use of the computer or cellular telephone is for a substantial business reason of your employer. All facts

must be considered in making this determination. The use of your computer or cellular phone during your regular working hours to carry on your employer's business is generally for the convenience of your employer.

"Required as a condition of your employment" means that you cannot properly perform your duties without it. Whether or not you can properly perform your duties without the computer or cellular telephone depends on all the facts and circumstances. It is not necessary that your employer explicitly requires you to use your computer or cellular telephone. But neither is it sufficient that your employer merely states that your use of these items is a condition of your employment.

Example
You are an engineer with an engineering firm. You occasionally take work home at night rather than work late at the office. You own and use a computer that is similar to the one you use at the office to complete your work at home. Because your use of the computer is not for the convenience of your employer and is not required as a condition of your employment, you cannot claim a deduction.

TaxAlert
Which depreciation method you may use depends on whether or not your computer or cellular telephone is used predominantly (more than 50%) for business or personal purposes. See Publication 529 for more information.

TaxAlert
The rules for depreciation on a computer that you use in your work as an employee differ from the rules for depreciation on a computer owned or leased and used only in your home office. See the section below relating to home office and Publication 529 for more information.

TaxPlanner
Personal computers. Home computers are frequently used for both business and personal purposes. Video games, children's homework, holiday card lists, and personal finances are considered personal uses. If you don't have a separate personal computer and a separate business computer, some type of allocation should be made between business use and personal use of the same computer.

The point to remember is that it is difficult to claim a deduction for your home computer. The IRS position is that no deduction will be allowed for a personal computer unless it meets the "for the convenience of your employer" and "required as a condition of your employment" tests described above.

TaxOrganizer
Records you should keep. Adequate records must be maintained to support your business use of the property in order to claim a depreciation expense deduction.

In case the IRS challenges your deductions for depreciation on home computers or cellular telephones, you should keep the following information to support your claim for home computer and cellular telephone depreciation deductions:

- Documentation from your employer that use of the home computer or cellular telephone is required by the employer
- A log of time spent using the computer or cellular phone and whether such time was for personal or business use

For details on allowable methods of depreciation, see Chapter 10, *Rental Income and Expenses.* The Section 179 deduction is explained in Chapter 39, *If You Are Self-Employed: How to File Schedule C.*

For more information about the rules and exceptions to the rules affecting the allowable deductions for a home computer or cellular telephone, see Publication 529.

Dues to Chambers of Commerce and Professional Societies
You may be able to deduct dues paid to professional organizations (such as bar associations and medical associations) and to chambers of commerce and similar organizations, if membership helps you carry out the duties of your job. Similar organizations include:

- Boards of trade,
- Business leagues,
- Civic or public service organizations,
- Real estate boards, and
- Trade associations.

You cannot deduct dues paid to an organization if one of its main purposes is to:

1. Conduct entertainment activities for members or their guests, or
2. Provide members or their guests with access to entertainment facilities.

Dues paid to airline, hotel, and luncheon clubs are not deductible. See *Club Dues* under *Nondeductible Expenses*, later.
Lobbying and political activities. You may not be able to deduct that part of your dues that is for certain lobbying and political activities. See *Dues used for lobbying* under *Lobbying Expenses,* later.

Educator Expenses Over Limit
If you were an educator in 2005 and you had qualified expenses that were more than you can deduct on Form 1040, line 23, you can deduct the rest as an itemized deduction subject to the 2% limit. See *Educator Expenses* in chapter 21.

Home Office
If you use a part of your home regularly and exclusively for business purposes, you may be able to deduct a part of the operating expenses and depreciation of your home.

TaxAlert
Home office deduction. It is now easier for taxpayers to claim a home office deduction. *Even if you were not able to claim a home office deduction in prior years and your business use of your home has not changed, you should check again to see if you are able to take a deduction.*

Explanation
Individuals claiming home office deductions on Schedule C are required to figure those deductions on Form 8829, *Expenses for Business Use of Your Home.* However, if you are an employee claiming unreimbursed job-related expenses, use Form 2106, *Employee Business Expenses,* if applicable, or include the amount directly on Schedule A.

You can claim this deduction for the business use of a part of your home only if you use that part of your home regularly and exclusively:

1. As your principal place of business for any trade or business,
2. As a place to meet or deal with your patients, clients, or customers in the normal course of your trade or business, or
3. In the case of a separate structure not attached to your home, in connection with your trade or business.

Explanation
A home may be a house, an apartment, a condominium, a mobile home, or even a boat. It may also be other structures on the same property as the house you live in, such as a studio, a barn, a greenhouse, or an unattached garage.

The regular and exclusive business use must be for the convenience of your employer and not just appropriate and helpful in your job. Get Publication 587 for more detailed information and a worksheet.

Explanation
A home office deduction will only be allowed if you use your home in connection with a **trade or business.** All profit-seeking activities are not trades or businesses (e.g., if you invest from home and are not a broker or dealer investing on behalf of clients or are not a "trader," you are not in the business of investing). However, you may take a home office deduction for a trade or business that is not your full-time occupation, as long as all of the appropriate tests are met (an example would be an attorney who uses his home office for the management of rental properties he owns).

Once the trade or business test is met, the remaining tests for qualifying for a home office deduction are:

1. The "principal place of business" test
2. The "regular and exclusive use" test
3. If an employee, the "for the convenience of your employer" test

The deduction is then limited to your gross income from your trade or business.

TAXPLANNER

Principal place of business. Administrative and management activities for your trade or business that are performed exclusively and regularly in your home will qualify your home as your **principal place of business** if you have no other fixed location where you perform substantial administrative or management activities. Activities that are considered administrative or managerial include billing clients, customers, or patients; keeping books and records; ordering supplies; setting up appointments; and writing reports.

In addition, certain administrative and management activities may be performed in other locations and *not* disqualify your home office as your principal place of business for purposes of meeting the above test. For example, you may hire another person or company to perform your administrative activities, such as computing employee payrolls, at locations other than your home. You may also conduct administrative and management activities at places that are not fixed locations, such as hotel rooms or airports, and you may occasionally conduct minimal administrative and managerial activities at a fixed location outside of your home. Also, performing substantial nonadministrative activities outside of your home, such as servicing clients or making sales calls, will not disqualify your home as your principal place of business. And, significantly, you may even have suitable space available to you outside your home for performing administrative and managerial tasks but choose to use your home in-stead. (Note, however, that if you are an employee, any use of your home must be for the convenience of your employer in order to qualify for the home office deduction.)

Example
Jeff is a self-employed anesthesiologist, working for three different local hospitals. One of the hospitals provides him with a small shared office where he could perform administrative or management activities. However, Jeff prefers to use a room in his home as an office. He regularly and exclusively uses this room to schedule patients, maintain patient logs, bill patients, and read medical journals.

Prior to 2000, Jeff's home office did not qualify as his principal place of business because his most important activity, administering anesthetics, was performed in the hospitals. Under the current rules, Jeff's office qualifies for the home office deduction in 2005 (i.e., his home office will qualify as his principal place of business) because he conducts administrative and managerial activities for his business there and has no other fixed location where these activities take place. Neither the fact that Jeff has available space at the hospital for performing administrative tasks nor the fact that his most important task is performed outside of his home disqualifies his home office as his principal place of business.

Explanation
To qualify for the **regular and exclusive use** test, you must use a specific area of your home *only* for your trade or business and on a continuing basis. The specific area can be a separate room or any identifiable space (the space does not need to be marked off by a permanent enclosure). Any personal use of the space will cause you to fail the requirements of the exclusive use test. Occasional or incidental use will cause you to fail the regular use test, even if that area of your house is not used for any other purposes.

Exceptions
Note that there is an exception to the regular and exclusive use test if you use part of your home as a day-care facility for children, persons age 65 or older, or individuals who are physically or mentally incapable of caring for themselves. The day-care provider must be licensed or certified under applicable state law, or exempt from licensing, for the exception to apply. There is also an exception to the regular and exclusive use test if you use part of your home to store inventory or product samples. If your home is the principal place of your business, the space used for inventory and sample storage qualifies for the home office deduction as long as it is used regularly, but not necessarily exclusively, for business.

TAXPLANNER

Many home sales operations require a great deal of personal time and attention but produce a minimum of deductible expenses. The storage use concept may produce valuable deductions for otherwise underutilized spaces, such as attics and basements. Remember, the storage space must be a specific area that is used as a part of your principal place of business.

TAXSAVER

Day-care providers. Day-care providers who operate businesses in their homes may benefit from a recent IRS ruling. The square footage of a room that is regularly used for day care and is available throughout the business day will be considered used for day care for the entire business day. Previously, taxpayers had to take partial days based on the hours of actual business use. The deduction for day-care providers is equal to the total costs of maintaining the home (e.g., electricity, gas, water, trash collection, general maintenance) to provide day care, multiplied by the following two fractions:

$$\frac{\text{Total square feet available and used regularly each day}}{\text{Total square feet of home}}$$

$$\frac{\text{Total hours each year home used for day-care business}}{\text{Total hours each year (8,760 hours in 2005)}}$$

The resulting deduction is subject to the income limitation, discussed below. IRS Form 8829 will help you work through this calculation.

Example
A day-care provider uses a bedroom (available for child care throughout the business day) for the children's morning and afternoon naps every day. Although the bedroom is not used during every hour of the business day, the total square footage of that room is considered as day-care usage for the entire business day when the total area for business is calculated.

Explanation
If you are an employee and you meet the above tests for the use of your home in your trade or business, you will only qualify for a home office deduction if your use of your home is for the **convenience of your employer** and you do not rent your home office to your employer. It is not sufficient that a home office is helpful to your job; it must be a requirement of your employer. Your home office must also be justified by the nature of your job, which depends on all the facts and circumstances.

How to figure the deduction. To figure the percentage of your home used for business, you may compare the square feet of space used for business to the total square feet in your home. Or, if the rooms in your home are approximately the same size, you may compare the number of rooms used for business to the total number of rooms in your home. You may also use any other reasonable method. Generally, you figure the business part of your expenses by applying the percentage to the total of each expense.

Example
The room in your home that you use for business measures 120 square feet. Your home measures 1,200 square feet. Therefore, you are using one-tenth, or 10%, of the total area for business.

If you use one room for business in a five-room house and the rooms in your home are about the same size, you are using one-fifth, or 20%, of the total area for business.

Basing the deduction on an approximation of the rental costs of comparable office space is not a proper method, according to one court ruling.

Explanation
The general rule is that the expenses you have for maintaining and running your entire home may be taken, in part, as deductions, because they benefit both the business and the personal parts of your home.

If you have purchased your home, you may deduct part of the interest you pay on your home mortgage as a business expense. To figure the business part of your mortgage interest, multiply the mortgage interest by the part of your home used for business. If you rent a home, you may deduct part of the rent you pay using a similar calculation.

If you have a casualty loss (see Chapter 27, *Casualty and Theft Losses*) on your home or other property that you use in business, you may deduct the business part of the loss as a business expense. The amount of the loss that qualifies for a deduction depends on what property is affected. If the loss is sustained on property that you use only in your business, the entire loss is treated as a business deduction. If the loss affects property used for both business and personal purposes, only the business part is a business deduction.

If you use part of your home for business, you may also deduct part of the expenses for utilities and services, such as electricity, gas, trash removal, and cleaning services. Expenses that are related only to your business, such as business long-distance telephone calls and depreciation of office furniture and equipment, are fully deductible.

Likewise, if you use part of your home for business, you may deduct part of your insurance on your home. However, if your insurance premium gives you coverage for a period that extends past the end of your tax year, you may deduct for business only the part of the premium that covers you for the tax year.

Example
If you paid a 2-year premium of $240 on September 1, 2005, only 4 months of the policy are included in your 2005 tax year. Therefore, only four twenty-fourths (1/6) of the premium may be used to figure your deduction in 2005. In 2006, you may use twelve twenty-fourths (1/2), and in 2007 eight twenty-fourths (1/3) would be used to figure your deduction. The premium must then be allocated between business and nonbusiness uses of your home.

Explanation
When it comes to repairs, you may deduct the cost of labor and supplies for the business part of your home. Your own labor, however, is not a deductible expense.

You can deduct part of the cost of painting the outside of your home or repairing the roof based on the percentage of your home used for business. However, you cannot deduct expenses for lawn care and landscaping.

Example
A repair to your furnace benefits the entire home. If 10% of the area of your home is used for business, 10% of the cost of the furnace repair is deductible.

Depreciation. You can deduct depreciation on the part of your home used for business subject to the *limit on the deduction* discussed above.

Home leased to employer. If you lease any part of your home to your employer, you cannot claim a home office deduction for that part for any period you use that part of your home to perform services for your employer. However, you may want to see Chapter 10, *Rental Income and Expenses,* as well as Publication 527, *Residential Rental Property,* for information on deducting rental expenses.

Income limitation. Deductions for the business use of your home may not create or add to a business loss. Therefore, if the total gross income for your business exceeds all of your business expenses (both direct business expenses and the expenses you have allocated for the use of a home office), you may deduct all of your expenses. However, if your business expenses exceed your gross business income, your deduction of certain expenses may be limited. You can carry any excess business expenses that are not currently deductible over to the next tax year, assuming that you have income from the business in the next tax year. If you do not have income from the business in the next tax year, the deductions may be carried to any later year in which you have gross income from the business.

Explanation
Your business deductions for the business use of your home are deducted in the following order:

1. The business percentage of the expenses that would otherwise be allowable as deductions, that is, mortgage interest, real estate taxes, and deductible casualty losses.
2. The direct expenses for your business in your home, such as expenses for supplies and compensation, but not the other expenses of the office in your home (such as those listed in item 3, below).
3. The other expenses for the business use of your home, such as maintenance, utilities, insurance, and depreciation. Deductions that adjust the basis in your home are taken last.

Example
Peggy Green is an employee who works in her home for the convenience of her employer. She uses 20% of her home regularly and exclusively for this business purpose. In 2005, her gross income, expenses for the business, and computation of the deduction for the business use of her home are as follows:

Gross income from business use of home		$7,500
Minus:		
Business percentage (20% of home use) of mortgage interest and real estate taxes	2,000	
Other business expenses (supplies, transportation, etc.)	5,000	$7,000
Modified net income		$ 500
Business use of home expenses		
Maintenance, insurance, utilities (20%)		$ 800
Depreciation (20%)		700
Total		$1,500
Deduction limited to modified net income		500
Carryover expenses to 2006 (subject to income limitation in 2006)		$1,000

The deduction of $500 is considered to be maintenance, insurance, and utilities. Peggy will not reduce the basis in her home for the $700 of depreciation until that amount is deducted in a future year.

TaxOrganizer

Records you should keep. If you intend to deduct home office expenses, it is extremely important that you keep adequate records. You should keep records of clients who come to your house, hours worked at home, type of work done at home, and office equipment purchases. Additionally, you should keep track of repairs that can be allocated to your home office. See the *Records You Should Keep* section at the front of this book for other items that you should keep.

For more information on using your home in your work and how to compute your allowable deduction, get Publication 587.

Job Search Expenses
You can deduct certain expenses you have in looking for a new job in your present occupation, even if you do not get a new job.

You cannot deduct these expenses if:

1. You are looking for a job in a new occupation,
2. There was a substantial break between the ending of your last job and your looking for a new one, or
3. You are looking for a job for the first time.

Examples
- A certified public accountant employed by a national accounting firm was permitted to deduct expenses incurred in investigating whether or not he could practice his profession as a **self-employed** person.
- A corporate executive could deduct expenses involved in seeking a position as a corporate executive with another corporation.
- An attorney for a state agency could deduct the costs of taking an examination for a position as an attorney in another city because the new position would be in the same trade or business.
- An unemployed electrician was allowed to deduct transportation costs for going to the union hall to check on potential job opportunities. He was considered to be in the electrical trade, even though he was unemployed at the time.

Employment and outplacement agency fees. You can deduct employment and outplacement agency fees you pay in looking for a new job in your present occupation.

Employer pays you back. If, in a later year, your employer pays you back for employment agency fees, you must include the amount you receive in your gross income up to the amount of your tax benefit in the earlier year. (See *Recoveries* in chapter 13.)

Employer pays the employment agency. If your employer pays the fees directly to the employment agency and you are not responsible for them, you do not include them in your gross income.

Explanation
Job search expenses and fees are deductible, even if the agency does not find you a suitable job.

Expenses for career counseling are deductible if they are incurred in your effort to find other employment in the same trade or business.

Résumé. You can deduct amounts you spend for typing, printing, and mailing copies of a résumé to prospective employers if you are looking for a new job in your present occupation.

Travel and transportation expenses. If you travel to an area and, while there, you look for a new job in your present occupation, you may be able to deduct travel expenses to and from the area. You can deduct the travel expenses if the trip is primarily to look for a new job. The amount of time you spend on personal activity compared to the amount of time you spend in looking for work is important in determining whether the trip is primarily personal or is primarily to look for a new job.

Even if you cannot deduct the travel expenses to and from an area, you can deduct the expenses of looking for a new job in your present occupation while in the area.

You may choose to use the standard mileage rate to figure your car expenses. The standard mileage rate for 2005 is 40.5 cents per mile through August, 48.5 cents per mile after August 31, 2005. See chapter 28 for more information.

TaxOrganizer

Records you should keep. In case the IRS challenges your deduction for job search expenses, you should keep the following information to support your claim for job search expense deductions:

- Evidence of your current occupation at the time the job search expenses were incurred
- Written records, such as a letter from a prospective employer or an employment agency contract, evidencing a search for employment and the nature of the job
- Receipts, canceled checks, credit card slips, plane tickets, and the like, evidencing the amount and payment of job search expenses
- Detailed records and evidence of costs, such as automobile mileage, for which a direct payment is not made
- A log allocating the time spent while traveling on personal activities compared to the time spent looking for a job

Licenses and Regulatory Fees
You can deduct the amount you pay each year to state or local governments for licenses and regulatory fees for your trade, business, or profession.

Occupational Taxes
You can deduct an occupational tax charged at a flat rate by a locality for the privilege of working or conducting a business in the locality. If you are an employee, you can claim occupational taxes only as a miscellaneous deduction subject to the 2% limit; you cannot claim them as a deduction for taxes elsewhere on your return.

Repayment of Income Aid Payment
An "income aid payment" is one that is received under an employer's plan to aid employees who lose their jobs because of lack of work. If you repay a lump-sum income aid payment that you received and included in income in an earlier year, you can deduct the repayment.

Research Expenses of a College Professor
If you are a college professor, you can deduct research expenses, including travel expenses, for teaching, lecturing, or writing and publishing on subjects that relate directly to the field of your teaching duties. You must have undertaken the research as a means of carrying out the duties expected of a professor and without expectation of profit apart from salary. However, you cannot deduct the cost of travel as a form of education.

Explanation
Travel as a form of education is never deductible. An example would be a French teacher who, in order to learn more about local customs in France, travels throughout the country. The travel in this case is not for research in writing or publishing and the person did not teach while traveling. Travel as a form of education tends to resemble travel for personal purposes, and the IRS will disallow a deduction for travel expenses as a form of educational expenses. See Chapter 29, *Tax Benefits for Work-Related Education,* for more information on educational expenses that are deductible.

Tools Used in Your Work
Generally, you can deduct amounts you spend for tools used in your work if the tools wear out and are thrown away within 1 year from the date of purchase. You can depreciate the cost of tools that have a useful life substantially beyond the tax year. For more information about depreciation, see Publication 946.

Union Dues and Expenses
You can deduct dues and initiation fees you pay for union membership.

You can also deduct assessments for benefit payments to unemployed union members. However, you cannot deduct the part of the assessments or contributions that provides funds for the payment of sick, accident, or death benefits. Also, you cannot deduct contributions to a pension fund, even if the union requires you to make the contributions.

You may not be able to deduct amounts you pay to the union that are related to certain lobbying and political activities. See *Lobbying Expenses* under *Nondeductible Expenses,* later.

Explanation
A fine paid by a union member is deductible if by not paying the fine the member would be dropped from the union:

If a union contract provides that all employees, regardless of whether or not they are union members, must pay union dues, the nonmembers may also deduct the union dues.

Work Clothes and Uniforms
You can deduct the cost and upkeep of work clothes if the following two requirements are met.

1. You must wear them as a condition of your employment.
2. The clothes are not suitable for everyday wear.

Caution. *It is not enough that you wear distinctive clothing. The clothing must be specifically required by your employer. Nor is it enough that you do not, in fact, wear your work clothes away from work. The clothing must not be suitable for taking the place of your regular clothing.*

Examples of workers who may be able to deduct the cost and upkeep of work clothes are: delivery workers, firefighters, health care workers, law enforcement officers, letter carriers, professional athletes, and transportation workers (air, rail, bus, etc.).

Musicians and entertainers can deduct the cost of theatrical clothing and accessories if they are not suitable for everyday wear.

However, work clothing consisting of white cap, white shirt or white jacket, white bib overalls, and standard work shoes, which a painter is required by his union to wear on the job, is not distinctive in character or in the nature of a uniform. Similarly, the costs of buying and maintaining blue work clothes worn by a welder at the request of a foreman are not deductible.

Protective clothing. You can deduct the cost of protective clothing required in your work, such as safety shoes or boots, safety glasses, hard hats, and work gloves.

Examples of workers who may be required to wear safety items are: carpenters, cement workers, chemical workers, electricians, fishing boat crew members, machinists, oil field workers, pipe fitters, steamfitters, and truck drivers.

Military uniforms. You generally cannot deduct the cost of your uniforms if you are on full-time active duty in the armed forces. However, if you are an armed forces reservist, you can deduct the unreimbursed cost of your uniform if military regulations restrict you from wearing it except while on duty as a reservist. In figuring the deduction, you must reduce the cost by any nontaxable allowance you receive for these expenses.

If local military rules do not allow you to wear fatigue uniforms when you are off duty, you can deduct the amount by which the cost of buying and keeping up these uniforms is more than the uniform allowance you receive.

You can deduct the cost of your uniforms if you are a civilian faculty or staff member of a military school.

Explanation
The initial expense and the costs of maintaining work clothes and business uniforms are deductible, not only if they must be worn as a condition of employment and they are not suitable for general or personal use but also if they are in fact not used for personal purposes. Taxpayers have been allowed to deduct costs relating to uniforms in the following cases:

- An art teacher deducted the costs of protective smocks.
- An airline clerk deducted the cost of "unfeminine, businesslike" shoes that she was required to wear and, in fact, wore only at work.
- A hospital worker deducted work clothes he kept in a locker at the hospital. He was in frequent contact with contagious persons and never brought the clothing home.
- A private-duty nurse deducted a uniform that served as a mark of her profession and was necessary for patient care.
- A member of the National Ski Patrol was allowed to deduct the cost of the parkas and ski trousers patrol members are required to wear.
- Scoutmasters, Red Cross volunteers, and others who wear uniforms while performing charitable activities may deduct the cost of the uniforms as charitable donations.

Tax Preparation Fees (Line 21)

You can usually deduct tax preparation fees in the year you pay them. Thus, on your 2005 return, you can deduct fees paid in 2005 for preparing your 2004 return. These fees include the cost of tax preparation software programs and tax publications. They also include any fee you paid for electronic filing of your return. However, if you paid your tax by credit card, you cannot deduct the convenience fee you were charged.

Deduct expenses of preparing tax schedules relating to profit or loss from business (Schedule C or C-EZ), rentals or royalties (Schedule E), or farm income and expenses (Schedule F) on the appropriate schedule. Deduct the expenses of preparing the remainder of the return on line 21, Schedule A (Form 1040).

Explanation
You may deduct expenses paid for the determination, collection, or refund of any tax—income tax, estate tax, gift tax, sales tax, or property tax. Fees paid to a consultant to advise you on the tax consequences of a transaction are deductible. If you contest a tax assessment, any fees you pay are deductible, even if the defense is unsuccessful. Professional fees incurred in obtaining federal tax rulings are deductible. However, the cost of filing a complaint in court relating to an IRS levy against property is considered a capital expenditure and therefore not currently deductible.

TaxPlanner

Business related. Generally, most tax preparation fees are only deductible on Schedule A and are subject to the 2% adjusted gross income floor and the overall limitation on itemized deductions. However, according to the IRS, business owners can deduct the portion of tax preparation fees relating to a business directly on Schedule C, E, or F (and related business schedules).

TaxOrganizer

In order to minimize controversy with the IRS over what portion of tax preparation fees applies to each activity, it's best to have your tax advisor give you a detailed breakdown of your bill, indicating the amounts attributable to each activity.

Example
Mark, an individual taxpayer, owns a consulting business and rental property. In 2005, he paid $900 in tax preparation fees, of which $400 was related to the consulting business, $300 to the rental property, and $200 to his individual return. Mark can deduct $400 as a business expense on Schedule C, $300 as a business expense on Schedule E, and $200 as a miscellaneous itemized deduction (subject to the 2%-adjusted-gross-income floor) on Schedule A.

Other Expenses (Line 22)

You can deduct certain other expenses as miscellaneous itemized deductions subject to the 2%-of-adjusted-gross-income limit. These are expenses you pay:

1. To produce or collect income that must be included in your gross income,
2. To manage, conserve, or maintain property held for producing such income, or
3. To determine, contest, pay, or claim a refund of any tax.

You can deduct expenses you pay for the purposes in (1) and (2) above only if they are reasonably and closely related to these purposes. Some of these other expenses are explained in the following discussions.

If the expenses you pay produce income that is only partially taxable, see *Tax-Exempt Income Expenses,* later, under *Nondeductible Expenses.*

Explanation
Deductions have also been allowed for the following:
- Monthly service charges paid to a bank to participate in an automatic investment service plan
- Service charges subtracted from cash dividends before the dividends are reinvested
- Premiums on indemnity bonds posted to secure replacement of lost taxable securities

- Trustee's commission for administering a revocable trust
- Expenses incurred by an official of the National Association of Investment Clubs in attending conventions
- Transportation and parking costs on trips to the taxpayer's stockbroker
- Packing, moving, and storage expenses of condominium furniture when the only tenant the taxpayer could find wanted the unit unfurnished
- Depreciation on a safe used to store securities and other financial certificates
- Expenses incurred in moving the office in which a taxpayer carries on his or her investment activities to a new location
- Postage related to investment activities
- A fee paid to a broker engaged to find another company that could be merged with the taxpayer's closely held company, even though no company was found
- Safe-deposit box rental when the box was used to store Series EE treasury bonds, even though no income is reportable in the tax year because the taxpayer elected to report the appreciation when the bonds matured (see Chapter 8, *Interest Income,* for details)
- Entertainment expenses in connection with taxable investments
- Investor's payment to a stockholders' committee that sought changes in corporate management
- Travel expenses to a directors' meeting of a director who was also a substantial minority shareholder (The taxpayer feared that the policies of the majority would endanger his investment. Because the expense was incurred to protect his investment, it was deductible.)
- Costs incurred in a proxy fight opposing management
- Fees paid to an attorney for estate planning (but not for the preparation of a will)

You may deduct a reward paid for the return of business property you have lost.

Example
A man left his briefcase on the train. A deduction was allowed for the reward given and for the cost of the ad offering the reward.

Appraisal Fees
You can deduct appraisal fees if you pay them to figure a casualty loss or the fair market value of donated property.

Certain Casualty and Theft Losses
You can deduct a casualty or theft loss as a miscellaneous itemized deduction subject to the 2% limit if you used the damaged or stolen property in performing services as an employee. First report the loss in Section B of Form 4684, Casualties and Thefts. You may also have to include the loss on Form 4797, Sales of Business Property, if you are otherwise required to file that form. To figure your deduction, add all casualty or theft losses from this type of property included on line 32 of Form 4684, line 38b of Form 4684, or line 18a of Form 4797. For other casualty and theft losses, see chapter 27.

Clerical Help and Office Rent
You can deduct office expenses, such as rent and clerical help, that you have in connection with your investments and collecting the taxable income on them.

Depreciation on Home Computer
You can deduct depreciation on your home computer if you use it to produce income (for example, to manage your investments that produce taxable income). You generally must depreciate the computer using the straight line method over the Alternative Depreciation System (ADS) recovery period. But if you work as an employee and also use the computer in that work, see Publication 946.

Excess Deductions of an Estate
If an estate's total deductions in its last tax year are more than its gross income for that year, the beneficiaries succeeding to the estate's property can deduct the excess. Do not include deductions for the estate's personal exemption and charitable contributions when figuring the estate's total deductions. The beneficiaries can claim the deduction only for the tax year in which, or with which, the estate terminates, whether the year of termination is a normal year or a short tax year. For more information, see *Termination of Estate* in Publication 559, Survivors, Executors, and Administrators.

Fees to Collect Interest and Dividends
You can deduct fees you pay to a broker, bank, trustee, or similar agent to collect your taxable bond interest or dividends on shares of stock. But you cannot deduct a fee you pay to a broker to buy investment property, such as stocks or bonds. You must add the fee to the cost of the property.

You cannot deduct the fee you pay to a broker to sell securities. You can use the fee only to figure gain or loss from the sale. See the instructions for columns (d) and (e) of Schedule D (Form 1040) for information on how to report the fee.

Hobby Expenses
You can generally deduct hobby expenses, but only up to the amount of hobby income. A hobby is not a business because it is not carried on to make a profit. See *Activity not for profit* in chapter 13 under *Other Income.*

Indirect Deductions of Pass-Through Entities
Pass-through entities include partnerships, S corporations, and mutual funds that are not publicly offered. Deductions of pass-through entities are passed through to the partners or shareholders. The partners or shareholders can deduct their share of passed-through deductions for investment expenses as miscellaneous itemized deductions subject to the 2% limit.

Example. You are a member of an investment club that is formed solely to invest in securities. The club is treated as a partnership. The partnership's income is solely from taxable dividends, interest, and gains from sales of securities. In this case, you can deduct your share of the partnership's operating expenses as miscellaneous itemized deductions subject to the 2% limit. However, if the investment club partnership has investments that also produce nontaxable income, you cannot deduct your share of the partnership's expenses that produce the nontaxable income.

Publicly offered mutual funds. Publicly offered mutual funds do not pass deductions for investment expenses through to shareholders. A mutual fund is "publicly offered" if it is:

1. Continuously offered pursuant to a public offering,
2. Regularly traded on an established securities market, or
3. Held by or for at least 500 persons at all times during the tax year.

A publicly offered mutual fund will send you a Form 1099-DIV, Dividends and Distributions, or a substitute form, showing the net amount of dividend income (gross dividends minus investment expenses). This net figure is the amount you report on your return as income. You cannot deduct investment expenses.

Information returns. You should receive information returns from pass-through entities.

Partnerships and S corporations. These entities issue Schedule K-1, which lists the items and amounts you must report and identifies the tax return schedules and lines to use.

Nonpublicly offered mutual funds. These funds will send you a Form 1099-DIV, or a substitute form, showing your share of gross income and investment expenses. You can claim the expenses only as a miscellaneous itemized deduction subject to the 2% limit.

Investment Fees and Expenses

You can deduct investment fees, custodial fees, trust administration fees, and other expenses you paid for managing your investments that produce taxable income.

TAXPLANNER

Courts have ruled that trustee fees and trust accounting fees required by state fiduciary law or the trust instrument are not subject to the 2% of adjusted gross income (AGI) rule.

Investment advisory fees paid by a trust may be deducted without consideration of the 2% limitation rule if the trustee could affirmatively establish that the fees would not have been incurred had the trust assets not been held in trust. The trust document has to be carefully structured and take into consideration different state law requirements. The IRS has been challenging this position and the courts are divided on this issue, so a knowledgeable tax advisor should be consulted when taking the deduction.

Legal Expenses

You can usually deduct legal expenses that you incur in attempting to produce or collect taxable income or that you pay in connection with the determination, collection, or refund of any tax.

You can also deduct legal expenses that are:

1. Related to either doing or keeping your job, such as those you paid to defend yourself against criminal charges arising out of your trade or business,
2. For tax advice related to a divorce, if the bill specifies how much is for tax advice and it is determined in a reasonable way, or
3. To collect taxable alimony.

You can deduct expenses of resolving tax issues relating to profit or loss from business (Schedule C or C-EZ), rentals or royalties (Schedule E), or farm income and expenses (Schedule F) on the appropriate schedule. You deduct expenses of resolving nonbusiness tax issues on Schedule A (Form 1040). See *Tax Preparation Fees,* earlier.

Contingent fees related to "civil-rights" type cases which were settled or paid after October 22, 2004 are deducted as an adjustment in calculating adjusted gross income.

TAXPLANNER

Professional fees. Legal, accounting, and professional fees often have deductible and nondeductible elements. Whether professional fees should be deducted, capitalized, or considered personal expenses depends on the reasons the fees were incurred. To be deductible as a miscellaneous expense on Schedule A, the expense must either be connected to producing income (advising you on your employment, collecting alimony, and the like) or be incurred for a tax-related matter.

TAXORGANIZER

Records you should keep. To minimize controversy with the IRS over what portion of a professional fee is deductible, it's best to have the professional give you a detailed breakdown of your bill, indicating which portions are tax-deductible.

TAXSAVER

A tax act in 2004 has made legal and other expenses deductible in calculating adjusted gross income for "civil rights" type lawsuits which are settled or paid after October 22, 2004. For lawsuits settled or paid before October 23, 2004, or non-civil rights type lawsuits, the Supreme Court has held that these expenses are miscellaneous itemized deductions subject to the 2% of adjusted gross income (AGI) floor.

Loss on Deposits

For information on whether, and if so, how, you may deduct a loss on your deposit in a qualified financial institution, see *Deposit in Insolvent or Bankrupt Financial Institution* in chapter 15.

Repayments of Income

If you had to repay an amount that you included in income in an earlier year, you may be able to deduct the amount you repaid. If the amount you had to repay was ordinary income of $3,000 or less, the deduction is subject to the 2% limit. If it was more than $3,000, see *Repayments Under Claim of Right* under *Deductions Not Subject to the 2% Limit,* later.

Repayments of Social Security Benefits

For information on how to deduct your repayments of certain social security benefits, see *Repayments More Than Gross Benefits* in chapter12.

Safe Deposit Box Rentals

You can deduct safe deposit box rent if you use the box to store taxable income-producing stocks, bonds, or investment-related papers and documents. You cannot deduct the rent if you use the box only for jewelry, other personal items, or tax-exempt securities.

Service Charges on Dividend Reinvestment Plans

You can deduct service charges you pay as a subscriber in a dividend reinvestment plan. These service charges include payments for:

1. Holding shares acquired through a plan,
2. Collecting and reinvesting cash dividends, and
3. Keeping individual records and providing detailed statements of accounts.

Trustee's Administrative Fees for IRA

Trustee's administrative fees that are billed separately and paid by you in connection with your individual retirement arrangement (IRA) are deductible (if they are ordinary and necessary) as a miscellaneous itemized deduction subject to the 2% limit. For more information about IRAs, see chapter 18.

TAXSAVER

Administrative fees paid to IRA trustees are deductible if the fees are billed to, and paid by, the account owner separate from any IRA contribution. If the trustee takes the fee out of your $4,000 contribution, your total deduction is less than what it could be (only $4,000 instead of $4,000 plus the trustee's fee); also, you then have less money remaining in the IRA account for investment. Because the income in the IRA account accumulates tax free, the difference in these two amounts—the full $4,000 and the remainder of that sum after fees—compounded annually, becomes significant over the years.

Deductions Not Subject to the 2% Limit

You can deduct the items listed below as miscellaneous itemized deductions. They are not subject to the 2% limit. Report these items on line 27, Schedule A (Form 1040).

List of Deductions

Each of the following items is discussed in detail after the list.

- Amortizable premium on taxable bonds.
- Casualty and theft losses from income-producing property.
- Federal estate tax on income in respect of a decedent.
- Gambling losses up to the amount of gambling winnings.
- Impairment-related work expenses of persons with disabilities.
- Repayments of more than $3,000 under a claim of right.
- Unrecovered investment in an annuity.

Amortizable Premium on Taxable Bonds

In general, if the amount you pay for a bond is greater than its stated principal amount, the excess is bond premium. You can elect to amortize the premium on taxable bonds. The amortization of the premium is generally an offset to interest income on the bond rather than a separate deduction item.

Part of the premium on some bonds may be a miscellaneous deduction not subject to the 2% limit. For more information, see *Amortizable Premium on Taxable Bonds* in Publication 529, and *Bond Premium Amortization* in chapter 3 of Publication 550, Investment Income and Expenses.

TaxORGANIZER

You should keep documentation that shows the date of purchase, face value, and the purchase price of the bond. The types of documents you may want to keep include your broker's confirmation or monthly account statement.

Certain Casualty and Theft Losses

You can deduct a casualty or theft loss as a miscellaneous itemized deduction not subject to the 2% limit if the damaged or stolen property was income-producing property (property held for investment, such as stocks, notes, bonds, gold, silver, vacant lots, and works of art). First, report the loss in Section B of Form 4684. You may also have to include the loss on Form 4797 if you are otherwise required to file that form. To figure your deduction, add all casualty or theft losses from this type of property included on line 32 of Form 4684, line 38b of Form 4684, or line 18a of Form 4797. For more information on casualty and theft losses, see chapter 27.

TaxALERT

Some taxpayers had attempted to take the position that losses from stock which resulted from corporate malfeasance, such as was the case with Enron or WorldCom, could be deducted as theft losses not subject to the 2% of AGI disallowance. The IRS has ruled that this position is incorrect. Because there was no direct relationship between shareholders and the executives of these companies there was no "theft." Instead, the losses would have to be claimed as capital losses subject to the $3,000 annual limit on such losses.

Federal Estate Tax on Income in Respect of a Decedent

You can deduct the federal estate tax attributable to income in respect of a decedent that you as a beneficiary include in your gross income. Income in respect of the decedent is gross income that the decedent would have received had death not occurred and that was not properly includible in the decedent's final income tax return. See Publication 559 for more information.

Gambling Losses Up to the Amount of Gambling Winnings

You must report the full amount of your gambling winnings for the year on Form 1040, line 21. You deduct your gambling losses for the year on line 27, Schedule A (Form 1040). You cannot deduct gambling losses that are more than your winnings.

Caution. *You cannot reduce your gambling winnings by your gambling losses and report the difference. You must report the full amount of your winnings as income and claim your losses (up to the amount of winnings) as an itemized deduction. Therefore, your records should show your winnings separately from your losses.*

Diary of winnings and losses.

You must keep an accurate diary or similar record of your losses and winnings.

Your diary should contain at least the following information.

1. The date and type of your specific wager or wagering activity.
2. The name and address or location of the gambling establishment.
3. The names of other persons present with you at the gambling establishment.
4. The amount(s) you won or lost.

See Publication 529 for more information.

Explanation

For specific wagering transactions, you can use the following items to support your winnings and losses:

Keno: Copies of the keno tickets you purchased that were validated by the gambling establishment, copies of your casino credit records, and copies of your casino check-cashing records.

Slot machines: A record of the machine number and all winnings by date and time the machine was played.

Table games (twenty-one [blackjack], craps, poker, baccarat, roulette, wheel of fortune, etc.): The number of the table at which you were playing and casino credit card data indicating whether the credit was issued in the pit or at the cashier's cage.

Bingo: A record of the number of games played, cost of tickets purchased, and amounts collected on winning tickets. Supplemental records include any receipts from the casino, parlor, and the like.

Racing (horse, harness, dog, etc.): A record of the races, amounts of wagers, amounts collected on winning tickets, and amounts lost on losing tickets. Supplemental records include unredeemed tickets and payment records from the racetrack.

Lotteries: A record of ticket purchases, dates, winnings, and losses. Supplemental records include unredeemed tickets, payment slips, and winnings statements.

TaxALERT

The cost of transportation, meals, and lodging related to gambling is not deductible for tax purposes.

Impairment-Related Work Expenses

If you have a physical or mental disability that limits your being employed, or substantially limits one or more of your major life activities, such as performing manual tasks, walking, speaking, breathing, learning, and working, you can deduct your impairment-related work expenses.

Impairment-related work expenses are ordinary and necessary business expenses for attendant care services at your place of work and for other expenses in connection with your place of work that are necessary for you to be able to work.

Where to report. If you are an employee, you enter impairment-related work expenses on Form 2106 or Form 2106-EZ. Enter on line 27, Schedule A (Form 1040), that part of the amount on line 10 of Form 2106, or line 6 of Form 2106-EZ, that is related to your impairment. Enter the amount that is unrelated to your impairment on line 20, Schedule A (Form 1040).

Repayments Under Claim of Right
If you had to repay more than $3,000 that you included in your income in an earlier year because at the time you thought you had an unrestricted right to it, you may be able to deduct the amount you repaid or take a credit against your tax. See *Repayments* in chapter 13 for more information.

Unrecovered Investment in Annuity
A retiree who contributed to the cost of an annuity can exclude from income a part of each payment received as a tax-free return of the retiree's investment. If the retiree dies before the entire investment is recovered tax free, any unrecovered investment can be deducted on the retiree's final income tax return. See chapter 11 for more information about the tax treatment of pensions and annuities.

TAXSAVER

Performing Artist
If you are a performing artist, you may qualify to deduct your employee business expenses as an adjustment to income rather than as a miscellaneous itemized deduction. To qualify to deduct your expenses as an adjustment income, you must meet all three of the following requirements:

1. You perform services in the performing arts for at least two employers during your tax year.
2. Your related performing-arts business expenses are more than 10% of your gross income from the performance of such services.
3. Your adjusted gross income is not more than $16,000 before deducting these business expenses.

Explanation
You are not considered to have performed services in the performing arts for an employer unless that employer paid you $200 or more.

If you do not meet all of the above requirements, you do not qualify to deduct your expenses as an adjustment to gross income and the expenses are subject to the 2% limit.

Special rules for married persons. If you are married, you must file a joint return unless you lived apart from your spouse at all times during the tax year.

If you file a joint return, you must figure requirements (1) and (2) separately for both you and your spouse. However, requirement (3) applies to your and your spouse's combined adjusted gross income.

Where to report. If you meet all of the above requirements, you should first complete Form 2106 or Form 2106-EZ. Then you include your performing arts–related expenses from line 10 of Form 2106 or from line 6 of 2106-EZ on line 32 of Form 1040. Then print "QPA" and the amount of your performing arts–related expenses on the dotted line next to line 36 (Form 1040).

Officials Paid on a Fee Basis
If you are a fee-basis official, you can claim your expenses in performing services in that job as an adjustment to income rather than as a miscellaneous itemized deduction. To qualify as a fee-basis official, you must be employed by a state or local government and be paid in whole or in part on a fee basis.

Where to report. If you qualify as a fee-basis official, you should first complete Form 2106 or Form 2106-EZ. Then include your expenses in performing services in that job (line 10 of Form 2106 or line 6 of Form 2106-EZ) on line 24 of Form 1040.

Armed Forces Reservists Traveling More Than 100 Miles From Home

If you are a member of a reserve component of the Armed Forces of the United States and you travel more than 100 miles away from home in connection with your performance of services as a member of the reserves, you can deduct your travel expenses as an adjustment to gross income rather than as a miscellaneous itemized deduction. The amount of expenses you can deduct as an adjustment to gross income is limited to the regular federal *per diem* rate (for lodging, meals, and incidental expenses) and the standard mileage rate (for car expenses) plus any parking fees, ferry fees, and tolls. For more information, see Publication 463.

Member of a reserve component. You are a member of a reserve component of the Armed Forces of the United States if you are in the Army, Naval, Marine Corps, Air Force, or Coast Guard Reserve, the Army National Guard of the United States, the Air National Guard of the United States, or the Reserve Corps of the Public Health Service.

Where to report. If you have reserve-related travel that takes you more than 100 miles from home, you should first complete Form 2106 or Form 2106-EZ. Then include your expenses for reserve travel over 100 miles from home, up to the federal rate, from line 10 of Form 2106 or line 6 of Form 2106-EZ in the total on line 24 of Form 1040. Subtract this amount from the total on line 10 of Form 2106 or line 6 of Form 2106-EZ and deduct the balance as an itemized deduction on line 20 of Schedule A (Form 1040).

You cannot deduct expenses of travel that does not take you more than 100 miles from home as an adjustment to gross income. Instead, you must complete Form 2106 or 2106-EZ and deduct those expenses as an itemized deduction on line 20 of Schedule A (Form 1040).

Nondeductible Expenses

Examples of nondeductible expenses are listed next. The list is followed by discussions of additional nondeductible expenses.

List of Nondeductible Expenses

- Broker's commissions that you paid in connection with your IRA or other investment property.
- Burial or funeral expenses, including the cost of a cemetery lot.
- Capital expenses.
- Fees and licenses, such as car licenses, marriage licenses, and dog tags.
- Hobby losses—But see *Hobby Expenses,* earlier.
- Home repairs, insurance, and rent.
- Illegal bribes and kickbacks—See *Bribes and kickbacks* in chapter 13 of Publication 535.
- Losses from the sale of your home, furniture, personal car, etc.
- Personal disability insurance premiums.
- Personal, living, or family expenses.
- The value of wages never received or lost vacation time.

Explanation
Expenses of a general search or preliminary investigation of a business or investment by an individual taxpayer are generally nondeductible.

Exception

While funeral and burial expenses may not be deducted on your personal income tax return, they may be deducted on your federal estate tax return (Form 706). Contributions to a not-for-profit cemetery company may be deductible as charitable contributions.

Adoption Expenses

You cannot deduct the expenses of adopting a child, but you may be able to take a credit for those expenses. See chapter 39.

Campaign Expenses

You cannot deduct campaign expenses of a candidate for any office, even if the candidate is running for reelection to the office. These include qualification and registration fees for primary elections.

Legal fees. You cannot deduct legal fees paid to defend charges that arise from participation in a political campaign.

Check-Writing Fees on Personal Account

If you have a personal checking account, you cannot deduct fees charged by the bank for the privilege of writing checks, even if the account pays interest.

Club Dues

Generally, you cannot deduct the cost of membership in any club organized for business, pleasure, recreation, or other social purpose. This includes business, social, athletic, luncheon, sporting, airline, hotel, golf, and country clubs. For exceptions, see *Dues to Chambers of Commerce and Professional Societies* under *Unreimbursed Employee Expenses,* earlier.

Explanation

No deduction is allowed for club dues if the club is organized for business, pleasure, recreation, or social purposes. These clubs include any organization whose principal purpose is the entertainment of its members or guests. The character of an organization is determined by its purposes and activities, not by its name. For example, no deduction is allowed for dues paid to country clubs, airline clubs, and hotel clubs.

The IRS has specified, however, that some club dues will continue to be deductible under the regular business-use rules. For example, dues paid to trade associations, bar and medical associations, and civic organizations—such as Rotary clubs or Kiwanis clubs—will continue to be deductible as long as the principal purpose of these organizations is not to conduct entertainment activities for their members.

TAXSAVER

Meals and entertainment. Specific business expenses, such as meals and entertainment that occur at a club, are deductible to the extent that they otherwise satisfy the standard for deductibility. For details, see Chapter 28, *Car Expenses and Other Employee Business Expenses.*

Commuting Expenses

You cannot deduct commuting expenses (the cost of transportation between your home and your main or regular place of work). If you haul tools, instruments, or other items, in your car to and from work, you can deduct only the additional cost of hauling the items such as the rent on a trailer to carry the items.

Explanation

Commuting to a temporary work site can be a deductible expense. A work assignment is temporary if the individual has the expectation that it will last less than 1 year, and it actually does last for 1 year or less. If you have a regular place of business away from home, then travel expenses from home to a temporary work site are deductible, regardless of the distance.

An individual who has no regular place of business outside the home (or a home office), but who works at several locations within a metropolitan area, can deduct travel expenses to a temporary work site that is outside the metropolitan area. However, many people now commute as many as 2 hours or more one way. Therefore, the IRS interpretation of a "metropolitan area" is also expanding.

Another increasingly common scenario is an individual who loses his full-time job due to downsizing or outsourcing and subsequently works for several different employers on a part-time basis. This individual has no regular place of business. It is not clear whether his travel to a temporary work site outside the metropolitan area is deductible. A strict interpretation of the rules would indicate that such travel is deductible, because a regular business location is not a consideration. However, the IRS may argue that he has merely extended his personal commute, because he is working for a different employer in each location.

TAXSAVER

If you drive to a location close to home to perform a bona fide job function and then drive to your regular work location, the second leg of the trip is deductible. See Chapter 28, *Car Expenses and Other Employee Business Expenses,* for details.

Example

An accountant drives to the local IRS office to represent clients and then goes to his office downtown later that day. The second leg of his travel is deductible.

TAXORGANIZER

Records you should keep:

- Purchase price of car
- Monthly lease payments on car
- Gas receipts
- Toll receipts
- Receipts for repairs and maintenance

You should keep a written record of these expenses and the dates they were incurred to verify deductibility.

Fines or Penalties

You cannot deduct fines or penalties you pay to a governmental unit for violating a law. This includes an amount paid in settlement of your actual or potential liability for a fine or penalty (civil or criminal). Fines or penalties include parking tickets, tax penalties, and penalties deducted from teachers' paychecks after an illegal strike.

Explanation

Although state taxes are deductible when itemizing your deductions, the penalties and interest related to the underpayment or late payment of taxes are not deductible.

Health Spa Expenses
You cannot deduct health spa expenses, even if there is a job requirement to stay in excellent physical condition, such as might be required of a law enforcement officer or a fireman.

Home Security System
You cannot deduct the cost of a home security system as a miscellaneous deduction. However, you may be able to claim a deduction for a home security system as a business expense if you have a home office. See *Home Office* under *Unreimbursed Employee Expenses,* earlier, and *Security System* under *Deducting Expenses* in Publication 587.

Homeowners' Insurance Premiums
You cannot deduct premiums that you pay or that are placed in escrow for insurance on your home, such as fire and liability or mortgage insurance.

Investment-Related Seminars
You cannot deduct any expenses for attending a convention, seminar, or similar meeting for investment purposes.

Life Insurance Premiums
You cannot deduct premiums you pay on your life insurance. You may be able to deduct, as alimony, premiums you pay on life insurance policies assigned to your former spouse. See chapter 20 for information on alimony.

Lobbying Expenses
You generally cannot deduct amounts paid or incurred for lobbying expenses. These include expenses to:

1. Influence legislation,
2. Participate or intervene in any political campaign for, or against, any candidate for public office,
3. Attempt to influence the general public, or segments of the public, about elections, legislative matters, or referendums, or
4. Communicate directly with covered executive branch officials in any attempt to influence the official actions or positions of those officials.

Lobbying expenses also include any amounts paid or incurred for research, preparation, planning, or coordination of any of these activities.

Dues used for lobbying. If a tax-exempt organization notifies you that part of the dues or other amounts you pay to the organization are used to pay nondeductible lobbying expenses, you cannot deduct that part. See *Lobbying Expenses* in Publication 529 for information on exceptions.

Lost or Mislaid Cash or Property
You cannot deduct a loss based on the mere disappearance of money or property. However, an accidental loss or disappearance of property can qualify as a casualty if it results from an identifiable event that is sudden, unexpected, or unusual. See chapter 27.

Example. A car door is accidentally slammed on your hand, breaking the setting of your diamond ring. The diamond falls from the ring and is never found. The loss of the diamond is a casualty.

Lunches with Coworkers
You cannot deduct the expenses of lunches with coworkers, except while traveling away from home on business. See chapter 28 for information on deductible expenses while traveling away from home.

Meals While Working Late
You cannot deduct the cost of meals while working late. However, you may be able to claim a deduction if the cost of meals is a deductible entertainment expense, or if you are traveling away from home. See chapter 28 for information on deductible entertainment expenses and expenses while traveling away from home.

Personal Legal Expenses
You cannot deduct personal legal expenses such as those for the following.

1. Custody of children.
2. Breach of promise (to marry) suit.
3. Civil or criminal charges resulting from a personal relationship.
4. Damages for personal injury.
5. Preparation of a title (or defense or perfection of a title).
6. Preparation of a will.
7. Property claims or property settlement in a divorce.

You cannot deduct these expenses even if a result of the legal proceeding is the loss of income-producing property.

Political Contributions
You cannot deduct contributions made to a political candidate, a campaign committee, or a newsletter fund. Advertisements in convention bulletins and admissions to dinners or programs that benefit a political party or political candidate are not deductible.

Professional Accreditation Fees
You cannot deduct professional accreditation fees such as the following.

1. Accounting certificate fees paid for the initial right to practice accounting.
2. Bar exam fees and incidental expenses in securing admission to the bar.
3. Medical and dental license fees paid to get initial licensing.

Professional Reputation
You cannot deduct expenses of radio and TV appearances to increase your personal prestige or establish your professional reputation.

Relief Fund Contributions
You cannot deduct contributions paid to a private plan that pays benefits to any covered employee who cannot work because of any injury or illness not related to the job.

Residential Telephone Service
You cannot deduct any charge (including taxes) for basic local telephone service for the first telephone line to your residence, even if it is used in a trade or business.

Stockholders' Meetings
You cannot deduct transportation and other expenses you pay to attend stockholders' meetings of companies in which you own stock but have no other interest. You cannot deduct these expenses even if you are attending the meeting to get information that would be useful in making further investments.

Explanation
The courts have allowed deductions for stockholders' meetings when the shareholders' interests are more extensive. Consider the following:

- A shareholder who went to a meeting to present a resolution that management stop diluting shareholder equity was entitled to deduct his travel expenses. (See Chapter 28, *Car Expenses and Other Employee Business Expenses.*)
- A court held that an investor's travel expenses to an investment convention were deductible because (1) the trip was part of a rationally planned, systematic investigation of business operations; (2) the costs were reasonable in relation to the size of the investment and the value of the information expected; (3) there was no disguised personal motive

for the trip; and (4) there was evidence of practical application of the information obtained on the trip.

Nevertheless, if a person owns only a very small interest in a large corporation and cannot reasonably expect that his or her attendance at a stockholders' meeting would affect his or her income or investment, the deduction of travel expenses probably would not be allowed.

Tax-Exempt Income Expenses

You cannot deduct expenses to produce tax-exempt income. You cannot deduct interest on a debt incurred or continued to buy or carry tax-exempt securities.

If you have expenses to produce both taxable and tax-exempt income, but you cannot identify the expenses that produce each type of income, you must divide the expenses based on the amount of each type of income to determine the amount that you can deduct.

Example. During the year, you received taxable interest of $4,800 and tax-exempt interest of $1,200. In earning this income, you had total expenses of $500 during the year. You cannot identify the amount of each expense item that is for each income item. Therefore, 80% ($4,800/$6,000) of the expense is for the taxable interest and 20% ($1,200/$6,000) is for the tax-exempt interest. You can deduct, subject to the 2% limit, expenses of $400 (80% of $500).

Travel Expenses for Another Individual

You generally cannot deduct travel expenses you pay or incur for a spouse, dependent, or other individual who accompanies you (or your employee) on business travel. See chapter 28 for more information on deductible travel expenses.

Voluntary Unemployment Benefit Fund Contributions

You cannot deduct voluntary unemployment benefit fund contributions you make to a union fund or a private fund. However, you can deduct contributions as taxes if state law requires you to make them to a state unemployment fund that covers you for the loss of wages from unemployment caused by business conditions.

Wristwatches

You cannot deduct the cost of a wristwatch, even if there is a job requirement that you know the correct time to properly perform your duties.

Explanation

The courts have found the following to be nondeductible expenses:

- Amounts paid to guard a personal residence against burglary attempts
- The cost of a home security system installed to protect a collector's stamps and coins. (The IRS reasoned that the activity was an investment activity and not a regular trade or business; consequently, the expense did not meet the home office rules, discussed earlier in this chapter.)
- Payments for general advice pertaining to a family trust
- Legal fees for defending a libel suit arising out of the purchase of the taxpayer's personal residence

TaxAlert

The cost of specific legal advice on the disposition of a stock is not deductible as a miscellaneous expense on Schedule A but must be treated as a selling expense and used to increase your basis in the stock.

TaxOrganizer

Records you should keep.

- Legal fees itemizing services performed
- Tax preparation fees that allocate amount between Schedules A, C, and E
- Financial account statements that indicate investment fees
- Logs substantiating the use of property (i.e., a cellular telephone, a home computer, an automobile) for both business and personal purposes
- Home office expenses and the calculation to allocate total expenses between business and personal use
- Evidence of job search expenses

For miscellaneous deductions, taxpayers' records should demonstrate:

- Why the expense is deductible due to its relationship to the production or collecting of income, or the determination of tax, and
- That the expense was clearly incurred in support of that deductible purpose

Limit on Itemized Deductions

Note: The 2004 IRS Publication 17 (Your Federal Income Tax) has been updated by Ernst & Young LLP for 2005. Dates and dollar amounts shown are for 2005. Gray type is used to indicate where IRS text has been updated or intentionally omitted. Unrevised IRS text is shown in black type.

Introduction

The tax law limits the amount of certain itemized deductions that individuals can use to reduce their taxable income. For example, the threshold for deducting medical expenses is 7.5% of adjusted gross income; miscellaneous deductions are limited to those in excess of 2% of adjusted gross income; and home mortgage interest expense is subject to various limitations.

Congress has placed an additional "overall" limitation on the deductibility of a certain group of itemized deductions. Itemized deductions that are subject to this limitation include taxes, home mortgage interest, charitable contributions, and miscellaneous itemized deductions.

The total of this group of deductions must be reduced by 3% of the amount of your adjusted gross income in excess of $145,950 ($72,975 if married filing separately). This limitation is applied after you have used any other limitations that exist in the law, such as the adjusted gross income limitation for charitable contributions and the mortgage interest expense limitations. The threshold amount is indexed annually for inflation.

Medical expenses, casualty and theft losses, investment interest expense, and gambling losses are not subject to this rule.

This chapter discusses the overall limit on itemized deductions on Schedule A (Form 1040). The topics include:

- Who is subject to the limit,
- Which itemized deductions are limited, and
- How to figure the limit.

Useful Items

You may want to see:

Form (and Instructions)

☐ **Schedule A (Form 1040)** Itemized Deductions

Are You Subject to the Limit?

You are subject to the limit on certain itemized deductions if your adjusted gross income (AGI) is more than $145,950 ($72,975 if you are married filing separately). Your AGI is the amount on Form 1040, line 37.

Which Itemized Deductions Are Limited?

The following Schedule A (Form 1040) deductions are subject to the overall limit on itemized deductions.

- Taxes—line 9.
- Interest—lines 10, 11, and 12.
- Gifts to charity—line 18.
- Job expenses and most other miscellaneous deductions—line 26.
- Other miscellaneous deductions—line 27, excluding gambling and casualty or theft losses.

Which Itemized Deductions Are Not Limited?

The following Schedule A (Form 1040) deductions are not subject to the overall limit on itemized deductions. However, they are still subject to other applicable limits.

- Medical and dental expenses—line 4.
- Investment interest expense—line 13.
- Casualty and theft losses from personal use property—line 19.
- Casualty and theft losses from income-producing property—line 27.
- Gambling losses—line 27.

Explanation
Whether a particular deduction will be limited or not depends on the character of the deduction.

Example 1
Martin and Judy Stone file a joint income tax return. They have an adjusted gross income of $345,950. The Stones' only itemized deductions are $20,000 of home

mortgage interest and $8,000 of real estate taxes. Because both of these itemized deductions are subject to the limitation, their total deductions of $28,000 must be reduced by 3% of $200,000 (the amount by which AGI exceeds $145,950), or $6,000. They may reduce their taxable income by total itemized deductions of $22,000 ($28,000 − $6,000).

Example 2

Assume the same facts as above, except that the Stones live in a downtown apartment, and their only itemized deduction is $28,000 of otherwise allowable investment interest expense. Because investment interest expense is not subject to the 3% limitation, the entire $28,000 will be deductible.

How Do You Figure the Limit?

If your itemized deductions are subject to the limit, the total of all your itemized deductions is reduced by the smaller of:

- 3% of the amount by which your AGI exceeds $145,950 ($72,975 if married filing separately), or
- 80% of your itemized deductions that are affected by the limit. See *Which Itemized Deductions Are Limited*, earlier.

Before you figure the overall limit on itemized deductions, you first must complete Schedule A (Form 1040), lines 1 through 27, including any related forms (such as Form 2106, Form 4684, etc.).

The overall limit on itemized deductions is figured after you have applied any other limit on the allowance of any itemized deduction. These other limits include charitable contribution limits (chapter 26), the limit on certain meals and entertainment (chapter 28), and the 2%-of-adjusted-gross-income limit on certain miscellaneous deductions (chapter 30).

Itemized Deductions Worksheet. After you have completed Schedule A (Form 1040) through line 27, you can use the Itemized Deductions Worksheet in the Form 1040 instructions for Schedule A to figure your limit. Enter the result on Schedule A (Form 1040), line 28. Keep the worksheet for your records.

Tip. *You should compare the amount of your standard deduction to the amount of your itemized deductions after applying the limit. Use the greater amount when completing Form 1040, line 40. See chapter 22 for information on how to figure your standard deduction.*

Example

For tax year 2005, Bill and Terry Willow are filing a joint return on Form 1040. Their adjusted gross income on line 37 is $259,600. Their Schedule A itemized deductions are as follows:

Taxes—line 9	$ 17,900
Interest—lines 10, 11, and 12	45,000
Investment interest expense—line 13	41,000
Gifts to charity—line 18	21,000
Job expenses—line 26	17,240
Total	**$142,140**

The Willows' investment interest expense deduction ($41,000 from Schedule A (Form 1040), line 13) is not subject to the overall limit on itemized deductions.

The Willows use the Itemized Deductions Worksheet in the Schedule A (Form 1040) instructions to figure their overall limit. Their completed worksheet is shown as Table 31-1.

Of their $142,140 total itemized deductions, the Willows can deduct only $138,730 ($142,140 − $3,410). They enter $138,730 on Schedule A (Form 1040), line 28.

Table 31-1. **Itemized Deductions Worksheet—Line 28**   *Keep for your records*

1. Enter the total of the amounts from Schedule A, lines 4, 9, 14, 18, 19, 26, and 27. . . . . **1.** 142,140
2. Enter the total of the amounts from Schedule A, lines 4, 13, and 19, plus any gambling and casualty or theft losses included on line 27. . . . . **2.** 41,000

> **CAUTION** Be sure your total gambling and casualty or theft losses are clearly identified on the dotted lines next to line 27.

3. Is the amount on line 2 less than the amount on line 1?
   ☐ **No.** (STOP) Your deduction is not limited. Enter the amount from line 1 above on Schedule A, line 28.
   ☑ **Yes.** Subtract line 2 from line 1 . . . . **3.** 101,140
4. Multiply line 3 by 80% (.80). **4.** 80,912
5. Enter the amount from Form 1040, line 37 . . . . **5.** 259,600
6. Enter: $145,950 ($72,975 if married filing separately) **6.** 145,950
7. Is the amount on line 6 less than the amount on line 5?
   ☐ **No.** (STOP) Your deduction is not limited. Enter the amount from line 1 above on Schedule A, line 28.
   ☑ **Yes.** Subtract line 6 from line 5 . . . . **7.** 113,650
8. Multiply line 7 by 3% (.03) **8.** 3,410
9. Enter the **smaller** of line 4 or line 8 . . . . **9.** 3,410
10. **Total itemized deductions.** Subtract line 9 from line 1. Enter the result here and on Schedule A, line 28 . . . . **10.** 138,730

Calculating the 3% limitation. In certain situations, it is possible for the 3% limitation to reduce allowable itemized deductions below the standard deduction amount. You should consider this possibility when you are choosing whether to itemize your deductions or to use the standard deduction.

Example
Arthur and Karen White have adjusted gross income of $245,950. They have no mortgage on their home; however, they pay annual real estate taxes of $5,500. Each year they contribute $2,500 to their favorite charity. The Whites would compute their taxable income as follows:

Adjusted gross income		$245,950
Itemized deductions		
Real estate taxes	$5,500	
Charitable contributions	2,500	
Total	$8,000	
Less 3% of AGI in excess of $145,950	3,000	
Allowable itemized deductions	$5,000	
Standard deduction if married, filing a joint return	$10,000	
Greater of standard deduction or allowable itemized deductions		(10,000)
Personal Exemptions		(4,992)
Taxable Income		$230,958

Note: The personal exemptions have been reduced according to the phaseout rules discussed in Chapter 3, *Personal Exemptions and Dependents.*

TAXALERT

The American Jobs Creation Act of 2004 provides the taxpayer with the opportunity to elect to deduct state and local general sales taxes instead of state and local income taxes as an itemized deduction (see chapter 24, *Taxes You May Deduct,* for details). Similar to state and local income taxes, state and local general sales taxes are also subject to the "overall itemized deduction limitation."

TAXPLANNER

Bunching. If your itemized deductions are subject to this 3% limitation, you may want to consider a technique called "bunching." Bunching is effective if you are able to accumulate deductions so that they are high in one year and low in the next. Bunching your itemized deductions so that they are higher in one year can help you take advantage of those itemized deductions if the limitation would normally cause the standard deduction to be higher.

Example
Assume the same facts as in the previous example. This time, however, the Whites are able to *postpone* payment of their 2005 real estate taxes until January 2006, and they can also pay $1,500 of their $2,500 charitable contributions in early 2006. Then next year, in December 2006, they will *accelerate* these payments to make sure that they fall in 2006 and not 2007. The Whites will end up with the following expenses for 2005 and 2006:

	2005	2006
2005 Real estate taxes	—	$5,500
2005 Charitable contributions	1,000	1,500
2006 Real estate taxes	—	$5,500
2006 Charitable contributions	—	2,500
Total	$1,000	$15,000

By bunching the expenses, the Whites may use the $10,000 standard deduction in 2005 and itemized deductions of $12,000 ($15,000 less the 3% limit of $3,000) in 2006. Total deductions equal $22,000 for the two years ($10,000 + $12,000). In 2006, they will have reduced their taxable income by an additional $2,000 ($12,000 − $10,000). Without bunching, the Whites would have been limited to the standard deduction in each year. (These calculations assume that the standard deduction and the itemized deduction limit will not change in 2006.)

PART VI

Figuring Your Taxes and Credits

The seven chapters in this part explain how to figure your tax and how to figure the tax of certain children who have more than $1,600 of investment income. They also discuss tax credits that, unlike deductions, are subtracted directly from your tax and reduce your tax, dollar for dollar.

Among other tax credits, Chapter 38 discusses the earned income credit and how you may be able to get part of the credit paid to you in advance throughout the year.

32

How to Figure Your Tax

Note: The 2004 IRS Publication 17 (Your Federal Income Tax) has been updated by Ernst & Young LLP for 2005. Dates and dollar amounts shown are for 2005. Gray type is used to indicate where IRS text has been updated or intentionally omitted. Unrevised IRS text is shown in black type.

Introduction

This chapter explains how to calculate your tax liability under all three available tax forms—Form 1040EZ, Form 1040A, and Form 1040. It will help you decide which of the forms to file.

In particular, you should review the section of this chapter on the alternative minimum tax to determine if that tax may apply to you.

After you have figured your income and deductions as explained in *Parts One* through *Five*, your next step is to figure your tax. This chapter discusses:

* The general steps you take to figure your tax,
* An additional tax you may have to pay called the alternative minimum tax, and
* The conditions you must meet if you want the IRS to figure your tax.

Figuring Your Tax

Your income tax is based on your taxable income. After you figure your income tax, subtract your tax credits and add any other taxes you may owe. The result is your total tax. Compare your total tax with your total payments to determine whether you are entitled to a refund or owe additional tax.

This section provides a general outline of how to figure your tax. You can find step-by-step directions in the instructions for Forms 1040EZ, 1040A, and 1040. If you are unsure of which tax form you should file, see *Which Form Should I Use?* in chapter 1.

Tax. Most taxpayers use either the Tax Table or the Tax Computation Worksheet to figure their income tax. However, there are special methods if your income includes any of the following items.

* A net capital gain. (See chapter 17.)
* Qualified dividends taxed at the same rates as a net capital gain. (See chapter 17.)
* Lump-sum distributions. (See chapter 11.)
* Farming or fishing income. (See Schedule J (Form 1040), Income Averaging for Farmers and Fishermen.)
* Investment income over $1,600 for children under age 14. (See chapter 33.)

Credits. After you figure your income tax, determine your tax credits. This chapter does not explain whether you are eligible for these credits. You can find that information in chapters 34 through 39 and your form instructions. See the following table for credits you may be able to subtract from your income tax.

CREDITS

For information on:	See chapter:
Adoption	39
Child and dependent care	34
Child tax credit	36
Education	37
Elderly or disabled	35
Foreign tax	39
Mortgage interest	39
Prior year minimum tax	39
Qualified electric vehicle	39
Qualified retirement savings contributions	39

Some credits (such as the earned income credit) are not listed above because they are treated as payments. See *Payments,* later.

There are other credits that are not discussed in this publication. These include the following items.

* General business credit, which is made up of several separate business-related credits. These generally are reported on Form 3800, General Business Credit, and are discussed in chapter 4 of Publication 334, Tax Guide for Small Business.
* Empowerment zone and renewal community employment credit, which is for certain employers who are engaged in a business in an empowerment zone, a renewal community, or the DC zone. See Publication 954, Tax Incentives for Distressed Communities. Also see the instructions for Form 8844, Empowerment Zone and Renewal Community Employment Credit.
* District of Columbia first-time homebuyer credit, which is for certain persons who buy a main home in the District. See the instructions for Form 8859, *District of Columbia First-Time Homebuyer Credit.*
* Credit for fuel from a nonconventional source, which is for the

person who sold the fuel. See the instructions for line 55 of Form 1040 and section 29 of the Internal Revenue Code.

Other taxes. After you subtract your tax credits, determine whether there are any other taxes you must pay. This chapter does not explain these other taxes. You can find that information in other chapters of this publication and your form instructions. See the following table for other taxes you may need to add to your income tax.

OTHER TAXES

For information on:	See chapter:
Additional taxes on qualified retirement plans and IRAs	11, 18
Advance earned income credit payments	38
Household employment taxes	34
Recapture of an education credit	37
Social Security and Medicare tax on unreported tips	7
Uncollected Social Security and Medicare tax on tips	7

Another tax you may have to pay, the alternative minimum tax, is discussed later in this chapter.

There are other taxes that are not discussed in this publication. These include the following items.

1. *Self-employment tax.* You must figure this tax if either of the following applies to you (or your spouse if you file a joint return).
   a. Your net earnings from self-employment from other than church employee income were $400 or more. The term "net earnings from self-employment" may include certain nonemployee compensation and other amounts reported to you on Form 1099-MISC, Miscellaneous Income. If you received a Form 1099-MISC, see the *Instructions to Recipients* on the back. Also see the instructions for Schedule SE (Form 1040), Self-Employment Tax, and Publication 533, Self-Employment Tax.
   b. You had church employee income of $108.28 or more.
2. *Recapture taxes.* You may have to pay these taxes if you previously claimed an investment credit, a low-income housing credit, a mortgage interest credit, a new markets credit, a qualified electric vehicle credit, a credit for employer-provided child care facilities, or an Indian employment credit. For more information, see the instructions for line 63 of Form 1040.
3. *Section 72(m)(5) excess benefits tax.* If you are (or were) a 5% owner of a business and you received a distribution that exceeds the benefits provided for you under the qualified pension or annuity plan formula, you may have to pay this additional tax. See *Tax on Excess Benefits* in chapter 4 of Publication 560, Retirement Plans for Small Business (SEP, SIMPLE, and Qualified Plans).
4. *Uncollected social security and Medicare tax on group-term life insurance.* If your former employer provides you with more than $50,000 of group-term life insurance coverage, you must pay the employee part of social security and Medicare taxes on those premiums. The amount should be shown in box 12 of your Form W-2 with codes M and N.
5. *Tax on golden parachute payments.* This tax applies if you received an "excess parachute payment" (EPP) due to a change in a corporation's ownership or control. See the instructions for line 63 of Form 1040.
6. *Tax on accumulation distribution of trusts.* This applies if you are the beneficiary of a trust that accumulated its income instead of distributing it currently. See the instructions for Form 4970, Tax on Accumulation Distribution of Trusts.
7. *Additional tax on HSAs or MSAs.* If amounts contributed to, or distributed from, your health savings account or medical savings account do not meet the rules for these accounts, you may have to pay additional taxes. See Publication 969, Health Savings Accounts and Other Tax-Favored Health Plans; Form 8853, Archer MSAs and Long-Term Care Insurance Contracts; Form 8889, Health Savings Accounts (HSAs); and Form 5329, Additional Taxes on Qualified Plans (Including IRAs) and Other Tax-Favored Accounts.
8. *Additional tax on Coverdell ESAs.* This applies if amounts contributed to, or distributed from, your Coverdell ESA do not meet the rules for these accounts. See Publication 970, Tax Benefits for Education, and Form 5329.
9. *Additional tax on qualified tuition programs.* This applies to amounts distributed from qualified tuition programs that do not meet the rules for these accounts. See Publication 970 and Form 5329.
10. *Tax on insider stock compensation from an expatriated corporation.* You may owe a 15% excise tax on the value of nonstatutory stock options and certain other stock-based compensation held by you or a member of your family from an expatriated corporation or its expanded affiliated group in which you were an officer, director, or more-than-10% owner. For more information, see the instructions for line 63 of Form 1040.

Payments. After you determine your total tax, figure the total payments you have already made for the year. Include credits that are treated as payments. This chapter does not explain these payments and credits. You can find that information in other chapters of this publication and your form instructions. See the following table for amounts you can include in your total payments.

PAYMENTS

For information on:	See chapter:
Child tax credit (additional)	36
Earned income credit	38
Estimated tax paid	5
Excess Social Security and RRTA tax withheld	39
Federal income tax withheld	5
Health coverage tax credit	39
Regulated investment company credit	39
Tax paid with extension	1

Another credit that is treated as a payment is the credit for federal excise tax paid on fuels. This credit is for persons who have a nontaxable use of certain fuels, such as diesel fuel and kerosene. It is claimed on line 70 of Form 1040. See Publication 378, Fuel Tax Credits and Refunds, and Form 4136, Credit for Federal Tax Paid on Fuels.

Refund or balance due. To determine whether you are entitled to a refund or owe additional tax, compare your total payments with your total tax. If you are entitled to a refund, see your form instructions for information on having it directly deposited into your checking or savings account instead of receiving a paper check.

Explanation

For information on how to elect to pay your 2005 tax in installments, see Chapter 1, *Filing Information*, under the section entitled *Amount You Owe*.

Alternative Minimum Tax

This section briefly discusses an additional tax you may have to pay.

The tax law gives special treatment to some kinds of income and allows special deductions and credits for some kinds of expenses. Taxpayers who benefit from the law in these ways may have to pay at least a minimum amount of tax through an additional tax. This additional tax is called the alternative minimum tax (AMT).

Explanation

The Alternative Minimum Tax (AMT) has been receiving a lot of attention recently. Why? Because more and more taxpayers are subject to it. Absent further law changes, approximately one-third of all taxpayers will be subject to the AMT by 2010, up considerably over the last decade.

Begun in 1978, the AMT was originally intended to ensure the "rich" made at least some minimum amount of tax. Until recently, however, the vast majority of taxpayers were not subject to the AMT. But the recent reduction in regular income tax rates without a corresponding reduction in AMT rates has caused more people to be subject to this tax.

How the AMT works: The simplest way to understand the AMT is to think of it as a separate tax system with its own allowable deductions and exclusions, many of which are different from those allowed for regular income tax purposes. Thus, although it is in many ways parallel to the "regular income tax" computation, some of the applicable rules are different. You first calculate your regular income tax as you always have, then you calculate your tax under the AMT system, and pay the greater of the two amounts. The following are some of the more common items treated differently under the two tax systems that can affect your exposure to AMT:

- State and local income and sales taxes
- Real estate and personal property taxes
- Large medical and dental expenses
- Miscellaneous itemized deductions (subject to the 2% of AGI floor)
- Interest expense from a mortgage or home equity loan that is not used for the purpose of acquiring, constructing or improving a principal residence or "second home"
- The "spread" on the exercise of incentive stock options (ISOs)
- Deductions for personal exemptions
- The standard deduction

Most of these items consist of deductions that are allowed in computing your regular income tax liability but are not allowed when you figure your AMT. Take, for example, state and local income and real estate taxes that you pay. They are allowable as a deduction against your income for regular tax purposes but not for AMT. (You'll find a more detailed explanation of how to figure your AMT later in this section.)

Example

The Smiths have two children and gross wages totaling $250,000. Their itemized deductions consist of state and local income taxes and real estate taxes totaling $22,500 and mortgage interest of $20,000. Assume as well that the Smiths have no interest, dividend or capital gain income. In 2002, their federal tax bill was $52,933, but they were not subject to AMT because that calculation was only $52,780. However, in 2005 the new lower tax rates cause their regular tax to drop to $46,971 while their AMT only drops to $50,260. The Smiths will be required to pay the AMT amount—$3,289 more than their regular tax amount. Note that, even with the AMT, their overall tax is lower thanks to the lower regular tax rates.

The same won't hold true in 2006 when their ATM exemption is scheduled to fall to $45,000 from $58,000. Assuming all income and deductions remain constant, and assuming no inflation adjustments, the Smiths's regular tax will be $46,262. Their AMT will be $53,900, $7,638 more than their regular tax amount. In other words, they'll be paying more in 2006 than they did in 2002—even though regular tax rates have decreased.

TaxPlanner

The AMT can not only affect the amount of tax you pay, but it can also potentially affect the most tax efficient way to invest your money.

For example, if part of your investment portfolio consists of municipal bond holdings, beware. Private activity bond interest is a preference item that can make it more likely that you will be subject to AMT. Generally, you earn a higher yield on private activity bonds than other municipals. However, if you're subject to the AMT, your effective yield will be slashed. If you're not sure what type of municipal bonds you have, ask your investment advisor.

Long-term capital gains and qualifying dividends are subject to the same maximum rate, 15%, for AMT purposes as they are for regular tax purposes. But because these items of income are included in AMTI, which could reduce your allowable exemption, the actual marginal AMT rate could be as high as 22%. Before deciding to invest in securities that generate these types of income, you should consider the effect of the AMT.

Example

Consider the Smiths again in the Example above. Assume that in addition to their other income ($250,000 in gross wages), the Smiths had a long-term capital gain in 2005 of $100,000. At first blush, you might expect that their federal tax bill would increase by about $15,000 (15% long-term capital gain rate on $100,000, assuming no state income tax). However, because they end up subject to AMT, the additional tax burden is actually $22,000.

This estimate does not include any additional state income tax. Considering that most states do impose income taxes on capital gains, the Smiths would be liable for additional tax. If, say, the Smiths lived in a state with an 8% tax rate, then after taking into account the state tax itself, there would be a total of $30,000 of federal and state taxes attributable to a long-term gain of $100,000!

You may have to pay the alternative minimum tax if your taxable income for regular tax purposes, combined with certain adjustments and tax preference items, is more than:

- $58,000 if your filing status is married filing a joint return (or qualifying widow(er) with dependent child),
- $40,250 if your filing status is single or head of household, or
- $29,000 if your filing status is married filing a separate return.

Explanation

Individuals, trusts, and estates must pay the alternative minimum tax (AMT) if it exceeds their regular tax liability for the year. The amount subject to the AMT will be determined by adding a number of preference items to your taxable income and making various adjustments to your regular taxable income. This amount is reduced by the exemption amounts, and the balance is subject to the following AMT rates:

Rate	Married filing separately	All other filers
26%	Up to $87,500 over exemption amount	Up to $175,000 over exemption amount
28%	Greater than $87,500 over exemption amount	Greater than $175,000 over exemption amount

Exemption amount

Filing status	Base amount	Less 25% of the amount by which AMTI* exceeds
Single	$40,250	$112,500
Married filing jointly, surviving spouses	58,000	150,000
Married filing separately, estates and trusts	29,000	75,000

*Alternative minimum taxable income

TaxAlert

In 2006, the exemption amount is scheduled to drop significantly: $45,000 for married couples filing jointly (from $58,000) and $33,750 for single filers (from $40,250). This means that an increasing number of taxpayers will be subject to the AMT.

TaxPlanner

The chart below should provide you with a better understanding of whether you might be affected by the AMT. Look at where your taxable income falls—then see how much you would need to have in preferences and adjustments (state and local taxes, personal exemptions, miscellaneous itemized deductions, standard deduction, etc.) to see whether you'd be subject to the AMT. For example, say you have ordinary taxable income of $100,000, claim 7 personal exemptions at $3,200 each ($22,400 in total) and take the standard deduction of $10,000. Your total preferences are $32,400 and you'd be subject to the AMT.

Regular taxable income	Adjustments & Preferences Needed to Trigger AMT	
	Joint	Single
$ 25,000	$44,618	$28,272
50,000	34,041	25,502
75,000	29,464	24,895
100,000	28,502	23,954
125,000	27,500	20,493
150,000	24,039	17,031
200,000	19,522	16,127
300,000	13,807	19,642
400,000	19,870	42,752
500,000	44,870	67,752

Analysis assumes ordinary income, no capital gains or qualifying dividends

Explanation

Once your alternative minimum taxable income ("AMTI") increases above a certain level, your AMT exemption begins to phase out.

If you are married and filing a joint return, for every dollar that your AMTI exceeds $150,000, you lose $.25 of your exemption until it's totally phased out at $382,000 in 2005 (for single taxpayers it's totally phased out at $273,500). In tax years after 2005, when the exemption amount is scheduled to drop back to $45,000, as mentioned in the Tax Alert above, the AMT exemption will be totally phased out once your AMTI reaches $330,000 for joint filers ($247,500 for singles.)

Adjustments and tax preference items. The more common adjustments and tax preference items include:

- Addition of personal exemptions,
- Addition of the standard deduction (if claimed),
- Addition of itemized deductions claimed for state and local taxes, certain interest, most miscellaneous deductions, and part of medical expenses,
- Subtraction of any refund of state and local taxes included in gross income,
- Changes to accelerated depreciation of certain property,
- Difference between gain or loss on the sale of property reported for regular tax purposes and AMT purposes,
- Addition of certain income from incentive stock options,
- Change in certain passive activity loss deductions,
- Private activity bond interest

TaxAlert

If your deduction for state taxes is unusually high—for example, perhaps you made a large payment with your 2004 state tax return when you filed in April of 2005; or perhaps you have substantial state tax withholding during 2005 on your regular income—you should take a closer look at the possibility of being subject to the AMT.

Explanation

Besides accounting for tax preference items, certain adjustments (increases or decreases) must be made to taxable income to arrive at alternative minimum taxable income. The adjustments are as follows:

1. An alternative depreciation deduction (using less accelerated methods and longer depreciable lives) is substituted for the regular tax depreciation deduction for real and personal property and certified pollution control facilities placed in service after 1986 and before 1999. Recomputations are done in the aggregate; that is, the amount of the adjustment is not determined on a property-by-property basis. *Note:* This adjustment does not apply if you have elected to apply the alternative depreciation system (ADS) for regular tax purposes. For tax years beginning in or after 1999, the recovery periods over which property is depreciated will be the same for regular and AMT purposes.
2. Mining exploration and development costs must be amortized over 10 years using the straight-line method.
3. The percentage-of-completion method of accounting must be used for long-term contracts entered into on or after March 1, 1986. Certain small construction contracts entered into on or after June 21, 1988, must use separate, simplified procedures for cost allocations in the percentage-of-completion calculation.
4. An alternative tax net operating loss deduction replaces the regular net operating loss deduction.
5 The installment method of accounting is disallowed for certain installment sales occurring after March 1, 1986.
6. The treatment of itemized deductions is modified as follows:

- Medical expenses are deductible only to the extent that they exceed 10% (instead of 7.5%) of the taxpayer's adjusted gross income.
- State, local, and foreign real property, sales and income taxes, and state and local personal property taxes, are deductible for AMT purposes only if they are deductible for regular tax purposes in computing adjusted gross income. *Note:* These are taxes related to business, rental property, and farming that are deducted on Schedule C, E, or F.
- Investment interest is deductible to the extent of net investment income that is adjusted for amounts relating to tax-exempt interest earned on certain private-activity bonds.
- Home mortgage interest is allowed as a deduction for AMT purposes. However, the definition of such interest is narrower than that of "qualified residence interest" for regular tax purposes. Refinanced home mortgage interest that is applicable to any mortgage in excess of the outstanding mortgage before refinancing is not deductible unless the excess was used for home improvements.
- No deduction is allowed for miscellaneous itemized deductions subject to the 2%-of-adjusted-gross-income limit.

7. No deduction is allowed for the standard deduction.
8. Circulation expenditures and research/experimental costs must be amortized over 3- and 10-year periods, respectively.
9. Deductions for passive farm losses are denied, except to the extent that the taxpayer is insolvent or the activity is disposed of during the year.
10. Rules limiting passive loss deductions also apply to the AMT, except that (a) otherwise disallowed losses are reduced by the amount by which the taxpayer is insolvent, and (b) all AMT adjustments and preferences are taken into consideration in computing income and/or losses from passive activities.
11. For beneficiaries of estates and trusts, the difference between a distribution included in income for regular tax and the AMT income shown on Schedule K-1 must be taken into account.
12. For property disposed of during the year, the gain or loss is refigured to take into consideration the impact that AMT adjustments, such as depreciation, have on the taxpayer's basis in the property.
13. For partners in partnerships and shareholders in S corporations, the income or loss is refigured to take into account AMT adjustments.
14. In exercising an incentive stock option (ISO), the taxpayer needs to adjust for the difference between the option price and the fair market value at the time the option is exercised. In calculating the AMT gain or loss on the subsequent sale of the ISO stock, the AMT basis in the stock is the sum of the option price paid and the AMT adjustment included in alternative minimum taxable income when the ISO was exercised.

TaxAlert

Incentive stock options present a unique AMT trap. While the "spread"—the difference between the fair market value of the stock at the time the option is exercised and the exercise price is not taxable for regular tax purposes, it is for the AMT. The larger the "spread," the more likely you will be liable for AMT.

In addition, you compute your "basis" (generally the amount you paid) for stock bought with incentive stock options one way for regular tax purposes and another way for figuring your AMT. Your basis for regular tax purposes will generally be the exercise price of the options. The basis for AMT will generally be the fair market value of the shares when exercised, assuming you sold the shares after the year in which you exercised your option. Figuring your basis is more complicated if you sell the shares within a year of exercising your options. You should consult your tax advisor.

If matters weren't complicated enough, the amount of AMT attributable to an incentive stock option can be credited against your regular tax liability in a future year. So, should your regular tax liability exceed your AMT tax calculation in a subsequent year, you can apply the credit against the difference between the two.

Example

In 2005 Martin and Fern Burns have $275,000 of ordinary income and $39,000 of itemized deductions— $10,000 of state income taxes, $4,000 of real estate taxes, $15,000 of mortgage interest, and $10,000 of charitable contributions. They also have two dependent children. Their regular tax would be $57,468. They would not be subject to the AMT since that amount ($57,260) would be less than their regular tax.

Now suppose that in 2005 Fern exercised 1,000 incentive stock options (ISOs) that had an exercise price of $10 a share and that the stock was worth $25 a share at the time of exercise. That results in a total spread of $15,000 (1,000 × $15) that has to be added back in calculating AMT. The Burns' AMT for 2005 would be $62,510, an additional tax of $5,042. But all is not lost. Since the additional $5,042 was a result of the ISO exercise that amount can be carried forward to a future year and credited against their tax to the extent their regular tax exceeds their AMT in that future year .

Let's say that in 2007 Fern sells the stock she got from the ISO exercise for $30 a share. The basis of the stock for regular tax purposes is $10 a share so she has a regular long-term capital gain of $20,000 (1,000 × $20). But her basis for AMT purposes is $25 a share— the value of the stock on the date of exercise—for an AMT long-term capital gain of $5,000 (1,000 × $5). So in calculating her AMT in 2007 she would reflect a **negative** adjustment on Form 6251 of $15,000.

- Addition of certain depletion that is more than the adjusted basis of the property,
- Addition of part of the deduction for certain intangible drilling costs, and

TaxSaver

To avoid treating excess intangible drilling costs as a tax preference item, you may elect to capitalize and amortize these expenses over a 10-year period in your regular tax calculation.

- Addition of tax-exempt interest on certain private activity bonds.

TaxAlert

If you plan to make a substantial gift of appreciated property (e.g., stock) to a charity, there is no adjustment to consider for the alternative minimum tax (AMT). You are able to recognize a charitable contribution deduction for the full fair market value of appreciated long-term capital gain property for both regular and AMT purposes (subject to adjusted gross income limitations).

TAXALERT

You only pay AMT if the tentative alternative tax calculation results in a higher tax liability than your regular tax calculation. For 2005, nonrefundable credits may be used to offset your AMT and regular tax liability. See Chapter 38, *Other Credits Including the Earned Income Credit* for a discussion of nonrefundable credits.

Explanation

The law provides a credit against the regular tax for all or a portion of the AMT you paid in previous years. The credit is the AMT attributable to deferral, rather than exclusion, items. Deferral items such as accelerated depreciation or the spread on incentive stock option (ISO), are those that have the effect of reducing your regular taxable income relative to alternative minimum taxable income in early years, but the situation reverses over time. Thus, the same total of deductions is eventually allowed under both tax systems. When you pay AMT as a result of deferral preferences or adjustments, the law gives you a credit that can be used to reduce your regular tax liability in the future. This avoids double taxation on the same income. Exclusion preferences, such as certain tax-exempt interest income, reduce your regular taxable income permanently. Because these preferences never reverse in the future, you are not given a credit for AMT paid. The credit is carried forward indefinitely from the year of payment and cannot be carried back.

Example

The following example demonstrates how you would calculate your regular tax and your AMT for calendar year 2005 assuming your filing status is married filing jointly.

	Regular tax	Alternative minimum tax
Salary	$150,000	$150,000
Interest	11,000	11,000
Long-term capital gains (15%)	80,000	80,000
Net passive losses	(25,000)	(25,000)
Passive losses disallowed by Tax Reform Act of 1986	25,000	25,000
Adjusted gross income	$241,000	$241,000
State taxes	(30,000)	n/a*
Charitable contributions	(40,000)	(40,000)
Interest expense—principal residence	(27,000)	(27,000)
Reduction in itemized deductions for adjusted gross income over $145,950	2,852	n/a
Exemptions (4)	(10,496)	n/a
Tax adjustment items:		

	Regular tax	Alternative minimum tax
Incentive stock options	n/a	25,000
Alternative taxable income before exemption	n/a	$199,000
Exemption ($58,000 less 25% of alternative taxable income in excess of $150,000)	n/a	($45,750)
Taxable income	$136,356	$153,250
Tax due	$19,418	$30,740

*n/a means "not applicable."

Because your regular tax is less than your AMT, you must pay the AMT of $30,740.

The $30,000 you paid in state income tax was not allowed as a deduction from alternative minimum taxable income. Because deductions are based on actual payments made during the calendar year, good planning would require minimizing your state income taxes and your miscellaneous deductions to the extent that you are able in a year when it is possible you will be subject to the AMT.

TAXPLANNER

Even if you have benefited from the tax preference items that generally subject you to the AMT, you may avoid the AMT by controlling the timing of certain transactions. The trick is not to exceed the amount exempt from the AMT for a given year. If you know that you will be subject to the AMT this year, and provided your current AMT situation is due to exclusion items, you should consider realizing income this year that otherwise would be realized next year so that it is taxed at 26% or 28% rather than at a higher rate next year. Likewise, consider deferring deductions, especially those that are not deductible for AMT purposes.

The $58,000 exemption for joint returns is phased out beginning at $150,000 of alternative minimum taxable income. For unmarried taxpayers, the exemption amount is $40,250, and it is phased out beginning at $112,500. You lose $1 of exemption for every $4 over the base amount. Consequently, the exemption amount is completely phased out at $382,000 for joint returns and $273,500 for unmarried taxpayers.

More information. For more information about the alternative minimum tax, see the instructions for Form 1040, line 45, and Form 6251, Alternative Minimum Tax—Individuals.

Tax Figured by IRS

If you file by April 17, 2006, you can have the IRS figure your tax for you on Form 1040EZ, Form 1040A, or Form 1040.

If the IRS figures your tax and you paid too much, you will receive a refund. If you did not pay enough, you will receive a bill for the balance. To avoid interest or the penalty for late payment, you must pay the bill within 30 days of the date of the bill or by the due date for your return, whichever is later.

TAXPLANNER

If you make a preliminary calculation and see that you owe money to the IRS, you might consider waiting until

April 15 to file your return and letting the IRS figure your tax. It will take the IRS some time to process your return and compute your tax. You will not have to come up with the money you owe until 30 days after the IRS sends you a bill. You will not have to pay any interest if you pay within 30 days of receiving your bill.

When the IRS cannot figure your tax. The IRS cannot figure your tax for you if any of the following apply.

1. You want your refund directly deposited.
2. You want any part of your refund applied to your 2006 estimated tax.
3. Any of your income for the year was from other than wages, salaries, tips, interest, dividends, taxable social security benefits, unemployment compensation, IRA distributions, pensions, and annuities.
4. Your taxable income is $100,000 or more.
5. You itemize deductions.
6. You file any of the following forms.
   a. Form 2555, Foreign Earned Income.
   b. Form 2555-EZ, Foreign Earned Income Exclusion.
   c. Form 4137, Social Security and Medicare Tax on Unreported Tip Income.
   d. Form 4970, Tax on Accumulation Distribution of Trusts.
   e. Form 4972, Tax on Lump-Sum Distributions.
   f. Form 6198, At-Risk Limitations.
   g. Form 6251, Alternative Minimum Tax—Individuals.
   h. Form 8606, Nondeductible IRAs.
   i. Form 8615, Tax for Children Under Age 14 With Investment Income of More Than $1,600.
   j. Form 8814, Parents' Election To Report Child's Interest and Dividends.
   k. Form 8839, Qualified Adoption Expenses.
   l. Form 8853, Archer MSAs and Long-Term Care Insurance Contracts.
   m. Form 8889, Health Savings Accounts (HSAs).

Filing the Return

After you complete the line entries for the tax form you are filing, as discussed next, attach the peel-off label. If you do not have a peel-off label, fill in your name and address. Enter your social security number in the space provided. If you are married, enter the social security numbers of both spouses. Sign and date your return and enter your occupation(s). If you are filing a joint return, both you and your spouse must sign it. Enter your daytime phone number in the space provided.

Attach a copy of each of your Forms W-2 to your return. Also attach any Form 1099-R you received that has withholding tax in box 4.

Mail your return to the Internal Revenue Service Center for the area where you live. A list of Service Center addresses is shown near the end of this publication.

Form 1040EZ Line Entries

Read lines 1 through 8b and fill in the lines that apply to you. Do not complete lines 9 through 12. If you are filing a joint return, use the space to the left of line 6 to separately show your taxable income and your spouse's taxable income.

Earned income credit. If you can take this credit, as discussed in chapter 38, the IRS can figure it for you. Print "EIC" in the space to the left of line 8a.

If your credit for any year after 1996 was reduced or disallowed by the IRS, you may also have to file Form 8862, Information To Claim Earned Income Credit After Disallowance, with your return. For details, see the Form 1040EZ instructions.

Form 1040A Line Entries

Read lines 1 through 27 and fill in the lines that apply to you. If you are filing a joint return, use the space to the left of line 27 to sepa-

rately show your taxable income and your spouse's taxable income. Do not complete line 28. Complete lines 29 through 34, 37, and 39 through 42 if they apply to you. Do not fill in lines 30 and 41a if you want the IRS to figure the credits shown on those lines. Also, enter any write-in information that applies to you in the space to the left of line 43. Do not complete lines 35, 36, 38, and 43 through 48.

Credit for child and dependent care expenses. If you can take this credit, as discussed in chapter 34, complete Schedule 2 and attach it to your return. Enter the amount of the credit on line 29 (Form 1040A). The IRS will not figure this credit.

Credit for the elderly or the disabled. If you can take this credit, as discussed in chapter 35, attach Schedule 3 (1040A), Credit for the Elderly or the Disabled for Form 1040A Filers. Print "CFE" next to line 30 (Form 1040A). The IRS will figure this credit for you. On Schedule 3, check the box in Part I for your filing status and age. Complete Part II and lines 11 and 13 of Part III if they apply.

Earned income credit. If you can take this credit, as discussed in chapter 38, the IRS will figure it for you. Print "EIC" to the left of the entry space for line 41a. If you have a qualifying child, you must fill in Schedule EIC, Earned Income Credit, and attach it to your return.

If your credit for any year after 1996 was reduced or disallowed by the IRS, you may also have to file Form 8862 with your return. For details, see the Form 1040A instructions.

Form 1040 Line Entries

Read lines 1 through 43 and fill in the lines that apply to you. Do not complete line 44.

If you are filing a joint return, use the space under the words "Adjusted Gross Income" on the front of your return to separately show your taxable income and your spouse's taxable income.

Read lines 45 through 70. Fill in the lines that apply to you, but do not fill in the "Total" lines. Also, do not complete line 57 and lines 71 through 76. Do not fill in lines 49 and 66a if you want the IRS to figure the credits shown on those lines.

Fill in any forms or schedules asked for on the lines you completed, and attach them to your return.

Credit for child and dependent care expenses. If you can take this credit, as discussed in chapter 34, complete Form 2441 and attach it to your return. Enter the amount of the credit on line 48. The IRS will not figure this credit.

Credit for the elderly or the disabled. If you can take this credit, as discussed in chapter 35, attach Schedule R, Credit for the Elderly or the Disabled. Print "CFE" on the dotted line next to line 49 of Form 1040. The IRS will figure the credit for you. On Schedule R check the box in Part I for your filing status and age. Complete Part II and lines 11 and 13 of Part III if they apply.

Earned income credit. If you can take this credit, as discussed in chapter 38, the IRS will figure it for you. Print "EIC" on the dotted line next to line 66a of Form 1040. If you have a qualifying child, you must fill in Schedule EIC and attach it to your return.

If your credit for any year after 1996 was reduced or disallowed by the IRS, you may also have to file Form 8862 with your return. For details, see the Form 1040 instructions.

TAXORGANIZER

Records you should keep.

- *W-2:* Wages, salaries, tips; allocated tips; advance EIC payments; dependent care benefits; adoption benefits; employer contributions to a medical savings account
- *W-2G:* Gambling winnings
- *1098:* Mortgage interest; points; refund of overpaid interest

- *1098-E:* Student loan interest
- *1099-A:* Acquisition or abandonment of secured property
- *1099-B:* Stocks and bonds; bartering; futures contracts
- *1099-C:* Canceled debt
- *1099-DIV:* Ordinary dividends; total capital gains distributions; nontaxable distributions; investment expenses; foreign tax paid
- *1099-G:* Unemployment compensation; state or local income tax refund; taxable grants; agriculture payments
- *1099-INT:* Interest income; early withdrawal penalty; interest on U.S. savings bonds and Treasury obligations

- *1099-LTC:* Long-term care and accelerated death benefits
- *1099-MISC:* Rents; royalties; other income (prizes, awards); nonemployee compensation
- *1099-MSA, 1099-HSA:* Distributions from medical savings accounts and health savings accounts
- *1099-OID:* Original issue discount; other periodic interest; early withdrawal penalty
- *1099-PATR:* Patronage dividends and other distributions from a cooperative; credits; patron's AMT adjustment
- *1099-R:* Distributions from IRAs; distributions from pensions, annuities; capital gain
- *1099-S:* Gross proceeds from real estate transactions; buyer's part of real estate tax

33

Tax on Investment Income of Certain Minor Children

Note: The 2004 IRS Publication 17 (Your Federal Income Tax) has been updated by Ernst & Young LLP for 2005. Dates and dollar amounts shown are for 2005. Gray type is used to indicate where IRS text has been updated or intentionally omitted. Unrevised IRS text is shown in black type.

Introduction

*There's nothing easy about bringing up children these days, and that applies to their tax returns as well. It is enormously complicated to determine the correct tax and fill out a proper tax return for children **under age 14** who have **unearned** income.*

Unearned income of children under age 14 is taxed at the marginal rate of their parents, as if the parents had received the income, rather than at the child's lower rate. This is commonly referred to as the "kiddie tax." Generally, this isn't going to give your child a break. Because most parents have a higher marginal tax rate than their children, these rules generally eliminate the benefits of transferring income-producing assets, such as stocks or bonds, to your minor children in order for the income to be taxed at the children's lower marginal rate.

The following are additional complications:

1. A child may not claim a personal exemption for himself or herself if he or she is eligible to be claimed on a parent's return.

2. A child's unearned income falls under special rules. The child can use $800 of his or her standard deduction to offset unearned income. The next $800 of unearned income is taxed at the child's tax rate. The balance of a child's unearned income will be taxed at the parent's marginal tax rate. This is accomplished by including the child's income on the parent's return (use Form 8814) OR by filing a tax return for the child (attach Form 8615).

3. If a child also has earned income, his or her tax return gets more complicated still. The earned income can increase his or her allowable standard deduction.

This chapter will help you sort through all the complications. Here's hoping that, while you're muddling through it, your children will be out having fun.

What's New

Investment income of child under age 14. The amount of taxable investment income a child under age 14 can have without it being subject to tax at the parent's rate remains at $1,600.

This chapter discusses the following two rules that may affect the tax on certain investment income of a child under age 14.

1. If the child's interest and dividend income total less than $8,000, the child's parent may be able to choose to include that income (including capital gain distributions) on the parent's return rather than file a return for the child. (See *Parent's Election To Report Child's Interest and Dividends,* later.)
2. If the child's interest, dividends, and other investment income total more than $1,600, part of that income may be taxed at the parent's tax rate instead of the child's tax rate. (See *Tax for Children Under Age 14 Who Have Investment Income of More Than $1,600,* later.)

For these rules, the term "child" includes a legally adopted child and a stepchild. These rules apply whether or not the child is a dependent.

These rules do not apply if:

- The child is not required to file a tax return, or
- Neither of the child's parents were living at the end of the tax year.

Explanation
For the 2005 tax year, "under age 14" means that the child has not reached age 14 by January 1, 2006. If your child reached age 14 at any time during 2005, this chapter will not apply.

TAXSAVER

The tax benefit of transferring investment property to your children is limited; however, some advantages still exist. First, keep in mind that the first $1,600 in investment income is taxed at a very low rate. Second, the child will eventually be 14 years old and have his or her own tax bracket (which will probably be lower than yours). Third, if the property appreciates in value while your child is a minor, the appreciation will not complicate your tax situation.

Useful Items

You may want to see:

Publication

☐ 929   Tax Rules for Children and Dependents

Forms (and Instructions)

☐ 8615   Tax for Children Under Age 14 With Investment Income of More Than $1,600
☐ 8814   Parents' Election To Report Child's Interest and Dividends

Which Parent's Return To Use

If a child's parents are married to each other and file a joint return, use the joint return to figure the tax on the investment income of a child under age 14. The tax rate and other return information from that return are used to figure the child's tax as explained later under *Tax for Children Under Age 14 Who Have Investment Income of More Than $1,600*.

Parents Who Do Not File a Joint Return

For parents who do not file a joint return, the following discussions explain which parent's tax return must be used to figure the tax. Only the parent whose tax return is used can make the election described under *Parent's Election To Report Child's Interest and Dividends*.

Parents are married. If the child's parents file separate returns, use the return of the parent with the greater taxable income.

Parents not living together. If the child's parents are married to each other but not living together, and the parent with whom the child lives (the custodial parent) is considered unmarried, use the return of the custodial parent. If the custodial parent is not considered unmarried, use the return of the parent with the greater taxable income.

For an explanation of when a married person living apart from his or her spouse is considered unmarried, see *Head of Household* in chapter 2.

Parents are divorced. If the child's parents are divorced or legally separated, and the parent who had custody of the child for the greater part of the year (the custodial parent) has not remarried, use the return of the custodial parent.

Custodial parent remarried. If the custodial parent has remarried, the stepparent (rather than the noncustodial parent) is treated as the child's other parent. Therefore, if the custodial parent and the stepparent file a joint return, use that joint return. Do not use the return of the noncustodial parent.

If the custodial parent and the stepparent are married, but file separate returns, use the return of the one with the greater taxable income. If the custodial parent and the stepparent are married but not living together, the earlier discussion under *Parents not living together* applies.

Explanation
When both parents have custody of a child with unearned income, the custodial parent is the parent with custody for the greater portion of the calendar year.

Parents never married. If a child's parents did not marry each other, but lived together all year, use the return of the parent with the greater taxable income. If the parents did not live together all year, the rules explained earlier under *Parents are divorced* apply.

Widowed parent remarried. If a widow or widower remarries, the new spouse is treated as the child's other parent. The rules explained earlier under *Custodial parent remarried* apply.

Parent's Election To Report Child's Interest and Dividends

You may be able to elect to include your child's interest and dividend income (including capital gain distributions) on your tax return. If you do, your child will not have to file a return.

You can make this election for 2005 only if all the following conditions are met.

- Your child was under age 14 at the end of 2005. (A child born on January 1,1992, is considered to be age 14 at the end of 2005. You cannot make the election for this child.)
- Your child is required to file a return for 2005, unless you make this election.
- Your child had income only from interest and dividends (including capital gain distributions and Alaska Permanent Fund dividends).
- The dividend and interest income was less than $8,000.
- No estimated tax payment was made for 2005 and no 2004 overpayment was applied to 2005 under your child's name and social security number.
- No federal income tax was taken out of your child's income under the backup withholding rules.
- You are the parent whose return must be used when applying the special tax rules for children under age 14. (See *Which Parent's Return To Use,* earlier.)

These conditions are also shown in Figure 33-A.

How to make the election. Make the election by attaching Form 8814 to your Form 1040 or Form 1040NR. (If you make this election, you cannot file Form 1040A or Form 1040EZ.) Attach a separate Form 8814 for each child for whom you make the election. You can make the election for one or more children and not for others.

Figure 33-A. **Can You Include Your Child's Income On Your Tax Return?**

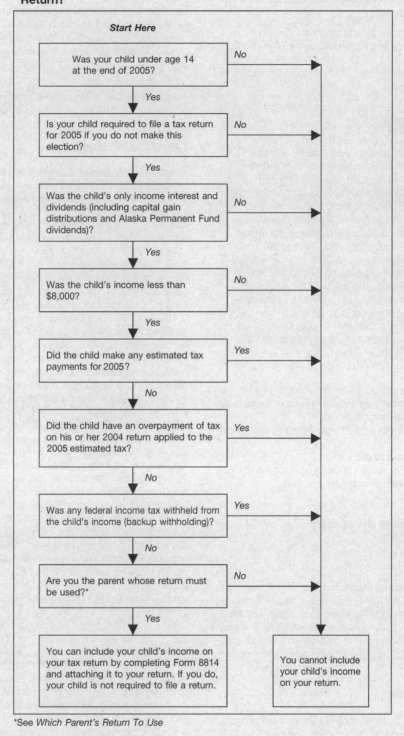

*See *Which Parent's Return To Use*

Effect of Making the Election

The federal income tax on your child's income may be more if you make the Form 8814 election.

Rate may be higher. If your child received qualified dividends or capital gain distributions, you may pay up to $40 more tax if you make this election instead of filing a separate tax return for the child. This is because the tax rate on the child's income between $800 and $1,600 is 10% if you make this election. However, if you file a separate return for the child, the tax rate may be as low as 5% because of the preferential tax rates for qualified dividends and capital gain distributions.

TAXSAVER

Most individuals will not want to elect to file Form 8814, because, as the IRS notes, in some cases it could result in more total tax.

Deductions you cannot take. By making the Form 8814 election, you cannot take any of the following deductions that the child would be entitled to on his or her return.

- The higher standard deduction for a blind child.
- The deduction for a penalty on an early withdrawal of your child's savings.
- Itemized deductions (such as your child's investment expenses or charitable contributions).

TaxSaver

If you use Form 8814 to add your child's income to yours, not only may your increased adjusted gross income reduce such items on your return as any itemized deductions for medical expenses, casualty and theft losses, and certain miscellaneous expenses, but it may also subject you to the personal exemption phase-out and the 3% reduction to itemized deductions (see Chapter 22, *Standard Deduction,* and Chapter 31, *Limit on Itemized Deductions*), as well as limit your deduction for IRA contributions (*see* Chapter 18, *Individual Retirement Arrangements* [IRAs]), and your ability to claim the favorable $25,000 rental loss allowance under the passive activity rules (see Chapter 13, *Other Income*). Finally, adding your child's income to yours also may increase your state and local tax liability. Consider this election carefully before filing Form 8814.

Reduced deductions or credits. If you use Form 8814, your increased adjusted gross income may reduce certain deductions or credits on your return including the following.

- Deduction for contributions to a traditional individual retirement arrangement (IRA).
- Deduction for student loan interest.
- Itemized deductions for medical expenses, casualty and theft losses, and certain miscellaneous expenses.
- Total itemized deductions.
- Personal exemptions.
- Credit for child and dependent care expenses.
- Child tax credit.
- Education tax credits.
- Earned income credit.

Penalty for underpayment of estimated tax. If you make this election for 2005 and did not have enough tax withheld or pay enough estimated tax to cover the tax you owe, you may be subject to a penalty. If you plan to make this election for 2006, you may need to increase your federal income tax withholding or your estimated tax payments to avoid the penalty. See chapter 5 for more information.

Figuring Child's Income

Use Part I of Form 8814 to figure your child's interest and dividend income to report on your return. Only the amount over $1,600 is added to your income. This amount is shown on line 6 of Form 8814. Include this amount on line 21 of Form 1040 or Form 1040NR. Enter "Form 8814" in the space next to line 21. If you file more than one Form 8814, include the total amounts from line 6 of all your Forms 8814 on line 21.

Capital gain distributions and qualified dividends. If your child's dividend income included any capital gain distributions see *Capital gain distributions* under *Figuring Child's Income* in Part 2 of Publication 929. If your child's dividend income included any qualified dividends, see *Qualified dividends* under *Figuring Child's Income* in Part 2 of Publication 929.

Figuring Additional Tax

Use Part II of Form 8814 to figure the tax on the $1,600 of your child's interest and dividends that you do not include in your income. This tax is added to the tax figured on your income.

This additional tax is the smaller of:

- 10% × (your child's gross income − $800), or $80.

Include the amount from line 9 of all your Forms 8814 in the total on Form 1040, line 44, or Form 1040NR, line 41. Check box a on Form 1040, line 44, or Form 1040NR, line 41.

Illustrated Example

David and Linda Parks are married and will file separate tax returns for 2005. Their only child, Philip, is 8. Philip received a Form 1099-INT showing $3,240 taxable interest income and a Form 1099-DIV showing $360 ordinary dividends. All the dividends were qualified dividends. His parents decide to include that income on one of their returns so they will not have to file a return for Philip.

First, David and Linda each figure their taxable income (Form 1040, line 43) without regard to Philip's income. David's taxable income is $41,700 and Linda's is $59,300. Because her taxable income is greater, Linda can elect to include Philip's income on her return. See *Which Parent's Return To Use,* earlier.

On Form 8814 (see illustrated form), Linda enters her name and social security number, then Philip's name and social security number. She enters Philip's taxable interest income, $3,240, on line 1a. Philip had no tax-exempt interest income, so she leaves line 1b blank. She enters Philip's ordinary dividends, $360, on line 2. Philip did not have any capital gain distributions, so she leaves line 3 blank.

Linda adds lines 1a and 2 and enters the result, $3,600, on line 4. Because Philip had qualified dividends, Linda must use the Child's Qualified Dividends and Capital Gain Distributions Worksheet to figure the amount to enter on line 6, instead of subtracting line 5 from line 4. The amount she enters on line 6 is $1,800, the amount from line 11 of the worksheet. On the dotted line next to line 6, she enters "QD−$200," the amount from line 8 of the worksheet. She includes that amount ($200) on lines 9a and 9b of her Form 1040. On the dotted line next to lines 9a and 9b, she enters "Form 8814−$200."

Linda includes $1,800 in the total on line 21 of her Form 1040 (not illustrated) and in the space next to that line enters "Form 8814−$1,800." Adding that amount, plus the $200 of qualified dividends, to her income increases each of the amounts on lines 22, 37, 38, 41, and 43 of her Form 1040 by $2,000. Linda is not claiming any deductions or credits that are affected by the increase to her income. Therefore, her revised taxable income on line 43 is $61,300 ($59,300 + $200 + $1,800).

On Form 8814, Linda subtracts the $800 shown on line 7 from the $3,600 on line 4 and enters the result, $2,800, on line 8. Because that amount is not less than $800, she enters $80 on line 9. This is the tax on the first $1,600 of Philip's income, which Linda did not have to add to her income. She must add this additional tax to the tax figured on her revised taxable income.

The tax on her $61,300 revised taxable income is $12,004. She adds $80, and enters the $12,084 total on line 44 of Form 1040, and checks box a.

Linda attaches Form 8814 to her Form 1040.

Tax for Children Under Age 14 Who Have Investment Income of More Than $1,600

Part of a child's 2005 investment income may be subject to tax at the parent's tax rate if all of the following statements are true.

- The child was under age 14 at the end of 2005. (A child born on January 1, 1992, is considered to be age 14 at the end of 2005. This child's investment income is not taxed at the parent's rate.)
- The child's investment income was more than $1,600.
- The child is required to file a return for 2005.

Figure 33-B. **Do You Have To Use Form 8615 To Figure Your Child's Tax?**

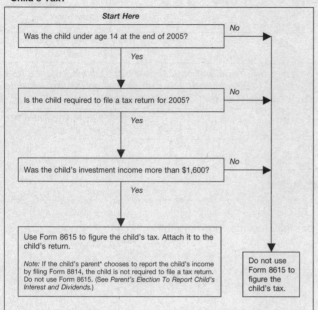

*See *Which Parent's Return To Use*

**Child's Qualified Dividends and
Capital Gain Distributions Worksheet**
(Keep for your records)

1. Enter the amount of qualified dividends included on Form 8814, line 2 . . . . $360
2. Enter the amount from Form 8814, line 3   0
3. Enter the amount from Form 8814, line 4   3,600
4. Divide line 1 by line 3. Enter the result as a decimal (rounded to at least 3 places)   .100
5. Divide line 2 by line 3. Enter the result as a decimal (rounded to at least 3 places)   .000
6. Base amount . . . . $ 1,600
7. Subtract line 6 from line 3 . . .   2,000
8. Multiply line 7 by line 4. Include this amount on Form 1040, lines 9a and 9b, or Form 1040NR, lines 10a and 10b. On the dotted lines next to those lines, enter "Form 8814" and this amount (unless you file Schedule B (Form 1040); in that case, follow the instructions in the **Note** on this line). Also, enter "QD" (for "qualified dividends") and this amount on the dotted line next to line 6 of Form 8814. **Note.** If this amount plus the parents' dividends is more than $1,500, report this amount on Schedule B (Form 1040). Show it as from "Form 8814"   200
9. Multiply line 7 by line 5. Include this amount on Schedule D, line 13; Form 1040, line 13, or Form 1040NR, line 14. Enter "Form 8814" and this amount on the dotted line next to line 13 of Schedule D, or in the space to the left of line 13 of Form 1040 or line 14 of Form 1040NR. Also, enter "CGD" (for "capital gain distribution") and this amount on the dotted line next to line 6 of Form 8814.   0
10. Add lines 8 and 9   200
11. Subtract line 10 from line 7. Enter the result here and on Form 8814, line 6   1,800

These conditions are also shown in Figure 33-B.

If neither parent was alive on December 31, 2005, do not use Form 8615. Instead, figure the child's tax in the normal manner.

If the parent does not or cannot choose to include the child's income on the parent's return, use Form 8615 to figure the child's tax. Attach the completed form to the child's Form 1040, Form 1040A, or Form 1040NR.

The following discussions explain the parental information needed for Form 8615 and the steps to follow in figuring the child's tax. Form 8615 is illustrated later.

Providing Parental Information (Form 8615, lines A–C)

On Form 8615, lines A and B, enter the parent's name and social security number. (If the parents filed a joint return, enter the name and social security number listed first on the joint return.) On line C, check the box for the parent's filing status.

See *Which Parent's Return To Use* at the beginning of this chapter for information on which parent's return information must be used on Form 8615.

Parent with different tax year. If the parent and the child do not have the same tax year, complete Form 8615 using the information on the parent's return for the tax year that ends in the child's tax year.

Parent's return information not known timely. If the information needed from the parent's return is not known by the time the child's return is due (usually April 15), you can file the return using estimates.

You can use any reasonable estimate. This includes using information from last year's return. If you use an estimated amount on Form 8615, enter "Estimated" on the line next to the amount.

When you get the correct information, file an amended return on Form 1040X, Amended U.S. Individual Income Tax Return.

Instead of using estimated information, you may want to request an extension of time to file. Extensions are discussed in chapter 1.

Step 1. Figuring the Child's Net Investment Income (Form 8615, Part I)

The first step in figuring a child's tax using Form 8615 is to figure the child's net investment income. To do that, use Form 8615, Part I. **Line 1 (investment income).** If the child had no earned income, enter on this line the adjusted gross income shown on the child's return. Adjusted gross income is shown on line 37 of Form 1040, line 22 of Form 1040A, or line 35 of Form 1040NR. Form 1040EZ and Form 1040NR-EZ cannot be used if Form 8615 must be filed.

If the child had earned income, figure the amount to enter on Form 8615, line 1, by using the worksheet in the instructions for the form.

However, if the child has excluded any foreign earned income or deducted either a loss from self-employment or a net operating loss from another year, use the Alternate Worksheet for Line 1 of Form 8615 in Publication 929 to figure the amount to enter on Form 8615, line 1.

Form **8814**	**Parents' Election To Report Child's Interest and Dividends**	OMB No. 1545-1128

Department of the Treasury
Internal Revenue Service

► See instructions.
► Attach to parents' Form 1040 or Form 1040NR.

2005

Attachment Sequence No. **40**

Name(s) shown on your return: Linda Parks

Your social security number: 111 : 00 : 1111

Caution: *The Federal income tax on your child's income, including qualified dividends and capital gain distributions, may be less if you file a separate tax return for the child instead of making this election. This is because you cannot take certain tax benefits that your child could take on his or her own return. For details, see* **Tax benefits you may not take** *on page 2.*

A Child's name (first, initial, and last): Philip Parks

B Child's social security number: 000 : 00 : 0000

C If more than one Form 8814 is attached, check here . . . . . . ►

Part I Child's Interest and Dividends To Report on Your Return

1a Enter your child's **taxable** interest. If this amount is different from the amounts shown on the child's Forms 1099-INT and 1099-OID, see the instructions	**1a**	3,500	
b Enter your child's **tax-exempt** interest. **Do not** include this amount on line 1a	**1b**		
2 Enter your child's ordinary dividends, including any Alaska Permanent Fund dividends. If your child received any ordinary dividends as a nominee, see the instructions	**2**		
3 Enter your child's capital gain distributions. If your child received any capital gain distributions as a nominee, see the instructions	**3**		
4 Add lines 1a, 2, and 3. If the total is $1,600 or less, skip lines 5 and 6 and go to line 7. If the total is $8,000 or more, **do not** file this form. Your child **must** file his or her own return to report the income	**4**	3,500	
5 Base amount	**5**	1,600	00
6 Subtract line 5 from line 4. See the instructions for where to report this amount. Go to line 7 below ►	**6**	1,900	

Part II Tax on the First $1,600 of Child's Interest and Dividends

7 Amount not taxed	**7**	800	00
8 Subtract line 7 from line 4. If the result is zero or less, enter -0-	**8**	2,700	
9 **Tax.** Is the amount on line 8 less than $800? ☑ **No.** Enter $80 here and see the **Note** below. ☐ **Yes.** Multiply line 8 by 10% (.10). Enter the result here and see the **Note** below.	**9**	80	

Note: *If you checked the box on line C above, see the instructions. Otherwise, include the amount from line 9 in the tax you enter on Form 1040, line 44, or Form 1040NR, line 41. Be sure to check box a on Form 1040, line 44, or Form 1040NR, line 41.*

For Paperwork Reduction Act Notice, see page 3.   Cat. No. 10750J   Form **8814** (2005)

Investment income defined. Investment income is generally all income other than salaries, wages, and other amounts received as pay for work actually done. It includes taxable interest, dividends, capital gains (including capital gain distributions), the taxable part of social security and pension payments, and certain distributions from trusts. Investment income includes amounts produced by assets the child obtained with earned income (such as interest on a savings account into which the child deposited wages).

Nontaxable income. For this purpose, investment income includes only amounts that the child must include in total income. Nontaxable investment income, such as tax-exempt interest and the nontaxable part of social security and pension payments, is not included.

Income from property received as a gift. A child's investment income includes all income produced by property belonging to the child. This is true even if the property was transferred to the child, regardless of when the property was transferred or purchased or who transferred it.

A child's investment income includes income produced by property given as a gift to the child. This includes gifts to the child from grandparents or any other person and gifts made under the Uniform Gift to Minors Act.

Example. Amanda Black, age 13, received the following income.

- Dividends — $600
- Wages — $2,100
- Taxable interest — $1,200
- Tax-exempt interest — $100
- Net capital gains — $100.

The dividends were on stock given to her by her grandparents.

Amanda's investment income is $1,900. This is the total of the dividends ($600), taxable interest ($1,200), and net capital gains ($100). Her wages are earned (not investment) income because they are received for work actually done. Her tax-exempt interest is not included because it is nontaxable.

Trust income. If a child is the beneficiary of a trust, distributions of taxable interest, dividends, capital gains, and other investment income from the trust are investment income to the child.

Line 2 (deductions). If the child does not itemize deductions on Schedule A (Form 1040 or Form 1040NR), enter $1,600 on line 2.

If the child does itemize deductions, enter on line 2 the larger of:

- $800 plus the child's itemized deductions that are directly connected with the production of investment income entered on line 1, or
- $1,600.

Directly connected. Itemized deductions are directly connected with the production of investment income if they are for expenses paid to produce or collect taxable income or to manage, conserve, or maintain property held for producing income. These expenses include custodian fees and service charges, service fees to collect taxable interest and dividends, and certain investment counsel fees.

These expenses are added to certain other miscellaneous itemized deductions on Schedule A (Form 1040). Only the amount greater than 2% of the child's adjusted gross income can be deducted. See chapter 30 for more information.

Explanation
Directly connected itemized deductions also include any investment interest expense deducted on the child's return that relates to debt incurred to finance the investments that produced the unearned income.

Example 1. Roger, age 12, has investment income of $8,000, no other income, no adjustments to income, and itemized deductions of $300 (net of the 2%-of-adjusted-gross-income limit) that are directly connected with his investment income. His adjusted gross income is $8,000, which is entered on Form 1040, line 37, and on Form 8615,

line 1. Line 2 is $1,600 because that is more than the sum of $800 and his directly connected itemized deductions of $300.

Example 2. Eleanor, 8, has investment income of $16,000 and an early withdrawal penalty of $100. She has no other income. She has itemized deductions of $1,050 (net of the 2%-of-adjusted-gross-income limit) that are directly connected with the production of her investment income. Her adjusted gross income, entered on line 1, is $15,900 ($16,000 − $100). The amount on line 2 is $1,850. This is the larger of:

- $800 plus the $1,050 of directly connected itemized deductions, or
- $1,600.

TAXSAVER

Children with investment income. If your child is under 14 years of age and has investment income and you are in the top income bracket, you may want to consider altering his or her investment strategy if it is financially appropriate. Because a child with over $1,600 in unearned income will be taxed at his or her parent's rate, it might be advisable to seek out deferred or tax-exempt income.

An example of deferred income might be generated by an investment in a growth-oriented stock or mutual fund. Such an investment may not pay high current dividends, and the realization of any appreciation in value may be deferred by holding the investment until the child reaches age 14. Tax-exempt income may be generated by municipal bonds or U.S. government EE bonds.

Line 3. Subtract line 2 from line 1 and enter the result on this line. If zero or less, do not complete the rest of the form. However, you must still attach Form 8615 to the child's tax return. Figure the tax on the child's taxable income in the normal manner.

Line 4 (child's taxable income). Enter on line 4 the child's taxable income from Form 1040, line 43; Form 1040A, line 27; or Form 1040NR, line 40.

Line 5 (net investment income). A child's net investment income cannot be more than his or her taxable income. Enter on line 5 the smaller of line 3 or line 4 of Form 8615. This is the child's net investment income.

If zero or less, do not complete the rest of the form. However, you must still attach Form 8615 to the child's tax return. Figure the tax on the child's taxable income in the normal manner.

Step 2. Figuring Tentative Tax at the Parent's Tax Rate (Form 8615, Part II)

The next step in completing Form 8615 is to figure a tentative tax on the child's net investment income at the parent's tax rate. The tentative tax at the parent's tax rate is the difference between the tax on the parent's taxable income figured with the child's net investment income (plus the net investment income of any other child whose Form 8615 includes the tax return information of that parent) and the tax figured without it.

When figuring the tentative tax at the parent's tax rate, do not refigure any of the exclusions, deductions, or credits on the parent's return because of the child's net investment income. For example, do not refigure the medical expense deduction.

Figure the tentative tax on Form 8615, lines 6 through 13.

Note. If the child has any capital gains or losses, get Publication 929 for help in completing Part II of Form 8615.

Line 7 (net investment income of other children). If the tax return information of the parent is also used on any other child's Form 8615, enter on line 7 the total of the amounts from line 5 of all the other children's Forms 8615. Do not include the amount from line 5 of the Form 8615 being completed.

Example. Paul and Jane Persimmon have three children, Sharon, Jerry, and Mike, who must attach Form 8615 to their tax returns. The children's net investment income amounts on line 5 of their Forms 8615 are:

- Sharon — $800
- Jerry — $600
- Mike — $1,000

Line 7 of Sharon's Form 8615 will show $1,600 ($600 + $1,000), the total of the amounts on line 5 of Jerry's and Mike's Forms 8615.

Line 7 of Jerry's Form 8615 will show $1,800 ($800 + $1,000).

Line 7 of Mike's Form 8615 will show $1,400 ($800 + $600).

Other children's information not available. If the net investment income of the other children is not available when the return is due, either file the return using estimates or get an extension of time to file. See *Parent's return information not known timely,* earlier.

Line 11 (tentative tax). Subtract line 10 from line 9 and enter the result on this line. This is the tentative tax.

If line 7 is blank, skip lines 12a and 12b and enter the amount from line 11 on line 13.

Lines 12a and 12b (dividing the tentative tax). If an amount is entered on line 7, divide the tentative tax shown on line 11 among the children according to each child's share of the total net investment income. This is done on lines 12a, 12b, and 13. Add the amount on line 7 to the amount on line 5 and enter the total on line 12a. Divide the amount on line 5 by the amount on line 12a and enter the result as a decimal on line 12b.

Example. In the earlier example under *Line 7 (net investment income of other children),* Sharon's Form 8615 shows $1,600 on line 7. The amount entered on line 12a is $2,400, the total of lines 5 and 7 ($800 + $1,600). The decimal on line 12b is .333, figured as follows and rounded to three places.

$$\frac{\$800}{\$2,400} = .333$$

Step 3. Figuring the Child's Tax (Form 8615, Part III)

The final step in figuring a child's tax using Form 8615 is to determine the larger of:

1. The total of:
   a. The child's share of the tentative tax based on the parent's tax rate, plus
   b. The tax on the child's taxable income in excess of net investment income, figured at the child's tax rate, or
2. The tax on the child's taxable income, figured at the child's tax rate.

This is the child's tax. It is figured on Form 8615, lines 14 through 18.

Alternative minimum tax. A child may be subject to alternative minimum tax (AMT) if he or she has certain items given preferential treatment under the tax law. See *Alternative Minimum Tax* in chapter 32.

For more information on who is liable for AMT and how to figure it, get Form 6251. For information on special limits that apply to a child who files Form 6251, Alternative Minimum Tax—Individuals, see *Alternative Minimum Tax* in Publication 929.

Illustrated Example

The following example includes a completed Form 8615. Form 1040A is not shown.

John and Laura Brown have one child, Sara. She is 13 and has $2,800 taxable interest income and $1,500 earned income. She does not itemize deductions. John and Laura file a joint return with John's name and social security number listed first. They claim three exemptions, including an exemption for Sara, on their return.

Because Sara is under age 14 and has more than $1,600 investment income, part of her income may be subject to tax at her parents' rate. A completed Form 8615 must be attached to her return. Sara's father, John, fills out Sara's return for her.

John enters his name and social security number on Sara's Form 8615 because his name and number are listed first on the joint return he and Laura are filing. He checks the box for married filing jointly.

He enters Sara's investment income, $2,800, on line 1. Sara does not itemize deductions, so John enters $1,600 on line 2. He enters $1,200 ($2,800 − $1,600) on line 3.

Sara's taxable income, as shown on line 27 of her Form 1040A, is $2,550. This is her total income ($4,300) minus her standard deduction ($1,750). Her standard deduction is limited to the amount of her earned income plus $250. John enters $2,550 on line 4.

John compares lines 3 and 4 and enters the smaller amount, $1,200, on line 5.

John enters $48,000 on line 6. This is the taxable income from line 43 of their joint Form 1040 return. Sara is an only child, so line 7 is blank. He adds line 5 ($1,200), line 6 ($48,000), and line 7 (blank), and enters $49,200 on line 8.

Using the column for married filing jointly in the Tax Table, John finds the tax on $49,200. He enters the tax, $6,650, on line 9. He enters $6,470 on line 10. This is the tax from line 44 of John and Laura's Form 1040. He enters $180 on line 11 ($6,650 − $6,470).

Because line 7 is blank, John skips lines 12a and 12b and enters $180 on line 13.

John subtracts line 5 ($1,200) from line 4 ($2,550) and enters the result, $1,350, on line 14. Using the column for single filing status in the Tax Table, John finds the tax on $1,350 and enters this tax, $136, on line 15. He adds lines 13 ($180) and 15 ($136) and enters $316 on line 16.

Using the column for single filing status in the Tax Table, John finds the tax on $2,550 (line 4) and enters this tax, $256, on line 17.

John compares lines 16 and 17 and enters the larger amount, $316, on line 18 of Sara's Form 8615. He also enters that amount on line 28 of Sara's Form 1040A.

John also completes Schedule 1 (Form 1040A) for Sara.

TaxOrganizer

Records you should keep. You should retain documentation for the following items:

1. *1099-INT or 1099-OID:* Child's interest income.
2. *1099-DIV:* Child's dividend investment income; child's capital gain investment income.
3. *W-2:* Child's earned income; child's estimated tax payments for the year (if any).

Form **8615**	**Tax for Children Under Age 14 With Investment Income of More Than $1,600** ► Attach only to the child's Form 1040, Form 1040A, or Form 1040NR. ► See separate instructions.	OMB No. 1545-0998 **2005** Attachment Sequence No. **33**

Department of the Treasury Internal Revenue Service (99)

Child's name shown on return	Child's social security number
Sara L. Brown	117 : 00 : 1111

Before you begin: If the child, the parent, or any of the parent's other children under age 14 must use the Schedule D Tax Worksheet or has income from farming or fishing, see **Pub. 929**, Tax Rules for Children and Dependents. It explains how to figure the child's tax using the **Schedule D Tax Worksheet** or **Schedule J** (Form 1040).

A	Parent's name (first, initial, and last). **Caution:** See instructions before completing.	B	Parent's social security number
	John J. Brown		007 : 00 : 0001

C Parent's filing status (check one):

☐ Single   ☑ Married filing jointly   ☐ Married filing separately   ☐ Head of household   ☐ Qualifying widow(er)

Part I   Child's Net Investment Income

1	Enter the child's investment income (see instructions)	**1**	2,800
2	If the child **did not** itemize deductions on **Schedule A** (Form 1040 or Form 1040NR), enter $1,600. Otherwise, see instructions	**2**	1,600
3	Subtract line 2 from line 1. If zero or less, **stop;** do not complete the rest of this form but **do** attach it to the child's return	**3**	1,200
4	Enter the child's **taxable income** from Form 1040, line 43; Form 1040A, line 27; or Form 1040NR, line 40	**4**	2,550
5	Enter the **smaller** of line 3 or line 4. If zero, **stop;** do not complete the rest of this form but **do** attach it to the child's return	**5**	1,200

Part II   Tentative Tax Based on the Tax Rate of the Parent

6	Enter the parent's **taxable income** from Form 1040, line 43; Form 1040A, line 27; Form 1040EZ, line 6; Form 1040NR, line 40; or Form 1040NR-EZ, line 14. If zero or less, enter -0-	**6**	48,000
7	Enter the total, if any, from Forms 8615, line 5, of **all other** children of the parent named above. **Do not** include the amount from line 5 above	**7**	
8	Add lines 5, 6, and 7 (see instructions)	**8**	49,200
9	Enter the tax on the amount on line 8 based on the **parent's** filing status above (see instructions). If the Qualified Dividends and Capital Gain Tax Worksheet, Schedule D Tax Worksheet, or Schedule J (Form 1040) is used to figure the tax, check here ► ☐	**9**	6,650
10	Enter the parent's tax from Form 1040, line 44; Form 1040A, line 28, minus any alternative minimum tax; Form 1040EZ, line 10; Form 1040NR, line 41; or Form 1040NR-EZ, line 15. **Do not** include any tax from **Form 4972** or **8814.** If the Qualified Dividends and Capital Gain Tax Worksheet, Schedule D Tax Worksheet, or Schedule J (Form 1040) was used to figure the tax, check here ► ☐	**10**	6,470
11	Subtract line 10 from line 9 and enter the result. If line 7 is blank, also enter this amount on line 13 and go to **Part III**	**11**	180
12a	Add lines 5 and 7	**12a**	
b	Divide line 5 by line 12a. Enter the result as a decimal (rounded to at least three places)	**12b**	× .
13	Multiply line 11 by line 12b	**13**	180

Part III   Child's Tax—If lines 4 and 5 above are the same, enter -0- on line 15 and go to line 16.

14	Subtract line 5 from line 4	**14** 1,350	
15	Enter the tax on the amount on line 14 based on the **child's** filing status (see instructions). If the Qualified Dividends and Capital Gain Tax Worksheet, Schedule D Tax Worksheet, or Schedule J (Form 1040) is used to figure the tax, check here ► ☐	**15**	136
16	Add lines 13 and 15	**16**	316
17	Enter the tax on the amount on line 4 based on the **child's** filing status (see instructions). If the Qualified Dividends and Capital Gain Tax Worksheet, Schedule D Tax Worksheet, or Schedule J (Form 1040) is used to figure the tax, check here ► ☐	**17**	256
18	Enter the **larger** of line 16 or line 17 here and on the **child's** Form 1040, line 44; Form 1040A, line 28; or Form 1040NR, line 41	**18**	316

For Paperwork Reduction Act Notice, see the instructions.   Cat. No. 64113U   Form **8615** (2005)

Draft as of 06/07/2005

Child and Dependent Care Credit

Note: The 2004 IRS Publication 17 (Your Federal Income Tax) has been updated by Ernst & Young LLP for 2005. Dates and dollar amounts shown are for 2005. Gray type is used to indicate where IRS text has been updated or intentionally omitted. Unrevised IRS text is shown in black type.

Introduction

*A credit that directly reduces your taxes is available for certain child and **dependent** care expenses that enable you to work. The credit may be as much as $1,050 if you have one qualifying individual or $2,100 if you have more than one qualifying individual. The credit is designed to help ease the tax burden of persons who must work and who also have the responsibility for the care of children or disabled dependents and spouses.*

*In general, to claim this credit, you must pay someone to care for a qualifying individual so that you can work or look for work. You must also have **earned income** from your work during the year and must have maintained a home for yourself and the qualifying individual. This chapter spells out all the details.*

What's New

Qualifying Individual. As of January 1, 2005, the definition of a qualifying individual for purposes of the child and dependent care credit has been substantially revised. Under these new rules the following individuals qualify a taxpayer for the child and dependent care credit:

(1) a dependent of yours, (i.e., a qualifying child, see chapter 3) who hasn't attained age 13

(2) a dependent of yours who is physically or mentally incapable of caring for himself and who has the same principal place of abode as you for more than half of the tax year

(3) your spouse, if the spouse is physically or mentally incapable of caring for himself or herself and has the same principal place of abode as you for more than half of the tax year

For a child of parents who are divorced, separated, or living apart, see below.

If a child turned 13 during the year, the child is a qualifying per-son only for the part of the year he or she was under age 13. A child attains a given age on the anniversary of the date the child was born.

The status of a person as a qualifying individual is determined on a daily basis. So if your dependent or the spouse loses his or her qualifying status on September 16, you can include employment-related expenses through September 15 in computing the credit.

An individual isn't treated as having the same principal place of abode as you if, at any time during the tax year, the relationship between you and the individual violates local law.

Combat pay election. If you elected to include nontaxable combat pay in earned income when figuring the earned income credit for 2005, also include it in earned income when you figure the amount of dependent care benefits you exclude or deduct from income. For more information, see chapter 38.

Maintenance of household. The requirement that you maintain a household in order to claim the child and dependent care credit has been eliminated as of January 1, 2005.

TaxAlert

Effective January 1, 2005, the Working Families Tax Relief Act of 2004 established a uniform definition for "qualifying child" for the purposes of the dependency exemption, the child tax credit, the earned income tax credit, the dependent care credit, and head of household filing status. This definition can be found at www.irs.gov and is intended to simplify the meaning of a "qualifying child" for purposes of several tax benefits, such as head of household filing status, the exemption for a dependent, the child tax credit, the child and dependent care credit, and the earned income tax credit. An explanation of this definition can also be found in chapter 3.

Reminders

Taxpayer identification number needed for each qualifying person. You must include on line 2 of Form 2441 or Schedule 2 (Form 1040A) the name and taxpayer identification number (generally the social security number) of each qualifying person. See *Taxpayer identification number* under *Qualifying Person Test,* later.

You may have to pay employment taxes. If you pay someone to come to your home and care for your dependent or spouse, you may be a household employer who has to pay employment taxes. Usually, you are not a household employer if the person who cares for your dependent or spouse does so at his or her home or place of business. See *Employment Taxes for Household Employers,* later.

Explanation
See Chapter 42, *What to Do if You Employ Domestic Help.*

This chapter discusses the credit for child and dependent care expenses and covers the following topics.

- Tests you must meet to claim the credit.
- How to figure the credit.
- How to claim the credit.
- Employment taxes you may have to pay as a household employer.

You may be able to claim the credit if you pay someone to care for your dependent who is under age 13 or for your spouse or dependent who is not able to care for himself or herself. The credit can be up to 35% of your expenses. To qualify, you must pay these expenses so you can work or look for work.

Caution. *This credit should not be confused with the child tax credit discussed in chapter 36.*

Dependent care benefits. If you received any dependent care benefits from your employer during the year, you may be able to exclude from your income all or part of them. You must complete Part III of Form 2441 or Schedule 2 (Form 1040A) before you can figure the amount of your credit. See *Dependent Care Benefits* under *How To Figure the Credit,* later.

Useful Items

You may want to see:

Publications

- ☐ **501** Exemptions, Standard Deduction, and Filing Information
- ☐ **503** Child and Dependent Care Expenses
- ☐ **926** Household Employer's Tax Guide

Forms (and Instructions)

- ☐ **2441** Child and Dependent Care Expenses
- ☐ **Schedule 2 (Form 1040A)** Child and Dependent Care Expenses for Form 1040A Filers
- ☐ **Schedule H (Form 1040)** Household Employment Taxes
- ☐ **W-7** Application for IRS Individual Taxpayer Identification Number
- ☐ **W-10** Dependent Care Provider's Identification and Certification

Tests To Claim the Credit

To be able to claim the credit for child and dependent care expenses, you must file Form 1040 or Form 1040A, not Form 1040EZ, and meet all the following tests.

1. The care must be for one or more qualifying persons who are identified on the form you use to claim the credit. (See *Qualifying Person Test.*)
2. You (and your spouse if you are married) must keep up a home that you live in with the qualifying person or persons. (See *Keeping Up a Home Test,* later.)
3. You (and your spouse if you are married) must have earned income during the year. (However, see *Rule for student-spouse or spouse not able to care for self* under *Earned Income Test,* later.)
4. You must pay child and dependent care expenses so you (and your spouse if you are married) can work or look for work. (See *Work-Related Expense Test,* later.)
5. You must make payments for child and dependent care to someone you (or your spouse) cannot claim as a dependent. If you make payments to your child, he or she cannot be your dependent and must be age 19 or older by the end of the year. (See *Payments to Relatives* under *Work-Related Expense Test,* later.)
6. Your filing status must be single, head of household, qualifying widow(er) with dependent child, or married filing jointly. You must file a joint return if you are married, unless an exception applies to you. (See *Joint Return Test,* later.)
7. You must identify the care provider on your tax return. (See *Provider Identification Test,* later.)
8. If you exclude or deduct dependent care benefits provided by a dependent care benefits plan, the total amount you exclude or deduct must be less than the dollar limit for qualifying expenses (generally, $3,000 if one qualifying person was cared for or $6,000 if two or more qualifying persons were cared for). (If two or more qualifying persons were cared for, the amount you exclude or deduct will always be less than the dollar limit, since the amount you can exclude or deduct is limited to $5,000. See *Reduced Dollar Limit* under *How To Figure the Credit,* later.)

These tests are presented in Figure 34-A and are also explained in detail in this chapter.

Qualifying Person Test

Your child and dependent care expenses must be for the care of one or more qualifying persons.

A qualifying person is:

1. Your qualifying child who was under age 13 when the care was provided,
2. Your spouse who was physically or mentally not able to care for himself or herself and who had the same principal place of abode as you for more than half the tax year, or
3. Your dependent who was physically or mentally not able to care for himself or herself and [IRS text intentionally omitted] who had the same principal place of abode as you for more than half the tax year.

If you are divorced or separated, see *Child of Divorced or Separated Parents,* later, to determine which parent may treat the child as a qualifying person.

Figure 34-A **Can You Claim the Child and Dependent Care Credit?**

In order to claim a child and dependent care credit you must meet the following requirements:

1. You must have one or more "qualifying individuals." A qualifying individual is anyone who is your dependent who is not yet 13 or your dependent who is physically or mentally incapable of caring for himself and who lives with you for more than half of the tax year or your spouse, if he is physically or mentally incapable of caring for himself and lives with you for more than half of the tax year.

   If you're divorced or separated, a special rule may apply. If you have a child who's under age 13 or is physically or mentally incapable of caring for himself that child is treated as your qualifying individual if you are the custodial parent even if the noncustodial parent can claim the child as a dependent. The noncustodial parent can't get the credit even though the noncustodial parent gets the dependency exemption.

2. You must have incurred qualifying expenses that enable you to be gainfully employed.

   Qualifying expenses are limited to the income you or your spouse earns from work, using the figure for whoever of you earns less. If one of you has no earned income, you won't be entitled to any credit. But if one spouse has no actual earned income and that spouse is a full-time student or disabled, that spouse is considered to have monthly income of $250 (if the couple has one qualifying child) or $500 (two or more qualifying children).

   Qualifying expenses can't be more than $3,000 per year if you have one qualifying individual, or $6,000 per year for two or more. If your employer has a dependent care assistance program under which you receive benefits excluded from gross income, the dollar limits ($3,000 or $6,000) are reduced by the excludable amounts you receive

3. To claim the credit, you and your spouse must file a joint return.

If a child turned 13 during the year, the child is a qualifying person only for the part of the year he was under age 13.
An individual isn't treated as living with you if, at any time during the year, the relationship between you and the individual violates local law.

Physically or mentally not able to care for oneself. Persons who cannot dress, clean, or feed themselves because of physical or mental problems are considered not able to care for themselves. Also, persons who must have constant attention to prevent them from injuring themselves or others are considered not able to care for themselves.

Explanation
For a person to be considered disabled, physical or mental incapacity must prevent the person from caring for himself or herself. The mere inability to engage in any substantial gainful activity, perform the normal household functions of a homemaker, or care for minor children does not necessarily establish that the person cannot care for himself or herself.

Person qualifying for part of year. You determine a person's qualifying status each day. For example, if the person for whom you pay child and dependent care expenses no longer qualifies on September 16, count only those expenses through September 15. Also see *Dollar Limit* under *How To Figure the Credit*, later.

Taxpayer identification number. You must include on your return the name and taxpayer identification number (generally the social security number) of the qualifying person(s). If the correct information is not shown, the credit may be reduced or disallowed.

Individual taxpayer identification number (ITIN) for aliens. If your qualifying person is a nonresident or resident alien who does not have and cannot get a social security number (SSN), use that person's ITIN. To apply for an ITIN, file Form W-7 with the IRS. The ITIN is entered wherever an SSN is requested on a tax return.

An ITIN is for tax use only. It does not entitle the holder to social security benefits or change the holder's employment or immigration status under U.S. law.

Adoption taxpayer identification number (ATIN). If your qualifying person is a child who was placed in your home for adoption and for whom you do not have an SSN, you must get an ATIN for the child. File Form W-7A, Application for Taxpayer Identification Number for Pending U.S. Adoptions.

Child of Divorced or Separated Parents
To be a qualifying person, your child usually must be your dependent. But there is an exception to this rule that applies to a child of divorced or separated parents.

A child who is under age 13, or is physically or mentally incapable of caring for himself, is treated as a qualifying person for a custodial parent and not the noncustodial parent even if the noncustodial parent can claim the child as a dependent under the release rules discussed in chapter 3 (the custodial parent released the right to claim the child as a dependent). The child is treated as a qualifying individual either as a dependent under age 13, or as a dependent who is physically or mentally incapable of self-care (whichever is appropriate), for the custodial parent.

The custodial parent means the parent with whom the child shared the same home for a greater portion of the calendar year where the child is in the custody of one or both parents for more than half the calendar year and receives over half of his support from the parents during the calendar year

Example: You are the custodial parent and provide all the support for your 8-year-old son, Sam. You pay for a babysitter to watch your son while you're at work. You are divorced, and you signed a declaration releasing the dependency exemption to your ex-wife. You are still entitled to claim the credit.

[IRS text intentionally omitted]

Explanation
To take the credit, you do not necessarily have to claim the child as a dependent. If you have custody of the child even though you have signed a statement that entitles your ex-spouse to the child's dependency exemption, you may still claim the credit. To receive the credit, however, you must write your child's name on line 2 of Form 2441, or Schedule 2 of Form 1040A. To avoid questions from the IRS, you may want to attach to your tax return a copy of the signed statement authorizing the release of your dependency claim.

Example

Charles and Katherine Collins are divorced and share custody of their 3-year-old son, Dieter. Dieter lives 10 months a year with Katherine and attends a day-care center while his mother works. Charles and Katherine provide all of Dieter's support. Dieter is a qualifying person, since he is under age 13, is in the custody of his parents for more than half the year, and receives more than half his support from his parents. He is a qualifying person for Katherine and not Charles, because Katherine has custody of him for a longer period than does Charles. Dieter is a qualifying person for Katherine, even if she has released her right to claim him as a dependent to Charles.

In no case may two taxpayers filing separate returns claim separate tax credits for the same qualifying individual.

[IRS text intentionally omitted]

Earned Income Test

To claim the credit, you (and your spouse if you are married) must have earned income during the year.

Earned income. Earned income includes wages, salaries, tips, other taxable employee compensation, and net earnings from self-employment. A net loss from self-employment reduces earned income. Earned income also includes strike benefits and any disability pay you report as wages.

Earned income also includes nontaxable employee compensation such as parsonage allowances, meals and lodging furnished for the convenience of the employer, voluntary salary deferrals, military basic quarters and subsistence allowances and in-kind quarters and subsistence, and military pay earned in a combat zone.

Members of certain religious faiths opposed to social security. Certain income earned by persons who are members of certain religious faiths that are opposed to participation in Social Security Act Programs and have an IRS-approved form that exempts certain income from social security and Medicare taxes may not be considered earned income for this purpose. See *Earned Income Test* in Publication 503.

Not earned income. Earned income does not include pensions or annuities, social security payments, workers' compensation, interest, dividends, or unemployment compensation. It also does not include scholarship or fellowship grants, except amounts paid to you (and reported on Form W-2) for teaching, research, or other services.

Rule for student-spouse or spouse not able to care for self. Your spouse is treated as having earned income for any month that he or she is:

1. A full-time student, or
2. Physically or mentally not able to care for himself or herself.

Figure the earned income of the nonworking spouse described under (1) or (2) above as explained under *Earned Income Limit,* later.

This rule applies to only one spouse for any one month. If, in the same month, both you and your spouse do not work and are either full-time students or physically or mentally not able to care for yourselves, only one of you can be treated as having earned income in that month.

Full-time student. You are a full-time student if you are enrolled at and attend a school for the number of hours or classes that the school considers full time. You must have been a student for some part of each of 5 calendar months during the

year. (The months need not be consecutive.) If you attend school only at night, you are not a full-time student. However, as part of your full-time course of study, you may attend some night classes.

School. The term "school" includes elementary schools, junior and senior high schools, colleges, universities, and technical, trade, and mechanical schools. It does not include on-the-job training courses, correspondence schools, and night schools.

Example

Ben Winston and Sarah G. Winston are married and file a joint return. Sarah works full-time. Ben was a full-time student from January through May and from September through December. Their 6-year-old son attends a day-care center while Ben is in school. Since Ben was a full-time student during at least 5 months of the year, the minimum required by the IRS, he is considered to have worked each of the 9 months he was a full-time student.

Assume the same facts, except that both Ben and Sarah were full-time students for 9 months during the year. Only one of them may be considered as having worked during the months they were students. They would not be able to claim a credit for child-care expenses.

Assume instead that while Ben and Sarah were full-time students, Ben also held a part-time job. Both may now be considered as having worked during the 9 months they were students—Ben because he was working and Sarah because she was a full-time student. They may claim a credit for child-care expenses.

Work-Related Expense Test

Child and dependent care expenses must be work related to qualify for the credit. Expenses are considered work related only if both of the following are true.

• They allow you (and your spouse if you are married) to work or look for work.
• They are for a qualifying person's care.

Working or Looking for Work

To be work related, your expenses must allow you to work or look for work. If you are married, generally both you and your spouse must work or look for work. Your spouse is treated as working during any month he or she is a full-time student or is physically or mentally not able to care for himself or herself.

Your work can be for others or in your own business or partnership. It can be either full time or part time.

Work also includes actively looking for work. However, if you do not find a job and have no earned income for the year, you cannot take this credit. See *Earned Income Test,* earlier.

Whether your expenses allow you to work or look for work depends on the facts. For example, the cost of a sitter while you and your spouse go out to eat is not normally a work-related expense.

An expense is not considered work related merely because you had it while you were working. The purpose of the expense must be to enable you to work.

Volunteer work. For this purpose, you are not considered to be working if you do unpaid volunteer work or volunteer work for a nominal salary.

Figure 34-B. **Is a Child of Divorced or Separated Parents a Qualifying Person?**

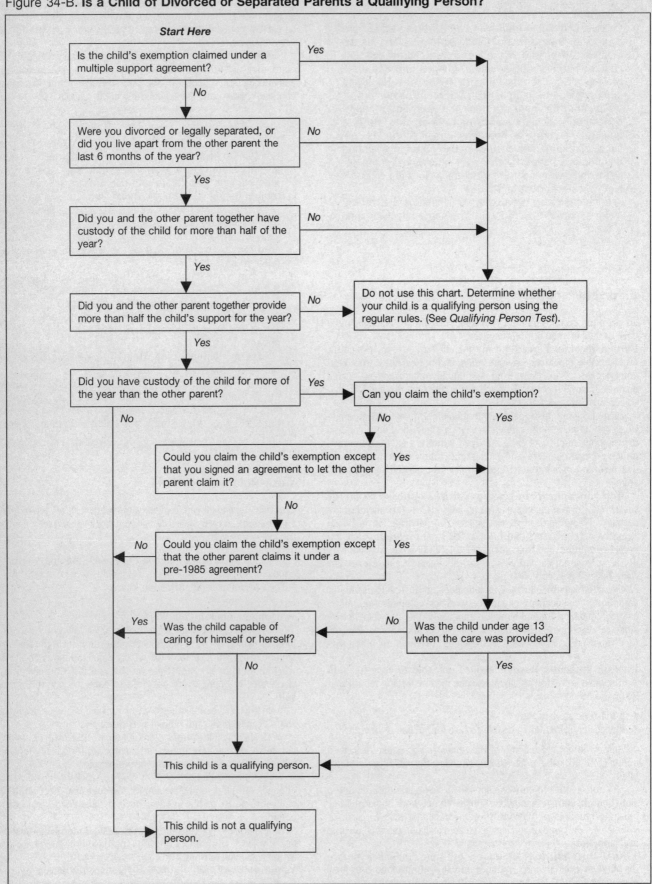

Example 1

Susan McMorris is single. She began looking for a job in November 2005. Prior to this time, she had not worked. While looking for a job, she paid a sitter to watch her 2-year-old daughter. She finally found a job in February 2006. Her child-care expenses during November and December 2005 were $125. Since Susan did not have income from work in 2005, she may not claim a credit for her child-care expenses for that year.

Assume the same facts, except that Susan had worked until October 2005 when she was laid off and began looking for a new job. In this instance, she did have income from work during the year, so she may claim a credit for her child care expenses incurred while looking for work.

Example 2

Missy Angelle works 12 hours per week as an unpaid volunteer in the local humane society. She pays a sitter to watch her 3-year-old twins while she is working. Since she is not compensated for her work, she may not claim a credit for her child-care expenses.

If Missy were paid $15 per week for her services in the library, she still could not claim a credit for her child-care expenses because her work is for a nominal salary. What is considered a nominal salary is determined by the facts and circumstances of each situation. As a general rule, however, if you are working for less than the minimum wage, you are probably working for a nominal salary.

Work for part of year. If you work or actively look for work during only part of the period covered by the expenses, then you must figure your expenses for each day. For example, if you work all year and pay care expenses of $250 a month ($3,000 for the year), all the expenses are work related. However, if you work or look for work for only 2 months and 15 days during the year and pay expenses of $250 a month, your work-related expenses are limited to $625 (2 1/2 months × $250).

Payments while you are out sick. Do not count as work-related expenses amounts you pay for child and dependent care while you are off work because of illness. These amounts are not paid to allow you to work. This applies even if you get sick pay and are still considered an employee.

Example

Chrissy Pietruskewicz, a single parent, has a housekeeper on weekdays to watch her 8-year-old daughter while Chrissy works. She pays the housekeeper $1,000 a month. As a result of illness, Chrissy was home 10 business days during September. Chrissy's work-related expenses for the month are $500 [(10 workdays ÷ 20 business days in September) × $1,000].

If you know that your total work-related expenses for the year will exceed the limits, it is not necessary to perform this calculation.

Care of a Qualifying Person

To be work related, your expenses must be to provide care for a qualifying person. You do not have to choose the least expensive way of providing the care.

Expenses are for the care of a qualifying person only if their main purpose is the person's well-being and protection.

Expenses for household services qualify if part of the services is for the care of qualifying persons. See *Household services,* later.

Expenses not for care. Expenses for care do not include amounts you pay for food, clothing, education, and entertainment. However, you can include small amounts paid for these items if they are incident to and cannot be separated from the cost of caring for the qualifying person.

Education. Expenses to attend first grade or a higher grade are not expenses for care. Do not use these expenses to figure your credit.

Explanation

You can use the total cost of schooling prior to first grade only if the cost of schooling cannot be separated from the cost of the child's care.

Example 1. You take your 3-year-old child to a nursery school that provides lunch and educational activities as a part of its preschool childcare service. You can count the total cost when you figure the credit.

Example 2. You place your 10-year-old child in a boarding school so you can work full time. Only the part of the boarding school expense that is for the care of your child is a work-related expense. You can count that part of the expense in figuring your credit if it can be separated from the cost of education. You cannot count any part of the amount you pay the school for your child's education.

Care outside your home. You can count the cost of care provided outside your home if the care is for your dependent under age 13 or any other qualifying person who regularly spends at least 8 hours each day in your home.

Dependent care center. You can count care provided outside your home by a dependent care center only if the center complies with all state and local regulations that apply to these centers.

A dependent care center is a place that provides care for more than six persons (other than persons who live there) and receives a fee, payment, or grant for providing services for any of those persons, even if the center is not run for profit.

Explanation

If a care center has six or fewer individuals enrolled on the day on which you enroll a qualified person, you may presume that it is not a dependent care center for the tax year. You may also presume that if a center was not a dependent care center in the prior year and has six or fewer individuals enrolled on January 1, it will not be considered a dependent care center during the current year.

As the IRS text notes, if care is provided by a dependent care center, the center must meet local and state regulations for your expenses to qualify for the credit. For example, most states stipulate the maximum permissible ratio of children to adult workers in a day-care center. You may wish to inquire at a center if it meets all state and local regulations. Ask to see a copy of the center's most recent certification from the proper authorities. However, if care is provided by a center that is not a dependent care center, the center need not meet local and state regulations for your expenses to qualify for the credit.

Example
Kitty Anderson attends a child-care center during the week while her mother works. The center regularly cares for 15 children and does not meet local and state regulations. The center is a dependent care center, but since the center does not meet the appropriate government regulations, expenses for Kitty's care do not qualify for the tax credit.

Assume the same facts, except that the center regularly cares for five children. Now the center is not a dependent care center. Expenses for Kitty's care qualify for the tax credit, although the center does not meet government regulations.

Camp. The cost of sending your child to an overnight camp is not considered a work-related expense.

Transportation. The cost of getting a qualifying person from your home to the care location and back, or from the care location to school and back, is not considered a work-related expense. This includes the costs of bus, subway, taxi, or private car. Also, if you pay the transportation cost for the care provider to come to your home, you cannot count this cost as a work-related expense.

Household services. Expenses you pay for household services meet the work-related expense test if they are at least partly for the well-being and protection of a qualifying person.

Household services are ordinary and usual services done in and around your home that are necessary to run your home. They include the services of a housekeeper, maid, or cook. However, they do not include the services of a chauffeur, bartender, or gardener. See *Household Services* in Publication 503 for more information.

TAXPLANNER

Allocating expenses. There are no hard-and-fast rules that govern when an allocation is reasonable or when the expense for other services is small in relation to the total expense. The facts and circumstances of each case are the determining factors. Use your best judgment. If you must make an allocation, you should document how the allocation is made. If you decide that an allocation is not necessary, you should also document the basis for your decision. A note in your personal records should be sufficient.

In this chapter, the term "housekeeper" refers to any household employee whose services include the care of a qualifying person.

Taxes paid on wages. The taxes you pay on wages for qualifying child and dependent care services are work-related expenses. See *Employment Taxes for Household Employers,* later.

Explanation
See Chapter 42, *What to Do if You Employ Domestic Help.*

Payments to Relatives
You can count work-related payments you make to relatives who are not your dependents, even if they live in your home. However, do not count any amounts you pay to:

1. A dependent for whom you (or your spouse if you are married) can claim an exemption, or
2. Your child who was under age 19 at the end of the year, even if he or she is not your dependent.

Example
Brandi McKenzie lives with her daughter Stacy and cares for her granddaughter Melissa after school while Stacy is at work. Stacy pays her mother $300 per month and cannot claim her as a dependent. These payments qualify as work-related expenses for Stacy.

Assume, instead, that Stacy pays her other daughter, Sarah, $150 per month to look after Melissa, Sarah's sister. Sarah turns 19 during the year and can be claimed as a dependent by Stacy. Stacy's payments to Sarah are not qualified work-related expenses.

Joint Return Test

Generally, married couples must file a joint return to take the credit. However, if you are legally separated or living apart from your spouse, you may be able to file a separate return and still take the credit.

Legally separated. You are not considered married if you are legally separated from your spouse under a decree of divorce or separate maintenance. You are eligible to take the credit on a separate return.

Married and living apart. You are not considered married and are eligible to take the credit if all the following apply.

1. You file a separate return.
2. Your home is the home of a qualifying person for more than half the year.
3. You pay more than half the cost of keeping up your home for the year.
4. Your spouse does not live in your home for the last 6 months of the year.

Example
Cole and Christine Lee separated in April. They are not **legally separated** at the end of the year and plan to file separate returns. Their two children lived with Christine for the entire year, and she provided more than half the costs of maintaining her household for the year. Christine may claim a credit on her separate return.

Assume, instead, that Cole and Christine were separated in August. Since Cole lived in Christine's home during part of the last 6 months of the year, a joint return must be filed to claim the credit.

Death of spouse. If your spouse died during the year and you do not remarry before the end of the year, you generally must file a joint return to take the credit. If you do remarry before the end of the year, the credit can be claimed on your deceased spouse's separate return.

Provider Identification Test

You must identify all persons or organizations that provide care for your child or dependent. Use Part I of Form 2441 or Schedule 2 (Form 1040A) to show the information.

Information needed. To identify the care provider, you must give the provider's:

1. Name,
2. Address, and
3. Taxpayer identification number.

If the care provider is an individual, the taxpayer identification number is his or her social security number or individual taxpayer identification number. If the care provider is an organization, then it is the employer identification number (EIN).

You do not have to show the taxpayer identification number if the care provider is one of certain tax-exempt organizations (such as a church or school). In this case, write "Tax-Exempt" in the space where the tax form calls for the number.

If you cannot provide all of the information or if the information you provide is incorrect you must be able to show that you used due diligence (discussed later) in trying to furnish the necessary information.

Getting the information. You can use Form W-10 to request the required information from the care provider. If you do not use Form W-10, you can get the information from:

1. A copy of the provider's social security card,
2. A copy of the provider's driver's license (in a state where the license includes the social security number),
3. A copy of the provider's completed Form W-4 if he or she is your household employee,
4. A copy of the statement furnished by your employer if the provider is your employer's dependent care plan, or
5. A letter or invoice from the provider if it shows the information.

Explanation
Also see *Records You Need* in Chapter 42, *What to Do if You Employ Domestic Help,* if the care provider does not have a social security number.

You should keep this information with your tax records. Do not send Form W-10 (or other document containing this information) to the Internal Revenue Service.

TAX ORGANIZER
Keep Form W-10 with your tax records to substantiate the name, address, and taxpayer identification number(s) of your day-care provider(s). If Form W-10 is not used, keep any other documents that substantiate the required information.

Due diligence. If the care provider information you give is incorrect or incomplete, your credit may not be allowed. However, if you can show that you used due diligence in trying to supply the information, you can still claim the credit.

You can show due diligence by getting and keeping the provider's completed Form W-10 or one of the other sources of information listed earlier. Care providers can be penalized if they do not provide this information to you or if they provide incorrect information.

Provider refusal. If the provider refuses to give you their identifying information, you should report whatever information you have (such as the name and address) on the form you use to claim the credit. Write "See page 2" in the columns calling for the information you do not have. On the bottom of page 2, explain that you requested the information from the care provider, but the provider did not give you the information. This statement will show

that you used due diligence in trying to furnish the necessary information.

How To Figure the Credit

Your credit is a percentage of your work-related expenses. Your expenses are subject to the earned income limit and the dollar limit. The percentage is based on your adjusted gross income.

Figuring Total Work-Related Expenses

To figure the credit for 2005 work-related expenses, count only those you paid by December 31, 2005.

Expenses prepaid in an earlier year. If you pay for services before they are provided, you can count the prepaid expenses only in the year the care is received. Claim the expenses for the later year as if they were actually paid in that later year.

Example
Martha Winters paid $1,800 in November 2005 to the day-care center her son attends. The payment was for the 6-month period from November 2005 through April 2006. She may use $600 (2/6 × $1,800) of this payment in calculating her credit for 2005. This amount represents payment for services rendered in November and December 2004. She may use $1,200 (4/6 × $1,800) of this payment in 2006. This amount represents payment for services rendered in January through April 2006.

Expenses not paid until the following year. Do not count 2004 expenses that you paid in 2005 as work-related expenses for 2005. You may be able to claim an additional credit for them on your 2005 return, but you must figure it separately. See *Payments for previous year's expenses* under *Amount of Credit* in Publication 503.

Tip. *If you had expenses in 2005 that you did not pay until 2006, you cannot count them when figuring your 2005 credit. You may be able to claim a credit for them on your 2006 return.*

TAXPLANNER
The general rule is that expenses used in computing your child-care credit are included in figuring your tax for the year in which the expenses are paid or for the year in which the services are provided, whichever is later. However, regardless of when they are paid, expenses are subject to the dollar limitation for the year in which the services are provided. You may not reap an additional tax advantage by paying your expenses in a year that is different from the one in which the services are provided.

Example
Bernadette Dryden, who is divorced and files a separate return, paid $300 in January 2005 for care provided for her daughter in November and December 2004. Her adjusted gross income and earned income in 2004 were $25,000, and she paid $1,200 for work-related expenses in 2004. Jennifer may increase her 2005 child care credit by $90 (as calculated in Column A, following).

	Column A	Column B
1) 2004 expenses paid in 2004	$1,200	$3,000
2) 2004 expenses paid in 2005	300	300
3) Total 2004 expenses	$1,500	$3,300
4) Limitation for one qualifying person	$3,000	$3,000
5) Earned income limitation	25,000	25,000
6) Smallest of lines 3, 4, and 5	1,500	3,000
7) Child care expenses used in calculating 2004 credit	(1,200)	(3,000)
8) 2004 expenses carried over to 2005	$300	$-0-
9) Credit percentage applicable for 2004 adjusted gross income	30%	30%
10) Increase in 2005 credit (line 8 × line 9)	$90	$-0-

Bernadette should attach a statement to her 2005 return, showing the above calculation in Column A as support for her inclusion of $90 on line 9, Form 2441.

Assume, instead, that Bernadette paid $3,000 in work-related expenses during 2004. No increase in her 2005 credit is available (see Column B above), since the maximum amount of expenses for 2004 is already used in calculating the credit. She receives no benefit for the $300 paid in 2005, as she would have received no benefit if it had been paid in 2004.

Expenses reimbursed. If a state social services agency pays you a nontaxable amount to reimburse you for some of your child and dependent care expenses, you cannot count the expenses that are reimbursed as work-related expenses.

Example. You paid work-related expenses of $3,000. You are reimbursed $2,000 by a state social services agency. You can use only $1,000 to figure your credit.

Medical expenses. Some expenses for the care of qualifying persons who are not able to care for themselves may qualify as work-related expenses and also as medical expenses. You can use them either way, but you cannot use the same expenses to claim both a credit and a medical expense deduction.

If you use these expenses to figure the credit and they are more than the earned income limit or the dollar limit, discussed later, you can add the excess to your medical expenses. However, if you use your total expenses to figure your medical expense deduction, you cannot use any part of them to figure your credit.

Example

During the year, you pay $3,350 to a private-duty nurse for the care of your physically handicapped dependent daughter, who is not able to care for herself. These expenses are for work done in your home and qualify as medical expenses. Your earned income for the year is $25,000. Because your work-related expenses are for one qualifying person, you may take a maximum of $3,000 of these expenses into account in figuring your tax credit. You may treat the remaining $350 as a medical expense.

Caution. *Amounts excluded from your income under your employer's dependent care benefits plan cannot be used to claim a medical expense deduction.*

Explanation

Keep copies of receipts and canceled checks to document the amount of dependent care expenses that you paid for the year. The fact that you have provided these to your employer's plan may not be sufficient without such records.

Dependent Care Benefits

If you receive dependent care benefits, your dollar limit for purposes of the credit may be reduced. See *Reduced Dollar Limit,* later. But, even if you cannot take the credit, you may be able to take an exclusion or deduction for the dependent care benefits.

Dependent care benefits. Dependent care benefits include:

1. Amounts your employer pays directly to either you or your care provider for the care of your qualifying person while you work, and
2. The fair market value of care in a day-care facility provided or sponsored by your employer.

Your salary may have been reduced to pay for these benefits. If you received benefits, they should be shown on your W-2 form. See *Statement for employee,* later.

Exclusion or deduction. If your employer provides dependent care benefits under a qualified plan, you may be able to exclude these benefits from your income. Your employer can tell you whether your benefit plan qualifies.

If you are self-employed and receive benefits from a qualified dependent care benefit plan, you are treated as both employer and employee. Therefore, you would not get an exclusion from wages but instead a deduction on Schedule C (Form 1040), line 14; Schedule E (Form 1040), line 18; or Schedule F (Form 1040), line 17. Partnerships would report a separately stated deduction on Schedule K-1 (Form 1065), line 11, that you enter on Schedule E (Form 1040), line 28.

If your plan qualifies, you must complete Part III of either Form 2441 or Schedule 2 (Form 1040A) to claim the exclusion or deduction. You cannot use Form 1040EZ.

The amount you can exclude or deduct is limited to the smallest of:

1. The total amount of dependent care benefits you received during the year,
2. The total amount of qualified expenses you incurred during the year,
3. Your earned income,
4. Your spouse's earned income, or
5. $5,000 ($2,500 if married filing separately).

The definition of earned income for this purpose is not exactly the same as the definition for the credit. See the instructions for Form 2441 or Schedule 2 (Form 1040A).

Explanation

You cannot claim any credit if your employer has reduced your income by the full $5,000 and you have been reimbursed the full $5,000. See *Reduced Dollar Limit* later.

TAXSAVER

Before you sign up for your employer's plan, you should determine which will give you the greater tax savings: the child-care credit or excluding the expenses from earnings under your employer's plan.

Statement for employee. Your employer must give you a Form W-2 (or similar statement) showing in box 10 the total amount of dependent care benefits provided to you during the year under a qualified plan. Your employer will also include any dependent care benefits over $5,000 in your wages shown on your Form W-2 in box 10.

Forfeitures. Forfeitures are amounts credited to your dependent care benefit account (flexible spending account) and included in the amount shown on your Form W-2 in box 10, but not received because you did not incur the expense. When figuring your exclusion, subtract any forfeitures from the total dependent care benefits reported by your employer. To do this, enter the forfeited amount on line 13 of Form 2441 or Schedule 2 (Form 1040A).

Caution. *Forfeitures do not include amounts that you expect to receive in the future.*

Effect of exclusion. If you exclude dependent care benefits from your income, the amount of the excluded benefits:

1. Is not included in your work-related expenses, and
2. Reduces the dollar limit, discussed later.

Earned Income Limit

The amount of work-related expenses you use to figure your credit cannot be more than:

1. Your earned income for the year if you are single at the end of the year, or
2. The smaller of your or your spouse's earned income for the year if you are married at the end of the year.

Earned income is defined under *Earned Income Test*, earlier.

Tip. *For purposes of item (2), use your spouse's earned income for the entire year, even if you were married for only part of the year.*

TAXPLANNER

At year-end, if you are self-employed, you should review your income and expenses for the year. To the extent it is possible, income and expenses for the remaining part of the year should be timed to take maximum advantage of the dependent care credit.

Separated spouse. If you are legally separated or married and living apart from your spouse (as described under *Joint Return Test*, earlier), you are not considered married for purposes of the earned income limit. Use only your income in figuring the earned income limit.

Surviving spouse. If your spouse died during the year and you file a joint return as a surviving spouse, you are not considered married for purposes of the earned income limit. Use only your income in figuring the earned income limit.

Community property laws. You should disregard community property laws when you figure earned income for this credit.

Example

Durwood and Sheila Dupuis are married and live in a community property state. Durwood earns $52,000 as an engineer, while Sheila earns $15,000 as a teaching assistant. Under community property laws, each is considered to have earned half the other's compensation. Hence, each is considered to bring in $33,500 [(50% × $52,000) + (50% × $15,000)]. For the purpose of calculating this tax credit, however, Durwood has $52,000 of earned income and Sheila has $15,000.

Student-spouse or spouse not able to care for self. Your spouse who is either a full-time student or not able to care for himself or herself is treated as having earned income. His or her earned income for each month is considered to be at least $250 if there is one qualifying person in your home, or at least $500 if there are two or more.

Spouse works. If your spouse works during that month, use the higher of $250 (or $500) or his or her actual earned income for that month.

Spouse qualifies for part of month. If your spouse is a full-time student or not able to care for himself or herself for only part of a month, the full $250 (or $500) still applies for that month.

Both spouses qualify. If, in the same month, both you and your spouse are either full-time students or not able to care for yourselves, only one spouse can be considered to have this earned income of $250 (or $500) for that month.

TAXALERT

As stated earlier under *Qualifying Person Test* (see page 469), if the dependent for whom you have work-related expenses is disabled for only part of a month, the total work-related expenses are limited to that part of the month.

Example 1

David and Donna are married and file a joint return. Because of an accident, David is incapable of self-care for the entire tax year. To keep working, Donna pays a neighbor $2,000 to take care of him. Donna's adjusted gross income is $29,000. The entire amount is earned income.

They figure their credit on the smallest of the following amounts:

1) Total work-related expenses	$ 2,000
2) Donna's earned income	$29,000
3) Income considered earned by David (12 × $250)	$3,000
Allowable credit (28% of $2,000)	$560

Example 2

Carlos works and keeps up a home for himself, his wife, Diana, and their two children (both under age 13). Carlos has adjusted gross income of $35,000. The entire amount is earned income.

Diana is a full-time student at State University from January 4 through June 10. She does not return to school after June 10.

They paid a neighbor $600 per month from January 4 to June 10 (total $3,600) to care for their two children in her home while the children are not in school.

They figure the credit on the smallest of the following amounts:

1) Total work-related expenses	$3,600
2) Carlos's earned income	$35,000
3) Income considered earned by Diana (6 × $500)	$3,000
Allowable credit (25% of $3,000)	$750

Dollar Limit

There is a dollar limit on the amount of your work-related expenses you can use to figure the credit. This limit is $3,000 for one qualifying person, or $6,000 for two or more qualifying persons.

Tip. *If you paid work-related expenses for the care of two or more qualifying persons, the $6,000 limit does not need to be divided equally among them. For example, if your work-related expenses for the care of one qualifying person are $3,200 and your work-related expenses for another qualifying person are $2,800, you can use the total, $6,000, when figuring the credit.*

Yearly limit. The dollar limit is a yearly limit. The amount of the dollar limit remains the same no matter how long, during the year, you have a qualifying person in your household. Use the $3,000 limit if you paid work-related expenses for the care of one qualifying person at any time during the year. Use $6,000 if you paid work-related expenses for the care of more than one qualifying person at any time during the year.

Example

Wendy Ackal employs a full-time housekeeper to care for her two children while she works. Her older child turned 13 years old during the year. The dollar limit on her work-related expenses is $6,000, since at some time during the year she had two qualifying persons.

Assume the same facts, except that Wendy has only one child, Paris, who turned 13 years old on August 31. The dollar limit on her work-related expenses is $3,000. Only her expenses through August 31 may be used. The limit is the maximum amount that may be used in calculating the credit. If her actual expenses through August are less than $3,000, she must use that amount in calculating her tax credit.

Reduced Dollar Limit

If you received dependent care benefits that you exclude or deduct from your income, you must subtract that amount from the dollar limit that applies to you. Your reduced dollar limit is figured on lines 28 through 32 of Form 2441 or lines 24 through 28 of Schedule 2 (Form 1040A). See *Dependent Care Benefits,* earlier, for information on excluding or deducting these benefits.

Example. George is a widower with one child and earns $24,000 a year. He pays work-related expenses of $2,900 for the care of his 4-year-old child and qualifies to claim the credit for child and dependent care expenses. His employer pays an additional $1,000 under a dependent care benefit plan. This $1,000 is excluded from George's income.

Although the dollar limit for his work-related expenses is $3,000 (one qualifying person), George figures his credit on only $2,000 of the $2,900 work-related expenses he paid. This is because his dollar limit is reduced as shown next.

George's Reduced Dollar Limit

1) Maximum allowable expenses for one qualifying person....................	$3,000
2) Minus: Dependent care benefits George excludes from income	−$1,000
3) Reduced dollar limit on expenses George can use for the credit	$2,000

Amount of Credit

To determine the amount of your credit, multiply your work-related expenses (after applying the earned income and dollar limits) by a percentage. This percentage depends on your adjusted gross income shown on Form 1040, line 37, or Form 1040A, line 22. The following table shows the percentage to use based on adjusted gross income.

IF your adjusted gross income is:		THEN the percentage is:
Over	**But not over**	
0	$15,000	35%
$15,000	17,000	34%
17,000	19,000	33%
19,000	21,000	32%
21,000	23,000	31%
23,000	25,000	30%
25,000	27,000	29%
27,000	29,000	28%
29,000	31,000	27%
31,000	33,000	26%
33,000	35,000	25%
35,000	37,000	24%
37,000	39,000	23%
39,000	41,000	22%
41,000	43,000	21%
43,000	No limit	20%

Example 1

Karl Dryden is single, has adjusted gross income of $23,500, and has $1,800 in qualified expenses for 2005. The credit available to him is $540 (30% × $1,800).

Assume, instead, that Karl has adjusted gross income of $28,500. Now his available tax credit is $504 (28% × $1,800).

Example 2

Joni Morris has a tax liability of $730 before credits and a potential child care credit of $1,050. She may use $730 of the child care credit to bring her tax liability to zero. The excess credit of $320 is effectively lost. It may not be refunded, carried forward to a future year, or carried back to a prior year.

How To Claim the Credit

To claim the credit, you can file Form 1040 or Form 1040A. You cannot claim the credit on Form 1040EZ.

Form 1040. You must complete Form 2441 and attach it to your Form 1040. Enter the credit on Form 1040, line 48. An example of a filled-in Form 2441 is at the end of this chapter.

Form 1040A. You must complete Schedule 2 (Form 1040A) and attach it to your Form 1040A. Enter the credit on your Form 1040A, line 29.

Limit on credit. The amount of credit you can claim is limited to the amount of your regular tax (after reduction by any allowable foreign tax credit) plus your alternative minimum tax, if any. For more information, see the instructions for Form 2441 or Schedule 2 (Form 1040A).

Tax credit not refundable. You cannot get a refund for any part of the credit that is more than this limit.

Recordkeeping. You should keep records of your work-related expenses. Also, if your dependent or spouse is not able to care for himself or herself, your records should show both the nature and the length of the disability. Other records you should keep to support your claim for the credit are described earlier under *Provider Identification Test.*

Explanation

Your records of work-related expenses may be either canceled checks or cash receipt tickets. A note in your files recording the nature and length of a person's disability should be sufficient documentation in most cases.

Example

The following example shows how to figure the credit for child and dependent care expenses for two children when employer-provided dependent care benefits are involved. The filled-in Form 2441 is shown at the end of this chapter.

Illustrated example. Joan Thomas is divorced and has two children, ages 3 and 9. She works at ACME Computers. Her adjusted gross income (AGI) is $29,000, and the entire amount is earned income.

Joan's younger child (Susan) stays at her employer's on-site childcare center while she works. The benefits from this childcare center qualify to be excluded from her income. Her employer reports the value of this service as $3,000 for the year. This $3,000 is shown in her Form W-2 in box 10 but is not included in taxable wages in box 1.

A neighbor cares for Joan's older child (Seth) after school, on holidays, and during the summer. Joan pays her neighbor $2,400 for this care.

Joan figures her credit on Form 2441 as follows.

1) Work-related expenses Joan paid	$2,400
2) Dollar limit (2 or more qualified individuals)	$6,000
3) Minus: Dependent care benefits excluded from Joan's income	−$3,000
4) Reduced dollar limit	$3,000
5) Lesser of expenses paid ($2,400) or dollar limit ($3,000) ...	$2,400
6) Percentage for AGI of $29,000	28%(.28)
7) Multiply the amount on line 5 by the percentage on line 6 ($2,400 × .28)	$ 672
8) Enter the amount from Form 1040, line 46	$1,376
9) Enter the amount from Form 1040, line 47	–0–
10) Subtract line 9 from line 8	1,376
11) Credit (Enter the smaller of line 7 or line 10)	$672

Explanation

Note: The dollar limit for two or more qualifying persons ($6,000) is reduced by the amount of excluded benefits, as discussed earlier under *Reduced Dollar Limit.*

Form **2441**

Department of the Treasury
Internal Revenue Service   (99)

Child and Dependent Care Expenses

▶ Attach to Form 1040.

▶ See separate instructions.

OMB No. 1545-0068

2005

Attachment
Sequence No. **21**

Name(s) shown on Form 1040

Joan Thomas

Your social security number

559 : 00 : 3436

Before you begin: You need to understand the following terms. See **Definitions** on page 1 of the instructions.

● **Dependent Care Benefits**   ● **Qualifying Person(s)**   ● **Qualified Expenses**

Part I **Persons or Organizations Who Provided the Care—**You **must** complete this part.
(If you need more space, use the bottom of page 2.)

1	(a) Care provider's name	(b) Address (number, street, apt. no., city, state, and ZIP code)	(c) Identifying number (SSN or EIN)	(d) Amount paid (see instructions)
	Pat Green	12 Ash Avenue Hometown, TX 75240	240-00-3811	2,400
	ACME Computers	(See W-2)		

Did you receive **dependent care benefits?**

No ——▶ Complete only Part II below.

Yes ——▶ Complete Part III on the back next.

Caution. If the care was provided in your home, you may owe employment taxes. See the instructions for Form 1040, line 62.

Part II **Credit for Child and Dependent Care Expenses**

2   Information about your **qualifying person(s).** If you have more than two qualifying persons, see the instructions.

(a) Qualifying person's name		(b) Qualifying person's social security number	(c) Qualified expenses you incurred and paid in 2005 for the person listed in column (a)
First	Last		
Seth	Thomas	559 : 00 : 1234	2,400
Susan	Thomas	559 : 00 : 5678	

3	Add the amounts in column (c) of line 2. **Do not** enter more than $3,000 for one qualifying person or $6,000 for two or more persons. If you completed Part III, enter the amount from line 32	**3**	2,400	
4	Enter your **earned income.** See instructions	**4**	29,000	
5	If married filing jointly, enter your spouse's earned income (if your spouse was a student or was disabled, see the instructions); **all others,** enter the amount from line 4	**5**	29,000	
6	Enter the **smallest** of line 3, 4, or 5	**6**	2,400	
7	Enter the amount from Form 1040, line 38 **7** 29,000			
8	Enter on line 8 the decimal amount shown below that applies to the amount on line 7			

If line 7 is:			If line 7 is:		
Over	But not over	Decimal amount is	Over	But not over	Decimal amount is
$0—15,000		.35	$29,000—31,000		.27
15,000—17,000		.34	31,000—33,000		.26
17,000—19,000		.33	33,000—35,000		.25
19,000—21,000		.32	35,000—37,000		.24
21,000—23,000		.31	37,000—39,000		.23
23,000—25,000		.30	39,000—41,000		.22
25,000—27,000		.29	41,000—43,000		.21
27,000—29,000		.28	43,000—No limit		.20

8   × .28

9	Multiply line 6 by the decimal amount on line 8. If you paid 2004 expenses in 2005, see the instructions	**9**	672	
10	Enter the amount from Form 1040, line 46, minus any amount on Form 1040, line 47	**10**	1,376	
11	**Credit for child and dependent care expenses.** Enter the **smaller** of line 9 or line 10 here and on Form 1040, line 48	**11**	672	

For Paperwork Reduction Act Notice, see page 4 of the instructions.   Cat. No. 11862M   Form **2441** (2005)

Draft as of 04/04/2005

Form 2441 (2005)   Page **2**

Part III   Dependent Care Benefits

12	Enter the total amount of **dependent care benefits** you received in 2005. Amounts you received as an employee should be shown in box 10 of your Form(s) W-2. **Do not** include amounts reported as wages in box 1 of Form(s) W-2. If you were self-employed or a partner, include amounts you received under a dependent care assistance program from your sole proprietorship or partnership	**12**	3,000
13	Enter the amount forfeited, if any (see the instructions)	**13**	
14	Subtract line 13 from line 12	**14**	3,000

15	Enter the total amount of **qualified expenses** incurred in 2005 for the care of the **qualifying person(s)**	**15**	5,400
16	Enter the **smaller** of line 14 or 15	**16**	3,000
17	Enter your **earned income.** See instructions	**17**	29,000
18	Enter the amount shown below that applies to you. • If married filing jointly, enter your spouse's earned income (if your spouse was a student or was disabled, see the instructions for line 5). • If married filing separately, see the instructions for the amount to enter. • All others, enter the amount from line 17.	**18**	29,000
19	Enter the **smallest** of line 16, 17, or 18	**19**	3,000

20	Enter the amount from line 12 that you received from your sole proprietorship or partnership. If you did not receive any such amounts, enter -0-	**20**	-0-
21	Subtract line 20 from line 14	**21**	3,000
22	Enter $5,000 ($2,500 if married filing separately **and** you were required to enter your spouse's earned income on line 18)	**22**	5,000
23	**Deductible benefits.** Enter the **smallest** of line 19, 20, or 22. Also, include this amount on the appropriate line(s) of your return (see the instructions)	**23**	-0-
24	Enter the **smaller** of line 19 or 22	**24**	3,000
25	Enter the amount from line 23	**25**	-0-
26	**Excluded benefits.** Subtract line 25 from line 24. If zero or less, enter -0-	**26**	3,000
27	**Taxable benefits.** Subtract line 26 from line 21. If zero or less, enter -0-. Also, include this amount on Form 1040, line 7. On the dotted line next to line 7, enter "DCB"	**27**	-0-

To claim the child and dependent care
credit, complete lines 28–32 below.

28	Enter $3,000 ($6,000 if two or more qualifying persons)	**28**	6,000
29	Add lines 23 and 26	**29**	3,000
30	Subtract line 29 from line 28. If zero or less, **stop.** You cannot take the credit. **Exception.** If you paid 2004 expenses in 2005, see the instructions for line 9	**30**	3,000
31	Complete line 2 on the front of this form. **Do not** include in column (c) any benefits shown on line 29 above. Then, add the amounts in column (c) and enter the total here	**31**	2,400
32	Enter the **smaller** of line 30 or 31. Also, enter this amount on line 3 on the front of this form and complete lines 4–11	**32**	2,400

Credit for the Elderly or the Disabled

Note: The 2004 IRS Publication 17 (Your Federal Income Tax) has been updated by Ernst & Young LLP for 2005. Dates and dollar amounts shown are for 2005. Gray type is used to indicate where IRS text has been updated or intentionally omitted. Unrevised IRS text is shown in black type.

Introduction

When Congress passed legislation giving the elderly a tax credit, the idea was to provide a measure of tax relief for older citizens who were not receiving adequate amounts of Social Security or other nontaxable **pensions.** *Consequently, if you or your spouse is 65 years old or older, you may be entitled to a credit of as much as $1,125 against your tax.*

Taxpayers under 65 years of age who are permanently and totally disabled may also be eligible for the credit.

In general, if you file as a **single** *individual, you do* **not** *qualify for the tax credit if (1) you receive nontaxable Social Security or other nontaxable pensions of $5,000 or more, (2) your* **adjusted gross income** *is $17,500 or more, or (3) your tax is zero.*

This chapter tells you specifically if you are eligible for the credit for the elderly and, if so, how you may claim it—whether you are single or married.

If you qualify, the law provides a number of credits that can reduce the tax you owe for a year. One of these credits is the credit for the elderly or the disabled.

This chapter explains:

• Who qualifies for the credit for the elderly or the disabled, and
• How to figure this credit.

You may be able to take this credit if you are:

• Age 65 or older, or
• Retired on permanent and total disability.

Useful Items

You may want to see:

Publications

☐ **524** Credit for the Elderly or the Disabled
☐ **554** Older Americans' Tax Guide
☐ **967** The IRS Will Figure Your Tax

Forms (and Instructions)

☐ **Schedule 3 (Form 1040A)** Credit for the Elderly or the Disabled for Form 1040A Filers
☐ **Schedule R (Form 1040)** Credit for the Elderly or the Disabled

Explanation
See Chapter 12, *Social Security and Equivalent Railroad Retirement Benefits,* for a discussion of how Social Security and equivalent railroad retirement benefits are taxed.

Can You Take the Credit?

You can take the credit for the elderly or the disabled if you meet both of the following requirements.

• You are a qualified individual.
• Your income is not more than certain limits.

You can use Figure 35-A and Figure 35-B as guides to see if you qualify.

Figure 35-A. **Are You a Qualified Individual?**

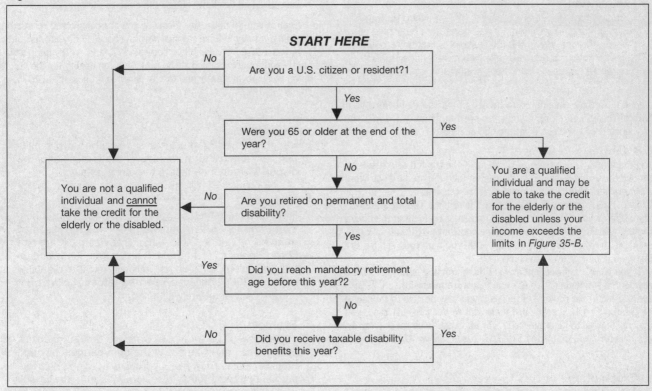

1If you were a nonresident alien at any time during the tax year and were married to a U.S. citizen or resident at the end of the tax year, see *U.S. Citizen or Resident* under *Qualified Individual*. If you and your spouse choose to treat you as a U.S. resident, answer "yes" to this question.
2Mandatory retirement age is the age set by your employer at which you would have been required to retire, had you not become disabled.

Figure 35-B. **Income Limits**

IF your filing status ...	THEN even if you qualify (see *Figure 35-A*), you CANNOT take the credit if ...	
	Your adjusted gross income (AGI)* is equal to or more than ...	OR the total of your nontaxable social security and other nontaxable pension(s) is equal to or more than ...
single, head of household, or qualifying widow(er) with dependent child	$17,500	$5,000
married filing a joint return and both spouses qualify in *Figure 35-A*	$25,000	$7,500
married filing a joint return and only one spouse qualifies in *Figure 35-A*	$20,000	$5,000
married filing a separate return and you did not live with your spouse at any time during the year	$12,500	$3,750

*AGI is the amount on Form 1040A, line 22, or Form 1040, line 37.

Use Figure 35-A first to see if you are a qualified individual. If you are, go to Figure 35-B to make sure your income is not too high to take the credit.
Tip. *You can take the credit only if you file Form 1040 or Form 1040A. You cannot take the credit if you file Form 1040EZ.*

Qualified Individual

You are a qualified individual for this credit if you are a U.S. citizen or resident and either of the following applies.

1. You were age 65 or older at the end of 2005.
2. You were under age 65 at the end of 2005 and all three of the following statements are true.
   a. You retired on permanent and total disability (explained later).
   b. You received taxable disability income for 2005.
   c. On January 1, 2005, you had not reached mandatory retirement age (defined later under Disability income).

Explanation
To qualify for the credit, you cannot have reached your employer's mandatory retirement age before the beginning of the year. The reason for the requirement is that any amount received from your employer *after* you have reached mandatory retirement age is *not* disability income.

Age 65. You are considered to be age 65 on the day before your 65th birthday. Therefore, if you were born on January 1, 1941, you are considered to be age 65 at the end of 2005.

U.S. Citizen or Resident
You must be a U.S. citizen or resident (or be treated as a resident) to take the credit. Generally, you cannot take the credit if you were a nonresident alien at any time during the tax year.
Exceptions. You may be able to take the credit if you are a nonresident alien who is married to a U.S. citizen or resident at the end of the tax year and you and your spouse choose to treat you as a U.S. resident. If you make that choice, both you and your spouse are taxed on your worldwide income.

If you were a nonresident alien at the beginning of the year and a resident at the end of the year, and you were married to a U.S. citizen or resident at the end of the year, you may be able to choose to be treated as a U.S. resident for the entire year. In that case, you may be allowed to take the credit. For information on these choices, see chapter 1 of Publication 519, *U.S. Tax Guide for Aliens*.

Explanation
For more information about resident and nonresident aliens, see Chapter 44, *Foreign Citizens Living in the United States*.

Married Persons
Generally, if you are married at the end of the tax year, you and your spouse must file a joint return to take the credit. However, if you and your spouse did not live in the same household at any time during the tax year, you can file either joint or separate returns and still take the credit.

Example 1
Don and Sylvia Fitch are both past the age of 65 and are married at year's end, but they have been living apart since May. They must file a joint return to claim the credit. Next year, if they remain married and live apart for the entire year, they may file separate returns and claim the credit.

Example 2
Sam and Leah Wilkins are married at year's end and have lived apart for the entire year. Leah is 63 years old and receives a disability pension from her former employer. Sam is 69 years old. They may file separate returns, and each may claim a credit, since both meet the basic tests for eligibility.

Head of household. You can file as head of household and qualify to take the credit, even if your spouse lived with you during the first 6 months of the year, if you meet all the tests. See *Head of Household* in chapter 2 for the tests you must meet.

Under Age 65
If you are under age 65 at the end of 2005, you can qualify for the credit only if you are retired on permanent and total disability. You are retired on permanent and total disability if:

- You were permanently and totally disabled when you retired, and
- You retired on disability before the close of the tax year.

Even if you do not retire formally, you are considered retired on disability when you have stopped working because of your disability.

If you retired on disability before 1977, and were not permanently and totally disabled at the time, you can qualify for the credit if you were permanently and totally disabled on January 1, 1976, or January 1, 1977.

Example 1
Ray Russell is 62 years old and receives a disability pension from his former employer. He is eligible for the disability credit if he meets the other tests.

Example 2
Fritz Hartman retired at age 60 and is receiving a pension from his former employer. Fritz was not disabled when he retired. In 2005, when Fritz was 62 years old, he was in an accident that left him permanently and totally disabled. Fritz is not eligible for the disability credit in 2005, because when he retired, he was not permanently and totally disabled.

Example 3
Joelle Bowes retired in 1976 at age 25 on disability, even though she was not at the time permanently and totally disabled. However, by January 1, 1977, she was permanently and totally disabled. In 2005, she is still receiving disability payments from her former employer and has not yet reached her employer's mandatory retirement age. Joelle is eligible for the credit in 2005.

Tip. *You are considered to be under age 65 at the end of 2005 if you were born after January 1, 1941.*
Permanent and total disability. You are permanently and totally disabled if you cannot engage in any substantial gainful activity because of your physical or mental condition. A physician must certify that the condition has lasted or can be expected to last continuously for 12 months or more, or that the condition can be expected to result in death. See *Physician's statement,* later.
Substantial gainful activity. Substantial gainful activity is the performance of significant duties over a reasonable period of time while working for pay or profit, or in work generally done for pay or profit. Full-time work (or part-time work done at your employer's convenience) in a competitive work situation for at least the minimum wage conclusively shows that you are able to engage in substantial gainful activity.

Substantial gainful activity is not work you do to take care of yourself or your home. It is not unpaid work on hobbies, institutional therapy or training, school attendance, clubs, social programs, and similar activities. However, doing this kind of work may show that you are able to engage in substantial gainful activity.

The fact that you have not worked for some time is not, of itself, conclusive evidence that you cannot engage in substantial gainful activity.

Explanation
The facts and circumstances of your particular situation determine whether you are able to "engage in substantial gainful activity" for purposes of claiming the credit. No strict rule governs every case. The most important question to remember is Did you hold a job that paid at least the minimum wage? This can mean any job, not just the job you held before your disability.

Sheltered employment. Certain work offered at qualified locations to physically or mentally impaired persons is considered sheltered employment. These qualified locations are in sheltered workshops, hospitals and similar institutions, homebound programs, and Department of Veterans Affairs sponsored homes.

Compared to commercial employment, pay is lower for sheltered employment. Therefore, one usually does not look for sheltered employment if he or she can get other employment. The fact that one has accepted sheltered employment is not proof of that person's ability to engage in substantial gainful activity.

Physician's statement. If you are under age 65, you must have your physician complete a statement certifying that you were permanently and totally disabled on the date you retired. You can use the statement in the instructions for Schedule R (Form 1040) or Schedule 3 (Form 1040A).

You do not have to file this statement with your Form 1040 or Form 1040A, but you must keep it for your records.

Veterans. If the Department of Veterans Affairs (VA) certifies that you are permanently and totally disabled, you can substitute VA Form 21-0172, Certification of Permanent and Total Disability, for the physician's statement you are required to keep. VA Form 21-0172 must be signed by a person authorized by the VA to do so. You can get this form from your local VA regional office.

Physician's statement obtained in earlier year. If you got a physician's statement in an earlier year and, due to your continued disabled condition, you were unable to engage in any substantial gainful activity during 2005, you may not need to get another physician's statement for 2005. For a detailed explanation of the conditions you must meet, see the instructions for Part II of Schedule R (Form 1040) or Schedule 3 (Form 1040A). If you meet the required conditions, check the box on line 2 of Part II of Schedule R (Form 1040) or Schedule 3 (Form 1040A).

If you checked box 4, 5, or 6 in Part I of either Schedule R or Schedule 3, enter, in the space above the box on line 2 in Part II, the first name(s) of the spouse(s) for whom the box is checked.

Disability income. If you are under age 65, you can qualify for the credit only if you have taxable disability income. Disability income must meet both of the following requirements.

- It must be paid under your employer's accident or health plan or pension plan.
- It must be included in your income as wages (or payments instead of wages) for the time you are absent from work because of permanent and total disability.

Payments that are not disability income. Any payment you receive from a plan that does not provide for disability retirement is not disability income. Any lump-sum payment for accrued annual leave that you receive when you retire on disability is a salary payment and is not disability income.

For purposes of the credit for the elderly or the disabled, disability income does not include amounts you receive after you reach mandatory retirement age. Mandatory retirement age is the age set by your employer at which you would have had to retire, had you not become disabled.

Example 1
Melissa Lee retired in June at age 55 with a total and permanent disability. At retirement, she received a $5,000 payment for accrued vacation and sick-leave days. The amount is not disability income, since it is not paid to her as wages or in lieu of wages because of her permanent and total disability.

Example 2
Adam LeBleu turned 62 years old on September 9, 2004. He had retired several years earlier as a result of a total and permanent disability. He has received disability payments from his employer since retirement. His former employer's mandatory retirement age is 62. As a result, any amount Adam receives after he reaches the age of 62 will *not* be disability income.

Income Limits

To determine if you can claim the credit, you must consider two income limits. The first limit is the amount of your adjusted gross income (AGI). The second limit is the amount of nontaxable social security and other nontaxable pensions you received. The limits are shown in Figure 35-B, later.

If both your AGI and nontaxable pensions are less than the income limits, you may be able to claim the credit. See *Figuring the Credit*, next.

Caution. *If either your AGI or your nontaxable pensions are equal to or more than the income limits, you cannot take the credit.*

Figuring the Credit

You can figure the credit yourself (see the explanation that follows) or the IRS will figure it for you. See *Credit Figured for You*, later.

TaxAlert
With the aid of this book, you should not have to rely on the IRS to calculate your credit. Although the IRS routinely checks the arithmetic on a return, it too can make computational errors. Also, as noted in Chapter 32, *How to Figure Your Tax*, you must still provide certain information to enable the IRS to calculate the credit. Therefore, our advice is to give the calculation of your credit a try.

Figuring the credit yourself. If you figure the credit yourself, fill out the front of either Schedule R (if you are filing Form 1040) or Schedule 3 (if you are filing Form 1040A). Next, fill out Part III of either Schedule R or Schedule 3.

There are four steps in Part III to determine the amount of your credit:

1. Determine your initial amount (lines 10–12).
2. Total any nontaxable social security and certain other nontaxable pensions and disability benefits you received (lines 13a, 13b, and 13c).
3. Determine your excess adjusted gross income (lines 14–17).
4. Determine your credit (lines 18–24 of Schedule R or lines 18–22 of Schedule 3).

These steps are discussed in more detail next.

Step 1. Determine Initial Amount

To figure the credit, you must first determine your initial amount. See Table 35-1.

Initial amounts for persons under age 65. If you are a qualified individual under age 65, your initial amount cannot be more than your taxable disability income.

Example 1
Ben Winston, who is 59 years old and single, retired during the year because of a total and permanent physical disability. He received $4,300 in income during the year from his prior employer because of his disability. He received no other income. The initial amount Ben uses in calculating his credit is $4,300.

Table 35-1. **Initial Amounts**

IF your filing status is ...	THEN enter on line 10 of Schedule R (Form 1040) or Schedule 3 (Form 1040A)...
Single, head of household, or qualifying widow(er) with dependent child and, by the end of 2005, you were	
• 65 or older	$5,000
• under 65 and retired on permanent and total disability[1]	$5,000
Married filing a joint return and by the end of 2005	
• both of you were 65 or older	$7,500
• both of you were under 65 and one of you retired on permanent and total disability[1]	$5,000
• both of you were under 65 and both of you retired on permanent and total disability[2]	$7,500
• one of you was 65 or older, and the other was under 65 and retired on permanent and total disability[3]	$7,500
• one of you was 65 or older, and the other was under 65 and not retired on permanent and total disability . . .	$5,000
Married filing a separate return and you did not live with your spouse at any time during the year and, by the end of 2005, you were	
• 65 or older	$3,750
• under 65 and retired on permanent and total disability[1]	$3,750

[1]Amount cannot be more than the taxable disability income.
[2]Amount cannot be more than your combined taxable disability income.
[3]Amount is $5,000 plus the taxable disability income of the spouse under age 65, but not more than $7,500.

If Ben had received $6,900 in disability income, his initial amount would be $5,000.

Example 2
David Jefferson is 72 years old and files a joint return with his wife, Donna. Donna is 63 years old and is permanently and totally disabled. She received $3,000 from her previous employer because of her disability. The initial amount they use in calculating their credit is $7,500, which is the lesser of (1) the $7,500 initial amount for married couples filing joint returns or (2) $5,000 plus the $3,000 disability income received by the person under the age of 65.

Step 2. Total Certain Nontaxable Pensions and Benefits

Step 2 is to figure the total amount of nontaxable social security and certain other nontaxable payments you received during the year. (See *Nontaxable payments,* later.)

Enter these nontaxable payments on lines 13a or 13b, and total them on line 13c. If you are married filing a joint return, you must enter the combined amount of nontaxable payments both you and your spouse receive.

Tip. *Worksheets are provided in the Form 1040 or Form 1040A instructions to help you determine if any part of your social security benefits (or equivalent railroad retirement benefits) is taxable.*
Nontaxable payments. Include the following nontaxable payments in the amounts you enter on lines 13a and 13b.

• Nontaxable social security payments. This is the nontaxable part of the amount of benefits shown in box 5 of Form SSA-1099, which includes disability benefits, before deducting any amounts withheld to pay premiums on supplementary Medicare insurance, and before any reduction because of receipt of a benefit under workers' compensation.

Do not include a lump-sum death benefit payment you may receive as a surviving spouse, or a surviving child's insurance benefit payments you may receive as a guardian.

Example 1
Tony and Sheila are married and file a joint return. He is 69 years old and she is 64, and each receives $1,000 in nontaxable social security. The initial amount used to figure their credit is $5,000, since only Tony is 65 years of age or older. This initial amount must be reduced by the $2,000 in nontaxable Social Security that they received during the year. Next year, when Sheila becomes 65 years old, their initial amount will rise to $7,500.

Example 2

Gail Goodson retired in January 2005 at age 62 because of a permanent disability and collected $4,600 from her former employer as a disability pension. She also received $3,600 in nontaxable Social Security benefits in 2005. Gail is single, and her adjusted gross income is less than $7,500. Gail must subtract the nontaxable Social Security income from her disability income in computing the adjusted initial amount. Her credit is $150 [15% × ($4,600 − $3,600)].

- Social security equivalent part of tier 1 railroad retirement pension payments that is not taxed. This is the nontaxable part of the amount of benefits shown in box 5 of Form RRB-1099.
- Nontaxable pension or annuity payments or disability benefits that are paid under a law administered by the Department of Veterans Affairs (VA).

  Do not include amounts received as a pension, annuity, or similar allowance for personal injuries or sickness resulting from active service in the armed forces of any country or in the National Oceanic and Atmospheric Administration, or the Public Health Service, or as a disability annuity under section 808 of the Foreign Service Act of 1980.

- Pension or annuity payments or disability benefits that are excluded from income under any provision of federal law other than the Internal Revenue Code.

  Do not include amounts that are a return of your cost of a pension or annuity. These amounts do not reduce your initial amount.

Caution. *You should be sure to take into account all of the nontaxable amounts you receive. These amounts are verified by the IRS through information supplied by other government agencies.*

Explanation

Do not reduce the initial amount used to figure your credit by any of the following:

- Amounts that are treated as a return of your cost of an annuity or a pension
- Veterans Administration service-connected disability compensation
- Payments from accident or health insurance policies
- Basic or supplementary Medicare benefits
- Death compensation paid by the Veterans Administration to the surviving spouse of a veteran who died from sickness or injury incurred in active service
- Life insurance payments received when the insured person dies

Step 3. Determine Excess Adjusted Gross Income

You also must reduce your initial amount by your excess adjusted gross income. Figure your excess adjusted gross income on lines 14 through 17.

You figure your excess adjusted gross income as follows:

1. Subtract from your adjusted gross income (line 37 of Form 1040 or line 22 of Form 1040A) the amount shown for your filing status in the following list:
   a. $7,500 if you are single, a head of household, or a qualifying widow(er) with a dependent child,
   b. $10,000 if you are married filing a joint return, or
   c. $5,000 if you are married filing a separate return and you and your spouse did not live in the same household at any time during the tax year.
2. Divide the result of (1) by 2.

Example 1

Raymond is over age 65 and single, with $8,900 in adjusted gross income, which is in excess of the $7,500 allowed for his single filing status. He must reduce his initial amount by $700 (one-half of the $1,400 difference between $8,900 and $7,500). Raymond also receives $1,000 in nontaxable Social Security payments. The adjusted initial amount he uses to compute his credit is $3,300, calculated as follows:

Initial amount	$5,000
Less:	
Nontaxable Social Security	1,000
Excess adjusted gross income	700
Adjusted initial amount	$3,300
Tentative credit (15% of $3,300)	$ 495

Note: 15% times the adjusted initial amount is the method you use in calculating your tentative credit.

Example 2

Horace and Prudence are married, both are over age 65, and they file a joint return. Their adjusted gross income for the year is $12,000. They receive $1,750 in nontaxable Social Security. Their adjusted initial amount used to figure their credit is $4,750, calculated as follows:

Initial amount	$7,500
Less:	
Nontaxable Social Security	1,750
Excess adjusted gross income [1/2 ($12,000 − $10,000)]	1,000
Adjusted initial amount	$4,750
Tentative credit (15% of $4,750)	$ 713

Step 4. Determine Your Credit

To determine if you can take the credit, you must add the amounts you figured in Step 2 and Step 3.

IF the total of Steps 2 and 3 is ...	THEN ...
Equal to or more than the amount in Step 1	You **cannot** take the credit.
Less than the amount in Step 1	You **can** take the credit.

Figuring the credit. If you can take the credit, subtract the total of Step 2 and Step 3 from the amount in Step 1 and multiply the result by 15%.

In certain cases, the amount of your credit may be limited. See *Limit on credit,* later.

Explanation

In summary, you may not claim the credit for the elderly and disabled if (1) your nontaxable Social Security and other nontaxable pensions or (2) 50% of your excess adjusted gross income or (3) the sum of (1) and (2) equals or exceeds your initial amount.

A simple way to compute your credit is as follows:

1. Subtract from your initial amount the sum of your nontaxable Social Security income, other nontaxable pensions, and your excess adjusted gross income.
2. Multiply the amount from step 1 by 15%. This is your credit for the year.

Example. You are 66 years old and your spouse is 64. Your spouse is not disabled. You file a joint return on Form 1040. Your adjusted gross income is $14,630. Together you received $3,200 from Social Security, which was nontaxable. You figure the credit as follows:

1) Initial amount $5,000

2) Subtract the total of: _____

  a) Nontaxable social security and other nontaxable pensions $3,200

  b) Excess adjusted gross income [($14,630 − $10,000) ÷ 2] 2,315

3) Balance (Not less then –0–) .... –0–

4) Credit .... –0–

You cannot take the credit since your nontaxable social security (line 2a) plus your excess adjusted gross income (line 2b) is more than your amount on line 1.

Limit on credit. The amount of credit you can claim may be limited.

Figure any limit on your credit on lines 21–24 of Schedule R or lines 21–22 of Schedule 3.

Credit Figured for You

If you choose to have the Internal Revenue Service (IRS) figure the credit for you, read the following discussion for the form you will file (Form 1040 or 1040A). If you want the IRS to figure your tax, see chapter 32.
Form 1040. If you want the IRS to figure your credit, see *Form 1040 Line Entries* under *Tax Figured by IRS* in chapter 32.
Form 1040A. If you want the IRS to figure your credit, see *Form 1040A Line Entries* under *Tax Figured by IRS* in chapter 32.

Examples

The following examples illustrate the credit for the elderly or the disabled. The initial amounts are taken from Table 35-1, shown earlier.

    Example 1. James Davis is 58 years old, single, and files Form 1040A. In 1999 he retired on permanent and total disability, and he

Instructions for Physician's Statement

Taxpayer

If you retired after 1976, enter the date you retired in the space provided on the statement below.

Physician

A person is permanently and totally disabled if **both** of the following apply:

1. He or she cannot engage in any substantial gainful activity because of a physical or mental condition, and
2. A physician determines that the disability has lasted or can be expected to last continuously for at least a year or can lead to death.

Physician's Statement (keep for your records)

I certify that _____ Helen A. White _____

Name of disabled person

was permanently and totally disabled on January 1, 1976, or January 1, 1977, **OR** was permanently and totally disabled on the date he or she retired. If retired after 1976, enter the date retired. _November 30, 2005_

Physician: Sign your name on **either** A or B below.

A The disability has lasted or can be expected to last continuously for at least a year

B There is no reasonable probability that the disabled condition will ever improve

Physician's signature | Date

Juanita D. Doctor   2/7/06
Physician's signature | Date

Physician's name
Juanita D. Doctor

Physician's address
1900 Green St., Hometown, MD 20000

is still permanently and totally disabled. He got the required physician's statement in 1999, and kept it with his records. His physician signed on line B of the statement. This year James checks the box in Part II of Schedule 3. He does not need to get another statement for 2005.

He received the following income for the year:

Nontaxable Social Security	$1,500
Interest (taxable)	100
Taxable disability pension	11,400

James' adjusted gross income is $11,500 ($11,400 + $100). He figures the credit on Schedule 3 as follows:

1) Initial amount		$5,000
2) Taxable disability pension		11,400
3) Smaller of (1) or (2)		5,000
4) Subtract the total of:		
a) Nontaxable disability benefits (Social Security)	$1,500	
(b) Excess adjusted gross income [($11,500 − $7,500) ÷ 2]	2,000	3,500
5) Balance (Not less than -0-)		1,500
6) Multiply line 5 by 15% (.15)		225
7) Enter the amount from Form 1040A, line 28		358
8) Enter any amounts from Form 1040A, line 29		−0−
9) Subtract line 8 from line 7		358
10) Credit (Enter the smaller of line 6 or line 9)		$225

His credit is $225. He enters $225 on line 30 of Form 1040A. The Schedule 3 for James Davis is not shown.

Example 2. William White is 53. His wife Helen is 49. William had a stroke 3 years ago and retired on permanent and total disability. He is still permanently and totally disabled because of the stroke. In November of last year, Helen was injured in an accident at work and retired on permanent and total disability.

William received nontaxable Social Security disability benefits of $3,000 during the year and a taxable disability pension of $6,000. Helen earned $9,200 from her job and received a taxable disability pension of $1,000. Their joint return on Form 1040 shows adjusted gross income of $16,200 ($6,000 + $9,200 + $1,000).

Helen got her doctor to complete the physician's statement in the instructions for Schedule R. Helen is not required to include the statement with her return for the year, but she must keep it for her records.

William got a physician's statement for the year he had the stroke. His doctor had signed on line B of that physician's statement to certify that William was permanently and totally disabled. William has kept the physician's statement with his records. He checks the box in Part II of Schedule R and writes his first name in the space above line 2.

William and Helen use Schedule R to figure their $31 credit for the elderly or the disabled. They attach Schedule R to their joint return and enter $31 on line 48 of Form 1040. See their filled-in Schedule R and Helen's filled-in physician's statement on the previous three pages.

Schedule R (Form 1040)	Credit for the Elderly or the Disabled	OMB No. 1545-0074

Schedule R (Form 1040)

Department of the Treasury
Internal Revenue Service   (99)

Credit for the Elderly or the Disabled

► **Attach to Form 1040.**   ► **See Instructions for Schedule R (Form 1040).**

OMB No. 1545-0074

2005

Attachment
Sequence No. **16**

Name(s) shown on Form 1040

William M. White and Helen A. White

Your social security number

220 : 00 : 3333

You may be able to take this credit and reduce your tax if by the end of 2005:

- You were age 65 or older   **or**   • You were under age 65, you retired on **permanent and total** disability, and you received taxable disability income.

But you must also meet other tests. See page R-1.

(TIP) In most cases, the IRS can figure the credit for you. See page R-1.

Part I   **Check the Box for Your Filing Status and Age**

If your filing status is:	And by the end of 2005:	Check only one box:
Single, Head of household, or Qualifying widow(er)	**1** You were 65 or older **1**	☐
	2 You were under 65 and you retired on permanent and total disability **2**	☐
Married filing jointly	**3** Both spouses were 65 or older **3**	☐
	4 Both spouses were under 65, but only one spouse retired on permanent and total disability **4**	☐
	5 Both spouses were under 65, and both retired on permanent and total disability **5**	☑
	6 One spouse was 65 or older, and the other spouse was under 65 and retired on permanent and total disability **6**	☐
	7 One spouse was 65 or older, and the other spouse was under 65 and **not** retired on permanent and total disability **7**	☐
Married filing separately	**8** You were 65 or older and you lived apart from your spouse for all of 2005 . . . . **8**	☐
	9 You were under 65, you retired on permanent and total disability, and you lived apart from your spouse for all of 2005 . . . . **9**	☐

Did you check box 1, 3, 7, or 8?	— **Yes** ──→ Skip Part II and complete Part III on back.
	— **No** ──→ Complete Parts II and III.

Part II   **Statement of Permanent and Total Disability** (Complete **only** if you checked box 2, 4, 5, 6, or 9 above.)

If: 1 You filed a physician's statement for this disability for 1983 or an earlier year, or you filed or got a statement for tax years after 1983 and your physician signed line B on the statement, **and**

William

2 Due to your continued disabled condition, you were unable to engage in any substantial gainful activity in 2005, check this box . . . . ► ☑

- If you checked this box, you do not have to get another statement for 2005.

- If you **did not** check this box, have your physician complete the statement on page R-4. You **must** keep the statement for your records.

For Paperwork Reduction Act Notice, see Form 1040 instructions.   Cat. No. 11359K   **Schedule R (Form 1040) 2005**

Part III	**Figure Your Credit**		

10 If you checked (in Part I):   **Enter:**

Box 1, 2, 4, or 7 . . . . $5,000

Box 3, 5, or 6 . . . . $7,500   **10**   7,500

Box 8 or 9 . . . . $3,750

Did you check box 2, 4, 5, 6, or 9 in Part I?	Yes ——————▶	You **must** complete line 11.
	No ——————▶	Enter the amount from line 10 on line 12 and go to line 13.

11 If you checked (in Part I):

• Box 6, add $5,000 to the taxable disability income of the spouse who was under age 65. Enter the total.

• Box 2, 4, or 9, enter your taxable disability income.   **11**   7,000

• Box 5, add your taxable disability income to your spouse's taxable disability income. Enter the total.

TIP For more details on what to include on line 11, see page R-3.

12 If you completed line 11, enter the **smaller** of line 10 or line 11; **all others,** enter the amount from line 10 . . . . **12**   7,000

13 Enter the following pensions, annuities, or disability income that you (and your spouse if filing a joint return) received in 2005.

  a Nontaxable part of social security benefits and

Nontaxable part of railroad retirement benefits treated as social security (see page R-3). . . . **13a** 3,000

  b Nontaxable veterans' pensions and

Any other pension, annuity, or disability benefit that is excluded from income under any other provision of law (see page R-3). . . . **13b**

  c Add lines 13a and 13b. (Even though these income items are not taxable, they **must** be included here to figure your credit.) If you did not receive any of the types of nontaxable income listed on line 13a or 13b, enter -0- on line 13c **13c** 3,000

14 Enter the amount from Form 1040, line 38 . . . . **14** 16,200

15 If you checked (in Part I):   **Enter:**

Box 1 or 2 . . . . . . $7,500

Box 3, 4, 5, 6, or 7 . . . $10,000   **15** 10,000

Box 8 or 9 . . . . . . $5,000

16 Subtract line 15 from line 14. If zero or less, enter -0- **16** 6,200

17 Enter one-half of line 16 . . . . **17** 3,100

18 Add lines 13c and 17 . . . . **18** 6,100

19 Subtract line 18 from line 12. If zero or less, **stop;** you **cannot** take the credit. Otherwise, go to line 20 . . . . **19** 900

20 Multiply line 19 by 15% (.15) **20** 135

21 Enter the amount from Form 1040, line 46 . . . . **21** 31

22 Add the amounts from Form 1040, lines 47 and 48, and enter the total . . . . **22** -0-

23 Subtract line 22 from line 21 . . . . **23** 31

24 **Credit for the elderly or the disabled.** Enter the **smaller** of line 20 or line 23 here and on Form 1040, line 49 . . . . **24** 31

36

Child Tax Credit

Note: The 2004 IRS Publication 17 (Your Federal Income Tax) has been updated by Ernst & Young LLP for 2005. Dates and dollar amounts shown are for 2005. Gray type is used to indicate where IRS text has been updated or intentionally omitted. Unrevised IRS text is shown in black type.

Introduction

A tax credit of $1,000 is available for each qualifying child under age 17. A qualifying child (defined in greater detail in Chapetr 3, Personal Exemptions and Dependants) is an individual for whom the taxpayer can claim a dependency exemption and who is the child, stepchild, or eligible foster child of the taxpayer or is a brother, sister, stepbrother, or stepsister of the taxpayer or a descendant of any of these relatives ("brother" and "sister" *include a brother or sister by half-blood). That means a "qualifying child" doesn't necessarily have to be your child! The credit is phased out depending on your adjusted gross income and the number of qualifying children. The child tax credit is not the same as the credit for child and dependent care expenses, which is explained in Chapter 34, Child and Dependent Care Credit.*

TAXALERT

The Working Families Tax Relief Act of 2004 established a maximum child tax credit of $1,000 per qualifying child for tax years 2005–2010. In addition, the same act increased the refundability of the child credit to 15% of the taxpayer's earned income in excess of $11,000 for 2005 (with indexing for inflation).

TAXALERT

The Working Families Tax Relief Act of 2004 established a uniform definition for "qualifying child" for the purposes of the dependency exemption, the child tax credit, the earned income tax credit, the dependent care credit, and head of household filing status. This definition became effective January 1, 2005, and can be found on the IRS website, www.irs.gov, by searching for "qualifying child."

The child tax credit is a credit that you may be able to take on your tax return. It may reduce your tax by as much as $1,000 for each of your qualifying children.

The additional child tax credit is a credit you may be able to take if you are not able to claim the full amount of the child tax credit.

This chapter explains:

• Who is a qualifying child.
• How much is the credit.
• How to claim the credit.
• Why you should check your tax withholding.

Caution. *The child tax credit and the additional child tax credit should not be confused with the* child and dependent care credit *discussed in chapter 34.*

If you have no tax. Credits, such as the child tax credit, the adoption credit, or the credit for child and dependent care expenses, are used to reduce tax. If your tax on Form 1040, line 46, or Form 1040A, line 28, is zero, do not figure the child tax credit because there is no tax to reduce. However, you may qualify for the additional child tax credit on line 68 (Form 1040) or line 42 (Form 1040A).

Useful Items

You may want to see:

Publication

☐ **972** Child Tax Credit

Forms (and Instructions)

☐ **8812** Additional Child Tax Credit
☐ **W-4** Employee's Withholding Allowance Certificate

Qualifying Child

A qualifying child for purposes of the child tax credit must be all of the following.

1. Claimed as your dependent on line 6c of Form 1040 or Form 1040A.
2. Under age 17 at the end of 2005.
3. Your:
   a. Son, daughter, adopted child, stepchild, or a descendant of any of them (for example, your grandchild),
   b. Brother, sister, stepbrother, stepsister, or a descendant of any of them (for example, your niece or nephew), or

c. Foster child (any child placed with you by an authorized placement agency).

4. A U.S. citizen or resident alien.

Example. Your son turned 17 on December 30, 2005. He is a citizen of the United States and you claimed him as a dependent on your return. He is not a qualifying child for the child tax credit because he was not under age 17 at the end of 2005.

Adopted child. An adopted child is always treated as your own child. An adopted child includes a child placed with you by an authorized placement agency for legal adoption even if the adoption is not final.

Kidnapped child. A kidnapped child is treated as a qualifying child for the child tax credit if both of the following statements are true.

1. The child is presumed by law enforcement authorities to have been kidnapped by someone who is not a member of your family or the child's family.
2. The child qualified as your dependent for the part of the year before the kidnapping.

This treatment applies for all years until the child is returned. However, the last year this treatment can apply is the earlier of:

1. The year there is a determination that the child is dead, or
2. The year the child would have reached age 18.

Amount of Credit

The maximum amount you can claim for the credit is $1,000 for each qualifying child.

Limits on the Credit

You must reduce your child tax credit if either (1) or (2) applies.

1. The amount on Form 1040, line 44 or Form 1040A, line 28 is less than the credit. If this amount is zero, you cannot take this credit because there is no tax to reduce. But you may be able to take the additional child tax credit. See *Additional Child Tax Credit,* later.
2. Your modified adjusted gross income (AGI) is above the amount shown below for your filing status.
   a. Married filing jointly – $110,000.
   b. Single, head of household, or qualifying widow(er) – $75,000.
   c. Married filing separately – $55,000.

Explanation

The maximum child credit you may claim is equal to $1,000 multiplied by the number of qualifying children you have. However, if your adjusted gross income (AGI) is greater than a specified amount, then there are limitations on the amount of child tax credit that you may claim. The amount of the credit allowable is reduced (but not below zero) by $50 for each $1,000 (or part of that amount) by which your AGI exceeds the threshold amounts. The threshold amounts for 2005 are $75,000 for single filers and head of household, $110,000 for couples filing jointly, and $55,000 for married persons filing separately).

Modified AGI. For purposes of the child tax credit, your modified AGI is your AGI plus the following amounts that may apply to you.

- Any amount excluded from income because of the exclusion of income from Puerto Rico.
- Any amount on line 43 or line 48 of Form 2555, Foreign Earned Income.
- Any amount on line 18 of Form 2555-EZ, Foreign Earned Income Exclusion.

- Any amount on line 15 of Form 4563, Exclusion of Income for Bona Fide Residents of American Samoa.

If you do not have any of the above, your modified AGI is the same as your AGI.

AGI. Your AGI is the amount on Form 1040, line 37, or Form 1040A, line 22.

Claiming the Credit

To claim the child tax credit, you must file Form 1040 or Form 1040A. You cannot claim the child tax credit on Form 1040EZ. You must provide the name and identification number (usually a social security number) on your tax return for each qualifying child.

Answer the *Questions* in your form instructions for Form 1040, line 52 or Form 1040A, line 33 to find out which child tax credit worksheet you can use to figure the credit.

If you answer "Yes" to question 1, 2, or 3 in your Form 1040 instructions or question 1 or 2 in your Form 1040A instructions, you must complete the child tax credit worksheet in Publication 972. Otherwise, you can use the *Child Tax Credit Worksheet* in your Form 1040 or Form 1040A instructions. (See the filled-in example, later.)

Example

Amy Brown files as head of household and has two dependent children under age 17. The children are qualifying children for purposes of the child tax credit. Amy's only income is her salary of $23,500. Amy chooses to itemize her deductions and files Form 1040. Her AGI, shown on line 37 of her Form 1040, is $23,500. This is her taxable earned income.

Amy does not file Form 2555, 2555-EZ, or 4563. She does not exclude income from Puerto Rico. Her modified AGI is $23,500.

Amy's tax, shown on line 46 of her Form 1040, is $708. She claims a $437 credit for child and dependent care expenses on line 48. She claims a $2,302 earned income credit on line 66a. She has no other credits.

After answering the *Questions* in the Form 1040 instructions for line 52, she completes the child tax credit worksheet to figure her child tax credit of $271. Amy's completed questions and child tax credit worksheet are shown later.

Amy reads the *TIP* in the worksheet and finds that she may be able to take the additional child tax credit. See *Additional Child Tax Credit* and Amy's completed Form 8812, later.

Additional Child Tax Credit

This credit is for certain individuals who get less than the full amount of the child tax credit. The additional child tax credit may give you a refund even if you do not owe any tax.

How to claim the additional child tax credit. To claim the additional child tax credit, follow the steps below.

1. Make sure you figured the amount, if any, of your child tax credit. See *Claiming the Credit,* earlier.
2. If you answered "Yes" on line 4 or line 5 of the *Child Tax Credit Worksheet* in the Form 1040 or Form 1040A instructions, or line 13 of the *Child Tax Credit Worksheet* in Publication 972, use Form 8812 to see whether you can take the additional child tax credit.
3. If you have an additional child tax credit on line 13 of Form 8812, carry it to Form 1040, line 68 or Form 1040A, line 42.

Checking Your Withholding

The child tax credit decreases your tax. You can check your tax withholding by using Publication 919, How Do I Adjust My Tax Withholding.

If you are having too much tax withheld, and you prefer to have the money during the year, you may be able to decrease your withholding. You do this by completing a new Form W-4 and giving it to your employer.

Filled-in Questions for Amy Brown
(Page references are to the Form 1040 instructions.)

Questions   **Who Must Use Pub. 972**

1. Are you excluding income from Puerto Rico or are you filing any of the following forms?

    ● Form 2555 or 2555-EZ (relating to foreign earned income)

    ● Form 4563 (exclusion of income for residents of American Samoa)

    ☑ **No.** *Continue* ⬎   ☐ **Yes.** (STOP) You must use Pub. 972 to figure your credit.

---

2. Is the amount on Form 1040, line 37, more than the amount shown below for your filing status?

    ● Married filing jointly – $110,000

    ● Single, head of household, or qualifying widow(er) – $75,000

    ● Married filing separately – $55,000

    ☑ **No.** *Continue* ⬎   ☐ **Yes.** (STOP) You must use Pub. 972 to figure your credit.

---

3. Are you claiming any of the following credits?

    ● Adoption credit, Form 8839 (see the instructions for Form 1040, line 53)

    ● Mortgage interest credit, Form 8396 (see the instructions for Form 1040, line 54)

    ● District of Columbia first-time homebuyer credit, Form 8859

    ☑ **No.** Use the worksheet on page 38 to figure your child tax credit.   ☐ **Yes.** You must use Pub. 972 to figure your child tax credit. You will also need the form(s) listed above for any credit(s) you are claiming.

Filled-in Child Tax Credit Worksheet—Amy Brown
(Page references are to the Form 1040 instructions.)

Child Tax Credit Worksheet—Line 52

Keep for Your Records

- To be a qualifying child for the child tax credit, the child must be **under age 17** at the end of 2005 and meet the other requirements listed on page 37.

- **Do not** use this worksheet if you answered "Yes" to question 1, 2, or 3 on page 37. Instead, use Pub. 972.

1. Number of qualifying children: _____2_____ × $1,000. Enter the result.

   | 1 | 2,000 |

2. Enter the amount from Form 1040, line 46.

   | 2 | 708 |

3. Add the amounts from Form 1040:

   Line 47   _____

   Line 48   + _____437_____

   Line 49   + _____

   Line 50   + _____

   Line 51   + _____   Enter the total.

   | 3 | 437 |

4. Are the amounts on lines 2 and 3 the same?

   ☐ **Yes.** (STOP)
   You cannot take this credit because there is no tax to reduce. However, you may be able to take the **additional child tax credit.** See the **TIP** below.

   ☑ **No.** Subtract line 3 from line 2.

   | 4 | 271 |

5. Is the amount on line 1 more than the amount on line 4?

   ☑ **Yes.** Enter the amount from line 4.
   Also, you may be able to take the **additional child tax credit.** See the **TIP** below.

   ☐ **No.** Enter the amount from line 1.

   This is your child tax credit.

   | 5 | 271 |

   Enter this amount on Form 1040, line 52.

TIP

You may be able to take the **additional child tax credit** on Form 1040, line 68, if you answered "Yes" on line 4 **or** line 5 above.

- First, complete your Form 1040 through line 67.

- Then, use Form 8812 to figure any additional child tax credit.

Form **8812**

Additional Child Tax Credit

OMB No. 1545-1620

2005

Department of the Treasury
Internal Revenue Service (99)

Complete and attach to Form 1040 or Form 1040A.

Attachment
Sequence No. **47**

Name(s) shown on return
Amy Brown

Your social security number
012 : 00 : 5678

Part I All Filers

1	Enter the amount from line 1 of your Child Tax Credit Worksheet on page 38 of the Form 1040 instructions or page 37 of the Form 1040A instructions. If you used Pub. 972, enter the amount from line 8 of the worksheet on page 4 of the publication	**1**	2,000
2	Enter the amount from Form 1040, line 52, or Form 1040A, line 33	**2**	271
3	Subtract line 2 from line 1. If zero, **stop**; you cannot take this credit	**3**	1,729

4a Earned income (see instructions on back) . . . **4a** 23,500

  b Nontaxable combat pay from Form(s) W-2, box 12, with code Q. If married filing jointly, include your spouse's amounts with yours. . . **4b**

5 Is the amount on line 4a more than $11,000?

  ☐ **No.** Leave line 5 blank and enter -0- on line 6.

  ☑ **Yes.** Subtract $11,000 from the amount on line 4a. Enter the result . . **5** 12,500

6 Multiply the amount on line 5 by 15% (.15) and enter the result **6** 1,875

  Next. Do you have three or more qualifying children?

  ☑ **No.** If line 6 is zero, **stop**; you cannot take this credit. Otherwise, skip Part II and enter the **smaller** of line 3 or line 6 on line 13.

  ☐ **Yes.** If line 6 is equal to or more than line 3, skip Part II and enter the amount from line 3 on line 13. Otherwise, go to line 7.

Part II Certain Filers Who Have Three or More Qualifying Children

7 Withheld social security and Medicare taxes from Form(s) W-2, boxes 4 and 6. If married filing jointly, include your spouse's amounts with yours. If you worked for a railroad, see instructions on back **7**

8 **1040 filers:** Enter the total of the amounts from Form 1040, lines 27 and 59, plus any uncollected social security and Medicare or tier 1 RRTA taxes included on line 63.

  1040A filers: Enter -0-. **8**

9 Add lines 7 and 8 . . . . **9**

10 **1040 filers:** Enter the total of the amounts from Form 1040, lines 66a and 67.

  1040A filers: Enter the total of the amount from Form 1040A, line 41a, plus any excess social security and tier 1 RRTA taxes withheld that you entered to the left of line 43 (see instructions on back). **10**

11 Subtract line 10 from line 9. If zero or less, enter -0- **11**

12 Enter the **larger** of line 6 or line 11 . . . . . . **12**

  Next, enter the **smaller** of line 3 or line 12 on line 13.

Part III Additional Child Tax Credit

13 **This is your additional child tax credit** **13** 1,729

Enter this amount on
Form 1040, line 68, or
Form 1040A, line 42.

37

Education Credits and Other Education Tax Benefits

Note: The 2004 IRS Publication 17 (Your Federal Income Tax) has been updated by Ernst & Young LLP for 2005. Dates and dollar amounts shown are for 2005. Gray type is used to indicate where IRS text has been updated or intentionally omitted. Unrevised IRS text is shown in black type.

Introduction

The deduction of educational expenses may be very limited. However, two tax credits broaden the tax benefits available for education costs. You can elect either a non-refundable Hope scholarship tax credit or a Lifetime Learning credit for eligible education expenses.

The credits are phased out for single taxpayers with modified adjusted gross income (AGI) of $43,000–$53,000 and for couples filing jointly with modified AGI between $87,000–$107,000.

For both the Hope scholarship credit and the Lifetime Learning credit, qualified tuition does not include any amounts otherwise excludable from gross income or amounts deductible as a business expense or as an education expense.

This chapter also discusses a variety of other education benefits that may be available to you—student loan deductions, deductions for higher education expenses, Coverdell education savings accounts, and employee provided educational assistance programs, among others.

What's New

Income limits increased. Beginning in 2005, the amount of your Hope or lifetime learning credit is gradually reduced (phased out) if your modified adjusted gross income (MAGI) is between $43,000 and $53,000 ($87,000 and $107,000 if you file a joint return). You cannot claim a credit if your MAGI is $53,000 or more ($107,000 or more if you file a joint return). This is an increase from the 2004 limits of $42,000 and $52,000 ($85,000 and $105,000 if filing a joint return). For more information, see *Effect of the Amount of Your Income on the Amount of Your Credit*, later.

This chapter discusses two tax credits (referred to here as education credits) available to persons who pay expenses for higher education.

• The Hope credit.
• The lifetime learning credit.

The chapter will:

• Give you general information that applies to both of the credits,
• Give you specific information about each of the credits,
• Help you choose which of the credits to claim, and
• Show you how to figure the credit you choose.

Can you claim both education credits this year? For each student, you can elect for any year only one of the credits. For exam-

ple, if you elect to take the Hope credit for a child on your 2005 tax return, you cannot, for that same child, also claim the lifetime learning credit for 2005.

If you are eligible to claim the Hope credit and you are also eligible to claim the lifetime learning credit for the same student in the same year, you can choose to claim either credit, but not both. For 2005, if the total qualified education expenses for a student are less than $7,500, it will generally be to your benefit to claim the Hope credit.

If you pay qualified education expenses for more than one student in the same year, you can choose to take credits on a per-student, per-year basis. This means that, for example, you can claim the Hope credit for one student and the lifetime learning credit for another student in the same year.

Differences between the Hope and lifetime learning credits. There are several differences between the Hope credit and the lifetime learning credit. For example, you can claim the Hope credit based on the same student's expenses for no more than 2 years. However, there is no limit on the number of years for which you can claim a lifetime learning credit based on the same student's expenses. The differences between the two credits are summarized in Table 37-1.

Tip. *You may be able to take a deduction for your education expenses instead of a credit. Choose the one that will give you the lower tax. See chapter 21 for details about the tuition and fees deduction.*

Table 37-1. **Comparison of Education Credits**

Hope Credit	Lifetime Learning Credit
Up to $1,500 credit per **eligible student**	Up to $2,000 credit per **return**
Available only until the first 2 years of postsecondary education are completed	Available for all years of postsecondary education and for courses to acquire or improve job skills
Available only for 2 years per eligible student	Available for an unlimited number of years
Student must be pursuing an undergraduate degree or other recognized educational credential	Student does not need to be pursuing a degree or other recognized educational credential
Student must be enrolled at least half time for at least one academic period beginning during the year	Available for one or more courses
No felony drug conviction on student's record	Felony drug conviction rule does not apply

Information for Both the Hope and Lifetime Learning Credits

Several rules are common to both education credits. These are discussed below.

Useful Items

You may want to see:

Publication

☐ **970** Tax Benefits for Education

Form (and Instructions)

☐ **8863** Education Credits (Hope and Lifetime Learning Credits)

Can You Claim a Credit

The following rules will help you determine if you are eligible to claim an education credit on your tax return.

Who Can Claim a Credit

Generally, you can claim an education credit for 2005 if all three of the following requirements are met.

1. You pay qualified education expenses of higher education.
2. You pay the education expenses for an eligible student.
3. The eligible student is either yourself, your spouse, or a dependent for whom you claim an exemption on your tax return.

"Qualified education expenses" are defined below under *What Expenses Qualify*. "Eligible students" are defined later under *Who Is an Eligible Student*. A "dependent for whom you claim an exemption" is defined later under *Who Can Claim a Dependent's Expenses*.

You may find Figure 37-A, later in this chapter, helpful in determining if you can claim an education credit on your tax return.

Who Cannot Claim a Credit

You cannot claim an education credit for 2005 if any of the following apply.

- Your filing status is married filing separately.
- You are listed as a dependent in the *Exemptions* section on another person's tax return (such as your parents'). See *Who Can Claim a Dependent's Expenses*, later.

- Your modified adjusted gross income (MAGI) is $53,000 or more ($107,000 or more in the case of a joint return). MAGI is explained later under *Effect of the Amount of Your Income on the Amount of Your Credit*.
- You (or your spouse) were a nonresident alien for any part of 2005 and the nonresident alien did not elect to be treated as a resident alien for tax purposes. More information on nonresident aliens can be found in Publication 519, U.S. Tax Guide for Aliens.
- You claim a tuition and fees deduction for the same student in 2005.

What Expenses Qualify

The education credits are based on qualified education expenses you pay for yourself, your spouse, or a dependent for whom you claim an exemption on your tax return. Generally, a credit is allowed for qualified education expenses paid in 2005 for an academic period beginning in 2005 or in the first 3 months of 2006.

For example, if you paid $1,500 in December 2005 for qualified tuition for the Spring 2006 semester beginning in January 2006, you may be able to use that $1,500 in figuring your 2005 credit.

Academic period. An academic period includes a semester, trimester, quarter, or other period of study (such as a summer school session) as reasonably determined by an educational institution. In the case of an educational institution that uses credit hours or clock hours and does not have academic terms, each payment period can be treated as an academic period.

Paid with borrowed funds. You can claim an education credit for qualified education expenses paid with the proceeds of a loan. You use the expenses to figure the education credit for the year in which the expenses are paid, not the year in which the loan is repaid. Treat loan payments sent directly to the educational institution as paid on the date the institution credits the student's account.

Student withdraws from class(es). You can claim an education credit for qualified education expenses not refunded when a student withdraws.

Qualified Education Expenses

For purposes of an education credit, qualified education expenses are tuition and certain related expenses required for enrollment or attendance at an eligible educational institution.

Eligible educational institution. An eligible educational institution is any college, university, vocational school, or other postsecondary educational institution eligible to participate in a student aid program administered by the Department of Education. It includes virtually all accredited, public, nonprofit, and proprietary (privately owned profit-making) postsecondary institutions. The educational institution should be able to tell you if it is an eligible educational institution.

Certain educational institutions located outside the United States also participate in the U.S. Department of Education's Federal Student Aid (FSA) programs. See chapter 2 or 3 of Publication 970 for more information.

Related expenses. Student-activity fees and expenses for course-related books, supplies, and equipment are included in qualified education expenses only if the fees and expenses must be paid to the institution as a condition of enrollment or attendance.

In the following examples, assume that each student is an eligible student at an eligible educational institution.

Example 1. Jackson is a sophomore in University V's degree program in dentistry. This year, in addition to tuition, he is required to pay a fee to the university for the rental of the dental equipment he will use in this program. Because the equipment rental fee must be paid to University V for enrollment and attendance, Jackson's equipment rental fee is a qualified expense.

Example 2. Donna and Charles, both first-year students at College W, are required to have certain books and other reading materials to use in their mandatory first-year classes. The college has no policy about how students should obtain these materials, but any student who purchases them from College W's bookstore will receive a bill directly from the college. Charles bought his books from a friend, so what he paid for them is not a qualified education expense. Donna bought hers at College W's bookstore. Although Donna paid College W directly for her first-year books and materials, her payment is not a qualified expense because the books and materials are not required to be purchased from College W for enrollment or attendance at the institution.

Example 3. When Marci enrolled at College X for her freshman year, she had to pay a separate student activity fee in addition to her tuition. This activity fee is required of all students, and is used solely to fund on-campus organizations and activities run by students, such as the student newspaper and the student government. No portion of the fee covers personal expenses. Although labeled as a student activity fee, the fee is required for Marci's enrollment and attendance at College X. Therefore, it is a qualified expense.

No Double Benefit Allowed
You cannot do any of the following.

- Deduct higher education expenses on your income tax return (as, for example, a business expense) and also claim an education credit based on those same expenses.
- Claim an education credit in the same year that you are claiming a tuition and fees deduction for the same student.
- Claim a Hope credit and a lifetime learning credit based on the same qualified education expenses.
- Claim an education credit based on the same expenses used to figure the tax-free portion of a distribution from a Coverdell education savings account (ESA) or qualified tuition program (QTP).
- Claim a credit based on qualified education expenses paid with tax-free scholarship, grant, or employer-provided educational assistance. See *Adjustments to Qualified Education Expenses*, next.

TAXALERT

One credit per customer. The Hope credit and Lifetime Learning credit are mutually exclusive. For each eligible student in each tax year, the taxpayer must elect either one of the tax credits. The Hope and Lifetime Learning credits can be claimed in the same year that a distribution from a Coverdell education savings account or qualified tuition program is made, as long as the distribution is not used to cover the same expenses for which the education credits are claimed.

The credits are phased out for single taxpayers with modified adjusted gross income (AGI) of $43,000 to $53,000 and for couples filing jointly with modified AGI between $87,000 and $107,000.

Adjustments to Qualified Education Expenses
If you pay qualified education expenses with certain tax-free funds, you cannot claim a credit for those amounts. You must reduce the qualified education expenses by the amount of any tax-free educational assistance and refund(s) you received.

Tax-free educational assistance. This includes:

- Tax-free part of scholarships and fellowships (see chapter 13 of this publication and chapter 1 of Publication 970),
- Pell grants (see chapter 1 of Publication 970),
- Employer-provided educational assistance (see chapter 11 of Publication 970),
- Veterans' educational assistance (see chapter 1 of Publication 970), and
- Any other nontaxable (tax-free) payments (other than gifts or inheritances) received as educational assistance.

Refunds. Qualified education expenses do not include expenses for which you, or someone else who paid qualified education expenses on behalf of a student, receive a refund. For more information, see *Refunds* in chapters 2 and 3 of Publication 970.

Amounts that do not reduce qualified education expenses. Do not reduce qualified education expenses by amounts paid with funds the student receives as:

- Payment for services, such as wages,
- A loan,
- A gift,
- An inheritance, or
- A withdrawal from the student's personal savings.

Do not reduce the qualified education expenses by any scholarship or fellowship reported as income on the student's tax return in the following situations.

- The use of the money is restricted to costs of attendance (such as room and board) other than qualified education expenses.
- The use of the money is not restricted and is used to pay education expenses that are not qualified (such as room and board).

Example 1. In 2005, Jackie paid $3,000 for tuition and $5,000 for room and board at University X. The university did not require her to pay any fees in addition to her tuition in order to enroll in or attend classes. To help pay these costs, she was awarded a $2,000 scholarship and a $4,000 student loan.

The terms of the scholarship state that it may be used to pay any of Jackie's college expenses. Because she applied it toward her tuition, the scholarship is tax-free. Therefore, for purposes of figuring an education credit (either Hope or lifetime learning), she must first use the $2,000 scholarship to reduce her tuition (her only qualified education expense). The student loan is not tax-free educational assistance, so she does not use it to reduce her qualified expenses. Jackie is treated as having paid $1,000 in qualified education expenses ($3,000 tuition − $2,000 scholarship) in 2005.

Example 2. The facts are the same as in *Example 1*, except that Jackie uses the $2,000 scholarship to pay room and board, and, therefore, reports her entire scholarship as income on her tax return. In this case, the scholarship is allocated to expenses other than qualified education expenses. Jackie is treated as paying the entire $3,000 tuition with other funds and can figure her education credit on the entire $3,000.

Expenses That Do Not Qualify
Qualified education expenses do not include amounts paid for:

- Insurance,
- Medical expenses (including student health fees),
- Room and board,
- Transportation, or
- Similar personal, living, or family expenses.

This is true even if the amount must be paid to the institution as a condition of enrollment or attendance.

Sports, games, hobbies, and noncredit courses. Qualified education expenses generally do not include expenses that relate to any course of instruction or other education that involves sports, games or hobbies, or any noncredit course. However, if the course of instruction or other education is part of the student's degree program, these expenses can qualify.

Comprehensive or bundled fees. Some eligible educational institutions combine all of their fees for an academic period into one amount. If you do not receive or do not have access to an allocation showing how much you paid for qualified education expenses and how much you paid for personal expenses, such as those listed above, contact the institution. The institution is required to make this allocation and provide you with the amount you paid (or were billed) for qualified education expenses on Form 1098-T, Tuition Statement. See *Figuring the Credit*, later, for more information about Form 1098-T.

Who Can Claim a Dependent's Expenses

If there are qualified education expenses for your dependent for a year, either you or your dependent, but not both of you, can claim an education credit for your dependent's expenses for that year.

For you to claim an education credit for your dependent's expenses, you must also claim an exemption for your dependent. You do this by listing your dependent's name and other required information on Form 1040 (or Form 1040A), line 6c.

IF you...	THEN only...
claim an exemption on your tax return for a dependent who is an eligible student	you can claim an education credit based on that dependent's expenses. The dependent cannot claim a credit.
do **not** claim an exemption on your tax return for a dependent who is an eligible student (even if entitled to the exemption)	the dependent can claim an education credit. You cannot claim a credit based on this dependent's expenses.

TAXALERT

Who should claim the education credit. If you claim your child as a dependent, only you may claim the education credit for the child's qualified tuition and related expenses. If, however, you are eligible to claim your child as a dependent but choose not to do so, your child may claim the education credit for his or her qualified tuition and related expenses *even if* the tuition and expenses were paid by you, the parent. It is important to note, however, that if a parent who is eligible to claim a dependency exemption for a student does not do so, the student is not allowed to take a personal exemption for himself or herself on his or her own return. As a result, the exemption for the student may be lost. Due to the phaseout of the dependency ex-

emption, however, this may not be of concern to higher income parents. If you are subject to the income phaseout limitation of the education credits, you should review the overall tax effect of not claiming an exemption for your child and allowing your child to claim the education credits. See Chapter 2, Personal Exemptions and Dependents for a detailed discussion regarding the change in definition of a dependent and the four tests that must be met for tax years beginning in 2005.

Expenses paid by dependent. If you claim an exemption on your tax return for an eligible student who is your dependent, treat any expenses paid (or deemed paid) by your dependent as if you had paid them. Include these expenses when figuring the amount of your education credit.

Tip. *Qualified education expenses paid directly to an eligible educational institution for your dependent under a court-approved divorce decree are treated as paid by your dependent.*

Expenses paid by you. If you claim an exemption for a dependent who is an eligible student, only you can include any expenses you paid when figuring the amount of an education credit. If neither you nor anyone else claims an exemption for the dependent, only the dependent can include any expenses you paid when figuring an education credit.

Expenses paid by others. Someone other than you, your spouse, or your dependent (such as a relative or former spouse) may make a payment directly to an eligible educational institution to pay for an eligible student's qualified education expenses. In this case, the student is treated as receiving the payment from the other person and, in turn, paying the institution. If you claim an exemption on your tax return for the student, you are considered to have paid the expenses.

Example. In 2005, Ms. Allen makes a payment directly to an eligible educational institution for her grandson Todd's qualified education expenses. For purposes of claiming an education credit, Todd is treated as receiving the money as a gift from his grandmother and, in turn, paying his qualified education expenses himself.

Unless an exemption for Todd is claimed on someone else's return, only Todd can use the payment to claim an education credit.

If anyone, such as Todd's parents, claims an exemption for Todd on his or her tax return, whoever claims the exemption may be able to use the expenses to claim an education credit. If anyone else claims an exemption for Todd, Todd cannot claim an education credit.

Tuition reduction. When an eligible educational institution provides a reduction in tuition to an employee of the institution (or spouse or dependent child of an employee), the amount of the reduction may or may not be taxable. If it is taxable, the employee is treated as receiving a payment of that amount and, in turn, paying it to the educational institution on behalf of the student. For more information on tuition reductions, see *Qualified Tuition Reduction* in chapter 1 of Publication 970.

Effect of the Amount of Your Income on the Amount of Your Credit

The amount of your education credit is phased out (gradually reduced) if your modified adjusted gross income (MAGI) is between $43,000 and $53,000 ($87,000 and $107,000 if you file a joint return). You cannot claim an education credit if your MAGI is $53,000 or more ($107,000 or more if you file a joint return).

Modified adjusted gross income (MAGI). For most taxpayers, MAGI is adjusted gross income (AGI) as figured on their federal income tax return.

MAGI when using Form 1040A. If you file Form 1040A, your MAGI is the AGI on line 22 of that form.

MAGI when using Form 1040. If you file Form 1040, your MAGI is the AGI on line 37 of that form, modified by adding back any:

Figure 37-A. **Can You Claim an Education Credit for 2005?**

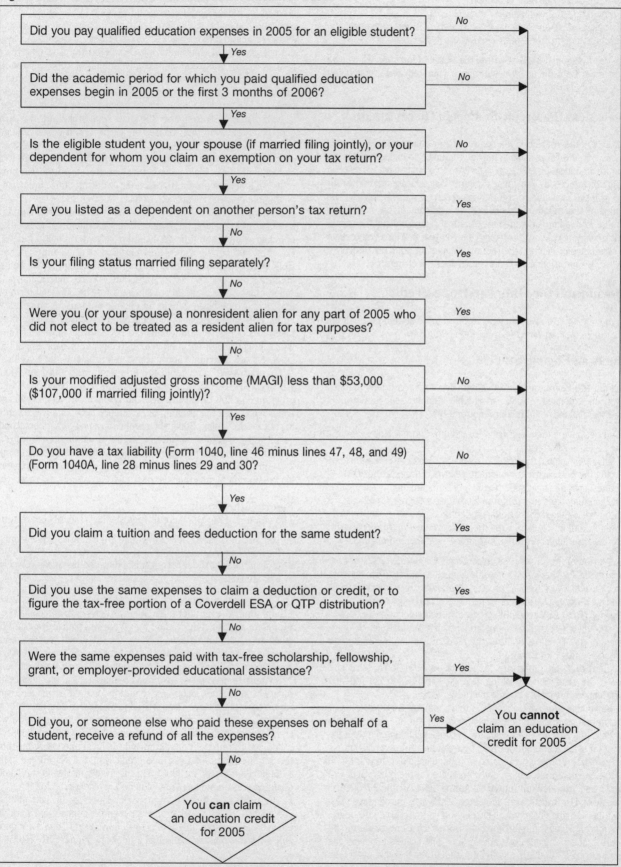

1. Foreign earned income exclusion,
2. Foreign housing exclusion,
3. Exclusion of income for *bona fide* residents of American Samoa, and
4. Exclusion of income from Puerto Rico.

Phaseout. If your MAGI is within the range of incomes where the credit must be reduced, you will figure your reduced credit using lines 8–14 of Form 8863.

When Must the Credit Be Repaid (Recaptured)

If, after you file your 2005 tax return, you or someone else receives tax-free educational assistance for, or a refund of, an expense you used to figure an education credit on that return, you may have to repay all or part of the credit. You must refigure your education credit(s) for 2005 as if the assistance or refund was received in 2005. Subtract the amount of the refigured credit from the amount of the credit you claimed. The result is the amount you must repay. You add the repayment (recapture) to your tax liability for the year in which you receive the assistance or refund (see the instructions for your tax return for that year). Your original 2005 tax return does not change.

Information for Only the Hope Credit

You may be able to claim a Hope credit of up to $1,500 for qualified education expenses paid for each eligible student.

Who Is an Eligible Student

To claim the Hope credit, the student for whom you pay qualified education expenses must be an eligible student. This is a student who meets all of the following requirements.

1. Did not have expenses that were used to figure a Hope credit in any 2 earlier tax years.
2. Had not completed the first 2 years of postsecondary education (generally, the freshman and sophomore years of college) before 2005.
3. For at least one academic period beginning in 2005, was enrolled at least half-time in a program leading to a degree, certificate, or other recognized educational credential.
4. Was free of any federal or state felony conviction for possessing or distributing a controlled substance as of the end of 2005.

Completion of first 2 years. A student who was awarded 2 years of academic credit for postsecondary work completed before 2005 has completed the first 2 years of postsecondary education. This student generally would not be an eligible student for purposes of the Hope credit.

Exception. Any academic credit awarded solely on the basis of the student's performance on proficiency examinations is disregarded in determining whether the student has completed 2 years of postsecondary education.

Enrolled at least half-time. A student was enrolled at least half-time if the student was taking at least half the normal full-time work load for his or her course of study.

The standard for what is half of the normal full-time work load is determined by each eligible educational institution. However, the standard may not be lower than any of those established by the Department of Education under the Higher Education Act of 1965.

Example 1. Marty graduated from high school in June 2004. In September, he enrolled in an undergraduate degree program at College U, and attended full time for both the 2004 fall and 2005 spring semesters. For the 2005 fall semester, Marty was enrolled less than half-time. Because Marty was enrolled in an undergraduate degree program on at least a half-time basis for at least one academic period that began during 2004 and at least one academic period that began during 2005, he is an eligible student for tax years 2004 and 2005 (including the 2005 fall semester when he enrolled at College U on less than a half-time basis).

Example 2. After taking classes at College V on a half-time basis for the 2004 spring and fall semesters, Sharon became a full-time student for the 2005 spring semester. College V classified Sharon as a second-semester sophomore for the 2005 spring semester and as a first-semester junior for the 2005 fall semester. Because College V did not classify Sharon as having completed the first two years of postsecondary education as of the beginning of 2005, Sharon is an eligible student for tax year 2005. Therefore, the qualified education expenses paid for the 2005 spring semester and the 2005 fall semester are taken into account in calculating any Hope credit for 2005.

Example 3. During the 2004 fall semester, Luis was a high school student who took classes on a half-time basis at College X. Luis was not enrolled as part of a degree program at College X because College X only admits students to a degree program if they have a high school diploma or equivalent. Because Luis was not enrolled in a degree program at College X during 2004, Luis was not an eligible student for tax year 2004.

Example 4. The facts are the same as in *Example 3*. During the 2005 spring semester, Luis again attended College X but not as part of a degree program. Luis graduated from high school in June 2005. For the 2005 fall semester, Luis enrolled as a full-time student in College X as part of a degree program, and College X awarded Luis credit for his prior coursework at College X. Because Luis was enrolled in a degree program at College X for the 2005 fall term on at least a half-time basis, Luis is an eligible student for all of tax year 2005. Therefore, the qualified education expenses paid for classes taken at College X during both the 2005 spring semester (during which Luis was not enrolled in a degree program) and the 2005 fall semester are taken into account in computing any Hope credit.

Example 5. Diana graduated from high school in June 2003. In January 2004, Diana enrolled in a one-year postsecondary certificate program on a full-time basis to obtain a certificate as a travel agent. Diana completed the program in December 2004, and was awarded a certificate. In January 2005, she enrolled in a one-year postsecondary certificate program on a full-time basis to obtain a certificate as a computer programmer. Diana is an eligible student for both tax years 2004 and 2005 because she meets the degree requirement, the work load requirement, and the year of study requirement for those years.

Figuring the Credit

The amount of the Hope credit (per eligible student) is the sum of:

1. 100% of the first $1,000 of qualified education expenses you paid for the eligible student, and
2. 50% of the next $1,000 of qualified education expenses you paid for that student.

The maximum amount of Hope credit you can claim in 2005 is $1,500 times the number of eligible students. You can claim the full $1,500 for each eligible student for whom you paid at least $2,000 of qualified education expenses. However, the credit may be reduced based on your modified adjusted gross income (MAGI). See *Effect of the Amount of Your Income on the Amount of Your Credit*, earlier.

Example. Jon and Karen Frost are married and file a joint tax return. For 2005, they claim an exemption for their dependent daughter on their tax return. Their MAGI is $70,000. Their daughter is in her sophomore (second) year of studies at the local university. Jon and Karen paid qualified education expenses of $4,300 in 2005.

Jon and Karen, their daughter, and the local university meet all of the requirements for the Hope credit. Jon and Karen can claim a $1,500 Hope credit in 2005. This is 100% of the first $1,000 of qualified education expenses, plus 50% of the next $1,000.

Form 1098-T. To help you figure your Hope credit, you should receive Form 1098-T. Generally, an eligible educational institution (such as a college or university) must send Form 1098-T (or acceptable substitute) to each enrolled student by January 31, 2006.

Claiming the Credit

You claim the Hope credit by completing Parts I and III of Form 8863 and submitting it with your Form 1040 or 1040A. Enter the credit on Form 1040, line 50, or on Form 1040A, line 31. An illustrated example using Form 8863 appears at the end of this chapter.

Information for Only the Lifetime Learning Credit

You may be able to claim a lifetime learning credit of up to $2,000 for qualified education expenses paid for all students enrolled in eligible educational institutions.

Who Is an Eligible Student

For purposes of the lifetime learning credit, an eligible student is a student who is enrolled in one or more courses at an eligible educational institution.

Figuring the Credit

The amount of the lifetime learning credit is 20% of the first $10,000 of qualified education expenses you paid for all eligible students. The maximum amount of lifetime learning credit you can claim for 2005 is $2,000 (20% × $10,000). However, that amount may be reduced based on your modified adjusted gross income (MAGI). See *Effect of the Amount of Your Income on the Amount of Your Credit*, earlier.

Example. Bruce and Toni are married and file a joint tax return. For 2005, their MAGI is $75,000. Toni is attending a local college (an eligible educational institution) to earn credits toward a degree in nursing. She already has a bachelor's degree in history and wants to become a nurse. In August 2005, Toni paid $6,000 of qualified education expenses for her fall 2005 semester. Bruce and Toni can claim a $1,200 (20% × $6,000) lifetime learning credit on their 2005 joint tax return.

Form 1098-T. To help you figure your lifetime learning credit, you should receive Form 1098-T. Generally, an eligible educational institution (such as a college or university) must send Form 1098-T (or acceptable substitute) to each enrolled student by January 31, 2006.

Claiming the Credit

You claim the lifetime learning credit by completing Parts II and III of Form 8863 and submitting it with your Form 1040 or 1040A. Enter the credit on Form 1040, line 50, or Form 1040A, line 31. An illustrated example using Form 8863 is shown at the end of this chapter.

Illustrated Example

Dave and Valerie Jones are married and file a joint tax return. For 2005, they claim exemptions for their two dependent children on their tax return. Their modified adjusted gross income is $88,000. Their tax, before credits, is $9,956. Their son, Sean, will receive his bachelor's degree in psychology from the state college in May 2006. Their daughter, Corey, enrolled full-time at that same college in August 2004, to begin working on her bachelor's degree in physical education. In July 2005, Dave and Valerie paid $2,200 in tuition costs for each child for the fall 2005 semester. In December 2005, they also paid $2,600 of tuition for each child for the spring 2006 semester that begins in January.

Dave and Valerie, their children, and the college meet all of the requirements for the higher education credits. Because Sean is beyond the second (sophomore) year of his postsecondary education, his expenses do not qualify for the Hope credit. But, amounts paid for Sean's expenses in 2005 for academic periods beginning in 2005 and the first 3 months of 2006 qualify for the lifetime learning credit. Corey is in her first two (freshman and sophomore) years of postsecondary education, and expenses paid for her in 2005, for academic periods beginning in 2005 and January 2006, qualify for the Hope credit.

Dave and Valerie figure their tentative education credits for 2005, $2,460, as shown in the completed Form 8863. They cannot claim the full amount because their modified adjusted gross income is more than $87,000. They carry the amount from line 20 of Form 8863, $2,091, to line 50 of Form 1040, and they attach the Form 8863 to their return.

Table 37-2. **Other Education Tax Benefits**

There are many education tax incentives in addition to the Hope and Lifetime Learning Credits. Some of the more popular incentives are summarized below.

Student loan interest deduction

Student loan interest paid is deductible if the interest was paid on a loan that you took out to pay for qualified higher education expenses at an eligible educational institution for yourself, your spouse, or your dependent. Qualified higher education expenses include the costs of tuition, fees, room and board, books, supplies, and equipment. You cannot deduct interest on a loan for which you are not legally obligated to make the payments nor can you deduct interest if you did not actually make the payments.

Benefit	If you paid interest on a qualified education loan in 2005, you may be able to deduct up to $2,500 of the interest paid on your 2005 tax return.
Qualifications	You can claim the deductions if the following requirements are met: 1) Your filing status is any filing status except married filing separately. 2) No one else can claim an exemption for you on his or her tax return. 3) You paid interest on a qualified student loan.
Income limits	For 2005 the phase-out range for single taxpayers is $50,000–$65,000. For taxpayers filing joint returns, the phase-out range is $105,000–$135,000.

For more information on the student loan interest deduction, see Chapter 25, *Interest Expense*.

Forgiveness of certain student loans

Benefit	When any loan for which you are responsible is forgiven, you generally must include the amount that was forgiven in your gross income. When certain student loans are forgiven, however, you may not have to include any amount in income.
Qualifications	Your loan must provide that all or a portion of the debt will be canceled if you work for a certain period of time, in certain professions, and for a designated class of employers. The loan must have been made by a qualified lender. A qualified lender includes: • The U.S., a state (or political subdivision), and any governmental agency or instrumentality. • Certain tax-exempt public benefit corporations • An educational institution in connection with certain programs. If you refinanced a student loan with a loan from an educational or tax-exempt organization, the refinanced loan may also be considered as having been made by a qualified lender. In order to qualify, it must have been made in connection with a program designed to encourage students to serve in occupations or areas with unmet needs, and the services required must be performed under the direction of a governmental unit or tax-exempt 501(c)(3) organization.
Income limits	There are no specific income limits restricting the use of this provision.

For more information on forgiveness of student loans, see Chapter 13, *Other Income*.

Deduction for higher-education expenses

The deduction for higher-education expenses are limited to those qualifying expenses paid during 2005 for 2005 enrollment periods, including any academic period that begins in 2005 or in the first three months of 2006.

Benefit	Certain taxpayers are eligible to deduct up to $4,000 paid for qualified tuition and related expenses. The deduction is an adjustment to gross income ("above-the-line") and is available even if you do not itemize deductions on Schedule A.
Qualifications	Qualified tuition and related expenses are tuition and fees paid for you, your spouse, or a dependent for whom you claim an exemption. The expenses must be required for enrollment or attendance at an "eligible educational institution." A college, university, vocational school, or other postsecondary educational institution, which is eligible to participate in a student aid program administered by the Department of Education generally will be considered an eligible educational institution. Student activity fees and fees for course-related books, supplies, and equipment generally do not qualify unless they are paid to the educational institution as a condition of enrollment or attendance. The cost of insurance, medical expenses, room and board, transportation, and similar personal expenses are not considered qualified tuition and related expenses even if paid to the institution as a condition of enrollment or attendance.
Income limits	For tax years beginning in 2005, you can deduct up to $4,000 if you are a qualifying taxpayer and your modified adjusted gross income is not more than $65,000, or $130,000 on a joint return. If your modified AGI is more than these amounts but not more than $160,000 ($80,000 for unmarrieds) you can deduct up to $2,000. These are absolute limits, not phase-outs. If your income is above those amounts, you cannot take any deduction.

Tax-free scholarships and fellowships

In general, scholarships and fellowships received to assist an individual with payment of educational expenses are not considered taxable income. See the chart below for more details.

Benefit	A candidate for a degree at an educational institution can exclude from income amounts received as a qualified scholarship or fellowship.

Qualifications	A candidate for a degree is defined as including a student who:
	
	1. Attends a primary or secondary school or is pursuing a degree at a college or university, or
	2. Attends a qualifying accredited educational organization that is authorized to provide a program:
	  a. That is acceptable for full credit toward a bachelor's or higher degree, or
	  b. That trains students for employment in a recognized occupation.
	
	A scholarship or fellowship grant is generally an amount paid for the benefit of an individual to aid such individual in the pursuit of study or research. A scholarship or fellowship grant does *not* include any amount provided by an individual to aid a relative, friend, or other individual if the grantor is motivated by family or philanthropic considerations.
	
	Amounts received that are used for qualified tuition and related expenses can be excluded from income. These expenses include tuition and fees required to enroll in, or to attend, an educational institution, and fees, books, supplies, and equipment required of all students in your course of instruction. Incidental expenses including room and board and travel expenses do not qualify. Although scholarships are usually taxable if they carry a future service requirement, qualified amounts received under the National Health Service Corps Scholarship Program or the Armed Forces Health Professions Scholarship and Financial Assistance Program will not be taxed.

Income limits	There are no specific income limits restricting the use of this provision.

For more information on scholarships and fellowships, see Chapter 13, *Other Income,* and IRS Publication 520.

Withdrawals from IRAs before age 59 1/2 to pay qualified higher educational expenses

Benefit	Generally, withdrawals from a traditional or Roth IRA before age 59 1/2 are subject to an additional 10% tax on the part of the distribution included in gross income. You will not be subject to the 10% additional tax, however, if for the year of withdrawal you have paid sufficient qualified higher education expenses for yourself, your spouse, or for your or your spouse's children or grandchildren.
Qualifications	N/A
Income limits	There are no specific income limits restricting the use of this provision.

For more information on withdrawals from IRAs before age 59 1/2, see Chapter 18, *Individual Retirement Arrangements (IRAs).*

Education savings bond program

Benefit	Interest earned on U.S. savings bonds is generally taxed either in the year the interest is earned or, more typically, in the year in which you cash in the bonds. Under the education savings bond program, when you cash in qualified U.S. savings bonds, you may be able to exclude from your income all or a portion of the interest earned.
Qualifications	Only Series EE bonds issued after 1989 and Series I savings bonds qualify. In addition, the owner of the bond must be at least 24 years old before the bond's issue date, and cannot have a filing status of married filing separately. To be able to exclude interest from your taxable income, you must pay "qualified higher education expenses" for yourself, your spouse, or a dependent for whom you claim an exemption on your return. If the total that you receive when you cash in the bonds is not more than the available qualified higher education expenses for the year, all interest earned on the bonds may be tax-free. If the total received is more than the qualifying expenses, part of the interest may be tax-free.
Income limits	The interest exclusion is phased out for higher income taxpayers. The phase-out range for single taxpayers in 2005 is $61,200–$76,200. For taxpayers filing joint returns, the phase-out range is $91,850–$121,850.

For more information on the education savings bond program, see Chapter 8, *Interest Income.*

Educational assistance as a working condition fringe benefit

Benefit	Certain educational expenses paid by your employer may be excludable from your income if the expenditures are considered a working condition fringe benefit.
Qualifications	Expenses qualify if the education you receive maintains or improves skills required in your employment or meets the express requirements of your employer or applicable law required as a condition of employment. Educational expenses that are incurred to meet minimum educational requirements or that qualify you for a new trade or business (such as a law or medical degree) do not qualify. Amounts paid by your employer will generally qualify as a working condition fringe benefit if the item would have been deductible as an employee business expense had you paid the expense. Treatment as a working condition fringe benefit is generally more beneficial than a deduction, however, since employee business expenses are deductible only if you itemize your deductions, and then only to the extent that they, in combination with other miscellaneous itemized deductions, exceed 2% of your adjusted gross income.
Income limits	There are no specific income limits restricting the use of this provision.

For more information about working condition fringe benefits, see IRS Publication 15-B.

Employer-provided educational assistance programs

Your employer may assist you with educational payments, a portion of which may be excludable from your income (see chart below). Qualified payments include payments for tuition, fees, books, supplies, and equipment (not including meals and transportation). Courses in sports, games or hobbies are not qualified expenses unless there is a reasonable relationship between the courses and the business of the employer or if the courses are required as part of a degree program.

Benefit	Up to $5,250 of employer-provided educational assistance payments may be excluded from your income each calendar year when provided under an employer-sponsored educational assistance program. Qualifying payments are excludable from income whether or not the courses taken are job-related. This benefit covers educational assistance for graduate level courses under a program leading to a law, business, medical, or other advanced degree.
Qualifications	Payments must be made under a qualifying written plan that does not discriminate in favor of highly compensated employees. Payments may be made for tuition, fees, books, supplies, and equipment. Payments made for meals, lodging, and transportation generally do not qualify.
Income limits	There are no specific income limits restricting the use of this provision.

For more information on education as a working condition fringe benefit and on employer-provided educational assistance programs, see Chapter 13, *Other Income*, and Chapter 29, *Tax Benefits for Work-Related Education*.

Coverdell education savings accounts

You may be eligible to set up a Coverdell Education Savings Account to assist a designated beneficiary with financing his or her qualified education expenses. Coverdell accounts may be used to pay qualifying elementary and secondary school expenses as well as higher education expenses.

Benefit	There is no federal income tax on earnings in these accounts when distributions are used to pay qualifying educational expenses.
Qualifications	Qualified educational expenses include tuition, fees, books, supplies, and equipment, and the costs of room and board. Qualified expenses include elementary and secondary school expenses. The purchase of computer equipment, internet access, and related technology, if used by the student or the student's family, also qualifies. There is no federal income tax deduction for contributions to Coverdell accounts. Except in the case of a special needs beneficiary, you cannot contribute to a Coverdell account after the beneficiary reaches age 18. To the extent that distributions are not used for qualifying educational expenses, an income and penalty tax may apply to the distributed earnings.
Income limits	The maximum contribution to a Coverdell account is $2,000 per year. The amount that a taxpayer is allowed to contribute to a Coverdell account is phased out for higher income taxpayers. In 2005 for joint returns, the phase-out range is $190,000–$220,000. For other taxpayers, the phase-out range is $95,000–$110,000.

Qualified Tuition (Section 529) Programs

A qualified tuition program allows you to prepay or contribute to an account that has been established to pay qualified higher education expenses. Unlike Coverdell Education Savings Accounts, there are no income limits restricting the use of these accounts. Although contributions are not deductible for federal income tax purposes, many states permit you to deduct a portion or all of your contribution on your state income tax return.

Benefit	There is no federal income tax imposed when distributions from Qualified Tuition Programs (popularly known as 529 plans) are used to pay qualifying higher education expenses.
Qualifications	There are two basic types of 529 plans. Under the prepaid educational service type of plan, you purchase tuition credits today for use in the future. The other type of plan (often referred to as a "college savings plan") permits you to contribute to a special higher education savings account for a designated beneficiary. In both types of plans, your initial investment is designed to grow over time and the value of that growth is not subject to federal income tax when distributions are made for qualifying higher education expenses. There is no federal income tax deduction for contributions to a 529 plan. Unlike distributions from Coverdell accounts, qualifying expenditures may only be made for *higher* education expenses. To the extent that distributions are not used for qualifying higher educational expenses, an income and penalty tax may apply.
Income limits	529 plans are not subject to income limits and permit you to make contributions far in excess of the $2,000 annual contribution permitted for Coverdell accounts. The combination of benefits and flexibility offered by these plans will likely make them the most widely used education tax incentive program. Be sure to discuss the investment options and limitations of the various programs with your financial advisor.

For more information on qualified tuition programs, Coverdell education savings accounts and other education incentives see IRS Publication 970 Tax Benefits for Education.

Form **8863**	**Education Credits** (Hope and Lifetime Learning Credits) ▶ See instructions. ▶ Attach to Form 1040 or Form 1040A.	OMB No. 1545-1618 **20**05
Department of the Treasury Internal Revenue Service (99)		Attachment Sequence No. **50**

Name(s) shown on return	Your social security number
Dave and Valerie Jones	987 00 6543

Caution: *You **cannot** take both an education credit and the tuition and fees deduction (Form 1040, line 34, or Form 1040A, line 19) for the **same student** in the same year.*

| **Part I** | **Hope Credit. Caution:** *You **cannot** take the Hope credit for more than 2 tax years for the **same student.*** |

1	(a) Student's name (as shown on page 1 of your tax return) First name / Last name	(b) Student's social security number (as shown on page 1 of your tax return)	(c) Qualified expenses (see instructions). **Do not** enter more than $2,000 for each student.	(d) Enter the **smaller** of the amount in column (c) or $1,000	(e) Add column (c) and column (d)	(f) Enter one-half of the amount in column (e)
	Corey Jones	137 00 9642	2,000	1,000	1,000	500

2	Tentative Hope credit. Add the amounts on line 1, column (f). If you are taking the lifetime learning credit for another student, go to Part II; otherwise, go to Part III . . . . . ▶	**2**	1,500

| **Part II** | **Lifetime Learning Credit** |

3	**Caution:** *You **cannot** take the Hope credit and the lifetime learning credit for the **same student** in the same year.*	(a) Student's name (as shown on page 1 of your tax return) First name / Last name	(b) Student's social security number (as shown on page 1 of your tax return)	(c) Qualified expenses (see instructions)
		Sean Jones	246 00 9731	4,800

4	Add the amounts on line 3, column (c), and enter the total	**4**	4,800
5	Enter the **smaller** of line 4 or $10,000	**5**	4,800
6	Tentative lifetime learning credit. Multiply line 5 by 20% (.20) and go to Part III . . ▶	**6**	960

| **Part III** | **Allowable Education Credits** |

7	Tentative education credits. Add lines 2 and 6	**7**	2,460
8	Enter: $107,000 if married filing jointly; $53,000 if single, head of household, or qualifying widow(er)	**8**	107,000
9	Enter the amount from Form 1040, line 38*, or Form 1040A, line 22	**9**	88,000
10	Subtract line 9 from line 8. If zero or less, **stop;** you cannot take any education credits	**10**	19,000
11	Enter: $20,000 if married filing jointly; $10,000 if single, head of household, or qualifying widow(er)	**11**	20,000
12	If line 10 is equal to or more than line 11, enter the amount from line 7 on line 13 and go to line 14. If line 10 is less than line 11, divide line 10 by line 11. Enter the result as a decimal (rounded to at least three places)	**12**	× .950
13	Multiply line 7 by line 12 . . . . ▶	**13**	2,337
14	Enter the amount from Form 1040, line 46, or Form 1040A, line 28 . . .	**14**	9,630
15	Enter the total, if any, of your credits from Form 1040, lines 47 through 49, or Form 1040A, lines 29 and 30	**15**	-0-
16	Subtract line 15 from line 14. If zero or less, **stop;** you cannot take any education credits . . . . ▶	**16**	9,630
17	**Education credits.** Enter the **smaller** of line 13 or line 16 here and on Form 1040, line 50, or Form 1040A, line 31 . . . . ▶	**17**	2,337

* If you are filing Form 2555, 2555-EZ, or 4563, or you are excluding income from Puerto Rico, see Pub. 970 for the amount to enter.

For Paperwork Reduction Act Notice, see page 3.	Cat. No. 25379M	Form **8863** (2005)

38

Other Credits Including the Earned Income Credit

Note: The 2004 IRS Publication 17 (Your Federal Income Tax) has been updated by Ernst & Young LLP for 2005. Dates and dollar amounts shown are for 2005. Gray type is used to indicate where IRS text has been updated or intentionally omitted. Unrevised IRS text is shown in black type.

Introduction

This chapter discusses ten credits you may use to reduce your tax liability. Six of these credits are nonrefundable; that is, although they may be used to bring your tax liability to zero, any credit in excess of your liability is not refunded to you. Four of these credits are refundable. That means that any unused credit is refunded to you.

The six nonrefundable credits are:

1. The Adoption Credit
2. The Foreign Tax Credit
3. The Mortgage Interest Credit
4. The Retirement Savings Contribution Credit
5. The Minimum Tax Credit
6. The Electric Vehicle Credit

Depending on the credit, part or all of a nonrefundable credit that is not utilized in the current year generally may be carried back or carried forward and utilized in another year.

The four refundable credits are:

1. The Excess Social Security or Railroad Retirement Tax Credit
2. The Regulated Investment Company Credit or Credit for Tax on Undistributed Capital Gain
3. The Health Coverage Tax Credit
4. The Earned Income Credit

What's New

Adoption credit. The maximum adoption credit increases to $10,630 in 2005. See *Adoption Credit,* later for more information.

Excess withholding of social security tax and tier 1 railroad retirement tax. Social security and tier 1 railroad retirement tax (RRTA) are both withheld at a rate of 6.2% of wages. The maximum wages subject to this tax increased to $90,000 in 2005. If you had two or more employers and they withheld too much social security or RRTA tax during 2005, you may be entitled to a credit of the excess withholding. For more information about the credit, see *Credit for Excess Social Security Tax or Railroad Retirement Tax Withheld* under *Refundable Credits,* later.

   This chapter discusses the following credits.

• Adoption credit.
• Foreign tax credit.

• Mortgage interest credit.
• Retirement savings contributions credit.
• Credit for prior year minimum tax.
• Credit for electric vehicles.
• Credit for excess social security tax or railroad retirement tax withheld.
• Credit for tax on undistributed capital gain.
• Health coverage tax credit.
• Earned income credit.

   Several other credits are discussed in other chapters in this publication.

• Child and dependent care credit (chapter 34).
• Credit for the elderly or the disabled (chapter 35).
• Child tax credit (chapter 36).
• Education credits (chapter 37).

Nonrefundable credits. The first part of this chapter, *Nonrefundable Credits,* covers six credits that you subtract directly from your tax. These credits may reduce your tax to zero. If these credits are more than your tax, the excess is not refunded to you.

Refundable credits. The second part of this chapter, *Refundable Credits,* covers three credits that are treated as payments and are refundable to you. These credits are added to the federal income tax withheld and any estimated tax payments you made. If this total is more than your total tax, the excess will be refunded to you.

Useful Items

You may want to see:

Publications

- ☐ 502 Medical and Dental Expenses
- ☐ 514 Foreign Tax Credit for Individuals
- ☐ 530 Tax Information for First-Time Homeowners
- ☐ 535 Business Expenses
- ☐ 590 Individual Retirement Arrangements (IRAs)
- ☐ 968 Tax Benefits for Adoption

Forms (and Instructions)

- ☐ 1116 Foreign Tax Credit (Individual, Estate, or Trust)
- ☐ 2439 Notice to Shareholder of Undistributed Long-Term Capital Gains
- ☐ 8396 Mortgage Interest Credit
- ☐ 8801 Credit For Prior Year Minimum Tax—Individuals, Estates, and Trusts
- ☐ 8828 Recapture of Federal Mortgage Subsidy
- ☐ 8834 Qualified Electric Vehicle Credit
- ☐ 8839 Qualified Adoption Expenses
- ☐ 8880 Credit for Qualified Retirement Savings Contributions
- ☐ 8885 Health Coverage Tax Credit

Nonrefundable Credits

The credits discussed in this part of the chapter can reduce your tax. However, if the total of these credits is more than your tax, the excess is not refunded to you.

Adoption Credit

You may be able to take a tax credit of up to $10,630 for qualifying expenses paid to adopt an eligible child. A credit of up to $10,630 may be allowed for the adoption of a child with special needs even if you do not have any qualifying expenses.

If your modified adjusted gross income (AGI) is more than $159,450, your credit is reduced. If your modified AGI is $199,450 or more, you cannot claim the credit.

Caution. *The amount of expenses paid or incurred before 2002 that can be taken into account is limited to the pre-2002 dollar limits. The limit on these expenses is $5,000 ($6,000 in the case of a child with special needs, defined later).*

> **TAXALERT**
>
> In the case of the adoption of a child with special needs, you may claim a credit of $10,630 when the adoption becomes finalized regardless of whether you have actually paid qualified adoption expenses.

Qualifying expenses. Qualifying adoption expenses are reasonable and necessary adoption fees, court costs, attorney fees, travel-

ing expenses (including amounts spent for meals and lodging) while away from home, and other expenses directly related to, and whose principal purpose is for, the legal adoption of an eligible child.

Nonqualifying expenses. Qualifying adoption expenses do not include expenses:

- That violate state or federal law,
- For carrying out any surrogate parenting arrangement,
- For the adoption of your spouse's child,
- Paid using funds received from any federal, state, or local program,
- Allowed as a credit or deduction under any other federal income tax rule, or
- Paid or reimbursed by your employer or any other person or organization.

Eligible child. The term "eligible child" means any individual:

1. Under 18 years old, or
2. Physically or mentally incapable of caring for himself or herself.

> **TAXALERT**
>
> Qualified adoption expenses eligible for the credit include expenses paid or incurred in an unsuccessful effort to adopt an otherwise eligible child who is a citizen or resident of the United States. In the case of a child who is not a citizen or resident of the United States, the credit is available only for adoptions that become final.

Child with special needs. An eligible child is a child with special needs if all three of the following apply.

1. He or she is a citizen or resident of the United States (including U.S. possessions).
2. A state (including the District of Columbia) determines that the child cannot or should not be returned to his or her parents' home.
3. The state has determined that the child will not be adopted unless assistance is provided to the adoptive parents. Factors used by the state to make this determination include:
   a. The child's ethnic background,
   b. The child's age,
   c. Whether the child is a member of a minority or sibling group, or
   d. Whether the child has a medical condition or physical, mental, or emotional handicap.

When to claim the credit. Generally, for any year before the adoption becomes final, you take the credit in the year after your qualified expenses are paid or incurred. See Publication 968 for more specific information on when to claim the credit.

Foreign child. If the child is not a U.S. citizen or resident, you cannot take the credit unless the adoption becomes final. You treat all adoption expenses paid or incurred in years before the adoption becomes final as paid or incurred in the year it becomes final.

> **TAXALERT**
>
> You may claim a credit for qualified adoption expenses of up to $10,630. The credit is phased out for taxpayers with an adjusted gross income between $159,450 and $199,450. Taxpayers with adjusted gross income of more than $199,450 are not entitled to the credit. Qualified adoption expenses include reasonable and necessary adoption fees, court costs, attorney fees, and other expenses that are directly related to the adoption of a child by the taxpayer. The principal purpose of the ex-

penses must be the adoption of an eligible child. An eligible child is an individual who has not attained the age of 18 or who is physically or mentally incapable of caring for himself or herself. The expenses cannot be in violation of federal or state law or for carrying out any surrogate parenting arrangement. You may not claim a credit for expenses incurred in adopting the child of your spouse. You may also not claim a credit for expenses reimbursed by a program of your employer; a federal, state, or local program; or other types. You are eligible for a separate credit for each child whom you adopt. Thus, you may claim a credit of up to $21,260 if you adopt two children and meet all of the other requirements.

How to claim the credit. To claim the credit, you must complete Form 8839 and attach it to your Form 1040 or Form 1040A. Enter the credit on Form 1040, line 53, or Form 1040A, line 34.

Foreign Tax Credit

You generally can choose to claim income taxes you paid or accrued during the year to a foreign country or U.S. possession as a credit against your U.S. income tax. Or, you can deduct them as an itemized deduction (see chapter 24).

   You cannot take a credit (or deduction) for foreign income taxes paid on income that you exclude from U.S. tax under any of the following.

1. Foreign earned income exclusion.
2. Foreign housing exclusion.
3. Possession exclusion.
4. Extraterritorial income exclusion.

Limit on the credit. Unless you can elect not to file Form 1116, your foreign tax credit cannot be more than your U.S. tax liability (Form 1040, line 44), multiplied by a fraction. The numerator of the fraction is your taxable income from sources outside the United States. The denominator is your total taxable income from U.S. and foreign sources. See Publication 514 for more information.

Explanation
To take the foreign tax credit, the foreign taxes must have been imposed on you, and you must have paid or accrued the taxes during your tax year. Furthermore, if you work overseas and elect to claim the foreign earned income exclusion or the foreign housing exclusion, the amount of foreign taxes eligible for credit is reduced. The foreign earned income exclusion allows U.S. citizens or residents who meet one of the tests for living abroad to exclude up to $80,000 of foreign earned income from their **gross income.** The foreign housing exclusion allows U.S. citizens or residents to exclude excess foreign housing costs from their gross income. See Chapter 43, *U.S. Citizens Working Abroad: Tax Treatment of Foreign Earned Income,* for a more complete discussion of these subjects.

   The amount you may claim as a foreign tax credit is limited. You can figure your maximum credit by performing the following calculation:

$$\frac{\text{Taxable income from sources outside the U.S.}}{\text{Taxable income from all sources}} \times \text{U.S. income tax} = \text{Maximum credit}$$

Separate foreign tax credit limitations must be calculated for passive income and several other categories.

However, while you are limited in the amount of credit for foreign taxes you may claim in any one year, you are able to carry back or carry forward the unused credits. See Chapter 43, *U.S. Citizens Working Abroad: Tax Treatment of Foreign Earned Income,* for a further discussion of how to calculate your foreign tax credit.

TaxAlert

For tax years beginning *before* October 23, 2004, you may carry back the unused credit for 2 years and carry forward the unused credit for 5 years. For tax years beginning *on* or *after* October 23, 2004, you may carry back the unused credits for 1 year and carry forward the unused credits for 10 years.

TaxPlanner

It is usually better to claim a credit for foreign taxes than to deduct them as itemized deductions. Credits reduce your U.S. tax on a dollar-for-dollar basis, whereas a deduction just reduces the amount of income subject to tax. (For an example of this point, see Chapter 24, *Taxes You May Deduct.*)

How to claim the credit. Complete Form 1116 and attach it to your Form 1040. Enter the credit on Form 1040, line 47.
   Election not to file Form 1116. You will not be subject to the limit and may be able to claim the credit without using Form 1116 if all the following requirements are met.

1. Your only foreign source income for the tax year is passive income (dividends, interest, royalties, etc.) that is reported to you on a payee statement (such as a Form 1099-DIV, Dividends and Distributions, or 1099-INT, Interest Income).
2. Your qualified foreign taxes for the tax year are not more than $300 ($600 if filing a joint return) and are reported on a payee statement.
3. You elect this procedure for the tax year.

   If you qualify and elect not to file Form 1116, enter the amount of your foreign taxes paid on Form 1040, line 47.
Caution. *If you make this election, you cannot carry back or carry over any unused foreign tax to or from this tax year.*

Mortgage Interest Credit

The mortgage interest credit is intended to help lower-income individuals afford home ownership. If you qualify, you can claim the credit each year for part of the home mortgage interest you pay.
Who qualifies. You may be eligible for the credit if you were issued a mortgage credit certificate (MCC) from your state or local government. Generally, an MCC is issued only in connection with a new mortgage for the purchase of your main home.
Amount of credit. Figure your credit on Form 8396. If your mortgage is equal to (or smaller than) the certified indebtedness amount (loan) shown on your MCC, enter on Form 8396, line 1, all the interest you paid on your mortgage during the year.

   If your mortgage loan amount is larger than the certified indebtedness amount shown on your MCC, you can figure the credit on only part of the interest you paid. To find the amount to enter on line 1, multiply the total interest you paid during the year on your mortgage by the following fraction.

$$\frac{\text{Certified indebtedness amount on your MCC}}{\text{Original amount of your mortgage}}$$

If two or more persons (other than a married couple filing a joint return) hold an interest in the home to which the MCC relates, the credit must be divided based on the interest held by each person. See Publication 530 for further information.

Caution. *If the certificate credit rate is higher than 20%, the credit you are allowed cannot be more than $2,000.*

Carryforward. If your allowable credit is reduced because of the limit based on your tax, you can carry forward the unused portion of the credit to the next 3 years or until used, whichever comes first.

If you are subject to the $2,000 limit because your certificate credit rate is more than 20%, you cannot carry forward any amount more than $2,000 (or your share of the $2,000 if you must divide the credit).

How to claim the credit. Figure your 2005 credit and any carryforward to 2006 on Form 8396, and attach it to your Form 1040. Be sure to include any credit carryforward from 2002, 2003, and 2004.

Include the credit in your total for Form 1040, line 54, and check box a.

Reduced home mortgage interest deduction. If you itemize your deductions on Schedule A (Form 1040), you must reduce your home mortgage interest deduction by the amount of the mortgage interest credit shown on line 3 of Form 8396. You must do this even if part of that amount is to be carried forward to 2005. For more information about the home mortgage interest deduction, see chapter 25.

Recapture of federal mortgage subsidy. If you received an MCC with your mortgage loan, you may have to recapture (pay back) all or part of the benefit you received from that program. The recapture may be required if you sell or dispose of your home at a gain during the first 9 years after the date you closed your mortgage loan. See Publication 523, Selling Your Home, for more information.

Retirement Savings Contributions Credit

You may be able to take a tax credit of up to $1,000 ($2,000 if married filing jointly) for making eligible contributions to an employer-sponsored retirement plan or to an individual retirement arrangement (IRA). The credit is a percentage of the qualifying contributions, with the highest rate for taxpayers with the least income.

You cannot claim this credit if any of the following apply.

1. The amount of your 2005 adjusted gross income (discussed next) is more than $25,000 ($37,500 if head of household, $50,000 if married filing jointly).
2. You were born after January 1, 1988.
3. You are claimed as a dependent on another person's 2005 tax return.
4. You were a full-time student in 2005.

The amount of credit you can take depends on your filing status, your adjusted gross income (AGI), and your eligible contributions.

Adjusted gross income (AGI). This is generally the amount on Form 1040, line 37, or Form 1040A, line 22. However, you must add to that amount any exclusion or deduction claimed for the year for:

- Foreign earned income,
- Foreign housing costs,
- Income for residents of American Samoa, and
- Income from Puerto Rico.

Eligible contributions. These include contributions to a traditional or Roth IRA and salary reduction contributions (elective deferrals) to most employer-sponsored retirement plans. They also include certain voluntary after-tax employee contributions.

Contributions reduced. Your eligible contributions must be reduced by certain taxable and nontaxable distributions made after 2001 and before the due date (including extensions) of your 2005 tax return.

See Publication 590, chapter 4, for more specific information on eligible contributions and the reductions you must make.

Limit on the credit. After your contributions are reduced, the maximum annual contributions on which you can base the credit is $2,000 per person. This makes the maximum possible credit $1,000 per return ($2,000 if married filing jointly).

How to figure and report the credit. The amount of the credit you can get is based on the contributions you make and your credit rate. Your credit rate can be as low as 10% or as high as 50%. Your credit rate depends on your income and your filing status. See Form 8880 to determine your credit rate.

The maximum contribution taken into account is $2,000 per person. On a joint return, up to $2,000 is taken into account for each spouse.

Figure the credit on Form 8880. Report the credit on line 51 of your Form 1040 or line 32 of your Form 1040A and attach Form 8880 to your return.

Credit for Prior Year Minimum Tax

The tax laws give special treatment to some kinds of income and allow special deductions and credits for some kinds of expenses. If you benefit from these laws, you may have to pay at least a minimum amount of tax in addition to any other tax on these items. This is called the alternative minimum tax.

The special treatment of some items of income and expenses only allows you to postpone paying tax until a later year. If in prior years you paid alternative minimum tax because of these tax deferral items, you may be able to claim a credit for prior year minimum tax against your current year's regular tax. The amount of the credit cannot reduce your current year's tax below your current year's tentative alternative minimum tax.

You may be able to take a credit against your 2005 regular tax if for 2004 you had:

- An alternative minimum tax liability and adjustments or preferences other than exclusion items,
- A minimum tax credit that you are carrying forward to 2005, or
- An unallowed nonconventional source fuel credit or qualified electric vehicle credits.

How to claim the credit. Figure your 2005 credit and any carryforward to 2006 on Form 8801, and attach it to your Form 1040. Include the credit in your total for Form 1040, line 55, and check box b. You can carry forward any unused credit for prior year minimum tax to later years until it is completely used.

For additional information about the credit, see the instructions for Form 8801.

TAXPLANNER

Taxpayers reporting varying income from year to year may find themselves in a regular tax position in one year and in an AMT position the next. By accelerating income into an AMT year and deferring expenses until a regular tax year, you may take advantage of the different tax rates between the regular tax and the AMT. The effect of such a strategy is reduced due to the AMT credit, which is designed to even out the effect of AMT over time. However, the AMT credit will be of no benefit for AMT arising from certain itemized deductions, certain tax-exempt interest, depletion, and the exclusion for gains on the sale of certain small business stock. This should be considered if you undertake any plans to defer or accelerate income or expenses.

TAXPLANNER

Where possible, you should arrange income and deductions so that any AMT incurred will result in an AMT credit that is quickly usable.

Qualified Electric Vehicle Credit

You may be allowed a tax credit if you placed a qualified electric vehicle in service during the year.

Qualified electric vehicle. This is a vehicle that:

- Has at least four wheels and is manufactured primarily for use on public streets, roads, and highways,
- Is powered primarily by an electric motor drawing current from rechargeable batteries, fuel cells, or other portable sources of electrical current,
- Is originally used by you,
- Is acquired for your own use, not for resale,
- Has never been used as a nonelectric vehicle, and
- Is used predominately in the United States.

Amount of credit. If you placed a qualified electric vehicle in service during 2005, the credit is generally 10% of the cost of the vehicle. However, if the vehicle is a depreciable business asset, you must reduce the cost of the vehicle by any section 179 deduction before figuring the credit. See Publication 463, Travel, Entertainment, Gift, and Car Expenses, for information on the section 179 deduction.

The credit is limited to $4,000 for each vehicle placed in service in 2005.

TAX ALERT

For property place in service during 2006, the otherwise allowable credit must be reduced by 75%.

Recapture. The credit will be subject to recapture if, within 3 years after the date you place the vehicle in service, the vehicle is used predominately outside the United States or is modified (or its use is modified) so that it is no longer eligible for the credit. You recapture the credit by adding part or all of it to your income tax for the year in which the recapture event occurs. See chapter 12 of Publication 535 for more information.

How to claim the credit. To claim the credit, complete Form 8834 and attach it to your Form 1040. Include the credit in your total for Form 1040, line 55. Check box c, and print "8834" on the line next to box c.

Caution. *Do not confuse this credit with the deduction for clean-fuel vehicles.*

Refundable Credits

The following credits are refundable and are treated as payments of tax.

- Credit for excess social security tax or railroad retirement tax withheld.
- Credit for tax on undistributed capital gain.
- Health coverage tax credit.
- Earned income credit.

Credit for Excess Social Security Tax or Railroad Retirement Tax Withheld

TAXALERT

Since 1994, there has not been a cap on wages subject to the 1.45% Medicare tax. However, there is still a cap for Social Security taxes. In 2005, employees are subject to the 6.2% Social Security tax on the first $90,000 of wages. If you worked for two or more employers in 2005, you may still claim a credit for any excess Social Security or railroad retirement taxes withheld on your wages.

Most employers must withhold social security tax from your wages. If you work for a railroad employer, that employer must withhold tier 1 railroad retirement (RRTA) tax and tier 2 RRTA tax.

If you worked for two or more employers in 2005, you may have had too much social security or RRTA tax withheld from your pay. You can claim the excess social security or RRTA tier 1 tax as a credit against your income tax. The following table shows the maximum amount of wages subject to tax and the maximum amount of tax that should have been withheld in 2005.

Type of Tax	Maximum wages subject to tax	Maximum tax that should have been withheld
Social Security or RRTA tier 1	$90,000	$5,580.00
RRTA tier 2	$65,100	$3,189.90

Caution. *All wages are subject to Medicare tax withholding.*
Tip. *Use Form 843, Claim for Refund and Request for Abatement, to claim a refund of excess RRTA tier 2 tax. See Publication 505, Tax Withholding and Estimated Tax, for details.*
One employer. If any one employer withheld social security or RRTA tax that exceeded the amounts in the preceding table, you cannot claim the extra amount withheld by that employer as a credit against your income tax. Your employer must adjust this for you.
Joint return. If you are filing a joint return, you cannot add the social security or RRTA tax withheld from your spouse's wages to the amount withheld from your wages. Figure the credit separately for you and your spouse to determine if either of you has excess withholding.

Example 1
Marie Gibson earned $95,000 during 2005. Her sole employer for the year inadvertently withheld $8,000 in Social Security and Medicare taxes from her salary. The amount that should have been withheld was $6,958 (6.2% × $90,000 plus 1.45% × $95,000). She may not claim the $1,042 overwithholding as a credit on her return. Instead, her employer should adjust her next check for this amount.

Example 2
Assume instead that Marie worked for two firms during the year and that her total withholding for Social Security and Medicare taxes was $8,000. She should now claim the $1,042 overwithholding as a credit.

How to figure the credit if you did not work for a railroad. If you did not work for a railroad during 2005, figure the credit as follows:

1. Add all Social Security tax withheld (but not more than $5,580.00 for each employer). Enter the total here .... ____
2. Enter any uncollected Social Security tax on tips or group-term life insurance included in the total on Form 1040, line 63 .... ____
3. Add lines 1 and 2. If $5,580.00 or less, stop here. You cannot claim the credit .... ____
4. Social security tax limit 5,580.00
5. Credit. Subtract line 4 from line 3. Enter the result here and on Form 1040, line 67 (or Form 1040A, line 43)................................ ____

Example. You are married and file a joint return with your spouse who had no gross income in 2005. During 2005, you worked for the Brown Shoe Company and earned $52,000 in wages. Social security tax of $3,224 was withheld. You also worked for another employer in 2005 and earned $40,200 in wages. $2,492.40 of social security tax was withheld from these wages. Because you worked for more than one employer and your total wages were more than $90,000, you can claim a credit of $136.40 for the excess social security tax withheld.

1. Add all social security tax withheld (but not more than $5,580.00 for each employer). Enter the total here	$5,716.40
2. Enter any uncollected social security tax on tips or group-term life insurance included in the total on Form 1040, line 63	–0–
3. Add lines 1 and 2. If $5,580.00 or less, stop here. You cannot claim the credit	5,716.40
4. Social security tax limit	5,580.00
5. Credit. Subtract line 4 from line 3. Enter the result here and on Form 1040, line 67 (or Form 1040A, line 43)	$136.40

How to figure the credit if you worked for a railroad. If you were a railroad employee during 2005, figure the credit as follows:

1. Add all social security and tier 1 RRTA tax withheld (but not more than $5,580.00 for each employer). Enter the total here	_____
2. Enter any uncollected social security and tier 1 RRTA tax on tips or group-term life insurance included in the total on Form 1040, line 63	_____
3. Add lines 1 and 2. If $5,580.00 or less, stop here. You cannot claim the credit	_____
4. Social security and tier 1 RRTA tax limit	5,580.00
5. Credit. Subtract line 4 from line 3. Enter the result here and on Form 1040, line 67 (or Form 1040A, line 43)	_____

Example

In 2005, Maurice Evans worked for a railroad for 7 months and had $2,573.00 in tier 1 railroad retirement tax, $601.75 in Medicare tax, and $2,033.50 in tier 2 railroad retirement tax withheld. He worked the remaining 5 months for a nonrailroad employer and had $4,705.00 in Social Security tax and $1,100.36 in Medicare tax withheld. He had no income from tips or group-term life insurance on either job. His credit is calculated as follows:

1. Total Social Security and tier 1 RRTA tax................... withheld (do not include more than $5,580.00 for each employer	$7,278.00
2. Total Social Security and tier 1 RRTA tax................... on tips or group-term life insurance included on line 63, Form 1040	0
3. Total: Add lines 1 and 2	7,278.00
4. Limit...	$5,580.00
5. Credit: Subtract line 4 from line 3........................	$1,698.00

How to claim the credit. Enter the credit on Form 1040, line 67. You cannot claim the credit on Form 1040A or Form 1040EZ.

Credit for Tax on Undistributed Capital Gain

You must include in your income any amounts that regulated investment companies (commonly called mutual funds) or real estate investment trusts (REITs) allocated to you as capital gain distributions, even if you did not actually receive them. If the mutual fund or REIT paid a tax on the capital gain, you are allowed a credit for the tax since it is considered paid by you. The mutual fund or REIT will send you Form 2439, *Notice to Shareholder of Undistributed Long-Term Capital Gains,* showing the undistributed capital gains and the tax paid, if any. Claim the credit for the tax paid by entering the amount on line 70, Form 1040, and checking box a. Attach Copy B of Form 2439 to your return. See *Capital Gain Distributions* in chapter 9 for more information on undistributed capital gains.

Health Coverage Tax Credit

There is a health coverage tax credit available to certain individuals who receive a pension benefit from the Pension Benefit Guaranty Corporation (PBGC) or are eligible to receive certain Trade Adjustment Assistance (TAA) or who are eligible for the Alternate Trade Adjustment Assistance (ATAA) program. You qualify for this credit if you:

1. Are an eligible individual,
2. Pay for qualified health insurance covering an eligible coverage month for yourself or for yourself and qualifying family members,
3. Do not have other specified coverage, and
4. Are not in prison.

You qualify for this credit on a month-by-month basis. If you qualify, you can claim a credit equal to 65% of the premiums you pay for qualified health insurance.

You can either take this credit on your tax return or have it paid on your behalf in advance to your insurance company. Your payments and any payments paid on your behalf in advance are treated as having been made on the first day of the month for which they are made. If the credit is paid on your behalf in advance, that amount will reduce the amount of the credit you can claim on your tax return. If you received National Emergency Grant (NEG) payments during 2005 for qualified health insurance, that amount will also reduce the amount of the credit you can claim.

Caution. *You are not entitled to the credit for a month, if on the first day of that month, you are either:*

- *Covered by Medicare, or*
- *Covered by a group health plan available through your or your spouse's employer if the employer contributes 50% or more of the premium.*

For a definition of an eligible individual, see the following discussion. For definitions of the terms in (2) and (3) earlier, including qualified health insurance and other specified coverage, see Publication 502.

Eligible Individual

You are an eligible individual for any month during which one of the following is true.

1. You receive a TAA for individuals under the Trade Act of 1974 for at least one day in the month.
2. You would receive a TAA but do not because you have not yet exhausted your unemployment benefits, and are covered under a TAA certification.
3. You are a worker receiving a supplemental wage allowance under section 246 of the Trade Act of 1974 for such month.
4. You are at least 55 years old as of the first day of the month and are receiving pension benefits from the PBGC.

Once you qualify under (1) or (2) above, you remain eligible for the first month that you otherwise cease to be eligible.

Example. You receive a TAA for individuals during May, but do not receive another for the rest of the year. You are eligible for the health coverage tax credit for both May and June.

You are not an eligible individual if an exemption can be claimed for you on another person's tax return.

ATAA workers. If you are eligible for the Alternative Trade Adjustment Assistance (ATAA) program, you are eligible for this credit for a period not to exceed two years if you:

1. Are covered by a qualifying certification,
2. Are reemployed not more than 26 weeks after the date of separation from the adversely-affected employment,
3. Are at least 50 years of age,
4. Do not earn more than $50,000 a year in wages from reemployment,
5. Are employed on a full-time basis, and
6. Do not return to the employment from which you were separated.

How To Claim the Credit
To claim the credit, complete Form 8885 and attach it to your Form 1040. Include your credit in the total for Form 1040, line 70, and check box c. You cannot claim the credit on Form 1040A or Form 1040EZ.

You must attach invoices and proof of payment for any amounts you include on line 2 of Form 8885 for which you did not receive an advance payment. For details, see Publication 502 or Form 8885.

Earned Income Credit

[IRS text intentionally omitted]
The amount you can earn and still get the credit has increased for 2005. The amount of income you earn must be less than:

- $30,338 ($32,338 for married filing jointly) with one qualifying child,
- $34,458 ($36,458 for married filing jointly) with more than one qualifying child, or
- $11,490 ($13,490 for married filing jointly) if you do not have a qualifying child.

Investment income amount is more. The maximum amount of investment income you can have and still get the credit has increased to $2,700. See *Rule 6*.

Form 8836. If you received Form 8836, Qualifying Children Residency Statement, you have been selected to participate in the EIC certification pilot program. File the form with the IRS, following the form instructions, to show that your child met the residency test described in *Rule 8*. If you did not receive the form, you do not need to get it or file it. You have to file Form 8836 only if it was mailed to you.

Reminders

Increased EIC on certain joint returns. A married person filing a joint return may get more EIC than someone with the same income but a different filing status. As a result, the EIC table has different columns for married persons filing jointly than for everyone else. When you look up your EIC in the EIC Table, be sure to use the correct column for your filing status and the number of children you have.

Advance payment of the earned income credit in your paycheck. If you expect to qualify for the earned income credit in 2006, you can receive part of it in each paycheck throughout the year. See *Advance Earned Income Credit*, later, for more information.

EIC questioned by IRS. The IRS may ask you to provide documents to prove you are entitled to claim the EIC. We will tell you what documents to send us. These may include: birth certificates, school records, medical records, etc. We will also send you a letter with the name, address and telephone number of the IRS employee assigned to your case. The process of establishing your eligibility will delay your refund.

Earned income credit has no effect on certain welfare benefits. Any refund you receive because of the EIC and any advance EIC payments you receive generally will not be considered income when determining whether you are eligible for the following benefit programs, or how much you can receive from these programs.

- Medicaid and supplemental security income (SSI).
- Food stamps.
- Low-income housing.

Temporary assistance for needy families (TANF) benefits may be affected. Please check with your state.

The earned income credit (EIC) is a tax credit for certain people who work and have earned income under $35,458. A tax credit usually means more money in your pocket. It reduces the amount of tax you owe. The EIC may also give you a refund.

How do you get the earned income credit? To claim the EIC, you must:

1. Qualify by meeting certain rules, and
2. File a tax return, even if you:
   a. Do not owe any tax,
   b. Did not earn enough money to file a return, or
   c. Did not have income taxes withheld from your pay.

When you complete your return, you can figure your EIC by using a worksheet in the instructions for Form 1040, Form 1040A, or Form 1040EZ. Or, if you prefer, you can let the IRS figure the credit for you.

TaxAlert
The earned income credit is a credit available to certain low-income taxpayers. For 2005, a taxpayer without any qualifying children (see later) may be eligible for a maximum credit of $399.

A taxpayer with one child may be eligible for a maximum credit of $2,662, while a taxpayer with two or more qualifying children may be eligible for a maximum credit of $4,400.

TaxAlert
You are not eligible to claim the earned income credit if your investment income exceeds $2,700. Investment income includes dividends, interest, tax-exempt interest, net capital gain, net passive income, and net rental and royalty income not derived in the ordinary course of a trade or business.

TaxAlert
Taxpayers claiming the earned income credit must include a taxpayer identification number for themselves, their spouses (if married), and any qualifying children on the return. For this purpose only, a taxpayer identification number is a Social Security number issued by the Social Security Administration, other than one issued to an individual for the purpose of applying for federally funded benefits.

How will this section help you? This section will explain the following:

- The rules you must meet to qualify for the EIC, and
- How to get advance payment of the EIC in your paycheck.

For information about how to figure the EIC, see Publication 17, Chapter 38, at www.irs.gov.

Table 38-1. **Earned Income Credit in a Nutshell**

First, you must meet all the rules in this column.		Second, you must meet all the rules in *one* of these columns, whichever applies.		Third, you must meet the rule in this column.
Part A Rules for Everyone		Part B. Rules If You Have a Qualifying Child	Part C. Rules If You Do Not Have a Qualifying Child	Part D. Figuring and Claiming the EIC
1. Your adjusted gross income (AGI) must be less than: •$35,263 ($37,263 for married filing jointly) if you have more than one qualifying child, •$31,030 ($33,030 for married filing jointly) if you have one qualifying child, or •$11,750 ($13,750 for married filing jointly) if you do not have a qualifying child.	**2.** You must have a valid social security number. **3.** Your filing status cannot be "Married filing separately." **4.** You must be a U.S. citizen or resident alien all year. **5.** You cannot file Form 2555 or Form 2555-EZ (relating to foreign earned income). **6.** Your investment income must be $2,700 or less. **7.** You must have earned income.	**8.** Your child must meet the relationship, age, and residency tests. **9.** Your qualifying child cannot be used by more than one person to claim the EIC. **10.** You cannot be a qualifying child of another person.	**11.** You must be at least age 25 but under age 65. **12.** You cannot be the dependent of another person. **13.** You cannot be a qualifying child of another person. **14.** You must have lived in the United States more than half of the year.	**15.** Your earned income must be less than: •$35,263 ($37,263 for married filing jointly) if you have more than one qualifying child, •$31,030 ($33,030 for married filing jointly) if you have one qualifying child, or •$11,750 ($13,750 for married filing jointly) if you do not have a qualifying child.

Useful Items

You may want to see:

Publication

☐ **596**   Earned Income Credit (EIC)

Forms (and Instructions)

☐ **Schedule EIC** Earned Income Credit (Qualifying Child Information)
☐ **W-5**   Earned Income Credit Advance Payment Certificate
☐ **8862**   Information to Claim Earned Income Credit After Disallowance

---

TAXSAVER

You *must* file a tax return to receive the earned income credit. If the tax you owe is less than the amount of the earned income credit, you will receive a refund from the government. Therefore, even if you are not required to file a tax return because your income is less than the income required to file, you still must do so in order to receive the credit.

Do You Qualify for the Credit?

To qualify to claim the EIC, you must first meet all of the rules explained in Part A, *Rules for Everyone.* Then you must meet the rules in Part B, *Rules If You Have a Qualifying Child,* or Part C, *Rules If You Do Not Have a Qualifying Child.* There is one final rule you must meet in Part D, *Figuring and Claiming the EIC.* You qualify for the credit if you meet all the rules in each part that applies to you.

• If you have a qualifying child, the rules in *Parts A, B,* and *D* apply to you.
• If you do not have a qualifying child, the rules in *Parts A, C,* and *D* apply to you.

Note: Parts A, B, C, and D are *not* included in this publication but can be found in Publication 17, Chapter 38, at www.irs.gov.

Table 38-1, Earned Income Credit in a Nutshell. Use Table 38-1 as a guide to *Parts A, B, C,* and *D.* The table is a summary of all the rules in each part. See Figure 38-1.

If Improper Claim Made in Prior Year

If your EIC for any year after 1996 was denied or reduced for any reason other than a math or clerical error, you must attach a completed Form 8862 to your next tax return to claim the EIC.

However, if your EIC was denied or reduced as a result of a math or clerical error, do not attach Form 8862 to your next tax return. For example, if your arithmetic is incorrect, the IRS can correct it. If you do not provide a correct social security number, the IRS can deny the EIC. These kinds of errors are called math or clerical errors.

If your EIC for any year after 1996 was denied and it was determined that your error was due to reckless or intentional disregard of the EIC rules, then you cannot claim the EIC for the next 2 years. If your error was due to fraud, then you cannot claim the EIC for the next 10 years.

More information. See chapter 5 in Publication 596 for more detailed information about the disallowance period and Form 8862.

Advance Earned Income Credit

Do you expect to be eligible for the EIC this year (2006) and to have a qualifying child? If so, you can choose to get payments of the EIC in your paycheck now instead of waiting to get your EIC all at once in 2007 when you file your tax return for the year 2006. These payments are called advance EIC payments. This chapter explains how you may be able to get them this year and how to report them on your tax return.

Who can get the advance payment of the earned income credit? To get part of the earned income credit paid to you throughout the year in your paycheck, you must meet all the following rules.

1. You must expect that your earned income and AGI will each be less than a certain amount. The amount in 2005 was $30,338 ($32,338 if you expected to file married filing jointly). The amount for 2006 will be higher. (See the 2006 Form W-5 for the 2006 amount.)
2. You must expect to have a qualifying child.

Figure 38-1. **Tests for Qualifying Child**

Relationship

A qualifying child is a child who is your...

Son, daughter, adopted child, stepchild, or a descendant of any of them (for example, your grandchild)

or

Brother, sister, stepbrother, stepsister, or a descendant of any of them (for example, your niece or nephew)

or

Foster child (any child placed with you by an authorized placement agency).

AND

Age

was at the end of 2005...

Under age 19

OR

Under age 24 and a student

OR

Permanently and totally disabled at any time during the year, regardless of age.

AND

Residency

who...

Lived with you in the United States for more than half of 2005.

3. You must expect to meet all the rules in *Parts A, B,* and *D* of Publication 17 or in the instructions for Form W-5.

Persons who are not entitled to receive advance payments. Under certain circumstances, even if you meet these rules, you may not be entitled to get EIC. If your wages are not subject to federal income tax, social security tax, or Medicare tax withholding, you cannot get the advance payment of the earned income credit. If you are a farm worker and are paid on a daily basis, your employer is not required to pay you the advance amount of the credit.

How To Get Advance Payments for 2006

If you meet the rules stated above under *Who can get the advance payment of the earned income credit,* give your employer a Form W-5, Earned Income Credit Advance Payment Certificate, for 2006.

After you have read the instructions and completed Form W-5, give the lower part of the form to your employer. Keep the top part for your records.

More than one employer. If you have more than one employer, give a certificate to only one of them. If you are married and both you and your spouse are employed and expect to qualify for the credit, you may give a Form W-5 to your employer and your spouse may give one to his or her employer.

If you receive advance payments of EIC in 2006, you must file a 2006 tax return (even if you would not otherwise have to file) to report the payments and claim any additional EIC. Box 9 of your Form W-2 will show the amount you received. See the instructions

for Form 1040 or Form 1040A for the line number on which you report advance payments of EIC.

Caution. *You cannot use Form 1040EZ to report your advance payments. You must file Form 1040 or Form 1040A.*

Receipt of advance payments you do not qualify for. If you receive advance payments of EIC in 2006, and later find out that you are not eligible for some or all of them, you still must report them on your tax return.

When to give your employer a new Form W-5. The 2006 Form W-5 you give to your employer is valid until December 31, 2006. If you expect to be eligible for EIC in 2007 and you want to receive advance payments, you must give your employer a new Form W-5 in 2007. Do this each year you expect to be eligible for the EIC.

If you no longer want to get advance payments or if your situation changes and you no longer qualify for the earned income credit, you must give your employer a new Form W-5. Check the "No" box on line 1 of the new form.

If your spouse files a Form W-5 with his or her employer, you must file a new Form W-5 with your employer. Check the "Yes" box on line 3.

Advance Payments Received in 2005

If you received advance payments of EIC in 2005, you must file Form 1040 or Form 1040A to report the payments. Your Form W-2, box 9, will show the amount you received. Report the amount on line 61 (Form 1040) or line 37 (Form 1040A).

Caution. *You cannot use Form 1040EZ to report your advance payments.*

PART VII

Special Situations and Tax Planning

The first four chapters in this part discuss some special situations. Chapter 39, *If You Are Self-Employed: How to File Schedule C,* is essential reading for anyone who is self-employed—freelancers, artists, and small business owners. Mutual fund investors will want to pay special attention to Chapter 40, *Mutual Funds.* It discusses what you need to know about the tax treatment of gains, losses, dividends, and distributions from a mutual fund. Generous-spirited readers will want to peruse Chapter 41, *Estate and Gift Tax Planning.* It explains the tax intricacies of giving assets to others while you are alive and also discusses the estate tax and various strategies you can use. Chapter 42, *What to Do If You Employ Domestic Help,* will be of interest to taxpayers who employ domestic help, whether it is to care for their children or a disabled or elderly dependent. Chapter 43, *U.S. Citizens Working Abroad: Tax Treatment of Foreign Earned Income,* discusses how U.S. citizens working abroad should handle their taxes. Among other matters, it explains how you can get a credit against your U.S. taxes for taxes you have paid to a foreign government. Chapter 44, *Foreign Citizens Living in the United States,* discusses the tax rules applicable to foreign citizens living in the United States. Chapter 45, *How to Prepare for Your Accountant,* tells you how to prepare your tax records for your accountant. Ernst & Young prepares tax returns for thousands of individuals, so you won't be surprised to learn this is a matter that we've considered quite carefully. The next chapters offer a further helping hand. Chapter 46, *Everything You Need to Know About E-filing,* leads you through the electronic filing process. With luck, you won't need to refer to Chapter 47, *If Your Return Is Examined,* but, in case your tax return is examined and you are subject to an audit, you will find it useful. Chapter 48, *Planning Ahead for 2006 and Beyond,* can help you save money on your taxes next year and beyond. It discusses tax developments in 2006 and after.

If You Are Self-Employed: How to File Schedule C

Introduction

Many people work for themselves. Whether a business—already existing or new—is your sole source of income or whether it supplements other income, you will face a number of perplexing tax questions that ordinary wage earners do not. What income do you report? What expenses can you deduct? What forms do you need to file?

Unlike a partnership or a regular corporation, a sole proprietorship is not a separate entity. (An LLC (limited liability company) which has only one member is treated as a sole proprietorship for tax purposes.) In a sole proprietorship, you and your business are one and the same. You report net profit or loss for the year from a

sole proprietorship on Form 1040, Schedule C (or Schedule C-EZ), and it becomes part of your adjusted gross income. In addition to owing income tax on such income, you, as the sole proprietor, usually will be liable for self-employment tax and will also be required to make payments of estimated taxes. A net loss from the business generally can be deducted when you compute your adjusted gross income (see Hobby Loss rules, later in this chapter).

This chapter concentrates on how a sole proprietorship recognizes business profit and losses on federal Form 1040, Schedule C and Schedule SE.

Who Must File Schedule C

If you are a sole proprietor, an independent contractor, a statutory employee, a statutory nonemployee, or a single member LLC, you may be required to report business income and expenses on Schedule C.

Sole proprietor. If you operate a business as a sole proprietor, you must file Schedule C to report your income and expenses from your business. If you operate more than one business, or if you and your spouse had separate businesses, you must prepare a separate Schedule C for each business.

Independent contractor. A person whose work hours and procedures are not controlled by another and who is therefore deemed to be self-employed for tax purposes must also file a Schedule C. (Refer to page 531 for further discussion on independent contractors.)

Statutory employee. If you are a statutory employee, you should file Schedule C. If you file Schedule C, you can deduct certain business expenses when computing your adjusted gross income. A statutory employee's business expenses will not be subject to the 2% reduction of his or her adjusted gross income that applies to business expenses reported as a part of Schedule A, Itemized Deductions. A statutory employee includes the following occupations:

1. Certain agent and commission drivers
2. Full-time life insurance sales representatives
3. Certain home workers performing work, according to specifications furnished by the person for whom the services are performed
4. Certain traveling or city salespeople who work full-time (except for sideline sales activities) for one firm or person, soliciting orders from customers

If you meet the definition of a statutory employee, your employer must indicate this classification by checking the "Statutory employee" box in box 13 on your Form W-2. This indicates to the IRS that you have the right to report your income and expenses on Schedule C.

As a statutory employee, you are considered an employee for Social Security and Medicare purposes. However, if you and your employer agree, federal income tax withholding is optional rather than mandatory.

A statutory employee reports his or her wages from box 1 of Form W-2 on line 1 of Schedule C. He or she then deducts allowable expenses on Part II of Schedule C to arrive at reportable income.

Statutory nonemployee. If you are a statutory nonemployee, you must file Schedule C to report your income and expenses.

Explanation

There are two categories of statutory nonemployees. The two categories are a direct seller of consumer products and a licensed real estate agent. They are treated as self-employed for federal income tax and employment tax purposes if:

1. Substantially all payments for their services as direct sellers or real estate agents are directly related to sales or other output, rather than to the number of hours worked; and
2. Their services are performed under a written contract providing that they will not be treated as employees for federal tax purposes.

Direct sellers. Direct sellers are persons:
1. Engaged in selling (or soliciting the sale of) consumer products in the home or at a place of business other than in a permanent retail establishment; or
2. Engaged in selling (or soliciting the sale of) consumer products to any buyer on a buy-sell basis, a deposit-commission basis, or any similar basis prescribed by regulations for resale in the home or at a place of business other than in a permanent retail establishment.

Direct selling also includes activities of individuals who attempt to increase direct sales activities of their direct sellers and who earn income based on the productivity of their direct sellers. Such activities include providing motivation and encouragement; imparting skills, knowledge, or experience; and recruiting.

Licensed real estate agents. This category includes individuals engaged in appraisal activities for real estate sales if they earn income based on sales or other output.

TAXALERT

Unlike a statutory employee, a statutory nonemployee is not subject to Social Security and Medicare withholding. Therefore, he or she is required to pay self-employment tax on net earnings. Additionally, federal income tax withholding is not required; therefore, estimated taxes must be paid.

Single Member LLC (limited liability company)—if you operate your business through a single member LLC (this is generally done for liability purposes), you should report your income and expenses with respect to the LLC activity on Schedule C.

What's Included on Schedule C

Schedule C is used to report income and related expenses applicable to the above activities. Income includes cash, property, and services received from all sources, unless specifically excluded under the tax code. Expenses include all ordinary and necessary expenses incurred in connection with the activity.

For sole proprietorships in the business of selling goods or inventory, the primary expense will be the cost of goods sold. The cost of goods sold represents the cost of materials, labor, and overhead included in the inventory sold during the year. Other expenses that you deduct on Schedule C include salaries and wages, interest on loans used in the activity, rent, depreciation, bad debts, travel, 50% of entertainment expenses, insurance, real estate taxes, state and local taxes, and an allocable portion of your tax return preparation fee.

TAXPLANNER

Schedule C-EZ. You may use Schedule C-EZ instead of Schedule C if you operated a business or practiced a profession as a sole proprietorship and you have met all of the requirements listed below:

- Had business expenses of $5,000 or less (Note: This amount has doubled from 2004)
- Used the cash method of accounting
- Did not have an inventory at any time during the year
- Did not have a net loss from your business
- Had only one business as a sole proprietor

and you:

- Had no employees during the year
- Are not required to file Form 4562, *Depreciation and Amortization,* for this business
- Do not deduct expenses for business use of your home
- Do not have prior year, unallowed passive activity losses from this business

Where to Report on Your Return

Adjusted gross income (AGI). The net income or net loss arrived at on Schedule C should be reported on page 1 of Form 1040. The net income or net loss (subject to certain limitations) generated on your Schedule C will cause either an increase or a decrease in your AGI.

TAXALERT

It is important to note that if you are filing Schedule C or Schedule C-EZ, you must use Form 1040, not Form 1040A or Form 1040-EZ.

Losses. If Schedule C expenses exceed Schedule C income, a loss will result. There is a possibility that the amount of Schedule C loss that can be deducted on your current year's income tax return may be limited. The amount of the loss that can be deducted on your return depends on whether or not you materially participate in the operation of the business or whether or not you have enough investment at risk to cover the loss.

TaxAlert

Reporting losses several years in a row on Schedule C may increase the risk that you will be subject to an IRS audit. The IRS monitors Schedule C filers to see if the "hobby loss" rules apply to their returns. Schedule C filers should make sure they understand the hobby loss rules (see below) when they enter into ventures that will produce losses in the early years of operation. The ability to prove material participation will most likely result in no change to the amount of loss you claim on Schedule C, should you be audited.

Defining material participation. You are treated as a material participant only if you are involved in the operations of the activity on a regular, continuous, and substantial basis. If you are not a material participant in an activity but your spouse is, you are treated as being a material participant and the activity is not considered passive. A passive activity involves the conduct of any trade or business in which you do not materially participate.

For more information about passive activities and the at-risk limitation, see Chapter 13, *Other Income,* and IRS Publication 925, *Passive Activity and At-Risk Rules.*

What is a Hobby Loss? *The IRS presumes that an activity which produces net income in 3 or more taxable years within a period of 5 consecutive years is engaged in for profit.. Therefore, if an activity produces a loss for 3 or more years in a consecutive 5 year period, the IRS may infer that the activity is not engaged in for profit and disallow the loss.*

Carrybacks and Carryforwards. If you have incurred a Schedule C loss, it is possible that the loss may be large enough to offset all taxable income reported on your Form 1040. If this is the case, you may have generated a net operating loss (NOL).

TaxAlert

Net operating loss. If you have incurred a net operating loss (NOL), you can carry back or carry forward the loss and utilize it to offset income in other years. Generally, an NOL can be carried back 2 years and forward 20 years.

Exceptions: NOLs incurred in 2001 and 2002 could be carried back 5 years instead of 2 years. Earlier NOLs from pre-1998 tax years expire after 15 carryforward years.

You may elect not to carry back your NOL. If you make this election, you may use your NOL only during the 20-year carryforward period with respect to losses arising for tax years beginning after August 5, 1997. To make this election, attach a statement to your tax return for the NOL year. This statement must show that you are electing to forgo the carryback period under Section 172(b)(3) of the Internal Revenue Code.

Victims of theft or casualty and proprietorships with less than $5 million in gross receipts that incurred losses attributable to presidentially declared disaster areas are subject to a 3-year carryback period.

Example:

In 2005, Robert Jones, the sole proprietor of a small business, has a net operating loss of $66,000. In past years, Jones reported the following amounts of taxable income: in 2003, $82,000 and in 2004, $10,000. The NOL can be carried back 2 years to 2003 and offset $66,000 of taxable income in that year.

TaxSaver

If your income was subject to tax at a lower tax bracket during the carryback period and you expect your future income to be subject to tax at a higher tax bracket, you may wish to elect to forgo the carryback of the NOL.

Example

In 2005, Mark's business incurs an NOL of $20,000. He has been profitable in the 2 previous years, and the profits have been taxed at a 15% tax rate. He expects to generate large income in future years, which will be taxed at a 35% tax rate. By electing to forgo the carryback of the NOL, he can save $4,000 in taxes [$20,000 × (35% − 15%)].

For more information on net operating losses, see Form 1045 and Publication 536, *Net Operating Losses.*

Self-Employment Income and Social Security Tax

Income reported on Schedule C is classified as self-employment income for the sole proprietor, the independent contractor, and the statutory nonemployee. It is not classified as self-employment income for a statutory employee and is therefore not subject to self-employment tax.

Self-employment tax is calculated on Form 1040, Schedule SE.

Self-employment tax is composed of a Social Security tax of 12.4% and a Medicare tax of 2.9%. For 2005, the maximum amount of wages and/or self-employment income subject to the Social Security part of the self-employment tax is $90,000. All net earnings are subject to the Medicare portion of self-employment tax. Therefore, if your salary income as an employee is $90,000 or above, you would have already paid all the Social Security tax you owe. Your self-employment income would, however, be subject to the Medicare tax of 2.9%. There is no limit on the amount of earnings subject to the Medicare portion of the self-employment tax. A comprehensive example at the end of this chapter shows you how to calculate your self-employment tax when you also have salary income.

You may be able to use the short Schedule SE if:

1. Your self-employment earnings and wages subject to Social Security were less than $90,000;
2. You did not receive tips reported to your employer;
3. You are not a minister or member of a religious order.

If your net self-employment income multiplied by 0.9235 is below $400, you are not subject to self-employment tax on your self-employment income.

TaxAlert

Estimated income taxes. You may be required to pay estimated tax on your self-employment income. This depends on how much income and self-employment tax you expect for the year and how much of your income will be subject to withholding tax. For more information, see Chapter 5, *Tax Withholding and Estimated Tax.*

TAXPLANNER

If you are a salaried employee as well, you may cover your estimated self-employment tax payments by having your employer increase the amount of income tax withheld from your pay.

TAXSAVER

If you have more than one trade or business, you must combine the net earnings from each business to determine your net self-employment income. A loss that you incur in one business will offset your income in another business.

When an individual's self-employment earnings are less than $400, he or she is not required to file Form 1040, Schedule SE, or to pay self-employment tax.

Joint returns show the name of the spouse with self-employment income on Schedule SE. If both spouses have self-employment income, each must file a separate Schedule SE. If one spouse qualifies to use Short Schedule SE and the other has to use Long Schedule SE, both can use one Schedule SE. One spouse should complete the front and the other the back.

Include the total profits or losses from all businesses on Form 1040, as appropriate. Enter the combined Schedule SE tax on Form 1040.

TAXSAVER

Self-employment tax deduction. You can deduct one-half of your self-employment tax in figuring your adjusted gross income. This is an income tax adjustment only. It does not affect either your net earnings from self-employment or your self-employment tax. To deduct the tax, enter on Form 1040, line 27 the amount shown on line 6 of short Form Schedule SE or line 13 of long Form Schedule SE.

What Is Included in Net Self-Employment Earnings?

In most cases, net earnings include your net profit from a farm or nonfarm business, plus the following items:

- Rental income from a farm if, as landlord, you materially participated in the production or management of the production of farm products on this land.
- Cash or a payment in kind from the Department of Agriculture for participating in a land diversion program.
- Payments for the use of rooms or other space when you also provided substantial services. Examples are hotel rooms, boarding houses, tourist camps or homes, parking lots, warehouses, and storage garages.
- Income from the retail sale of newspapers and magazines if you were age 18 or older and kept the profits.
- Amounts received by current or former self-employed insurance agents that are:
  1. Paid after retirement but calculated as a percentage of commissions received from the paying company before retirement;
  2. Renewal commissions; or
  3. Deferred commissions paid after retirement for sales made before retirement.

- Fees as a state or local government employee if you were paid only on a fee basis and the job was not covered under a federal-state Social Security coverage agreement.
- Interest received in the course of any trade or business, such as interest on notes or accounts receivable.
- Fees and other payments received by you for services as a director of a corporation.
- Fees you received as a professional fiduciary.
- Gain or loss from Section 1256 contracts or related property by an options or commodities dealer in the normal course of dealing in or trading Section 1256 contracts.

Income and Losses Not Included in Net Earnings From Self-Employment

- Salaries, fees, and so on, subject to Social Security or Medicare tax that you received for performing services as an employee.
- Income you received as a retired partner under a written partnership plan that provides for lifelong periodic retirement payments if you had no other interest in the partnership and did not perform services for it during the year.
- Income from real estate rentals (including rentals paid in crop shares), if you did not receive the income in the course of a trade or business as a real estate dealer. This includes cash and crop shares received from a tenant or sharefarmer.
- Dividends on shares of stock and interest on bonds, notes, and so on, if you did not receive the income in the course of your trade or business as a dealer in stocks or securities.
- Gain or loss from:

  1. The sale or exchange of a capital asset;
  2. The sale, exchange, involuntary conversion, or other disposition of property unless the property is stock in trade or other property that would be considered inventory, or held primarily for sale to customers in the ordinary course of the business; or
  3. Certain transactions in timber, coal, or domestic iron ore.

- Net operating losses from other years.

Statutory employee income. If you were a statutory employee, **do not** include the net profit or loss from that Schedule C (or the net profit from Schedule C-EZ) on Schedule SE. A statutory employee is defined above.

Self-Employment Tax Calculation

Self-employment tax can be calculated under one of the following methods: the regular method, the farm optional method, and the nonfarm optional method.

Regular Method. Under the regular method, your self-employment tax should be calculated as follows:

1. Figure your net self-employment income. The net profit from your business or profession is generally your net self-employment income.
2. After you figure your net self-employment income, determine how much is subject to self-employment tax. The amount subject to self-employment tax is called net earnings from self-employment. It is figured on Short Schedule SE, line 4, or Long Schedule SE, line 4a. It is generally 92.35% of net self-employment income.
3. Figure your self-employment tax as follows:

- If, for 2005, your net earnings from self-employment plus any wages and tips are not more than $90,000 and you do not have to use Long Schedule SE, use Short Schedule SE. On line 5, multiply your net earnings by 15.3% (0.153). The result is the amount of your self-employment tax.
- If you had no wages or tips in 2005, your net earnings from self-employment are more than $90,000, and you do not have to use Long Schedule SE, use Short Schedule SE. On line 5, multiply the line 4 net earnings by 2.9% (0.029) Medicare tax and add the result to $11,160 (12.4% of $90,000). The total is the amount of your self-employment tax.
- If you received wages or tips in 2005 and your net earnings from self-employment *plus* any wages and tips are more than $90,000, you must use Long Schedule SE. Subtract your total wages and tips from $90,000 to find the maximum amount of earnings subject to the 12.4% Social Security part of the tax. If more than zero, multiply the amount by 12.4% (0.124). The result is the Social Security tax amount. Then multiply your net earnings from self-employment by 2.9% (0.029). The result is the Medicare tax amount. The total of the Social Security tax amount and the Medicare tax amount is your self-employment tax.

Optional Methods. Generally, you can use the optional methods when you have a loss or small amount of net income from self-employment and:

1. You want to receive credit for Social Security benefit coverage;
2. You incurred child or dependent care expenses for which you could claim a credit (this method will increase your earned income, which could increase your credit); or
3. You are entitled to the earned income credit (this method will increase your earned income, which could increase your credit).

How to Determine Items of Income and Expenses

Start-up and Pre-operating Expenses. Start-up expenditures are the costs of getting started in business before you actually begin doing business. Start-up costs may include expenses for such things as advertising, travel, utilities, repairs, or employees' wages. These are often the same kinds of costs that can be deducted when they occur after you open for business.

Start-up costs include what you pay for both investigating a prospective business and getting the business started. For example, they may include costs for the following items:

- A survey of potential markets
- An analysis of available facilities, labor, supplies, etc.
- Advertisements for the opening of the business
- Salaries and wages for employees who are being trained and their instructors
- Travel and other necessary costs for securing prospective distributors, suppliers, or customers
- Salaries and fees for executives and consultants or for other professional services

Start-up costs do not include deductible interest, taxes, and research and experimental costs. Therefore, subject to other limitations, these items are currently deductible.

Whether or not you can deduct your start-up expenditures depends on whether you actually begin the active trade or business.

If you go into business, start-up expenses of a trade or business are not deductible unless you elect to deduct them in accordance with the following rules. You can elect a current deduction for a limited amount (up to $5,000) of start-up expenditures in the tax year in which the trade or business begins. However, this $5,000 amount is reduced (but not below zero) by the amount by which the cumulative cost of start-up expenditures exceeds $50,000. The remainder of the start-up expenditures can be claimed as a deduction ratably over a 15-year period

You are allowed a deduction for the year in which the active trade or business begins in an amount equal to the lesser of:

1. The amount of start-up expenditures for the active trade or business; or
2. $5,000, reduced (but not below zero) by the amount by which the start-up expenditures exceed $50,000.

All start-up expenditures related to a particular trade or business, whether incurred before or after October 22, 2004, are considered in determining whether the cumulative cost of start-up expenditures exceeds $50,000.

If your start-up expenses are $5,000 or less, you can deduct those expenses in full in the year you begin the active trade or business.

Example

Tony's repair shop started business on June 1, 2005. Prior to starting business, Tony incurred various expenses totaling $6,000 to set up shop. Tony can deduct $5,000 of these expenses in 2005 and deduct the balance of $1,000 ratably over 15 years.

TaxAlert

Although the IRS has been instructed to do so, it has not issued any guidance as to when a trade or a business begins. When it does, the IRS is likely to take a conservative stance. In the meantime, there has been substantial litigation about this issue. The generally accepted rule seems to be that even though a taxpayer has made a firm decision to enter into a business and over a considerable period of time has spent money in preparation for entering that business, he or she still has not engaged in carrying on any trade or business until such time as the business has begun to function as a going concern and has performed those activities for which it was organized.

Failure to go into business. If your attempt to go into business is not successful, whether or not you can deduct the expenses you incurred in trying to establish yourself in business depends on the type of expenses you incurred.

Investigatory expenses. The costs you incurred before making a decision to acquire or to begin a specific business are classified as personal and therefore are not deductible. Investigatory expenses include costs incurred in the course of a general search for, or preliminary investigation of, a business prior to reaching a decision to acquire or enter any business. Examples include expenses incurred for the analysis or survey of potential markets, products, labor supply, transportation facilities, and so on.

Start-up expenses. The costs that you incur after you've made a decision to acquire or to establish a particular business and prior to its actual operation are classified as capital expenditures and may be deductible in the year in which your attempt to go into business fails.

Business sold. If you completely dispose of a trade or a business before the end of the amortization period you have selected, any deferred start-up costs for the trade or business that have not yet been deducted may be deducted to the extent that they qualify as a loss from a trade or a business.

Tax Year

Every taxpayer must determine taxable income and file a tax return on the basis of an annual accounting period. The term "*tax year*" is the annual accounting period you use for keeping your records and for reporting your income and expenses. The accounting periods you can use are as follows:

1. A calendar year
2. A fiscal year

You adopt a tax year when you file your first income tax return. It cannot be longer than 12 months.

Calendar tax year. If you adopt the calendar year for your annual accounting period, you must maintain your books and records, and report your income and expenses for the period from January 1 through December 31 of each year.

TAXALERT

If you filed your first return using the calendar tax year and you later begin business as a sole proprietor, you must continue to use the calendar tax year, unless you get permission from the IRS to change. You must report your income from all sources, including your sole proprietorship, using the same tax year.

Fiscal tax year. A regular fiscal tax year is 12 consecutive months, ending on the last day of any month except December.

If you adopt a fiscal tax year, you must maintain your books and records, and report your income and expenses using the same tax year.

Accounting Methods

Accounting methods are described in Chapter 1, *Filing Information*. The discussion that follows relates mainly to self-employed entrepreneurs, sole proprietors, and others who file Schedule C. No single accounting method is required for all taxpayers. Generally, you may figure your taxable income under any one of the following accounting methods:

1. Cash method
2. Accrual method
3. Special methods of accounting for certain items of income and expenses
4. Combination (hybrid) method using elements of (1), (2), or (3)

Cash method. The cash method of accounting is used by most individuals and many small businesses with no inventories. However, if inventories are necessary in accounting for your income, you must use the accrual method for your sales and purchases. If you are not required to maintain inventories, it is often more advantageous to use the cash method, because it allows you more flexibility and control over your income.

Income. Under the cash method, your gross income includes all items of income you actually receive during the year. You must include in your income property and services you receive at their fair market value.

Expenses. Usually, you must deduct expenses in the tax year in which you actually pay them. However, you may be required to postpone the deduction for expenses you pay in advance. In addition, you may have to capitalize certain costs.

Accrual method. Under an accrual method of accounting, income generally is reported in the year in which it is earned, regardless of when the income is actually collected, and expenses generally are deducted in the year in which they are incurred, regardless of when the expenses are paid. The purpose of an accrual method of accounting is to match your income and your expenses. If inventories are necessary in your business, only the accrual method of accounting can be used for purchases and sales.

Income. All items of income are generally included in your gross income when you earn them, even though you may receive payment in another tax year. All events that fix your right to receive the income must have happened, and you must be able to determine the amount with reasonable accuracy.

Example

You are a calendar year taxpayer. You sold a radio on November 28, 2005. You billed the customer 3 days later but did not receive payment until February 2006. You must include the amount of the sale in your income for 2005 because you earned the income in 2005.

Income received in advance. Prepaid income is generally included in gross income in the year you receive it. Your method of accounting does not matter as long as the income is available to you. Prepaid income includes rents or interest received in advance and compensation for services to be performed later.

If, under an agreement, you receive advance payment for services to be performed by the end of the next tax year, you can defer the inclusion in income of the payments received until you earn them by performing the service. You **must** be an accrual method taxpayer to defer recognition of income on advance payments for services. You cannot defer the income beyond the year after the year you receive the payment.

Example 1

You are in the television repair business. In 2005, you received payment for 1-year contracts under which you agree to repair or replace certain parts that fail to function properly in television sets that were sold by an unrelated party. You include the payments in gross income as you earn them (which is by performing the contracted services).

If for any reason you do not perform part of the services by the end of the following tax year, 2006, you must include in gross income for 2006 the amount of the advance payments that are for services yet to be performed).

Example 2

You own a dance studio. On November 4, 2005, you received payment for a 1-year contract, beginning on that date and providing for 48 1-hour lessons. You gave 8 lessons in 2005. If you recognize income under the accrual method of including advance payments, you must include one-sixth (8/48) of the payment in income for 2005 and five-sixths (40/48) of the payment in 2006.

Expenses. You deduct expenses when you become liable for them, whether or not you pay them in the same year. Before you can deduct expenses, all of the events that set the amount of the liability must have happened, you must be able to determine the amount of the liability with reasonable accuracy, and economic performance (see below) must occur.

Economic performance rule. Even if all of the events that determine the amount of your expenses have occurred, you still cannot deduct business expenses until economic performance occurs. If your expense is for property or services provided to you, or for use of property by you, economic performance occurs as the property or services are provided or as the property is used. If your expense is for property or services that you provide to others, economic performance occurs as the property or services are provided or as the property is used.

Special rules for related persons. An accrual basis taxpayer cannot deduct business expenses and interest owed to a related cash basis taxpayer until the amount is actually paid.

For purposes of applying this rule, related persons include, but are not limited to:

1. Members of the immediate family, including only brothers and sisters, husband and wife, ancestors, and lineal descendants
2. An individual and a corporation, if more than 50% in value of the outstanding stock is owned, directly or indirectly, by or for such individual
3. An S corporation and any individual who owns any of the stock of such S corporation
4. A partnership and any person who owns any capital interest or profits interest of such partnership

Special methods. In addition to the cash or accrual methods, certain items of income or expenses are accounted for under special methods. They include:

- Depreciation
- Amortization and depletion
- Bad debts
- Installment sales

The method of accounting for depreciation and bad debts is discussed later in this chapter. Methods for deducting amortization and depletion are discussed in IRS Publication 535, *Business Expenses.* Methods for reporting installment sales are discussed in IRS Publication 537, *Installment Sales.*

Combination (hybrid) method. Any combination of cash, accrual, and special methods of accounting can be used if the combination clearly reflects income and is consistently used. As an example, if you maintain inventory, the accrual method of accounting for purchases and sales must be used; however, you may use the cash method for all other items of income and expenses.

Two or more businesses. If you operate more than one business, you generally may use a different accounting method for each separate and distinct business if the method you use for each clearly reflects your income. For example, if you operate a personal-service business and a manufacturing business, you may use the cash method for the personal-service business, but you must use the accrual method for the manufacturing business.

How to Complete Schedule C

Schedule C is divided into five parts:

Part I: Income
Part II: Expenses
Part III: Cost of Goods Sold
Part IV: Information on Your Vehicle
Part V: Other Expenses

In addition, Schedule C requires that you answer a number of general questions about the activity.

General Information

Line A asks for the principal business or profession, including the product or service that provided your principal source of income.

Line B asks for the four-digit code that identifies your principal business or professional activity. The instructions to Schedule C contain a list of the principal business or professional activity codes that you should use.

Line C asks for your business name. If none, leave this line blank.

Line D asks for your employer identification number (EIN). An EIN is needed only if you had a Keogh plan (discussed later in this chapter and in Chapter 18, *Individual Retirement Arrangements [IRAs]*) or if you were required to file an employment or excise tax return. If you do not have an EIN, do not enter your Social Security number. To apply for an EIN, you must file Form SS-4 with the IRS where you file your individual tax return. For your convenience, Form SS-4 is found in the back of this book.

Line E requests your business address. If you conducted business out of your home, you do not have to complete this line.

Line F asks for your accounting method, as discussed earlier in this chapter and in Chapter 1, *Filing Information.*

Line G asks whether or not you "materially participated" in the business. If you did not, your losses from the business that you can deduct currently may be limited. See Chapter 13, *Other Income.*

Line H must be checked if this is the initial Schedule C filed for this particular business.

In addition, Part III of the form asks two additional questions. Line 33 asks for the method used to value closing inventory, if your business maintains inventory. The inventory can be valued under any one of the following three methods: (1) cost, (2) lower of cost or market, or (3) any other method approved by the IRS. Methods of valuing inventory will be discussed later in this chapter.

Line 34 does not need to be answered if your business does not have inventory. If the business does maintain inventory and there was a change in determining quantities, costs, or valuations between opening and closing inventories, answer the question "yes" and attach an explanation for the change.

Income

Part I of Schedule C is used to report the gross income from the business. You should include on line 1 gross receipts or sales from your business. Do not combine receipts from two separate businesses on this line. Remember that you must file a separate Schedule C for each business. Statutory employees enter the amount from box 1 of Form W-2 and check the box on line 1.

On line 2, report such items as sales returns, rebates, and allowances. For example, if an item you previously sold is returned for a cash refund, the cash refund should be reported here and not included as a reduction of the gross receipts or sales reported on line 1.

Subtract line 2 from line 1, and enter the difference

on line 3. From this amount, deduct the cost of goods sold. After deducting the cost of goods sold, you arrive at the gross profit from the business.

Costs of Goods Sold

Part III of Schedule C is used to determine your cost of goods sold. If you make or buy goods to sell, you are entitled to deduct the cost of the goods sold on your tax return. One of the most important costs that must be determined is the cost of your inventory.

Inventories are required to be determined at the beginning and end of each tax year for manufacturers, wholesalers, retailers, and every other business that makes, buys, or sells goods to produce income. Inventories include goods held for sale in the normal course of business, work in process, and raw materials and supplies that will physically become a part of merchandise intended for sale.

Add to your beginning inventory the cost of inventory items purchased during the year, including all other items entering into the cost of obtaining or producing the inventory. From this total, subtract your inventory at the end of the year. The remainder represents the cost of goods sold during the tax period. It should not include selling expenses or any other expenses that are not directly related to obtaining or producing the goods sold.

Inventory methods. To determine the value of your inventory, you need a method for identifying the items in your inventory and a method for valuing these items. In general, there are three methods of identifying items in inventory: (1) specific identification; (2) first in, first out (FIFO); and (3) last in, first out (LIFO).

The specific identification method is used to identify the cost of each inventoried item by matching the item with its cost of acquisition in addition to other allocable costs, such as labor and transportation. This method is most often used by retailers of unique items.

If there is no specific identification of items with their costs, you must make an assumption to decide which items were sold and which remain in inventory. You make this identification by either the FIFO or the LIFO method.

The FIFO method assumes that the items you purchased or produced first are the first items you sold, consumed, or otherwise disposed of.

The LIFO method assumes that the items of inventory that you purchased or produced last are sold or removed from inventory first.

The FIFO method and the LIFO method produce different results in income, depending on the trend of price levels of the goods included in those inventories. In times of inflation, when prices are rising, LIFO will produce a larger cost of goods sold and a lower closing inventory. Under FIFO, the cost of goods sold will be lower and the closing inventory will be higher. However, in times of falling prices, LIFO will produce a smaller cost of goods sold and a higher closing inventory. Under FIFO, the reverse will be true.

Valuing inventory. Valuing the items in your inventory is a major factor in figuring your taxable income. The two common ways to value your inventory if you use the FIFO method are the specific-cost identification method and the lower-of-cost-or-market method.

Adopting LIFO method. To adopt the LIFO method, you are required to file Form 970, *Application to Use LIFO Inventory Method,* or a statement that has all the information required in Form 970. You must file the form (or the statement) with your timely filed tax return for the year in which you first use LIFO.

Once a method is selected you may not change to another method without the permission of the IRS. For a further discussion of inventory, see Publication 334, *Tax Guide for Small Business.*

Expenses

Part II of Schedule C is used to report expenses associated with your business. To be deductible, a business expense must be both ordinary and necessary. An ordinary expense is one that is common and accepted in your field of business, trade, or profession. A necessary expense is one that is helpful and appropriate for your trade, business, or profession. An expense does not have to be indispensable to be considered necessary. Examples of deductible business expenses include (1) reasonable allowance for salaries and other compensation, (2) traveling expenses while away from home, and (3) rentals or other payments for property used in a trade or a business.

You must keep business expenses separate from personal expenses. If you have any expense that is partly business and partly personal, a reasonable allocation should be made to separate the personal part from the business part.

Capital expenditures. A capital expenditure is defined as an expense that must be capitalized rather than deducted. These costs are considered a part of your investment in your business. There are, in general, three types of costs that must be capitalized: (1) costs of going into business, (2) costs to purchase business assets, and (3) cost of improvements.

Although you generally cannot directly deduct a capital expenditure, you may be able to take deductions for the amount you spend through a method of depreciation, amortization, or depletion.

A discussion of some of the more common expenses you will encounter in your business follows.

Bad Debts. If someone owes you money that you cannot collect, you have a bad debt. You may be able to deduct the amount owed to you when you figure your business income in the year in which the debt becomes worthless. There are two kinds of bad debts: business bad debts and nonbusiness bad debts. A business bad debt generally is one that comes from your trade or business. All other bad debts are nonbusiness bad debts. For a discussion of nonbusiness bad debts and when a debt becomes worthless, see Chapter 15, *Sale of Property.*

Business bad debts usually occur because of credit sales to customers. They can also be loans to suppliers, employees, and others associated with your trade or business. These debts are usually shown on your books as either accounts receivable or notes receivable. If you are unable to collect any part of these accounts or notes receivable, the uncollectible part is a business bad debt.

You may take a bad debt deduction on your accounts and notes receivable only if you have basis in the debt; that is, you already included the amount you are owed in your current or earlier gross income (*i.e.*, accounts receivable), or you actually loaned the money (i.e., notes receivable). Only individuals filing a Schedule C using either the accrual or hybrid (cash accrual) accounting method will be able to deduct bad debts relating to accounts receivable. Cash method taxpayers do not report income that is due them until they actually receive payment. Therefore, they cannot take a bad debt deduction on payments they cannot collect.

Example 1

Paul, who uses the accrual method on his Schedule C, reported income in 2004 of $1,000 related to an account receivable from a customer. In 2005, that account receivable became worthless. Because Paul is on the accrual method and has already included the $1,000 in income, he is permitted to recognize a bad debt deduction in 2005.

Example 2

Assume the same facts as in Example 1, except that Paul is on the cash method. Because Paul has not recognized the $1,000 income in 2004, he cannot take a bad debt deduction when the debt becomes worthless in 2005.

The net effect on Paul's income in either situation is the same.

	Accrual	Cash
Income recognized in 2004	$1,000	-0-
Less bad debt deduction in 2005	1,000	-0-
Net effect	-0-	-0-

Methods of treating bad debts. The method of accounting for bad debts is referred to as the "specific charge-off method," because it requires the specific identification of the debt that has become worthless. Using the specific charge-off method, you can deduct specific business bad debts that become either partly or totally worthless during the tax year.

Partially worthless debts. You may deduct specific bad debts that are partially uncollectible. To take the deduction, however, the amount must be written off on your books; that is, you must eliminate the worthless portion of the debt from your books as an asset. You do not have to write off and deduct your partially worthless debts annually. Instead, you may delay the write-off until a later year. Also, you may wait until more of the debt has become worthless or until you have collected all you can on the debt and it is totally worthless. You may not, however, deduct any part of the bad debt in a year after the year in which the debt becomes totally worthless. This rule affords you the opportunity to select the year in which to claim the partial bad debt deduction.

Totally worthless debts. A totally worthless debt is deducted only in the tax year in which it becomes totally worthless. The deduction for the debt must not include any amount deducted in an earlier tax year when the debt was only partially worthless. You are not required to make an actual write-off on your books to claim a bad debt deduction for a totally worthless debt. However, you may want to do so. If a debt you claim to be totally worthless is not written off on your books and the IRS later rules that the debt is only partially worthless, you will not be allowed a deduction until the amount is actually written off your books.

Recovery of bad debt. If you deducted a bad debt and in a later tax year recover (collect) all or part of it, you may have to include the amount you recover in your gross income. However, you may exclude from gross income the amount recovered, up to the amount of the deduction that did not reduce your tax in the year in which it was deducted.

Example

In 2004, Beatriz had a $25,000 bad debt loss relating to her Schedule C. She also had $25,000 of income from the activity. Beatriz had no taxable income for 2004.

In 2005 Beatriz recovered the entire $25,000 debt.

To figure how much she should include in her 2005 income, see the calculation below.

	2004 with bad debt	2005 without bad debt
Income:		
Schedule C	$25,000	$25,000
Bad debt loss	(25,000)	-0-
Adjusted gross income	-0-	25,000
Less:		
Standard deductions	-0-	5,000
Personal exemption	-0-	3,200
Taxable income	-0-	16,800

The calculations show that Beatriz's 2004 taxable income was reduced by $16,800 by including the bad debt. Therefore, $16,800 is included in Beatriz's taxable income for 2005, the year in which she collected the $25,000 debt.

Automobile and Truck Expenses

If you use your automobile for business purposes, you may be able to deduct expenses associated with the business use of the automobile. You generally can use one of two methods to figure your expense: actual expenses or the standard mileage rate. Refer to Chapter 28, *Car Expenses and Other Employee Business Expenses,* for more information on expenses for business use of your automobile.

TaxAlert

You can report business vehicle information on Part IV of Schedule C instead of Form 4562 if you are claiming the standard mileage rate, (which is 40.5 cents in 2005), you lease your vehicle, or your vehicle is fully depreciated. However, if you wish to deduct actual automobile expenses or if you must file Form 4562 for any other reason, you must continue to use Part V of Form 4562 to report the vehicle information.

Depreciating and Expensing Certain Assets

When you use property in your business, you are permitted to recover your investment in the property through tax deductions. You do this by "depreciating" the property—that is, deducting some of your cost on your income tax return each year. You can depreciate "tangible" property, such as a car, a building, or machinery, and amortize "intangible" property, such as a copyright or a patent. Your depreciation deduction is generally based on the cost of the qualifying property. However, the total amount you can elect to deduct is subject to a dollar limit and a business income limit. These limits apply to each taxpayer, not to each business. Depreciation is reported on Part II or Part III of Form 4562, whereas amortization is reported on Part VI of Form 4562. You cannot depreciate land, property you rent, or inventory.

Property is depreciable if it meets the following requirements:

1. It must be used in business or held for the production of income.
2. It must have a determinable life, and that life must be longer than 1 year.
3. It must be something that wears out, decays, gets

used up, becomes obsolete, or loses value from natural causes.

In general, if property does not meet all three of these conditions, it is not depreciable.

The amount of depreciation you can deduct depends on (1) how much the property costs, (2) when you began using it, (3) how long it will take to recover your cost, and (4) which one of the several depreciation methods you use.

You begin to claim depreciation on property when you place it in service in your trade or business or for the production of income. You continue to depreciate the property until you recover your basis (generally the cost) in it, dispose of it, or stop using it for business or investment purposes.

Form 4562, *Depreciation and Amortization,* is used to report your depreciation. For a further discussion of depreciation, see Chapter 10, *Rental Income and Expenses.* Additional information can be found in Publication 534, *Depreciation.*

TaxAlert

Expensing certain assets (Section 179 deduction). For tax years beginning in 2005, you can elect to treat all or part of the cost, not to exceed $105,000, of certain qualifying property as an expense in the year in which the property is purchased, rather than capitalize the cost and depreciate it over its life. This means that you can deduct all or part of the cost in 1 year rather than take depreciation deductions spread out over several years. You must decide for each item of qualifying property whether to deduct, subject to the yearly limit, or capitalize and depreciate its cost.

Qualifying property is property purchased for use in your trade or business and property that would have qualified for the investment tax credit.

TaxAlert

The American Jobs Creation Act of 2004 increased the Section 179 deduction for the expense of property place in service before 2008. The $100,000 limit was adjusted for inflation to $105,000 for 2005. This amount will be adjusted for inflation again in 2006 and 2007. For tax years beginning in 2008 and beyond, the maximum Section 179 deduction is scheduled to fall back to only $25,000.

The maximum dollar amount under Section 179 for sport utility vehicles is limited to $25,000 for vehicles purchased after October 22, 2004. A "sport utility vehicle" is any 4-wheeled vehicle designed primarily for, or that can be used to carry passengers over public streets, roads, or highways, that is not considered a "luxury vehicle" within the definitions set forth in the Internal Revenue Code, and is rated at 14,000 pounds gross vehicle weight or less (in place of the present law 6,000 pound rating). Certain vehicles are excluded from the reduced Section 179 expense (e.g., vehicles with a seating capacity behind the driver 9 persons or more).

Basis of qualifying property. The amount you elect to deduct is subtracted from the basis of the qualifying property. If you elect the Section 179 deduction, the amount of your allowable ACRS or MACRS deduction for this property will be reduced. If you and your spouse file separate returns, you can each deduct only $52,500, unless you and your spouse agree on a different split of the $105,000.

Other restrictions. The amount of the Section 179 de-

duction cannot be greater than the income derived from the active conduct by the taxpayer of any business during such taxable year (computed without regard to the property to be expensed). This rule prevents you from generating or adding to a net operating loss due to the Section 179 expense. Any Section 179 deductions disallowed under this income limitation are carried forward to the succeeding taxable year and added to the allowable amount for such year. Therefore, in the following year, you are eligible to receive the $105,000 deduction plus the carryover from the preceding year, limited to the amount of income. Also, the $105,000 amount is reduced dollar for dollar for property investments in excess of $420,000.

Cost. The cost of property for the Section 179 deduction does not include any part of the basis of the property that is determined by reference to the basis of other property held at any time by the person acquiring this property. For example, if you buy a new truck to use in your business, your cost for purposes of the Section 179 deduction does not include the adjusted basis of the truck you trade in on the new vehicle.

Example

You buy a new piece of equipment, paying $2,500 cash and trading in your old equipment, which had an undepreciated cost to you of $4,000. Even though the new equipment has a tax basis to you of $6,500, you may claim the Section 179 deduction only on the $2,500 you paid out.

When to elect. You must make an election to take the Section 179 deduction. You can only make this election in the first tax year in which the property is placed in service.

If you elect to deduct the cost of qualifying property, you must specify the items to which the election applies and the part of the cost of each you elect to deduct. If in 2005, you purchase and place in service two items of qualifying property costing $87,000 and $18,300, and you want to elect the $105,000 deduction, you must specify what part of the $87,000 property and the $18,300 property you want to deduct. You may arbitrarily allocate the maximum $105,000 between the two properties. Your remaining basis of $300 ($105,300 total cost of property placed in service, less $105,000 maximum Section 179 expense) may be depreciated.

Use Form 4562 to make your election and report your Section 179 deduction. You make the election by taking the deduction on Form 4562, filed with your original tax return. The election can be made on an amended tax return filed after the due date (including extensions), and can be revoked as long as the statute of limitations for the return is still open.

You should consult your tax advisor regarding the Section 179 rules, particularly when you acquire or dispose of assets.

Computers. If you use a computer for both business and personal use, there are special rules that may limit the amount of depreciation that can be deducted.

The amount of depreciation you are allowed to deduct depends on what percentage of use was business and what percentage was personal. The allocation is made on the basis of the most appropriate unit of time. For example, determine the percentage of use in a trade or a business for a tax year by dividing the number of hours the computer is used for business purposes by the total number of hours the computer is used for any purpose for that tax year.

Luxury automobiles. See Chapter 28, *Car Expenses and Other Employee Business Expenses,* for a discussion of luxury cars and depreciation.

Amortization. Capitalized costs of certain intangible property that is acquired and is held in connection with the conduct of a trade or business or an activity engaged in for the production of income may be amortized. The amount of the deduction is determined by amortizing the adjusted basis (generally the cost) of the intangible property ratably over a 15-year period. The amortization period begins with the month that the intangible property is acquired.

These amortization rules apply to "Section 197 intangible" property. "Section 197 intangible" property is defined as any property that is included in any one or more of the following categories:

1. Goodwill and going concern value
2. Certain specified types of intangible property that generally relate to workforce, information base, know-how, customers, suppliers, or other similar items
3. Any license, permit, or other right granted by a governmental unit or an agency or instrumentality thereof
4. Any covenant not to compete (or other arrangement to the extent that the arrangement has substantially the same effect as a covenant not to compete) entered into in connection with the direct or indirect acquisition of an interest in a trade or business (or substantial portion thereof)
5. Any franchise, trademark, or trade name

Special rules apply if a taxpayer disposes of some, but not all, of "Section 197 intangible" property that was acquired in a transaction. No loss is to be recognized by reason of such a disposition. Instead, the adjusted bases of the retained "Section 197 intangible" properties that were acquired in connection with such transaction are increased by the amount of any loss that is not recognized.

Leasing Business Assets

Many sole proprietors decide to lease a business asset, rather than purchase it. This is ideal if the asset is only needed for a limited period of time. For example, a tax practitioner may only need a computer for the months of February through April. Instead of incurring the large capital outlay required to purchase the asset, he or she can free up cash by leasing a computer.

Generally, the entire expense for leasing a business asset is deductible. This assumes that the asset is used 100% of the time for business purposes. If, however, the asset is used for both business and personal use, only the portion attributable to business use is allowed as a deduction. The most common business asset that is leased by a sole proprietor and a statutory employee is an automobile.

If you lease an automobile, you can deduct the part of each lease payment that is for the use of the automobile in your business or work. You cannot deduct any part of a lease payment that is for commuting to your regular job or other personal use of the automobile. You must amortize any advance payments made on the lease over the entire lease period.

If you leased an automobile after December 31, 1986, that you use in your business, for a lease term of 30 days or more, you may have to include in your income for each tax year in which you lease the car an "inclusion amount." If the fair market value of the automobile when the lease began was more than $12,800 ($13,400 for leases beginning

in 1991; $13,700 for leases beginning in 1992; $14,300 for leases beginning in 1993; $14,600 for leases beginning in 1994; $15,500 for leases beginning in 1995 and 1996; $15,800 for leases beginning in 1997 and 1998; $15,500 for leases beginning in 1999, 2000, 2001, and 2002; $18,000 for leases beginning in 2003; $17,500 for leases beginning in 2004; and $15,200 for leases beginning in 2005), you must include in your gross income an inclusion amount each tax year during which you lease the automobile. For more about leasing, see Chapter 28, Car Expenses and Other Employee Business Expenses.

Health Insurance

Self-employed individuals, including those filing Schedule C, may deduct the amount paid for health insurance premiums on behalf of themselves, their spouses, and dependents. This deduction is only available if you had net profits from self-employment for the year and were not eligible to participate in a subsidized health plan maintained by you or your spouse's employer. The determination of whether a self-employed individual or his or her spouse may be eligible for employer-provided health benefits is made on a monthly basis.

The allowable deduction is limited to the lesser of (1) 100% of the amount paid for health insurance premiums during 2005 for the self-employed individual, spouse, and dependent, or (2) the net profit from the trade or business less the amount claimed for a Keogh plan or a SEP deduction on Form 1040, line 28.

The deduction is not claimed on Schedule C and is not allowed as a deduction for self-employment tax purposes. However, the deduction is claimed on Form 1040, line 29, as an adjustment to income. Any medical insurance expenses in excess of the allowable deduction may be claimed as an itemized deduction on Schedule A (Form 1040), subject to the 7.5% (10% in the case of alternative minimum tax) of adjusted gross income floor for medical expenses.

Employees

Who are employees? Before you can know how to treat payments that you make for services rendered to you, you must first know the business relationship that exists between you and the person performing those services. The person performing the services may be: (1) an independent contractor, (2) a common-law employee, (3) a statutory employee, or (4) a statutory independent contractor.

The determination of a worker's classification can have significant tax consequences to an employer. When workers are not treated as employees, the employer can avoid employment tax and wage withholding responsibilities, as well as costs related to pension plans, health insurance, and other fringe benefits.

Independent contractors. People, such as lawyers, contractors, subcontractors, public stenographers, auctioneers, and so on, who follow an independent trade, business, or profession in which they offer their services to the general public are generally not employees. However, whether such people are employees or independent contractors depends on the facts in each case. The general rule is that an individual is an independent contractor if you, the employer, have the right to control or direct only the result of the work and not the means and methods of accomplishing the result.

You do not have to withhold or pay taxes on payments that you make to independent contractors.

Common-law employees. Under common-law rules, every individual who performs services subject to the will and control of an employer, as to both what must be done and how it must be done, is an employee. It does not matter that the employer allows the employee discretion and freedom of action, so long as the employer has the legal right to control both the method and the result of the services.

Two usual characteristics of an employer-employee relationship are that the employer has the right to discharge the employee and that the employer supplies the employee with tools and a place to work.

No distinction is made between classes of employees. Superintendents, managers, and other supervisory personnel are all employees. An officer of a corporation is generally an employee, but a director is not. An officer who performs no services or only minor services, and neither receives nor is entitled to receive any pay, is not considered an employee.

You generally must withhold and pay federal, Social Security, and Medicare taxes on wages you pay to common-law employees.

Statutory employees and statutory independent contractors are discussed at the beginning of this chapter.

Salaries, wages, and other forms of pay that you make to employees are generally deductible business expenses. However, a deduction for salaries and wages must be reduced by any work opportunity credit determined for the tax year. This will be discussed later in this chapter.

Tests for Deductibility

To be deductible, employees' pay must meet all of the following four tests:

Test 1—Ordinary and necessary. You must be able to show that salaries, wages, and other payments for employees' services are ordinary and necessary expenses directly connected with your trade or business.

Test 2—Reasonable. What is reasonable pay is determined by the facts. Generally, it is the amount that would ordinarily be paid for these services by like enterprises under similar circumstances.

Test 3—For services performed. You must be able to prove that the payments were made for services actually performed.

Test 4—Paid or incurred. You must have actually made the payments or incurred the expense during the tax year.

If you use the cash method of accounting, the expense for salaries and wages can be deducted only in the year in which the salaries and wages were paid. If you use the accrual method of accounting, the expense for salaries and wages is deducted when your obligation to make the payments is established and economic performance occurs (generally, when an employee performs his or her services for you). In addition, the expense must be paid within 2 1/2 months after the end of the tax year. However, the deduction of an accrual of salary to an owner may be limited. (See the previous discussion on the deduction of an accrual to a related party.)

Payroll Taxes

General Rules for Withholding

As an employer, you must generally withhold income taxes, Social Security, and Medicare taxes from wages that you pay employees. In addition, the amounts withheld with respect to Social Security and Medicare taxes will have to be matched by you, the employer. Also, unemployment tax payments may be required.

For information about the payroll tax deposit rules, see Publication 15, as well as IRS Circular E, *Employer's Tax Guide.*

TaxSaver

You may find it helpful to remember the following general rules for withholding:

1. *Independent contractors.* You do not withhold income tax or Social Security and Medicare taxes from amounts you pay an independent contractor.
2. *Common-law employees.* You generally have to withhold income tax, Social Security tax, and Medicare tax from the wages you pay common-law employees. You also have to pay federal unemployment tax and your share of Social Security and Medicare taxes on these wages.
3. *Statutory employees.* You are not required to withhold income tax from the wages of statutory employees. You must withhold and pay Social Security and Medicare taxes. Unless they are full-time life insurance sales agents or work at home, you must also pay federal unemployment tax on their wages.
4. *Statutory nonemployees.* You do not withhold or pay taxes on payments to statutory nonemployees.

Reporting payments to independent contractors and statutory nonemployees. If you pay an independent contractor or a statutory nonemployee $600 or more during the year in the course of your trade or business, you must file with the IRS and provide the independent contractor a Form 1099-MISC, *Miscellaneous Income.*

Reporting payments to common-law employees. To report wages paid to a common-law employee, you must complete a Form W-2. The Form W-2 must show the total wages and other compensation paid, total wages subject to Social Security taxes, total wages subject to Medicare taxes, the amounts deducted for income, Social Security, and Medicare taxes, and any other information required on the statement. For information on preparing Form W-2, see the Instructions that come with Form W-2.

Reporting payments to statutory employees. To report wages paid to a statutory employee, you must complete a Form W-2. You must report the same information that you reported for common-law employees. If the statutory employee and employer have elected not to withhold income tax, this information does not have to be furnished. Also, the employer must check the box for "statutory employee" on Form W-2.

When hiring new employees, you are required to have the employee complete a Form W-4, *Employee's Withholding Allowance Certificate,* and a Form I-9, *Employment Eligibility Verification Form.* In addition, the employee is required to file various payroll forms with the government. For more information on which payroll forms the employee must file, see IRS Circular E, *Employer's Tax Guide.*

Office in the Home and Form 8829

It is not unusual for a person filing a Schedule C to use part of his or her home for business. If you use part of your home regularly and exclusively for business, you may be able to deduct certain operating and depreciation expenses on your home.

Requirements for claiming the deduction. You may deduct certain expenses for operating out of a part of your home only if that part of your home is used regularly and exclusively as:

1. Your principal place of business for any trade or business in which you engage
2. A place to meet or deal with your patients, clients, or customers in the normal course of your trade or business

For tax years beginning before January 1, 1999, the U.S. Supreme Court had established a very restrictive approach to determine if a home office constituted a principal place of business. Under the Supreme Court's approach, the primary considerations in determining if a home office constituted a principal place of business were (1) the relative importance of activities performed at each business location, and (2) the time spent at each business location.

For example, under this approach a plumber's principal place of business was generally considered to be the customers' kitchens and bathrooms, so no home office deductions were allowed.

TaxAlert

The Taxpayer Relief Act of 1997 overruled the U.S. Supreme Court by providing that for tax years beginning after December 31, 1998, a home office qualifies as the principal place of business if:

1. You use the office to conduct administrative or management activities of a trade or business, and
2. There is no other fixed location of the trade or business where you conduct substantial administrative or management activities

Example

John Smith is a salesperson. His only office is a room in his house used regularly and exclusively to set up appointments and write up orders and other reports for the companies whose products he sells. John's tax year is the calendar year.

John's business is selling products to customers at various locations within the metropolitan area where he lives. To make these sales, he regularly visits the customers to explain the available products and to take orders. John makes only a few sales from his home office. John spends an average of 30 hours a week visiting customers and 12 hours a week working at his home office.

The essence of John's business as a salesperson requires him to meet with customers primarily at the customer's place of business. The home office activities are less important to John's business than the sales activities he performs when visiting customers. Prior to 1999, John would not have been allowed to deduct expenses of a home office. Now, John will be entitled to deduct home office expenses.

You may also deduct certain expenses for operating out of a separate structure that is not attached to your home, if you use it regularly and exclusively for your trade or business. (See Chapter 30, *Miscellaneous Deductions,* for more about deducting these expenses.)

TaxSaver

Even if you do *not* qualify for a business use of the home deduction, you may be allowed to take a depreciation deduction or elect a Section 179 deduction for furniture and equipment you use in your home for business or work as an employee.

If you use part of your home for business and meet the requirements discussed earlier, you must divide the expenses of operating out of your home between personal and business use. Some expenses are divided on an area basis. Some of these are further divided on a time–usage basis. If neither of these methods is appropriate, you can choose any other reasonable method to figure the business part of the expense.

What to deduct. Some expenses you pay to maintain your home are directly related to its business use; others are indirectly related; some are unrelated. You can deduct direct expenses and part of your indirect expenses, both subject to certain limitations. If you are a cash-basis taxpayer, you can deduct only the expenses you pay during the tax year.

TaxAlert

The deduction for expenses related to a storage unit in the taxpayer's home that is regularly used for inventory of the taxpayer's business of selling products in which the home is the sole fixed location of the business has been expanded to cover product samples as well as inventory.

Taxpayers are not required to use the space *exclusively* for the storage of inventory or product samples in order to be eligible for the deduction. The new rule adds "product samples" to clarify the current rule, so taxpayers need not attempt to distinguish between inventory and product samples.

Example

Joe Smith is in the business of selling cosmetics. Joe's residence is the only location of his business. He uses space in the study of his home to store cosmetic samples. Joe may deduct the expenses related to the portion of his residence used to store the product samples. It does not matter if Joe uses the study for additional purposes.

Direct Expenses

Direct expenses benefit only the business part of your home. They include painting or repairs made to the specific area or room used for business. You can deduct direct expenses in full.

Indirect Expenses

Indirect expenses are for keeping up and running your entire home. They benefit both the business and personal parts of your home. Examples of indirect expenses include:

Real estate taxes
Deductible mortgage interest
Casualty losses
Rent
Utilities and services
Insurance
Repairs
Security systems
Depreciation

You can deduct the business percentage of your indirect expenses.

Figuring the business percentage. To figure deductions for the business use of your home, find the business percentage. You can do this by dividing the area used for business by the total area of your home. You may measure the area in square feet. To figure the percentage of your home used for business, divide the number of square feet of space used for business by the total number of square feet of space in your home. If the rooms in your home are about the same size, figure the business percentage by dividing the number of rooms used for business by the number of rooms in the home. You can also use any other reasonable method to determine the business percentage.

Example 1. Your home measures 1,200 square feet. You use one room that measures 240 square feet for business.

Therefore, you use one-fifth (240 ÷ 1,200), or 20%, of the total area for business.

Example 2. If the rooms in your home are about the same size, and you use one room in a 5-room house for business, you use one-fifth, or 20%, of the total area for business.

Real Estate Taxes

If you own your home, you can deduct part of the real estate taxes on your home as a business expense. To figure the business part of your real estate taxes, multiply the real estate taxes paid by the percentage of your home used for business.

Deductible Mortgage Interest

If you pay deductible mortgage interest, you can generally deduct part of it as a business expense. To figure the business part of your deductible mortgage interest, multiply this interest by the percentage of your home used in business. You can include interest on a second mortgage in this computation.

Casualty Losses

If you have a casualty loss on your home or other property you use in business, you can deduct the business part of the loss as a business expense. Treat a casualty loss as an unrelated expense, a direct expense, or an indirect expense depending on the property affected.

In a partial destruction, the deductible loss is the decrease in fair market value of the property or the adjusted basis of the property, whichever is less. You must reduce this amount by any insurance or other reimbursement you receive or expect to receive.

If your business property is completely destroyed (becomes totally worthless), your deductible loss is the adjusted basis of the property, minus any salvage value and any insurance or other reimbursement you receive or expect to receive. Figure the loss without taking into account any decrease in fair market value.

Rent

If you rent, rather than own, a home and meet the requirements for business use of the home, you can deduct part of the rent you pay. To figure your deduction, multiply your rent payments by the percentage of your home used for business.

Utilities and Services

Expenses for utilities and services, such as electricity, gas, trash removal, and cleaning services, are primarily personal expenses. However, if you use part of your home for business, you can deduct the business part of these expenses.

Telephone

The basic local telephone service charge, including taxes, for the first telephone line into your home is a nondeductible personal expense. However, charges for business long-distance phone calls on that line, as well as the cost of a second line into your home used exclusively for business, are deductible business expenses for the business use of your home. Deduct these charges separately on the appropriate schedule. Do not include them in your home office deduction.

Insurance

You can deduct the cost of insurance that covers the business part of your home.

Repairs

The cost of repairs and supplies that relate to your business, including labor (other than your own labor), is a deductible expense. For example, a furnace repair benefits the entire home. If you use 10% of your home for business, you can deduct 10% of the cost of the furnace repair.

Repairs keep your home in good working order over its useful life. Examples of common repairs are patching walls and floors, painting, wallpapering, repairing roofs and gutters, and mending leaks.

Security System

If you install a security system that protects all the doors and windows in your home, you can deduct the business part of the expenses you incur to maintain and monitor the system. You can also take a depreciation deduction for the part of the cost of the security system relating to the business use of your home.

Depreciation

The cost of property that can be used for more than 1 year, such as a building, a permanent improvement, or furniture, is a capital expenditure.

Land is not depreciable property. You generally cannot recover the cost of land until you dispose of it.

Permanent improvements. A permanent improvement increases the value of property, adds to its life, or gives it a new or different use. Examples of improvements are replacement of electric wiring or plumbing, a new roof, an addition, paneling, remodeling, or major modifications.

Depreciating your home. If you use part of your home for business, depreciate that part as nonresidential real property under the Modified Accelerated Cost Recovery System (MACRS). Under MACRS, nonresidential real property is depreciated using the straight-line method over 39 years.

To figure depreciation on the business part of your home, you need to know:

1. The business-use percentage of your home
2. The first month in your tax year for which you can deduct business use of your home expenses
3. The adjusted basis and fair market value of your home at the time you qualify for a deduction

Adjusted basis of home. The adjusted basis of your home is generally its cost plus the cost of any permanent improvements that you made to it minus any casualty losses deducted in earlier tax years.

When you change part of your home from personal to business use, your basis for depreciation is the business-use percentage times the lesser of:

1. The adjusted basis of your home (excluding land) on the date of change; or
2. The fair market value of your home (excluding land) on the date of change.

Unrelated expenses benefit only the parts of your home that you do not use for business. These include repairs to personal areas of your home, lawn care, and landscaping. You cannot deduct unrelated expenses. For more information, also see Chapter 30, *Miscellaneous Deductions*.

Recordkeeping. You do not have to use a particular method of recordkeeping, but you must keep records that provide the information needed to figure your deductions for the business use of your home. Your records must show the following:

1. The part of your home you use for business
2. That you use this part of your home exclusively and regularly for business as either your principal place of business or as the place where you meet or deal with clients or customers in the normal course of your business

3. The depreciation and expenses for the business part of your home

Generally, you must keep your records for at least 3 years from the date the return was filed or 2 years from the date the tax was paid, whichever is later. Keep records that support your basis in your home for as long as they are needed to figure the correct basis of your home.

Deduction Limit

If your gross income from the business use of your home equals or exceeds your total business expenses (including depreciation), you can deduct all of your expenses for the business use of your home. But if your gross income from that use is less than your total business expenses, your deduction for certain expenses for the business use of your home is limited. The total of your deductions for otherwise nondeductible expenses, such as utilities, insurance, and depreciation (with depreciation taken last) cannot be more than your gross income from the business use of your home minus the sum of:

1. The business percentage of the otherwise deductible mortgage interest, real estate taxes, and casualty and theft losses, and
2. The business expenses that are not attributable to the business use of your home (e.g., salaries or supplies).

If you are self-employed, do not include in (2) above your deduction for half of your self-employment tax.

You can carry forward to your next tax year deductions over the current year's limit. These deductions are subject to the gross income limit from the business use of your home for the next tax year. The amount carried forward will be allowable only up to your gross income in the next tax year from the business in which the deduction arose, whether or not you live in the home during the year.

Figuring deduction limit and carryover. If you file Schedule C (Form 1040), figure your deduction limit on Form 8829, *Expenses for Business Use of Your Home.* Enter the amount from line 34 of Form 8829 on Schedule C, line 30.

Deductible mortgage interest. After you have figured the business part of the mortgage interest on Form 8829, subtract that amount from the total mortgage interest. The *remainder* is deductible on Schedule A; do not deduct any of the business part on Schedule A. If the amount of interest you deduct on Schedule A for your home mortgage is limited, enter the excess on Form 8829.

Real estate taxes. If you file Schedule C, enter all your deductible real estate taxes on Form 8829. After you have figured the business part of your taxes on Form 8829, subtract that amount from your total real estate taxes. The *remainder* is deductible on Schedule A; do not deduct any of the business part of real estate taxes on Schedule A.

Day-Care Facility

You can deduct expenses for using part of your home on a regular basis to provide day-care services if you meet the following requirements:

1. You must be in the trade or business of providing day care for children, for persons age 65 or older, or for persons who are physically or mentally unable to care for themselves.
2. You must have applied for, been granted, or be exempt from having a license, certification, registra-

tion, or approval as a day-care center or as a family or group day-care home under applicable state law. You do not meet this requirement if your application was rejected or your license or other authorization was revoked.

Meals. If you provide food for your day-care business, do not include the expense as a cost of using your home for business. Claim it as a separate deduction on your Schedule C. You can deduct 100% of the cost of food consumed by your day-care recipients and 50% of the cost of food consumed by your employees as a business expense. You cannot deduct the cost of food consumed by you and your family.

Do not deduct the cost of meals for which you were reimbursed under the Child and Adult Care Food Program administered by the Department of Agriculture. The reimbursements are not included in your income to the extent you used them to provide food for the eligible children.

Retirement Plans

If you are self-employed, you can take an income tax deduction for certain contributions that you make for yourself to a retirement plan. You can also deduct a trustee's fees if contributions to the plan do not cover them.

TAXALERT

Small businesses with 100 or fewer employees who have received a mimimun of $5,000 from the business in the preceding year are eligible for a tax credit for 50% of the expenses of establishing a new retirement plan. The maximum allowable credit is $500 for the first year and each of the 3 succeeding years. Deductible contributions plus the plan's earnings on them are tax-free until you receive distributions from the plan in later years. If you are a sole proprietor, you can deduct contributions you make for your common-law employees, as well as contributions you make for yourself. A common-law employee cannot take a deduction for your contributions.

The two types of plans that a self-employed person most commonly may set up are a Keogh plan or a Simplified Employee Pension (SEP) plan.

Keogh Plans

A Keogh (HR 10) plan is a retirement plan that can be established by a sole proprietor. The plan must be for the exclusive benefit of employees or their beneficiaries. As an employer, you can usually deduct, subject to limits, contributions you make to a Keogh plan, including those made for your own retirement.

For further information about Keogh plans, see Chapter 18, *Individual Retirement Arrangements (IRAs).*

Where to deduct on Form 1040. Take the deduction for contributions for yourself on line 28 of Form 1040. Deduct the contributions for your common-law employees on Schedule C.

Because the deduction for your contribution to a Keogh plan for your benefit is reported on Form 1040, line 28, not on Schedule C, the contribution does not reduce your self-employment income that is subject to tax.

Reporting requirements. As the Keogh plan administrator or the employer, you may have to file an annual return or report form by the last day of the seventh month following the end of the plan year.

Simplified Employee Pension (SEP)

A simplified employee pension (SEP) is a written plan that allows an employer to make contributions toward an employee's retirement, and his or her own, if the employer is self-employed, without becoming involved in a more complex Keogh retirement plan.

For further information about SEPs, see Chapter 18, *Individual Retirement Arrangements (IRAs)*.

Individual Retirement Arrangements (IRAs)

In addition to the retirement plans already discussed, a self-employed person may also make a contribution, which may or may not be deductible, to an Individual Retirement Arrangement (IRA).

TaxAlert

The earnings on your contributions generated by the plan are generally not subject to tax. The distributions of your deductible contributions and the earnings from the plan, which are subject to certain limitations, may be taxable to you upon withdrawal.

For further information about IRAs, see Chapter 18, *Individual Retirement Arrangements (IRAs)*.

SIMPLE Retirement Plan. Small businesses that normally employ 100 or fewer employees, paid them at least $5,000 in compensation in the preceding year, and do not maintain another qualified plan may establish a Savings Incentive Match Plan for Employees (SIMPLE plan). A SIMPLE plan can be in the form of either an individual retirement arrangement (IRA) for each employee or part of a qualified cash or deferred arrangement [401(k) plan]. Employees may make elective contributions of up to $10,000 for 2005 to a SIMPLE plan, and employers must make matching contributions. Employees are not taxed on account assets until distributions are made, and employers generally may deduct their contributions to the plan.

For more information about tax credits for small businesses related to retirement plans, see IRS Publication 560, available at www.irs.gov

Travel and Entertainment

Business travel and meals and entertainment expenses are deductible, subject to certain limits, assuming that these amounts are both ordinary and necessary, as defined earlier in the chapter.

For a self-employed person, the meals and entertainment expenses to be deducted are subject to the 50% limit and certain documentation requirements as discussed in Chapter 28, *Car Expenses and Other Employee Business Expenses*. (Also see Chapter 28 for a more complete discussion of the deductibility of both travel and meals and entertainment expenses.)

Other Schedule C Deductions

Various other expenses not previously mentioned are allowed as a deduction on Schedule C. Examples of these expenses are advertising, commissions and fees, insurance (other than health), interest, legal and professional services, office expenses, including supplies and other items used in the office, general rent, repairs and maintenance, taxes, utilities, and any other business expense that can be classified as ordinary and necessary.

Sales of Business Property Used in Your Business
How Different Assets Are Treated

A sole proprietorship usually has many assets. When sold, these assets must be classified as either depreciable personal property used in the business, real property used in the business, or property held for sale to customers, such as inventory or stock in trade or capital assets.

The gain or loss on each asset is figured separately. The sale of inventory results in ordinary income or loss and is reported on Schedule C. The sale of a capital asset results in a capital gain or loss and is reported on Schedule D. The sale of depreciable personal property and real property used in the business results in Section 1231 gains or losses and is reported on Form 4797. (For further information about Section 1231 transactions, see Chapter 17, *Reporting Gains and Losses*.)

Any gain realized on sales and certain other dispositions of depreciable personal property and, under certain circumstances depreciable real property, is treated as ordinary income to the extent of depreciation deductions taken prior to the sale. The amount of depreciation recapture is the lesser of (1) the gain recognized or (2) depreciation taken on the property. For more information, see Chapters 14, *Basis of Property,* 15, *Sale of Property,* and 17, *Reporting Gains and Losses.*

Section 1231 business gain or loss. Once you have determined your gain or loss on your personal and real property that is not subject to depreciation recapture, you must combine all gains and losses from the sale and disposition of Section 1231 property for the tax year including Section 1231 gains and losses reported to you through partnerships and S corporations in which you have an interest. In general, if all of your Section 1231 transactions resulted in a net gain, the gain is treated as a long-term capital gain. If all of your Section 1231 transactions resulted in a net loss, the loss is treated as an ordinary loss. See Chapter 17, *Reporting Gains and Losses,* for a further discussion of how to treat Section 1231 gains and losses.

Recapture of net ordinary losses. A net Section 1231 gain is treated as ordinary income to the extent that it does not exceed your nonrecaptured net Section 1231 losses taken in prior years. Nonrecaptured losses are net Section 1231 losses deducted for your 5 most recent tax years that have not yet been applied (recaptured) against any net Section 1231 gains in a tax year beginning after 1984. Your losses are recaptured, beginning with the earliest year that is subject to recapture.

Sale of the Entire Business

Because a sole proprietorship is not a separate entity, a sale of the business will be treated as if each asset in the business had been sold separately. The gain or loss on such a sale is the total of the gains or losses as separately computed for each individual asset.

Both the buyer and the seller of a group of assets constituting a trade or a business must report to the IRS on Form 8594 various information about the acquisition of assets, including the following:

1. The name of the buyer and seller of the assets
2. The fair market value of the assets transferred
3. The allocation of the sales price to the assets transferred

4. Whether the buyer purchased a license, covenant not to compete or entered into a lease agreement, employment contract, management contract, or similar arrangement with the seller

Business Tax Credit
Tax credits are distinguished from deductions in that a deduction reduces taxable income and a credit reduces tax liability. Consequently, $1 in tax credit is more valuable than $1 in tax deduction.

Form 3800. The general business tax credit includes the following:

1. The investment credit (Form 3468)
2. The work opportunity credit (Form 5884)
3. The credit for increasing research activities (Form 6765)
4. The low-income housing credit (Form 8586)
5. The welfare-to-work credit (Form 8861)
6. The credit for small employer pension plan start-up costs (Form 8881)

If you have more than one of these credits, if you have a carryback or carryforward of any of these credits, or if any of these credits is from a passive activity, you must attach the appropriate credit forms and summarize them on Form 3800. If you have only one of these credits and that credit is not from a passive activity, you do not have to file Form 3800. Instead, use the applicable form to claim the credit. For example, if you have only a 2005 work opportunity credit, you may use Form 5884, Work Opportunity Credit. You do not have to file Form 3800.

TaxAlert

Work opportunity credit. The work opportunity tax credit provides an incentive to hire persons from targeted groups that have a particularly high unemployment rate or other special employment needs. The employer is entitled to a credit equal to 25% of qualified first-year wages for hiring an eligible employee who works 120 to 399 hours and a 40% credit for employees who work 400 hours or more.

This program is subject to yearly Congressional renewal. The tax credit is extended to December 31, 2005. The credit is also retroactive to December 31, 2003.

TaxAlert

Credit for hiring long-term family assistance recipients. A credit, called the welfare-to-work credit, is available for employers who paid wages to long-term family assistance recipients who began work after 1997. The amount of the credit for a tax year is 35% of the qualified first-year wages for such year plus 50% of the qualified second-year wages for such year. The credit applies only to the first $10,000 of wages in each year with respect to any individual. Thus, the maximum total credit per qualified employee is $8,500 for the 2 years.

Any unused credit can be carried back 1 year or forward 20 tax years as part of the general business credit for years beginning after December 31, 1997.

Special Situations
Artists and Authors
The proper way for artists and authors to account for their expenses has been the topic of much debate in recent years. A special exception excludes authors and artists from the uniform capitalization rules for certain qualified creative expenses that they incur in their trade or business. As a result, these expenses can be currently deducted and not capitalized. A "qualified creative expense" is defined as any expense that is paid or incurred by an individual in the trade or business of being a writer or an artist and that would be allowable as a deduction for the taxable year.

Although you are allowed currently to deduct those expenses that are classified as qualified creative expenses, there are some expenses that need to be capitalized. Examples of such expenses include any expense related to printing, photographic plates, motion pictures, videotapes, and similar items.

There is an alternative way for an artist or an author to treat his or her qualified creative expenses. If the artist or author so chooses, he or she can capitalize all qualified creative costs. In the current year he or she is able to deduct 50% of the eligible costs and then deduct the remaining 50% ratably over the next 2 years. The reason one may choose this method over deducting all qualified creative expenses currently is that the meaning of a qualified creative cost is broader in this instance. It includes the costs of films, sound recordings, videotapes, and books. These expenses would normally need to be capitalized and amortized over their estimated useful lives.

How to Complete Schedule SE
Line by Line, Briefly
Self-employed individuals filing Schedule C may be required to pay self-employment tax. Self-employment income and the related tax are discussed earlier in this chapter.

When completing Form 1040, Schedule SE, you must first determine whether you need to file the short Schedule SE form or the long Schedule SE form. You must use the long Schedule SE form if any of the following apply:

- You received wages or tips and the total of all of your wages (and tips) subject to Social Security, Medicare, or railroad retirement taxes plus your net earnings from self-employment are more than $90,000.
- You use either "optional method" to figure your net earnings from self-employment.
- You are a minister, a member of a religious order, or a Christian Science practitioner and you received IRS approval (by filing Form 4361) not to be taxed on your earnings from these sources, but you owe self-employment tax on other earnings.
- You had church employee income of $108.28 or more that was reported to you on Form W-2.
- You received tips subject to Social Security, Medicare, or railroad retirement taxes, but you did not report those tips to your employer.

If none of these conditions exist, you are able to use the Short Schedule SE form.

As a Schedule C filer, you would report your Schedule C income on line 2 of Section A for the Short form Schedule SE or Section B for the Long form Schedule SE (remember, do not include the income reported on Schedule C as a statutory employee).

Example

Peter Doyle is single. He is employed as a full-time Latin professor at a university. His wages from this job were $81,500. Dr. Doyle also gives lectures around the country on a free-lance basis. His net profit from these lectures was $15,000, which he reported on Schedule C-EZ (Form 1040).

His net profit from lecturing and his wages total more than $90,000, so he must fill out Long Schedule SE.

1. On his Long Schedule SE, Doyle has no farm income, so he leaves line 1 blank.
2. Doyle enters the net profit from his Schedule C-EZ, $15,000.
3. Doyle has no farm income, so he enters the same amount on line 3, $15,000.
4a. Doyle multiplies the $15,000 by 92.35% (.9235) to get his net earnings and enters $13,853.
4b. Doyle did not elect an optional method, so he leaves this line blank.
4c. Line 4b is blank, so he enters the same amount he entered on line 4a, $13,853.
5a.-b Doyle had no church employee income, so he leaves these lines blank.
6. Line 5b is blank, so Doyle enters the same amount he entered on line 4c, $13,853.
8a. Doyle enters his total wages, $81,500.
8b. This line does not apply to him, so Doyle leaves it blank.
8c. Line 8b is blank, so he enters the same amount he entered on line 8a, $81,500.
9. He subtracts line 8c ($81,500) from line 7 and enters the result, $6,400.
10. Doyle multiplies the smaller of line 6 ($13,853) or line 9 ($6,400) by 12.4% (.124) and enters the result, $794.
11. Doyle multiplies line 6 ($13,853) by 2.9% (.029) and enters the result, $402.
12. Doyle adds lines 10 and 11 and enters the total, $1,196, here and on line 58 of Form 1040 (not illustrated).
13. Doyle multiples line 12 (his SE tax) by 50% (.5) and enters the result ($598) on: Line 13 of this schedule, and Line 27 of Form 1040. This is the amount of SE tax he can deduct.

Comprehensive Schedule C/ Self-Employment Example

Paul Jones is a self-employed comic book salesman. He does business as JPJ Comics. The majority of his business consists of retail sales of comic books. Paul works out of his home, located at 64-09 79th Street,, Queens, New York 11379, where he has been running the business since 1992. One-fourth of his home is used solely for the purpose of running his business. Paul accounts for his purchases and sales on the accrual method. All other income and expense items are accounted for by use of the cash method. He is also a professor of civil law studies and has $54,000 of W-2 wages in 2005.

Paul Jones had the following income and expenses during 2005:

Gross receipts from sales of comic books—accrual basis..	$35,000
Beginning inventory	2,200
Purchases	13,000
Ending inventory	2,700
Business subscriptions	350
Advertising	1,700
Legal Fees	200
Supplies	1,200
Meals and entertainment	600
Travel	900
Telephone	300
Annual home insurance	900
Annual mortgage interest	6,000
Annual real estate taxes	4,000
Annual utilities	1,200
Basis of home purchased on 6/1/89	220,000
Amount attributable to land	40,000
Amount attributable to house	180,000

Paul Jones has established a profit-sharing plan, providing for a maximum contribution of 25% of compensation. For 2005, he has made the maximum contribution before filing his tax return.

| SCHEDULE C
(Form 1040)

Department of the Treasury
Internal Revenue Service | **Profit or Loss From Business**
(Sole Proprietorship)
▶ Partnerships, joint ventures, etc., must file Form 1065 or 1065-B.
▶ Attach to Form 1040 or 1041.   ▶ See Instructions for Schedule C (Form 1040). | OMB No. 1545-0074
20**05**
Attachment
Sequence No. **09** |

Name of proprietor	Social security number (SSN)
John Paul Jones	111 : 22 : 3344

A Principal business or profession, including product or service (see page C-2 of the instructions)
Retail sales of comic books

B Enter code from pages C-7, 8, & 9
▶ | | 5 | 0 | 1 | 7

C Business name. If no separate business name, leave blank.
JPJ Comics

D Employer ID number (EIN), if any
1 | 3 : 2 | 9 | 9 | 9 | 9 | 0 | 9

E Business address (including suite or room no.) ▶ 64-09 79th Street
City, town or post office, state, and ZIP code   Queens, NY 11379

F Accounting method: **(1)** ☐ Cash   **(2)** ☐ Accrual   **(3)** ☒ Other (specify) ▶ Hybrid

G Did you "materially participate" in the operation of this business during 2005? If "No," see page C-3 for limit on losses   ☒ Yes ☐ No

H If you started or acquired this business during 2005, check here . . . . ▶ ☐

Part I   Income

1	Gross receipts or sales. **Caution.** If this income was reported to you on Form W-2 and the "Statutory employee" box on that form was checked, see page C-3 and check here . . . . . . ▶ ☐	**1**	35,000
2	Returns and allowances	**2**	
3	Subtract line 2 from line 1	**3**	35,000
4	Cost of goods sold (from line 42 on page 2)	**4**	12,500
5	**Gross profit.** Subtract line 4 from line 3	**5**	22,500
6	Other income, including Federal and state gasoline or fuel tax credit or refund (see page C-3) . . .	**6**	
7	**Gross income.** Add lines 5 and 6 . . . . ▶	**7**	22,500

Part II   Expenses. Enter expenses for business use of your home **only** on line 30.

8	Advertising	**8**	1,700	18	Office expense	**18**	
9	Car and truck expenses (see page C-3)	**9**		19	Pension and profit-sharing plans	**19**	
10	Commissions and fees . .	**10**		20	Rent or lease (see page C-5):		
11	Contract labor (see page C-4)	**11**			a Vehicles, machinery, and equipment	**20a**	
12	Depletion	**12**			b Other business property . .	**20b**	
13	Depreciation and section 179 expense deduction (not included in Part III) (see page C-4)	**13**		21	Repairs and maintenance . .	**21**	
				22	Supplies (not included in Part III)	**22**	1,200
				23	Taxes and licenses . . .	**23**	
				24	Travel, meals, and entertainment:		
14	Employee benefit programs (other than on line 19). .	**14**			a Travel	**24a**	900
15	Insurance (other than health) .	**15**			b Deductible meals and entertainment (see page C-5)	**24b**	300
16	Interest:			25	Utilities	**25**	600
a	Mortgage (paid to banks, etc.)	**16a**		26	Wages (less employment credits)	**26**	
b	Other	**16b**		27	Other expenses (from line 48 on page 2)	**27**	350
17	Legal and professional services	**17**	200				

28	**Total expenses** before expenses for business use of home. Add lines 8 through 27 in columns . ▶	**28**	5,250
29	Tentative profit (loss). Subtract line 28 from line 7	**29**	17,250
30	Expenses for business use of your home. Attach **Form 8829**	**30**	4,229
31	**Net profit or (loss).** Subtract line 30 from line 29. • If a profit, enter on **Form 1040, line 12,** and **also** on **Schedule SE, line 2** (statutory employees, see page C-6). Estates and trusts, enter on Form 1041, line 3. • If a loss, you **must** go to line 32.	**31**	12,521

32 If you have a loss, check the box that describes your investment in this activity (see page C-6).
• If you checked 32a, enter the loss on **Form 1040, line 12,** and **also** on **Schedule SE, line 2** (statutory employees, see page C-6). Estates and trusts, enter on Form 1041, line 3.
• If you checked 32b, you **must** attach **Form 6198.** Your loss may be limited.

32a ☐ All investment is at risk.
32b ☐ Some investment is not at risk.

For Paperwork Reduction Act Notice, see Form 1040 instructions.   Cat. No. 11334P   Schedule C (Form 1040) 2005

Draft as of 05/31/2005

Schedule C (Form 1040) 2005   Page **2**

Part III	**Cost of Goods Sold** (see page C-6)		

33   Method(s) used to value closing inventory: **a** ☒ Cost   **b** ☐ Lower of cost or market   **c** ☐ Other (attach explanation)

34   Was there any change in determining quantities, costs, or valuations between opening and closing inventory? If "Yes," attach explanation . . . . ☐ **Yes**   ☒ **No**

35	Inventory at beginning of year. If different from last year's closing inventory, attach explanation . .	**35** 2,200
36	Purchases less cost of items withdrawn for personal use	**36** 13,000
37	Cost of labor. Do not include any amounts paid to yourself	**37**
38	Materials and supplies	**38**
39	Other costs	**39**
40	Add lines 35 through 39	**40** 15,200
41	Inventory at end of year	**41** 2,700
42	**Cost of goods sold.** Subtract line 41 from line 40. Enter the result here and on page 1, line 4 . .	**42** 12,500

Part IV	**Information on Your Vehicle.** Complete this part **only** if you are claiming car or truck expenses on line 9 and are not required to file Form 4562 for this business. See the instructions for line 13 on page C-4 to find out if you must file Form 4562.

43   When did you place your vehicle in service for business purposes? (month, day, year) ▶ . . . . / . . . . . . / . . . . . .

44   Of the total number of miles you drove your vehicle during 2005, enter the number of miles you used your vehicle for:

a Business . . . . **b** Commuting (see instructions) . . . . **c** Other . . . .

45   Do you (or your spouse) have another vehicle available for personal use? . . . . ☐ **Yes**   ☐ **No**

46   Was your vehicle available for personal use during off-duty hours? . . . . ☐ **Yes**   ☐ **No**

47a   Do you have evidence to support your deduction? . . . . ☐ **Yes**   ☐ **No**

   b   If "Yes," is the evidence written? . . . . ☐ **Yes**   ☐ **No**

Part V	**Other Expenses.** List below business expenses not included on lines 8–26 or line 30.	
	Business subscriptions	350
48	**Total other expenses.** Enter here and on page 1, line 27	**48**

✳ *Printed on recycled paper*   **Schedule C (Form 1040) 2005**

SCHEDULE SE
(Form 1040)

Department of the Treasury
Internal Revenue Service

OMB No. 1545-0074

Self-Employment Tax

▶ **Attach to Form 1040.** ▶ **See Instructions for Schedule SE (Form 1040).**

20**05**

Attachment
Sequence No. **17**

Name of person with **self-employment** income (as shown on Form 1040)

John Paul Jones

Social security number of person
with **self-employment** income ▶ 111 : 22 : 3344

Who Must File Schedule SE

You must file Schedule SE if:

● You had net earnings from self-employment from **other than** church employee income (line 4 of Short Schedule SE or line 4c of Long Schedule SE) of $400 or more **or**

● You had church employee income of $108.28 or more. Income from services you performed as a minister or a member of a religious order **is not** church employee income (see page SE-1).

Note. Even if you had a loss or a small amount of income from self-employment, it may be to your benefit to file Schedule SE and use either "optional method" in Part II of Long Schedule SE (see page SE-3).

Exception. If your only self-employment income was from earnings as a minister, member of a religious order, or Christian Science practitioner **and** you filed Form 4361 and received IRS approval not to be taxed on those earnings, **do not** file Schedule SE. Instead, write "Exempt–Form 4361" on Form 1040, line 58.

May I Use Short Schedule SE or Must I Use Long Schedule SE?

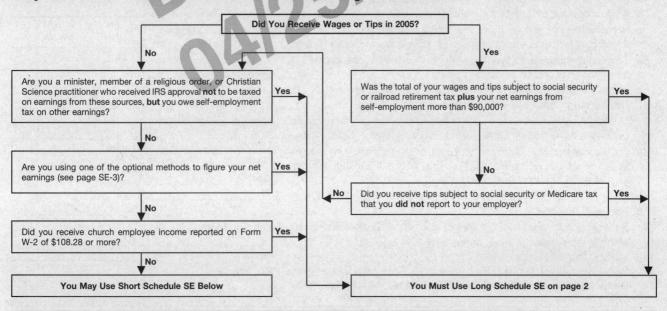

Section A—Short Schedule SE. Caution. Read above to see if you can use Short Schedule SE.

1	Net farm profit or (loss) from Schedule F, line 36, and farm partnerships, Schedule K-1 (Form 1065), box 14, code A	**1**
2	Net profit or (loss) from Schedule C, line 31; Schedule C-EZ, line 3; Schedule K-1 (Form 1065), box 14, code A (other than farming); and Schedule K-1 (Form 1065-B), box 9. Ministers and members of religious orders, see page SE-1 for amounts to report on this line. See page SE-2 for other income to report	**2**
3	Combine lines 1 and 2	**3**
4	**Net earnings from self-employment.** Multiply line 3 by 92.35% (.9235). If less than $400, **do not** file this schedule; you do not owe self-employment tax . . . . ▶	**4**
5	**Self-employment tax.** If the amount on line 4 is: ● $90,000 or less, multiply line 4 by 15.3% (.153). Enter the result here and on **Form 1040, line 58.** ● More than $90,000, multiply line 4 by 2.9% (.029). Then, add $11,160.00 to the result. Enter the total here and on **Form 1040, line 58.**	**5**
6	**Deduction for one-half of self-employment tax.** Multiply line 5 by 50% (.5). Enter the result here and on **Form 1040, line 27** **6**	

For Paperwork Reduction Act Notice, see Form 1040 instructions.   Cat. No. 11358Z   **Schedule SE (Form 1040) 2005**

Schedule SE (Form 1040) 2005   Attachment Sequence No. **17**   Page **2**

Name of person with **self-employment** income (as shown on Form 1040)	Social security number of person with **self-employment** income ►

Section B—Long Schedule SE

Part I   Self-Employment Tax

Note. If your only income subject to self-employment tax is **church employee income,** skip lines 1 through 4b. Enter -0- on line 4c and go to line 5a. Income from services you performed as a minister or a member of a religious order **is not** church employee income. See page SE-1.

A   If you are a minister, member of a religious order, or Christian Science practitioner **and** you filed Form 4361, but you had $400 or more of **other** net earnings from self-employment, check here and continue with Part I . . . . ▶ ☐

1	Net farm profit or (loss) from Schedule F, line 36, and farm partnerships, Schedule K-1 (Form 1065), box 14, code A. **Note.** Skip this line if you use the farm optional method (see page SE-4)	**1**	
2	Net profit or (loss) from Schedule C, line 31; Schedule C-EZ, line 3; Schedule K-1 (Form 1065), box 14, code A (other than farming); and Schedule K-1 (Form 1065-B), box 9. Ministers and members of religious orders, see page SE-1 for amounts to report on this line. See page SE-2 for other income to report. **Note.** Skip this line if you use the nonfarm optional method (see page SE-4)	**2**	12,521
3	Combine lines 1 and 2	**3**	12,521
4a	If line 3 is more than zero, multiply line 3 by 92.35% (.9235). Otherwise, enter amount from line 3	**4a**	11,563
b	If you elect one or both of the optional methods, enter the total of lines 15 and 17 here	**4b**	
c	Combine lines 4a and 4b. If less than $400, **stop;** you do not owe self-employment tax. **Exception.** If less than $400 and you had **church employee income,** enter -0- and continue. . . . . . . ▶	**4c**	11,563
5a	Enter your **church employee income** from Form W-2. See page SE-1 for definition of church employee income **5a**		
b	Multiply line 5a by 92.35% (.9235). If less than $100, enter -0- . . .	**5b**	
6	**Net earnings from self-employment.** Add lines 4c and 5b	**6**	11,563
7	Maximum amount of combined wages and self-employment earnings subject to social security tax or the 6.2% portion of the 7.65% railroad retirement (tier 1) tax for 2005	**7**	90,000 00
8a	Total social security wages and tips (total of boxes 3 and 7 on Form(s) W-2) and railroad retirement (tier 1) compensation. If $90,000 or more, skip lines 8b through 10, and go to line 11 **8a**		
b	Unreported tips subject to social security tax (from Form 4137, line 9) **8b**		
c	Add lines 8a and 8b	**8c**	54,000
9	Subtract line 8c from line 7. If zero or less, enter -0- here and on line 10 and go to line 11 ▶	**9**	36,000
10	Multiply the **smaller** of line 6 or line 9 by 12.4% (.124) . . .	**10**	1,434
11	Multiply line 6 by 2.9% (.029)	**11**	335
12	**Self-employment tax.** Add lines 10 and 11. Enter here and on **Form 1040, line 58**	**12**	1,769
13	**Deduction for one-half of self-employment tax.** Multiply line 12 by 50% (.5). Enter the result here and on **Form 1040, line 27** **13** 885		

Part II   Optional Methods To Figure Net Earnings (see page SE-3)

Farm Optional Method. You may use this method **only** if **(a)** your gross farm income[1] was not more than $2,400 **or (b)** your net farm profits[2] were less than $1,733.

14	Maximum income for optional methods	**14**	1,600 00
15	Enter the **smaller** of: two-thirds (⅔) of gross farm income[1] (not less than zero) **or** $1,600. Also include this amount on line 4b above	**15**	

Nonfarm Optional Method. You may use this method **only** if **(a)** your net nonfarm profits[3] were less than $1,733 and also less than 72.189% of your gross nonfarm income[4] **and (b)** you had net earnings from self-employment of at least $400 in 2 of the prior 3 years.

Caution. You may use this method no more than five times.

16	Subtract line 15 from line 14	**16**	
17	Enter the **smaller** of: two-thirds (⅔) of gross nonfarm income[4] (not less than zero) **or** the amount on line 16. Also include this amount on line 4b above	**17**	

[1] From Sch. F, line 11, and Sch. K-1 (Form 1065), box 14, code B.

[2] From Sch. F, line 36, and Sch. K-1 (Form 1065), box 14, code A.

[3] From Sch. C, line 31; Sch. C-EZ, line 3; Sch. K-1 (Form 1065), box 14, code A; and Sch. K-1 (Form 1065-B), box 9.

[4] From Sch. C, line 7; Sch. C-EZ, line 1; Sch. K-1 (Form 1065), box 14, code C; and Sch. K-1 (Form 1065-B), box 9.

Schedule SE (Form 1040) 2005

Form **8829**

Department of the Treasury
Internal Revenue Service (99)

Expenses for Business Use of Your Home

▶ File only with Schedule C (Form 1040). Use a separate Form 8829 for each home you used for business during the year.

▶ See separate instructions.

OMB No. 1545-1266

2005

Attachment
Sequence No. **66**

Name(s) of proprietor(s)   John Paul Jones

Your social security number   111 : 22 : 3344

Part I   Part of Your Home Used for Business

1	Area used regularly and exclusively for business, regularly for daycare, or for storage of inventory or product samples (see instructions)	**1**	200 SF
2	Total area of home	**2**	800 SF
3	Divide line 1 by line 2. Enter the result as a percentage	**3**	25%

• **For daycare facilities not used exclusively for business, also complete lines 4–6.**

• **All others, skip lines 4–6 and enter the amount from line 3 on line 7.**

4	Multiply days used for daycare during year by hours used per day	**4**	hr.
5	Total hours available for use during the year (365 days × 24 hours) (see instructions)	**5**	8,760 hr.
6	Divide line 4 by line 5. Enter the result as a decimal amount	**6**	.
7	Business percentage. For daycare facilities not used exclusively for business, multiply line 6 by line 3 (enter the result as a percentage). All others, enter the amount from line 3. ▶	**7**	%

Part II   Figure Your Allowable Deduction

		(a) Direct expenses	(b) Indirect expenses		
8	Enter the amount from Schedule C, line 29, **plus** any net gain or (loss) derived from the business use of your home and shown on Schedule D or Form 4797. If more than one place of business, see instructions			**8**	17,250
	See instructions for columns (a) and (b) before completing lines 9–20.				
9	Casualty losses (see instructions)	**9**			
10	Deductible mortgage interest (see instructions)	**10**	6,000		
11	Real estate taxes (see instructions)	**11**	4,000		
12	Add lines 9, 10, and 11	**12**	10,000		
13	Multiply line 12, column (b) by line 7	**13**	2,500		
14	Add line 12, column (a) and line 13			**14**	2,500
15	Subtract line 14 from line 8. If zero or less, enter -0-			**15**	14,750
16	Excess mortgage interest (see instructions)	**16**			
17	Insurance	**17**	900		
18	Repairs and maintenance	**18**			
19	Utilities	**19**	300		
20	Other expenses (see instructions)	**20**			
21	Add lines 16 through 20	**21**	1,200		
22	Multiply line 21, column (b) by line 7	**22**	300		
23	Carryover of operating expenses from 2004 Form 8829, line 41	**23**			
24	Add line 21 in column (a), line 22, and line 23			**24**	300
25	Allowable operating expenses. Enter the **smaller** of line 15 or line 24			**25**	300
26	Limit on excess casualty losses and depreciation. Subtract line 25 from line 15			**26**	13,950
27	Excess casualty losses (see instructions)	**27**			
28	Depreciation of your home from Part III below	**28**	1,429		
29	Carryover of excess casualty losses and depreciation from 2004 Form 8829, line 42	**29**			
30	Add lines 27 through 29			**30**	1,429
31	Allowable excess casualty losses and depreciation. Enter the **smaller** of line 26 or line 30			**31**	1,429
32	Add lines 14, 25, and 31			**32**	4,229
33	Casualty loss portion, if any, from lines 14 and 31. Carry amount to **Form 4684,** Section B			**33**	
34	Allowable expenses for business use of your home. Subtract line 33 from line 32. Enter here and on Schedule C, line 30. If your home was used for more than one business, see instructions ▶			**34**	4,229

Part III   Depreciation of Your Home

35	Enter the **smaller** of your home's adjusted basis or its fair market value (see instructions)	**35**	
36	Value of land included on line 35	**36**	
37	Basis of building. Subtract line 36 from line 35	**37**	
38	Business basis of building. Multiply line 37 by line 7	**38**	
39	Depreciation percentage (see instructions)	**39**	%
40	Depreciation allowable (see instructions). Multiply line 38 by line 39. Enter here and on line 28 above	**40**	

Part IV   Carryover of Unallowed Expenses to 2006

41	Operating expenses. Subtract line 25 from line 24. If less than zero, enter -0-	**41**	
42	Excess casualty losses and depreciation. Subtract line 31 from line 30. If less than zero, enter -0-	**42**	

For Paperwork Reduction Act Notice, see page 4 of separate instructions.   Cat. No. 13232M   Form **8829** (2005)

40

Mutual Funds

Introduction

Mutual funds come in all shapes and sizes. Generally, mutual funds are classified according to their investment objectives. Aggressive growth funds, for example, are characterized by high risk and high potential return. These funds typically seek long-term capital appreciation and do not produce significant interest income or dividends. The objectives of balanced funds, on the other hand, are to conserve an investor's initial principal, pay high current income through dividends, and promote the long-term growth of both principal and income. While aggressive growth funds generally invest only in stocks, balanced funds typically invest in both bonds and stocks. There are many other kinds of mutual funds—growth and income funds, bond funds, sector funds, index funds, and the like—all with different investing objectives and different strategies to achieve them. A general rule to keep in mind: The higher the potential reward from your investment, the greater the risk that you may not achieve the expected return.

*A **money market fund** is a mutual fund that tries to increase current income available to shareholders by purchasing short-term market investments.*

This chapter explains how differing distributions that you may receive from a mutual fund are taxed as well as the different methods by which you may calculate your gain or loss when you sell your mutual fund shares. It also discusses some of the expenses you may incur when investing in mutual funds.

Kinds of Mutual Funds

A mutual fund is a regulated investment company generally created by "pooling" funds of investors to allow them to take advantage of a diversity of investments and professional management.

The advantages that investment companies can offer you are numerous, including:

- Professional investment management of assets at a relatively low cost
- Ownership in a diversified portfolio
- Potentially lower commissions, because the investment company buys and sells in large blocks
- Prospectuses and reports of various periodicals to assist people in readily accessing information needed to perform fund comparisons
- Other special services, such as dividend reinvestment plans, periodic withdrawal and investment plans, the ability to switch between funds by telephone or over the Internet, and in some cases, check writing privileges

Investment Objectives

Mutual funds are classified according to their investment objectives. Following is a summary of the various types of funds categorized by their investment objective.

Aggressive Growth Funds. These funds are characterized by high risk and high potential return: They typically seek capital appreciation and do not produce significant interest income or dividends.

Growth Funds. Growth funds aim to achieve an increase in the value of their investments over the long term (capital gains) rather than paying dividends.

Growth and Income Funds. Also called "equity-income" and "total return" funds, these funds aim to balance the objectives of long-term growth and current income.

Balanced Funds. These funds have three objectives: to conserve investors' initial principal, to pay high current income through dividends and interest, and to promote long-term growth of both principal and income. Balanced funds invest in both bonds and stocks.

Bond Funds. Bond mutual funds invest primarily in bonds. Some funds may concentrate on short-term bonds, others on intermediate-term bonds, and still others on long-term bonds.

Sector Funds. Sector funds invest in one industry, such as biotechnology or retail, and therefore do not offer the diversity you generally receive from a diversified growth mutual fund, which might invest a portion of the fund assets in a variety of sectors.

Index Funds. Index mutual funds re-create a particular market index (e.g., the S&P 500). The holdings and the return should mirror that of the index.

Types of Regulated Investment Companies

In addition to categorizing investment companies by their investment objectives, investment companies are classified according to their capital structure. The three types are:

- Closed-end funds
- Unit investment trusts
- Open-end funds

Closed-End Funds. Closed-end investment companies have a set capital structure with a specified number of shares. For this reason, investors must generally purchase existing shares of closed-end funds from current stockholders. Investors who wish to liquidate their position in closed-end investment companies must sell their shares to other investors. Shares in closed-end funds are therefore traded on the open market just like the stock of publicly held corporations. As a result, closed-end funds have an additional risk that isn't present in open-end funds—their price does not necessarily equal their net asset value. Therefore, there is a risk that the fund's shares could sell for less than the value of the underlying investments. However, closed-end funds that are purchased at a discount from the value of the underlying investments can produce an opportunity for greater return.

Unit Investment Trusts. Unit investment trusts are a variation of closed-end funds. Unit investment trusts typically invest in a fixed portfolio of bonds that are held until maturity rather than managed and traded, as is the case with bond mutual funds. As an investor you purchase units that represent an ownership in the trust assets. Because the bonds are not actively traded, the annual fees charged for unit trusts may be lower than those charged by bond mutual funds. The unit trust collects the interest income and repayment of principal of the bonds held in the portfolio and distributes these funds to the unit holders. Unit investment trusts can provide you with a portfolio of bonds that have different maturity dates and an average holding period that meets your objectives. Cash flow is relatively predictable, because the intention is to hold the bonds until maturity.

Open-End Funds. Commonly referred to as mutual funds, open-end funds differ from closed-end funds in that they do not have a fixed number of shares to issue. Instead, the number of shares outstanding varies as investors purchase and redeem them directly from the open-end investment company. An investor who wants a position in a particular mutual fund purchases the shares from the fund either through a brokerage firm or by contacting the fund company directly. Conversely, mutual fund shareholders who want to liquidate their position sell their shares back to the company. The value of a share in a mutual fund is determined by the net asset value (NAV). Funds compute NAV by dividing the value of the fund's total net assets by the number of shares outstanding.

Mutual Funds Fees

The costs associated with open-end fund shares resemble those for closed-end funds. Like closed-end funds, open-end funds bear the trading costs and investment management fees of the investment company. However, mutual fund investors may or may not be subject to a sales charge referred to as a "load."

Depending on the type of load charged (if any), open-end mutual funds are classified as:

- No-load funds
- 12b-1 funds
- Load funds

No-Load Funds. No-load funds don't impose a sales charge on their investors. Purchases and sales of shares in a no-load fund are made at the fund's NAV per share. Consequently, every dollar invested gets allocated to the fund for investment rather than having a portion permanently kept back to cover sales charges.

12b-1 Funds. 12b-1 funds are a variation on no-load funds. While every dollar paid into the fund is committed to investment, the 12b-1 fund shareholders indirectly pay an annual fee to cover the fund's sales and marketing costs. This 12b-1 fee typically ranges from 0.1% to the maximum 1% of total fund assets. [*Note:* The 12b-1 fee is assessed every year (instead of only once); thus, the longer you hold your 12b-1 fund shares, the greater the sales charge you will bear.]

Load Funds. Load funds charge the shareholder a direct commission at the time of purchase and/or when the shares are redeemed and may also assess ongoing 12b-1 fees. "Front-end loads" are charged to the investor at the time of purchase and can be as high as 8.5% of the gross amount invested. On the other hand, some load funds charge their shareholders the load at the time their shares are redeemed. This cost will be either a "back-end load" or a "redemption fee." A back-end load is based on the lesser of the initial cost or final value of the shares redeemed and may disappear after a certain number of years. A redemption fee is similar to a back-end load, but is based on the value of the shares you choose to redeem rather than your initial investment. It typically applies if the investor sells within a very short period of time (usually 30 to 90 days). The purpose of such fees is to discourage shareholders from short-term trading of fund shares.

All fees, loads, and charges reduce your investment return. Therefore, you should consider not only a fund's return, but all of the expenses that affect this return.

Foreign Stock Mutual Funds

Many stock mutual funds invest in foreign stocks. They are divided into the following categories:

- *Global or world funds.* These funds invest anywhere in the world, including the United States.
- *International or foreign funds.* Such funds invest anywhere in the world except the United States.

- *Regional funds.* These invest in specific geographic areas, such as Europe, Latin America, or the Pacific Rim.
- *Country funds.* Funds of this sort invest entirely in a specific country. For the most part, single country funds are closed-end mutual funds that typically trade on either the New York Stock Exchange or the American Stock Exchange.
- *International index funds.* These are mutual funds that parallel the concept of a domestic equity index fund. They are designed and operated so that their portfolios mirror the composition of the market index after which the funds are named.

Foreign Bond Mutual Funds

In addition to foreign stock funds, numerous foreign bond funds are available for investment. Because economic conditions differ from country to country, interest rates vary as well. At any given time, you can usually find several countries with interest rates higher than those in the United States. There is a downside to consider, though. Overseas interest rates may be more attractive, but language barriers, differing regulations, and illiquid markets all increase the challenge of foreign investments. Fluctuating currency values, although a potential advantage, can work against you if the currency of your foreign investment loses value relative to the U.S. dollar.

For more about mutual fund investing see *Ernst & Young's Personal Financial Planning Guide, Special Tax Edition.*

Tax Treatment of Distributions

A mutual fund will send you a Form 1099-DIV, *Dividends and Distributions,* or a substitute form containing substantially the same language, to tell you what you must report or take into account on your income tax return. See *How to Report,* later.

TAXPLANNER

How mutual funds are taxed. Which mutual fund or funds you choose will depend largely on your own investment objectives. But one factor you should definitely consider is how your mutual fund investment will be taxed. Generally, a mutual fund is a conduit for tax purposes—that is, the fund does not ordinarily pay income taxes, but its shareholders do. Interest, dividends, gains, and losses are generally passed through to shareholders in a fund in the form of dividends and capital gains distributions. As a shareholder, you are liable for any taxes due on these distributions. Consequently, it can matter enormously how those gains and losses are taxed.

Dividends declared at the end of one year but not paid until the next. Often, a mutual fund will declare a dividend at the end of the calendar year but not pay it until January of the following year. Nevertheless, you are treated as having received the dividend in the year in which it was declared.

Example

A fund declares a dividend in December 2005 payable to shareholders owning stock on that date. This is known as the record date. The dividend is not paid until January 2006. You are treated as having received the dividend on December 31, 2005.

TAXSAVER

Timing your purchase of a mutual fund. You should pay close attention to the timing of your purchase of a mutual fund. For example, if you invest in a fund near the end of the year and the fund shortly thereafter makes a year-end distribution, you will have to pay tax on the distribution even though from your point of view you are simply getting back the capital you just invested in the fund. In effect, all you've done is "bought" taxable income that the fund earned earlier in the year but had not yet paid out to shareholders. Typically, the fund's share price drops by the amount of the distribution. Your cost basis in the mutual fund, however, will be the predistribution price you paid for the shares.

There is one consolation. Your higher basis will reduce any capital gain on a later sale. Moreover, if you sell the fund at a loss, it will increase your capital loss. If you want to limit your current tax liability and lower your basis in the shares, you should delay your purchase of fund shares until after the record date for the distribution. Usually, a fund can tell you when distributions, if any, for the year are expected. Alternatively, you can consult investment publications, such as *Morningstar Mutual Funds,* which indicate distribution dates for the previous year.

Example

ABC Fund declares and distributes a $1 dividend on December 1. If you had purchased 1,000 shares at $10 per share on November 30, you will have to report $1,000 of income for 2005. If instead you bought the shares on December 2, after the record date, you will pay $9 per share and have no taxable income to report in 2005. Of course, for the shares bought on November 30, your basis would be $10 per share instead of $9.

TAXSAVER

Year end selling. If you are thinking of selling shares in a mutual fund, particularly near the end of the year when many funds pay dividends, you should consider redeeming your shares before any upcoming dividend is paid by the fund. If your shares are worth more than you paid and are held for more than one year, it might be to your advantage to sell the shares before a dividend is declared to take advantage of the 15% maximum long-term capital gains tax rate. If you wait until after the dividend is declared to sell, there is the possibility that some portion of the dividend may not be qualified dividend income and therefore be taxed at the higher ordinary income tax rates. Additionally, if your shares are worth more than you paid and if you have capital losses available in the current year, it might be to your advantage to sell the shares before a dividend is declared. The gain on the sale of the mutual fund shares, unlike the dividend income, can be offset by the capital losses. However, if your shares are worth less than what you paid for them, you can minimize your capital losses by selling the shares before the dividend is paid. Remember, the net asset value per share of the fund (that is, the amount you would receive on the redemption of your shares) decreases by the amount of the dividend.

Community property states. If you are married and receive a distribution that is community income, one-half of the distribution is generally considered to be received by each spouse. If you file separate returns, you must each report one-half of any taxable distribution. Get Publication 555, *Community Property,* for more information on community income.

If the distribution is not considered community income under state law and you and your spouse file separate returns, each of you must report your separate taxable distributions.

Kinds of Distributions

There are several kinds of distributions that you, as a shareholder, may receive from a mutual fund. They include:

- Ordinary dividends,
- Capital gain distributions,
- Exempt-interest dividends, and
- Return of capital (nontaxable) distributions.

Tax-exempt mutual fund. Distributions from a tax-exempt mutual fund (one that invests primarily in tax-exempt securities) may consist of ordinary dividends, capital gain distributions, undistributed capital gains, or return of capital like any other mutual fund. These distributions generally are treated the same as distributions from a regular mutual fund. Distributions designated as exempt-interest dividends are not taxable.

All other distributions generally follow the same rules as a regular mutual fund. Regardless of what type of mutual fund you have (whether regular or tax-exempt), when you dispose of your shares (sell, exchange, or redeem), you usually will have a taxable gain or a deductible loss to report.

For more information on figuring taxable gains and losses see *Sales Exchanges and Redemptions,* later. Also see Chapter 17, *Reporting Gains and Losses,* for further information.

Ordinary Dividends

An ordinary dividend is a distribution by a mutual fund out of its earnings and profits. Include ordinary dividends that you receive from a mutual fund as dividend income on your individual income tax return.

TaxAlert

Dividend distributions from a mutual fund, such as dividends earned from the fund's investment securities, are generally treated as a net capital gain for purposes of applying the capital gain tax rates for both the regular tax and the alternative minimum tax. In order to be eligible for the lower capital gain (versus ordinary) income tax rate, the mutual fund must hold the underlying stock for a specified time period. Each year the mutual fund will be required to report to each shareholder the amount of dividends that qualify for the favorable capital gain and/or ordinary income tax treatment.

Ordinary dividends are the most common type of dividends. They will be reported in box 1 of the Form 1099-DIV or on a similar statement you receive from the mutual fund.

Qualified Dividends.

Many ordinary dividends you received in 2005 are also classified as qualified dividends. The amount of your qualified dividends will be shown in box 1b of Form 1099–DIV or on a similar statement you get from the mutual fund.

Qualified dividends are taxed at the same lower rates that apply to a net capital gain. They are taxed at 15% if the regular tax rate that would apply is 25% or higher. They are taxed at 5% if the regular tax rate that would apply is 10% or 15%.

To be a qualified dividend subject to the 5% or 15% rate, a dividend must meet all of the following requirements.

1. The dividend must have been paid by a U.S. corporation or a qualified foreign corporation. See chapter 1 of Publication 550 for the definition of a qualified foreign corporation.
2. The dividend must not be of a type excluded by law from the definition of a qualified dividend. See chapter 1 of Publication 550 for a list of these types of dividends.
3. You must meet the holding period requirement (discussed next).

Holding period.

You must have held the stock for more than 60 days during the 121-day period that begins 60 days before the ex-dividend date. The ex-dividend date is the first date following the declaration of a dividend on which the buyer of a stock will not receive the next dividend payment. Instead, the seller will get the dividend.

When counting the number of days you held the stock, include the day you disposed of the stock, but not the day you acquired it. See chapter 1 of Publication 550 for more information about qualified dividends.

TaxAlert

Mutual funds that pass through dividend income to their shareholders must meet the holding period test for the dividend-paying stocks that they hold in order for the amounts they pay out to be reported as qualified dividends on Form 1099-DIV. In addition, investors must then meet the holding period test for the shares owned in the mutual fund in order for the qualified dividends reported to them to be taxed at the lower rates. If investors do not meet the holding period test, they can not claim the lower tax rate on the qualified dividend income reported to them on Form 1099-DIV and must classify the qualified dividends as ordinary dividends.

Capital Gain Distributions

Capital gain distributions (also called capital gain dividends) are paid to you or credited to your account by *regulated investment companies* (commonly called *mutual funds*) and *real estate investment trusts (REITs).* They will be shown in box 2a of the Form 1099-DIV you receive from the mutual fund or REIT.

Report capital gain distributions as long-term capital gains regardless of how long you owned your shares in the mutual fund or REIT.

Explanation

A capital gains distribution from a fund represents net long-term capital gains realized by the fund. While a fund may also realize net long-term losses from the sale of securities, it is not permitted to pass through these losses to shareholders. Instead, the fund must carry net capital losses forward to offset any future capital gains. Generally, all dividend and capital gains distributions from a fund are subject to federal and state income taxes. Dividends from municipal bond or municipal money market funds are the exception. These dividends are usually exempt from federal income tax and may also be exempt from state and local income taxes, depending on where you live and your state's tax law. See the above discussion on tax-exempt mutual funds. For more information on reporting capital gains and losses from the sale of mutual fund shares, see the discussion on gains and losses later in this chapter.

☐ CORRECTED (if checked)

PAYER'S name, street address, city, state, ZIP code, and telephone no.		1a Total ordinary dividends $	OMB No. 1545-0110	Dividends and Distributions
		1b Qualified dividends $	20**05** Form **1099-DIV**	
		2a Total capital gain distr. $	2b Unrecap. Sec. 1250 gain $	Copy B For Recipient
PAYER'S Federal identification number	RECIPIENT'S identification number			
RECIPIENT'S name		2c Section 1202 gain $	2d Collectibles (28%) gain $	This is important tax information and is being furnished to the Internal Revenue Service. If you are required to file a return, a negligence penalty or other sanction may be imposed on you if this income is taxable and the IRS determines that it has not been reported.
		3 Nondividend distributions $	4 Federal income tax withheld $	
Street address (including apt. no.)			5 Investment expenses $	
City, state, and ZIP code		6 Foreign tax paid $	7 Foreign country or U.S. possession	
Account number (see instructions)		8 Cash liquidation distributions $	9 Noncash liquidation distributions $	

Form **1099-DIV** (keep for your records) Department of the Treasury - Internal Revenue Service

---

TAXSAVER

High-turnover funds. Before you invest in a mutual fund, you should consider the rate at which the fund turns over its assets. A fund with a high turnover rate will generate frequent gains and losses, increasing the chances that capital distributions will be short term, rather than long term. Short-term capital gain distributions are reported and taxed as ordinary income dividends; long-term capital gains are eligible for the lower long-term capital gain rate.

Undistributed capital gains of mutual funds and REITs. Some mutual funds and REITs keep their long-term capital gains and pay tax on them. You must treat your share of these gains as distributions, even though you did not actually receive them. However, they are not included on Form 1099-DIV. Instead, they are reported to you on **Form 2439,** *Notice to Shareholder of Undistributed Long-Term Capital Gains.*

Report undistributed capital gains shown in box la of Form 2439 as long-term capital gains in column (f) on line 11 of Schedule D (Form 1040). If there is an amount shown in box 1b of Form 2439, report that amount in column (g) on line 11 of Schedule D. The tax paid on these gains by the mutual fund or REIT is shown in box 2 of Form 2439. You take credit for this tax by including it on line 70, Form 1040, and checking box a on that line. Attach Copy B of Form 2439 to your return, and keep Copy C for your records.

TAXORGANIZER

Undistributed capital gains. A mutual fund will report the amount of undistributed capital gains to you on Form 2439, not on Form 1099-DIV.

A special rule exists for capital gain distributions you receive when you sell your shares in the fund at a loss within 6 months of the date of original purchase. In this case, the portion of your capital loss attributable to the capital gain dividend is treated as a long-term— not a short-term—capital loss.

Basis adjustment. You should increase your basis in your mutual fund or your interest in a REIT by the difference between the gain you report and the credit you claim for the tax paid.
Additional information. For more information on the treatment of distributions from mutual funds, see Publication 564.

Exempt-Interest Dividends

A mutual fund may pay exempt-interest dividends to its shareholders if it meets certain requirements. These dividends are paid from tax-exempt interest earned by the fund. Since the exempt-interest dividends keep their tax-exempt character, do not include them in income. However, you may need to report them on your return. See *Information reporting requirement,* next. The mutual fund will send you a statement within 60 days after the close of its tax year showing your exempt-interest dividends. Exempt-interest dividends are not shown on Form 1099-DIV.
Information reporting requirement. Although exempt-interest dividends are not taxable, you must report them on your tax return if you are required to file. This is an information reporting requirement and does ***not*** convert tax-exempt interest to taxable interest. In addition, you may be required to add the tax-exempt interest back to your state income tax return if it is interest paid by a state other than your state of residence.

TAXPLANNER

"Tax-preference" dividends. Some or all of your tax-exempt dividends may be treated as a "tax preference item" and may be subject to the alternative minimum tax (AMT). The mutual fund company will let you know what percentage of your dividends is a tax preference. If you receive exempt-interest dividends, you should obtain Form 6251, *Alternative Minimum Tax—Individuals,* for more information.

Return of Capital (Nontaxable) Distributions

A distribution that is not out of earnings and profits is a return of your investment, or capital, in the mutual fund and is shown in box 3 of Form 1099-DIV. These returns of capital distributions are not taxed as ordinary dividends and are sometimes called tax-free dividends or nontaxable distributions. However, they may be fully or partly taxable as capital gains.

A return of capital distribution reduces your basis in the shares. Basis is explained in Chapter 14, *Basis of Property.* Your basis cannot be reduced below zero. If your basis is reduced to zero, you must report the return of capital distribution on your tax return as a capital gain. The distribution is taxable if it, when added to all return of capital distributions received in past years, is more than your basis in the shares. Report this capital gain on Schedule D (Form 1040). Whether it is a long-term or short-term capital gain depends on how long you held the shares.

Table 40-1. **Reporting Mutual Fund Distributions on Form 1040**

TYPE OF DISTRIBUTION	WHERE TO REPORT IF TOTAL DIVIDENDS FROM ALL PAYERS ARE:	
	$ 1,500 OR LESS	**MORE THAN $ 1,500**
Ordinary Dividends Form 1099-DIV, box 1a	Form 1040, line 9a	Schedule B, line 5
Qualified Dividends Form 1099-DIV, box 1b	Form 1040, line 9b, and Qualified Dividends and Capital Gain Tax Worksheet, line 2	Form 1040, line 9b, and Schedule D Tax Worksheet, line 2
Capital Gain Distributions Form 1099-DIV, Boxes 2a-2d	Schedule D, line 13, column (f) (Form 1040, line 13 if no other capital gains)	Schedule D, line 13, column (f) (Form 1040, line 13 if no other capital gains)
Nontaxable Distributions Form 1099-DIV, Box 3	Basis of shares reduced to zero? No - Nontaxable until zero Yes - Report on Schedule D	Basis of shares reduced to zero? No - Nontaxable until zero Yes - Report on Schedule D
Exempt-Interest Dividends Not Included on Form 1099-DIV	Form 1040, line 8b	Form 1040, line 8b
Undistributed Capital Gains Form 2439, Box 1a	Gain - Schedule D, line 11, column (f)	Gain - Schedule D, line 11, column (f)

Example

In 1993, Jane Smith bought shares in ABC Mutual Fund for $10 a share. In 1994, she received a return of capital distribution of $2 a share, which reduces her basis in each share by $2 to an adjusted basis of $8. In 1995, Jane received a return of capital of $4 per share, reducing her basis in each share from $8 to $4. In 2005, the return of capital distribution from the mutual fund is $5 a share. Jane will report the $1 excess per share as a long-term capital gain on Schedule D.

Reinvestment of dividends. Many mutual funds offer dividend reinvestment plans in which you may use your dividends to buy more shares of stock in the mutual fund instead of receiving the dividends in cash. If you reinvest your dividends, you still must report the dividends on your return. Whether you include the reinvested dividends in income depends on the nature of the dividend. For example, if you reinvest your tax-exempt dividends, you do not have to include them in income. On the other hand, if you reinvest your ordinary dividends, you will need to report dividend income.

How To Report

You must report mutual fund distributions on Form 1040 or Form 1040A. You cannot report mutual fund distributions on Form 1040EZ.

You **cannot** use Form 1040A and **must** use Form 1040 in either of the following situations.

• You received a return of capital distribution that must be reported as a capital gain because it is more than your basis in your mutual fund shares.
• You must report an undistributed capital gain.

Table 40-1, *Reporting Mutual Fund Distributions on Form 1040,* explains where on Form 1040 or its related schedules to report distributions from mutual funds.

If your only capital gains are from mutual funds distributions, you should report them on line 13 of Form 1040 and not on Schedule D. In addition, check the box on line 13 that you are not required to file Schedule D. Make sure you calculate the tax using the table in the instructions.

TAXSAVER

If you did not have any capital gain or nontaxable distributions, you may be able to file Form 1040A rather than Form 1040. See Chapter 1, *Filing Information,* for further details.

Foreign tax deduction or credit. Some mutual funds invest in foreign securities or other instruments. Your mutual fund may choose to allow you to claim a deduction or credit for the taxes it paid to a foreign country or U.S. possession. The fund will notify you if this applies to you. The notice will include your share of the foreign taxes paid to each country or possession and the part of the dividend derived from sources in each country or possession.

Explanation

You must complete Form 1116 if you choose to claim the credit for income tax paid to a foreign country. You do not have to complete Form 1116 if your total foreign taxes paid is $300 or less for the year ($600 if married filing jointly). You can claim the credit for the full amount of the taxes paid as long as your foreign income is all passive (i.e., interest dividends, etc.). Under certain circumstances, however, it may be to your benefit to treat the tax as an itemized deduction on Schedule A (Form 1040).

For a discussion of the foreign tax credit and whether you should claim the credit or a tax deduction, see Chapter 24, *Taxes You May Deduct.*

Sales, Exchanges, and Redemptions

When you sell or exchange your mutual fund shares, or if they are redeemed (a redemption), you will generally have a taxable gain or a deductible loss. This also applies to shares of a tax-exempt mutual fund. Sales, exchanges, and redemptions are all treated as sales of capital assets. The amount of the gain or loss is the difference between your adjusted basis (defined earlier) in the shares and the amount you realize from the sale, exchange, or redemption.

In general, a sale is a transfer of shares for money only. An exchange is a transfer of shares in return for other shares. A redemption occurs when a fund reacquires its shares from you in exchange for money or other property.

Information returns. Brokers must report to the Internal Revenue Service the proceeds from sales, exchanges, or redemptions. Brokers must give each customer a written statement with that information by January 31 of the year following the calendar year the transaction occurred. Form 1099-B, *Proceeds From Broker and Barter Exchange Transactions,* or a substitute, may be used for this purpose. Report your sales shown on Form(s) 1099-B (or substitute) on Schedule D (Form 1040) along with your other gains and losses. If the total sales reported on Form(s) 1099-B is more than the total you report on Schedule D, attach a statement to your return explaining the difference.

Taxpayer identification number. You must give the broker your correct taxpayer identification number (TIN). Generally, an individual will use his or her social security number as the TIN. If you do not provide your TIN, your broker is required to withhold tax at a rate of 30% on the gross proceeds of a transaction, and you may be penalized.

Keeping Track of Your Basis

You should keep track of your basis in mutual fund shares because you need the basis to figure any gain or loss on the shares when you sell, exchange, or redeem them. The basis depends on how the shares were acquired.

Shares Acquired by Purchase

The original basis of mutual fund shares you bought is usually their cost or purchase price. The purchase price usually includes any commissions or load charges paid for the purchase.

broker for the purchase. His cost basis for each share is $10.50 ($2,100 ÷ 200).

Commissions and load charges. The fees and charges you pay to acquire or redeem shares of a mutual fund are not deductible. You can usually add acquisition fees and charges to your cost of the shares and thereby increase your basis. A fee paid to redeem the shares is usually a reduction in the redemption price (sales price).

You cannot add your entire acquisition fee or load charge to the cost of mutual fund shares if *all* of the following conditions apply.

1) You get a reinvestment right because of the purchase of the shares or the payment of the fee or charge.
2) You dispose of the shares within 90 days of the purchase date.
3) You acquire new shares in the same mutual fund or another mutual fund, for which the fee or charge is reduced or waived because of the reinvestment right.

The amount of the original load charge in excess of the reduction in (3) is added to the cost of the original shares. The rest of the original load charge is added to the cost basis of the new shares (unless all three conditions above apply to the purchase of the new shares).

Reinvestment right. This is the right to acquire mutual fund shares in the same or another mutual fund without paying a fee or load charge, or by paving a reduced fee or load charge.

Shares Acquired by Reinvestment

The original cost basis of mutual fund shares you acquire by reinvesting your distributions is the amount of the distributions used to purchase each full or fractional share. This rule applies even if the distribution is an exempt-interest dividend that you do not report as income.

Shares Acquired by Gift or Inheritance

See Chapter 14, *Basis of Property.*

Adjusted Basis

After you acquire mutual fund shares, you may need to make adjustments to your basis. The adjusted basis of your shares is your original basis (defined earlier), increased or reduced as described here.
Addition to basis. Increase the basis in your shares by the difference between the amount of undistributed capital gain you include in income and the tax considered paid by you on that income.

The mutual fund reports the amount of your undistributed capital gain in box 1a of Form 2439. You should keep Copy C of all Forms 2439 to show increases in the basis of your shares.

Reduction of basis. You must reduce your basis in your shares by any return of capital distributions that you receive from the fund.

No reduction of basis. You do not reduce your basis for distributions from the fund that are exempt-interest dividends.

Identifying the Shares Sold

To figure your gain or loss when you dispose of mutual fund shares, you need to determine which shares were sold and the basis of those shares. If your shares in a mutual fund were acquired all on the same day and for the same price, figuring their basis is not difficult. However, shares are generally acquired at various times, in various quantities, and at various prices. Therefore, figuring your basis can be more difficult. You can choose to use either a cost basis or an average basis to figure your gain or loss. See Table 40-2, *Choosing a Basis Method.*

Table 40-2. **Choosing a Basis Method**

Basis Method	Advantages/Disadvantages
Specific identification	The most flexible way to determine your gains and losses. But there are important restrictions governing its use.
FIFO (first-in first-out)	The simplest approach. But it may mean a large gain if your shares have appreciated significantly and you are redeeming only part of your account.
Average cost (single category)	The middle ground. A more modest tax burden than the FIFO method but more tedious calculations if you sell shares frequently.
Average cost (double category)	Only makes sense if (1) you have elected it in the past and are required to continue using it and (2) there is a tax benefit from maintaining separate short- and long-term average costs.

Cost Basis

Under the *cost basis,* you can choose one of the following methods:

• Specific share identification, or
• FIFO

Specific share identification. If you can definitely identify the shares you sold, you can use the adjusted basis of those particular shares to figure your gain or loss.

You will adequately identify your mutual fund shares, even if you bought the shares in different lots at various prices and times, if you:

1) Specify to your broker or other agent the particular shares to be sold or transferred at the time of the sale or transfer, and

2) Receive confirmation of your specification from your broker in writing within a reasonable time.

The confirmation by the mutual fund must confirm that you instructed your broker to sell particular shares. You continue to have the burden of proving that you owned the specified shares at the time of sale or transfer.

First-in first-out (FIFO). If the shares were acquired at different times or at different prices and you cannot identify which shares you sold, use the basis of the shares you acquired first as the basis of the shares sold. Therefore, the oldest shares still available are considered sold first. You should keep a separate record of each purchase and any dispositions of the shares until all shares purchased at the same time have been disposed of completely. Table 40-3, *How to Figure Basis of Shares Sold,* shows how to figure a gain or loss on a sale of shares in a mutual fund using the FIFO method.

Average Basis

You may choose to use an average basis to figure your gain or loss when you sell all or part of your shares in a regulated investment company, if you acquired the shares at various times and prices, and you left the shares on deposit in an account handled by a custodian or agent who acquires or redeems those shares.

Once you elect to use an average basis, you must continue to use it for all accounts in the same fund. However, you may specify cost basis for shares in other funds, even those within the same family of funds.

Example
You own two accounts in the income fund issued by Company A. You also own 100 shares of the growth fund issued by Company A. If you elect to use average basis for the first account of the income fund, you must use average basis for the second account. However, you may use cost basis for the growth fund.

To figure average basis, you can use one of the following methods:

• Single-category method
• Double-category method

Single-category method. All shares are included in a single category. The adjusted basis of each share is the total adjusted basis of all shares in the category at the time of a disposition, divided by the number of shares in the category. In determining the holding period, the shares disposed of are considered to be those shares acquired first.

Example
John Smith bought the following shares in the GLM Mutual Fund: 100 shares in 2003 at $10 per share, 100 shares in 2004 at $12 a share, and 100 shares in 2005 at $26 a share. The 300 shares cost a total of $4,800. The average basis per share is $16 ($4,800 ÷ 300).

Remaining shares. The basis of your shares determined under average basis is the basis of *all* your shares in the account. That is, the basis of the remaining shares is the same as the basis of the shares sold.

Double-category method. All shares in an account at the time of each disposition are divided into two categories: short-term and long-term. Shares held one year or less are short-term. Shares held longer than one year are long-term.

The adjusted basis of each share in a category is the total adjusted

Table 40-3. **How to Figure Basis of Shares Sold**

This is an example showing two different ways to figure basis. It compares the cost basis using the FIFO method and the average basis using the single-category method.				
Date	**Action**	**Share Price**	**No. of Shares**	**Total Shares Owned**
02/4/04	Invest $4,000	$25	160	160
08/5/04	Invest $4,800	$20	240	400
12/16/04	Reinvest $300 dividend	$30	10	410
09/29/05	Sell $6,720	$32	210	200

COST BASIS (FIFO)

To figure the basis of the 210 shares sold on 9/29/05, use the share price of the first 210 shares you bought, namely the 160 shares you purchased on 2/4/04 and 50 of those purchased on 8/5/04.

	$4,000	(cost of 160 shares on 2/4/04)
+	$1,000	(cost of 50 shares on 8/5/04)
Basis =	$5,000	

AVERAGE BASIS (single-category)

To figure the basis of the 210 shares sold on 9/29/05 use the average basis of all 410 shares owned on 9/29/05.

	$9,100	(cost of 410 shares)
÷	410	(number of shares)
	$22.20	(average basis per share)
	$22.20	
×	210	
Basis =	$4,662	

basis of all shares in that category at the time of disposition divided by the total shares in the category. You may specify, to the custodian or agent handling your account, from which category the shares are to be sold or transferred. The custodian or agent must confirm *in writing* your specification. If you do not specify or receive confirmation, you must first charge the shares sold against the long-term category and then, any remaining shares sold against the short-term category.

Changing categories. After you have held a mutual fund share for more than one year, you must transfer that share from the short-term category to the long-term category. When you make the change, the basis of a transferred share is its actual cost or adjusted basis to you, or if some of the shares in the short-term category have been disposed of, its basis under the average basis method. The basis of the undisposed shares left in the short-term category that are changed to the long-term category is the average basis of the shares in the short-term category at the time of the most recent disposition from this category.

Making the choice. You choose to use the average basis of mutual fund shares by clearly showing on your income tax return, for each year the choice applies, that you used an average basis in reporting gain or loss from the sale or transfer of the shares. You must specify whether you used the single-category method or the double-category method in determining average basis. This choice is effective until you get permission from the IRS to revoke it.

Making the choice for gift shares. If your account includes shares that you received by gift, and the fair market value of the shares at the time of the gift was less than the donor's basis, special rules apply. To use the average basis, you must submit a statement with your initial choice to use one of the average basis methods. It must state that the basis used in figuring the average basis of the

gift shares under either method will be the FMV at the time of the gift. This statement applies to gift shares you receive before and after making the choice, as long as the choice to use the average basis is in effect. If you do not make this statement, you cannot choose to use the average basis for any account that contains gift shares.

Gains and Losses

You figure gain or loss on the disposition of your shares by comparing the **amount you realize** with the **adjusted basis** of your shares. If the amount you realize is more than the adjusted basis of the shares, you have a gain. If the amount you realize is less than the adjusted basis of the shares, you have a loss.

Amount you realize. The amount you realize from a disposition of your shares is the money and value of any property you receive for the shares disposed of, minus your expenses of sale (such as redemption fees, sales commissions, sales charges, or exit fees).

Adjusted basis. Adjusted basis is explained under *Keeping Track of Your Basis,* earlier.

Reporting on Schedule D. Mutual funds and brokers report dispositions of mutual fund shares on Form 1099-B, or a substitute form containing substantially the same language. The form shows the amount of the sales price and indicates whether the amount reported is the gross amount or the net amount (gross amount minus commissions).

If your Form 1099-B or similar statement from the payer shows the gross sales price, do not subtract the expenses of sale from it when reporting your sales price in column (d) on Schedule D. Instead, report the gross amount in column (d) and increase your cost or other basis, column (e), by any expense of the sale. If your Form 1099-B shows that the gross sales price less commissions was reported to IRS, enter the net amount in column (d) of Schedule D and *do not* increase your basis in column (e) by the sales commission.

Example 1
Linda Jones sold 200 shares of Fund B for $5,000. She paid a $150 commission to the broker for handling the sale. Her Form 1099-B shows that the net sales proceeds, $4,850 ($5,000 − $150), were reported to the IRS. Report this amount in column (d) of Schedule D.

Example 2
Joe Green sold 100 shares of Fund KLM for $5,000. He paid a $50 commission to the broker for handling the sale. He bought the shares for $2,500. Joe's broker reported the gross proceeds to the IRS on Form 1099-B, so he must increase his basis in column (e) of Schedule D to $2,550.

Holding Period

When you dispose of your mutual fund shares, you must determine your holding period. Your holding period determines whether the gain or loss is a short-term capital gain or loss or a long-term capital gain or loss.

Short-term gain or loss. If you hold the shares for one year or less, your gain or loss will be a short-term gain or loss.

Long-term gain or loss. If you hold the shares for more than one year, your gain or loss will be a long-term gain or loss.

Determining period held. Determine your holding period by using the trade dates of your purchases and your sales. The *trade date* is the date on which you contract to buy or sell shares. Most mutual funds will show the trade dates on confirmation statements showing your purchases and sales.

To find out how long you have held your shares, begin counting on the day after the trade date on which you bought the shares. (Do not count the trade date itself.) The trade date on which you dispose of the shares is counted as part of your holding period.

Example
Assume Lori Hill bought shares in XYZ Mutual Fund on January 13, 2004 (trade date). She starts counting on January 14, and the 14th of each following month is the beginning of a new month. Therefore, if she sells the shares on January 13, 2005 (trade date), her holding period would not be more than 1 year. However, if she sells them on January 14, 2005, her holding period would be more than 1 year (12 months plus 1 day).

Mutual fund shares received as a gift. If you receive a gift of mutual fund shares and your basis is determined by the donor's basis, your holding period is considered to have started on the same day that the donor's holding period started.

Inherited mutual fund shares. If you inherit mutual fund shares, you are considered to have held the shares for more than 1 year (even if you disposed of the shares within 1 year after the decedent's death). Your basis in the shares is:

1. The fair market value at the date of the decedent's death (or the alternate valuation date), or
2. The decedent's adjusted basis (in the case of shares decedent received as a gift from you in the year prior to decedent's death).

Report the sale of inherited mutual fund shares on line 8 of Schedule D and write "Inherited" in column (b) instead of the date you acquired the shares.

Reinvested distributions. If your dividends and capital gain distributions are reinvested in new shares, the holding period of each new share begins the day after that share was purchased. Therefore, if you sell both the new shares and the original shares, you might have both short-term and long-term gains and losses.

Certain short-term losses. Special rules may apply if you have a short-term loss on the sale of shares on which you received an exempt-interest dividend or a capital gain distribution.

Exempt-interest dividends before short-term loss. If you received exempt-interest dividends on mutual fund shares that you held for 6 months or less and sold at a loss, you may claim only the part of the loss that is more than the exempt-interest dividends. On Schedule D, column (d), increase the sales price by the amount of exempt-interest dividends. Report the loss as a short-term capital loss.

Example
On January 6, 2005, you bought a mutual fund share for $50. On February 2, 2005, the mutual fund paid a $3 dividend from tax-exempt interest, which is not taxable to you. On February 9, 2005, you sold the share for $45. If it were not for the tax-exempt dividend, your loss would be $5 ($50 − $45). However, you can deduct only $2, the part of the loss that is more than the exempt-interest dividend ($5 − $3). On Schedule D, column (d), increase the sales price from $45 to $48 (the $3 portion of the loss that is not deductible). You may deduct only $2 as a short-term capital loss.

Capital gain distribution before short-term loss. Generally, if you received capital gain distributions (or had to report undistributed capital gains) on mutual fund shares that you held for 6 months or less and sold at a loss, report only the part of the loss that is more than the capital gain distribution (or undistributed capital gain) as a short-term capital loss. The rest of the loss is reported as a long-term capital loss.

Example
On April 12, 2005, Ben Simms bought one share of ABC Mutual Fund for $25. On June 29, 2005, the mutual fund paid a capital gain distribution of $1 a share, which is taxed as a long-term capital gain. On July 12, 2005, he sold the share for $22.50. If it were not for the capital gain distribution, Ben would have had a $2.50 ($25 − $22.50) short-term loss. However, the part of the loss that is not more than the capital gain distribution ($1) must be reported as a long-term capital loss. The remaining $1.50 of the loss can be reported as a short-term capital loss.

Wash sales. If you sell mutual fund shares at a loss and within 30 days before or after the sale you buy, acquire in a taxable exchange, or acquire a contract or option to buy substantially identical property, you have a wash sale. You cannot deduct losses from wash sales. In determining whether the shares are substantially identical, you must consider all the facts and circumstances. Ordinarily, shares issued by one company are not considered to be substantially identical to shares issued by another company.

How to Figure Gains and Losses on Schedule D

Separate your short-term gains and losses from your long-term gains and losses on all the mutual fund shares and other capital assets you disposed of during the year. Then determine your net short-term gain or loss and your net long-term gain or loss.

Explanation
Net capital loss. If you have a net capital loss, your allowable capital loss deduction is the smaller of:

1. $3,000 ($1,500 if you are married and filing a separate return)
2. Your net capital loss

Enter your allowable loss on line 13 of Form 1040.

Example 1
Margaret has capital gains and losses for the year as follows:

	Short-term	Long-term
Gains	$700	$400
Losses	(800)	(2,000)

Margaret's deductible capital loss is $1,700, which she figures as follows:

Short-term capital losses	($800)
Subtract short-term capital gains	700
Net short-term capital loss	($100)
Long-term capital losses	($2,000)
Subtract long-term capital gains	400
Net long-term capital loss	($1,600)
Deductible capital loss	($1,700)

Example 2
Art and Karen file a joint return. They have a net long-term capital loss of $5,600 and a net short-term capital gain of $450. Their net capital loss is $5,150 ($5,600 − $450). Because their net capital loss exceeds $3,000, the amount they can deduct for the current year is limited to $3,000; however, the capital loss carryover is $2,150.

Capital loss carryovers. If your net capital losses are more than your allowable net capital loss deduction, you may carry over the excess to later years until it is completely used up. To determine your capital loss carryover, subtract from your capital loss the lesser of:

1) Your allowable capital loss deduction for the year, or
2) Your taxable income increased by your allowable capital loss deduction for the year and by your deduction for personal exemptions.

If your deductions exceed your gross income, you start the computation with a negative number.

When carried over, the loss will keep its original character as long-term or short-term. Therefore, a long-term capital loss carried over from a previous year will offset long-term gains of the current year before it offsets short-term gains of the current year.

In determining your capital loss carryover, apply your capital loss deduction to reduce your net short-term losses first. If after applying the short-term losses, the capital loss limit has not been reached, then apply the long-term losses until you reach the limit.

Use the *Capital Loss Carryover Worksheet* at the end of Chapter 17, *Reporting Gains and Losses,* to figure your capital loss carryover.

Capital loss carryovers from separate returns are combined if you file a joint return for the current year. However, if you once filed jointly and are now filing separately, a capital loss carryover from the joint return can be deducted only on the separate return of the spouse who actually had the loss.

Investment Expenses
You can generally deduct the expenses of producing investment income. These include expenses for investment counseling and advice, legal and accounting fees, and investment newsletters. These expenses are deductible as miscellaneous itemized deductions to the extent that they exceed 2% of your adjusted gross income. See Chapter 30, *Miscellaneous Deductions,* for further information.

Publicly offered mutual funds. Generally, mutual funds are publicly offered funds. These mutual funds report only the net amount of investment income after your share of the investment expenses has been deducted.

TAXSAVER
If you own shares in a publicly offered mutual fund, you do not have to pay tax on your share of the fund's expenses. There should be no entry in box 5 of Form 1099-DIV. However, expenses of a nonpublicly offered fund may be subject to tax. You should consult your tax advisor for details.

TAXSAVER
Front-end fees. "Front-end," or purchase, fees (also known as "load charges") reduce your investment in a mutual fund, but they are still considered part of your cost basis for tax purposes.

Example
You invest $10,000 in a fund that charges a 1% load on portfolio transaction (purchase) fee. Your account statement reports a net balance of $9,900 ($10,000 minus the 1% fee). For tax purposes, however, your cost remains at $10,000.

Exception
Your basis in mutual fund shares does not include load charges (sales fees) paid after October 3, 1989, on the purchase of shares if you held the shares for 90 days or less and then reinvested the proceeds in a fund within the same fund family with a reduced load charge. Instead, the load charges become part of your basis in the shares of the new fund into which you put your investment.

TAXSAVER
Sales charges and redemption fees. Before you buy a mutual fund, you should examine the sales charges and redemption fees it charges, if any. No-load funds do not have a sales charge. Mutual fund listings in newspapers generally indicate whether there is a sales charge. No-load funds have the same purchase and redemption price for fund shares. Your broker or financial advisor should be able to tell you which funds charge commissions.

Explanation
Back-end fees. Fees may also be deducted from your fund when you redeem or sell shares. These are gener-

ally called redemption or "back-end" fees. (Certain back-end fees called "contingent deferred sales charges" or "contingent deferred sales loads" typically decline and eventually disappear over a set period of time.) If your mutual fund reports all proceeds net of redemption fees on your Form 1099-B, you do not need to adjust your tax cost. However, if your mutual fund reports gross proceeds before any redemption fees on Form 1099-B, you should increase your cost basis by the amount of the fee you paid when calculating your capital gain or loss.

Other fees. Custodial and account maintenance fees are deductible as investment expenses on Schedule A of your income tax return, subject to certain caveats. See Investment Expenses, above, and Chapter 2, *Filing Status*.

Nonpublicly Offered Mutual Funds
If you own shares in a nonpublicly offered mutual fund during the year, you can deduct your share of the investment expenses on your Schedule A (Form 1040) as a miscellaneous itemized deduction to the extent your miscellaneous deductions exceed 2% of your adjusted gross income. Your share of the expenses will be shown in box 5 of Form 1099-DIV. A nonpublicly offered mutual fund is one that:

1. Is not continuously offered pursuant to a public offering
2. Is not regularly traded on an established securities market
3. Is not held by at least 500 persons at all times during the tax year

Contact your mutual fund if you are not sure whether it is nonpublicly offered.

Expenses allocable to exempt-interest dividends. You cannot deduct expenses that are for the collection or production of exempt-interest dividends. Expenses must be allocated if they were partly for both taxable and tax-exempt income. One accepted method for allocating expenses is to divide them in the same proportion that your tax-exempt income from the mutual fund is to your total income from the fund.

Limit on Investment Interest Expense

The amount you can deduct as an investment interest expense may be limited. See Chapter 25, *Interest Expense.*

TaxOrganizer

Records you should keep.
- *Confirmation statements.* You should keep a copy of all mutual fund confirmation statements reflecting all purchases and sales, as well as records of dividends that are automatically reinvested in your account.
- *Form 1099-DIV.* You should keep a copy of Form 1099-DIV, *Dividends and Distributions,* or a substitute form supplied by the mutual fund or brokerage firm containing substantially the same language. This form will tell you what you must report or take into account on your income tax return.
- *Form 1099-B.* You should keep a copy of Form 1099-B, *Proceeds from Broker and Barter Exchange Transactions,* or a substitute form supplied by the mutual fund or brokerage firm containing substantially the same language. This form will summarize the proceeds from sales, exchanges, or redemptions.
- *Confirmation from mutual fund company on specific share identification method.* This confirmation by the mutual fund company must confirm that you instructed them to sell particular mutual fund shares.
- *Form 2439.* You should keep a copy of Form 2439, *Notice to Shareholders of Undistributed Long-Term Capital Gains,* showing your share of undistributed capital gains and any tax paid by the mutual fund.

41

Estate and Gift Tax Planning

Introduction

Although it is not possible to take it with you, with careful thought and astute planning it is possible to provide your heirs, loved ones, and friends with a significant portion of your wealth. This chapter discusses the estate tax, the gift tax, and the generation-skipping transfer tax. The chapter also contains some ideas and techniques in estate planning that may aid you in making your plans for the future.

Frequent tax law changes continue to have a significant impact on estate planning. This makes it more difficult to protect your assets from the ravages of time unless you plan effectively. For example, the tax bill enacted in 2001 contained significant changes with regard to the estate, gift, and generation-skipping transfer taxes.

As a result of these changes, and because your goals and expectations constantly change as you go through life, you should periodically review your estate and gift tax plan. A review will help you (1) discover how your objectives may have changed;

(2) assess whether your plan can still achieve your objectives; and (3) determine how legislative changes may affect existing plans and whether you can accomplish your goals more advantageously.

This chapter is intended as an introduction to estate and gift tax planning. You should seek professional advice especially if your financial or family situation is complicated; if you own interests in closely held corporations or other illiquid assets; or if your spouse is not a U.S. citizen.

Getting Started

A periodic review of your personal financial plan makes sense. Filing an annual income tax return forces most taxpayers to look over their situation. Yet many—perhaps most—individuals allow years to go by without adequately considering possible changes in property holdings or key provisions in wills and trusts. To be on the safe side, you should periodically examine the following six basic tax and financial considerations:

1. Have there been any changes in the tax laws or rulings that might adversely affect your present estate plan?
2. Does your estate have sufficient cash or other liquid assets to take care of debts, taxes, funeral expenses, and estate administration expenses?
3. Have there been any changes in your family's circumstances—births, adoptions, deaths, marriages, illness or disability, special schooling needs, and so on—that might call for revisions in your estate plan?
4. Should you initiate a plan to give away some of your assets as gifts to your children, to other family members, or to charitable institutions? If you have already been giving gifts, should you continue to do so? Which assets are most appropriate for such a gift program?

5. Is the current form of ownership of your family assets appropriate for saving taxes and expenses and providing you the flexibility you need to deal with unexpected situations?
6. Have you designated a beneficiary for, and decided on the form of payment of, distributions from qualified employee benefit programs and IRAs?

Do You Need a Will?

A will is a legal document that specifies who receives what at your death and who will manage your estate. Even if you die without a will, you already have an estate plan of sorts. Generally, assets you own jointly with another person—a bank account, stock, personal residence, or business interest, or where you have designated a particular beneficiary, as under an insurance policy or IRA — will be passed on to the joint tenant or designated beneficiary. But, assets you own in your name alone will be passed on in accordance with your state's laws.

If you die without a will—*intestate* is the legal term—state laws determine how your estate is divided up among your surviving spouse, children, and parents—and what happens when there is no surviving spouse. State law may not conform to your wishes. Often, the biggest problem is not the distribution of the property but rather the guardianship of minor children. If both parents die without a will that directs who will be guardian of a minor child, the court and the state social welfare department will make the decision. So, even if you do not have enough assets to have to pay federal estate tax, it's a good idea to draw up a will.

Estate Tax Fundamentals

Who Has to Pay Federal Estate Tax?

Current law provides two major exemptions from federal estate tax:

1. There is no federal tax on the first $1.5 million of assets for 2005 ($2.0 million for 2006–2008, $3.5 million for 2009).
2. There is an unlimited marital deduction for assets passing to a spouse who is a U.S. citizen. Any amount given or left at death to a surviving spouse, whether given outright or in certain types of trusts, is exempt from federal estate tax. For more information, see the discussion later in this chapter.

TaxAlert

Under the current tax law, the federal estate tax rate is gradually reduced to 45% between 2005 and 2007 while the amount exempt from tax is gradually increased (see the Table below), after which the tax is repealed for the year 2010 only. Unless Congress acts in the interim to permanently repeal the estate tax, the estate tax will be reinstated starting in 2011 and revert back to the law as it was before the 2001 Tax Act was passed.

TaxPlanner

The two major exemptions, discussed above, along with the gradual phaseout and (temporary) repeal of the estate tax, certainly make planning easier for many Americans, but they should not lull you into thinking that estate planning is unnecessary. Given the uncertainty about which party will control Congress and the White House and questions regarding future budgetary constraints, it is questionable whether the estate tax will be permanently repealed. In addition, you may be worth more than you think. Many middle-class families now own homes that are worth several times what they cost. Moreover, despite the ups and downs in the stock market, the value of real estate has still increased significantly in recent years. And, in many cases, the proceeds of life insurance are also included in your taxable estate regardless of the beneficiary.

Even if your assets do not currently exceed $1.5 million (or the future increased exemption amount), they might at the time of your death. Therefore, it is prudent to focus on strategies that help freeze the value of assets in your estate.

How to Value Your Estate

Assets Subject to Estate Tax. Federal estate tax is a levy on the transfer of property at death. Your gross estate will include the value of all property to the extent of your interest in it at the time of death. Following are types of property included in your gross estate by law:

Tangible Personal Property, Real Estate, and Other Assets. This category includes property you own that is transmitted at death according to provisions of a will or state intestacy laws. Such property is commonly referred to as the probate estate. Examples: real estate, stocks, bonds, furniture, personal effects, jewelry, works of art, an interest in a partnership, an interest in a sole proprietorship, a bank account, and a promissory note or other evidence of indebtedness you hold.

Jointly Owned Property. In general. one-half of the value of property owned by a husband and wife jointly will be included in the estate of the first spouse to die. The unlimited marital deduction allows the transfer of the property from the deceased to the surviving spouse without being subject to federal estate tax. Upon the survivor's death, however, the entire property will be subject to tax (assuming it is still held at the time of death).

If two people who are not married own property jointly, the entire value of the property is included in the gross estate of the first to die, unless the estate can prove that all or part of the payment for acquiring the property was actually furnished by the other joint owner. If you and another joint owner acquired property by gift or inheritance, only your fractional share of the property is included.

Jointly held property passes to the other owner automatically on death without regard to whether or not you have a will. In many states, Transfer on Death (TOD), or Totten Trust accounts, allow securities and bank accounts to pass directly to a beneficiary even if the property is not held in joint name.

Life Insurance. Your gross estate will include life insurance proceeds that are received (1) by or for the benefit

Table 41-1 **Estate Tax, Gift Tax, and Generation-Skipping Tax (GST) Rates and Unified Credit**

Exemption Amount Calendar Year	Estate and GST tax deathtime transfer exemption	Highest estate and gift tax rates (GST tax rate)
2004	$1.5 million	48%
2005	$1.5 million	47%
2006	$2 million	46%
2007	$2 million	45%
2008	$2 million	45%
2009	$3.5 million	45%
2010	N/A (estate and GST taxes repealed)	only gift tax at 35%
2011	$1 million for estate tax; $1.1 million indexed from 2002 for GST tax	55% (plus 5% surtax on certain estates over $10 million)

The gift tax exemption amount remains at $1 million throughout this period. Gift tax remains, equal to top individual income tax rate of 35%

of your estate or (2) by other beneficiaries if you own all or part of the policies at the time of your death. "Ownership" includes the power to change the beneficiary of the policy, the right to cancel the policy and receive the cash value, the right to borrow against the policy, and the right to assign the policy, among other things.

TaxSaver

You can transfer ownership of a life insurance policy to your children or to a trust for your family's benefit and reap significant tax advantages. To be effective in keeping the proceeds out of your estate, the gift must be made more than three years before death. The three-year waiting period can be avoided for a newly purchased policy if proper steps are taken to have someone else (e.g., a trustee of an irrevocable trust) apply for the policy and own the policy from its inception. These types of irrevocable life insurance trusts can be structured so that you contribute money each year to the trust for paying premiums. Frequently, your payments can qualify for the annual gift tax exclusion (explained below). Setting up such a trust can be an effective way to get insurance proceeds to your heirs without incurring gift or estate tax.

Employee Benefits. The value of payments from qualified pension plans, IRAs and other retirement plans payable to surviving beneficiaries or the estate of an employee (or the owner, in the case of a Keogh/HR 10 plan) generally is included in your gross estate.

Certain Gifts and Gift Tax Paid within Three Years of Death. Gifts of property made during your lifetime are generally not included in your gross estate, but must be figured in the estate tax calculation if they exceed the $11,000 annual gift tax exclusion (discussed later). However, life insurance proceeds are included in your estate if the policies or ownership of the policies were given away within three years of your death. Also included is any gift tax you have paid within three years of your death. Lifetime gifts that a decedent retains some interest in (e.g., a life income interest) or control over (e.g., voting rights in closely held stock given as a gift) will be included in the decedent's gross estate.

Allowable Deductions and Exclusions. Deductions are allowed for funeral and administration expenses of the estate, and debts, unpaid mortgages, and other indebtedness on property included in the gross estate. Also allowed are such special deductions as the marital deduction and the charitable deduction. (See later sections for more details on the marital deduction.)

Funeral and Administration Expenses. Deductible funeral expenses include burial costs, costs for a burial lot, costs for future care of a grave site, and so on. Deductible administration costs include executor's commissions, attorney's fees, accounting fees, appraisal fees, and court costs.

Other Deductible Estate Expenses. To be deductible, debts must be enforceable personal obligations of the decedent, such as outstanding mortgages or personal bank loans, auto loans, credit card balances, utility bills, and so on. The deductible amount also includes any interest accrued on such debt at the date of death. Transfers made under a marital property settlement because of a divorce may be treated as estate expenses. Taxes are also deductible debts if they are accrued and unpaid at date of death. Deductible taxes include accrued property taxes, gift taxes unpaid at death, and income taxes.

Valuing Estate Property. Property is included in an estate at its "fair market value," which is the price at which property would change hands between a willing buyer and a willing seller. Property that trades on an established market may be valued easily. For example, publicly traded stocks and bonds are valued based on the average of the high and low selling price on the date of death (or, if elected, the date six months after death). However, interests in closely held businesses or partnerships must generally be appraised, taking into account the business's assets, earning capacity, and other factors. An accountant can assist you in appraising business interests for estate or gift tax valuation purposes.

Your gross estate is valued as of the date of your death or six months later (also known as the alternative valuation date), whichever your personal representative elects. An election to value the estate six months after date of death will generally apply to all assets in the estate, but is available only if the election results in a decrease in your gross estate and estate tax liability.

Your taxable estate. The amount remaining after subtracting any allowable deductions is your taxable estate. The federal estate tax is computed on this amount. Gifts made after 1976 are also factored in and can increase the marginal tax bracket of the estate.

If You Are the Beneficiary of an Estate

Property acquired from a decedent generally gets a new basis. Basis is generally the cost of an asset or the amount you will use to figure your tax. And since the new basis is usually greater than the old basis, this is known as your "stepped-up basis." In most cases, the new basis is the fair market value at date of death or alternative valuation date, whichever is used for estate tax purposes.

TaxAlert

Under the tax law, however, property acquired from a decedent who dies in year 2010 will not get a "stepped-up" basis. Consequently, if you inherit property from a decedent, you will generally receive a basis equal to the lesser of the fair market value of the property on the decedent's date of death or the decedent's adjusted basis in the property. This is known as "carryover basis." This new rule—if it goes into effect—would make it that much more important to keep accurate basis records so they will be available for your heir.

Exception. There is one key exception to this new rule: A decedent's executor can increase the basis of assets transferred by a total of $1.3 million plus any unused capital losses and net operating losses. An additional $3 million basis increase is allowed for property transferred to a surviving spouse, which means that property transferred to a spouse will be allowed a basis increase of $4.3 million. This could put the executor in an awkward spot: deciding which family members or other heirs get tax-free assets and which ones gets assets with built-in capital gain.

Certain types of assets are not eligible for the basis increase. Nonresident aliens would only be allowed a basis increase of $60,000 indexed for inflation after 2010.

In addition, under the current law, the $250,000 exclusion for the gain on the sale of a principal residence is extended to estates and heirs, provided the decedent used the property as a principal residence for 2 or more years during the 5-year period before the sale. The decedent's period of occupancy may also be added to any subsequent period of occupancy by the heir in determining whether the property was owned and occupied for 2 years as a principal residence.

How Your Estate Is Taxed

Tax Rates. The federal estate tax is progressive, ranging from a marginal rate of 18% to 47% in 2005.

The current 47% top rate applies to estates and gifts larger than $2.0 million. (See the table of rates at the end of this chapter.). As noted previously, the first $1.5 million (for 2005) of transfers at death are exempt from estate tax because of the estate tax exemption (see below).

Credits and Exemptions. Your estate can claim certain credits and exemptions before figuring the amount of federal estate tax owed. These items include:

Estate Tax Exemption. Each individual is entitled to an estate tax exemption. For 2005, the exemption is $1.5 million. In other words, no federal estate tax will be assessed on the first $1.5 million of an individual's combined taxable gifts and transfers at death. To the extent that the exemption has been used to offset gifts the decedent made during his or her lifetime, the exemption against the estate tax is reduced.

Example: Mary had a estate valued at $2 million at the time of her death in 2005. Two years before she died, she gave her son Bill a gift of $250,000 to help him buy a house. Instead of an estate tax exemption of $1.5 million, only $1.25 million of Mary's estate will qualify for the exemption.

Under the tax law, the amount of the exemption increases each year as follows:

Year	Exemption
2005	1.5 million
2006–2008	2 million
2009	3.5 million
2010	N/A (estate tax repealed)

TaxSaver

While you should have your will reviewed on a regular basis, it is especially important to be sure it is drafted to take advantage of the estate tax exemption available under the law in existence at the time of your death.

TaxAlert

State Death Tax Credit. Under the current tax law, the state death tax credit is eliminated for decedents dying in 2005 through 2009, and replaced with an unlimited state death tax deduction. Because many states' laws prior to the change in the tax law in 2002 imposed a state estate tax equal to the maximum allowable federal credit for state death taxes, many states have passed legislative changes to "decouple" their state estate tax from the federal state death tax credit. As a result, even as the federal estate tax decreases or is repealed, your estate may still be subject to state estate tax.

Foreign Death Tax Credit. A credit is allowed against the federal estate tax for any death taxes actually paid to a foreign country, Puerto Rico, or the Virgin Islands on property that is also subject to the federal estate tax. The credit is limited to the U.S. tax attributable to the property taxed by the foreign country.

Credit for Tax on Prior Transfers. Under certain circumstances a credit is allowed against the federal estate tax for part or all of any estate tax paid on property transferred to the present decedent.

State Tax Considerations. All states impose some kind of inheritance or estate tax. In some states, the estate tax is simply the amount of the federal credit for state death taxes. Consequently, in these states, if there is no federal tax, due to the estate tax exemption, there is also no state tax. However, as noted above, many states are enacting estate taxes that are not tied to the federal credit. Furthermore, some states do not allow an unlimited marital deduction, as the federal government does. In these states, state death tax considerations may influence how your estate plan should be structured.

The Marital Deduction. One of the most significant tax-saving provisions of the law is the marital deduction. As its name implies, it is a special deduction available only to married persons, where the spouse transferring the assets is a U.S. citizen. An estate is allowed an unlimited deduction for the value of property transferred to the spouse of the deceased. Thus, in effect, the marital deduction permits a couple to postpone paying any estate tax until the surviving spouse dies.

TaxSaver

While the estate tax remains in effect (until it is repealed in 2010), most married individuals will want to take advantage of both the estate tax exemption and the unlimited marital deduction. This will reduce the federal estate tax to zero for the estate of the first spouse to die. See the following examples about several ways this can be done.

TaxSaver

By placing property in a special marital trust, you can arrange for your spouse to receive a lifetime income interest in certain property. After your spouse dies, the property will be passed on to whomever you have stipulated in the trust document.

The marital deduction is unavailable for property transferred by gift or at death to a surviving spouse who is not a U.S. citizen at the time the transfer is made. Instead, the law provides that tax-free gifts to a non-U.S. citizen spouse can only total $117,000 (for 2005) per year, adjusted for inflation. There is, however, no lifetime limit to the total value of gifts you can give tax-free to a spouse who is not a U.S. citizen.

TaxSaver

Your will can be drafted so that your property is placed in a special type of trust that benefits a spouse who is not a U.S. citizen. The trust enables estate tax on the property to be postponed until the property is distributed out of the trust or the surviving spouse dies. This type of trust is called a Qualified Domestic Trust (QDOT). It permits property to qualify for the marital deduction if certain requirements—which provide that the property will eventually be subject to estate tax—are met.

Examples: Here are three examples for computing the gross estate, the taxable estate, and the estate tax due for three different size estates of married individuals who are assumed to die in 2005, each of whom is the first of the two spouses to die. The assets of these three individuals are listed in Step 1 below. As you can see, Sue's gross estate is larger then Michael's, and Dan's is the largest of the three.

Step 1: Computing the gross estate.

	Michael	Sue	Dan
Assets			
Cash	$ 600,000	$ 900,000	$ 800,000
Marketable securities	300,000	600,000	2,850,000
Business equity	0	0	800,000
Residence	300,000	400,000	1,300,000
Vacation residence	0	0	750,000
Personal property	110,000	100,000	600,000
Deferred compensation	110,000	100,000	400,000
Ordinary life insurance	20,000	100,000	1,000,000
Group-term insurance	60,000	300,000	1,500,000
Gross estate	$1,500,000	$2,500,000	$10,000,000

Step 2: Computing your taxable estate.

The executor of your estate will subtract from the total value of your gross estate all those deductions allowable under the tax law, including the marital deduction.

Michael's will provided that his wife was to receive his total estate after payment of debts, thereby reducing the taxable value of the estate to zero. He could do this because of the unlimited marital deduction (discussed above).

In Sue's case, the size of her estate's marital deduction was the product of some planning. The deduction was designed to dovetail with the estate tax exemption available in the year of her death in order to eliminate any estate tax liability.

Dan's estate planned to use less than the full amount of the marital deduction that could have been used. He and his wife, Elaine, decided that with his bequest and her separate assets, she would not require ownership of all of Dan's estate. Thus, because of their children's needs, a decision was made to give a trust for the children's benefit enough assets to soak up not only the $1,500,000 exemption, but also the lower estate tax brackets, even though taxes would be paid by his estate. The plan could have been structured to pay no taxes at the time of Dan's death if he were to leave only $1,500,000 to the children with the rest going to Elaine. The children could have then received the additional assets from Elaine as gifts or from her estate. Whether the amount of taxes on Elaine's estate would be more or less than those paid under the plan described above, would ultimately depend on the size of Elaine's estate.

	Michael	Sue	Dan
Gross estate	$ 1,500,000	$ 2,500,000	$ 10,000,000
Deductions			
Funeral expenses	(5,000)	(10,000)	(20,000)
Estate administration expenses	(40,000)	(60,000)	(150,000)
Debts	(100,000)	(70,000)	(300,000)
Mortgages	(125,000)	(160,000)	(530,000)
Marital deduction	(1,200,000)	(700,000)	(4,500,000)
Charitable deductions	(30,000)	0	(1,000,000)
Total deductions	$(1,500,000)	$(1,000,000)	$(6,500,000)
Taxable estate	$0	$1,500,000	$3,500,000

Step 3: Computing the federal estate tax.

Computing federal estate tax is straightforward in 2005. The taxable estate is reduced by the exemption and a tentative estate tax is calculated. The state tax credit is then allowed.

	Michael	Sue	Dan
Gross estate	$1,500,000	$2,500,000	$10,000,000
Deductions	(1,500,000)	(1,000,000)	(6,500,000)
Taxable estate	0	1,500,000	3,500,000
Estate exemption	0	(1,500,000)	(1,500,000)
Taxable estate after exemption	0	0	2,000,000
Tentative estate tax	0	0	929,200
Federal estate tax	$0	$0	$929,200

The Fundamentals of the Gift Tax

You might think that the government would make it easy to give money away to noncharitable recipients. In some respects it does. You can give up to $11,000 annually ($22,000 if you file a joint gift tax return and your spouse consents) to as many individuals as you want without paying any gift tax. But, above that amount, gifts consume the gift tax exemption amount of $1 million (this exemption does not increase) and then can result in gift tax. The reason is that without such a tax people could escape death taxes—assuming they were willing to give away a large portion of their property before death. You should think carefully before making significant gifts that would result in a gift tax payable in light of the possible permanent repeal of the estate tax.

TAXALERT

Under the tax law, the highest gift tax rate is gradually reduced to 45% between 2003 and 2007; however, the gift tax is **not** repealed (see the Table above). Beginning in 2010, the highest gift tax rate will be equal to the highest individual income tax rate, which by then is scheduled to be 35%. The gift tax was retained largely to limit the amount of income tax that taxpayers can avoid by gifting income-producing and appreciated assets to family members in lower income tax brackets. The $1 million gift tax exemption will remain constant and will not be indexed to the inflation rate. Therefore, the gift and estate tax systems are no longer completely "unified."

Any gift you give above the annual amount that is exempt from tax is, in effect, included in your estate when you die. The value of the gift is not the value at the date of your death but the value at the time you gave the gift. In addition, there are some special rules. A gift of life insurance, for example, made within three years of your death will be included in your gross estate at its full face value. Any gift tax you pay on gifts made within three years of your death is also added to the value of your taxable estate. Nevertheless, giving gifts can substantially reduce your overall gift and estate transfer taxes as well as fulfill other desires. But gift-giving does require careful planning—and the commitment to make the gifts before it is too late. In addition, given the uncertainty that currently exists as to whether the federal estate tax will be permanently repealed, it is generally prudent to consider gift-giving strategies that minimize the size of the taxable gift and that avoid gift tax to the extent possible.

Basis to the Recipient of a Gift

In general, the basis of appreciated property acquired by gift is the donor's basis for tax purposes. If a gift tax return was filed, the recipient—or donee—should examine it for information regarding the donor's basis, the holding period, and the amount of depreciation. The basis of gifts received after 1976 is increased by the amount of the federal gift tax attributable to the difference between the donor's basis and the gift's fair market value, if higher as of the date of gift.

How to Give Tax-Free Gifts

The Gift Tax Annual Exclusion. As noted above, you may give up to $11,000 each year to as many individuals as you want without incurring any gift tax (the $11,000 exclusion is indexed for inflation). And, if your spouse joins in making the gift (by signing a consent on a gift tax return), you may give $22,000 to each person annually without paying any tax. But this annual gift tax exclusion applies only to gifts of "present interests"—items that can be used, possessed, and enjoyed presently. Examples of a gift of a present interest include gifts of money, holiday presents, and so forth.

Gifts of "future interests" do not qualify for the annual exclusion. Gifts of future interests include remainder interests, reversions, or any other interest that won't give the recipient the right to possess, enjoy, or profit from the gift until some future date or time. An exception: Gifts in trust to minors are subject to special rules that may allow an otherwise future interest to qualify for the annual exclusion.

Gifts to Pay Medical or Educational Expenses. In addition to the annual exclusion, an unlimited gift tax exclusion is available to pay someone's medical or educational expenses. The beneficiary does not have to be your dependent or even related to you, although payment of a grandchild's expenses is perhaps the most common use of the exclusion. Also, contributions to a Section 529 plan or a qualified tuition program (QTP) will be eligible for the regular $11,000 exclusion. (See *Qualified Tuition Programs* under *Giving Gifts to Minors*, below.)

TAXSAVER

In order for a gift to be exempt from taxes, you must make the payment directly to the medical or educational institution providing the service. The beneficiary of the gift should not actually receive the payment. In addition, educational expenses include only tuition. Room and board, books, and other fees will not qualify for the unlimited exclusion, although they can, of course, qualify for the annual gift tax exclusion.

TAXSAVER

You can reduce your taxable estate substantially through a planned annual program of $11,000 (or $22,000 if you are married) gifts. All gifts within the exclusion limits are exempt from federal estate taxes. In addition, outright gifts that qualify for the annual exclusion are also protected from generation-skipping transfer taxes (see below). Obviously, you cannot hope to significantly reduce the tax your estate will pay by making gifts in a single year. But, the estate tax savings can be substantial if you embark upon a carefully planned gift-giving program that extends for a number of years before your death.

TAXSAVER

A donor who makes contributions to a qualified tuition program (commonly known as a "529 plan") in excess of the $11,000 annual exclusion amount may elect to take the contributions into account ratably over the five-year period starting with the year of the contributions. This means a donor can make a $55,000 tax-free contribution in one year (or $110,000 if the donor is married and the donor's spouse consents to gift-splitting). If the donor dies before the end of the five-year period, the portion of the contribution allocable to the period after the donor's date of death is included in the donor's gross estate.

TAXSAVER

Another major tax advantage of making a gift is that future appreciation in the gift's value and after-tax income earned on the property are not included in your estate. Example: Suppose you give stocks worth $50,000 to your children now. If you die in 10 years and the stock is worth $130,000, the $80,000 of appreciation will not be included in your estate. Nor will you (or your estate) include any dividends paid on the stock after the gift.

Gift Tax Charitable Contribution Deduction. An unlimited gift tax deduction is available for gifts to certain charitable organizations.

The Gift Tax Marital Deduction. The gift tax marital deduction allows you to transfer unlimited amounts of property during your lifetime to your spouse without gift tax. Property can be transferred outright or in trust Also, a gift of a lifetime income interest in property to your spouse can qualify for the marital deduction, if it is structured properly. You should consult with your tax advisor.

TAXSAVER

The gift tax marital deduction can help you lower the taxes on your estate. Consider: In order for one spouse to make full use of his or her estate tax exemption, it may be desirable to make gifts to that spouse so that he or she will have an estate at least equal to the estate tax exemption equivalent—$1.5 million in 2005. Since the gift tax marital deduction allows you to make unlimited tax-free transfers to your spouse, you can build up his or her assets without worrying that your gifts will be taxable.

Some words of caution: The unlimited marital deduction is not allowed for gifts to a spouse who is not a U.S. citizen, although tax-free transfers of up to $117,000 (in 2005) are permitted each year. (See the section on marital deduction under Estate Tax Fundamentals earlier in this chapter.) Furthermore, the amount of the gift tax marital deduction for a particular state may differ from the federal amount. It is therefore vital to get professional advice before making any significant gifts.

Example: Giving Gifts without Paying Gift Tax. This example illustrates how you can set up a substantial gift program and avoid paying any gift tax. Note, however, that part of the gift tax exemption is being used.

During 2005, James made outright gifts of $100,000 to his wife, Helen, and $40,000 to each of his three children, for a total of $220,000.

James incurred no gift tax on Helen's gift because of the unlimited marital deduction. James and Helen were entitled to a total of $66,000 in annual exclusions (based on $22,000 for each child) because they elected to treat one-half of those gifts as made by Helen. That still leaves, however, a taxable gift of $54,000 to the three children. By applying a portion of their gift tax exemptions, James and Helen can entirely eliminate paying gift tax. Assuming that this was their first gift using their exemptions, they will have reduced the remaining assets in their estates that will be considered tax-free from $1.5 million to $1,473,000, respectively.

Giving Gifts to Minors

Before a parent or grandparent gives a gift to a minor child, certain legal and practical matters need to be considered. Because a child typically cannot manage his or her own affairs and because parents usually do not want to give young children unfettered control over gift property, some special arrangements need to be made. The tax law, too, poses some challenges since only gifts of a "present interest"—property for the beneficiary's immediate enjoyment—qualify for the $11,000 annual gift tax exclusion. Furthermore, state laws frequently discourage outright gifts to minors. Many states commonly prohibit or discourage the registration of securities in the name of a minor and impose supervisory restrictions upon the sale of a minor's property. Consequently, gifts to minors can take different forms and have different tax consequences.

Outright Gifts. The $11,000 annual gift tax exclusion is available for these gifts unless the property being given as a gift is a "future interest." Income from the property is taxed to the minor, and the property is included in the minor's estate if he or she should die. However, because of the "kiddie tax," which requires that a child's unearned income be taxed at the parent's rate until the child reaches age 14, your child may actually be taxed at your rates on any income he or she receives from the property.

Guardianship. A guardianship is an arrangement where property is under a guardian's legal control subject to formal (and possibly burdensome) accounting to a court. The gift, income, and estate tax consequences are the same as for outright gifts. Thus, such gifts also qualify for the $11,000 gift tax exclusion.

Custodial Arrangements. To overcome the legal disability minors have in owning property outright, all 50 states, the District of Columbia, and the Virgin Islands have adopted the Uniform Gifts (or Transfers) to Minors Act. Under this act, a custodian may hold both cash and securities for a minor until he or she reaches adulthood. Securities may be registered in the name of any bank, trust company, or adult as custodian for the minor. Custodial gifts to minors are considered completed gifts for gift tax purposes, and such gifts are eligible for the annual gift tax exclusion. The income from the gift property during the custodial period is taxable to the minor (subject to kiddie tax provisions). However, if you use the income for your minor child's maintenance and support, it is taxable to you because you are the person legally obligated to support the minor.

TaxSaver

Generally, you should not act as custodian of your own gifts to your minor child. If you do and if you die before your child becomes an adult, the value of the custodial account maintained for your child's benefit will be included in your estate. Instead, your spouse may be the custodian. If you and your spouse both make gifts to your minor child, in essence splitting your gifts to take advantage of the annual gift tax exclusion, you should consider making a third party the custodian for the child.

Present Interest Trust. Special rules enacted by Congress provide a method of making gifts to minors that qualify for the annual exclusion. A gift to a qualifying trust established for an individual under the age of 21 will be considered a gift of a present interest and qualify for the $11,000 annual gift tax exclusion. The trust instrument must provide that the gift property and its income:

- May be expended for the benefit of the beneficiary before reaching age 21, and
- To the extent not so expended, will pass to the beneficiary upon becoming age 21.

If the child dies before reaching age 21, the funds must be payable to the child's estate or as the child may designate under a general power of appointment. This rule applies to trusts for children under the age of 21, even if a state law has reduced the age of majority to age 19 or 18.

Crummey Trust. This is a type of trust to which you can transfer property and have the gift qualify for the annual gift tax exclusion. The distinguishing characteristic of a Crummey trust (which takes its name from a court case) is that it gives the beneficiary the annual right to demand distributions from the trust equal to the lesser of the amount of the contributions to the trust during the year or some specified amount (i.e., $5,000 or 5% of the trust's value). The beneficiary (or legal guardian) must be notified of the power to withdraw the body of the trust, although the power is permitted to lapse or terminate after a short period of time, such as 30 days. If the beneficiary fails to make a demand during the window period, after being notified that a contribution was made, the right lapses for that year's contributions. To the extent the beneficiary (or guardian) has the right to demand distribution of the year's contribution, that contribution is considered a "present interest" and, therefore, qualifies for the annual gift tax exclusion.

A Crummey trust is very flexible. The trustee can be required to accumulate income until the child reaches a specified age above age 21. The trustee also can be restricted to using trust assets and income for specific purposes (e.g., college expenses). The trust is useful as a vehicle for permanently removing assets from the parents' gross estates.

Totten Trust. An "In Trust For" or so-called Totten Trust is created when a donor deposits his or her own money into a bank account for the benefit of a minor and names himself or herself as trustee. Under the laws of certain states, this is an informal and revocable arrangement. Upon the donor-trustee's death, the funds avoid probate and pass directly to the minor. However, the trust is not considered a separate entity for tax purposes because the donor retains complete control over any property in the trust. Accordingly, the donor will be taxed on the income as if the trust were not in existence. Also, assets in the trust account will be included in the donor's estate.

Qualified Tuition Programs (Section 529 Plans). Section 529 plans allow a donor to either buy tuition credits or contribute to a special higher-education savings account for a designated beneficiary. A donor can leverage the $11,000 annual gift tax exclusion under a special gift tax rule that allows the donor to treat any contribution to a qualified tuition program in excess of the annual exclusion amount as if it were made ratably over five years. This permits a donor to contribute up to $55,000 in one year (or $110,000 if gift-splitting with spouse) per beneficiary, free of gift tax.

Although treated as a completed gift, you can retain ownership and control over the funds in a Section 529 account. This unique provision allows you to decide when to distribute funds to the beneficiary. Subject to certain guidelines, you can even substitute a different beneficiary or revoke the account and take back the funds.

Earnings in the account are permitted to grow on a tax-deferred basis. In addition, under current law, no federal income tax is imposed on the earnings, provided that the funds are used to pay for qualifying higher education expenditures. Although contributions to Section 529 plans are not deductible for federal income tax purposes, a number of states offer a deduction against state income tax for contributions made to their programs.

Do You Need to File a Gift Tax Return?

Only individuals are required to file a gift tax return. If a trust, estate, partnership, or corporation makes a gift, the individual beneficiaries, partners, or stockholders are considered donors and may be liable for the gift tax. If a donor dies before filing a return, the donor's executor must file the gift tax return.

Although you may have made gifts during the year, you do not need to file a gift tax return so long as you meet all of the following requirements:

1. You made no gifts during the year to your spouse;
2. You gave no more than $11,000 during the year to any one recipient; and
3. All of the gifts you made were of present interests.

Additionally, except in limited circumstances, you do not have to file a gift tax return solely to report gifts to your spouse (regardless of the amount of these gifts and regardless of whether the gifts are present or future interests).

You must file a gift tax return, however, if:

- Your spouse is not a U.S. citizen and the total gifts you made to your spouse during the year exceed $117,000;
- You make any gift of a terminable interest to your spouse that does not meet certain exceptions;
- You make a Qualified Terminable Interest Property election;
- You gave gifts to any donee other than your spouse that are not fully excluded under the $11,000 annual exclusion. Thus, you must file a gift tax return to report any gift of a future interest (regardless of amount) or to report gifts to any donee that total more than $11,000 for the year; or
- You elect to split gifts with your spouse (regardless of the amount of the gifts).

If you are required to file a gift tax return, use Form 709, *United States Gift Tax Return,* unless, as explained later, you are entitled to use Form 709-A, *United States Short Form Gift Tax Return* in lieu of Form 709.

When to File the Gift Tax Return

The gift tax return is an annual return. In general, you must file a gift tax return on or after January 1 but not later than April 15 (without extensions) of the year following the calendar year when the gifts were made. If the donor of the gifts died during the year in which the gifts were made, the executor must file the donor's gift tax return not later than the earlier of (1) the due date (with extensions) for filing the donor's estate tax return; or (2) April 15 of the year following the calendar year when the gifts were made. If no estate tax return is required to be filed, the due date for the gift tax return (without extensions) is April 15.

Extension of Time to File

You can extend the time to file the gift tax return in either of two ways. First, you can request an extension by filing Form 8892 if you are not extending your Form 1040. Second, you can request an extension by using one of the extension forms used to extend the filing of your income tax return. Income tax return extensions are made by using

Forms 4868 or 2350. Any extension of time to file your income tax return will also extend the time to file your gift tax return.

TAXPLANNER

Like the income tax return, an extension to file a gift tax return does not extend the time to pay the gift tax due. If you want an extension of time to pay the gift tax, you must make a separate request.

Gift Tax Return—Form 709

Form 709 is used to report transfers subject to the federal gift tax (as well as the generation-skipping transfer tax, not discussed here) and also to compute the tax, if any, due on those transfers. A married couple may not file a joint Form 709, even if the spouses elect gift splitting. Instead, both the donor spouse and the consenting spouse must each file a separate gift tax return unless either of two situations are met:

Situation 1. During the calendar year:

- Only one spouse made any gifts;
- The total value of these gifts to each third-party donee does not exceed $22,000; and
- All of the gifts were of present interests.

Situation 2. During the calendar year:
- Only one spouse (the donor spouse) made gifts of more than $11,000 but not more than $22,000 to any third-party donee;
- The only gifts made by the other spouse (the consenting spouse) were gifts of not more than $11,000 to third-party donees other than those to whom the donor spouse made gifts; and
- All of the gifts by both spouses were of present interests.

If either of these two situations is met, only the donor spouse must file a return and the consenting spouse signifies consent on that return.

Gift Tax Return—Form 709-A

When You May File a Form 709-A instead of a Form 709. Form 709-A is the short form gift tax return and may be used only by certain married couples to report nontaxable gifts that they consent to split. If you were married during the entire calendar year, you may use Form 709-A instead of Form 709, so long as all of the following requirements are met:

1. You are a citizen or resident of the United States, and were married during the entire calendar year to one individual who is also a citizen or resident of the United States. Both you and your spouse must have been alive at the end of the calendar year.
2. Your only gifts (other than gifts for tuition or medical care) to a third party consisted entirely of present interests in tangible personal property, cash, U.S. Savings Bonds, or stocks and bonds listed on a stock exchange. You cannot use Form 709-A to report gifts of closely held stock, partnership interests, fractional interests in real estate, or gifts for which the value has been reduced to reflect a valuation discount.
3. Your gifts to any one individual (other than gifts for tuition or medical care) during the calendar year did not total more than $22,000. If the recipient of the gift is a charity, no part of that gift may be given to a noncharitable entity.

4. During the calendar year, you did not make any gifts of terminable interests to your spouse.
5. During the calendar year, your spouse did not make any gifts to any of the donees listed on the form, did not make gifts of terminable interests to you, did not make gifts (other than gifts for tuition or medical care) of over $11,000 to any other donee, and did not make any gifts of future interests to any other donee.
6. You and your spouse agree to split all of the gifts either of you made during the calendar year.
7. You did not file a Form 709 for the calendar year in which you are filing the Form 709-A.

TaxOrganizer

Records you should keep.

- You should retain all gift tax returns filed by you and your spouse.

The Generation-Skipping Tax

An additional tax may apply to gifts or bequests that skip a generation. For example, a gift of property directly from a grandparent to a grandchild (which effectively "skips" the intervening generation) would be subject to the generation-skipping transfer tax.

The reason for the tax is simple. It's designed to impose the equivalent of the gift or estate tax that would have been paid if the intervening generation had received the gift or bequest. So for a direct gift from a grandparent to a grandchild, the generation-skipping transfer tax represents the amount of tax that would have been paid if the property had first been transferred to the child, who then died leaving the property to the grandchild.

The Generation-Skipping Transfer Tax Is Stiff. In 2005, this tax is imposed at the maximum estate and gift tax rate of 47%. It is payable in addition to any estate or gift tax otherwise payable as a result of the transfer. Fortunately, most individuals will escape paying it. First, $11,000 ($22,000 if made with the consent of a spouse) outright gifts from a grandparent to grandchildren that qualify for the annual exclusion are exempt from this tax. Furthermore, each individual is entitled to an aggregate $1.5 million exemption from the tax for lifetime gifts and transfers at death. Since a married couple can "gift-split," they can make up to $3.0 million in generation-skipping transfers without incurring the tax. In addition, any subsequent appreciation on the transferred property after it is given will escape the generation-skipping transfer tax.

TaxAlert

Under the tax law, the generation-skipping transfer tax rate is gradually reduced to 45% between 2003 and 2007, after which the tax is repealed for the year 2010 only. However, unless Congress acts in the interim to permanently repeal the generation-skipping transfer tax, it will be reinstated and revert back to prior law starting in 2011.

TaxSaver

A wealthy individual can maximize his or her opportunity to avoid the imposition of the generation-skipping tax on transfers to grandchildren and later generations by allocating the $1.5 million exemption for gifts during his or her lifetime.

If your living descendants are already well provided for, you may want to consider establishing a "dynasty trust." As its name implies, the trust can benefit future descendants by sheltering assets from estate, gift, and generation-skipping transfer taxes for several generations.

How to Use Trusts

A trust is one of the most useful personal financial planning tools available. A trust is an arrangement under which one person or institution holds legal title to real or personal property for the benefit of another person or persons, usually under the terms of a written document setting forth the rights and responsibilities of all parties. Its primary virtue is that it can hold property for the benefit of other persons, now or in the future, and often avoid some taxes that otherwise would have to be paid.

Irrevocable Trusts. An irrevocable trust may not be changed or revoked after its creation. It is usually created to remove property and its future income and appreciation from the estate of the creator of the trust. A present interest trust and a Crummey trust, both of which are discussed above, are irrevocable trusts. You might also use an irrevocable trust if you want to make a gift to someone but want to prevent the assets from being spent too quickly. An irrevocable trust also can be used to protect assets you give from your beneficiary's creditors.

However, property placed in an irrevocable trust will not be removed from your estate if you retain certain interests or powers in the trust—such as an interest that entitles you to receive the income from the trust for the rest of your life or the power to determine which beneficiaries will receive distributions. In addition, any transfer to an irrevocable trust will be subject to gift tax to the extent you relinquish control over the property. If someone else will receive the current income from the trust, or if it is a present income trust, the $11,000 annual gift tax exclusion can shield at least part of the property transfer to the trust from gift tax.

Besides saving you estate tax, irrevocable trusts created for your children can cut your income taxes. The amount of income tax savings depends on how much other income your children already receive and whether the "kiddie tax" applies to them. Also, there are very strict rules that limit the amount of control you or your spouse may keep over the trust in order for you not to include the trust's income on your tax return. The income from the trust will be taxed to you if the trust is used to pay for an item that you are legally obligated to provide as support for the beneficiary.

Revocable Trusts. A revocable trust (also known as a "living trust") is created during your lifetime, and you may amend or revoke it at any time. The trust instrument stipulates how the assets held by the trust are to be managed during your lifetime. This type of trust can also act very much like a will; the trust instrument can include instructions about how the assets in the trust should be distributed after your death.

What distinguishes a revocable trust from other kinds of trust arrangements is that you keep the power to reclaim the trust assets or contribute additional property to the trust at any time and for any reason. Thus, in effect, if you set up a revocable trust you really have not committed yourself to anything—at least until you die and the trust becomes irrevocable. For all practical purposes, you continue to own the trust property; the trust merely gets legal title. Since you keep complete control over the trust and its assets, the property held in it will be included in your gross estate for estate tax purposes. Also, all income and deductions attributable to the property in the trust will be included on your income tax return. On the other hand, you will not be liable for any gift tax when you contribute assets to the trust. This is the case even though the trust names the beneficiaries who will inherit the property upon your death. However, a gift will occur if you give up your power to revoke or amend the trust, or if income or principal is actually paid to someone else.

Essentially, there are no tax advantages gained by establishing a revocable trust. But there can be some real financial and administrative advantages, including:

Avoiding Probate and Ancillary Administration. Revocable trust assets pass to the beneficiaries you name in the trust document and are not controlled by your will. This cuts out the costs and delays arising from the probate process, but first check the laws in your state. Many states have streamlined the probate process and reduced the associated costs. Also, unlike probate, with a revocable trust the identity and instructions for distributing estate property are not part of the public record. Further, if you own real property in a state other than your state of domicile, a revocable trust will avoid the ancillary probate administration in that state that would otherwise be required.

Avoiding Legal Guardianship. If you become incapacitated, the assets kept in your living trust would be managed by a trustee you named in the trust document. Otherwise, the determination of whether and to what extent you are disabled or incompetent and who is going to handle your affairs could be left to public, and potentially costly, guardianship proceedings. A durable power of attorney can also be an effective tool for prearranging the management of your affairs in the event you become incapacitated.

Relief from Financial Responsibility. If desired, an independent trustee can be used immediately to relieve you of the details of managing your property and investments, record- keeping chores, and the preparation and filing of income tax returns.

Living trusts have some drawbacks and are not suited for everyone:

- Expect to pay legal fees and other expenses, such as recording fees, to set up the trust and transfer property to it. You will also owe recurring trustee and administrative charges if you use a corporate trustee rather than managing the trust yourself.
- You will not necessarily save on other legal, accounting, and executor's fees paid to handle your estate. Whether your assets are held in a living trust or pass through probate, the same sort of work will generally be needed to value your assets, prepare federal and state tax returns, settle creditors' claims, and resolve disputes among beneficiaries.

TAXSAVER

Two reminders: (1) If you establish a living trust, be sure that any property covered by the trust is legally titled in the trustee's name. This is a straightforward, but often overlooked, point. (2) After setting up a living trust, you must remember to conduct your personal business affairs through the trust. This is not difficult but can be a burden. Property held outside the trust at your death will be subject to probate—except for life insurance proceeds (payable to a beneficiary other than your estate) and prop-

erty held jointly with right of survivorship, which by law would avoid probate.

How to Raise Cash to Pay Estate Taxes

In many instances, the estate of an owner of a closely held business—or for that matter, any estate—may not have sufficient cash to pay all the estate's obligations, including estate taxes. Without sufficient liquidity, the estate may be forced to sell a portion of the business to raise the necessary cash. But there are special rules for the estates of owners of closely held businesses. The techniques described below can help alleviate these problems.

Stock Redemptions to Pay Death Taxes

A special tax provision (Section 303 of the Internal Revenue Code) allows certain redemptions or partial redemptions of closely held stock to be treated as a sale or exchange, not as a dividend. Since the estate's basis in the decedent's stock will be the stock's fair market value at the date of death (for decedents dying prior to 2010), only post-death appreciation will be taxed upon the redemption and only up to the maximum long-term capital gains tax rate (generally 15% for sales and exchanges before 2009). To qualify for what is called a Section 303 redemption, the value of all the stock of the corporation included in the decedent's gross estate must exceed 35% of the decedent's adjusted gross estate. The adjusted gross estate is the gross estate less the allowable deductions for funeral and administration expenses, debts, the family-owned business deduction, and certain losses (but before any charitable deduction or marital deduction). A qualifying redemption under Section 303 is limited in amount to the sum of the following items:

- Federal and state death taxes,
- Funeral expenses, and
- Estate administration expenses.

TAXALERT

The advantages of sale and exchange treatment under Section 303 may be somewhat diminished under the tax law, which taxes certain qualified dividends at the lower capital gains (vs. ordinary income) rate. As long as the redemption by the estate results in qualified dividend treatment, the estate would be taxed at 15% on post-death appreciation without meeting the Section 303 requirements.

TAXSAVER

An estate does not actually have to be illiquid in order to qualify for this special redemption. The estate may redeem stock up to the maximum amount referred to above, if the estate otherwise has sufficient liquid assets to take care of its expenses and taxes.

Installment payment of estate tax. The estate taxes attributable to a decedent's closely held business can be paid over a 14-year period if certain conditions are met. This 14-year pay-out offers a very favorable interest rate plus a 5-year deferral on the first installment of estate taxes. The deferral provision only applies to an "interest in a closely held business." To qualify, the value of the closely held business must exceed 35% of the adjusted gross estate. The amount of estate tax that qualifies for a deferred payout is limited to the portion of the total tax that is attributable to the decedent's business interest. Thus, if the decedent's qualifying stock constitutes 62% of the adjusted gross estate, then 62% of the total estate tax liability may be deferred.

Even though none of the tax attributable to the closely held business interest is paid for five years, the interest on the tax for the first four years must be paid annually. Starting in the fifth year, the estate tax due plus interest may be paid in up to 10 yearly installments.

The interest rate charged on the deferred estate tax attributable to the first $1 million in value of the closely held business interest is 2%. An interest rate equal to 45% of the rate applicable to tax underpayments applies to the deferred estate tax in excess of that amount.

Concerns Regarding Community Property

Community property is most often property acquired by spouses while they are married and domiciled in a community property state. But not *all* property acquired during the marriage is community property. If one spouse individually receives a gift or inheritance, it is not community property but rather is "separate property" owned solely by the recipient. Property acquired or otherwise owned by each spouse prior to marriage is also considered separate property.

Community property and marital property are treated differently from noncommunity property when someone dies. In a noncommunity property state, the basis of the decedent's property is increased or decreased for tax purposes to fair market value as of the date generally of the decedent's death. However, when one spouse in a community property state dies, the basis of *both* spouses' interest in all community property is stepped up or down, that is, increased or decreased to the fair market value at date of death.

TAXPLANNER

Estate Planning—Steps to Take Now
Here's a handy checklist of estate planning measures you need to consider:

- Review with your spouse your current financial situation and your entire personal financial plan (including plans for your retirement as well as plans for the years after one of you has died).
- If any adult member of your family does not have a will, or if any wills have not been reviewed within the last three years, contact your attorney. This is especially important because of the frequency of tax law changes.
- Compile a list documenting where all your important financial and legal papers are located. Inform all appropriate persons of your list. If you have not already done so, be sure your spouse or whomever you designate as your personal representative knows your attorney, accountant, trust officer, broker, insurance advisor, and other appropriate individuals.
- Compile information on the cost and approximate purchase date of all your assets, including your residence.
- To reduce federal estate taxes, consider assigning ownership rights of your group term life insurance to children, a trust, or other appropriate recipient.
- Review whom you have designated as a beneficiary for your employee retirement or Keogh plan and other employee benefits.
- Review how your assets will be passed on to your beneficiaries.

- Make sure that you have provided for the legal guardianship and personal custody of your minor children.
- Review your will or any trust you have set up with your attorney. In particular, you and your spouse should check the provisions in your wills that pertain to what would happen to your estates if both of you died at the same time. Have you, for example, properly divided your assets to take maximum advantage of the marital deduction and the estate tax exemption?
- If you and your spouse do not have durable powers of attorney, health care proxies, or living wills, consider having them drawn up soon. If the answer to any of the following questions is yes, you may need professional assistance to help you determine whether there are tax problems on the horizon. Remember: A "yes" answer is a warning flag, but not necessarily a signal that there is a problem.

Are you:
- Making significant cash gifts to members of your family that are likely to continue indefinitely?
- Planning to make gifts to grandchildren within the next few years? In your will?
- Anticipating a significant inheritance? Is your spouse?

Do you:
- Hold assets jointly with your spouse, other than your residence and a working banking account?
- Have a simple will that leaves all property you own at the date of your death outright to your spouse?
- Own any real property in a state other than the state of your residence?
- Have a child or other relative with a serious medical problem that may require special consideration in your will or trust instrument?
- Have substantially more or less property than your spouse?

Have you:
- Moved your residence to a different state since you last executed your will?
- Named your estate as the beneficiary of your life insurance or your retirement plan benefits?

Table for Computing Estate and Gift Tax

Column A — Taxable Amount Over—	Column B — Taxable Amount Not Over—	Column C — Tax on Amount in Column A [1]	Column D — Rate of Tax on Excess Over Amount in Column A
—	$10,000	—	18%
0,000	20,000	$1,800	20%
20,000	40,000	3,800	22%
40,000	60,000	8,200	24%
60,000	80,000	13,000	26%
80,000	100,000	18,200	28%
100,000	150,000	23,800	30%
150,000	250,000	38,800	32%
250,000	500,000	70,800	34%
500,000	750,000	155,800	37%
750,000	1,000,000	248,300	39%
1,000,000	1,250,000	345,800	41%
1,250,000	1,500,000	448,300	43%
1,500,000	2,000,000	555,800	45%
2,000,000	—	780,800	48%

[1] Before credits

42

What to Do If You Employ Domestic Help

Note: The 2004 IRS Publication 17 (Your Federal Income Tax) has been updated by Ernst & Young LLP for 2005. Dates and dollar amounts shown are for 2005. Gray type is used to indicate where IRS text has been updated or intentionally omitted. Unrevised IRS text is shown in black type.

Introduction

If you have a domestic helper who qualifies as your **employee,** *you may have to pay Social Security and Medicare taxes, as well as federal and state unemployment taxes. You may also have to withhold federal income tax and make* **earned income credit** *advance payments. In general, a person who works in or around your house qualifies as your employee if you control his or her working conditions—pay, work schedule, conduct, and appearance. This chapter spells out what federal tax rules govern domestic help and advises you on how to comply with them.*

Both you and your employee are subject to Social Security and Medicare taxes if you pay your employee $1,400 or more during any calendar year. If you have paid any employee $1,000 or more in any calendar quarter during the current or preceding year, you are subject to federal unemployment taxes on every employee during the current year.

Your employee may ask you to withhold federal income tax from compensation. If you decide to do so, you must withhold the proper amount from each paycheck. This withholding must be remitted to the IRS.

Use Schedule H (Form 1040) to compute federal taxes for your household employees and attach it to your personal income tax return.

If you pay your income taxes late, penalties and interest will be due by you on the taxes described in this chapter as well as on your personal income taxes.

This chapter only discusses the federal taxes applying to household employees. There may be additional taxes due depending on the state and city where the services are rendered.

You may also be subject to federal and/or state rules regarding employees' pay and benefits. For example, state laws may dictate the maximum number of hours an employee may work, the amount to be paid for overtime, and/or or the number of days of paid vacation and holidays the employee is entitled to.

Even if your domestic employee does not have legal authorization to work in the United States, you are still liable for the payroll taxes discussed in this chapter.

TAXPLANNER

The rules in this chapter relate to someone who works for you in the United States or who is a U.S. citizen or green card holder. If you are employing someone to work outside of the United States, you will need to investigate your responsibilities under the laws of that country.

Employment Taxes for Household Employers

If you pay someone to come to your home and care for your dependent or spouse, you may be a household employer. If you are a household employer, you will need an employer identification number (EIN) and you may have to pay employment taxes. If the individuals who work in your home are self-employed, you are not liable for any of the taxes discussed in this section. Self-employed persons who are in business for themselves are not household employees. Usually, you are **not** a household employer if the person who cares for your dependent or spouse does so at his or her home or place of business.

Exception

Babysitters and yard workers under the age of 18 are exempt, regardless of how much they earn, provided that is not their main job. In addition, the wages that they earn in the year in which they turn 18 are also exempted.

TaxPlanner

Paying the "nanny" tax. Employers are required to report the Social Security and federal unemployment taxes due on domestic workers' wages on the employers' Form 1040, Schedule H. The taxes must be paid through the employers' estimated tax payments. Alternatively, the employer could increase federal withholding on his or her own wages and pay the Social Security tax on the domestic worker in that manner. Federal unemployment taxes on domestics are payable the same way.

If you use a placement agency that exercises control over what work is done and how it will be done by a babysitter or companion who works in your home, that person is not your employee. This control could include providing rules of conduct and appearance and requiring regular reports. In this case, you do not have to pay employment taxes. But, if an agency merely gives you a list of sitters and you hire one from that list, the sitter may be your employee.

If you have a household employee you may be subject to:

1) Social Security and Medicare taxes,
2) Federal unemployment tax, and
3) Federal income tax withholding.

Social Security and Medicare taxes are generally withheld from the employee's pay and matched by the employer. Federal unemployment (FUTA) tax is paid by the employer only and provides for payments of unemployment compensation to workers who have lost their jobs. Federal income tax is withheld from the employee's total pay if the employee asks you to do so and you agree.

For more information on a household employer's tax responsibilities. see Publication 926 and Schedule H (Form 1040) and its instructions. **State employment tax.** You may also have to pay state unemployment tax. Contact your state unemployment tax office for information. You should also find out whether you need to pay or collect other state employment taxes or carry workers' compensation and/or disability insurance. A list of state employment tax agencies, including addresses and phone numbers, is in Publication 926.

Explanation
You may be able to claim a Child and Dependent Care credit for the expenses you incur for domestic help.

Example
Janice Johnson is single and works to keep up a home for herself and her dependent father. Her adjusted gross income of $25,000 is entirely earned income. Her father was disabled and incapable of self-care for 6 months. To keep working, she paid a housekeeper $600 per month to care for her father, prepare lunch and dinner, and do housework.

Her credit is as follows:

Total work-related expenses (6 × $600)	$3,600
Maximum allowable expenses	$3,000
Amount of credit (30% of $3,000)	$ 900

Explanation
Employee or independent contractor? Whether or not a person who provides services in and around your house is your employee depends on the facts and circumstances of the situation. In general, a person is your employee if you control his or her working conditions and compensation. A person does not have to work for you full-time to qualify as your employee.

Generally, workers are classified based on how they perform their work and their accountability for it. By definition, independent contractors are responsible for *results,* not how their tasks are accomplished. On the other hand, individuals who are instructed as to when, where, and how to complete their jobs would probably be considered employees. If you determine that your domestic helpers are employees, you must withhold and match Social Security payments and may be subject to paying federal and state unemployment taxes as well.

To gain a better understanding of the distinction between an independent contractor and an employee, consider the person who mows your lawn. If the person works for an independent lawn service and is supervised by the lawn company that also provides its own equipment—all you provide is the grass—there's little question that the provider is an independent contractor. However, if a college student cuts your lawn using your mower, and you give specific instructions as to how and when to do the job, he or she will be considered your employee.

To enable you to determine whether a person is indeed an independent contractor, there are certain common indicators that can help. An independent contractor:

• Works for several homeowners
• Provides his or her own tools and supplies to perform the job
• Can bring in additional help if he or she deems necessary
• Determines how the results will be accomplished
• Is paid by the job, not by the hour
• Advertises his or her services
• May be fired at will
• Can set his or her own hours and leave when the job is completed

If you have reason to believe that a person is an independent contractor and not your employee, you should not withhold Social Security tax from his or her compensation. You may want to get a signed letter from this person indicating that he or she is an independent contractor and is responsible for his or her own employment taxes.

TaxPlanner

Records you need. When you hire a household employee, make a record of that person's name and Social Security number exactly as it appears on his or her Social Security card. You will need this information when you remit Social Security, Medicare, federal unemployment, and withholding of federal income taxes.

An employee who does not have a Social Security number should apply for one on Form SS-5, *Application for a Social Security Card.* This form is available at all Social Security Administration offices, or on the Internet at www.irs.gov as well as at most IRS offices and post offices.

If your employee is not eligible to obtain a Social Security number, he or she may obtain an individual taxpayer identification number (ITIN) by filing Form W-7 with the IRS. The ITIN can be used on a tax return wherever a Social Security number should be used. You should note that the ITIN is for IRS records only. It does not change the employee's status with the Immigration and Naturalization Service or his or her entitlement to Social Security or other employment benefits.

Table 42-1. **IRS Offices for EIN Application**

Your residence location	IRS address and phone/fax number
Connecticut, Delaware, District of Columbia, Florida, Georgia, Maine, Maryland, Massachusetts, New Hampshire, New Jersey, New York, North Carolina, Ohio, Pennsylvania, Rhode Island, South Carolina, Vermont, Virginia, West Virginia	Attn: EIN Operation P. O. Box 9003 Holtsville, NY 11742-9003 Fax-TIN 631-447-8960
Illinois, Indiana, Kentucky, Michigan	Attn: EIN Operation Cincinnati, OH 45999 Fax-TIN 859-669-5760
Alabama, Alaska, Arizona, Arkansas, California, Colorado, Hawaii, Idaho, Iowa, Kansas, Louisiana, Minnesota, Mississippi, Missouri, Montana, Nebraska, Nevada, New Mexico, North Dakota, Oklahoma, Oregon, Puerto Rico, South Dakota, Tennessee, Texas, Utah, Washington, Wisconsin, Wyoming	Attn: EIN Operation Philadelphia, PA 19255 Fax-TIN 215-516-3990
If you have no legal residence, principal place of business, or principal office or agency in any state:	Attn: EIN Operation Philadelphia, PA 19255 Telephone 215-516-6999 Fax-TIN 215-516-3990

Employer identification Number (EIN). In order to pay federal taxes for your household employee, you will need an employer identification number (EIN). This is a nine-digit number issued by the IRS. It is not the same as your Social Security number. If you already have an EIN, use that number. If you do not have an EIN, use Form SS-4, *Application for Employer Identification Number,* from Chapter 50, *2005 Federal Tax Forms and Schedules You Can Use or at www.irs.gov.* You will need to send it to the IRS office listed in Table 42-1 for your location or you can file it while on the IRS Web site. If you need further information regarding the IRS process for issuing an EIN number, call or fax the IRS office in your area or see the IRS Web site.

Social Security and Medicare Taxes

If you pay a household employee cash wages of $1,400 or more during a calendar year, those wages are subject to Social Security and Medicare taxes. Payments in kind (meals, transportation, etc.) are not used to figure the $1,400 amount or to figure the taxes. The taxes are figured on all cash wage payments in the year, regardless of when they were earned.

What is taxable compensation? Table 42-2 may help to clarify what is reportable income to your employee. Remember that state and local income tax and unemployment or disability and other employment tax rules may be different.

Family members. Social Security and Medicare taxes do not apply to household services performed by your spouse or by your child under 21. However, Social Security and Medicare taxes **apply** to wages you pay your parents for household services if:

1. you are a surviving spouse or a divorced individual who hasn't remarried or have a spouse living in the home who has a mental or physical condition which results in the spouse's being incapable of caring for a child or stepchild for at least four continuous weeks in the quarter in which the service is performed; and
2. your child or stepchild is living in the home; and
3. your child or stepchild is under age 18 or has a mental or physical condition which requires the personal care of an adult for at least four continuous weeks in the quarter in which the service is performed

TAXALERT

If a person is an employee whom you pay a total of $1,400 or more per year, you have tax filing and payment responsibilities.

TAXPLANNER

Babysitters. If the babysitter watches your children in your house at the time you specify, IRS rulings conclude that the person is an employee. It's not enough to stop giving the sitter a ride home in an attempt to make him or her appear more independent. You would need to use sitters who watch children in *their* homes or other facilities during set business hours. Or you can rotate sitters to avoid paying anyone more than $1,400 per year. As previously noted, sitters under age 18 who are full-time students are exempt from Social Security taxes.

Paying the tax. Both you and the employee pay a share of the Social Security and Medicare taxes on the employee's wages. For 2005, the tax rate for Social Security is 6.2% for both you and the employee (a total of 12.4%). The tax rate for Medicare is 1.45% for both you and the employee (a total of 2.9%). The 6.2% Social Security tax applies only to the first $90,000 you paid each employee during calendar year 2005. The 1.45% Medicare tax applies to all wages.

TAXALERT

For 2006, the Social Security and Medicare tax rates will not change. The 2006 Social Security wage base amount has not yet been determined. The 2005 OASDI Trustees Report estimates that the FICA wage base will be $93,000 in 2006. You can confirm the actual wage base for 2006 at http://www.ssa.gov/OACT/COLA/cbb.html.

You must pay the total of these taxes (your employee's and your share) yourself if you do not deduct the employee's share from his or her wages. Any of the employee's share you pay is added income to the employee. This income must be included in box 1, *Wages, tips, other compensation,* on Form W-2, *Wage and Tax Statement,* but do not count it as cash wages for Social Security and Medicare purposes. You must also include the employee Social Security and Medicare taxes you pay in boxes 4 and 6 of the employee's Form W-2, even though the taxes were not actually withheld.

TAXPLANNER

If you would rather pay your employee's share of Social Security and Medicare taxes without deducting it from wages, you may do so. Any portion you do pay, however, is added to the compensation to your employee, even though it does not constitute cash wages for Social Security and Medicare purposes. Although it may be easier if you pay your employee's share of Social Security and Medicare taxes, it does raise *your* cost. You should come to an agreement with your employee on this issue before he or she begins work.

Table 42-2. **What Is Taxable Compensation?**

	Federal Income Tax	Social Security and Medicare (FICA)	Federal Unemployment Tax (FUTA)
Salary paid by cash, check, or other means	Yes	Yes	Yes
Cash bonus (overtime, holiday, etc.)[1]	Yes	Yes	Yes
Cash gifts (holiday, birthday, wedding, etc.)[1]	Yes	Yes	Yes
Gifts of property (holiday, birthday, etc.)[1],[2]	Yes	Yes	Yes
Vacation Pay	Yes	Yes	Yes
Sign-on bonus	Yes	Yes	Yes
Value of meals & lodging on your premises as part of job and for your convenience	No	No	No
Car provided to employee for commutation	Yes	Yes	Yes
Value of public transit tokens provided (less than $100 per month)	No	No	No
Car provided to employee to do work for you only	No	No	No
Insurance for employee's own car	Yes	Yes	Yes
Employee's medical insurance bills you pay	No	No	No
Uniforms you give to employee to wear on your premises	No	No	No
Cash uniform allowance	Yes	Yes	Yes
Value of vacation when nanny accompanies family to care for children	No	No	No
Employee's legal fees you pay	Yes	Yes	Yes
Employee's social security taxes you pay	Yes	No	Yes
Employee's income taxes you pay	Yes	Yes	Yes

[1]Unless less than $30, then nontaxable.

[2]Taxable value is lesser of cost or fair market value. Gifts valued at less than $30 are not taxable.

TAXPLANNER

If you and your employee agree that the employee will be responsible for his or her own share of the Social Security and Medicare taxes, you should also reach agreement on how it is to be paid. To minimize difficulties, you may want to start withholding immediately rather than wait until $1,400 has been earned each year. This avoids the problem of the employee having to pay you $107.10 (7.65% × $1,400) once the threshold has been met.

Example

Meredith Cabot pays her full-time housekeeper a $15,000 salary. She also pays both the employer's share of the Social Security and Medicare taxes (7.65% of $15,000, or $1,147.50) and the employee's share (7.65% of $15,000, or $1,147.50). For federal income tax purposes, the housekeeper's total compensation for the year is $16,147.50 ($15,000 plus $1,147.50), even though only $15,000 is subject to Social Security and Medicare taxes.

Federal Income Tax Withholding

If your household employee requests income tax withholding, and you agree, you must withhold an amount from each payment based on the information shown on the **Form W-4,** *Employee's Withholding Allowance Certificate,* given to you by the employee. See Chapter 6, *Wages, Salaries, and Other Earnings,* for more information about Form W-4. Publication 15 (Circular E), *Employer's Tax Guide,* explains how to figure the amount to withhold.

TAXPLANNER

It is your decision whether or not to withhold income tax from your employee's compensation, even if withholding is requested by your employee. However, if you do withhold for an employee, everything that you pay your employee—whether cash or noncash—is income subject to withholding. Some of the more common forms of compensation for household employees are (1) salaries; (2) over-

time and bonuses; (3) meals, unless provided in your home and for your convenience; and (4) lodging, unless provided in your home, for your convenience, and as a condition of employment. As a general rule, if you have live-in domestic help, any meals and lodging you provide are *not* considered compensation. A car that you provide solely for use in transporting family members and doing household errands would not be considered compensation. However, a car provided to a domestic employee for his or her personal use (including getting to and from your house) would be considered income to him or her. Other forms of compensation include cash reimbursement for the employee's personal expenses, such as car insurance and vacation expenses. However, up to $105 per month in public transit passes and up to $200 per month for qualified parking can be provided to an employee without any federal tax effect. State tax laws may be different.

Any income tax withholding you pay for an employee without deducting it from the employee's wages is added income to the employee and subject to income, Social Security, and Medicare taxes.

Form W-4 and Publication 15 can be requested by calling 1-800-TAX-FORM (1-800-829-3676) or downloaded at **www.irs.gov**.

Earned income credit advance payment. You must make advance payments of the earned income credit to any employee who is eligible to claim the earned income credit and requests advance payment of it. Who is eligible to claim the credit is explained in Chapter 38, *Other Credits Including the Earned Income Credit.*

The employee makes the request by giving you a completed **Form W-5,** *Earned Income Credit Advance Payment Certificate.* Each payday, you make the payments to your employee from the Social Security, Medicare, and withheld income taxes that you would otherwise pay to the Internal Revenue Service. For more information, see Publication 15.

You must notify any employees not having federal income tax withheld that they may be eligible for an income tax refund because of the earned income credit.

For more information about employment taxes, see Publication 926, *Household Employer's Tax Guide*.

Federal Unemployment Tax (FUTA)

Federal unemployment tax (FUTA) is for your employee's unemployment insurance. If you paid cash wages of $1,000 or more to household employees in any calendar quarter this year or last year, you are liable for FUTA for any employees you have this year. However, the tax does not apply to wages paid to your spouse, your parents, or your children under 21 years old.

Rate. The rate for 2005 and 2006 is 6.2% on the first $7,000 of cash wages paid to each employee during the calendar year.

The tax is imposed on you as the employer. Unlike Social Security, Medicare, and federal income tax, federal unemployment tax is *solely* an employer's responsibility. It is an additional cost to you of having domestic help. You must not collect or deduct it from the wages of your employees.

You may claim a credit against your federal unemployment tax for the state unemployment tax you paid by the due date for filing your Form 1040. The credit can be up to 5.4% of the federal tax. So your net federal tax may be as low as 0.8% if you pay the state tax on time.

When you hire a household employee, you should contact your state employment tax office to get information on how to file the state return and to get a state reporting number. The state will help you to figure the amount of tax you will pay the state. See the instructions to Schedule H for how to claim the credit.

Example 1

George Darby paid his housekeeper $3,000 in cash during the first quarter of 2005. He must pay federal unemployment tax (FUTA) for any employees he has during any part of 2005. Since he was liable for FUTA in 2005, any cash wages he pays to his employees in 2006 will also be subject to FUTA.

Example 2

George Darby paid his housekeeper and sole employee $12,000 for all of 2005. Since FUTA is assessed only on the first $7,000 of cash compensation paid to each employee during the calendar year, George's FUTA liability (before any credit for state unemployment taxes) was $434 ($7,000 × 6.2%).

Reporting and paying taxes on wages paid to household employees. Unless you own a business as a sole proprietor, you should report these taxes on Schedule H attached to your 2005 Form 1040. These taxes are added to your income taxes. The total must be paid during the course of the year. See Chapter 5, *Tax Withholding and Estimated Tax.*

If you are a sole proprietor who has nonhousehold employees, you should be filing Form 940 (or 940-EZ) annually to report FUTA (unemployment taxes) and Form 941 quarterly to report and remit federal income tax and FICA (Social Security and Medicare) tax withholdings. The IRS gives sole proprietors the option of including withholdings and taxes paid for domestic employees with withholdings and taxes paid for nondomestic employees on Forms 940 and 941. Alternatively, sole proprietors can exclude domestic employees from Forms 940 and 941 and file Schedule H with their own income tax returns.

Whether or not you are a sole proprietor, once you withhold tax from an employee, you must remit the tax to the IRS. If you do not, you could be responsible for substantial fines and penalties.

Example

Paul and Irene Jurgens employ Emily Whitney as a housekeeper and babysitter. Emily's weekly salary is $200, which is paid by Paul in cash each Friday. In addition, Irene pays Emily $50 for helping once a month on weekends when the Jurgens entertain. Emily uses her own car to drive to and from the Jurgens' home but is reimbursed weekly by Irene for gas to drive the children to school. Emily gives Irene a list of the actual miles driven and Irene pays her 40.5 cents per mile. Four times a year Paul pays $400 for Emily's medical insurance. Irene pays Emily's $300 vacation airfare in June and gives her a $500 bonus in December. Since Emily's annual compensation is expected to be over $1,400, the Jurgens decide to deduct FICA from Emily's salary from the beginning of the year. Emily completes and provides to the Jurgens a Form W-4. The Jurgens agree to deduct income tax from Emily's compensation. Emily does not qualify for the earned income credit. The state in which they reside has a flat income tax of 4% and unemployment taxes of 2% to be paid by Emily, and 7% to be paid by the Jurgens on income up to $7,000.

Since Emily has provided documentation indicating how many miles were driven, for what purpose and when, and since the reimbursement is within the IRS guideline of 40.5 cents per mile, Emily's reimbursement for gas is not taxable income to her. Also, since Emily does not have the option of receiving cash for the medical insurance premiums, the reimbursement for medical insurance is not taxable to her. The following worksheet (Table 42-3) summarizes the taxable compensation paid to Emily and the taxes required to be deducted from her pay. The Jurgens would provide a Form W-2 to Emily showing taxable earnings of $11,800 and withholdings as indicated on Table 42-3. A copy would be sent to the Social Security Administration. They would report the federal income tax withholding and FICA and pay the required FUTA and their portion of Social Security ($902) with their Form 1040, reflected on Schedule H. The state income tax and unemployment tax withholdings would be remitted as required by the state authorities. In addition, the Jurgens would be liable for $490 of state unemployment tax, which would also be remitted as required but not later than the due date for filing the Jurgens' Form 1040. The employer is responsible for FUTA, which in this case would be $56 ($7,000 × 6.2% less 5.4% maximum credit).

The Jurgens will have to either increase the withholding from their wages or increase their estimated tax payments by $2,875 in order to pay their household employee's taxes during the course of the year.

A sample of a completed Schedule H is included in this chapter for this example. You may want to see the IRS instructions to Schedule H for further information.

TAXORGANIZER

Forms you will need. You will need the following federal tax forms if you employ household help:

Schedule H
Form W-2, Wage and Tax Statement

Table 42-3. **Worksheet for Domestic Employee's Wages**

Employee's Name **Emily Whitney**   Employee's Social Security Number **123-45-6789**

	Cash Paid Directly to Employee	Cash Paid to Third Parties	Non-Cash Amounts	Taxes Paid on Behalf of Employee	Total Earnings for W-2 Purposes	Social Security and Medicare Tax Deducted	Federal Income Tax Deducted	State Income Tax Deducted	Other State Taxes Deducted	Earned Income Credit Advanced
January	$850				$850	$65	$65	$34	$17	
February	850				850	65	65	34	17	
March	1,050				1,050	80	95	42	21	
April	850				850	65	65	34	17	
May	850				850	65	65	34	17	
June	1,050		$300		1,350	103	137	54	27	
July	850				850	65	65	34	17	
August	850				850	65	65	34	7	
September	1,050				1,050	80	95	42		
October	850				850	65	65	34		
November	850				850	65	65	34		
December	1,550				1,550	119	167	62		
Total	$11,500		$300		$11,800	$902	$1,014	$472	$140	

Form W-3, Transmittal of Wage and Tax Statements
Form W-4, Employees' Withholding Allowance Certificate

You will need to contact your state tax authorities for applicable state tax forms.

As an employer, you must keep records of any cash or noncash wages paid to your employee as well as any taxes withheld from those wages. Table 42-3 is designed to help you accumulate this information. You will need this information at year-end to prepare the employee's Form W-2, which must be given to the employee by January 31 of the following year. If you are preparing more than one Form W-2, you also will need Form W-3, *Transmittal of Wage and Tax Statements*, to send copies to the Social Security Administration. The government copies must be sent by the last day of February of the following year.

TAX ORGANIZER

Records you should keep

- Employee's name and Social Security Number exactly as it appears on the SSN card
- Employer Identification Number from the IRS
- Records of payments made to domestic help
- Copies of payroll tax forms (W-2, W-3, etc.) filed for domestic help

SCHEDULE H
(Form 1040)

Department of the Treasury
Internal Revenue Service (99)

Household Employment Taxes
(For Social Security, Medicare, Withheld Income, and Federal Unemployment (FUTA) Taxes)
▶ Attach to Form 1040, 1040NR, 1040-SS, or 1041.
▶ See separate instructions.

OMB No. 1545-0074

2005

Attachment
Sequence No. **44**

Name of employer

Paul and Irene Jurgens

Social security number
923 : 45 : 6789

Employer identification number
1 1 : 1 : 1 1 1 1 1 1 1

A Did you pay **any one** household employee cash wages of $1,400 or more in 2005? (If any household employee was your spouse, your child under age 21, your parent, or anyone under age 18, see the line A instructions on page H-3 before you answer this question.)

- ☒ **Yes.** Skip lines B and C and go to line 1.
- ☐ **No.** Go to line B.

B Did you withhold Federal income tax during 2005 for any household employee?

- ☐ **Yes.** Skip line C and go to line 5.
- ☐ **No.** Go to line C.

C Did you pay **total** cash wages of $1,000 or more in **any** calendar **quarter** of 2004 or 2005 to **all** household employees? (**Do not** count cash wages paid in 2004 or 2005 to your spouse, your child under age 21, or your parent.)

- ☐ **No.** **Stop.** Do not file this schedule.
- ☐ **Yes.** Skip lines 1-9 and go to line 10 on the back. (Calendar year taxpayers having no household employees in 2005 **do not** have to complete this form for 2005.)

Part I   Social Security, Medicare, and Income Taxes

1	Total cash wages subject to social security taxes (see page H-3)	**1** 11,800	
2	Social security taxes. Multiply line 1 by 12.4% (.124)	**2**	1,463
3	Total cash wages subject to Medicare taxes (see page H-3)	**3** 11,800	
4	Medicare taxes. Multiply line 3 by 2.9% (.029)	**4**	342
5	Federal income tax withheld, if any	**5**	1,014
6	**Total social security, Medicare, and income taxes** (add lines 2, 4, and 5)	**6**	2,819
7	Advance earned income credit (EIC) payments, if any	**7**	—
8	**Net taxes** (subtract line 7 from line 6)	**8**	2,819

9 Did you pay **total** cash wages of $1,000 or more in **any** calendar **quarter** of 2004 or 2005 to household employees? (**Do not** count cash wages paid in 2004 or 2005 to your spouse, your child under age 21, or your parent.)

- ☐ **No.** **Stop.** Enter the amount from line 8 above on Form 1040, line 62. If you are not required to file Form 1040, see the line 9 instructions on page H-4.
- ☒ **Yes.** Go to line 10 on the back.

For Paperwork Reduction Act Notice, see Form 1040 instructions.   Cat. No. 12187K   Schedule H (Form 1040) 2005

Schedule H (Form 1040) 2005   Page **2**

Part II   Federal Unemployment (FUTA) Tax

		Yes	No
10	Did you pay unemployment contributions to only one state? (If you paid contributions to the states of XXXXXXX, XXXXXXX, or XXXXXXX, check "No.") **10**	X	
11	Did you pay all state unemployment contributions for 2005 by April 17, 2006? Fiscal year filers, see page H-4 **11**	X	
12	Were all wages that are taxable for FUTA tax also taxable for your state's unemployment tax? **12**	X	

Next: If you checked the **"Yes"** box on **all** the lines above, complete Section A.

If you checked the **"No"** box on **any** of the lines above, skip Section A and complete Section B.

Section A

13	Name of the state where you paid unemployment contributions ▶	Any State	
14	State reporting number as shown on state unemployment tax return ▶	22-222	

15	Contributions paid to your state unemployment fund (see page H-4)	**15**	490	
16	Total cash wages subject to FUTA tax (see page H-4)	**16**	7,000
17	**FUTA tax.** Multiply line 16 by .008. Enter the result here, skip Section B, and go to line 26 . .	**17**	56

Section B

18   Complete all columns below that apply (if you need more space, see page H-4):

(a) Name of state	(b) State reporting number as shown on state unemployment tax return	(c) Taxable wages (as defined in state act)	(d) State experience rate period		(e) State experience rate	(f) Multiply col. (c) by .054	(g) Multiply col. (c) by col. (e)	(h) Subtract col. (g) from col. (f). If zero or less, enter -0-.	(i) Contributions paid to state unemployment fund
			From	To					

19	Totals	**19**		
20	Add columns (h) and (i) of line 19 . . . . **20**		**20**	
21	Total cash wages subject to FUTA tax (see the line 16 instructions on page H-4)	**21**	
22	Multiply line 21 by 6.2% (.062)	**22**	
23	Multiply line 21 by 5.4% (.054) **23**		**23**	
24	Enter the **smaller** of line 20 or line 23 . . . . **24**	
	XXXXXXX, XXXXXXX, and XXXXXXX employers must use the worksheet on page X of the instructions and check the applicable box). XXXXXXX ☐ XXXXXXX ☐ XXXXXXX ☐		
25	**FUTA tax.** Subtract line 24 from line 22. Enter the result here and go to line 26	**25**	

Part III   Total Household Employment Taxes

26	Enter the amount from line 8	**26**	2,819
27	Add line 17 (or line 25) and line 26	**27**	2,875

28   Are you required to file Form 1040?

☒ **Yes.   Stop.** Enter the amount from line 27 above on Form 1040, line 62. **Do not** complete Part IV below.

☐ **No.**   You may have to complete Part IV. See page H-4 for details.

Part IV   Address and Signature—Complete this part only if required. See the line 28 instructions on page H-4.

Address (number and street) or P.O. box if mail is not delivered to street address	Apt., room, or suite no.
City, town or post office, state, and ZIP code	

Under penalties of perjury, I declare that I have examined this schedule, including accompanying statements, and to the best of my knowledge and belief, it is true, correct, and complete. No part of any payment made to a state unemployment fund claimed as a credit was, or is to be, deducted from the payments to employees.

▶ _____   ▶ _____
Employer's signature   Date

43

U.S. Citizens Working Abroad: Tax Treatment of Foreign Earned Income

Introduction

U.S. citizens and **resident aliens** *are taxed on their worldwide income regardless of where it is earned, paid, or received. But U.S. citizens living abroad get certain tax benefits that are not available back home.* **Employees** *and* **self-employed** *individuals living abroad may elect to exclude up to $80,000 of their foreign-earned*

income from taxation in 2005. Employees and self-employed individuals may also exclude or deduct part of their housing costs from **taxable** *income. This chapter tells you about all the tax benefits you get from living abroad and what you have to do to qualify for them.*

How to Qualify for the Foreign Earned Income Exclusion

You qualify for the foreign earned income exclusion if you are a U.S. citizen, you have a **tax home** in a foreign country, and you meet either the foreign residence test or the physical presence test, described below.

Generally, if you are a resident alien of the United States, you may qualify for the foreign earned income exclusion if you satisfy the physical presence test. This assumes that you have not permanently left the United States and that you plan to continue your resident alien status.

Tax home. Your tax home generally is the location of your principal place of employment, which may or may not coincide with the location of your family's residence. Among the factors that are important in determining whether or not your tax home is outside the United States are the anticipated duration of your overseas assignment and whether or not you will return to the same employment location in the United States. Under IRS guidelines, an anticipated short-term (less than 1-year) assignment overseas, followed by a return to the same place of em-

ployment in the United States, would indicate that you do not have a tax home outside the United States.

If you meet either the foreign residence test or the physical presence test, you are eligible for two exclusions—the foreign earned income exclusion and the foreign housing exclusion. Self-employed individuals are eligible for a housing **deduction** rather than the housing exclusion (see the discussion later in this chapter).

Foreign residence test. The foreign residence test requires that you be a "bona fide resident" of a foreign country (or more than one foreign country) for an uninterrupted period that includes an entire tax year. Whether or not you are a bona fide resident is a subjective question of your intent, the answer to which is determined by the facts and circumstances of your particular situation, including the purpose of your trip and the nature and length of your stay abroad.

The following factors are considered by the IRS in determining your intent to be a "bona fide" resident in a specific place.

1. The type of quarters you occupy (hotel or rooming house, rented quarters, purchased quarters, or quarters furnished by your employer)

2. How long your family resided with you during the tax year
3. The length of the uninterrupted period of time during which you have been living outside the United States
4. The nature of any conditions or limitations concerning your employment agreement and the type and term of your visa to live/work in the foreign country
5. Whether you maintain a home in the United States and, if so, its rental status and the relationship of any tenants to you

If you make a statement to the authorities of a foreign country that you are not a resident of that country, and if you are not taxed as a resident of that country, you do not qualify as a bona fide resident of that country.

Once you have met the foreign residence test for an entire tax year, your qualification is retroactive to the first day you established your bona fide residence. Occasional trips to the United States for business or vacation do not affect your qualification.

Example 1
You moved from the United States to a foreign country, arriving on September 15, 2005. You entered the country under a resident visa with your family for a 3-year assignment. You did not declare to the foreign authorities that you were not a resident of that country. You qualify as a bona fide resident of the foreign country if these facts remain the same through December 31, 2006. You may file your 2005 U.S. income tax return (or amend your original 2005 tax return) to claim the benefits of being a bona fide resident of a foreign country for the period September 15, 2005, through December 31, 2005.

Example 2
George has been a resident of the United Kingdom for 5 consecutive years. If he moves to France this year, he continues to be a bona fide resident of a foreign country. An uninterrupted period of bona fide residence may include residence in more than one foreign country in a given year.

Example 3
Amy moved to France with her family on June 15, 2004, for a job assignment of indefinite length. On December 3, 2005, she was transferred back to the United States. She did not satisfy the bona fide residence test in either year, since she did not maintain a bona fide residence in a foreign country for a period that includes a complete tax year. However, she may qualify for the foreign exclusions under the physical presence test.

Physical presence test. This test simply requires that you be physically present in a foreign country (or countries) for 330 full days during any consecutive 12-month period. This is a purely objective test. There is no reference to your intentions or to any other factors that determine bona fide residence abroad.

Two important rules to keep in mind regarding this test are as follows:

1. A full day is a 24-hour period commencing at midnight. Thus, a day in which you travel *to or from the United States* is not a full day in a foreign country.
2. When you travel *between foreign countries,* the travel days will qualify as full days in a foreign country, provided that the time spent outside of either foreign country during the journey (*i.e.,* time spent over international waters and/or time spent in the United States) is less than 24 hours.

TAXORGANIZER

Keep a calendar. Keep a record of your travel days in and out of the United States and retain it with your other important tax records. The calendar should be supported by airline tickets, stamped passports, or other evidence of arrival and departure dates.

The Foreign Earned Income Exclusion
If you qualify, you may elect to exclude a maximum of $80,000 in foreign earned income from your U.S. taxable income in 2005. The amount of the exclusion will be indexed for inflation beginning in 2008.

The amount of earned income you may exclude depends on either (1) the number of days during the year in which you were a bona fide resident of a foreign country or (2) the number of days you were physically present in a foreign country during a 12-month period. These are known as your "qualifying days." If you are out of the U.S. for the entire year, you may exclude all of your earned income up to the $80,000 limit. However, if you are out of the U.S. for only part of the year, you generally must prorate the exclusion based on your number of qualifying days during the taxable year.

Example
You were a bona fide resident of a foreign country for 300 days during 2005. The maximum amount of income you may exclude from U.S. taxes is 300/365 × $80,000, or $65,753. Your exclusion is, of course, limited by the amount of foreign income you earn. If you earn less than the maximum allowed, you may exclude only that lower amount.

Only foreign earned income is eligible for the exclusion. Earned income is income you receive for the performance of personal services. It does *not* include **dividends, interest, capital gains, rental property income, and other kinds of unearned income.** For example, interest paid on a bank account in the United Kingdom by a U.S. expatriate on assignment in London is not eligible for the exclusion, since it is not foreign *earned* income.

Earned income may be received in cash or as benefits-in-kind and include the following:

- Salaries, wages, bonuses, commissions, overseas incentive premiums, and so on.
- A housing allowance. This may take the form of a cash payment to you, a cash payment by your employer directly to a landlord, or housing provided by your employer. When a cash payment is made, you must report the full amount as income. When housing is provided, your employer should furnish you with an estimate of its **fair market value, which is used for income-reporting purposes.**
- An automobile allowance. A cash allowance for an automobile should be included in your income. When an automobile is provided by your employer, an amount representing the value of its personal use to you should be included in your income.
- A cost-of-living allowance.
- An education allowance (*e.g.,* for the cost of schooling your children).
- Home leave. The value of home leave benefits provided to you and your family is included in your income. However, if you spend a significant portion of your home leave on business, you may be justified in characterizing your portion of the trip as a business trip and thereby exclude your travel expenses from income.

- Rest and relaxation airfare.
- A moving expense reimbursement or allowance, in certain cases.
- A tax reimbursement or allowance.

Source of earned income. The source of earned income depends on the place where the services are rendered. If the services are performed in the United States, the income is considered U.S. source income. On the other hand, if the services are performed in a foreign country, the income is foreign source. For the income to be excluded on your tax return, the earned income must be from sources within a foreign country (or countries).

How to compute your foreign source income. To compute your foreign source income for purposes of the foreign earned income exclusion, you must determine your earned income from sources outside the United States.

Foreign source earned income includes *all* income received for personal services performed outside the United States. The place of payment is irrelevant: a payment made into a U.S. bank account by a U.S.-based employer for services performed outside the United States is foreign source income. If you perform services both inside and outside the United States during the tax year, you must determine what portion of your income is from U.S. sources and what portion is from foreign sources.

Example 1

You received $50,000 for services performed in 2005. You worked a total of 240 days during the year, 235 days in the United Kingdom on foreign assignment and 5 days in the United States for a technical meeting. The source of your earned income is as follows:

$$\frac{\text{5 days worked in the United States}}{\text{240 days worked worldwide}} \times \$50,000 = \$1,042$$

$$\frac{\text{235 days worked outside the United States}}{\text{240 days worked worldwide}} \times \$50,000 = \$48,958$$

Your U.S. source income is $1,042, and your foreign source income is $48,958.

There are several other considerations to keep in mind when you are figuring out the source of your income:

1. If there has been a significant change in your rate of compensation during the year, it may be appropriate to allocate your compensation separately for the days worked and income earned in the respective periods.
2. If a payment is received during the year for services performed in a prior year, it may be appropriate to compute the foreign source portion of that payment based on the days worked in the prior year. It is not possible to exclude this prior year foreign source income using the current year's foreign earned income exclusion, but it might be possible to exclude some or all of the income on your current year's tax return to the extent that last year's exclusion was not fully used up.
3. Do not take into account vacation or holiday travel to the U.S. as part of your workday calculation.

Example 2

In 2004, you were eligible for the full $80,000 foreign earned income exclusion but only had $70,000 of foreign source earned income that was excluded on your 2004 tax return. Therefore, you have $10,000 of unused exclusion from 2004. In 2005, your compensation includes $12,000 of foreign source income earned in 2004 (in this case, a bonus payment). You are able to exclude $10,000 of the $12,000 of income on your 2005 tax return. The $10,000 exclusion is in addition to any exclusion you might have for foreign compensation earned and received in 2005.

The Foreign Housing Exclusion

If you qualify as a U.S. citizen living abroad, you may elect to exclude from your U.S. taxable income the excess of reasonable housing expenses over a "base housing amount." The base housing amount ($12,191 for 2005) is 16% of the salary for a U.S. government employee at the GS-14, step 1 level. The base amount is prorated by the ratio of the number of qualifying days to the total days in the year.

Example

You had $18,000 of qualified housing expenses in your 2005 qualifying period. Based on an allocation of your earned income, you determine that you had $98,000 of foreign source income. Furthermore, you had a qualifying period of 330 days in the tax year. Assume that the base housing amount is $12,191. Your housing exclusion is computed as follows:

1) Housing expenses	$18,000
2) Number of qualifying days	330
3) Total days in the tax year	365
4) Base housing amount	$12,191
5) 330/365 × $12,191	$11,022
6) Housing exclusion (line 1 − line 5)	$6,978

Assuming the same facts, you calculate your foreign earned income exclusion as follows:

1) Maximum foreign earned income exclusion	$80,000
2) Number of qualifying days	330
3) Total days in tax year	365
4) 330/365 × $80,000	$72,329
5) Total foreign source income	$98,000
6) Less: Housing exclusion	($6,978)
7) Total foreign source income available for exclusion	$91,022
8) Smaller of line 4 or 7	$72,329

Your foreign earned income exclusion is $72,329. In addition, your foreign housing exclusion is $6,978. Your total exclusion is $79,307.

Foreign housing deduction for self-employed individuals. If you are a self-employed individual and you do not have an employer to provide housing, you may *deduct* the cost of foreign housing, net of the base housing amount, in computing your **adjusted gross income.** Your housing deduction is limited to the amount by which your foreign earned income exceeds your foreign earned income exclusion for that year.

If you are both an employee and a self-employed individual during the same tax year, see Publication 54, *Tax Guide for U.S. Citizens and Resident Aliens Abroad.*

TaxPlanner

When to elect the foreign earned income exclusion and the foreign housing exclusion. You elect and calculate the foreign earned income exclusion and the foreign housing exclusion separately using Form 2555 or, in some cases, Form 2555-EZ. The elections can be made on a tax return that you file on time, on an amended tax return, or on a late-filed tax return that is filed within 1 year of the original due date. The IRS also allows the elections to be made later under certain circumstances. When you are deciding whether or not to use the exclusions, you should take into account a number of factors, including the level of taxation in the foreign country in which you are living, the type of foreign assignment you are on, and your employer's policies concerning individuals on foreign assignment.

When you elect the foreign income exclusion, you are required to reduce your otherwise deductible expenses that are associated with the excluded income. Similarly, foreign taxes available for the foreign tax credit must also be reduced (see *Foreign Tax Credit,* later).

If you are living in a foreign country with a high tax rate, you may be better off forgoing the exclusions and claiming a larger foreign tax credit. In this case, forgoing the exclusions might result in a higher current tax liability but may also create larger foreign tax credits that you might be able to use in other years to offset tax on foreign source income. In countries with moderate or low tax rates, it is usually to your advantage to claim the exclusions. In any event, you should calculate your taxes with and without the exclusions to see which is more beneficial to you.

Once you elect the exclusion(s), you may revoke either or both of them by attaching a statement to your return or your amended return stating that you do not wish to claim the exclusion(s). Once revoked, you may not claim the exclusions again for the next 5 years without obtaining IRS approval.

Employer-Provided Meals and Lodging

Meals and lodging provided in kind by, or on behalf of, an employer to an employee or to his or her spouse or **dependents** are excluded from taxable income if certain requirements are met:

1. The meals are provided on the business premises of, and for the convenience of, the employer.
2. Lodging is furnished on the premises of, and for the convenience of, the employer, and the employee is required to accept this lodging as a condition of employment.

The IRS has taken a narrow view of the lodging exclusion. As a result, most employer-provided lodging is not excludable from your income. However, the exclusion applies if the employee resides in a camp that is provided by the employer because the employee's work site is in a remote area where satisfactory housing is not available on the open market. The camp has to be located as near as is practicable to the work site and should be furnished with a common area or enclave that is not available to the general public and normally accommodates 10 or more employees.

TaxAlert

You do not have to be living abroad to take advantage of this exclusion for employer-provided meals and lodging. All taxpayers are entitled to exclude the value of meals and lodging from taxable income when they are provided on the employer's premises for the employer's convenience and when the lodging must be accepted as a condition of employment.

Foreign Tax Credit

You may elect to claim a credit for foreign income taxes paid or accrued during the tax year, or you may claim the taxes paid as an itemized deduction. Generally, claiming a credit is more beneficial, since it results in a dollar-for-dollar reduction in your tax bill. The foreign tax credit on your U.S. return is limited to the lesser of (1) the actual foreign income taxes paid or accrued during the year (including carrybacks or carryforwards) or (2) the amount of U.S. tax attributable to foreign source taxable income for the year. The foreign tax credit is elected and calculated on Form 1116 (see Chapter 38, *Other Credits Including the Earned Income Credit*).

As mentioned above, if you elect either the foreign earned income exclusion or the foreign housing exclusion, the amount of foreign taxes that is available for credit is reduced.

TaxOrganizer

Keep a copy of your foreign tax return and receipts for taxes paid in order to support the foreign tax credit calculations. This may be needed if your return is audited by the IRS.

Example 1

You had $98,000 of foreign source income and $18,000 of qualified housing expenses in 2005. The total amount you may exclude from your income is $79,307. (See the foreign housing exclusion example above to learn how this number is calculated.) You paid $4,000 in foreign taxes for the year. You figure the amount that you may claim as a foreign tax credit as follows:

$$\frac{\$79,307}{\$98,000} \times \$4,000 = \$3,237$$

A maximum of $763 ($4,000 − $3,237) may be claimed as a foreign tax credit.

Example 2

You are an unmarried U.S. citizen currently residing in the United Kingdom. Your total **gross income** for the year is $120,000, all of which is compensation. You qualify for a foreign earned income exclusion of $80,000 and a housing exclusion of $5,000, for a total of $85,000. You spent 10% of your working days in the United States. You have $6,200 of **itemized deductions**, none of which directly relate to a particular class of income. The amount you may claim as a foreign tax credit is computed as follows:

Compensation from foreign sources (90% of $120,000)	$108,000
Deductions allocated to foreign source compensation: ($6,200 × 90%)	($5,580)
Less: Foreign earned income and housing exclusions	($85,000)
Foreign source taxable income	$17,420
U.S. source compensation (10% of $120,000)	$12,000
Balance of itemized deductions ($6,200 minus $5,580)	($620)
Total taxable income before personal exemptions	$ 28,800

The foreign tax credit limitation is calculated by determining the ratio of foreign source taxable income to total taxable income (as shown above). The ratio in the above example would be

$$\frac{\$17,420}{\$28,800} = 0.6049$$

This ratio is then multiplied by the U.S. tax liability for the year to determine the maximum amount of foreign tax credit usable for the year. If we assume that the U.S. tax is $3,475, the maximum credit would be $2,102 (0.6049 × $3,475).

Carryback and carryforward of foreign tax credit. Example 1 (above) shows how to determine the amount of foreign taxes that may be used as a credit. Example 2 shows how to determine the maximum amount of foreign tax credit that may be currently used as a credit against your U.S. taxes. If the amount of the foreign tax credit that is generated exceeds the amount that can be used currently, you may carry back the excess one year. The remainder, if any, may be carried forward for up to ten years. The excess credit must be carried back first, and used in the preceding year if possible, before it can be carried forward.

TaxPlanner

Planning tips for individuals on international assignment. Here is a list of items you should consider in planning your tax affairs and preparing your tax return:

1. **Sale of your principal residence.** A taxpayer may claim an exclusion of up to $250,000 for single taxpayers ($500,000 for joint filers) once every 2 years if the taxpayer owned the residence and occupied it as a principal residence for at least 2 of the 5 years before the sale or exchange.

   There are no special rules for U.S. home sales by expatriates. If you have a significant gain built up in your home and you expect your assignment to last more than 3 years, you should give consideration to selling your home. Otherwise, if you decide to sell at a later date, you may fail the 2-year out of 5-year test and some or all of the exclusion may be lost (see Chapter 16, *Selling Your Home*).

   Keep in mind that if you purchase your primary residence in a foreign country, the amount of any gain will be affected by changes in the foreign exchange rate.

2. **Individual retirement arrangements (IRAs).** An expatriate who contributes to an IRA (see Chapter 18, *Individual Retirement Arrangements [IRAs]*) must have earned income in excess of the total of his or her foreign earned income and foreign housing exclusions if he or she elects to use the exclusions.

   If you are covered by a company pension plan, your modified **adjusted gross income** must be below a certain level for your IRA contribution to be tax deductible. Similarly, your modified **adjusted gross income** must be below a certain level in order to make a contribution to a **Roth IRA** or an **education IRA.** Note that for purposes of computing modified **adjusted gross income,** the foreign earned income exclusion and the foreign housing exclusion amounts must be disregarded. For a more detailed discussion of IRAs, please refer to Chapter 18, *Individual Retirement Arrangements (IRAs)*.

3. **Alternative minimum tax (AMT).** For taxable years beginning after December 31, 1986, the maximum amount of AMT (see Chapter 32, *How to Figure Your Tax*) that can be offset with foreign tax credits is 90%.

   The American Jobs Creation Act of 2004 repealed the 90% limit on the AMT foreign tax credit beginning in tax year 2005. This is a positive change that will benefit taxpayers living in high-tax countries, in particular.

4. **Report of Foreign Bank and Financial Accounts.** You should become familiar with the filing requirements of Form TD F 90-22.1, which is a form that is used to provide information concerning foreign bank and financial accounts if in the aggregate their value exceeds $10,000. Significant penalties apply for noncompliance.

TaxOrganizer

Records you should keep.

- Keep a calendar of travel days to track workdays and non-workdays in the United States, the assignment country, and any other country. The calendar can be supported by airline tickets, stamped passports, or other evidence documenting arrival and departure dates.
- Keep a list of housing expenses in the host country.
- Keep a copy of your foreign tax returns and receipts for foreign taxes paid or accrued during the tax year, depending on the method used for claiming the foreign tax credit.

Foreign Citizens Living in the United States

Introduction

Almost everybody living in the United States—whether a U.S. citizen or not—is subject to U.S. income tax laws.

Foreign nationals working in the United States are either **resident aliens** *or* **nonresident aliens.** *Resident aliens, like U.S. citizens, are subject to U.S. tax on their worldwide income. Nonresident aliens are subject to U.S. tax only on certain types of their U.S. source income. Some foreign citizens living in the United States are not taxed at all—at least not by the U.S. government. A foreign citizen resident in the United States who*

works for a foreign government doing normal diplomatic work is exempt from the U.S. tax laws, provided that U.S. government employees working in that foreign country are exempt from its tax laws. Tax treaties between the United States and some foreign countries contain numerous other exceptions that alter the normal domestic U.S. tax laws.

This chapter tells you how to determine if you are a resident alien or a nonresident alien and how you should calculate your tax.

Determining Your Status

Whether you are a resident alien or a nonresident alien is of critical importance when you compute how much U.S. income tax you will pay. Your residency status will determine your filing status, the tax rate schedule applicable to your income, and the amount of your income that will be subject to U.S. income tax. Under rules that became effective in 1985, an alien must meet *either* one of the two following tests in order to be considered a resident of the United States for tax purposes:

1. **The green card test.** Have you been lawfully admitted to the United States for permanent residency? In other words, do you have a green card?
2. **The substantial presence test.** Have you been present in the United States for a substantial period of time? If you have been present in the United States for at least 31 days in the current year and if the total days you are present in the United States during the current year, plus one-third of the days present in the preceding calendar year, plus one-sixth of the

days present in the second preceding calendar year, are equal to at least 183 days, you will meet the substantial presence test and be considered a resident alien in the current year.

If you are considered a U.S. resident under the substantial presence test (and you were not a U.S. resident in the prior year), your residency period generally begins on the first day you were present in the United States in the current year. However, if you have a brief visit (or visits) to the United States, and the total days you spend in the United States during the visit (or visits) amount to 10 days or less, you may, under certain circumstances, ignore those days for purposes of determining when your residency period begins.

Example

You move to the United States on June 1, 2005, and spend a sufficient number of days in this country in 2005 to meet the substantial presence test. Prior to your actual arrival on June 1, you spent 10 days in the

United States from February 2 through February 11 to house hunt and to meet with your U.S. employer while you maintained your tax home in a foreign country. Your U.S. residency period begins on June 1. In the event you had stayed in the United States until February 12 (11 days), your U.S. residency period would have begun on February 2.

A similar rule applies in the year in which your U.S. residency terminates. Your residency period generally ends on the 31st of December. However, if you can show that you have closer connections to a foreign country for the remainder of the year, your U.S. residency generally ends on the last day you are present in the United States. Visits to the United States totaling 10 days or less following your departure may be disregarded in determining the last day of your U.S. residency.

TaxAlert

To take advantage of this closer connection rule and terminate your residency on the last day you are present in the United States, you may be required to attach a statement to your U.S. tax return for that year detailing the facts that support your closer connection to a foreign country.

Example
In 2005 you lived in the United States continuously from January 1 through October 31, when you moved to a foreign country and established a closer connection to it. Generally, you are considered to be a resident of the United States through October 31. If you return to the United States on business trips or on vacation during November and December and spend 10 days or less in total in the United States, your residency period terminates on October 31. If you spend more than 10 days in total in the United States in November and December, your U.S. residency period will be extended beyond October 31. The actual termination date will depend on the specific dates of your visits. You would also want to take into consideration any tax treaty benefits that might be available to you.

TaxOrganizer

Arrival and departure dates. To substantiate your arrival and departure dates to and from the United States, copies of travel tickets (airline, boat, etc.), stamped passports, and other relevant documentation should be retained in your tax files.

TaxAlert

Resident alien status. Even if you meet the substantial presence test, you can avoid being considered a resident alien if you are present in the United States for less than 183 days in the current year *and* you can show closer ties to a tax home in a foreign country (or, in the case of a move, no more than two foreign countries) than to the United States for the entire year. Whether you have closer ties to the United States or to a foreign country depends on the facts and circumstances of your situation. Consult a tax advisor for details. You will be required to furnish a statement with detailed information to the IRS if you take this closer connection position.

Election to Be Treated as a Resident
The tax law contains a provision that allows an alien to elect to be treated as a resident of the United States

for tax purposes (a "first year election"), even though he or she does not meet the green card or substantial presence test. The first year election allows an alien with significant U.S. presence toward the end of year 1 and who meets the substantial presence test in year 2 to elect to be treated as a U.S. resident alien in year 1. The alien can only make this first year election after he or she has met the substantial presence test in year 2. This may require filing an extension for the year 1 tax return. This election will be advantageous to some aliens, such as those who incur significant expenses when they first arrive in the United States (such as interest, deductible mortgage points, and real estate taxes related to a purchased home in the U.S.), which would be deductible for a resident but not for a nonresident. In addition, this election could also benefit married aliens who would otherwise be required to file using the married filing separate rates that apply to nonresidents. As U.S. residents under this election, they would be permitted to make a further election to be treated as residents for the entire year, thus permitting the filing of a joint return and the use of the more favorable joint return rates. An alien who meets the following criteria may make the election (please see the following Example):

1. Doesn't meet the green card or substantial presence tests for the current year,
2. Was not a resident alien in the prior year,
3. Meets the substantial presence test in the following year,
4. Is present in the United States for at least 31 consecutive days in the current year, and
5. Spends at least 75% of the days between the first of the 31 consecutive days and year-end in the United States. *(Note:* Up to 5 non–U.S. days will be counted as U.S. days for the purposes of this test.)

An alien who makes the election to be treated as a resident may also make a similar election on his or her tax return on behalf of dependent children if the children are not required to file tax returns on their own, assuming, of course, that the children also meet the requirements of the election. The filing of the election will enable an alien to take dependent exemptions for the children.

Example
Assume that an alien is present in the United States for the following periods:

7/4–8/15	43 days
9/16–11/25	71 days
12/16–12/31	16 days

During the testing period of July 4 through December 31, the individual is in the United States 130 days out of 181 days total. Including the 5 additional non-U.S. days, which can be counted as U.S. days, the individual is present in the United States on less than 75% of the days and cannot make the election for this period.

$$\frac{130 \text{ plus } 5}{181} = 74.6\%$$

However, since, during the testing period of September 16 through December 31, the individual was in the United States 87 days out of 107, which exceeds 75%, the individual could elect to be treated as a resident for the period of September 16 through December 31 (assuming that the other tests regarding the prior and subsequent years are also met).

TAXPLANNER

If you have a green card, you should be aware that you are considered a resident alien and that you are subject to tax on all of your worldwide income. If you have substantial U.S. or foreign investment income, you may want to transfer the income-producing assets to somebody else, for example, a spouse or other close relative who is still living abroad. Before making any transfers, however, you should consult with a tax advisor to consider possible gift tax and foreign tax implications.

TAXPLANNER

Substantial presence test. If you meet the substantial presence test described above, but you are present in the United States less than 183 days each year, you should examine your ties to another country. You might qualify for an exception to the substantial presence test if you can demonstrate that your ties to another country are stronger than your ties to the United States. You must file a statement with your tax return supporting your claim, or, if no return is required, a statement alone must be filed with the IRS.

If your ties are weak and you want to try to strengthen them, consider:

1. Maintaining a home in that country
2. Obtaining a driver's license issued by that country
3. Joining a religious, political, or cultural organization in that country
4. Maintaining or establishing a membership in a social organization in that country
5. Having a bank account in that country
6. Having personal property in that country such as cars, clothing, or jewelry
7. Continuing to vote in that country

If you spend a significant amount of time in the United States each year, you should carefully monitor the days to keep them below the 183-day threshold during the 3-year period considered under the substantial presence test.

TAXPLANNER

Do not assume that nonresident alien filing status necessarily results in greater savings than resident alien status. Resident alien status may result in a lower U.S. tax if you can use the lower joint return rates (for married resident aliens), if you are eligible for greater itemized deductions, and/or if you can benefit from the foreign tax credit.

Income tax treaties. Income tax treaties may have the effect of overriding the provisions of U.S. law. Consult a tax advisor for details.

Generally, tax treaties are consulted when an individual is a dual resident, that is, a resident of both the United States and a foreign country under each country's tax rules. When a treaty is used to claim that an individual is a nonresident of the United States, the individual must file Form 1040-NR and attach Form 8833, *Treaty-Based Return Position Disclosure,* to the return, presenting facts to support the claim of U.S. nonresidency.

An election to be treated as a nonresident of the United States under a treaty will apply for *all* purposes in computing the individual's income tax liability for the dual residency period.

TAXALERT

Filing Form 1040-NR may influence the determination by the Immigration and Naturalization Service as to whether you continue to qualify as a U.S. resident for immigration purposes if you hold a green card. Consult with immigration counsel to evaluate the impact of this tax position on your immigration situation. In addition, you should consult with a tax advisor so that you understand all the implications of a treaty-based nonresident filing position.

Dual-status aliens. A dual-status alien is a person who is considered a resident alien and a nonresident alien during the same tax year.

You are most likely to have dual status in the year of your arrival in or departure from the United States. You could, for example, be a resident alien until your departure from the United States. Thereafter, you would be a nonresident alien.

For purposes of computing your tax liability, different rules apply to the time when you are a resident alien and the time when you are a nonresident alien. However, it is necessary to fill out only one tax return. You may make a special election that may decrease your taxes for some years in which you have dual status. This election is discussed in the following section.

TAXPLANNER

An alien's residency status may not be the same for all purposes. The definition discussed above applies for federal income tax laws. Different rules apply in determining residency for state income tax and for federal gift and estate tax purposes.

How Resident Aliens Are Taxed

Like U.S. citizens, resident aliens are subject to tax on the worldwide income they receive, regardless of its source. Resident aliens compute their **taxable income** and income tax liability the same way U.S. citizens do. They include the same items in income and are entitled to take the same **deductions** as U.S. citizens.

TAXALERT

Rules for Individuals Giving up U.S. Citizenship or U.S. Residency

The American Jobs Creation Act of 2004 introduced significant changes to the rules for individuals giving up U.S. citizenship or U.S. residency. The new tax law applies to individuals who relinquish U.S. citizenship or terminate long-term residency after June 3, 2004.

Prior tax law contains a provision that treats long-term resident aliens who terminate their U.S. residency similarly to individuals who relinquish their U.S. citizenship. Under these rules, these individuals will continue to be subject to U.S. tax for 10 years on certain categories of U.S. source income and gains, provided they terminated residency principally for the purpose of avoiding U.S. income tax.

An individual (other than a U.S. citizen) is a long-term U.S. resident if the individual is a lawfully permanent U.S. resident in at least 8 out of 15 tax years ending with the tax year of expatriation. An individual is presumed to have a tax avoidance motive if the individual's average annual net income tax liability for 5 tax years ending before the loss of long-term residence is greater than $124,000 or if his/her net worth on such date is $622,000 or more. However, individuals may challenge the presumption of tax avoidance by submitting a complete and good faith request for a ruling to the IRS.

The 2004 tax law revises the rules applicable to expatriated individuals as follows:

- Objective standards replace the subjective "tax avoidance motive" standard to determine whether expatriated individuals are subject to U.S. tax on certain types of income. Under the new tax law, an expatriated individual is subject to U.S. tax on certain types of income unless the individual has an average annual U.S. federal income tax liability over the preceding five years of $127,000 (for tax year 2005) and a net worth of not more than $2 million. Limited exceptions apply. In addition, the expatriated individual has to certify that he has complied with all U.S. federal tax obligations for the preceding five years, and prove this if required. The ruling request procedure under prior law is no longer available.

- An expatriated individual continues to be treated as a U.S. citizen or long-term resident until he gives notice of an expatriating act or termination of residency to the Secretary of State or the Secretary of Homeland Security, and provides an information statement in accordance with the law.

- An expatriated individual subject to U.S. tax on certain types of income is subject to full U.S. federal taxation for any year in the 10 years following expatriation in which he is present in the U.S. for more than 30 days.

- Expatriated individuals are required to file annual returns for each year after expatriation that they are subject to U.S. tax on certain types of income, even if no U.S. federal tax is due.

- In addition, there may be U.S. gift and estate tax implications to the expatriated individual.

Note: If you are contemplating terminating residency or relinquishing U.S. citizenship, consult your tax advisor and immigration attorney. The rules are very complex, and special filings may be required.

Dual-Status Aliens

Dual-status aliens who are resident aliens for part of the tax year are taxed somewhat differently from U.S. citizens.

If you file a single return, you are taxed on your worldwide income for the part of the year in which you are a resident alien. For the part of the year in which you are a nonresident alien, only certain types of your U.S. source income is taxed.

Dual-status aliens who are married may not file a **joint return** or claim the standard deduction. Married taxpayers are taxed on their worldwide income for the part of the year in which they are resident aliens and only on certain types of their U.S. source income for the part of the year in which they are nonresidents. They are not, however, able to file a joint return and take advantage of the joint return rate schedule.

Exceptions. Dual-status aliens who are married have two other alternatives in the year in which they arrive in the United States:

1. **The Section 6013(h) election.** This election is available only in cases in which a U.S. citizen or resident alien is married to an individual who is a resident alien at the close of the tax year. An alien choosing this alternative is treated as a resident of the United States for the *entire tax year.* The most significant consequences of making this choice are:
a) All income, both U.S. and foreign source, is subject to tax, including any income you had during the period in which you were not a resident of the United States. This income would have been exempt from U.S. taxes, or taxed at a reduced rate, if you had not made the Section 6013(h) election.
b) You may claim **itemized deductions** for the period in which you were not a resident of the United States, if such items would otherwise qualify for deduction. Some examples are foreign real property taxes, mortgage interest, and medical expenses.
c) You may deduct, or elect to claim as a credit, foreign income taxes attributable to the period during which you were not a U.S. resident, which may substantially reduce or even eliminate U.S. income tax. Other benefits, however, like being able to file a joint return and thus be taxed at accordingly lower rates, are left intact. The result is that your net U.S. tax liability may be reduced.

2. **The Section 6013(g) election.** Under the Section 6013(g) election, a married couple may file a joint return as full-year residents of the United States if, at the end of the tax year, one spouse is a nonresident alien and the other is a citizen or resident of the United States.

The effects of making this election are the same as choosing the Section 6013(h) election, with one very significant distinction. The Section 6013(g) election is valid for all subsequent years in which you and your spouse qualify, including the year in which the resident alien leaves the United States. Once made, the Section 6013(g) election can be revoked. However, if you revoke the election, you cannot make another such election in the future. On the other hand, the Section 6013(h) election cannot be made by the same two individuals in any future tax year.

Example

You and your spouse became U.S. residents on April 1, 2005. Prior to your arrival in the United States, you earned $5,000 in wages and your spouse earned $1,000 in wages. Both of you also had $500 in joint interest income for the first 3 months of the year. Once in the United States, you earned $75,000 from April through December. Your spouse did not work in the United States. You had an additional $700 in joint interest income. Your itemized deductions equal the standard deduction. Your tax liabilities are computed as follows:

Alternative 1: Dual-status return, married filing separately (for period while a U.S. resident)

Salary	$75,000
Interest	350
Itemized deductions	(5,000)
Exemptions	(3,200)
Taxable income	$67,150
Tax	$13,668

You would not be taxed on your non-U.S. source income.

Alternative 2: Full-year election, joint return

Salary	$81,000
Interest	1,200

Itemized deductions	(10,000)
Exemptions	(6,400)
Taxable income	$65,800
Tax	$9,780

By electing to be treated as a resident alien for the entire tax year, you save $3,888 in federal income taxes. Note that your spouse could not be claimed as a dependent under Alternative 1, since your spouse had income during the U.S. residency period. Your spouse does not need to file a return under Alternative 1, since your spouse's income did not exceed the amount that requires you to file. (See Chapter 1, *Filing Information*.)

The $6,500 in income that you and your spouse had in your home country would probably be subject to tax there. If so, you would be eligible for the foreign tax credit if you filed under Alternative 2. The tax credit would further lower your taxes. See Chapter 38, *Other Credits Including the Earned Income Credit*, for a discussion of the foreign tax credit.

TAXPLANNER

In order to claim exemptions for a resident alien's spouse and/or children who are not eligible to obtain a Social Security number, an individual taxpayer identification number (an "ITIN") is required for each person. Obtaining such a tax ID number no longer necessitates going to the Social Security office with the family. Rather, these numbers are now obtained directly from the IRS. Alternatively, certain tax advisors are registered with the IRS to review your original documentation and obtain the ITIN for you.

How Nonresident Aliens Are Taxed

A nonresident alien is taxed as follows:

Compensation for services rendered in the United States or other income that is effectively connected with a U.S. trade or business is generally taxed at graduated rates, using the appropriate tax rate schedules. A nonresident alien may deduct certain expenses incurred in producing that income, such as business-related expenses and state and local income taxes. In addition, he or she may deduct casualty losses and qualifying charitable contributions. However, a nonresident alien may not claim the standard deduction.

TAXALERT

For taxable years beginning after 1986, income that is effectively connected with a U.S. trade or business at the time it is earned will be considered "effectively connected" at the time it is received, even if receipt occurs in a different tax year.

A nonresident alien is generally able to claim a personal exemption only for himself or herself. However, a nonresident alien who is a resident of Mexico or Canada, or a national of the United States (such as certain American Samoans or Northern Mariana Islanders) is also entitled to claim personal exemptions for

1. A spouse, if the spouse had no gross income for U.S. tax purposes and was not the dependent of another taxpayer
2. Other dependents, if they meet the same requirements as a U.S. citizen

In addition, certain tax treaties allow for personal exemptions for a spouse and dependents in specific cases.

A married nonresident alien is taxed under the "married filing separately" Tax Rate Schedule, which is the highest Tax Rate Schedule applicable to individuals. You may not claim **head of household** status if you are a nonresident alien. A nonresident alien who is **single** would use the "unmarried" Tax Rate Schedule.

Dividends, interest, royalties, pensions, annuities, and other types of U.S. source income that are not effectively connected with a U.S. trade or business are usually subject to a flat 30% tax rate unless a tax treaty allows for a lower rate of tax. No deductions or exemptions are allowed against this income. Interest earned on U.S. bank accounts, as well as certain other investments (known as "portfolio" debt instruments), is exempt from U.S. taxes.

Gains and losses from the sale of **capital assets,** other than real property situated in the U.S., may be taxed in either of two ways. If the gains and losses are not connected with a trade or business in the United States, any gain (after deducting losses) is taxed at a 30% rate if the nonresident alien is in the United States for 183 days or more during the tax year. If a gain is derived from the sale of capital assets effectively connected with a trade or a business in the United States, it is taxed in the same manner as it would be for a U.S. citizen. Capital gains from the sale of real property located in the United States are considered to be connected with a U.S. trade or business and are subject to special U.S. tax laws. (For a more detailed discussion of the tax treatment of gains and losses, see IRS Publication 519, *U.S. Tax Guide for Aliens*.)

Foreign students. Foreign students who enter the U.S. under an "F" visa (academic or language student) or a "J" visa (educational and cultural exchange visitor) are generally nonresidents for U.S. income tax purposes, as long as they substantially comply with the terms of their visa.

TAXPLANNER

Foreign nationals who become U.S. residents. Foreign nationals who become U.S. residents are taxed on their worldwide income from the day on which they become residents. You may, however, take several steps before you become a U.S. resident in order to limit your U.S. tax liability. Consider the following:

1. If you anticipate receiving a payment of compensation for past services, such as a bonus, arrange to receive this payment before becoming a resident of the United States. If this payment is received after you become a U.S. resident alien, it will be taxable in full by the United States, even though the related services were rendered prior to coming to the United States. Review tax treaty and foreign tax credit rules for possible relief if it is received after becoming a U.S. tax resident.
2. If you anticipate incurring expenses that will be deductible for U.S. income tax purposes, such as mortgage points, interest, or certain charitable contributions, consider deferring these payments until after you are a resident of the United States.
3. If you sell shares in a corporation for a gain prior to your arrival in the United States, the entire gain is not subject to U.S. tax. However, if you sell shares at a profit after you become a U.S. resident, the entire gain is subject to U.S. tax, even if the entire ap-

preciation of the shares occurred before you became a U.S. resident. You should consider selling shares and other investments in which you have a profit before you become a U.S. resident.

By the same token, if you hold an investment that has a loss and the entire loss was generated before you became a U.S. resident, but you did not realize the loss until after you took up residency, you may deduct the loss on your U.S. tax return, subject to the normal rules.

4. If you receive a **lump-sum distribution** from a government or private retirement plan after you have become a U.S. resident, the entire amount may be subject to U.S. tax. If at all possible, arrange to receive the payment before you become a U.S. resident, when it is not subject to U.S. tax. In addition, note that the American Jobs Creation Act of 2004 provides that distributions from foreign pension plans made on or after October 22, 2004, will be taxable in the hands of a U.S. resident to the extent that the amount distributed has not been subject to U.S. or foreign tax previously. Again, review tax treaty and foreign tax credit rules for possible relief if it is received after becoming a U.S. tax resident.

5. If you sell your principal residence before becoming a U.S. resident, the proceeds are not normally subject to any U.S. tax. However, if you become a U.S. resident and elect to be taxed as a resident alien for the entire year to take advantage of lower joint filing rates (see *Exceptions,* earlier), you may end up paying tax on the sale of your principal residence, as well as tax on any exchange gain associated with the payoff of the mortgage. Be sure to consider this fact before you elect to be taxed as a resident alien for the entire year.

There is a $250,000 exclusion for single taxpayers ($500,000 for married taxpayers filing jointly) on the gain from the sale of a home if you have **owned the home and lived** in the home as your principal residence for 2 of the last 5 years. The use of the exclusion by foreign nationals who have ceased to be residents of the United States is permitted if the expatriation provisions do not apply (see *Rules for Individuals Giving Up U.S. Citizenship or U.S. Residency,* earlier in this chapter). Given the fact that this area of law is complex, you should seek tax advice prior to disposing of your primary residence.

6. You may be able to take advantage of a "window between tax residencies," a situation in which certain income is never taxed. This requires analyzing the tax laws of your home country and the United States. A window may be created, for example, if you come from a country that does not tax income of its nonresident citizens.

Example

Humphrey Benson is a citizen of a country that does not tax its nonresident citizens, and he decides to move permanently to the United States. He owns securities that have appreciated by $10,000. On his move to the United States, Humphrey goes to Bermuda for 2 weeks. While there, he sells all his securities. The result is that he does not have to pay any tax in his home country, in the United States, or in Bermuda.

TAX**PLANNER**

Minimizing your tax burden. The main point to remember is that the best time for you to minimize your U.S. tax burden is *before* you make an investment in the United States and *before* you become a U.S. resident.

Departing from the United States

Before you depart from the United States, you must obtain a certificate of compliance, indicating that you have satisfied your federal tax liability. This certificate, frequently referred to as a "sailing permit" or a "departure permit," is obtained by filing Form 1040C or Form 2063. To get the permit, you must either pay all of the U.S. income tax due prior to departure or demonstrate that your departure from the United States will not impair the collection of the tax. The forms may be obtained from your nearest IRS office. An exit permit is valid only for 30 days. If you postpone your departure, you probably have to apply for a new exit permit. See IRS Publication 519, *U.S. Tax Guide for Aliens,* for more details and for certain categories of individuals who are exempt from the "sailing permit" requirements.

TAX**ORGANIZER**

Sailing permits. The IRS representative must see actual departure tickets in order to issue your "sailing permit." Make sure you bring these along to the IRS office. *A certificate of compliance is not a substitute for an annual income tax return.* A federal tax return still must be filed in accordance with regular filing procedures. Any payment in conjunction with the filing of Form 1040C is treated as a payment on your annual tax return.

TAX**PLANNER**

Income from employment that is paid in a tax year after the individual's year of departure will be considered effectively connected with a U.S. business and taxed at the regular graduated rates. There could be significant U.S. tax savings if, for example, the individual was in the highest tax bracket in the year in which the income was earned, and if a portion of the income is foreign-source income. The receipt of the income in a subsequent year will cause it to be taxed at lower marginal tax rates. Care should be taken to understand any non-U.S. tax implications of deferring the receipt of income.

TAX**ORGANIZER**

Records you should keep.

- Keep a calendar of travel days in and out of the United States as well as work days in and out of the United States. Also retain copies of travel tickets, stamped passports, and other documentation to substantiate the dates. In some cases, you may need calendars for the current calendar year plus the two previous years.
- If you will be taxed as a resident of the United States and you have income/deductions from sources outside the United States, you will need to include those items on your U.S. return. Therefore, evidence of those items should be maintained. Note that the United States may tax certain items of income differently than other countries; you should consult a tax advisor to confirm proper U.S. tax treatment.
- Keep a copy of your visa and permanent residence card (*i.e.,* green card) if applicable.
- Keep a copy of your foreign tax returns and receipts for foreign taxes paid or accrued during the tax year, depending on the method used for the foreign tax credit.
- Keep a copy of your Social Security card or individual taxpayer identification number (ITIN) card(s) for yourself, your spouse, and your dependents.

How to Prepare for Your Accountant

Introduction

Millions of Americans prepare their own tax returns every year, while others rely on accountants to do the work for them. In fact, over half of those filing individual tax returns seek some kind of professional assistance. Which path you should take depends primarily on how complicated your financial affairs are and, of course, your willingness to puzzle through IRS forms. This chapter will help you organize your financial affairs, whether or not you have an accountant.

Who Needs an Accountant?

You will probably benefit from the advice and expertise of an accountant if you find yourself in one or more of the following conditions:

1. You have more than one source of income.
2. You think you are eligible for a lot of deductions.
3. You want to take advantage of a tax credit.
4. You are involved in partnerships or own rental properties.
5. You are not familiar with the current income tax laws.

You probably do *not* need an accountant if your return appears to be relatively simple. *If you are planning to file using Form 1040EZ, there is probably no reason for you to seek professional help.*

Choosing an Accountant

Finding an accountant. Choosing an accountant is not something that should be done casually. There are over 300,000 certified public accountants in the United States. Most of them are single practitioners or in business with a few other people. The bread and butter of their work is preparing tax returns for individuals. The rest of the nation's accountants work mostly for larger accounting firms or for individual companies.

Questions to ask your tax return preparer. Before choosing your tax preparer, you may want to get satisfactory answers to the following questions:

1. Are you a certified public accountant? What are your professional qualifications? Are you affiliated with any financial institution or investment company?
2. Do you have experience in preparing returns for others in my occupation and in handling federal, state and, possibly, international tax issues similar to mine?
3. How much will it cost to prepare my tax return?
4. Is there anything I can do to reduce the cost of return preparation?
5. What type of information do you need to prepare my return? In what format would you like it submitted and by what date?
6. If I am owed a refund, when can I expect to receive it?
7. Will you inform me if any items on my return are likely to be challenged by the IRS or state authorities?
8. Will you inform me if I am passing up any opportunities to reduce my tax liability?
9. What should I do if I receive a notice from the IRS or state authorities concerning my return? Will I be billed additionally for responses to tax notices?
10. Will you represent me before the IRS or state authorities if my return is audited?
11. Who in your office would work on my return? Do you use outside computer service firms to help prepare tax returns?
12. Can you give me the names of clients who would be references for your work?

What an accountant should do for you. You should be able to rely on your accountant for more than preparing your annual tax return. As your accountant becomes increasingly familiar with your personal and financial affairs, he or she should become a valuable and trusted financial advisor.

Any time you are entering into a major financial transaction, it is a good idea to give your accountant a call and review the alternatives available. Your accountant should advise you of any possibilities that will minimize your taxes. If you're buying or selling a house, for example, your accountant should be consulted regarding certain procedures that may have significant tax consequences. Investment decisions can also have significant income tax consequences. For example, the difference between long-term and short-term capital gains and taxable versus tax-free interest can have a significant impact on your overall tax situation.

The cost of an accountant. The cost of having your tax return prepared by an accountant can vary widely. Although some charge a fixed fee for the preparation of a return, the cost usually depends on the time your accountant spends on your return. You can help reduce this time by gathering, organizing, and summarizing your information yourself.

While you do not need to furnish your accountant with supporting cancelled checks or other documents, you should provide those documents about which you have questions. Considerable time may have to be spent on your return if the law governing some of your transactions is particularly difficult or unclear.

The hourly rates charged by national accounting firms are ordinarily higher than those charged by local firms. However, the fees charged by some of the larger local firms approximate those of the national firms. *The fee structure should be discussed and agreed on before your accountant begins work.* Cost is an important consideration but does not displace professional competence as a key criterion for selection.

Getting good service. You should expect good service from your accountant. Your telephone calls should be returned promptly. Your questions should be answered willingly and in understandable language. Your return should be completed and available to you with adequate time for you to review it before it must be filed.

It is important to understand whether or not your accountant is "independent." For example, you should know the relationship, if any, that your accountant has to any investment he or she recommends to you. Does your accountant have a significant financial interest in the investment that he or she recommends? Is your accountant an officer, director, or otherwise related to the investment? In addition, you should know the nature and amount of compensation, if any, that your accountant receives from any other person for his or her recommendations.

Switching accountants. If you are dissatisfied with your present accountant, you may wish to consider switching to another. As a matter of professional courtesy, most accountants will cooperate with a new accountant to make the transition as smooth as possible.

You may want your new accountant to have copies of your prior accountant's work papers. Although these work papers are the property of the prior accountant, most will make them available to you or your new accountant. It is important for you to collect information that may impact future tax years, such as the cost basis of stocks you own. If your files with your prior accountant are extensive, you should discuss an acceptable billing arrangement to cover the cost of providing them to your new accountant.

Preparing for Your Accountant

When to see your accountant. It may not be necessary to see your accountant more than once a year, especially if he or she has prepared your return in prior years.

However, it may benefit you to do some tax planning for the coming year, especially if your income or deductions have changed significantly. In addition, if you have a significant tax event, such as a sale of stock in which you have a large position or a residence, you may want to touch base with your accountant during the year. If you have a new accountant you might also want to get together for an initial meeting to go over your personal situation before your return is prepared.

A good time to meet with your accountant is after you have received substantially all of your tax reporting documents and have organized your tax information. If your accountant is already familiar with your tax situation, you can alternatively send whatever documentation is necessary to prepare your return and talk on the telephone.

You may want to wait to meet with your accountant after he or she has prepared your return so that you can go over it together. It is usually wise to do this as soon as possible so that if any changes need to be made they can be done before the filing deadline.

TaxOrganizer

Documents you will need. The remainder of this chapter discusses the documentation you should keep to support the information contained in your tax return.

What to bring to your accountant. Whether you prepare your own tax return or let an accountant do the work, the task of gathering your tax information together is unavoidable. The better prepared you are to discuss your affairs with your accountant, the more efficient the entire process of preparing your return will be. In general, you should have documentation that supports all income, deductions, and credits that will appear on your return. In addition, if you are using a new accountant, you should also bring a copy of your prior year's returns.

In most instances, your payors (except as noted below) have a January 31 deadline to furnish you with appropriate tax documentation. Therefore, all the information you need to give your accountant may not be available before that date.

Supporting documentation comes in many forms. The most common types of documentation and the items they substantiate are outlined in the following table.

Item	Documentation
1) Wages and salaries	W-2 forms; usually provided by your employer
2) Dividends and interest	Form 1099-DIV and Form 1099-INT; usually provided by the bank or company paying the dividend or interest
3) Capital gains and losses	Form 1099-B for sale of assets during the year and trade confirmations or account statements for the purchase dates; usually provided by the broker handling the sale
4) Business income from sole proprietorships, rents and royalties	Books and records (Form 1099-MISC *may* also be provided by the payor of the income)
5) Business expenses	Receipts and cancelled checks
6) Income from partnerships, estates, trusts, and S corporations	Form K-1; usually provided by the partnership, etc.

Check Analysis

Date	Check #	Payee	Amount	Medical	Taxes	Interest Expense	Charitable Contributions	Other	Description
2/17	1459	Dr. Broline	$ 55.00	$ 55.00					
3/04	1502	Cancer Society	25.00				$25.00		
3/26	1542	State Comptroller	494.00		$494.00				
4/20	1590	First National Bank	350.00			$350.00			
5/16	1630	Church	75.00				75.00		
6/12	1665	Acme Trucking	783.00					$783.00	Moving
7/18	1721	Dr. Broline	40.00	40.00					
7/18	1722	Ace Pharmacy	27.00	27.00					
10/22	1853	Church	75.00				75.00		
11/15	1902	First National Bank	300.00			300.00			
Totals			$2,224.00	$122.00	$494.00	$650.00	$175.00	$783.00	

7) Unemployment compensation	Form 1099-G; usually provided by the governmental agency paying the unemployment compensation	20) Other taxes	Receipts and cancelled checks
8) Social Security benefits	Form SSA-1099; usually provided by the federal government	21) Contributions	Receipts, cancelled checks; written acknowledgment from the charitable organization is generally required for contributions of $250 or more, Form 1098-C. Detailed acknowledgment required for vehicle donation (see Chapter 26, *Contributions*, for details).
9) State and local income tax refunds	Form 1099-G; usually provided by the state or city that refunded the taxes		
10) Original issue discount	Form 1099-OID; usually provided by the issuer of the debt obligation	22) Estimated tax payments	Cancelled checks
11) All distributions, both total and partial, from pensions, annuities, insurance contracts, retirement or profit-sharing plans, and Individual Retirement Arrangements (IRAs)	Form 1099-R; usually provided by the trustee for the plan making the distribution	23) Tuition and fees	Receipts and cancelled checks

What not to bring to your accountant. You need not bring all of your documentation to your accountant. For example, if you prepare a summary of your dividends or charitable contributions, just provide your accountant with the summary. If you are providing a summary of your capital gains and losses to your accountant, make sure that the total of all your sales proceeds agrees to the total reported to you on Form 1099-B(s). If you do give your accountant all of your documentation, he or she will probably feel obligated to verify the accuracy of your summaries, which, as you well know, can be a time-consuming process. Your fee increases accordingly. However, you should be able to provide full documentation on request.

Collecting Your Tax Information

1. **Study last year's tax return.** A good place to start when you are gathering information is your prior year's tax return. This return is a record of your taxable transactions during the previous year. If your economic activities have not significantly changed during the current year, then your prior year's return will give you a good indication of the kinds of documentation you should gather for your accountant. The old return may also serve as a powerful re-

12) Barter income	Form 1099-B; usually provided by the barter exchange through which property or services were exchanged
13) Sale of your home	Form 1099-S; provided by the person responsible for closing a real estate transaction
14) IRA contributions	Form 5498; provided by the trustee or custodian of the IRA
15) Moving and employee business expenses	Receipts and cancelled checks
16) Medical expenses	Receipts and cancelled checks
17) Mortgage interest and points paid on the purchase of a principal residence	Form 1098 or mortgage company statement; usually provided by mortgage company
18) Business and investment interest	Canceled checks and brokers' statements
19) Real estate taxes	Receipts, cancelled checks, and mortgage company statements, Form 1098 (if applicable)

minder of a little-used bank account that paid you interest or some other source of income, great or small, that you otherwise might forget. Your old return is also a reference point for information on capital losses carried forward from previous years and any other carry-forward items. You should retain copies of prior years' returns for future reference.

2. **Review all checks.** At some point, you should be sure to review all the checks you have written during the year to search for possible tax deductions. To simplify your task, it's wise, if possible, to pay all of your checks from a single account. If, for example, you have a money market account and a checking account at your bank, it might be easier for record-keeping purposes to transfer money into your checking account as necessary rather than to write checks on both accounts. If you want to be absolutely certain not to miss anything, prepare a worksheet like the one above. Do so each month throughout the year as you reconcile your bank statement. Various computer software programs are also available to help simplify the task of record-keeping.

3. **Fill out a tax questionnaire.** To make sure that you don't miss anything, many accountants use questionnaires or checklists to obtain information about all of your taxable transactions during the year. Even if you're not planning to use an accountant, it might be a good idea to fill out an accountant's questionnaire. Some accountants may ask for this information in electronic format to facilitate preparation of your return. For a sample questionnaire, refer to the Individual Tax Organizer in the front of this book.

A final reminder: The common goal that you share with your accountant is the preparation of a complete and accurate return. The closer you work together, the more likely it is that your return will be satisfactory. Just as important, the closer you work together, the better your chances will be of saving money on your taxes.

46

Everything You Need to Know About E-filing

Introduction

E-filing has been a tremendous success. The IRS reports that for the 2005 filing season, more than 66,000,000 returns were filed electronically, a 11% increase from the prior year. Almost 17,000,000 taxpayers filed from a home computer, up 17%. Overall, 65 percent of all returns were e-filed—up from 60% for the same period in the prior year.

E-filing can offer a number of advantages. It's easy and efficient and, of course, eliminates having to fill out paper forms. If you owe money, you can e-file and authorize an electronic funds withdrawal or pay by credit card. Generally, you receive an electronic proof of receipt within 48 hours that the IRS has received your return. Your return can be quickly and automatically checked for errors and other missing information. The error rate for e-filed returns, according to the IRS, is less than one percent. If you are entitled to a refund, you can get one in half the time paper filers do. Your chance of being audited does not differ whether you e-file or file a paper tax return. Finally, your bank account information, as well as your other tax return information, is safeguarded.

E-filing is available for all individual income tax returns but it might not be the right choice for you. This may be true if you prefer the familiarity of paper and pencil or if you're simply not comfortable with computers and the Internet. The IRS doesn't require e-filing for any individual taxpayers, so the choice is entirely yours.

This chapter discusses the four options available for e-filing and which one, if any, might be right for you.

TAXALERT

TeleFile, which allowed you to submit your return using a telephone, has been eliminated for the 2006 filing season.

Information You'll Need to E-file

Whether you decide to e-file or not, your first step is to get all your tax information together. That way you'll save time and won't have to stop in the middle of preparing your return to find a missing document. Here's what you'll need:

- Social Security numbers for yourself, your spouse, and any dependents.
- Forms W-2 from all employers are required for yourself and your spouse. If you are filing electronic returns using a personal computer, you enter the data from the forms into the electronic filing software yourself. This is similar to the attachment of Form W-2, Form W-2G, and Form 1099-R to the face of paper tax returns. However, if you chose to use an "authorized IRS e-file Provider" (explained below), you must provide Form W-2, Form W-2G, and Form 1099-R to the authorized IRS e-file provider before the provider sends the electronic return to the IRS. Providers are prohibited from submitting electronic returns to the IRS prior to receipt of all Form W-2, Form W-2G, and Form 1099-R from the taxpayer.
- Forms 1099 for Dividends, Retirement, or other income, or any Forms 1099 with income tax withholding.
- Receipts for expenses for itemized deductions (Schedule A).
- Receipts and records for other income or expenses.
- Bank account numbers (for a fast refund, or to pay electronically).

Note: For a brief explanation of some of the details of e-filing, also see Chapter 1, *Filing Information, Does My Return Have to Be on Paper?*

Signing your electronic tax return

You sign your electronic tax return by either using a Self-Select PIN (see the discussion below) for *e-file* for a completely paperless return, or by signing Form 8453, *U.S. Individual*

Income Tax Declaration for an IRS e-file Return. (If you use a personal computer to e-file your return and don't use a Self-Select PIN you'll have to file Form 8453-OL, *U.S. Individual Income Tax Declaration for e-file Online Return.*)

Self-Select PIN

The Self-Select PIN (Personal Identification Number) method allows you to electronically sign your *e-filed* return by selecting a five-digit PIN as your signature. The five-digit PIN can be any five numbers except all zeros. If you use the Self-Select PIN you won't have to file Form 8453, *U.S. Individual Income Tax Declaration for an IRS e-file Return* or Form 8453-OL, *U.S. Individual Income Tax Declaration for e-file Online Return.* You can use your PIN whether you do your own taxes using a personal computer (described below) or have a tax professional prepare them for you.

You create your own PIN. You do not register the PIN with the IRS before filing or need to contact the IRS to get it. When you use one of the commercially available tax software packages on your personal computer that support the Self-Select PIN option, you will be guided through the process of entering your own PIN. If you use a tax professional, the preparer will help you. If filing a joint return, a PIN is needed for each taxpayer.

The following taxpayers are eligible to use the Self-Select PIN method:

- Taxpayers who are eligible to file Form 1040, Form 1040A, Form 1040EZ.
- Taxpayers who filed Form 1040-PR for TY 2004, who are eligible to file Form 1040 for Tax Year 2005.
- Taxpayers who did not file for Tax Year 2004, but have filed previously.
- Taxpayers who are age 16 or older on or before December 31, 2005, who have never filed a tax return.
- Taxpayers under age 16, filing as "Primary" taxpayers, who have filed previously. A Primary taxpayer is the taxpayer whose name appears on the first name line of the return.
- Taxpayers under age 16, filing as "Secondary" taxpayers (spouse), who filed in the immediate prior year. A Secondary taxpayer is the person whose name appears in the spouse line of the return.
- Military personnel residing overseas with APO/FPO addresses.
- U.S. citizens and resident aliens residing in the American Possessions of the Virgin Islands, Puerto Rico, American Samoa, Guam and Northern Marianas, or with foreign country addresses.
- Taxpayers filing a Form 4868 (*automatic extension of time to file*) or Form 2350 (*extension for certain U.S. citizens living abroad*).
- Those who are filing on behalf of deceased taxpayers.

The following taxpayers are *not* eligible to use the Self-Select PIN method:

- Primary Taxpayers under age 16 who have never filed.
- Secondary Taxpayers (spouse) under age 16 who did not file in the immediate prior year.
- Taxpayers who filed Form 1040-NR or Form 1040-SS for tax year 2004.
- Taxpayers whose returns require attachments other than Form W-2, Form W-2G, or Form 1099-R.
- Taxpayers required to file the following forms:
  - Form 3115, *Application for Change in Accounting Method*

- Form 3468, *Investment Credit* (if Historic Structure Certificate is required)
- Form 5713, *International Boycott Report*
- Form 8283, *Non-Cash Charitable Contributions* (if using Part B)
- Form 8332, *Release of Claim to Exemption for Children of Divorced or Separated Parents*
- Form 8885, *Health Coverage Tax Credit*

All of the above-listed forms must be submitted with Form 8453, *U.S. Individual Income Tax Declaration for e-file Return* (if you use an electronic return originator [ERO] or Form 8453-OL, *U.S. Individual Income Tax Declaration for e-file Online Return* (if you don't). (An ERO is a tax firm that files income tax returns electronically with the IRS under the "IRS *e-file*" brand name.)

After you sign the return using a Self-Select PIN or Form 8453, the ERO transmits the return to the IRS or to a third-party transmitter who then forwards the entire electronic record to the IRS for processing. (A third-party transmitter just sends information; it does not do any calculations or provide any tax services.) Once received at the IRS, the return is automatically checked by computers for errors and missing information. If it cannot be processed, it is sent back to the originating transmitter (usually the ERO) to clarify any necessary information. After correction, the transmitter retransmits the return to the IRS.

Within 48 hours of electronically sending your return to IRS, the IRS sends an acknowledgment to the transmitter stating the return is accepted for processing. This is your proof of filing and assurance that the IRS has your return information. The Authorized IRS *e-file* Provider then sends Form 8453, if required, to the IRS.

Refunds. If you're due a refund, you can expect to receive it in approximately three weeks from the acknowledgment date—even faster with Direct Deposit (half the time as when filed on paper).

Making tax payments. If you owe money, you can make payment in one of three convenient ways:

1. By authorizing an electronic funds withdrawal from a checking or savings account. For electronic funds withdrawal, you include your bank routing information and account number on the Form 1040 when you file electronically. You can designate the exact date (up to and including April 17, 2006) that you want the payment to be withdrawn (by the Department of Treasury financial agents) from either your checking or savings account at your bank.
2. By credit card (American Express®, Discover®, MasterCard®, or VISA®), or
3. By mailing a check or money order (made out to the United States Treasury) using Form 1040-V, Payment Voucher.

One of the advantages of Options 1 and 2 is that you receive an immediate acknowledgment when IRS accepts your payment. A downside of using a credit card is that the credit card company will charge a separate fee for this service, in addition to any interest that might be charged on any outstanding balance.

Errors. IRS *e-file* returns are virtually error-proof with an error rate of less than one percent. IRS *e-file* greatly reduces the chance that you will get an error letter from the IRS.

When to file and pay any tax due. Your tax professional can file your return electronically any time during the filing season; however, sending the payment for a balance due by April 17, 2006 is still your responsibility. You may file electronically as soon as you are ready and will receive a confirmation from the IRS within 48 hours of receipt of your return. All balance-due payments, regardless of method of payment, must be authorized or sent to the IRS by April 17, 2006 to avoid late payment penalties or interest charges.

E-file for your state tax returns. Federal/State *e-file*, an extension of IRS *e-file*, is offered in most states and the District of Columbia. However, not all Authorized IRS *e-file* providers provide this service. Your Authorized IRS *e-file* Provider can tell you if they participate in the Federal/State *e-file* program.

Extra fees for e-filing. The IRS does not charge a fee for electronic filing. Some Authorized IRS *e-file* Providers (EROs) charge a fee for providing this service to their clients while others may offer it free of charge. However, this fee cannot be based on any figure from the tax return. Fees vary depending upon the tax professional you choose and the specific services you request.

With IRS *e-file* you can prepare your own return and pay a professional only to transmit it electronically, or you can pay to have your return both prepared and transmitted. Whichever you choose, shop around for a tax professional who offers the services you need at an acceptable cost to you.

Methods of E-filing.

There are three basic methods: using a tax professional, using your personal computer and the Free File option. (TeleFile, which allowed you to submit your return using a telephone, has been eliminated for 2005 returns.) We'll explain each of these methods in detail.

Tax Professional

Tax professionals who are accepted into the electronic filing program are called "Authorized IRS *e-file* Providers." You, or your tax professional, prepare your tax return. In many cases, the tax professional is also the Electronic Return Originator (ERO) who is authorized to file your return electronically to the IRS. If you've prepared the return, the tax professional will convert it into the appropriate format for e-filing. You ask your tax professional to file your return through IRS *e-file*.

Many tax professionals offer IRS *e-file* to their clients. To find a tax professional to file your return electronically, search for the Authorized IRS *e-file* Provider nearest you or look in your local telephone directory under "Tax Return Preparation" for an "Authorized IRS *e-file* Provider" that meets your needs. Also, look for the "Authorized IRS *e-file* Provider" sign or decal in storefront windows.

Personal Computer

Instead of using the services of a tax professional, you can quickly and conveniently *e-file* your return using a personal computer. To do this you can:

- Purchase commercially available software,
- Download software from an Internet site and prepare your return offline, or
- Prepare and file your return online.

NOTE: The IRS cannot compete with private enterprise and does not offer free *e-file* software or direct filing. A number of companies, tested and approved by the IRS, do offer free use of their software and free filing, while others will charge nominal fees. Terms and conditions vary among companies and you are advised to review the information on each company's Web site and choose for yourself the product that is right for you.

Any way you choose, however, it's a simple process. **Who can file using a computer.** Anyone can use this method of filing. Obviously, access to a personal computer is necessary. Software can be purchased, downloaded off the Internet or accessed online. A modem is used to conveniently, quickly, and safely transmit your return and receive proof of acknowledgment.

Using this method, you prepare your tax return on a personal computer and transmit the information via modem to an electronic return transmitter. You can transmit a maximum of five returns using tax preparation software, so you can prepare returns for family and friends as well.

The electronic return transmitter converts the file you send to a format that meets IRS specifications, and transmits it to the IRS. The IRS checks the return and notifies the transmitter (who then informs you) whether the return has been accepted or rejected. If your return is not accepted, the electronic return transmitter will provide you with customer support to correct your return and resubmit it.

Signing your return. You can sign the return using the Self-Select Pin, if you meet the eligibility requirements described above. If you have to file Form 8453-OL, instead, you are not required to attach Form W-2, *Wage and Tax Statement*, Form W-2G, *Certain Gambling Winnings*, and Form 1099-R, *Distribution From Pensions, Annuities, Retirement or Profit-Sharing Plans, IRAs, Insurance Contracts*, etc., with Form8453-OL. However, it makes sense for you to continue to maintain copies of these attachments for your records.

Extra fees for e-filing from a personal computer. The IRS does not charge a fee for *e-file* using a personal computer. However, an electronic return transmitter offering this service to taxpayers may charge a fee for transmission. Check out the IRS e-file Partners IRS e-file Partners or Online Filing Software Companies pages on the IRS Web site to learn about free and low cost *e-file* opportunities.

Payment methods and refunds. The same payment methods available using a Tax Professional are available with personal computer e-filing—check or money order, electronic fund withdrawal, and credit card. Refunds should be in your savings or checking account within 2 weeks if you choose direct deposit; in about 3 weeks if you choose a paper check.

If you have additional questions, you can also contact the IRS's toll-free customer service at 1-800-829-1040.

IRS Free File

This program is in its third year, and for the 2005 filing season over 5,000,000 returns were filed using it.

Through a public-private partnership between the IRS and the tax software industry (i.e., Free File Alliance, LLC), you may access free, online tax preparation and electronic filing services through www.irs.gov. Eligible taxpayers may prepare and file their federal income tax returns using online software provided by the Free File Alliance companies—not the IRS.

The partnership agreement calls for the Free File Alliance to provide free tax preparation and filing to at least 60 percent of all taxpayers, or approximately 78 million individuals who file an individual tax return.

Each participating software company has its own eligibility requirements.

The difference between Free File and the first two methods is that the entire filing process takes place over the Internet—there is no need to visit a tax professional or purchase or download software. You just input data while you're on the provider's Web site to complete your return.

Privacy and security concerns. Your tax information and data will be protected. To ensure your data's safety, the IRS requires participating companies to obtain both privacy and security seal certifications. These certification programs, administered by third-party providers, certify your tax return information is protected from unauthorized access during the tax preparation process. In addition:

- Tax return preparation is accomplished using proprietary software approved by the IRS; transmittal is through the established IRS *e-file* system.
- Alliance companies must comply with all federal rules and regulations on taxpayer privacy for paying and free customers. These rules prohibit use of tax return data for purposes not specifically authorized by the taxpayer.
- The IRS monitors the progress of each of the companies. If any problems develop, the companies are required to alert the IRS. If appropriate, the IRS will remove the company from the IRS.gov site until the problem is resolved.

For more information, you should visit the company's privacy and security policy located on the company's Web site.

Step 1. How to Get Started: You start at an IRS Web site page—"Free File Home—Your link to Free Online Filing" (http://www.irs.gov/efile/article/0,,id=118986,00.html). Click on the **"Start Now"** button. You will go to an IRS.gov Free File page where you may start your search for a Free File company.

Step 2. Determine Your Eligibility: You must first determine your eligibility for using a particular company. Each company has a simple description of its eligibility criteria for using its free service. You may also find additional information on IRS.gov Free File pages under the "more details" links.

Step 3. Link to Free File Company Service: After choosing a company, click on the company's title, which sends you directly to the company's Web site *(you will be notified you are leaving IRS.gov and being sent to a commercial Web site).* Follow the instructions on that company's Web site to begin the preparation of your tax return.

Alternatively, if you are having trouble choosing by scanning the list of Free File companies, you may want to use the interactive help tool, "Guide Me to a Service" to narrow down the possible companies offering free preparation and e-filing for you. Click on the button "Guide Me to a Service" to start searching for the companies that may provide free services for you.

If you are uncertain about your answers for the questions contained, you may want to view the complete list of companies and their services. The accuracy of the results is dependent on the accuracy of the information you provide the "Guide Me to a Service" tool.

Step 4. If you do not qualify for the selected company's free offer, you may want to check other Free File company offers by accessing the IRS.gov Free File page. If you are on the company's Web site, look for the link that takes you back to IRS.gov and search for another Free File service. Go back and scan the listing of free company services as described in Step 3.

If you do **not** qualify for the company's free offer but continue with the preparation and e-filing process with this company, please be aware you will be charged a fee for preparing and e-filing your federal tax return.

Example: If you select a company whose free services are provided to individuals with an Adjusted Gross Income (AGI) of $26,000 or less and, based on your tax data, the company determines your AGI exceeds the $26,000 limit, you will be notified you may be subject to a fee. It is important you understand each of the company's eligibility criteria before selecting a company. You may find the fee by looking under "more details" next to the company's description on the Free File pages.

Step 5. Prepare and e-File Your Federal Income Tax Return: The company's software prepares and e-files your income tax returns using proprietary processes and systems right over the Internet. Electronically filed returns are transmitted by the company to the IRS using the established e-file system, which uses secure telephone lines. An acknowledgment file, notifying you that the return has been either accepted or rejected, is sent via e-mail from the company.

Refunds and payments using Free File are handled the same way as they are for the other e-filing options.

If Your Return Is Examined

Note: The 2004 IRS Publication 17 (Your Federal Income Tax) has been updated by Ernst & Young LLP for 2005. Dates and dollar amounts shown are for 2005. Gray type is used to indicate where IRS text has been updated or intentionally omitted. Unrevised IRS text is shown in black type.

Introduction

This chapter is probably not for you. Overall, the IRS examines only a small fraction of all tax returns that are filed. However, if you are contacted by the IRS about your tax return, this material may be very important to you. Just how important will depend on how carefully your return was prepared and the sources and amount of your income.

An IRS examination is nothing to be feared, if you have kept accurate records to support your deductions and all of your income has been reported. In most cases, IRS audits are rather routine. In fact, in about 25% of the cases, the IRS makes no changes or issues a refund. Whatever the result, you won't do yourself much good by making things difficult for the IRS. An IRS examiner has the legal power to force a taxpayer to produce books and records to complete the examination. The best strategy is almost invariably one of concluding

the examination as quickly as possible by providing the facts needed and by meeting deadlines.

On the other hand, an IRS examination is nothing to take lightly. You should be prepared, and that preparation starts with keeping receipts and records, followed by careful preparation of your return. The IRS examiner must follow certain rules in conducting the examination. Since you'd be well advised to know what they are, this chapter tells you about them.

You will find a summary of your rights as a taxpayer at the beginning of this chapter. It may be especially helpful in cases that involve the delinquent payment of assessed taxes. This chapter tells you about your rights when your return is examined. You should know these rights, since they affect you and your pocketbook. You should also read IRS Publication 1, Your Rights as a Taxpayer.

The first part of this section explains some of your most important rights as a taxpayer. The second part explains the examination, appeal, collection, and refund processes.

Declaration of Taxpayer Rights

Protection of your rights. IRS employees will explain and protect your rights as a taxpayer throughout your contact with us.

Privacy and confidentiality. The IRS will not disclose to anyone the information you give us, except as authorized by law. You have the right to know why we are asking you for information, how we will use it, and what happens if you do not provide requested information.

Professional and courteous service. If you believe that an IRS employee has not treated you in a professional, fair, and courteous manner, you should tell that employee's supervisor. If the supervisor's response is not satisfactory, you should write to the IRS director for your area or the center where you filed your return.

Representation. You may either represent yourself or, with proper written authorization, have someone else represent you in your place. Your representative must be a person allowed to practice be-

fore the IRS, such as an attorney, certified public accountant, or enrolled agent. If you are in an interview and ask to consult such a person, then we must stop and reschedule the interview in most cases.

You can have someone accompany you at an interview. You may make sound recordings of any meetings with our examination, or collection personnel, provided you tell us in writing 10 days before the meeting.

Payment of only the correct amount of tax. You are responsible for paying only the correct amount of tax due under the law—no more, no less. If you cannot pay all of your tax when it is due, you may be able to make monthly installment payments.

Help with unresolved tax problems. See *How to Get Tax Help.*

Appeals and judicial review. If you disagree with us about the amount of your tax liability or certain collection actions, you have the right to ask the Appeals Office to review your case. You may also ask a court to review your case.

Relief from certain penalties and interest. The IRS will waive penalties when allowed by law if you can show you acted reasonably and in good faith or relied on the incorrect advice of an IRS employee. We will waive interest that is the result of certain errors or delays caused by an IRS employee.

Examinations, Appeals, Collections, and Refunds

Examinations (Audits)

We accept most taxpayers' returns as filed. If we inquire about your return or select it for examination, it does not suggest that you are dishonest. The inquiry or examination may or may not result in more tax. We may close your case without change; or, you may receive a refund.

The process of selecting a return for examination usually begins in one of two ways. First, we use computer programs to identify returns that may have incorrect amounts. These programs may be based on information returns, such as Forms 1099 and W-2, on studies of past examinations, or on certain issues identified by compliance projects. Second, we use information from outside sources that indicates that a return may have incorrect amounts. These sources may include newspapers, public records, and individuals. If we determine that the information is accurate and reliable, we may use it to select a return for examination.

Publication 556, *Examination of Returns, Appeal Rights, and Claims for Refund*, explains the rules and procedures that we follow in examinations. The following sections give an overview of how we conduct examinations.

By mail. We handle many examinations and inquiries by mail. We will send you a letter with either a request for more information or a reason why we believe a change to your return may be needed. You can respond by mail or you can request a personal interview with an examiner. If you mail us the requested information or provide an explanation, we may or may not agree with you, and we will explain the reasons for any changes. Please do not hesitate to write to us about anything you do not understand.

By interview. If we notify you that we will conduct your examination through a personal interview, or you request such an interview, you have the right to ask that the examination take place at a reasonable time and place that is convenient for both you and the IRS. If our examiner proposes any changes to your return, he or she will explain the reasons for the changes. If you do not agree with these changes, you can meet with the examiner's supervisor.

Repeat examinations. If we examined your return for the same items in either of the 2 previous years and proposed no change to your tax liability, please contact us as soon as possible so we can see if we should discontinue the examination.

The Explanation Process

The IRS examines returns for correctness of income, exemptions, credits, and deductions.

Who gets audited? The odds that your return will be examined by the IRS are, in fact, quite low. According to the most recent Treasury tables, the IRS examined approximately 1% of all individual returns, down from about 5% in the mid-1960s. The odds shift substantially, depending on your income level and types of income. However, recent pressure by the U.S. Congress to block the Taxpayer Compliance Measurement Program (TCMP) has prevented the IRS from updating its individual return selection systems, so for the time being the IRS is using old data and relying more heavily on supplemental systems. This may alter the traditional odds of getting audited.

TaxPlanner

Here is a list of some items or circumstances that can frequently draw the IRS's attention:

- Reported income does not agree with information on information returns, Forms 1099 and W-2.
- Married taxpayers filing separately. Many such taxpayers do not report items consistently between returns (e.g., itemized deductions, zero bracket or standard deduction amount elections).
- Returns with significant items that may trigger alternative minimum tax (e.g., significant miscellaneous itemized deductions and state, local, and property taxes).
- Taxpayers who may receive substantial cash payments in the normal course of business (e.g., doctors, lawyers, retail establishments, waiters).
- Deductions that seem unusually large compared to your income level.
- Total Schedule C (business income) gross receipts of $100,000 or more. According to one recent study, the IRS has concluded that individuals filing Schedule C are most likely not to report income.
- Large business expenses in relation to your income.
- A return submitted by an accountant or a tax preparer who is on an IRS list of problem preparers because they have repeatedly violated the law.
- Complex investment or business transactions without clear explanations.
- Schedule F (farm) losses, particularly where the taxpayer has significant salary income.
- Earned income credit. Because there is the perception of potential abuse in this area, returns claiming the earned income credit are more closely scrutinized.
- Taxpayers' returns that fall in an area included in the IRS Market Segment Specialization Program (MSSP) such as automobile dealers, taxi services, air charters, attorneys, gas retailers, and others in a series of businesses or occupations that the IRS believes to need examination attention.

In addition, a local IRS district may undertake an Information Gathering Project (IGP) to more specifically focus on what they perceive as local compliance problems.

TaxAlert

The IRS is realigning its audit resources to focus on key areas of noncompliance with the tax laws. This strategy represents a new direction for the agency's compliance effort. The new approach will focus on high-risk areas of noncompliance. The IRS effort will generally focus first on promoters and then on participants in these various schemes. The initiative will feature new and enhanced efforts on several priority areas, including:

- Offshore credit card users
- High-risk, high-income taxpayers
- Abusive schemes and promoter investigations
- High-income non-filers
- Unreported income
- The National Research Program (NRP)

The strategy reflects a new way of doing business at the IRS. Several of these efforts—such as the National Research Program and the credit-card initiative—reflect innovative approaches to tackle long-standing tax problems.

Fairness If Your Return Is Examined

Most taxpayers' returns are accepted as filed. But if your return is selected for examination, it does not suggest that you are dishonest. The inquiry or examination may or may not result in more tax. Your case may be closed without change. Or, you may receive a refund.

Courtesy and consideration. You are entitled to courteous and considerate treatment from IRS employees at all times. If you ever feel that you are not being treated with fairness, courtesy, and consideration by an IRS employee, you should tell the employee's supervisor. Publication 1, *Your Rights as a Taxpayer,* explains the many rights you have as a taxpayer. You can get free publications by calling 1-800-829-3676.

Your rights as a taxpayer. While the taxpayer bill of rights did not break new legal ground, it did create a single document that informs you of your rights. It is useful to review it to be aware of the rights you have. A summary of the most important points follows.

Pay only the required tax. You have the right to plan your business and personal finances in such a way that you will pay the least tax that is due under the law. You are liable only for the correct amount of tax. The IRS's purpose is to apply the law consistently and fairly to all taxpayers.

Privacy and confidentiality. You have the right to have your tax case kept confidential. Under the law, the IRS must protect the privacy of your tax information. However, if a lien or a lawsuit is filed, certain aspects of your tax case will become public record. People who prepare your return or represent you must also keep your information confidential.

You also have the right to know why the IRS is asking you for the information, exactly how the agency will use it, and what might happen if you do not give it.

Examination of Returns

An examination usually begins when the IRS notifies you that your return has been selected. The IRS will tell you which records you will need. If you gather your records before the examination, it can be completed with the least amount of effort.

How returns are selected. The IRS selects returns for examination by several methods. A computer program called the Discriminant Function System (DIF) is used to select most returns. In this method, the computer uses historical data to give parts of the return a score. IRS personnel then screen the return.

Some returns are selected at random. The IRS uses the results of examining these returns to update and improve its selection process.

The IRS also selects returns by examining claims for credit or refund and by matching information documents, such as Forms W-2 and the 1099 series, with returns.

In addition, your return can be selected as a result of information received from other sources on potential noncompliance with the tax laws or inaccurate filing. This information can come from a number of sources, including the media, public records, or possibly informants. The information is evaluated for reliability and accuracy before it is used as the basis of an examination or investigation.

Verification methods for proper payment. The IRS uses several methods and techniques to attempt to verify that the proper amount of tax is being paid by taxpayers:

1. **Document perfection.** Every return is checked for mathematical, tax calculation, and clerical errors in initial processing. If a mistake is discovered, a recalculation of the tax due and a notice of explanation are sent to the taxpayer. This procedure is not an **audit**—an important distinction.

   The IRS determines whether the return is in "processible form." The law lets the IRS avoid payment of interest on any refund until the return contains the taxpayer's name, address, identifying number, and required signature. Furthermore, the return must be on the permitted form and contain sufficient information to permit the mathematical verification of the tax liability shown on the return. The IRS has carried this to extremes by sending tax returns back to taxpayers for failing to check a box, not attaching all required forms, and not making alternative minimum tax computations when it is obvious no such action is due. While the IRS concentrates on refund returns with small errors that permit them to avoid large refunds, it has also sent balance-due returns back after depositing any checks attached. If the return is not perfected and returned before the due date, the IRS says the return is delinquent. The IRS has lost this issue in the Tax Court but persists in its position.

2. **Discriminant Function System (DIF).** Basically, DIF assigns a numerical value to certain items on your return. If the total of all the values equals or exceeds a minimum set by the IRS, the computer will single out the return for a possible audit. IRS agents will then check the return to see if it is worth the IRS's time to conduct an audit. This will depend on, among other things, staffing in your IRS district office. Even if your return is selected for an audit, it is likely that only specific items, such as charitable contributions or employee business expenses, would be examined, not your entire return.

   It's a closely guarded secret what weight DIF assigns to which items. Some things this computer program is on the lookout for include:

   - Large amounts of income not subject to withholding
   - More deductions than seem to be reasonable for your income level
   - Claims for an unusual number of dependency deductions as compared to withholding and other items on the return
   - Discrepancies such as a change of address combined with deductions claimed for owning a residence when you have not reported that you sold your old residence

   The DIF system is being used less as a selection source in recent years, especially in the case of Schedule C filers. The Audit Specialization Program is taking its place (see later in this chapter).

3. **The National Research Program (NRP).** The NRP examinations, which began in the fall of 2003, measure reporting compliance and identify compliance issues. The NRP will enable the IRS to improve the examination selection process. NRP is very different from its predecessor, the Taxpayer Compliance Measurement Program (TCMP). The NRP no longer relies heavily on time-intensive, "line-by-line" audits for establishing a baseline measure of reporting compliance.

   The IRS has not conducted updated research on the distribution of errors on returns for more than 13 years, a period when the economy and the tax law have changed dramatically. Without the information that will be gathered through the NRP, the IRS will have less ability to direct examinations and other compliance activities with accuracy and precision. With updated information, the NRP effort will prevent thousands of "no change" audits each year.

   The NRP effort will review a small, statistically valid sample of individual returns, less than 50,000 returns out of 132 million individual returns filed.

4. **Document-matching program.** The IRS matches the information supplied by your bank, your employer, and others on Forms W-2 and 1099 and other information documents with the information supplied on your return. If an item is omitted from your return or conflicts with what is reported to the IRS, the IRS computer will generate a notice that recalculates your tax with corrections for the omitted income or overstated deduction. The Revenue Reconciliation Act of 1989 repealed the section of the tax law that gave the IRS the presumption of being correct in asserting a negligence penalty if you fail to report correctly relevant amounts reflected on information returns. The change applies to returns filed after December 31, 1989. It is probable that the IRS will continue to assert not only the negligence penalty but also the substantial understatement penalty. This procedure does not technically constitute a formal examination.

5. **The Market Segment Specialization Program (MSSP) and other special projects.** In 1991, the Internal Revenue Service began a project in the Los Angeles District Office focusing on developing highly trained revenue agents for a particular business market segment. Prior to this initiative, the IRS had not been training their revenue agents to be specialists within any certain business market segment. From that initiative in Los Angeles, the IRS has expanded the program to cover more business market segments and has formally named the program the Market Segment Specialization Program (MSSP). The following is a list of these market segments:

IRC Section 936 corporations	Electronic components
Air charter	Emergency care clinics
Alaska commercial fishing	Employment tax—pizza drivers
Alaska placer gold mining	Entertainment industry:
Architectural services	• Contracts—audit applications
Art dealers	• Foreign athletes and entertainers
Attorneys	• Motion pictures/television
Auto body shops	• Music (Nashville)
Auto repair shops	• Theater—live performances
Bail bondsmen	Escort service
Bankruptcy	Federal excise tax, coal mining
Beauty shops/barber shops	Financial institutions
Bed & breakfast	Foreign tourism
Building maintenance services	Form 1042S withholding agents
Cable TV	Furniture manufacturing
Carwashing and detailing	Garment industry
Casino gambling	Gas retailers
Cattle	Golf courses
Check cashing establishments	Grain and milo growers
Child Care	Grocery stores
Citrus industry	Health care
Commercial baking	Insurance agencies
Community banks	Jewelry dealers
Construction/general building contractors	
Construction industry	
Cooperative housing corporations	

Laundromat	Recycling
Life insurance	Reforestation
Liquor stores	Rehabilitation credit
Low-income housing credit	Rent to own
Ministers	Restaurants/bars/eating places
Mobile cart vendors	RTC project (forgiveness of debt)
Mortuaries	Scrap metal
Motor fuel tax	Seafood purchases
Nursing/rest homes	Selling door-to-door/telephone
Offshore captive insurance co.	Taxicabs
Oil and gas operators	Timber sales
Parking lots	Time-sharing
Passive activity losses	Tobacco
Pawn shops	Tour bus industry
Petroleum contamination cleanup	Travel agency
Pizza parlors	Trucking industry
Plastic surgeons	Used auto dealers
Port of Houston	Wine industry
Poultry	
Printing	
Real estate agents/brokers	
Real estate developers	

The scope of the MSSP will affect virtually every taxpayer who has a Schedule C attached to his or her return whose business operations come under one of the many business market segments. Once a business market segment is identified, the IRS issues detailed audit guidelines to their specialists as a guide to conduct an audit of the tax return. These guidelines will detail various issues and practices within a market segment that should be scrutinized by all revenue agents for potential adjustment. The IRS has issued formal audit guidelines to their examiners with respect to 27 market segments, including, but not limited to, gas retailers, attorneys, trucking, mortuaries, air charters, bed and breakfasts, taxicabs, the music industry, foreign athletes and entertainers, architectural services, bars and restaurants, mobile food vendors, resolution trust corporations, the wine industry, passive activity losses, and the rehabilitation credit.

In addition, the IRS initiates compliance projects on an area-by-area basis to identify areas of noncompliance. For example, one area examined all the drywall contractors in a major metro area and claims to have found widespread underreporting of gross receipts as well as nonfilers. Another area selected returns of individuals who had renegotiated loans and examined them to determine if they were subject to tax because an indebtedness had been forgiven.

IRS service centers conduct other projects. Several service centers screened returns to determine if taxpayers who requested extensions of time to file were understating the tax that would be due. The IRS then treated extensions as invalid when the difference between the tax shown on the return and the extension exceeded certain tolerances. Other IRS service centers screened tax returns to detect failure to report gain on residences that were not replaced.

6. **Economic reality audits.** The IRS has a program of gathering information about a taxpayer that is a reflection of the individual's financial status. This technique involves

an examination of the taxpayer's lifestyle as an additional check on whether the taxpayer had unreported income. Areas of inquiry may include standard of living, accumulated wealth, economic history, business environment, and potential nontaxable income. The intent is to audit the taxpayer and not just the tax return.

Problems can arise when the examiner decides that the taxpayer cannot afford the style in which the taxpayer lives, if such a decision is made without knowledge of what mortgage indebtedness (if any) the taxpayer may owe. If the taxpayer has nontaxable trust, or other income, determinations based on inadequate information can be the start of a troublesome IRS investigation that is unwarrantedly seeking criminal evasion evidence. Because of the delicate balance between what is and what is not a proper subject of inquiry of the IRS examiner, some care should be exercised. Particular attention should be given if there is any indication that the matter could be tied to a Market Segment inquiry (see above). The issues are serious to the IRS and the inquiry is a serious matter.

With the passage of the Internal Revenue Service Restructuring and Reform Act of 1998, economic reality audits have been severely restricted. These audit techniques were extremely intrusive and their use has been limited to situations where the IRS already has indications of unreported income. In these cases, the examiners have been instructed to tell the taxpayer that there appears to be a problem regarding income and give him an opportunity to explain and/or resolve any discrepancies. However, due to the potential serious nature of this type of issue, the well-informed taxpayer should consider contacting a tax advisor.

Arranging the examination. Many examinations are handled by mail. However, if the IRS notifies you that your examination is to be conducted through a personal interview, or if you request an interview, you have the right to ask that the examination take place at a reasonable time and place that are convenient for both you and the IRS. If the time or place the IRS suggests is not convenient, the examiner will try to work out something more suitable. However, the IRS will make the final determination on how, when, and where an examination takes place. The difference between the correspondence and office audit is as follows:

Correspondence audit. After a tax return is initially selected for examination, the IRS may first conduct a correspondence audit, requesting that documentation of a specific item on your tax return be submitted by mail. If it is more convenient, you may request that the audit be held at the IRS's local district office. However, by law, the IRS has the right to make the final decision on where and how an examination will be conducted, as long as it is not unreasonable in exercising its discretion. The Taxpayer Bill of Rights directed the IRS to publish regulations defining reasonable time and place. These regulations were published in temporary form, effective June 4, 1990.

Office audit. If the examination is conducted at an IRS office, its scope may be expanded to cover all questionable items. Although correspondence audits may be resolved more quickly than examinations conducted at an IRS office, there is no rule of thumb for which type of audit would be more beneficial to you. However, it is generally to your disadvantage to request that a correspondence audit be changed to an office audit or a field audit. Correspondence audits are limited in scope. You open the opportunity for the examiner to question other items if you request an interview audit at an IRS office or an audit at your place of business.

The easier you make the IRS's job, the less the amount of time required to conclude the audit and the greater the likelihood that you will avoid any arbitrary adjustments.

An examination verifies the accuracy of your tax liability on a specific item as reported on a tax return, claim, or other filing. An examination is generally limited to the study of those matters bearing directly on the tax question at hand. The IRS has the authority to examine information that may not appear to be directly related to your tax liability. For example, the IRS may study your living expenses to determine if your reported income can support your lifestyle or whether you may have unreported income.

Transfers to another district. Generally, your individual return is examined in the IRS district office nearest your home. However, not all offices have examination facilities. Your business return is examined where your books and records are maintained. If the place of examination is not convenient, you may ask to have the examination done in another office or transferred to a different district.

Representation. Throughout the examination, you may represent yourself, have someone else accompany you, or, with proper written authorization, have someone represent you in your absence. If you want to consult an attorney, an enrolled agent, a CPA, or any other person permitted to represent a taxpayer during an examination, the IRS will stop and reschedule the interview. The IRS cannot suspend the interview if you are there because of an administrative summons.

If you use Form 8821, *Tax Information Authorization,* to name a representative for you, the representative is only authorized to receive information and cannot fully represent you by taking action on the information. If you use Form 2848, *Power of Attorney,* to name your representative, the representative is fully authorized to represent you and take any action necessary, including signing an agreement for a deficiency or overassessment of tax to conclude the case.

In recent years, some districts and some examiners have been very aggressive in demanding that the taxpayer, even though represented by a qualified practitioner with a power of attorney, appear personally to answer questions. This practice was admittedly to probe for unreported income and to establish if the taxpayer's lifestyle might suggest other problems in compliance with tax laws. The Taxpayer Bill of Rights now specifies that the IRS "may not require a taxpayer to accompany the representative in the absence of an administrative summons," and a properly qualified practitioner with a power of attorney is authorized to represent a client in any interview without the taxpayer's presence, except for criminal cases or matters involving the integrity of an IRS employee. Furthermore, the law specifies that "if a taxpayer clearly states at any time during an interview," except where an administrative summons has been enforced or accepted, "that the taxpayer wishes to consult with an attorney, certified public accountant, enrolled agent, enrolled actuary, or any other person permitted to represent the taxpayer," the IRS "shall suspend such interview, regardless of whether the taxpayer may have answered one or more questions."

TAXPLANNER

Do you need professional help? The answer is: It depends on the issues involved and your ability to represent yourself.

If the amounts involved are small, it may not be worth it to pay for an advisor's time. If your return was prepared by a certified public accountant or a lawyer, you will want to inquire whether his or her fee included representing you at an audit. If it didn't and you want him or her to represent you, you should agree on a fee at the beginning of the process. You will certainly want an accountant or a lawyer to represent you if (1) the law involved in the audit is unclear or complicated, (2) highly technical supporting information may be required, (3) you think other issues may come up, or (4) you are too nervous or emotionally involved to handle the matter yourself.

Tape recording meetings with the IRS. You can generally make an audio recording of an interview with an IRS examination officer. Your request to record the interview should be made in writing. You must notify the IRS at least 10 days before the meeting and bring your own recording equipment. The IRS also can record an interview. If the IRS initiates the recording, it will notify you 10 days before the meeting, and you can get a copy of the recording at your expense.

Repeat examinations. The IRS tries to avoid repeat examinations of the same items, but sometimes this happens. If the IRS examines your tax return for the same items in either of the 2 previous years and proposed no change to your tax liability, please contact it as soon as possible so that the agency can see if it should discontinue the examination.

Generally, in connection with auditing your return for a particular year, the IRS may inspect your books only once. But there may be a second examination if you request it or if the IRS notifies you in writing that an additional audit is necessary. A further investigation could be considered necessary simply if the IRS suspects that additional tax is owed.

You may refuse the IRS's request to make a second examination. In fact, if you do not object, you have, in effect, given your consent for the examination to take place. If you refuse to produce records, the IRS must issue a summons. If you still resist, the IRS will be forced to obtain court assistance to enforce the summons.

The ban on second examinations does not apply:

1. When the original audit, although prolonged and characterized by IRS staffing changes, is still going on.
2. When the examination is not considered an examination as such (e.g., when the IRS contacts you to verify the amount of dividends or interest on your return because that figure does not match what was otherwise reported).
3. When the second examination is for a different kind of tax (e.g., employment or excise tax, instead of income tax) than was dealt with in the first examination.
4. When a mere visual inspection of the return has taken place, not an examination of your books and records.
5. In cases involving the year of deduction of a net operating loss carryback (or similar type of carryback).
6. In cases in which there have been involuntary conversions and the taxpayer has not recomputed the tax liability after the replacement period has expired.

In sum, it is difficult for the IRS to justify a second examination of your books and records for the same year, but if there is a legitimate reason to do so, the IRS is usually within its rights.

Explanation of changes. If the IRS proposes any changes to your return, it will explain the reasons for the changes. It is important that you understand the reasons for any proposed change. You should not hesitate to ask about anything that is unclear to you.

Agreement with changes. If you agree with the proposed changes, you may sign an agreement form and pay any additional tax you may owe. You must pay interest on any additional tax. If you pay when you sign the agreement, the interest is generally figured from the due date of your return to the date you paid.

The IRS uses misleading language when it describes this consent form as an "agreement form." When you sign a Form 870 or Form 4549, you are simply permitting the IRS to make its assessment of tax without waiting 90 days, as required by law, and you are forfeiting your right to go to the Tax Court. You are not bound to follow the IRS position in subsequent years and may even file a claim for a refund for the years covered by the Form 870 after the tax has been paid.

If you do not pay the additional tax when you sign the agreement, you will receive a bill. The interest on the additional tax is generally figured from the due date of your return to the billing date. However, you will not be billed for more than 30 days' additional interest, even if the bill is delayed. Also, you will not have to pay any additional interest or penalties if you pay the amount due within 10 days of the billing date.

If you are due a refund, the IRS can refund your money more quickly if you sign the agreement form. You will be paid interest on the refund.

An IRS examiner's authority. An IRS examiner has virtually unlimited authority to determine the facts. Since most examination issues concern factual matters, the examiner has considerable discretion in accepting secondary evidence and in deciding what constitutes acceptable proof. On technical legal issues, though, he or she must adhere to established IRS policy. Therefore, even if certain court cases support your argument, the examiner must disallow it if the IRS has decided not to follow the precedents established by these cases.

In theory, IRS examiners are also not permitted to trade off items, letting you take one deduction in return for disallowing another. In practice, negotiations with the IRS are commonplace.

An important reminder. IRS examiners are under considerable pressure to close cases by reaching an agreement at the initial examination. An agent is given high marks for explaining the IRS position in a convincing manner. Contrary to popular belief, examiners are not rated by the amount of money they bring in or by the number of cases they close.

While all examination reports have a chance of being reviewed, except for cases that fall into a mandatory review category, the review is on a sample basis, so only a small percentage of cases are actually reviewed. The mandatory categories include cases involving refunds in excess of $1 million, tax shelters, NRP, and fraud. All unagreed cases are subject to a limited review on receipt of a protest asking for an Appeals hearing. This review is primarily focused on perfecting the IRS case based on your arguments in the protest.

Appeals

If you do not agree with the examiner's proposed changes, you can appeal them to the Appeals Office of the IRS. Most differences can be settled without expensive and time-consuming court trials. Your appeal rights are explained in detail in both Publication 5, *Your Appeal Rights and How to Prepare a Protest If You Don't Agree,* and Publication 556, *Examination of Returns, Appeal Rights, and Claims for Refund.*

If you do not wish to use the Appeals Office or disagree with its findings, you may be able to take your case to the U.S. Tax Court, U.S. Court of Federal Claims, or the U.S. District Court where you live. If you take your case to court, the IRS will have the burden of proving certain facts if you kept adequate records to show your tax liability, cooperated with the IRS, and meet certain other conditions. If the court agrees with you on most issues in your case and finds that our position was largely unjustified, you may be able to recover some of your administrative and litigation costs. You will not be eligible to recover these costs unless you tried to resolve your case administratively, including going through the appeals system, and you gave us the information necessary to resolve the case.

Explanation

Appealing the Examination Findings

If you and the IRS auditor reach an agreement on the issue under examination, the auditor will be on your side if his or her report is reviewed by his or her boss.

If you do not agree with the examiner's report, you can meet with the examiner's supervisor to discuss your case further. If you still do not agree after receiving the examiner's findings, you have the right to appeal them. The examiner will explain your appeal rights and give you a copy of Publication 5, *Appeal Rights and Preparation of Protests for Unagreed Cases.* This free publication explains your appeal rights in detail and tells you exactly what to do if you want to appeal.

The IRS now offers fast-track mediation services to help taxpayers resolve many disputes. Most cases that are not docketed in any court qualify for fast-track mediation. Mediation can take place as early as the conference you requested with the examiner's supervisor. The process involves an Appeals Officer who has been trained in mediation.

If you disagree with the IRS. If you and the IRS examiner disagree over the proper interpretation of a point of law, either you or the examiner may request technical advice from the IRS national office. Technical advice will be given only if the issue is unusual or complex, or if there is a lack of uniformity within the IRS about its treatment. If you ask for technical advice and the examiner denies the request, you may appeal to the Chief of the Examination Division. If he or she also denies the request and you disagree with the denial, all data will be forwarded to the Assistant Commissioner (Examination) in the national office for review. Action on the disputed issue generally will be suspended until it is decided whether or not technical advice will be issued.

Technical disagreements may be resolved by taking them to the agent's supervisor. However, this course of action is not recommended unless you are absolutely certain you are correct. The supervisor could point out an alternative position that might be more favorable to the examining agent.

Appeals. There is a single level of administrative appeal within the IRS. You make your appeal about the findings of the examiner to the Appeals Office in your region. Appeals conferences are conducted as informally as possible.

If you want an appeals conference, address your request to your District Director, according to the instructions in the IRS letter to you. Your District Director will forward your request to the Appeals Office, which will arrange for a conference at a convenient time and place. You or your representative should be prepared to discuss all disputed issues and to present your views at this meeting in order to save the time and expense of additional conferences. Most differences are resolved at this level.

If agreement is not reached at your appeals conference, you may, at any stage of the proceedings, take your case to court. See *Appeals to the Courts,* later.

Written protests. Along with your request for a conference, you may be required to file a written protest with your District Director.

You do not have to file a written protest if:

1. The proposed increase or decrease in tax, or claimed refund, is not more than $25,000 for any of the tax periods involved.
2. Your examination was conducted by correspondence or in an IRS office by a tax auditor.

To request an appeal, follow the instructions in the letter to you by sending a letter requesting Appeals consideration, indicating the changes you don't agree with, and the reasons why you don't agree.

If a written protest is required, you should send it within the period granted in the letter that you received with the examination report. Your protest should contain all of the following:

1. A statement that you want to appeal the findings of the examiner to the Appeals Office
2. Your name and address and a daytime phone number
3. The date and symbols from the letter, showing the adjustments and findings you are protesting
4. The tax periods or years involved
5. An itemized schedule of the adjustments with which you do not agree and why you do not agree
6. A statement of facts supporting your position in any issue with which you do not agree
7. A statement outlining the law or other authority on which you rely

You must sign the written protest, stating that it is true, under penalties of perjury as follows:

"Under the penalties of perjury, I declare that I have examined the facts stated in this protest and in any accompanying schedules and, to the best of my knowledge and belief, they are true, correct, and complete."

If your representative submits the protest for you, he or she may substitute a declaration stating the following:

1. That he or she prepared the protest and accompanying documents
2. Whether he or she knows personally that the statement of facts contained in the protest and accompanying documents is true and correct

Representation. You may represent yourself at your appeals conference, or you may be represented by an attorney, a certified public accountant, or a person enrolled to practice before the IRS.

If your representative attends a conference without you, he or she may receive or inspect confidential information only if a power of attorney or a tax information authorization has been filed. Form 2848, *Power of Attorney and Declaration of Representative,* or Form 8821, *Tax Information Authorization,* or any other properly written power of attorney or authorization may be used for this purpose.

You may also bring witnesses to support your position. You should consider consulting an attorney specializing in tax law before you do this.

Bargaining with the IRS. Whereas an IRS examiner must follow established IRS policy on statutory and procedural points, the appeals officer may bargain with you. He or she may consider whether litigation is worthwhile, given the strength of the views at odds with the IRS's position. If you make an unsuitable good faith settlement offer, the appeals officer may reject it but indicate a settlement he or she would recommend be accepted. In arriving at a figure, the appeals officer may calculate the chances of the IRS prevailing in court. Generally, however, the IRS will not settle a case just because it is a nuisance to continue to pursue it.

Appeals officers do not have final settlement authority in all cases and for all issues. Accordingly, it is good practice in negotiating a settlement to ask the appeals officer if any part of a settlement proposed is subject to a supervisory review.

If no agreement can be reached at the appeals conference, you have two options:

1. Pay the additional tax generated by the disputed issue and sue for the refund of this payment in your District Court or the U.S. Court of Federal Claims (formerly the U.S. Claims Court; see *Appeals to the courts,* below).
2. Wait for the arrival of your closing letter, and select a course of action at that point. If you do not pay the disputed amount, you will receive from the IRS a notice of deficiency, which is also known as a 90-day letter. This notice authorizes you to file a petition in the U.S. Tax Court without first having to pay the tax. A Tax Court suit may not be filed before receipt of the 90-day letter.

TaxAlert

Partnerships and S Corporations. Special procedures apply to certain partnerships and S corporations. The amount of any adjustment is determined at the partnership or S corporation level. The procedures are complex, regular statutory notices are not issued, and you should consult a professional if you want to contest a partnership or S corporation issue raised in the examination of your return.

Appeals to the courts. Depending on whether you first pay the disputed tax, you can take your case to the U.S. Tax Court, the U.S. Court of Federal Claims, or your U.S. District Court. These courts are entirely independent of the IRS. However, a U.S. Tax Court case is generally reviewed by an Appeals Office before it is heard by the Tax Court. As always, you can represent yourself or have someone admitted to practice before the court represent you.

Tax Court. If your case involves a disagreement over whether you owe additional income tax, estate tax, gift tax, windfall profit tax on domestic crude oil, or certain excise taxes of private foundations, public charities, qualified pension and other retirement plans, or real estate investment trusts, you may take it to the U.S. Tax Court. For you to appeal your case to the Tax Court, the IRS must first issue a formal letter, called a *notice of deficiency.* You have 90 days from the date this notice is mailed to you to file a petition with the Tax Court (150 days if it is addressed to you outside the United States). If you do not file your petition within the 90 or 150 days, you lose your opportunity to appeal to the Tax Court.

Generally, the Tax Court hears cases only if the tax has not been assessed and paid; however, you may pay the tax after the notice of deficiency has been issued and still petition the Tax Court for review. You must be sure that your petition to the Tax Court is filed on time. If it is not, the proposed liability will be automatically assessed against you. Once the tax is assessed, a notice of tax due (a bill) will be sent to you, and you may no longer take your case to the Tax Court. Once the assessment has been made, collection of the full amount due may proceed, even if you believe that the assessment was excessive. Publication 586A, *The Collection Process (Income Tax Accounts),* explains IRS collection procedures.

If you filed your petition on time, the Tax Court will schedule your case for trial at a location that is convenient to you. You may represent yourself before the Tax Court, or you may be represented by anyone admitted to practice before the Tax Court.

If your case involves a dispute of not more than $50,000 for any 1 tax year, the Tax Court provides a simple alternative for resolving disputes. At your request, and with the approval of the Tax Court, your case may be handled under the *small case* procedures, whereby you can present your own case to the Tax Court for a binding decision. If your case is handled under this procedure, the decision of the Tax Court is final and cannot be appealed. You can get more information about the small case procedures and other Tax Court matters from the U.S. Tax Court, 400 Second Street, N.W., Washington, D.C. 20217.

TaxAlert

Representing yourself. Since many taxpayers represent themselves in small cases, the IRS has a very high win record. Filing your own petition may not be a good idea, especially if the amount is substantial to you. In any event, be careful in following the instructions *to the letter,* especially regarding the date for filing, the required fee, and the address of the Tax Court. The date of mailing a petition to the Tax Court is the filing date, but you should use certified mail and carefully retain the receipt with a legible postmark.

District Court and U.S. Court of Federal Claims. Generally, the District Court and the U.S. Court of Federal Claims hear tax cases only after you have paid the tax and have filed a claim for a credit or a refund. As explained later under *Claims for Refund,* you may file a claim for a credit or a refund with the IRS if, after you pay your tax, you believe that the tax is incorrect or too high. If your claim is rejected, you will receive a notice of disallowance of the claim, unless you signed a Form 2297, *Waiver of Statutory Notification of Claim Disallowance.* If the IRS has not acted on your claim within 6 months from the date on which you filed it, you may then file suit for refund. You must file suit for a credit or a refund no later than 2 years after the IRS disallows your claim or a Form 2297 is issued.

You may file your credit or refund suit in your U.S. District Court or in the U.S. Court of Federal Claims. However, the U.S. Court of Federal Claims does not have jurisdiction if your claim was filed after July 18, 1984, and is for credit or refund of a penalty that relates to promoting an abusive tax shelter or to aiding and abetting the understatement of tax liability on someone else's return.

For information about procedures for filing suit in either court, contact the Clerk of your U.S. District Court or the Clerk of the U.S. Court of Federal Claims. The addresses of the District Courts and the U.S. Court of

Federal Claims are in Publication 556, *Examination of Returns, Appeal Rights, and Claims for Refund.*

Before you file suit. Here are some of the factors that you might want to consider before you decide to file your suit in Tax Court, District Court, or U.S. Court of Federal Claims:

1. Which court has most recently arrived at favorable rulings on similar disputed issues.
2. The amount of tax involved. You may file a suit in Tax Court without paying the IRS the amount it claims you owe. If the tax has already been paid and you wish to file suit to obtain a refund, the U.S. District Court and the U.S. Court of Federal Claims are your only choices. However, to stop the accumulation of interest, you can at any time make a deposit in the nature of a cash bond of the tax that an examiner says you owe. *Note:* Such a remittance must be clearly labeled as a deposit. If you are successful in an appeal, you will draw no interest on the deposits returned. A deposit does not prevent you from going to the Tax Court. Once you file a suit in Tax Court, you may then pay the alleged tax deficiency and your suit will not be thrown out of court. If you do make the payment at this point in the process, you will not be liable for interest charges past the payment date. If you win, the government will then owe you interest from the date on which you made the payment. A deposit will be converted to a payment of the tax when you file a petition with the Tax Court. It is important to distinguish between payments of tax and deposits to stop the accumulation of interest.
3. Jury trials are available only in the District Courts. If your case rests on a question of equity, rather than on a finer point of tax law, a jury might be more responsive to your arguments. Remember, however, that both parties may appeal a District Court or a Tax Court decision.
4. A representative who is not an attorney may appear before the Tax Court if admitted to practice before that court.
5. Filing a suit before the Tax Court suspends the statute of limitation for assessment on the tax return that you are contesting. Consequently, if the IRS chooses, it could raise new issues and assert additional tax while your case is pending in court.
6. You're more likely to avoid embarrassing publicity before the Court of Federal Claims. The U.S. Court of Federal Claims is located in Washington, D.C. There is a U.S. District Court near your hometown. The Tax Court tries cases on a circuit-riding basis in most major cities.
7. You may file suit in Tax Court within 90 days (150 days if outside the United States) after the IRS issues a statutory notice of deficiency. You have more time to file before the U.S. District Court and the U.S. Court of Federal Claims.
8. In Tax Court, attorneys from the Office of Chief Counsel represent the IRS. In District Court and U.S. Court of Federal Claims, attorneys from the Tax Division of the Department of Justice will oppose your case.
9. Tax Court and District Court cases are appealed to the Circuit Court of Appeals and then to the Supreme Court. U.S. Court of Federal Claims decisions may be appealed to the Court of Appeals for the Federal Circuit and then to the Supreme Court.
10. Any court of the United States may now award attorney's fees and other costs for cases initiated after December 31, 1985, including certain costs incurred in an administrative appeal if the IRS's position was not substantially justified.

Recovering litigation expenses. If the court agrees with you on most of the issues in your case and finds the IRS's position to be largely unjustified, you may be able to recover some of your litigation expenses from the IRS. But to do this, you must have used up all the administrative remedies available to you within the IRS, including going through the appeals system. You may also be able to recover administrative expenses from the IRS. Free Publication 556, *Examination of Returns, Appeal Rights, and Claims for Refund,* explains your appeal rights.

The Taxpayer Bill of Rights corrects an inequity in prior law by permitting the courts to award costs, not only for litigating but also for administrative proceedings once a taxpayer's administrative appeal rights have been exhausted and a "notice of decision" by the IRS or a statutory notice of deficiency has been issued, whichever occurs earlier. The prior law had been interpreted to permit recovery only after the IRS's attorneys had taken a position before the courts. To recover, a taxpayer must substantially prevail through a determination in an administrative proceeding, after the point specified above, or in a court of law and must establish that the position of the United States in the proceeding was not substantially justified. In collection matters, when neither notice is issued, only litigation costs are recoverable.

Reasonable administrative costs include the following:

- Fees or charges imposed by the IRS
- Reasonable expert witness fees
- Reasonable costs of studies and analyses
- Costs associated with engineering or test reports
- Reasonable fees (generally not in excess of $150 per hour) for a qualified representative of the taxpayer in connection with the administrative action

Collections

Publication 594, *The IRS Collection Process,* explains your rights and responsibilities regarding payment of federal taxes. It describes:

- What to do when you owe taxes. It describes what to do if you get a tax bill and what to do if you think your bill is wrong. It also covers making installment payments, delaying collection action, and submitting an offer in compromise.
- IRS collection actions. It covers liens, releasing a lien, levies, releasing a levy, seizures and sales, and release of property.

Your collection appeal rights are explained in detail in Publication 1660, *Collection Appeal Rights.*

Innocent spouse relief. Generally, both you and your spouse are responsible, jointly and individually, for paying the full amount of any tax, interest, or penalties due on your joint return. However, if you qualify for innocent spouse relief, you may not have to pay the tax, interest, and penalties related to your spouse (or former spouse). For information on innocent spouse relief and two other ways to get relief, see Publication 971, *Innocent Spouse Relief,* and Form 8857, *Request for Innocent Spouse Relief (And Separation of Liability and Equitable Relief).*

Claims for Refund

You may file a claim for refund if you think you paid too much tax. You must generally file the claim within 3 years from the date you filed your original return or 2 years from the date you paid the tax, whichever is later. The law generally provides for interest on your refund if it is not paid within 45 days of the date you filed your return or claim for refund. Publication 556, *Examination of Returns, Appeals Rights, and Claims for Refund,* has more information on refunds.

If you were due a refund but you did not file a return, you must file within 3 years from the date the return was originally due to get that refund.

Explanation. If you believe that tax, penalty, or interest was unjustly charged, you have rights that can remedy the situation.

Claims for refund. Once you have paid your tax, you have the right to file a claim for a credit or refund if you believe the tax is too much. Be aware that informal claims that mention vague and general future possibilities to justify a refund will not be considered valid. The procedure for filing a claim is explained in Chapter 1, *Filing Information.*

Some courts have held that an informal claim for a refund will, under certain circumstances, prevent the statutory period from expiring before you can accumulate and submit all your data. An informal claim should be in writing, should notify the IRS that a right to a refund is being asserted, and should tell as fully as possible the reasons why you feel the refund would be valid. A formal claim for the refund filed on official IRS forms should be made as soon as practical thereafter.

If you file with the wrong IRS center. If you file an amended return with the wrong IRS Service Center, it is under no obligation to forward that return to the correct Service Center. If you do not hear from the IRS within 6 months of filing Form 1040X, you should make a point of contacting it to determine the source of the delay.

Claims (Form 1040X) should always ask for a specific dollar amount or "for such greater amount as is legally refundable" to ensure that you receive a refund of interest and interest on such interest where appropriate.

Cancellation of penalties. You have the right to ask that certain penalties (but not interest, as discussed later) be cancelled (abated) if you can show reasonable cause for the failure that led to the penalty (or can show that you exercised due diligence, if that is the standard for the penalty).

If you relied on wrong advice from IRS employees given to you by phone, the agency will cancel certain penalties that may result. But you have to show that your reliance on the advice was reasonable.

Reduction of interest. If the IRS's error caused a delay in your case, and this is grossly unfair, you may be entitled to a reduction of the interest that would otherwise be due. Only delays caused by procedural or mechanical acts that do not involve exercising judgment or discretion qualify. If you think the IRS caused such a delay, please discuss it with the examiner and file a claim.

TaxSaver

If the IRS makes an error. If the IRS made an error, sent you a refund check, and then made you pay interest when you repaid it, you now can strike back. According to the Tax Reform Act of 1986, the IRS may not charge you interest from the date of the erroneous refund to the date they demanded you repay it. The law

has also given the IRS the discretion to refund or abate excessive interest that you may have paid on an underpayment of your tax if an IRS employee was dilatory or made an error in processing it. To qualify, you must not have caused the error in any way. The erroneous refund must have been less than $50,000. Use Form 843 to file your claim.

Past-due taxes. The Taxpayer Bill of Rights recognized that taxpayers occasionally may have problems paying taxes due on their returns because of unanticipated changes on examination or other unexpected difficulties. To ensure fair treatment, the Taxpayer Bill of Rights made some changes in how notices are issued, how much time is allowed for payment, how taxpayers can get help, and so on. The key provisions relating to past-due taxes are as follows:

1. The period from when the IRS provides written notice to a taxpayer to the first permissible date on which the IRS can levy on bank accounts, wages, and so on is increased from 10 days to 30 days. The IRS also cannot levy on property on any day on which the person appears before the IRS in response to a summons, unless the IRS determines the collection of the tax is in jeopardy. In addition, financial institutions are required to hold accounts garnished by the IRS for 21 days after receipt of the notice of levy.

2. The IRS established a formal system for the appeal of liens similar to that existing in the income tax deficiency area. The appeals procedures are printed on the notice of lien. See Publication 1660, *Collection Appeal Rights.*

3. The IRS now has the legal right to enter into installment agreements with taxpayers so that they can more easily pay delinquent taxes. The agreement will remain in effect unless the taxpayer has provided inaccurate information, does not pay an installment when it is due, fails to respond to a reasonable request for updated financial information, or the collection of the balance is in jeopardy. In addition, the IRS may only modify or terminate an agreement if the taxpayer's financial condition has significantly changed. Notification of the reason for the action has to be given at least 30 days prior to any action.

4. The Taxpayer Advocate is authorized to issue a taxpayer assistance order (TAO) in any situation in which the taxpayer is suffering or about to suffer a significant hardship as a result of the manner in which the IRS laws are being administered. During the period in which the order is in effect, the statute of limitations is suspended and any further IRS action is halted. Only the Commissioner, Deputy Commissioner, or Taxpayer Advocate can modify or rescind the order. The Taxpayer Advocate administers the IRS Problem Resolution Program, which was created to resolve problems not remedied through normal operating channels.

The IRS has designed a form (Form 911) to assist taxpayers in applying for a TAO.

The Taxpayer Bill of Rights and the Taxpayer Bill of Rights 2, which passed August 1996, have many other provisions that may be helpful to you. If you have further problems with the IRS and believe that you are being treated unfairly, you should contact the district Problem Resolution Officer or a knowledgeable professional.

48

Planning Ahead for 2006 and Beyond

Introduction

The Working Families Tax Relief Act of 2004, the American Jobs Creation Act of 2004 and the Energy Tax Incentives Act of 2005 are the most recent major pieces of tax legislation that impact the amount of taxes paid by individuals. The new laws provide extensions for many expiring or soon-to-expire provisions that offer tax relief, as well as retroactively reinstate expired credits from previous tax acts and provide for new tax incentives. Among the important provisions for individuals are:

- *An extension of the increased child tax credit,*
- *Continuation of marriage penalty relief for those married taxpayers who file joint returns using the standard deduction,*
- *A new alternative motor vehicle credit consisting of the sum of four new tax credits for the purchase of alternative power vehicles, and*
- *A new personal tax credit for the purchase of residential energy efficient property.*

The 2004 Working Families Act also extended the increased size of the 15% rate bracket for joint returns and the 10% rate bracket for individuals through the 2010 tax year.

In order to limit the projected cost of the new laws on the federal budget, many of the provisions in the bills will only be in effect for a few years—unless Congress acts to extend them. So while the new legislation may provide an immediate financial benefit to many taxpayers, it may also make planning ahead for years beyond 2005 more challenging.

Prudent taxpayers need to begin planning even before their taxes are due. You should consult your tax advisor to determine how the new tax provisions will affect your individual tax situation. In the meantime, here is a summary of some of the major items from recent tax legislation that may affect your tax returns in the future.

Reduction of Individual Tax Rates
Continuing through 2010, the regular individual income tax rates above 10% and 15% are 25%, 28%, 33%, and 35%, the top individual rate. Unless Congress acts, however, these reduced rates will expire starting for tax years beginning after December 31, 2010. These rates also apply to trusts.

Taxable Income Levels for 10% Rate Bracket
The Working Families Tax Relief Act of 2004 extended the size of the 10% rate bracket through 2010. The size of the 10% rate bracket for 2005 through 2010 is set at $7,000 for single individuals, with annual indexing for inflation for all years after 2003 (it was $7,150 in 2004 and $7,300 in 2005). After 2010 the 10% bracket will expire entirely.

Tax Rate on Capital Gains

The top individual rate on long term capital gains, which generally used to be 20% (10% for taxpayers in the 10% and 15% brackets), is reduced to 15% (5% for taxpayers with income in the lower brackets) through 2008. These lower rates apply to both the regular tax and the alternative minimum tax. The lower rates apply to assets held more than one year. For taxpayers with income in the lower brackets, the 5% rate is reduced to zero in 2008. After 2008 these rates revert back the old ones.

Tax Rate for Qualifying Dividends

Certain dividend income, "qualified dividend income," is taxed at a rate of 15% until 2009. Prior to 2003, both dividends and interest were taxed at ordinary income tax rates. The top tax rate on "qualified dividend income" (but not interest) is now 15% for the purposes of computing both the regular tax and the alternative minimum tax. Unless there is further legislation, in 2009 dividends will again be subject to tax at ordinary income rates.

For a dividend to be eligible for the 15% reduced tax rate, you must own the underlying stock for more than 60 days during the 121-day period beginning 60 days before the "ex-dividend date," the day on which the stock starts trading without its next dividend. In the case of certain preferred stock, the holding period is increased to more than 90 days during the 181-day period beginning 90 days before the ex-dividend date.

Limitation on the Personal Exemption Deduction Starts to Ease.

Starting in 2006, higher-income taxpayers may be able to claim more of a deduction for their personal exemptions. First, they will determine the amount they must reduce their personal exemption deduction by, using the inflation-adjusted phaseout formula. Then they will multiply that reduction amount by 2/3. The net result is the amount that reduces their personal exemption deduction. For example, assume a married couple has two children, that the personal exemption deduction in 2006 is $3,300, that the deduction phaseout begins at $220,000 and that their adjusted gross income (AGI) is $250,000. Using the phaseout formula their deduction is initially reduced by 24% or $3,168 ($3,300 × 4 × .24). But their deduction will only be reduced by $2,112 ($3,168 × 2/3). The phaseout reduction remains at 2/3 in 2007. See Chapter 3, Personal Exemptions and Dependents for a discussion on how the inflation-adjusted phaseout formula works.

For 2008 and 2009, the reduction will be 1/3 of the amount determined under the inflation-adjusted formula. In 2010, the personal exemption phaseout will be repealed and higher-income taxpayers will be able to deduct the full amount of their personal exemptions. After 2010, the old phaseout rule returns in full force.

Limitation on Itemized Deductions Starts to Ease

Starting in 2006, higher-income taxpayers will be able to claim more of their total itemized deductions.

Two computations will have to be done in order to determine the amount of itemized deductions that will be deductible starting in 2006:

1. Determine what the regular limitation on itemized deductions is, using the 3% and 80% formulas. See Chapter 31, Limit on Itemized Deductions for a discussion on how these formulas work.

2. Determine the new amount that can be deducted from adjusted gross income for the tax year. This is done by taking the amount calculated under computation 1 and multiplying it by 2/3.

Example: For the 2006 tax year, Mary and John Barker compute their regular limitation on itemized deductions to be $17,600. They multiply this figure by 2/3 to arrive at $11,733, the amount they must reduce their total itemized deductions by. This calculation is the same for 2007.

For tax years 2008 and 2009, two computations will also be required:

1. Determine what the regular limitation on itemized deductions is, using the 3% and 80% formulas.
2. Determine the new amount that can be deducted from adjusted gross income for the tax year. This is done by taking the amount calculated under computation 1 and multiplying it by 1/3.

Example: For the 2008 tax year, Mary and John Barker compute their regular limitation on itemized deductions to be $17,600. They multiply this figure by 1/3 to arrive at $5,867, the amount they must ultimately reduce their total itemized deductions by.

For tax year 2010, the itemized deduction phaseout is repealed and higher-income taxpayers will not have to reduce their total itemized deductions based on an adjusted gross income limitation. After 2010, the old phaseout rule returns in full force.

Decrease in the Alternative Minimum Tax Exemption

The tax laws give preferential treatment to certain kinds of income and allow special deductions and credits for certain kinds of expenses. The alternative minimum tax attempts to ensure that anyone who benefits from these tax advantages pays at least a minimum amount of tax.

The alternative minimum tax ("MT") is a separately computed tax that eliminates many deductions and credits that are allowed in computing your regular tax liability. The AMT is the government's mechanism through which taxpayers with a large amount of deductions still pay some income tax. The tentative minimum tax rates on ordinary income are 26% and 28%. The regular capital gains tax rates apply for capital gains.

If your taxable income for regular tax purposes, plus any adjustments and preference items you have, total more than the exemption amount, then you may have to pay the AMT. The exemption amounts in effect for 2005 are:

1. $58,000 for married filing jointly/qualified widow or widower.
2. $40,250 for single or head of household.
3. $29,000 for married filing separately.

The AMT exemption amounts are phased out for higher-income taxpayers. The exemptions are phased out by an amount equal to 25% of the amount by which the taxpayer's AMT exceeds $150,000 in the case of married individuals filing a joint return and surviving spouses, and $112,500 in the case of other unmarried taxpayers.

Married individuals filing jointly and surviving spouses in 2005 will have the exemption fully phased out once income exceeds $382,000. At $273,500 the exemption will be phased out for other unmarried taxpayers.

As of the date of publication, the AMT exemption is scheduled to decrease dramatically in 2006 and beyond as follows:

1. $45,000 (down from $58,000) for married filing jointly/qualified widow or widower.
2. $33,750 (down from $40,250) for single or head of household
3. $22,500 (down from $29,000) for married filing separately.

Unless Congress acts to extend the higher exemption amounts into 2006 and beyond, substantially more taxpayers are going to be subject to the AMT as a result of these decreased exemption amounts.

Partial "Marriage Penalty" Relief

Although married couples may elect to file separate returns, the rate schedules and other tax provisions are structured so that a married couple filing separate returns usually has a higher combined tax than when filing a joint return. Different rate schedules and tax provisions apply to single taxpayers. A "marriage penalty" is said to exist when the tax liability of a married couple filing jointly is greater than the sum of the tax liabilities that would apply if each taxpayer were single.

A 2003 tax act increased the basic standard deduction amount for joint returns to twice the basic standard deduction amount for single returns for 2003 and 2004. The Working Families Tax Relief Act of 2004 extended the law so that the basic standard deduction amount for joint returns will continue to equal twice the basic standard deduction amount for single returns effective for the 2005–2010 tax years.

The 2003 tax act also provided relief for the marriage penalty that resulted due to the fact that the upper band on the 15% tax bracket was considerably lower for married filing jointly taxpayers than it was for unmarried taxpayers. Two unmarried individuals thus could have a greater amount of income taxed at the lower 15% tax rate than a married couple with similar income.

The Working Families Tax Relief Act of 2004 extends the size of the 15% rate bracket for joint returns to twice the size of the corresponding rate bracket for single returns effective for tax years 2005–2010. Therefore, the size of the 15% rate bracket for joint returns is twice the size of the corresponding rate bracket for single returns for tax years 2005–2010

Increase in the Child Tax Credit

A child tax credit is available for each qualifying child under the age of 17. The credit is phased out for higher-income taxpayers. The credit begins to phase out at $75,000 of modified adjusted gross income for single individuals and $110,000 for married individuals filing joint returns.

The Working Families Tax Relief Act of 2004 extended the child tax credit at the $1,000 per qualifying child level for tax years 2005–2009.

Under prior law, the maximum child tax credit was to be $1,000 per qualifying child for the 2010 tax year. As a result, the maximum child tax credit is $1,000 per child for tax years 2005–2010. For 2005, the taxpayer's earned income in excess of $11,000 (with indexing for inflation) will be eligible for the 15% refundable child credit.

Deduction for Higher-Education Expenses Expires

Eligible taxpayers are able to claim an annual deduction for up to $4,000 in 2005 of qualified higher education expenses. This deduction is also an adjustment to gross income and available even if you do not claim itemized deductions. The deductions are available to a single taxpayer with adjusted gross income up to $65,000, or $130,000 if married and filing jointly. **This deduction expires on December 31, 2005, and will not be available in 2006 unless extended by Congress.**

Deduction for Educator Expenses Expires

In 2005, regardless of whether you itemize your deductions or not, and regardless of the 2%-of-adjusted-gross-income limit, if you qualify as an "eligible educator," you are allowed a classroom expense deduction of up to $250 for expenses that you pay in connection with books, certain supplies, computer equipment (including related software and services), other equipment, and supplementary materials that you use in the classroom. An eligible educator is an individual who is a kindergarten through twelfth grade teacher, instructor, counselor, principal, or aide in a school for at least 900 hours during a school year, and a school is any school which provides elementary education or secondary education (kindergarten through twelfth grade), as determined under state law.

This deduction expires on December 31, 2005, and will not be available in 2006 unless extended by Congress.

Saver's Credit Expires After 2006

The saver's tax credit can save a taxpayer up to $1,000 in taxes just for putting money aside for retirement. The credit is a reward you receive for putting up to $2,000 a year in an individual retirement account (IRA), Roth IRA, 401(k) plan, or other plan. The credit is an additional tax benefit on top of any other benefits available for the contribution. And, unlike deductions that only reduce taxable income, the credit reduces your actual tax bill dollar for dollar (but not below zero).

This credit expires on December 31, 2006 and will not be available in 2007 unless extended by Congress.

Higher IRA Contribution Limits

Taxpayers' annual tax-free contributions to an IRA are limited to the amount of compensation they receive in a tax year or a statutory limit. The statutory annual contribution limits to both traditional and Roth IRAs will gradually rise from the current $4,000 to $5,000 by 2008 with annual inflation adjustments after 2008. Taxpayers who have attained age 50 by the end of the year will be able to make additional "catch-up" contributions of $1,000 for 2006 and thereafter.

TABLE 1
TRADITIONAL AND ROTH IRA ANNUAL CONTRIBUTION LIMITS

CALENDAR YEAR	INDIVIDUALS UNDER AGE 50	INDIVIDUALS AGE 50 AND ABOVE
2005	$4,000	$4,500
2006–2007	$4,000	$5,000
2008	$5,000	$6,000

Deduction for IRA Contribution Income Limitations

The modified adjusted gross income (AGI) limit for the deduction of contributions to traditional IRAs will increase. For

2006, if you are covered by a retirement plan at work and also contribute to an IRA, your deduction is reduced (phased out) when your modified adjusted gross income is:

- More than $75,000 and less than $85,000 for married couples filing joint returns/qualifying widow(er)s,
- More than $50,000 but less than $60,000 for a single individual or head of household, or
- More than $0 but less than $10,000 for a married individual filing a separate return.

Defined Benefit Plans
The maximum annual benefit for years ending after 2005 is based on cost of living and has not yet been determined. For years ending after 2004, the maximum annual benefit for a participant under a defined benefit plan is the smaller of these amounts:

- 100% of the participant's average compensation for his highest three consecutive calendar years, or
- $170,000, which is subject to cost-of-living increases.

Defined Contribution Plans
The maximum annual contribution for years ending after 2005 is based on cost of living and has not yet been determined. For years beginning after 2004, a defined contribution plan's maximum annual contributions and other additions, excluding earnings, to the account of a participant is the smaller of these amounts:

- 100% of compensation actually paid to the participant, or
- $42,000, subject to cost of living increases.

Roth 401(k) Plans
Starting in 2006, if your employer's plan allows it, you'll be able to designate part or all of your 401(k) contributions as "Roth 401(k)" contributions. As with a Roth IRA, your contributions to a Roth 401(k) are nondeductible, but all of the income in the plan will be tax-free to you when distributed if you meet the same requirements that apply to Roth IRAs—5 years of participation and distribution after age 59, death, disability, or for up to $10,000 for a first-time home purchase.

Elective Deferral Limits
The dollar limit on the amount you can contribute on an elective deferral basis to your 401(k) or other defined contribution plan increases to $15,000 by 2006, after which it will be indexed for inflation. The applicable dollar limit is larger for taxpayers who are age 50 by the end of the year. Table 2 shows the limits.

TABLE 2
DEFINED CONTRIBUTION PLAN: ANNUAL ELECTIVE DEFERRAL LIMITS

CALENDAR YEAR	INDIVIDUALS UNDER AGE 50	INDIVIDUALS AGE 50 AND ABOVE
2005	$14,000	$18,000
2006	$15,000	$20,000

SIMPLE Plans
A SIMPLE plan is an arrangement under which an employer with fewer than 100 employees makes contributions to employees' SIMPLE retirement accounts. The two types of SIMPLE plans are the SIMPLE IRA and SIMPLE 401(k) plans.

The maximum annual elective deferral that may be made to a SIMPLE plan is $10,000 in 2005. For taxpayers who reach age 50 before the end of the plan year, this limit is increased to $12,000 for 2005 and $12,500 for 2006.

Sales Tax Deduction Expires
In 2005, you can choose between either taking state sales taxes or state income taxes as an itemized deduction on your federal tax return. Unless Congress extends this provision, you will not be able to deduct sales taxes after 2005.

New Alternative Motor Vehicle Credit
For vehicles placed in service after 2005, there is an alternative motor vehicle credit available which consists of the following four new credits:

1. Qualified Fuel Cell Motor Vehicle credit
2. Advanced Lean Burn Technology Motor Vehicle credit
3. Qualified Hybrid Motor Vehicle credit
4. Qualified Alternative Fuel Motor Vehicle credit

The alternative motor vehicle credit is allowed to the vehicle owner, including the lessor of a vehicle subject to a lease. It is allowed in the year the vehicle is placed in service. The vehicle must be used pre-dominantly in the United States to qualify for the credit. If you claim this credit, you must reduce any deduction otherwise allowable under Code Section 179A. No credit is allowed for the portion of the cost of any property taken into account under Code Section 179.

The portion of the alternative motor vehicle credit attributable to vehicles that are subject to depreciation is treated as part of the general business credit. Any remaining credit is treated as a personal credit and may offset the excess of the regular tax over the alternative minimum tax. The credit is not allowed against AMT.

New Personal Tax Credit for the Purchase of Residential Energy Efficient Property
This credit applies to property placed in service after December 31, 2005, and before January 1, 2008. The credit is equal to the sum of the following:

1. 30% of the amount paid for qualified photovoltaic property, with a maximum credit of $2,000,
2. 30% of the amount paid for qualified solar water heating property, with a maximum credit of $2,000, and
3. 30% of the amount paid for qualified fuel cell property, with a maximum credit of $500 for each 0.5 kilowatt of capacity.

The credit is nonrefundable and reduces the basis in the depreciable property it relates to. If the credit is limited (due to an overall limit on the various nonrefundable personal credits that are allowed in a tax year), it may be carried forward to the next tax year.

Exclusion of Gain from Sale of Principal Residence after Like-Kind Exchange
Formerly, if a principal residence was sold after being owned for just two years after a tax-free like-kind exchange, the owner could exclude up to $250,000 (single) or $500,000 (joint) of the gain. Under the American Jobs Creation Act of 2004, if sale of a principal residence occur after October 22, 2004, and the residence was previously acquired in a like-kind exchange, the exclusion is available only if the residence was owned for five years prior to sale, rather than the two-year rule which applies to a regular sale.

Substantiation Requirements for Charitable Contribution of Vehicles

Under the 2004 American Jobs Creation Act, and new 2005 guidelines, taxpayers are required to obtain more substantiation than ever before when claiming a deduction of more than $500 for the donation of a vehicle. First, written acknowledgment of the donation from the organization receiving the vehicle is required. Second, the acknowledgment must include the name and taxpayer identification number of the donor; the vehicle identification number, and certain certifications, depending on the disposition of the vehicle by the donee organization. Third, if the charitable organization sells the vehicle, the donor's charitable deduction is generally limited to proceeds received by the organization upon sale. Taxpayers who plan to donate vehicles and claim this deduction, are well advised to heed these substantiation requirements, as the IRS has expressed concern over abuses of the deduction. The IRS will be closely monitoring these deductions, so you should become very familiar with the new rules. For more information, see Publication 4303—A Donor's Guide to Car Donations.

Form 4868—Automatic Extension of Time to File U.S. Individual Income Tax Return

The IRS has issued the 2005 Form 4868, which extends the automatic time to file an individual income tax return from 4 months to 6 months. This change in the automatic extension period was made in response to taxpayers' concerns over the ever-increasing paperwork burdens that they face.

PART VIII

2005 Draft Tax Forms and Filling Out Your Tax Return

The chapters in this part provide you with draft forms and tax rate schedules. Chapter 49, 2005 Draft Federal Tax Forms, includes many of the draft 2005 Federal Tax Forms. Final forms were not yet available when this book went to press in late September 2005 but the draft forms provide a useful reference. *Any additional final forms that you may need to complete your return are easily available at the IRS Web site at www.irs.gov.* Chapter 50, Filling Out Form 1040, has line-by-line instructions for filling out Form 1040. The final chapter includes tax rate schedules that you need to complete your tax return. The 2005 Tax Tables, which were not available at press time, can be easily viewed and printed out at *www.irs.gov*. The tax tables must be used by taxpayers with taxable income of less than $100,000. Taxpayers with taxable income of $100,000 or more should use the tax rate schedules.

49

2005 Draft Federal Tax Forms

Introduction

This Chapter contains many of the 2005 **draft** IRS tax forms referred to in this book. The draft forms cannot be used to file your return but are included here as a helpful reference. The final 2005 forms were not yet available as this book went to press in September 2005 but are easily found at www.irs.gov. Click on Forms and Publications.

It is perfectly acceptable to print out the forms from the IRS website to complete your return. In fact, many of these forms can be completed right on your computer screen and then printed out with all your entered tax information. You can then save the completed form on your computer. We also recommend that you print out a copy for your files.

A listing of all the tax forms included in this book—some of which are samples—can be found in the Contents.

Here are the draft forms that are included in this chapter:

Form SS-4: Application for Employer Identification Number

Form 1040X: Amended U.S. Individual Income Tax Return

Form 1040EZ: Income Tax Return for Single and Joint Filers with No Dependents

Form 1040A: U.S. Individual Income Tax Return

  Schedule 1: Interest and Ordinary Dividends for Form 1040A Filers

  Schedule 2: Child and Dependent Care Expenses for Form 1040A Filers

  Schedule 3: Credit for the Elderly or the Disabled for Form 1040A Filers

Form 1040: U.S. Individual Income Tax Return

  Schedule A: Itemized Deductions

  Schedule B: Interest and Ordinary Dividends

  Schedule C: Profit or Loss from Business (Sole Proprietorship)

  Schedule D: Capital Gains and Losses

  Schedule E: Supplemental Income and Loss

  Schedule F: Profit or Loss from Farming

  Schedule H: Household Employment Taxes

  Schedule R: Credit for the Elderly or the Disabled

  Schedule SE: Self-Employment Tax

Form 1040-V: Payment Voucher

Form 1098-C: Contributions of Motor Vehicles, Boats, and Airplanes

Form 2106: Employee Business Expenses

Form 2441: Child and Dependent Care Expenses

Form 4562: Depreciation and Amortization

Form 4684: Casualties and Thefts

Form 4797: Sale of Business Property

Form 4952: Investment Interest Expense Deduction

Form 5329: Additional Taxes on Qualified Plans (Including IRAs) and Other Tax-Favored Accounts

Form 6251: Alternative Minimum Tax—Individuals

Form 8606: Nondeductible IRAs

Form 8283: Noncash Charitable Contributions

Form 8615: Tax for Children Under Age 14 With Investment Income of More Than $1,600

Form 8812: Additional Child Tax Credit

Form 8814: Parents' Election to Report Child's Interest and Dividends

Form 8829: Expenses for Business Use of Your Home

Form 8863: Education Credits (Hope and Lifetime Learning Credits)

Form 8880: Credit for Qualified Retirement Savings Contributions

NOTE: Form SS-4 and Form 1098-C are final forms.

Form **SS-4**

(Rev. December 2001)

Department of the Treasury
Internal Revenue Service

Application for Employer Identification Number

(For use by employers, corporations, partnerships, trusts, estates, churches, government agencies, Indian tribal entities, certain individuals, and others.)

▶ See separate instructions for each line.   ▶ Keep a copy for your records.

EIN

OMB No. 1545-0003

Type or print clearly.

1 Legal name of entity (or individual) for whom the EIN is being requested	

2 Trade name of business (if different from name on line 1)	**3** Executor, trustee, "care of" name

4a Mailing address (room, apt., suite no. and street, or P.O. box)	**5a** Street address (if different) (Do not enter a P.O. box.)
4b City, state, and ZIP code	**5b** City, state, and ZIP code

6 County and state where principal business is located

7a Name of principal officer, general partner, grantor, owner, or trustor	**7b** SSN, ITIN, or EIN

8a **Type of entity** (check only one box)

☐ Sole proprietor (SSN) _____
☐ Partnership
☐ Corporation (enter form number to be filed) ▶ _____
☐ Personal service corp.
☐ Church or church-controlled organization
☐ Other nonprofit organization (specify) ▶ _____
☐ Other (specify) ▶

☐ Estate (SSN of decedent) _____
☐ Plan administrator (SSN) _____
☐ Trust (SSN of grantor) _____
☐ National Guard   ☐ State/local government
☐ Farmers' cooperative   ☐ Federal government/military
☐ REMIC   ☐ Indian tribal governments/enterprises
Group Exemption Number (GEN) ▶ _____

8b If a corporation, name the state or foreign country (if applicable) where incorporated

State	Foreign country

9 **Reason for applying** (check only one box)

☐ Started new business (specify type) ▶ _____
_____
☐ Hired employees (Check the box and see line 12.)
☐ Compliance with IRS withholding regulations
☐ Other (specify) ▶

☐ Banking purpose (specify purpose) ▶ _____
☐ Changed type of organization (specify new type) ▶ _____
☐ Purchased going business
☐ Created a trust (specify type) ▶ _____
☐ Created a pension plan (specify type) ▶ _____

10 Date business started or acquired (month, day, year)	**11** Closing month of accounting year

12 First date wages or annuities were paid or will be paid (month, day, year). **Note:** *If applicant is a withholding agent, enter date income will first be paid to nonresident alien. (month, day, year)* . . . . ▶

13 Highest number of employees expected in the next 12 months. **Note:** *If the applicant does not expect to have any employees during the period, enter "-0-."* . . . . ▶	Agricultural	Household	Other

14 Check **one** box that best describes the principal activity of your business.

☐ Construction   ☐ Rental & leasing   ☐ Transportation & warehousing
☐ Real estate   ☐ Manufacturing   ☐ Finance & insurance

☐ Health care & social assistance   ☐ Wholesale–agent/broker
☐ Accommodation & food service   ☐ Wholesale–other   ☐ Retail
☐ Other (specify)

15 Indicate principal line of merchandise sold; specific construction work done; products produced; or services provided.

16a Has the applicant ever applied for an employer identification number for this or any other business? . . . .   ☐ **Yes**   ☐ **No**
Note: *If "Yes," please complete lines 16b and 16c.*

16b If you checked "Yes" on line 16a, give applicant's legal name and trade name shown on prior application if different from line 1 or 2 above.
Legal name ▶   Trade name ▶

16c Approximate date when, and city and state where, the application was filed. Enter previous employer identification number if known.

Approximate date when filed (mo., day, year)	City and state where filed	Previous EIN

Third Party Designee	Complete this section **only** if you want to authorize the named individual to receive the entity's EIN and answer questions about the completion of this form.	
	Designee's name	Designee's telephone number (include area code) ( )
	Address and ZIP code	Designee's fax number (include area code) ( )

Under penalties of perjury, I declare that I have examined this application, and to the best of my knowledge and belief, it is true, correct, and complete.

Applicant's telephone number (include area code) ( )

Name and title (type or print clearly) ▶

Applicant's fax number (include area code) ( )

Signature ▶   Date ▶

For Privacy Act and Paperwork Reduction Act Notice, see separate instructions.   Cat. No. 16055N   Form **SS-4** (Rev. 12-2001)

Department of the Treasury—Internal Revenue Service

Amended U.S. Individual Income Tax Return

► See separate instructions.

OMB No. 1545-0091

This return is for calendar year ►   , or fiscal year ended ►   ,   .

Your first name and initial	Last name	**Your social security number**
If a joint return, spouse's first name and initial	Last name	**Spouse's social security number**
Home address (no. and street) or P.O. box if mail is not delivered to your home	Apt. no.	Phone number ( )
City, town or post office, state, and ZIP code. If you have a foreign address, see page 2 of the instructions.		**For Paperwork Reduction Act Notice, see page 6.**

Please print or type

A If the address shown above is different from that shown on your last return filed with the IRS and you would like us to change it, check here . . . . ► ☐

B Filing status. Be sure to complete this line. **Note.** You cannot change from joint to separate returns after the due date.

On original return ► ☐ Single ☐ Married filing jointly ☐ Married filing separately ☐ Head of household ☐ Qualifying widow(er)

On this return ► ☐ Single ☐ Married filing jointly ☐ Married filing separately ☐ Head of household* ☐ Qualifying widow(er)

* If the qualifying person is a child but not your dependent, see page 2 of the instructions.

Use Part II on the back to explain any changes

Income and Deductions (see instructions)

			A. Original amount or as previously adjusted (see page 3)	B. Net change— amount of increase or (decrease)— explain in Part II	C. Correct amount
1	Adjusted gross income (see page 3)	1			
2	Itemized deductions or standard deduction (see page 3).	2			
3	Subtract line 2 from line 1	3			
4	Exemptions. If changing, fill in Parts I and II on the back	4			
5	Taxable income. Subtract line 4 from line 3	5			

Tax Liability

6	Tax (see page 4). Method used in col. C_____	6			
7	Credits (see page 4)	7			
8	Subtract line 7 from line 6. Enter the result but not less than zero .	8			
9	Other taxes (see page 4)	9			
10	Total tax. Add lines 8 and 9	10			

Payments

11	Federal income tax withheld and excess social security and tier 1 RRTA tax withheld. If changing, see page 4	11			
12	Estimated tax payments, including amount applied from prior year's return	12			
13	Earned income credit (EIC)	13			
14	Additional child tax credit from Form 8812	14			
15	Credits from Form 2439, Form 4136, or Form 8885 . .	15			
16	Amount paid with request for extension of time to file (see page 5)		16		
17	Amount of tax paid with original return plus additional tax paid after it was filed		17		
18	Total payments. Add lines 11 through 17 in column C		18		

Refund or Amount You Owe

19	Overpayment, if any, as shown on original return or as previously adjusted by the IRS . . .	19	
20	Subtract line 19 from line 18 (see page 5)	20	
21	**Amount you owe.** If line 10, column C, is more than line 20, enter the difference and see page 5	21	
22	If line 10, column C, is less than line 20, enter the difference	22	
23	Amount of line 22 you want **refunded to you**	23	
24	Amount of line 22 you want **applied to your** estimated tax	24		

Sign Here

Joint return?
See page 2.
Keep a copy for your records.

Under penalties of perjury, I declare that I have filed an original return and that I have examined this amended return, including accompanying schedules and statements, and to the best of my knowledge and belief, this amended return is true, correct, and complete. Declaration of preparer (other than taxpayer) is based on all information of which the preparer has any knowledge.

► Your signature   Date   ► Spouse's signature. If a joint return, **both** must sign.   Date

Paid Preparer's Use Only

Preparer's signature ►	Date	Check if self-employed ☐	Preparer's SSN or PTIN
Firm's name (or yours if self-employed), address, and ZIP code ►		EIN	
		Phone no. ( )	

Cat. No. 11360L   Form **1040X** (Rev. 11-2005)

615

Part I　Exemptions. See Form 1040 or 1040A instructions.

If you are **not changing your exemptions,** do not complete this part.
If claiming **more exemptions,** complete lines 25–31.
If claiming **fewer exemptions,** complete lines 25–30.

		A. Original **number** of exemptions reported or as previously adjusted	B. Net change	C. Correct **number** of exemptions
25	Yourself and spouse . . . . **Caution.** If someone can claim you as a dependent, you cannot claim an exemption for yourself.	**25**		
26	Your dependent children who lived with you	**26**		
27	Your dependent children who did not live with you due to divorce or separation	**27**		
28	Other dependents.	**28**		
29	Total number of exemptions. Add lines 25 through 28	**29**		

30　Multiply the number of exemptions claimed on line 29 by the amount listed below for the tax year you are amending. Enter the result here and on line 4.

Tax year	Exemption amount	But see the instructions for line 4 on page 3 if the amount on line 1 is over:
2005	$3,200	$109,475
2004	3,100	107,025
2003	3,050	104,625
2002	3,000	103,000

		30		

31　Dependents (children and other) not claimed on original (or adjusted) return:

(a) First name　　　　Last name	(b) Dependent's social security number	(c) Dependent's relationship to you	(d) ✓ if qualifying child for child tax credit (see page 5)
			☐
			☐
			☐
			☐
			☐
			☐

No. of children on 31 who:
- lived with you . . ▶ ☐
- **did not** live with you due to divorce or separation (see page 5) . . ▶ ☐

Dependents on 31 not entered above ▶ ☐

Part II　Explanation of Changes

Enter the line number from the front of the form for each item you are changing and give the reason for each change. Attach only the supporting forms and schedules for the items changed. If you do not attach the required information, your Form 1040X may be returned. Be sure to include your name and social security number on any attachments.

If the change relates to a net operating loss carryback or a general business credit carryback, attach the schedule or form that shows the year in which the loss or credit occurred. See page 2 of the instructions. Also, check here. . . . . . ▶ ☐

_____

_____

_____

_____

_____

_____

Part III　Presidential Election Campaign Fund. Checking below will not increase your tax or reduce your refund.

If you did not previously want $3 to go to the fund but now want to, check here . . . . ▶ ☐
If a joint return and your spouse did not previously want $3 to go to the fund but now wants to, check here . . . . . ▶ ☐

Form **1040X** (Rev. 11-2005)

Form
1040EZ

Department of the Treasury—Internal Revenue Service
**Income Tax Return for Single and
Joint Filers With No Dependents** (99) **2005**

OMB No. 1545-0675

Label
(See page 11.)
Use the IRS label.
Otherwise, please print or type.

L A B E L   H E R E

Your first name and initial   Last name

If a joint return, spouse's first name and initial   Last name

Home address (number and street). If you have a P.O. box, see page 11.   Apt. no.

City, town or post office, state, and ZIP code. If you have a foreign address, see page 11.

Your social security number

Spouse's social security number

▲ You **must** enter your SSN(s) above. ▲

Checking a box below will not change your tax or refund.

Presidential Election Campaign (page 11) ▶

Check here if you, or your spouse if a joint return, want $3 to go to this fund? . . . ▶ ☐ **You**   ☐ **Spouse**

Income

Attach Form(s) W-2 here.
Enclose, but do not attach, any payment.

1	Wages, salaries, and tips. This should be shown in box 1 of your Form(s) W-2. Attach your Form(s) W-2.	1
2	Taxable interest. If the total is over $1,500, you cannot use Form 1040EZ.	2
3	Unemployment compensation and Alaska Permanent Fund dividends (see page 13).	3
4	Add lines 1, 2, and 3. This is your **adjusted gross income.**	4
5	If someone can claim you (or your spouse if a joint return) as a dependent, check the applicable box(es) below and enter the amount from the worksheet on back. ☐ **You** ☐ **Spouse** If someone cannot claim you (or your spouse if a joint return), enter $8,200 if **single;** $16,400 if **married filing jointly.**	5
6	Subtract line 5 from line 4. If line 5 is larger than line 4, enter -0-. This is your **taxable income.** ▶	6

Payments and tax

7	Federal income tax withheld from box 2 of your Form(s) W-2.	7
8a	**Earned income credit (EIC).**	8a
b	Nontaxable combat pay election. 8b	
9	Add lines 7 and 8a. These are your **total payments.** ▶	9
10	**Tax.** Use the amount on **line 6 above** to find your tax in the tax table on pages 24–32 of the booklet. Then, enter the tax from the table on this line.	10

Refund

Have it directly deposited! See page 18 and fill in 11b, 11c, and 11d.

11a	If line 9 is larger than line 10, subtract line 10 from line 9. This is your **refund.** ▶	11a

▶ **b** Routing number ☐☐☐☐☐☐☐☐☐   ▶ **c** Type: ☐ Checking ☐ Savings

▶ **d** Account number ☐☐☐☐☐☐☐☐☐☐☐☐☐☐☐☐☐

Amount you owe

12	If line 10 is larger than line 9, subtract line 9 from line 10. This is the **amount you owe.** For details on how to pay, see page 19. ▶	12

Third party designee

Do you want to allow another person to discuss this return with the IRS (see page 19)? ☐ **Yes.** Complete the following. ☐ **No**

Designee's name ▶   Phone no. ▶ (   )   Personal identification number (PIN) ▶ ☐☐☐☐☐

Sign here

Joint return? See page 11. Keep a copy for your records.

Under penalties of perjury, I declare that I have examined this return, and to the best of my knowledge and belief, it is true, correct, and accurately lists all amounts and sources of income I received during the tax year. Declaration of preparer (other than the taxpayer) is based on all information of which the preparer has any knowledge.

Your signature	Date	Your occupation	Daytime phone number ( )
Spouse's signature. If a joint return, **both** must sign.	Date	Spouse's occupation	

Paid preparer's use only

Preparer's signature ▶	Date	Check if self-employed ☐	Preparer's SSN or PTIN
Firm's name (or yours if self-employed), address, and ZIP code ▶		EIN	
		Phone no. ( )	

For Disclosure, Privacy Act, and Paperwork Reduction Act Notice, see page 23.   Cat. No. 11329W   Form **1040EZ** (2005)

Form
1040A

Department of the Treasury—Internal Revenue Service
U.S. Individual Income Tax Return (99) **2005** IRS Use Only—Do not write or staple in this space.

OMB No. 1545-0085

Label

(See page 18.)

Use the IRS label.

Otherwise, please print or type.

Presidential Election Campaign ▶

L A B E L   H E R E

Your first name and initial	Last name

Your social security number

If a joint return, spouse's first name and initial	Last name

Spouse's social security number

Home address (number and street). If you have a P.O. box, see page 18.	Apt. no.

▲ You **must** enter your SSN(s) above. ▲

City, town or post office, state, and ZIP code. If you have a foreign address, see page 18.

Checking a box below will not change your tax or refund.

Check here if you, or your spouse if filing jointly, want $3 to go to this fund (see page 18) ▶ ☐ **You** ☐ **Spouse**

Filing status

Check only one box.

1 ☐ Single
2 ☐ Married filing jointly (even if only one had income)
3 ☐ Married filing separately. Enter spouse's SSN above and full name here. ▶
4 ☐ Head of household (with qualifying person). (See page 19.) If the qualifying person is a child but not your dependent, enter this child's name here. ▶
5 ☐ Qualifying widow(er) with dependent child (see page 19)

Exemptions

If more than six dependents, see page 20.

6a ☐ **Yourself.** If someone can claim you as a dependent, **do not** check box 6a.

b ☐ **Spouse**

c Dependents:

(1) First name Last name	(2) Dependent's social security number	(3) Dependent's relationship to you	(4) ✓ if qualifying child for child tax credit (see page 21)
			☐
			☐
			☐
			☐
			☐
			☐

Boxes checked on 6a and 6b

No. of children on 6c who:
• **lived with you**
• **did not live with you due to divorce or separation (see page 21)**

Dependents on 6c not entered above

Add numbers on lines above ▶

d Total number of exemptions claimed.

Income

Attach Form(s) W-2 here. Also attach Form(s) 1099-R if tax was withheld.

If you did not get a W-2, see page 22.

Enclose, but do not attach, any payment.

7	Wages, salaries, tips, etc. Attach Form(s) W-2.	**7**	
8a	**Taxable** interest. Attach Schedule 1 if required.	**8a**	
b	**Tax-exempt** interest. **Do not** include on line 8a.	8b	
9a	Ordinary dividends. Attach Schedule 1 if required.	**9a**	
b	Qualified dividends (see page 23).	9b	
10	Capital gain distributions (see page 23).	**10**	
11a	IRA distributions.	11a		**11b** Taxable amount (see page 23).	**11b**	
12a	Pensions and annuities.	12a		**12b** Taxable amount (see page 24).	**12b**	
13	Unemployment compensation and Alaska Permanent Fund dividends.	**13**	
14a	Social security benefits.	14a		**14b** Taxable amount (see page 26).	**14b**	
15	Add lines 7 through 14b (far right column). This is your **total income.** ▶	**15**	

Adjusted gross income

16	Educator expenses (see page 26).	16	
17	IRA deduction (see page 26).	17	
18	Student loan interest deduction (see page 29).	18	
19	Tuition and fees deduction (see page 29).	19	
20	Add lines 16 through 19. These are your **total adjustments.**	**20**	
21	Subtract line 20 from line 15. This is your **adjusted gross income.** ▶	**21**	

For Disclosure, Privacy Act, and Paperwork Reduction Act Notice, see page 57.   Cat. No. 11327A   Form **1040A** (2005)

Tax, credits, and payments	**22**	Enter the amount from line 21 (adjusted gross income).	22

Standard Deduction for—

- People who checked any box on line 23a or 23b **or** who can be claimed as a dependent, see page 31.
- All others:

Single or Married filing separately, $5,000

Married filing jointly or Qualifying widow(er), $10,000

Head of household, $7,300

23a Check if: ☐ **You** were born before January 2, 1941, ☐ Blind / **Spouse** was born before January 2, 1941, ☐ Blind } **Total boxes checked** ▶ 23a

b If you are married filing separately and your spouse itemizes deductions, see page 30 and check here ▶ 23b ☐

24 Enter your **standard deduction** (see left margin).   24

25 Subtract line 24 from line 22. If line 24 is more than line 22, enter -0-.   25

26 If line 22 is $109,475 or less, multiply $3,200 by the total number of exemptions claimed on line 6d. If line 22 is over $109,475, see the worksheet on page 32.   26

27 Subtract line 26 from line 25. If line 26 is more than line 25, enter -0-. This is your **taxable income.** ▶ 27

28 **Tax,** including any alternative minimum tax (see page 31).   28

29 Credit for child and dependent care expenses. Attach Schedule 2.   29

30 Credit for the elderly or the disabled. Attach Schedule 3.   30

31 Education credits. Attach Form 8863.   31

32 Retirement savings contributions credit. Attach Form 8880.   32

33 Child tax credit (see page 36). Attach Form 8901 if required.   33

34 Adoption credit. Attach Form 8839.   34

35 Add lines 29 through 34. These are your **total credits.**   35

36 Subtract line 35 from line 28. If line 35 is more than line 28, enter -0-.   36

37 Advance earned income credit payments from Form(s) W-2.   37

38 Add lines 36 and 37. This is your **total tax.** ▶ 38

39 Federal income tax withheld from Forms W-2 and 1099.   39

40 2005 estimated tax payments and amount applied from 2004 return.   40

If you have a qualifying child, attach Schedule EIC.

41a **Earned income credit (EIC).**   41a

b Nontaxable combat pay election.   41b

42 Additional child tax credit. Attach Form 8812.   42

43 Add lines 39, 40, 41a, and 42. These are your **total payments.** ▶ 43

Refund

Direct deposit? See page 50 and fill in 45b, 45c, and 45d.

44 If line 43 is more than line 38, subtract line 38 from line 43. This is the amount you **overpaid.**   44

45a Amount of line 44 you want **refunded to you.** ▶ 45a

▶ **b** Routing number   ▶ c Type: ☐ Checking ☐ Savings

▶ **d** Account number

46 Amount of line 44 you want **applied to your 2006 estimated tax.**   46

Amount you owe

47 **Amount you owe.** Subtract line 43 from line 38. For details on how to pay, see page 51. ▶ 47

48 Estimated tax penalty (see page 51).   48

Third party designee

Do you want to allow another person to discuss this return with the IRS (see page 52)? ☐ **Yes.** Complete the following. ☐ **No**

Designee's name ▶   Phone no. ▶ ( )   Personal identification number (PIN) ▶

Sign here

Under penalties of perjury, I declare that I have examined this return and accompanying schedules and statements, and to the best of my knowledge and belief, they are true, correct, and accurately list all amounts and sources of income I received during the tax year. Declaration of preparer (other than the taxpayer) is based on all information of which the preparer has any knowledge.

Joint return? See page 18. Keep a copy for your records.

Your signature	Date	Your occupation	Daytime phone number ( )
Spouse's signature. If a joint return, **both** must sign.	Date	Spouse's occupation	

Paid preparer's use only

Preparer's signature ▶	Date	Check if self-employed ☐	Preparer's SSN or PTIN
Firm's name (or yours if self-employed), address, and ZIP code ▶		EIN	
		Phone no. ( )	

✶ Printed on recycled paper   Form **1040A** (2005)

Schedule 1

(Form 1040A)

Department of the Treasury—Internal Revenue Service

Interest and Ordinary Dividends for Form 1040A Filers   (99)   **2005**

OMB No. 1545-0085

Name(s) shown on Form 1040A

Your social security number

Part I

Interest

(See back of schedule and the instructions for Form 1040A, line 8a.)

Note. If you received a Form 1099-INT, Form 1099-OID, or substitute statement from a brokerage firm, enter the firm's name and the total interest shown on that form.

1   List name of payer. If any interest is from a seller-financed mortgage and the buyer used the property as a personal residence, see back of schedule and list this interest first. Also, show that buyer's social security number and address.

	Amount
1	

2   Add the amounts on line 1.   2

3   Excludable interest on series EE and I U.S. savings bonds issued after 1989. Attach Form 8815.   3

4   Subtract line 3 from line 2. Enter the result here and on Form 1040A, line 8a.   4

Part II

Ordinary dividends

(See back of schedule and the instructions for Form 1040A, line 9a.)

Note. If you received a Form 1099-DIV or substitute statement from a brokerage firm, enter the firm's name and the ordinary dividends shown on that form.

5   List name of payer.

	Amount
5	

6   Add the amounts on line 5. Enter the total here and on Form 1040A, line 9a.   6

For Paperwork Reduction Act Notice, see Form 1040A instructions.   Cat. No. 12075R   Schedule 1 (Form 1040A) 2005

621

Schedule 2
(Form 1040A)

Department of the Treasury—Internal Revenue Service

Child and Dependent Care Expenses for Form 1040A Filers (99) 2005

OMB No. 1545-0085

Name(s) shown on Form 1040A

Your social security number

Before you begin: You need to understand the following terms. See **Definitions** on page 1 of the separate instructions.
- **Dependent care benefits**
- **Qualifying person(s)**
- **Qualified expenses**

Part I

Persons or organizations who provided the care

You **must** complete this part.

	(a) Care provider's name	(b) Address (number, street, apt. no., city, state, and ZIP code)	(c) Identifying number (SSN or EIN)	(d) Amount paid (see instructions)
1				

(If you need more space, use the bottom of page 2.)

Did you receive **dependent care benefits?**
- No ———→ Complete only Part II below.
- Yes ———→ Complete Part III on the back next.

Caution. If the care was provided in your home, you may owe employment taxes. If you do, you must use Form 1040. See **Schedule H** and its instructions for details.

Part II

Credit for child and dependent care expenses

2 Information about your **qualifying person(s).** If you have more than two qualifying persons, see the instructions.

(a) Qualifying person's name		(b) Qualifying person's social security number	(c) Qualified expenses you incurred and paid in 2005 for the person listed in column (a)
First	Last		

3	Add the amounts in column (c) of line 2. **Do not** enter more than $3,000 for one qualifying person or $6,000 for two or more persons. If you completed Part III, enter the amount from line 26.	3	
4	Enter your **earned income.** See the instructions.	4	
5	If married filing jointly, enter your spouse's earned income (if your spouse was a student or was disabled, see the instructions); **all others,** enter the amount from line 4.	5	
6	Enter the **smallest** of line 3, 4, or 5.	6	
7	Enter the amount from Form 1040A, line 22.	7	

8 Enter on line 8 the decimal amount shown below that applies to the amount on line 7.

If line 7 is:			If line 7 is:		
Over	But not over	Decimal amount is	Over	But not over	Decimal amount is
$0—15,000		.35	$29,000—31,000		.27
15,000—17,000		.34	31,000—33,000		.26
17,000—19,000		.33	33,000—35,000		.25
19,000—21,000		.32	35,000—37,000		.24
21,000—23,000		.31	37,000—39,000		.23
23,000—25,000		.30	39,000—41,000		.22
25,000—27,000		.29	41,000—43,000		.21
27,000—29,000		.28	43,000—No limit		.20

8 ✕ .

9	Multiply **line 6** by the decimal amount on line 8. If you paid 2004 expenses in 2005, see the instructions.	9	
10	Enter the amount from Form 1040A, line 28.	10	
11	**Credit for child and dependent care expenses.** Enter the **smaller** of line 9 or line 10 here and on Form 1040A, line 29.	11	

For Paperwork Reduction Act Notice, see Form 1040A instructions. Cat. No. 10749I **Schedule 2 (Form 1040A) 2005**

623

Part III

Dependent care benefits

12   Enter the total amount of **dependent care benefits** you received for 2005. This amount should be shown in box 10 of your Form(s) W-2. **Do not** include amounts that were reported to you as wages in box 1 of Form(s) W-2.   12

13   Enter the amount forfeited, if any. See the instructions.   13

14   Subtract line 13 from line 12.   14

15   Enter the total amount of **qualified expenses** incurred in 2005 for the care of the qualifying person(s).   15

16   Enter the **smaller** of line 14 or 15.   16

17   Enter your **earned income.** See the instructions.   17

18   Enter the amount shown below that applies to you.
- If married filing jointly, enter your spouse's earned income (if your spouse was a student or was disabled, see the instructions for line 5).
- If married filing separately, see the instructions for the amount to enter.
- All others, enter the amount from line 17.   18

19   Enter the **smallest** of line 16, 17, or 18.   19

20   **Excluded benefits.** Enter here the **smaller** of the following:
- The amount from line 19, or
- $5,000 ($2,500 if married filing separately **and** you were required to enter your spouse's earned income on line 18).   20

21   **Taxable benefits.** Subtract line 20 from line 14. Also, include this amount on Form 1040A, line 7. In the space to the left of line 7, enter "DCB."   21

To claim the child and dependent care credit, complete lines 22–26 below.

22   Enter $3,000 ($6,000 if two or more qualifying persons).   22

23   Enter the amount from line 20.   23

24   Subtract line 23 from line 22. If zero or less, **stop.** You cannot take the credit. **Exception.** If you paid 2004 expenses in 2005, see the instructions for line 9.   24

25   Complete line 2 on the front of this schedule. **Do not** include in column (c) any benefits shown on line 20 above. Then, add the amounts in column (c) and enter the total here.   25

26   Enter the **smaller** of line 24 or 25. Also, enter this amount on line 3 on the front of this schedule and complete lines 4–11.   26

Schedule 3
(Form 1040A)

Department of the Treasury—Internal Revenue Service

Credit for the Elderly or the Disabled
for Form 1040A Filers

(99) **2005**

OMB No. 1545-0085

Name(s) shown on Form 1040A

Your social security number

You may be able to take this credit and reduce your tax if by the end of 2005:

- You were age 65 or older **or** • You were under age 65, you retired on **permanent and total** disability, and you received taxable disability income.

But you must also meet other tests. See the separate instructions for Schedule 3.

TIP In most cases, the IRS can figure the credit for you. See the instructions.

Part I

Check the box for your filing status and age

If your filing status is:	And by the end of 2005:	Check only one box:
Single, Head of household, or Qualifying widow(er)	**1** You were 65 or older	1 ☐
	2 You were under 65 and you retired on permanent and total disability	2 ☐
Married filing jointly	**3** Both spouses were 65 or older	3 ☐
	4 Both spouses were under 65, but only one spouse retired on permanent and total disability	4 ☐
	5 Both spouses were under 65, and both retired on permanent and total disability	5 ☐
	6 One spouse was 65 or older, and the other spouse was under 65 and retired on permanent and total disability	6 ☐
	7 One spouse was 65 or older, and the other spouse was under 65 and **not** retired on permanent and total disability	7 ☐
Married filing separately	**8** You were 65 or older and you lived apart from your spouse for all of 2005	8 ☐
	9 You were under 65, you retired on permanent and total disability, and you lived apart from your spouse for all of 2005	9 ☐

Did you check box 1, 3, 7, or 8?

— **Yes** ——➤ Skip Part II and complete Part III on the back.

— **No** ——➤ Complete Parts II and III.

Part II

Statement of permanent and total disability

Complete this part **only** if you checked box 2, 4, 5, 6, or 9 above.

If: **1** You filed a physician's statement for this disability for 1983 or an earlier year, or you filed or got a statement for tax years after 1983 and your physician signed line B on the statement, **and**

2 Due to your continued disabled condition, you were unable to engage in any substantial gainful activity in 2005, check this box . . . . ➤ ☐

- If you checked this box, you do not have to get another statement for 2005.

- If you **did not** check this box, have your physician complete the statement on page 4 of the instructions. You **must** keep the statement for your records.

For Paperwork Reduction Act Notice, see Form 1040A instructions.

Cat. No. 12064K

Schedule 3 (Form 1040A) 2005

Part III

Figure your credit

10	**If you checked (in Part I):**		**Enter:**	
	Box 1, 2, 4, or 7		$5,000	
	Box 3, 5, or 6		$7,500	
	Box 8 or 9		$3,750	**10**

> **Did you check box 2, 4, 5, 6, or 9 in Part I?** — Yes ➝ You **must** complete line 11.
>
> — No ➝ Enter the amount from line 10 on line 12 and go to line 13.

11 **If you checked (in Part I):**

- Box 6, add $5,000 to the taxable disability income of the spouse who was under age 65. Enter the total.

- Box 2, 4, or 9, enter your taxable disability income.

- Box 5, add your taxable disability income to your spouse's taxable disability income. Enter the total.

(TIP) For more details on what to include on line 11, see the instructions.   **11**

12 If you completed line 11, enter the **smaller** of line 10 or line 11; **all others,** enter the amount from line 10.   **12**

13 Enter the following pensions, annuities, or disability income that you (and your spouse if filing a joint return) received in 2005.

a Nontaxable part of social security benefits and

Nontaxable part of railroad retirement benefits treated as social security (see the instructions).   **13a**

b Nontaxable veterans' pensions and

Any other pension, annuity, or disability benefit that is excluded from income under any other provision of law (see the instructions).   **13b**

c Add lines 13a and 13b. (Even though these income items are not taxable, they **must** be included here to figure your credit.) If you did not receive any of the types of nontaxable income listed on line 13a or 13b, enter -0- on line 13c.   **13c**

14 Enter the amount from Form 1040A, line 22.   **14**

15	**If you checked (in Part I):**	**Enter:**		
	Box 1 or 2	$7,500		
	Box 3, 4, 5, 6, or 7	$10,000		
	Box 8 or 9	$5,000	**15**	

16 Subtract line 15 from line 14. If zero or less, enter -0-.   **16**

17 Enter one-half of line 16.   **17**

18 Add lines 13c and 17.   **18**

19 Subtract line 18 from line 12. If zero or less, **stop; you cannot** take the credit. Otherwise, go to line 20.   **19**

20 Multiply line 19 by 15% (.15).   **20**

21 Enter the amount from Form 1040A, line 28, minus any amount on Form 1040A, line 29.   **21**

22 **Credit for the elderly or the disabled.** Enter the **smaller** of line 20 or line 21 here and on Form 1040A, line 30.   **22**

Form 1040

Department of the Treasury—Internal Revenue Service

U.S. Individual Income Tax Return 2005

(99)   IRS Use Only—Do not write or staple in this space.

For the year Jan. 1–Dec. 31, 2005, or other tax year beginning _____ , 2005, ending _____ , 20 _____

OMB No. 1545-0074

Label
(See instructions on page 16.)

Use the IRS label. Otherwise, please print or type.

L A B E L   H E R E

Your first name and initial | Last name | Your social security number

If a joint return, spouse's first name and initial | Last name | Spouse's social security number

Home address (number and street). If you have a P.O. box, see page 16. | Apt. no.

▲ You **must** enter your SSN(s) above. ▲

City, town or post office, state, and ZIP code. If you have a foreign address, see page 16.

Checking a box below will not change your tax or refund.

Presidential Election Campaign ▶ Check here if you, or your spouse if filing jointly, want $3 to go to this fund (see page 16) ▶ ☐ **You** ☐ **Spouse**

Filing Status

Check only one box.

1 ☐ Single

2 ☐ Married filing jointly (even if only one had income)

3 ☐ Married filing separately. Enter spouse's SSN above and full name here. ▶

4 ☐ Head of household (with qualifying person). (See page 17.) If the qualifying person is a child but not your dependent, enter this child's name here. ▶

5 ☐ Qualifying widow(er) with dependent child (see page 17)

Exemptions

6a ☐ **Yourself.** If someone can claim you as a dependent, **do not** check box 6a

b ☐ **Spouse**

c Dependents:

(1) First name Last name	(2) Dependent's social security number	(3) Dependent's relationship to you	(4) ✓ if qualifying child for child tax credit (see page 18)
			☐
			☐
			☐
			☐

If more than four dependents, see page 18.

d Total number of exemptions claimed

Boxes checked on 6a and 6b _____

No. of children on 6c who:
- lived with you _____
- did not live with you due to divorce or separation (see page 18) _____

Dependents on 6c not entered above _____

Add numbers on lines above ▶ ☐

Income

Attach Form(s) W-2 here. Also attach Forms W-2G and 1099-R if tax was withheld.

If you did not get a W-2, see page 19.

Enclose, but do not attach, any payment. Also, please use **Form 1040-V.**

7 Wages, salaries, tips, etc. Attach Form(s) W-2 | 7 |

8a **Taxable** interest. Attach Schedule B if required | 8a |

b **Tax-exempt** interest. **Do not** include on line 8a | 8b | |

9a Ordinary dividends. Attach Schedule B if required | 9a |

b Qualified dividends (see page 20) | 9b | |

10 Taxable refunds, credits, or offsets of state and local income taxes (see page 20) | 10 |

11 Alimony received | 11 |

12 Business income or (loss). Attach Schedule C or C-EZ | 12 |

13 Capital gain or (loss). Attach Schedule D if required. If not required, check here ▶ ☐ | 13 |

14 Other gains or (losses). Attach Form 4797 | 14 |

15a IRA distributions | 15a | | b Taxable amount (see page 22) | 15b |

16a Pensions and annuities | 16a | | b Taxable amount (see page 22) | 16b |

17 Rental real estate, royalties, partnerships, S corporations, trusts, etc. Attach Schedule E | 17 |

18 Farm income or (loss). Attach Schedule F | 18 |

19 Unemployment compensation | 19 |

20a Social security benefits | 20a | | b Taxable amount (see page 24) | 20b |

21 Other income. List type and amount (see page 24) _____ | 21 |

22 Add the amounts in the far right column for lines 7 through 21. This is your **total income** ▶ | 22 |

Adjusted Gross Income

23 Educator expenses (see page 26) | 23 |

24 Certain business expenses of reservists, performing artists, and fee-basis government officials. Attach Form 2106 or 2106-EZ | 24 |

25 Health savings account deduction. Attach Form 8889 | 25 |

26 Moving expenses. Attach Form 3903 | 26 |

27 One-half of self-employment tax. Attach Schedule SE | 27 |

28 Self-employed SEP, SIMPLE, and qualified plans | 28 |

29 Self-employed health insurance deduction (see page XX) | 29 |

30 Penalty on early withdrawal of savings | 30 |

31a Alimony paid b Recipient's SSN ▶ _____ | 31a |

32 IRA deduction (see page XX) | 32 |

33 Student loan interest deduction (see page XX) | 33 |

34 Tuition and fees deduction (see page XX) | 34 |

35 Domestic production activities deduction. Attach Form 8903 | 35 |

36 Add lines 23 through 31a and 32 through 35 | 36 |

37 Subtract line 36 from line 22. This is your **adjusted gross income** ▶ | 37 |

Tax and Credits	38	Amount from line 37 (adjusted gross income)		38	
	39a	Check { ☐ **You** were born before January 2, 1941, ☐ Blind. } **Total boxes** if: { ☐ **Spouse** was born before January 2, 1941, ☐ Blind. } checked ▶ 39a			
Standard Deduction for—	b	If your spouse itemizes on a separate return or you were a dual-status alien, see page 31 and check here ▶ 39b ☐			
• People who checked any box on line 39a or 39b **or** who can be claimed as a dependent, see page 31.	40	**Itemized deductions** (from Schedule A) **or** your **standard deduction** (see left margin) . .		40	
	41	Subtract line 40 from line 38		41	
	42	If line 38 is $109,475 or less, multiply $3,200 by the total number of exemptions claimed on line 6d. If line 38 is over $109,475, see the worksheet on page 33		42	
	43	**Taxable income.** Subtract line 42 from line 41. If line 42 is more than line 41, enter -0-		43	
• All others:	44	**Tax** (see page 33). Check if any tax is from: **a** ☐ Form(s) 8814 **b** ☐ Form 4972		44	
Single or Married filing separately, $5,000	45	**Alternative minimum tax** (see page 35). Attach Form 6251		45	
	46	Add lines 44 and 45 . . . . ▶		46	
	47	Foreign tax credit. Attach Form 1116 if required . . .	47		
Married filing jointly or Qualifying widow(er), $10,000	48	Credit for child and dependent care expenses. Attach Form 2441	48		
	49	Credit for the elderly or the disabled. Attach Schedule R .	49		
	50	Education credits. Attach Form 8863	50		
	51	Retirement savings contributions credit. Attach Form 8880 .	51		
Head of household, $7,300	52	Child tax credit (see page 37). Attach Form 8901 if required	52		
	53	Adoption credit. Attach Form 8839	53		
	54	Credits from: **a** ☐ Form 8396 **b** ☐ Form 8859 .	54		
	55	Other credits. Check applicable box(es): **a** ☐ Form 3800 **b** ☐ Form 8801 **c** ☐ Specify	55		
	56	Add lines 47 through 55. These are your **total credits**		56	
	57	Subtract line 56 from line 46. If line 56 is more than line 46, enter -0- . . . . . ▶		57	
Other Taxes	58	Self-employment tax. Attach Schedule SE		58	
	59	Social security and Medicare tax on tip income not reported to employer. Attach Form 4137 . .		59	
	60	Additional tax on IRAs, other qualified retirement plans, etc. Attach Form 5329 if required		60	
	61	Advance earned income credit payments from Form(s) W-2		61	
	62	Household employment taxes. Attach Schedule H		62	
	63	Add lines 57 through 62. This is your **total tax** . . . . ▶		63	
Payments	64	Federal income tax withheld from Forms W-2 and 1099 . . .	64		
	65	2005 estimated tax payments and amount applied from 2004 return	65		
If you have a qualifying child, attach Schedule EIC.	66a	**Earned income credit (EIC)**	66a		
	b	Nontaxable combat pay election ▶	66b		
	67	Excess social security and tier 1 RRTA tax withheld (see page 54)	67		
	68	Additional child tax credit. Attach Form 8812	68		
	69	Amount paid with request for extension to file (see page 54)	69		
	70	Payments from: **a** ☐ Form 2439 **b** ☐ Form 4136 **c** ☐ Form 8885 .	70		
	71	Add lines 64, 65, 66a, and 67 through 70. These are your **total payments** . . . . ▶		71	
Refund	72	If line 71 is more than line 63, subtract line 63 from line 71. This is the amount you **overpaid**		72	
Direct deposit? See page 54 and fill in 73b, 73c, and 73d.	73a	Amount of line 72 you want **refunded to you** . . . . ▶		73a	
	▶ b	Routing number ⬚⬚⬚⬚⬚⬚⬚⬚⬚ ▶ **c** Type: ☐ Checking ☐ Savings			
	▶ d	Account number ⬚⬚⬚⬚⬚⬚⬚⬚⬚⬚⬚⬚⬚⬚⬚⬚⬚			
	74	Amount of line 72 you want **applied to your 2006 estimated tax** ▶	74		
Amount You Owe	75	**Amount you owe.** Subtract line 71 from line 63. For details on how to pay, see page 55 ▶		75	
	76	Estimated tax penalty (see page 55)	76		

Third Party Designee

Do you want to allow another person to discuss this return with the IRS (see page 56)? ☐ **Yes.** Complete the following. ☐ **No**

Designee's name ▶	Phone no. ▶ ( )	Personal identification number (PIN) ▶ ⬚⬚⬚⬚⬚

Sign Here

Under penalties of perjury, I declare that I have examined this return and accompanying schedules and statements, and to the best of my knowledge and belief, they are true, correct, and complete. Declaration of preparer (other than taxpayer) is based on all information of which preparer has any knowledge.

Joint return? See page 17.

Keep a copy for your records.

Your signature	Date	Your occupation	Daytime phone number ( )
Spouse's signature. If a joint return, **both** must sign.	Date	Spouse's occupation	

Paid Preparer's Use Only

Preparer's signature ▶	Date	Check if self-employed ☐	Preparer's SSN or PTIN
Firm's name (or yours if self-employed), address, and ZIP code ▶		EIN Phone no. ( )	

Form **1040** (2005)

SCHEDULES A&B
(Form 1040)

Department of the Treasury
Internal Revenue Service (99)

Schedule A—Itemized Deductions

(Schedule B is on back)

► **Attach to Form 1040.** ► **See Instructions for Schedules A and B (Form 1040).**

OMB No. 1545-0074

20**05**

Attachment
Sequence No. **07**

Name(s) shown on Form 1040 | Your social security number

Medical and Dental Expenses		**Caution.** Do not include expenses reimbursed or paid by others.	
	1	Medical and dental expenses (see page A-2) . . .	**1**
	2	Enter amount from Form 1040, line 38	**2**
	3	Multiply line 2 by 7.5% (.075)	**3**
	4	Subtract line 3 from line 1. If line 3 is more than line 1, enter -0-	**4**
Taxes You Paid (See page A-2.)	5	State and local **(check only one box):** a ☐ Income taxes, **or** b ☐ General sales taxes (see page A-2)	**5**
	6	Real estate taxes (see page A-3)	**6**
	7	Personal property taxes	**7**
	8	Other taxes. List type and amount ►	**8**
	9	Add lines 5 through 8	**9**
Interest You Paid (See page A-3.) **Note.** Personal interest is not deductible.	10	Home mortgage interest and points reported to you on Form 1098	**10**
	11	Home mortgage interest not reported to you on Form 1098. If paid to the person from whom you bought the home, see page A-4 and show that person's name, identifying no., and address ►	**11**
	12	Points not reported to you on Form 1098. See page A-4 for special rules	**12**
	13	Investment interest. Attach Form 4952 if required. (See page A-4.)	**13**
	14	Add lines 10 through 13	**14**
Gifts to Charity If you made a gift and got a benefit for it, see page A-4.	15	Gifts by cash or check. If you made any gift of $250 or more, see page A-4	**15**
	16	Other than by cash or check. If any gift of $250 or more, see page A-4. You **must** attach Form 8283 if over $500	**16**
	17	Carryover from prior year	**17**
	18	Add lines 15 through 17	**18**
Casualty and Theft Losses	19	Casualty or theft loss(es). Attach Form 4684. (See page A-5.)	**19**
Job Expenses and Most Other Miscellaneous Deductions (See page A-5.)	20	Unreimbursed employee expenses—job travel, union dues, job education, etc. Attach Form 2106 or 2106-EZ if required. (See page A-6.) ►	**20**
	21	Tax preparation fees	**21**
	22	Other expenses—investment, safe deposit box, etc. List type and amount ►	**22**
	23	Add lines 20 through 22	**23**
	24	Enter amount from Form 1040, line 38	**24**
	25	Multiply line 24 by 2% (.02)	**25**
	26	Subtract line 25 from line 23. If line 25 is more than line 23, enter -0-	**26**
Other Miscellaneous Deductions	27	Other—from list on page A-6. List type and amount ►	**27**
Total Itemized Deductions	28	Is Form 1040, line 38, over $145,950 (over $72,975 if married filing separately)? ☐ **No.** Your deduction is not limited. Add the amounts in the far right column for lines 4 through 27. Also, enter this amount on Form 1040, line 40. } ☐ **Yes.** Your deduction may be limited. See page A-6 for the amount to enter. } ►	**28**
	29	If you elect to itemize deductions even though they are less than your standard deduction, check here ► ☐	

For Paperwork Reduction Act Notice, see Form 1040 instructions.   Cat. No. 11330X   **Schedule A (Form 1040) 2005**

629

Draft as of 06/06/2005

Name(s) shown on Form 1040. Do not enter name and social security number if shown on other side.

Your social security number

Schedule B—Interest and Ordinary Dividends

Attachment
Sequence No. **08**

Part I
Interest

(See page B-1 and the instructions for Form 1040, line 8a.)

Note. If you received a Form 1099-INT, Form 1099-OID, or substitute statement from a brokerage firm, list the firm's name as the payer and enter the total interest shown on that form.

1 List name of payer. If any interest is from a seller-financed mortgage and the buyer used the property as a personal residence, see page B-1 and list this interest first. Also, show that buyer's social security number and address ▶

	Amount
1	

2 Add the amounts on line 1 . . . . | **2** |

3 Excludable interest on series EE and I U.S. savings bonds issued after 1989. Attach Form 8815 . . . . | **3** |

4 Subtract line 3 from line 2. Enter the result here and on Form 1040, line 8a ▶ | **4** |

Note. If line 4 is over $1,500, you must complete Part III.

Part II
Ordinary Dividends

(See page B-2 and the instructions for Form 1040, line 9a.)

Note. If you received a Form 1099-DIV or substitute statement from a brokerage firm, list the firm's name as the payer and enter the ordinary dividends shown on that form.

5 List name of payer ▶

	Amount
5	

6 Add the amounts on line 5. Enter the total here and on Form 1040, line 9a . ▶ | **6** |

Note. If line 6 is over $1,500, you must complete Part III.

Part III
Foreign Accounts and Trusts

(See page B-2.)

You must complete this part if you **(a)** had over $1,500 of taxable interest or ordinary dividends; or **(b)** had a foreign account; or **(c)** received a distribution from, or were a grantor of, or a transferor to, a foreign trust.

	Yes	No

7a At any time during 2005, did you have an interest in or a signature or other authority over a financial account in a foreign country, such as a bank account, securities account, or other financial account? See page B-2 for exceptions and filing requirements for Form TD F 90-22.1. . . . . . .

b If "Yes," enter the name of the foreign country ▶

8 During 2005, did you receive a distribution from, or were you the grantor of, or transferor to, a foreign trust? If "Yes," you may have to file Form 3520. See page B-2 . . . .

For Paperwork Reduction Act Notice, see Form 1040 instructions.   Schedule B (Form 1040) 2005

SCHEDULE C (Form 1040) Department of the Treasury Internal Revenue Service	**Profit or Loss From Business** (Sole Proprietorship) ▶ Partnerships, joint ventures, etc., must file Form 1065 or 1065-B. ▶ Attach to Form 1040 or 1041. ▶ See Instructions for Schedule C (Form 1040).	OMB No. 1545-0074 20**05** Attachment Sequence No. **09**

Name of proprietor	Social security number (SSN)

A	Principal business or profession, including product or service (see page C-2 of the instructions)	B Enter code from pages C-7, 8, & 9 ▶

C	Business name. If no separate business name, leave blank.	D Employer ID number (EIN), if any

E Business address (including suite or room no.) ▶ --
   City, town or post office, state, and ZIP code

F Accounting method: (1) ☐ Cash   (2) ☐ Accrual   (3) ☐ Other (specify) ▶ ----------

G Did you "materially participate" in the operation of this business during 2005? If "No," see page C-3 for limit on losses   ☐ Yes   ☐ No

H If you started or acquired this business during 2005, check here . . . . ▶ ☐

Part I   Income

1	Gross receipts or sales. **Caution.** If this income was reported to you on Form W-2 and the "Statutory employee" box on that form was checked, see page C-3 and check here . . . . . ▶ ☐	1	
2	Returns and allowances	2	
3	Subtract line 2 from line 1	3	
4	Cost of goods sold (from line 42 on page 2)	4	
5	**Gross profit.** Subtract line 4 from line 3	5	
6	Other income, including Federal and state gasoline or fuel tax credit or refund (see page C-3) . . .	6	
7	**Gross income.** Add lines 5 and 6 . . . . ▶	7	

Part II   Expenses. Enter expenses for business use of your home **only** on line 30.

8	Advertising	8		18	Office expense	18	
9	Car and truck expenses (see page C-3)	9		19	Pension and profit-sharing plans	19	
10	Commissions and fees . .	10		20	Rent or lease (see page C-5):		
11	Contract labor (see page C-4)	11		a	Vehicles, machinery, and equipment .	20a	
12	Depletion	12		b	Other business property . . .	20b	
13	Depreciation and section 179 expense deduction (not included in Part III) (see page C-4)	13		21	Repairs and maintenance . .	21	
				22	Supplies (not included in Part III) .	22	
				23	Taxes and licenses	23	
				24	Travel, meals, and entertainment:		
14	Employee benefit programs (other than on line 19) .	14		a	Travel	24a	
				b	Deductible meals and entertainment (see page C-5)	24b	
15	Insurance (other than health) .	15		25	Utilities	25	
16	Interest:			26	Wages (less employment credits) .	26	
a	Mortgage (paid to banks, etc.) .	16a		27	Other expenses (from line 48 on page 2)	27	
b	Other	16b					
17	Legal and professional services	17					

28	**Total expenses** before expenses for business use of home. Add lines 8 through 27 in columns . ▶	28	

29	Tentative profit (loss). Subtract line 28 from line 7	29	
30	Expenses for business use of your home. Attach **Form 8829**	30	

31	**Net profit or (loss).** Subtract line 30 from line 29. ● If a profit, enter on **Form 1040, line 12,** and **also** on **Schedule SE, line 2** (statutory employees, see page C-6). Estates and trusts, enter on Form 1041, line 3. ● If a loss, you **must** go to line 32.	31	

32	If you have a loss, check the box that describes your investment in this activity (see page C-6). ● If you checked 32a, enter the loss on **Form 1040, line 12,** and **also** on **Schedule SE, line 2** (statutory employees, see page C-6). Estates and trusts, enter on Form 1041, line 3. ● If you checked 32b, you **must** attach **Form 6198.** Your loss may be limited.	32a ☐ All investment is at risk. 32b ☐ Some investment is not at risk.

For Paperwork Reduction Act Notice, see Form 1040 instructions.   Cat. No. 11334P   Schedule C (Form 1040) 2005

Part III   **Cost of Goods Sold** (see page C-6)

33   Method(s) used to
value closing inventory: **a** ☐ Cost   **b** ☐ Lower of cost or market   **c** ☐ Other (attach explanation)

34   Was there any change in determining quantities, costs, or valuations between opening and closing inventory? If
"Yes," attach explanation . . . . ☐ **Yes**   ☐ **No**

35 Inventory at beginning of year. If different from last year's closing inventory, attach explanation . .	**35**	
36 Purchases less cost of items withdrawn for personal use	**36**	
37 Cost of labor. Do not include any amounts paid to yourself	**37**	
38 Materials and supplies	**38**	
39 Other costs	**39**	
40 Add lines 35 through 39	**40**	
41 Inventory at end of year	**41**	
42 **Cost of goods sold.** Subtract line 41 from line 40. Enter the result here and on page 1, line 4 . .	**42**	

Part IV   **Information on Your Vehicle.** Complete this part **only** if you are claiming car or truck expenses on line 9 and are not required to file Form 4562 for this business. See the instructions for line 13 on page C-4 to find out if you must file Form 4562.

43   When did you place your vehicle in service for business purposes? (month, day, year) ▶ ..../......../........ .

44   Of the total number of miles you drove your vehicle during 2005, enter the number of miles you used your vehicle for:

   a Business .... **b** Commuting (see instructions) .... **c** Other ....

45   Do you (or your spouse) have another vehicle available for personal use?. . . . . ☐ **Yes**   ☐ **No**

46   Was your vehicle available for personal use during off-duty hours? . . . . ☐ **Yes**   ☐ **No**

47a   Do you have evidence to support your deduction? . . . . ☐ **Yes**   ☐ **No**

   b   If "Yes," is the evidence written? . . . . ☐ **Yes**   ☐ **No**

Part V   **Other Expenses.** List below business expenses not included on lines 8–26 or line 30.

....		
....		
....		
....		
....		
....		
....		
....		
48 **Total other expenses.** Enter here and on page 1, line 27	**48**	

✹ *Printed on recycled paper*

Schedule C (Form 1040) 2005

Capital Gains and Losses

▶ **Attach to Form 1040.**   ▶ **See Instructions for Schedule D (Form 1040).**

▶ **Use Schedule D-1 to list additional transactions for lines 1 and 8.**

OMB No. 1545-0074

2005

Attachment
Sequence No. **12**

Name(s) shown on Form 1040

Your social security number

Part I — Short-Term Capital Gains and Losses—Assets Held One Year or Less

(a) Description of property (Example: 100 sh. XYZ Co.)	(b) Date acquired (Mo., day, yr.)	(c) Date sold (Mo., day, yr.)	(d) Sales price (see page D-6 of the instructions)	(e) Cost or other basis (see page D-6 of the instructions)	(f) Gain or (loss) Subtract (e) from (d)
1					

2 Enter your short-term totals, if any, from Schedule D-1, line 2 . . . . **2**

3 **Total short-term sales price amounts.** Add lines 1 and 2 in column (d) **3**

4 Short-term gain from Form 6252 and short-term gain or (loss) from Forms 4684, 6781, and 8824 . . . . . . **4**

5 Net short-term gain or (loss) from partnerships, S corporations, estates, and trusts from Schedule(s) K-1 . . . . **5**

6 Short-term capital loss carryover. Enter the amount, if any, from line 8 of your **Capital Loss Carryover Worksheet** on page D-6 of the instructions . . . . **6** ( )

7 **Net short-term capital gain or (loss).** Combine lines 1 through 6 in column (f) **7**

Part II — Long-Term Capital Gains and Losses—Assets Held More Than One Year

(a) Description of property (Example: 100 sh. XYZ Co.)	(b) Date acquired (Mo., day, yr.)	(c) Date sold (Mo., day, yr.)	(d) Sales price (see page D-6 of the instructions)	(e) Cost or other basis (see page D-6 of the instructions)	(f) Gain or (loss) Subtract (e) from (d)
8					

9 Enter your long-term totals, if any, from Schedule D-1, line 9 . . . . **9**

10 **Total long-term sales price amounts.** Add lines 8 and 9 in column (d) **10**

11 Gain from Form 4797, Part I; long-term gain from Forms 2439 and 6252; and long-term gain or (loss) from Forms 4684, 6781, and 8824 . . . . **11**

12 Net long-term gain or (loss) from partnerships, S corporations, estates, and trusts from Schedule(s) K-1 . . . . **12**

13 Capital gain distributions. See page D-1 of the instructions **13**

14 Long-term capital loss carryover. Enter the amount, if any, from line 13 of your **Capital Loss Carryover Worksheet** on page D-6 of the instructions . . . . **14** ( )

15 **Net long-term capital gain or (loss).** Combine lines 8 through 14 in column (f). Then go to Part III on the back **15**

For Paperwork Reduction Act Notice, see Form 1040 instructions.   Cat. No. 11338H   Schedule D (Form 1040) 2005

633

Draft as of 05/17/2005

Part III   **Summary**

16   Combine lines 7 and 15 and enter the result. If line 16 is a loss, skip lines 17 through 20, and go to line 21. If a gain, enter the gain on Form 1040, line 13, and then go to line 17 below . . | **16** |

17   Are lines 15 and 16 **both** gains?
☐ **Yes.** Go to line 18.
☐ **No.** Skip lines 18 through 21, and go to line 22.

18   Enter the amount, if any, from line 7 of the **28% Rate Gain Worksheet** on page D-7 of the instructions . . . . ▶ | **18** |

19   Enter the amount, if any, from line 18 of the **Unrecaptured Section 1250 Gain Worksheet** on page D-8 of the instructions . . . . ▶ | **19** |

20   Are lines 18 and 19 **both** zero or blank?
☐ **Yes.** Complete Form 1040 through line 43, and then complete the **Qualified Dividends and Capital Gain Tax Worksheet** on page 34 of the Instructions for Form 1040. **Do not** complete lines 21 and 22 below.
☐ **No.** Complete Form 1040 through line 43, and then complete the **Schedule D Tax Worksheet** on page D-9 of the instructions. **Do not** complete lines 21 and 22 below.

21   If line 16 is a loss, enter here and on Form 1040, line 13, the **smaller** of:
● The loss on line 16 or
● ($3,000), or if married filing separately, ($1,500)   . . . . | **21** | (|) |

Note. When figuring which amount is smaller, treat both amounts as positive numbers.

22   Do you have qualified dividends on Form 1040, line 9b?
☐ **Yes.** Complete Form 1040 through line 43, and then complete the **Qualified Dividends and Capital Gain Tax Worksheet** on page 34 of the Instructions for Form 1040.
☐ **No.** Complete the rest of Form 1040.

Printed on recycled paper

Schedule D (Form 1040) 2005

634

SCHEDULE E
(Form 1040)

Department of the Treasury
Internal Revenue Service   (99)

Supplemental Income and Loss

**(From rental real estate, royalties, partnerships,
S corporations, estates, trusts, REMICs, etc.)**

▶ **Attach to Form 1040 or Form 1041.**   ▶ **See Instructions for Schedule E (Form 1040).**

OMB No. 1545-0074

2005

Attachment
Sequence No. **13**

Name(s) shown on return

Your social security number

Draft as of 05/24/2005

Part I   **Income or Loss From Rental Real Estate and Royalties**   **Note.** If you are in the business of renting personal property, use **Schedule C** or **C-EZ** (see page E-3). Report farm rental income or loss from **Form 4835** on page 2, line 40.

1	List the type and location of each **rental real estate property:**	2 For each rental real estate property listed on line 1, did you or your family use it during the tax year for personal purposes for more than the greater of: ● 14 days **or** ● 10% of the total days rented at fair rental value? (See page E-3.)		Yes	No
A			A		
B			B		
C			C		

Income:		Properties			Totals (Add columns A, B, and C.)
		A	B	C	
3 Rents received	3				3
4 Royalties received	4				4
Expenses:					
5 Advertising	5				
6 Auto and travel (see page E-4)	6				
7 Cleaning and maintenance	7				
8 Commissions	8				
9 Insurance	9				
10 Legal and other professional fees	10				
11 Management fees	11				
12 Mortgage interest paid to banks, etc. (see page E-4)	12				12
13 Other interest	13				
14 Repairs	14				
15 Supplies	15				
16 Taxes	16				
17 Utilities	17				
18 Other (list) ▶	18				
19 Add lines 5 through 18	19				19
20 Depreciation expense or depletion (see page E-4)	20				20
21 Total expenses. Add lines 19 and 20	21				
22 Income or (loss) from rental real estate or royalty properties. Subtract line 21 from line 3 (rents) or line 4 (royalties). If the result is a (loss), see page E-4 to find out if you must file **Form 6198**	22				
23 Deductible rental real estate loss. **Caution.** Your rental real estate loss on line 22 may be limited. See page E-4 to find out if you must file **Form 8582.** Real estate professionals must complete line 43 on page 2	23	( )	( )	( )	
24 **Income.** Add positive amounts shown on line 22. **Do not** include any losses					24
25 **Losses.** Add royalty losses from line 22 and rental real estate losses from line 23. Enter total losses here					25 ( )
26 **Total rental real estate and royalty income or (loss).** Combine lines 24 and 25. Enter the result here. If Parts II, III, IV, and line 40 on page 2 do not apply to you, also enter this amount on Form 1040, line 17. Otherwise, include this amount in the total on line 41 on page 2					26

For Paperwork Reduction Act Notice, see Form 1040 instructions.   Cat. No. 11344L   **Schedule E (Form 1040) 2005**

Name(s) shown on return. Do not enter name and social security number if shown on other side.	Your social security number
	⋮ ⋮

Caution. The IRS compares amounts reported on your tax return with amounts shown on Schedule(s) K-1.

Part II — Income or Loss From Partnerships and S Corporations

Note. If you report a loss from an at-risk activity for which **any** amount is **not** at risk, you **must** check the box in column (e) on line 28 and attach **Form 6198.** See page E-1.

27 Are you reporting any loss not allowed in a prior year due to the at-risk or basis limitations, a prior year unallowed loss from a passive activity (if that loss was not reported on Form 8582), or unreimbursed partnership expenses? ☐ **Yes** ☐ **No**
  If you answered "Yes," see page E-6 before completing this section.

28	**(a)** Name	**(b)** Enter **P** for partnership; **S** for S corporation	**(c)** Check if foreign partnership	**(d)** Employer identification number	**(e)** Check if any amount is not at risk
A			☐		☐
B			☐		☐
C			☐		☐
D			☐		☐

	Passive Income and Loss		Nonpassive Income and Loss		
	(f) Passive loss allowed (attach **Form 8582** if required)	**(g)** Passive income from **Schedule K–1**	**(h)** Nonpassive loss from **Schedule K–1**	**(i)** Section 179 expense deduction from **Form 4562**	**(j)** Nonpassive income from **Schedule K–1**
A					
B					
C					
D					
29a Totals					
b Totals					

30	Add columns (g) and (j) of line 29a	30	
31	Add columns (f), (h), and (i) of line 29b	31	( )
32	**Total partnership and S corporation income or (loss).** Combine lines 30 and 31. Enter the result here and include in the total on line 41 below	32	

Part III — Income or Loss From Estates and Trusts

33	**(a)** Name	**(b)** Employer identification number
A		
B		

	Passive Income and Loss		Nonpassive Income and Loss	
	(c) Passive deduction or loss allowed (attach **Form 8582** if required)	**(d)** Passive income from **Schedule K–1**	**(e)** Deduction or loss from **Schedule K–1**	**(f)** Other income from **Schedule K–1**
A				
B				
34a Totals				
b Totals				

35	Add columns (d) and (f) of line 34a	35	
36	Add columns (c) and (e) of line 34b	36	( )
37	**Total estate and trust income or (loss).** Combine lines 35 and 36. Enter the result here and include in the total on line 41 below	37	

Part IV — Income or Loss From Real Estate Mortgage Investment Conduits (REMICs)—Residual Holder

38	**(a)** Name	**(b)** Employer identification number	**(c)** Excess inclusion from **Schedules Q,** line 2c (see page E-6)	**(d)** Taxable income (net loss) from **Schedules Q,** line 1b	**(e)** Income from **Schedules Q,** line 3b

39	Combine columns (d) and (e) only. Enter the result here and include in the total on line 41 below	39	

Part V — Summary

40	Net farm rental income or (loss) from **Form 4835.** Also, complete line 42 below	40	
41	**Total income or (loss).** Combine lines 26, 32, 37, 39, and 40. Enter the result here and on Form 1040, line 17 ▶	41	

42 **Reconciliation of farming and fishing income.** Enter your **gross** farming and fishing income reported on Form 4835, line 7; Schedule K-1 (Form 1065), box 14, code B; Schedule K-1 (Form 1120S), box 17, code N; and Schedule K-1 (Form 1041), line 14 (see page E-6)   **42** _____

43 **Reconciliation for real estate professionals.** If you were a real estate professional (see page E-1), enter the net income or (loss) you reported anywhere on Form 1040 from all rental real estate activities in which you materially participated under the passive activity loss rules . . .   **43** _____

 Printed on recycled paper

SCHEDULE F
(Form 1040)

Department of the Treasury
Internal Revenue Service (99)

Profit or Loss From Farming

► Attach to Form 1040, Form 1041, Form 1065, or Form 1065-B.

► See Instructions for Schedule F (Form 1040).

OMB No. 1545-0074

2005

Attachment
Sequence No. **14**

Name of proprietor

Social security number (SSN)

A Principal product. Describe in one or two words your principal crop or activity for the current tax year.

B Enter code from Part IV
►

C Accounting method: **(1)** ☐ Cash   **(2)** ☐ Accrual

D Employer ID number (EIN), if any

E Did you "materially participate" in the operation of this business during 2005? If "No," see page F-2 for limit on passive losses.   ☐ Yes   ☐ No

Part I   Farm Income—Cash Method. Complete Parts I and II (Accrual method. Complete Parts II and III, and Part I, line 11.)

Do not include sales of livestock held for draft, breeding, sport, or dairy purposes; report these sales on Form 4797.

1	Sales of livestock and other items you bought for resale	**1**	
2	Cost or other basis of livestock and other items reported on line 1	**2**	
3	Subtract line 2 from line 1		**3**
4	Sales of livestock, produce, grains, and other products you raised		**4**
5a	Cooperative distributions (Form(s) 1099-PATR) **5a**	**5b** Taxable amount	**5b**
6a	Agricultural program payments (see page F-2) **6a**	**6b** Taxable amount	**6b**
7	Commodity Credit Corporation (CCC) loans (see page F-3):		
a	CCC loans reported under election		**7a**
b	CCC loans forfeited **7b**	**7c** Taxable amount	**7c**
8	Crop insurance proceeds and Federal crop disaster payments (see page F-3):		
a	Amount received in 2005 **8a**	**8b** Taxable amount	**8b**
c	If election to defer to 2006 is attached, check here ► ☐	**8d** Amount deferred from 2004	**8d**
9	Custom hire (machine work) income		**9**
10	Other income, including Federal and state gasoline or fuel tax credit or refund (see page F-3)		**10**
11	**Gross income.** Add amounts in the right column for lines 3 through 10. If you use the accrual method, enter the amount from Part III, line 51 ►		**11**

Part II   Farm Expenses—Cash and Accrual Method.

Do not include personal or living expenses such as taxes, insurance, repairs, etc., on your home.

12	Car and truck expenses (see page F-4—also attach **Form 4562**)	**12**	25	Pension and profit-sharing plans	**25**
13	Chemicals	**13**	26	Rent or lease (see page F-5):	
14	Conservation expenses (see page F-4)	**14**	a	Vehicles, machinery, and equipment	**26a**
15	Custom hire (machine work)	**15**	b	Other (land, animals, etc.)	**26b**
16	Depreciation and section 179 expense deduction not claimed elsewhere (see page F-4)	**16**	27	Repairs and maintenance	**27**
			28	Seeds and plants	**28**
			29	Storage and warehousing	**29**
17	Employee benefit programs other than on line 25	**17**	30	Supplies	**30**
18	Feed purchased	**18**	31	Taxes	**31**
19	Fertilizers and lime	**19**	32	Utilities	**32**
20	Freight and trucking	**20**	33	Veterinary, breeding, and medicine	**33**
21	Gasoline, fuel, and oil	**21**	34	Other expenses (specify):	
22	Insurance (other than health)	**22**	a	....	**34a**
23	Interest:		b	....	**34b**
			c	....	**34c**
a	Mortgage (paid to banks, etc.)	**23a**	d	....	**34d**
b	Other	**23b**	e	....	**34e**
24	Labor hired (less employment credits)	**24**	f	....	**34f**

35	**Total expenses.** Add lines 12 through 34f ►	**35**
36	**Net farm profit or (loss).** Subtract line 35 from line 11. • If a profit, enter on **Form 1040, line 18,** and also on **Schedule SE, line 1.** • If a loss, you **must** go on to line 37. Estates, trusts, and partnerships, see page F-6.	**36**

37 If you have a loss, you **must** check the box that describes your investment in this activity (see page F-6).
   • If you checked 37a, enter the loss on **Form 1040, line 18,** and also on **Schedule SE, line 1.**
   • If you checked 37b, you **must** attach Form 6198. Your loss may be limited.

37a ☐ All investment is at risk.

37b ☐ Some investment is not at risk.

For Paperwork Reduction Act Notice, see Form 1040 instructions.   Cat. No. 11346H   Schedule F (Form 1040) 2005

Part III   **Farm Income—Accrual Method** (see page F-6).

Do not include sales of livestock held for draft, breeding, sport, or dairy purposes; report these sales on Form 4797 and do not include this livestock on line 46 below.

38	Sales of livestock, produce, grains, and other products	38
39a	Cooperative distributions (Form(s) 1099-PATR). . **39a** **39b** Taxable amount	39b
40a	Agricultural program payments . . . . . **40a** **40b** Taxable amount	40b
41	Commodity Credit Corporation (CCC) loans:	
a	CCC loans reported under election	41a
b	CCC loans forfeited . . . . **41b** **41c** Taxable amount	41c
42	Crop insurance proceeds	42
43	Custom hire (machine work) income	43
44	Other income, including Federal and state gasoline or fuel tax credit or refund	44
45	Add amounts in the right column for lines 38 through 44	45
46	Inventory of livestock, produce, grains, and other products at beginning of the year **46**	
47	Cost of livestock, produce, grains, and other products purchased during the year **47**	
48	Add lines 46 and 47 . . . . **48**	
49	Inventory of livestock, produce, grains, and other products at end of year **49**	
50	Cost of livestock, produce, grains, and other products sold. Subtract line 49 from line 48*	50
51	**Gross income.** Subtract line 50 from line 45. Enter the result here and on Part I, line 11 . . . . . ▶	51

*If you use the unit-livestock-price method or the farm-price method of valuing inventory and the amount on line 49 is larger than the amount on line 48, subtract line 48 from line 49. Enter the result on line 50. Add lines 45 and 50. Enter the total on line 51 and on Part I, line 11.

Part IV   **Principal Agricultural Activity Codes**

 *File Schedule C (Form 1040) or Schedule C-EZ (Form 1040) instead of Schedule F if **(a)** your principal source of income is from providing agricultural services such as soil preparation, veterinary, farm labor, horticultural, or management for a fee or on a contract basis, or **(b)** you are engaged in the business of breeding, raising, and caring for dogs, cats, or other pet animals.*

These codes for the Principal Agricultural Activity classify farms by the type of activity they are engaged in to facilitate the administration of the Internal Revenue Code. These six-digit codes are based on the North American Industry Classification System (NAICS).

Select the code that best identifies your primary farming activity and enter it on page 1, line B.

Crop Production

111100   Oilseed and grain farming
111210   Vegetable and melon farming
111300   Fruit and tree nut farming
111400   Greenhouse, nursery, and floriculture production
111900   Other crop farming

Animal Production

112111   Beef cattle ranching and farming
112112   Cattle feedlots
112120   Dairy cattle and milk production
112210   Hog and pig farming
112300   Poultry and egg production
112400   Sheep and goat farming
112510   Animal aquaculture
112900   Other animal production

Forestry and Logging

113000   Forestry and logging (including forest nurseries and timber tracts)

Printed on recycled paper

SCHEDULE H (Form 1040) Department of the Treasury Internal Revenue Service (99)	**Household Employment Taxes** (For Social Security, Medicare, Withheld Income, and Federal Unemployment (FUTA) Taxes) ▶ **Attach to Form 1040, 1040NR, 1040-SS, or 1041.** ▶ **See separate instructions.**	OMB No. 1545-0074 20**05** Attachment Sequence No. **44**

Name of employer	Social security number
	Employer identification number

A Did you pay **any one** household employee cash wages of $1,400 or more in 2005? (If any household employee was your spouse, your child under age 21, your parent, or anyone under age 18, see the line A instructions on page H-3 before you answer this question.)

☐ **Yes.** Skip lines B and C and go to line 1.
☐ **No.** Go to line B.

B Did you withhold Federal income tax during 2005 for any household employee?

☐ **Yes.** Skip line C and go to line 5.
☐ **No.** Go to line C.

C Did you pay **total** cash wages of $1,000 or more in **any** calendar **quarter** of 2004 or 2005 to **all** household employees? (**Do not** count cash wages paid in 2004 or 2005 to your spouse, your child under age 21, or your parent.)

☐ **No.** **Stop.** Do not file this schedule.
☐ **Yes.** Skip lines 1-9 and go to line 10 on the back. (Calendar year taxpayers having no household employees in 2005 **do not** have to complete this form for 2005.)

Part I **Social Security, Medicare, and Income Taxes**

1	Total cash wages subject to social security taxes (see page H-3)	**1**	
2	Social security taxes. Multiply line 1 by 12.4% (.124)	**2**	
3	Total cash wages subject to Medicare taxes (see page H-3) . . .	**3**	
4	Medicare taxes. Multiply line 3 by 2.9% (.029)	**4**	
5	Federal income tax withheld, if any	**5**	
6	**Total social security, Medicare, and income taxes** (add lines 2, 4, and 5)	**6**	
7	Advance earned income credit (EIC) payments, if any	**7**	
8	**Net taxes** (subtract line 7 from line 6)	**8**	

9 Did you pay **total** cash wages of $1,000 or more in **any** calendar **quarter** of 2004 or 2005 to household employees? (**Do not** count cash wages paid in 2004 or 2005 to your spouse, your child under age 21, or your parent.)

☐ **No.** **Stop.** Enter the amount from line 8 above on Form 1040, line 62. If you are not required to file Form 1040, see the line 9 instructions on page H-4.

☐ **Yes.** Go to line 10 on the back.

For Paperwork Reduction Act Notice, see Form 1040 instructions.   Cat. No. 12187K   **Schedule H (Form 1040) 2005**

Part II Federal Unemployment (FUTA) Tax

		Yes	No
10	Did you pay unemployment contributions to only one state? (If you paid contributions to the states of XXXXXXX, XXXXXXX, or XXXXXXX, check "No.") **10**		
11	Did you pay all state unemployment contributions for 2005 by April 17, 2006? Fiscal year filers, see page H-4 **11**		
12	Were all wages that are taxable for FUTA tax also taxable for your state's unemployment tax? **12**		

Next: If you checked the **"Yes"** box on **all** the lines above, complete Section A.

If you checked the **"No"** box on **any** of the lines above, skip Section A and complete Section B.

Section A

13	Name of the state where you paid unemployment contributions ▶	
14	State reporting number as shown on state unemployment tax return ▶	
15	Contributions paid to your state unemployment fund (see page H-4)	**15**
16	Total cash wages subject to FUTA tax (see page H-4)	**16**
17	**FUTA tax.** Multiply line 16 by .008. Enter the result here, skip Section B, and go to line 26 . .	**17**

Section B

18 Complete all columns below that apply (if you need more space, see page H-4):

(a) Name of state	(b) State reporting number as shown on state unemployment tax return	(c) Taxable wages (as defined in state act)	(d) State experience rate period		(e) State experience rate	(f) Multiply col. (c) by .054	(g) Multiply col. (c) by col. (e)	(h) Subtract col. (g) from col. (f). If zero or less, enter -0-.	(i) Contributions paid to state unemployment fund
			From	To					

19	Totals	**19**		
20	Add columns (h) and (i) of line 19	**20**		
21	Total cash wages subject to FUTA tax (see the line 16 instructions on page H-4)	**21**		
22	Multiply line 21 by 6.2% (.062)	**22**		
23	Multiply line 21 by 5.4% (.054)	**23**		
24	Enter the **smaller** of line 20 or line 23	**24**		
	XXXXXXX, XXXXXXX, and XXXXXXX employers must use the worksheet on page X of the instructions and check the applicable box). XXXXXXX ☐ XXXXXXX ☐ XXXXXXX ☐			
25	**FUTA tax.** Subtract line 24 from line 22. Enter the result here and go to line 26	**25**		

Part III Total Household Employment Taxes

26	Enter the amount from line 8	**26**	
27	Add line 17 (or line 25) and line 26	**27**	
28	Are you required to file Form 1040?		
	☐ **Yes.** **Stop.** Enter the amount from line 27 above on Form 1040, line 62. **Do not** complete Part IV below.		
	☐ **No.** You may have to complete Part IV. See page H-4 for details.		

Part IV Address and Signature—Complete this part **only** if required. See the line 28 instructions on page H-4.

Address (number and street) or P.O. box if mail is not delivered to street address	Apt., room, or suite no.

City, town or post office, state, and ZIP code

Under penalties of perjury, I declare that I have examined this schedule, including accompanying statements, and to the best of my knowledge and belief, it is true, correct, and complete. No part of any payment made to a state unemployment fund claimed as a credit was, or is to be, deducted from the payments to employees.

▶ _____ ▶ _____

Employer's signature   Date

✪ Printed on recycled paper   **Schedule H (Form 1040) 2005**

Schedule R
(Form 1040)

Department of the Treasury
Internal Revenue Service   (99)

Credit for the Elderly or the Disabled

▶ Attach to Form 1040.   ▶ See Instructions for Schedule R (Form 1040).

OMB No. 1545-0074

2005

Attachment
Sequence No. **16**

Name(s) shown on Form 1040

Your social security number

You may be able to take this credit and reduce your tax if by the end of 2005:

- You were age 65 or older **or**
- You were under age 65, you retired on **permanent and total** disability, and you received taxable disability income.

But you must also meet other tests. See page R-1.

TIP In most cases, the IRS can figure the credit for you. See page R-1.

Part I   Check the Box for Your Filing Status and Age

If your filing status is:	And by the end of 2005:	Check only one box:
Single, Head of household, or Qualifying widow(er)	**1** You were 65 or older **1**	☐
	2 You were under 65 and you retired on permanent and total disability **2**	☐
Married filing jointly	**3** Both spouses were 65 or older **3**	☐
	4 Both spouses were under 65, but only one spouse retired on permanent and total disability **4**	☐
	5 Both spouses were under 65, and both retired on permanent and total disability **5**	☐
	6 One spouse was 65 or older, and the other spouse was under 65 and retired on permanent and total disability **6**	☐
	7 One spouse was 65 or older, and the other spouse was under 65 and **not** retired on permanent and total disability **7**	☐
Married filing separately	**8** You were 65 or older and you lived apart from your spouse for all of 2005 . . . . **8**	☐
	9 You were under 65, you retired on permanent and total disability, and you lived apart from your spouse for all of 2005 . . . . **9**	☐

Did you check box 1, 3, 7, or 8?	—— Yes ——▶	Skip Part II and complete Part III on back.
	—— No ——▶	Complete Parts II and III.

Part II   Statement of Permanent and Total Disability (Complete **only** if you checked box 2, 4, 5, 6, or 9 above.)

If: 1 You filed a physician's statement for this disability for 1983 or an earlier year, or you filed or got a statement for tax years after 1983 and your physician signed line B on the statement, **and**

2 Due to your continued disabled condition, you were unable to engage in any substantial gainful activity in 2005, check this box . . . . ▶ ☐

- If you checked this box, you do not have to get another statement for 2005.

- If you **did not** check this box, have your physician complete the statement on page R-4. You **must** keep the statement for your records.

For Paperwork Reduction Act Notice, see Form 1040 instructions.   Cat. No. 11359K   Schedule R (Form 1040) 2005

641

Part III   **Figure Your Credit**

10   If you checked (in Part I):   **Enter:**
     Box 1, 2, 4, or 7 . . . . $5,000
     Box 3, 5, or 6 . . . . $7,500 }   . . .   **10**
     Box 8 or 9 . . . . $3,750

> | Did you check | ── Yes ──➤ | You **must** complete line 11. |
> | box 2, 4, 5, 6, | | |
> | or 9 in Part I? | ── No ──➤ | Enter the amount from line 10 on line 12 and go to line 13. |

11   If you checked (in Part I):
     ● Box 6, add $5,000 to the taxable disability income of the spouse who was under age 65. Enter the total.
     ● Box 2, 4, or 9, enter your taxable disability income. }   **11**
     ● Box 5, add your taxable disability income to your spouse's taxable disability income. Enter the total.

(TIP) For more details on what to include on line 11, see page R-3.

12   If you completed line 11, enter the **smaller** of line 10 or line 11; **all others,** enter the amount from line 10 . . . .   **12**

13   Enter the following pensions, annuities, or disability income that you (and your spouse if filing a joint return) received in 2005.

  a Nontaxable part of social security benefits and
     Nontaxable part of railroad retirement benefits treated as social security (see page R-3).   } . . . **13a**

  b Nontaxable veterans' pensions and
     Any other pension, annuity, or disability benefit that is excluded from income under any other provision of law (see page R-3).   } . . . **13b**

  c Add lines 13a and 13b. (Even though these income items are not taxable, they **must** be included here to figure your credit.) If you did not receive any of the types of nontaxable income listed on line 13a or 13b, enter -0- on line 13c **13c**

14   Enter the amount from Form 1040, line 38 . . . .   **14**

15   If you checked (in Part I):   **Enter:**
     Box 1 or 2 . . . . . . $7,500
     Box 3, 4, 5, 6, or 7 . . . $10,000 }   **15**
     Box 8 or 9 . . . . . . $5,000

16   Subtract line 15 from line 14. If zero or less, enter -0- **16**

17   Enter one-half of line 16 . . . .   **17**

18   Add lines 13c and 17 . . . .   **18**

19   Subtract line 18 from line 12. If zero or less, **stop; you cannot** take the credit. Otherwise, go to line 20 . . . .   **19**

20   Multiply line 19 by 15% (.15) **20**

21   Enter the amount from Form 1040, line 46 . . . .   **21**

22   Add the amounts from Form 1040, lines 47 and 48, and enter the total **22**

23   Subtract line 22 from line 21 . . . .   **23**

24   **Credit for the elderly or the disabled.** Enter the **smaller** of line 20 or line 23 here and on Form 1040, line 49 . . . .   **24**

(✿) *Printed on recycled paper*   **Schedule R (Form 1040) 2005**

SCHEDULE SE (Form 1040) Department of the Treasury Internal Revenue Service	Self-Employment Tax ► **Attach to Form 1040.** ► **See Instructions for Schedule SE (Form 1040).**	OMB No. 1545-0074 20**05** Attachment Sequence No. **17**

Name of person with **self-employment** income (as shown on Form 1040)	Social security number of person with **self-employment** income ►		

Who Must File Schedule SE

You must file Schedule SE if:

- You had net earnings from self-employment from **other than** church employee income (line 4 of Short Schedule SE or line 4c of Long Schedule SE) of $400 or more **or**
- You had church employee income of $108.28 or more. Income from services you performed as a minister or a member of a religious order **is not** church employee income (see page SE-1).

Note. Even if you had a loss or a small amount of income from self-employment, it may be to your benefit to file Schedule SE and use either "optional method" in Part II of Long Schedule SE (see page SE-3).

Exception. If your only self-employment income was from earnings as a minister, member of a religious order, or Christian Science practitioner **and** you filed Form 4361 and received IRS approval not to be taxed on those earnings, **do not** file Schedule SE. Instead, write "Exempt–Form 4361" on Form 1040, line 58.

May I Use Short Schedule SE or Must I Use Long Schedule SE?

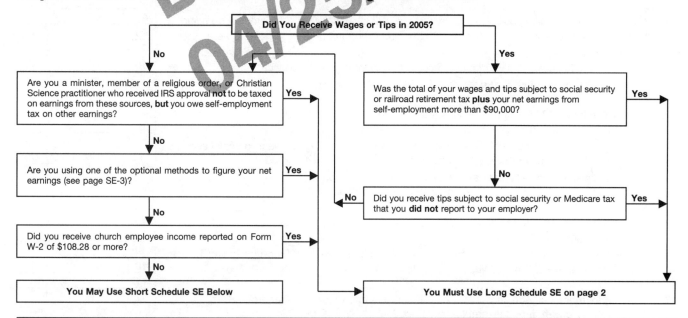

Section A—Short Schedule SE. Caution. Read above to see if you can use Short Schedule SE.

1	Net farm profit or (loss) from Schedule F, line 36, and farm partnerships, Schedule K-1 (Form 1065), box 14, code A	**1**		
2	Net profit or (loss) from Schedule C, line 31; Schedule C-EZ, line 3; Schedule K-1 (Form 1065), box 14, code A (other than farming); and Schedule K-1 (Form 1065-B), box 9. Ministers and members of religious orders, see page SE-1 for amounts to report on this line. See page SE-2 for other income to report	**2**		
3	Combine lines 1 and 2	**3**		
4	**Net earnings from self-employment.** Multiply line 3 by 92.35% (.9235). If less than $400, **do not** file this schedule; you do not owe self-employment tax . . . . ►	**4**		
5	**Self-employment tax.** If the amount on line 4 is: • $90,000 or less, multiply line 4 by 15.3% (.153). Enter the result here and on **Form 1040, line 58.** • More than $90,000, multiply line 4 by 2.9% (.029). Then, add $11,160.00 to the result. Enter the total here and on **Form 1040, line 58.**	**5**		
6	**Deduction for one-half of self-employment tax.** Multiply line 5 by 50% (.5). Enter the result here and on **Form 1040, line 27**	**6**		

For Paperwork Reduction Act Notice, see Form 1040 instructions.   Cat. No. 11358Z   **Schedule SE (Form 1040) 2005**

Schedule SE (Form 1040) 2005 | Attachment Sequence No. **17** | Page **2**

Name of person with **self-employment** income (as shown on Form 1040)

Social security number of person with **self-employment** income ▶

Section B—Long Schedule SE

Part I Self-Employment Tax

Note. If your only income subject to self-employment tax is **church employee income,** skip lines 1 through 4b. Enter -0- on line 4c and go to line 5a. Income from services you performed as a minister or a member of a religious order **is not** church employee income. See page SE-1.

A If you are a minister, member of a religious order, or Christian Science practitioner **and** you filed Form 4361, but you had $400 or more of **other** net earnings from self-employment, check here and continue with Part I . . . . . ▶ ☐

1 Net farm profit or (loss) from Schedule F, line 36, and farm partnerships, Schedule K-1 (Form 1065), box 14, code A. **Note.** Skip this line if you use the farm optional method (see page SE-4) | **1** |

2 Net profit or (loss) from Schedule C, line 31; Schedule C-EZ, line 3; Schedule K-1 (Form 1065), box 14, code A (other than farming); Schedule K-1 (Form 1065-B), box 9. Ministers and members of religious orders, see page SE-1 for amounts to report on this line. See page SE-2 for other income to report. **Note.** Skip this line if you use the nonfarm optional method (see page SE-4) | **2** |

3 Combine lines 1 and 2 | **3** |

4a If line 3 is more than zero, multiply line 3 by 92.35% (.9235). Otherwise, enter amount from line 3 | **4a** |

b If you elect one or both of the optional methods, enter the total of lines 15 and 17 here . . . | **4b** |

c Combine lines 4a and 4b. If less than $400, **stop;** you do not owe self-employment tax. **Exception.** If less than $400 and you had **church employee income,** enter -0- and continue. . . . . . ▶ | **4c** |

5a Enter your **church employee income** from Form W-2. See page SE-1 for definition of church employee income . . . | **5a** |

b Multiply line 5a by 92.35% (.9235). If less than $100, enter -0- . . . | **5b** |

6 **Net earnings from self-employment.** Add lines 4c and 5b . . . | **6** |

7 Maximum amount of combined wages and self-employment earnings subject to social security tax or the 6.2% portion of the 7.65% railroad retirement (tier 1) tax for 2005 . . . . . . | **7** | 90,000 | 00 |

8a Total social security wages and tips (total of boxes 3 and 7 on Form(s) W-2) and railroad retirement (tier 1) compensation. If $90,000 or more, skip lines 8b through 10, and go to line 11 . . . . | **8a** |

b Unreported tips subject to social security tax (from Form 4137, line 9) | **8b** |

c Add lines 8a and 8b . . . . | **8c** |

9 Subtract line 8c from line 7. If zero or less, enter -0- here and on line 10 and go to line 11 ▶ | **9** |

10 Multiply the **smaller** of line 6 or line 9 by 12.4% (.124) . . . . | **10** |

11 Multiply line 6 by 2.9% (.029) . . . . | **11** |

12 **Self-employment tax.** Add lines 10 and 11. Enter here and on **Form 1040, line 58** . . . | **12** |

13 **Deduction for one-half of self-employment tax.** Multiply line 12 by 50% (.5). Enter the result here and on **Form 1040, line 27** . . . . | **13** |

Part II Optional Methods To Figure Net Earnings (see page SE-3)

Farm Optional Method. You may use this method **only** if **(a)** your gross farm income[1] was not more than $2,400 **or (b)** your net farm profits[2] were less than $1,733.

14 Maximum income for optional methods . . . . | **14** | 1,600 | 00 |

15 Enter the **smaller** of: two-thirds (⅔) of gross farm income[1] (not less than zero) **or** $1,600. Also include this amount on line 4b above . . . . | **15** |

Nonfarm Optional Method. You may use this method **only** if **(a)** your net nonfarm profits[3] were less than $1,733 and also less than 72.189% of your gross nonfarm income[4] **and (b)** you had net earnings from self-employment of at least $400 in 2 of the prior 3 years.

Caution. You may use this method no more than five times.

16 Subtract line 15 from line 14 . . . . | **16** |

17 Enter the **smaller** of: two-thirds (⅔) of gross nonfarm income[4] (not less than zero) **or** the amount on line 16. Also include this amount on line 4b above . . . . | **17** |

[1] From Sch. F, line 11, and Sch. K-1 (Form 1065), box 14, code B.

[2] From Sch. F, line 36, and Sch. K-1 (Form 1065), box 14, code A.

[3] From Sch. C, line 31; Sch. C-EZ, line 3; Sch. K-1 (Form 1065), box 14, code A; and Sch. K-1 (Form 1065-B), box 9.

[4] From Sch. C, line 7; Sch. C-EZ, line 1; Sch. K-1 (Form 1065), box 14, code C; and Sch. K-1 (Form 1065-B), box 9.

Schedule SE (Form 1040) 2005

644

2005 Form 1040-V

What Is Form 1040-V and Do You Have To Use It?

It is a statement you send with your check or money order for any balance due on line 75 of your 2005 Form 1040. Using Form 1040-V allows us to process your payment more accurately and efficiently. We strongly encourage you to use Form 1040-V, but there is no penalty if you do not.

How To Fill In Form 1040-V

Line 1. Enter your social security number (SSN). If you are filing a joint return, enter the SSN shown first on your return.

Line 2. If you are filing a joint return, enter the SSN shown second on your return.

Line 3. Enter the amount you are paying by check or money order.

Line 4. Enter your name(s) and address exactly as shown on your return. Please print clearly.

How To Prepare Your Payment

● Make your check or money order payable to the **"United States Treasury."** Do not send cash.

● Make sure your name and address appear on your check or money order.

● Enter "2005 Form 1040," your daytime phone number, and your SSN on your check or money order. If you are filing a joint return, enter the SSN shown first on your return.

● To help process your payment, enter the amount on the right side of your check like this: $ XXX.XX. Do not use dashes or lines (for example, do not enter "$ XXX—" or "$ XXX$\frac{XX}{100}$").

How To Send In Your 2005 Tax Return, Payment, and Form 1040-V

● Detach Form 1040-V along the dotted line.

● Do not staple or otherwise attach your payment or Form 1040-V to your return or to each other. Instead, just put them loose in the envelope.

● Mail your 2005 tax return, payment, and Form 1040-V in the envelope that came with your 2005 Form 1040 instruction booklet.

Note. If you do not have that envelope or you moved or used a paid preparer, mail your return, payment, and Form 1040-V to the Internal Revenue Service at the address shown on the back that applies to you.

Paperwork Reduction Act Notice. We ask for the information on Form 1040-V to help us carry out the Internal Revenue laws of the United States. If you use Form 1040-V, you must provide the requested information. Your cooperation will help us ensure that we are collecting the right amount of tax.

You are not required to provide the information requested on a form that is subject to the Paperwork Reduction Act unless the form displays a valid OMB control number. Books or records relating to a form or its instructions must be retained as long as their contents may become material in the administration of any Internal Revenue law. Generally, tax returns and return information are confidential, as required by Internal Revenue Code section 6103.

The time needed to complete and mail Form 1040-V will vary depending on individual circumstances. The estimated average time is 12 minutes. If you have comments about the accuracy of this time estimate or suggestions for making Form 1040-V simpler, we would be happy to hear from you. See the Instructions for Form 1040.

Cat. No. 20975C

▼ **Detach Here and Mail With Your Payment and Return** ▼

Form **1040-V** (2005)

Form 1040-V

Department of the Treasury
Internal Revenue Service (99)

Payment Voucher

▶ **Do not staple or attach this voucher to your payment or return.**

OMB No. 1545-0074

2005

1 Your social security number (SSN)	2 If a joint return, SSN shown second on your return	3 Amount you are paying by check or money order	Dollars	Cents

4 Your first name and initial	Last name
If a joint return, spouse's first name and initial	Last name

Home address (number and street)	Apt. no.

City, town or post office, state, and ZIP code

Cat. No. 20975C

645

□ CORRECTED (if checked)

DONEE'S name, street address, city, state, ZIP code, and telephone no.		OMB No. 1545-1959	Attachment Sequence No. 55A
	1 Date of contribution	20**05** Form **1098-C**	**Contributions of Motor Vehicles, Boats, and Airplanes**
	2 Make, model, and year of vehicle		**Copy C**

DONEE'S federal identification number	DONOR'S identification number	**3** Vehicle or other identification number	**For Donor's Records**

DONOR'S name	**4a** □ Donee certifies that vehicle was sold in arm's length transaction to unrelated party	This information is being furnished to the Internal Revenue Service.
Street address (including apt. no.)	**4b** Date of sale	
City, state, and ZIP code	**4c** Gross proceeds from sale (see instructions) $	

5a □ Donee certifies that vehicle will not be transferred for money, other property, or services before completion of material improvements or significant intervening use	**5b** □ Donee certifies that vehicle is to be transferred to a needy individual for significantly below fair market value in furtherance of donee's charitable purpose

5c Donee certifies the following detailed description of material improvements or significant intervening use and duration of use

Form **1098-C**   (keep for your records)   Department of the Treasury - Internal Revenue Service

647

Form **2106**	**Employee Business Expenses**	OMB No. 1545-0139

Form 2106

Department of the Treasury
Internal Revenue Service (99)

Employee Business Expenses

▶ See separate instructions.

▶ Attach to Form 1040.

OMB No. 1545-0139

2005

Attachment
Sequence No. **54**

Your name	Occupation in which you incurred expenses	Social security number

Part I — Employee Business Expenses and Reimbursements

Step 1 Enter Your Expenses

		Column A — Other Than Meals and Entertainment		Column B — Meals and Entertainment
1	Vehicle expense from line 22 or line 29. (Rural mail carriers: See instructions.)	**1**		
2	Parking fees, tolls, and transportation, including train, bus, etc., that **did not** involve overnight travel or commuting to and from work . .	**2**		
3	Travel expense while away from home overnight, including lodging, airplane, car rental, etc. **Do not** include meals and entertainment.	**3**		
4	Business expenses not included on lines 1 through 3. **Do not** include meals and entertainment.	**4**		
5	Meals and entertainment expenses (see instructions)	**5**		
6	**Total expenses.** In Column A, add lines 1 through 4 and enter the result. In Column B, enter the amount from line 5	**6**		

Note: *If you were not reimbursed for any expenses in Step 1, skip line 7 and enter the amount from line 6 on line 8.*

Step 2 Enter Reimbursements Received From Your Employer for Expenses Listed in Step 1

7	Enter reimbursements received from your employer that were **not** reported to you in box 1 of Form W-2. Include any reimbursements reported under code "L" in box 12 of your Form W-2 (see instructions)	**7**	

Step 3 Figure Expenses To Deduct on Schedule A (Form 1040)

8	Subtract line 7 from line 6. If zero or less, enter -0-. However, if line 7 is greater than line 6 in Column A, report the excess as income on Form 1040, line 7	**8**	
	Note: *If **both** columns of line 8 are zero, you cannot deduct employee business expenses. Stop here and attach Form 2106 to your return.*		
9	In Column A, enter the amount from line 8. In Column B, multiply line 8 by 50% (.50). (Employees subject to Department of Transportation (DOT) hours of service limits: Multiply meal expenses incurred while away from home on business by 70% (.70) instead of 50%. For details, see instructions.)	**9**	
10	Add the amounts on line 9 of both columns and enter the total here. **Also, enter the total on Schedule A (Form 1040), line 20.** (Reservists, qualified performing artists, fee-basis state or local government officials, and individuals with disabilities: See the instructions for special rules on where to enter the total.) . . . . ▶	**10**	

For Paperwork Reduction Act Notice, see instructions.

Cat. No. 11700N

Form **2106** (2005)

Part II Vehicle Expenses

Section A—General Information (You must complete this section if you are claiming vehicle expenses.)

		(a) Vehicle 1	(b) Vehicle 2
11	Enter the date the vehicle was placed in service	11 / /	/ /
12	Total miles the vehicle was driven during 2005	12 miles	miles
13	Business miles included on line 12	13 miles	miles
14	Percent of business use. Divide line 13 by line 12	14 %	%
15	Average daily roundtrip commuting distance	15 miles	miles
16	Commuting miles included on line 12	16 miles	miles
17	Other miles. Add lines 13 and 16 and subtract the total from line 12	17 miles	miles
18	Do you (or your spouse) have another vehicle available for personal use?	☐ Yes	☐ No
19	Was your vehicle available for personal use during off-duty hours?	☐ Yes	☐ No
20	Do you have evidence to support your deduction?	☐ Yes	☐ No
21	If "Yes," is the evidence written?	☐ Yes	☐ No

Section B—Standard Mileage Rate (See the instructions for Part II to find out whether to complete this section or Section C.)

22	Multiply line 13 by 40.5¢ (.405)	22	

Section C—Actual Expenses

		(a) Vehicle 1		(b) Vehicle 2	
23	Gasoline, oil, repairs, vehicle insurance, etc.	23			
24a	Vehicle rentals	24a			
b	Inclusion amount (see instructions)	24b			
c	Subtract line 24b from line 24a	24c			
25	Value of employer-provided vehicle (applies only if 100% of annual lease value was included on Form W-2—see instructions)	25			
26	Add lines 23, 24c, and 25	26			
27	Multiply line 26 by the percentage on line 14	27			
28	Depreciation (see instructions)	28			
29	Add lines 27 and 28. Enter total here and on line 1	29			

Section D—Depreciation of Vehicles (Use this section only if you owned the vehicle and are completing Section C for the vehicle.)

		(a) Vehicle 1		(b) Vehicle 2	
30	Enter cost or other basis (see instructions)	30			
31	Enter section 179 deduction (see instructions)	31			
32	Multiply line 30 by line 14 (see instructions if you claimed the section 179 deduction or special allowance)	32			
33	Enter depreciation method and percentage (see instructions)	33			
34	Multiply line 32 by the percentage on line 33 (see instructions)	34			
35	Add lines 31 and 34	35			
36	Enter the applicable limit explained in the line 36 instructions	36			
37	Multiply line 36 by the percentage on line 14	37			
38	Enter the **smaller** of line 35 or line 37. If you skipped lines 36 and 37, enter the amount from line 35. Also enter this amount on line 28 above	38			

Printed on recycled paper

Form **2106** (2005)

650

Form **2441**

Department of the Treasury
Internal Revenue Service (99)

Child and Dependent Care Expenses

▶ Attach to Form 1040.

▶ See separate instructions.

OMB No. 1545-0068

2005

Attachment
Sequence No. **21**

Name(s) shown on Form 1040

Your social security number

Before you begin: You need to understand the following terms. See **Definitions** on page 1 of the instructions.

- **Dependent Care Benefits**
- **Qualifying Person(s)**
- **Qualified Expenses**

Part I **Persons or Organizations Who Provided the Care—You must complete this part.**
(If you need more space, use the bottom of page 2.)

1	(a) Care provider's name	(b) Address (number, street, apt. no., city, state, and ZIP code)	(c) Identifying number (SSN or EIN)	(d) Amount paid (see instructions)

Did you receive **dependent care benefits?**   **No** ▶ Complete only Part II below.

Yes ▶ Complete Part III on the back next.

Caution. If the care was provided in your home, you may owe employment taxes. See the instructions for Form 1040, line 62.

Part II **Credit for Child and Dependent Care Expenses**

2 Information about your **qualifying person(s).** If you have more than two qualifying persons, see the instructions.

(a) Qualifying person's name		(b) Qualifying person's social security number	(c) Qualified expenses you incurred and paid in 2005 for the person listed in column (a)
First	Last		

3 Add the amounts in column (c) of line 2. **Do not** enter more than $3,000 for one qualifying person or $6,000 for two or more persons. If you completed Part III, enter the amount from line 32 . . . . **3**

4 Enter your **earned income.** See instructions **4**

5 If married filing jointly, enter your spouse's earned income (if your spouse was a student or was disabled, see the instructions); **all others,** enter the amount from line 4 . . . **5**

6 Enter the **smallest** of line 3, 4, or 5 . . . . **6**

7 Enter the amount from Form 1040, line 38 . . . . | **7** |

8 Enter on line 8 the decimal amount shown below that applies to the amount on line 7

If line 7 is:			If line 7 is:		
Over	But not over	Decimal amount is	Over	But not over	Decimal amount is
$0—15,000		.35	$29,000—31,000		.27
15,000—17,000		.34	31,000—33,000		.26
17,000—19,000		.33	33,000—35,000		.25
19,000—21,000		.32	35,000—37,000		.24
21,000—23,000		.31	37,000—39,000		.23
23,000—25,000		.30	39,000—41,000		.22
25,000—27,000		.29	41,000—43,000		.21
27,000—29,000		.28	43,000—No limit		.20

8 ✕ .

9 Multiply line 6 by the decimal amount on line 8. If you paid 2004 expenses in 2005, see the instructions **9**

10 Enter the amount from Form 1040, line 46, minus any amount on Form 1040, line 47 . **10**

11 **Credit for child and dependent care expenses.** Enter the **smaller** of line 9 or line 10 here and on Form 1040, line 48 . . . . **11**

For Paperwork Reduction Act Notice, see page 4 of the instructions.   Cat. No. 11862M   Form **2441** (2005)

Part III Dependent Care Benefits

12 Enter the total amount of **dependent care benefits** you received in 2005. Amounts you received as an employee should be shown in box 10 of your Form(s) W-2. **Do not** include amounts reported as wages in box 1 of Form(s) W-2. If you were self-employed or a partner, include amounts you received under a dependent care assistance program from your sole proprietorship or partnership **12**

13 Enter the amount forfeited, if any (see the instructions) **13**

14 Subtract line 13 from line 12 . . . . **14**

15 Enter the total amount of **qualified expenses** incurred in 2005 for the care of the **qualifying person(s)** . . **15**

16 Enter the **smaller** of line 14 or 15 . . . . . . **16**

17 Enter your **earned income.** See instructions . . . **17**

18 Enter the amount shown below that applies to you.
   - If married filing jointly, enter your spouse's earned income (if your spouse was a student or was disabled, see the instructions for line 5).
   - If married filing separately, see the instructions for the amount to enter.
   - All others, enter the amount from line 17. } . . . **18**

19 Enter the **smallest** of line 16, 17, or 18 . . . . . **19**

20 Enter the amount from line 12 that you received from your sole proprietorship or partnership. If you did not receive any such amounts, enter -0- **20**

21 Subtract line 20 from line 14 . . . . **21**

22 Enter $5,000 ($2,500 if married filing separately **and** you were required to enter your spouse's earned income on line 18) **22**

23 **Deductible benefits.** Enter the **smallest** of line 19, 20, or 22. Also, include this amount on the appropriate line(s) of your return (see the instructions) **23**

24 Enter the **smaller** of line 19 or 22 . . . . . . **24**

25 Enter the amount from line 23 . . . . **25**

26 **Excluded benefits.** Subtract line 25 from line 24. If zero or less, enter -0- **26**

27 **Taxable benefits.** Subtract line 26 from line 21. If zero or less, enter -0-. Also, include this amount on Form 1040, line 7. On the dotted line next to line 7, enter "DCB" . . . **27**

To claim the child and dependent care
credit, complete lines 28–32 below.

28 Enter $3,000 ($6,000 if two or more qualifying persons) **28**

29 Add lines 23 and 26 . . . . **29**

30 Subtract line 29 from line 28. If zero or less, **stop.** You cannot take the credit. **Exception.** If you paid 2004 expenses in 2005, see the instructions for line 9 . . . . **30**

31 Complete line 2 on the front of this form. **Do not** include in column (c) any benefits shown on line 29 above. Then, add the amounts in column (c) and enter the total here **31**

32 Enter the **smaller** of line 30 or 31. Also, enter this amount on line 3 on the front of this form and complete lines 4–11 . . . . **32**

Form **2441** (2005)

652

Form **4562**	**Depreciation and Amortization** **(Including Information on Listed Property)**	OMB No. 1545-0172 **2005**
Department of the Treasury Internal Revenue Service	▶ See separate instructions. ▶ Attach to your tax return.	Attachment Sequence No. **67**

Name(s) shown on return	Business or activity to which this form relates	**Identifying number**

Part I Election To Expense Certain Property Under Section 179

Note: *If you have any listed property, complete Part V before you complete Part I.*

1	Maximum amount. See the instructions for a higher limit for certain businesses	**1**	$105,000
2	Total cost of section 179 property placed in service (see instructions)	**2**	
3	Threshold cost of section 179 property before reduction in limitation	**3**	$420,000
4	Reduction in limitation. Subtract line 3 from line 2. If zero or less, enter -0-	**4**	
5	Dollar limitation for tax year. Subtract line 4 from line 1. If zero or less, enter -0-. If married filing separately, see instructions	**5**	

(a) Description of property	(b) Cost (business use only)	(c) Elected cost
6		

7	Listed property. Enter the amount from line 29 **7**		
8	Total elected cost of section 179 property. Add amounts in column (c), lines 6 and 7	**8**	
9	Tentative deduction. Enter the **smaller** of line 5 or line 8	**9**	
10	Carryover of disallowed deduction from line 13 of your 2004 Form 4562	**10**	
11	Business income limitation. Enter the smaller of business income (not less than zero) or line 5 (see instructions)	**11**	
12	Section 179 expense deduction. Add lines 9 and 10, but do not enter more than line 11	**12**	
13	Carryover of disallowed deduction to 2006. Add lines 9 and 10, less line 12 ▶ **13**		

Note: *Do not use Part II or Part III below for listed property. Instead, use Part V.*

Part II Special Depreciation Allowance and Other Depreciation (Do not include listed property.) (See instructions.)

14	Special allowance for certain aircraft, certain property with a long production period, and qualified New York Liberty Zone property (other than listed property) placed in service during the tax year	**14**	
15	Property subject to section 168(f)(1) election	**15**	
16	Other depreciation (including ACRS)	**16**	

Part III MACRS Depreciation (Do not include listed property.) (See instructions.)

Section A

17	MACRS deductions for assets placed in service in tax years beginning before 2005	**17**	
18	If you are electing to group any assets placed in service during the tax year into one or more general asset accounts, check here ▶ ☐		

Section B—Assets Placed in Service During 2005 Tax Year Using the General Depreciation System

(a) Classification of property	(b) Month and year placed in service	(c) Basis for depreciation (business/investment use only—see instructions)	(d) Recovery period	(e) Convention	(f) Method	(g) Depreciation deduction
19a 3-year property						
b 5-year property						
c 7-year property						
d 10-year property						
e 15-year property						
f 20-year property						
g 25-year property			25 yrs.		S/L	
h Residential rental property			27.5 yrs.	MM	S/L	
			27.5 yrs.	MM	S/L	
i Nonresidential real property			39 yrs.	MM	S/L	
				MM	S/L	

Section C—Assets Placed in Service During 2005 Tax Year Using the Alternative Depreciation System

20a Class life					S/L	
b 12-year			12 yrs.		S/L	
c 40-year			40 yrs.	MM	S/L	

Part IV Summary (see instructions)

21	Listed property. Enter amount from line 28	**21**	
22	**Total.** Add amounts from line 12, lines 14 through 17, lines 19 and 20 in column (g), and line 21. Enter here and on the appropriate lines of your return. Partnerships and S corporations—see instr.	**22**	
23	For assets shown above and placed in service during the current year, enter the portion of the basis attributable to section 263A costs **23**		

For Paperwork Reduction Act Notice, see separate instructions.   Cat. No. 12906N   Form **4562** (2005)

Part V　**Listed Property** (Include automobiles, certain other vehicles, cellular telephones, certain computers, and property used for entertainment, recreation, or amusement.)

Note: *For any vehicle for which you are using the standard mileage rate or deducting lease expense, complete **only** 24a, 24b, columns (a) through (c) of Section A, all of Section B, and Section C if applicable.*

Section A—Depreciation and Other Information (Caution: *See the instructions for limits for passenger automobiles.***)**

24a　Do you have evidence to support the business/investment use claimed? ☐ Yes ☐ No	24b　If "Yes," is the evidence written? ☐ Yes ☐ No

(a) Type of property (list vehicles first)	(b) Date placed in service	(c) Business/ investment use percentage	(d) Cost or other basis	(e) Basis for depreciation (business/investment use only)	(f) Recovery period	(g) Method/ Convention	(h) Depreciation deduction	(i) Elected section 179 cost
25　Special allowance for qualified New York Liberty Zone listed property placed in service during the tax year and used more than 50% in a qualified business use (see instructions)					**25**			
26　Property used more than 50% in a qualified business use:								
		%						
		%						
		%						
27　Property used 50% or less in a qualified business use:								
		%				S/L –		
		%				S/L –		
		%				S/L –		
28　Add amounts in column (h), lines 25 through 27. Enter here and on line 21, page 1. ‥					**28**			
29　Add amounts in column (i), line 26. Enter here and on line 7, page 1. ‥‥‥‥‥							**29**	

Section B—Information on Use of Vehicles

Complete this section for vehicles used by a sole proprietor, partner, or other "more than 5% owner," or related person.

If you provided vehicles to your employees, first answer the questions in Section C to see if you meet an exception to completing this section for those vehicles.

	(a) Vehicle 1		(b) Vehicle 2		(c) Vehicle 3		(d) Vehicle 4		(e) Vehicle 5		(f) Vehicle 6	
30　Total business/investment miles driven during the year (**do not** include commuting miles) ‥‥‥												
31　Total commuting miles driven during the year												
32　Total other personal (noncommuting) miles driven ‥‥‥												
33　Total miles driven during the year. Add lines 30 through 32 ‥‥‥												
	Yes	No	Yes	No	Yes	No	Yes	No	Yes	No	Yes	No
34　Was the vehicle available for personal use during off-duty hours? ‥‥												
35　Was the vehicle used primarily by a more than 5% owner or related person?												
36　Is another vehicle available for personal use? ‥‥‥‥‥												

Section C—Questions for Employers Who Provide Vehicles for Use by Their Employees

Answer these questions to determine if you meet an exception to completing Section B for vehicles used by employees who **are not** more than 5% owners or related persons (see instructions).

		Yes	No
37	Do you maintain a written policy statement that prohibits all personal use of vehicles, including commuting, by your employees? ‥‥‥‥‥‥‥‥		
38	Do you maintain a written policy statement that prohibits personal use of vehicles, except commuting, by your employees? See the instructions for vehicles used by corporate officers, directors, or 1% or more owners ‥‥‥		
39	Do you treat all use of vehicles by employees as personal use? ‥‥‥‥‥‥‥‥		
40	Do you provide more than five vehicles to your employees, obtain information from your employees about the use of the vehicles, and retain the information received? ‥‥‥‥‥		
41	Do you meet the requirements concerning qualified automobile demonstration use? (See instructions.) ‥‥‥		
	Note: *If your answer to 37, 38, 39, 40, or 41 is "Yes," do not complete Section B for the covered vehicles.*		

Part VI　**Amortization**

(a) Description of costs	(b) Date amortization begins	(c) Amortizable amount	(d) Code section	(e) Amortization period or percentage	(f) Amortization for this year
42　Amortization of costs that begins during your 2005 tax year (see instructions):					
43　Amortization of costs that began before your 2005 tax year. ‥‥‥‥‥ **43**					
44　**Total.** Add amounts in column (f). See the instructions for where to report. ‥‥‥ **44**					

♻ *Printed on recycled paper*　　　　　　　　　　　　　　　　　　　　　　　　　　Form **4562** (2005)

Form **4684**	**Casualties and Thefts**	OMB No. 1545-0177

Form **4684**

Department of the Treasury
Internal Revenue Service

Casualties and Thefts

► See separate instructions.
► Attach to your tax return.
► Use a separate Form 4684 for each casualty or theft.

OMB No. 1545-0177

2005

Attachment
Sequence No. **26**

Name(s) shown on tax return

Identifying number

SECTION A—Personal Use Property (Use this section to report casualties and thefts of property **not** used in a trade or business or for income-producing purposes.)

1 Description of properties (show type, location, and date acquired for each property). Use a separate line for each property lost or damaged from the same casualty or theft.

Property **A** _____

Property **B** _____

Property **C** _____

Property **D** _____

		Properties			
		A	**B**	**C**	**D**
2	Cost or other basis of each property . . .				
3	Insurance or other reimbursement (whether or not you filed a claim) (see instructions)				
	Note: *If line 2 is more than line 3, skip line 4.*				
4	Gain from casualty or theft. If line 3 is **more** than line 2, enter the difference here and skip lines 5 through 9 for that column. See instructions if line 3 includes insurance or other reimbursement you did not claim, or you received payment for your loss in a later tax year				
5	Fair market value **before** casualty or theft . . .				
6	Fair market value **after** casualty or theft. . . .				
7	Subtract line 6 from line 5				
8	Enter the **smaller** of line 2 or line 7				
9	Subtract line 3 from line 8. If zero or less, enter -0-				

10	Casualty or theft loss. Add the amounts on line 9 in columns A through D	10	
11	Enter the **smaller** of line 10 or $100	11	
12	Subtract line 11 from line 10	12	
	Caution: *Use only one Form 4684 for lines 13 through 18.*		
13	Add the amounts on line 12 of all Forms 4684	13	
14	Add the amounts on line 4 of all Forms 4684	14	
15	● If line 14 is **more** than line 13, enter the difference here and on Schedule D. **Do not** complete the rest of this section (see instructions). ● If line 14 is **less** than line 13, enter -0- here and go to line 16. ● If line 14 is **equal** to line 13, enter -0- here. **Do not** complete the rest of this section.	15	
16	If line 14 is **less** than line 13, enter the difference	16	
17	Enter 10% of your adjusted gross income from Form 1040, line 38. Estates and trusts, see instructions . .	17	
18	Subtract line 17 from line 16. If zero or less, enter -0-. Also enter the result on Schedule A (Form 1040), line 19. Estates and trusts, enter the result on the "Other deductions" line of your tax return	18	

For Paperwork Reduction Act Notice, see page 4 of the instructions.   Cat. No. 12997O   Form **4684** (2005)

655

(Watermark: Draft as of 05/18/2005)

Name(s) shown on tax return. Do not enter name and identifying number if shown on other side. | Identifying number

SECTION B—Business and Income-Producing Property

Part I　Casualty or Theft Gain or Loss (Use a separate Part I for each casualty or theft.)

19 Description of properties (show type, location, and date acquired for each property). Use a separate line for each property lost or damaged from the same casualty or theft.

Property **A** _____

Property **B** _____

Property **C** _____

Property **D** _____

		Properties			
		A	**B**	**C**	**D**
20	Cost or adjusted basis of each property	**20**			
21	Insurance or other reimbursement (whether or not you filed a claim). See the instructions for line 3 . . . **Note:** *If line 20 is **more** than line 21, skip line 22*	**21**			
22	Gain from casualty or theft. If line 21 is **more** than line 20, enter the difference here and on line 29 or line 34, column (c), except as provided in the instructions for line 33. Also, skip lines 23 through 27 for that column. See the instructions for line 4 if line 21 includes insurance or other reimbursement you did not claim, or you received payment for your loss in a later tax year.	**22**			
23	Fair market value **before** casualty or theft . . .	**23**			
24	Fair market value **after** casualty or theft	**24**			
25	Subtract line 24 from line 23	**25**			
26	Enter the **smaller** of line 20 or line 25 . . . . **Note:** *If the property was totally destroyed by casualty or lost from theft, enter on line 26 the amount from line 20.*	**26**			
27	Subtract line 21 from line 26. If zero or less, enter -0-	**27**			
28	Casualty or theft loss. Add the amounts on line 27. Enter the total here and on line 29 **or** line 34 (see instructions)			**28**	

Part II　Summary of Gains and Losses (from separate Parts I)

(a) Identify casualty or theft	**(b)** Losses from casualties or thefts		**(c)** Gains from casualties or thefts includible in income
	(i) Trade, business, rental or royalty property	**(ii)** Income-producing and employee property	

Casualty or Theft of Property Held One Year or Less

29	_____	( )	( )	
		( )	( )	
30	Totals. Add the amounts on line 29	**30** ( )	( )	

31 Combine line 30, columns (b)(i) and (c). Enter the net gain or (loss) here and on Form 4797, line 14. If Form 4797 is not otherwise required, see instructions . . . . | **31** |

32 Enter the amount from line 30, column (b)(ii) here. Individuals, enter the amount from income-producing property on Schedule A (Form 1040), line 27, and enter the amount from property used as an employee on Schedule A (Form 1040), line 22. Estates and trusts, partnerships, and S corporations, see instructions . . . . | **32** |

Casualty or Theft of Property Held More Than One Year

33	Casualty or theft gains from Form 4797, line 32	**33**	
34	_____	( )	( )	
		( )	( )	
35	Total losses. Add amounts on line 34, columns (b)(i) and (b)(ii) . . .	**35** ( )	( )	
36	Total gains. Add lines 33 and 34, column (c)	**36**	
37	Add amounts on line 35, columns (b)(i) and (b)(ii)	**37**	

38 If the loss on line 37 is **more** than the gain on line 36:

a Combine line 35, column (b)(i) and line 36, and enter the net gain or (loss) here. Partnerships (except electing large partnerships) and S corporations, see the note below. All others, enter this amount on Form 4797, line 14. If Form 4797 is not otherwise required, see instructions . . . . | **38a** |

b Enter the amount from line 35, column (b)(ii) here. Individuals, enter the amount from income-producing property on Schedule A (Form 1040), line 27, and enter the amount from property used as an employee on Schedule A (Form 1040), line 22. Estates and trusts, enter on the "Other deductions" line of your tax return. Partnerships (except electing large partnerships) and S corporations, see the note below. Electing large partnerships, enter on Form 1065-B, Part II, line 11. | **38b** |

39 If the loss on line 37 is **less** than or **equal** to the gain on line 36, combine lines 36 and 37 and enter here. Partnerships (except electing large partnerships), see the note below. All others, enter this amount on Form 4797, line 3 . . . | **39** |

Note: *Partnerships, enter the amount from line 38a, 38b, or line 39 on Form 1065, Schedule K, line 11.*
S corporations, enter the amount from line 38a or 38b on Form 1120S, Schedule K, line 10.

Form **4797**

Department of the Treasury
Internal Revenue Service (99)

Sales of Business Property

(Also Involuntary Conversions and Recapture Amounts
Under Sections 179 and 280F(b)(2))

▶Attach to your tax return. ▶See separate instructions.

OMB No. 1545-0184

2005

Attachment
Sequence No. **27**

Name(s) shown on return | Identifying number

1 Enter the gross proceeds from sales or exchanges reported to you for 2005 on Form(s) 1099-B or 1099-S (or substitute statement) that you are including on line 2, 10, or 20 (see instructions). **1**

Part I **Sales or Exchanges of Property Used in a Trade or Business and Involuntary Conversions From Other Than Casualty or Theft—Most Property Held More Than 1 Year** (see instructions)

(a) Description of property	(b) Date acquired (mo., day, yr.)	(c) Date sold (mo., day, yr.)	(d) Gross sales price	(e) Depreciation allowed or allowable since acquisition	(f) Cost or other basis, plus improvements and expense of sale	(g) Gain or (loss) Subtract (f) from the sum of (d) and (e)
2						

3 Gain, if any, from Form 4684, line 39 . . . . **3**

4 Section 1231 gain from installment sales from Form 6252, line 26 or 37 . . . . **4**

5 Section 1231 gain or (loss) from like-kind exchanges from Form 8824 . . . . **5**

6 Gain, if any, from line 32, from other than casualty or theft **6**

7 Combine lines 2 through 6. Enter the gain or (loss) here and on the appropriate line as follows: **7**

Partnerships (except electing large partnerships) and S corporations. Report the gain or (loss) following the instructions for Form 1065, Schedule K, line 10, or Form 1120S, Schedule K, line 9. Skip lines 8, 9, 11, and 12 below.

Individuals, partners, S corporation shareholders, and all others. If line 7 is zero or a loss, enter the amount from line 7 on line 11 below and skip lines 8 and 9. If line 7 is a gain and you did not have any prior year section 1231 losses, or they were recaptured in an earlier year, enter the gain from line 7 as a long-term capital gain on the Schedule D filed with your return and skip lines 8, 9, 11, and 12 below.

8 Nonrecaptured net section 1231 losses from prior years (see instructions) **8**

9 Subtract line 8 from line 7. If zero or less, enter -0-. If line 9 is zero, enter the gain from line 7 on line 12 below. If line 9 is more than zero, enter the amount from line 8 on line 12 below and enter the gain from line 9 as a long-term capital gain on the Schedule D filed with your return (see instructions). **9**

Part II **Ordinary Gains and Losses** (see instructions)

10 Ordinary gains and losses not included on lines 11 through 16 (include property held 1 year or less):

11 Loss, if any, from line 7 . . . . **11** ( )

12 Gain, if any, from line 7 or amount from line 8, if applicable **12**

13 Gain, if any, from line 31 . . . . **13**

14 Net gain or (loss) from Form 4684, lines 31 and 38a **14**

15 Ordinary gain from installment sales from Form 6252, line 25 or 36 . . . . **15**

16 Ordinary gain or (loss) from like-kind exchanges from Form 8824 . . . . **16**

17 Combine lines 10 through 16 . . . . **17**

18 For all except individual returns, enter the amount from line 17 on the appropriate line of your return and skip lines a and b below. For individual returns, complete lines a and b below:

a If the loss on line 11 includes a loss from Form 4684, line 35, column (b)(ii), enter that part of the loss here. Enter the part of the loss from income-producing property on Schedule A (Form 1040), line 27, and the part of the loss from property used as an employee on Schedule A (Form 1040), line 22. Identify as from "Form 4797, line 18a." See instructions **18a**

b Redetermine the gain or (loss) on line 17 excluding the loss, if any, on line 18a. Enter here and on Form 1040, line 14 . . . . **18b**

For Paperwork Reduction Act Notice, see separate instructions.   Cat. No. 13086I   Form **4797** (2005)

Part III Gain From Disposition of Property Under Sections 1245, 1250, 1252, 1254, and 1255
(see instructions)

19	(a) Description of section 1245, 1250, 1252, 1254, or 1255 property:		**(b)** Date acquired (mo., day, yr.)	**(c)** Date sold (mo., day, yr.)
A				
B				
C				
D				

	These columns relate to the properties on lines 19A through 19D. ▶		Property A	Property B	Property C	Property D
20	Gross sales price (**Note:** *See line 1 before completing.*) .	20				
21	Cost or other basis plus expense of sale	21				
22	Depreciation (or depletion) allowed or allowable .	22				
23	Adjusted basis. Subtract line 22 from line 21 . .	23				
24	Total gain. Subtract line 23 from line 20	24				
25	**If section 1245 property:**					
a	Depreciation allowed or allowable from line 22 . .	25a				
b	Enter the **smaller** of line 24 or 25a	25b				
26	**If section 1250 property:** If straight line depreciation was used, enter -0- on line 26g, except for a corporation subject to section 291.					
a	Additional depreciation after 1975 (see instructions) . .	26a				
b	Applicable percentage multiplied by the **smaller** of line 24 or line 26a (see instructions)	26b				
c	Subtract line 26a from line 24. If residential rental property **or** line 24 is not more than line 26a, skip lines 26d and 26e	26c				
d	Additional depreciation after 1969 and before 1976 . .	26d				
e	Enter the **smaller** of line 26c or 26d	26e				
f	Section 291 amount (corporations only)	26f				
g	Add lines 26b, 26e, and 26f	26g				
27	**If section 1252 property:** Skip this section if you did not dispose of farmland or if this form is being completed for a partnership (other than an electing large partnership).					
a	Soil, water, and land clearing expenses	27a				
b	Line 27a multiplied by applicable percentage (see instructions)	27b				
c	Enter the **smaller** of line 24 or 27b	27c				
28	**If section 1254 property:**					
a	Intangible drilling and development costs, expenditures for development of mines and other natural deposits, and mining exploration costs (see instructions)	28a				
b	Enter the **smaller** of line 24 or 28a	28b				
29	**If section 1255 property:**					
a	Applicable percentage of payments excluded from income under section 126 (see instructions)	29a				
b	Enter the **smaller** of line 24 or 29a (see instructions) . .	29b				

Summary of Part III Gains. Complete property columns A through D through line 29b before going to line 30.

30	Total gains for all properties. Add property columns A through D, line 24	30	
31	Add property columns A through D, lines 25b, 26g, 27c, 28b, and 29b. Enter here and on line 13	31	
32	Subtract line 31 from line 30. Enter the portion from casualty or theft on Form 4684, line 33. Enter the portion from other than casualty or theft on Form 4797, line 6	32	

Part IV Recapture Amounts Under Sections 179 and 280F(b)(2) When Business Use Drops to 50% or Less
(see instructions)

			(a) Section 179	**(b)** Section 280F(b)(2)
33	Section 179 expense deduction or depreciation allowable in prior years	33		
34	Recomputed depreciation (see instructions).	34		
35	Recapture amount. Subtract line 34 from line 33. See the instructions for where to report . .	35		

✿ *Printed on recycled paper*   Form **4797** (2005)

Form **4952**

Department of the Treasury
Internal Revenue Service (99)

Investment Interest Expense Deduction

▶ **Attach to your tax return.**

OMB No. 1545-0191

2005

Attachment
Sequence No. **51**

Name(s) shown on return

Identifying number

Part I	**Total Investment Interest Expense**		
1	Investment interest expense paid or accrued in 2005 (see instructions)	**1**	
2	Disallowed investment interest expense from 2004 Form 4952, line 7	**2**	
3	**Total investment interest expense.** Add lines 1 and 2	**3**	

Part II	**Net Investment Income**				
4a	Gross income from property held for investment (excluding any net gain from the disposition of property held for investment)	**4a**			
b	Qualified dividends included on line 4a	**4b**			
c	Subtract line 4b from line 4a			**4c**	
d	Net gain from the disposition of property held for investment	**4d**			
e	Enter the **smaller** of line 4d or your net capital gain from the disposition of property held for investment (see instructions)	**4e**			
f	Subtract line 4e from line 4d			**4f**	
g	Enter the amount from lines 4b and 4e that you elect to include in investment income (see instructions)			**4g**	
h	Investment income. Add lines 4c, 4f, and 4g			**4h**	
5	Investment expenses (see instructions)			**5**	
6	**Net investment income.** Subtract line 5 from line 4h. If zero or less, enter -0-			**6**	

Part III	**Investment Interest Expense Deduction**		
7	Disallowed investment interest expense to be carried forward to 2006. Subtract line 6 from line 3. If zero or less, enter -0-	**7**	
8	**Investment interest expense deduction.** Enter the **smaller** of line 3 or 6. See instructions.	**8**	

Section references are to the Internal Revenue Code unless otherwise noted.

General Instructions

Purpose of Form

Use Form 4952 to figure the amount of investment interest expense you can deduct for 2005 and the amount you can carry forward to future years. Your investment interest expense deduction is limited to your net investment income.

For more information, see Pub. 550, Investment Income and Expenses.

Who Must File

If you are an individual, estate, or a trust, you must file Form 4952 to claim a deduction for your investment interest expense.

Exception. You do not have to file Form 4952 if all of the following apply.

● Your investment interest expense is not more than your investment income from interest and ordinary dividends minus any qualified dividends.

● You have no other deductible investment expenses.

● You have no disallowed investment interest expense from 2004.

Allocation of Interest Expense

If you paid or accrued interest on a loan and used the loan proceeds for more than one purpose, you may have to allocate the interest. This is necessary because different

rules apply to investment interest, personal interest, trade or business interest, home mortgage interest, and passive activity interest. See Pub. 535, Business Expenses.

Specific Instructions

Part I—Total Investment Interest Expense

Line 1

Enter the investment interest expense paid or accrued during the tax year, regardless of when you incurred the indebtedness. Investment interest expense is interest paid or accrued on a loan or part of a loan that is allocable to property held for investment (as defined on this page).

Include investment interest expense reported to you on Schedule K-1 from a partnership or an S corporation. Include amortization of bond premium on taxable bonds purchased after October 22, 1986, but before January 1, 1988, unless you elected to offset amortizable bond premium against the interest payments on the bond. A taxable bond is a bond on which the interest is includible in gross income.

Investment interest expense does not include any of the following:

● Home mortgage interest.

● Interest expense that is properly allocable to a passive activity. Generally, a passive activity is any business activity in which you do not materially participate and any rental activity. See the Instructions for Form 8582, Passive Activity Loss Limitations, for details.

● Any interest expense that is capitalized, such as construction interest subject to section 263A.

● Interest expense related to tax-exempt interest income under section 265.

● Interest expense, disallowed under section 264, on indebtedness with respect to life insurance, endowment, or annuity contracts issued after June 8, 1997, even if the proceeds were used to purchase any property held for investment.

Property held for investment. Property held for investment includes property that produces income, not derived in the ordinary course of a trade or business, from interest, dividends, annuities, or royalties. It also includes property that produces gain or loss, not derived in the ordinary course of a trade or business, from the disposition of property that produces these types of income or is held for investment. However, it does not include an interest in a passive activity.

Exception. A working interest in an oil or gas property that you held directly or through an entity that did not limit your liability is property held for investment, but only if you did not materially participate in the activity.

Part II—Net Investment Income

Line 4a

Gross income from property held for investment includes income, unless derived in the ordinary course of a trade or business, from interest, ordinary dividends (except Alaska Permanent Fund dividends), annuities, and royalties.

Cat. No. 13177Y

Form **4952** (2005)

Form **5329**

Department of the Treasury
Internal Revenue Service   (99)

Additional Taxes on Qualified Plans
(Including IRAs) and Other Tax-Favored Accounts

▶ Attach to Form 1040.

▶ See separate instructions.

OMB No. 1545-0203

2005

Attachment
Sequence No. **29**

Name of individual subject to additional tax. If married filing jointly, see instructions.

Your social security number

**Fill in Your Address Only
If You Are Filing This
Form by Itself and Not
With Your Tax Return**

Home address (number and street), or P.O. box if mail is not delivered to your home

Apt. no.

City, town or post office, state, and ZIP code

If this is an amended
return, check here ▶ ☐

If you **only** owe the additional 10% tax on early distributions, you may be able to report this tax directly on Form 1040, line 60, without filing Form 5329. See the instructions for Form 1040, line 60.

Part I **Additional Tax on Early Distributions**

Complete this part if you took a taxable distribution, before you reached age 59½, from a qualified retirement plan (including an IRA) or modified endowment contract (unless you are reporting this tax directly on Form 1040—see above). You may also have to complete this part to indicate that you qualify for an exception to the additional tax on early distributions or for certain Roth IRA distributions (see instructions).

1	Early distributions included in income. For Roth IRA distributions, see instructions	1	
2	Early distributions included on line 1 that are not subject to the additional tax (see instructions). Enter the appropriate exception number from the instructions: _____	2	
3	Amount subject to additional tax. Subtract line 2 from line 1	3	
4	**Additional tax.** Enter 10% (.10) of line 3. Include this amount on Form 1040, line 60	4	

Caution: *If any part of the amount on line 3 was a distribution from a SIMPLE IRA, you may have to include 25% of that amount on line 4 instead of 10% (see instructions).*

Part II **Additional Tax on Certain Distributions From Education Accounts**

Complete this part if you included an amount in income, on Form 1040, line 21, from a Coverdell education savings account (ESA) or a qualified tuition program (QTP).

5	Distributions included in income from Coverdell ESAs and QTPs	5	
6	Distributions included on line 5 that are not subject to the additional tax (see instructions) . .	6	
7	Amount subject to additional tax. Subtract line 6 from line 5	7	
8	**Additional tax.** Enter 10% (.10) of line 7. Include this amount on Form 1040, line 60	8	

Part III **Additional Tax on Excess Contributions to Traditional IRAs**

Complete this part if you contributed more to your traditional IRAs for 2005 than is allowable or you had an amount on line 17 of your 2004 Form 5329.

9	Enter your excess contributions from line 16 of your 2004 Form 5329 (see instructions). If zero, go to line 15	9	
10	If your traditional IRA contributions for 2005 are less than your maximum allowable contribution, see instructions. Otherwise, enter -0-	10	
11	2005 traditional IRA distributions included in income (see instructions)	11	
12	2005 distributions of prior year excess contributions (see instructions)	12	
13	Add lines 10, 11, and 12	13	
14	Prior year excess contributions. Subtract line 13 from line 9. If zero or less, enter -0-	14	
15	Excess contributions for 2005 (see instructions)	15	
16	Total excess contributions. Add lines 14 and 15	16	
17	**Additional tax.** Enter 6% (.06) of the **smaller** of line 16 **or** the value of your traditional IRAs on December 31, 2005 (including 2005 contributions made in 2006). Include this amount on Form 1040, line 60 . . .	17	

Part IV **Additional Tax on Excess Contributions to Roth IRAs**

Complete this part if you contributed more to your Roth IRAs for 2005 than is allowable or you had an amount on line 25 of your 2004 Form 5329.

18	Enter your excess contributions from line 24 of your 2004 Form 5329 (see instructions). If zero, go to line 23	18	
19	If your Roth IRA contributions for 2005 are less than your maximum allowable contribution, see instructions. Otherwise, enter -0- . . .	19	
20	2005 distributions from your Roth IRAs (see instructions)	20	
21	Add lines 19 and 20	21	
22	Prior year excess contributions. Subtract line 21 from line 18. If zero or less, enter -0-	22	
23	Excess contributions for 2005 (see instructions)	23	
24	Total excess contributions. Add lines 22 and 23	24	
25	**Additional tax.** Enter 6% (.06) of the **smaller** of line 24 **or** the value of your Roth IRAs on December 31, 2005 (including 2005 contributions made in 2006). Include this amount on Form 1040, line 60	25	

For Paperwork Reduction Act Notice, see page 5 of the instructions.   Cat. No. 13329Q   Form **5329** (2005)

Part V **Additional Tax on Excess Contributions to Coverdell ESAs**

Complete this part if the contributions to your Coverdell ESAs for 2005 were more than is allowable or you had an amount on line 33 of your 2004 Form 5329.

26	Enter the excess contributions from line 32 of your 2004 Form 5329 (see instructions). If zero, go to line 31	**26**	
27	If the contributions to your Coverdell ESAs for 2005 were less than the maximum allowable contribution, see instructions. Otherwise, enter -0-	**27**	
28	2005 distributions from your Coverdell ESAs (see instructions)	**28**	
29	Add lines 27 and 28	**29**	
30	Prior year excess contributions. Subtract line 29 from line 26. If zero or less, enter -0-	**30**	
31	Excess contributions for 2005 (see instructions)	**31**	
32	Total excess contributions. Add lines 30 and 31	**32**	
33	**Additional tax.** Enter 6% (.06) of the **smaller** of line 32 **or** the value of your Coverdell ESAs on December 31, 2005 (including 2005 contributions made in 2006). Include this amount on Form 1040, line 60	**33**	

Part VI **Additional Tax on Excess Contributions to Archer MSAs**

Complete this part if you or your employer contributed more to your Archer MSAs for 2005 than is allowable or you had an amount on line 41 of your 2004 Form 5329.

34	Enter the excess contributions from line 40 of your 2004 Form 5329 (see instructions). If zero, go to line 39	**34**	
35	If the contributions to your Archer MSAs for 2005 are less than the maximum allowable contribution, see instructions. Otherwise, enter -0-	**35**	
36	2005 distributions from your Archer MSAs from Form 8853, line 10	**36**	
37	Add lines 35 and 36	**37**	
38	Prior year excess contributions. Subtract line 37 from line 34. If zero or less, enter -0-.	**38**	
39	Excess contributions for 2005 (see instructions)	**39**	
40	Total excess contributions. Add lines 38 and 39	**40**	
41	**Additional tax.** Enter 6% (.06) of the **smaller** of line 40 **or** the value of your Archer MSAs on December 31, 2005 (including 2005 contributions made in 2006). Include this amount on Form 1040, line 60	**41**	

Part VII **Additional Tax on Excess Contributions to Health Savings Accounts (HSAs)**

Complete this part if you, someone on your behalf, or your employer contributed more to your HSAs for 2005 than is allowable or you had an amount on line 43 of your 2004 Form 5329.

42	Enter the excess contributions from line 42 of your 2004 Form 5329. If zero, go to line 47	**42**	
43	If the contributions to your HSAs for 2005 are less than the maximum allowable contribution, see instructions. Otherwise, enter -0-	**43**	
44	2005 distributions from your HSAs from Form 8889, line 14	**44**	
45	Add lines 43 and 44	**45**	
46	Prior year excess contributions. Subtract line 45 from line 42. If zero or less, enter -0-	**46**	
47	Excess contributions for 2005 (see instructions)	**47**	
48	Total excess contributions. Add lines 46 and 47	**48**	
49	**Additional tax.** Enter 6% (.06) of the **smaller** of line 48 **or** the value of your HSAs on December 31, 2005 (including 2005 contributions made in 2006). Include this amount on Form 1040, line 60	**49**	

Part VIII **Additional Tax on Excess Accumulation in Qualified Retirement Plans (Including IRAs)**

Complete this part if you did not receive the minimum required distribution from your qualified retirement plan.

50	Minimum required distribution for 2005 (see instructions)	**50**	
51	Amount actually distributed to you in 2005	**51**	
52	Subtract line 51 from line 50. If zero or less, enter -0-	**52**	
53	**Additional tax.** Enter 50% (.50) of line 52. Include this amount on Form 1040, line 60	**53**	

Signature. Complete **only** if you are filing this form by itself and not with your tax return.

Please Sign Here

Under penalties of perjury, I declare that I have examined this form, including accompanying schedules and statements, and to the best of my knowledge and belief, it is true, correct, and complete. Declaration of preparer (other than taxpayer) is based on all information of which preparer has any knowledge.

▶ Your signature   ▶ Date

Paid Preparer's Use Only

Preparer's signature ▶	Date	Check if self-employed ☐	Preparer's SSN or PTIN
Firm's name (or yours if self-employed), address, and ZIP code ▶		EIN	
		Phone no. ( )	

♻ *Printed on recycled paper*

Form **5329** (2005)

Form **6251**	**Alternative Minimum Tax—Individuals**	OMB No. 1545-0227
Department of the Treasury Internal Revenue Service (99)	▶ See separate instructions. ▶ Attach to Form 1040 or Form 1040NR.	**2005** Attachment Sequence No. **32**

Name(s) shown on Form 1040 | Your social security number

Part I Alternative Minimum Taxable Income (See instructions for how to complete each line.)

1	If filing Schedule A (Form 1040), enter the amount from Form 1040, line 41, and go to line 2. Otherwise, enter the amount from Form 1040, line 38, and go to line 7. (If less than zero, enter as a negative amount.)	**1**	
2	Medical and dental. Enter the **smaller** of Schedule A (Form 1040), line 4, **or** 2½% of Form 1040, line 38	**2**	
3	Taxes from Schedule A (Form 1040), line 9	**3**	
4	Enter the home mortgage interest adjustment, if any, from line 6 of the worksheet on page 2 of the instructions	**4**	
5	Miscellaneous deductions from Schedule A (Form 1040), line 26	**5**	
6	If Form 1040, line 38, is over $145,950 (over $72,975 if married filing separately), enter the amount from line 9 of the **Itemized Deductions Worksheet** on page B-1 of the Instructions for Schedules A & B (Form 1040)	**6** (	)
7	Tax refund from Form 1040, line 10 or line 21	**7** (	)
8	Investment interest expense (difference between regular tax and AMT)	**8**	
9	Depletion (difference between regular tax and AMT)	**9**	
10	Net operating loss deduction from Form 1040, line 21. Enter as a positive amount	**10**	
11	Interest from specified private activity bonds exempt from the regular tax	**11**	
12	Qualified small business stock (7% of gain excluded under section 1202)	**12**	
13	Exercise of incentive stock options (excess of AMT income over regular tax income)	**13**	
14	Estates and trusts (amount from Schedule K-1 (Form 1041), box 12, code A)	**14**	
15	Electing large partnerships (amount from Schedule K-1 (Form 1065-B), box 6)	**15**	
16	Disposition of property (difference between AMT and regular tax gain or loss)	**16**	
17	Depreciation on assets placed in service after 1986 (difference between regular tax and AMT)	**17**	
18	Passive activities (difference between AMT and regular tax income or loss)	**18**	
19	Loss limitations (difference between AMT and regular tax income or loss)	**19**	
20	Circulation costs (difference between regular tax and AMT)	**20**	
21	Long-term contracts (difference between AMT and regular tax income)	**21**	
22	Mining costs (difference between regular tax and AMT)	**22**	
23	Research and experimental costs (difference between regular tax and AMT)	**23**	
24	Income from certain installment sales before January 1, 1987	**24** (	)
25	Intangible drilling costs preference	**25**	
26	Other adjustments, including income-based related adjustments	**26**	
27	Alternative tax net operating loss deduction	**27** (	)
28	**Alternative minimum taxable income.** Combine lines 1 through 27. (If married filing separately and line 28 is more than $191,000, see page 6 of the instructions.)	**28**	

Part II Alternative Minimum Tax

29	Exemption. (If this form is for a child under age 14, see page 6 of the instructions.)		

IF your filing status is . . .	AND line 28 is not over . . .	THEN enter on line 29 . . .	
Single or head of household	$112,500	$40,250	
Married filing jointly or qualifying widow(er)	150,000	58,000	**29**
Married filing separately	75,000	29,000	

If line 28 is **over** the amount shown above for your filing status, see page 6 of the instructions.

30	Subtract line 29 from line 28. If zero or less, enter -0- here and on lines 33 and 35 and stop here	**30**	
31	• If you reported capital gain distributions directly on Form 1040, line 13; you reported qualified dividends on Form 1040, line 9b; **or** you had a gain on both lines 15 and 16 of Schedule D (Form 1040) (as refigured for the AMT, if necessary), complete Part III on the back and enter the amount from line 55 here. • **All others:** If line 30 is $175,000 or less ($87,500 or less if married filing separately), multiply line 30 by 26% (.26). Otherwise, multiply line 30 by 28% (.28) and subtract $3,500 ($1,750 if married filing separately) from the result.	**31**	
32	Alternative minimum tax foreign tax credit (see page 7 of the instructions)	**32**	
33	Tentative minimum tax. Subtract line 32 from line 31	**33**	
34	Tax from Form 1040, line 44 (minus any tax from Form 4972 and any foreign tax credit from Form 1040, line 47). If you used Schedule J to figure your tax, the amounts for lines 44 and 47 of Form 1040 must be refigured without using Schedule J (see page 8 of the instructions)	**34**	
35	**Alternative minimum tax.** Subtract line 34 from line 33. If zero or less, enter -0-. Enter here and on Form 1040, line 45	**35**	

For Paperwork Reduction Act Notice, see page 8 of the instructions.   Cat. No. 13600G   Form **6251** (2005)

663

Part III **Tax Computation Using Maximum Capital Gains Rates**

36	Enter the amount from Form 6251, line 30	**36**		
37	Enter the amount from line 6 of the Qualified Dividends and Capital Gain Tax Worksheet in the instructions for Form 1040, line 44, or the amount from line 13 of the Schedule D Tax Worksheet on page D-9 of the instructions for Schedule D (Form 1040), whichever applies (as refigured for the AMT, if necessary) (see page 8 of the instructions)	**37**	
38	Enter the amount from Schedule D (Form 1040), line 19 (as refigured for the AMT, if necessary) (see page 8 of the instructions)	**38**	
39	If you did not complete a Schedule D Tax Worksheet for the regular tax or the AMT, enter the amount from line 37. Otherwise, add lines 37 and 38, and enter the **smaller** of that result or the amount from line 10 of the Schedule D Tax Worksheet (as refigured for the AMT, if necessary)	**39**	
40	Enter the **smaller** of line 36 or line 39	**40**	
41	Subtract line 40 from line 36	**41**	
42	If line 41 is $175,000 or less ($87,500 or less if married filing separately), multiply line 41 by 26% (.26). Otherwise, multiply line 41 by 28% (.28) and subtract $3,500 ($1,750 if married filing separately) from the result . . . . ▶	**42**	
43	Enter: • $59,400 if married filing jointly or qualifying widow(er), • $29,700 if single or married filing separately, or • $39,800 if head of household.	**43**	
44	Enter the amount from line 7 of the Qualified Dividends and Capital Gain Tax Worksheet in the instructions for Form 1040, line 44, or the amount from line 14 of the Schedule D Tax Worksheet on page D-9 of the instructions for Schedule D (Form 1040), whichever applies (as figured for the regular tax). If you did not complete either worksheet for the regular tax, enter -0- . . .	**44**	
45	Subtract line 44 from line 43. If zero or less, enter -0-	**45**	
46	Enter the **smaller** of line 36 or line 37	**46**	
47	Enter the **smaller** of line 45 or line 46	**47**	
48	Multiply line 47 by 5% (.05) . . . . ▶	**48**	
49	Subtract line 47 from line 46	**49**	
50	Multiply line 49 by 15% (.15) . . . . ▶	**50**	
	If line 38 is zero or blank, skip lines 51 and 52 and go to line 53. Otherwise, go to line 51.		
51	Subtract line 46 from line 40	**51**	
52	Multiply line 51 by 25% (.25) . . . . ▶	**52**	
53	Add lines 42, 48, 50, and 52	**53**	
54	If line 36 is $175,000 or less ($87,500 or less if married filing separately), multiply line 36 by 26% (.26). Otherwise, multiply line 36 by 28% (.28) and subtract $3,500 ($1,750 if married filing separately) from the result	**54**	
55	Enter the **smaller** of line 53 or line 54 here and on line 31	**55**	

Printed on recycled paper

Form **6251** (2005)

664

Form **8606**

Department of the Treasury
Internal Revenue Service (99)

Nondeductible IRAs

▶ See separate instructions.

▶ Attach to Form 1040, Form 1040A, or Form 1040NR.

OMB No. 1545-1007

2005

Attachment
Sequence No. **48**

Name. If married, file a separate form for each spouse required to file Form 8606. See page 5 of the instructions.

Your social security number

Fill in Your Address Only if You Are Filing This Form by Itself and Not With Your Tax Return

Home address (number and street, or P.O. box if mail is not delivered to your home)

Apt. no.

City, town or post office, state, and ZIP code

Part I **Nondeductible Contributions to Traditional IRAs and Distributions From Traditional, SEP, and SIMPLE IRAs**

Complete this part only if:

- You made nondeductible contributions to a traditional IRA for 2005,
- You took distributions from a traditional, SEP, or SIMPLE IRA in 2005 (other than a rollover, conversion, recharacterization, or return of certain contributions) **and** you made nondeductible contributions to a traditional IRA in 2005 or an earlier year, **or**
- You converted part, but not all, of your traditional, SEP, and SIMPLE IRAs to Roth IRAs in 2005 (excluding any portion you recharacterized) **and** you made nondeductible contributions to a traditional IRA in 2005 or an earlier year.

1   Enter your nondeductible contributions to traditional IRAs for 2005, including those made for 2005 from January 1, 2006, through April 17, 2006 (see page 5 of the instructions) **1**

2   Enter your total basis in traditional IRAs (see page 5 of the instructions) **2**

3   Add lines 1 and 2 . . . . **3**

In 2005, did you take a distribution from traditional, SEP, or SIMPLE IRAs or make a Roth IRA conversion?

— No ——▶ Enter the amount from line 3 on line 14. Do not complete the rest of Part I.

— Yes ——▶ Go to line 4.

4   Enter those contributions included on line 1 that were made from January 1, 2006, through April 17, 2006 . . . . **4**

5   Subtract line 4 from line 3 . . . . **5**

6   Enter the value of **all** your traditional, SEP, and SIMPLE IRAs as of December 31, 2005, plus any outstanding rollovers (see page 6 of the instructions). **6**

7   Enter your distributions from traditional, SEP, and SIMPLE IRAs in 2005. **Do not** include rollovers, conversions to a Roth IRA, certain returned contributions, or recharacterizations of traditional IRA contributions (see page 6 of the instructions) **7**

8   Enter the net amount you converted from traditional, SEP, and SIMPLE IRAs to Roth IRAs in 2005. **Do not** include amounts converted that you later recharacterized (see page 6 of the instructions). Also enter this amount on line 16 . . . . **8**

9   Add lines 6, 7, and 8 . . . . **9**

10 Divide line 5 by line 9. Enter the result as a decimal rounded to at least 3 places. If the result is 1.000 or more, enter "1.000" . . . **10** × .

11 Multiply line 8 by line 10. This is the nontaxable portion of the amount you converted to Roth IRAs. Also enter this amount on line 17 . . . **11**

12 Multiply line 7 by line 10. This is the nontaxable portion of your distributions that you did not convert to a Roth IRA **12**

13 Add lines 11 and 12. This is the nontaxable portion of all your distributions **13**

14 Subtract line 13 from line 3. This is **your total basis in traditional IRAs for 2005 and earlier years** **14**

15 **Taxable amount.** Subtract line 12 from line 7. Also include this amount on Form 1040, line 15b; Form 1040A, line 11b; or Form 1040NR, line 16b **15**

Note: You may be subject to an additional 10% tax on the amount on line 15 if you were under age 59½ at the time of the distribution (see page 7 of the instructions).

For Paperwork Reduction Act Notice, see page 8 of the instructions.

Cat. No. 63966F

Form **8606** (2005)

Part II   **2005 Conversions From Traditional, SEP, or SIMPLE IRAs to Roth IRAs**

Complete this part if you converted part or all of your traditional, SEP, and SIMPLE IRAs to a Roth IRA in 2005 (excluding any portion you recharacterized).

Caution: *If your modified adjusted gross income is over $100,000 **or** you are married filing separately and you lived with your spouse at any time in 2005, you **cannot** convert any amount from traditional, SEP, or SIMPLE IRAs to Roth IRAs for 2005. If you erroneously made a conversion, you must recharacterize (correct) it (see page 7 of the instructions).*

16	If you completed Part I, enter the amount from line 8. Otherwise, enter the net amount you converted from traditional, SEP, and SIMPLE IRAs to Roth IRAs in 2005. **Do not** include amounts you later recharacterized back to traditional, SEP, or SIMPLE IRAs in 2005 or 2006 (see page 7 of the instructions) **16**	
17	If you completed Part I, enter the amount from line 11. Otherwise, enter your basis in the amount on line 16 (see page 7 of the instructions) **17**	
18	**Taxable amount.** Subtract line 17 from line 16. Also include this amount on Form 1040, line 15b; Form 1040A, line 11b; or Form 1040NR, line 16b **18**	

Part III   **Distributions From Roth IRAs**

Complete this part only if you took a distribution from a Roth IRA in 2005 (other than a rollover, recharacterization, or return of certain contributions—see page 7 of the instructions).

19	Enter your total nonqualified distributions from Roth IRAs in 2005 including any qualified first-time homebuyer distributions (see page 7 of the instructions) **19**	
20	Qualified first-time homebuyer expenses (see page 7 of the instructions). **Do not** enter more than $10,000 . . . . **20**	
21	Subtract line 20 from line 19. If zero or less, enter -0- and skip lines 22 through 25 . . . . . . **21**	
22	Enter your basis in Roth IRA contributions (see page 7 of the instructions) **22**	
23	Subtract line 22 from line 21. If zero or less, enter -0- and skip lines 24 and 25. If more than zero, you may be subject to an additional tax (see page 8 of the instructions) **23**	
24	Enter your basis in Roth IRA conversions (see page 8 of the instructions) **24**	
25	**Taxable amount.** Subtract line 24 from line 23. If zero or less, enter -0-. Also include this amount on Form 1040, line 15b; Form 1040A, line 11b; or Form 1040NR, line 16b **25**	

Sign Here Only if You Are Filing This Form by Itself and Not With Your Tax Return	Under penalties of perjury, I declare that I have examined this form, including accompanying attachments, and to the best of my knowledge and belief, it is true, correct, and complete.
	▶ _____ ▶ _____
	Your signature Date

Form **8606** (2005)

 Printed on recycled paper

Form **8283**
(Rev. December 2004)

Department of the Treasury
Internal Revenue Service

Noncash Charitable Contributions

▶ Attach to your tax return if you claimed a total deduction
of over $500 for all contributed property.

▶ See separate instructions.

OMB No. 1545-0908

Attachment
Sequence No. **55**

Name(s) shown on your income tax return | Identifying number

Note: *Figure the amount of your contribution deduction before completing this form. See your tax return instructions.*

Section A—List in this section **only** items (or groups of similar items) for which you claimed a deduction of $5,000 or less. Also, list certain publicly traded securities even if the deduction is over $5,000 (see instructions).

Part I	**Information on Donated Property**—If you need more space, attach a statement.

1	(a) Name and address of the donee organization	(b) Description of donated property (For a donated vehicle, enter the year, make, model, and mileage.)
A		
B		
C		
D		
E		

Note: *If the amount you claimed as a deduction for an item is $500 or less, you do not have to complete columns (d), (e), and (f).*

	(c) Date of the contribution	(d) Date acquired by donor (mo., yr.)	(e) How acquired by donor	(f) Donor's cost or adjusted basis	(g) Fair market value	(h) Method used to determine the fair market value
A						
B						
C						
D						
E						

Part II	**Other Information**—Complete line 2 if you gave less than an entire interest in property listed in Part I. Complete line 3 if conditions were placed on a contribution listed in Part I.

2 If, during the year, you contributed less than the entire interest in the property, complete lines a through e.

a Enter the letter from Part I that identifies the property ▶ _____ . If Part II applies to more than one property, attach a separate statement.

b Total amount claimed as a deduction for the property listed in Part I: **(1)** For this tax year ▶ _____ .

(2) For any prior tax years ▶ _____ .

c Name and address of each organization to which any such contribution was made in a prior year (complete only if different from the donee organization above):

Name of charitable organization (donee)

Address (number, street, and room or suite no.)

City or town, state, and ZIP code

d For tangible property, enter the place where the property is located or kept ▶ _____

e Name of any person, other than the donee organization, having actual possession of the property ▶ _____

3 If an agreement between the donor and donee places conditions on any contribution listed in Part I, answer questions a through c and attach the required statement (see instructions).

		Yes	No
a	Is there a restriction, either temporary or permanent, on the donee's right to use or dispose of the donated property?		
b	Did you give to anyone (other than the donee organization or another organization participating with the donee organization in cooperative fundraising) the right to the income from the donated property or to the possession of the property, including the right to vote donated securities, to acquire the property by purchase or otherwise, or to designate the person having such income, possession, or right to acquire?		
c	Is there a restriction limiting the donated property for a particular use?		

For Paperwork Reduction Act Notice, see page 4 of separate instructions.   Cat. No. 62299J   Form **8283** (Rev. 12-2004)

667

Name(s) shown on your income tax return | Identifying number

Section B—Appraisal Summary—List in this section only items (or groups of similar items) for which you claimed a deduction of more than $5,000 per item or group. **Exception.** Report contributions of certain publicly traded securities only in Section A.

| **Part I** | **Information on Donated Property**—To be completed by the taxpayer and/or appraiser. |

4   Check type of property:

☐ Art* (contribution of $20,000 or more)   ☐ Qualified Conservation Contribution   ☐ Computer Equipment

☐ Art* (contribution of less than $20,000)   ☐ Other Real Estate   ☐ Other

☐ Collectibles**   ☐ Intellectual Property (patents, etc.)

*Art includes paintings, sculptures, watercolors, prints, drawings, ceramics, antiques, decorative arts, textiles, carpets, silver, rare manuscripts, historical memorabilia, and other similar objects.

**Collectibles include coins, stamps, books, gems, jewelry, sports memorabilia, dolls, etc., but not art.

Note: *If your total art contribution deduction was $20,000 or more, you must attach a complete copy of the signed appraisal. See instructions.*

5	**(a)** Description of donated property (if you need more space, attach a separate statement)	**(b)** If tangible property was donated, give a brief summary of the overall physical condition at the time of the gift	**(c)** Appraised fair market value
A			
B			
C			
D			

| | **(d)** Date acquired by donor (mo., yr.) | **(e)** How acquired by donor | **(f)** Donor's cost or adjusted basis | **(g)** For bargain sales, enter amount received | **See instructions** | |
					(h) Amount claimed as a deduction	**(i)** Average trading price of securities
A						
B						
C						
D						

| **Part II** | **Taxpayer (Donor) Statement**—List each item included in Part I above that the appraisal identifies as having a value of $500 or less. See instructions. |

I declare that the following item(s) included in Part I above has to the best of my knowledge and belief an appraised value of not more than $500 (per item). Enter identifying letter from Part I and describe the specific item. See instructions. ▶ _____

Signature of taxpayer (donor) ▶   Date ▶

| **Part III** | **Declaration of Appraiser** |

I declare that I am not the donor, the donee, a party to the transaction in which the donor acquired the property, employed by, or related to any of the foregoing persons, or married to any person who is related to any of the foregoing persons. And, if regularly used by the donor, donee, or party to the transaction, I performed the majority of my appraisals during my tax year for other persons.

Also, I declare that I hold myself out to the public as an appraiser or perform appraisals on a regular basis; and that because of my qualifications as described in the appraisal, I am qualified to make appraisals of the type of property being valued. I certify that the appraisal fees were not based on a percentage of the appraised property value. Furthermore, I understand that a false or fraudulent overstatement of the property value as described in the qualified appraisal or this appraisal summary may subject me to the penalty under section 6701(a) (aiding and abetting the understatement of tax liability). I affirm that I have not been barred from presenting evidence or testimony by the Director of Practice.

Sign Here

Signature ▶   Title ▶   Date of appraisal ▶

Business address (including room or suite no.) | Identifying number

City or town, state, and ZIP code

| **Part IV** | **Donee Acknowledgment**—To be completed by the charitable organization. |

This charitable organization acknowledges that it is a qualified organization under section 170(c) and that it received the donated property as described in Section B, Part I, above on ▶ _____
                                                                                                                                                        (Date)

Furthermore, this organization affirms that in the event it sells, exchanges, or otherwise disposes of the property described in Section B, Part I (or any portion thereof) within 2 years after the date of receipt, it will file **Form 8282,** Donee Information Return, with the IRS and give the donor a copy of that form. This acknowledgment does not represent agreement with the claimed fair market value.

Does the organization intend to use the property for an unrelated use? . . . . ▶ ☐ Yes   ☐ No

Name of charitable organization (donee)	Employer identification number
Address (number, street, and room or suite no.)	City or town, state, and ZIP code
Authorized signature	Title	Date

✪ *Printed on recycled paper*

668

Form **8615**

Department of the Treasury
Internal Revenue Service (99)

Tax for Children Under Age 14
With Investment Income of More Than $1,600
▶ Attach only to the child's Form 1040, Form 1040A, or Form 1040NR.
▶ See separate instructions.

OMB No. 1545-0998

2005

Attachment
Sequence No. **33**

Child's name shown on return

Child's social security number

Before you begin: If the child, the parent, or any of the parent's other children under age 14 must use the Schedule D Tax Worksheet or has income from farming or fishing, see **Pub. 929**, Tax Rules for Children and Dependents. It explains how to figure the child's tax using the **Schedule D Tax Worksheet** or **Schedule J** (Form 1040).

A Parent's name (first, initial, and last). **Caution:** See instructions before completing.

B Parent's social security number

C Parent's filing status (check one):

☐ Single ☐ Married filing jointly ☐ Married filing separately ☐ Head of household ☐ Qualifying widow(er)

Part I Child's Net Investment Income

1	Enter the child's investment income (see instructions)	**1**	
2	If the child **did not** itemize deductions on **Schedule A** (Form 1040 or Form 1040NR), enter $1,600. Otherwise, see instructions	**2**	
3	Subtract line 2 from line 1. If zero or less, **stop;** do not complete the rest of this form but **do** attach it to the child's return	**3**	
4	Enter the child's **taxable income** from Form 1040, line 43; Form 1040A, line 27; or Form 1040NR, line 40	**4**	
5	Enter the **smaller** of line 3 or line 4. If zero, **stop;** do not complete the rest of this form but **do** attach it to the child's return	**5**	

Part II Tentative Tax Based on the Tax Rate of the Parent

6	Enter the parent's **taxable income** from Form 1040, line 43; Form 1040A, line 27; Form 1040EZ, line 6; Form 1040NR, line 40; or Form 1040NR-EZ, line 14. If zero or less, enter -0-	**6**	
7	Enter the total, if any, from Forms 8615, line 5, of **all other** children of the parent named above. **Do not** include the amount from line 5 above	**7**	
8	Add lines 5, 6, and 7 (see instructions)	**8**	
9	Enter the tax on the amount on line 8 based on the **parent's** filing status above (see instructions). If the Qualified Dividends and Capital Gain Tax Worksheet, Schedule D Tax Worksheet, or Schedule J (Form 1040) is used to figure the tax, check here ▶ ☐	**9**	
10	Enter the parent's tax from Form 1040, line 44; Form 1040A, line 28, minus any alternative minimum tax; Form 1040EZ, line 10; Form 1040NR, line 41; or Form 1040NR-EZ, line 15. **Do not** include any tax from **Form 4972** or **8814**. If the Qualified Dividends and Capital Gain Tax Worksheet, Schedule D Tax Worksheet, or Schedule J (Form 1040) was used to figure the tax, check here ▶ ☐	**10**	
11	Subtract line 10 from line 9 and enter the result. If line 7 is blank, also enter this amount on line 13 and go to **Part III**	**11**	
12a	Add lines 5 and 7 .... **12a**		
b	Divide line 5 by line 12a. Enter the result as a decimal (rounded to at least three places)	**12b**	× .
13	Multiply line 11 by line 12b	**13**	

Part III Child's Tax—If lines 4 and 5 above are the same, enter -0- on line 15 and go to line 16.

14	Subtract line 5 from line 4 .... **14**		
15	Enter the tax on the amount on line 14 based on the **child's** filing status (see instructions). If the Qualified Dividends and Capital Gain Tax Worksheet, Schedule D Tax Worksheet, or Schedule J (Form 1040) is used to figure the tax, check here ▶ ☐	**15**	
16	Add lines 13 and 15	**16**	
17	Enter the tax on the amount on line 4 based on the **child's** filing status (see instructions). If the Qualified Dividends and Capital Gain Tax Worksheet, Schedule D Tax Worksheet, or Schedule J (Form 1040) is used to figure the tax, check here ▶ ☐	**17**	
18	Enter the **larger** of line 16 or line 17 here and on the **child's** Form 1040, line 44; Form 1040A, line 28; or Form 1040NR, line 41	**18**	

For Paperwork Reduction Act Notice, see the instructions.

Cat. No. 64113U

Form **8615** (2005)

669

Form **8812**

Department of the Treasury
Internal Revenue Service (99)

Additional Child Tax Credit

Complete and attach to Form 1040 or Form 1040A.

OMB No. 1545-1620

2005

Attachment
Sequence No. **47**

Name(s) shown on return

Your social security number

Part I   All Filers

1 Enter the amount from line 1 of your Child Tax Credit Worksheet on page 38 of the Form 1040 instructions or page 37 of the Form 1040A instructions. If you used Pub. 972, enter the amount from line 8 of the worksheet on page 4 of the publication **1**

2 Enter the amount from Form 1040, line 52, or Form 1040A, line 33 **2**

3 Subtract line 2 from line 1. If zero, **stop**; you cannot take this credit **3**

4a Earned income (see instructions on back) **4a**

 b Nontaxable combat pay from Form(s) W-2, box 12, with code Q. If married filing jointly, include your spouse's amounts with yours. **4b**

5 Is the amount on line 4a more than $11,000?
☐ **No.** Leave line 5 blank and enter -0- on line 6.
☐ **Yes.** Subtract $11,000 from the amount on line 4a. Enter the result **5**

6 Multiply the amount on line 5 by 15% (.15) and enter the result **6**
Next. Do you have three or more qualifying children?
☐ **No.** If line 6 is zero, **stop;** you cannot take this credit. Otherwise, skip Part II and enter the **smaller** of line 3 or line 6 on line 13.
☐ **Yes.** If line 6 is equal to or more than line 3, skip Part II and enter the amount from line 3 on line 13. Otherwise, go to line 7.

Part II   Certain Filers Who Have Three or More Qualifying Children

7 Withheld social security and Medicare taxes from Form(s) W-2, boxes 4 and 6. If married filing jointly, include your spouse's amounts with yours. If you worked for a railroad, see instructions on back **7**

8 **1040 filers:** Enter the total of the amounts from Form 1040, lines 27 and 59, plus any uncollected social security and Medicare or tier 1 RRTA taxes included on line 63.
1040A filers: Enter -0-. **8**

9 Add lines 7 and 8 **9**

10 **1040 filers:** Enter the total of the amounts from Form 1040, lines 66a and 67.
1040A filers: Enter the total of the amount from Form 1040A, line 41a, plus any excess social security and tier 1 RRTA taxes withheld that you entered to the left of line 43 (see instructions on back). **10**

11 Subtract line 10 from line 9. If zero or less, enter -0- **11**

12 Enter the **larger** of line 6 or line 11 **12**

Next, enter the **smaller** of line 3 or line 12 on line 13.

Part III   Additional Child Tax Credit

13 **This is your additional child tax credit** **13**

Enter this amount on Form 1040, line 68, or Form 1040A, line 42.

For Paperwork Reduction Act Notice, see back of form.

Cat. No. 10644E

Form **8812** (2005)

671

Form **8814**

Department of the Treasury
Internal Revenue Service

**Parents' Election To Report
Child's Interest and Dividends**
▶ See instructions.
▶ **Attach to parents' Form 1040 or Form 1040NR.**

OMB No. 1545-1128

2005

Attachment
Sequence No. **40**

Name(s) shown on your return

Your social security number

Caution: *The Federal income tax on your child's income, including qualified dividends and capital gain distributions, may be less if you file a separate tax return for the child instead of making this election. This is because you cannot take certain tax benefits that your child could take on his or her own return. For details, see* **Tax benefits you may not take** *on page 2.*

A   Child's name (first, initial, and last)

B Child's social security number

C   If more than one Form 8814 is attached, check here . . . . ▶ ☐

Part I	Child's Interest and Dividends To Report on Your Return

1a Enter your child's **taxable** interest. If this amount is different from the amounts shown on the child's Forms 1099-INT and 1099-OID, see the instructions . . . . | **1a** | |

  b Enter your child's **tax-exempt** interest. **Do not** include this amount on line 1a . . . . | **1b** | |

2 Enter your child's ordinary dividends, including any Alaska Permanent Fund dividends. If your child received any ordinary dividends as a nominee, see the instructions . . . . | **2** | |

3 Enter your child's capital gain distributions. If your child received any capital gain distributions as a nominee, see the instructions . . . . | **3** | |

4 Add lines 1a, 2, and 3. If the total is $1,600 or less, skip lines 5 and 6 and go to line 7. If the total is $8,000 or more, **do not** file this form. Your child **must** file his or her own return to report the income . . . . | **4** | |

5 Base amount . . . . | **5** | 1,600 | 00 |

6 Subtract line 5 from line 4. See the instructions for where to report this amount. Go to line 7 below . . . . ▶ | **6** | |

Part II	Tax on the First $1,600 of Child's Interest and Dividends

7 Amount not taxed . . . . | **7** | 800 | 00 |

8 Subtract line 7 from line 4. If the result is zero or less, enter -0- . . . . | **8** | |

9   **Tax.** Is the amount on line 8 less than $800?
    ☐ **No.** Enter $80 here and see the **Note** below.
    ☐ **Yes.** Multiply line 8 by 10% (.10). Enter the result here and see the **Note** below. | **9** | |

Note: *If you checked the box on line C above, see the instructions. Otherwise, include the amount from line 9 in the tax you enter on Form 1040, line 44, or Form 1040NR, line 41. Be sure to check box* **a** *on Form 1040, line 44, or Form 1040NR, line 41.*

For Paperwork Reduction Act Notice, see page 3.   Cat. No. 10750J   Form **8814** (2005)

673

Form **8829**

Department of the Treasury
Internal Revenue Service   (99)

Expenses for Business Use of Your Home

▶ File only with Schedule C (Form 1040). Use a separate Form 8829 for each home you used for business during the year.

▶ See separate instructions.

OMB No. 1545-1266

2005

Attachment
Sequence No. **66**

Name(s) of proprietor(s)

Your social security number

Part I   Part of Your Home Used for Business

1	Area used regularly and exclusively for business, regularly for daycare, or for storage of inventory or product samples (see instructions)	1	
2	Total area of home	2	
3	Divide line 1 by line 2. Enter the result as a percentage	3	%

- **For daycare facilities not used exclusively for business, also complete lines 4–6.**
- **All others, skip lines 4–6 and enter the amount from line 3 on line 7.**

4	Multiply days used for daycare during year by hours used per day	4	hr.
5	Total hours available for use during the year (365 days × 24 hours) (see instructions)	5	8,760 hr.
6	Divide line 4 by line 5. Enter the result as a decimal amount	6	.
7	Business percentage. For daycare facilities not used exclusively for business, multiply line 6 by line 3 (enter the result as a percentage). All others, enter the amount from line 3 . . . . . ▶	7	%

Part II   Figure Your Allowable Deduction

8	Enter the amount from Schedule C, line 29, **plus** any net gain or (loss) derived from the business use of your home and shown on Schedule D or Form 4797. If more than one place of business, see instructions		8	

See instructions for columns (a) and (b) before completing lines 9–20.

		(a) Direct expenses	(b) Indirect expenses	
9	Casualty losses (see instructions)	9			
10	Deductible mortgage interest (see instructions)	10			
11	Real estate taxes (see instructions)	11			
12	Add lines 9, 10, and 11	12			
13	Multiply line 12, column (b) by line 7		13		
14	Add line 12, column (a) and line 13			14	
15	Subtract line 14 from line 8. If zero or less, enter -0-			15	
16	Excess mortgage interest (see instructions) . .	16			
17	Insurance	17			
18	Repairs and maintenance	18			
19	Utilities	19			
20	Other expenses (see instructions)	20			
21	Add lines 16 through 20	21			
22	Multiply line 21, column (b) by line 7	22			
23	Carryover of operating expenses from 2004 Form 8829, line 41 . .	23			
24	Add line 21 in column (a), line 22, and line 23			24	
25	Allowable operating expenses. Enter the **smaller** of line 15 or line 24			25	
26	Limit on excess casualty losses and depreciation. Subtract line 25 from line 15			26	
27	Excess casualty losses (see instructions)	27			
28	Depreciation of your home from Part III below	28			
29	Carryover of excess casualty losses and depreciation from 2004 Form 8829, line 42	29			
30	Add lines 27 through 29			30	
31	Allowable excess casualty losses and depreciation. Enter the **smaller** of line 26 or line 30 . .			31	
32	Add lines 14, 25, and 31			32	
33	Casualty loss portion, if any, from lines 14 and 31. Carry amount to **Form 4684,** Section B . .			33	
34	Allowable expenses for business use of your home. Subtract line 33 from line 32. Enter here and on Schedule C, line 30. If your home was used for more than one business, see instructions ▶			34	

Part III   Depreciation of Your Home

35	Enter the **smaller** of your home's adjusted basis or its fair market value (see instructions) . .	35	
36	Value of land included on line 35	36	
37	Basis of building. Subtract line 36 from line 35	37	
38	Business basis of building. Multiply line 37 by line 7	38	
39	Depreciation percentage (see instructions)	39	%
40	Depreciation allowable (see instructions). Multiply line 38 by line 39. Enter here and on line 28 above	40	

Part IV   Carryover of Unallowed Expenses to 2006

41	Operating expenses. Subtract line 25 from line 24. If less than zero, enter -0-	41	
42	Excess casualty losses and depreciation. Subtract line 31 from line 30. If less than zero, enter -0-	42	

For Paperwork Reduction Act Notice, see page 4 of separate instructions.   Cat. No. 13232M   Form **8829** (2005)

Form **8863**

Department of the Treasury
Internal Revenue Service (99)

Education Credits
(Hope and Lifetime Learning Credits)
▶ See instructions.
▶ **Attach to Form 1040 or Form 1040A.**

OMB No. 1545-1618

2005

Attachment
Sequence No. **50**

Name(s) shown on return

Your social security number

Caution: You **cannot** take both an education credit and the tuition and fees deduction (Form 1040, line 34, or Form 1040A, line 19) for the **same student** in the same year.

Part I	Hope Credit. **Caution:** You **cannot** take the Hope credit for more than **2** tax years for the **same student.**

1	**(a)** Student's name (as shown on page 1 of your tax return) First name / Last name	**(b)** Student's social security number (as shown on page 1 of your tax return)	**(c)** Qualified expenses (see instructions). **Do not** enter more than $2,000 for each student.	**(d)** Enter the **smaller** of the amount in column (c) or $1,000	**(e)** Add column (c) and column (d)	**(f)** Enter one-half of the amount in column (e)

2	Tentative Hope credit. Add the amounts on line 1, column (f). If you are taking the lifetime learning credit for another student, go to Part II; otherwise, go to Part III . . . . ▶	2	

Part II	Lifetime Learning Credit

3	**Caution:** You **cannot** take the Hope credit and the lifetime learning credit for the **same student** in the same year.	**(a)** Student's name (as shown on page 1 of your tax return) First name Last name	**(b)** Student's social security number (as shown on page 1 of your tax return)	**(c)** Qualified expenses (see instructions)

4	Add the amounts on line 3, column (c), and enter the total	4	
5	Enter the **smaller** of line 4 or $10,000	5	
6	Tentative lifetime learning credit. Multiply line 5 by 20% (.20) and go to Part III . . ▶	6	

Part III	Allowable Education Credits

7	Tentative education credits. Add lines 2 and 6		7	
8	Enter: $107,000 if married filing jointly; $53,000 if single, head of household, or qualifying widow(er)	8		
9	Enter the amount from Form 1040, line 38*, or Form 1040A, line 22	9		
10	Subtract line 9 from line 8. If zero or less, **stop;** you cannot take any education credits	10		
11	Enter: $20,000 if married filing jointly; $10,000 if single, head of household, or qualifying widow(er)	11		
12	If line 10 is equal to or more than line 11, enter the amount from line 7 on line 13 and go to line 14. If line 10 is less than line 11, divide line 10 by line 11. Enter the result as a decimal (rounded to at least three places)	12	× .	
13	Multiply line 7 by line 12 . . . . ▶	13		
14	Enter the amount from Form 1040, line 46, or Form 1040A, line 28	14		
15	Enter the total, if any, of your credits from Form 1040, lines 47 through 49, or Form 1040A, lines 29 and 30	15		
16	Subtract line 15 from line 14. If zero or less, **stop;** you cannot take any education credits . . . . ▶	16		
17	**Education credits.** Enter the **smaller** of line 13 or line 16 here and on Form 1040, line 50, or Form 1040A, line 31 . . . . ▶	17		

* If you are filing Form 2555, 2555-EZ, or 4563, or you are excluding income from Puerto Rico, see Pub. 970 for the amount to enter.

For Paperwork Reduction Act Notice, see page 3.

Cat. No. 25379M

Form **8863** (2005)

Form **8880**

Department of the Treasury
Internal Revenue Service

Credit for Qualified Retirement Savings Contributions

▶ Attach to Form 1040 or Form 1040A.

▶ See instructions on back.

OMB No. 1545-1805

2005

Attachment
Sequence No. **129**

Name(s) shown on return | Your social security number

 CAUTION

You **cannot** take this credit if **either** of the following applies.

● The amount on Form 1040, line 38, or Form 1040A, line 22, is more than $25,000 ($37,500 if head of household; $50,000 if married filing jointly).

● The person(s) who made the qualified contribution or elective deferral **(a)** was born after January 1, 1988, **(b)** is claimed as a dependent on someone else's 2005 tax return, or **(c)** was a **student** (see instructions).

		(a) You		(b) Your spouse
1	Traditional and Roth IRA contributions for 2005. **Do not** include rollover contributions **1**			
2	Elective deferrals to a 401(k) or other qualified employer plan, voluntary employee contributions, and 501(c)(18)(D) plan contributions for 2005 (see instructions) **2**			
3	Add lines 1 and 2 **3**			
4	Certain distributions received **after** 2002 and **before** the due date (including extensions) of your 2005 tax return (see instructions). If married filing jointly, include **both** spouses' amounts in **both** columns. See instructions for an exception **4**			
5	Subtract line 4 from line 3. If zero or less, enter -0- . . . **5**			
6	In each column, enter the **smaller** of line 5 or $2,000 . . . . . **6**			
7	Add the amounts on line 6. If zero, **stop**; you cannot take this credit **7**			
8	Enter the amount from Form 1040, line 38*, or Form 1040A, line 22 . **8**			

9 Enter the applicable decimal amount shown below:

If line 8 is—		And your filing status is—		
Over—	But not over—	Married filing jointly	Head of household	Single, Married filing separately, or Qualifying widow(er)
		Enter on line 9—		
---	$15,000	.5	.5	.5
$15,000	$16,250	.5	.5	.2
$16,250	$22,500	.5	.5	.1
$22,500	$24,375	.5	.2	.1
$24,375	$25,000	.5	.1	.1
$25,000	$30,000	.5	.1	.0
$30,000	$32,500	.2	.1	.0
$32,500	$37,500	.1	.1	.0
$37,500	$50,000	.1	.0	.0
$50,000	---	.0	.0	.0

9 X .

Note: *If line 9 is zero, **stop**; you cannot take this credit.*

10	Multiply line 7 by line 9 . . . . **10**		
11	Enter the amount from Form 1040, line 46, or Form 1040A, line 28 **11**		
12	Enter the total of your credits from Form 1040, lines 47 through 50, or Form 1040A, lines 29 through 31 . . . . **12**		
13	Subtract line 12 from line 11. If zero, **stop**; you cannot take this credit **13**		
14	**Credit for qualified retirement savings contributions.** Enter the **smaller** of line 10 or line 13 here and on Form 1040, line 51, or Form 1040A, line 32 . . . . . . **14**		

*See Pub. 590 for the amount to enter if you are filing Form 2555, 2555-EZ, or 4563 or you are excluding income from Puerto Rico.

For Paperwork Reduction Act Notice, see back of form.   Cat. No. 33394D   Form **8880** (2005)

Filling Out Form 1040

Note: The 2004 IRS Publication 17 (Your Federal Income Tax) has been updated by Ernst & Young LLP for 2005. Dates and dollar amounts shown are for 2005. Gray type is used to indicate where IRS text has been updated or intentionally omitted. Unrevised IRS text is shown in black type.

Introduction

Form 1040 is designed to handle every taxpayer's situation regardless of the size and complexity of his or her economic activity.

The line-by-line instructions that follow should guide you through the process of filling out your tax return. If you have to cope with a situation that is not covered in the following pages, you should turn to the appropriate chapter in the book.

Line Instructions for Form 1040

IRS *e-file* takes the guesswork out of preparing your return. You may also be eligible to use free online commercial tax preparation software to file your federal income tax return. Visit *www.irs.gov/efile* for details.

Name and Address

Use the Peel-Off Label

Using your peel-off name and address label on the back of this booklet will speed the processing of your return. It also prevents common errors that can delay refunds or result in unnecessary notices. Put the label on your return after you have finished it. Cross out any incorrect information and print the correct information. Add any missing items, such as your apartment number.

Address Change

If the address on your peel-off label is not your current address, cross out your old address and print your new address. If you plan to move after filing your return, use Form 8822 to notify the IRS of your new address.

Name Change

If you changed your name because of marriage, divorce, etc., be sure to report the change to your local Social Security Administration office before filing your return. This prevents delays in processing your return and issuing refunds. It also safeguards your future social security benefits. If you received a peel-off label, cross out your former name and print your new name.

What if You Do Not Have a Label?

Print or type the information in the spaces provided. If you are married filing a separate return, enter your husband's or wife's name on line 3 instead of below your name.

Tip. *If you filed a joint return for 2004 and you are filing a joint return for 2005 with the same spouse, be sure to enter your names and SSNs in the same order as on your 2004 return.*

P.O. Box

Enter your box number only if your post office does not deliver mail to your home.

Foreign Address

Enter the information in the following order: City, province or state, and country. Follow the country's practice for entering the postal code. Do not abbreviate the country name.

Death of a Taxpayer

See Instructions for Form 1040 at www.irs.gov.

Social Security Number (SSN)

An incorrect or missing SSN may increase your tax or reduce your refund. To apply for an SSN, fill in Form SS-5 and return it to the Social Security Administration (SSA). You can get Form SS-5 online at *www.socialsecurity.gov*, from your local SSA office, or by calling the SSA at 1-800-772-1213. It usually takes about 2 weeks to get an SSN.

Check that your SSN on your Forms W-2 and 1099 agrees with your social security card.

IRS Individual Taxpayer Identification Numbers (ITINs) for Aliens

If you are a nonresident or resident alien and you do not have and are not eligible to get an SSN, you must apply for an ITIN. For details on how to do so, see Form W-7 and its instructions. It usually takes about 4–6 weeks to get an ITIN.

If you already have an ITIN, enter it wherever your SSN is requested on your tax return.

Note. An ITIN is for tax use only. It does not entitle you to social security benefits or change your employment or immigration status under U.S. law.

Nonresident Alien Spouse

If your spouse is a nonresident alien and you file a joint or separate return, your spouse must have either an SSN or an ITIN.

Presidential Election Campaign Fund

This fund helps pay for Presidential election campaigns. The fund reduces candidates' dependence on large contributions from individuals and groups and places candidates on an equal financial footing in the general election. If you want $3 to go to this fund, check the "Yes" box. If you are filing a joint return, your spouse may also have $3 go to the fund. If you check "Yes," your tax or refund will not change.

Filing Status

Check only the filing status that applies to you. The ones that will usually give you the lowest tax are listed last.

- Married filing separately.
- Single.
- Head of household.
- Married filing jointly or qualifying widow(er) with dependent child.

Tip. *More than one filing status can apply to you. Choose the one that will give you the lowest tax.*

Exemptions

You usually can deduct $3,200 on line 42 for each exemption you can take.

Line 6b
Spouse

Check the box on line 6b if either of the following apply.

1. Your filing status is married filing jointly.
2. You were married as of December 31, 2005, your filing status is married filing separately or head of household, and both of the following apply.

   a. Your spouse had no income and is not filing a return.
   b. Your spouse cannot be claimed as a dependent on another person's return.

If your filing status is head of household and you check the box on line 6b, enter the name of your spouse on the dotted line next to line 6b. Also, enter your spouse's social security number in the space provided at the top of your return.

Line 6c
Dependents

You can take an exemption for each of your dependents. A dependent must be either a qualifying relative or a qualifying child. The following is a brief description of the requirements that must be met for a person to qualify as your dependent. If you have more than four dependents, attach a statement to your return with the required information.

Qualifying child.

In general, a qualifying child must meet all of the following conditions.

- The child must be your child (including an adopted child, stepchild, or eligible foster child), brother, sister, stepbrother, stepsister, or a descendant of any of them.
- The child must have lived with you for more than half of 2005. But an exception applies, in certain cases, for children of divorced or separated parents.

- At the end of 2005, the child must be under age 19, or under age 24 and a full-time student, or any age and permanently and totally disabled.
- The child must not have provided over half of his or her own support in 2005.

Qualifying relative.

In general, a qualifying relative must meet all of the following conditions.

- The person must be either your relative or any other person (other than your spouse) who lived in your home all year as a member of your household. If the person is not your relative, your relationship must not violate local law.
- The person cannot be the qualifying child of another person in 2005 (see above).
- The person must have gross income of less than $3,200. If the person is permanently and totally disabled, certain income from a sheltered workshop may be excluded for this purpose.
- You must have provided over half of the person's support in 2005. But exceptions apply, in certain cases, for children of divorced or separated parents and for a person supported by two or more taxpayers.

The following rules also apply in determining if a person is your dependent.

1. If you are a dependent of another person in 2005, you cannot claim any dependents on your return.
2. If the dependent is married, he or she cannot file a joint return unless the return is filed only as a claim for refund and no tax liability would exist for either spouse if they had filed separate returns.
3. A dependent generally must be a U.S. citizen, U.S. national, or a resident of the United States, Canada, or Mexico.
4. New tie-breaker rules apply if a child meets the conditions to be a qualifying child of two or more people and more than one person claims the child as a qualifying child.

Certain tax benefits, such as qualifying widow(er) filing status and medical and dental expenses, can still be claimed based on a person who is not your dependent if the only reason that person is not your dependent is because he or she is a qualifying relative who has gross income of $3,200 or more or because of items (1) or (2) above.

[IRS text intentionally omitted]

Tip. *For more details about the tests, including any exceptions that apply, see Pub. 501.*

Line 6c, Column (2)

You must enter each dependent's social security number (SSN). Be sure the name and SSN entered agree with the dependent's social security card. Otherwise, at the time we process your return, we may disallow the exemption claimed for the dependent and reduce or disallow any other tax benefits (such as the child tax credit) based on that dependent. If the name or SSN on the dependent's social security card is not correct, call the Social Security Administration at 1-800-772-1213.

If your dependent child was born and died in 2005 and you do not have an SSN for the child, you may attach a copy of the child's birth certificate instead and enter "Died" in column (2).

Adoption taxpayer identification numbers (ATINs). If you have a dependent who was placed with you by an authorized placement agency and you do not know his or her SSN, you must get an ATIN for the dependent from the IRS. An authorized placement agency includes any person authorized by state law to place children for legal adoption. See Form W-7A for details.

Line 6c, Column (4)

Check the box in this column if your dependent is a qualifying child for the child tax credit (defined below). If you have a qualifying child, you may be able to take the child tax credit on line 52 and the additional child tax credit on line 68.

Qualifying child for child tax credit. A qualifying child for purposes of the child tax credit is a qualifying child who [IRS text intentionally omitted] was under age 17 at the end of 2005.

Children Who Did Not Live With You Due to Divorce or Separation

If you are claiming a child who did not live with you under the rules explained in Pub. 501 for children of divorced or separated parents, attach Form 8332 or similar statement to your return. But see the *Exception* below.

If your divorce decree or separation agreement went into effect after 1984, you can attach certain pages from the decree or agreement instead of Form 8332. To be able to do this, the decree or agreement must state all three of the following:

1. You can claim the child as your dependent without regard to any condition (such as payment of support).
2. The other parent will not claim the child as a dependent.
3. The years for which the claim is released.

Attach all of the following pages from the decree or agreement.

- Cover page (include the other parent's SSN on that page).
- The pages that include all of the information identified in (1) through (3) above.
- Signature page with the other parent's signature and date of agreement.

Caution. *You must attach the required information even if you filed it with your return in an earlier year.*

Exception. You do not have to attach Form 8332 or similar statement if your divorce decree or written separation agreement went into effect before 1985 and it states that you can claim the child as your dependent.

Other Dependent Children

Include the total number of children who did not live with you for reasons other than divorce or separation on the line labeled "Dependents on 6c not entered above." Include dependent children who lived in Canada or Mexico during 2005.

Income

Foreign-Source Income

You must report unearned income, such as interest, dividends, and pensions, from sources outside the United States unless exempt by law or a tax treaty. You must also report earned income, such as wages and tips, from sources outside the United States.

If you worked abroad, you may be able to exclude part or all of your earned income. For details, see Pub. 54 and Form 2555 or 2555-EZ.

Foreign retirement plans. If you were a beneficiary of a foreign retirement plan, you may have to report the undistributed income earned in your plan. However, if you were the beneficiary of a Canadian registered retirement plan, see Form 8891 to find out if you can elect to defer tax on the undistributed income.

Report distributions from foreign pension plans on lines 16a and 16b.

Community Property States

Community property states are Arizona, California, Idaho, Louisiana, Nevada, New Mexico, Texas, Washington, and Wisconsin. If you and your spouse lived in a community property state, you must usually follow state law to determine what is community income and what is separate income. For details, see Pub. 555.

Rounding Off to Whole Dollars

You may round off cents to whole dollars on your return and schedules. If you do round to whole dollars, you must round all amounts. To round, drop amounts under 50 cents and increase amounts from 50 to 99 cents to the next dollar. For example, $1.39 becomes $1 and $2.50 becomes $3.

If you have to add two or more amounts to figure the amount to enter on a line, include cents when adding the amounts and round off only the total.

Line 7
Wages, Salaries, Tips, etc.

Enter the total of your wages, salaries, tips, etc. If a joint return, also include your spouse's income. For most people, the amount to enter on this line should be shown in Form(s) W-2, box 1. But the following types of income must also be included in the total on line 7.

- Wages received as a household employee for which you did not receive a Form W-2 because your employer paid you less than $1,400 in 2005. Also, enter "HSH" and the amount not reported on Form W-2 on the dotted line next to line 7.
- Tip income you did not report to your employer. Also include allocated tips shown on your Form(s) W-2 unless you can prove that you received less. Allocated tips should be shown in Form(s) W-2, box 8. They are not included as income in box 1. See Pub. 531 for more details.

Caution. *You may owe social security and Medicare tax on unreported or allocated tips. See the instructions for line 59.*

- Dependent care benefits, which should be shown in Form(s) W-2, box 10. But first complete Form 2441 to see if you may exclude part or all of the benefits.
- Employer-provided adoption benefits, which should be shown in Form(s) W-2, box 12, with code T. But see the Instructions for Form 8839 to find out if you can exclude part or all of the benefits. You may also be able to exclude amounts if you adopted a child with special needs and the adoption became final in 2005.
- Scholarship and fellowship grants not reported on Form W-2. Also, enter "SCH" and the amount on the dotted line next to line 7. However, if you were a degree candidate, include on line 7 only the amounts you used for expenses other than tuition and course-related expenses. For example, amounts used for room, board, and travel must be reported on line 7.
- Excess salary deferrals. The amount deferred should be shown in Form W-2, box 12, and the "Retirement plan" box in box 13 should be checked. If the total amount you (or your spouse if filing jointly) deferred for 2005 under all plans was more than $14,000 (excluding catch-up contributions as explained below), include the excess on line 7. This limit is increased to $17,000 for section 403(b) plans if you qualify for the 15-year rule in Pub. 571.

A higher limit may apply to participants in section 457(b) deferred compensation plans for the 3 years before retirement age. Contact your plan administrator for more information.

If you were age 50 or older at the end of 2005, your employer may have allowed an additional deferral (catch-up contributions) of up to $4,000 ($2,000 for SIMPLE plans). This additional deferral amount is not subject to the overall limit on elective deferrals.

Caution. *You cannot deduct the amount deferred. It is not included as income in Form W-2, box 1.*

- Disability pensions shown on Form 1099-R if you have not reached the minimum retirement age set by your employer. Disability pensions received after you reach that age and other payments shown on Form 1099-R (other than payments from an IRA*) are reported on lines 16a and 16b. Payments from an IRA are reported on lines 15a and 15b.
- Corrective distributions from a retirement plan shown on Form 1099-R of excess salary deferrals, and excess contributions (plus

earnings). But do not include distributions from an IRA* on line 7. Instead, report distributions from an IRA on lines 15a and 15b.

This includes a Roth, SEP, or SIMPLE IRA.

Were You a Statutory Employee?

If you were, the "Statutory employee" box in Form W-2, box 13, should he checked. Statutory employees include full-time life insurance salespeople, certain agent or commission drivers and traveling salespeople, and certain homeworkers. If you have related business expenses to deduct, report the amount shown in Form W-2, box 1, on Schedule C or C-EZ along with your expenses.

Missing or Incorrect Form W-2?

Your employer is required to provide or send Form W-2 to you no later than January 31, 2006. If you do not receive it by early February, use TeleTax topic 154 (see page 8) to find out what to do. Even if you do not get a Form W-2, you must still report your earnings on line 7. If you lose your Form W-2 or it is incorrect. ask your employer for a new one.

Line 8a
Taxable Interest

Each payer should send you a Form 1099-INT or Form 1099-OID. Enter your total taxable interest income on line 8a. But you must fill in and attach Schedule B if the total is over $1,500 or any of the other conditions listed at the beginning of the Schedule B instructions apply to you.

Interest credited in 2005 on deposits that you could not withdraw because of the bankruptcy or insolvency of the financial institution may not have to be included in your 2005 income. For details, see Pub. 550.

Tip. *If you get a 2005 Form 1099-INT for U.S. savings bond interest that includes amounts you reported before 2005, see Pub. 550.*

Line 8b
Tax-Exempt Interest

If you received any tax-exempt interest, such as from municipal bonds, report it on line 8b. Include any exempt-interest dividends from a mutual fund or other regulated investment company. Do not include interest earned on your IRA or Coverdell education savings account.

Line 9a
Ordinary Dividends

Each payer should send you a Form 1099-DIV. Enter your total ordinary dividends on line 9a. This amount should be shown in Form(s) 1099-DIV, box 1a. But you must fill in and attach Schedule B if the total is over $1,500 or you received, as a nominee, ordinary dividends that actually belong to someone else.

Nondividend Distributions

Some distributions are a return of your cost (or other basis). They will not be taxed until you recover your cost (or other basis). You must reduce your cost (or other basis) by these distributions. After you get back all of your cost (or other basis), you must report these distributions as capital gains on Schedule D. For details, see Pub. 550.

Tip. *Dividends on insurance policies are a partial return of the premiums you paid. Do not report them as dividends. Include them in income only if they exceed the total of all net premiums you paid for the contract.*

Line 9b
Qualified Dividends

Enter your total qualified dividends on line 9b. Qualified dividends are eligible for a lower tax rate than other ordinary income. Gener-

ally, these dividends are shown in Form(s) 1099-DIV, box 1b. See Pub. 550 for the definition of qualified dividends if you received dividends not reported on Form 1099-DIV.

Exception. Some dividends may be reported as qualified dividends in box 1b of Form 1099-DIV but are not qualified dividends. These include:

- Dividends you received as a nominee. See the Instructions for Schedule B.
- Dividends you received on any share of stock that you held for less than 61 days during the 121-day period that began 60 days before the ex-dividend date. The ex-dividend date is the first date following the declaration of a dividend on which the purchaser of a stock is not entitled to receive the next dividend payment. When counting the number of days you held the stock, include the day you disposed of the stock but not the day you acquired it. See the examples below. Also, when counting the number of days you held the stock, you cannot count certain days during which your risk of loss was diminished. See Pub. 550 for more details.
- Dividends attributable to periods totaling more than 366 days that you received on any share of preferred stock held for less than 91 days during the 181-day period that began 90 days before the ex-dividend date. When counting the number of days you held the stock, you cannot count certain days during which your risk of loss was diminished. See Pub. 550 for more details. Preferred dividends attributable to periods totaling less than 367 days are subject to the 61-day holding period rule above.
- Dividends on any share of stock to the extent that you are under an obligation (including a short sale) to make related payments with respect to positions in substantially similar or related property.
- Payments in lieu of dividends, but only if you know or have reason to know that the payments are not qualified dividends.

Example 1. You bought 5,000 shares of XYZ Corp. common stock on July 1, 2005. XYZ Corp. paid a cash dividend of 10 cents per share. The ex-dividend date was July 9, 2005. Your Form 1099-DIV from XYZ Corp. shows $500 in box 1a (ordinary dividends) and in box 1b (qualified dividends). However, you sold the 5,000 shares on August 4, 2005. You held your shares of XYZ Corp. for only 34 days of the 121-day period (from July 2, 2005, through August 4, 2005). The 121-day period began on May 10, 2005 (60 days before the ex-dividend date), and ended on September 7, 2005. You have no qualified dividends from XYZ Corp. because you held the XYZ stock for less than 61 days.

Example 2. Assume the same facts as in Example 1 except that you bought the stock on July 8, 2005 (the day before the ex-dividend date), and you sold the stock on September 9, 2005. You held the stock for 63 days (from July 9, 2005, through September 9, 2005). The $500 of the qualified dividends shown in Form 1099-DIV, box 1b, are all qualified dividends because you held the stock for 61 days of the 121-day period (from July 9, 2005, through September 7, 2005).

Example 3. You bought 10,000 shares of ABC Mutual Fund common stock on July 1, 2005. ABC Mutual Fund paid a cash dividend of 10 cents a share. The ex-dividend date was July 9, 2005. The ABC Mutual Fund advises you that the portion of the dividend eligible to be treated as qualified dividends equals 2 cents per share. Your Form 1099-DIV from ABC Mutual Fund shows total ordinary dividends of $1,000 and qualified dividends of $200. However, you sold the 10,000 shares on August 4, 2005. You have no qualified dividends from ABC Mutual Fund because you held the ABC Mutual Fund stock for less than 61 days.

Tip. *Be sure you use the Qualified Dividends and Capital Gain Tax Worksheet or the Schedule D Tax Worksheet, whichever applies, to figure your tax. Your tax may be less if you use the worksheet that applies. See the instructions for line 44 for details.*

Line 10
Taxable Refunds, Credits, or Offsets of State and Local Income Taxes

Tip. *None of your refund is taxable if, in the year you paid the tax, you did not itemize deductions.*

If you received a refund, credit, or offset of state or local income taxes in 2005, you may receive a Form 1099-G. If you chose to apply part or all of the refund to your 2005 estimated state or local income tax, the amount applied is treated as received in 2005.

Exception. See *Recoveries* in Pub. 525 if any of the following apply.

- You received a refund in 2005 that is for a tax year other than 2004.
- You received a refund other than an income tax refund, such as a real property tax refund, in 2005 of an amount deducted or credit claimed in an earlier year.
- Your 2004 taxable income was less than zero.
- You made your last payment of 2004 estimated state or local income tax in 2005.
- You owed alternative minimum tax in 2004.
- You could not deduct the full amount of credits you were entitled to in 2004 because the total credits exceeded the amount shown on your 2004 Form 1040, line 43.
- You could be claimed as a dependent by someone else in 2004.

Also, see *Tax benefit rule* in Pub. 525 if all of the following apply.

- You had to use the Itemized Deductions Worksheet in the 2004 Schedule A instructions because your 2004 adjusted gross income was over $143,700 ($71,850 if married filing separately).
- You could not deduct all of the amount on the 2004 Itemized Deductions Worksheet line 1.
- The amount on line 8 of that 2004 worksheet would be more than the amount on line 4 of that worksheet if the amount on line 4 were reduced by 80% of the refund you received in 2005.

Line 11
Alimony Received

Enter amounts received as alimony or separate maintenance. You must let the person who made the payments know your social security number. If you do not, you may have to pay a $50 penalty. For more details, use TeleTax topic 406 or see Pub. 504.

Line 12
Business Income or (Loss)

If you operated a business or practiced your profession as a sole proprietor, report your income and expenses on Schedule C or C-EZ.

Line 13
Capital Gain or (Loss)

If you had a capital gain or loss, including any capital gain distributions or a capital loss carryover from 2004, you must complete and attach Schedule D.

Exception. You do not have to file Schedule D if both of the following apply.

- The only amounts you have to report on Schedule D are capital gain distributions from Form(s) 1099-DIV, box 2a, or substitute statements.
- None of the Forms 1099-DIV or substitute statements have an amount in box 2b (unrecaptured section 1250 gain), box 2c (section 1202 gain), or box 2d (collectibles (28%) gain).

If both of the above apply, enter your total capital gain distributions (from box 2a of Form(s) 1099-DIV) on line 13 and check the box on that line. If you received capital gain distributions as a nominee (that is, they were paid to you but actually belong to someone else), report on line 13 only the amount that belongs to you. Attach a statement showing the full amount you received and the amount you received as a nominee. See the Instructions for Schedule B for filing requirements for Forms 1099-DIV and 1096.

Line 14
Other Gains or (Losses)

If you sold or exchanged assets used in a trade or business, see the Instructions for Form 4797.

Lines 15a and 15b
IRA Distributions

You should receive a Form 1099-R showing the amount of any distribution from your individual retirement arrangement (IRA). Unless otherwise noted in the line 15a and 15b instructions, an IRA includes a traditional IRA, Roth IRA, simplified employee pension (SEP) IRA, and a savings incentive match plan for employees (SIMPLE) IRA. Except as provided below, leave line 15a blank and enter the total distribution on line 15b.

Exception 1. Enter the total distribution on line 15a if you rolled over part or all of the distribution from one:

- IRA to another IRA of the same type (for example, from one traditional IRA to another traditional IRA), or
- SEP or SIMPLE IRA to a traditional IRA.

Also, put "Rollover" next to line 15b. If the total distribution was rolled over in a qualified rollover, enter -0- on line 15b. If the total distribution was not rolled over in a qualified rollover, enter the part not rolled over on line 15b unless *Exception 2* applies to the part not rolled over. Generally, a qualified rollover must be made within 60 days after the day you received the distribution. For more details on rollovers, see Pub. 590.

If you rolled over the distribution (a) in 2006, or (b) from an IRA into a qualified plan (other than an IRA), attach a statement explaining what you did.

Exception 2. If any of the following apply, enter the total distribution on line 15a and see Form 8606 and its instructions to figure the amount to enter on line 15b.

1. You received a distribution from an IRA (other than a Roth IRA) and you made nondeductible contributions to any of your traditional or SEP IRAs for 2005 or an earlier year. If you made nondeductible contributions to these IRAs for 2005, also see Pub. 590.
2. You received a distribution from a Roth IRA. But if either (a) or (b) below applies, enter -0- on line 15b; you do not have to see Form 8606 or its instructions.
   a. Distribution code T is shown in Form 1099-R, box 7, and you made a contribution (including a conversion) to a Roth IRA for 1999 or 2000.
   b. Distribution code Q is shown in Form 1099-R, box 7.
3. You converted part or all of a traditional, SEP, or SIMPLE IRA to a Roth IRA in 2005.
4. You had a 2004 or 2005 IRA contribution returned to you, with the related earnings or less any loss, by the due date (including extensions) of your tax return for that year.
5. You made excess contributions to your IRA for an earlier year and had them returned to you in 2005.
6. You recharacterized part or all of a contribution to a Roth IRA as a traditional IRA contribution, or vice versa.

Note. If you (or your spouse if filing jointly) received more than one distribution, figure the taxable amount of each distribution and enter the total of the taxable amounts on line 15b. Enter the total amount of those distributions on line 15a.

Caution. *You may have to pay an additional tax if (a) you received an early distribution from your IRA and the total was not rolled over, or (b) you were born before July 1, 1934, and received less than the minimum required distribution from your traditional, SEP, and SIMPLE IRAs. See the instructions for line 60 for details.*

Lines 16a and 16b
Pensions and Annuities

You should receive a Form 1099-R showing the amount of your pension and annuity payments. See page 23 and 24 for details on rollovers and lump-sum distributions. Do not include the following payments on lines 16a and 16b. Instead, report them on line 7.

- Disability pensions received before you reach the minimum retirement age set by your employer.
- Corrective distributions of excess salary deferrals or excess contributions to retirement plans.

Tip. *Attach Form(s) 1099-R to Form 1040 if any federal income tax was withheld.*

Fully Taxable Pensions and Annuities

If your pension or annuity is fully taxable, enter it on line 16b; do not make an entry on line 16a. Your payments are fully taxable if (a) you did not contribute to the cost (see page 23) of your pension or annuity, or (b) you got your entire cost back tax free before 2005.

Fully taxable pensions and annuities also include military retirement pay shown on Form 1099-R. For details on military disability pensions, see Pub. 525. If you received a Form RRB-1099-R, see Pub. 575 to find out how to report your benefits.

Partially Taxable Pensions and Annuities

Enter the total pension or annuity payments you received in 2005 on line 16a. If your Form 1099-R does not show the taxable amount, you must use the General Rule explained in Pub. 939 to figure the taxable part to enter on line 16b. But if your annuity starting date (defined below) was after July 1, 1986, see *Simplified Method* below to find out if you must use that method to figure the taxable part.

You can ask the IRS to figure the taxable part for you for a $95 fee. For details, see Pub. 939.

If your Form 1099-R shows a taxable amount, you may report that amount on line 16b. But you may be able to report a lower taxable amount by using the General Rule or the Simplified Method.

Annuity Starting Date

Your annuity starting date is the later of the first day of the first period for which you received a payment or the date the plan's obligations became fixed.

Simplified Method

You must use the Simplified Method if either of the following applies.

1. Your annuity starting date (defined above) was after July 1, 1986, and you used this method last year to figure the taxable part.
2. Your annuity starting date was after November 18, 1996, and both of the following apply.

   a. The payments are from a qualified employee plan, a qualified employee annuity, or a tax-sheltered annuity.
   b. On your annuity starting date, either you were under age 75 or the number of years of guaranteed payments was fewer than 5. See Pub. 575 for the definition of guaranteed payments.

If you must use the Simplified Method, complete the worksheet on page 23 to figure the taxable part of your pension or annuity. For more details on the Simplified Method, see Pub. 575 or Pub. 721 for U.S. Civil Service retirement benefits.
Caution. *If you received U.S. Civil Service retirement benefits and you chose the alternative annuity option, see Pub. 721 to figure the taxable part of your annuity.*

Age (or Combined Ages) at Annuity Starting Date

If you are the retiree, use your age on the annuity starting date. If you are the survivor of a retiree, use the retiree's age on his or her annuity starting date. But if your annuity starting date was after 1997 and the payments are for your life and that of your beneficiary, use your combined ages on the annuity starting date.

If you are the beneficiary of an employee who died, see Pub. 575. If there is more than one beneficiary, see Pub. 575 or Pub. 721 to figure each beneficiary's taxable amount.

Cost

Your cost is generally your net investment in the plan as of the annuity starting date. It does not include pre-tax contributions. Your net investment should be shown in Form 1099-R, box 9b, for the first year you received payments from the plan.

Rollovers

Generally, a qualified rollover is a tax-free distribution of cash or other assets from one retirement plan that is contributed to another plan within 60 days of receiving the distribution. Use lines 16a and 16b to report a qualified rollover, including a direct rollover, from one qualified employer's plan to another or to an IRA or SEP.

Enter on line 16a the total distribution before income tax or other deductions were withheld. This amount should be shown in Form 1099-R, box 1. From the total on line 16a, subtract any contributions (usually shown in box 5) that were taxable to you when made. From that result, subtract the amount of the qualified rollover. Enter the remaining amount, even if zero, on line 16b. Also, enter "Rollover" next to line 16b.

Special rules apply to partial rollovers of property. For more details on rollovers, including distributions under qualified domestic relations orders, see Pub. 575.

Lump-Sum Distributions

If you received a lump-sum distribution from a profit-sharing or retirement plan, your Form 1099-R should have the "Total distribution" box in box 2b checked. You may owe an additional tax if you received an early distribution from a qualified retirement plan and the total amount was not rolled over in a qualified rollover.

Enter the total distribution on line 16a and the taxable part on line 16b.
Tip. *You may be able to pay less tax on the distribution if you were born before January 2, 1936, or you are the beneficiary of a deceased employee who was born before January 2, 1936. For details, see Form 4972.*

Line 19
Unemployment Compensation

You should receive a Form 1099-G showing the total unemployment compensation paid to you in 2005.

If you received an overpayment of unemployment compensation in 2005 and you repaid any of it in 2005, subtract the amount you repaid from the total amount you received. Enter the result on line 19. Also, enter "Repaid" and the amount you repaid on the dotted line next to line 19. If, in 2005, you repaid unemployment compensation that you included in gross income in an earlier year, you may deduct the amount repaid on Schedule A, line 22. But if you repaid more than $3,000, see *Repayments* in Pub. 525 for details in how to report the repayment.

Lines 20a and 20b
Social Security Benefits

You should receive a Form SSA-1099 showing in box 3 the total social security benefits paid to you. Box 4 will show the amount of any benefits you repaid in 2005. If you received railroad retirement benefits treated as social security, you should receive a Form RRB-1099.

Exception. Do not use the worksheet on page 25 if any of the following apply.

- You made contributions to a traditional IRA for 2005 and you or your spouse were covered by a retirement plan at work or through self-employment. Instead, use the worksheets in Pub. 590 to see if any of your social security benefits are taxable and to figure your IRA deduction.
- You repaid any benefits in 2005 and your total repayments (box 4) were more than your total benefits for 2005 (box 3). None of your benefits are taxable for 2005. Also, you may be able to take an itemized deduction or a credit for part of the excess repayments if they were for benefits you included in gross income in an earlier year. For more details, see Pub. 915.
- You file Form 2555, 2555-EZ, 4563, or 8815, or you exclude employer-provided adoption benefits or income from sources within Puerto Rico. Instead, use the worksheet in Pub. 915.

Line 21
Other Income

Caution. *Do not report on this line any income from self-employment or fees received as a notary public. Instead, you must use Schedule C, C-EZ, or F, even if you do not have any business expenses. Also, do not report on line 21 any nonemployee compensation shown on Form 1099-MISC.*

Use line 21 to report any income not reported elsewhere on your return or other schedules. See the examples below. List the type and amount of income. If necessary, show the required information on an attached statement. For more details, see *Miscellaneous Income* in Pub. 525.

Tip. *Do not report any nontaxable amounts on line 21, such as child support; money or property that was inherited, willed to you, or received as a gift; or life insurance proceeds received because of a person's death.*

Examples of income to report on line 21 are:

- Taxable distributions from a Coverdell education savings account (ESA) or a qualified tuition program (QTP). Distributions from these accounts may be taxable if (a) they are more than the qualified higher education expenses of the designated beneficiary in 2005, and (b) they were not included in a qualified rollover. See Pub. 970.

Caution. *You may have to pay an additional tax if you received a taxable distribution from a Coverdell ESA or a QTP. See the Instructions for Form 5329.*

- Taxable distributions from a health savings account (HSA) or an Archer MSA. Distributions from these accounts may be taxable if (a) they are more than the unreimbursed qualified medical expenses of the account beneficiary or account holder in 2005, and (b) they were not included in a qualified rollover. See Pub. 969.

Caution. *You may have to pay an additional tax if you received a taxable distribution from an HSA or an Archer MSA. See the Instructions for Form 8889 for HSAs or the Instructions for Form 8853 for Archer MSAs.*

- Prizes and awards.
- Gambling winnings, including lotteries, raffles, a lump-sum payment from the sale of a right to receive future lottery payments, etc. For details on gambling losses, see the instructions for Schedule A, line 27.

Tip. *Attach Form(s) W-2G to Form 1040 if any federal income tax was withheld.*

- Jury duty fees. Also, see the instructions for line 36.
- Alaska Permanent Fund dividends.
- Reimbursements or other amounts received for items deducted in an earlier year, such as medical expenses, real estate taxes, or home mortgage interest. See Recoveries in Pub. 525 for details on how to figure the amount to report.
- Income from the rental of personal property if you engaged in the rental for profit but were not in the business of renting such property. Also, see the instructions for line 36.
- Income from an activity not engaged in for profit. See Pub. 535.
- Loss on certain corrective distributions of excess deferrals. See Retirement Plan Contributions in Pub. 525.

Adjusted Gross Income

Line 23
Educator Expenses

If you were an eligible educator in 2005, you can deduct up to $250 of qualified expenses you paid in 2005. If you and your spouse are filing jointly and both of you were eligible educators, the maximum deduction is $500. However, neither spouse can deduct more than $250 of his or her qualified expenses. An eligible educator is a kindergarten through grade 12 teacher, instructor, counselor, principal, or aide in a school for at least 900 hours during a school year.

Qualified expenses include ordinary and necessary expenses paid in connection with books, supplies, equipment (including computer equipment, software, and services), and other materials used in the classroom. An ordinary expense is one that is common and accepted in your educational field. A necessary expense is one that is helpful and appropriate for your profession as an educator. An expense does not have to be required to be considered necessary.

Qualified expenses do not include expenses for home schooling or for nonathletic supplies for courses in health or physical education. You must reduce your qualified expenses by the following amounts.

- Excludable U.S. series EE and I savings bond interest from Form 8815.
- Nontaxable qualified state tuition program earnings.
- Nontaxable earnings from Coverdell education savings accounts.
- Any reimbursements you received for these expenses that were not reported to you in Form W-2, box 1.
  For more details, use TeleTax topic 458.

Line 24
Certain Business Expenses of Reservists, Performing Artists, and Fee-Basis Government Officials

Include the following deductions on line 24.

- Certain business expenses of National Guard and reserve members who traveled more than 100 miles from home to perform services as a National Guard or reserve member.
- Performing-arts-related expenses as a qualified performing artist.
- Business expenses of fee-basis state or local government officials.

  For more details, see Form 2106 or 2106-EZ.

Line 25
Health Savings Account Deduction

If contributions (other than employer contributions) were made to your health savings account for 2005, you may be able to take this deduction. See Form 8889.

Line 26
Moving Expenses

If you moved in connection with your job or business or started a new job, you may be able to take this deduction. But your new workplace must be at least 50 miles farther from your old home than your old home was from your old workplace. If you had no former workplace, your new workplace must be at least 50 miles from your old home. Use TeleTax topic 455 or see Form 3903.

Line 27
One-Half of Self-Employment Tax

If you were self-employed and owe self-employment tax, fill in Schedule SE to figure the amount of your deduction.

Line 28
Self-Employed SEP, SIMPLE, and Qualified Plans

If you were self-employed or a partner, you may be able to take this deduction. See Pub. 560 or, if you were a minister, Pub. 517.

Line 29
Self-Employed Health Insurance Deduction

You may be able to deduct the amount you paid for health insurance for yourself, your spouse, and your dependents if any of the following apply.

- You were self-employed and had a net profit for the year.
- You used one of the optional methods to figure your net earnings from self-employment on Schedule SE.
- You received wages in 2005 from an S corporation in which you were a more-than-2% shareholder. Health insurance benefits paid for you may be shown in Form W-2, box 14.

The insurance plan must be established under your business. But if you were also eligible to participate in any subsidized health plan maintained by your or your spouse's employer for any month or part of a month in 2005, amounts paid for health insurance coverage for that month cannot be used to figure the deduction. For example, if you were eligible to participate in a subsidized health plan maintained by your spouse's employer from September 30 through December 31, you cannot use amounts paid for health insurance coverage for September through December to figure your deduction.

For more details, see Pub. 535.

Note. If, during 2005, you were an eligible trade adjustment assistance (TAA) recipient, alternative TAA recipient, or Pension Benefit Guaranty Corporation pension recipient, you must complete Form 8885 before completing the worksheet. When figuring the amount to enter on line 1 of the worksheet, do not include any health coverage tax credit advance payments shown in Form 1099-H, box 1. Also, subtract the amount shown on Form 8885, line 4, (reduced by any advance payments shown on line 6 of that form) from the total insurance premiums you paid.

If you qualify to take the deduction, use the worksheet to figure the amount you can deduct.

Exception. Use Pub. 535 instead of the worksheet to find out how to figure your deduction if any of the following apply.

- You had more than one source of income subject to self-employment tax.
- You file Form 2555 or 2555-EZ.
- You are using amounts paid for qualified long-term care insurance to figure the deduction.

Line 30
Penalty on Early Withdrawal of Savings

The Form 1099-INT or Form 1099-OID you received will show the amount of any penalty you were charged.

Lines 31a and 31b
Alimony Paid

If you made payments to or for your spouse or former spouse under a divorce or separation instrument, you may be able to take this deduction. Use TeleTax topic 452 or see Pub. 504.

Line 32
IRA Deduction

Tip. *If you made any nondeductible contributions to a traditional individual retirement arrangement (IRA) for 2005, you must report them on Form 8606.*

If you made contributions to a traditional IRA for 2005, you may be able to take an IRA deduction. But you, or your spouse if filing a joint return, must have had earned income to do so. For IRA purposes, earned income includes alimony and separate maintenance payments reported on line 11. A statement should be sent to you by May 31, 2006, that shows all contributions to your traditional IRA for 2005.

Use the worksheet in the instructions to figure the amount, if any, of your IRA deduction. But read the following list before you fill in the worksheet.

- If you were age 70 1/2 or older at the end of 2005, you cannot deduct any contributions made to your traditional IRA for 2005 or treat them as nondeductible contributions.
- You cannot deduct contributions to a Roth IRA. But you may be able to take the retirement savings contributions credit. See the instructions for line 51.

Caution. *If you made contributions to both a traditional IRA and a Roth IRA for 2005, see Pub. 590 to figure the amount, if any, of your IRA deduction.*

- You cannot deduct elective deferrals to a 401(k)plan, section 457 plan, SIMPLE plan, or the Federal Thrift Savings Plan. These amounts are not included as income in Form W-2, box 1. But you may be able to take the retirement savings contributions credit. See the instructions for line 51.
- If you made contributions to your IRA in 2005 that you deducted for 2004, do not include them in the worksheet.
- If you received a distribution from a nonqualified deferred compensation plan or nongovernmental section 457 plan that is included in Form W-2, box 1, do not include that distribution on line 8 of the worksheet. The distribution should be shown in Form W-2, box 11. If it is not, contact your employer for the amount of the distribution.
- You must file a joint return to deduct contributions to your spouse's IRA. Enter the total IRA deduction for you and your spouse on line 32.
- Do not include qualified rollover contributions in figuring your deduction. Instead, see the instructions for lines 15a and 15b.
- Do not include trustees' fees that were billed separately and paid by you for your IRA. These fees can be deducted only as an itemized deduction on Schedule A.
- If the total of your IRA deduction on line 32 plus any nondeductible contribution to your traditional IRAs shown on Form 8606 is less than your total traditional IRA contributions for 2005, see Pub. 590 for special rules.

Tip. *By April 1 of the year after the year in which you turn age 70 1/2, you must start taking minimum required distributions from your traditional IRA. If you do not, you may have to pay a 50% additional tax on the amount that should have been distributed. For details, including how to figure the minimum required distribution, see Pub. 590.*

Were You Covered by a Retirement Plan?
If you were covered by a retirement plan (qualified pension, profit-sharing (including 401(k)), annuity, SEP, SIMPLE, etc.) at work or

through self-employment, your IRA deduction may be reduced or eliminated. But you can still make contributions to an IRA even if you cannot deduct them. In any case, the income earned on your IRA contributions is not taxed until it is paid to you.

The "Retirement plan" box in Form W-2, box 13, should be checked if you were covered by a plan at work even if you were not vested in the plan. You are also covered by a plan if you were self-employed and had a SEP, SIMPLE, or qualified retirement plan.

If you were covered by a retirement plan and you file Form 2555, 2555-EZ, or 8815, or you exclude employer-provided adoption benefits, see Pub. 590 to figure the amount, if any, of your IRA deduction.

Married Persons Filing Separately. If you were not covered by a retirement plan but your spouse was, you are considered covered by a plan unless you lived apart from your spouse for all of 2005.

Line 33
Student Loan Interest Deduction

You can take this deduction only if all of the following apply.

- You paid interest in 2005 on a qualified student loan.
- Your filing status is any status except married filing separately.
- Your modified adjusted gross income (AGI) is less than: $65,000 if single, head of household, or qualifying widow(er); $135,000 if married filing jointly. Use lines 2 through 4 of the worksheet in the instructions to figure your modified AGI.
- You are not claimed as a dependent on someone's (such as your parent's) 2005 tax return.

Use the worksheet in the instructions to figure your student loan interest deduction.
Exception. Use Pub. 970 instead of the worksheet in the instructions to figure your student loan interest deduction if you file Form 2555, 2555-EZ, or 4563, or you exclude income from sources within Puerto Rico.

A qualified student loan is any loan you took out to pay the qualified higher education expenses for yourself, your spouse, or anyone who was your dependent when the loan was taken out. The person for whom the expenses were paid must have been an eligible student (see this page). However, a loan is not a qualified student loan if (a) any of the proceeds were used for other purposes, or (b) the loan was from either a related person or a person who borrowed the proceeds under a qualified employer plan or a contract purchased under such a plan. To find out who is a related person, see Pub. 970.

Qualified higher education expenses generally include tuition, fees, room and board, and related expenses such as books and supplies. The expenses must be for education in a degree, certificate, or similar program at an eligible educational institution. An eligible educational institution includes most colleges, universities, and certain vocational schools. You must reduce the expenses by the following benefits.

- Employer-provided educational assistance benefits that are not included in Form(s) W-2, box 1.
- Excludable U.S. series EE and I savings bond interest from Form 8815.
- Nontaxable qualified state tuition program earnings.
- Nontaxable earnings from Coverdell education savings accounts.
- Any scholarship, educational assistance allowance, or other payment (but not gifts, inheritances, etc.) excluded from income.

For more details on these expenses, see Pub. 970.
An eligible student is a person who:

- Was enrolled in a degree, certificate, or other program (including a program of study abroad that was approved for credit by the institution at which the student was enrolled) leading to a recognized educational credential at an eligible educational institution, and
- Carried at least half the normal full-time workload for the course of study he or she was pursuing.

Line 34
Tuition and Fees Deduction

You can take this deduction only if all of the following apply.

- You paid qualified tuition and fees (see this page) in 2005 for yourself, your spouse, or your dependent(s).
- Your filing status is any status except married filing separately.
- Your modified adjusted gross income (AGI) is not more than: $80,000 if single, head of household, or qualifying widow(er); $160,000 if married filing jointly. Use lines 1 through 3 of the worksheet in the instructions to figure your modified AGI.
- You cannot be claimed as a dependent on someone's (such as your parent's) 2005 tax return.
- You are not claiming an education credit for the same student. See the instructions for line 50.
- You were a U.S. citizen or resident alien for all of 2005 or you were a nonresident alien for any part of 2005 and you are filing a joint return.

Use the worksheet in the instructions to figure your tuition and fees deduction.
Exception. Use Pub. 970 instead of the worksheet in the instructions to figure your tuition and fees deduction if you file Form 2555, 2555-EZ, or 4563, or you exclude income from sources within Puerto Rico.

Qualified tuition and fees are amounts paid in 2005 for tuition and fees required for the student's enrollment or attendance at an eligible educational institution during 2005. Tuition and fees paid in 2005 for an academic period that begins in the first 3 months of 2006 can also be used in figuring your deduction. Amounts paid include those paid by credit card or with borrowed funds. An eligible educational institution includes most colleges, universities, and certain vocational schools.

Qualified tuition and fees do not include amounts paid for the following amounts:

- Room and board, insurance, medical expenses (including student health fees), transportation, or other similar personal, living, or family expenses.
- Course-related books, supplies, equipment, and nonacademic activities, except for fees required to be paid to the institution as a condition of enrollment or attendance.
- Any course involving sports, games, or hobbies, unless such course is part of the student's degree program.

Qualified tuition and fees must be reduced by the following benefits.

- Excludable U.S. series EE and I savings bond interest from Form 8815.
- Nontaxable qualified state tuition program earnings.
- Nontaxable earnings from Coverdell education savings accounts.
- Any scholarship, educational assistance allowance, or other payment (but not gifts, inheritances, etc.) excluded from income.

For more details, use TeleTax topic 457 or see Pub. 970.
Tip. *You may be able to take a credit for your educational expenses instead of a deduction. See the instructions for line 50 for details.*

Line 35
Domestic production activities deduction.

You can deduct 3% of the smaller of:

1. Your adjusted gross income determined without regard to this deduction, or
2. Your qualified production activities income from the following trade or business activities.
   a. Construction performed in the United States.
   b. Engineering or architectural services performed in the United States for construction projects in the United States.

c. Any lease, rental, license, sale, exchange, or other disposition of:
   i. Tangible personal property, computer software, and sound recordings that you manufactured, produced, grew, or extracted in whole or in significant part within the United States.
   ii. Any qualified film (defined later) you produced.

   iii. Electricity, natural gas, or potable water you produced in the United States.

The deduction does not apply to income derived from the sale of food and beverages you prepare at a retail establishment; property you leased, licensed, or rented for use by any related person; or the transmission or distribution of electricity, natural gas, or potable water.

See the instructions for Form 8903.

[IRS text intentionally omitted]

Line 36

Include in the total on line 36 any of the following write-in adjustments. To find out if you can take the deduction, see the form or publication indicated. On the dotted line next to line 36, enter the amount of your deduction and identify it as indicated.

- Archer MSA deduction (see Form 8853). Identify as "MSA."
- Jury duty pay if you gave the pay to your employer because your employer paid your salary while you served on the jury. Identified as "Jury Pay."
- Deductible expenses related to income reported on line 21 from the rental of personal property engaged in for profit. Identify as "PPR."
- Reforestation amortization and expenses (see Pub. 535). Identify as "RFST."
- Repayment of supplemental unemployment benefits under the Trade Act of 1974 (see Pub. 525). Identify as "Sub-Pay TRA."
- Contributions to section 501(c)(18)(D) pension plans (see Pub. 525). Identify as "501(c)(18)(D)."
- Contributions by certain chaplains to section 403(b) plans (see Pub. 517). Identify as "403(b)."
- Attorney fees and court costs paid after October 22, 2004, for actions settled or decided after that date involving certain unlawful discrimination claims, but only to the extent of gross income from such actions (see Pub. 525). Identify as "UDC."
- Deduction for clean-fuel vehicles. If you placed a qualified clean-fuel vehicle in service in 2005, you can deduct $2,000 on line 36 if you did not use the vehicle in your business (other than as an employee). Identify this deduction on line 36 as "Clean-Fuel."

If you used a qualified clean-fuel vehicle or other clean-fuel vehicle property in your business (other than as an employee), claim the business portion of the deduction on the applicable line of Schedule C, E, or F.

Tip. *There are higher deduction amounts for heavy trucks, vans, and buses.*

A qualified clean-fuel vehicle:

1. Must be acquired new and for your own use.
2. Must satisfy any federal and state emissions standards.
3. Is designed to be propelled by a clean-burning fuel, such as natural gas, liquefied natural gas, liquefied petroleum gas, hydrogen, or electricity.

A qualified clean-fuel vehicle includes certain gasoline-electric hybrid vehicles such as the Honda Insight, Honda Civic Hybrid, and Toyota Prius. It does not include electric vehicles.

Tip. *You may be able to take a credit if you placed a new electric vehicle in service in 2005. See Form 8834 for details.*

You may also be able to take this deduction for certain new property installed on a motor vehicle to enable it to be propelled by a clean-burning fuel.

For more details, see Pub. 535.

Line 37

If line 37 is less than zero, you may have a net operating loss that you can carry to another tax year. See the Instructions for Form 1045 for details.

Tax and Credits
Line 39a

If you were born before January 2, 1941, or were blind at the end of 2005, check the appropriate box(es) on line 39a. If you were married and checked the box on Form 1040, line 6b, and your spouse was born before January 2, 1941, or was blind at the end of 2005, also check the appropriate box(es) for your spouse. Be sure to enter the total number of boxes checked.

Blindness

If you were partially blind as of December 31, 2005, you must get a statement certified by your eye doctor or registered optometrist that:

- You cannot see better than 20/200 in your better eye with glasses or contact lenses, or
- Your field of vision is 20 degrees or less.

If your eye condition is not likely to improve beyond the conditions listed above, you can get a statement certified by your eye doctor or registered optometrist to this effect instead.

You must keep the statement for your records.

Line 39b

If your spouse itemizes deductions on a separate return or if you were a dual-status alien, check the box on line 39b. But if you were a dual-status alien and you file a joint return with your spouse who was a U.S. citizen or resident at the end of 2005 and you and your spouse agree to be taxed on your combined worldwide income, do not check the box.

Line 40
Itemized Deductions or Standard Deduction

In most cases, your federal income tax will be less if you take the larger of your itemized deductions or standard deduction.

Caution. *If you checked the box on line 39b, your standard deduction is zero.*

Itemized Deductions

To figure your itemized deductions, fill in Schedule A.

Standard Deduction

Most people can find their standard deduction by looking at the amounts listed under "All others" to the left of Form 1040, line 40. But if you, or your spouse if filing jointly, can be claimed as a dependent on someone's 2005 return or you checked any box on line 39a, use the worksheet or the chart in the instructions, whichever applies, to figure your standard deduction. Also, if you checked the box on line 39b, your standard deduction is zero, even if you were born before January 2, 1941, or were blind.

Electing To Itemize for State Tax or Other Purposes

If you itemize even though your itemized deductions are less than your standard deduction, enter "IE" on the dotted line next to line 40.

Line 44
Tax

Do you want the IRS to figure your tax for you?

❑ **Yes.** See Pub. 967 for details, including who is eligible and what to do. If you have paid too much, we will send you a refund. If you did not pay enough, we will send you a bill.

❑ **No.** Use one of the following methods to figure your tax. Also include in the total on line 44 any of the following taxes.

1. Tax from Forms 8814 and 4972. Be sure to check the appropriate box(es).
2. Tax from recapture of an education credit. You may owe this tax if (a) you claimed an education credit in an earlier year, and (b) you, your spouse if filing jointly, or your dependent received in 2005 either tax-free educational assistance or a refund of qualified expenses. See Form 8863 for more details. If you owe this tax, enter the amount and "ECR" on the dotted line next to line 44.

Tax Table or Tax Computation Worksheet. If your taxable income is less than $100,000, you must use the Tax Table in the instructions to figure your tax. Be sure you use the correct column. If your taxable income is $100,000 or more, use the Tax Computation Worksheet available in Pub. 17 at www.irs.gov.

However, do not use the Tax Table or Tax Computation Worksheet to figure your tax if any of the following apply.

Form 8615. Form 8615 must generally be used to figure the tax for any child who was under age 14 at the end of 2005, and who had more than $1,600 of investment income, such as taxable interest, ordinary dividends, or capital gains (including capital gain distributions). But if neither of the child's parents was alive at the end of 2005, do not use Form 8615 to figure the child's tax. Also, a child born on January 1, 1992, is considered to be age 14 at the end of 2005. Do not use Form 8615 for such a child.

Schedule D Tax Worksheet. If you have to file Schedule D and Schedule D, line 18 or 19, is more than zero, use the Schedule D Tax Worksheet on page D-9 of the Instructions for Schedule D to figure your tax.

Qualified Dividends and Capital Gain Tax Worksheet. If you do not have to use the Schedule D Tax Worksheet (see above), use the worksheet available in Pub. 17 at www.irs.gov to figure your tax if any of the following apply.

• You reported qualified dividends on Form 1040, line 9b.
• You do not have to file Schedule D and you reported capital gain distributions on Form 1040, line 13.
• You are filing Schedule D and Schedule D, lines 15 and 16, are both more than zero.

Schedule J. If you had income from farming or fishing, your tax may be less if you choose to figure it using income averaging on Schedule J.

Line 45
Alternative Minimum Tax

Use the worksheet in the instructions to see if you should fill in Form 6251.
Exception. Fill in Form 6251 instead of using the worksheet in the instructions if you claimed or received any of the following items.

• Accelerated depreciation.
• Stock by exercising an incentive stock option and you did not dispose of the stock in the same year.
• Tax-exempt interest from private activity bonds.
• Intangible drilling, circulation, research, experimental, or mining costs.
• Amortization of pollution-control facilities or depletion.
• Income or (loss) from tax-shelter farm activities or passive activities.

• Income from long-term contracts not figured using the percentage-of-completion method.
• Interest paid on a home mortgage not used to buy, build, or substantially improve your home.
• Investment interest expense reported on Form 4952.
• Net operating loss deduction.
• Alternative minimum tax adjustments from an estate, trust, electing large partnership, or cooperative.
• Section 1202 exclusion.
• A general business credit.

Caution. *Form 6251 should be filled in for a child who was under age 14 at the end of 2005 if the child's adjusted gross income from Form 1040, line 38, exceeds the child's earned income by more than $5,850.*

Line 47
Foreign Tax Credit

If you paid income tax to a foreign country, you may be able to take this credit. Generally, you must complete and attach Form 1116 to do so.
Exception. You do not have to complete Form 1116 to take this credit if all five of the following apply.

1. All of your gross foreign source income was from interest and dividends and all of that income and the foreign tax paid on it were reported to you on Form 1099-INT or Form 1099-DIV, or Schedule K-1 (or substitute statement).
2. If you have dividend income from shares of stock, you held those shares for at least 16 days.
3. You are not filing Form 4563 or excluding income from sources within Puerto Rico.
4. The total of your foreign taxes was not more than $300 (not more than $600 if married filing jointly).
5. All of your foreign taxes were:
   a. Legally owed and not eligible for a refund, and
   b. Paid to countries that are recognized by the United States and do not support terrorism.

For more details on these requirements, see the Instructions for Form 1116.
Do you meet all five requirements above?

❑ **Yes.** Enter on line 47 the smaller of (a) your total foreign taxes, or (b) the amount on Form 1040, line 44.
❑ **No.** See Form 1116 to find out if you can take the credit and, if you can, if you have to file Form 1116.

Line 48
Credit for Child and Dependent Care Expenses

You may be able to take this credit if you paid someone to care for your child under age 13 or your dependent or spouse who could not care for himself or herself. For details, use TeleTax topic 602 or see Form 2441.

Line 49
Credit for the Elderly or the Disabled

You may be able to take this credit if by the end of 2005 (a) you were age 65 or older, or (b) you retired on permanent and total disability and you had taxable disability income. But you usually cannot take the credit if the amount on Form 1040, line 38, is $17,500 or more ($20,000 or more if married filing jointly and only one spouse is eligible for the credit; $25,000 or more if married filing jointly and both spouses are eligible; $12,500 or more if married filing separately). See Schedule R and its instructions for details.
Credit Figured by the IRS. If you can take this credit and you want us to figure it for you, see the Instructions for Schedule R.

Line 50
Education Credits

If you (or your dependent) paid qualified expenses in 2005 for yourself, your spouse, or your dependent to enroll in or attend an eligible educational institution, you may be able to take an education credit. See Form 8863 for details. However, you cannot take an education credit if any of the following apply.

- You are claimed as a dependent on someone's (such as your parent's) 2005 tax return.
- Your filing status is married filing separately.
- The amount on Form 1040, line 38, is $53,000 or more ($107,000 or more if married filing jointly).
- You are taking a deduction for tuition and fees on Form 1040, line 34, for the same student.
- You (or your spouse) were a nonresident alien for any part of 2005 unless your filing status is married filing jointly.

Line 51
Retirement Savings Contributions Credit

You may be able to take this credit if you, or your spouse if filing jointly, made (a) contributions to a traditional or Roth IRA; (b) elective deferrals to a 401(k), 403(b), governmental 457, SEP, or SIMPLE plan; (c) voluntary employee contributions to a qualified retirement plan (including the federal Thrift Savings Plan); or (d) contributions to a 501(c)(18)(D) plan.
  However, you cannot take the credit if either of the following applies.

1. The amount on Form 1040, line 38, is more than $25,000 ($37,500 if head of household; $50,000 if married filing jointly).
2. The person(s) who made the qualified contribution or elective deferral (a) was born after January 1, 1988, (b) is claimed as a dependent on someone else's 2005 tax return, or (c) was a student (defined below).

You were a student if during any 5 months of 2005 you:

- Were enrolled as a full-time student at a school, or
- Took a full-time, on-farm training course given by a school or a state, county, or local government agency.

A school includes technical, trade, or mechanical schools. It does not include an on-the-job training course, correspondence school, or night school.
  For more details, use TeleTax topic 610 or see Form 8880.

Line 52—Child Tax Credit
What is the Child Tax Credit?

This credit is for people who have a qualifying child (defined below). It is in addition to the credit for child and dependent care expenses on Form 1040, line 48, and the earned income credit on Form 1040, line 66a.

Three Steps To Take the Child Tax Credit!

Step 1. Make sure you have a qualifying child for the child tax credit (defined below).
Step 2. Make sure you checked the box on Form 1040, line 6c, column (4), for each qualifying child.
Step 3. Answer the questions on this page to see if you may use the worksheet in the instructions to figure your credit or if you must use Pub. 972, Child Tax Credit available at www.irs.gov.

Qualifying Child for Child Tax Credit

A qualifying child for purposes of the child tax credit is a qualifying child as defined for purposes of the dependency deduction, who [IRS text intentionally omitted] was under age 17 at the end of 2005.

Line 53
Adoption Credit

You may be able to take this credit if either of the following applies.

- You paid expenses to adopt a child.
- You adopted a child with special needs and the adoption became final in 2005.

  See the Instructions for Form 8839 for details.

Line 54

Include the following credits on line 54 and check the appropriate box(es). To find out if you can take the credit, see the form indicated.

- Mortgage interest credit. If a state or local government gave you a mortgage credit certificate, see Form 8396.
- District of Columbia first-time homebuyer credit. See Form 8859.

Line 55
Other Credits

Include the following credits on line 55 and check the appropriate box(es). If box c is checked, also enter the form number, if applicable. To find out if you can take the credit, see the form or publication indicated.

- Credit for prior year minimum tax. If you paid alternative minimum tax in a prior year, see Form 8801.
- Qualified electric vehicle credit. If you placed a new electric vehicle in service in 2005, see Form 8834.
- General business credit. This credit consists of a number of credits that usually apply only to individuals who are partners, shareholders in an S corporation, self-employed, or who have rental property. See Form 3800 or Pub. 334.
- Empowerment zone and renewal community employment credit. See Form 8844.
- New York Liberty Zone business employee credit. See Form 8884.
- Nonconventional source fuel credit. If you sold fuel produced from a nonconventional source, or you were an owner of royalty interests and you received income from the sale of fuel produced from a nonconventional source, you may be able to take this credit. See Internal Revenue Code section 29 and, if an owner of royalty interests, Rev. Proc. 2004-27, 2004-17 I.R.B. 831. You can find Rev. Proc. 2004-27 on page 831 of Internal Revenue Bulletin 2004-17 at *www.irs.gov/pub/irs-irbs/irb04-17.pdf*. Attach a schedule showing how you figured the credit. Check box c and enter "FNS" on the line to the right of box c.
- Qualified zone academy bond credit. This credit applies only to S corporation shareholders. See Form 8860.

Other Taxes

Line 59
Social Security and Medicare Tax on Tip Income Not Reported to Employer

If you received tips of $20 or more in any month and you did not report the full amount to your employer, you must pay the social security and Medicare or railroad retirement (RRTA) tax on the unreported tips. You must also pay this tax if your Form(s) W-2 shows allocated tips that you are including in your income on Form 1040, line 7.
  To figure the social security and Medicare tax, use Form 4137. If you owe RRTA tax, contact your employer. Your employer will figure and collect the RRTA tax.
Caution. *You may be charged a penalty equal to 50% of the social security and Medicare tax due on tips you received but did not report to your employer.*

Line 60
Additional Tax on IRAs, Other Qualified Retirement Plans, etc.

If any of the following apply, see Form 5329 and its instructions to find out if you owe this tax and if you must file Form 5329.

1. You received any early distributions from (a) an IRA or other qualified retirement plan, (b) an annuity, or (c) a modified endowment contract entered into after June 20, 1988, and the total distribution was not rolled over in a qualified rollover contribution.
2. Excess contributions were made to your IRAs, Coverdell education savings accounts (ESAs), Archer MSAs, or health savings accounts.
3. You received taxable distributions from Coverdell ESAs or qualified tuition programs.
4. You were born before July 1, 1934, and did not take the minimum required distribution from your IRA or other qualified retirement plan.

Exception. If only item 1 applies to you and distribution code 1 is correctly shown in Form 1099-R, box 7, you do not have to file Form 5329. Instead, multiply the taxable amount of the distribution by 10% (.10) and enter the result on line 60. The taxable amount of the distribution you reported on Form 1040, line 15b or line 16b, or on Form 4972. Also, put "No" under the heading *Other Taxes* to the left of line 60 to indicate that you do not have to file Form 5329. But if distribution code 1 is incorrectly shown in Form 1099-R, box 7, or you qualify for an exception for qualified medical expenses, qualified higher education expenses, or qualified first-time homebuyer distributions, you must file Form 5329.

Line 61
Advance Earned Income Credit Payments

Enter the total amount of advance earned income credit (EIC) payments you received. These payments are shown in Form(s) W-2, box 9.

Line 62
Household Employment Taxes

If any of the following apply, see Schedule H and its instructions to find out if you owe these taxes.

1. You paid any one household employee (defined below) cash wages of $1,400 or more in 2005. Cash wages include wages paid by check, money order, etc.
2. You withheld federal income tax during 2005 at the request of any household employee.
3. You paid total cash wages of $1,000 or more in any calendar quarter of 2004 or 2005 to household employees.

Tip. *For item (1), do not count amounts paid to an employee who was under age 18 at any time in 2005 and was a student.*
Household Employee. Any person who does household work is a household employee if you can control what will be done and how it will be done. Household work includes work done in or around your home by babysitters, nannies, health aides, maids, yard workers, and similar domestic workers.

Line 63
Total Tax

Include in the total on line 63 any of the following taxes. To find out if you owe the tax, see the form or publication indicated. On the dotted line next to line 63, enter the amount of the tax and identify it as indicated.

1. Additional tax on health savings account distributions (see Form 8889). Identify as "HSA."
2. Additional tax on Archer MSA distributions (see Form 8853). Identify as "MSA."
3. Additional tax on Medicare Advantage MSA distributions (see Form 8853). Identify as "Med MSA."
4. Recapture of the following credits.
   a. Investment credit (see Form 4255). Identify as "ICR."
   b. Low-income housing credit (see Form 8611). Identify as "LIHCR."
   c. Qualified electric vehicle credit (see Pub. 535). Identify as "QEVCR."
   d. Indian employment credit (see Form 8845). Identify as "IECR."
   e. New markets credit (see Form 8874). Identify as "NMCR."
   f. Credit for employer-provided child care facilities (see Form 8882). Identify as "ECCFR."
5. Recapture of federal mortgage subsidy. If you sold your home in 2005 and it was financed (in whole or in part) from the proceeds of any tax-exempt qualified mortgage bond or you claimed the mortgage interest credit, see Form 8828. Identify as "FMSR."
6. Section 72(m)(5) excess benefits tax (see Pub. 560). Identify as "Sec. 72(m)(5)."
7. Uncollected social security and medicare or RRTA tax on tips or group-term life insurance. This tax should be shown in Form W-2, box 12, with codes A and B or M and N. Identify as "UT."
8. Golden parachute payments. If you received an excess parachute payment (EPP), you must pay a 20% tax on it. This tax should be shown in Form W-2, box 12, with code K. If you received a Form 1099-MISC, the tax is 20% of the EPP shown in box 13. Identify as "EPP."
9. Tax on accumulation distribution of trusts (see Form 4970). Identify as "ADT."
10. Excise tax on insider stock compensation from an expatriated corporation. You may owe a 15% excise tax on the value of nonstatutory stock options and certain other stock-based compensation held by you or a member of your family from an expatriated corporation or its expanded affiliated group in which you were an officer, director, or more-than-10% owner. See Internal Revenue Code section 4985. Identify as "ISC."
11. Nonqualified deferred compensation. If you are a participant in a nonqualified deferred compensation plan which fails to meet the requirements of Section 409A of the Internal Revenue Code, you must pay a 20% tax, plus interest in certain cases. The amount subject to the tax should be shown in Form W-2, box 12, with code Z. Identify as "409A."

Payments
Line 64
Federal Income Tax Withheld

Add the amounts shown as Federal income tax withheld on your Forms W-2, W-2G, and 1099-R. Enter the total on line 64. The amount withheld should be shown in Form W-2 or W-2G, box 2, and in Form 1099-R, box 4. Attach Forms W-2G and 1099-R to the front of your return if federal tax was withheld.

If you received a 2005 Form 1099 showing federal income tax withheld on dividends, interest income, unemployment compensation, social security benefits, or other income you received, include the amount withheld in the total on line 64. This should be shown in Form 1099, box 4, or Form SSA-1099, box 6.

Line 65
2005 Estimated Tax Payments

Enter any estimated federal income tax payments you made using Form 1040-ES for 2005. Include any overpayment from your 2004 return that you applied to your 2005 estimated tax.

If you and your spouse paid joint estimated tax but are now filing separate income tax returns, you can divide the amount paid in any way you choose as long as you both agree. If you cannot agree, you must divide the payments in proportion to each spouse's individual tax as shown on your separate returns for 2005. For an example of how to do this, see Pub. 505. Be sure to show both social security numbers (SSNs) in the space provided on the separate returns. If you or your spouse paid separate estimated tax but you are now filing a joint return, add the amounts you each paid. Follow these instructions even if your spouse died in 2005 or in 2006 before filing a 2005 return.

Divorced Taxpayers

If you got divorced in 2005 and you made joint estimated tax payments with your former spouse, put your former spouse's SSN in the space provided on the front of Form 1040. If you were divorced and remarried in 2005, put your present spouse's SSN in the space provided on the front of Form 1040. Also, under the heading *Payments* to the left of line 65, put your former spouse's SSN, followed by "DIV."

Name Change

If you changed your name because of marriage, divorce, etc., and you made estimated tax payments using your former name, attach a statement to the front of Form 1040. On the statement, explain all the payments you and your spouse made in 2005 and the name(s) and SSN(s) under which you made them.

Line 67
Excess Social Security and Tier 1 RRTA Tax Withheld

If you, or your spouse if filing a joint return, had more than one employer for 2005 and total wages of more than $90,000, too much social security or tier 1 railroad retirement (RRTA) tax may have been withheld. You can take a credit on this line for the amount withheld in excess of $5,5580. But if any one employer withheld more than $5,580, you must ask that employer to refund the excess to you. You cannot claim it on your return. Figure this amount separately for you and your spouse.

You cannot claim a refund for excess tier 2 RRTA tax on Form 1040. Instead, use Form 843.

For more details, see Pub. 505.

Line 68
Additional Child Tax Credit

What is the Additional Child Tax Credit?

This credit is for certain people who have at least one qualifying child as defined in the instructions for line 52. The additional child tax credit may give you a refund even if you do not owe any tax.

Two Steps To Take the Additional Child Tax Credit!

Step 1. Be sure you figured the amount, if any, of your child tax credit. See the instructions for line 52.
Step 2. Read the **TIP** at the end of your Child Tax Credit Worksheet. Use Form 8812 to see if you can take the additional child tax credit, but only if you meet the condition given in that TIP.

Line 69
Amount Paid With Request for Extension To File

If you filed Form 4868 to get an automatic extension of time to file Form 1040, enter any amount you paid with that form or by electronic funds withdrawal or credit card. If you paid by credit card, do not include on line 69 the convenience fee you were charged. Also, include any amounts paid with Form 2350.

Line 70
Other Payments

Check the box(es) on line 70 to report any credit from Form 2439, 4136, or 8885.

Refund

Line 72
Amount Overpaid

If line 72 is under $1, we will send a refund only on written request.

If you want to check the status of your refund, please wait at least 6 weeks (3 weeks if you filed electronically) from the date you filed your return to do so. But if you filed Form 8379 with your return, allow 14 weeks (11 weeks if you filed electronically).

Tip. *If the amount you overpaid is large, you may want to decrease the amount of income tax withheld from your pay be filing new Form W-4.*

Refund Offset

If you owe past-due federal tax, state income tax, child support, spousal support, or certain federal non-tax debts, such as student loans, all or part of the overpayment on line 72 may be used (offset) to pay the past-due amount. Offsets for federal taxes are made by the IRS. All other offsets are made by the Treasury Department's Financial Management Service (FMS). For federal tax offsets, you will receive a notice from the IRS. For all other offsets, you will re-

Sample Check—Lines 73b Through 73d

 The routing and account numbers may be in different places on your check.

ceive a notice from FMS. To find out if you may have an offset or if you have any questions about it, contact the agency to which you owe the debt.

Injured Spouse Claim

If you file a joint return and your spouse has not paid past-due federal tax, state income tax, child support, spousal support, or a federal nontax debt, such as a student loan, part or all of the overpayment on line 72 may be used (offset) to pay the past-due amount. But your part of the overpayment may be refunded to you if certain conditions apply and you complete Form 8379. For details, use TeleTax topic 203 or see Form 8379.

Lines 73b Through 73d
DIRECT DEPOSIT *Simple. Safe. Secure.*

Fast Refunds! Choose direct deposit—a fast, simple, safe, secure way to have your refund deposited automatically into your checking or savings account.

Complete lines 73b through 73d if you want us to directly deposit the amount shown on line 73a into your checking or savings account at a bank or other financial institution (such as a mutual fund, brokerage firm, or credit union) in the United States instead of sending you a check.
Note. If you do not want your refund directly deposited into your account, draw a line through the boxes on lines 73b and 73d.

Why Use Direct Deposit?

- You get your refund fast—in half the time as paper filers if you *e-file*.
- Payment is more secure—there is no check to get lost.
- More convenient. No trip to the bank to deposit your check.
- Saves tax dollars. A refund by direct deposit costs less than a check.

Tip. *You can check with your financial institution to make sure your direct deposit will be accepted and to get the correct routing and account numbers. The IRS is not responsible for a lost refund if you enter the wrong account information.*

If you file a joint return and fill in lines 73b through 73d, you are appointing your spouse as an agent to receive the refund. This appointment cannot be changed later.

Line 73b

The routing number must be nine digits. The first two digits must be 01 through 12 or 21 through 32. Otherwise, the direct deposit will be rejected and a check sent instead. On the sample check on the previous page, the routing number is 250250025.

Your check may state that it is payable through a financial institution different from the one at which you have your checking account. If so, do not use the routing number on that check. Instead, contact your financial institution for the correct routing number to enter on line 73b.

Line 73d

The account number can be up to 17 characters (both numbers and letters). Include hyphens but omit spaces and special symbols. Enter the number from left to right and leave any unused boxes blank. On the sample check on the previous page, the account number is 20202086. Do not include the check number.
Caution. *Some financial institutions will not allow a joint refund to be deposited into an individual account. If the direct deposit is rejected, a check will be sent instead. The IRS is not responsible if a financial institution rejects a direct deposit.*

Line 74
Applied to Your 2006 Estimated Tax

Enter on line 74 the amount, if any, of the overpayment on line 72 you want applied to your 2006 estimated tax. We will apply this amount to your account unless you attach a statement requesting us to apply it to your spouse's account. Include your spouse's social security number in the attached statement.
Caution. *This election to apply part or all of the amount overpaid to your 2006 estimated tax cannot be changed later.*

Amount You Owe

IRS *e-file* offers an additional payment option: Electronic funds withdrawal. This option allows you to file your return early and schedule your payment for withdrawal from your checking or savings account on a future date up to and including April 17, 2006. IRS *e-file* also provides proof of receipt of your return and payment by email or through your software package. Visit *www.irs.gov/efile* for details.

Line 75
Amount You Owe

Tip. *Pay your taxes in full by April 17, 2006, to save interest and penalties. You do not have to pay if line 75 is under $1.*
Include any estimated tax penalty from line 76 in the amount you enter on line 75.
You can pay by check, money order, or credit card. Do not include any estimated tax payment for 2006 in your check, money order, or amount you charge. Instead, make the estimated tax payment separately.
To pay by check or money order. Make your check or money order payable to the **"United States Treasury"** for the full amount due. Do not send cash. Do not attach the payment to your return. Write "2005 Form 1040" and your name, address, daytime phone number, and social security number (SSN) on your payment. If you are filing a joint return, enter the SSN shown first on your tax return.
To help process your payment, enter the amount on the right side of the check like this: $ XXX.XX. Do not use dashes or lines (for example, do not enter "$ XXX–" or "$ XXX xx/100").
Then, please complete Form 1040-V following the instructions on that form and enclose it in the envelope with your tax return and payment. Although you do not have to use Form 1040-V, doing so allows us to process your payment more accurately and efficiently.
To pay by credit card. You may use your American Express® Card, Discover® Card, Mastercard® card, or Visa® card. To pay by credit card, call toll free or visit the website of either service provider listed on this page and follow the instructions. A convenience fee will be charged by the service provider based on the amount you are paying. Fees may vary between the providers. You will be told what the fee is during the transaction and you will have the option to either continue or cancel the transaction. You can also find out what the fee will be by calling the provider's toll-free automated customer service number or visiting the provider's website shown below. If you pay by credit card before filing your return, please enter on page 1 of Form 1040 in the upper left corner the confirmation number you were given at the end of the transaction and the amount you charged (not including the convenience fee).

Official Payments Corporation
1-800-2PAY-TAX℠ (1-800-272-9829)
1-877-754-4413 (Customer Service)
www.officialpayments.com

Link2Gov Corporation
1-888-PAY-l040℠ (1-888-729-1040)
1-888-658-5465 (Customer Service)
www.PAY1040.com

Tip. *You may need to (a) increase the amount of income tax withheld from your pay by filing a new Form W-4 or (b) make estimated tax payments for 2006. See* Income Tax Withholding and Estimated Tax Payments for 2006.

What if You Cannot Pay?

If you cannot pay the full amount shown on line 75 when you file, you may ask to make monthly installment payments for the full or partial amount. You may have up to 60 months to pay. However, you will be charged interest and may be charged a late payment penalty on the tax not paid by April 17, 2006, even if your request to pay in installments is granted. You must also pay a fee. To limit the interest and penalty charges, pay as much of the tax as possible when you file. But before requesting an installment agreement, you should consider other less costly alternatives, such as a bank loan or credit card payment.

To ask for an installment agreement, use Form 9465. You should receive a response to your request for installments within 30 days. But if you file your return after March 31, it may take us longer to reply.

Line 76
Estimated Tax Penalty

You may owe this penalty if:

- Line 75 is at least $1,000 and it is more than 10% of the tax shown on your return, or
- You did not pay enough estimated tax by any of the due dates. This is true even if you are due a refund.

For most people, the "tax shown on your return" is the amount on line 63 minus the total of any amounts shown on lines 66a and 68 and Forms 8828, 4137, 4136, 5329 (Parts III through VIII only), and 8885. When figuring the amount on line 63, include the amount on line 62 only if line 64 is more than zero or you would owe the penalty even if you did not include those taxes. But if you entered an amount on Schedule H, line 7, include the total of that amount plus the amount on Form 1040, line 62.

Exception. You will not owe the penalty if your 2004 tax return was for a tax year of 12 full months and either of the following applies.

1. You had no tax liability for 2004 and you were a U.S. citizen or resident for all of 2004, or
2. The total of lines 64, 65, and 67 on your 2005 return is at least as much as the tax liability shown on your 2004 return. Your estimated tax payments for 2005 must have been made on time and for the required amount.

Caution. *If your 2004 adjusted gross income was over $150,000 (over $75,000 if your 2005 filing status is married filing separately), item 2 above applies only if the total of lines 64, 65, and 67 on your 2005 return is at least 110% of the tax liability shown on your 2004 return. This rule does not apply to farmers and fishermen.*

Figuring the Penalty

If the *Exception* above does not apply and you choose to figure the penalty yourself, see Form 2210 (or 2210-F for farmers and fishermen) to find out if you owe the penalty. If you do, you can use the form to figure the amount.

Enter the penalty on line 76. Add the penalty to any tax due and enter the total on line 75. If you are due a refund, subtract the penalty from the overpayment you show on line 72. Do not file Form 2210 with your return unless Form 2210 indicates that you must do so. Instead, keep it for your records.

Tip. *Because Form 2210 is complicated, if you want to, you can* leave line 76 blank and the IRS will figure the penalty and send you a bill. We will not charge you interest on the penalty if you pay by the date specified on the bill. If your income varied during the year, the annualized income installment method may reduce the amount of your penalty. But you must file Form 2210 because the IRS cannot figure your penalty under this method. See the Instructions for Form 2210 for other situations in which you may be able to lower your penalty by filing Form 2210.

Third Party Designee

If you want to allow a friend, family member, or any other person you choose to discuss your 2005 tax return with the IRS, check the "Yes" box in the "Third Party Designee" area of your return. Also, enter the designee's name, phone number, and any five digits the designee chooses as his or her personal identification number (PIN). But if you want to allow the paid preparer who signed your return to discuss it with the IRS, just enter "Preparer" in the space for the designee's name. You do not have to provide the other information requested.

If you check the "Yes" box, you, and your spouse if filing a joint return, are authorizing the IRS to call the designee to answer any questions that may arise during the processing of your return. You are also authorizing the designee to:

- Give the IRS any information that is missing from your return,
- Call the IRS for information about the processing of your return or the status of your refund or payment(s),
- Receive copies of notices or transcripts related to your return, upon request, and
- Respond to certain IRS notices about math errors, offsets, and return preparation.

You are not authorizing the designee to receive any refund check, bind you to anything (including any additional tax liability), or otherwise represent you before the IRS. If you want to expand the designee's authorization, see Pub. 947.

The authorization will automatically end no later than the due date (without regard to extensions) for filing your 2006 tax return. This is April 16, 2007, for most people. If you wish to revoke the authorization before it ends, see Pub. 947.

Sign Your Return

Form 1040 is not considered a valid return unless you sign it. If you are filing a joint return, your spouse must also sign. If your spouse cannot sign the return, see Pub. 501. Be sure to date your return and enter your occupation(s). If you have someone prepare your return, you are still responsible for the correctness of the return. If your return is signed by a representative for you, you must have a power of attorney attached that specifically authorizes the representative to sign your return. To do this, you can use Form 2848. If you are filing a joint return as a surviving spouse, see *Death of a Taxpayer.*

Child's Return

If your child cannot sign the return, either parent can sign the child's name in the space provided. Then, add "By (your signature), parent for minor child."

Daytime Phone Number

Providing your daytime phone number may help speed the processing of your return. We may have questions about items on your return, such as the earned income credit, credit for child and dependent care expenses, etc. By answering our questions over the phone, we may be able to continue processing your return without mailing you a letter. If you are filing a joint return, you may enter either your or your spouse's daytime phone number.

Paid Preparer Must Sign Your Return

Generally, anyone you pay to prepare your return must sign it in the space provided. The preparer must give you a copy of the return for your records. Someone who prepares your return but does not charge you should not sign your return.

Electronic Return Signatures!

Create your own personal identification number (PIN) and file a paperless return electronically or use a tax professional. If you are married filing jointly, you and your spouse will each need to create a PIN and enter these PINs as your electronic signatures.

A PIN is any combination of five digits you choose except five zeros. If you use a PIN, there is nothing to sign and nothing to mail—not even your Form W-2.

To verify your identity, you will be prompted to enter your adjusted gross income (AGI) from your originally filed 2004 federal income tax return, if applicable. Do not use your AGI from an amended return (Form 1040X), a math error notice, or an IRS examination report. AGI is the amount shown on your 2004 Form 1040, line 35; Form 1040A, line 21; Form 1040EZ, line 4; or on the TeleFile Tax Record, line I. If you do not have your 2004 income tax return, call the IRS at 1-800-829-1040 to get a free transcript of your return. You will also be prompted to enter your date of birth (DOB). Make sure your DOB is accurate and matches the information on record with the Social Security Administration by checking your annual social security statement.

Caution. *You cannot sign your return electronically if you are a first-time filer under age 16 at the end of 2005 or if you are filing Form 3115, 3468 (if attachments are required), 5713, 8283 (if Section B is completed), 8332, or 8885.*

For more details, visit *www.irs.gov/efile* and click on *"e-file for Individual Taxpayers."*

Forms 8453 and 8453-OL. Your return is not complete without your signature. If you are not eligible or choose not to sign your return electronically, you must complete, sign, and file Form 8453 or Form 8453-OL, whichever applies.

If you use a paid preparer, ask to sign your return electronically!

Assemble Your Return

Assemble any schedules and forms behind Form 1040 in order of the "Attachment Sequence No." shown in the upper right corner of the schedule or form. If you have supporting statements, arrange them in the same order as the schedules or forms they support and attach them last. Do not attach correspondence or other items unless required to do so. Attach a copy of Forms W-2 and 2439 to the front of Form 1040. Also attach Form(s) W-2G and 1099-R to the front of Form 1040 if tax was withheld.

Tax Rate Schedules

Introduction

This chapter contains the 2005 final Tax Rate Schedules, which taxpayers with taxable income of $100,000 or more must use. The 2005 Tax Tables, which were not available at press time, must be used by taxpayers with taxable income of less than $100,000. These Tax Tables can be found at www.irs.gov.

2005
Tax Rate
Schedules

Schedule X—Single

If your taxable income is:		The tax is:	of the amount over—
Over—	But not over—		
$0	$7,300	.... 10%	$0
7,300	29,700	$730.00 + 15%	7,300
29,700	71 950	4,090.00 + 25%	29,700
71 950	150,150	14,652.50 + 28%	71,950
150,150	326,450	36,548.50 + 33%	150,150
326,450	no limit	94,727.50 + 35%	326,450

Schedule Y-1—Married Filing Jointly or Qualifying Widow(er)

If your taxable income is:		The tax is:	of the amount over—
Over—	But not over—		
$0	$14,600	.... 10%	$0
14,600	59,400	$1,460.00 + 15%	14,600
59,400	119,950	8,180.00 + 25%	59,400
119,950	182,800	23,317.50 + 28%	119,950
182,800	326,450	40,915.50 + 33%	182,800
326,450	no limit	88,320.00 + 35%	326,450

Schedule Y-2—Married Filing Separately

If your taxable income is:		The tax is:	of the amount over—
Over—	But not over—		
$0	$7,300	.... 10%	$0
7,300	29,700	$730.00 + 15%	7,300
29,700	59,975	4,090.00 + 25%	29,700
59,975	91,400	11,658.75 + 28%	59,975
91,400	163,225	20,457.75 + 33%	91,400
163,225	no limit	44,160.00 + 35%	163,225

Schedule Z—Head of Household

If your taxable income is:		The tax is:	of the amount over—
Over—	But not over—		
$0	$10,450	.... 10%	$0
10,450	39,800	$1,045.00 + 15%	10,450
39,800	102,800	5,447.50 + 25%	39,800
102,800	166,450	21,197.50 + 28%	102,800
166,450	326,450	39,019.50 + 33%	166,450
326,450	no limit	91,819.50 + 35%	326,450

Order Blank for Forms and Publications

The most frequently ordered forms and publications are listed on the order blank below. We will mail you two copies of each form and one copy of each publication you order. To help reduce waste, please order only the items you need to prepare your return.

For faster ways of getting the items you need, such as by Internet or fax, see page 7.

How To Use the Order Blank

Circle the items you need on the order blank below. Use the blank spaces to order items not listed. If you need more space, attach a separate sheet of paper.

Print or type your name and address accurately in the space provided below. An accurate address will ensure delivery of your order. Cut the order blank on the dotted line. Enclose the order blank in your own envelope and send it to the IRS address shown below that applies to you. You should receive your order within 10 days after we receive your request.

Do not send your tax return to any of the addresses listed on this page. Instead, see the back cover.

Where To Mail Your Order Blank for Free Forms and Publications

IF you live in the . . .	THEN mail to . . .	AT this address . . .
Western United States	Western Area Distribution Center	Rancho Cordova, CA 95743-0001
Central United States	Central Area Distribution Center	P.O. Box 8903 Bloomington, IL 61702-8903
Eastern United States or a foreign country	Eastern Area Distribution Center	P.O. Box 85074 Richmond, VA 23261-5074

▲ *Cut here* ▲

Order Blank

Fill in your name and address.

Name

Postal mailing address ___ Apt./Suite/Room

City ___ State ___ ZIP code

Foreign country ___ International postal code

Daytime phone number
(   )

Circle the forms and publications you need. The instructions for any form you order will be included.

You can download all these items from the Internet at www.irs.gov or place an electronic order for them. The items in bold can be picked up at many IRS offices, post offices, and libraries.

1040	Schedule F (1040)	Schedule 3 (1040A)	4506	8822	Pub. 501	Pub. 535	Pub. 970
Schedules A&B (1040)	Schedule H (1040)	**1040EZ**	4562	8829	Pub. 502	Pub. 550	Pub. 972
Schedule C (1040)	Schedule J (1040)	1040-ES (2005)	4868	8863	Pub. 505	Pub. 554	
Schedule C-EZ (1040)	Schedule R (1040)	1040-V	6251	9465	Pub. 523	Pub. 575	
Schedule D (1040)	Schedule SE (1040)	1040X	8283	Pub. 1	Pub. 525	Pub. 590	
Schedule D-1 (1040)	**1040A**	2106	8582	Pub. 17	Pub. 527	Pub. 596	
Schedule E (1040)	**Schedule 1 (1040A)**	2106-EZ	8606	Pub. 334	Pub. 529	Pub. 910	
Schedule EIC (1040A or 1040)	**Schedule 2 (1040A)**	2441	8812	Pub. 463	Pub. 533	Pub. 926	

Refund Information

You can check on the status of your 2005 refund if it has been at least 6 weeks from the date you filed your return (3 weeks if you filed electronically). But if you filed Form 8379 with your return, allow 14 weeks (11 weeks if you filed electronically).

Be sure to have a copy of your 2005 tax return available because you will need to know the filing status and the exact whole-dollar amount of your refund. Then, do one of the following.

- Go to *www.irs.gov* and click on *Where's My Refund.*
- Call 1-800-829-4477 24 hours a day, 7 days a week, for automated refund information.

- Call 1-800-829-1954 during the hours shown on page 10.

Refunds are sent out weekly on Fridays. If you check the status of your refund and are not given the date it will be issued, please wait until the next week before checking back.

Do not send in a copy of your return unless asked to do so.

To get a refund, you generally must file your return within 3 years from the date the return was due (including extensions).

What Is TeleTax?

Recorded Tax Information

Recorded tax information is available 24 hours a day, 7 days a week. Select the number of the topic you want to hear. Then, call 1-800-829-4477. Have paper and pencil handy to take notes.

Topics by Internet

TeleTax topics are also available through the IRS website at *www.irs.gov.*

TeleTax Topics

All topics are available in Spanish.

Topic No.	Subject
	IRS Help Available
101	IRS services—Volunteer tax assistance, toll-free telephone, walk-in assistance, and outreach programs
102	Tax assistance for individuals with disabilities and the hearing impaired
103	Intro. to federal taxes for small businesses/self-employed
104	Taxpayer Advocate program—Help for problem situations
105	Public libraries—Tax information and reproducible tax forms
	IRS Procedures
151	Your appeal rights
152	Refunds—How long they should take
153	What to do if you haven't filed your tax return
154	2004 Form W-2 and Form 1099-R—What to do if not received
155	Forms and publications—How to order

Topic No.	Subject
156	Copy of your tax return—How to get one
157	Change of address—How to notify IRS
158	Ensuring proper credit of payments
159	Prior year(s) Form W-2—How to get a copy of
	Collection
201	The collection process
202	What to do if you can't pay your tax
203	Failure to pay child support and federal nontax and state income tax obligations
204	Offers in compromise
205	Innocent spouse relief (and separation of liability and equitable relief)
	Alternative Filing Methods
251	Electronic signatures
252	Electronic filing
253	Substitute tax forms
254	How to choose a paid tax preparer
255	TeleFile
256	Filing business returns electronically
	General Information
301	When, where, and how to file
302	Highlights of tax changes

Topic No.	Subject
303	Checklist of common errors when preparing your tax return
304	Extensions of time to file your tax return
305	Recordkeeping
306	Penalty for underpayment of estimated tax
307	Backup withholding
308	Amended returns
309	Roth IRA contributions
310	Coverdell education savings accounts
311	Power of attorney information
312	Disclosure authorizations
313	Qualified tuition programs (QTPs)
	Filing Requirements, Filing Status, and Exemptions
351	Who must file?
352	Which form—1040, 1040A, or 1040EZ?
353	What is your filing status?
354	Dependents
355	Estimated tax
356	Decedents
357	Tax information for parents of kidnapped children
	Types of Income
401	Wages and salaries

TeleTax Topics

(Continued)

Topic No.	Subject
402	Tips
403	Interest received
404	Dividends
405	Refunds of state and local taxes
406	Alimony received
407	Business income
408	Sole proprietorship
409	Capital gains and losses
410	Pensions and annuities
411	Pensions—The general rule and the simplified method
412	Lump-sum distributions
413	Rollovers from retirement plans
414	Rental income and expenses
415	Renting residential and vacation property
416	Farming and fishing income
417	Earnings for clergy
418	Unemployment compensation
419	Gambling income and expenses
420	Bartering income
421	Scholarship and fellowship grants
422	Nontaxable income
423	Social security and equivalent railroad retirement benefits
424	401(k) plans
425	Passive activities—Losses and credits
426	Other income
427	Stock options
428	Roth IRA distributions
429	Traders in securities (information for Form 1040 filers)
430	Exchange of policyholder interest for stock

Adjustments to Income

Topic No.	Subject
451	Individual retirement arrangements (IRAs)
452	Alimony paid
453	Bad debt deduction
454	Tax shelters
455	Moving expenses
456	Student loan interest deduction
457	Tuition and fees deduction
458	Educator expense deduction

Itemized Deductions

Topic No.	Subject
501	Should I itemize?
502	Medical and dental expenses
503	Deductible taxes
504	Home mortgage points
505	Interest expense
506	Contributions
507	Casualty and theft losses
508	Miscellaneous expenses

Topic No.	Subject
509	Business use of home
510	Business use of car
511	Business travel expenses
512	Business entertainment expenses
513	Educational expenses
514	Employee business expenses
515	Casualty, disaster, and theft losses

Tax Computation

Topic No.	Subject
551	Standard deduction
552	Tax and credits figured by the IRS
553	Tax on a child's investment income
554	Self-employment tax
555	Ten-year tax option for lump-sum distributions
556	Alternative minimum tax
557	Tax on early distributions from traditional and Roth IRAs
558	Tax on early distributions from retirement plans

Tax Credits

Topic No.	Subject
601	Earned income credit (EIC)
602	Child and dependent care credit
603	Credit for the elderly or the disabled
604	Advance earned income credit
605	Education credits
606	Child tax credits
607	Adoption credit
608	Excess social security and RRTA tax withheld
610	Retirement savings contributions credit

IRS Notices

Topic No.	Subject
651	Notices—What to do
652	Notice of underreported income—CP 2000
653	IRS notices and bills, penalties, and interest charges

Basis of Assets, Depreciation, and Sale of Assets

Topic No.	Subject
701	Sale of your home
703	Basis of assets
704	Depreciation
705	Installment sales

Employer Tax Information

Topic No.	Subject
751	Social security and Medicare withholding rates
752	Form W-2—Where, when, and how to file
753	Form W-4—Employee's Withholding Allowance Certificate
754	Form W-5—Advance earned income credit

Topic No.	Subject
755	Employer identification number (EIN)—How to apply
756	Employment taxes for household employees
757	Form 941—Deposit requirements
758	Form 941—Employer's Quarterly Federal Tax Return
759	Form 940 and 940-EZ—Deposit requirements
760	Form 940 and Form 940-EZ—Employer's Annual Federal Unemployment Tax Returns
761	Tips—Withholding and reporting
762	Independent contractor vs. employee

Magnetic Media Filers—1099 Series and Related Information Returns

Topic No.	Subject
801	Who must file magnetically
802	Applications, forms, and information
803	Waivers and extensions
804	Test files and combined federal and state filing
805	Electronic filing of information returns

Tax Information for Aliens and U.S. Citizens Living Abroad

Topic No.	Subject
851	Resident and nonresident aliens
852	Dual-status alien
853	Foreign earned income exclusion—General
854	Foreign earned income exclusion—Who qualifies?
855	Foreign earned income exclusion—What qualifies?
856	Foreign tax credit
857	Individual taxpayer identification number (ITIN)—Form W-7
858	Alien tax clearance

Tax Information for Puerto Rico Residents (in Spanish only)

Topic No.	Subject
901	Who must file a U.S. income tax return in Puerto Rico
902	Deductions and credits for Puerto Rico filers
903	Federal employment taxes in Puerto Rico
904	Tax assistance for Puerto Rico residents

Topic numbers are effective January 1, 2005.

Calling the IRS

If you cannot find the answer to your question using one of the methods listed on page 7, please call us for assistance at 1-800-829-1040. You will not be charged for the call unless your phone company charges you for toll-free calls. Our normal hours of operation are Monday through Friday from 7:00 a.m. to 10:00 p.m. local time. Beginning January 29, 2005, through April 9, 2005, assistance will also be available on Saturday from 10:00 a.m. to 3:00 p.m. local time. Assistance provided to callers from Alaska and Hawaii will be based on the hours of operation in the Pacific time zone.

 If you want to check the status of your 2005 refund, see Refund Information *on page 8.*

Before You Call

IRS representatives care about the quality of the service provided to you, our customer. You can help us provide accurate, complete answers to your questions by having the following information available.

- The tax form, schedule, or notice to which your question relates.
- The facts about your particular situation. The answer to the same question often varies from one taxpayer to another because of differences in their age, income, whether they can be claimed as a dependent, etc.
- The name of any IRS publication or other source of information that you used to look for the answer.

To maintain your account security, you may be asked for the following information, which you should also have available.

- Your social security number.
- The amount of refund and filing status shown on your tax return.
- The "Caller ID Number" shown at the top of any notice you received.
- Your personal identification number (PIN) if you have one.
- Your date of birth.
- The numbers in your street address.
- Your ZIP code.

If you are asking for an installment agreement to pay your tax, you will be asked for the highest amount you can pay each month and the date on which you can pay it.

Evaluation of services provided. The IRS uses several methods to evaluate our telephone service. One method is to record telephone calls for quality purposes only. A random sample of recorded calls is selected for review through the quality assurance process. Other methods include listening to live calls in progress and random selection of customers for participation in a customer satisfaction survey.

Making the Call

Call 1-800-829-1040 (for TTY/TDD help, call 1-800-829-4059). Our menus allow callers with pulse or rotary dial telephones to speak their responses when requested to do so. First, you will be provided a series of options that will request touch-tone responses. If a touch-tone response is not received, you will then hear a series of options and be asked to speak your selections. After your touch-tone or spoken response is received, the system will direct your call to the appropriate assistance. You can do the following within the system.

- Order tax forms and publications.
- Find out what you owe.
- Determine if we have adjusted your account or received payments you made.
- Request a transcript of your tax return or account.
- Find out where to send your tax return or payment.
- Request more time to pay or set up a monthly installment agreement.
- Find out if you qualify for innocent spouse relief.

Before You Hang Up

If you do not fully understand the answer you receive, or you feel our representative may not fully understand your question, our representative needs to know this. He or she will be happy to take additional time to be sure your question is answered fully.

By law, you are responsible for paying your share of federal income tax. If we should make an error in answering your question, you are still responsible for the payment of the correct tax. Should this occur, however, you will not be charged any penalty.

A Glossary of Tax and Financial Terms

Accelerated Cost Recovery System (ACRS). A method of **depreciation** that allows for faster deduction of the cost of a **capital asset** than previously possible. This method is used for almost all **assets** that began depreciating between 1981 and 1986. See Chapter 10, *Rental Income and Expenses.*

Accelerated death benefit. Payments received from a life insurance policy before the death of a terminally or chronically ill individual.

Accelerated depreciation. A method of **depreciation** that allows for faster deduction of the cost of a property than **straight-line depreciation.** Both **Accelerated Cost Recovery System (ACRS)** and **Modified Accelerated Cost Recovery System (MACRS)** contain accelerated depreciation rates. See Chapter 10, *Rental Income and Expenses.*

Accountable plan. Plan for reimbursing employees for business-related expenses that requires itemized validation of expenses and the return of any excess reimbursement. Note that valid reimbursements are generally excluded from wages and are not subject to employment taxes. See Chapter 28, *Car Expenses and Other Employee Business Expenses.*

Accounting to an employer. Providing an employer with documents (a diary, a statement of expenses, etc.) that support expenses the employee has incurred. See Chapter 28, *Car Expenses and Other Employee Business Expenses.*

Accrual method of accounting. A method of accounting with income reported in the year it is earned and expenses reported in the year they are incurred. Compare with **cash method of accounting.** See Chapter 1, *Filing Information.*

ACRS. See **Accelerated Cost Recovery System.**

Adjusted basis. The measure used for determining a gain or a loss on the sale or exchange of property. Adjusted basis is generally the cost of property adjusted by certain increases (e.g., **capital expenditures**) or decreases (e.g., **depreciation**). See Chapter 14, *Basis of Property.*

Adjusted gross income. Gross income reduced by certain adjustments allowed by law. For example, **gross income** may be reduced by deductible **IRA** contributions. See Chapter 32, *How to Figure Your Tax Including the Alternative Minimum Tax.*

Administrator. Person appointed by the court if (1) no will exists; (2) no **executor** was named in the will; or (3) the named **executor** cannot or will not serve. This person is responsible for overseeing the estate by distributing properties and/or settling debts.

ADS. See **Alternative Depreciation System.**

Alimony. Periodic payments made under (1) a decree of divorce or **separate maintenance;** (2) a written separation agreement; or (3) a decree of **support.** Note that payments made may be taken as a deduction in **adjusted gross income** and payments received must be included as income in **adjusted gross income.** See Chapter 20, *Alimony.*

Alternative Depreciation System (ADS). A method of depreciating assets using **straight-line depreciation** that has longer recovery periods than are available under **Modified Accelerated Cost Recovery System (MACRS).** This method is mandatory for such items as foreign assets, luxury automobiles, and tax-exempt use property. See Chapter 10, *Rental Income and Expenses.*

Alternative Minimum Tax (AMT). A tax that may apply in addition to regular income tax when a taxpayer has **tax preference items** or certain deductions allowed in determining regular **taxable income.** See Chapter 32, *How to Figure Your Tax Including the Alternative Minimum Tax.*

Amended return. A return (Form 1040X) filed within a 3-year period to correct a mistake or to claim a refund on an original income tax return.

Amortization. A deductible expense used as a means of recovering an investment in an intangible asset. Compare with **depreciation.**

Amount realized. The actual amount received on the sale or exchange of property.

AMT. See **Alternative Minimum Tax.**

Annuity. A sum of money paid periodically that includes the return of invested capital plus the income generated by it. Annuities are often purchased by individuals as investments and are used by retirement plans to pay **pensions.** See Chapter 11, *Retirement Plans, Pensions, and Annuities.*

Applicable federal rate. Interest rates published by the IRS used in determining the imputed interest on transactions providing for below-market interest.

Asset. Any property with value.

At-risk limitations. Generally, losses are deductible up to the amount at risk in the activity. This includes any amounts personally borrowed for use in the activity. See Chapter 13, *Other Income.*

Audit. An examination of financial records, whether performed by the IRS or another entity. See Chapter 47, *If Your Return Is Examined.*

Away from home overnight. A period of time spent away from an individual's **tax home** that is both substantially longer than an ordinary workday and also includes time for sleep or rest. See Chapter 28, *Car Expenses and Other Employee Business Expenses.*

B

Bad debt. An amount owed that cannot be collected by the lender. See Chapter 15, *Sale of Property.*

Basis. Generally, the cost of an **asset.** See Chapter 14, *Basis of Property.*

C

Calendar Year. The 12-month period ending on December 31. Most individual taxpayers are required to file their returns on the basis of such a year. Compare with **fiscal year.**

Cafeteria plan. Under a cafeteria plan, an employer may offer a "menu" of fringe benefits and cash from which participating employees may select. Under such a plan, the value of nontaxable qualified benefits that an employee selects is not includible in income.

Capital asset. Property held for personal purposes or investment, rather than for business purposes.

Capital expenditures. The cost of improvements that increase the value or **useful life** of a property.

Capital gain dividend (capital gain distribution). A **mutual fund** distribution to shareholders of a **capital gain** realized on the sale of a part of the fund's investment portfolio. See Chapter 9, *Dividends and Other Corporate Distributions.*

Capital gain or loss. A gain or a loss arising from the sale or exchange of **capital assets** that is computed by comparing the amount realized against the **adjusted basis** of the **asset.** See Chapter 17, *Reporting Gains and Losses.*

Capital loss carryover. The excess of **capital losses** over **capital gains** that cannot be deducted in a particular year and must be carried over to the following year.

Capitalize. To treat an expenditure as a cost of a property that increases the property's **basis** rather than treating the expenditure as a current deduction.

Cash method of accounting. A method of accounting with income reported when it is actually or **constructively received** and expenses reported when they are paid. Compare with **accrual method of accounting.** See Chapter 1, *Filing Information.*

Casualty loss. A loss arising from fire, storm, shipwreck, or other similar and unexpected occurrences sometimes referred to as an "Act of God." See Chapter 27, *Casualty and Theft Losses.*

Child support. Payments made to support a minor child following a divorce or separation. The payments cannot be deducted from **gross income** and are not taxable to the recipient parent. The parent with custody of the child is entitled to the dependency exemption unless such a right is expressly waived. See Chapter 20, *Alimony.*

Child tax credit. A tax credit is allowed against income for each qualifying child for taxpayers with modified **gross income** below certain thresholds. See Chapter 34, *Child and Dependent Care Credit.*

Community income. Income treated as belonging equally to each spouse, regardless of which spouse actually earns or receives it. See **community property.**

Community property. Property that belongs equally to husband and wife; this concept is used in the states of Arizona, California, Idaho, Louisiana, Nevada, New Mexico, Texas, Washington, and Wisconsin.

Condemnation. The seizure of property by a government agency for a public purpose.

Constructive receipt. Income that is taxable because it was available even if it was not actually received.

Consumer interest. Interest on personal and consumer purchases; also called personal interest.

Conversion transaction. A transaction in which the acquirer of a property agrees contemporaneously to sell the property at a determinable price to another taxpayer in the future. A conversion transaction requires the calculation of imputed loan interest before any allocation of gain as a capital gain.

Corporation. A business entity owned by shareholders that is generally treated as a separate tax entity. The shareholders of a corporation do not have personal liability.

Coverdell education savings account. A **trust** or custodial account created to pay for the qualified education expenses of the designated beneficiary.

D

Decedent. A deceased individual.

Declining balance depreciation. A method of **accelerated depreciation** that calculates each year's **depreciation** as a percentage of the reduced **basis** of the **asset.** See Chapter 10, *Rental Income and Expenses.*

Deductions. Expenses allowed by law that reduce **gross income. Gross income** minus deductible expenses results in **adjusted gross income** or **taxable income.** See S**standard deduction** and **Itemized deductions.**

Deferred gain. A gain realized but not recognized as **taxable income** until a later time.

Deficiency. The shortfall between the correct tax liability and the amount reported on a return.

Dependency exemption. An **exemption** allowed to a taxpayer for a qualifying child or a qualifying relative. See Chapter 3, *Personal Exemptions and Dependents.*

Dependent. An individual who is a qualifying child or qualifying relative such that the taxpayer is entitled to claim an **exemption** allowance on his or her tax return. See Chapter 3, *Personal Exemptions and Dependents.*

Dependent care credit. A credit that reduces taxes dollar-for-dollar based on expenses incurred in caring for a **dependent** so that the caregiver may become gainfully employed. See Chapter 34, *Child and Dependent Care Credit.*

Depletion. A deductible expense that reflects the decrease of a depletable natural resource (e.g., oil and gas) as it is extracted. See Chapter 13, *Other Income.*

Depreciable asset. Property used by a business or held for the production of income with a **useful life** of more than one year.

Depreciation. A deductible expense that reflects a reasonable allowance for wear and tear of tangible property. Only property that has a **useful life** of more than one year and is used for business purposes can be depreciated. Note that there are different methods used in accounting for depreciation. Compare with **amortization**. See Chapter 10, *Rental Income and Expenses*.

Direct rollover. A rollover distribution that is paid directly to an eligible retirement plan. See Chapter 11, *Retirement Plans, Pensions, and Annuities*.

Discount income. Income on a debt instrument such as a bond purchased at a discount and maturing at face value. See **Original Issue Discount (OID)**. See Chapter 8, *Interest Income*.

Dividend. A share of a corporation's profits that is distributed to shareholders and is then considered **taxable income** to the shareholder. See Qualified dividend.

Dividend Reinvestment Plan (DRIP). A plan that reinvests dividends by buying more shares of stock rather than paying out in cash.

Domestic production activities deduction. Starting in 2005, the tax law provides a deduction that is equal to a percentage of the income earned from manufacturing (and certain other production activity) in the United States. The deduction equals the lesser of (1) 3% of the lesser of (a) the "qualified production activities income" of the taxpayer for the tax year or (b) taxable income (modified adjusted gross income, for individual taxpayers) without regard to this deduction. The percentage stays at 3% for tax years beginning in 2006, increases to 6% for tax years beginning in 2007-2009, and to 9% afterward; or

(2) 50% of the sum of (a) wages paid and (b) the elective deferrals (e.g., 401(k) deferrals), that are made by the taxpayer during year.

Domicile. The place that an individual intends to be his or her permanent residence.

DRIP. See *Dividend Reinvestment Plan*

Dual-status alien. An individual who is a **nonresident alien** for part of the year and a **resident alien** or U.S. citizen for the rest of the year. See Chapter 44, *Foreign Citizens Living in the United States*.

E

Earned income. Compensation for personal services rendered. Earned income does not include amounts received from an **annuity** or a **pension**.

Earned income credit. A refundable credit available to low-income taxpayers based on **earned income**.

Eligible retirement plan. A **qualified retirement plan**, an **individual retirement account**, or an **individual retirement annuity**. See also **Qualified plan** and **Individual Retirement Arrangement (IRA)**.

Eligible rollover distribution. Any distribution, whether full or partial, to an individual that can be rolled over to a **qualified retirement plan or IRA**.

Employee. An individual whose work is performed under the control or direction of an employer. Compare with **Independent contractor**.

Estimated tax. A direct quarterly tax payment that is required when withheld taxes are inadequate to meet an individual's full tax liability. See Chapter 5, *Tax Withholding and Estimated Tax*.

Exclusion. Any amount that is excluded from **gross income**.

Executor. Person named in the decedent's will who is responsible for overseeing the estate by acting as the **decedent** has directed by distributing properties and/or settling debts. See also **Administrator**.

Exemption. A **deduction** allowed to a taxpayer for himself or herself and for each qualifying child and qualifying relative. See Chapter 3, *Personal Exemptions and Dependents*.

F

Fair market value. The price a willing buyer would pay and a willing seller would accept if neither was under any compulsion to enter into a transaction. This concept is used when determining the presumed value of an **asset** that is not actually being bought or sold.

Fiduciary. An individual with the discretionary authority to manage another person's property. Also, an individual who holds assets in a **trust** in which another person has an interest.

Finance charges. Interest or other charges paid on purchases made on a deferred-payment basis.

Fiscal year. Any 12-month period ending on the last day of any month other than December. A fiscal year may also be a 52–53 week, year ending on a specific date. Compare with **Calendar year**.

Flexible spending account. An optional feature of a cafeteria plan (see above) under which an employee elects to contribute pretax dollars for qualified expenses (either medical or dependent care) at the beginning of the plan year. As the employee incurs qualified expenses, he or she is reimbursed up to the total amount he or she elected to contribute at the beginning of the plan year.

Foreign corporation. A **corporation** organized outside the laws of the United States.

Foreign tax credit. A credit allowed for income taxes paid to a foreign country to mitigate double taxation.

401(k) plan. A qualified employer plan under which a portion of an employee's salary is withheld on a pretax basis and allowed to earn income on a tax-deferred basis until withdrawal upon the employee reaching age 59 1/2, separation from service, or other qualifying event. See Chapter 11, *Retirement Plans, Pensions, and Annuities*.

G

Gross income. All of a taxpayer's yearly income before subtracting any allowable adjustments or **deductions**.

H

Head of household. An unmarried taxpayer who pays more than 50% of the cost of maintaining a residence for the entire year for a qualifying individual. Note that heads of household qualify for special tax rates. See Chapter 2, *Filing Status*.

Holding period. The length of time an **asset** is held. This length of time determines whether a sale or exchange results in a **long-term** or **short-term capital gain** or **loss**. See Chapter 17, *Reporting Gains and Losses*.

Home acquisition debt. Loan used to acquire, construct, or substantially improve a principal residence or a second home, the interest on which is fully deductible (subject to limitations based on the amount of the debt). See Chapter 25, *Interest Expense*.

Home equity debt. Debt secured by a principal or secondary residence in excess of **acquisition debt**. Interest on home equity debt not in excess of $100,000 is generally fully deductible.

Hope scholarship credit. An income tax credit based on the qualified tuition and related expenses of each eligible student. This credit is only allowed for the first two years of undergraduate education. See Chapter 37, *Education Credits.*

I

Imputed interest. Interest deemed to have been earned or charged on a debt if the stated interest rate is below the rate set by law.

Incentive Stock Option (ISO). A type of **stock option** that can be received and exercised without recognition of income until the optioned stock is sold. The spread on the exercise of an ISO is an adjustment for Alternative Minimum Tax purposes. See Chapter 6, *Wages, Salaries, and Other Earnings.*

Income in respect of a decedent. Income earned by an individual before his or her death but taxed to the survivor who receives it.

Independent contractor. A person whose work hours and procedures (as opposed to end product) are not controlled by another and who is therefore deemed to be self-employed for tax purposes. Compare with **employee.** See Chapter 39, *If You Are Self-Employed: How to File Schedule C.*

Individual Retirement Account. See **Individual Retirement Arrangement.**

Individual Retirement Annuity. See **Individual Retirement Arrangement.**

Individual Retirement Arrangement (IRA). A retirement plan under which individuals are generally permitted to contribute up to $4,000 per person, per year ($4,500 for those age 50 or older). The deduction of these contributions is subject to income limitations and other rules. See Chapter 18, *Individual Retirement Arrangements (IRAs).*

Inflation adjustment. The annual adjustment to tax rate brackets, the standard deduction, personal exemption amounts, and other items due to inflation.

Installment sale method of accounting. A method of accounting under which a gain from a sale is reported when the installment payments are received instead of the entire amount being reported in the year of the sale.

Intangible personal property. Property (e.g., patents, notes receivable, and accounts receivable) whose value consists of rights rather than material attributes. Compare with **tangible personal property** and **real property.**

Internal Revenue Service (IRS). The division of the U.S. Treasury Department that is responsible for the enforcement of the tax laws.

Involuntary conversion. The forced disposition of property as a result of casualty, theft, or **condemnation.** Upon conversion, one usually receives payment through insurance proceeds or **condemnation** awards.

IRA. See **Individual Retirement Arrangement.**

IRS. See **Internal Revenue Service.**

Itemized deductions. Individually listed expenses claimed on Schedule A (Form 1040) that reduce the overall tax liability. Examples include medical expenses, interest, taxes, and charitable contributions. Compare with **standard deduction.** See *Part IV, Standard Deduction and Itemized Deductions.*

J

Joint return. A tax return filed by a married couple that combines both of their incomes and **deductions.**

K

Keogh plan. A retirement plan for the **self-employed.** Contributions are deductible within limits and the income accumulates tax-free until it is withdrawn. Keogh plans are sometimes known as HR 10 plans

Kiddie tax. A colloquial term for the tax on the investment income of a child under age 14, based on the parents' marginal tax rate. See Chapter 33, *Tax on Investment Income of Certain Minor Children.*

L

Legally separated. A husband and wife who live apart under a decree of separate maintenance.

Lifetime learning credit. An income tax credit based on qualified tuition and related expenses of undergraduate or graduate courses. See Chapter 37, *Education Credits and Other Education Benefits.*

Like-kind exchange. A tax-free exchange of properties held for either productive use in a trade or a business, or for investment that are of the same nature and character; sometimes used in connection with **involuntary conversions.**

Limited Liability Company (LLC). An LLC is owned by investors known as members. It is managed either by the members themselves or by designated managers. Like shareholders of a corporation, the members' liability is limited to the amount of their investment. For tax purposes, LLCs that are owned by more than one person are generally treated as partnerships. LLCs that are owned by one person are disregarded for tax purposes, with the result that the income of the LLC is taxed to the owner directly.

Long-term capital gain or loss. Gain or loss on the sale or exchange of a **capital asset** that has been held for more than 12 months. Compare with **short-term gain or loss.** See Chapter 17, *Reporting Gains and Losses.*

Long-term care insurance contract. Insurance policy that provides coverage for qualified long-term care services.

Lump-sum distribution. The full distribution of an individual's employer-funded qualified **pension** or profit-sharing plan account or benefit within one taxable year. Normally triggered by retirement or separation from service.

M

MACRS. See **Modified Accelerated Cost Recovery System.**

Marginal tax rate. The tax rate at which each additional dollar of income over a specified ceiling is taxed.

Market discount. The discount from face value of a debt instrument such as a bond purchased in the secondary market. Generally caused by an increase in interest rates or a similar change in other factors lessening the quality of the debt.

Marital deduction. Provision that allows for the unlimited transfer of assets to a spouse free of estate and gift tax.

Material participant. A taxpayer who participates in a business activity on a regular, continuous, and substantial basis. The term is sometimes used in connection with **passive activity losses.**

Miscellaneous itemized deductions. Most miscellaneous itemized deductions (e.g., investment expenses, fees for tax advice, union dues) that are deductible only to the extent that the total exceeds 2% of **adjusted gross income.**

Modified Accelerated Cost Recovery System (MACRS). A method of **depreciation** used for assets acquired after 1986 that allows for more rapid **depreciation** than **straight-line depreciation.** See **accelerated depreciation.** See Chapter 10, *Rental Income and Expenses.*

Mutual fund. A company that invests its shareholder's funds, usually in stocks and bonds. Sometimes known as a **regulated investment company.**

N

Net operating loss. A business loss that exceeds current income. A net operating loss may be carried backward or forward to reduce taxes in one or more of those years.

Nominee. Someone who receives income that belongs to another person.

Nonqualified stock option. A type of **stock option** that creates **ordinary income** for the taxpayer when exercised.

Nonrecourse financing. A type of debt that prohibits the lender from seeking personal recovery from the borrower upon default.

Nonrecovery property. A term that applies to most tangible depreciable property that was in use prior to 1981. See Chapter 10, *Rental Income and Expenses.*

Nonresident alien. An individual who is not a citizen or permanent resident of the United States. See Chapter 44, *Foreign Citizens Living in the United States.*

Nontaxable exchange. An exchange of property in which no gain or loss is recognized for tax purposes.

O

OID. See *original issue discount.*

Ordinary gain or loss. Any gain or loss other than a **capital gain or loss.** See Chapter 15, *Sale of Property.*

Ordinary income. Any income that does not come from the sale or exchange of a **capital asset** or a **Section 1231 asset** and is not subject to any preferential tax treatment.

Original Issue Discount (OID). The difference between face value and the actual amount paid for a debt instrument such as a bond, initially sold for less than face value. Generally the discount must be included in **taxable income** over the life of the debt instrument. See Chapter 8, *Interest Income.*

Owner-employee. An **employee** who is also the **proprietor** of a business. Also, a partner who owns more than 10% of either the capital or the profit interest of a partnership.

P

Passive activity loss. A loss from a business in which the individual is not a **material participant.** Passive activity losses are subject to deduction limitations and include rental activities and investments in limited partnerships. See Chapter 13, *Other Income.*

Patronage dividend. A taxable distribution from a cooperative to its members or patrons.

Pension. Payments made to retired employees for past services from an employer-funded retirement plan.

Percentage depletion. A method of calculating **depletion** that applies a fixed percentage to the gross income generated by the mineral property. See Chapter 13, *Other Income.*

Personal use property. Property that is not held for investment or for use by a business.

Points. Costs paid by a borrower that are calculated as a percentage of the loan proceeds; each point is 1%. Also called loan origination fees, maximum loan charges, or premium charges. See Chapter 25, *Interest Expense.*

Proprietor. An individual who is the sole owner of a business.

Q

QTIP Trust. See **Qualified Terminal Interest Property Trust.**

Qualified charitable organization. A nonprofit organization specifically recognized by the **IRS** as a valid recipient of charitable contributions that are tax deductible by the donor. See Chapter 26, *Contributions.*

Qualified dividend. A qualified dividend is a dividend received from a domestic corporation or qualified foreign corporation which is taxed at the maximum capital gains rate of 15% but only if certain holding period requirements are satisfied.

Qualified plan. An **employee** retirement plan that meets all legal requirements and qualifies for certain tax benefits. Two examples are **pension** and profit-sharing plans.

Qualified real estate professionals. Individuals who may offset rental real estate losses against all sources of **taxable income** by satisfying certain eligibility thresholds and materially participating in the rental real estate activities.

Qualified residence interest. Deductible interest, subject to limits, paid or accrued during the taxable year on **acquisition debt** and/or **home equity debt.** See Chapter 25, *Interest Expense.*

Qualified retirement plan. See **Qualified plan.**

Qualified Small Business Stock (QSBS). Certain stock issued after August 10, 1993, and held for more than 5 years. Note that the **capital gain** from the sale of this stock is eligible for a 50% exclusion from **gross income.**

Qualified Terminal Interest Trust (QTIP). A trust established to provide income for a surviving spouse. At the death of the surviving spouse, the trust assets are distributed to other beneficiaries according to the terms of the trust. A properly structured QTIP qualifies for the unlimited marital deduction and is not subject to estate taxation upon the death of the first spouse.

Qualified Tuition Program (QTP) (also called Section 529 Plan). Programs under which an individual may (1) prepay tuition (into an account or toward a waiver) on behalf of a beneficiary for use toward qualified higher education expenses, or (2) contribute to an account established for paying qualified higher education expenses on behalf of a beneficiary.

Qualifying widow(er). A surviving spouse with dependents whose status allows him or her to use the same tax rates and tables used for a **joint return.**

R

Real estate. See **real property.**

Real Estate Investment Trust (REIT). A **trust** that invests principally in **real estate** and mortgages and is taxed only on the income that is not distributed to its shareholders.

Real property (real estate). Physical property, such as land or buildings, that is permanent and nonmovable in nature. Compare with **tangible** and **intangible personal property.**

Realized gain or loss. The difference between the amount received for a property sold or exchanged and the **adjusted basis** of the property.

Recognized gain or loss. An amount of gain or loss realized that must be included as **taxable income.**

Recovery property. A term that applies to most tangible depreciable property in use after 1980 and before 1987.

Regulated investment company. An investment company subject to Security and Exchange Commission regulations that is taxed only on income not distributed to its shareholders. See also **Mutual fund.**

Reinvested dividends. Dividends that are used to purchase more stock rather than being distributed as cash. These dividends are **taxable income** in the year in which they are **constructively received.** See also **Dividend Reinvestment Plan (DRIP).**

REIT. See **real estate investment trust.**

Remainder interest. An interest in property or a **trust** that is left after the beneficiaries have received their income interest.

Resident alien. An individual who is not a citizen of the United States but is a permanent resident.

Rollover. A distribution from a **qualified plan** that is reinvested tax-free in another **qualified plan** or **IRA** within 60 days. See Chapter 18, *Individual Retirement Arrangements (IRAs).*

Roth IRA. Retirement plan under which contributions are nondeductible and qualified distributions may be tax-free. Contributions are limited by certain threshold amounts. See Chapter 18, *Individual Retirement Arrangements (IRAs).*

Royalty income. Income received for the use of certain kinds of properties, such as mineral and literary properties or patents.

S

S corporation. A **corporation** organized under the principles of Subchapter S of the Internal Revenue Code. Acting as a conduit, this type of **corporation** generally distributes all of its **taxable income** to its shareholders. See Chapter 13, *Other Income.*

Salvage value. The estimated **fair market value** of an asset at the end of its **useful life.**

Section 179 deduction. A tax rule under which an individual may deduct, rather than depreciate, all or a portion of the cost of a business property for the year the property is placed in service. See Chapter 39, *If You Are Self-Employed: How to File Schedule C.*

Section 1231 assets. Depreciable assets used for a business that are held for the required long-term **holding period.** After the recapture of **depreciation,** net gains from the sale of these assets are treated as **capital gains** and net losses are treated as **ordinary losses.** See Chapter 17, *Reporting Gains and Losses.*

Self-employed. An individual who works for him or herself. Compare with **employee** and see **independent contractor.** See also Chapter 39, *If You Are Self-Employed: How to File Schedule C.*

SEP. See *Simplified Employee Pension.*

Separate maintenance payments. Payments made from one separated spouse to another in accordance with a court order or an agreement between the parties. See Chapter 20, *Alimony.*

Service business. A business that derives income from providing personal services such as a law or accounting firm.

Short sale. The sale of borrowed securities at the current market price made either to fix a gain to be reported in a subsequent year or to profit from an expected decline in price.

Short-term capital gain or loss. Gain or loss on the sale or exchange of a **capital asset** that has not been held for more than 12 months. Compare with **long-term gain or loss.** See Chapter 17, *Reporting Gains and Losses.*

Simplified Employee Pension (SEP). An **Individual Retirement Arrangement (IRA)** to which an employer may contribute toward an employee's retirement. See Chapter 18, *Individual Retirement Arrangements (IRAs).*

Single. The filing status of an individual who is unmarried on the last day of the calendar year.

Single premium annuity contract. A policy issued by an insurance company that returns periodic **annuity** payments in exchange for a single premium.

Specialized Small Business Investment Company. (SSBIC). A licensed partnership or corporation under the Small Business Administration's Small Business Investment Act of 1958. Corporations or individuals may roll over the **capital gain** from the sale of securities into the purchase of stock or a partnership interest in a SSBIC without paying any **capital gain** tax.

Standard deduction. A **deduction** used to reduce **taxable income** by those who do not itemize their **deductions.** The amount of the **deduction** depends on the individual's tax status; specifically, whether they are (1) married or qualifying widow(er)s, single, or heads of household; (2) 65 or older; (3) blind, and/or; (4) eligible to be claimed as a **dependent** on another taxpayer's return. Compare with **itemized deductions.** See Chapter 22, *Standard Deduction.*

Standard mileage rate. An IRS-approved amount used to claim a deduction for business, medical, charitable, and moving automobile expenses in lieu of deducting actual expenses (not including parking, tolls, interest, and taxes). See Chapter 28, *Car Expenses and Other Employee Business Expenses.*

Statute of limitations. The time period during which the **IRS** can collect taxes and taxpayers can file for refunds.

Stock Appreciation Right (SAR). A form of compensation granted to an employee based on an increase in value of the company's stock between the date the right is granted and the date the right is exercised.

Stock dividend. A distribution of additional shares by a corporation to its shareholders.

Stock option. An option to buy stock at a specified price.

Straddle. Offsetting investment positions. Generally, a combination of an equal number of put and call options with the same strike price and exercise date on a stock, stock index, or commodity future.

Straight-line depreciation. A method of **depreciation** with the **basis** of the asset deducted in equal amounts over the property's **useful life.** Compare with **accelerated depreciation.** See Chapter 10, *Rental Income and Expenses.*

Sum of the years' digits depreciation. A method of **accelerated depreciation** that is based on a formula developed from the expected **useful life** of the property. See Chapter 10, *Rental Income and Expenses.*

Support. Payments made for the care of a **dependent** toward needs such as food, lodging, medical expenses, and the like.

Surviving Spouse. See **Qualifying widow(er)**

T

Tangible personal property. Physical property that can be moved, such as machinery and automobiles. Compare with **intangible personal property** and **real property.**

Tax credit carryforward (or carryover). A tax credit that was unusable for the reduction of a prior year's tax but can be applied to offset future taxes.

Tax-exempt income. Income that is not subject to federal income tax, such as income from state and municipal bonds, or not subject to state income tax, such as income from Treasury bonds.

Tax home. Generally, a taxpayer's place of business or employment that is used to determine if certain travel expenses are deductible as being incurred away from home. See **Away from home overnight.** See Chapter 28, *Car Expenses and Other Employee Business Expenses.*

Tax loss carryforward (or carryover). A net operating loss that an individual was not able to apply toward a prior year's income.

Tax preference items. Certain items (e.g., **state and local taxes and private activity bond interest**) that must be included when calculating the **Alternative Minimum Tax (AMT).**

Tax rate schedules. Schedules issued by the IRS used to determine individual income tax for individuals who may not use **tax tables** because their income exceeds a certain amount.

Tax-sheltered annuities (Section 403(b) plans). A tax-favored, deferred compensation plan for employees of tax-exempt organizations and public schools. Under a 403(b) plan, a portion of the employee's salary is withheld on a pretax basis and allowed to earn income until authorized withdrawal at age 59 1/2, separation of service, or other qualifying event.

Tax tables. Tables issued by the IRS used in determining individual income tax for individuals with **taxable income** below a certain amount.

Taxable income. An individual's **gross income** minus all allowable adjustments and **deductions** and **exemptions.** This amount is used for determining income tax before applying valid tax credits.

Tenants by the entirety. Married couple who own property jointly. In the event of the death of one, the survivor owns the entire property.

Tenants in common. Two or more parties, each of whom holds an undivided share of the entire property. In the event of the death of one, the survivors do not own the entire property; rather, the decedent's will or state law determines the final disposition of the decedent's share.

Tip Reporting Alternative Commitment Program (TRAC). A voluntary **IRS** program for reporting gratuities by food and beverage establishments. The program was established to increase tip reporting and compliance by both employees and employers.

Trade date. The date a purchase or sale of securities occurred; used in determining the **holding period** of a security.

Trust. An entity to which assets are transferred for protection, management, and potential distribution to its beneficiaries.

U

Useful life. The number of years a **depreciable asset** is reasonably expected to remain in use for a business.

W

Wash sale. A transaction in which an individual sells stock or securities at a loss and repurchases substantially identical stock or securities within 30 days before or 30 days after the sale. Losses are not deductible.

INDEX

NOTE: Boldface numerals indicate Ernst & Young Explanations, TaxAlerts, TaxPlanners and TaxSavers

NOTE: Boldface numerals indicate Ernst & Young Explanations, TaxAlerts, TaxPlanners and TaxSavers

E

NOTE: Boldface numerals indicate Ernst & Young Explanations, TaxAlerts, TaxPlanners and TaxSavers

insurance policy exchanges, 224
insurance premiums
  dividends, 104, **104,** 127–128
  group life, **85,** 85–87
  home, 443
  life, 298, **298–299,** 443
  long-term care, 85, 93, **327**
  medical, 327, **327**
  mortgage, 443
  paid in advance, 104, 327
  as part of alimony, 298, **298–299**
  rental, 136
  self-employed persons, 332, **332, 531**
insurance proceeds
  accelerated death benefits, 178–179
  accident and health, **186–187,** 188, 330, **330–331,** 331
  endowment, 178, **178**
  installment payments, 112
  interest on, **178**
  life, 112, 177, 178
  medical reimbursements, 330, **330–331,** 331
  property, **381,** 381–382
  veterans, 91
intangible property, **529, 531**
intellectual property, donations of, **360.** *See also* copyrights;
    patents
interest
  allocating, 353, **353–354**
  applicable federal rate (AFR), **220**
  below-market loans, 105, **105–106**
  business vs. personal, 353, **353–354**
  calculating after-tax rate of return, **104**
  condemnation awards, 104, **104**
  family members, **342**
  frozen deposits, 105
  how to report income, 116–117
  imputed, **220–221**
  investment, 349–350, **350–351,** 351
  joint accounts, **101–102**
  mortgage, **15,** 342–343, 342–349, **344, 345, 346, 348, 349**
  nondeductible, 350, 351, **351–352**
  passive activity, 351, **353**
  paying with borrowed funds, **352**
  personal, 352, **352**
  points, 345, **345,** 346, **346,** 347, **348,** 348–349
  purchased, 111–112, **112**
  reduction, **603**
  reporting, 355, **355**
  student loans, 310–312
  tax-exempt, 115, **115**
  taxability flowchart, 344
  Treasury bills, 111, **111**
  on unpaid taxes, 20
  U.S. obligations, 106–110, 111, **111**
  when to report income, 116
interest expense, 341–355
interest income, 100–117
Internal Revenue Service. *See IRS*
invalid divorces, **28**
inventions, **232–233**
inventory, **528**
investment clubs, **193–194**
investment income. *See also* bonds; mutual funds; stock
  deducting interest on indebtedness, 349–350, **350–351,** 351,
    353, **353–354**
  dividends and other corporate distributions, 118–131
  recordkeeping, 101, **101**
  reporting gains and losses, 248–260

reporting interest, 116–117, 254, **254–255**
  tax on child's, 101, **101,** 120, **120,** 351, 459–467
investment interest, 116–117, 254, **254–255,** 349–350, **350–351,**
    351
involuntary conversion, 208, 209, **209**
Iraq war. *See* Armed Forces; combat zones
IRAs. *See* individual retirement arrangements (IRAs)
irrevocable trusts, **564**
IRS
  allowing to figure your taxes, 456, **456–457,** 457
  calling, 705
  e-file, 9–11, **10,** 12, **590–594**
  examination of returns, 595–603
IRS Free File, 11, **592–593**
itemizing deductions. *See also particular type*
  changing your mind, 320
  and Form 1040-EZ, **8**
  and Form 1040A, **8**
  limits on, 445, **445–446,** 446, **447**
  recoveries, 182, **182–183**
  tax planning, **605**

job hunting. *See* new job
job-related expenses. *See* employee expenses
job search expenses, 435, **435,** 436, **436.** *See also* outplacement
    services
job transfers. *See* moving expenses
joint accounts, 101, **101–102**
  with children, **101–102**
  stock, 121, **121**
joint returns. *See* returns
joint tenancy, 101, **101–102,** 121, **304, 557**
jury duty, 194, **194**

Katrina, Hurricane, xvi–xviii. *See also* disaster areas
Keogh (H.R. 10) plans, 156, **275, 535**
kickbacks, 194

land, sale of lots, **232**
leases
  automobiles, 407, **407**
  canceled or transferred, 133, **133, 231–232**
  in lieu of purchase, **531**
  vs. sales, **136, 218**
legal expenses, 439, **439,** 443
legally separated taxpayers, 300
licenses and similar fees, 441
life insurance
  accelerated death benefits, 178–179
  premiums as alimony, 298, **298–299**
  premiums, **85,** 85–87, 443
  proceeds, 112, 177, 178, **557–558**
lifetime learning tax credit, **499,** 503, 508
"like-kind" property, 209–210, **210, 219,** 222, **222–223,** 223
limited liability companies, **179**
limits
  capital losses, 253–254, **254**
  casualty and theft losses, 383, **383–384,** 384–385, **385**
  charitable contributions, 368–369, **369**

NOTE: Boldface numerals indicate Ernst & Young Explanations, TaxAlerts, TaxPlanners and TaxSavers

S